KING OF HELL

VOLUMES 1-3

BY
RA IN-SOO

&

JAE-HWAN KIM

TOKYOPOP®

HAMBURG • LONDON • LOS ANGELES • TOKYO

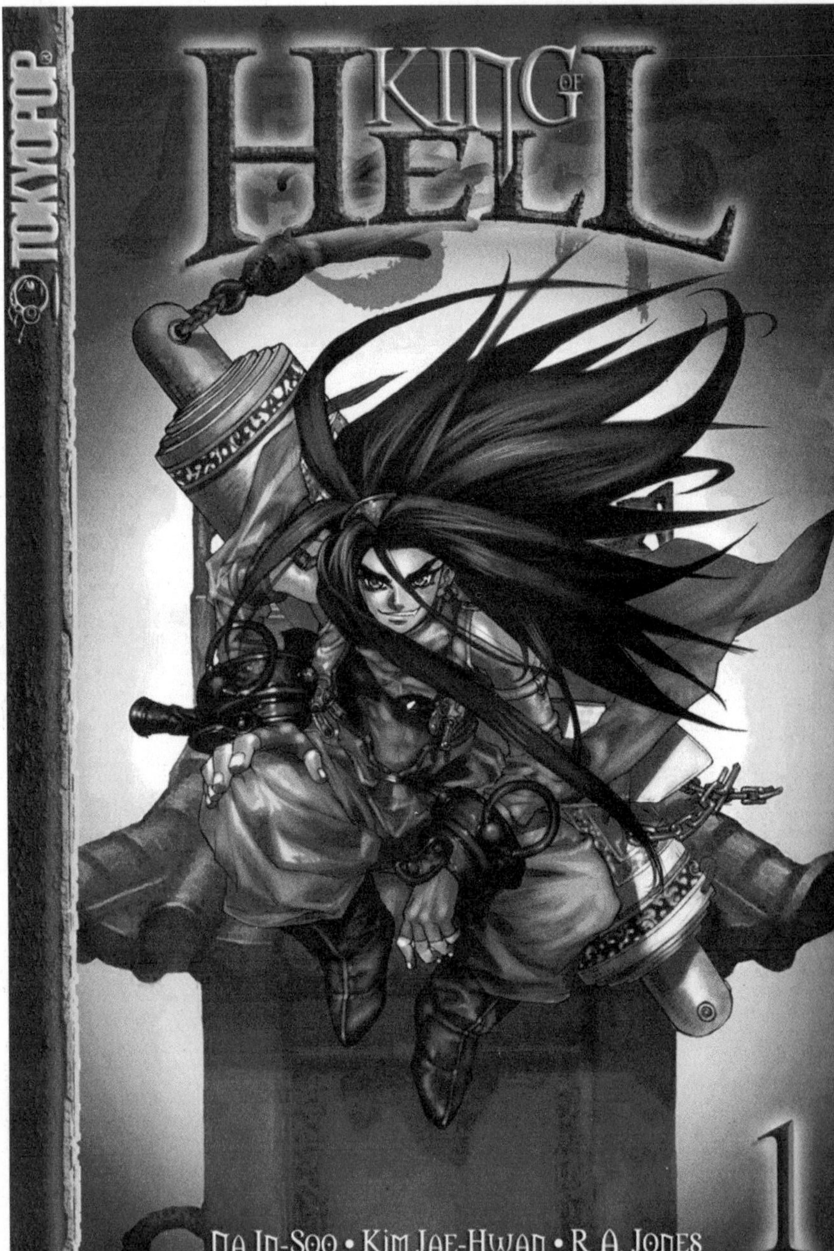
TOKYOPOP
KING OF HELL
1
NA IN-SOO • KIM JAE-HWAN • R.A. JONES

KING OF HELL™

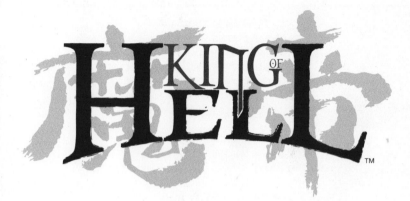

King of Hell -- Vols 1-3 Collection
Story By RA IN-SOO
Art By JAE-HWAN KIM

Translation - Lauren Na
English Adaptation - R.A. Jones
Retouch and Lettering - Star Print Brokers
Production Artist - Vicente Rivera, Jr.
Graphic Designer - Patrick Hook & Al-Insan Lashley
Contributing Editors - Mark Paniccia, Marco Pavia,
Jessica Chavez & Shannon Watters

Editor - Tim Beedle
Digital Imaging Manager - Chris Buford
Pre-Production Supervisor - Erika Terriquez
Production Manager - Elisabeth Brizzi
Managing Editor - Vy Nguyen
Creative Director - Anne Marie Horne
Editor-in-Chief - Rob Tokar
Publisher - Mike Kiley
President and C.O.O. - John Parker
C.E.O. and Chief Creative Officer - Stuart Levy

A  Manga

TOKYOPOP and 🐸 are trademarks or registered trademarks of TOKYOPOP Inc.

TOKYOPOP Inc.
5900 Wilshire Blvd. Suite 2000
Los Angeles, CA 90036

E-mail: info@TOKYOPOP.com
Come visit us online at www.TOKYOPOP.com

ISBN: 978-1-4278-1043-4
First TOKYOPOP printing: April 2008
10 9 8 7 6 5 4 3 2 1
Printed in the USA

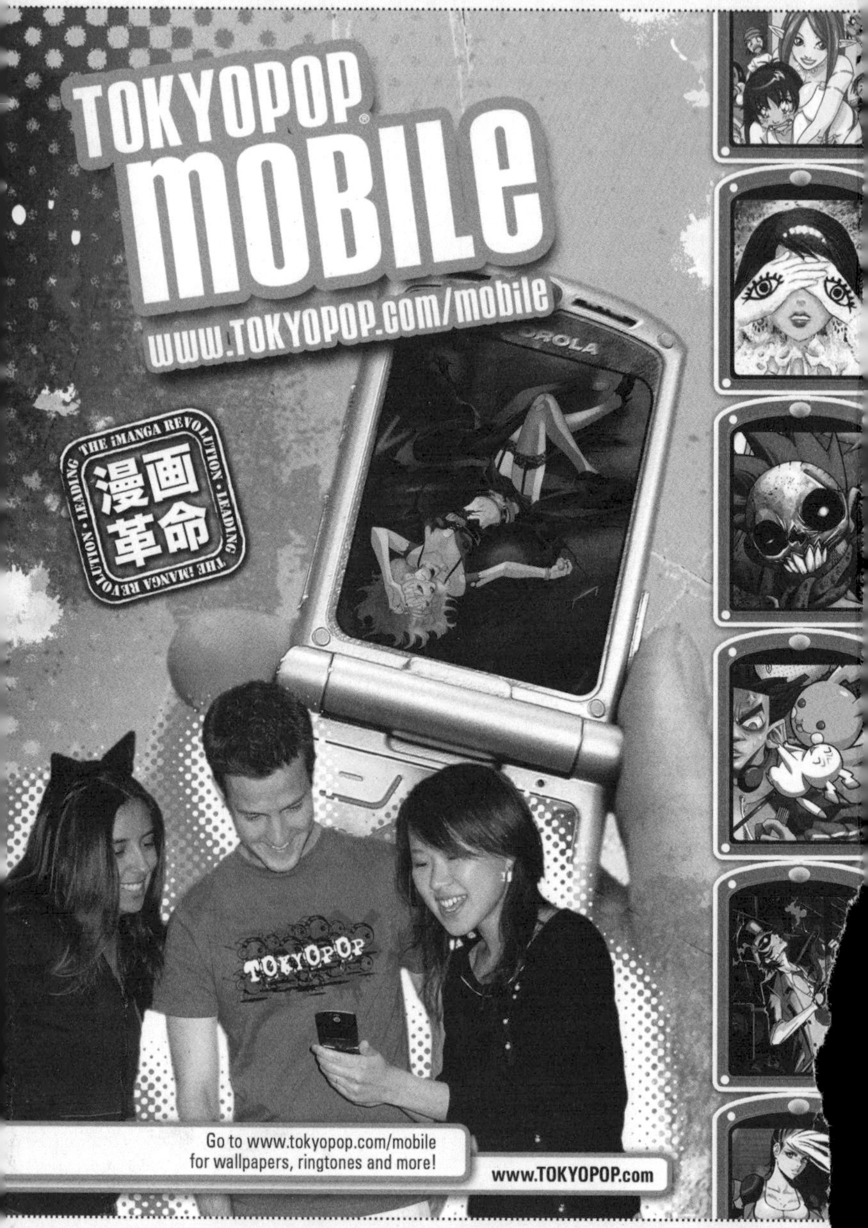
TOKYOPOP®
MOBILE
www.TOKYOPOP.com/mobile
THE iMANGA REVOLUTION · LEADING
漫画革命
THE iMANGA REVOLUTION · LEADING
TOKYOPOP
Go to www.tokyopop.com/mobile
for wallpapers, ringtones and more!
www.TOKYOPOP.com

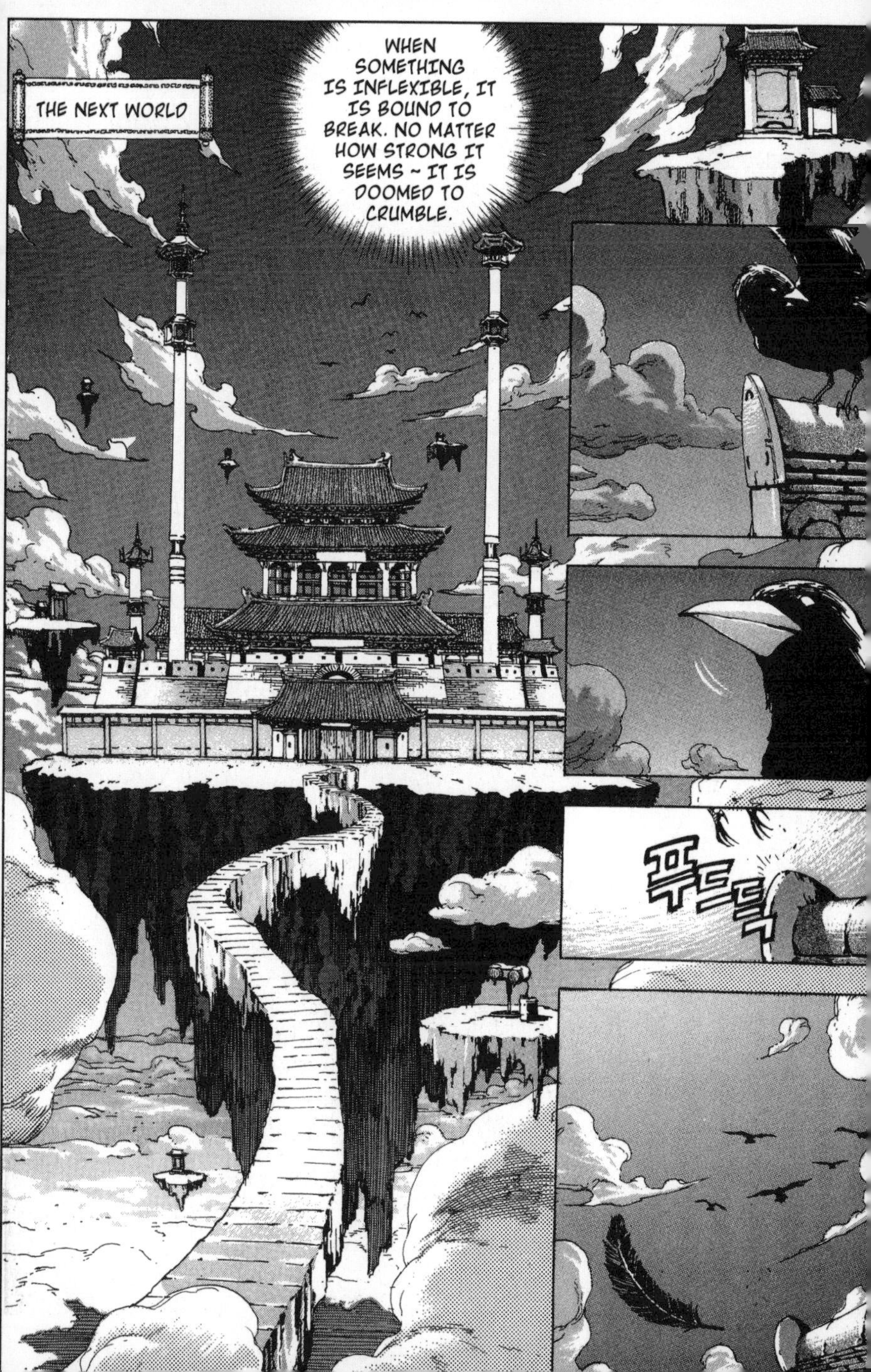
THE NEXT WORLD
WHEN SOMETHING IS INFLEXIBLE, IT IS BOUND TO BREAK. NO MATTER HOW STRONG IT SEEMS ~ IT IS DOOMED TO CRUMBLE.
푸드득

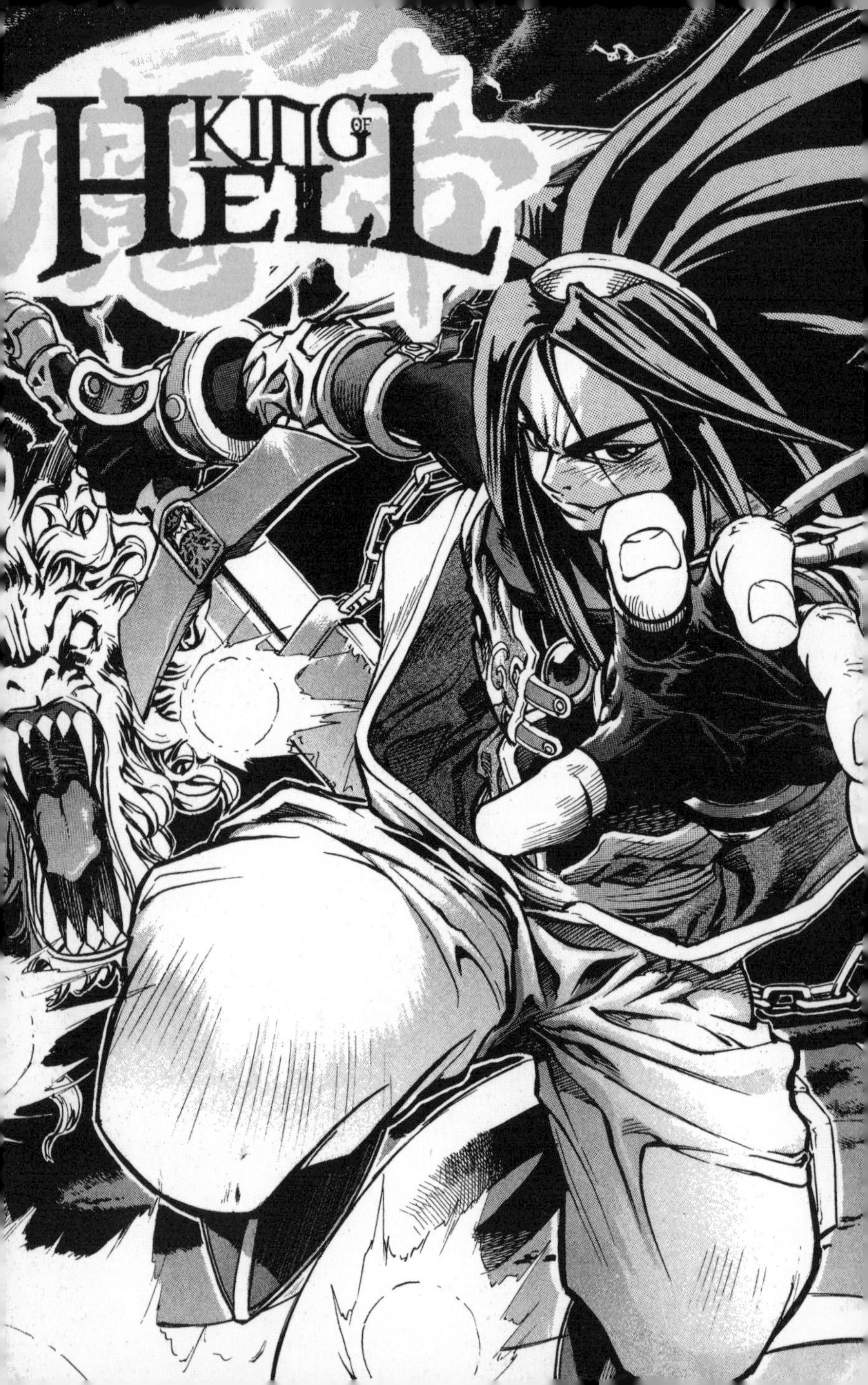
KING OF HELL

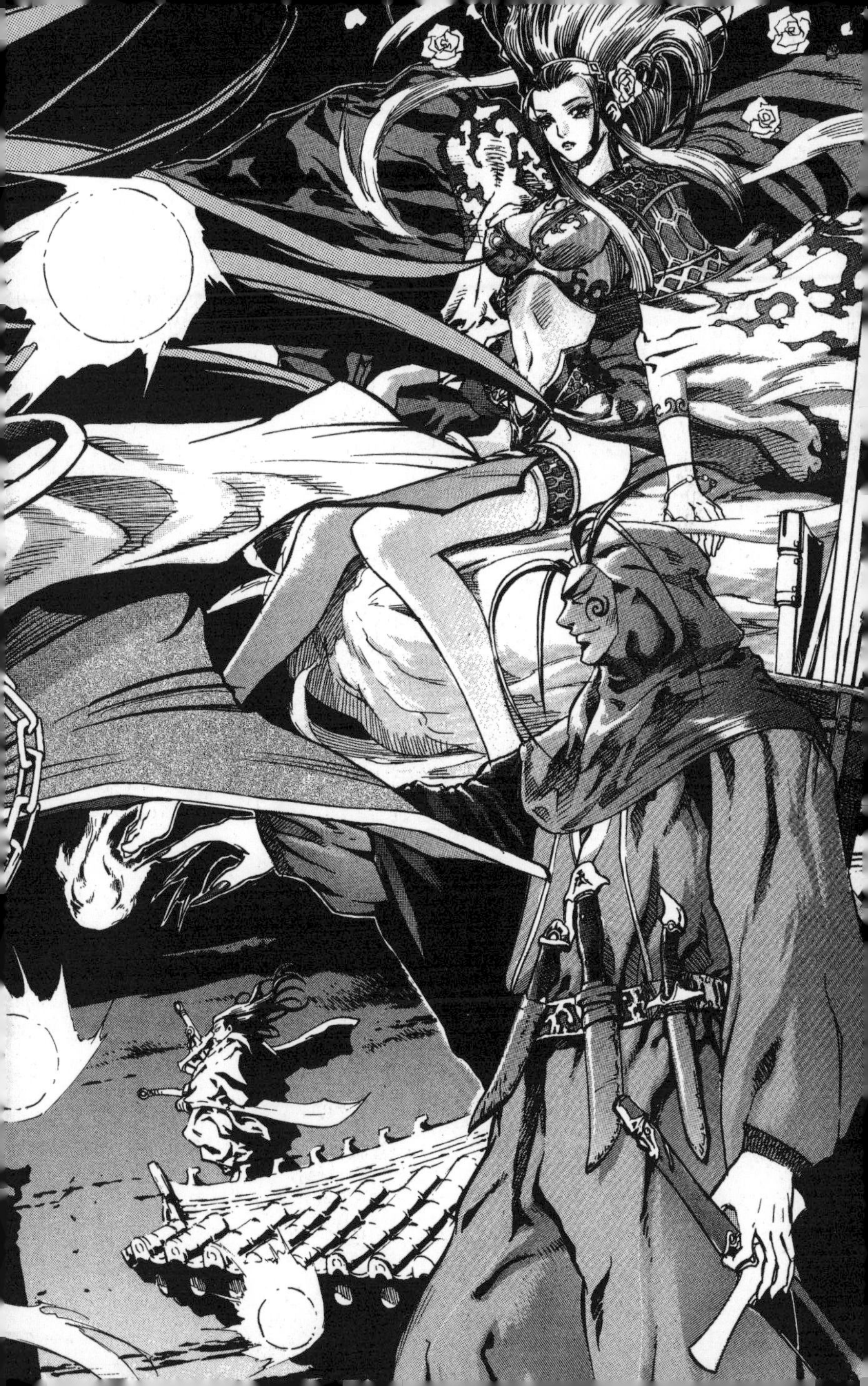

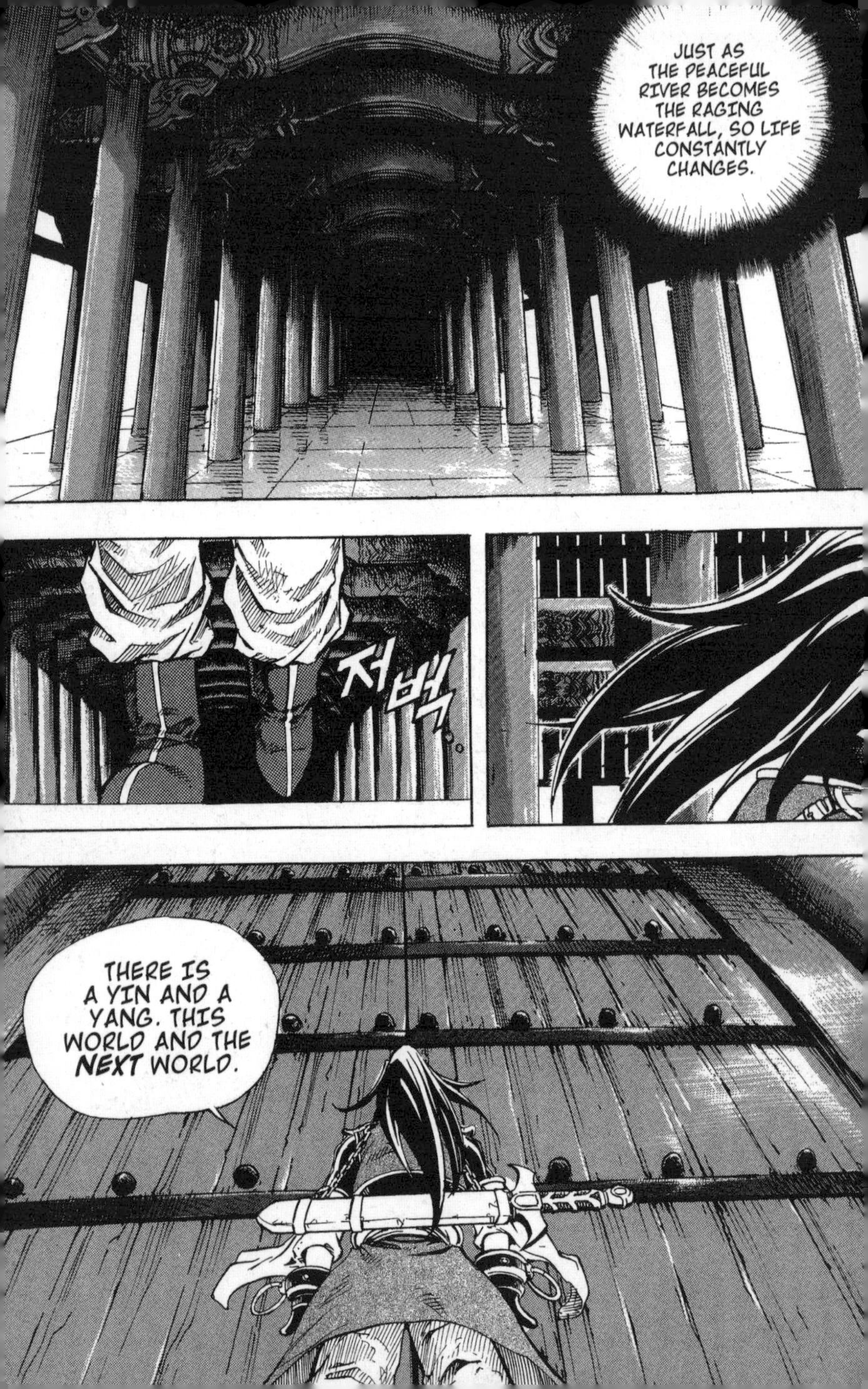
JUST AS THE PEACEFUL RIVER BECOMES THE RAGING WATERFALL, SO LIFE CONSTANTLY CHANGES.
저벅
THERE IS A YIN AND A YANG. THIS WORLD AND THE NEXT WORLD.

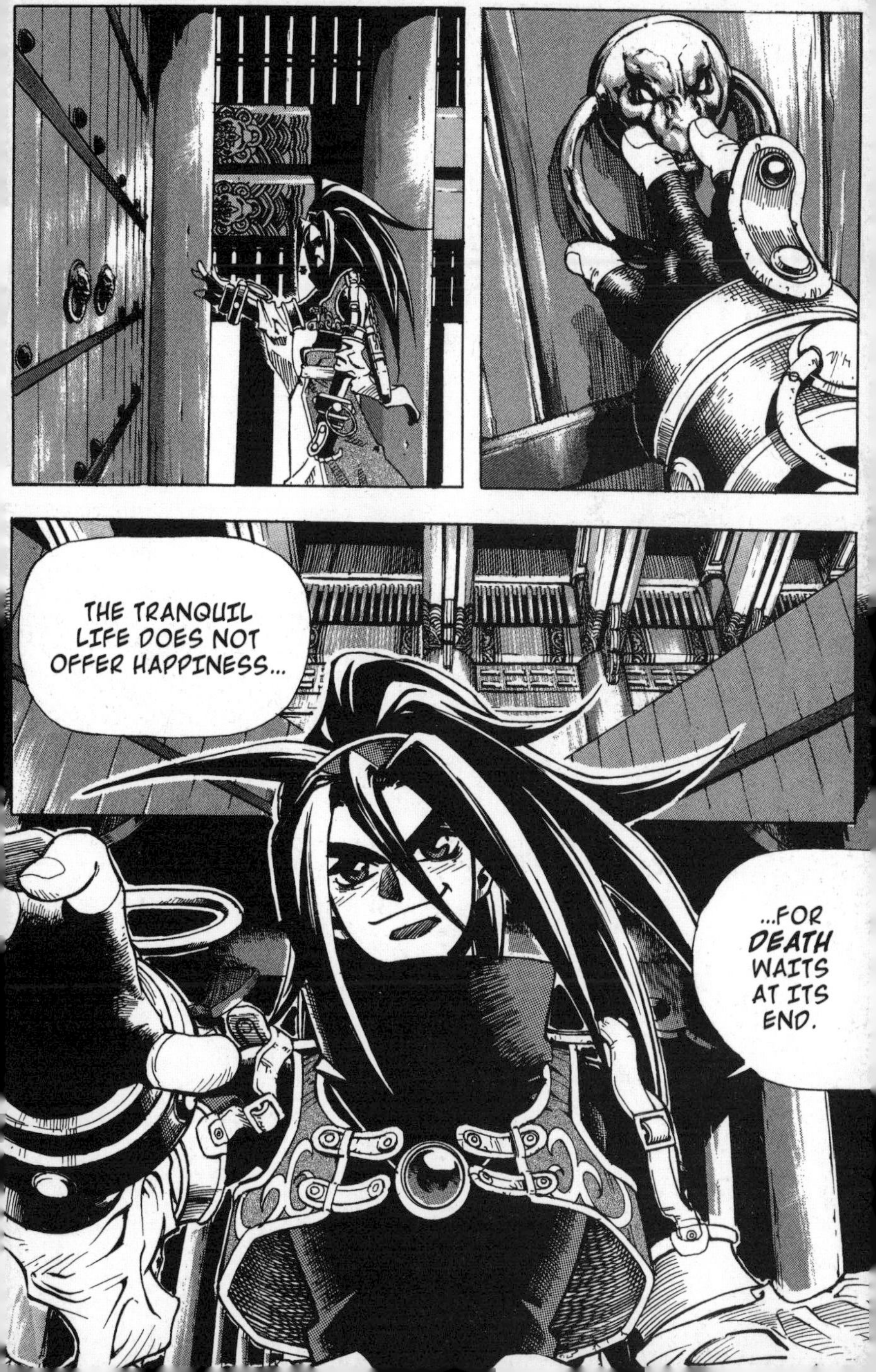
THE TRANQUIL LIFE DOES NOT OFFER HAPPINESS...
...FOR DEATH WAITS AT ITS END.

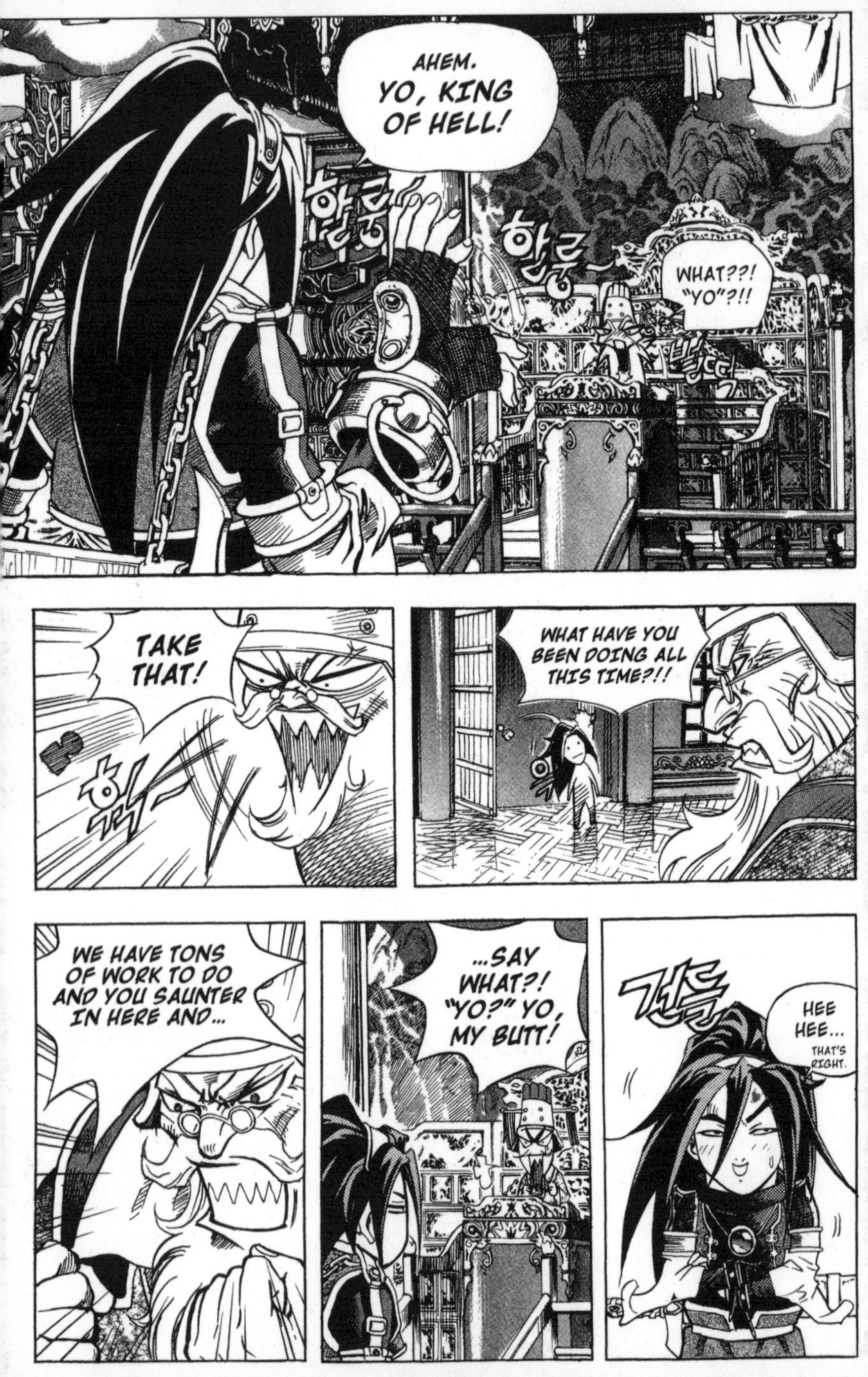
AHEM. YO, KING OF HELL!
WHAT??! "YO"?!!
TAKE THAT!
WHAT HAVE YOU BEEN DOING ALL THIS TIME?!!
WE HAVE TONS OF WORK TO DO AND YOU SAUNTER IN HERE AND...
...SAY WHAT?! "YO?" YO, MY BUTT!
HEE HEE...
THAT'S RIGHT.

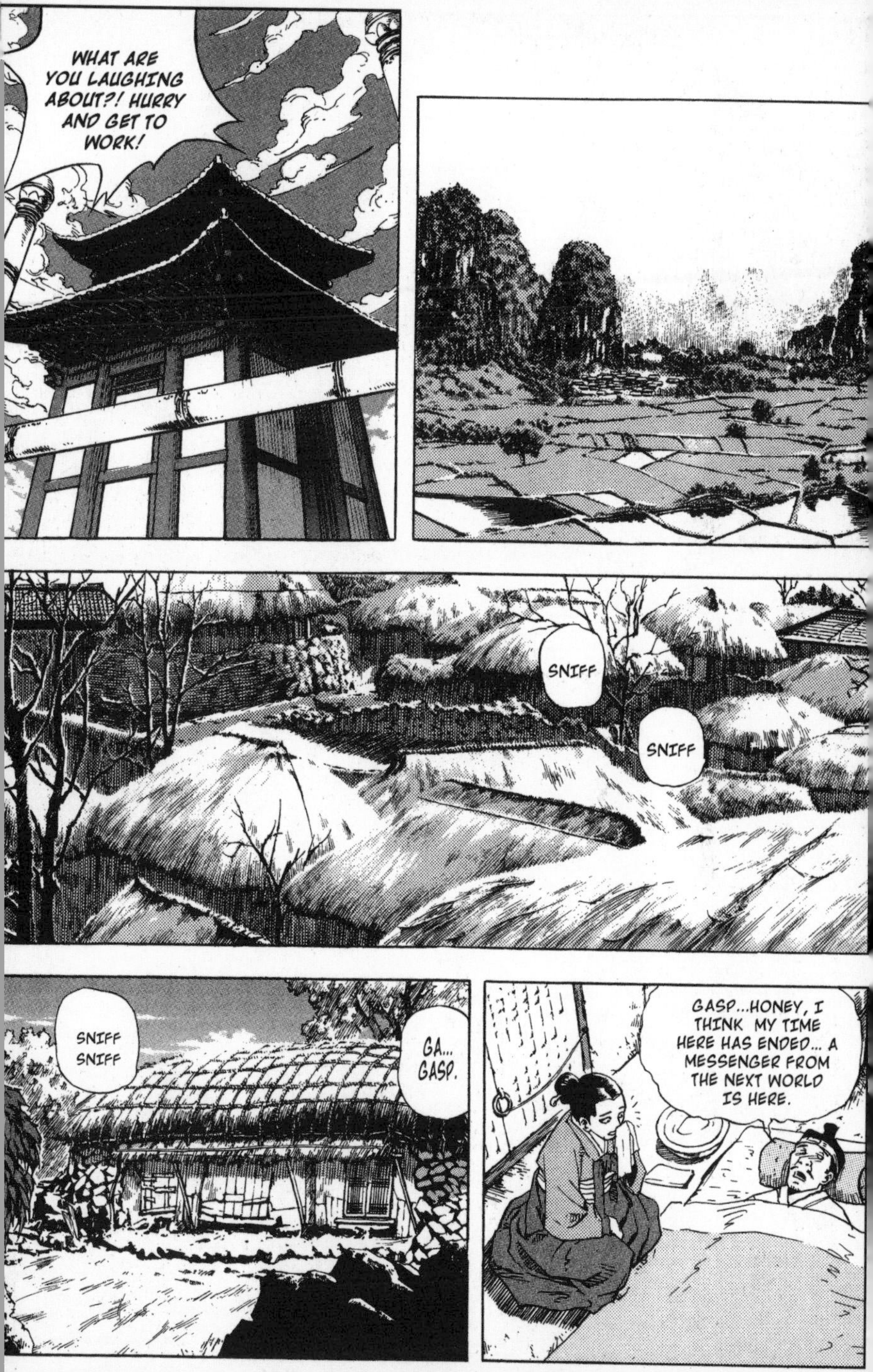
WHAT ARE YOU LAUGHING ABOUT?! HURRY AND GET TO WORK!
SNIFF
SNIFF
SNIFF SNIFF
GA... GASP.
GASP...HONEY, I THINK MY TIME HERE HAS ENDED... A MESSENGER FROM THE NEXT WORLD IS HERE.

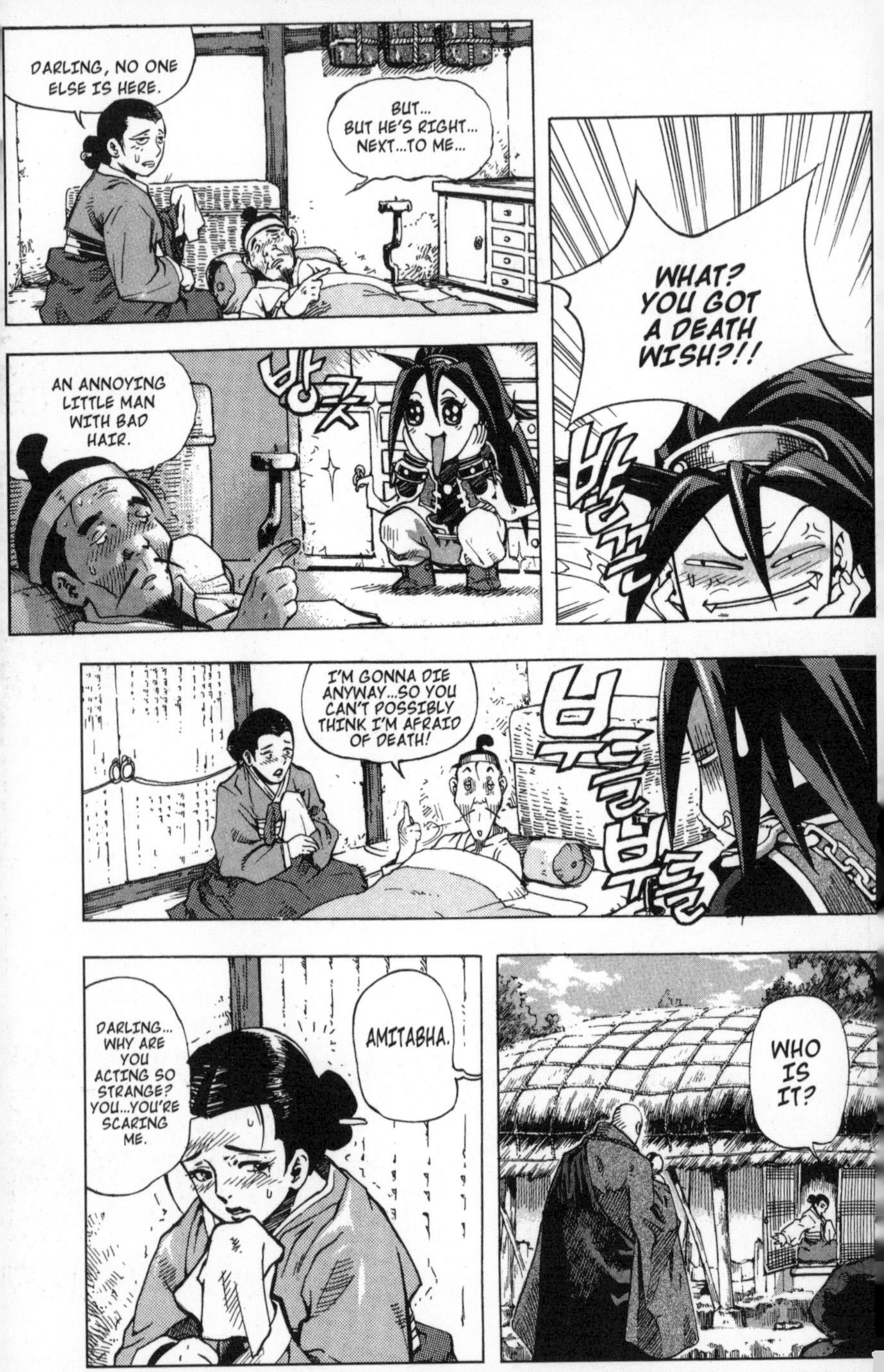
DARLING, NO ONE ELSE IS HERE.
BUT... BUT HE'S RIGHT... NEXT...TO ME...
AN ANNOYING LITTLE MAN WITH BAD HAIR.
WHAT? YOU GOT A DEATH WISH?!!
I'M GONNA DIE ANYWAY...SO YOU CAN'T POSSIBLY THINK I'M AFRAID OF DEATH!
DARLING... WHY ARE YOU ACTING SO STRANGE? YOU...YOU'RE SCARING ME.
AMITABHA.
WHO IS IT?

WOULD YOU PLEASE GIVE AN OFFERING?

AMITABHA.

WHY DON'T YOU ASK THE MONK TO PRAY TO BUDDHA FOR YOU? YOU NEVER KNOW! YOU MIGHT BE ABLE TO GET INTO PARADISE.

ALTHOUGH JUDGING BY YOUR ATTITUDE, I'D SAY YOU'RE BOUND FOR HELL... HEH, HEH...!

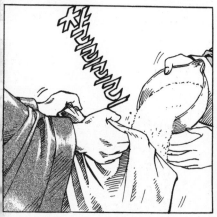

THANK YOU VERY MUCH.

13

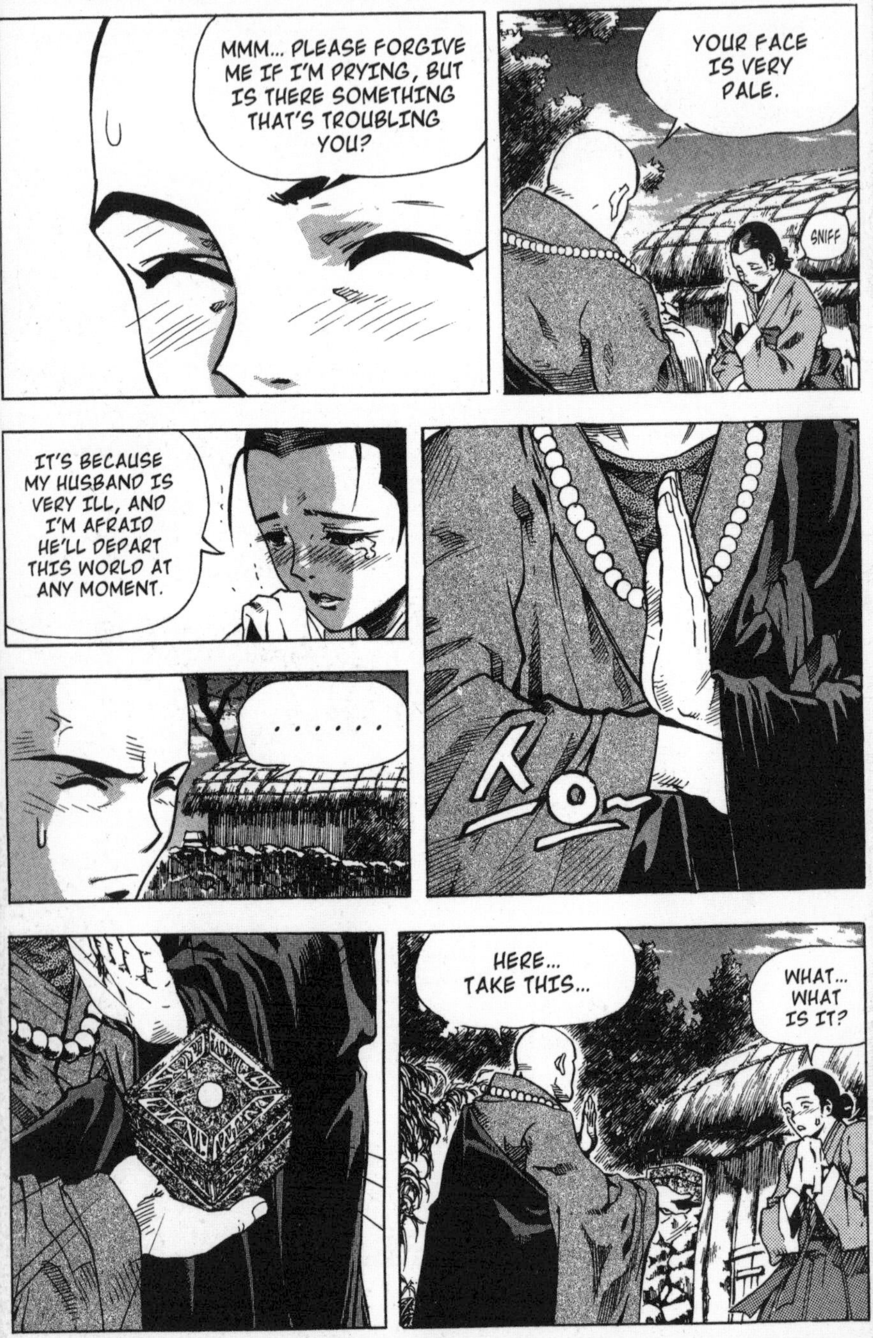
MMM... PLEASE FORGIVE ME IF I'M PRYING, BUT IS THERE SOMETHING THAT'S TROUBLING YOU?
YOUR FACE IS VERY PALE.
SNIFF
IT'S BECAUSE MY HUSBAND IS VERY ILL, AND I'M AFRAID HE'LL DEPART THIS WORLD AT ANY MOMENT.
....
HERE... TAKE THIS...
WHAT... WHAT IS IT?

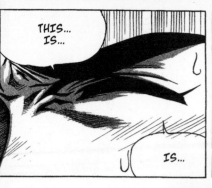

THIS...
IS...

IS...

...SOMETHING POWERFUL... SOMETHING THAT CAN EVEN RAISE THE DEAD...

...MEDICINE FROM THE SORIM TEMPLE!!!

GASP!

MEDICINE... FROM THE SORIM TEMPLE...? YOU MUST BE...

A MEDICINE SELLER.

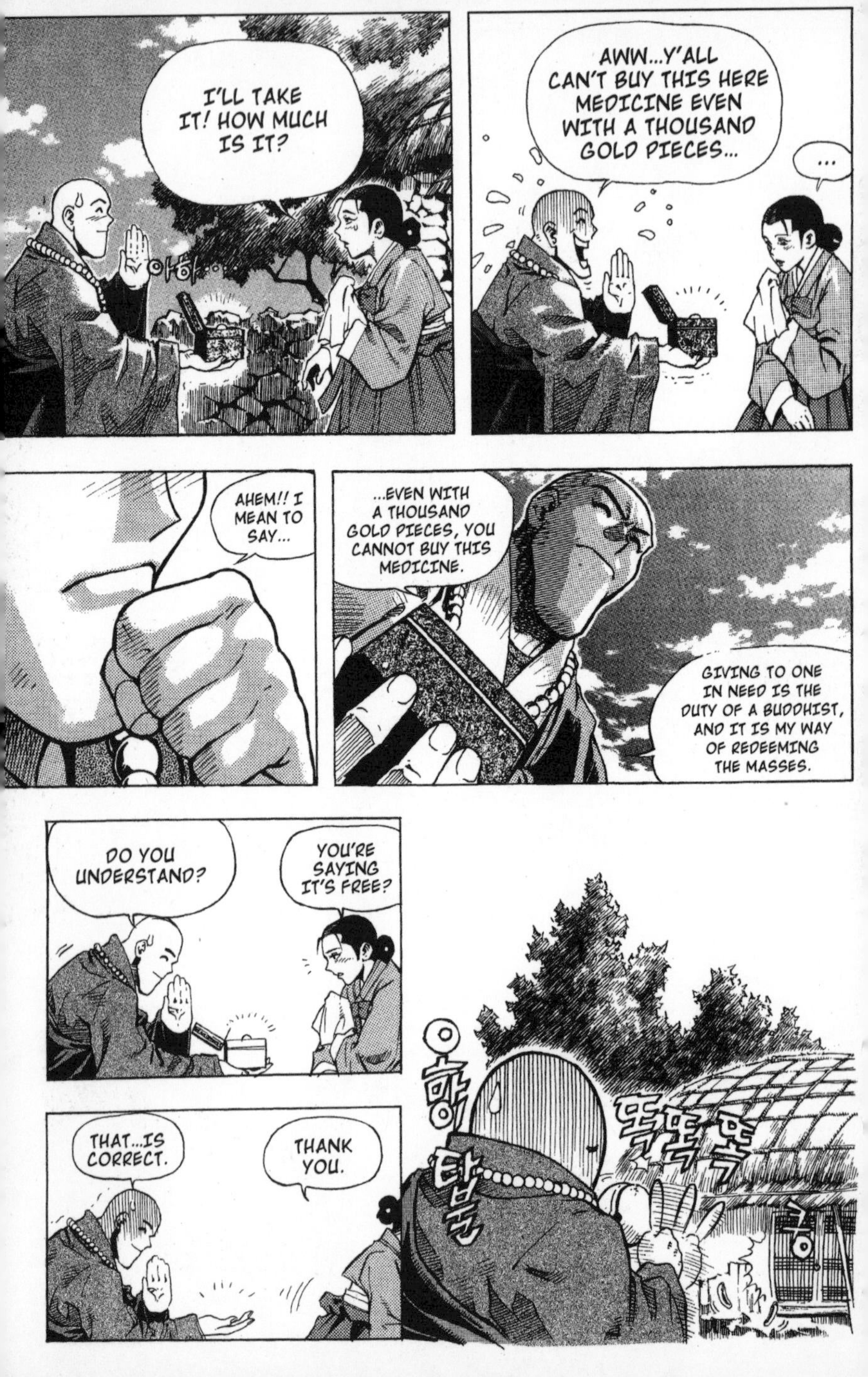
I'LL TAKE IT! HOW MUCH IS IT?
아하....
AWW...Y'ALL CAN'T BUY THIS HERE MEDICINE EVEN WITH A THOUSAND GOLD PIECES...
...
AHEM!! I MEAN TO SAY...
...EVEN WITH A THOUSAND GOLD PIECES, YOU CANNOT BUY THIS MEDICINE.
GIVING TO ONE IN NEED IS THE DUTY OF A BUDDHIST, AND IT IS MY WAY OF REDEEMING THE MASSES.
DO YOU UNDERSTAND?
YOU'RE SAYING IT'S FREE?
THAT...IS CORRECT.
THANK YOU.
똑똑똑
쿵

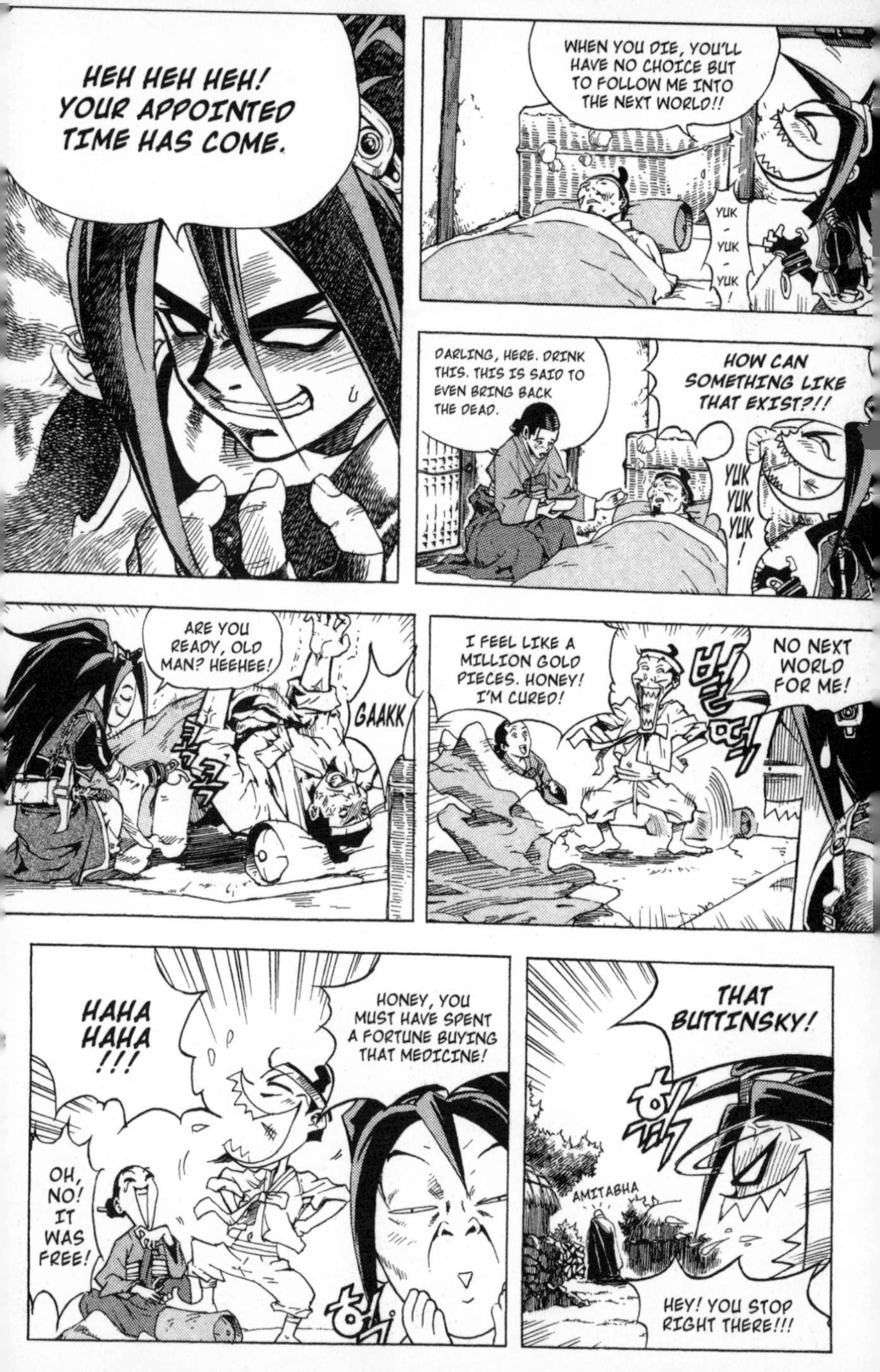
HEH HEH HEH! YOUR APPOINTED TIME HAS COME.
WHEN YOU DIE, YOU'LL HAVE NO CHOICE BUT TO FOLLOW ME INTO THE NEXT WORLD!!
YUK - YUK - YUK!
DARLING, HERE. DRINK THIS. THIS IS SAID TO EVEN BRING BACK THE DEAD.
HOW CAN SOMETHING LIKE THAT EXIST?!!
YUK YUK YUK!
ARE YOU READY, OLD MAN? HEEHEE!
GAAKK
I FEEL LIKE A MILLION GOLD PIECES. HONEY! I'M CURED!
벌떡
NO NEXT WORLD FOR ME!
HAHA HAHA !!!
HONEY, YOU MUST HAVE SPENT A FORTUNE BUYING THAT MEDICINE!
OH, NO! IT WAS FREE!
THAT BUTTINSKY!
AMITABHA
HEY! YOU STOP RIGHT THERE!!!

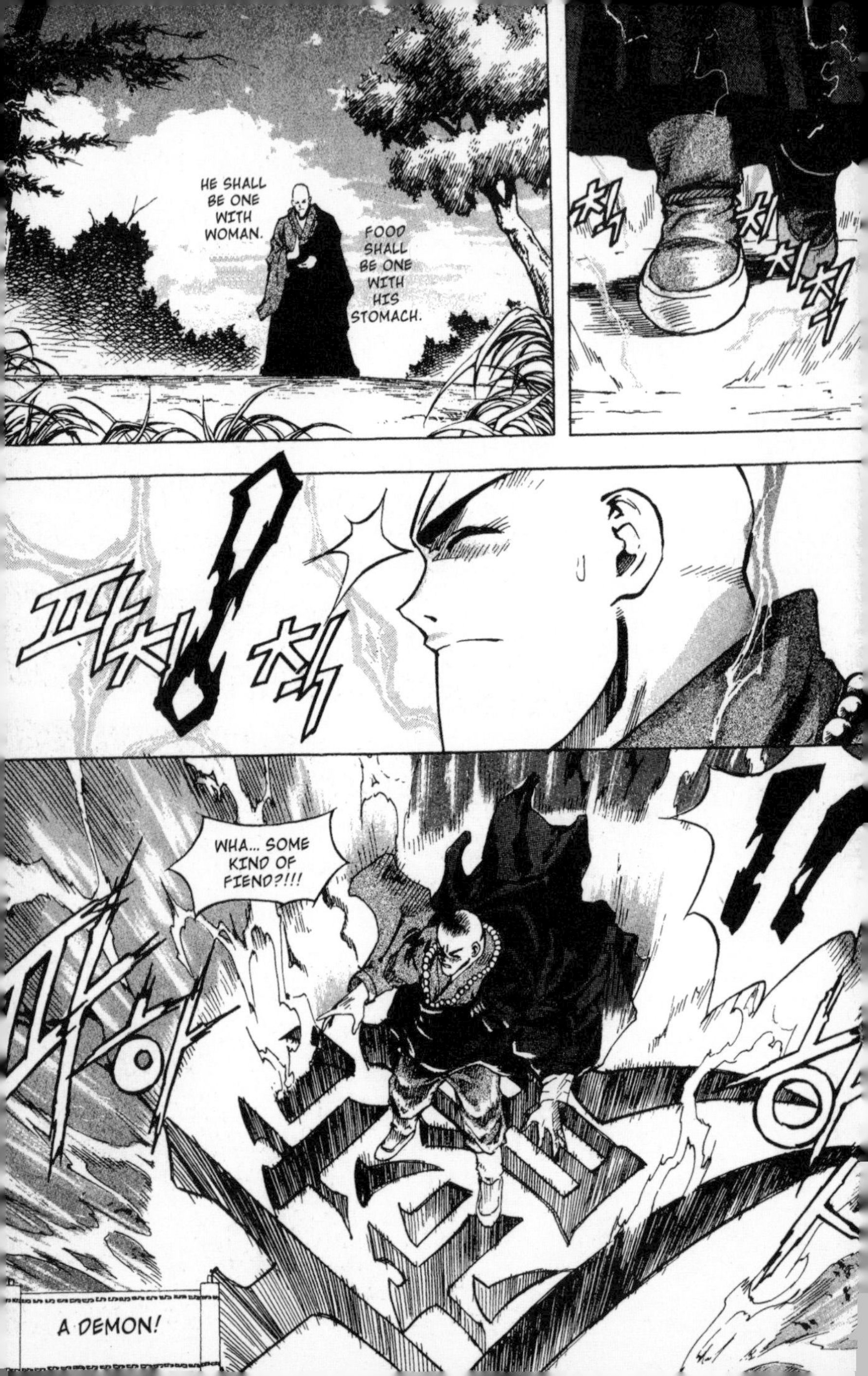
HE SHALL BE ONE WITH WOMAN.
FOOD SHALL BE ONE WITH HIS STOMACH.
WHA... SOME KIND OF FIEND?!!!
A DEMON!

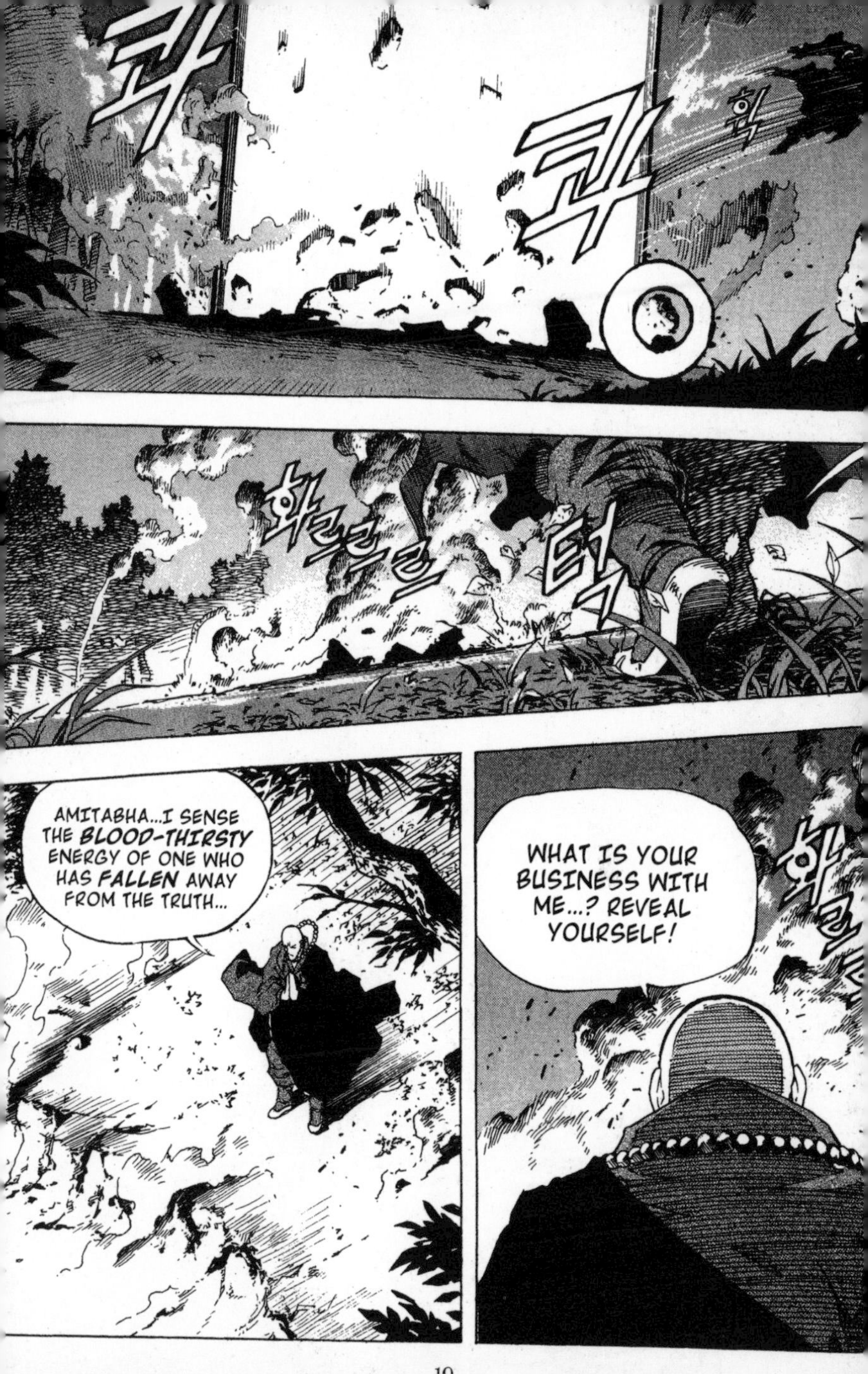
AMITABHA...I SENSE THE BLOOD-THIRSTY ENERGY OF ONE WHO HAS FALLEN AWAY FROM THE TRUTH...
WHAT IS YOUR BUSINESS WITH ME...? REVEAL YOURSELF!

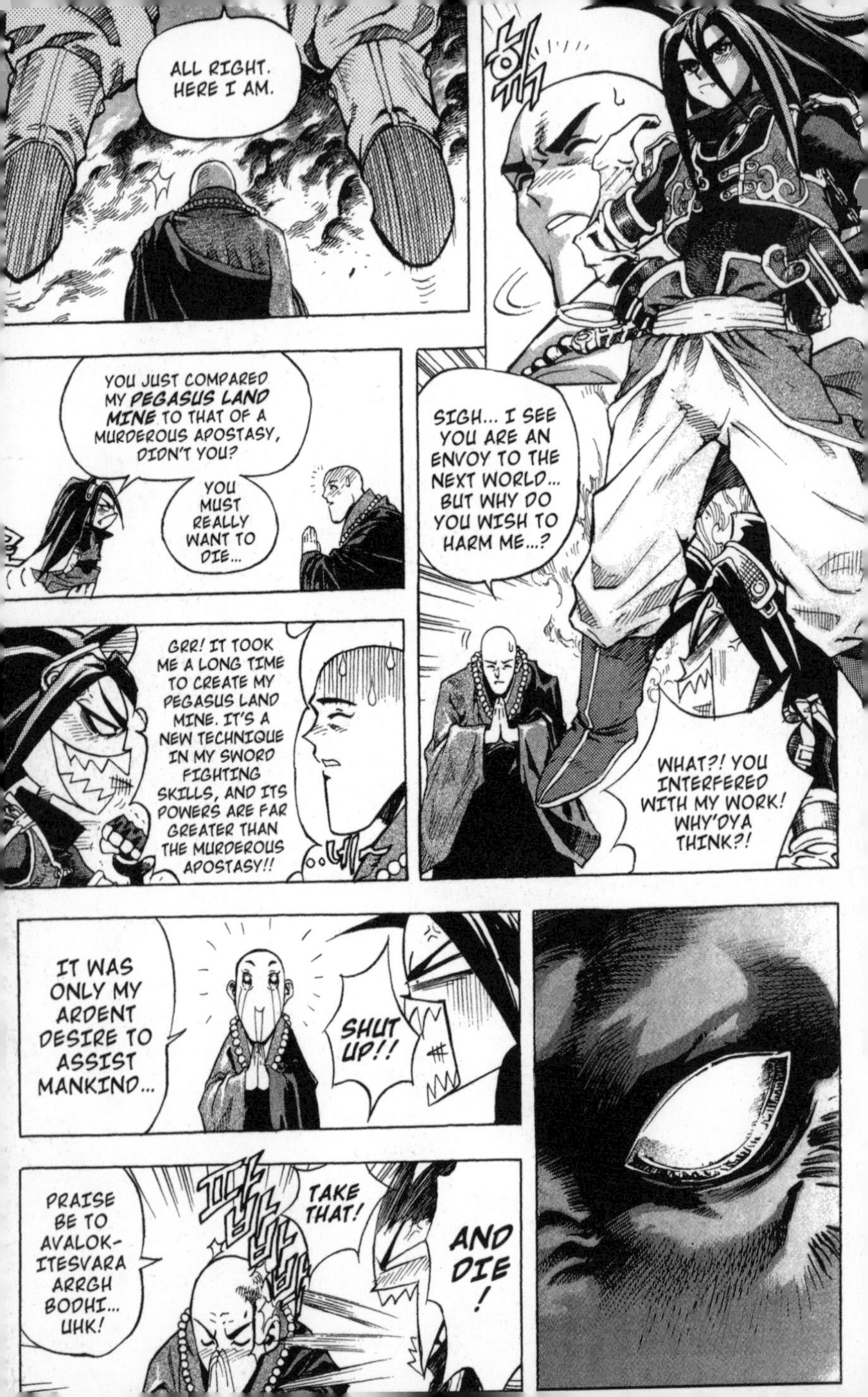
ALL RIGHT. HERE I AM.
YOU JUST COMPARED MY **PEGASUS LAND MINE** TO THAT OF A MURDEROUS APOSTASY, DIDN'T YOU?
YOU MUST REALLY WANT TO DIE...
GRR! IT TOOK ME A LONG TIME TO CREATE MY PEGASUS LAND MINE. IT'S A NEW TECHNIQUE IN MY SWORD FIGHTING SKILLS, AND ITS POWERS ARE FAR GREATER THAN THE MURDEROUS APOSTASY!!
SIGH... I SEE YOU ARE AN ENVOY TO THE NEXT WORLD... BUT WHY DO YOU WISH TO HARM ME...?
WHAT?! YOU INTERFERED WITH MY WORK! WHY'DYA THINK?!
IT WAS ONLY MY ARDENT DESIRE TO ASSIST MANKIND...
SHUT UP!!
PRAISE BE TO AVALOK-ITESVARA ARRGH BODHI... UHK!
TAKE THAT!
AND DIE!

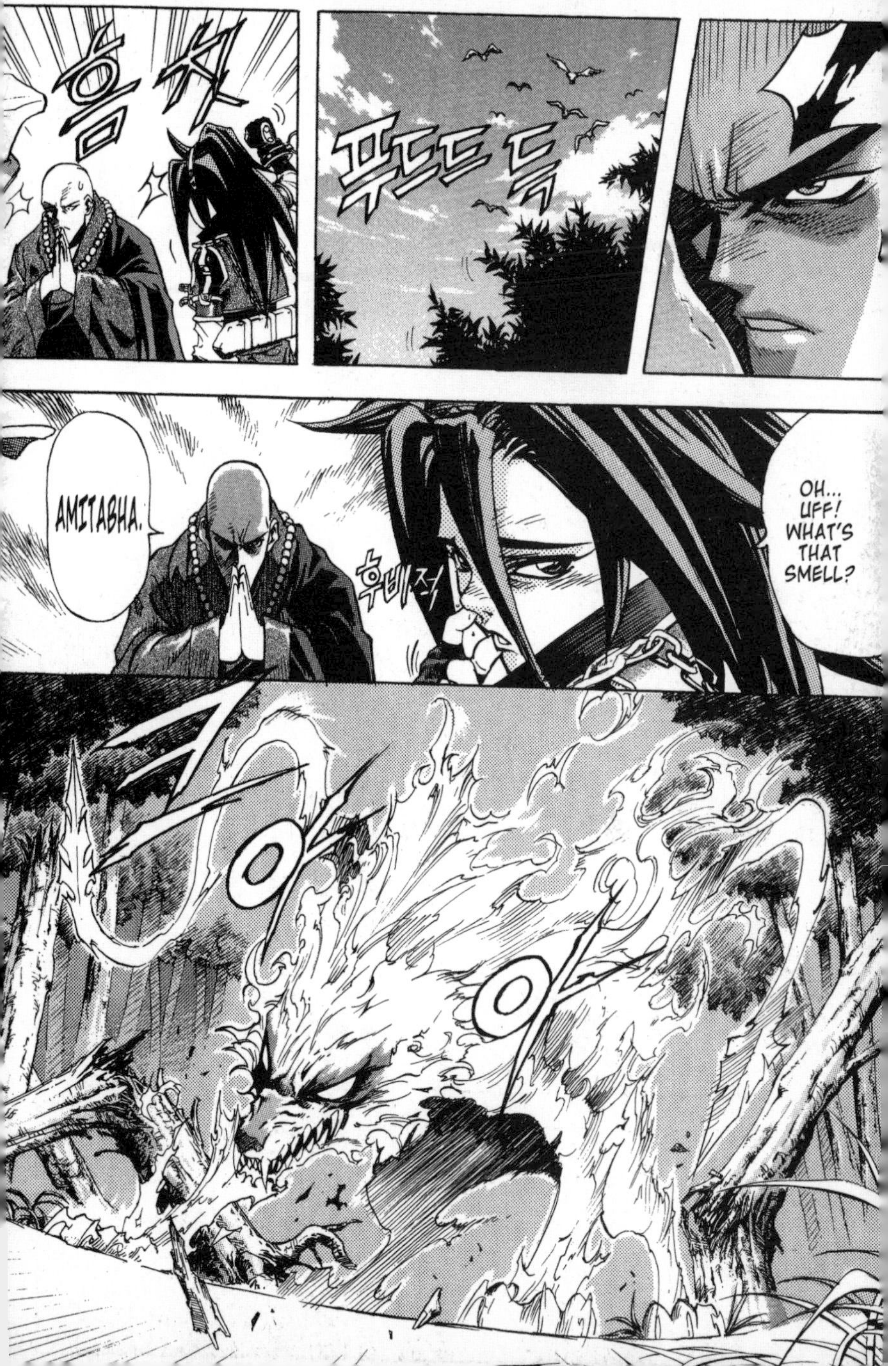

흠칫
푸드드득
AMITABHA.
후비적
OH... UFF! WHAT'S THAT SMELL?

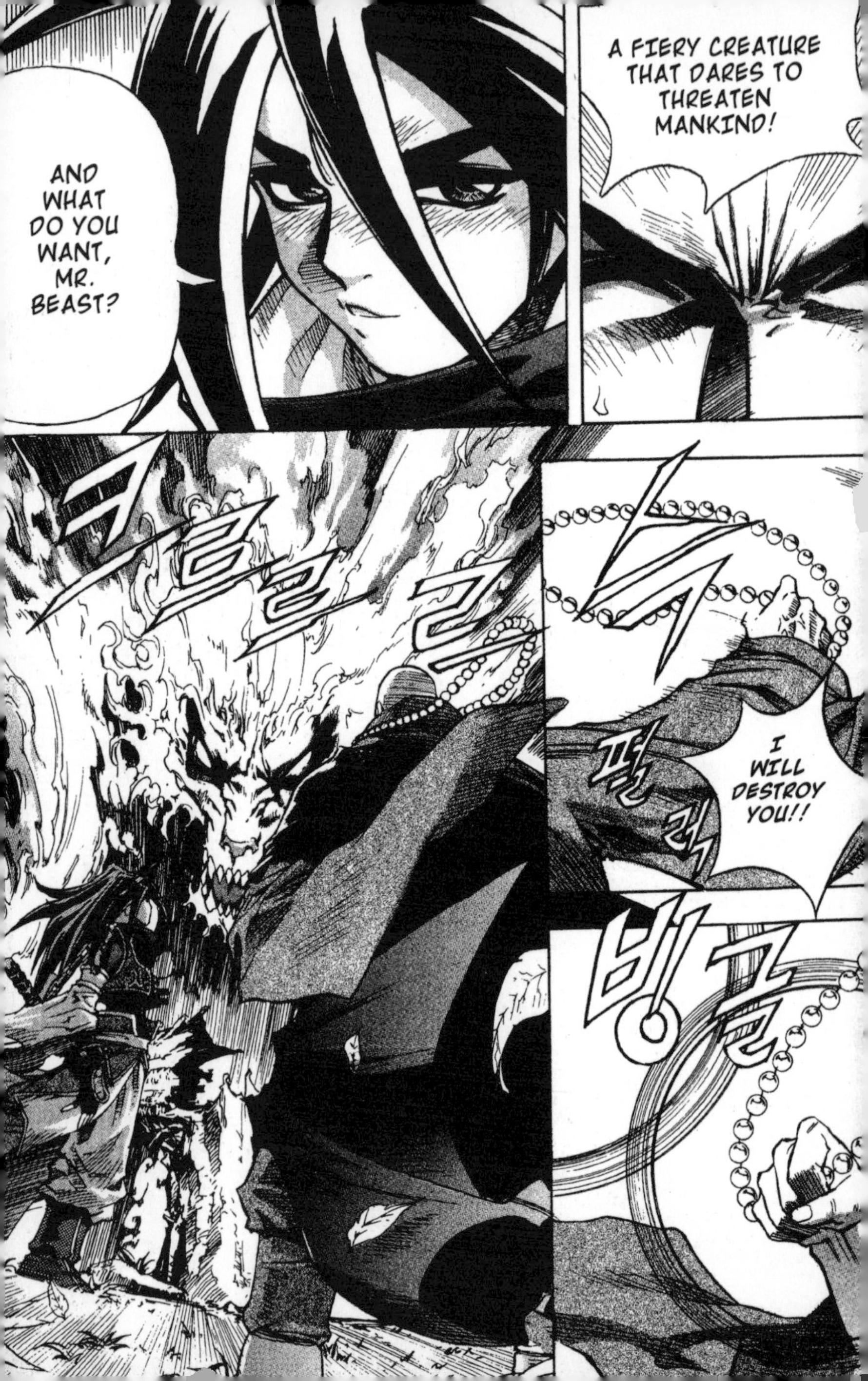
AND WHAT DO YOU WANT, MR. BEAST?
A FIERY CREATURE THAT DARES TO THREATEN MANKIND!
I WILL DESTROY YOU!!

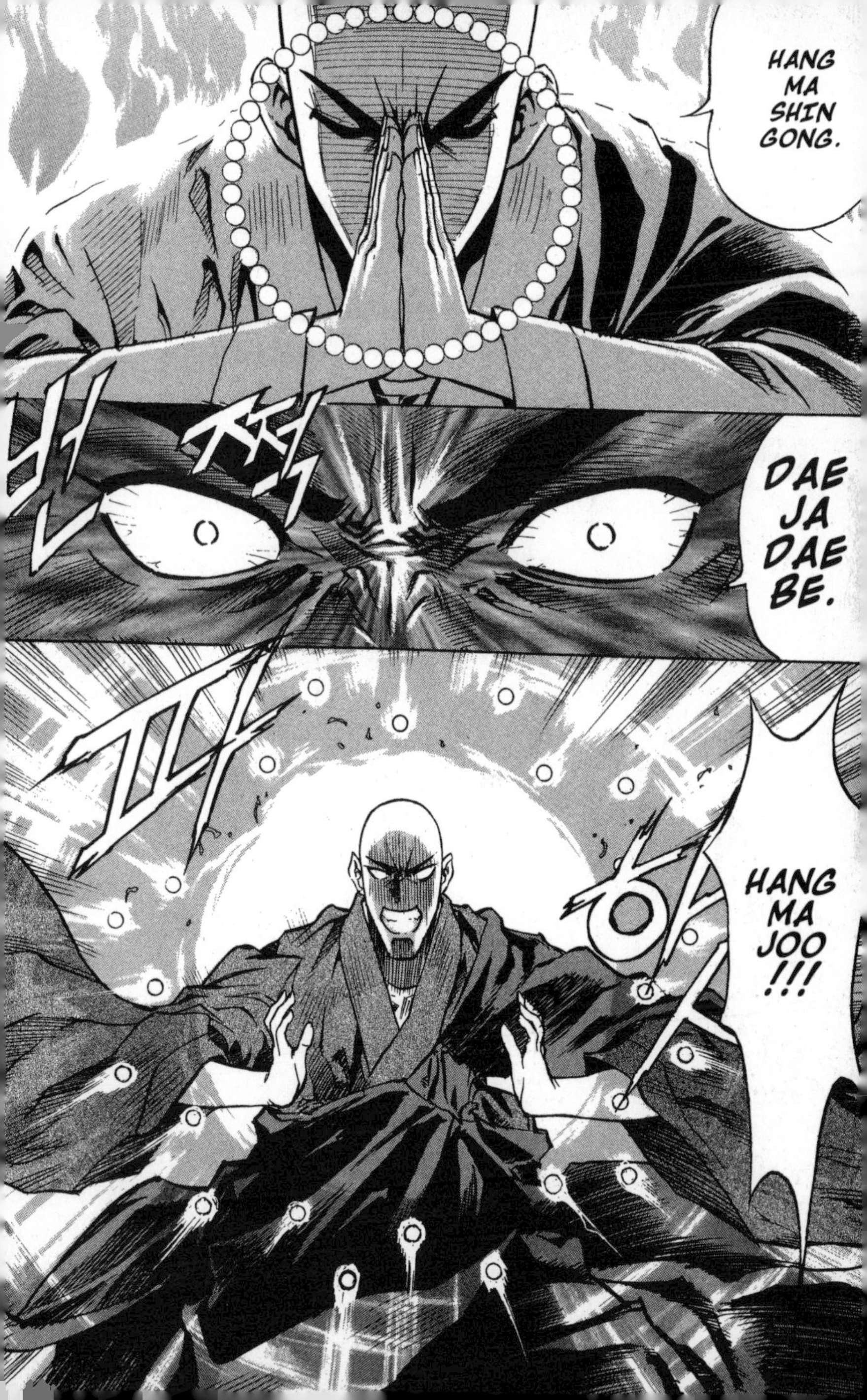
HANG MA SHIN GONG.
DAE JA DAE BE.
HANG MA JOO!!!

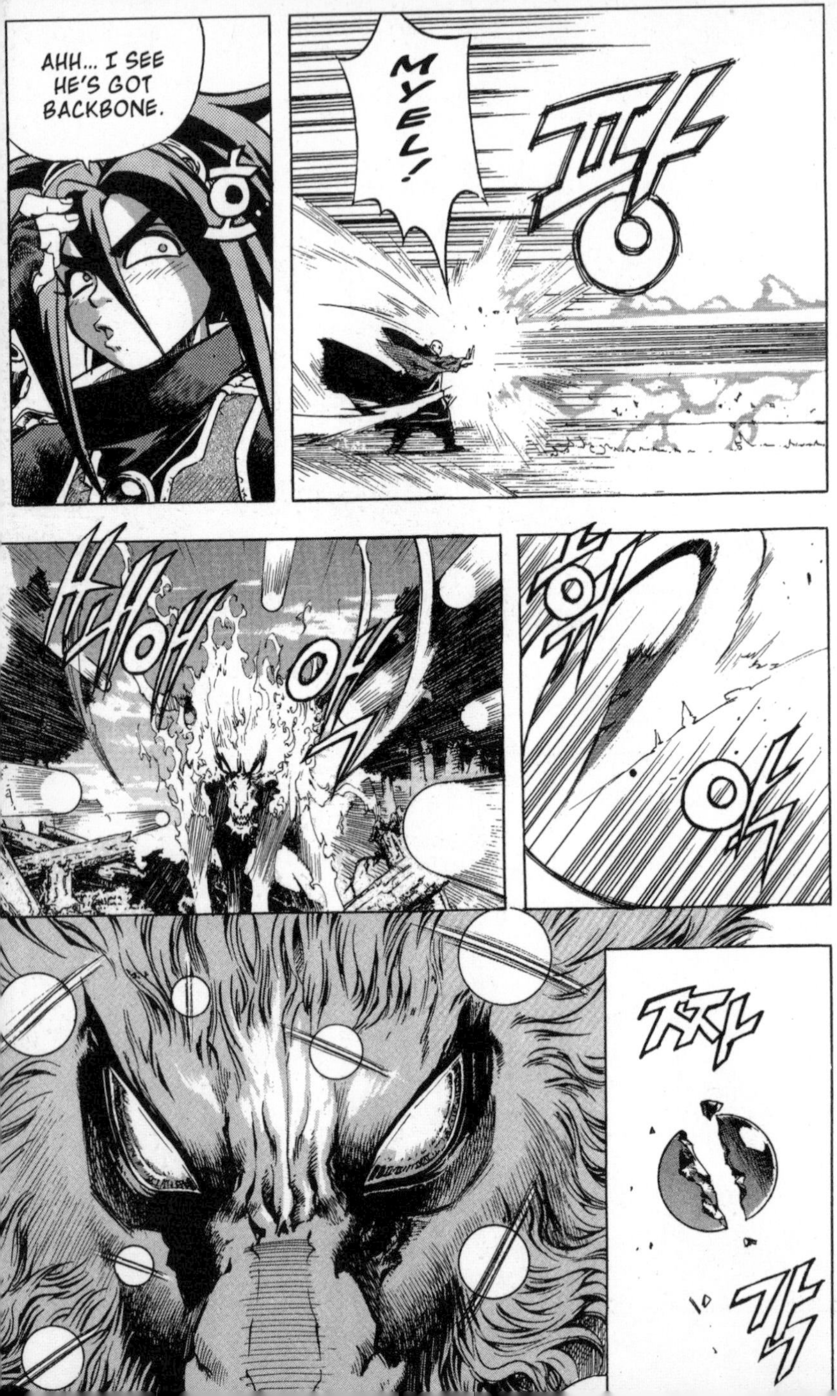
AHH... I SEE HE'S GOT BACKBONE.
MYEL!

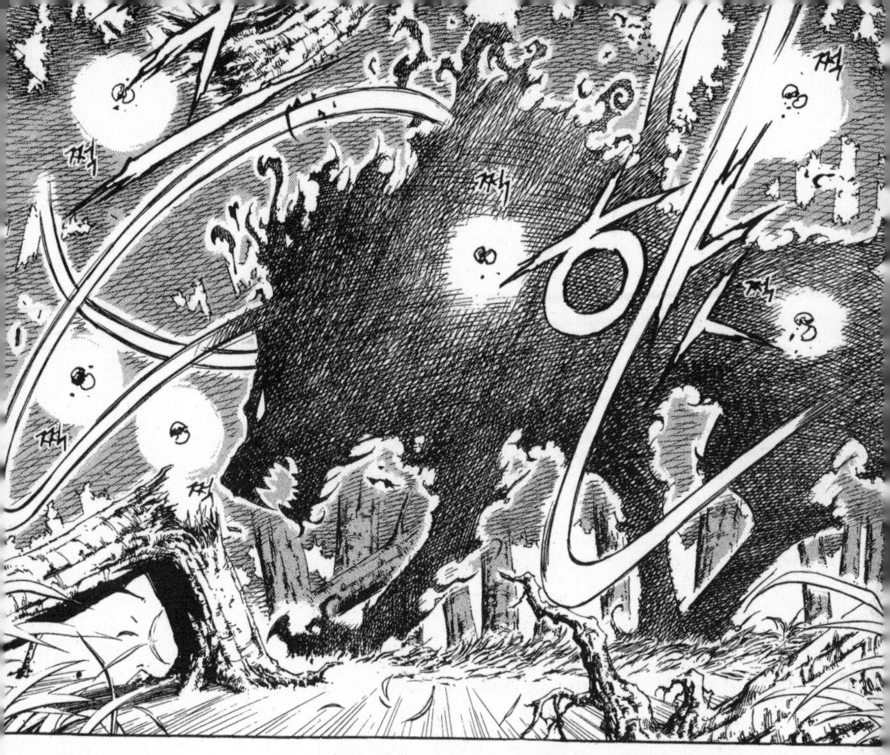

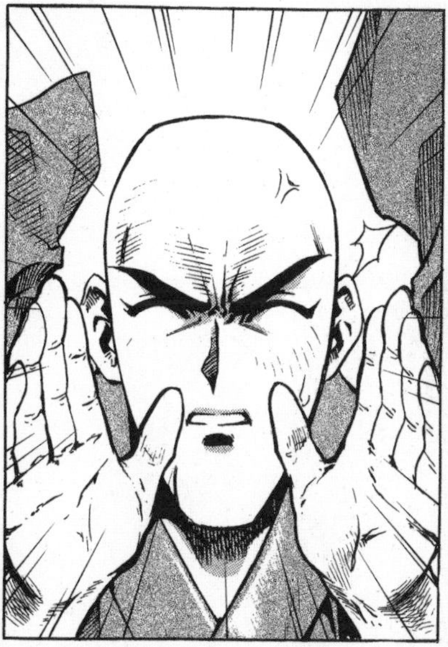

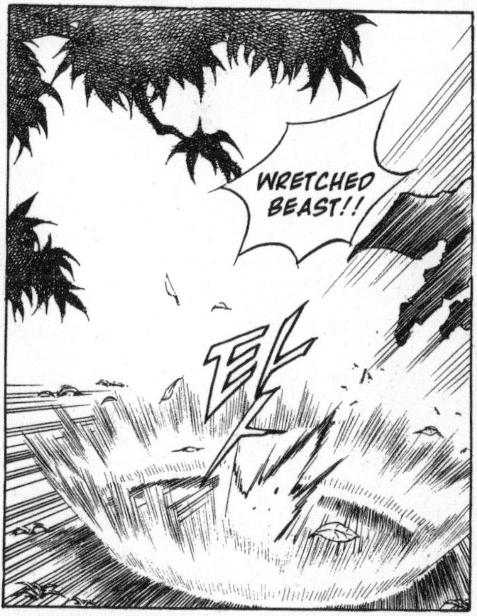
WRETCHED BEAST!!

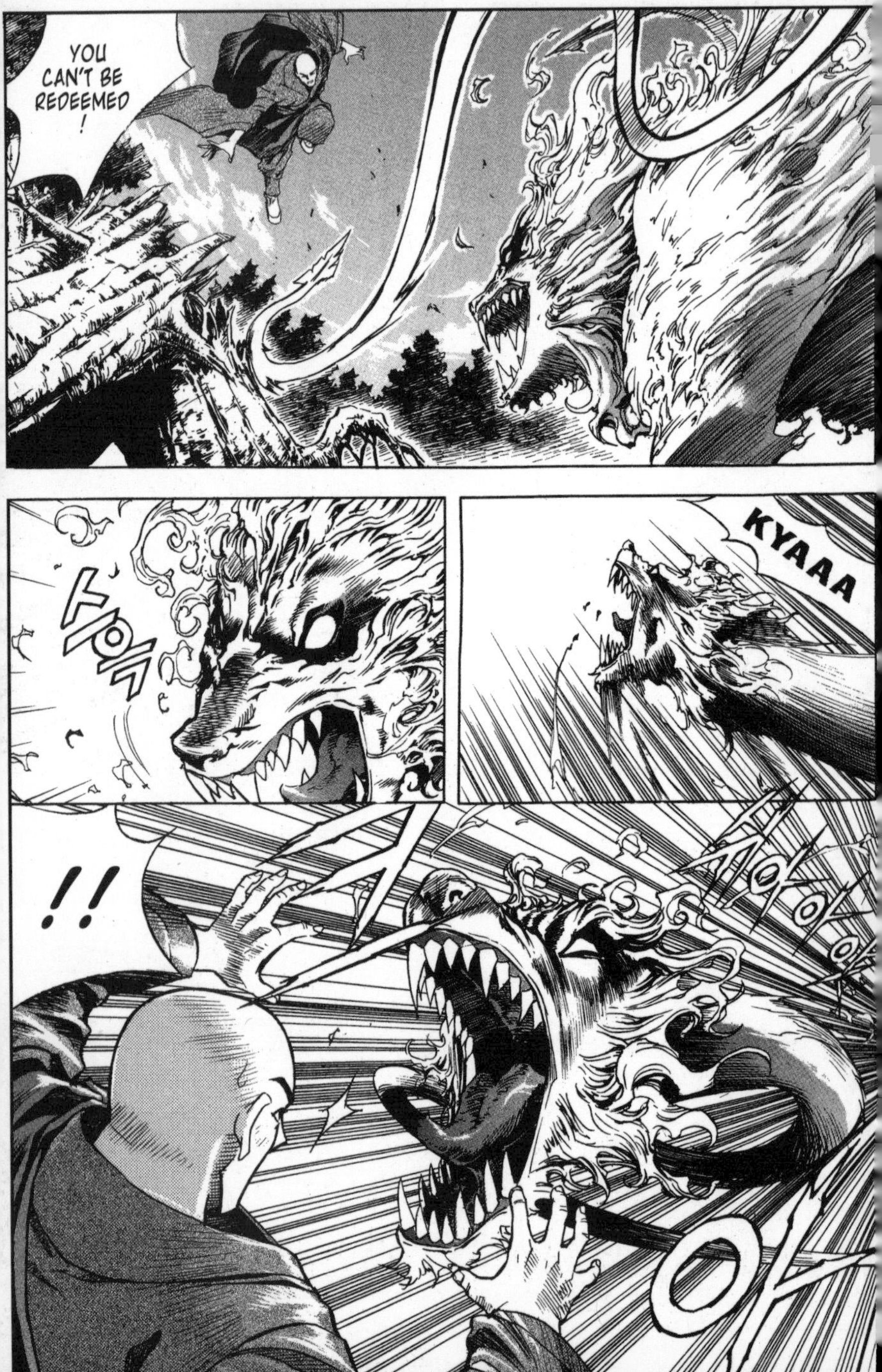
YOU CAN'T BE REDEEMED !
KYAAA
!!

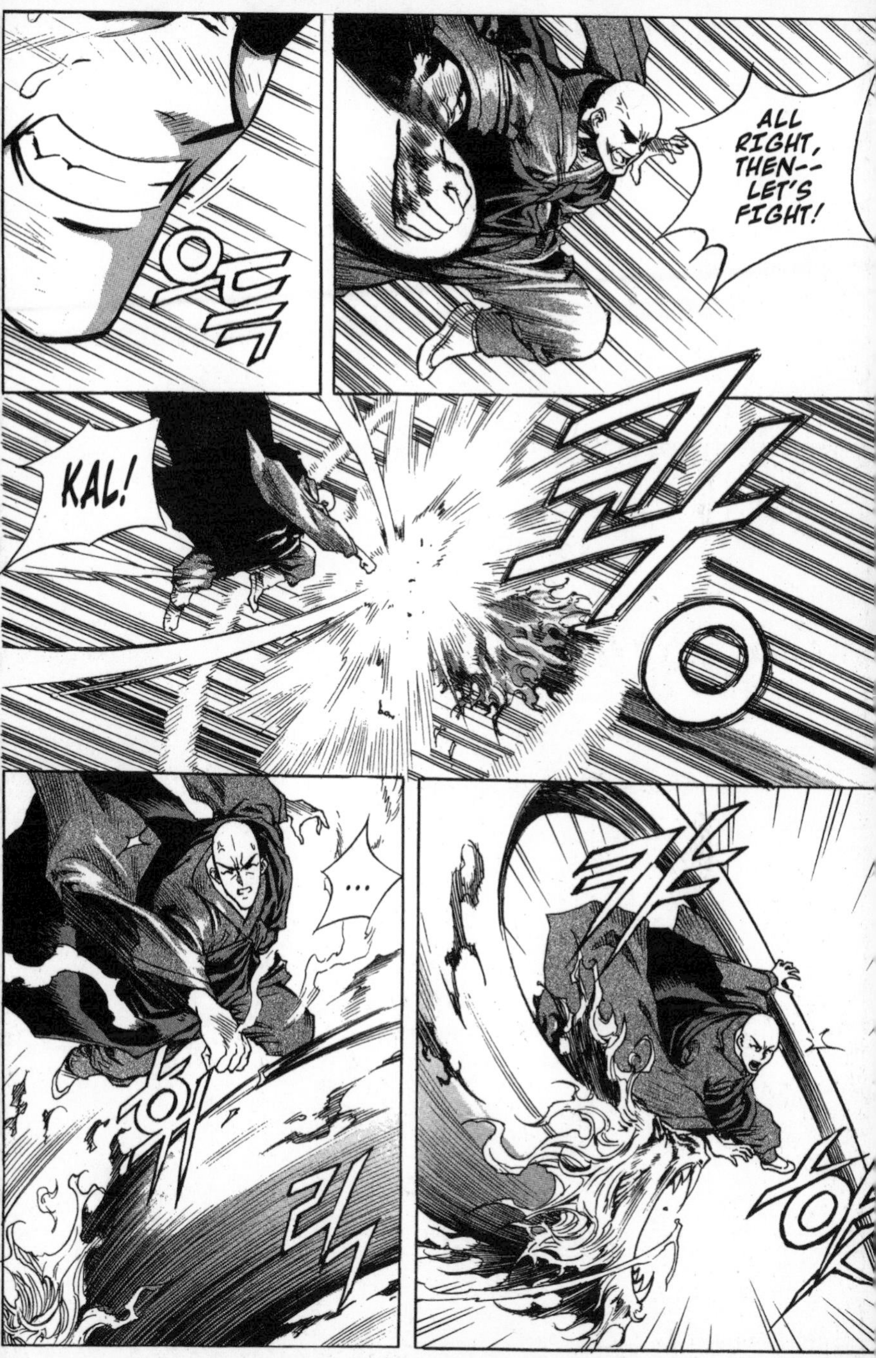
ALL RIGHT, THEN--LET'S FIGHT!
KAL!
...

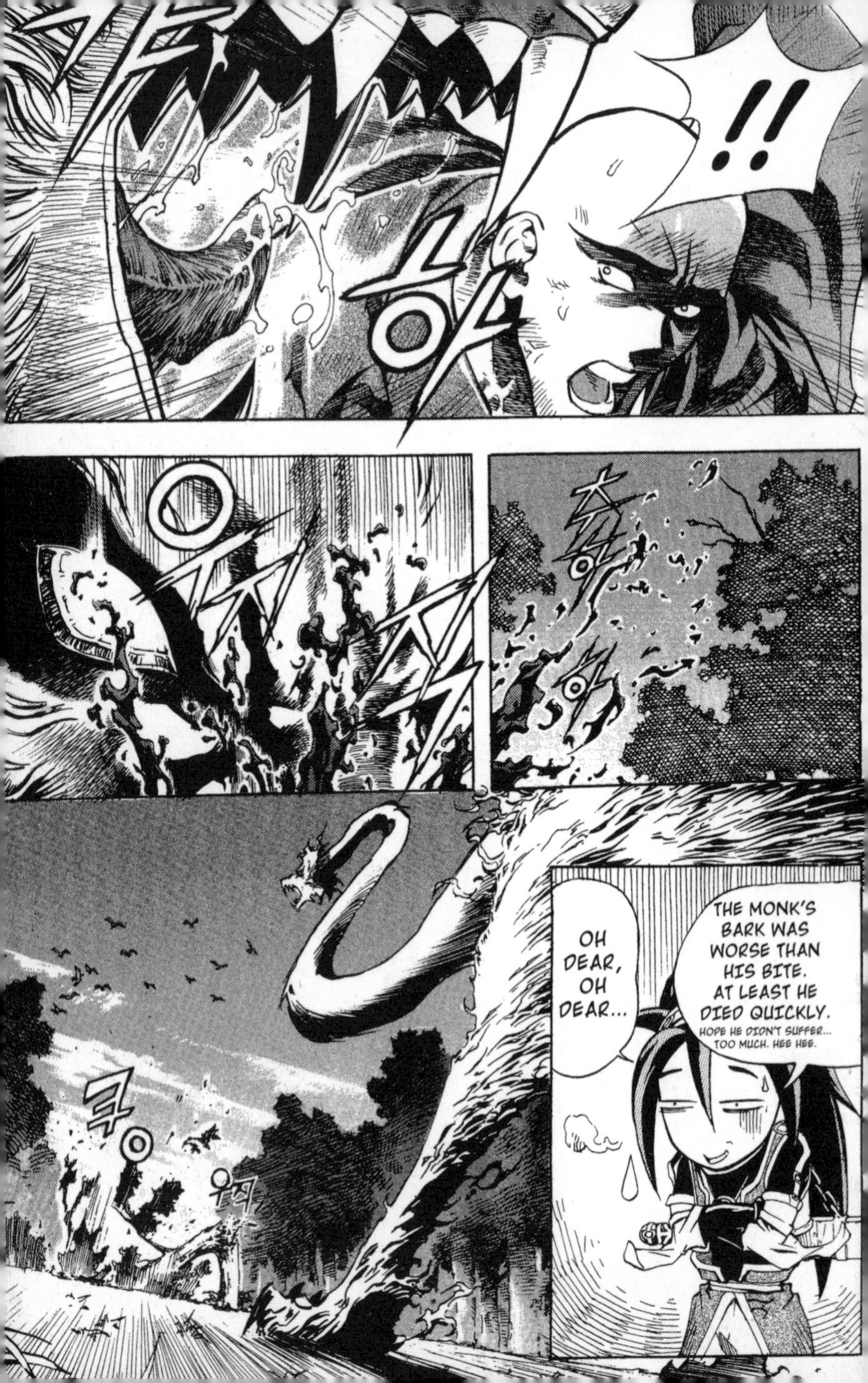
!!
OH DEAR, OH DEAR...
THE MONK'S BARK WAS WORSE THAN HIS BITE. AT LEAST HE DIED QUICKLY.
HOPE HE DIDN'T SUFFER... TOO MUCH. HEE HEE.

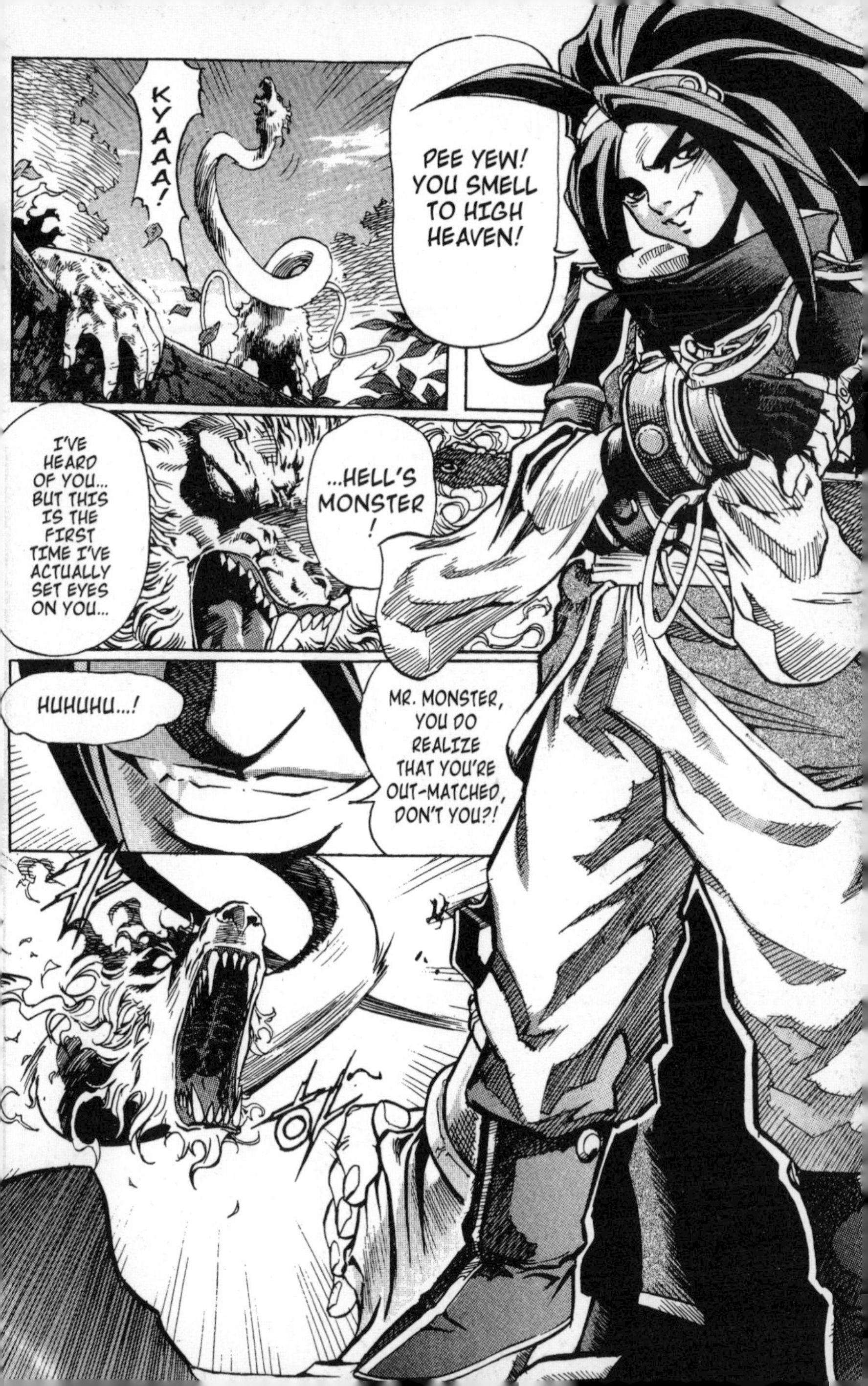
KYAAA!
PEE YEW! YOU SMELL TO HIGH HEAVEN!
I'VE HEARD OF YOU... BUT THIS IS THE FIRST TIME I'VE ACTUALLY SET EYES ON YOU...
...HELL'S MONSTER!
HUHUHU...!
MR. MONSTER, YOU DO REALIZE THAT YOU'RE OUT-MATCHED, DON'T YOU?!

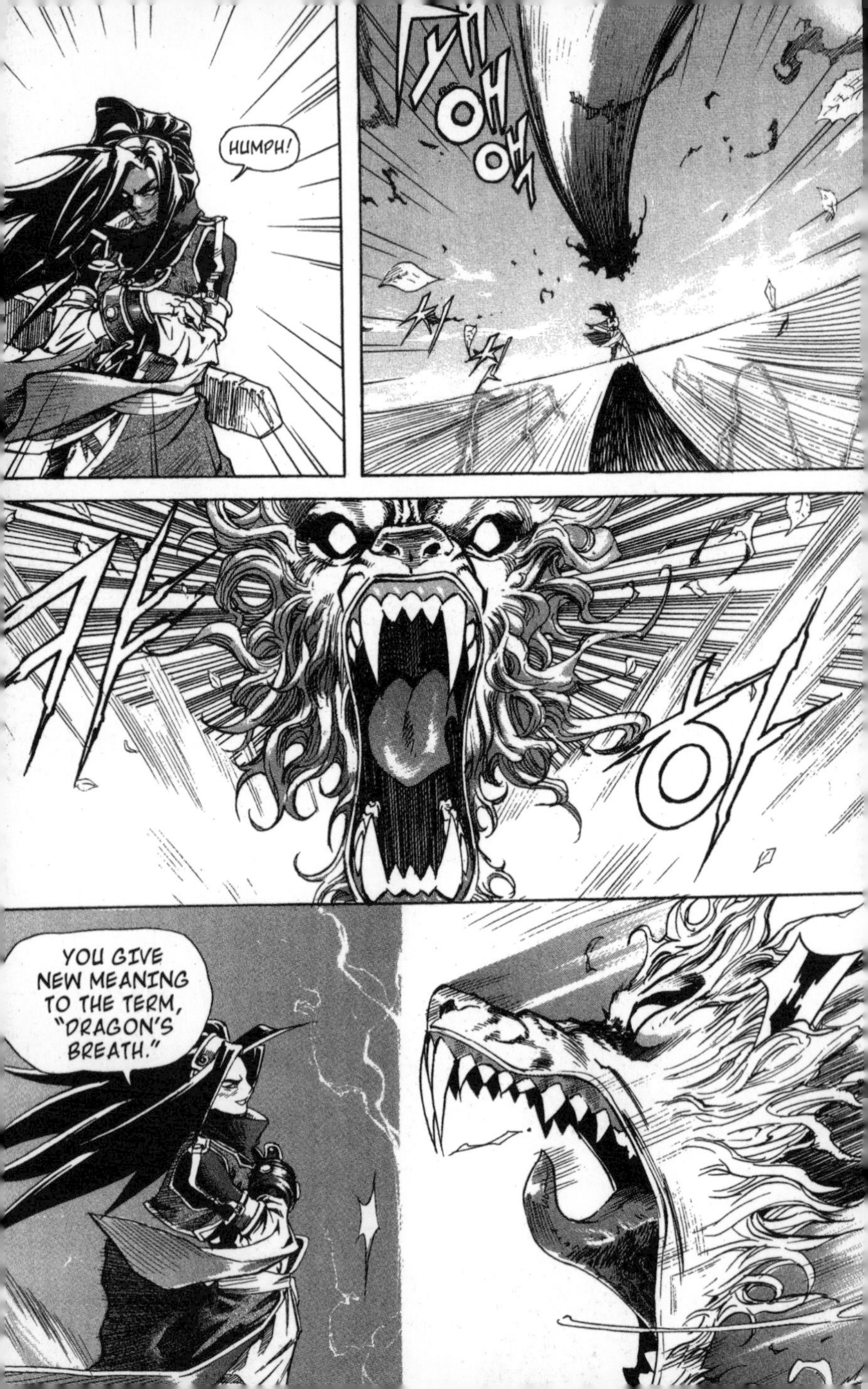
HUMPH!
YOU GIVE NEW MEANING TO THE TERM, "DRAGON'S BREATH."

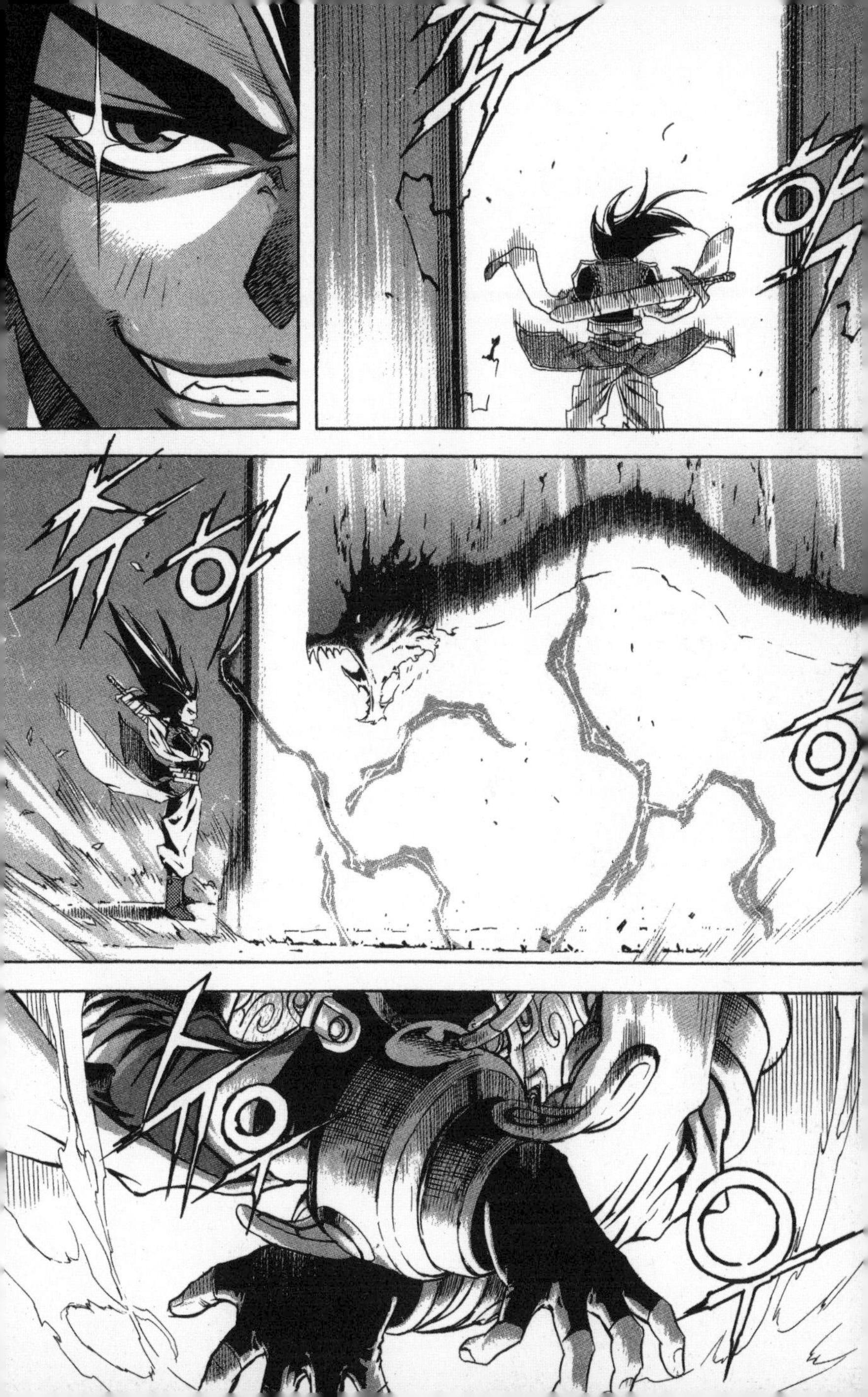

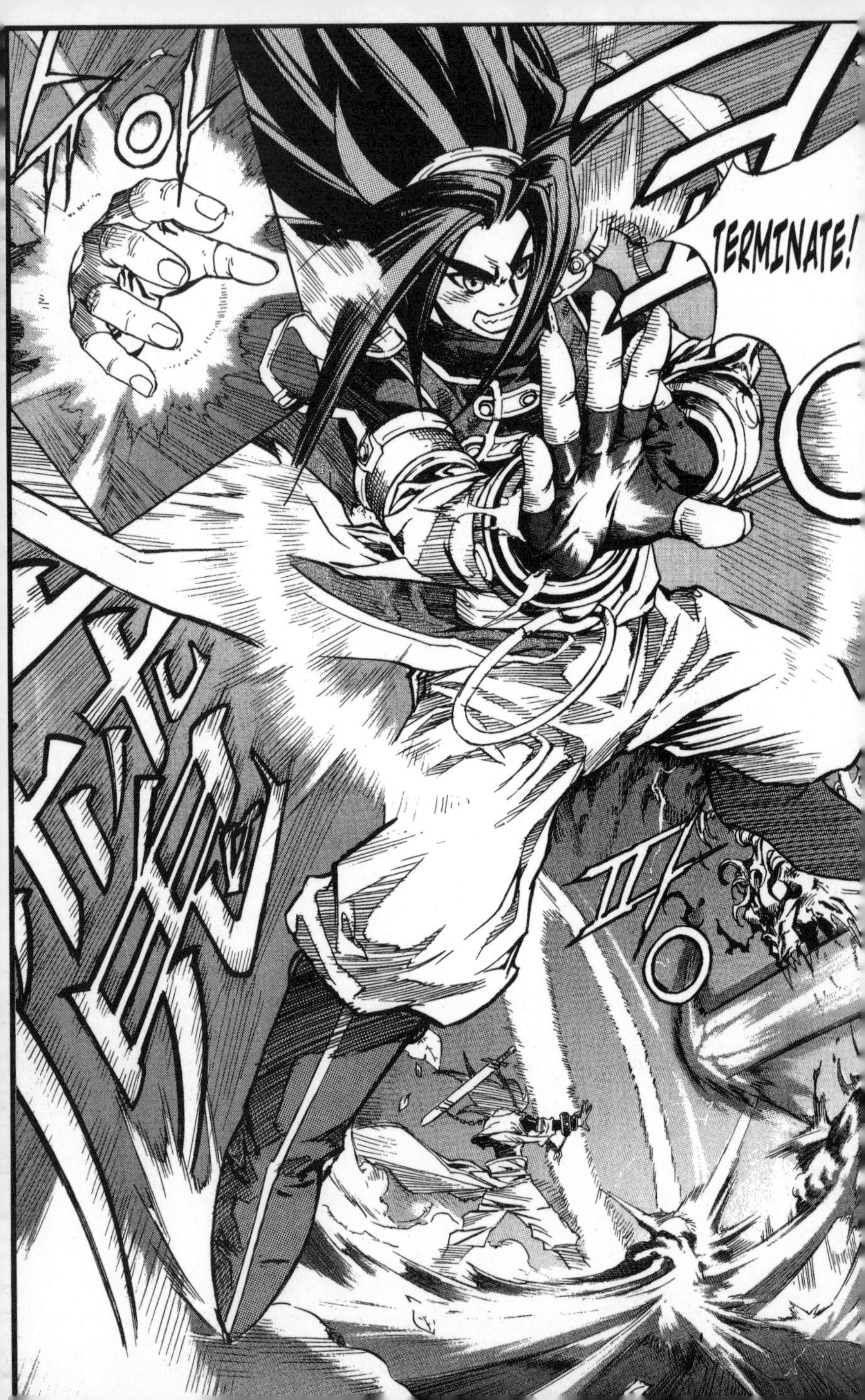
TERMINATE!

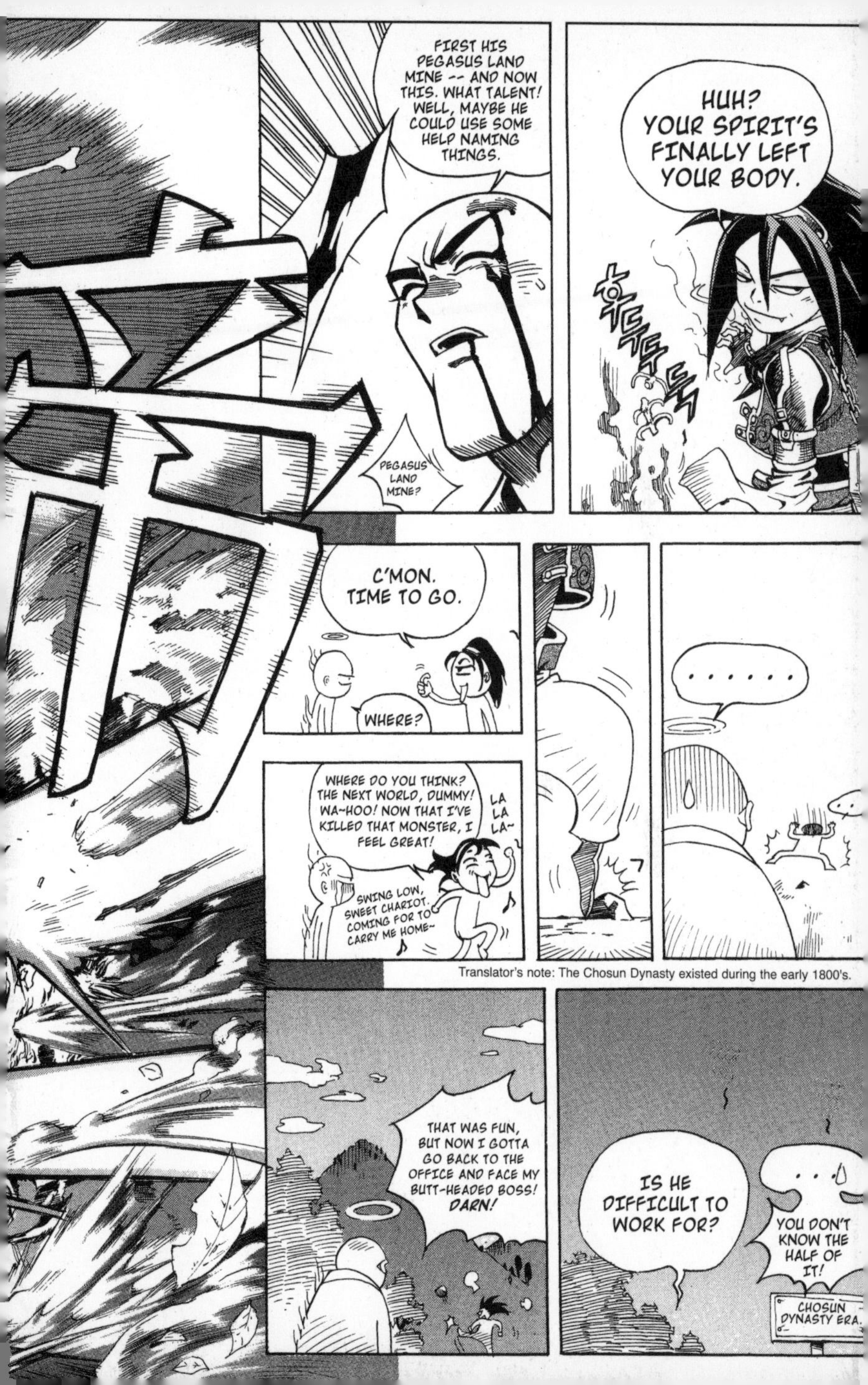
FIRST HIS PEGASUS LAND MINE -- AND NOW THIS. WHAT TALENT! WELL, MAYBE HE COULD USE SOME HELP NAMING THINGS.
PEGASUS LAND MINE?
HUH? YOUR SPIRIT'S FINALLY LEFT YOUR BODY.
C'MON. TIME TO GO.
WHERE?
WHERE DO YOU THINK? THE NEXT WORLD, DUMMY! WA~HOO! NOW THAT I'VE KILLED THAT MONSTER, I FEEL GREAT!
LA LA LA~
SWING LOW, SWEET CHARIOT. COMING FOR TO CARRY ME HOME~
......
THAT WAS FUN, BUT NOW I GOTTA GO BACK TO THE OFFICE AND FACE MY BUTT-HEADED BOSS! DARN!
IS HE DIFFICULT TO WORK FOR?
...
YOU DON'T KNOW THE HALF OF IT!
CHOSUN DYNASTY ERA.

Translator's note: The Chosun Dynasty existed during the early 1800's.

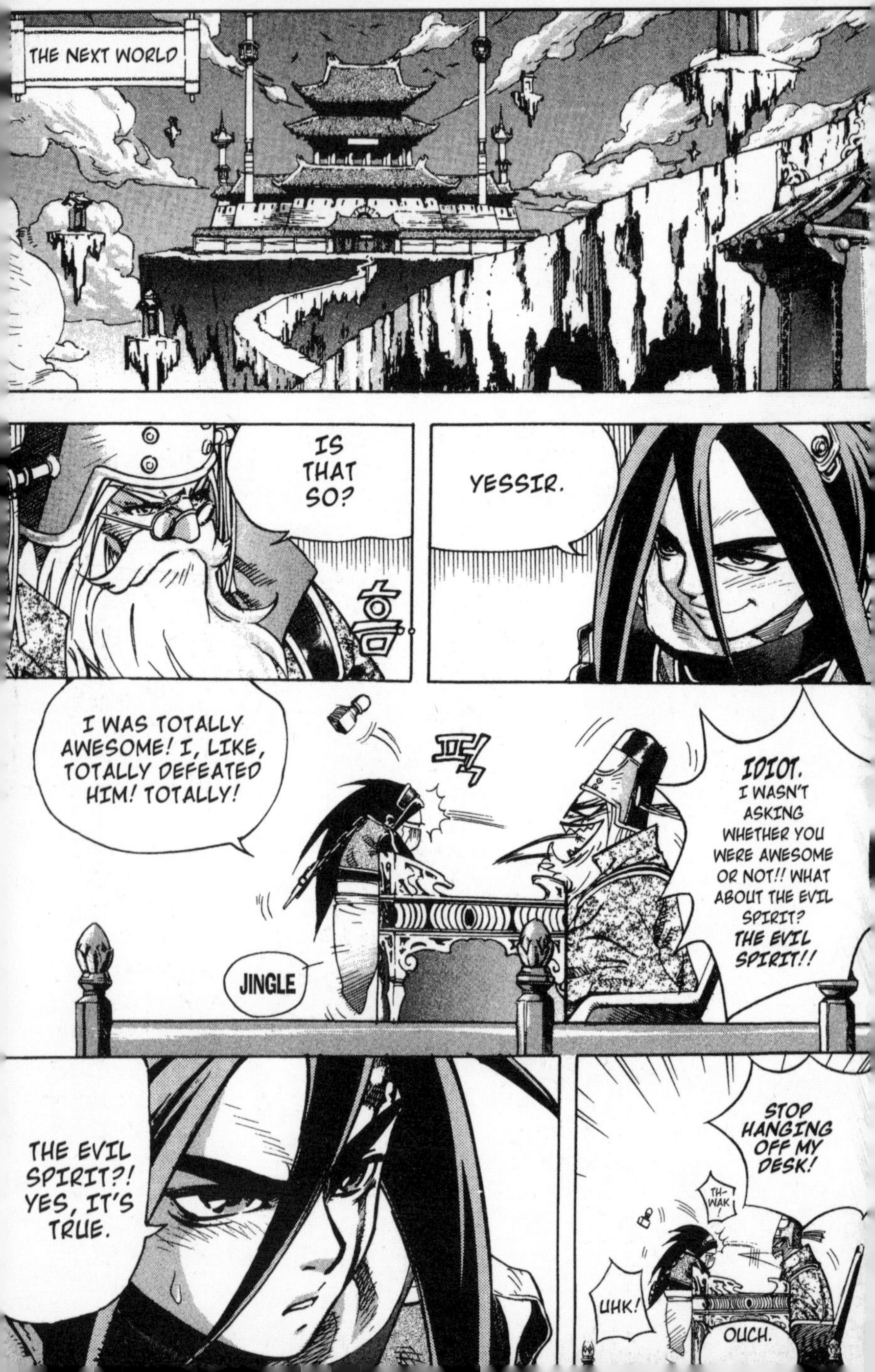
THE NEXT WORLD
IS THAT SO?
흠
YESSIR.
I WAS TOTALLY AWESOME! I, LIKE, TOTALLY DEFEATED HIM! TOTALLY!
JINGLE
IDIOT. I WASN'T ASKING WHETHER YOU WERE AWESOME OR NOT!! WHAT ABOUT THE EVIL SPIRIT? THE EVIL SPIRIT!!
THE EVIL SPIRIT?! YES, IT'S TRUE.
STOP HANGING OFF MY DESK!
TH-WAK!
UHK!
OUCH.

UH, SIR...ABOUT THE EVIL SPIRIT. IT APPEARS THERE'S A RIFT BETWEEN WORLDS. IT NEEDS CLOSING, DON'T YOU THINK?

HM...

...

OKAY, THEN...

UH-OH! I'VE GOT A BAD FEELING ABOUT THIS.

I'M NOT LISTENING.

FROM THIS MOMENT FORTH, YOU WILL BE RESPONSIBLE FOR FINDING ALL THE EVIL SPIRITS THAT ESCAPED FROM THIS WORLD INTO THE NEXT WORLD -- AND YOU MUST ERADICATE THEM!

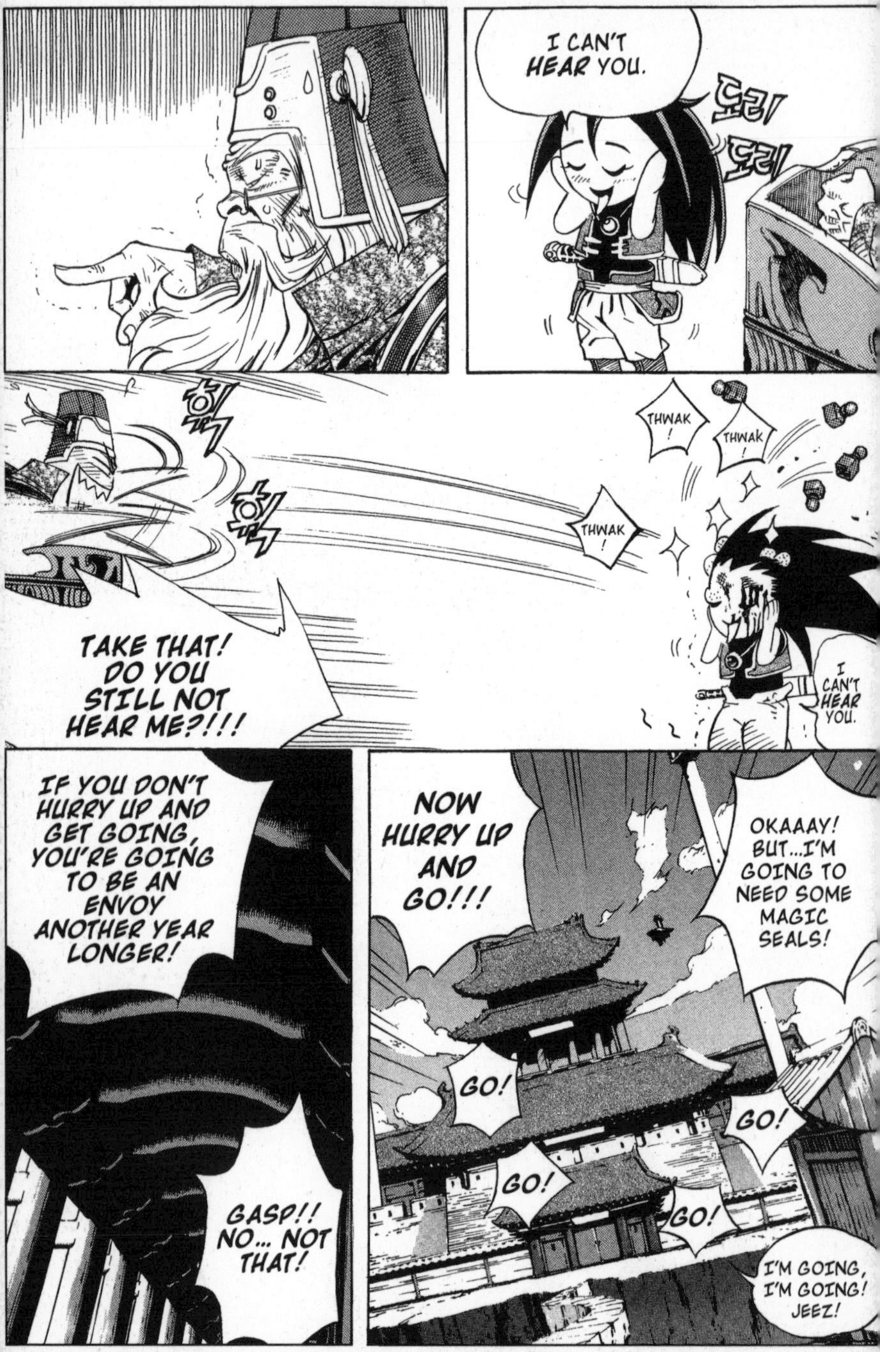
I CAN'T HEAR YOU.
TAKE THAT! DO YOU STILL NOT HEAR ME?!!!
THWAK!
THWAK!
THWAK!
I CAN'T HEAR YOU.
IF YOU DON'T HURRY UP AND GET GOING, YOU'RE GOING TO BE AN ENVOY ANOTHER YEAR LONGER!
GASP!! NO... NOT THAT!
NOW HURRY UP AND GO!!!
OKAAAY! BUT...I'M GOING TO NEED SOME MAGIC SEALS!
GO!
GO!
GO!
GO!
I'M GOING, I'M GOING! JEEZ!

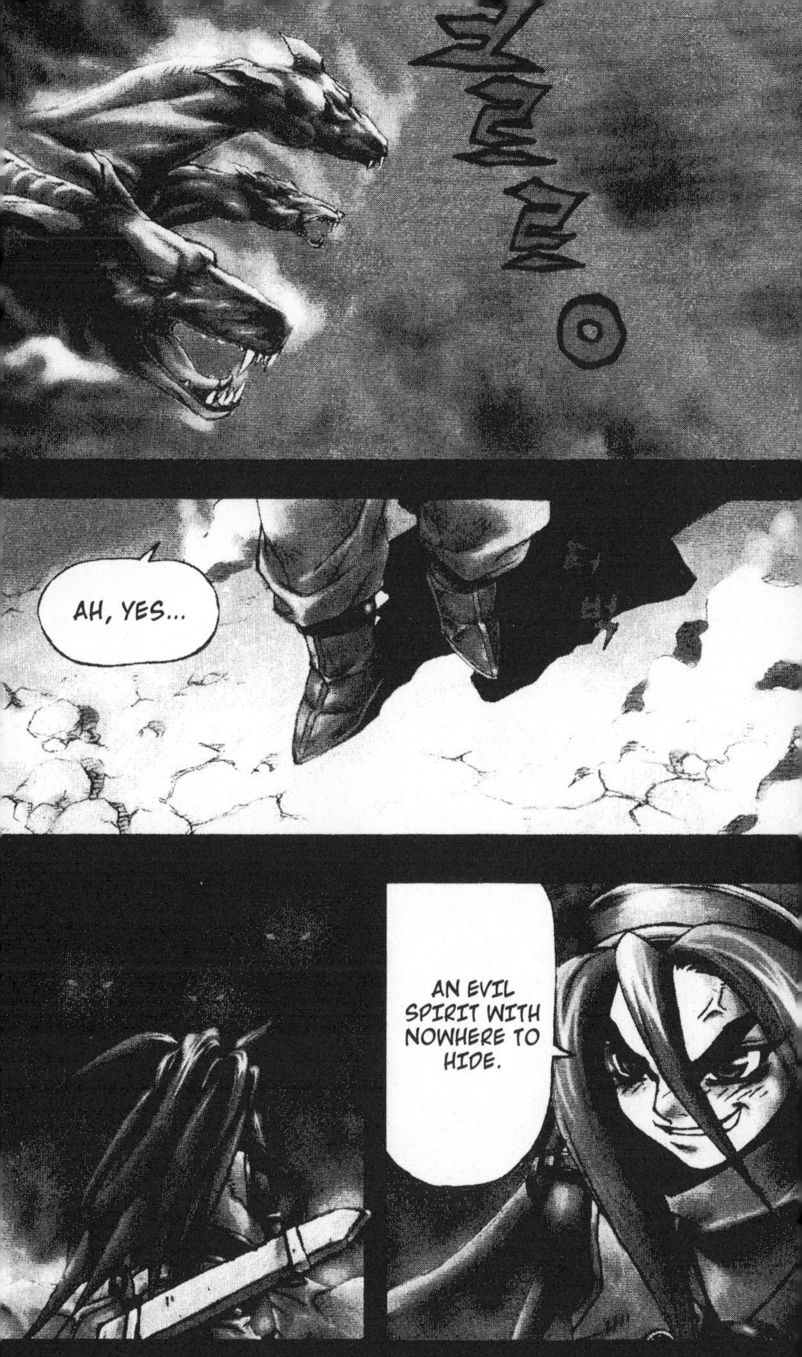
AH, YES...
AN EVIL SPIRIT WITH NOWHERE TO HIDE.

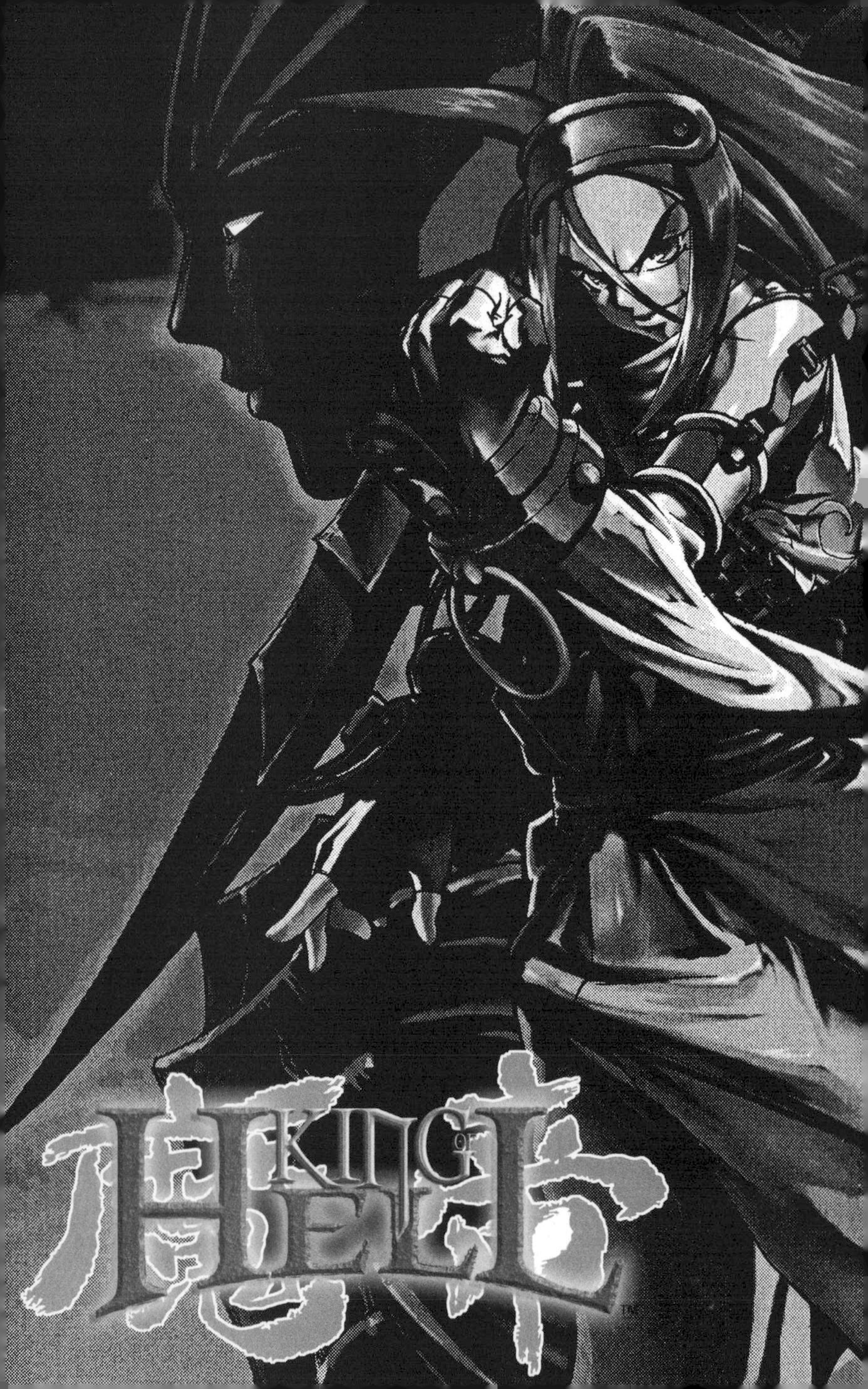
KING OF HELL™

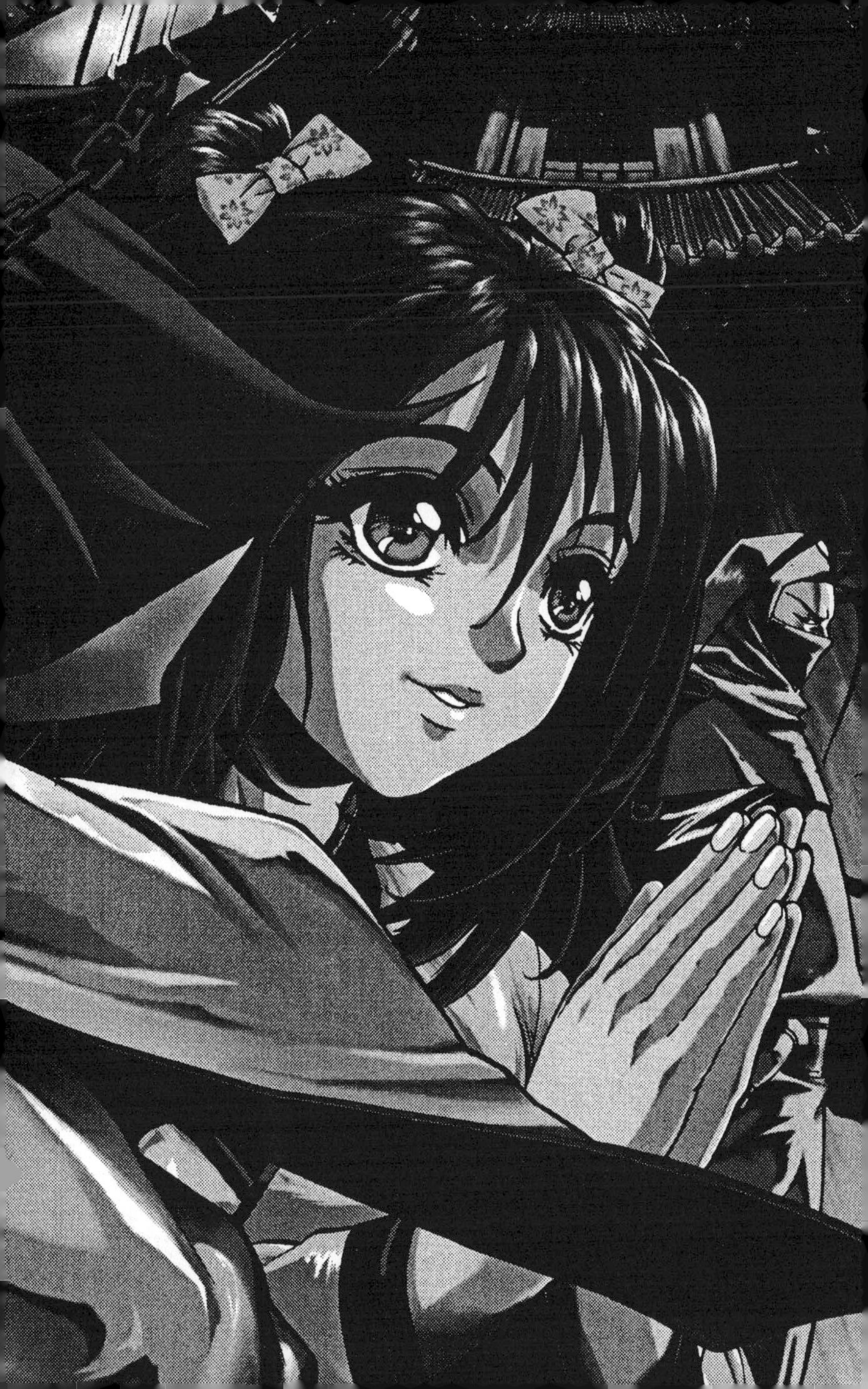

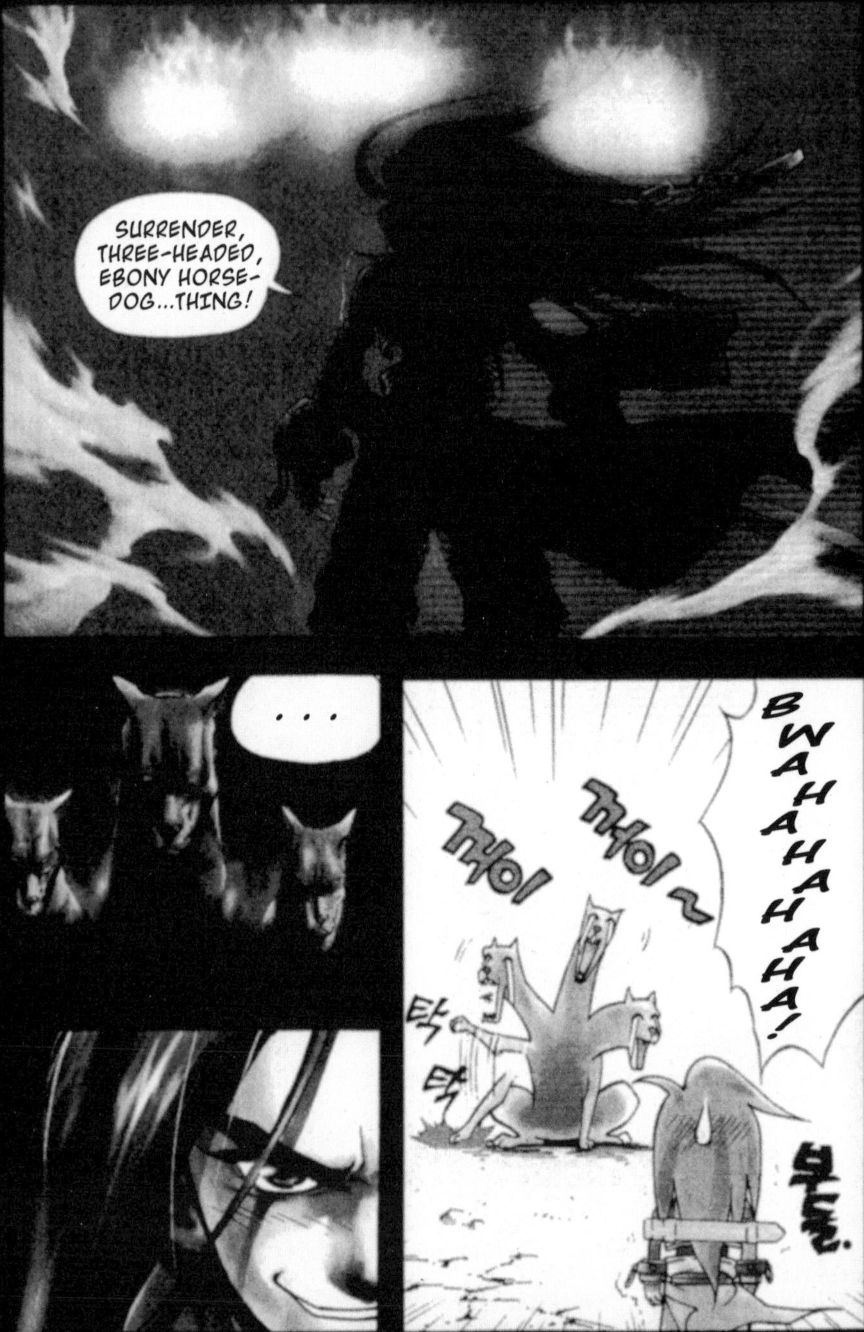
SURRENDER, THREE-HEADED, EBONY HORSE-DOG...THING!
...
깨이
깨이~
탁
탁
BWAHAHAHAHAHA!
부들

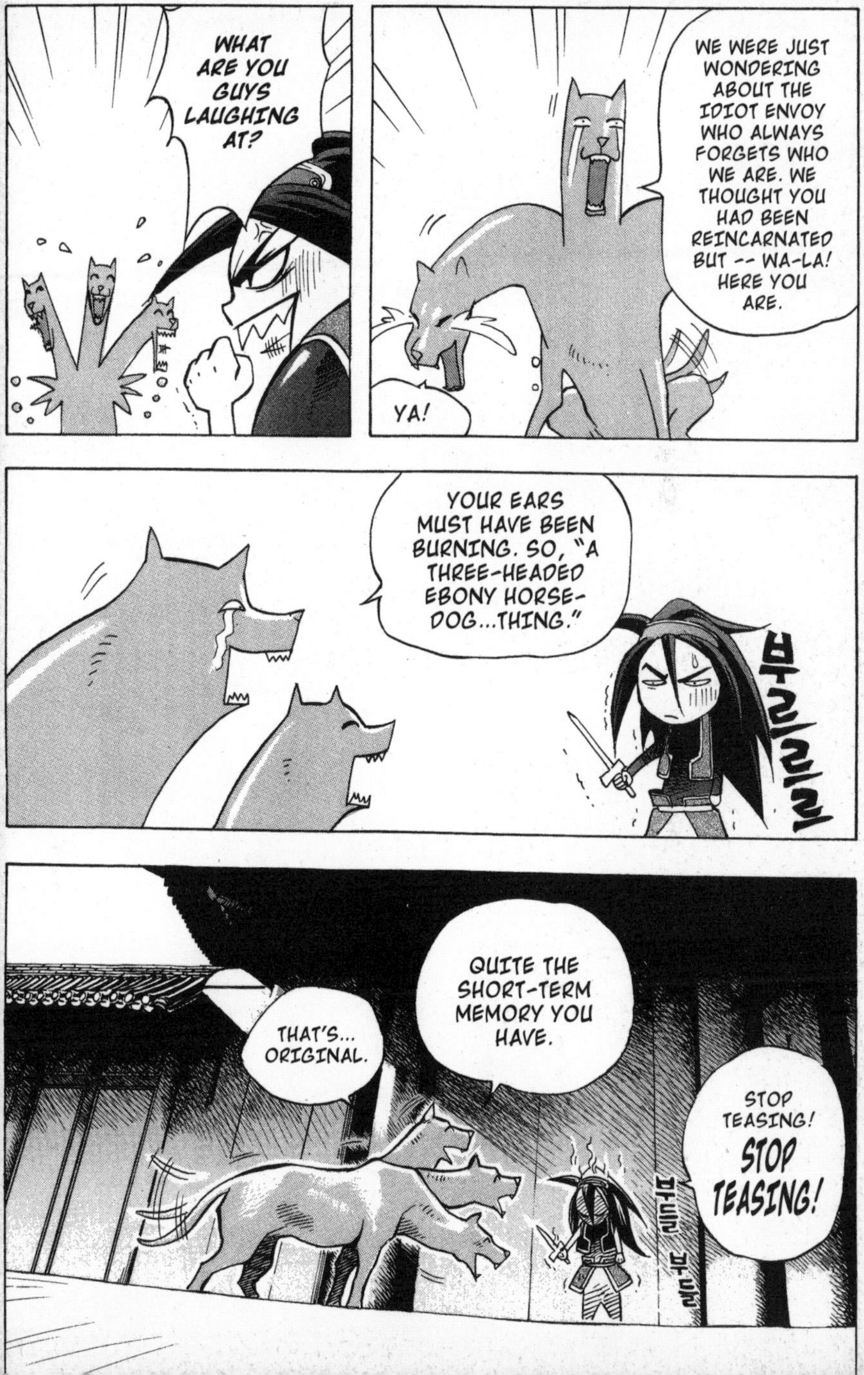
WHAT ARE YOU GUYS LAUGHING AT?
WE WERE JUST WONDERING ABOUT THE IDIOT ENVOY WHO ALWAYS FORGETS WHO WE ARE. WE THOUGHT YOU HAD BEEN REINCARNATED BUT -- WA-LA! HERE YOU ARE.
YA!
YOUR EARS MUST HAVE BEEN BURNING. SO, "A THREE-HEADED EBONY HORSE-DOG...THING."
THAT'S... ORIGINAL.
QUITE THE SHORT-TERM MEMORY YOU HAVE.
STOP TEASING! STOP TEASING!

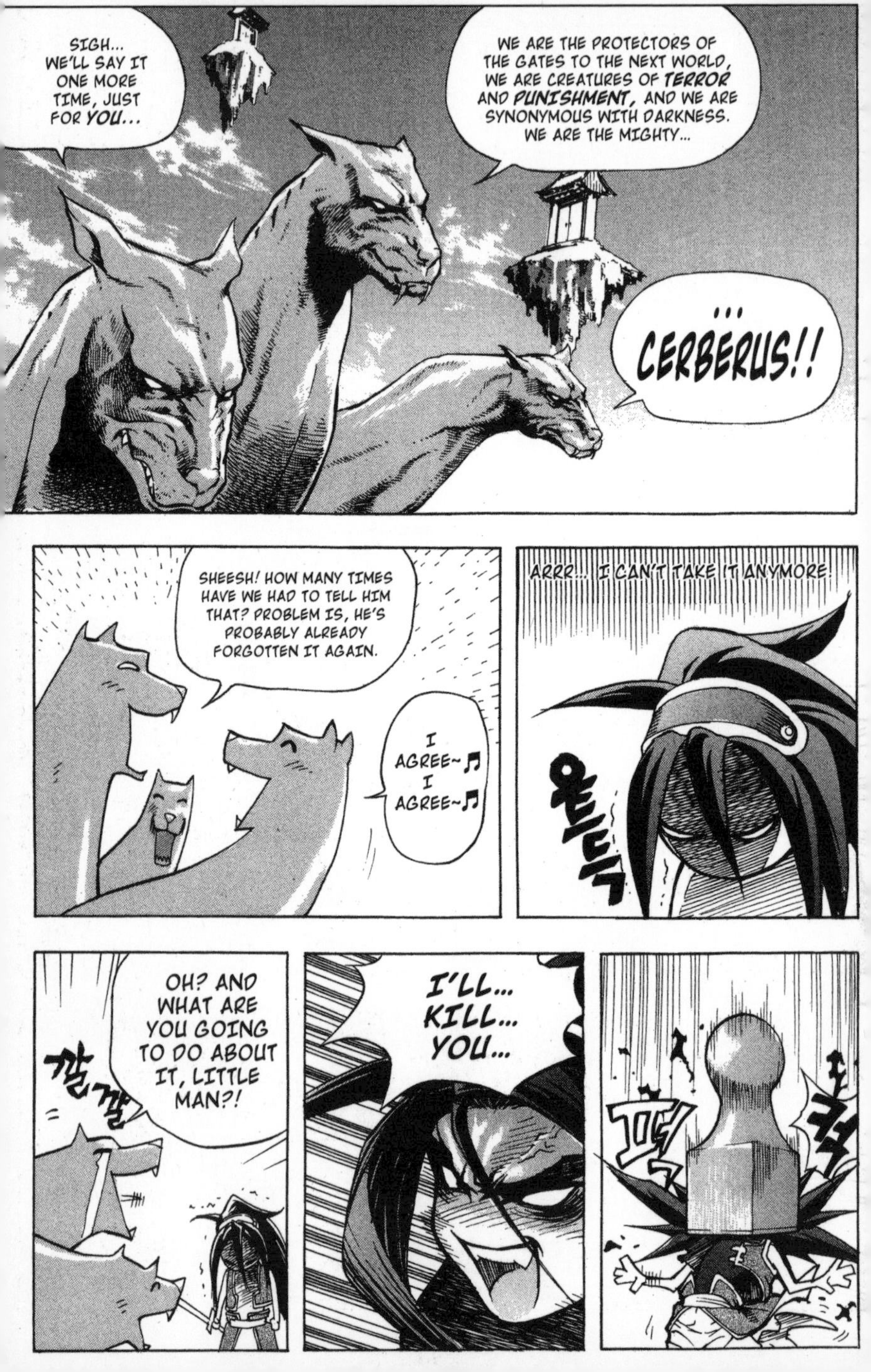
SIGH... WE'LL SAY IT ONE MORE TIME, JUST FOR *YOU*...
WE ARE THE PROTECTORS OF THE GATES TO THE NEXT WORLD, WE ARE CREATURES OF *TERROR* AND *PUNISHMENT*, AND WE ARE SYNONYMOUS WITH DARKNESS. WE ARE THE MIGHTY...
...CERBERUS!!
SHEESH! HOW MANY TIMES HAVE WE HAD TO TELL HIM THAT? PROBLEM IS, HE'S PROBABLY ALREADY FORGOTTEN IT AGAIN.
I AGREE~♫ I AGREE~♫
ARRR... I CAN'T TAKE IT ANYMORE.
OH? AND WHAT ARE YOU GOING TO DO ABOUT IT, LITTLE MAN?!
I'LL... KILL... YOU...

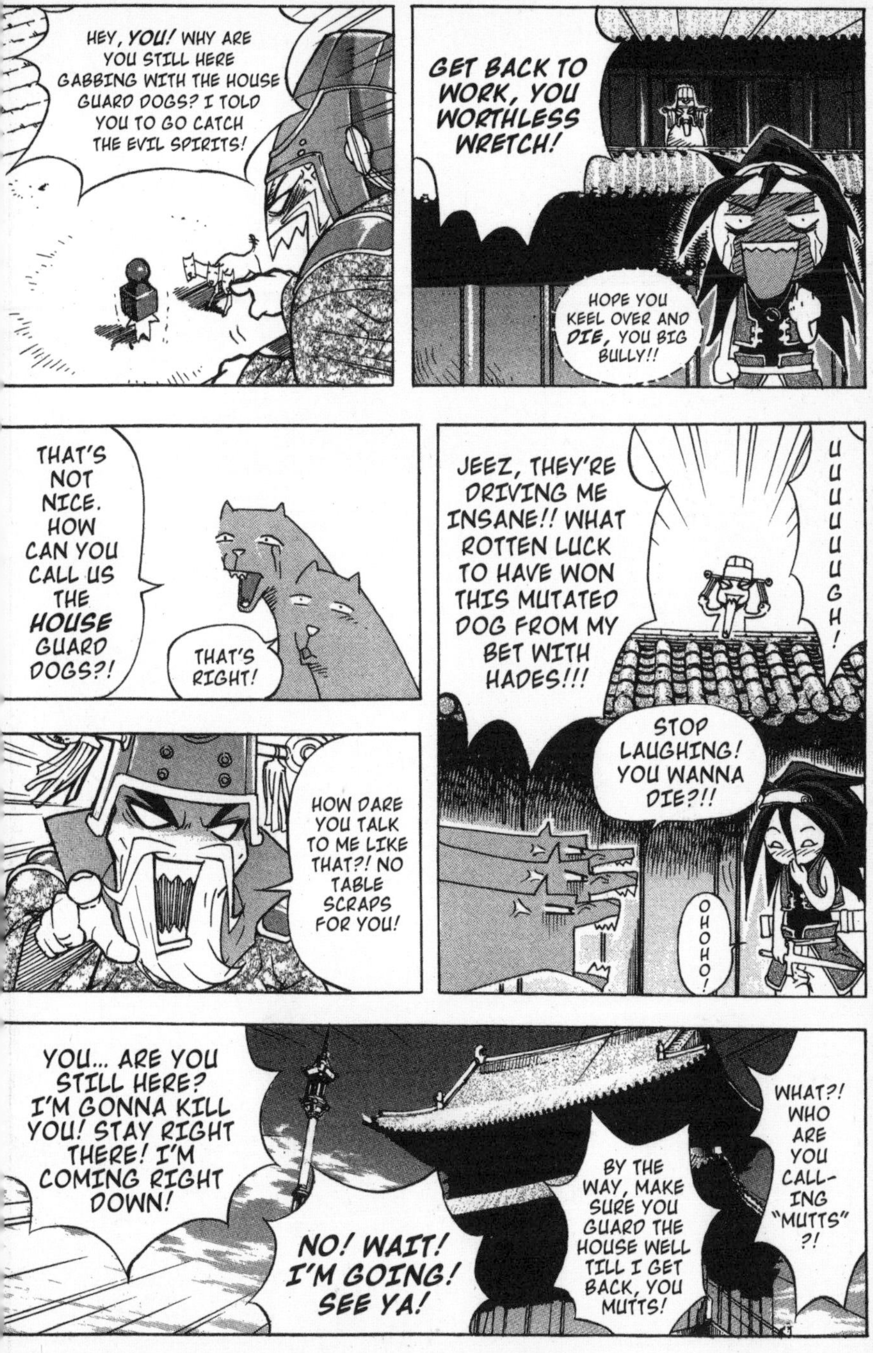
HEY, YOU! WHY ARE YOU STILL HERE GABBING WITH THE HOUSE GUARD DOGS? I TOLD YOU TO GO CATCH THE EVIL SPIRITS!
GET BACK TO WORK, YOU WORTHLESS WRETCH!
HOPE YOU KEEL OVER AND DIE, YOU BIG BULLY!!
THAT'S NOT NICE. HOW CAN YOU CALL US THE HOUSE GUARD DOGS?!
THAT'S RIGHT!
HOW DARE YOU TALK TO ME LIKE THAT?! NO TABLE SCRAPS FOR YOU!
JEEZ, THEY'RE DRIVING ME INSANE!! WHAT ROTTEN LUCK TO HAVE WON THIS MUTATED DOG FROM MY BET WITH HADES!!!
UUUUUUUUGH!
STOP LAUGHING! YOU WANNA DIE?!!
OHOHO!
YOU... ARE YOU STILL HERE? I'M GONNA KILL YOU! STAY RIGHT THERE! I'M COMING RIGHT DOWN!
NO! WAIT! I'M GOING! SEE YA!
BY THE WAY, MAKE SURE YOU GUARD THE HOUSE WELL TILL I GET BACK, YOU MUTTS!
WHAT?! WHO ARE YOU CALLING "MUTTS"?!

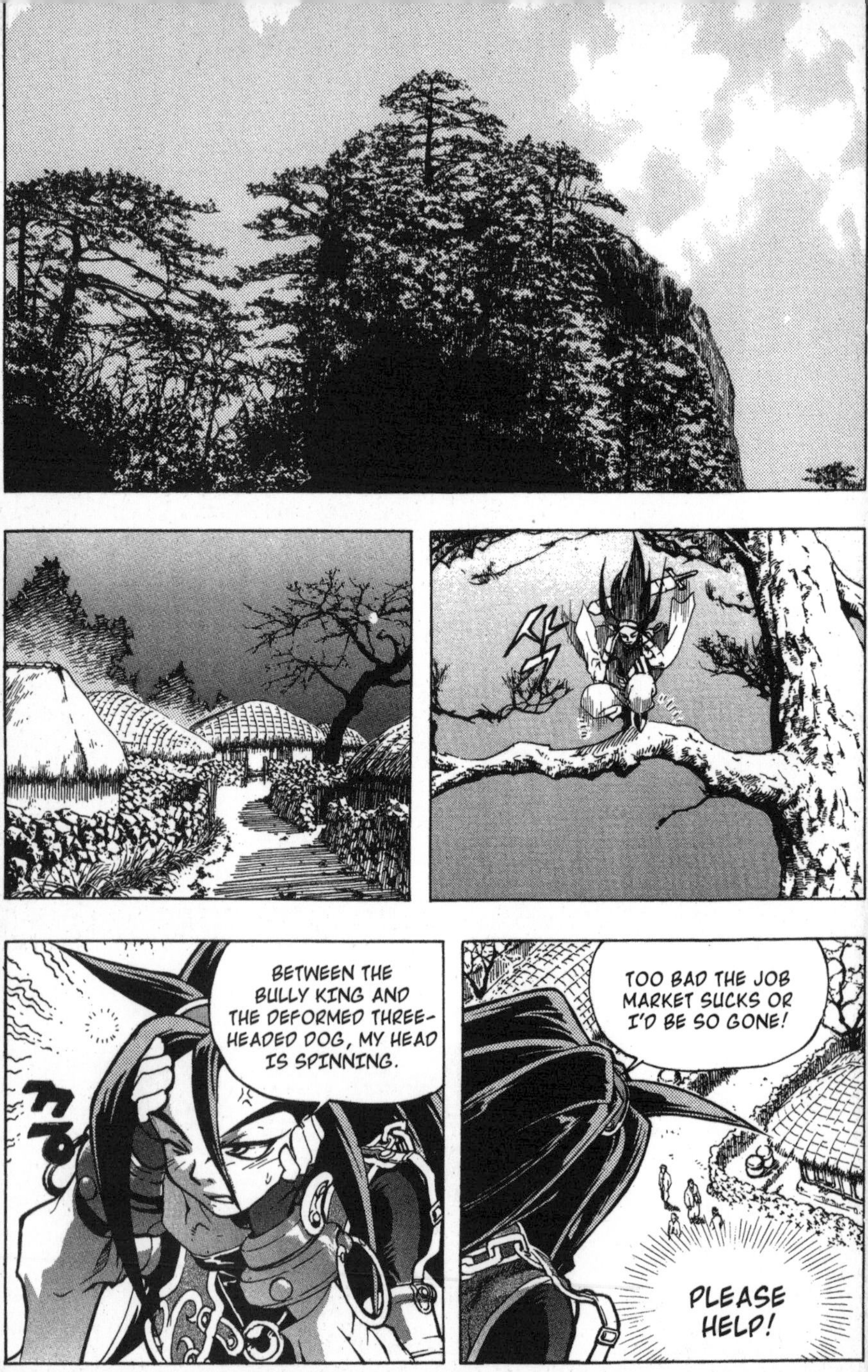
BETWEEN THE BULLY KING AND THE DEFORMED THREE-HEADED DOG, MY HEAD IS SPINNING.
TOO BAD THE JOB MARKET SUCKS OR I'D BE SO GONE!
PLEASE HELP!

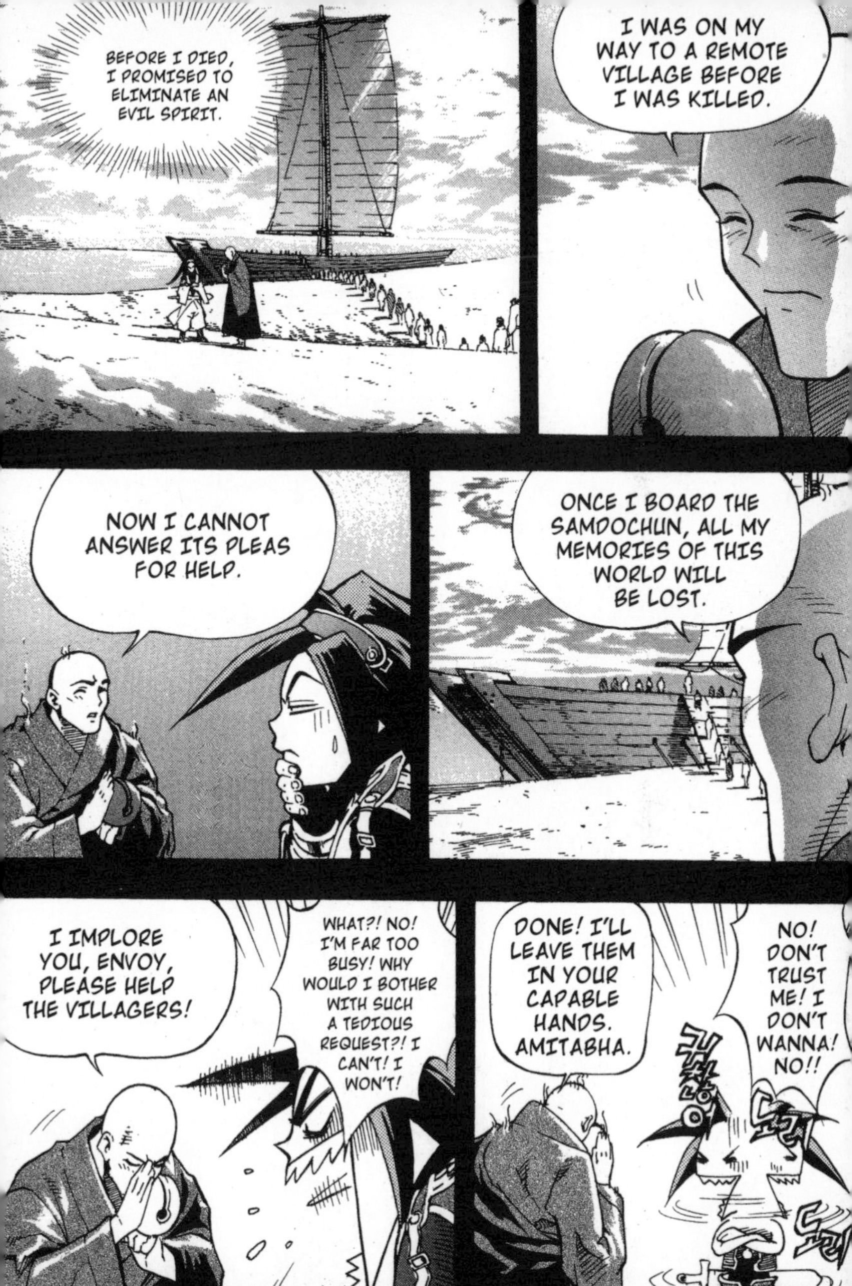
BEFORE I DIED, I PROMISED TO ELIMINATE AN EVIL SPIRIT.
I WAS ON MY WAY TO A REMOTE VILLAGE BEFORE I WAS KILLED.
NOW I CANNOT ANSWER ITS PLEAS FOR HELP.
ONCE I BOARD THE SAMDOCHUN, ALL MY MEMORIES OF THIS WORLD WILL BE LOST.
I IMPLORE YOU, ENVOY, PLEASE HELP THE VILLAGERS!
WHAT?! NO! I'M FAR TOO BUSY! WHY WOULD I BOTHER WITH SUCH A TEDIOUS REQUEST?! I CAN'T! I WON'T!
DONE! I'LL LEAVE THEM IN YOUR CAPABLE HANDS. AMITABHA.
NO! DON'T TRUST ME! I DON'T WANNA! NO!!

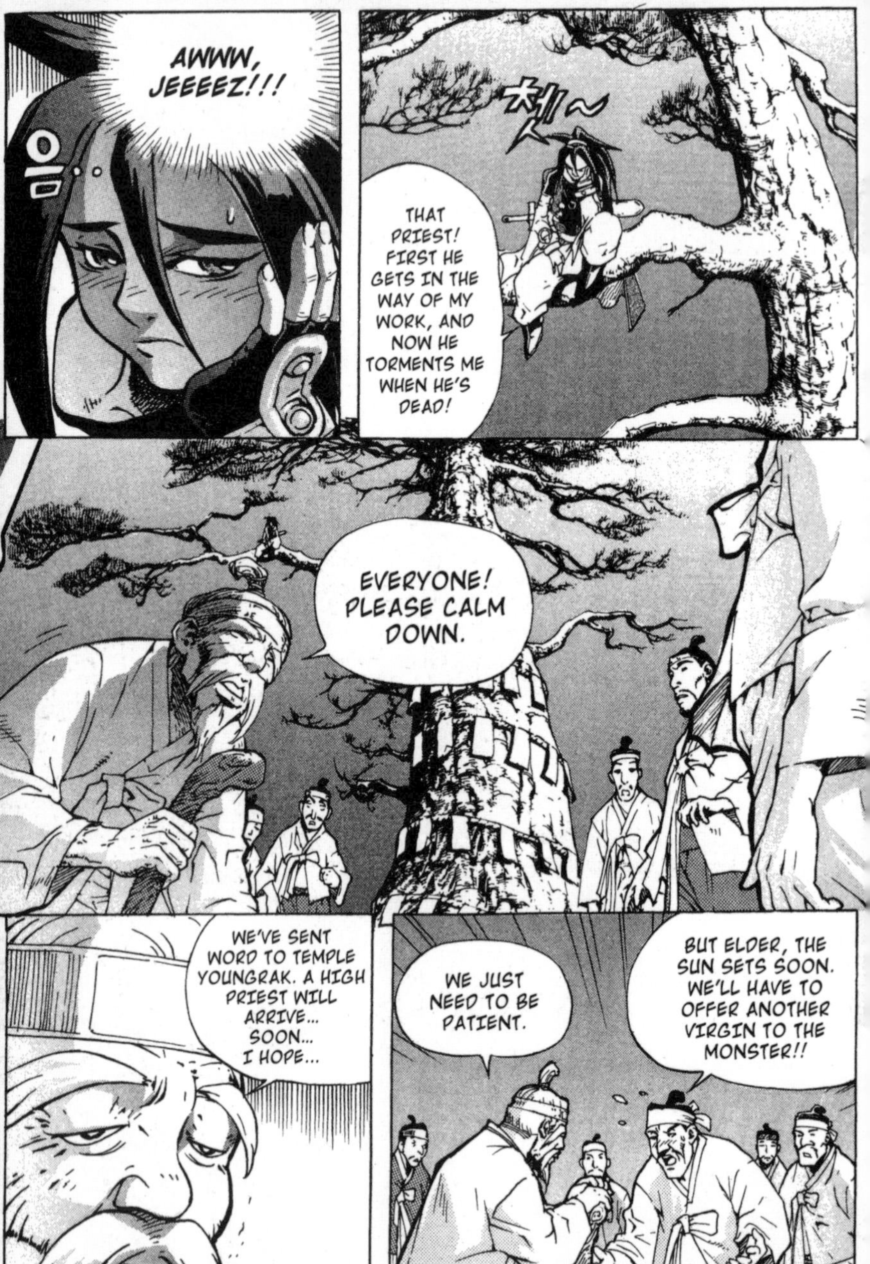
AWWW, JEEEEZ!!!
음
THAT PRIEST! FIRST HE GETS IN THE WAY OF MY WORK, AND NOW HE TORMENTS ME WHEN HE'S DEAD!
EVERYONE! PLEASE CALM DOWN.
WE'VE SENT WORD TO TEMPLE YOUNGRAK. A HIGH PRIEST WILL ARRIVE... SOON... I HOPE...
WE JUST NEED TO BE PATIENT.
BUT ELDER, THE SUN SETS SOON. WE'LL HAVE TO OFFER ANOTHER VIRGIN TO THE MONSTER!!

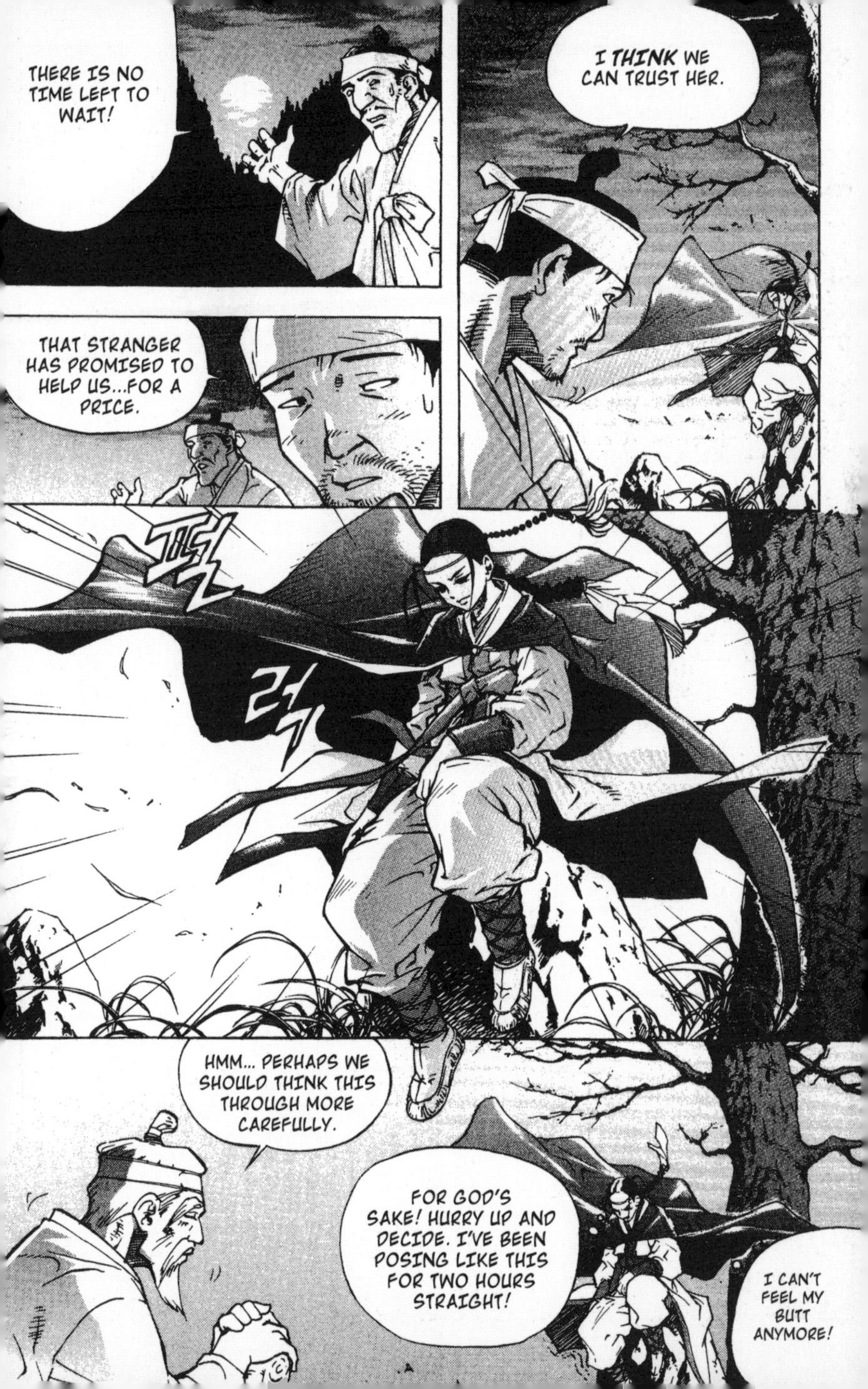
THERE IS NO TIME LEFT TO WAIT!
THAT STRANGER HAS PROMISED TO HELP US...FOR A PRICE.
I *THINK* WE CAN TRUST HER.
펄
럭
HMM... PERHAPS WE SHOULD THINK THIS THROUGH MORE CAREFULLY.
FOR GOD'S SAKE! HURRY UP AND DECIDE. I'VE BEEN POSING LIKE THIS FOR TWO HOURS STRAIGHT!
I CAN'T FEEL MY BUTT ANYMORE!

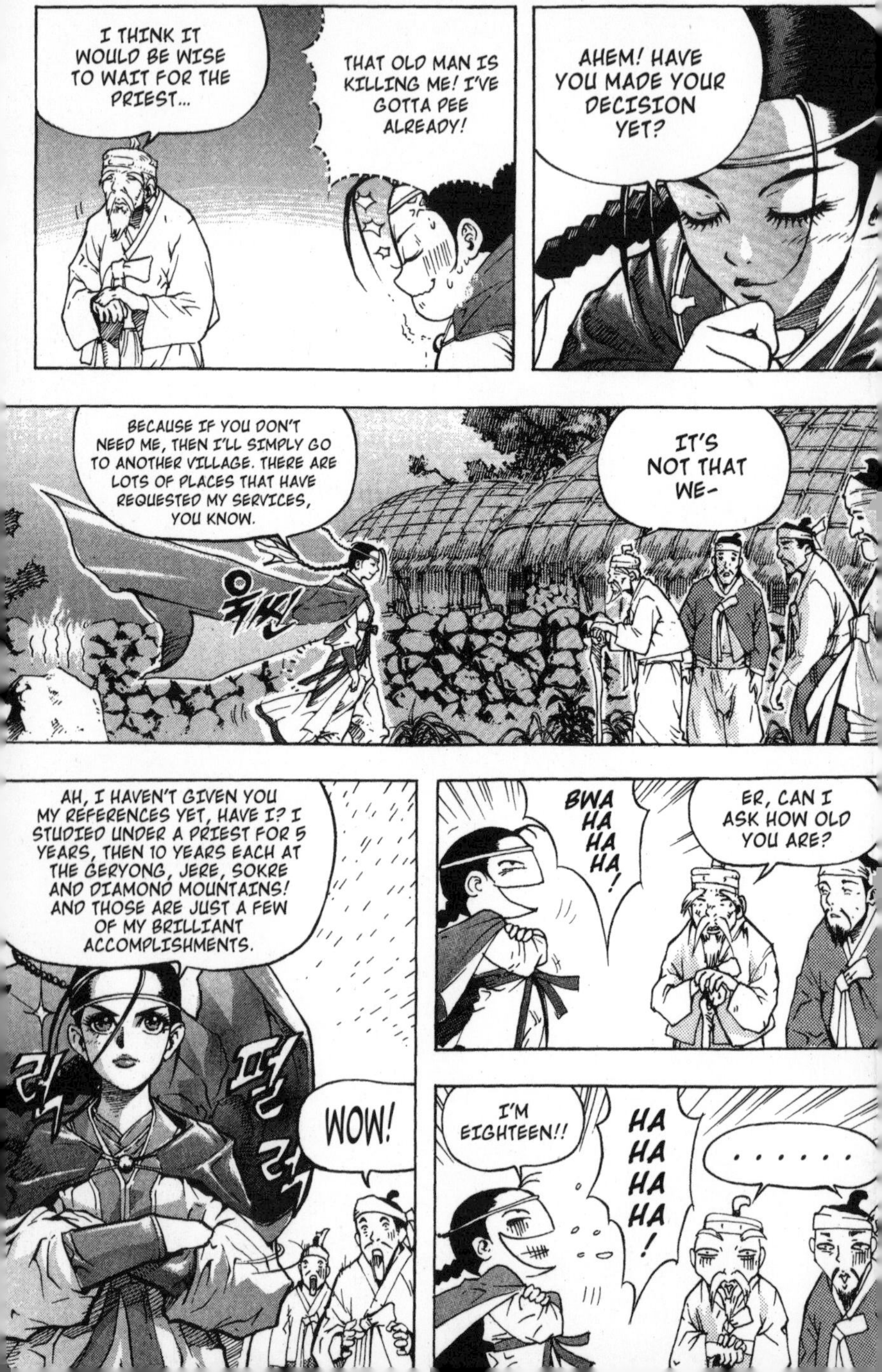
I THINK IT WOULD BE WISE TO WAIT FOR THE PRIEST...
THAT OLD MAN IS KILLING ME! I'VE GOTTA PEE ALREADY!
AHEM! HAVE YOU MADE YOUR DECISION YET?
BECAUSE IF YOU DON'T NEED ME, THEN I'LL SIMPLY GO TO ANOTHER VILLAGE. THERE ARE LOTS OF PLACES THAT HAVE REQUESTED MY SERVICES, YOU KNOW.
IT'S NOT THAT WE-
AH, I HAVEN'T GIVEN YOU MY REFERENCES YET, HAVE I? I STUDIED UNDER A PRIEST FOR 5 YEARS, THEN 10 YEARS EACH AT THE GERYONG, JERE, SOKRE AND DIAMOND MOUNTAINS! AND THOSE ARE JUST A FEW OF MY BRILLIANT ACCOMPLISHMENTS.
WOW!
BWA HA HA HA HA!
ER, CAN I ASK HOW OLD YOU ARE?
I'M EIGHTEEN!!
HA HA HA HA HA!
......

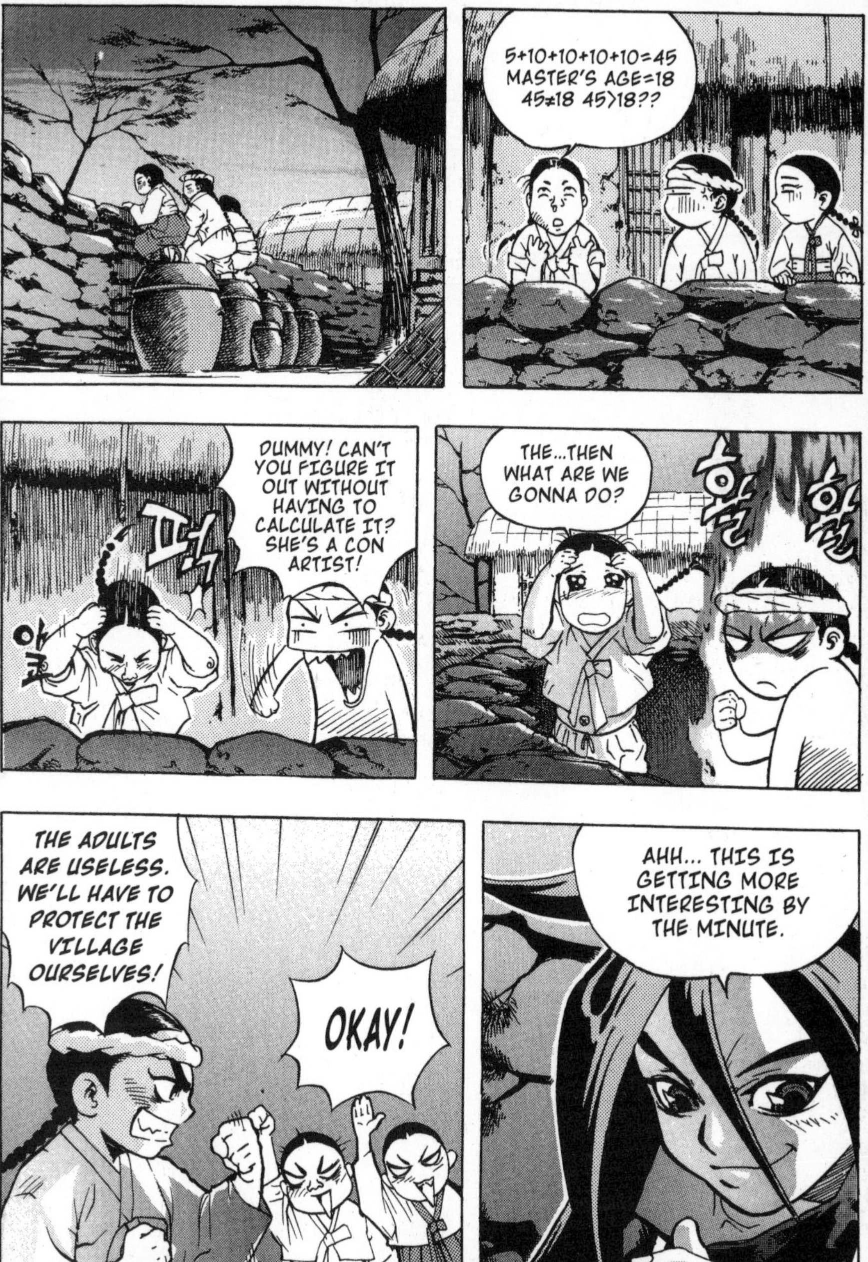
5+10+10+10+10=45
MASTER'S AGE=18
45≠18 45>18??
DUMMY! CAN'T YOU FIGURE IT OUT WITHOUT HAVING TO CALCULATE IT? SHE'S A CON ARTIST!
THE...THEN WHAT ARE WE GONNA DO?
THE ADULTS ARE USELESS. WE'LL HAVE TO PROTECT THE VILLAGE OURSELVES!
OKAY!
AHH... THIS IS GETTING MORE INTERESTING BY THE MINUTE.

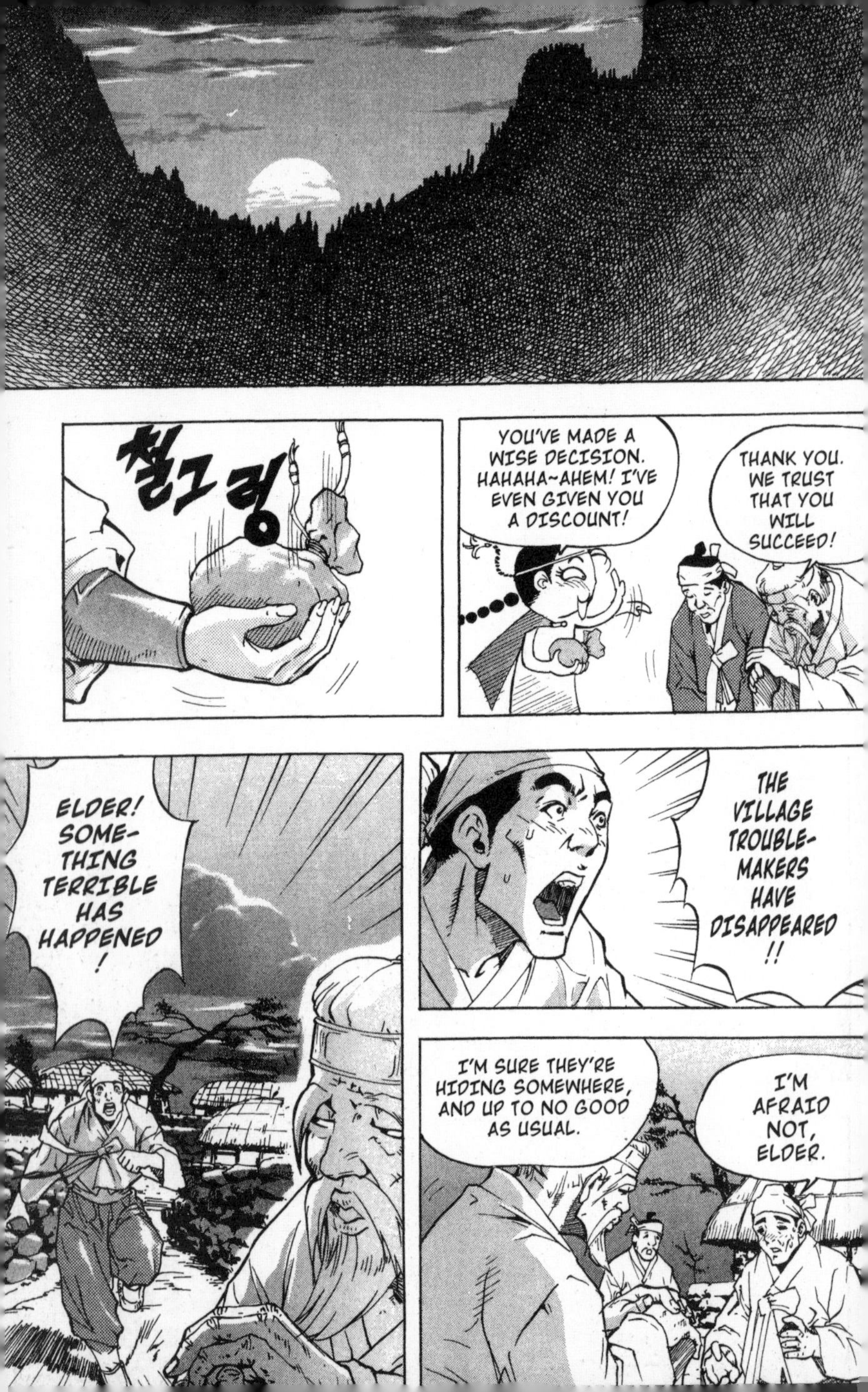
철그렁
YOU'VE MADE A WISE DECISION. HAHAHA~AHEM! I'VE EVEN GIVEN YOU A DISCOUNT!
THANK YOU. WE TRUST THAT YOU WILL SUCCEED!
ELDER! SOMETHING TERRIBLE HAS HAPPENED!
THE VILLAGE TROUBLEMAKERS HAVE DISAPPEARED!!
I'M SURE THEY'RE HIDING SOMEWHERE, AND UP TO NO GOOD AS USUAL.
I'M AFRAID NOT, ELDER.

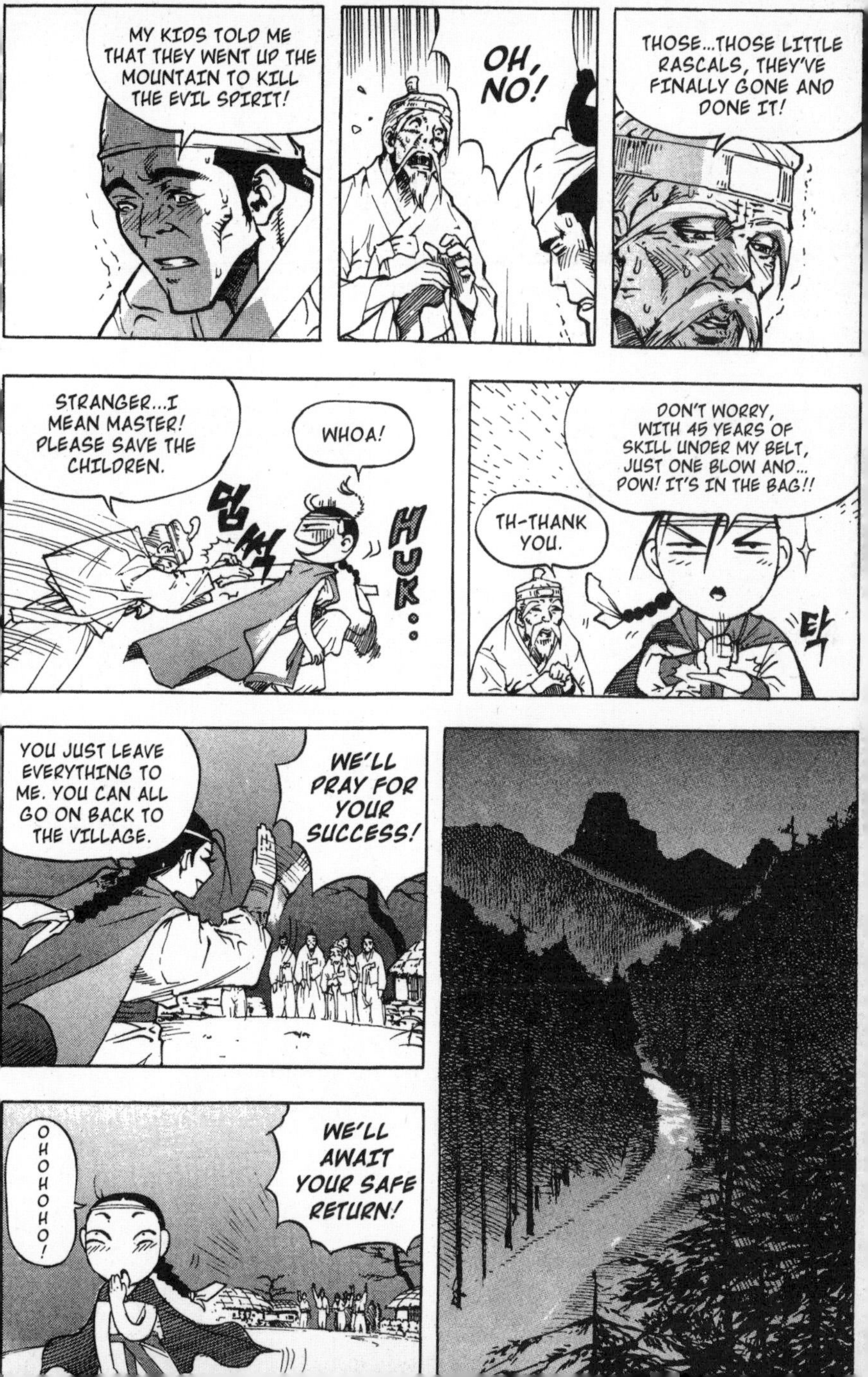

MY KIDS TOLD ME THAT THEY WENT UP THE MOUNTAIN TO KILL THE EVIL SPIRIT!
OH, NO!
THOSE...THOSE LITTLE RASCALS, THEY'VE FINALLY GONE AND DONE IT!
STRANGER...I MEAN MASTER! PLEASE SAVE THE CHILDREN.
WHOA!
덥석
HUK..
DON'T WORRY, WITH 45 YEARS OF SKILL UNDER MY BELT, JUST ONE BLOW AND... POW! IT'S IN THE BAG!!
TH-THANK YOU.
탁
YOU JUST LEAVE EVERYTHING TO ME. YOU CAN ALL GO ON BACK TO THE VILLAGE.
WE'LL PRAY FOR YOUR SUCCESS!
OHOHOHO!
WE'LL AWAIT YOUR SAFE RETURN!

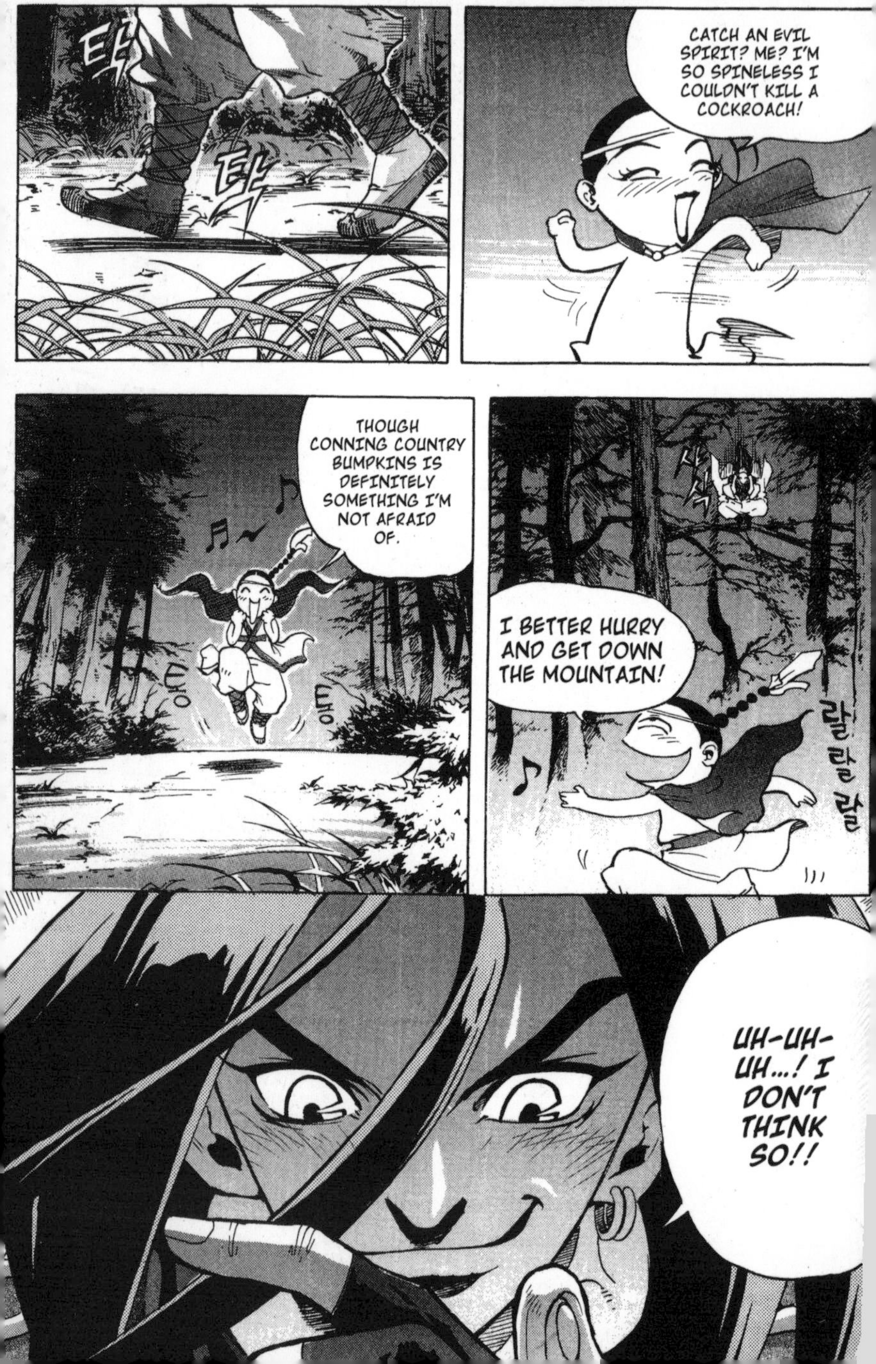
탁
탁
CATCH AN EVIL SPIRIT? ME? I'M SO SPINELESS I COULDN'T KILL A COCKROACH!
THOUGH CONNING COUNTRY BUMPKINS IS DEFINITELY SOMETHING I'M NOT AFRAID OF.
I BETTER HURRY AND GET DOWN THE MOUNTAIN!
랄 랄 랄
UH-UH-UH...! I DON'T THINK SO!!

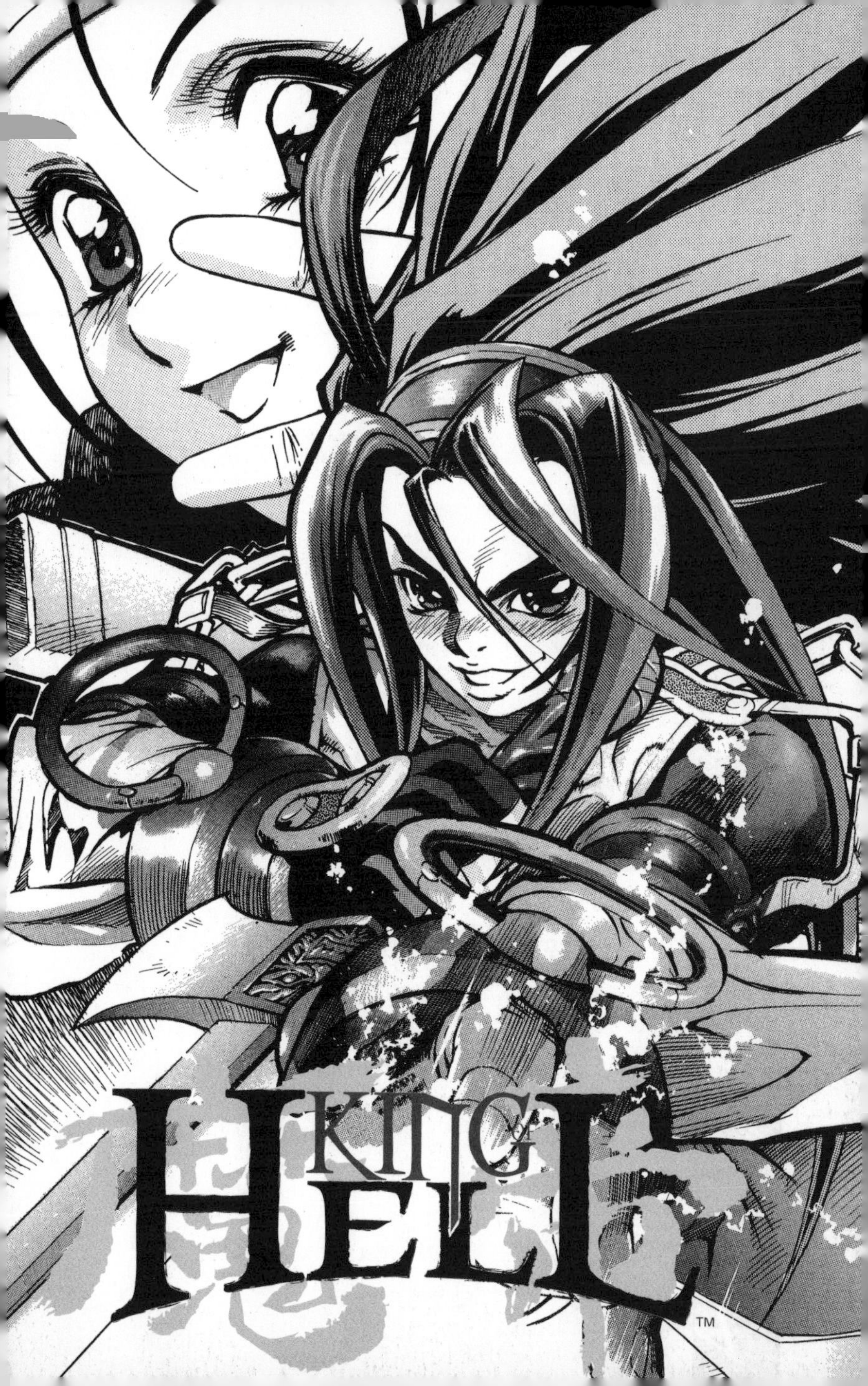

KING
HELL
™

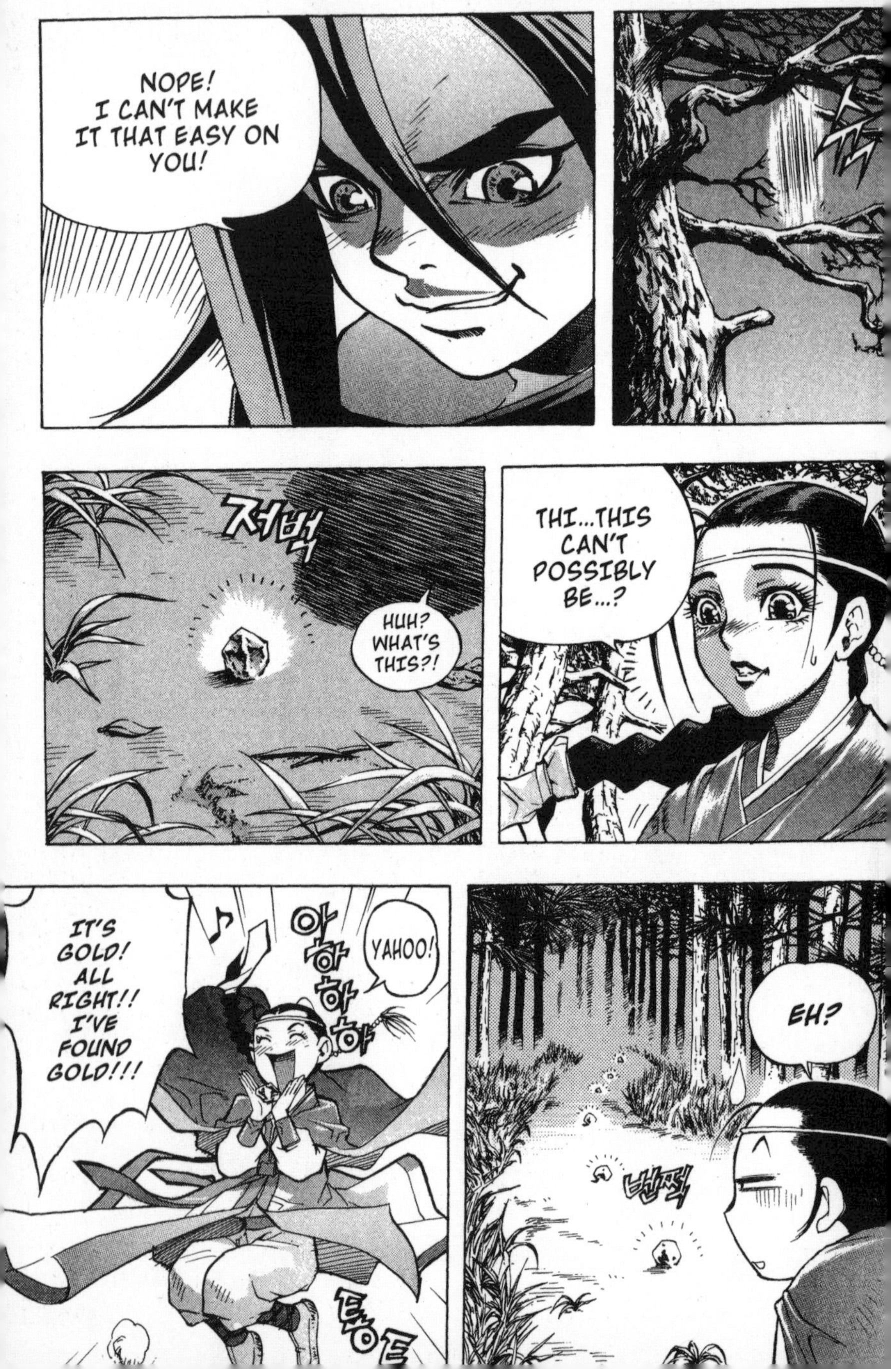
NOPE! I CAN'T MAKE IT THAT EASY ON YOU!
저벅
HUH? WHAT'S THIS?!
THI...THIS CAN'T POSSIBLY BE...?
IT'S GOLD! ALL RIGHT!! I'VE FOUND GOLD!!!
아하하하
YAHOO!
EH?
번쩍

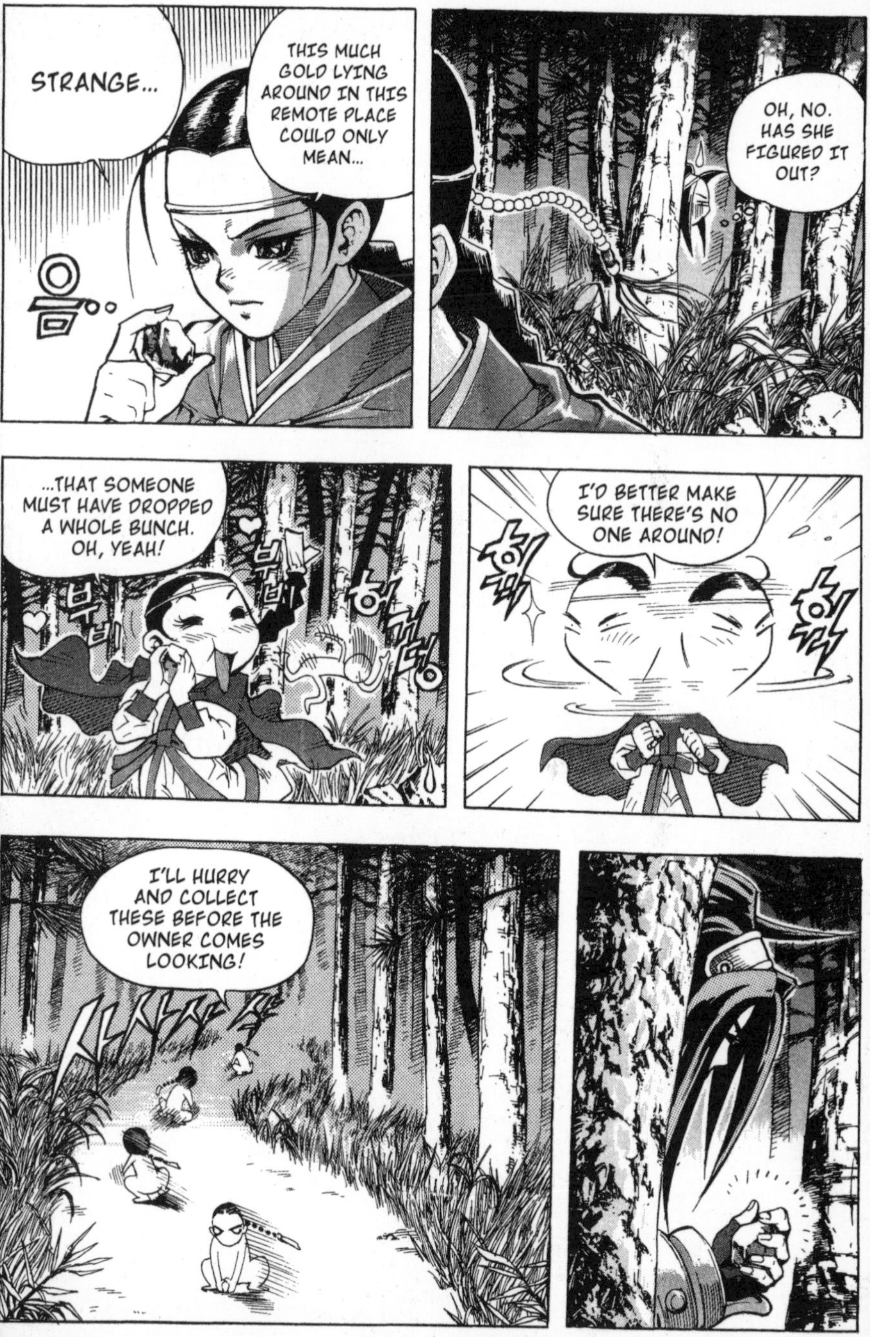
STRANGE...
THIS MUCH GOLD LYING AROUND IN THIS REMOTE PLACE COULD ONLY MEAN...
음...
OH, NO. HAS SHE FIGURED IT OUT?
...THAT SOMEONE MUST HAVE DROPPED A WHOLE BUNCH. OH, YEAH!
I'D BETTER MAKE SURE THERE'S NO ONE AROUND!
I'LL HURRY AND COLLECT THESE BEFORE THE OWNER COMES LOOKING!

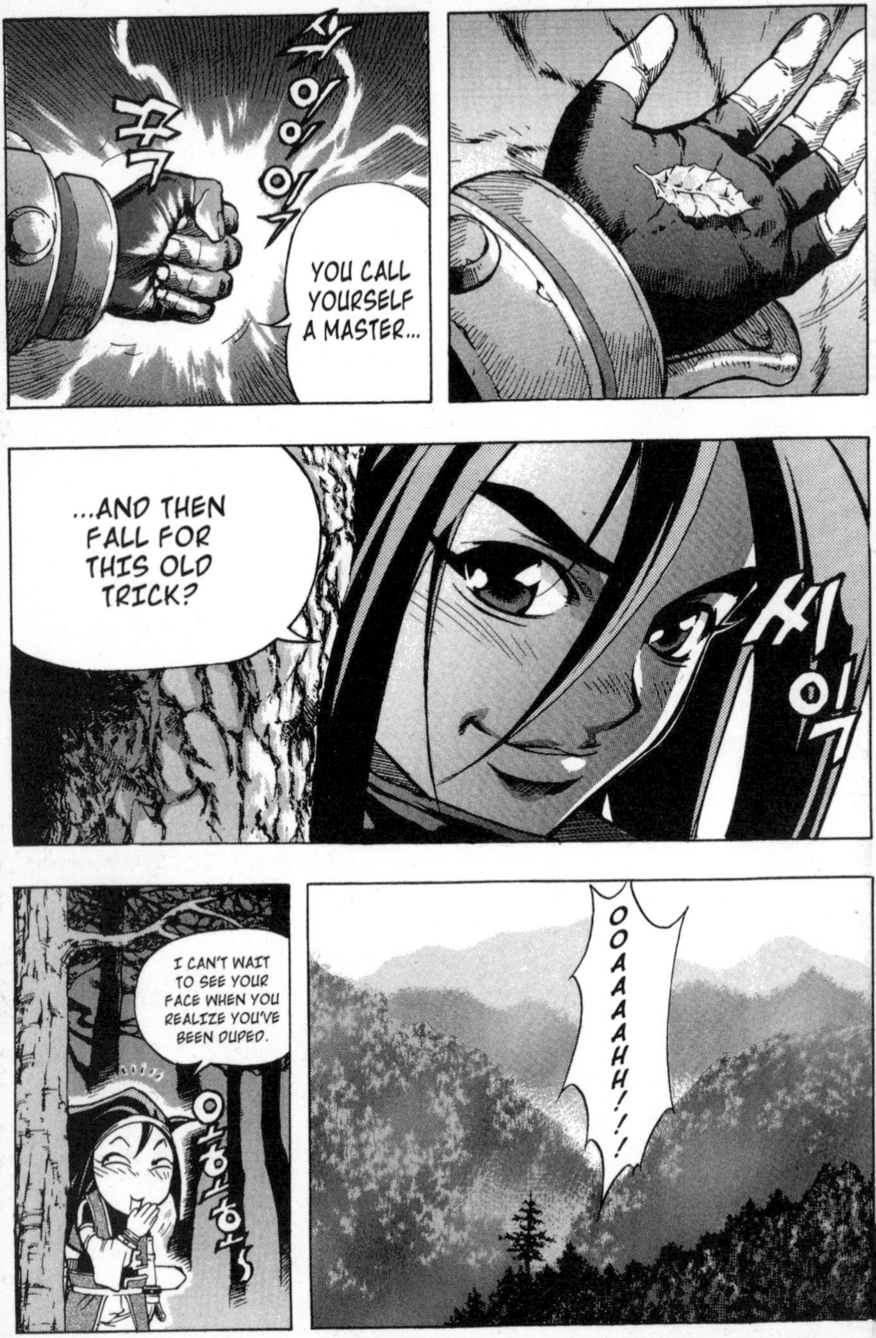
YOU CALL YOURSELF A MASTER...
...AND THEN FALL FOR THIS OLD TRICK?
I CAN'T WAIT TO SEE YOUR FACE WHEN YOU REALIZE YOU'VE BEEN DUPED.
OOAAAAAAH!!!

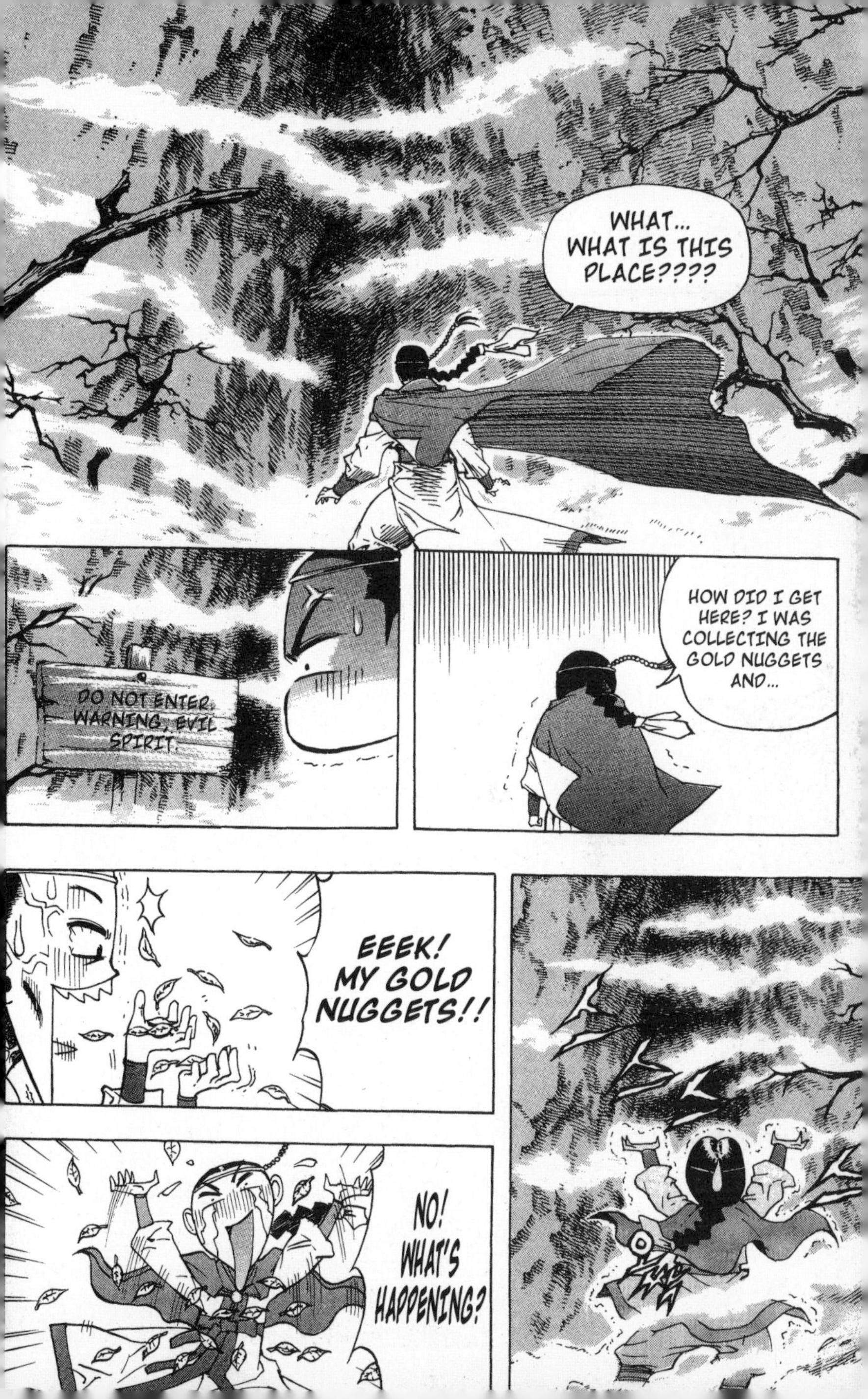
WHAT... WHAT IS THIS PLACE????
DO NOT ENTER. WARNING, EVIL SPIRIT.
HOW DID I GET HERE? I WAS COLLECTING THE GOLD NUGGETS AND...
EEEK! MY GOLD NUGGETS!!
NO! WHAT'S HAPPENING?

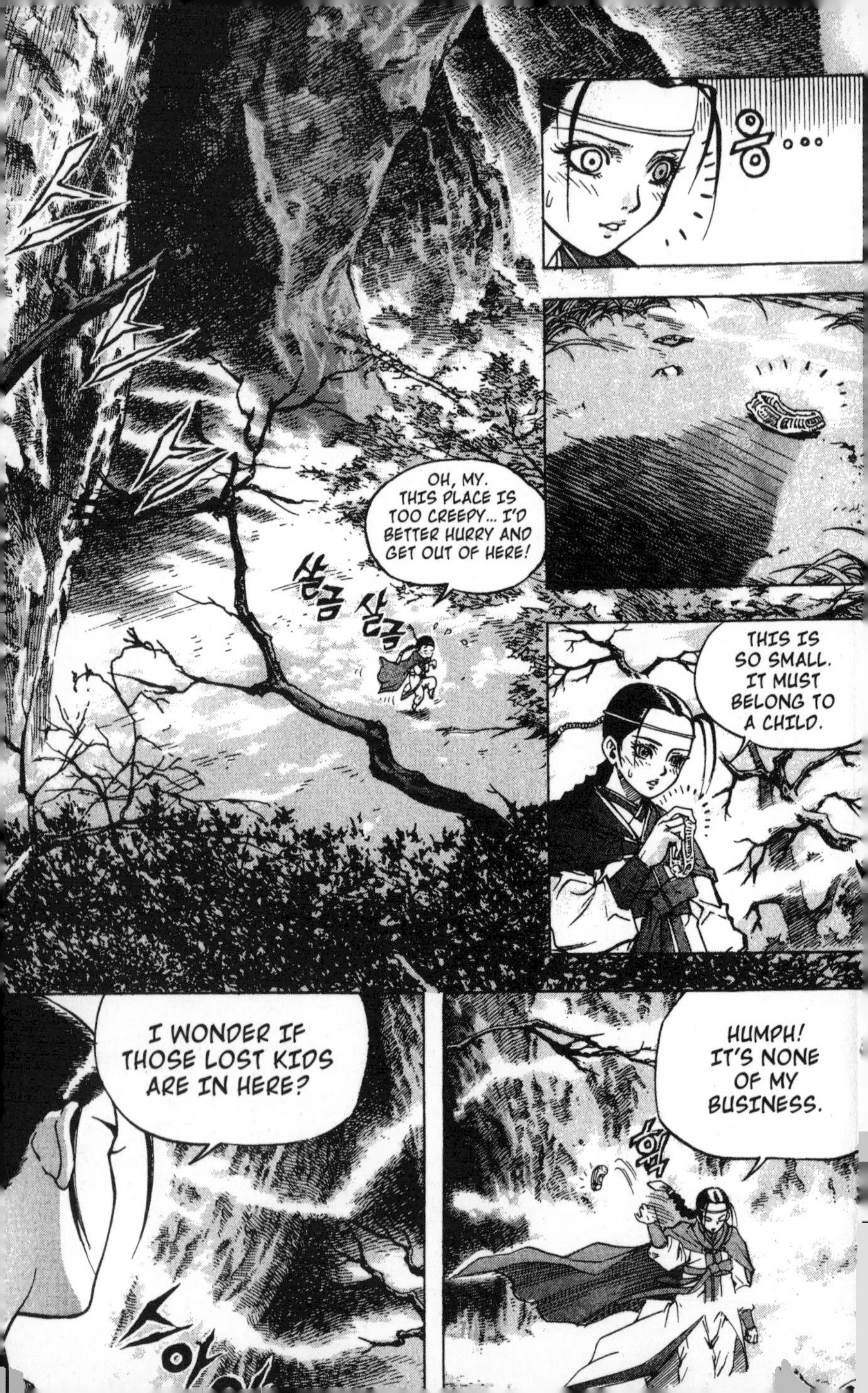
OH, MY. THIS PLACE IS TOO CREEPY... I'D BETTER HURRY AND GET OUT OF HERE!
살금 살금
응...
THIS IS SO SMALL. IT MUST BELONG TO A CHILD.
I WONDER IF THOSE LOST KIDS ARE IN HERE?
HUMPH! IT'S NONE OF MY BUSINESS.
휙

PLEASE, I BEG YOU!

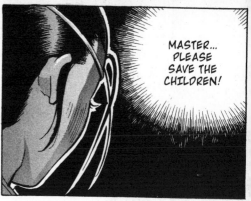

MASTER... PLEASE SAVE THE CHILDREN!

DAMN!

THE CHILDREN...

I'M NOTHING BUT A CON ARTIST!

I HAVE NO POWERS AND I'M SPINELESS TO BOOT!

SO, DON'T RELY ON ME...

...BECAUSE I CAN'T HANDLE IT.

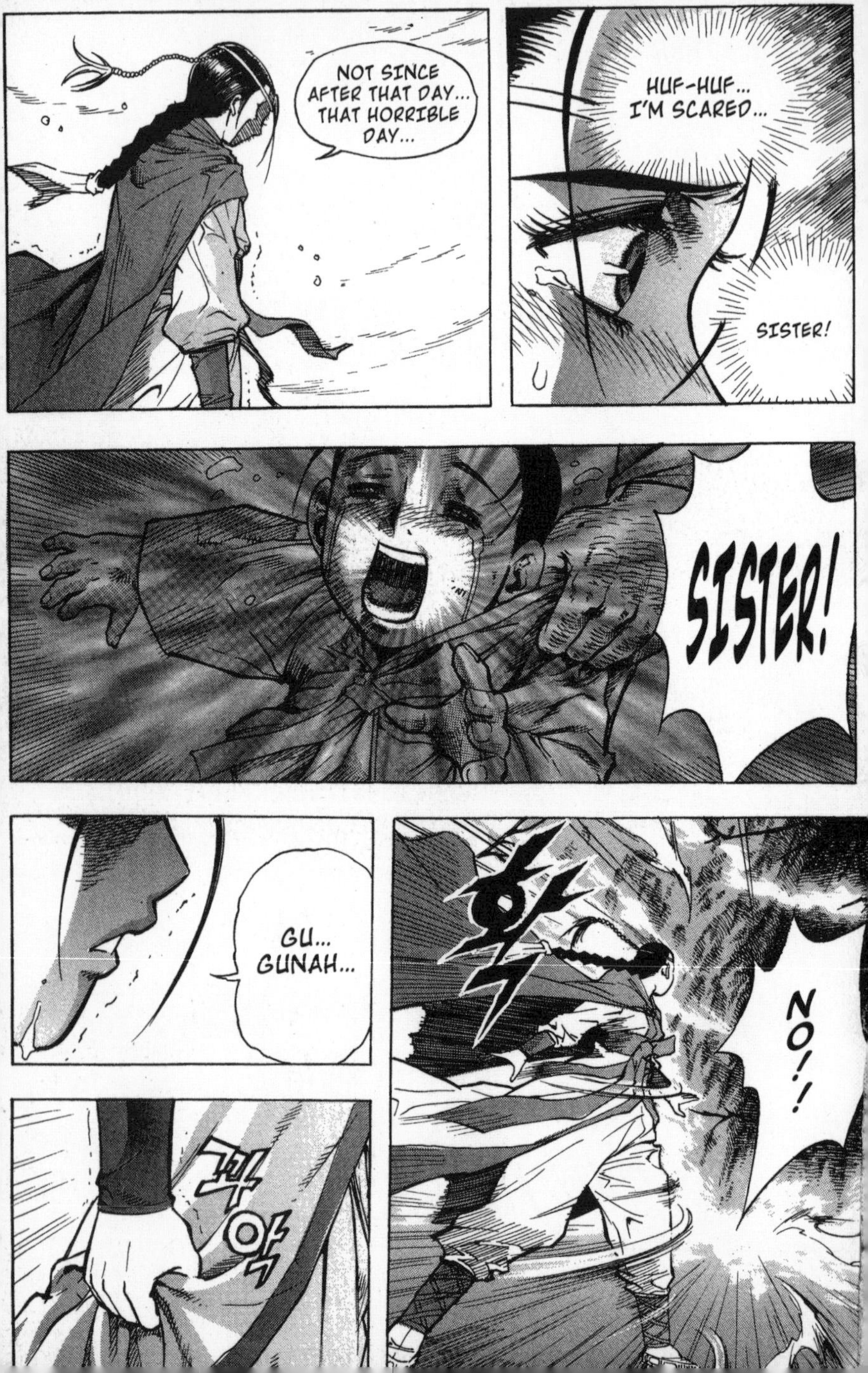
NOT SINCE AFTER THAT DAY... THAT HORRIBLE DAY...
HUF-HUF... I'M SCARED...
SISTER!
SISTER!
GU... GUNAH...
NO!!

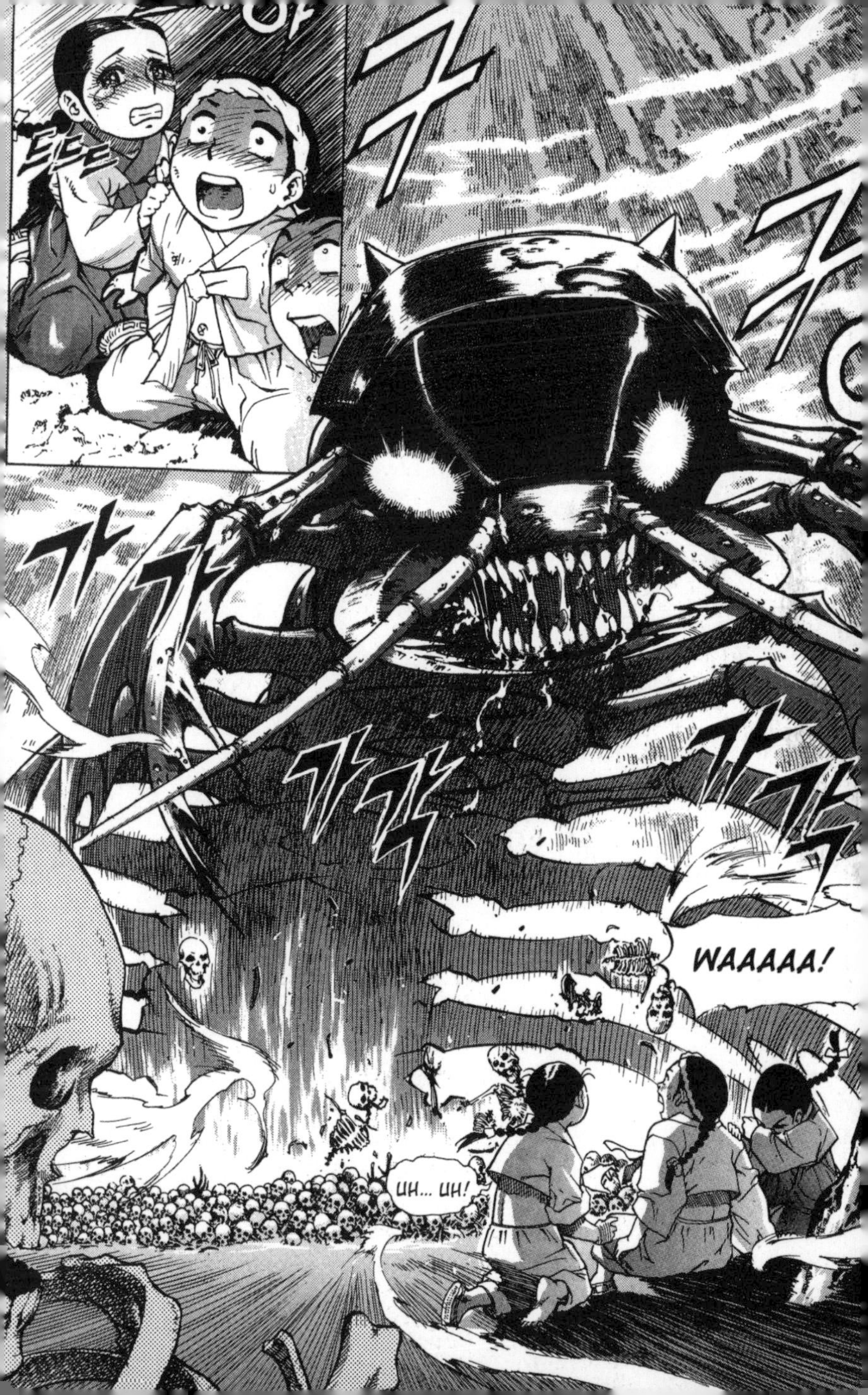
WAAAAA!
UH... UH!

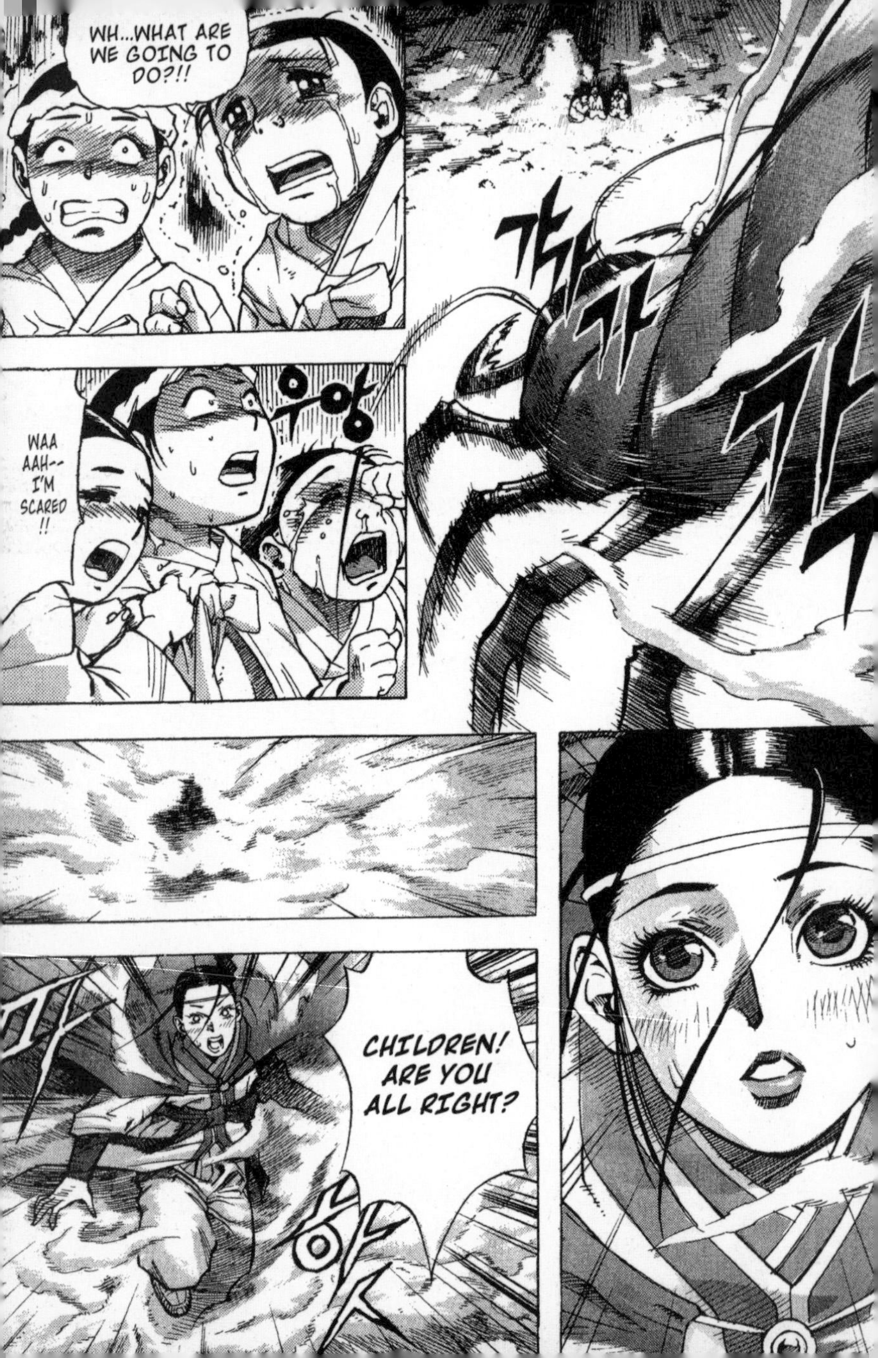
WH...WHAT ARE WE GOING TO DO?!!
WAA AAH-- I'M SCARED !!
CHILDREN! ARE YOU ALL RIGHT?

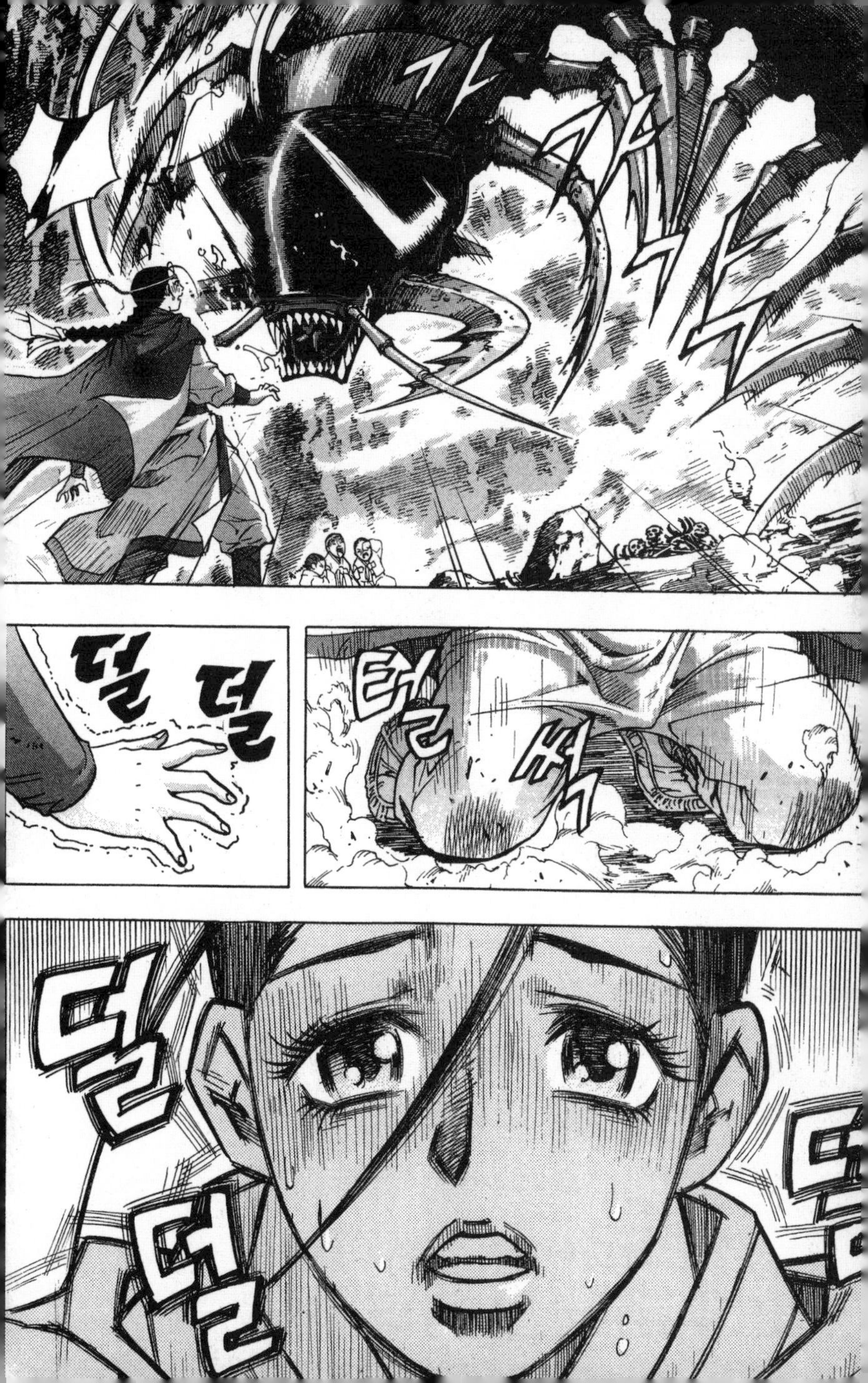
가샤샤
덜덜
털썩
덜덜
덜

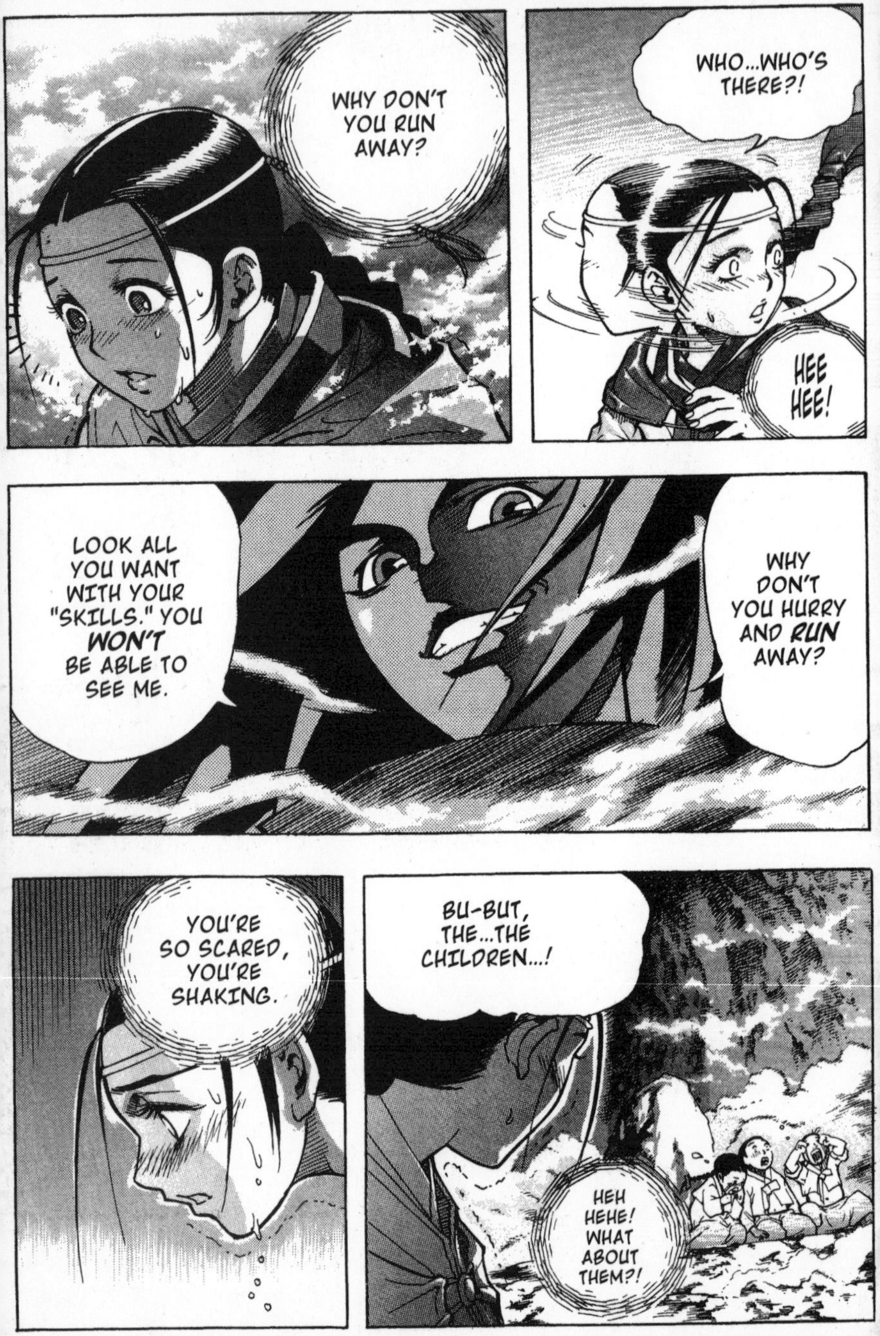
WHY DON'T YOU RUN AWAY?
WHO...WHO'S THERE?!
HEE HEE!
LOOK ALL YOU WANT WITH YOUR "SKILLS." YOU WON'T BE ABLE TO SEE ME.
WHY DON'T YOU HURRY AND RUN AWAY?
YOU'RE SO SCARED, YOU'RE SHAKING.
BU-BUT, THE...THE CHILDREN...!
HEH HEHE! WHAT ABOUT THEM?!

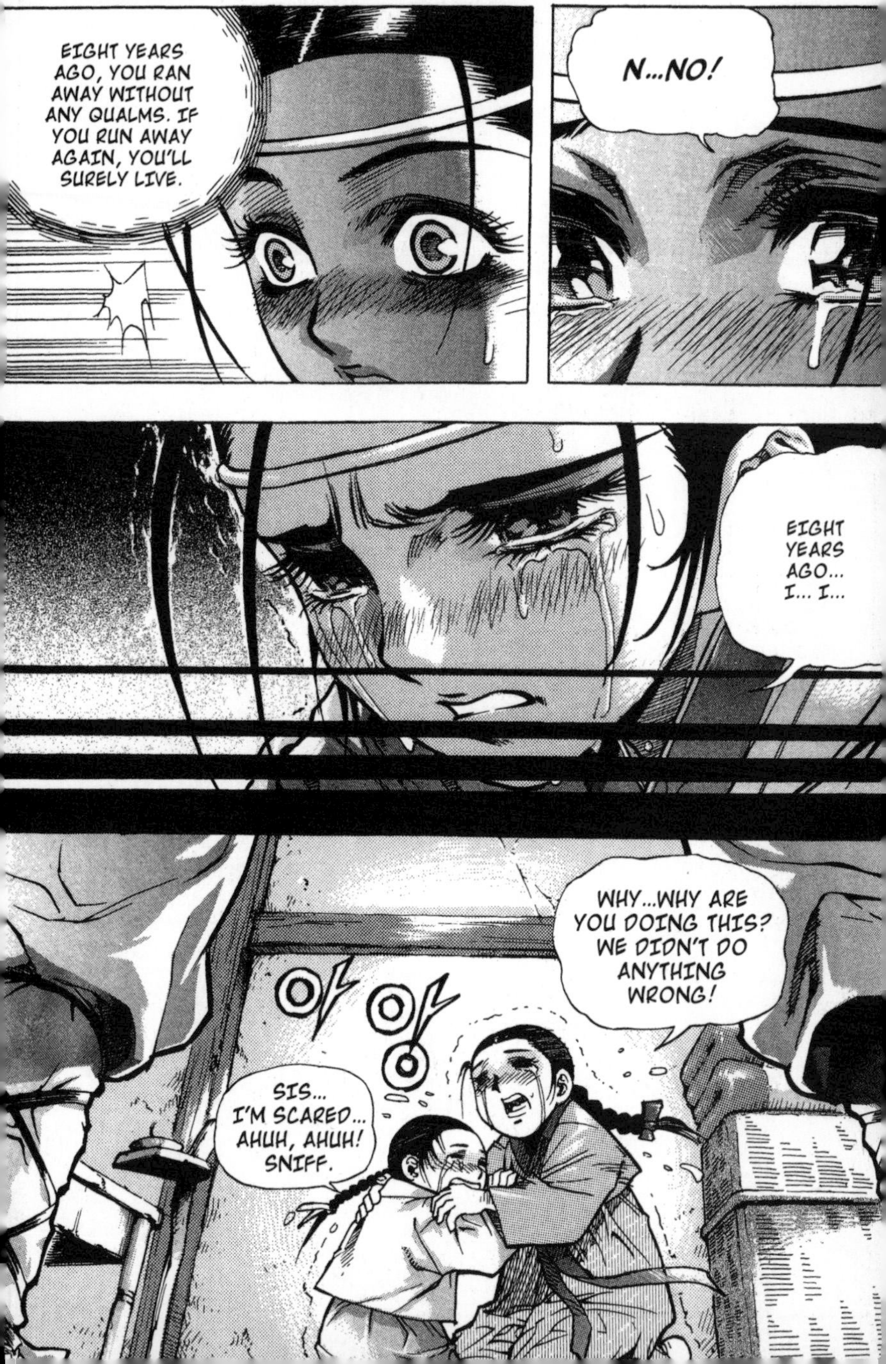
EIGHT YEARS AGO, YOU RAN AWAY WITHOUT ANY QUALMS. IF YOU RUN AWAY AGAIN, YOU'LL SURELY LIVE.
N...NO!
EIGHT YEARS AGO... I... I...
WHY...WHY ARE YOU DOING THIS? WE DIDN'T DO ANYTHING WRONG!
SIS... I'M SCARED... AHUH, AHUH! SNIFF.

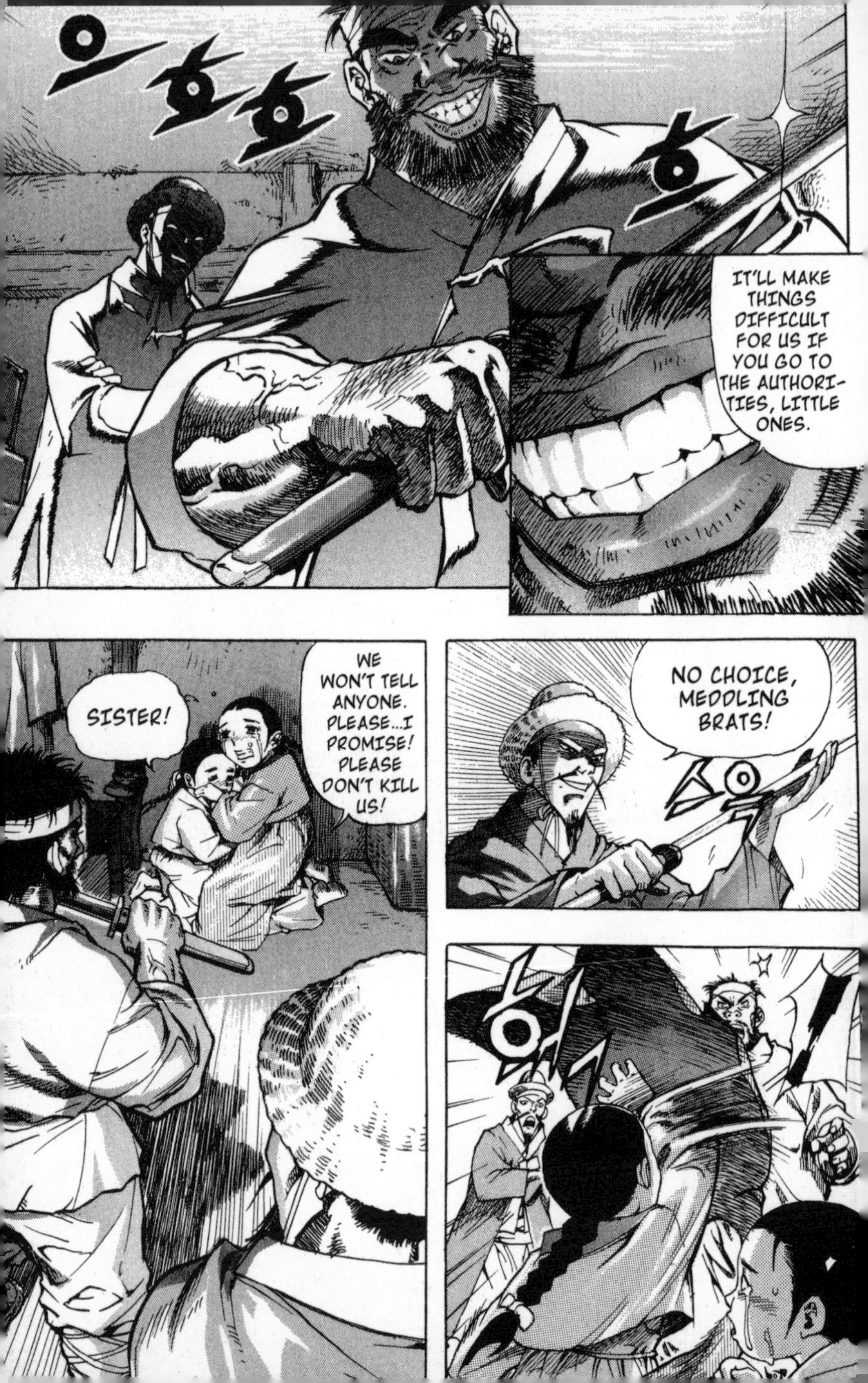
IT'LL MAKE THINGS DIFFICULT FOR US IF YOU GO TO THE AUTHORITIES, LITTLE ONES.
SISTER!
WE WON'T TELL ANYONE. PLEASE...I PROMISE! PLEASE DON'T KILL US!
NO CHOICE, MEDDLING BRATS!

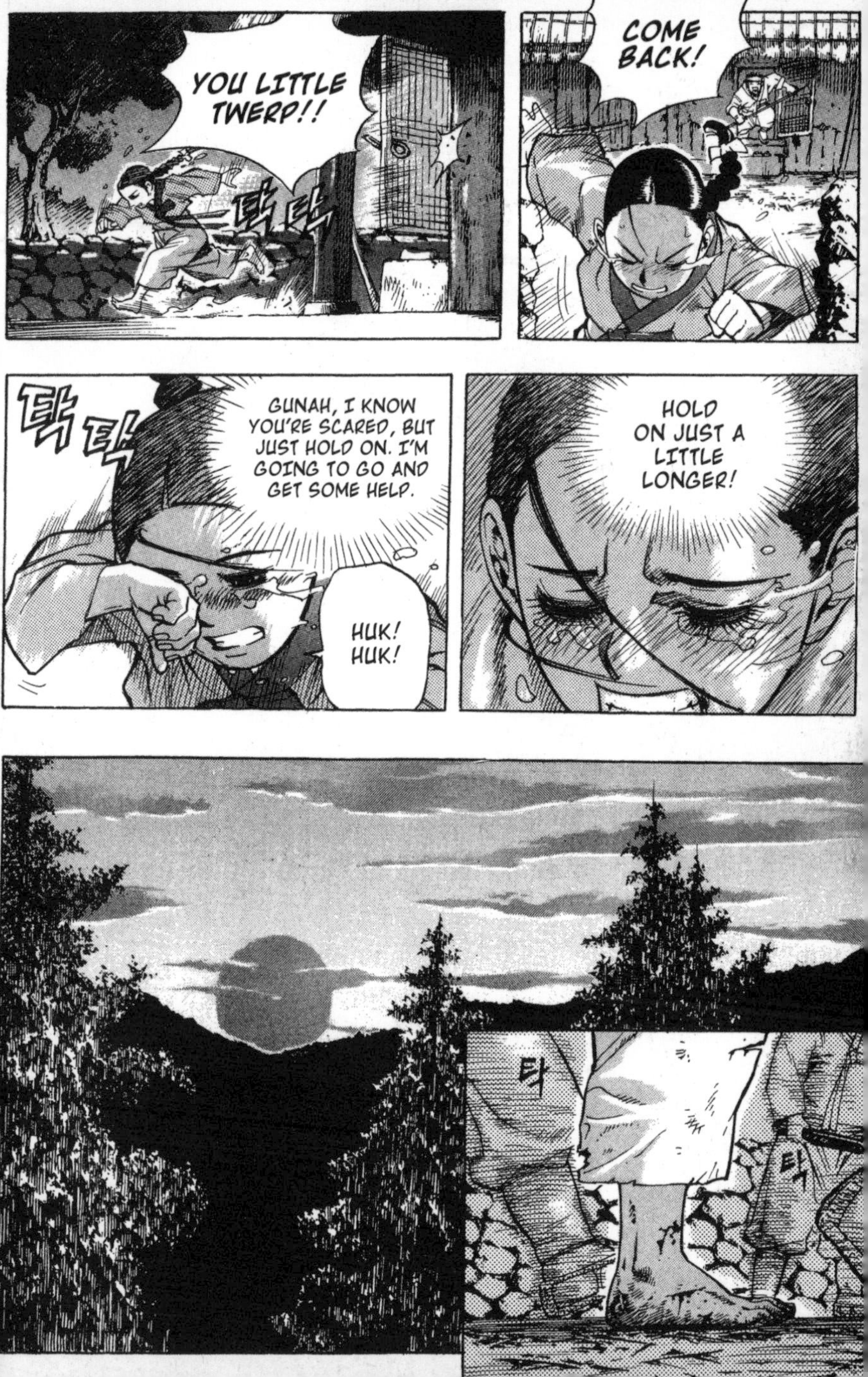
YOU LITTLE TWERP!!
COME BACK!
GUNAH, I KNOW YOU'RE SCARED, BUT JUST HOLD ON. I'M GOING TO GO AND GET SOME HELP.
HUK! HUK!
HOLD ON JUST A LITTLE LONGER!
타
탁

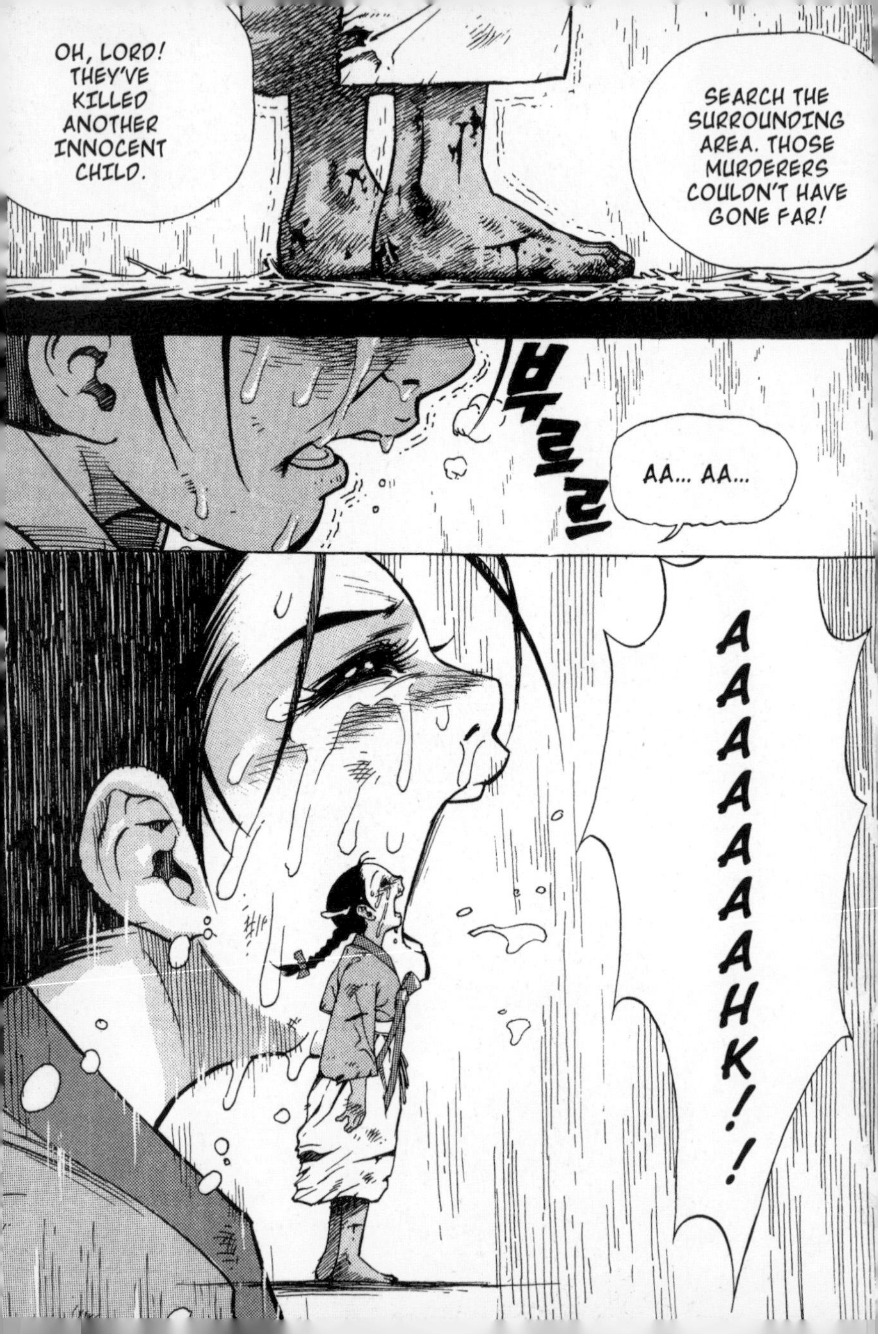
OH, LORD! THEY'VE KILLED ANOTHER INNOCENT CHILD.
SEARCH THE SURROUNDING AREA. THOSE MURDERERS COULDN'T HAVE GONE FAR!
부르르
AA... AA...
AAAAAAAAAHK!!

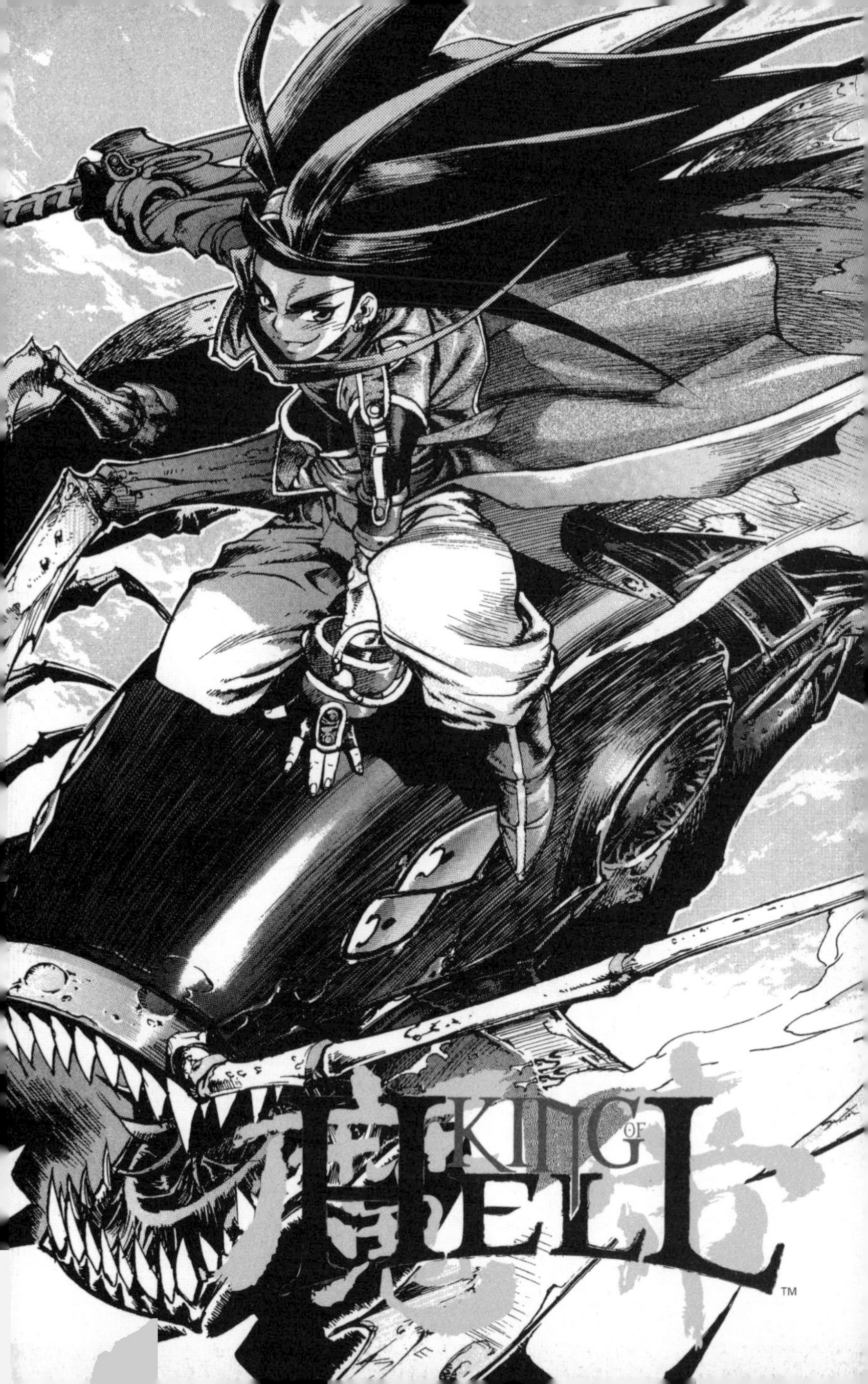
KING OF HELL
™

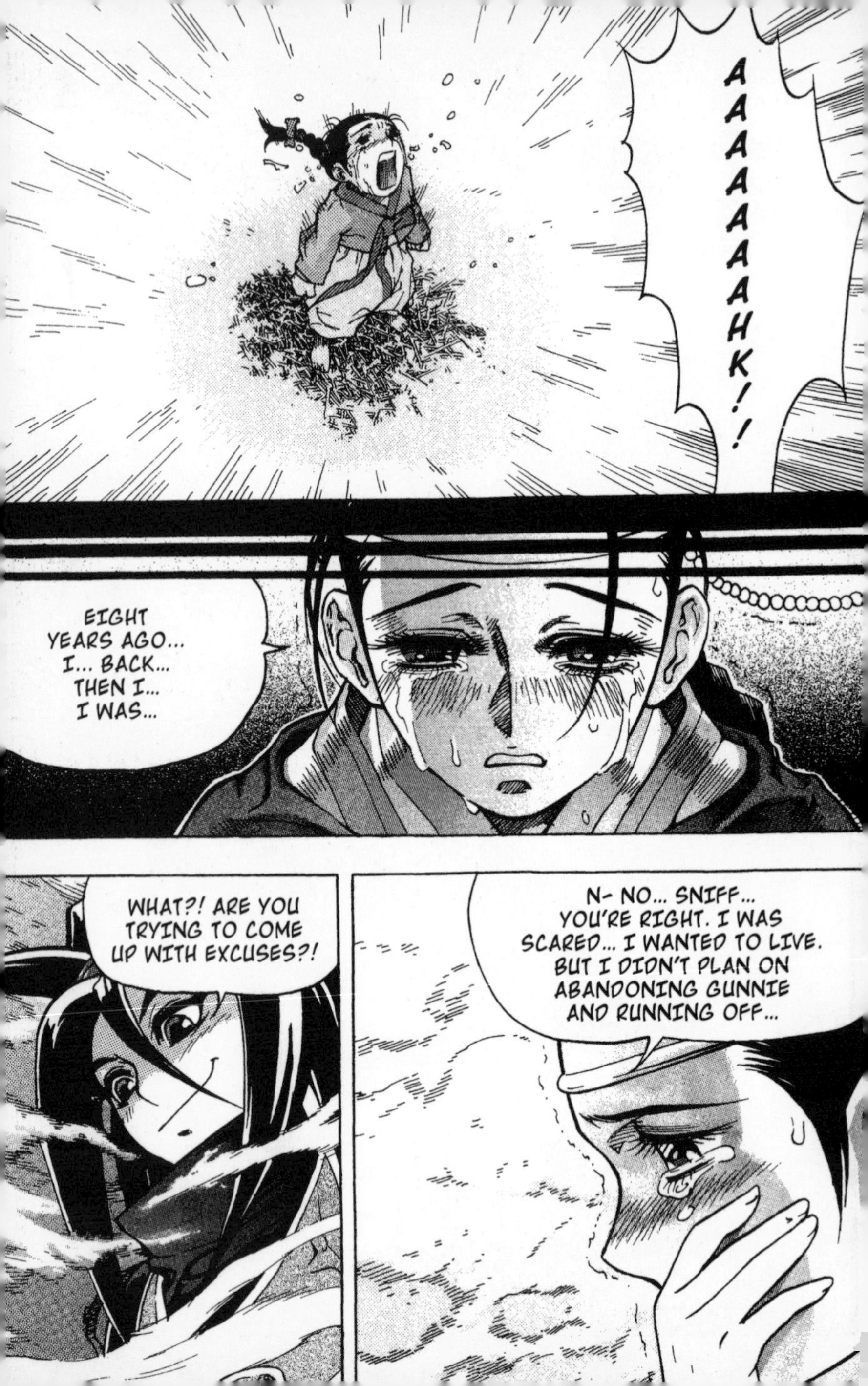
AAAAAAAAAHK!!
EIGHT YEARS AGO... I... BACK... THEN I... I WAS...
WHAT?! ARE YOU TRYING TO COME UP WITH EXCUSES?!
N- NO... SNIFF... YOU'RE RIGHT. I WAS SCARED... I WANTED TO LIVE. BUT I DIDN'T PLAN ON ABANDONING GUNNIE AND RUNNING OFF...

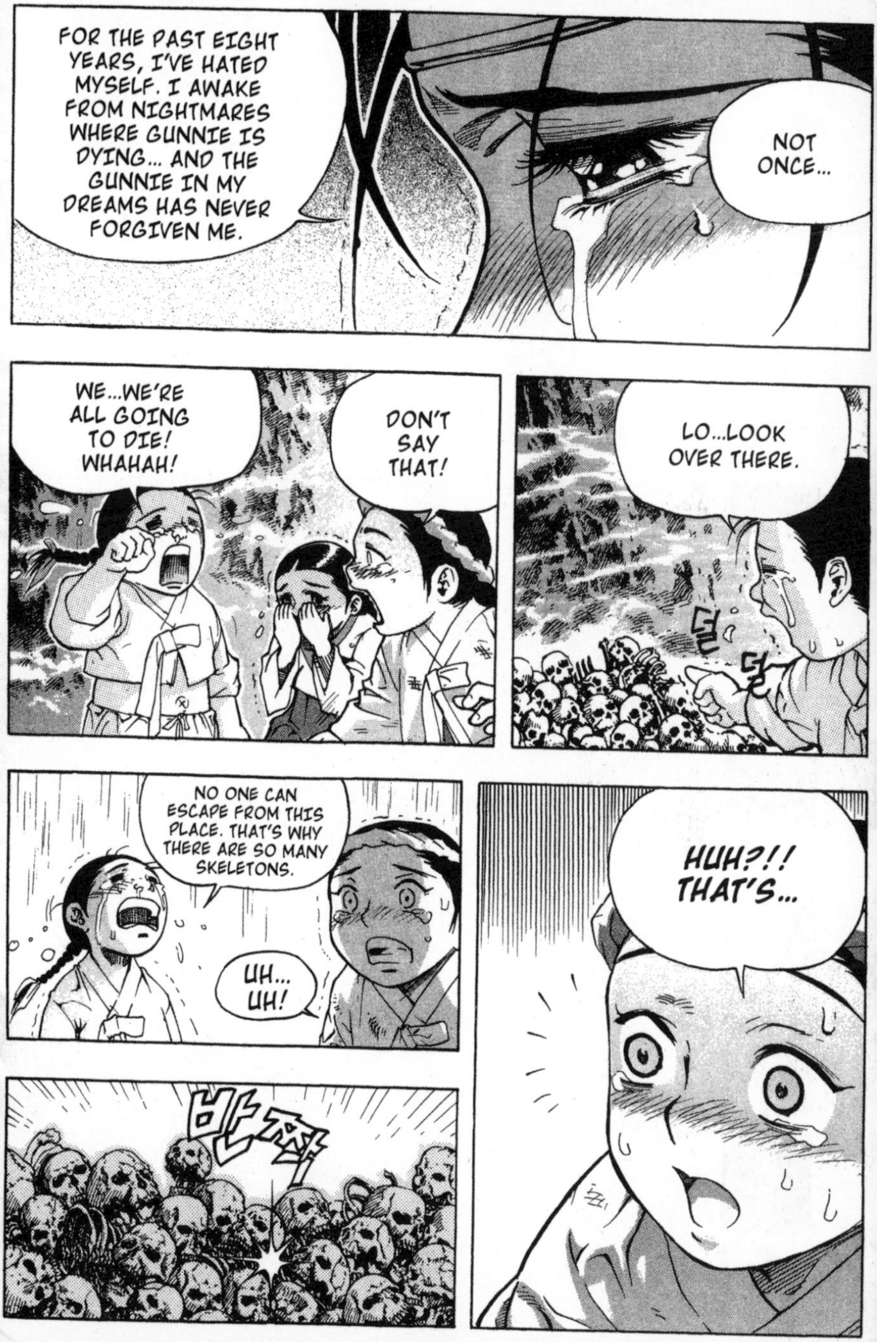
FOR THE PAST EIGHT YEARS, I'VE HATED MYSELF. I AWAKE FROM NIGHTMARES WHERE GUNNIE IS DYING... AND THE GUNNIE IN MY DREAMS HAS NEVER FORGIVEN ME.
NOT ONCE...
WE...WE'RE ALL GOING TO DIE! WHAHAH!
DON'T SAY THAT!
LO...LOOK OVER THERE.
덜 덜
NO ONE CAN ESCAPE FROM THIS PLACE. THAT'S WHY THERE ARE SO MANY SKELETONS.
UH... UH!
반짝
HUH?!! THAT'S...

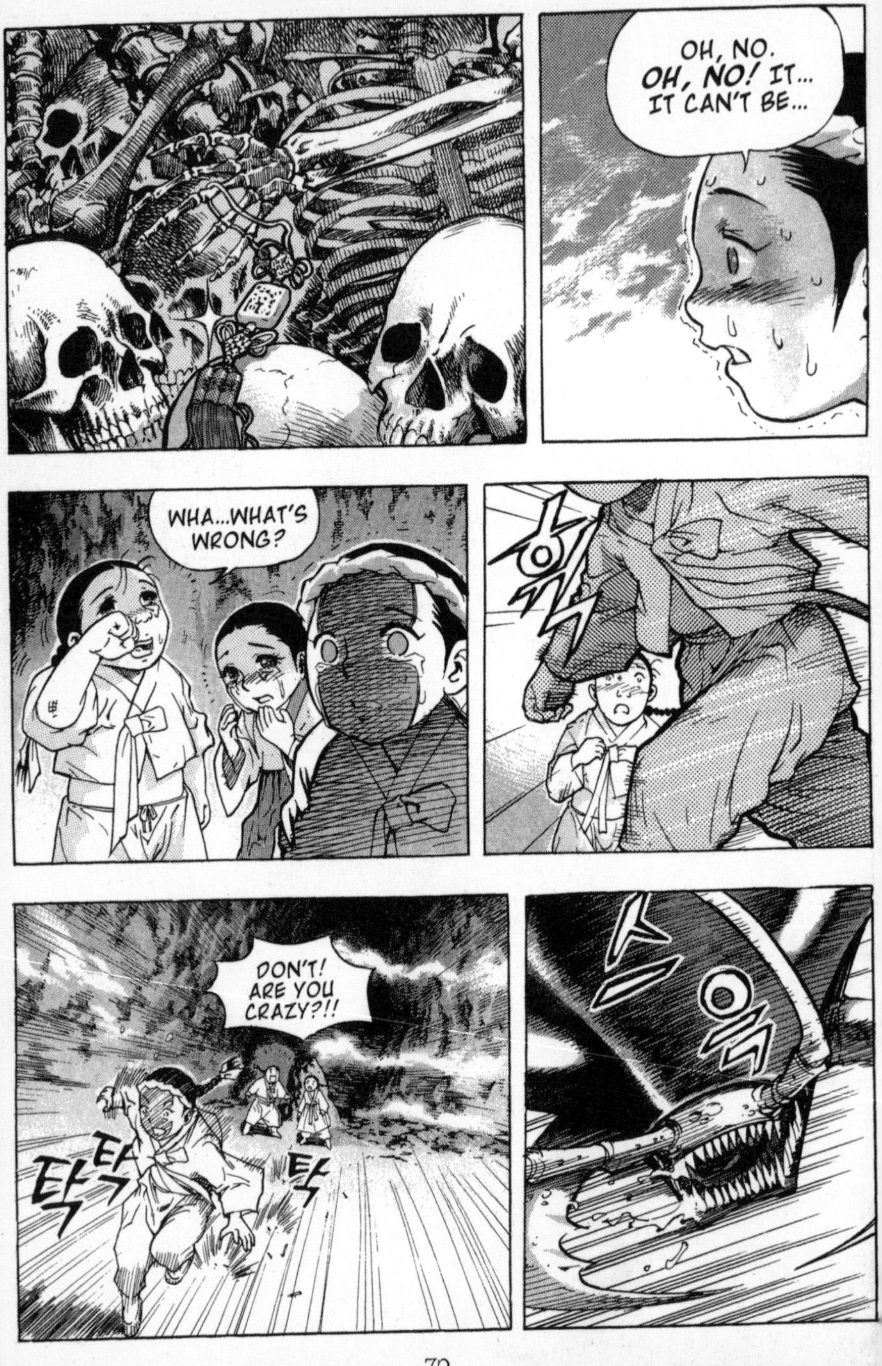
OH, NO.
OH, NO! IT... IT CAN'T BE...
WHA...WHAT'S WRONG?
DON'T! ARE YOU CRAZY?!!

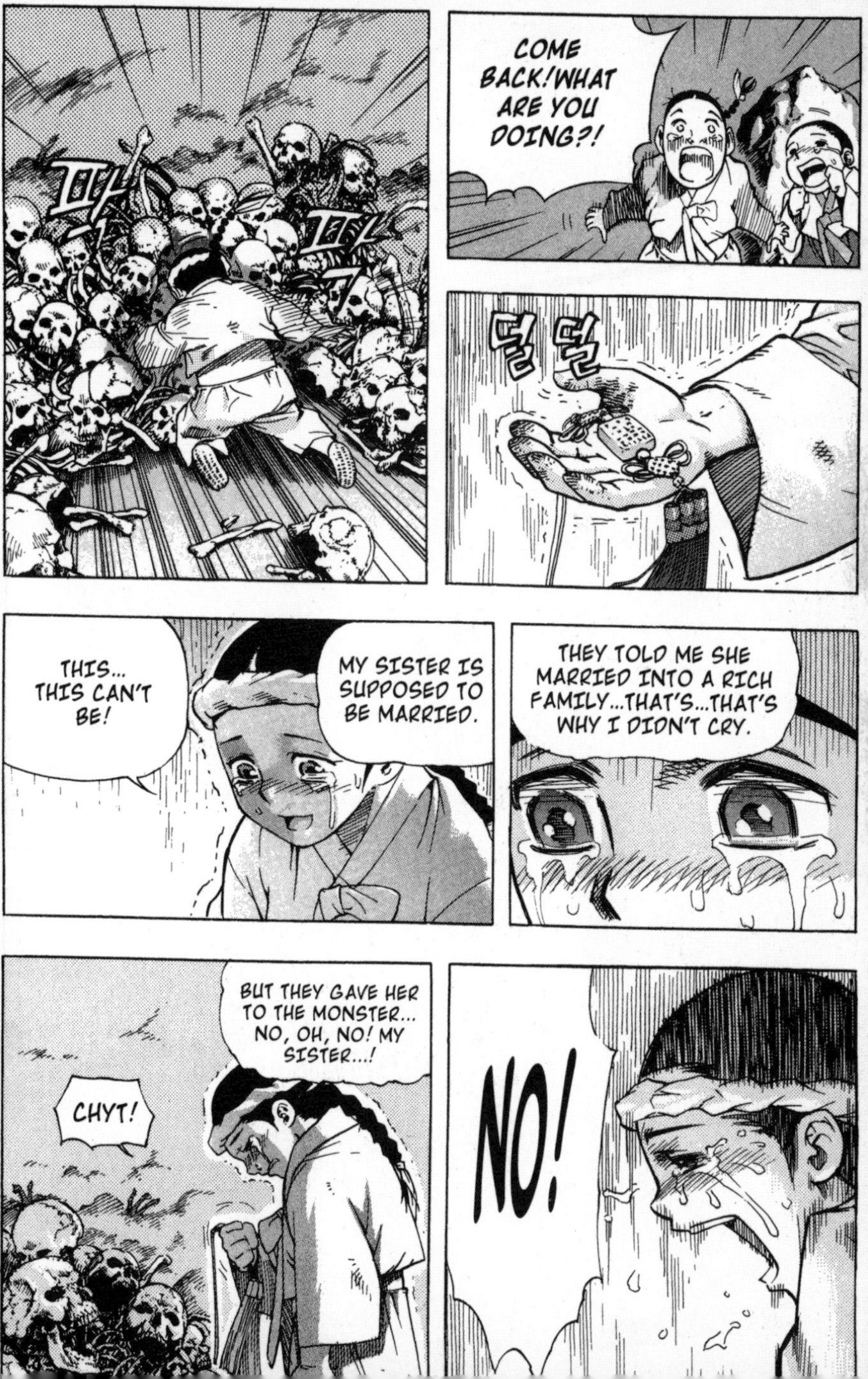
COME BACK! WHAT ARE YOU DOING?!
덜덜
THIS... THIS CAN'T BE!
MY SISTER IS SUPPOSED TO BE MARRIED.
THEY TOLD ME SHE MARRIED INTO A RICH FAMILY...THAT'S...THAT'S WHY I DIDN'T CRY.
BUT THEY GAVE HER TO THE MONSTER... NO, OH, NO! MY SISTER...!
CHYT!
NO!

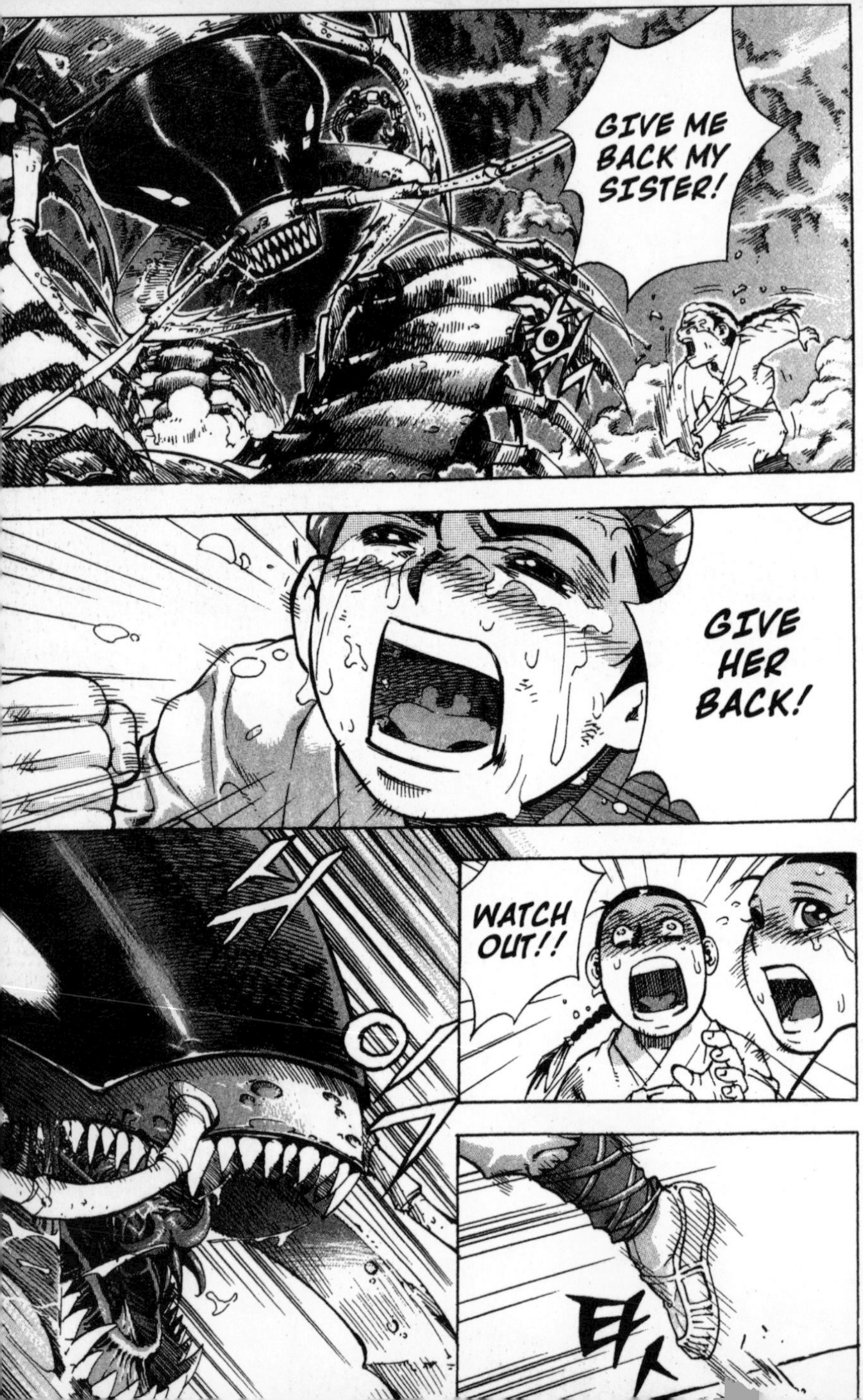
GIVE ME BACK MY SISTER!
GIVE HER BACK!
WATCH OUT!!

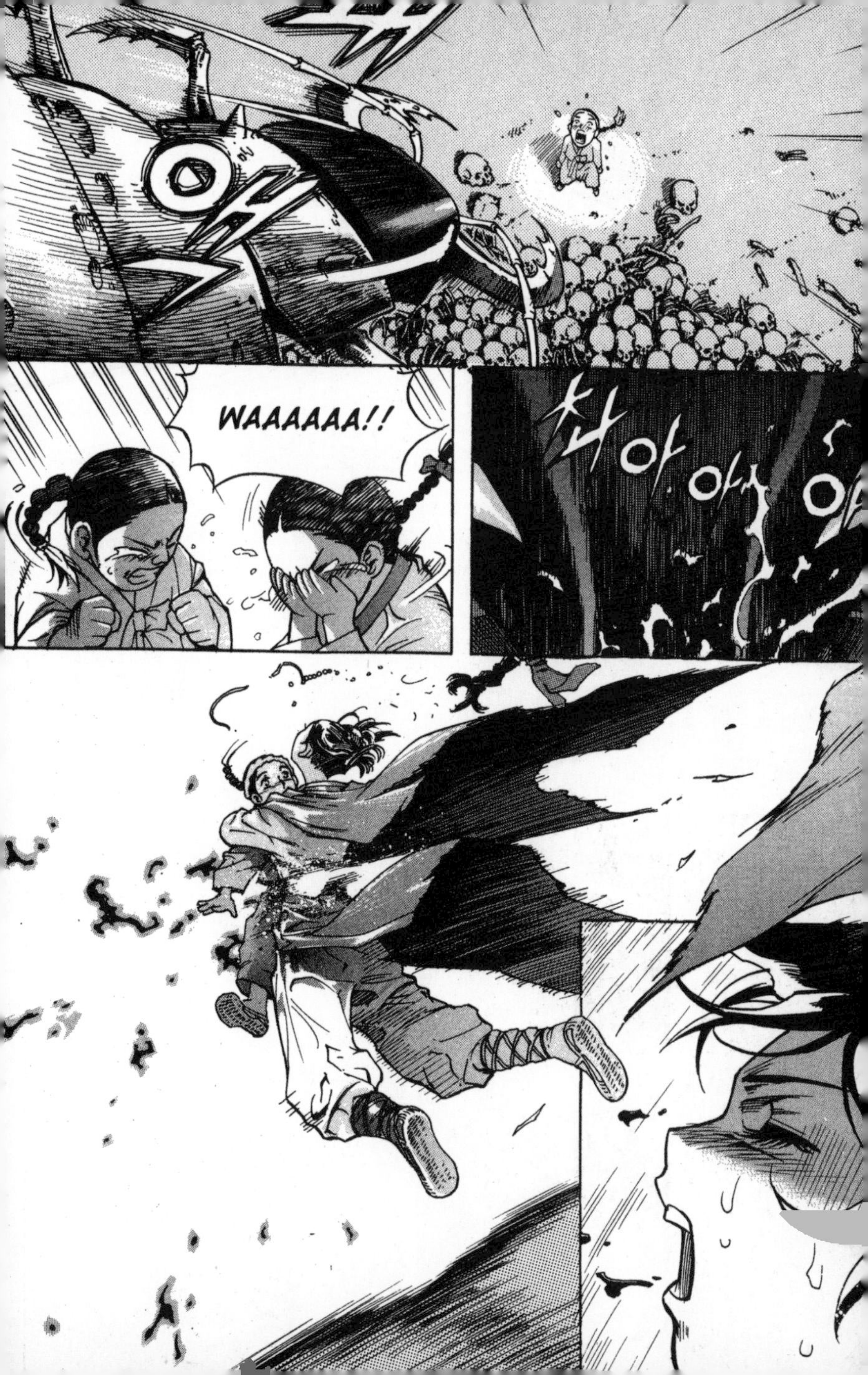
WAAAAAA!!

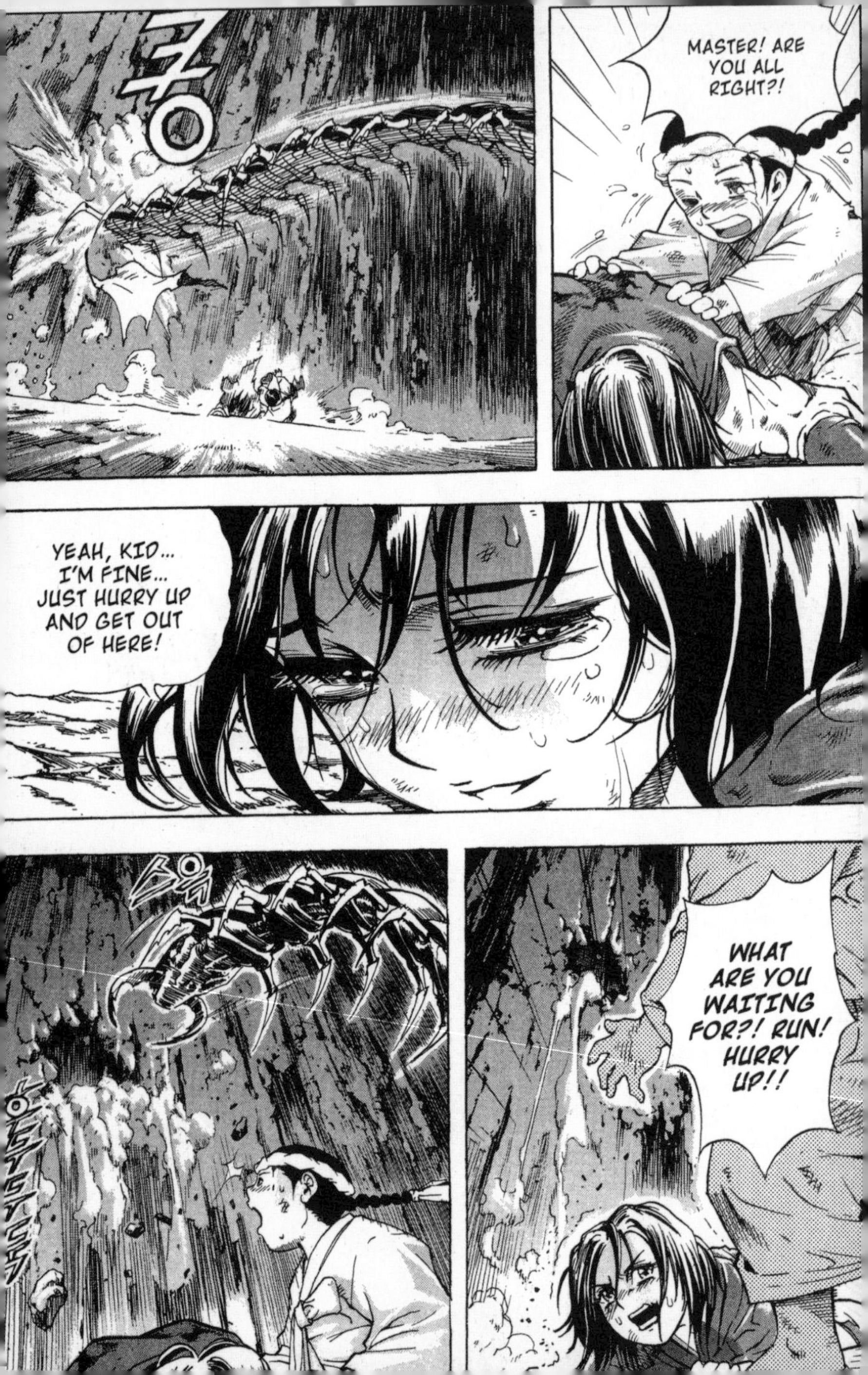
MASTER! ARE YOU ALL RIGHT?!
YEAH, KID... I'M FINE... JUST HURRY UP AND GET OUT OF HERE!
WHAT ARE YOU WAITING FOR?! RUN! HURRY UP!!

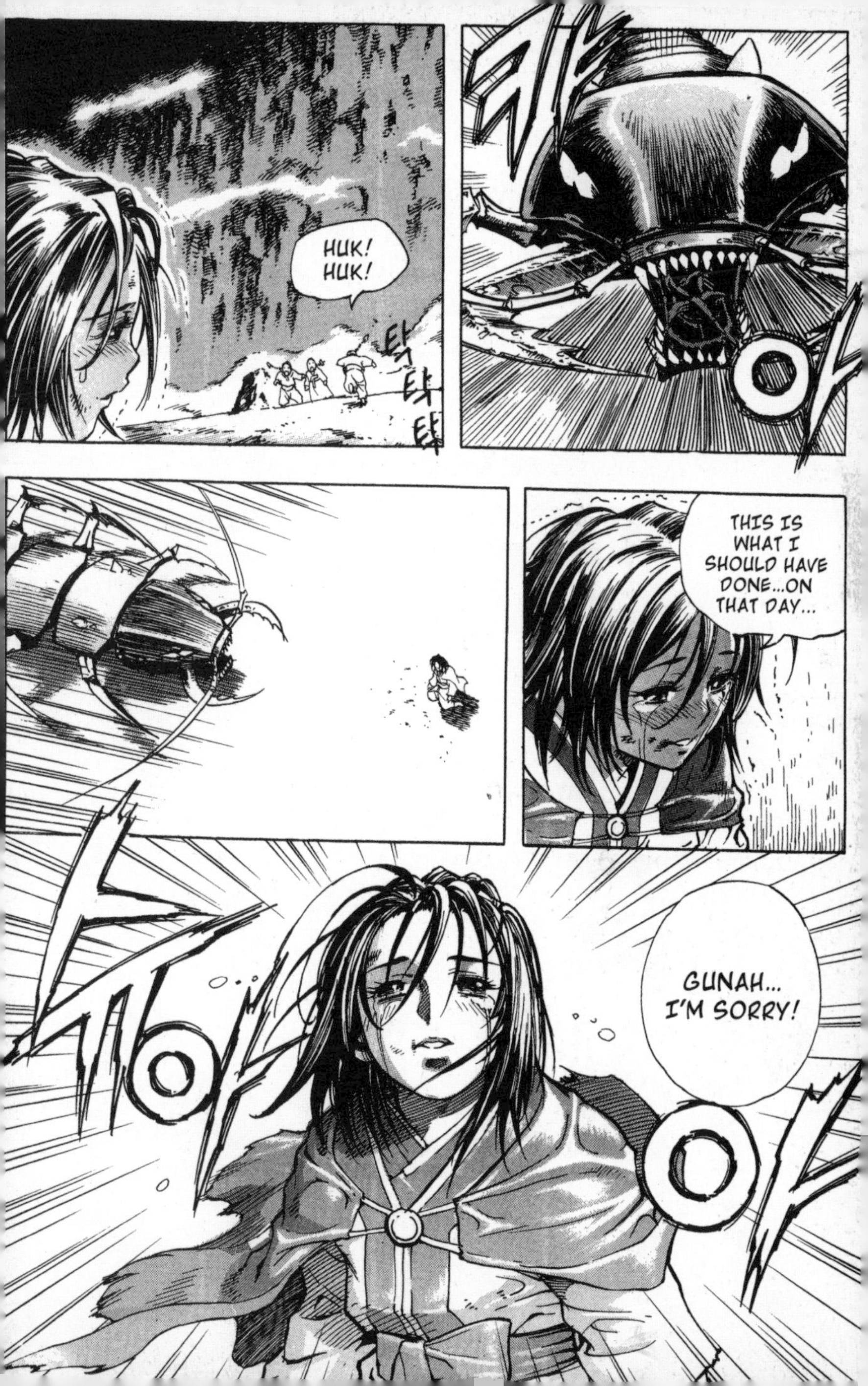
HUK! HUK!
탁
탁
탁
THIS IS WHAT I SHOULD HAVE DONE...ON THAT DAY...
GUNAH... I'M SORRY!

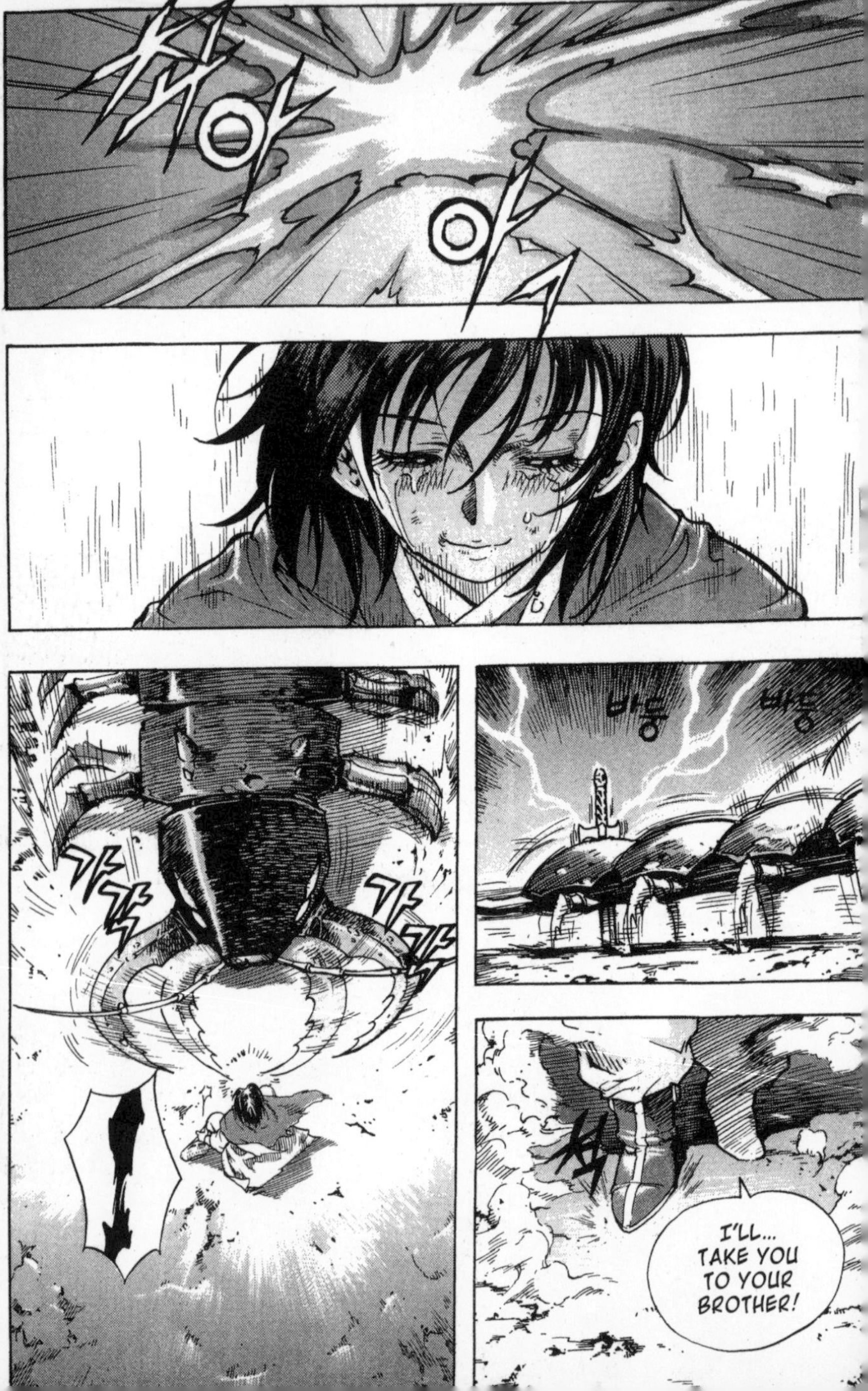
가각
가각
바둥
바둥
I'LL... TAKE YOU TO YOUR BROTHER!

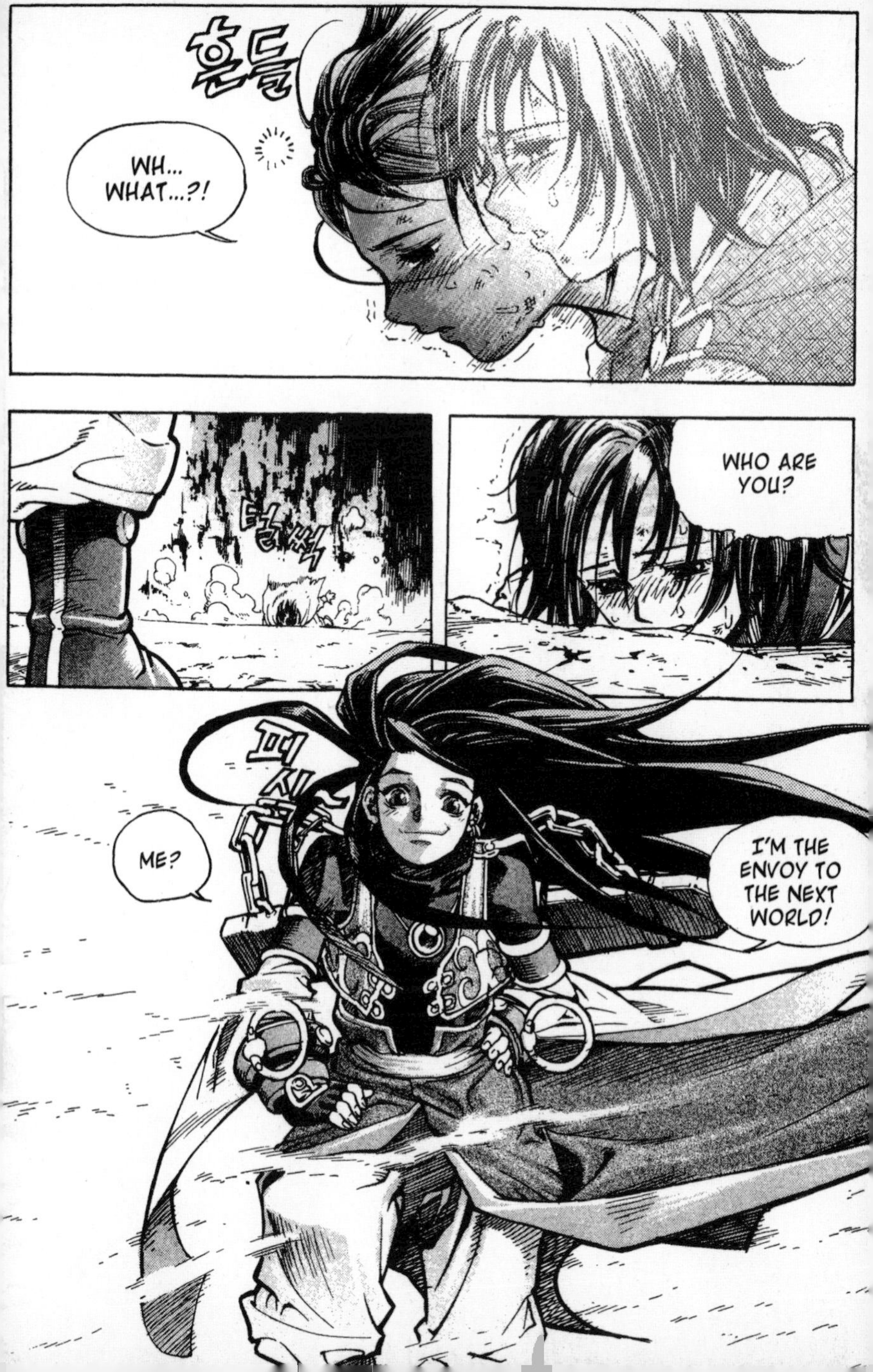

흔들
WH... WHAT...?!
WHO ARE YOU?
ME?
I'M THE ENVOY TO THE NEXT WORLD!

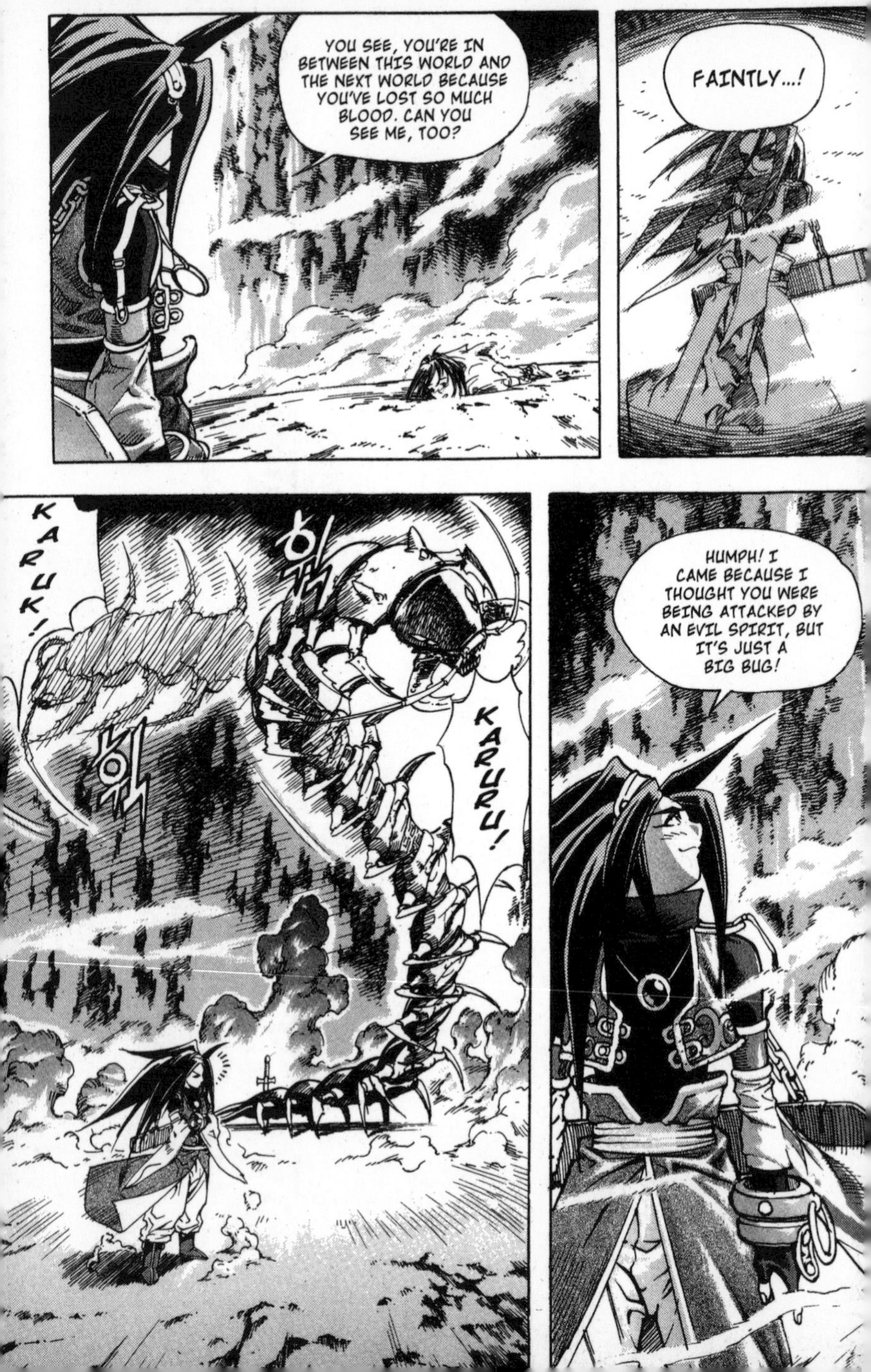
YOU SEE, YOU'RE IN BETWEEN THIS WORLD AND THE NEXT WORLD BECAUSE YOU'VE LOST SO MUCH BLOOD. CAN YOU SEE ME, TOO?
FAINTLY...!
KARUK!
KARURU!
HUMPH! I CAME BECAUSE I THOUGHT YOU WERE BEING ATTACKED BY AN EVIL SPIRIT, BUT IT'S JUST A BIG BUG!

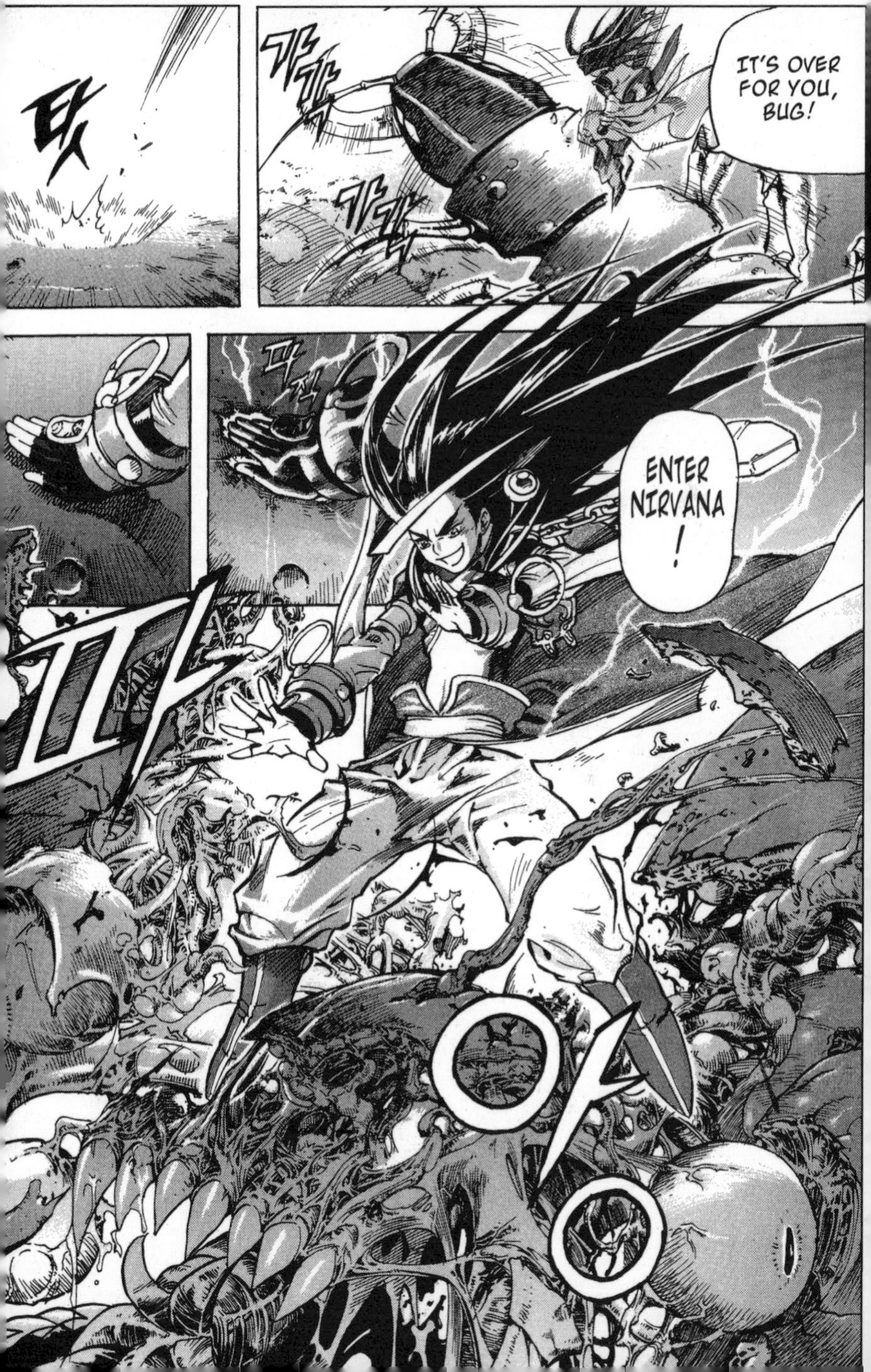
IT'S OVER FOR YOU, BUG!
ENTER NIRVANA!

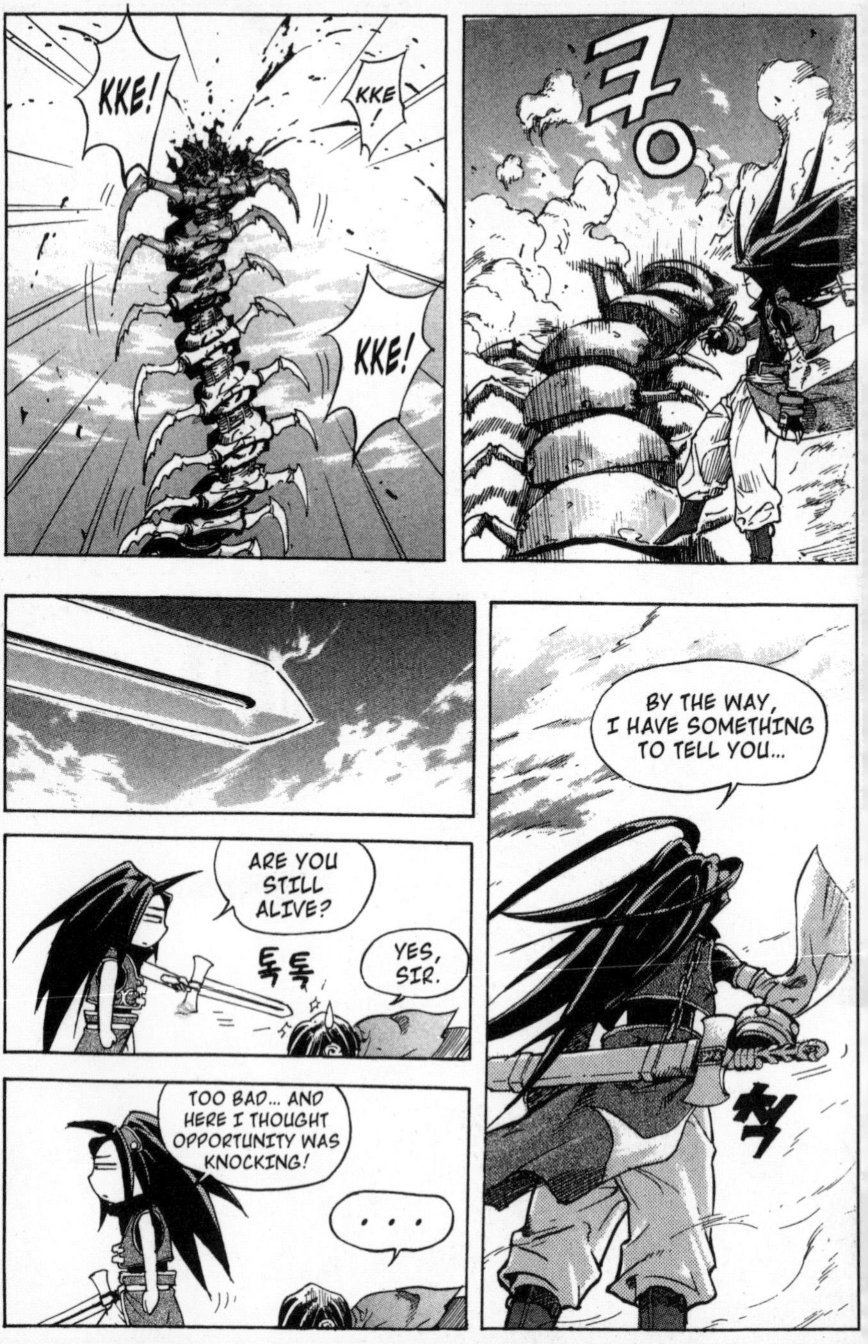
KKE!
KKE
KKE!
ARE YOU STILL ALIVE?
톡톡
YES, SIR.
TOO BAD... AND HERE I THOUGHT OPPORTUNITY WAS KNOCKING!
...
BY THE WAY, I HAVE SOMETHING TO TELL YOU...

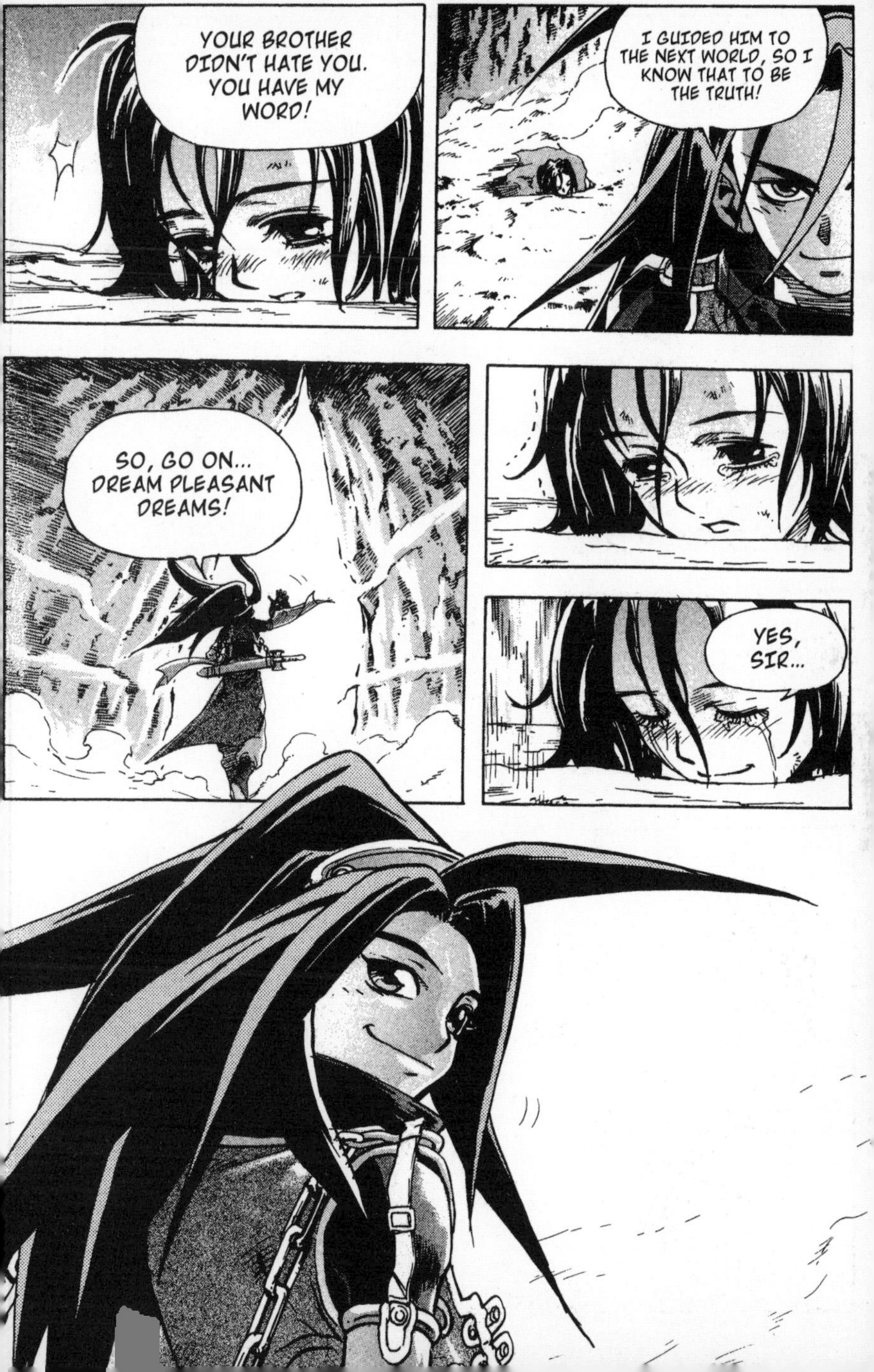
YOUR BROTHER DIDN'T HATE YOU. YOU HAVE MY WORD!
I GUIDED HIM TO THE NEXT WORLD, SO I KNOW THAT TO BE THE TRUTH!
SO, GO ON... DREAM PLEASANT DREAMS!
YES, SIR...

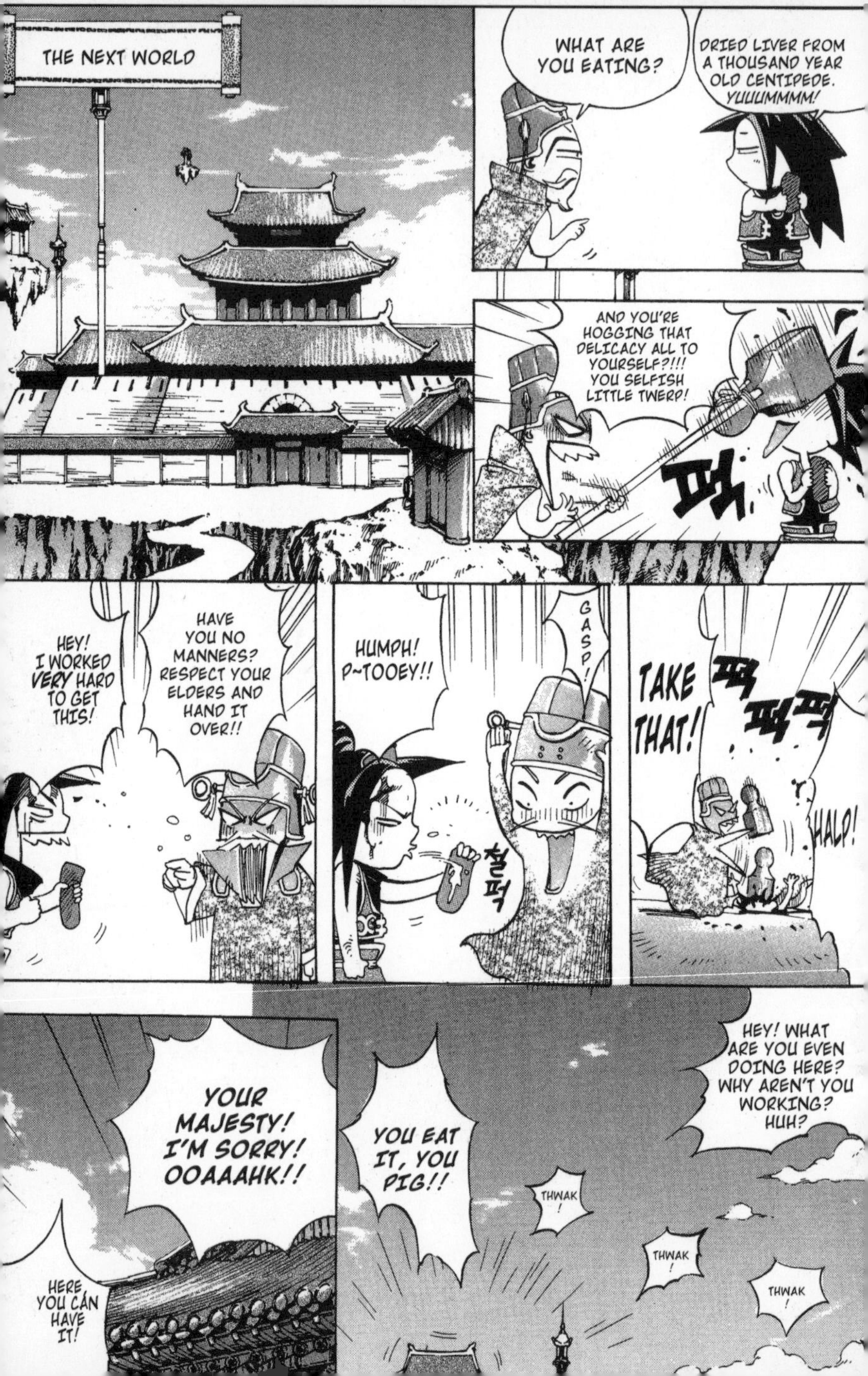
THE NEXT WORLD
WHAT ARE YOU EATING?
DRIED LIVER FROM A THOUSAND YEAR OLD CENTIPEDE. YUUUMMMM!
AND YOU'RE HOGGING THAT DELICACY ALL TO YOURSELF?!!! YOU SELFISH LITTLE TWERP!
퍽
HAVE YOU NO MANNERS? RESPECT YOUR ELDERS AND HAND IT OVER!!
HEY! I WORKED VERY HARD TO GET THIS!
HUMPH! P~TOOEY!!
GASP!
철퍽
TAKE THAT!
퍽
퍽퍽
HALP!
YOUR MAJESTY! I'M SORRY! OOAAAHK!!
HERE YOU CAN HAVE IT!
HEY! WHAT ARE YOU EVEN DOING HERE? WHY AREN'T YOU WORKING? HUH?
YOU EAT IT, YOU PIG!!
THWAK!
THWAK!
THWAK!

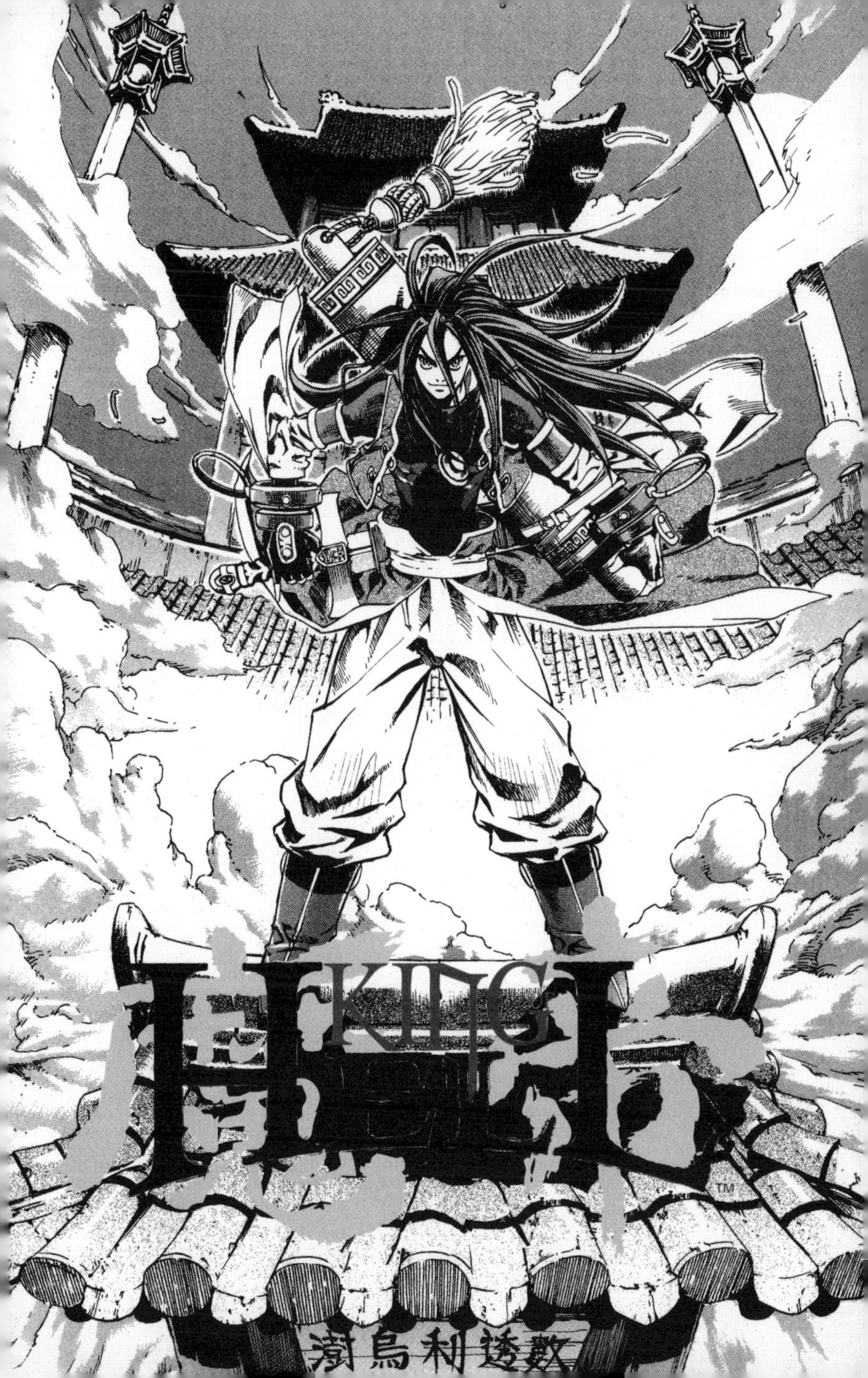
KING
TM
澍鳥利透數

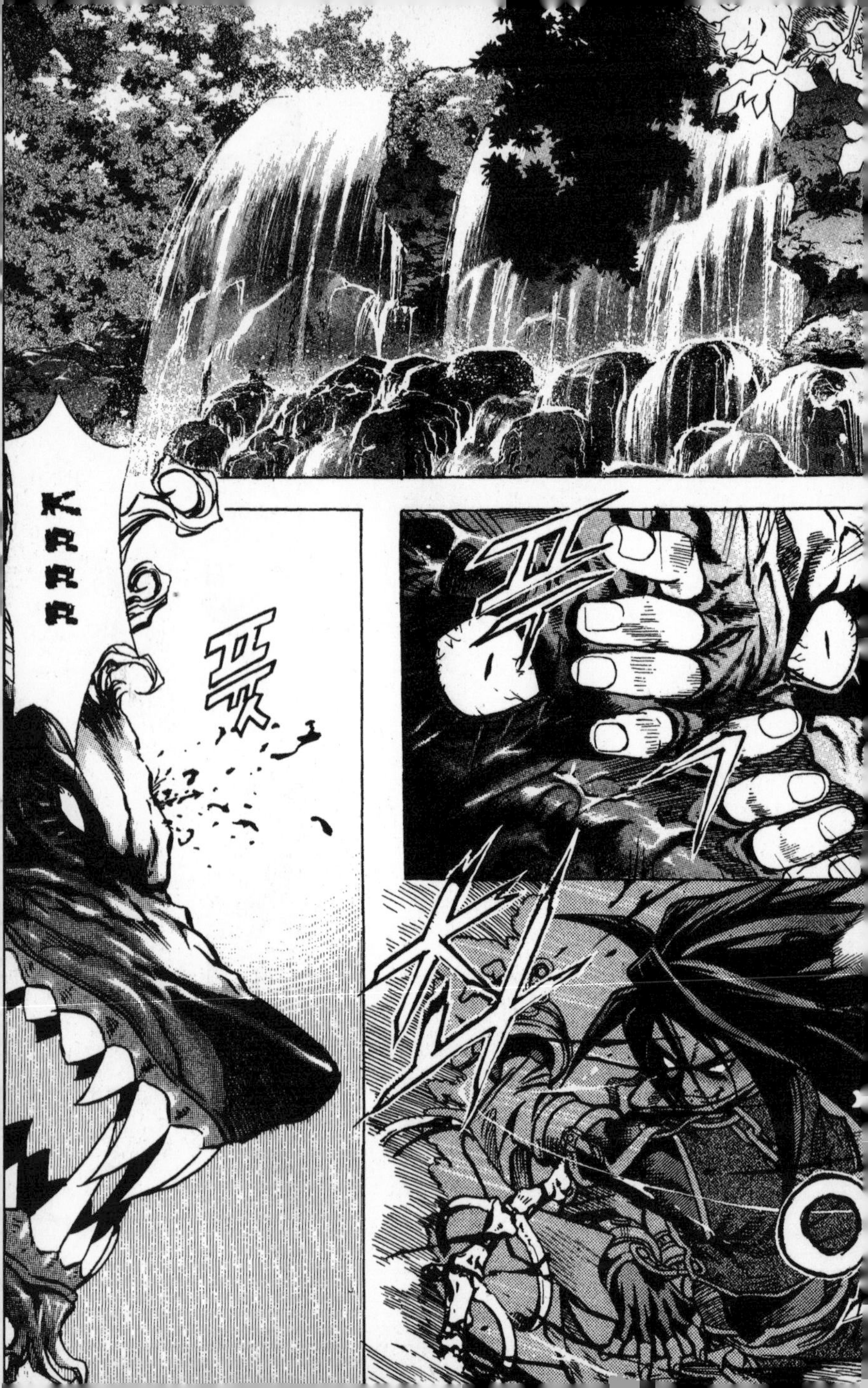
KRRRR

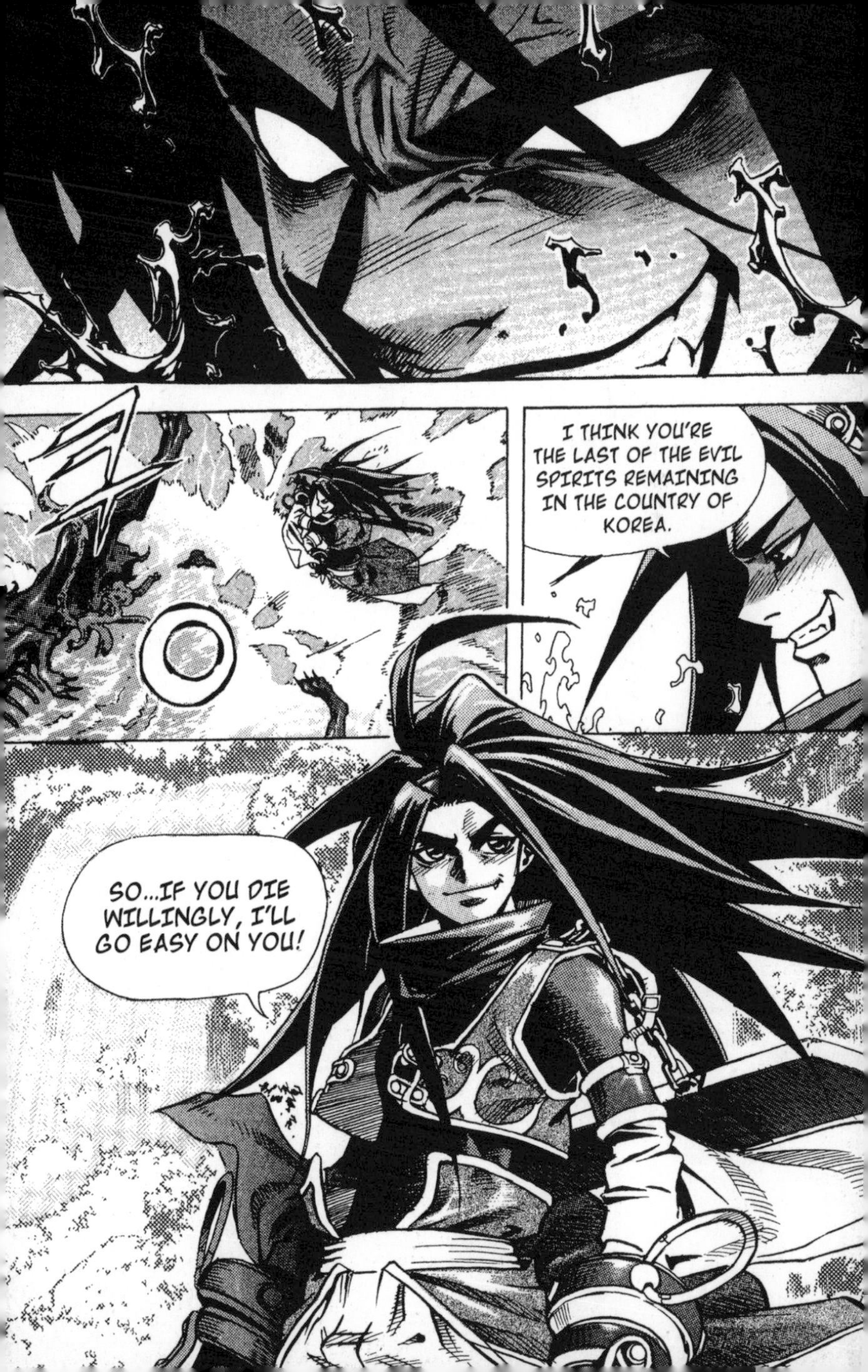
I THINK YOU'RE THE LAST OF THE EVIL SPIRITS REMAINING IN THE COUNTRY OF KOREA.
SO...IF YOU DIE WILLINGLY, I'LL GO EASY ON YOU!

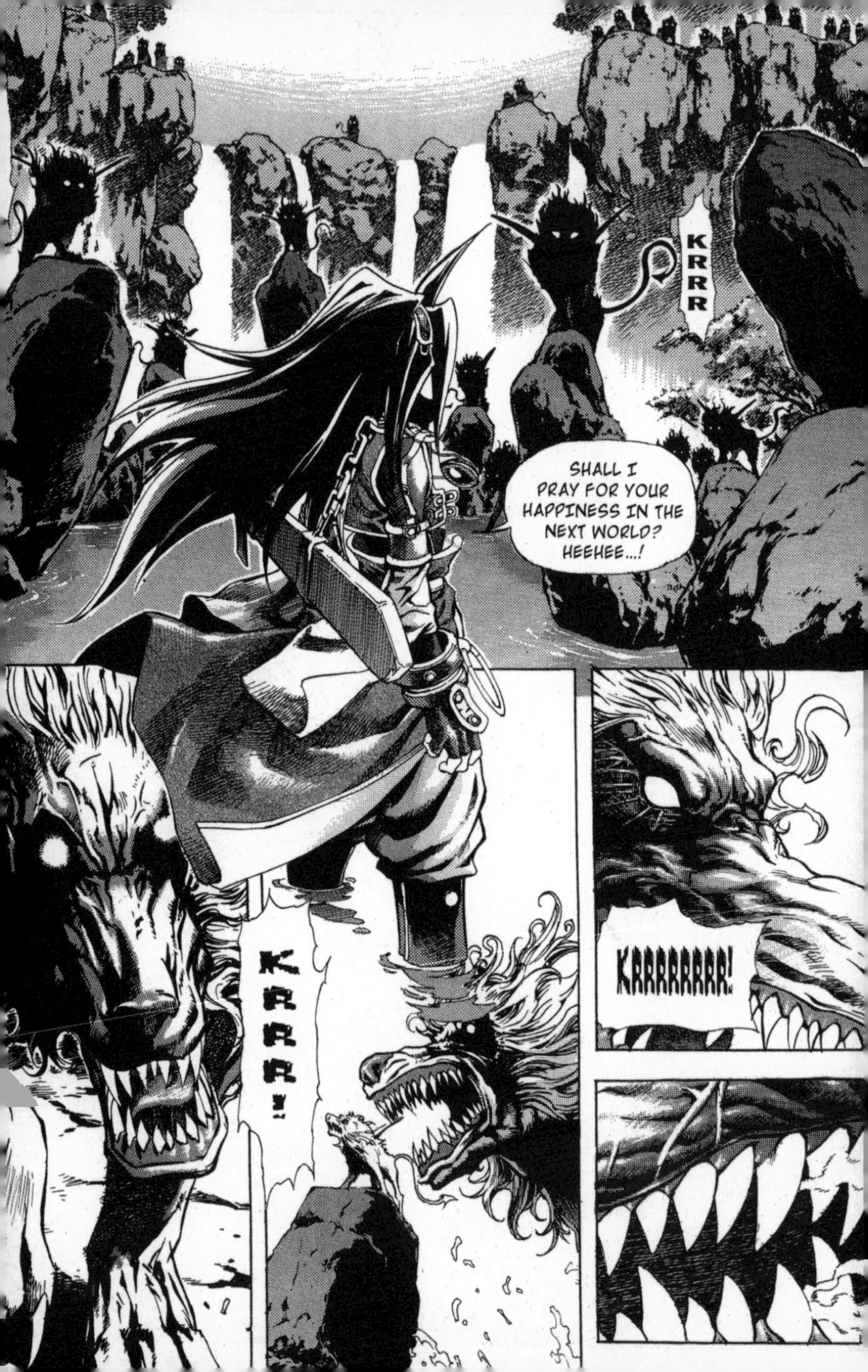
KRRR
SHALL I PRAY FOR YOUR HAPPINESS IN THE NEXT WORLD? HEEHEE...!
KRRR!!
KRRRRRRRR!

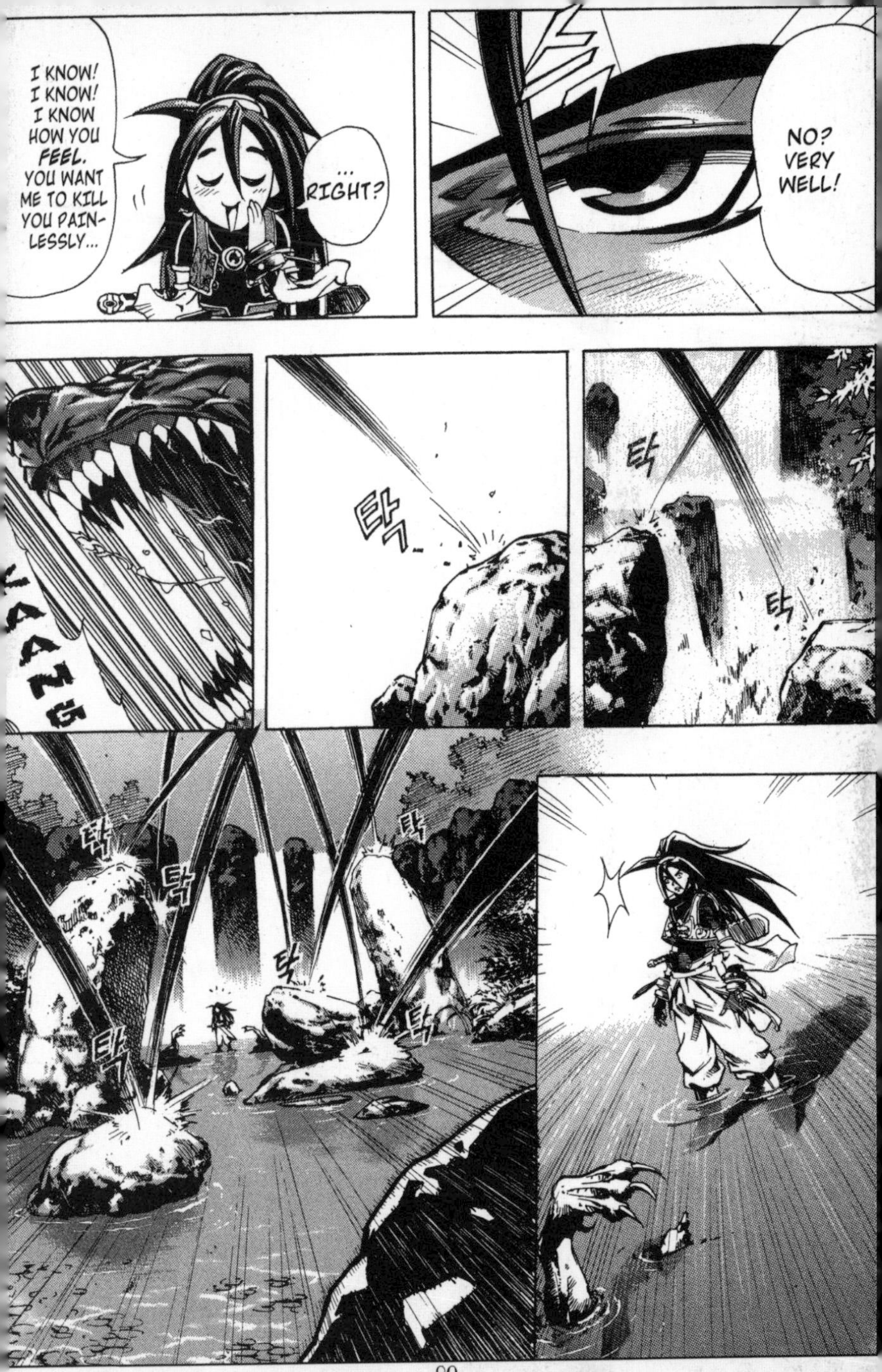
I KNOW! I KNOW! I KNOW HOW YOU FEEL. YOU WANT ME TO KILL YOU PAIN-LESSLY...
... RIGHT?
NO? VERY WELL!
AAANG
탁
탁
탁
탁
탁
탁
탁
탁
탁

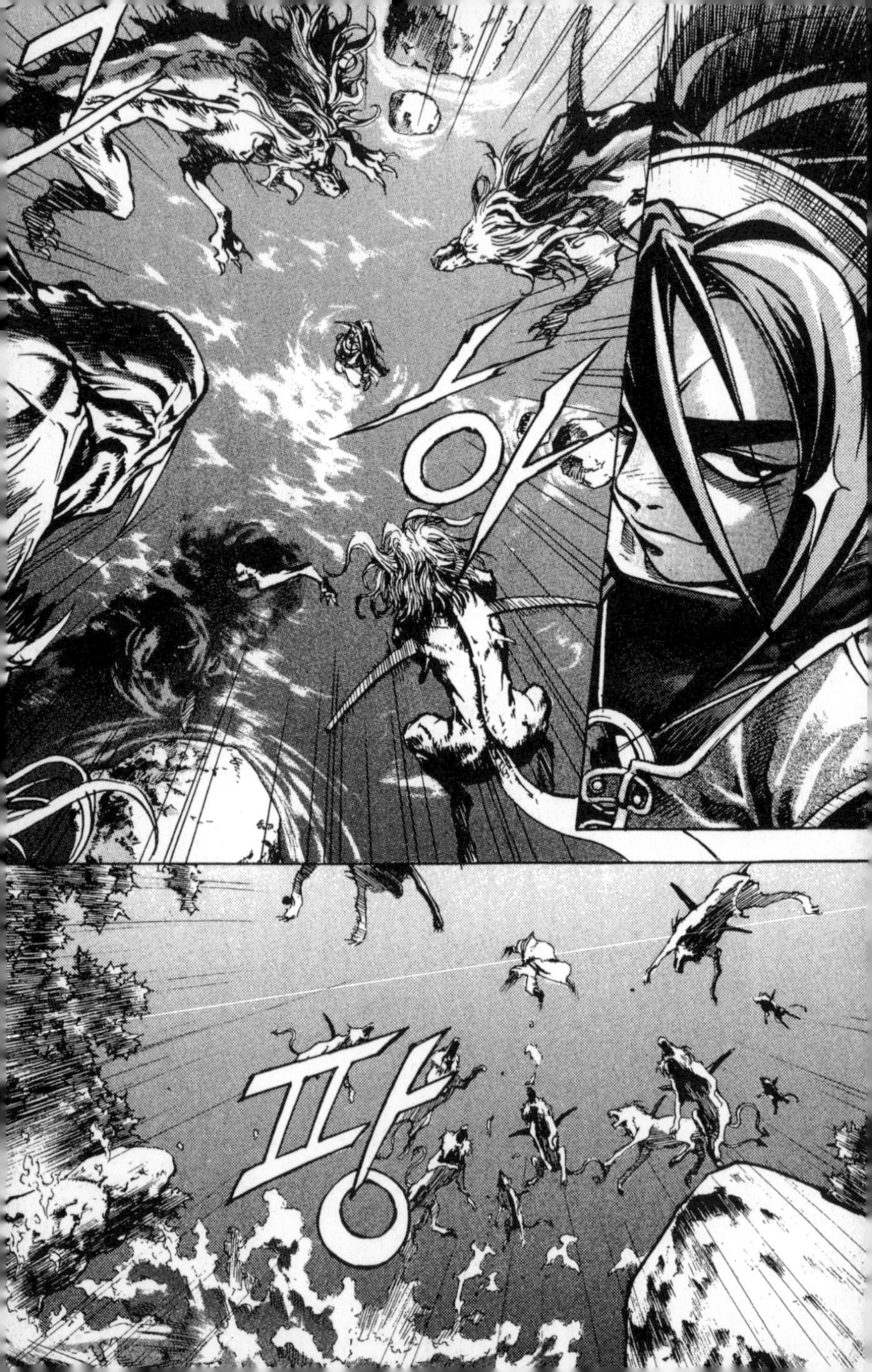
팡

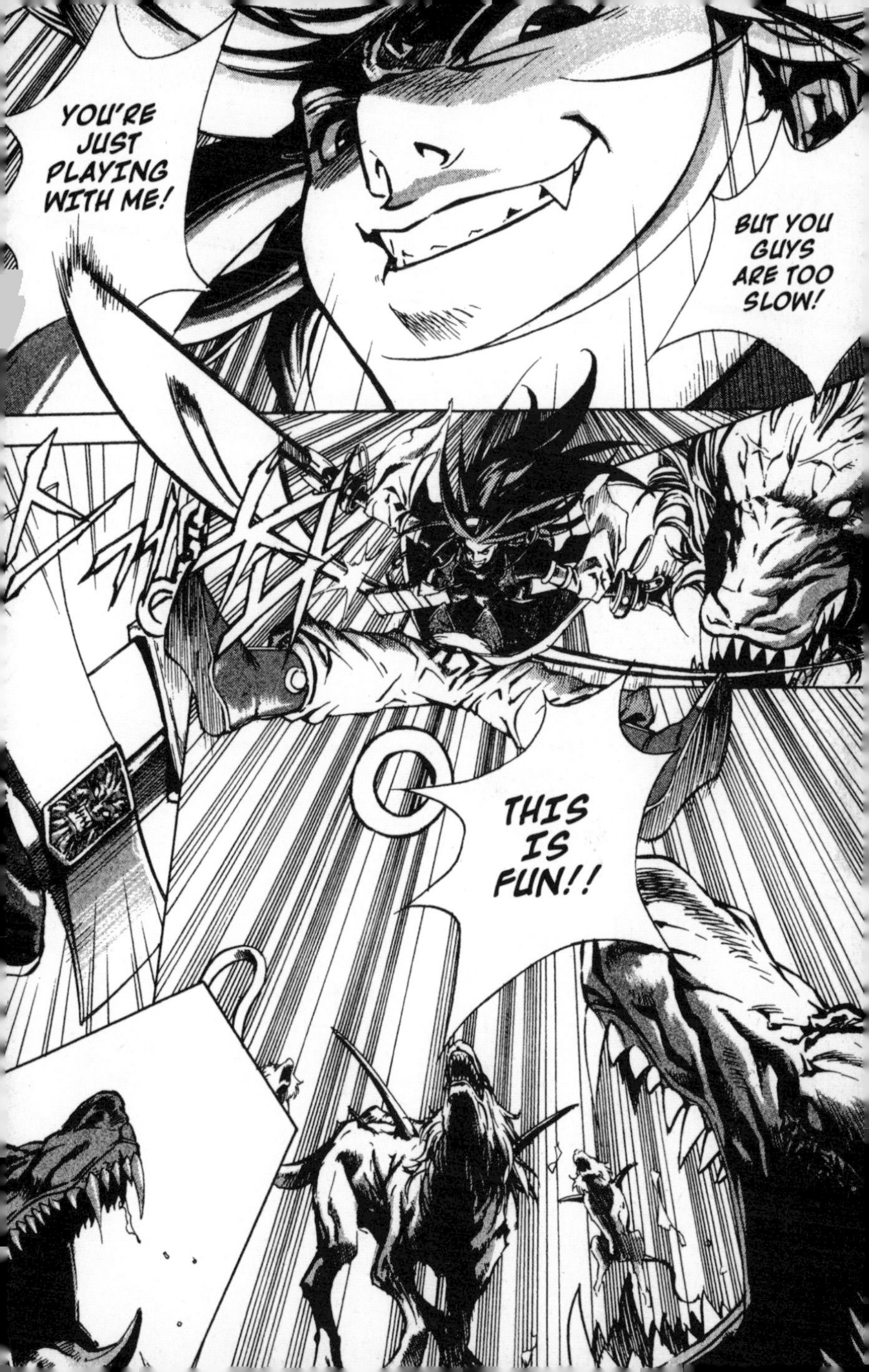
YOU'RE JUST PLAYING WITH ME!
BUT YOU GUYS ARE TOO SLOW!
THIS IS FUN!!

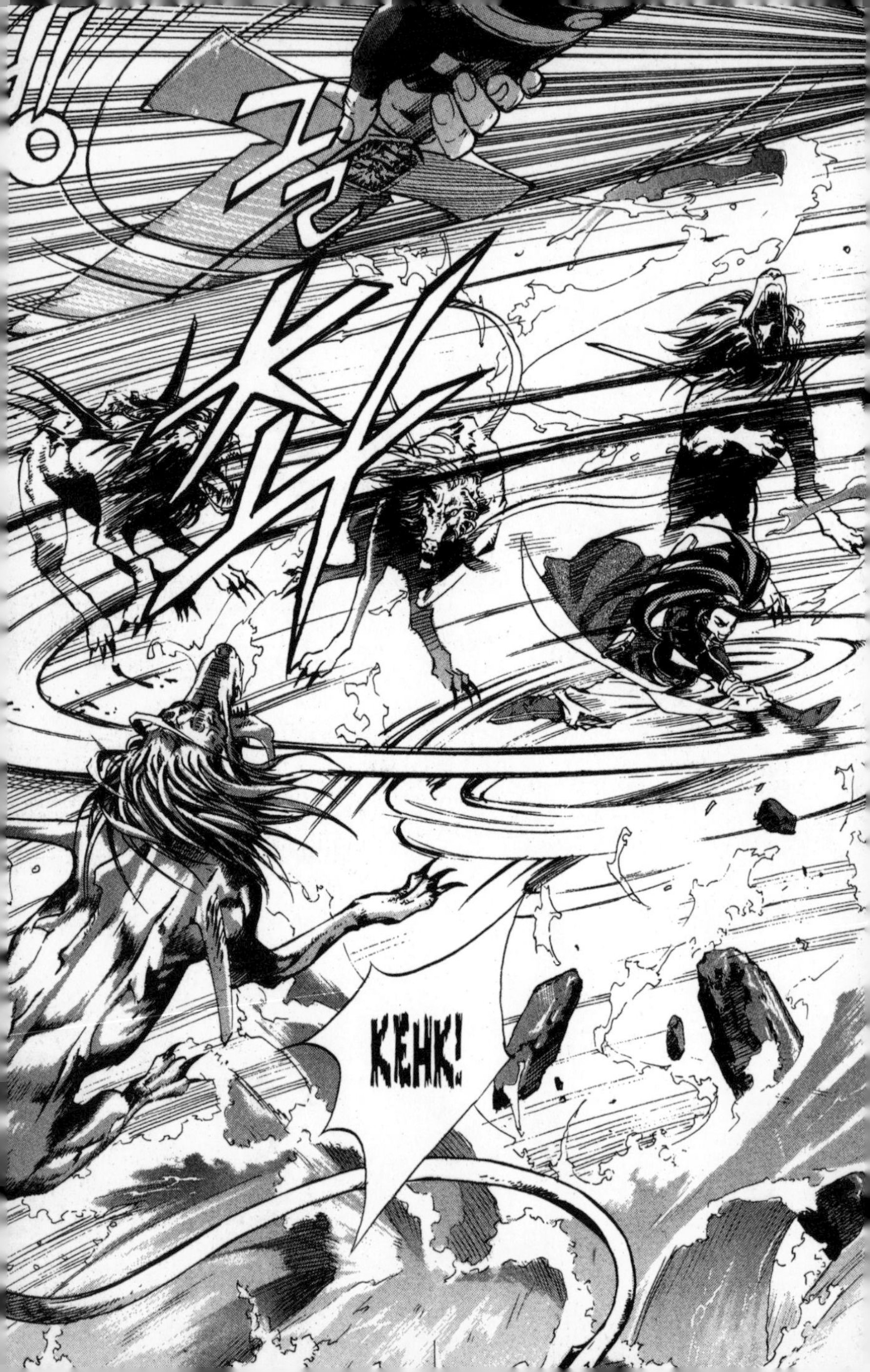
KEHK!

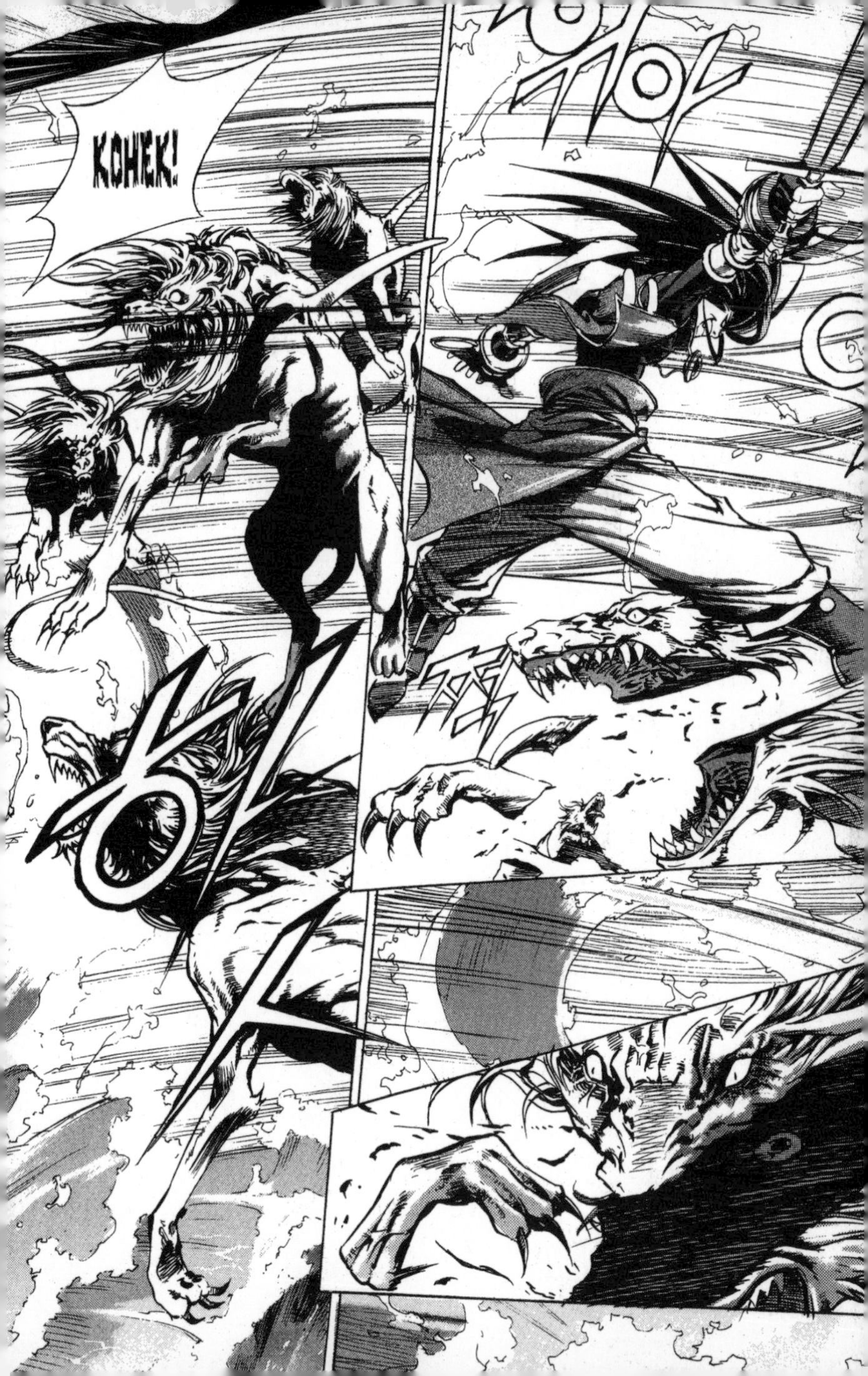
KOHEK!

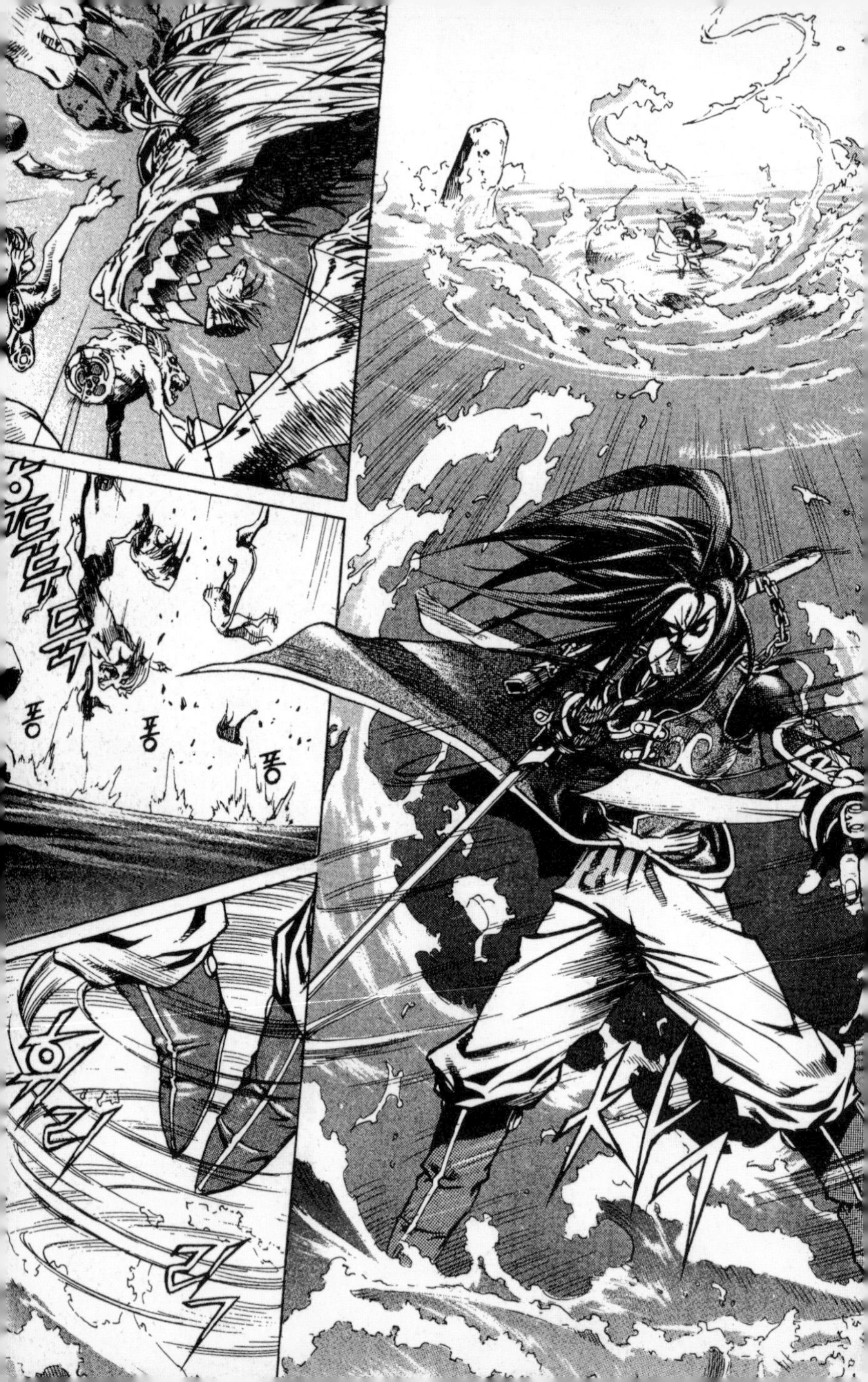
퐁
퐁
퐁

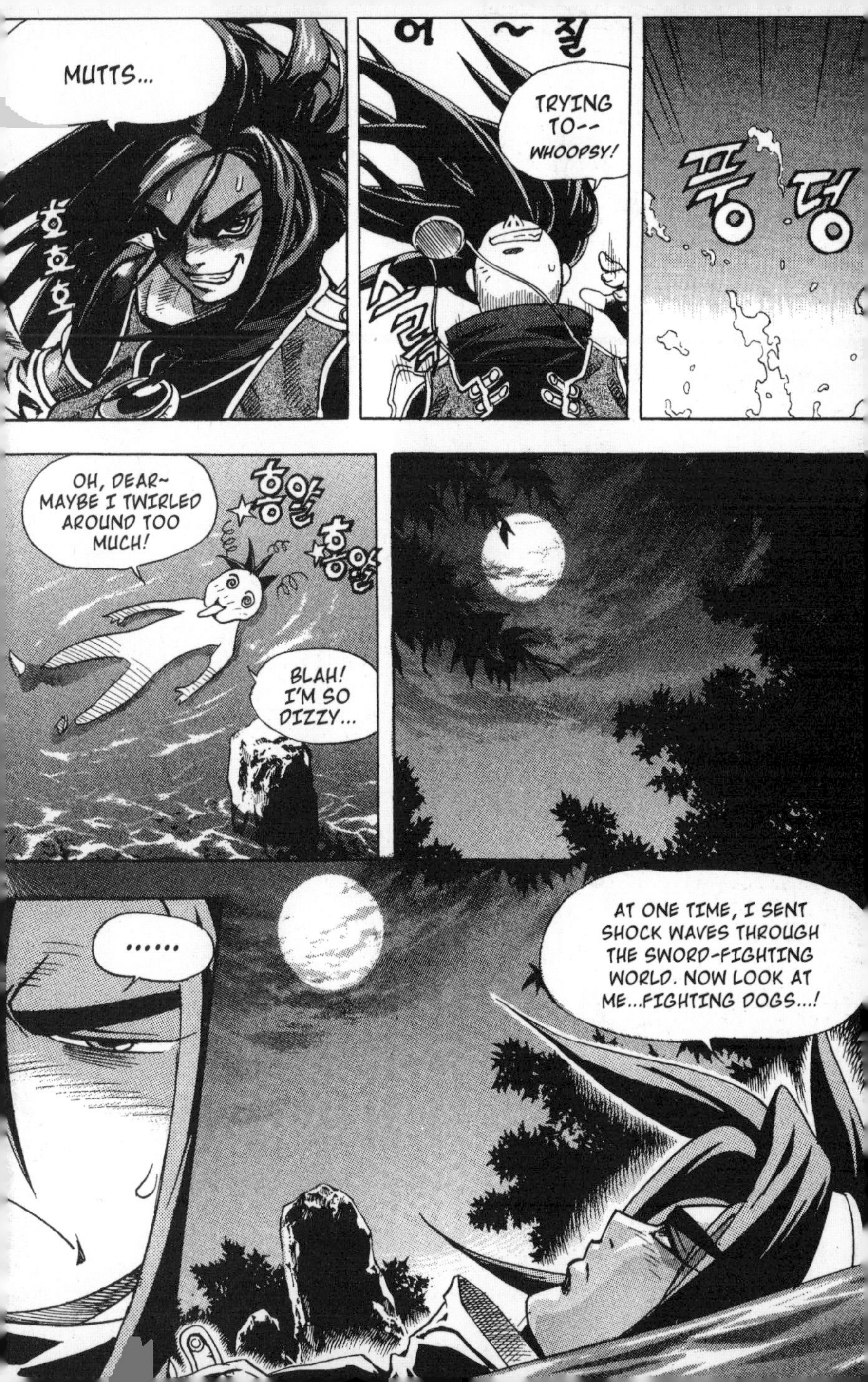
MUTTS...
어 ~ 질
TRYING TO-- WHOOPSY!
풍덩
OH, DEAR~ MAYBE I TWIRLED AROUND TOO MUCH!
BLAH! I'M SO DIZZY...
......
AT ONE TIME, I SENT SHOCK WAVES THROUGH THE SWORD-FIGHTING WORLD. NOW LOOK AT ME...FIGHTING DOGS...!

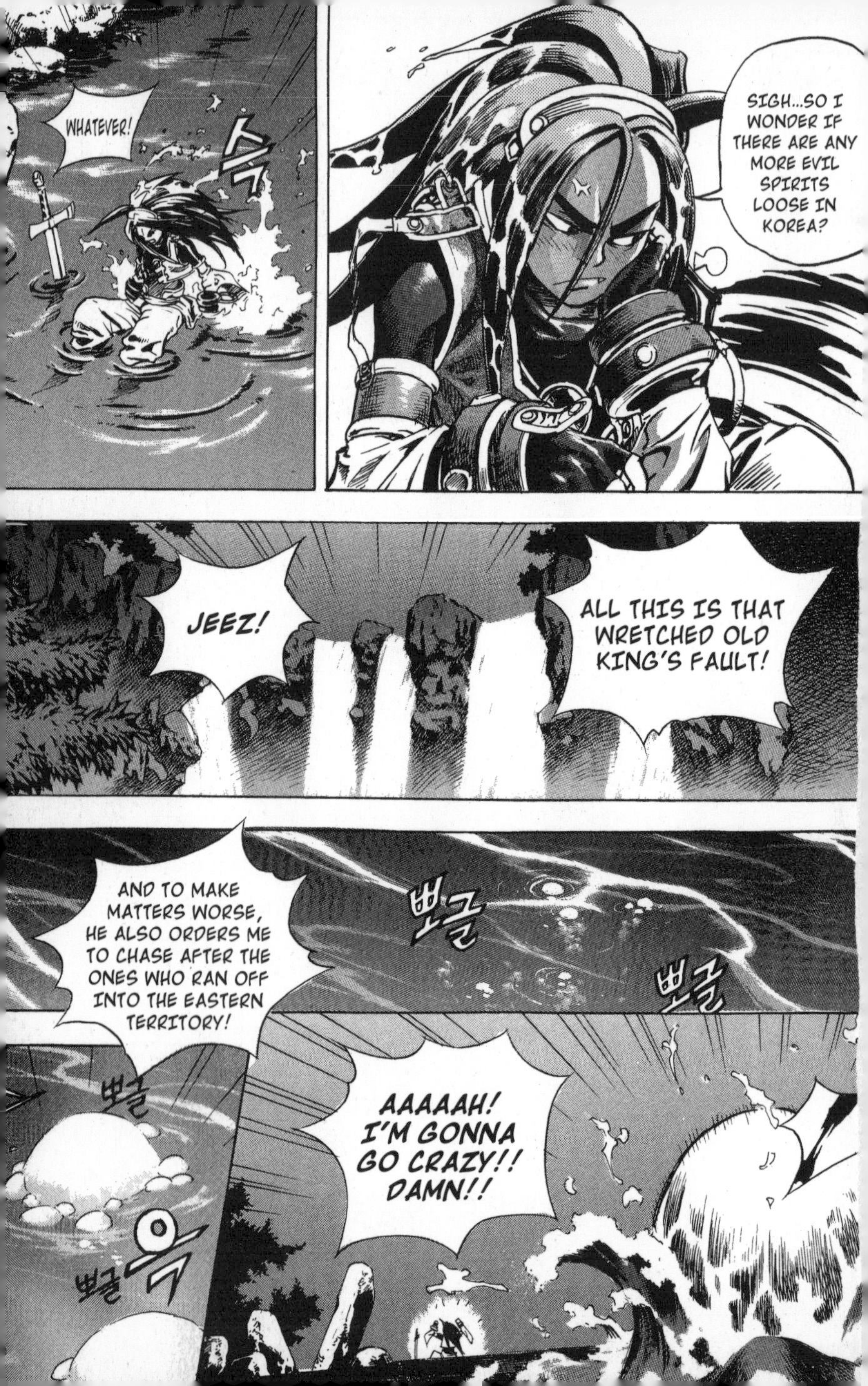
WHATEVER!
슥
SIGH...SO I WONDER IF THERE ARE ANY MORE EVIL SPIRITS LOOSE IN KOREA?
JEEZ!
ALL THIS IS THAT WRETCHED OLD KING'S FAULT!
AND TO MAKE MATTERS WORSE, HE ALSO ORDERS ME TO CHASE AFTER THE ONES WHO RAN OFF INTO THE EASTERN TERRITORY!
뽀글
뽀글
보글
욱
보글
AAAAAH! I'M GONNA GO CRAZY!! DAMN!!

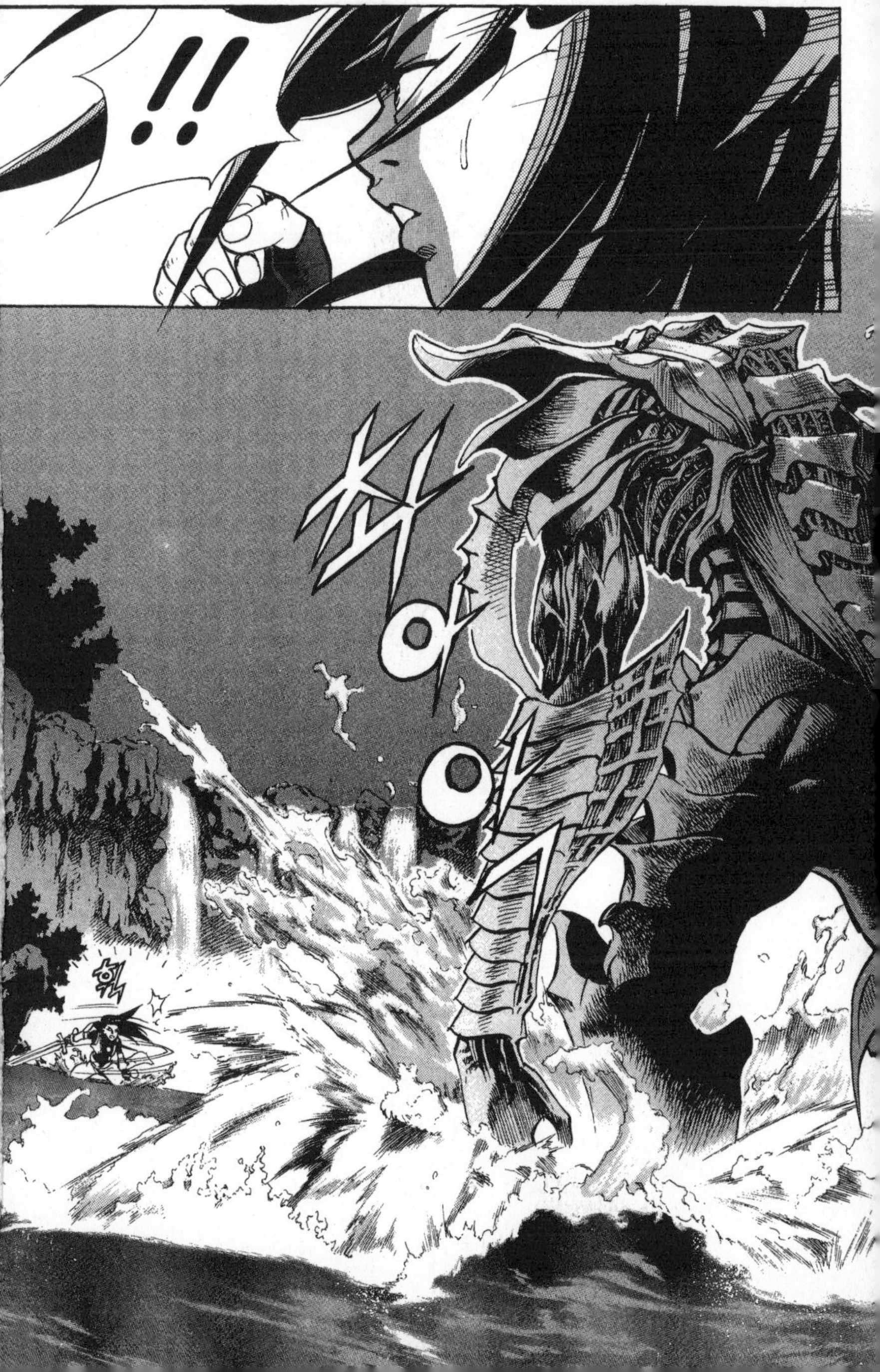
!!

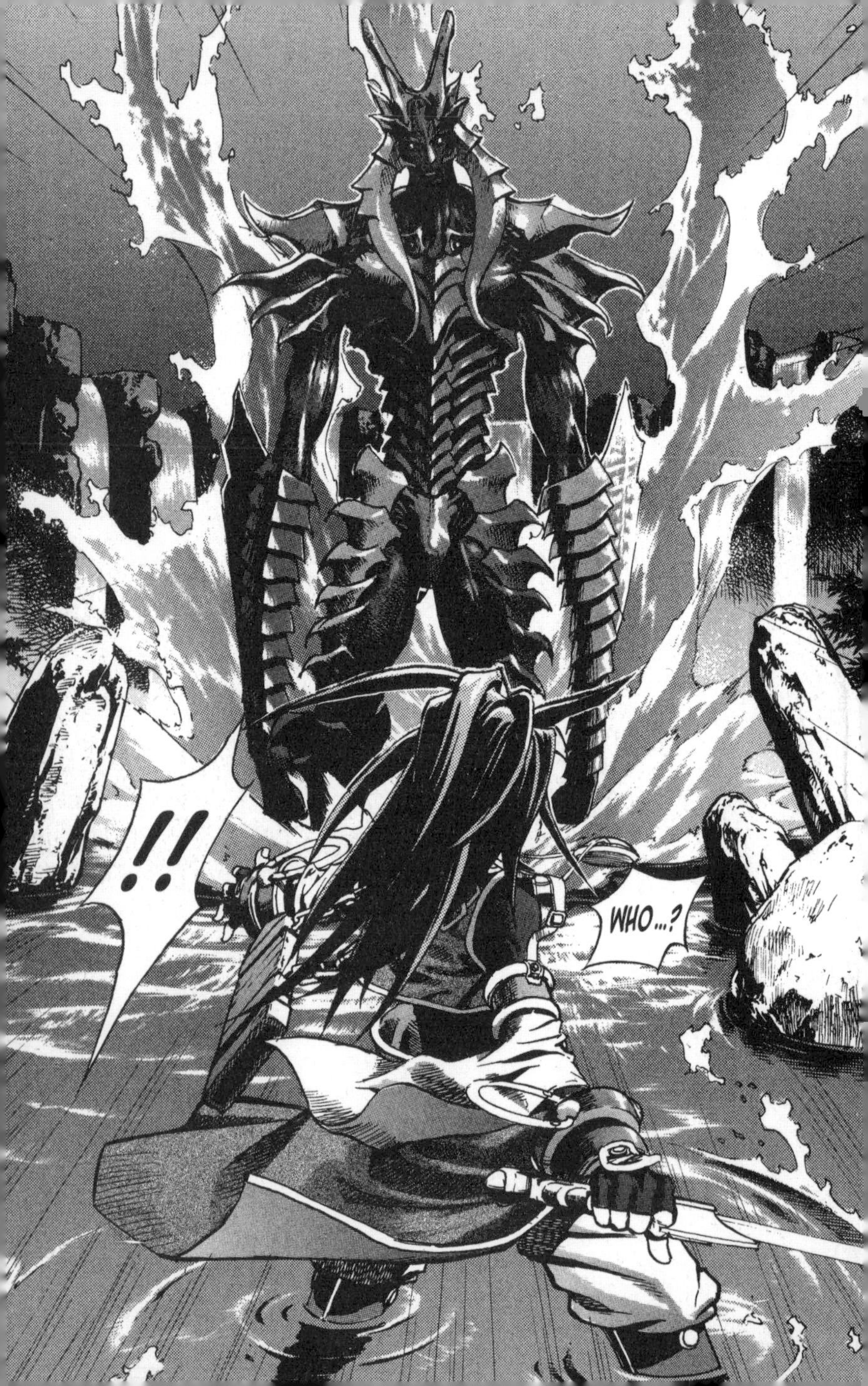
!!
WHO...?

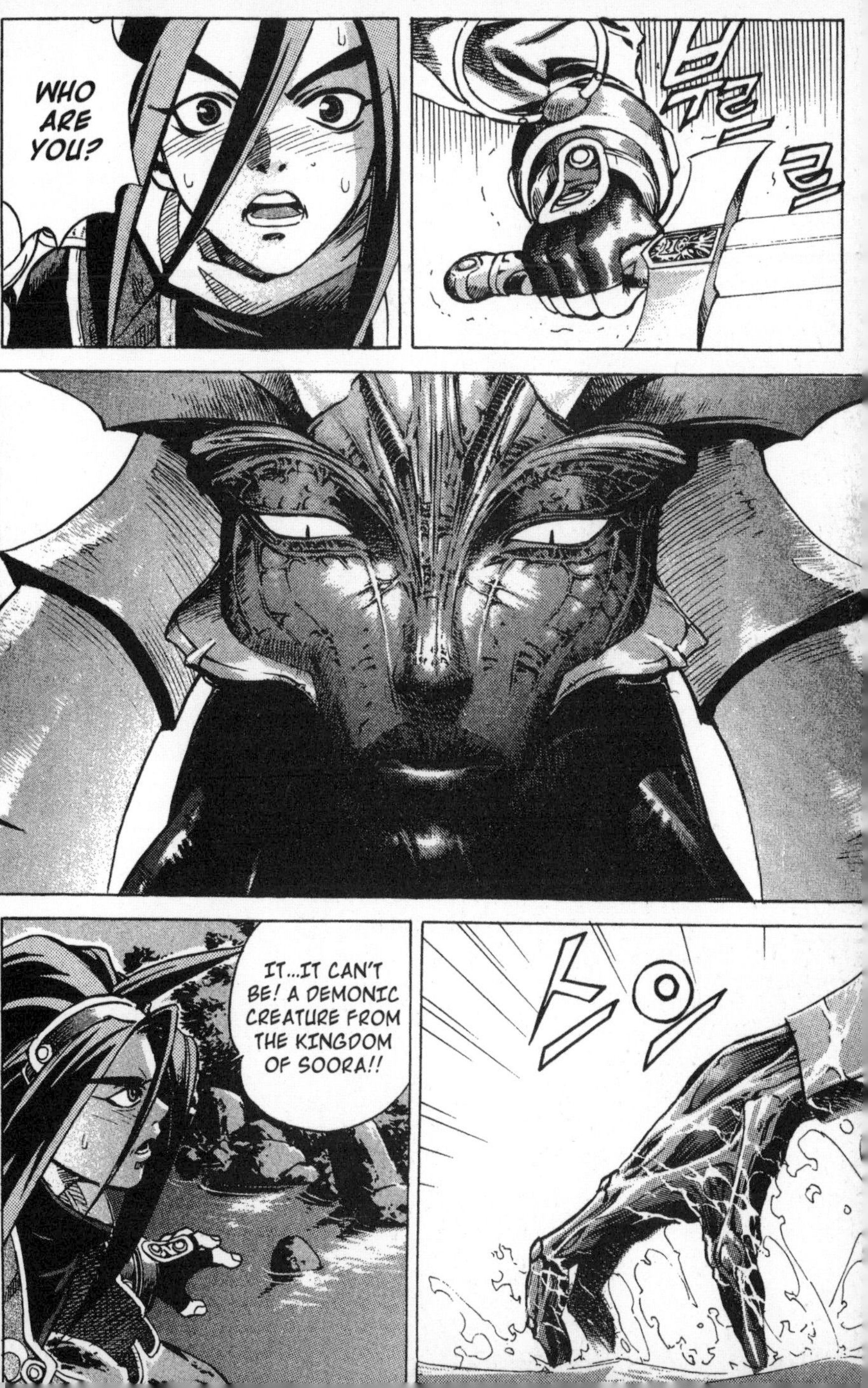
WHO ARE YOU?
부르르
IT...IT CAN'T BE! A DEMONIC CREATURE FROM THE KINGDOM OF SOORA!!
스으

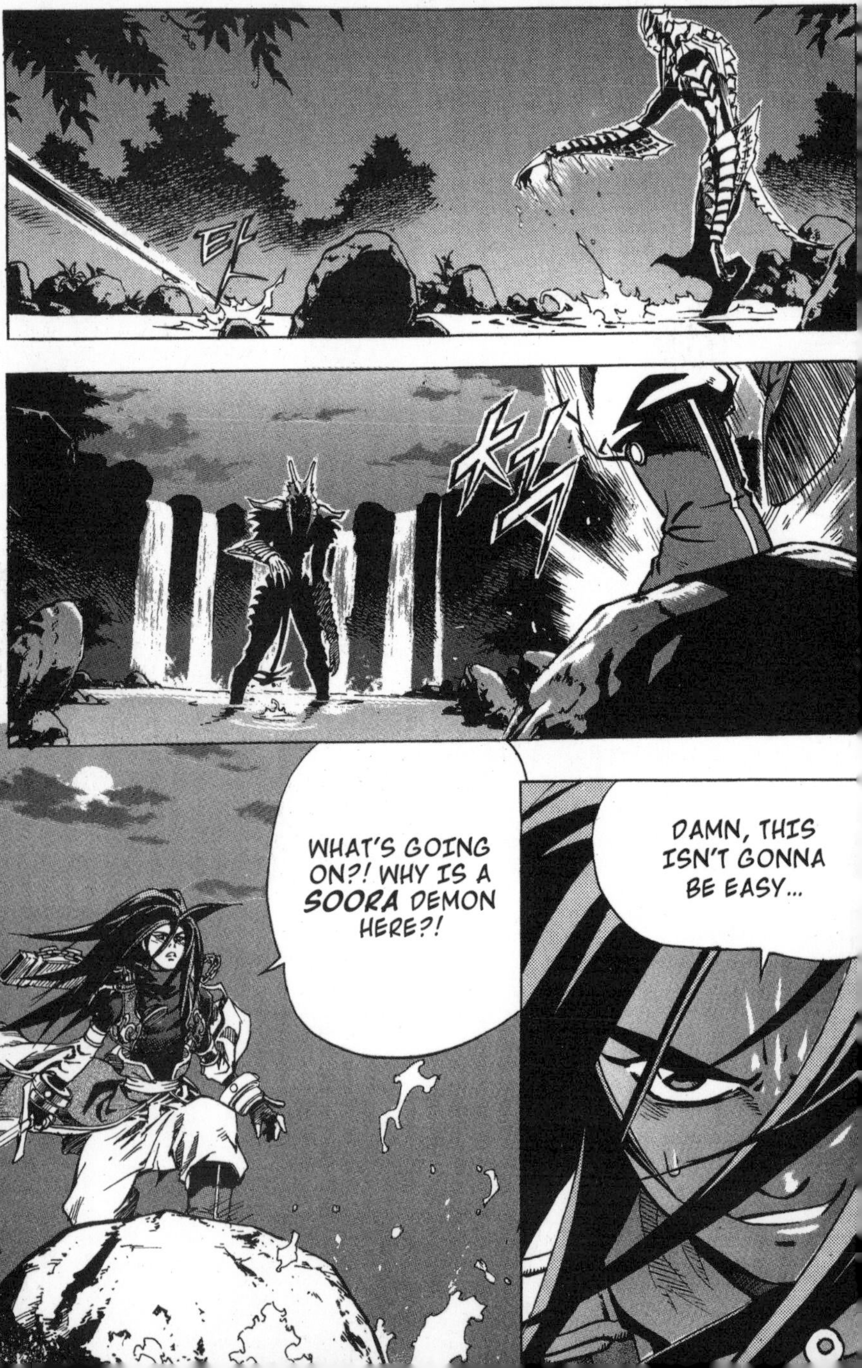
WHAT'S GOING ON?! WHY IS A SOORA DEMON HERE?!
DAMN, THIS ISN'T GONNA BE EASY...

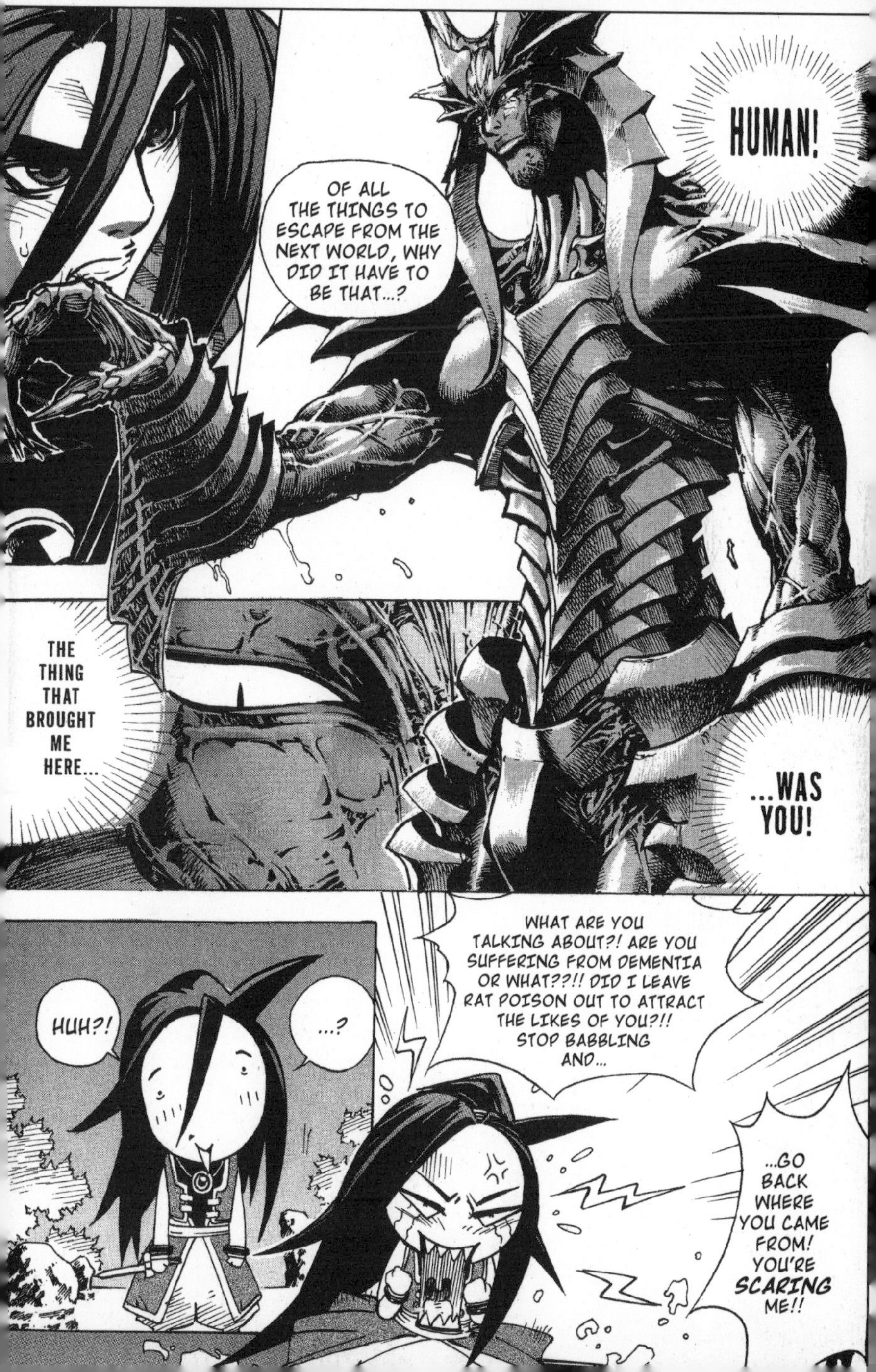
OF ALL THE THINGS TO ESCAPE FROM THE NEXT WORLD, WHY DID IT HAVE TO BE THAT...?
HUMAN!
THE THING THAT BROUGHT ME HERE...
...WAS YOU!
HUH?!
...?
WHAT ARE YOU TALKING ABOUT?! ARE YOU SUFFERING FROM DEMENTIA OR WHAT??!! DID I LEAVE RAT POISON OUT TO ATTRACT THE LIKES OF YOU?!! STOP BABBLING AND...
...GO BACK WHERE YOU CAME FROM! YOU'RE SCARING ME!!

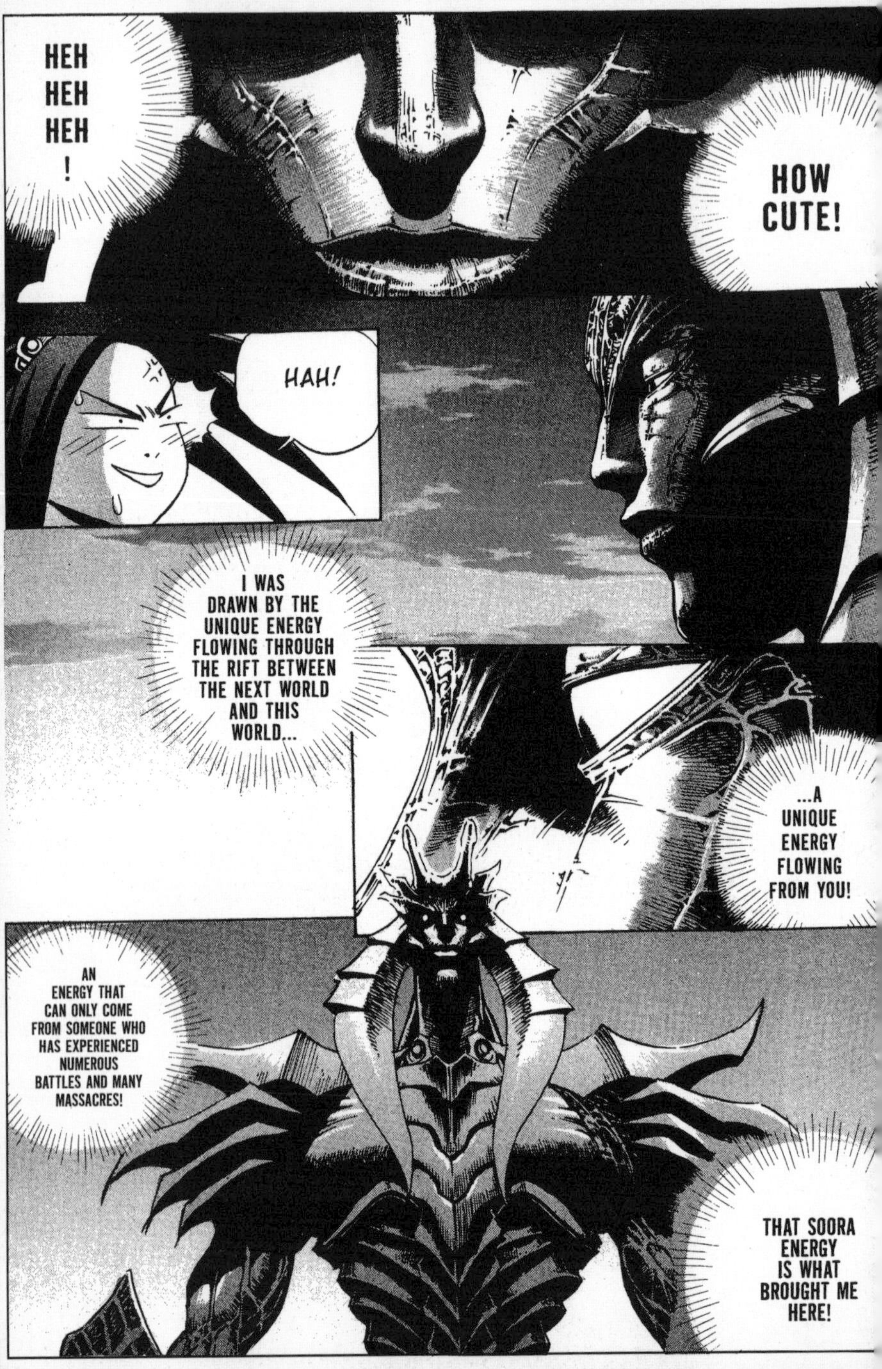
HEH HEH HEH !
HOW CUTE!
HAH!
I WAS DRAWN BY THE UNIQUE ENERGY FLOWING THROUGH THE RIFT BETWEEN THE NEXT WORLD AND THIS WORLD...
...A UNIQUE ENERGY FLOWING FROM YOU!
AN ENERGY THAT CAN ONLY COME FROM SOMEONE WHO HAS EXPERIENCED NUMEROUS BATTLES AND MANY MASSACRES!
THAT SOORA ENERGY IS WHAT BROUGHT ME HERE!

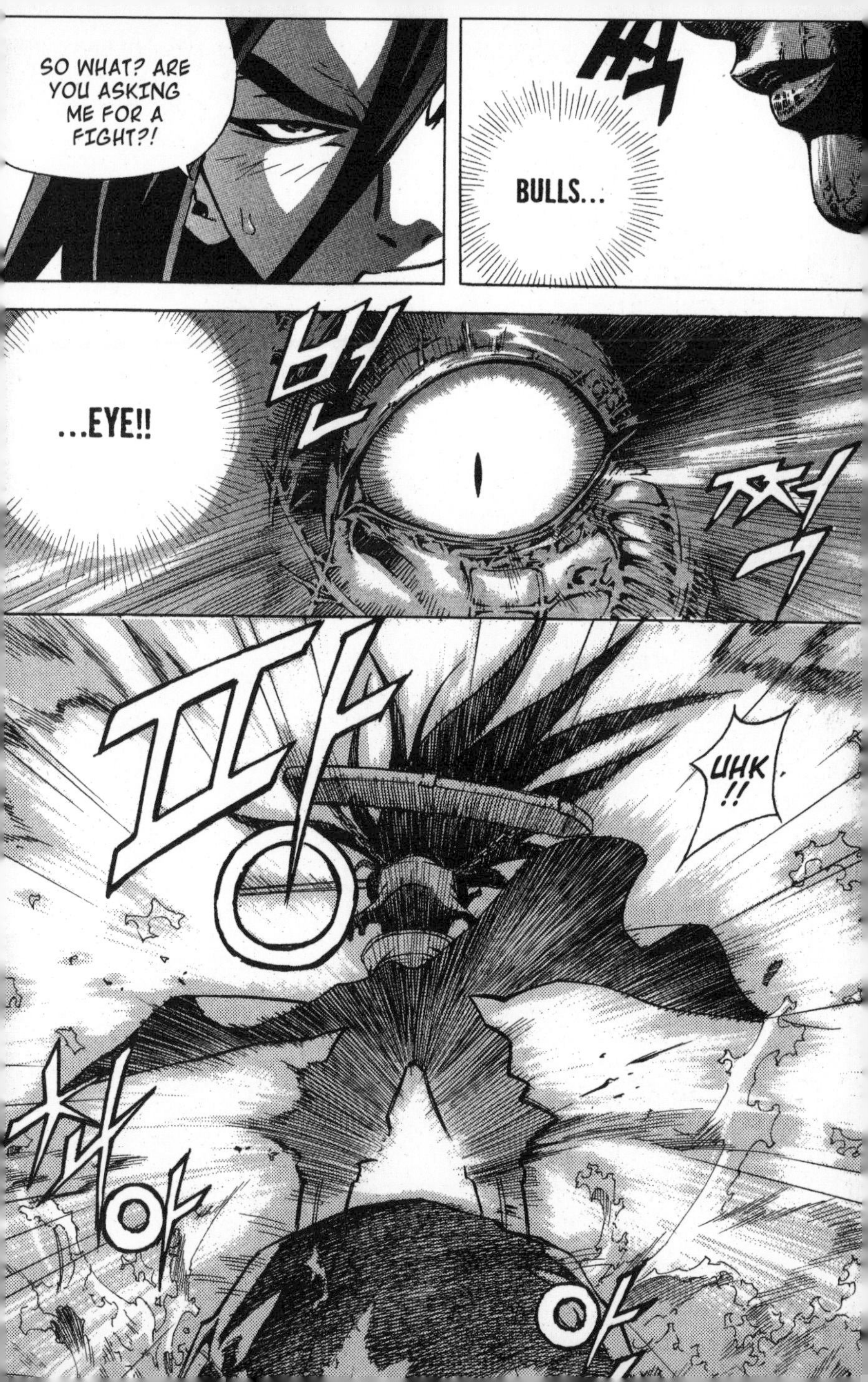

SO WHAT? ARE YOU ASKING ME FOR A FIGHT?!
BULLS...
...EYE!!
UHK!!

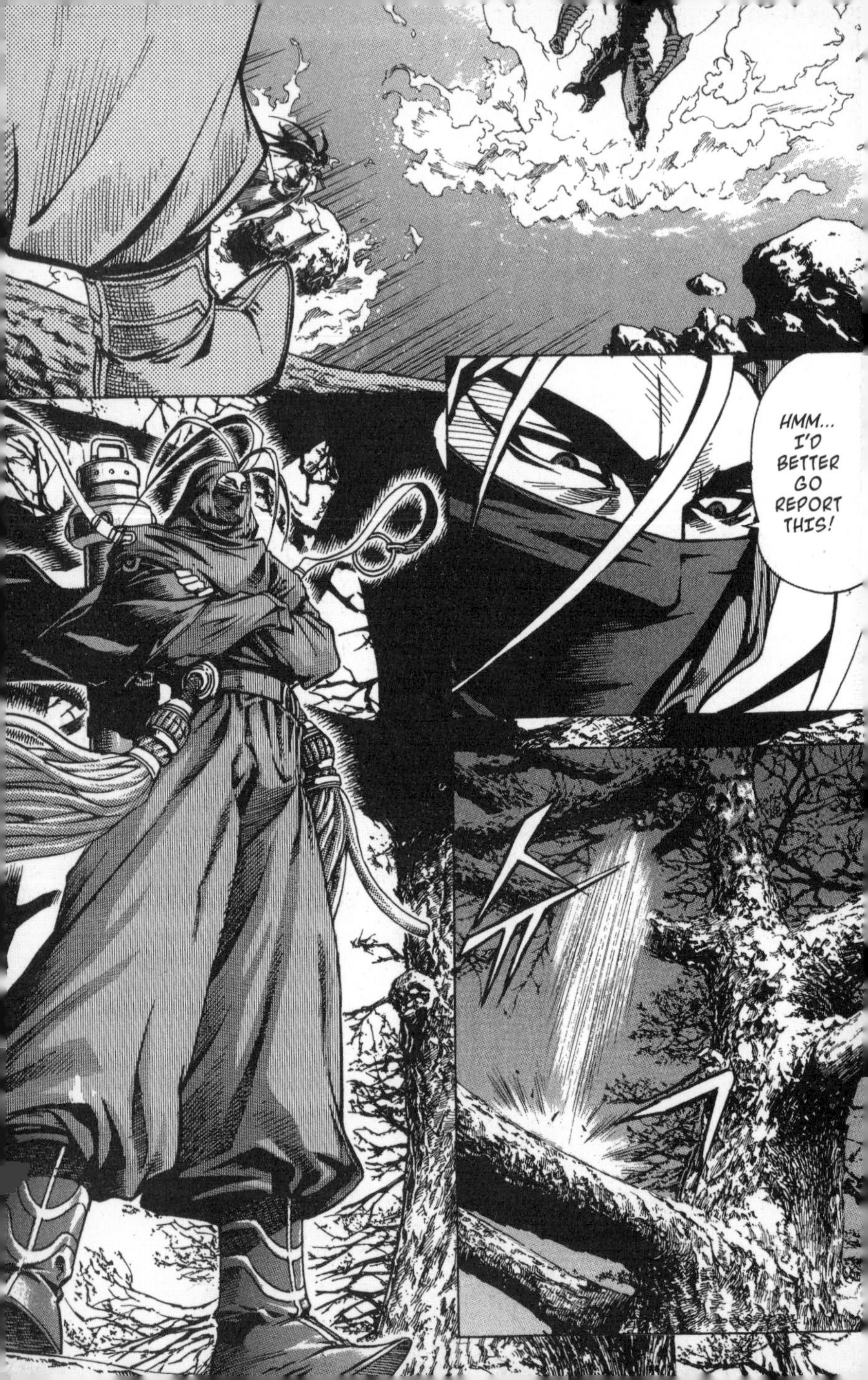
HMM... I'D BETTER GO REPORT THIS!

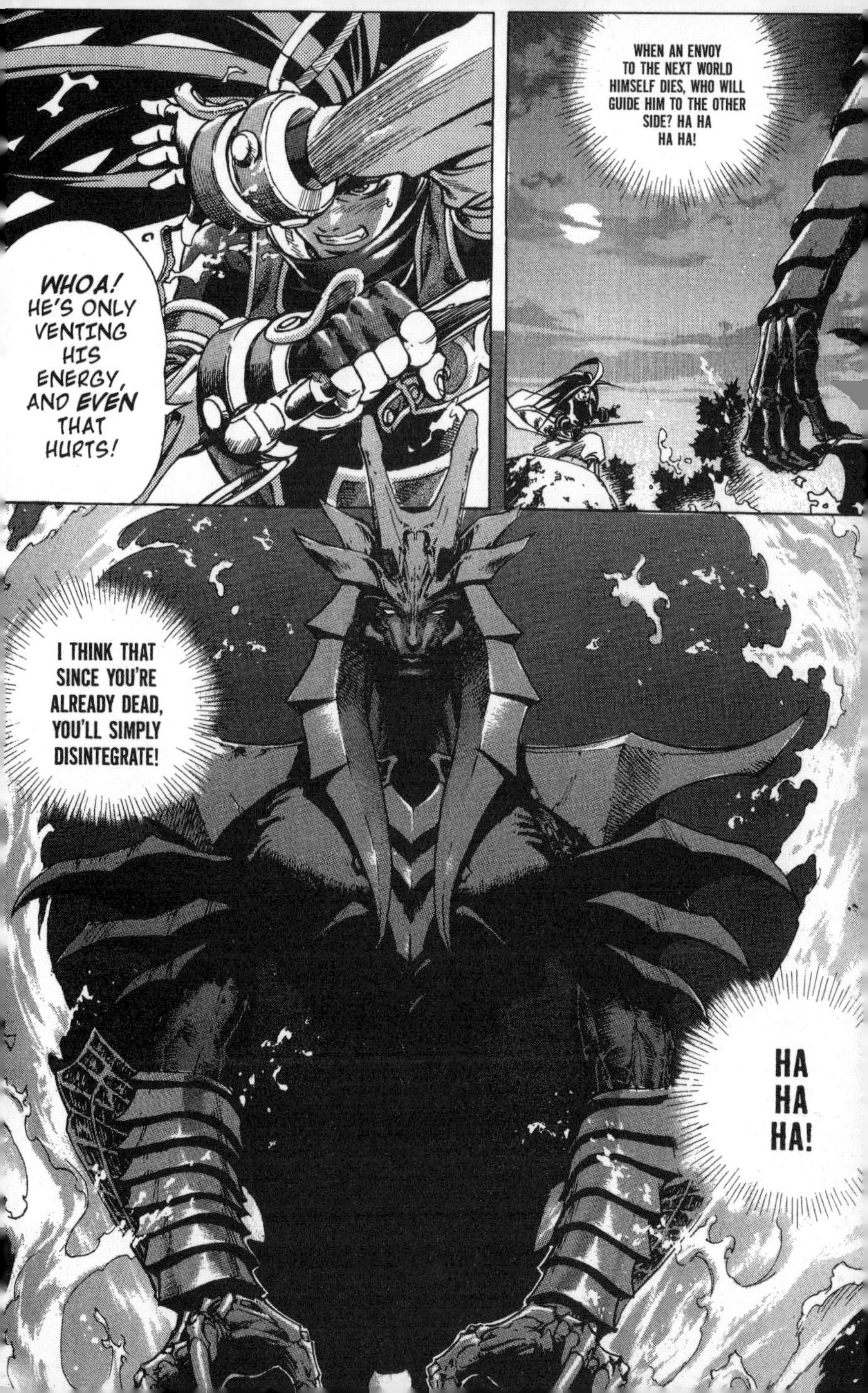
WHOA! HE'S ONLY VENTING HIS ENERGY, AND EVEN THAT HURTS!
WHEN AN ENVOY TO THE NEXT WORLD HIMSELF DIES, WHO WILL GUIDE HIM TO THE OTHER SIDE? HA HA HA HA!
I THINK THAT SINCE YOU'RE ALREADY DEAD, YOU'LL SIMPLY DISINTEGRATE!
HA HA HA!

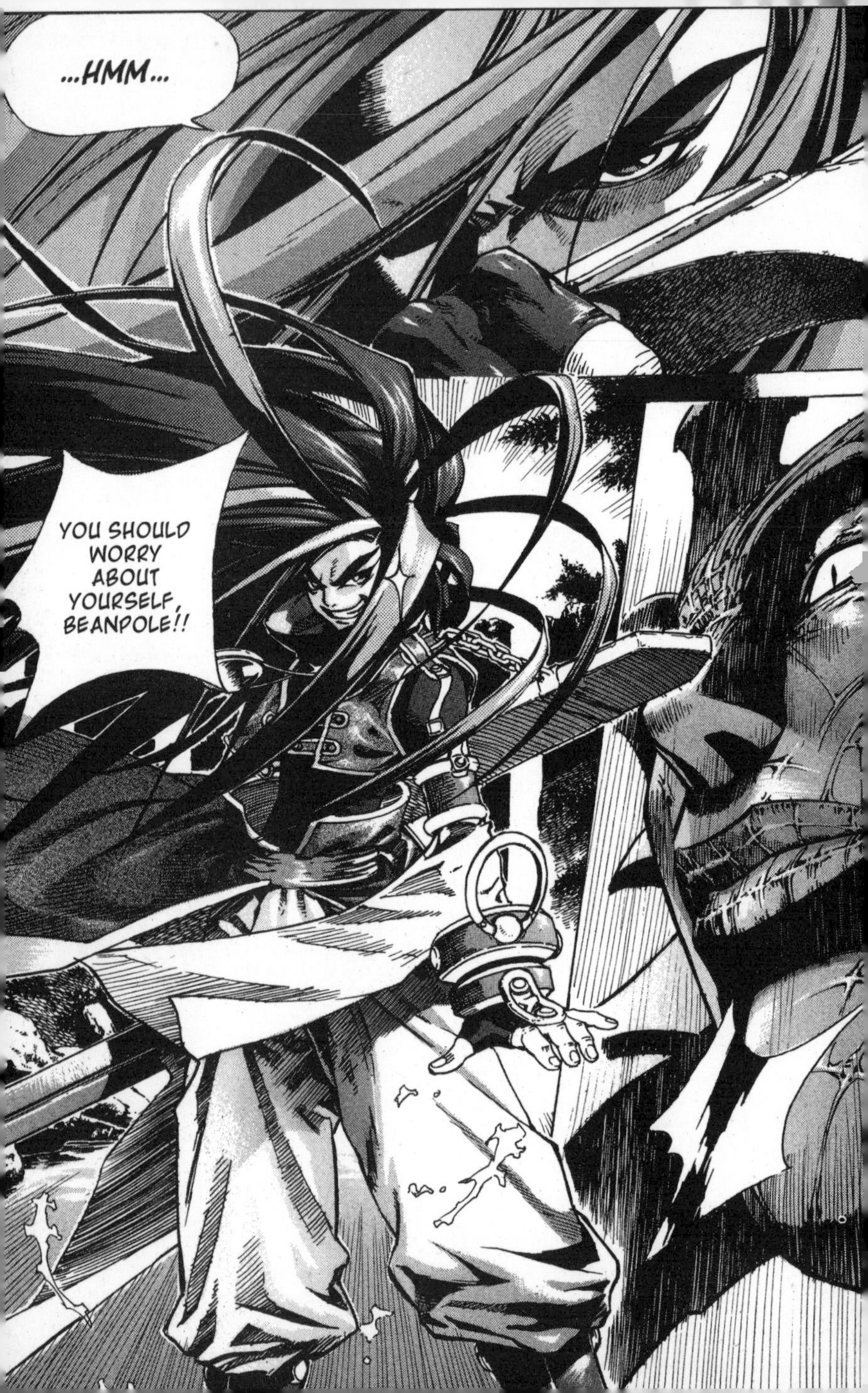
...HMM...
YOU SHOULD WORRY ABOUT YOURSELF, BEANPOLE!!

A SOORA DEMON?!

YES, SIR.

HMM... HE'S MET A FORMIDABLE FOE.

NEVERTHELESS... IF IT'S A DEMON FROM THE KINGDOM OF SOORA, WE HAVE NOTHING TO WORRY ABOUT.

THE TREATY BETWEEN THE KINGDOM OF HELL AND THE KINGDOM OF SOORA IS STILL VALID.

BY THE WAY, ARE ALL THE EVIL SPIRITS IN KOREA TAKEN CARE OF?!

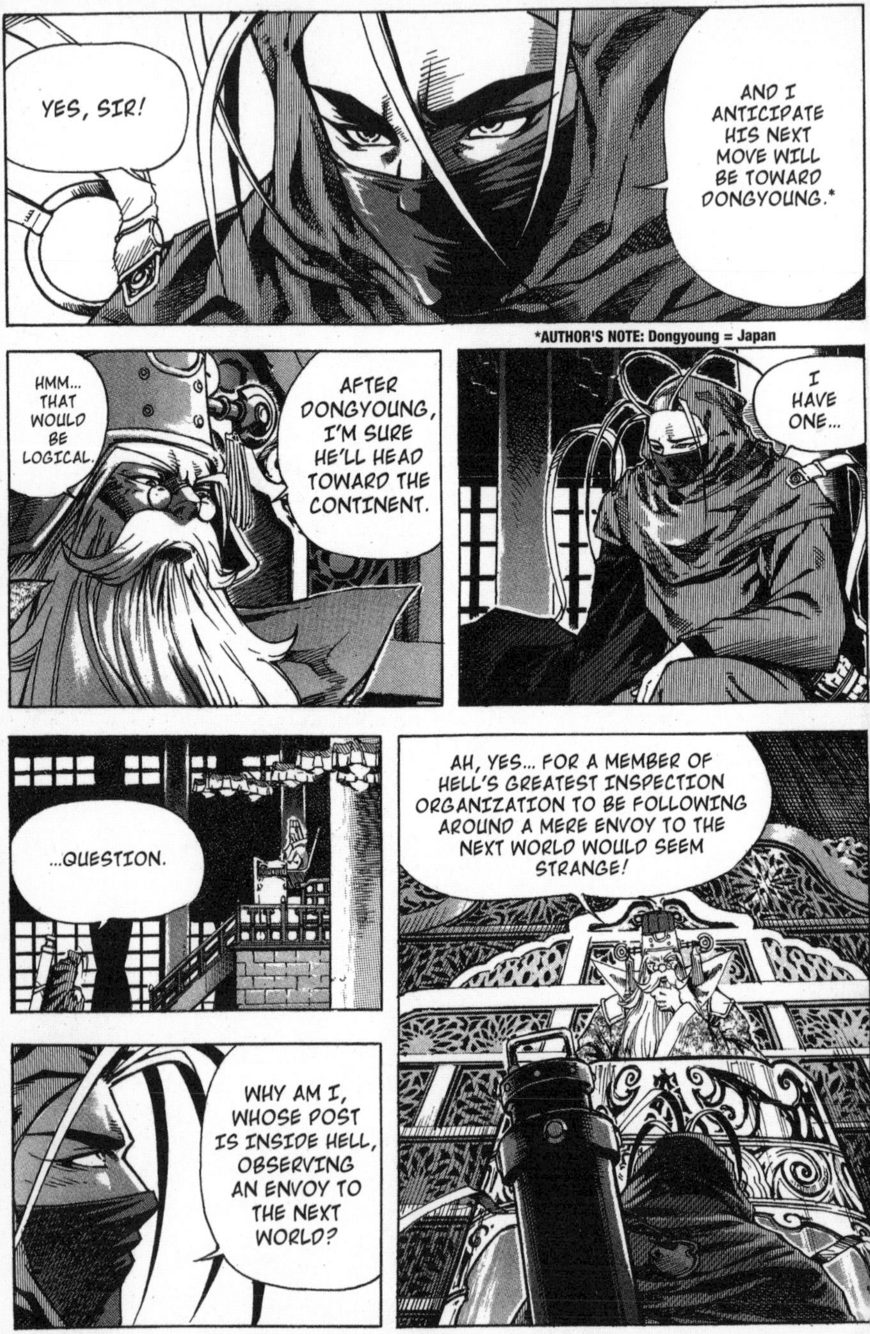
YES, SIR!
AND I ANTICIPATE HIS NEXT MOVE WILL BE TOWARD DONGYOUNG.*
*AUTHOR'S NOTE: Dongyoung = Japan
HMM... THAT WOULD BE LOGICAL.
AFTER DONGYOUNG, I'M SURE HE'LL HEAD TOWARD THE CONTINENT.
I HAVE ONE...
...QUESTION.
WHY AM I, WHOSE POST IS INSIDE HELL, OBSERVING AN ENVOY TO THE NEXT WORLD?
AH, YES... FOR A MEMBER OF HELL'S GREATEST INSPECTION ORGANIZATION TO BE FOLLOWING AROUND A MERE ENVOY TO THE NEXT WORLD WOULD SEEM STRANGE!

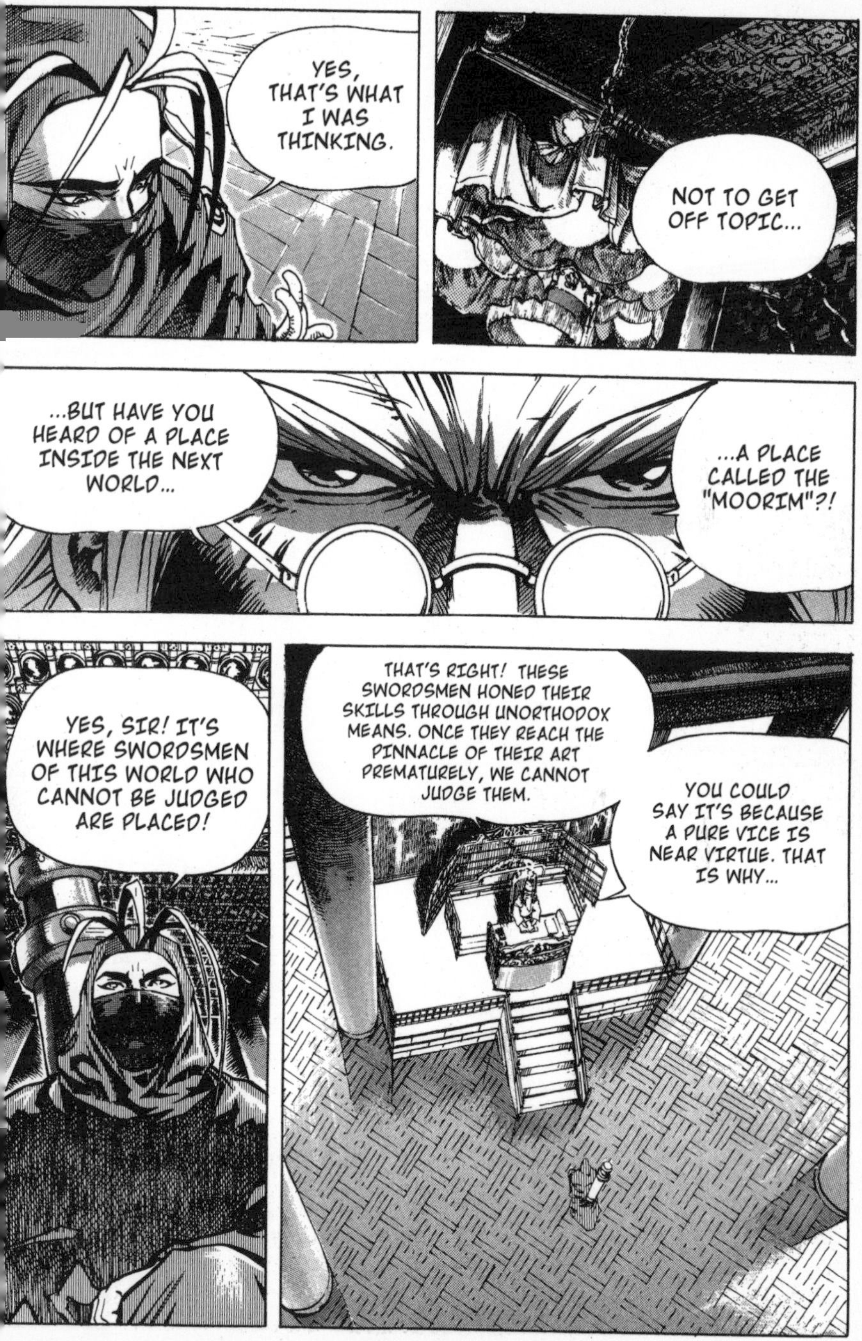
YES, THAT'S WHAT I WAS THINKING.
NOT TO GET OFF TOPIC...
...BUT HAVE YOU HEARD OF A PLACE INSIDE THE NEXT WORLD...
...A PLACE CALLED THE "MOORIM"?!
YES, SIR! IT'S WHERE SWORDSMEN OF THIS WORLD WHO CANNOT BE JUDGED ARE PLACED!
THAT'S RIGHT! THESE SWORDSMEN HONED THEIR SKILLS THROUGH UNORTHODOX MEANS. ONCE THEY REACH THE PINNACLE OF THEIR ART PREMATURELY, WE CANNOT JUDGE THEM.
YOU COULD SAY IT'S BECAUSE A PURE VICE IS NEAR VIRTUE. THAT IS WHY...

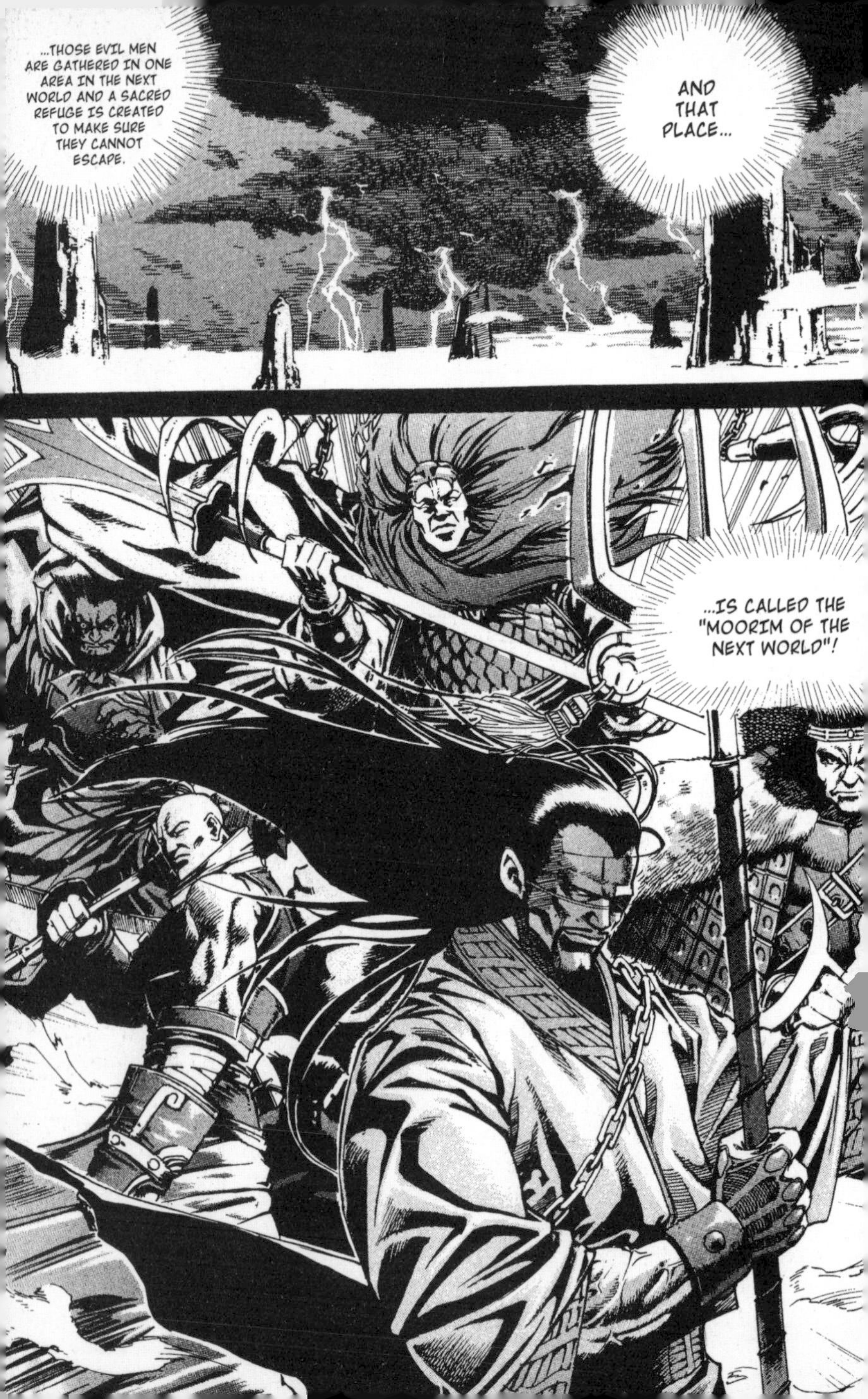
...THOSE EVIL MEN ARE GATHERED IN ONE AREA IN THE NEXT WORLD AND A SACRED REFUGE IS CREATED TO MAKE SURE THEY CANNOT ESCAPE.
AND THAT PLACE...
...IS CALLED THE "MOORIM OF THE NEXT WORLD"!

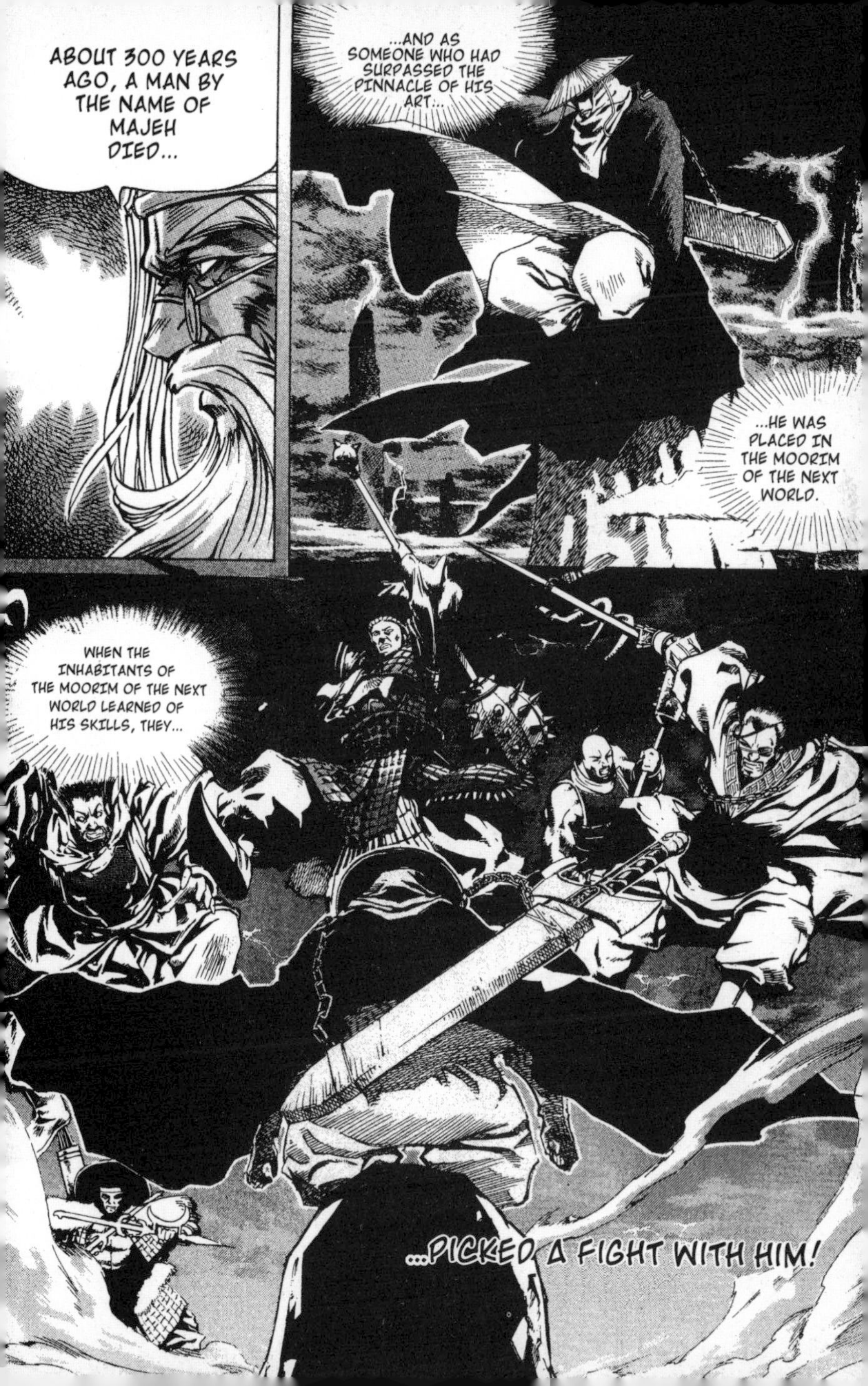
ABOUT 300 YEARS AGO, A MAN BY THE NAME OF MAJEH DIED...
...AND AS SOMEONE WHO HAD SURPASSED THE PINNACLE OF HIS ART...
...HE WAS PLACED IN THE MOORIM OF THE NEXT WORLD.
WHEN THE INHABITANTS OF THE MOORIM OF THE NEXT WORLD LEARNED OF HIS SKILLS, THEY...
...PICKED A FIGHT WITH HIM!

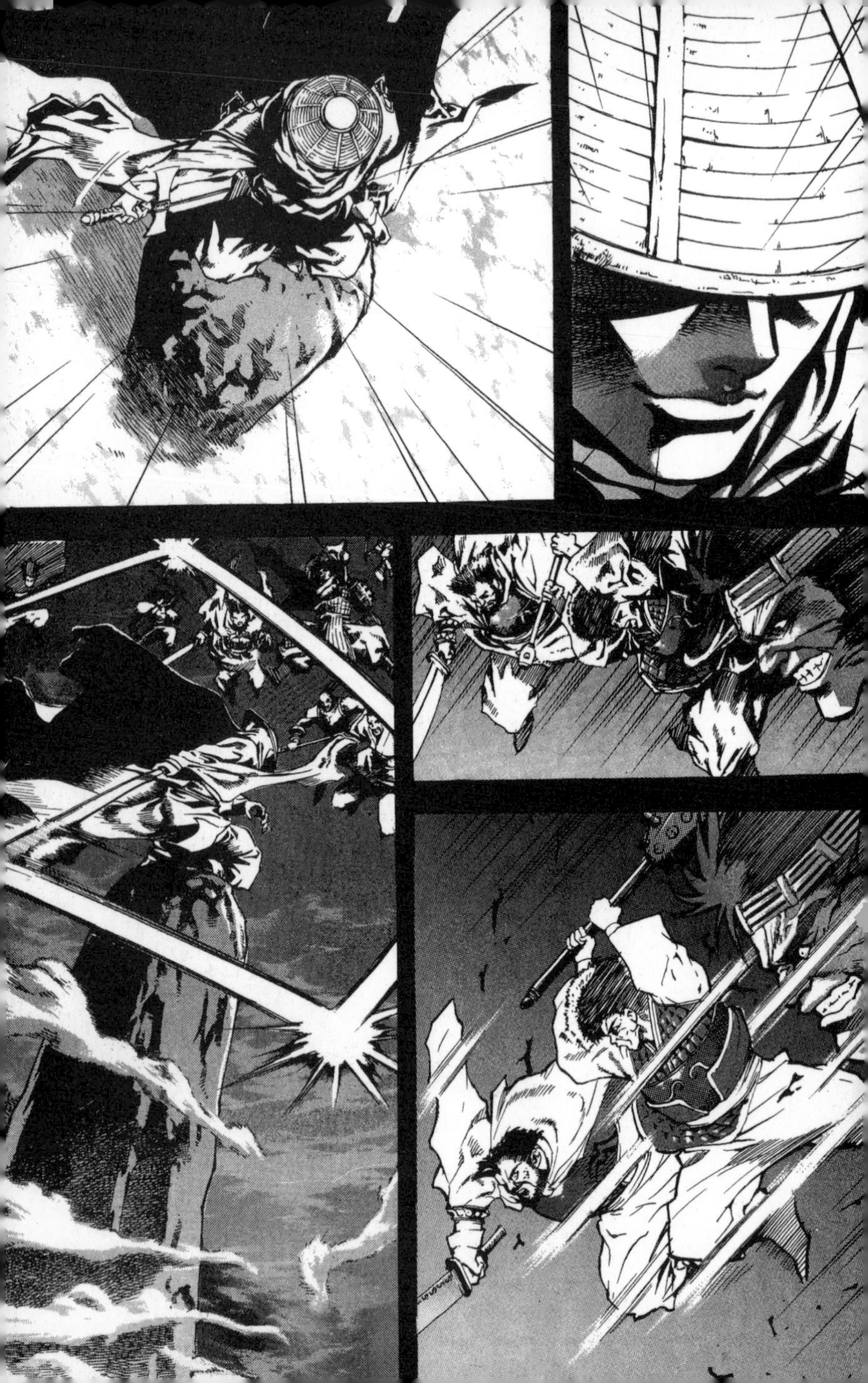

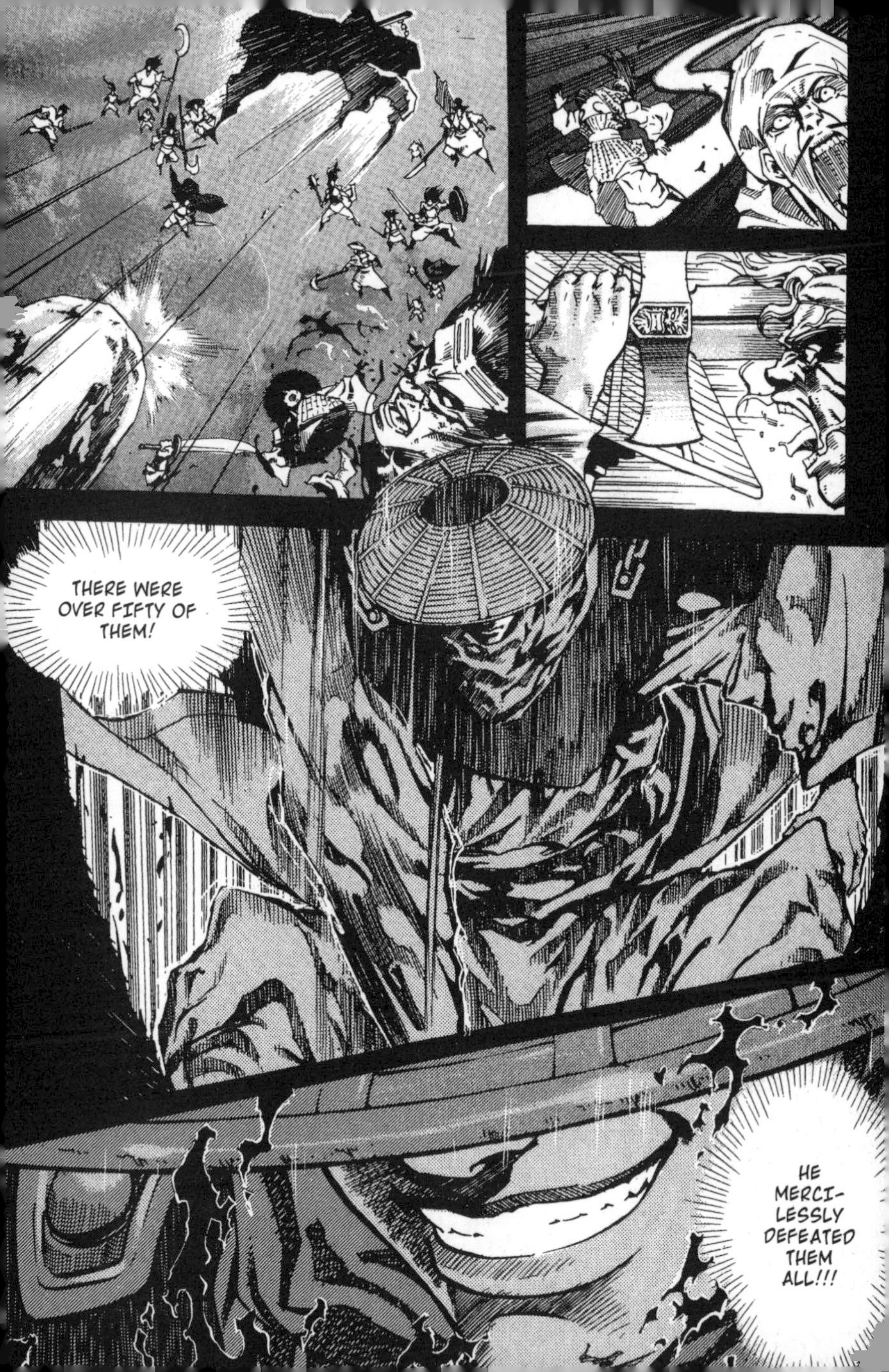
THERE WERE OVER FIFTY OF THEM!
HE MERCI-LESSLY DEFEATED THEM ALL!!!

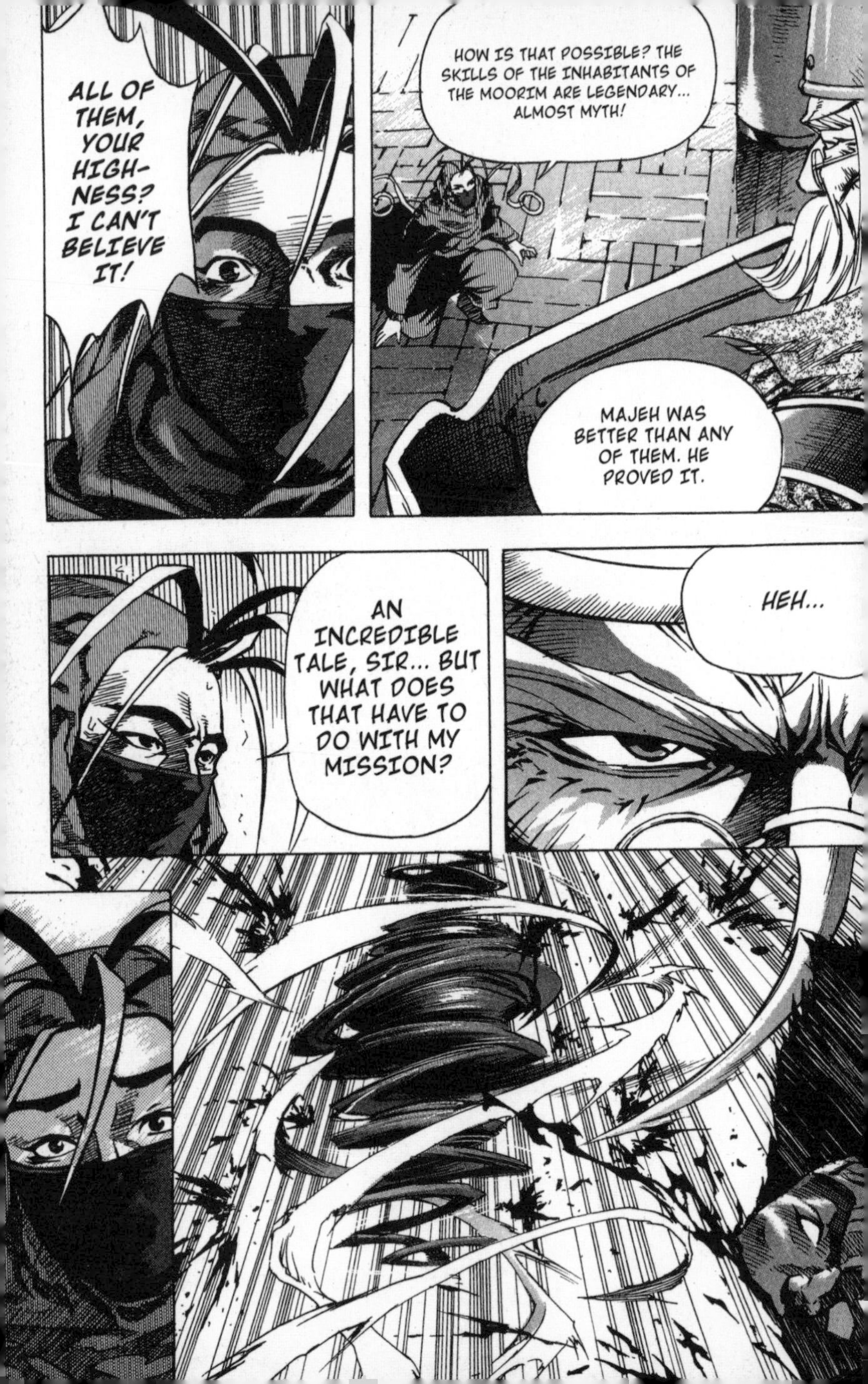
ALL OF THEM, YOUR HIGHNESS? I CAN'T BELIEVE IT!
HOW IS THAT POSSIBLE? THE SKILLS OF THE INHABITANTS OF THE MOORIM ARE LEGENDARY... ALMOST MYTH!
MAJEH WAS BETTER THAN ANY OF THEM. HE PROVED IT.
AN INCREDIBLE TALE, SIR... BUT WHAT DOES THAT HAVE TO DO WITH MY MISSION?
HEH...

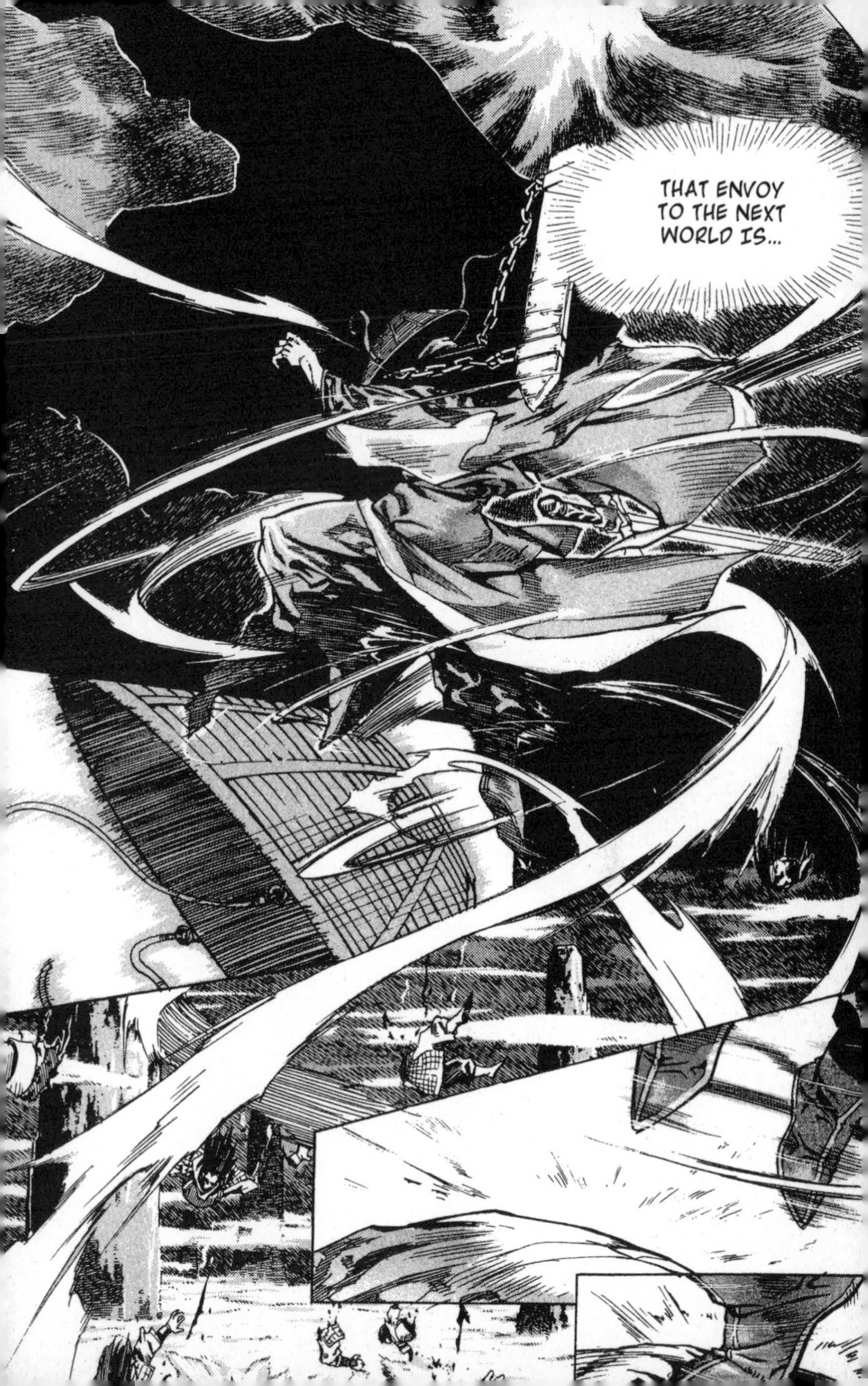
THAT ENVOY TO THE NEXT WORLD IS...

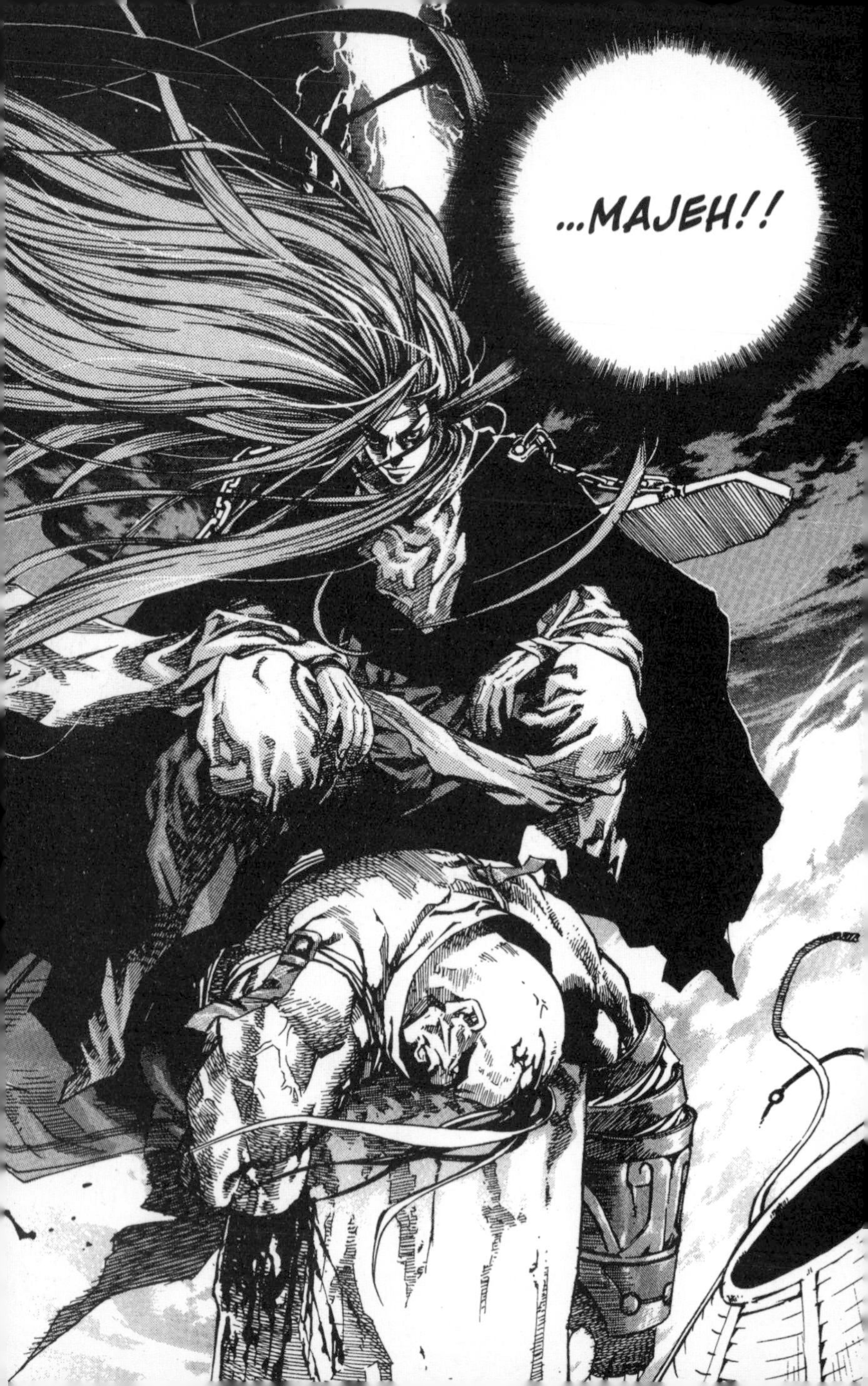
...MAJEH!!

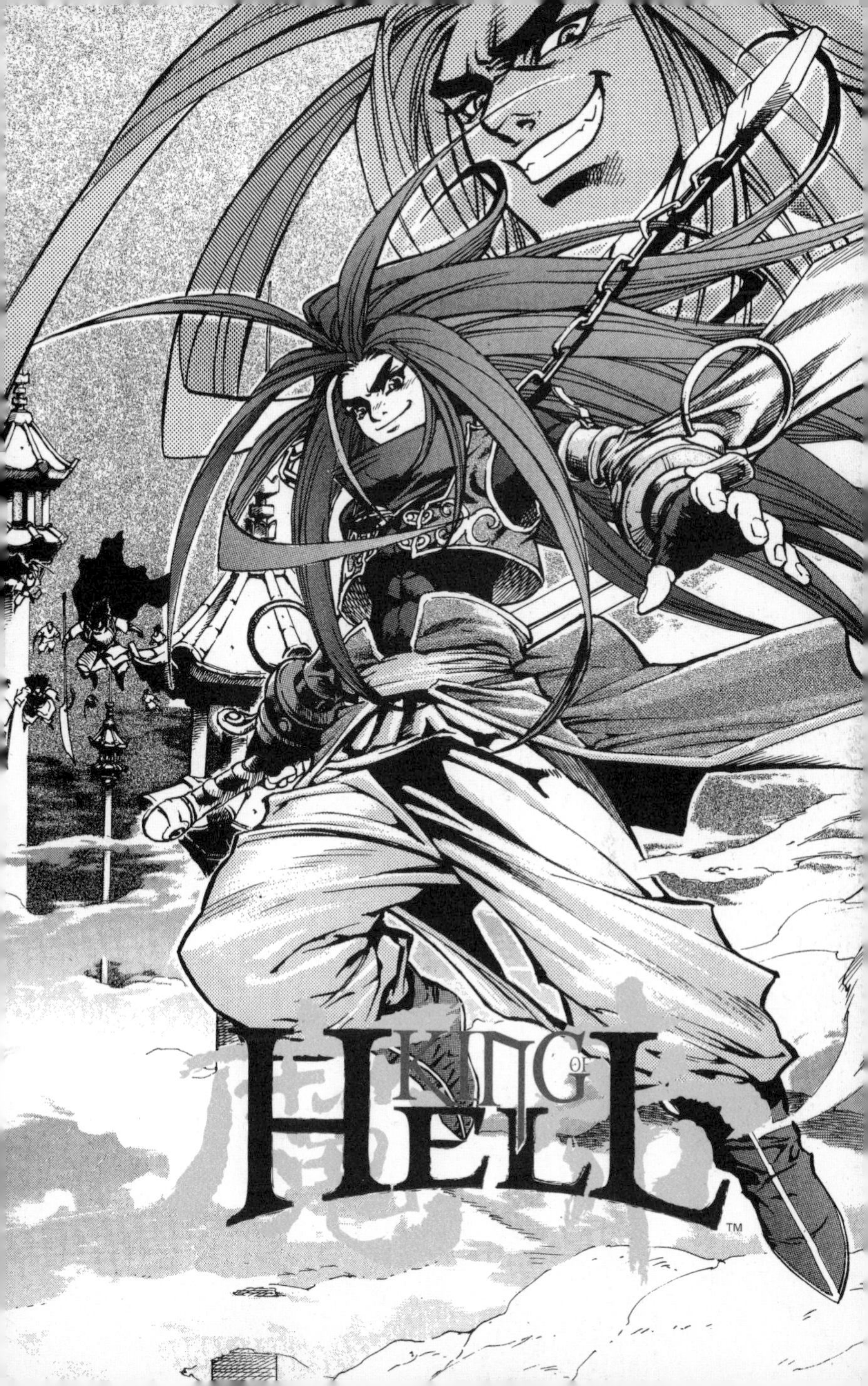
KING OF HELL™

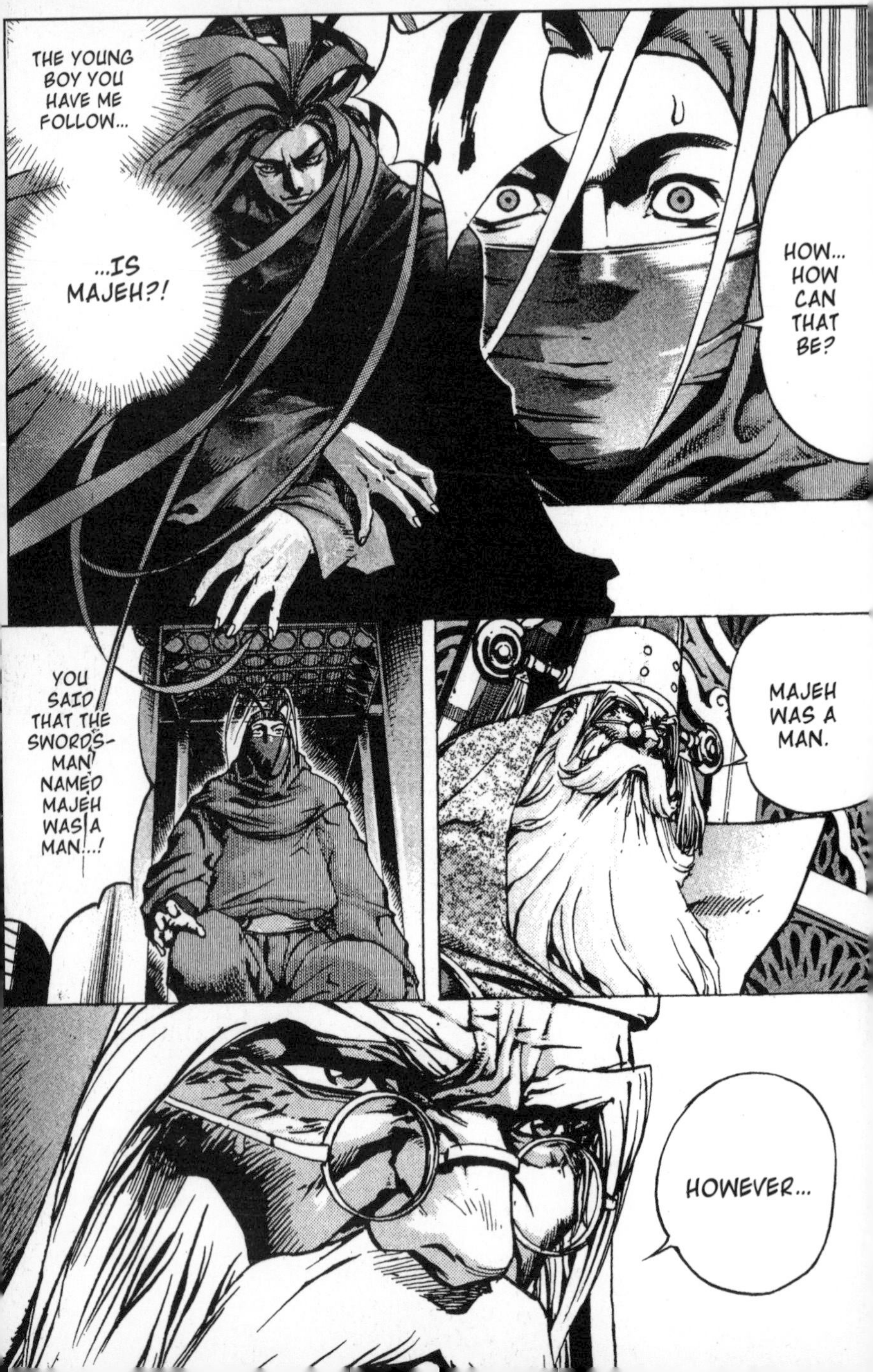
THE YOUNG BOY YOU HAVE ME FOLLOW...
...IS MAJEH?!
HOW... HOW CAN THAT BE?
YOU SAID THAT THE SWORDSMAN NAMED MAJEH WAS A MAN...!
MAJEH WAS A MAN.
HOWEVER...

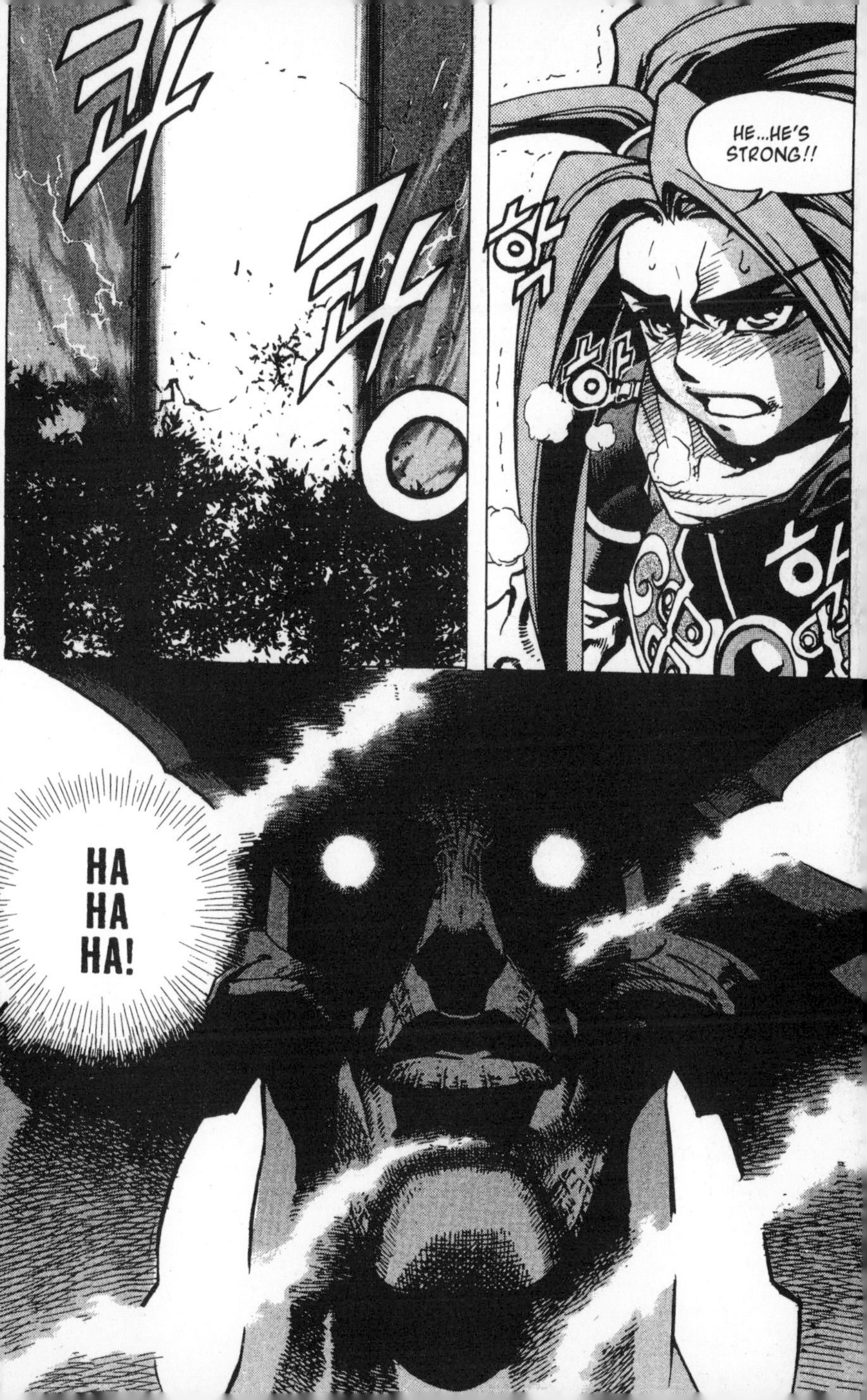
콰
콰
HE...HE'S STRONG!!
학
학
학
HA
HA
HA!

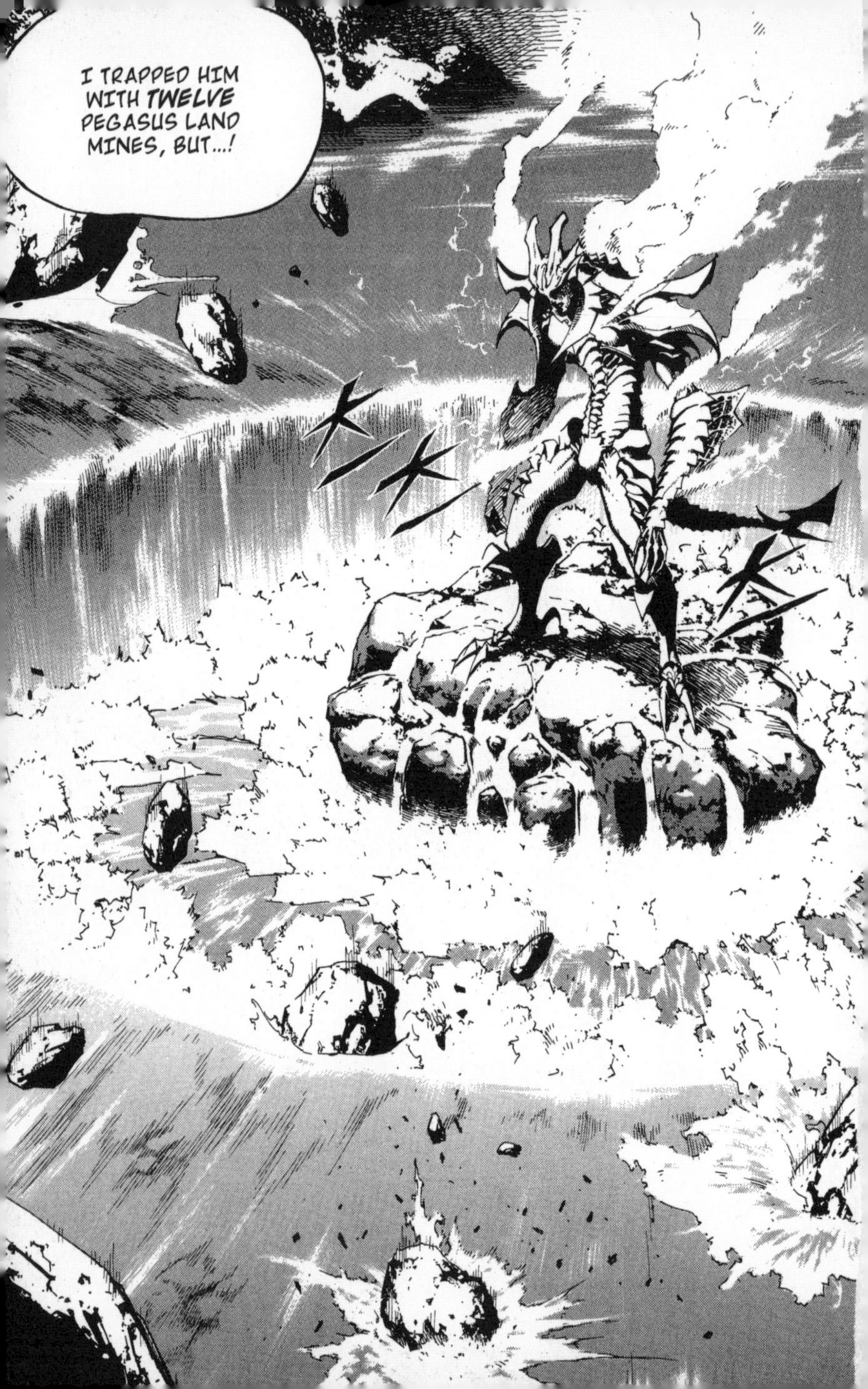
I TRAPPED HIM WITH TWELVE PEGASUS LAND MINES, BUT...!

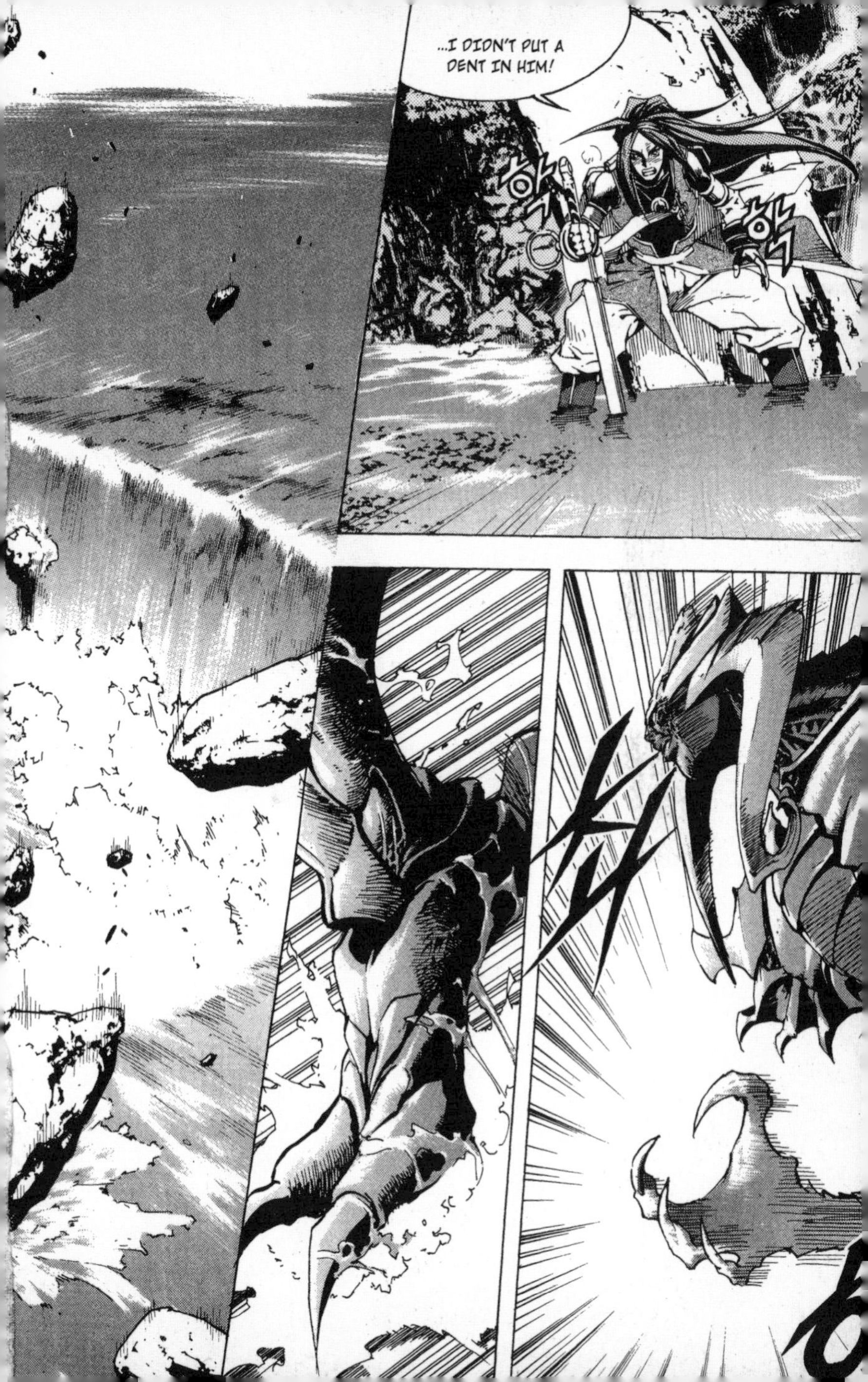
...I DIDN'T PUT A DENT IN HIM!

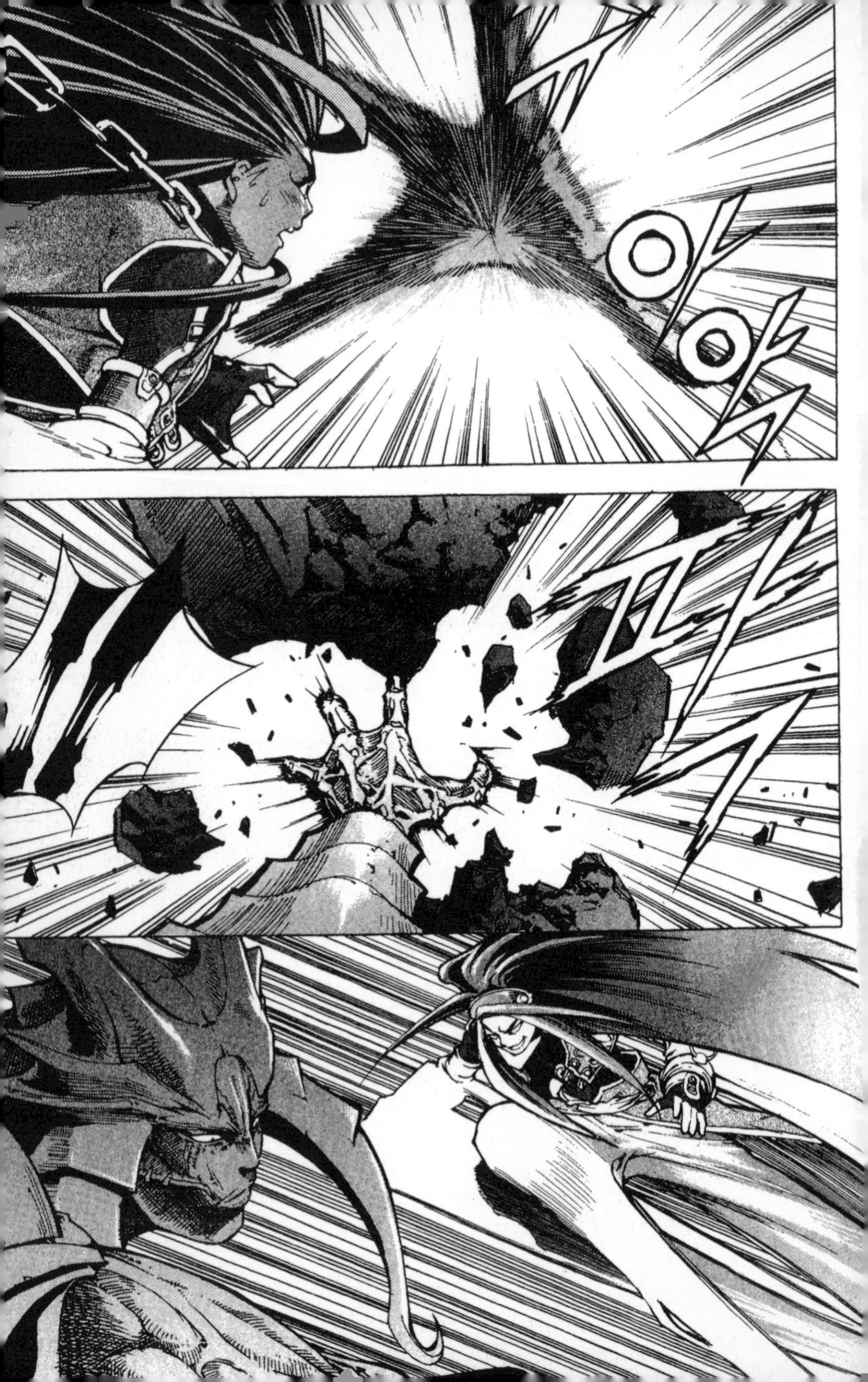
야앗

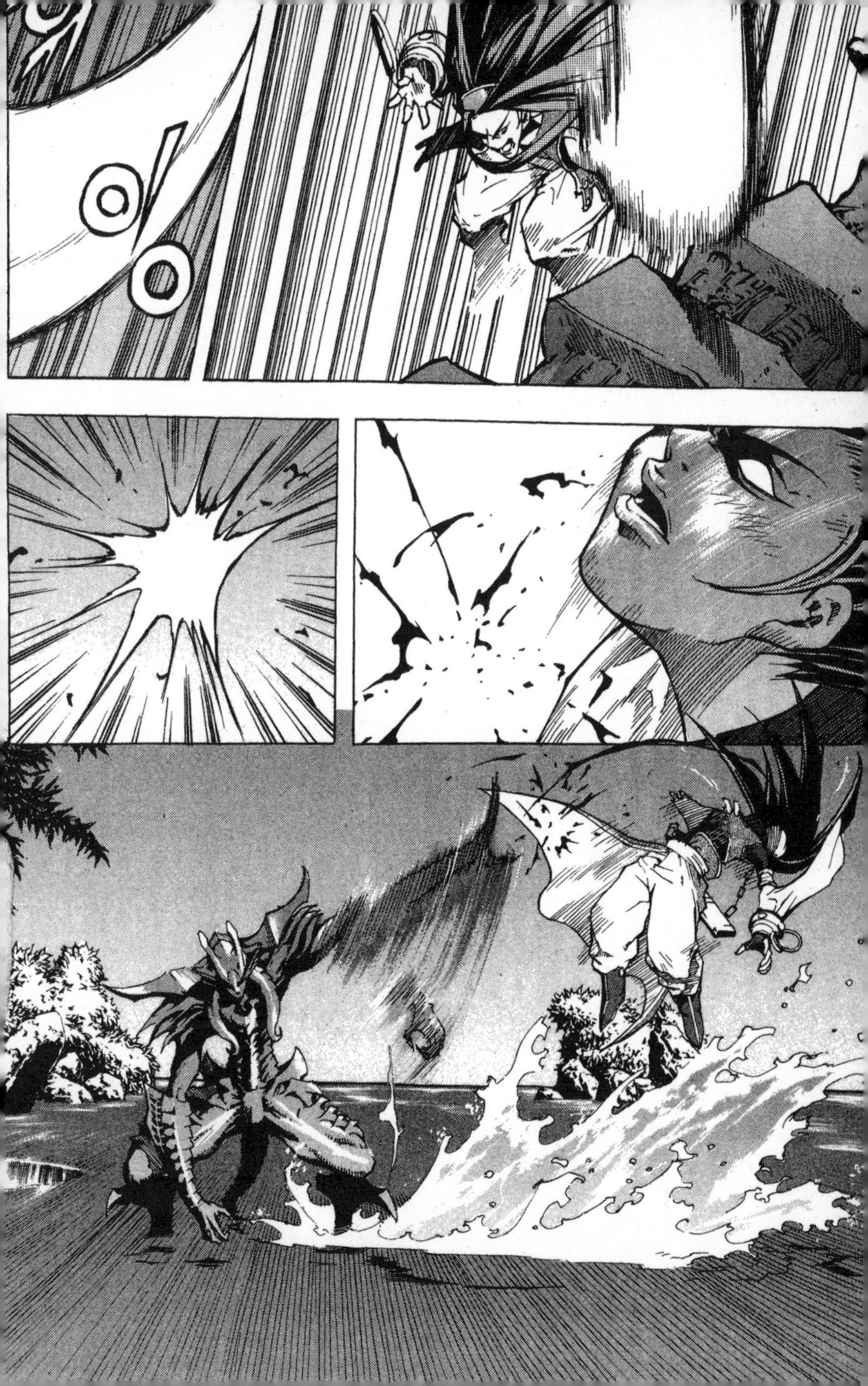

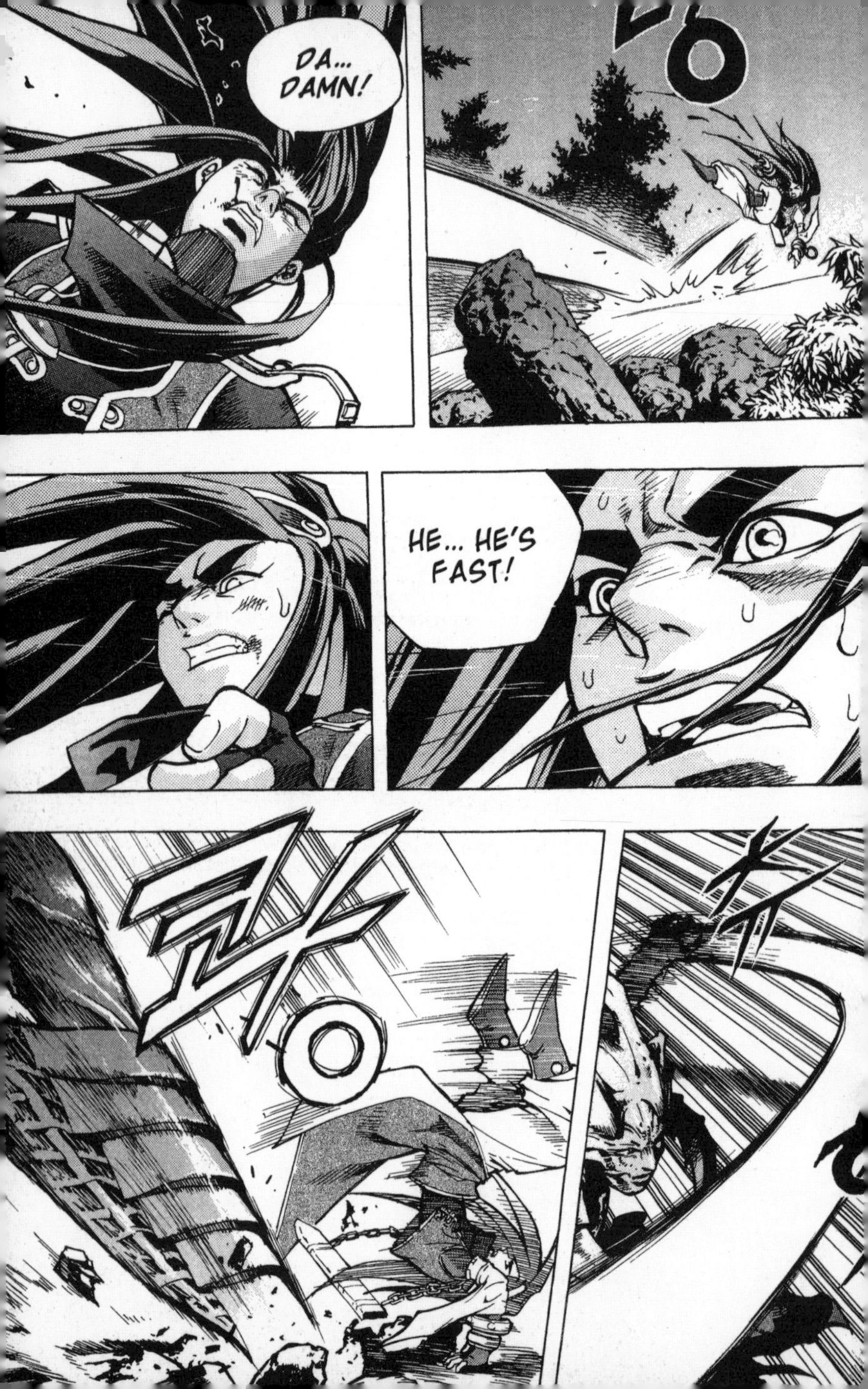
DA... DAMN!
HE... HE'S FAST!

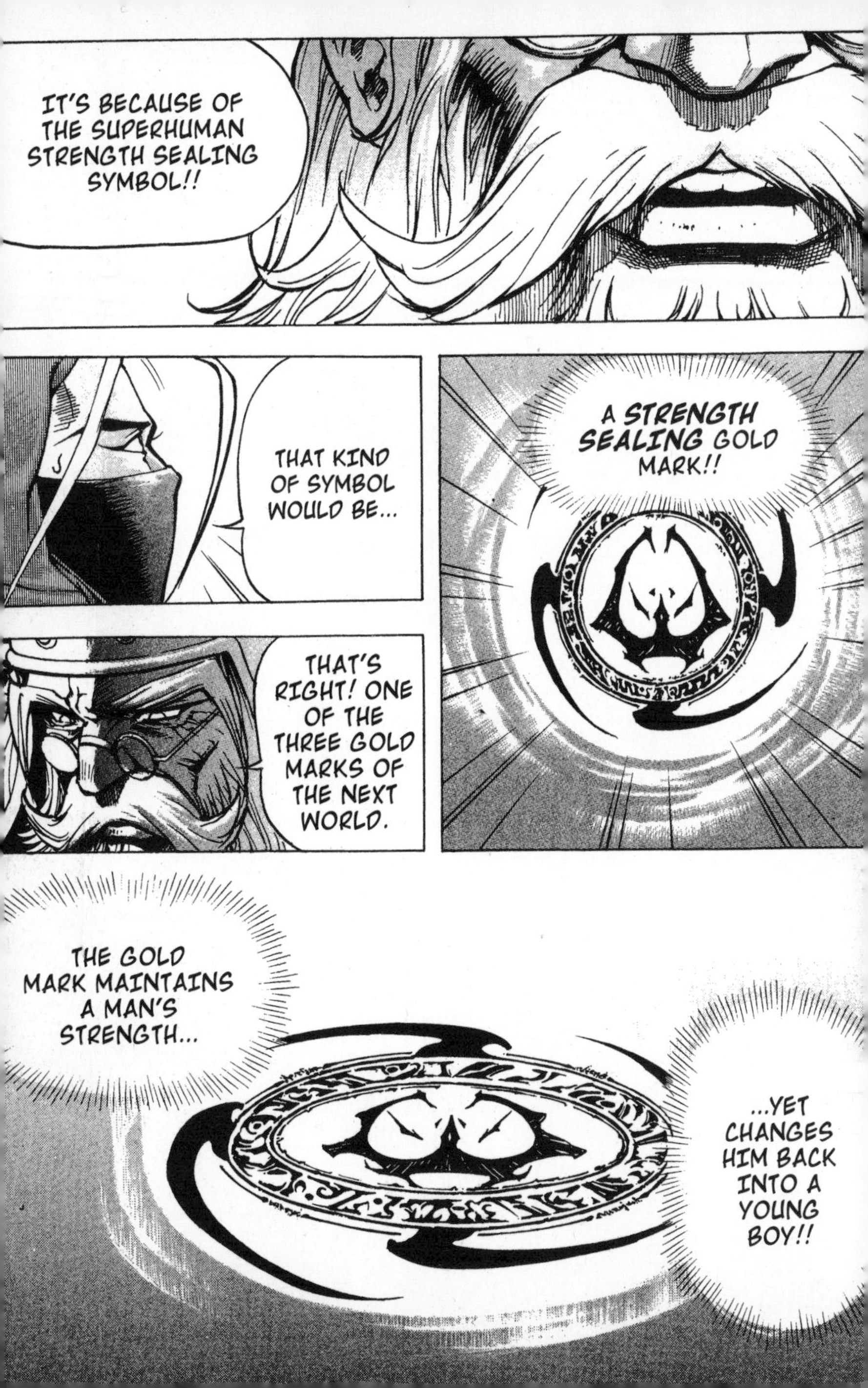
IT'S BECAUSE OF THE SUPERHUMAN STRENGTH SEALING SYMBOL!!
THAT KIND OF SYMBOL WOULD BE...
A STRENGTH SEALING GOLD MARK!!
THAT'S RIGHT! ONE OF THE THREE GOLD MARKS OF THE NEXT WORLD.
THE GOLD MARK MAINTAINS A MAN'S STRENGTH...
...YET CHANGES HIM BACK INTO A YOUNG BOY!!

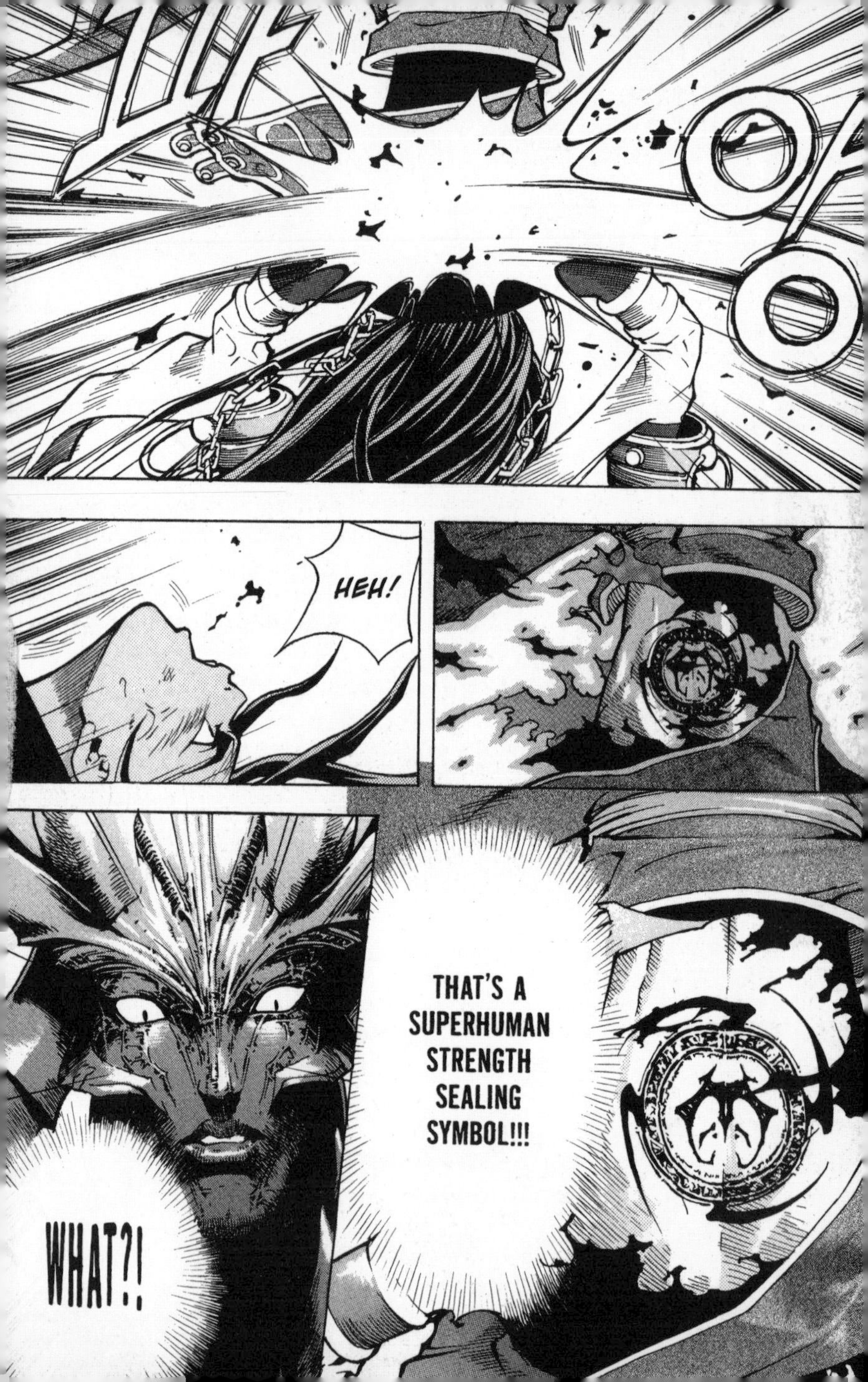
HEH!
THAT'S A SUPERHUMAN STRENGTH SEALING SYMBOL!!!
WHAT?!

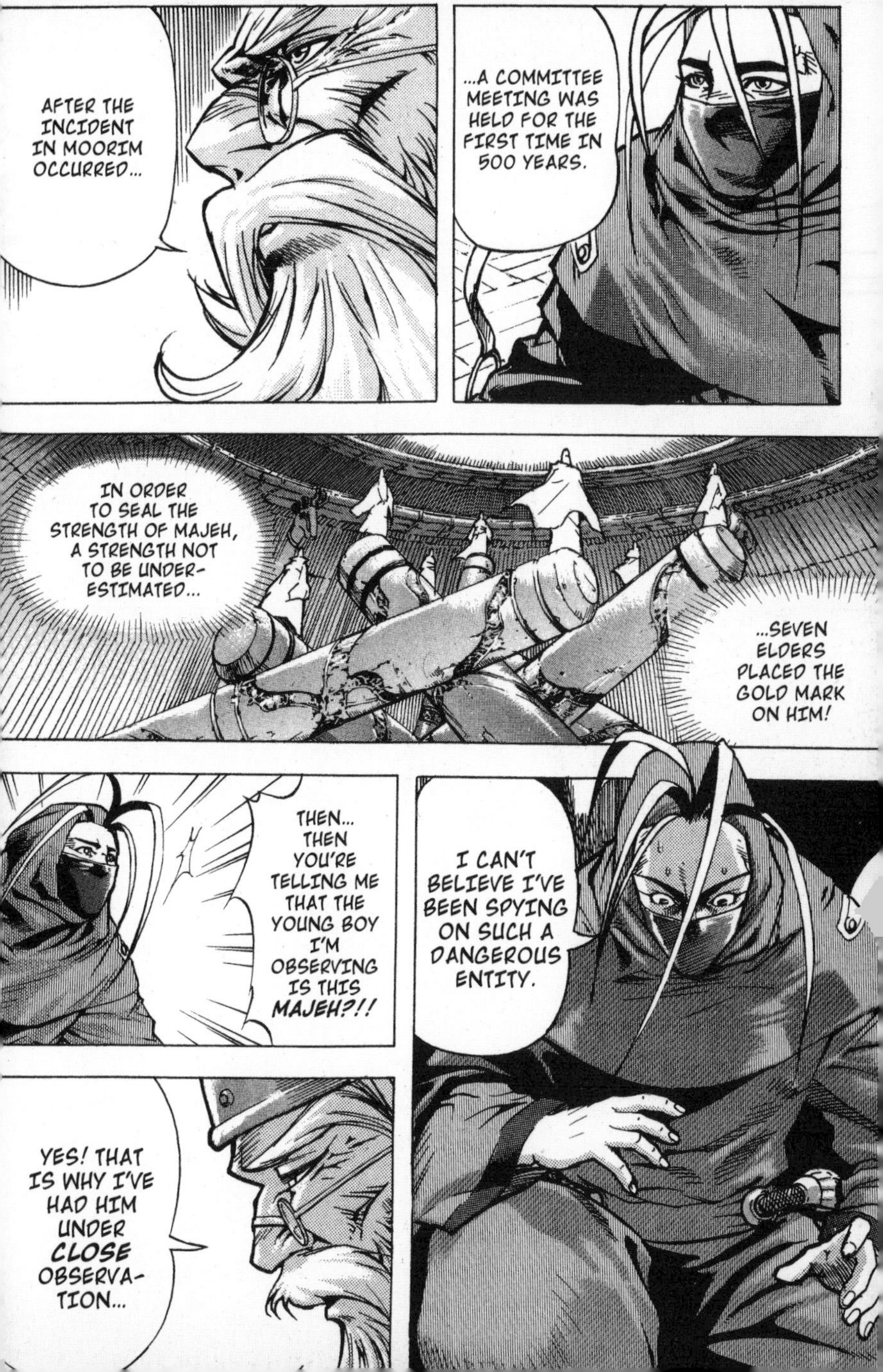
AFTER THE INCIDENT IN MOORIM OCCURRED...
...A COMMITTEE MEETING WAS HELD FOR THE FIRST TIME IN 500 YEARS.
IN ORDER TO SEAL THE STRENGTH OF MAJEH, A STRENGTH NOT TO BE UNDER-ESTIMATED...
...SEVEN ELDERS PLACED THE GOLD MARK ON HIM!
THEN... THEN YOU'RE TELLING ME THAT THE YOUNG BOY I'M OBSERVING IS THIS MAJEH?!!
I CAN'T BELIEVE I'VE BEEN SPYING ON SUCH A DANGEROUS ENTITY.
YES! THAT IS WHY I'VE HAD HIM UNDER CLOSE OBSERVA-TION...

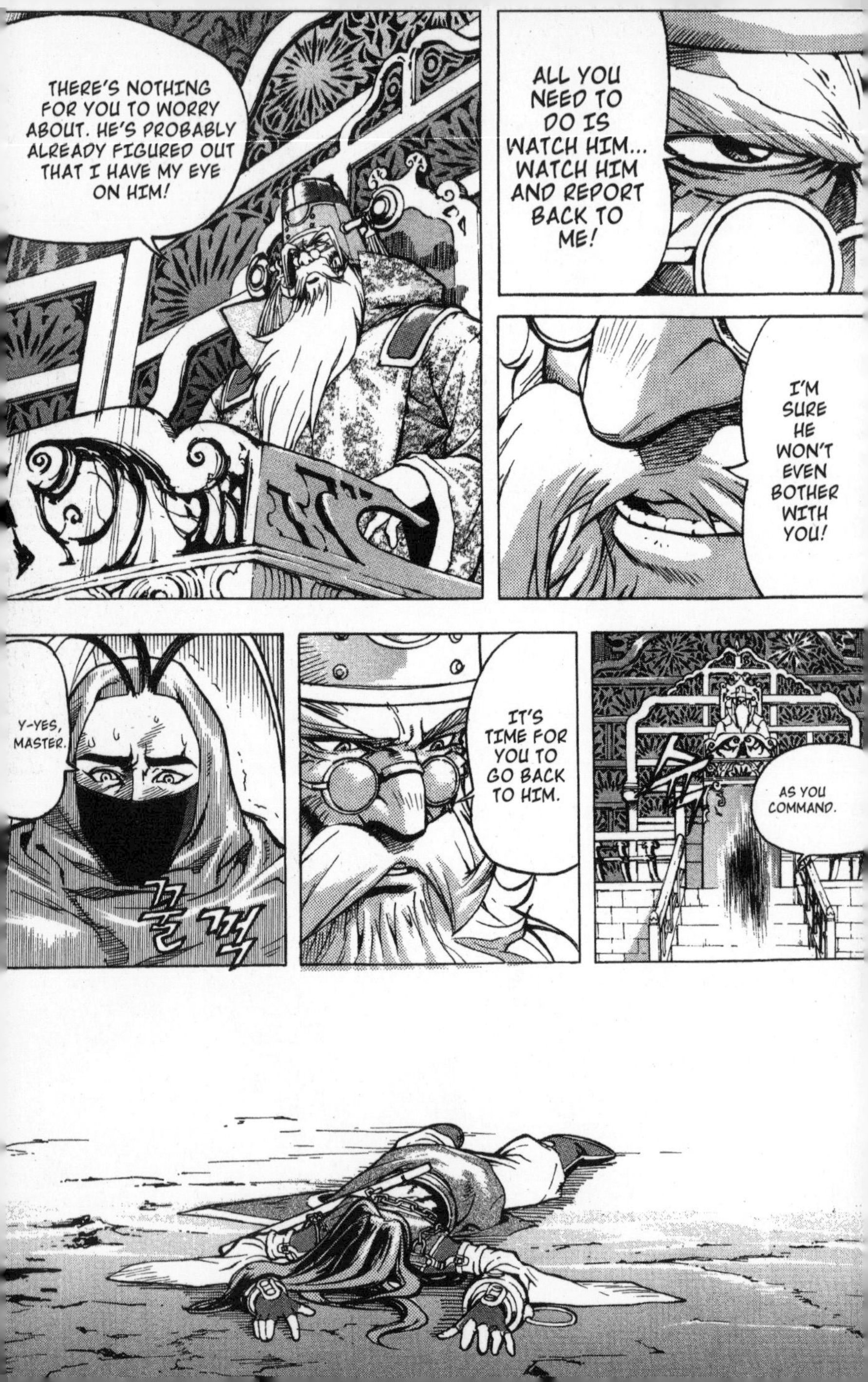

THERE'S NOTHING FOR YOU TO WORRY ABOUT. HE'S PROBABLY ALREADY FIGURED OUT THAT I HAVE MY EYE ON HIM!
ALL YOU NEED TO DO IS WATCH HIM... WATCH HIM AND REPORT BACK TO ME!
I'M SURE HE WON'T EVEN BOTHER WITH YOU!
Y-YES, MASTER.
IT'S TIME FOR YOU TO GO BACK TO HIM.
AS YOU COMMAND.

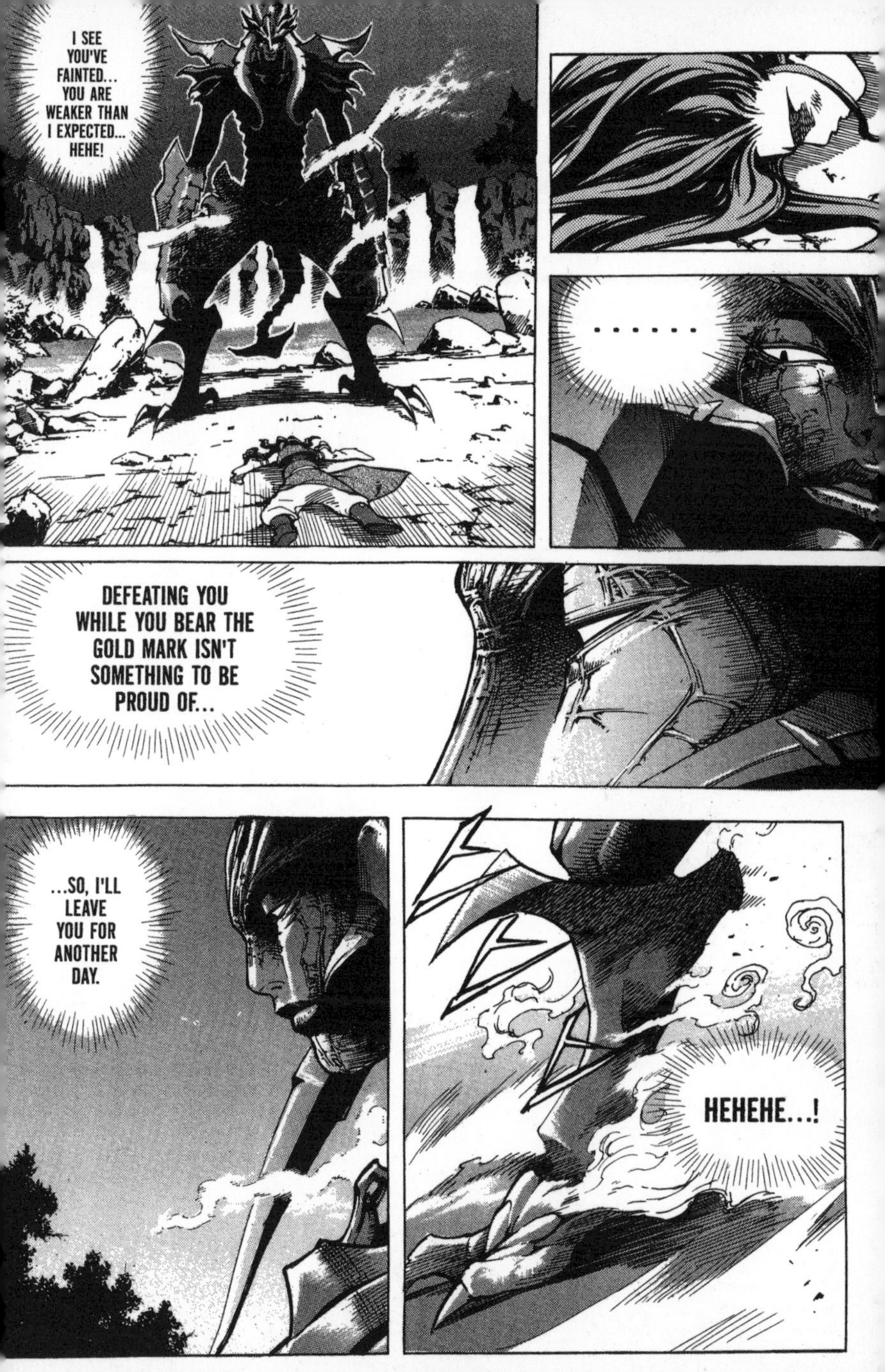
I SEE YOU'VE FAINTED... YOU ARE WEAKER THAN I EXPECTED... HEHE!
......
DEFEATING YOU WHILE YOU BEAR THE GOLD MARK ISN'T SOMETHING TO BE PROUD OF...
...SO, I'LL LEAVE YOU FOR ANOTHER DAY.
HEHEHE...!

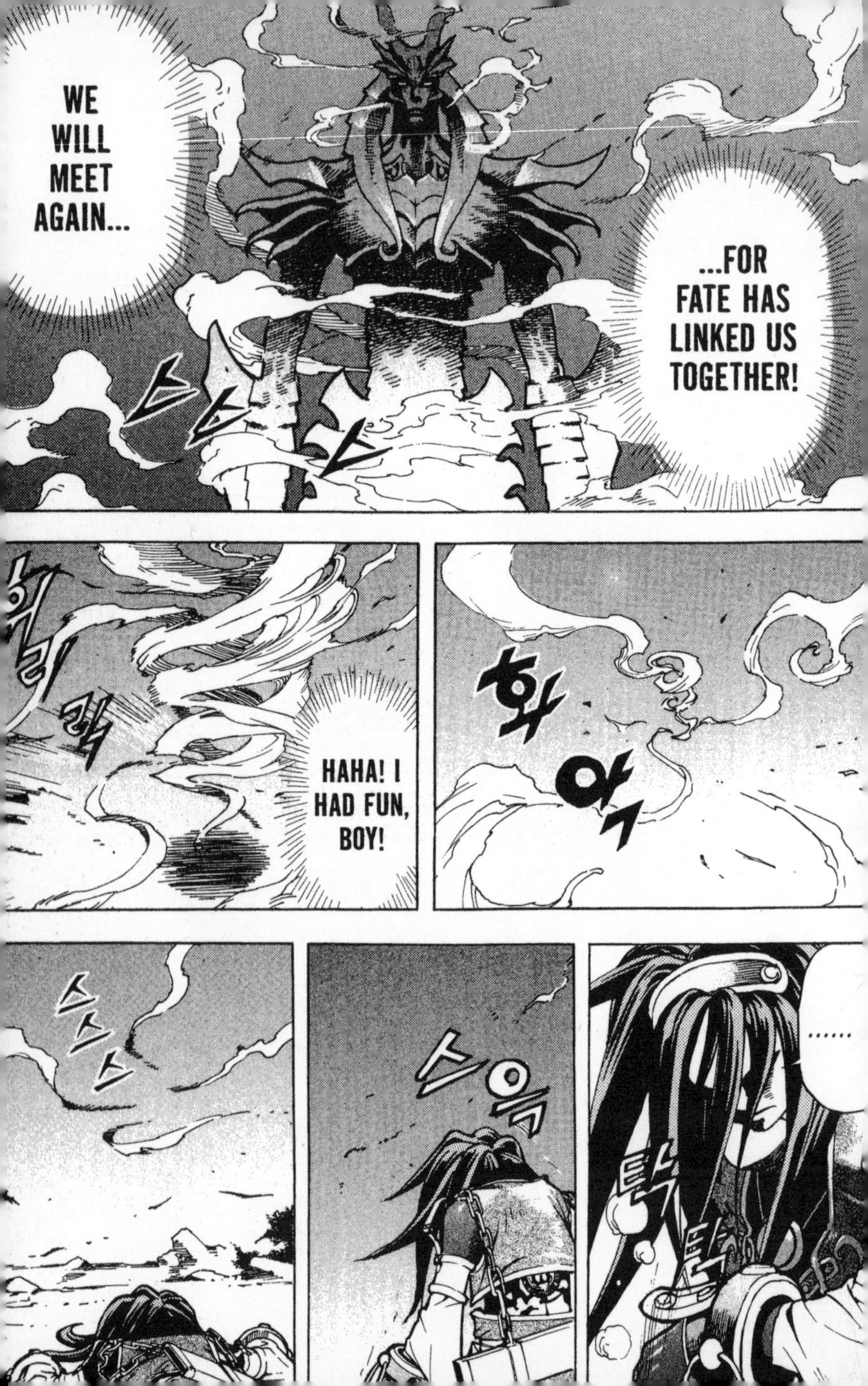
WE WILL MEET AGAIN...
...FOR FATE HAS LINKED US TOGETHER!
HAHA! I HAD FUN, BOY!
......

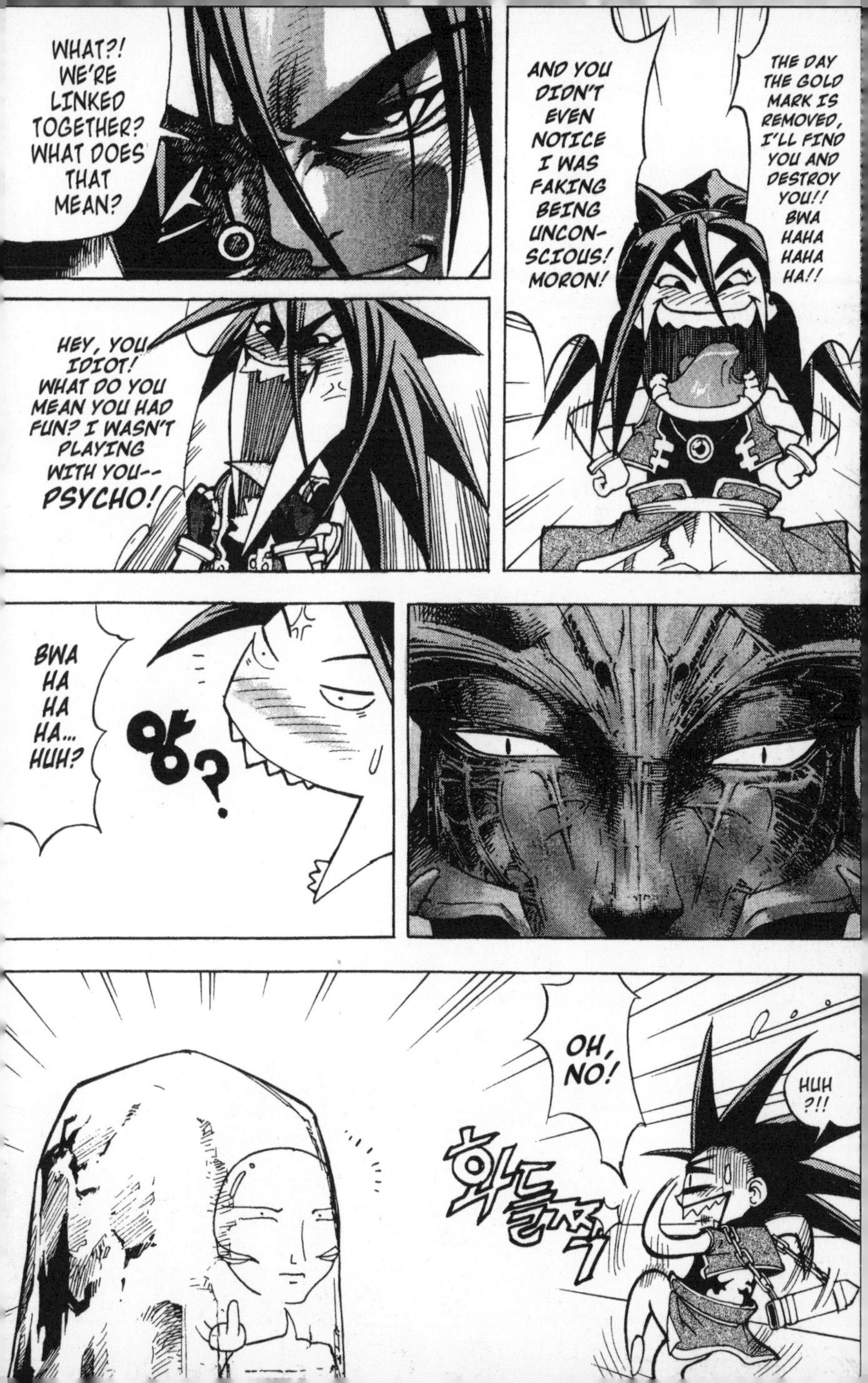
WHAT?! WE'RE LINKED TOGETHER? WHAT DOES THAT MEAN?
HEY, YOU IDIOT! WHAT DO YOU MEAN YOU HAD FUN? I WASN'T PLAYING WITH YOU-- PSYCHO!
AND YOU DIDN'T EVEN NOTICE I WAS FAKING BEING UNCONSCIOUS! MORON!
THE DAY THE GOLD MARK IS REMOVED, I'LL FIND YOU AND DESTROY YOU!! BWA HAHA HAHA HA!!
BWA HA HA HA... HUH?
앙?
OH, NO!
HUH ?!!
화들짝

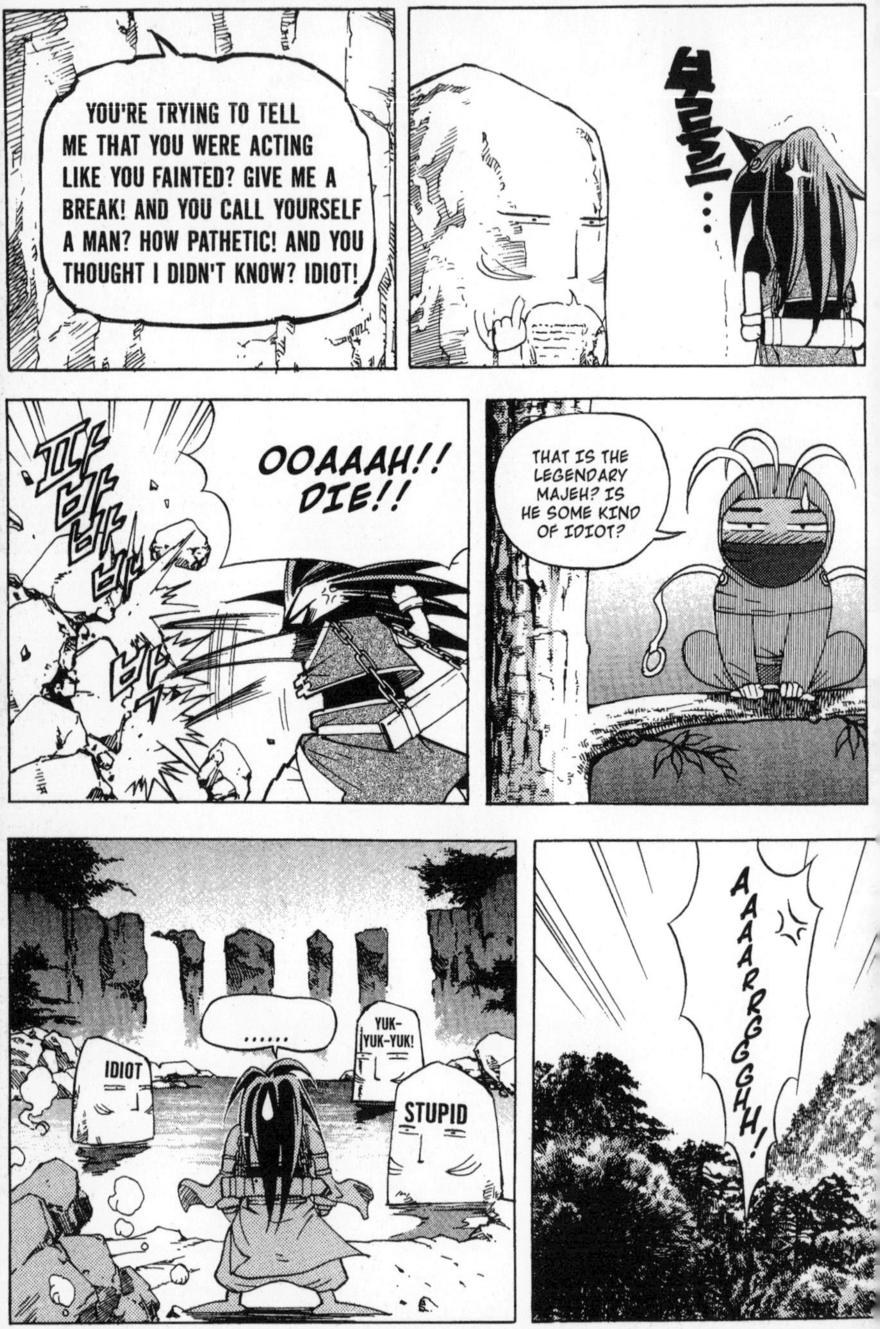
YOU'RE TRYING TO TELL ME THAT YOU WERE ACTING LIKE YOU FAINTED? GIVE ME A BREAK! AND YOU CALL YOURSELF A MAN? HOW PATHETIC! AND YOU THOUGHT I DIDN'T KNOW? IDIOT!
부르르...
파바바박
OOAAAH!! DIE!!
THAT IS THE LEGENDARY MAJEH? IS HE SOME KIND OF IDIOT?
IDIOT
......
YUK-YUK-YUK!
STUPID
AAAARRGGGHH!

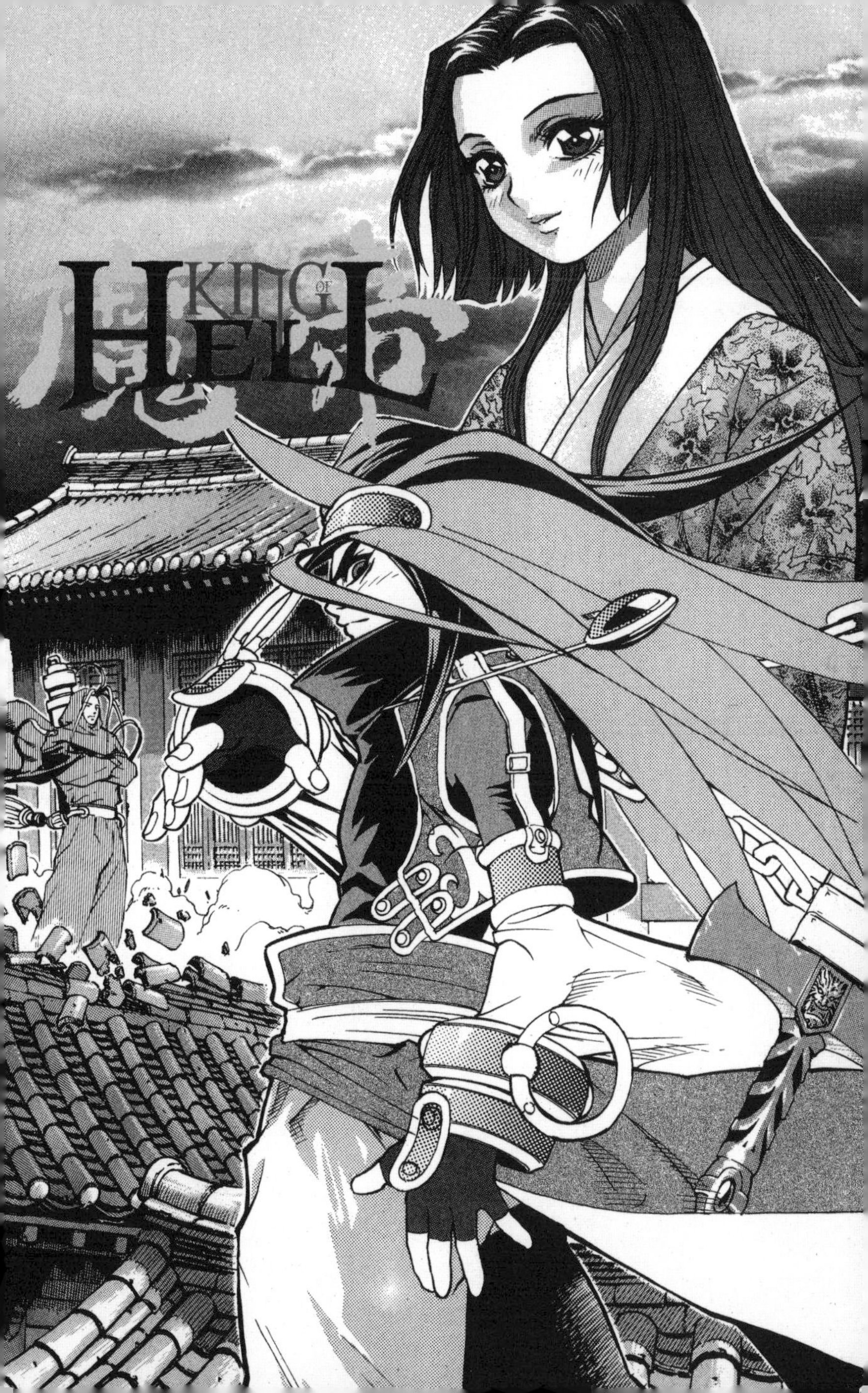
KING OF HELL

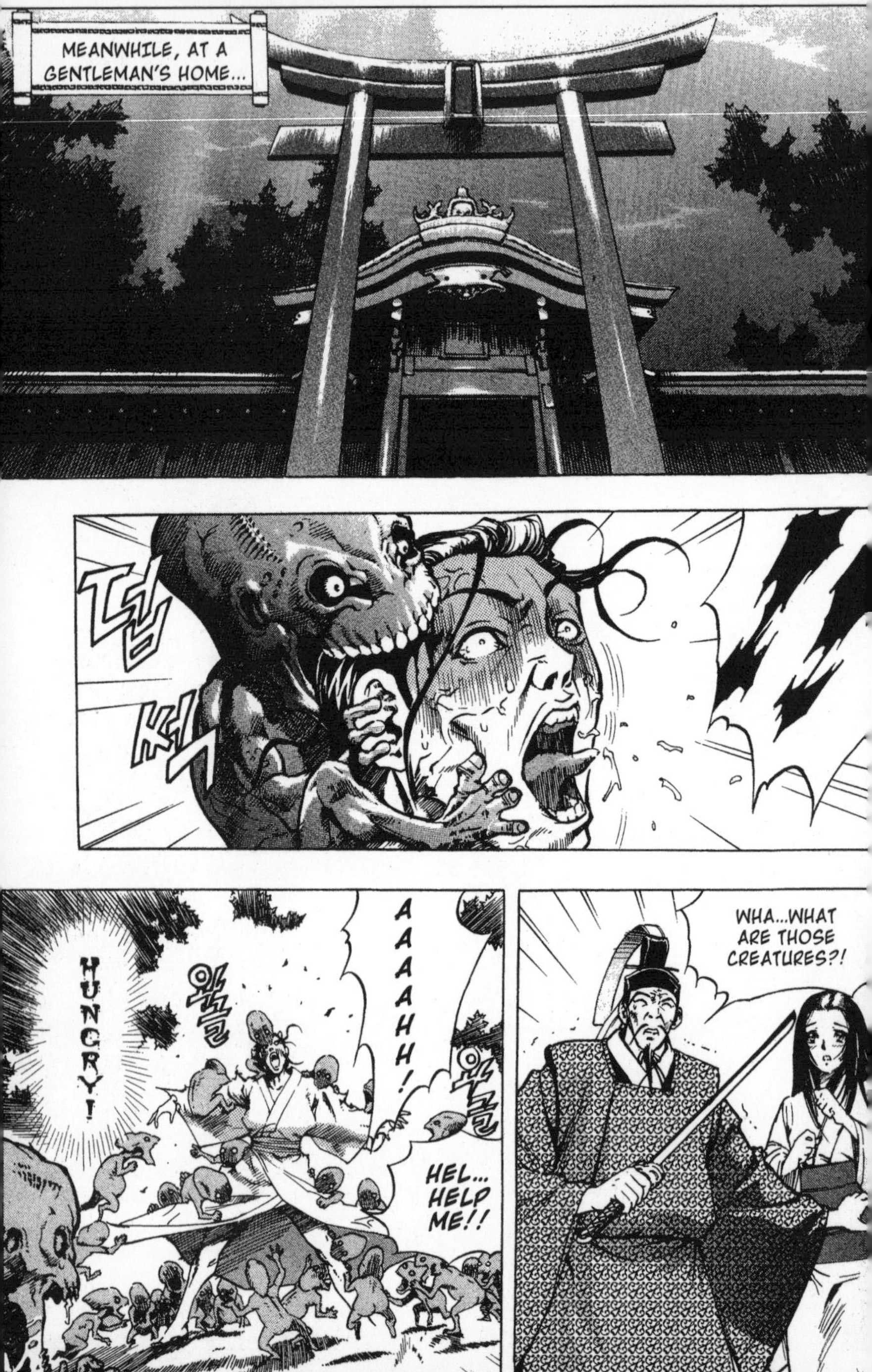
MEANWHILE, AT A GENTLEMAN'S HOME...
덥석
HUNGRY!
와글
AAAAAHH!
와글
HEL... HELP ME!!
WHA...WHAT ARE THOSE CREATURES?!

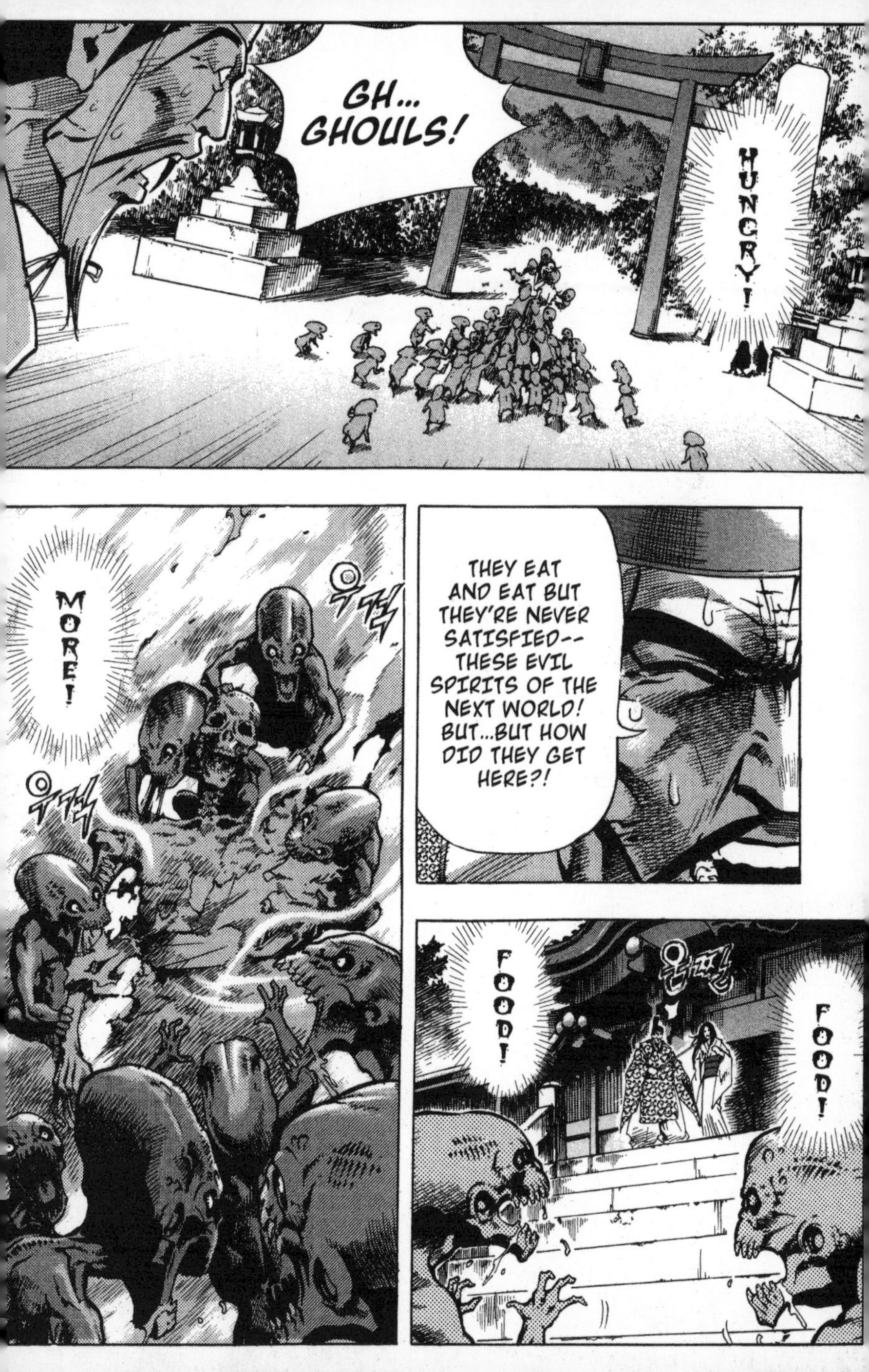
GH... GHOULS!
HUNGRY!
MORE!
THEY EAT AND EAT BUT THEY'RE NEVER SATISFIED-- THESE EVIL SPIRITS OF THE NEXT WORLD! BUT...BUT HOW DID THEY GET HERE?!
FOOD!
FOOD!

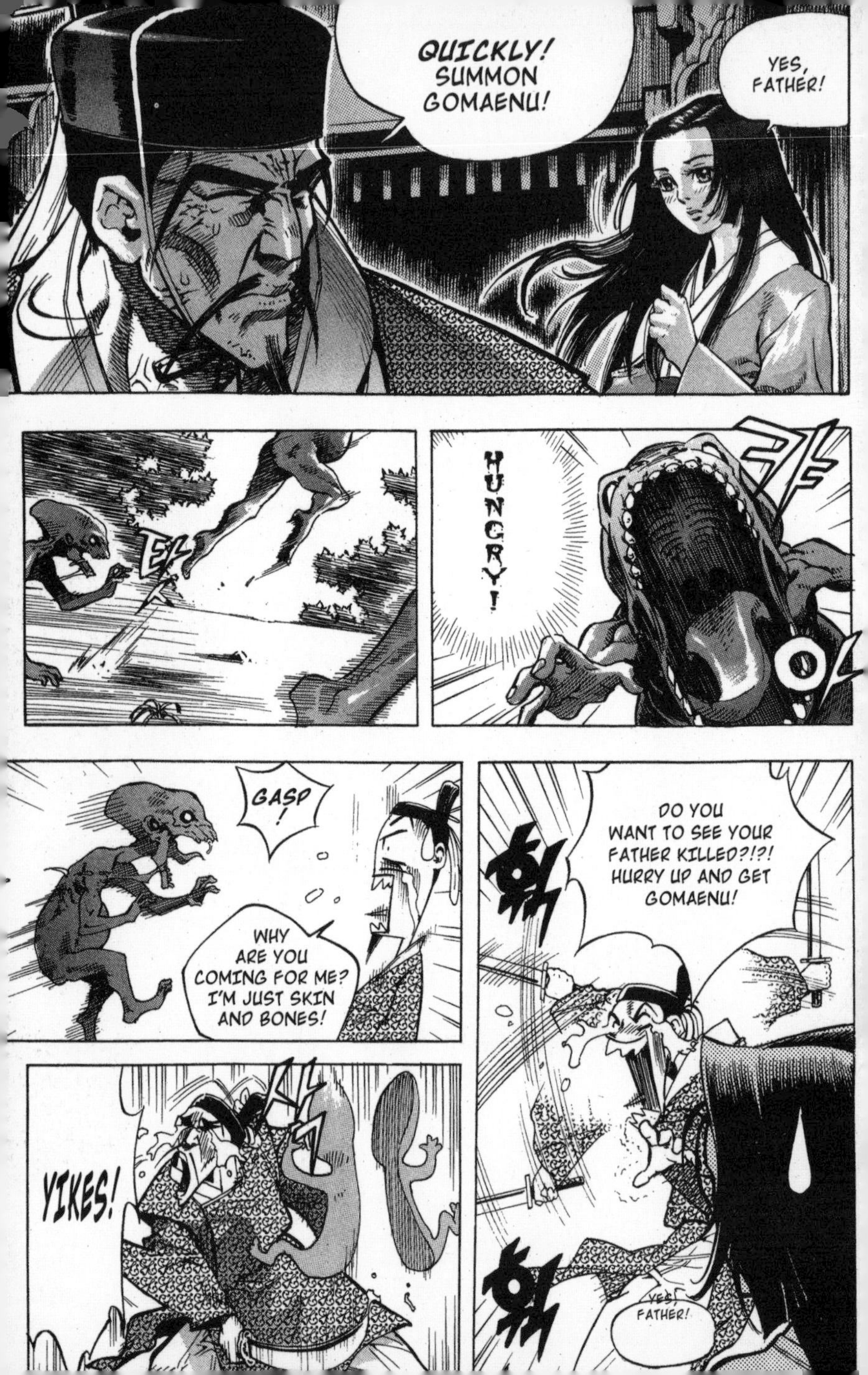
QUICKLY! SUMMON GOMAENU!
YES, FATHER!
HUNGRY!
GASP!
WHY ARE YOU COMING FOR ME? I'M JUST SKIN AND BONES!
YIKES!
DO YOU WANT TO SEE YOUR FATHER KILLED?!?! HURRY UP AND GET GOMAENU!
YES! FATHER!

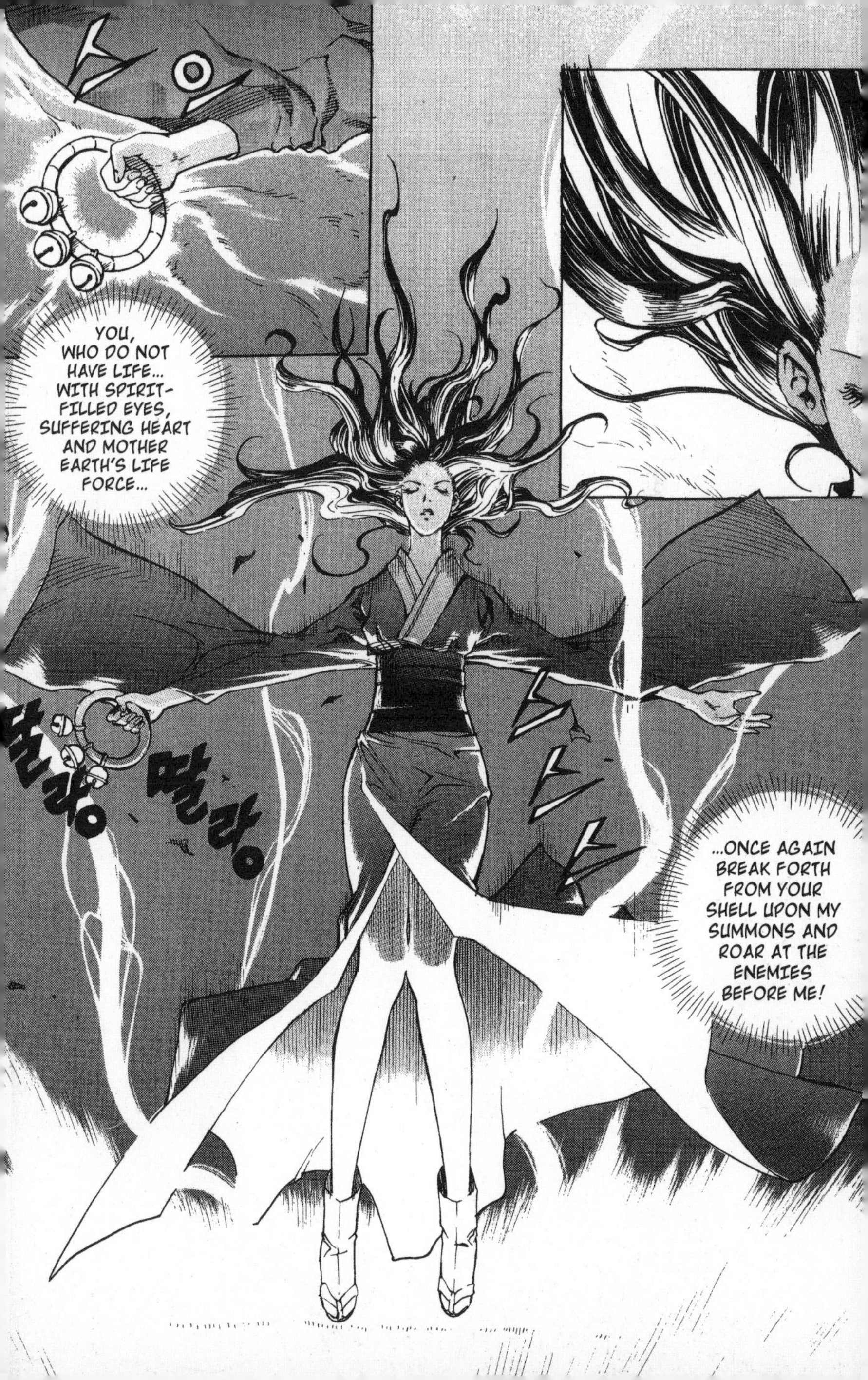
YOU, WHO DO NOT HAVE LIFE... WITH SPIRIT-FILLED EYES, SUFFERING HEART AND MOTHER EARTH'S LIFE FORCE...
...ONCE AGAIN BREAK FORTH FROM YOUR SHELL UPON MY SUMMONS AND ROAR AT THE ENEMIES BEFORE ME!

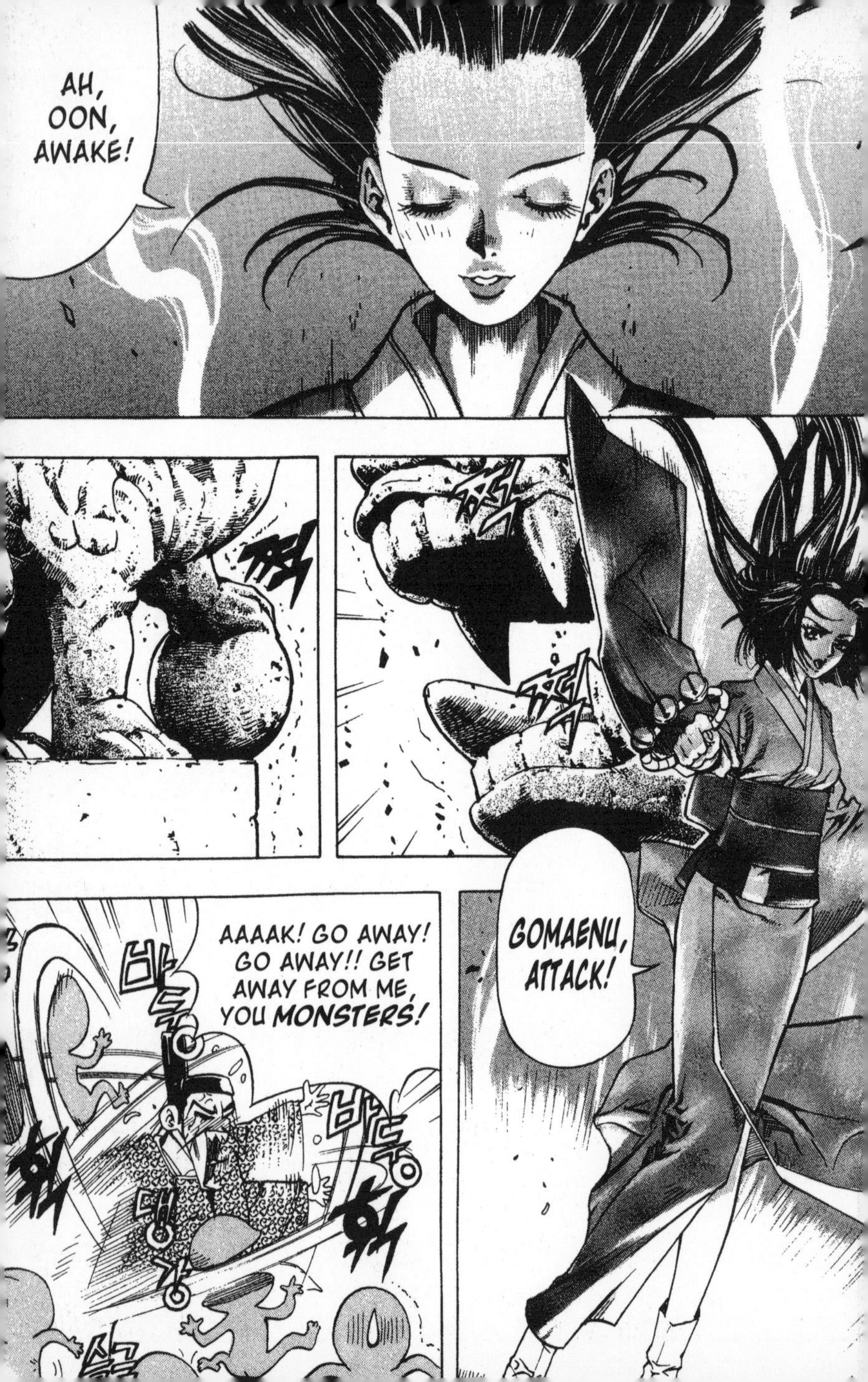
AH, OON, AWAKE!
AAAAK! GO AWAY! GO AWAY!! GET AWAY FROM ME, YOU MONSTERS!
GOMAENU, ATTACK!

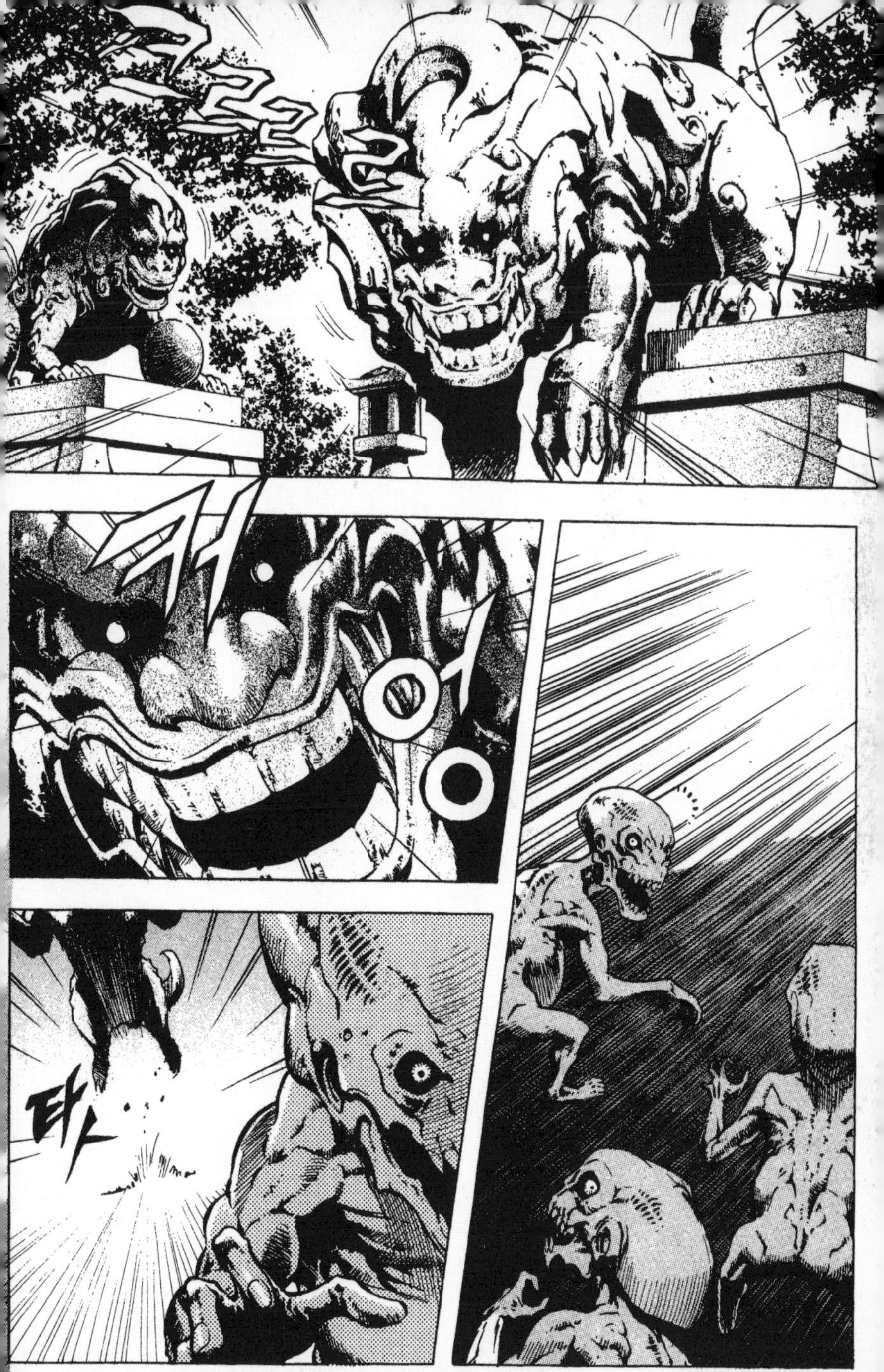
그르르르
샤아아
탓

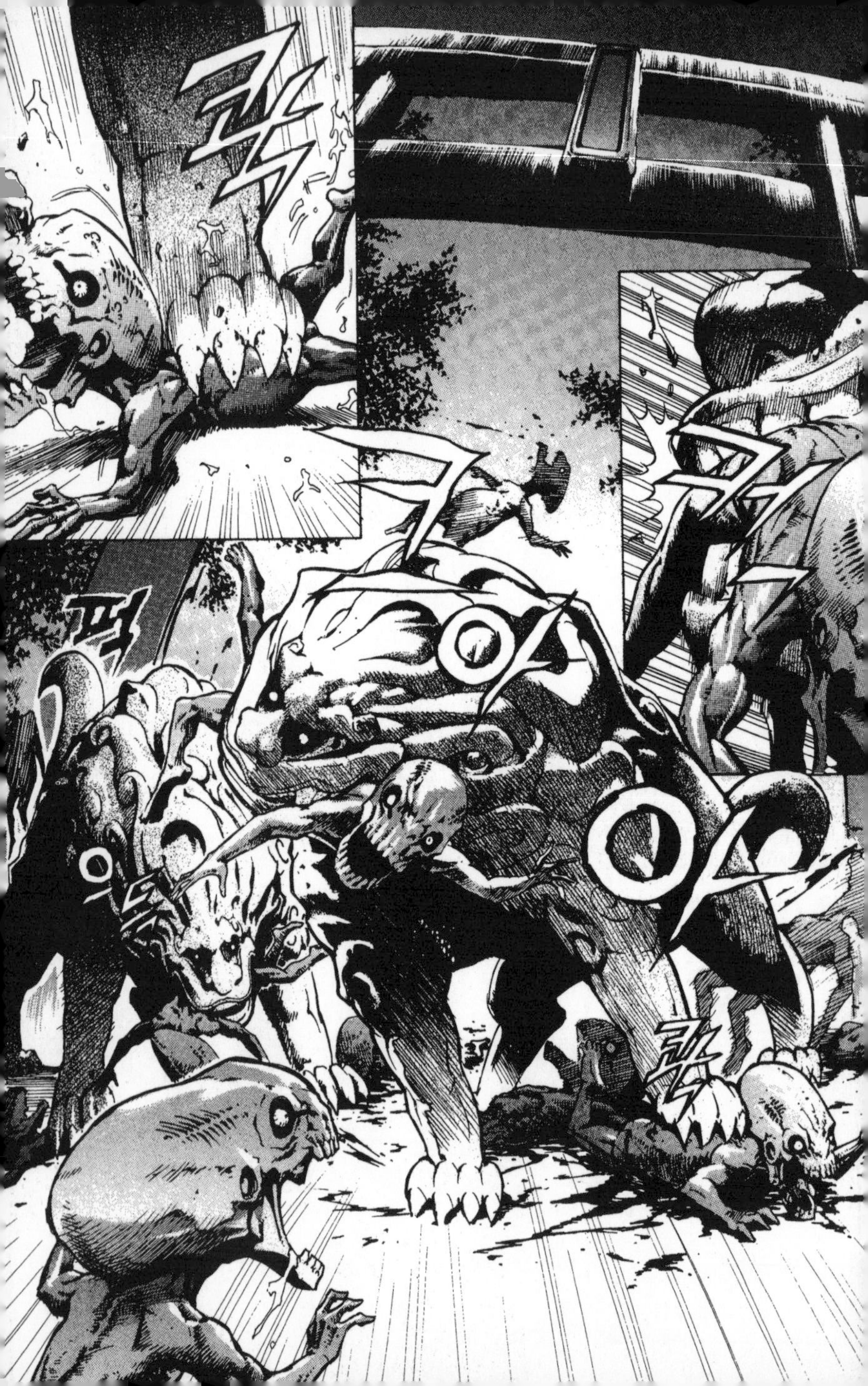
퍽

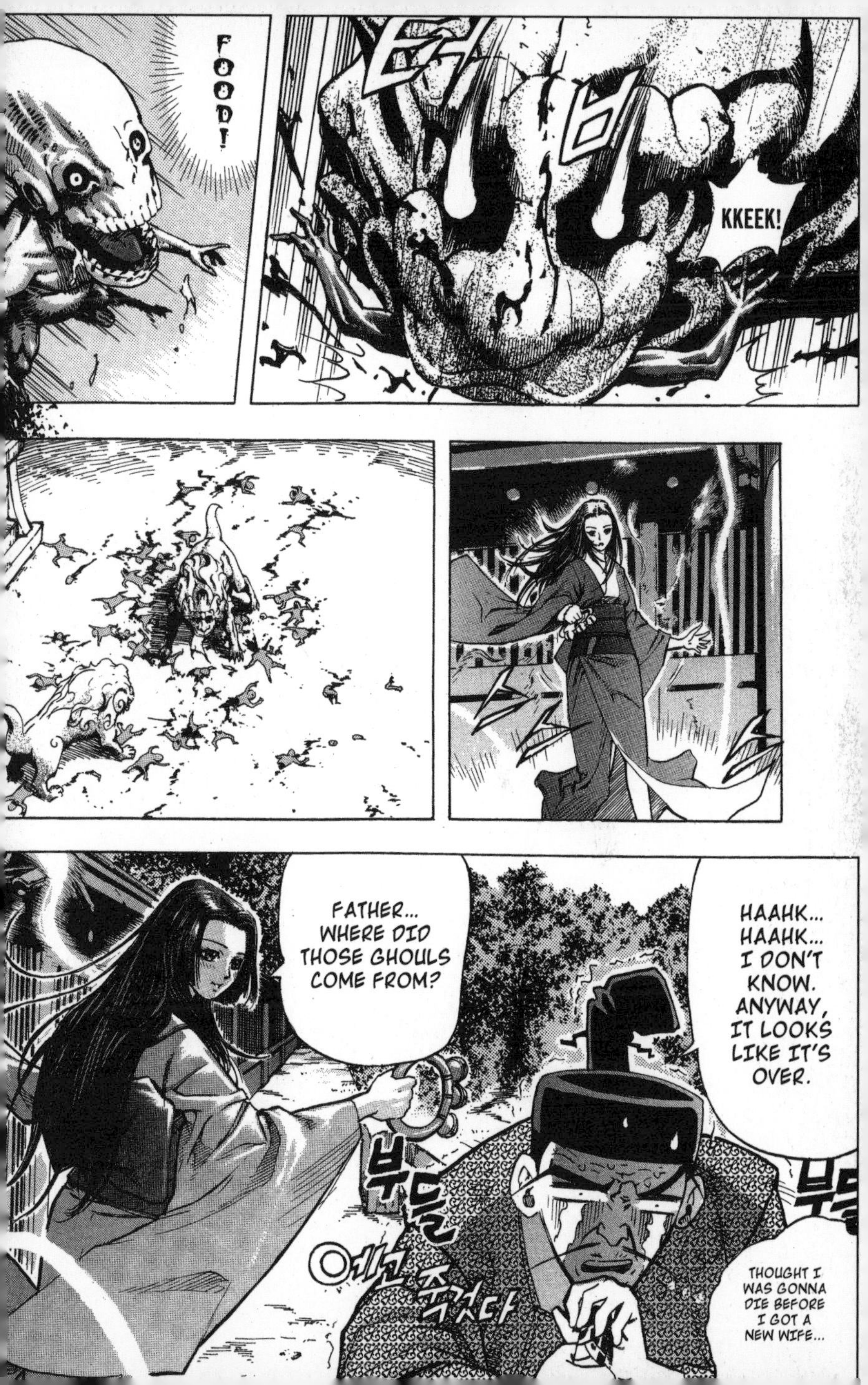

FOOD!
KKEEK!
FATHER... WHERE DID THOSE GHOULS COME FROM?
HAAHK... HAAHK... I DON'T KNOW. ANYWAY, IT LOOKS LIKE IT'S OVER.
부들
THOUGHT I WAS GONNA DIE BEFORE I GOT A NEW WIFE...

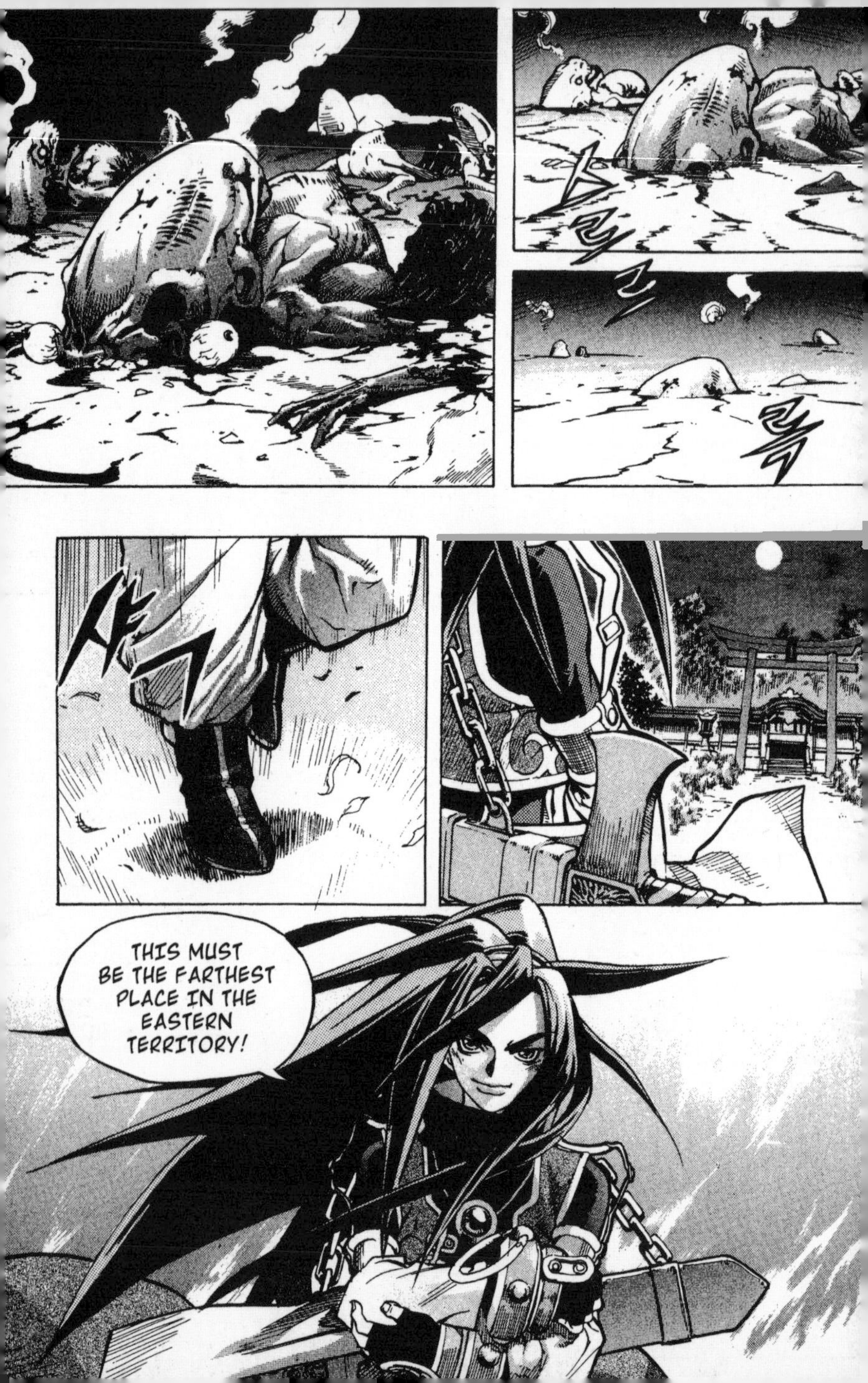
THIS MUST BE THE FARTHEST PLACE IN THE EASTERN TERRITORY!

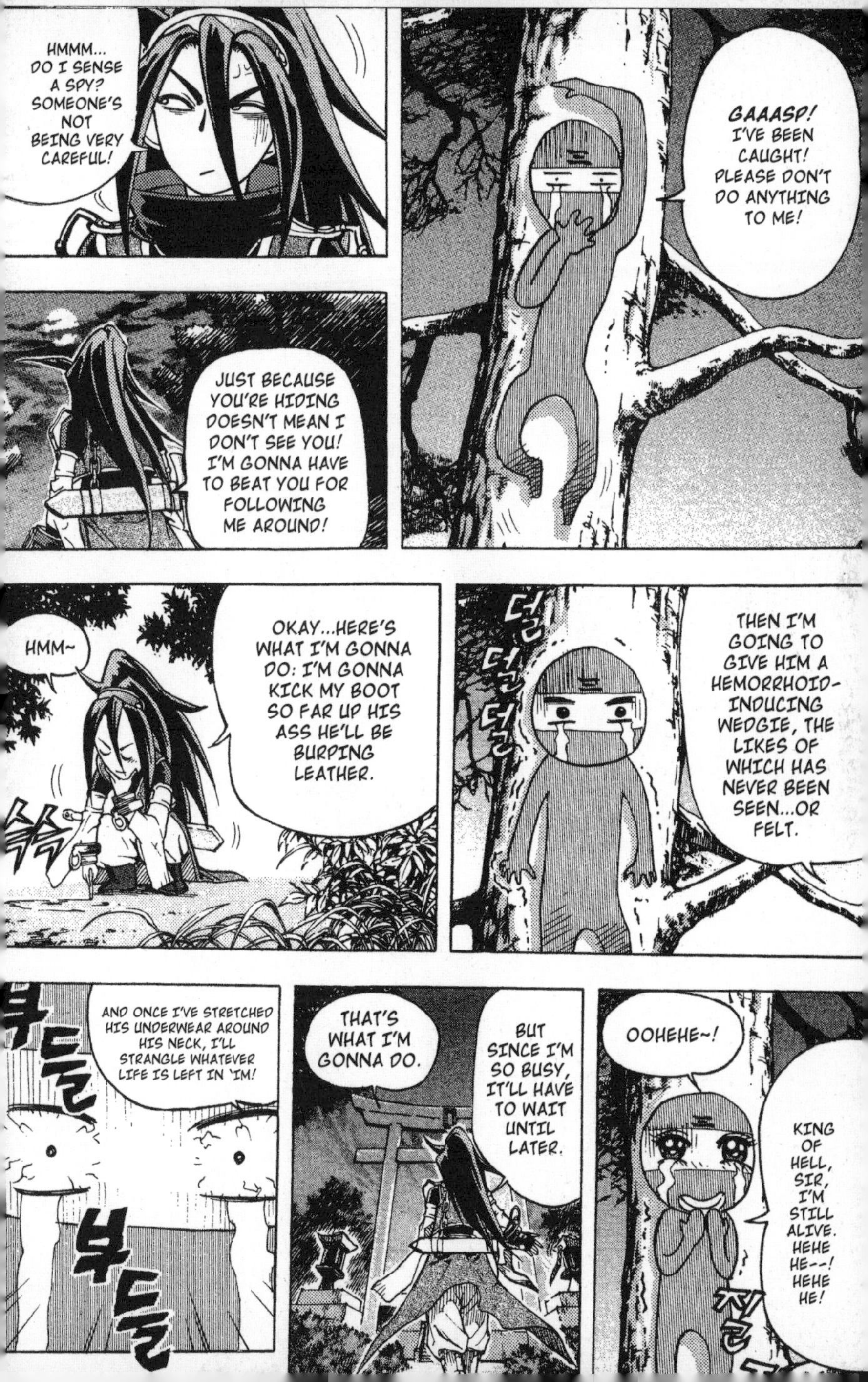
HMMM... DO I SENSE A SPY? SOMEONE'S NOT BEING VERY CAREFUL!
JUST BECAUSE YOU'RE HIDING DOESN'T MEAN I DON'T SEE YOU! I'M GONNA HAVE TO BEAT YOU FOR FOLLOWING ME AROUND!
GAAASP! I'VE BEEN CAUGHT! PLEASE DON'T DO ANYTHING TO ME!
HMM~
OKAY...HERE'S WHAT I'M GONNA DO: I'M GONNA KICK MY BOOT SO FAR UP HIS ASS HE'LL BE BURPING LEATHER.
덜덜덜덜
THEN I'M GOING TO GIVE HIM A HEMORRHOID-INDUCING WEDGIE, THE LIKES OF WHICH HAS NEVER BEEN SEEN...OR FELT.
부들 부들
AND ONCE I'VE STRETCHED HIS UNDERWEAR AROUND HIS NECK, I'LL STRANGLE WHATEVER LIFE IS LEFT IN 'IM!
THAT'S WHAT I'M GONNA DO.
BUT SINCE I'M SO BUSY, IT'LL HAVE TO WAIT UNTIL LATER.
OOHEHE~!
KING OF HELL, SIR, I'M STILL ALIVE. HEHE HE--! HEHE HE!

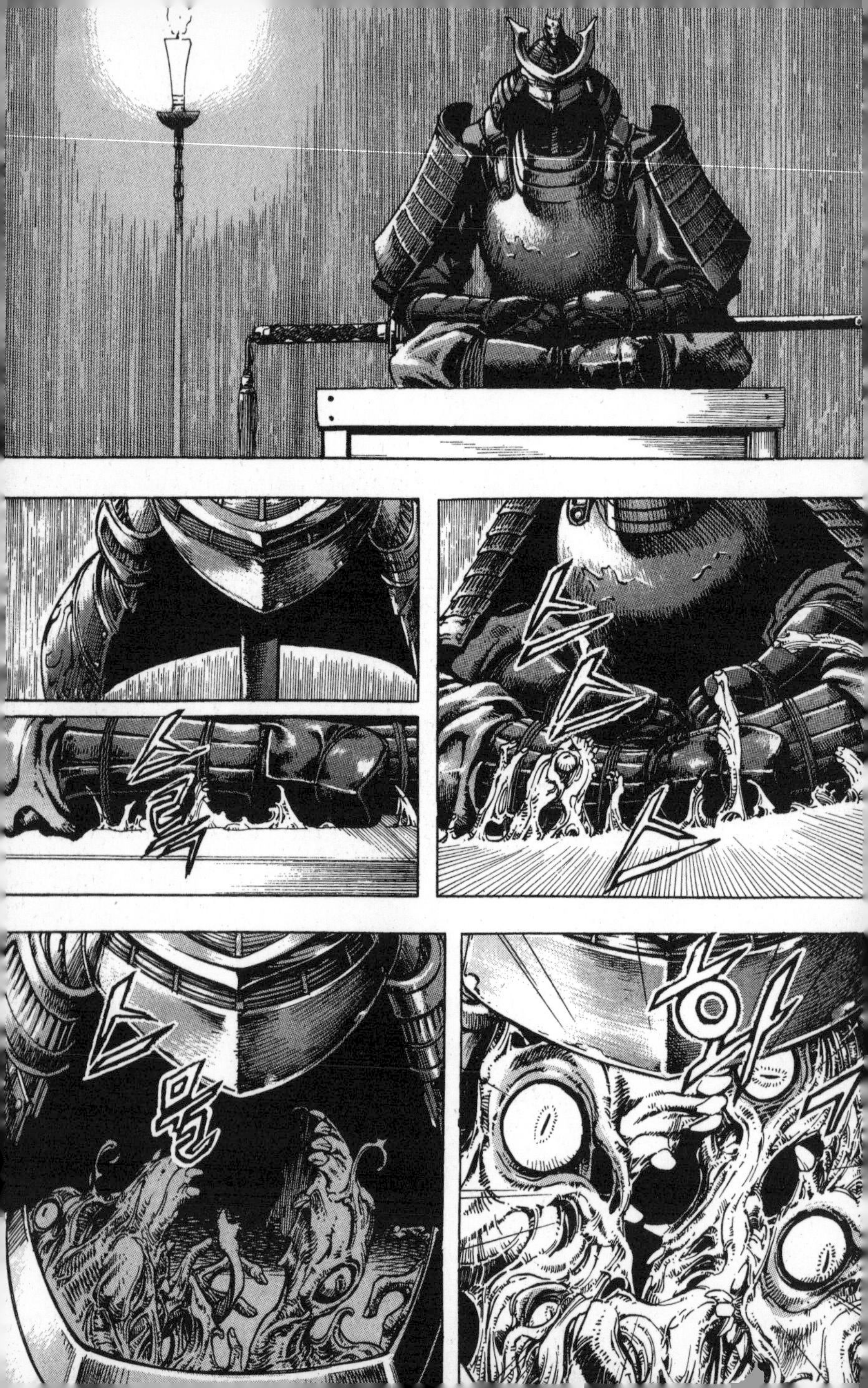

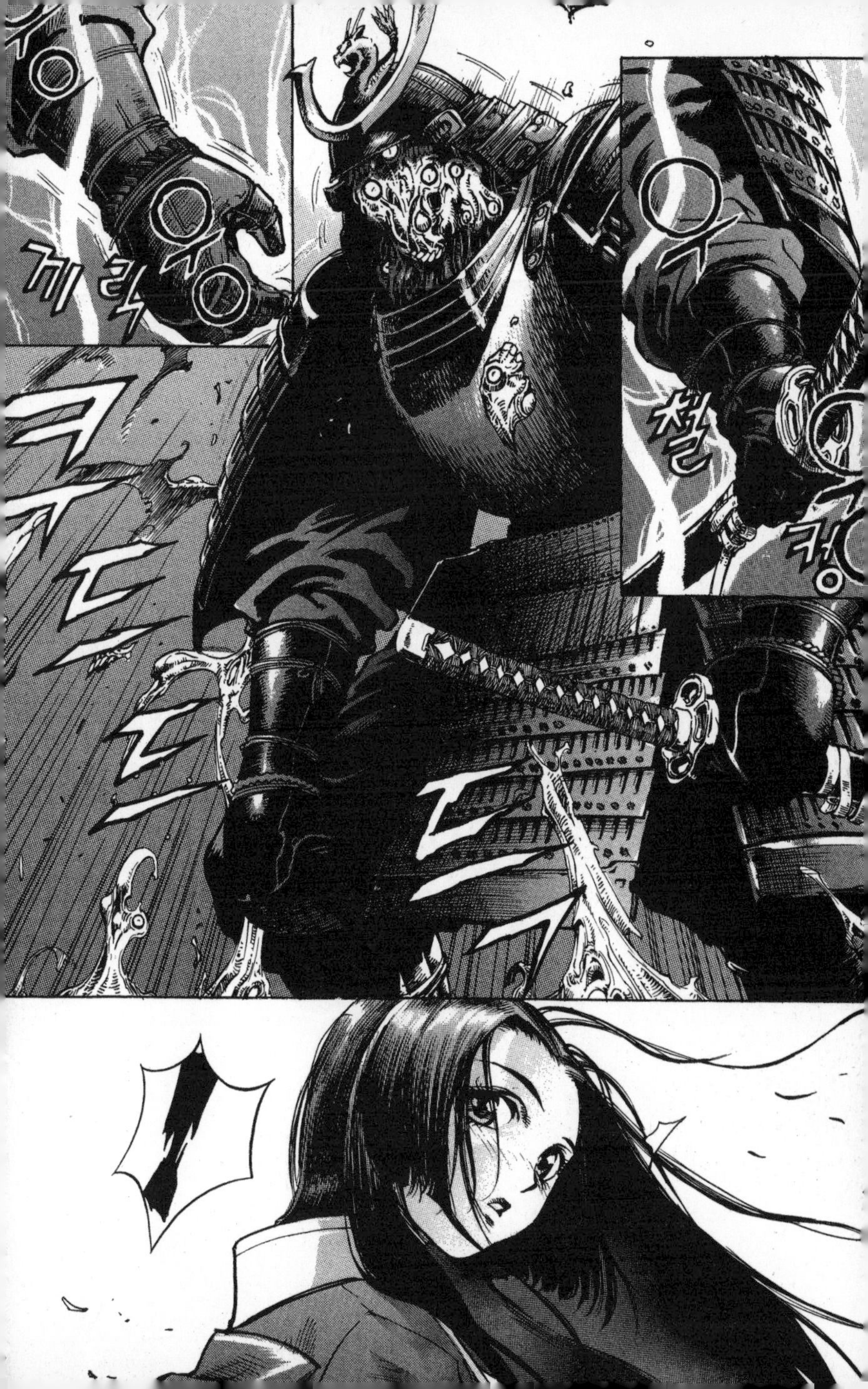
철컹

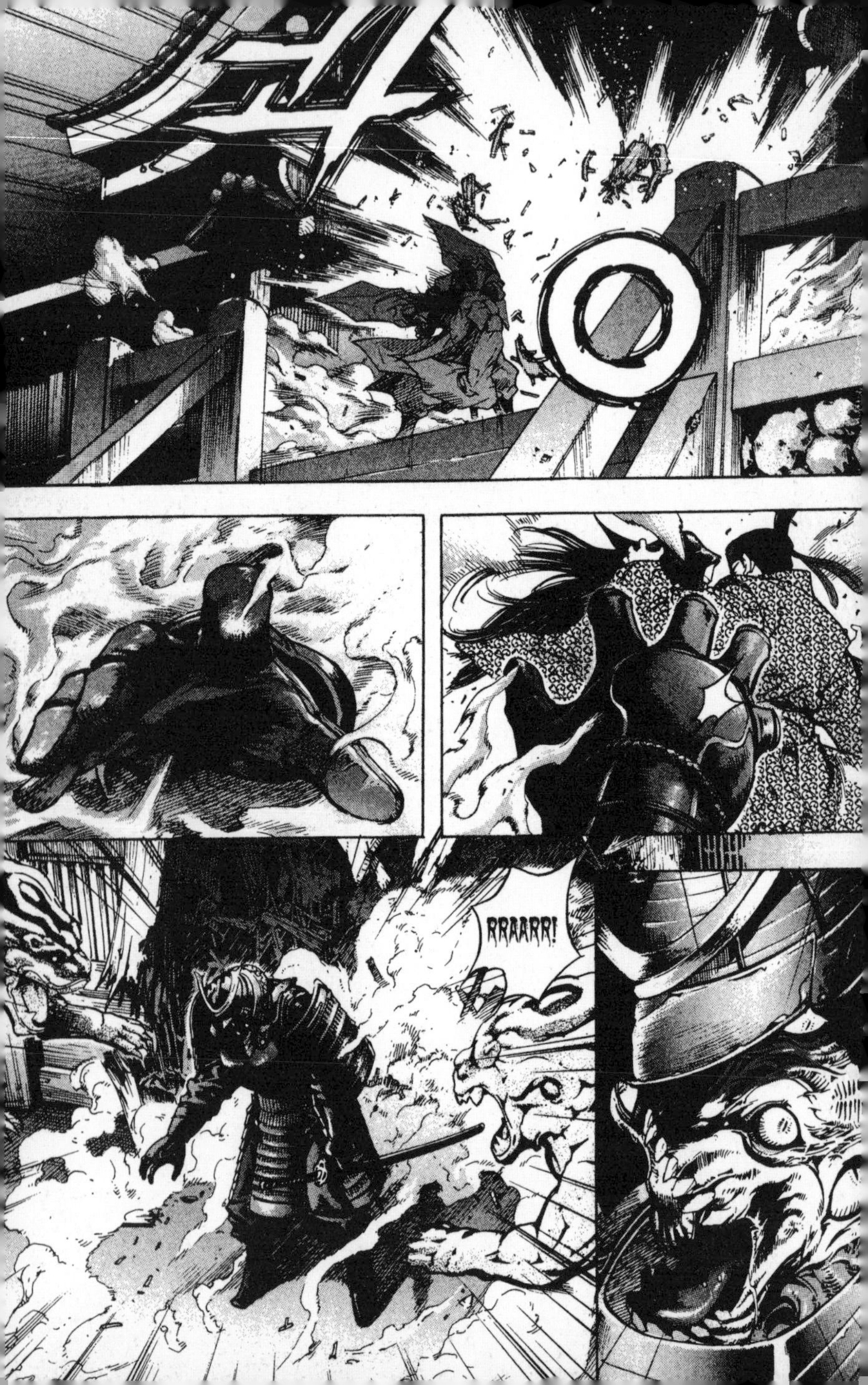
RRAARR!

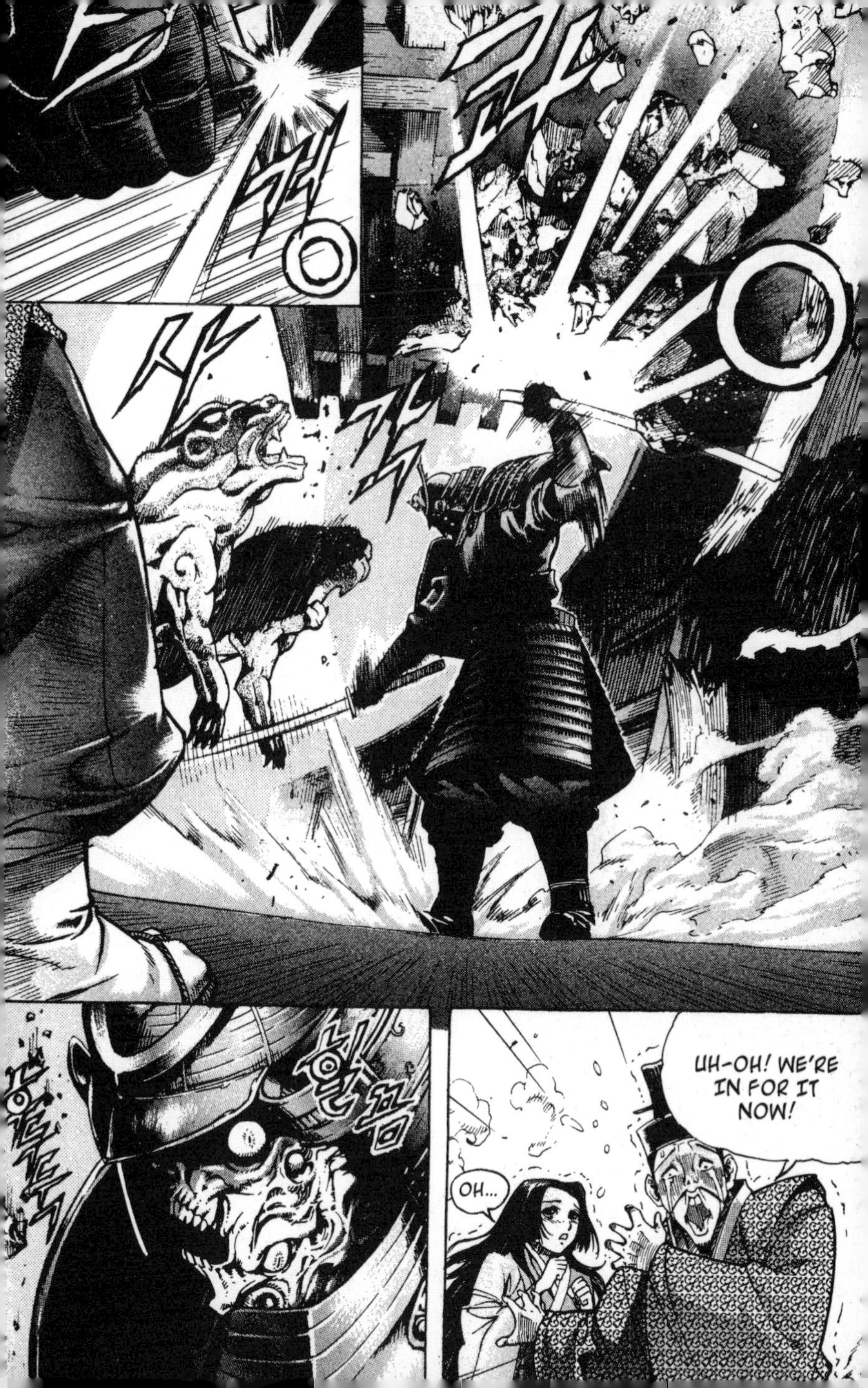
UH-OH! WE'RE IN FOR IT NOW!
OH...

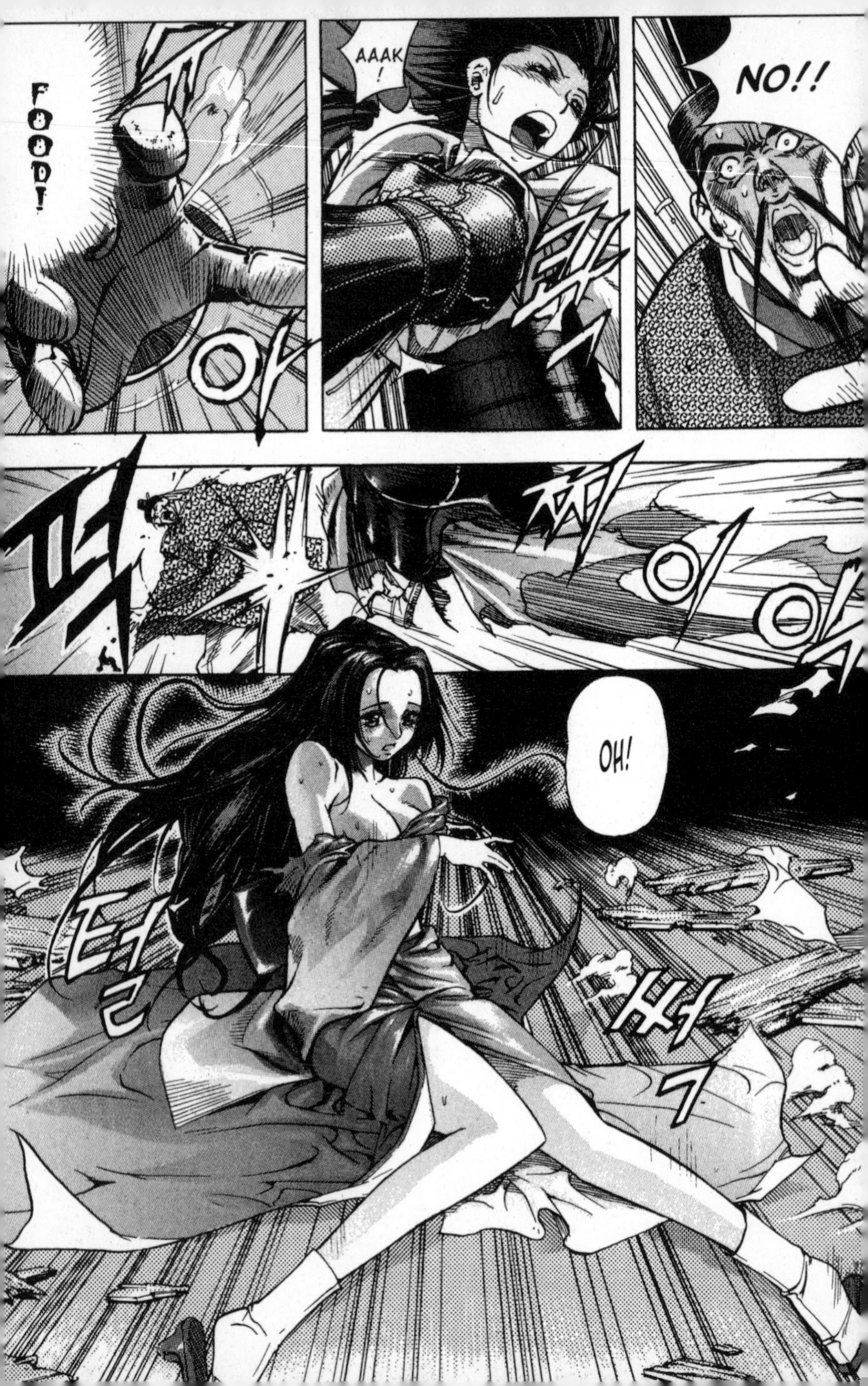
FOOD!
AAAK!
NO!!
OH!

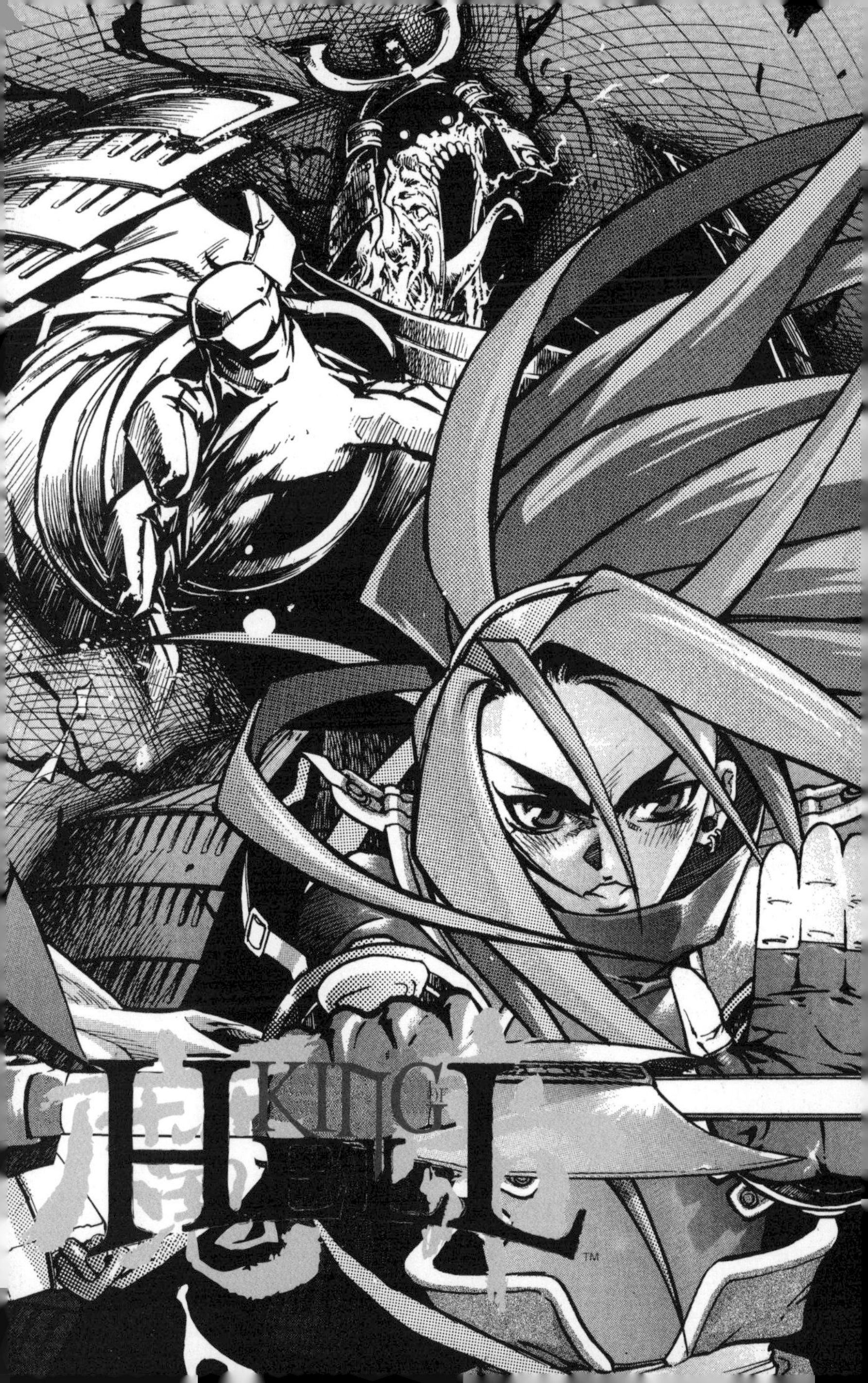
KING
OF

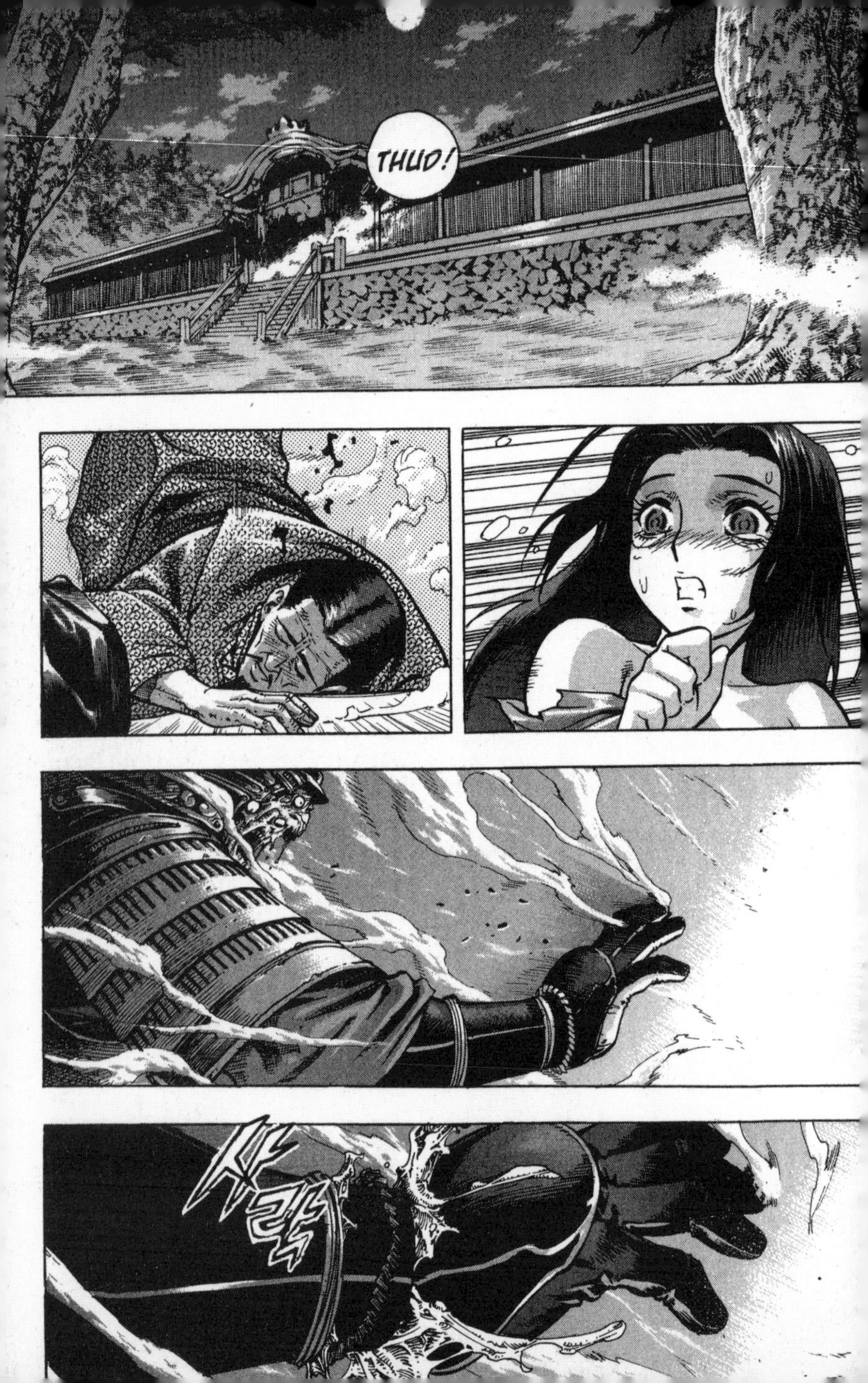
THUD!

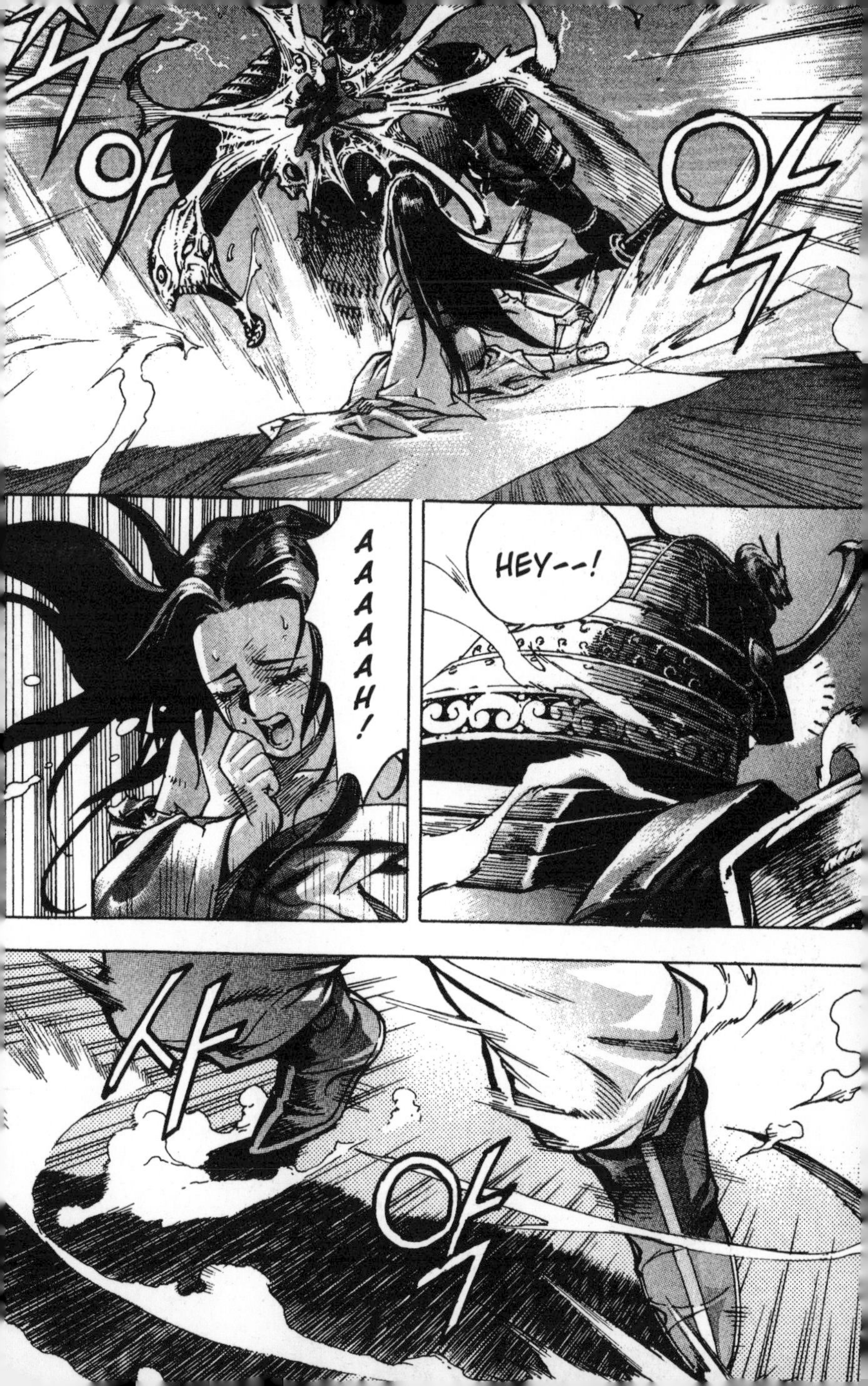
AAAAAAH!
HEY--!

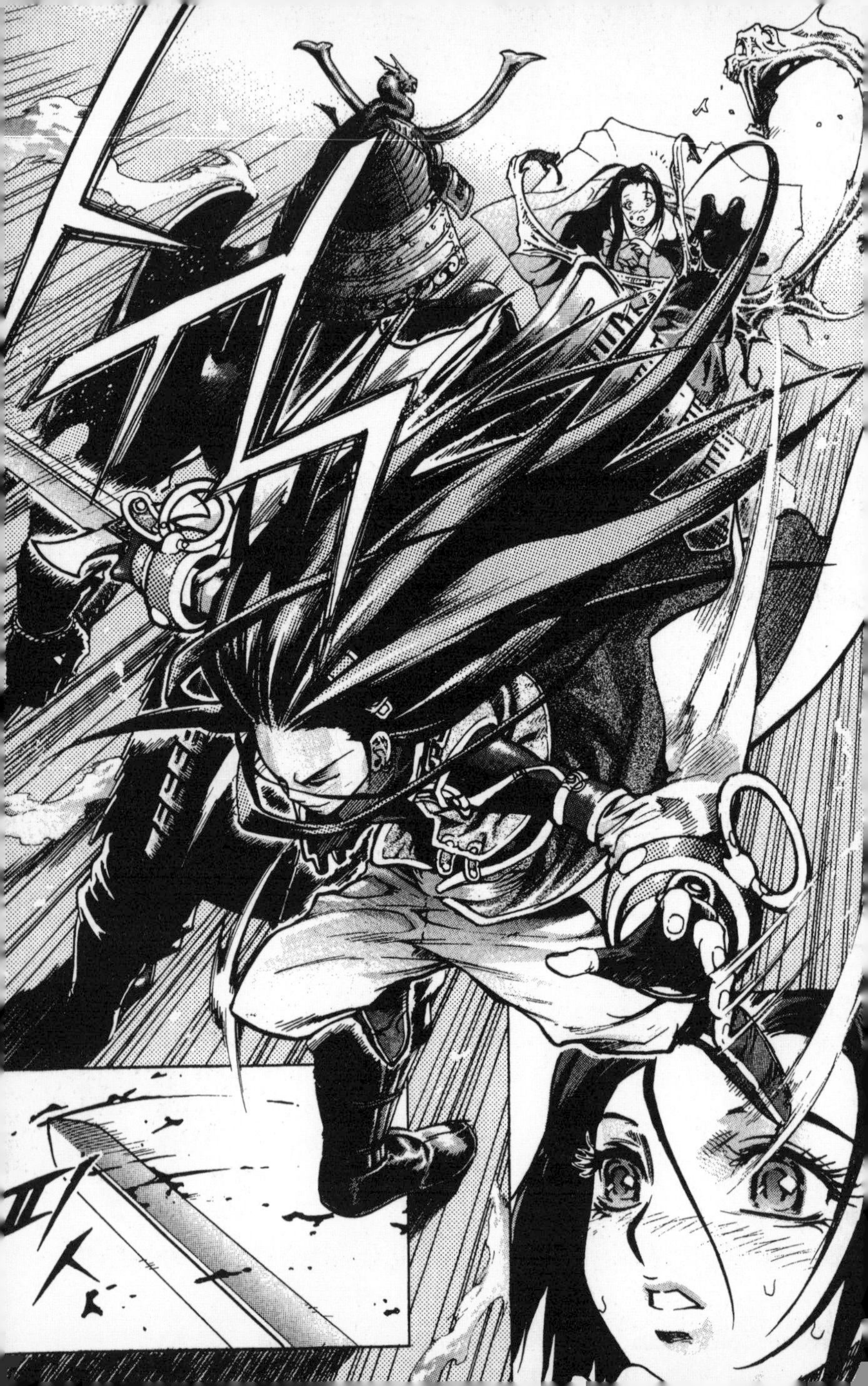

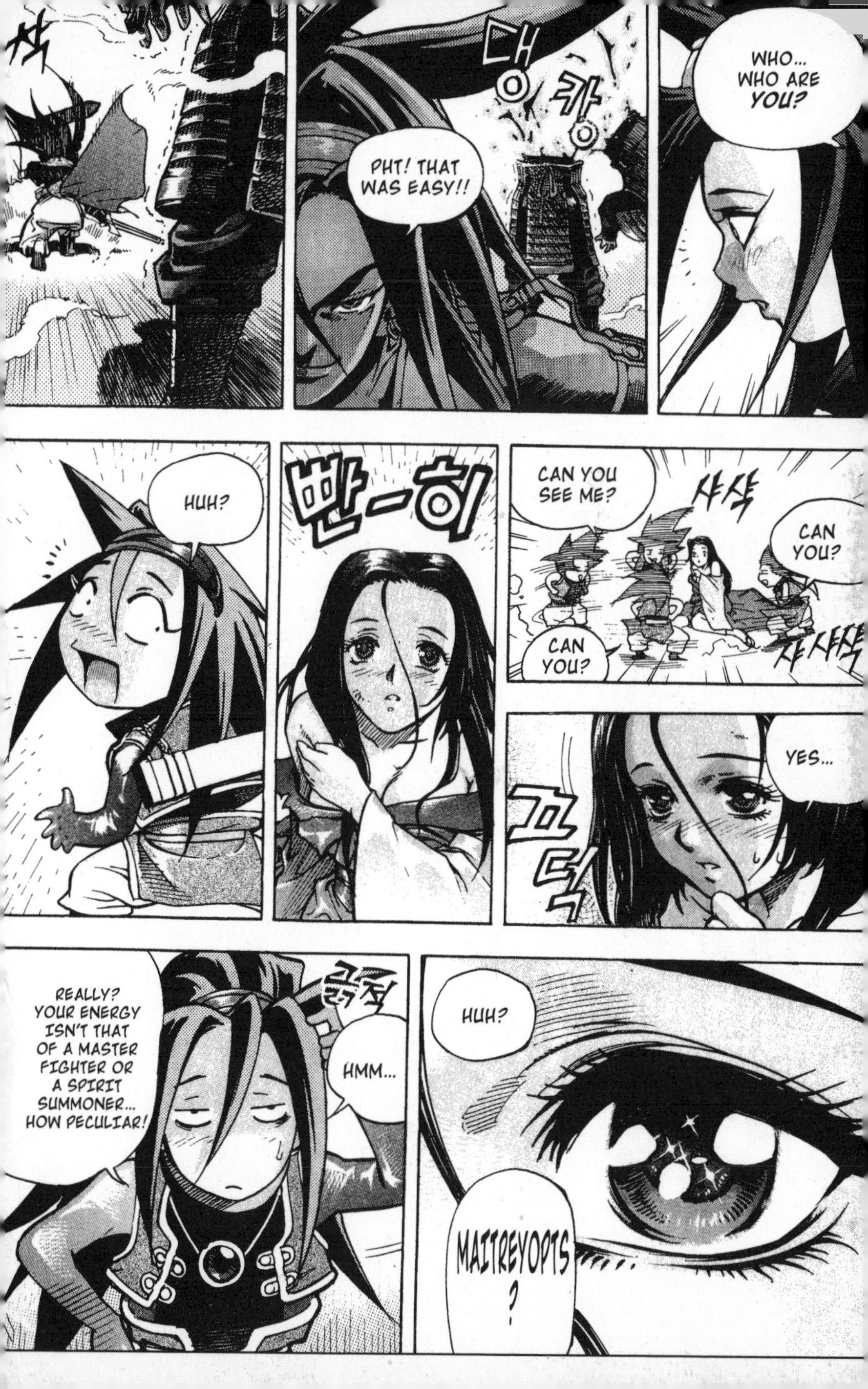
PHT! THAT WAS EASY!!
WHO... WHO ARE YOU?
HUH?
빤-히
CAN YOU SEE ME?
샤샥
CAN YOU?
CAN YOU?
YES...
끄덕
REALLY? YOUR ENERGY ISN'T THAT OF A MASTER FIGHTER OR A SPIRIT SUMMONER... HOW PECULIAR!
HMM...
HUH?
MAITREYOPTS ?

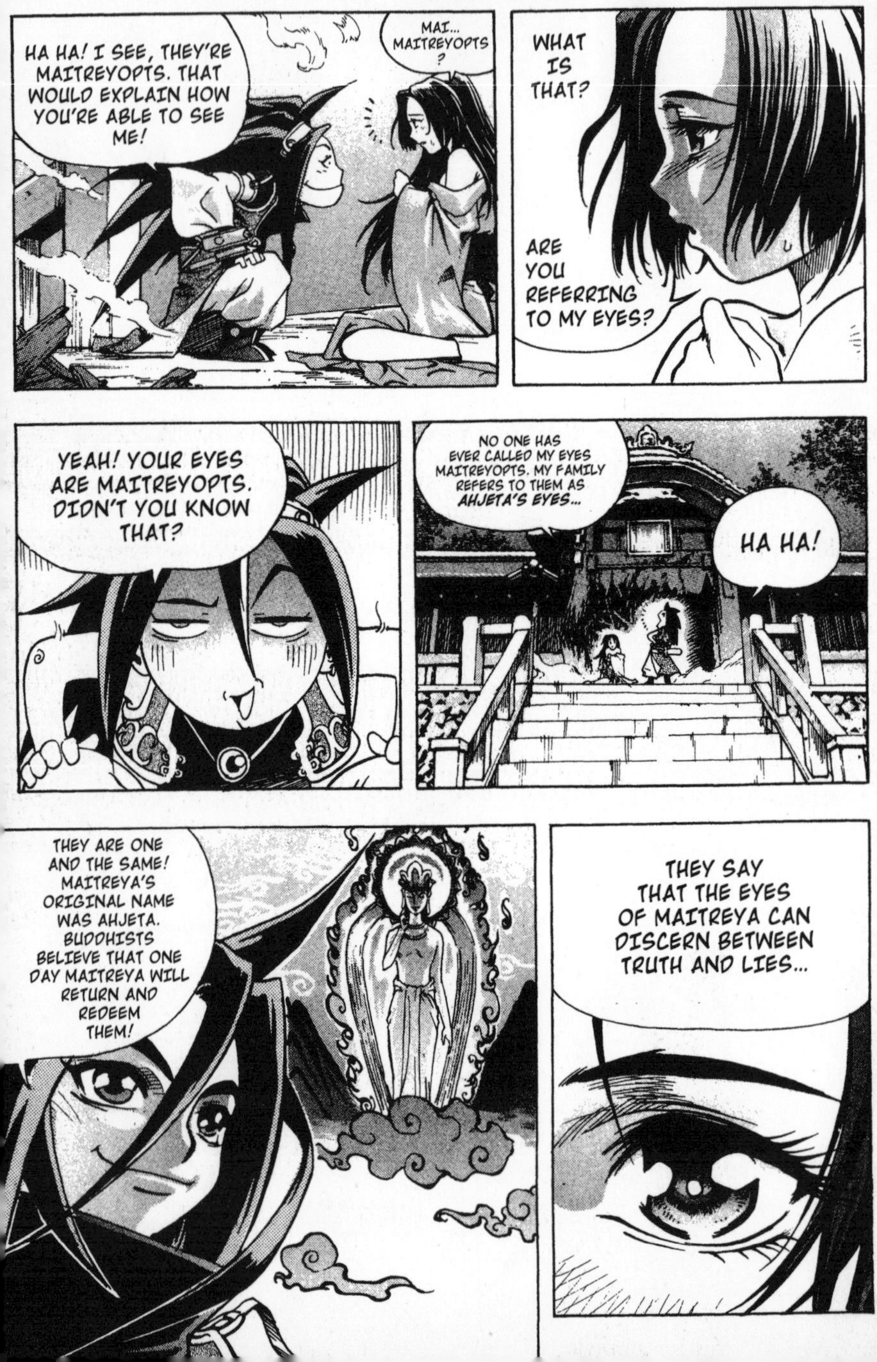
HA HA! I SEE, THEY'RE MAITREYOPTS. THAT WOULD EXPLAIN HOW YOU'RE ABLE TO SEE ME!
MAI... MAITREYOPTS?
WHAT IS THAT?
ARE YOU REFERRING TO MY EYES?
YEAH! YOUR EYES ARE MAITREYOPTS. DIDN'T YOU KNOW THAT?
NO ONE HAS EVER CALLED MY EYES MAITREYOPTS. MY FAMILY REFERS TO THEM AS *AHJETA'S EYES*...
HA HA!
THEY ARE ONE AND THE SAME! MAITREYA'S ORIGINAL NAME WAS AHJETA. BUDDHISTS BELIEVE THAT ONE DAY MAITREYA WILL RETURN AND REDEEM THEM!
THEY SAY THAT THE EYES OF MAITREYA CAN DISCERN BETWEEN TRUTH AND LIES...

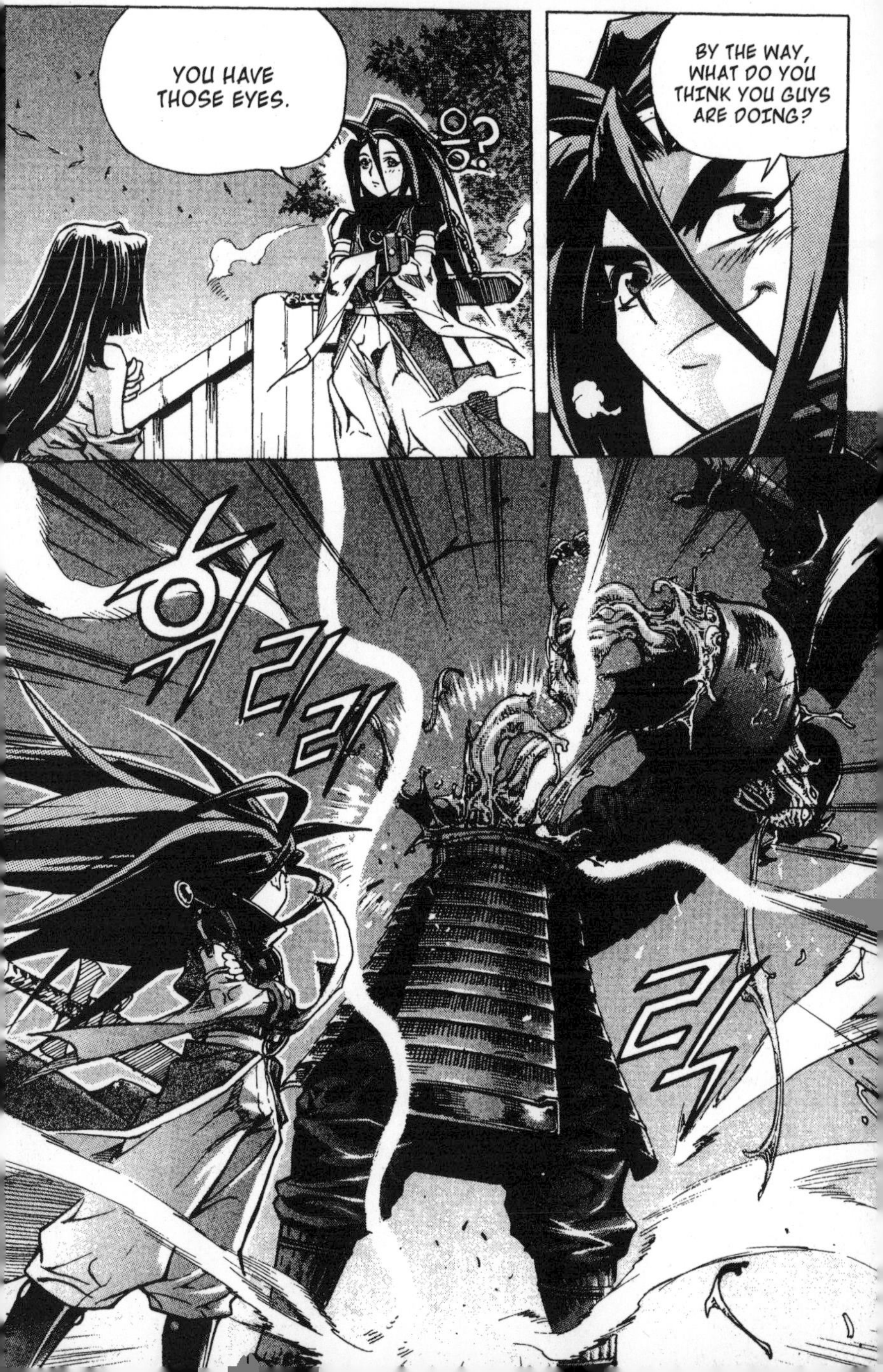
YOU HAVE THOSE EYES.
?
BY THE WAY, WHAT DO YOU THINK YOU GUYS ARE DOING?

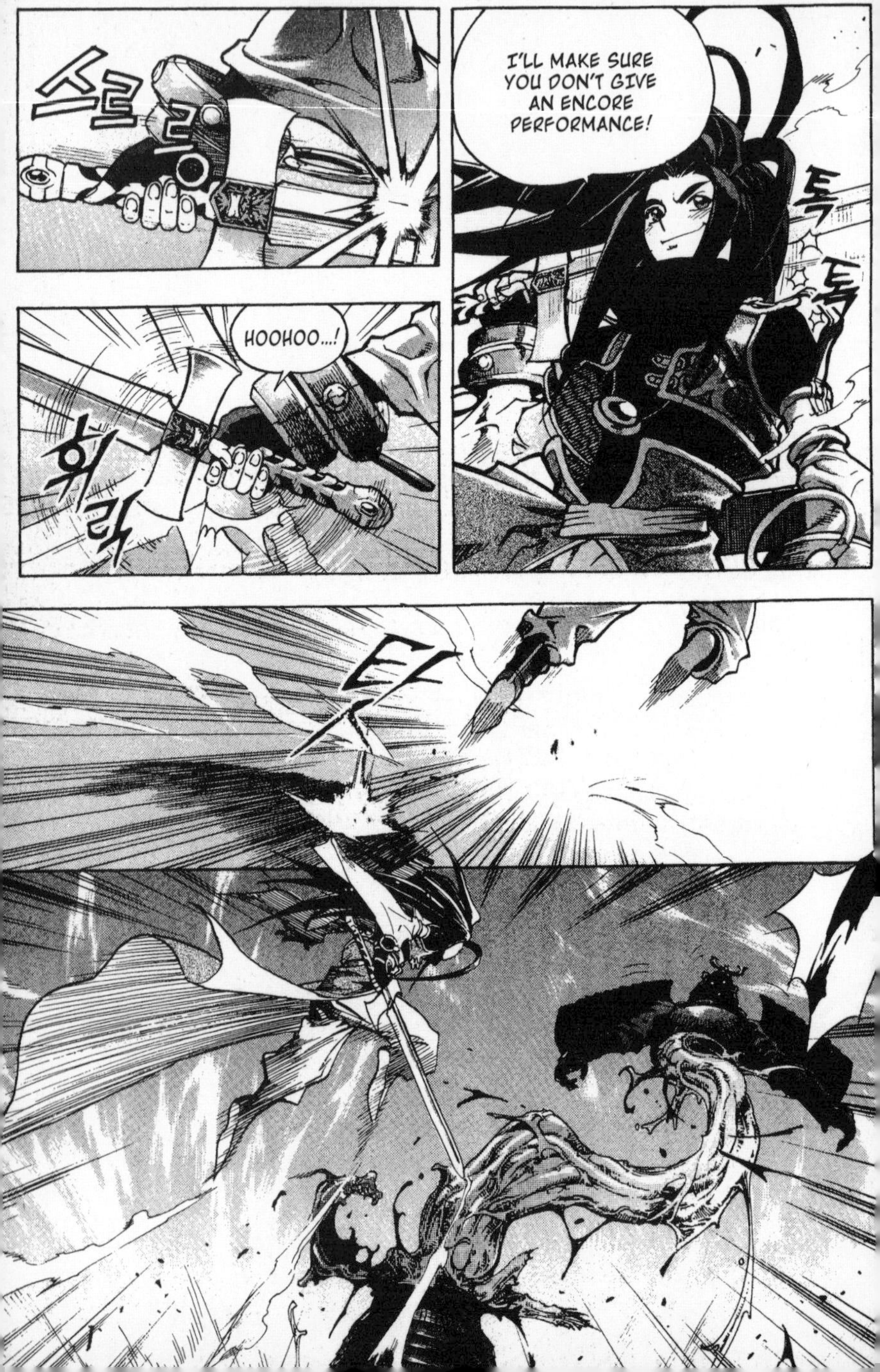
HOOHOO...!
I'LL MAKE SURE YOU DON'T GIVE AN ENCORE PERFORMANCE!
톡
톡

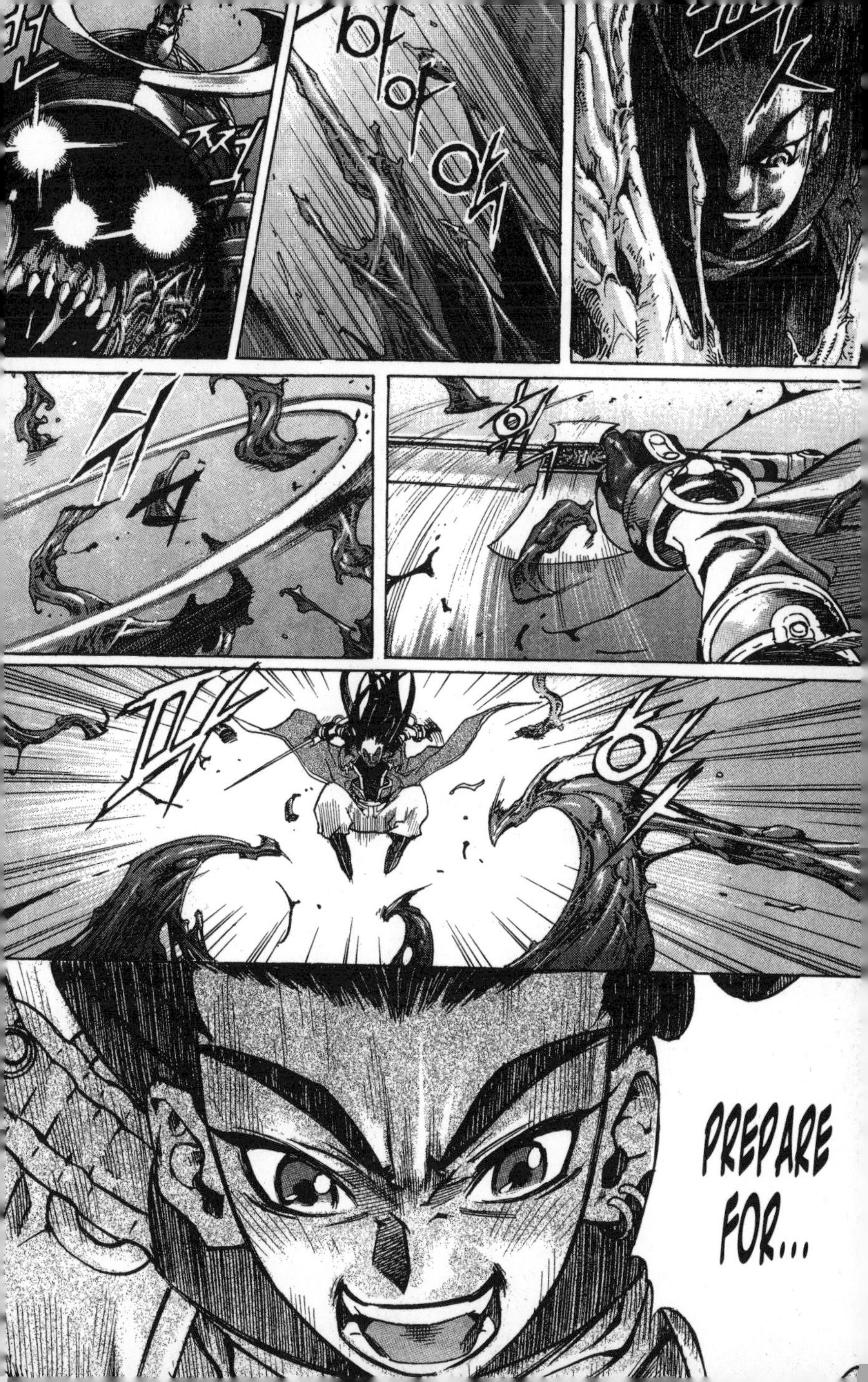
PREPARE FOR...

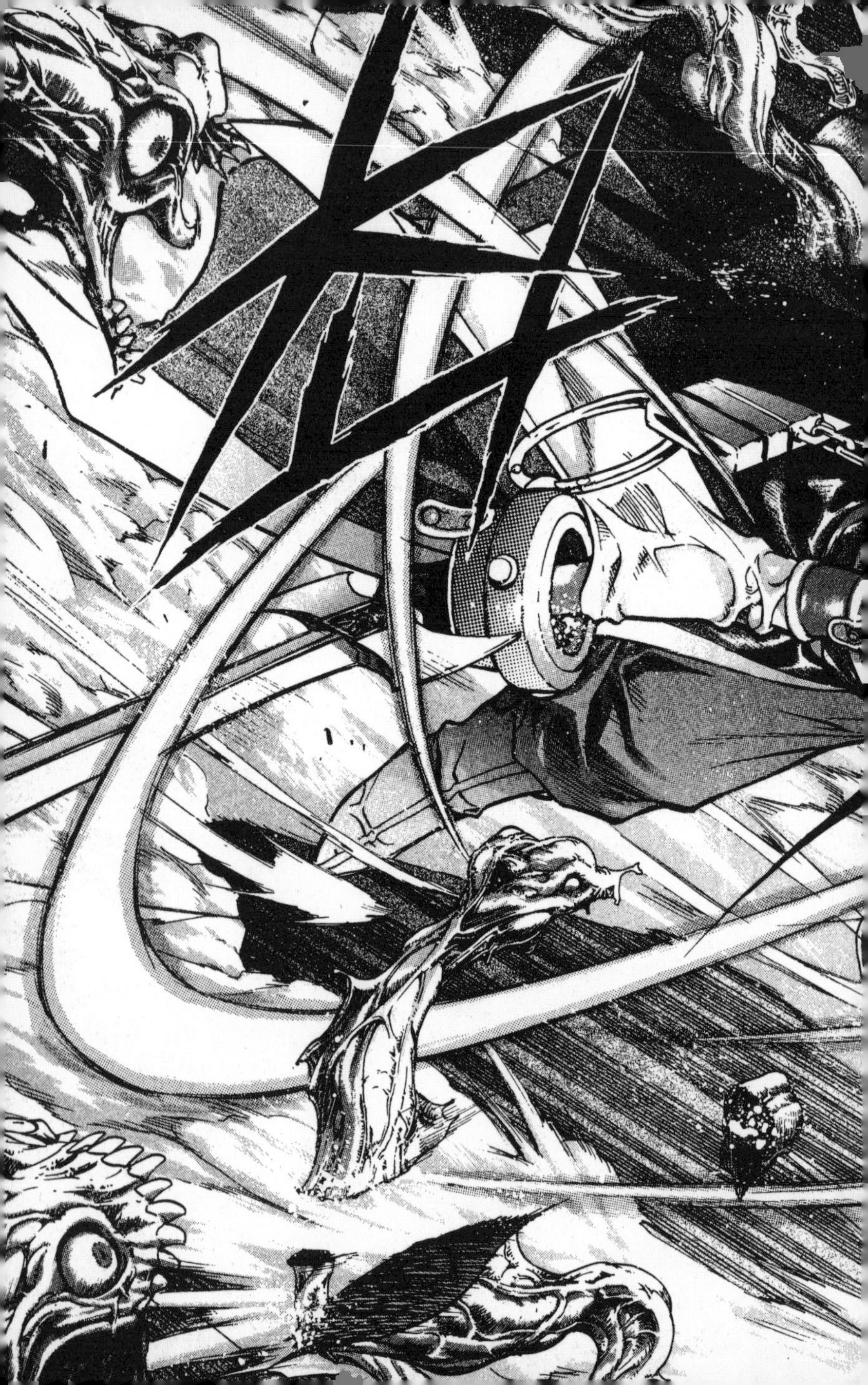

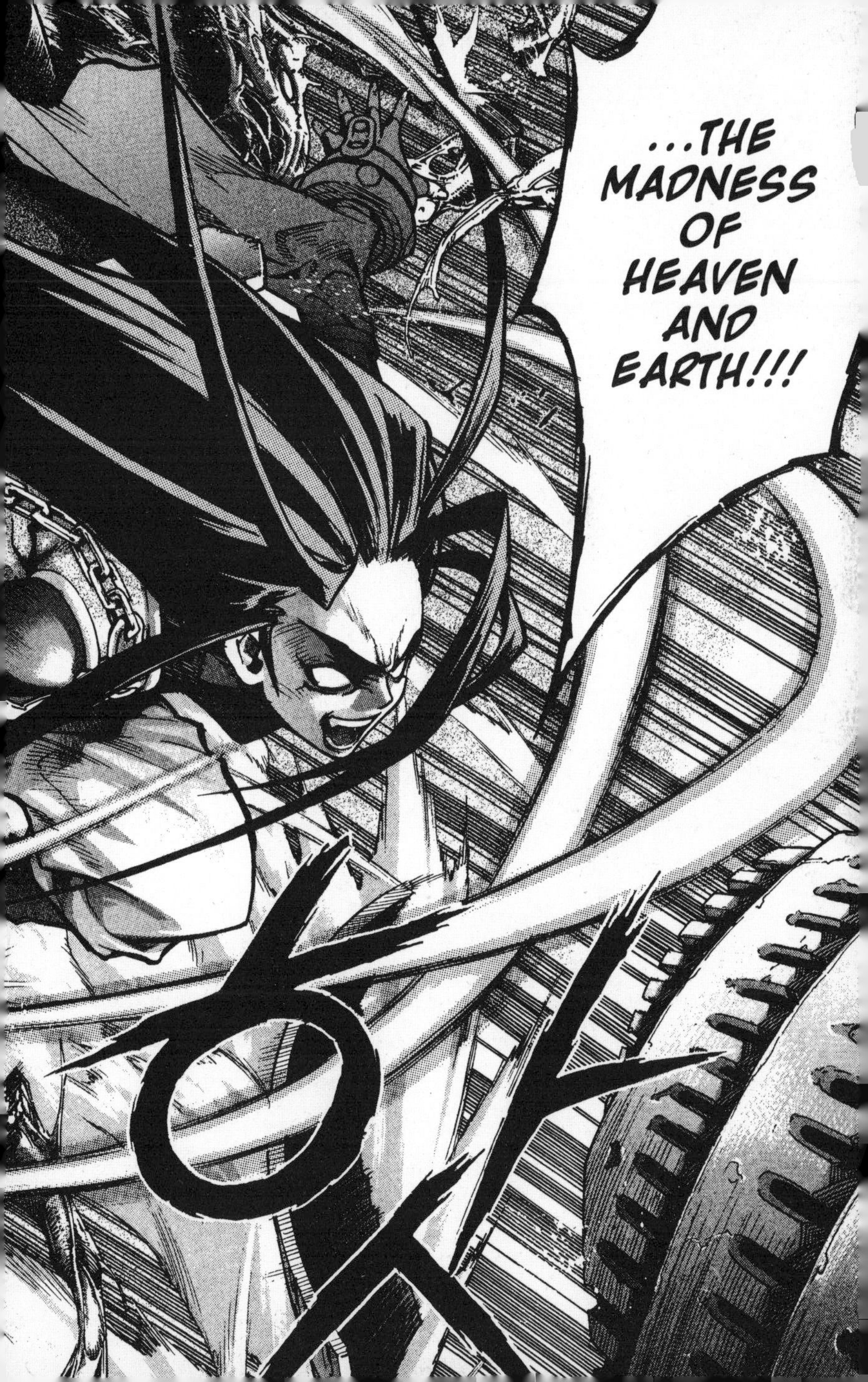
...THE MADNESS OF HEAVEN AND EARTH!!!

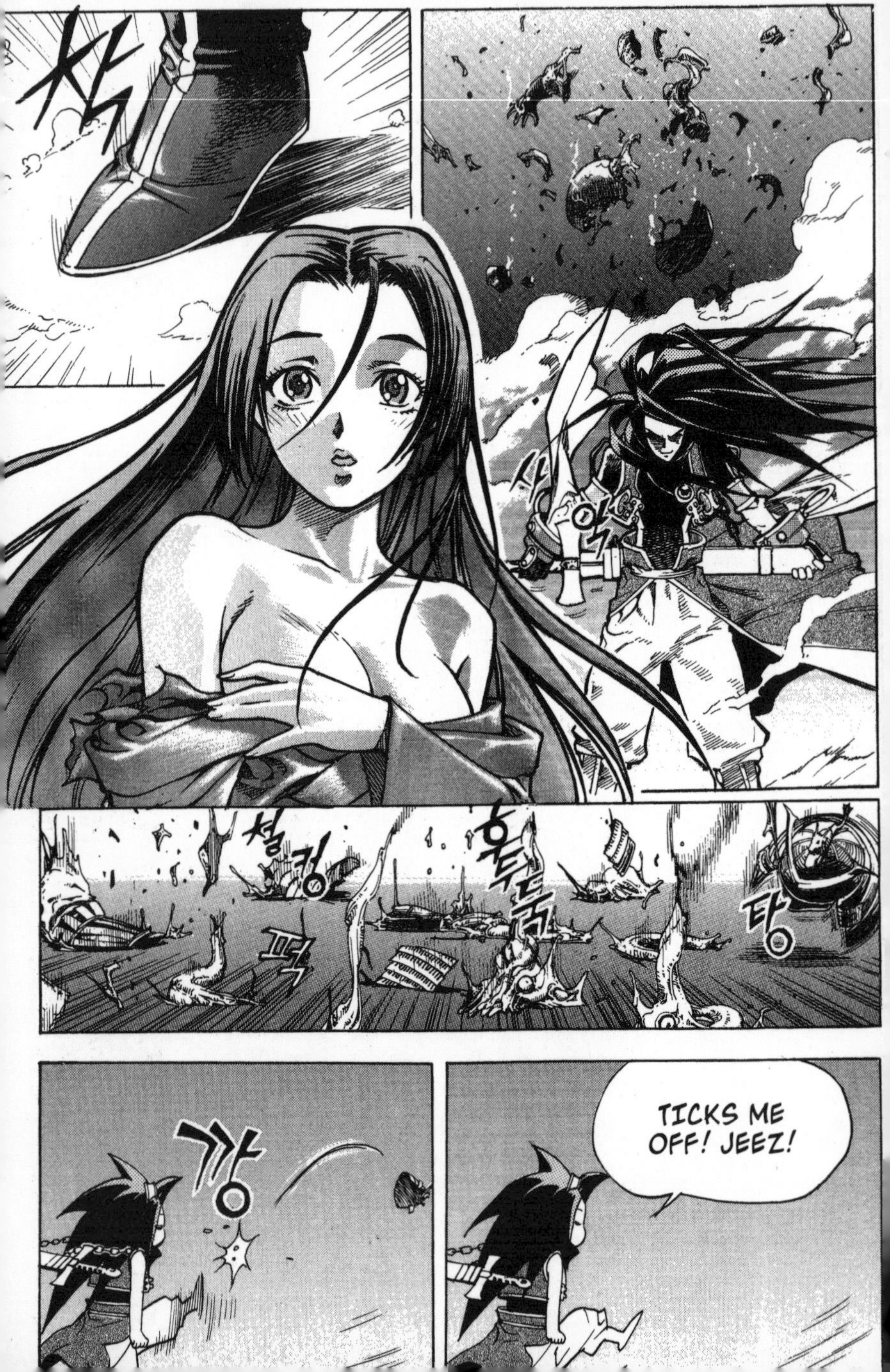

철컹
퍽
후두둑
탕
깡
TICKS ME OFF! JEEZ!

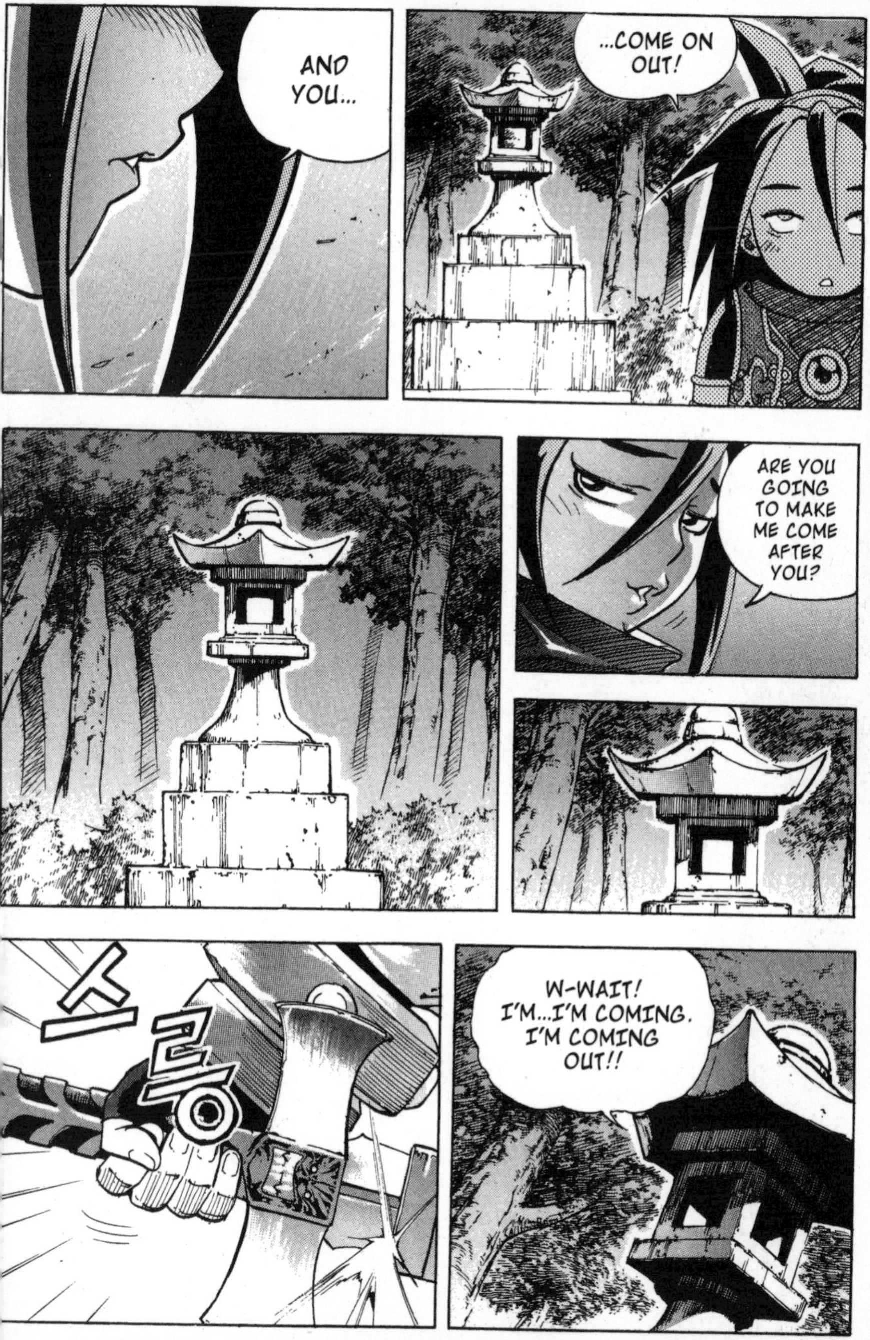
AND YOU...
...COME ON OUT!
ARE YOU GOING TO MAKE ME COME AFTER YOU?
W-WAIT! I'M...I'M COMING. I'M COMING OUT!!

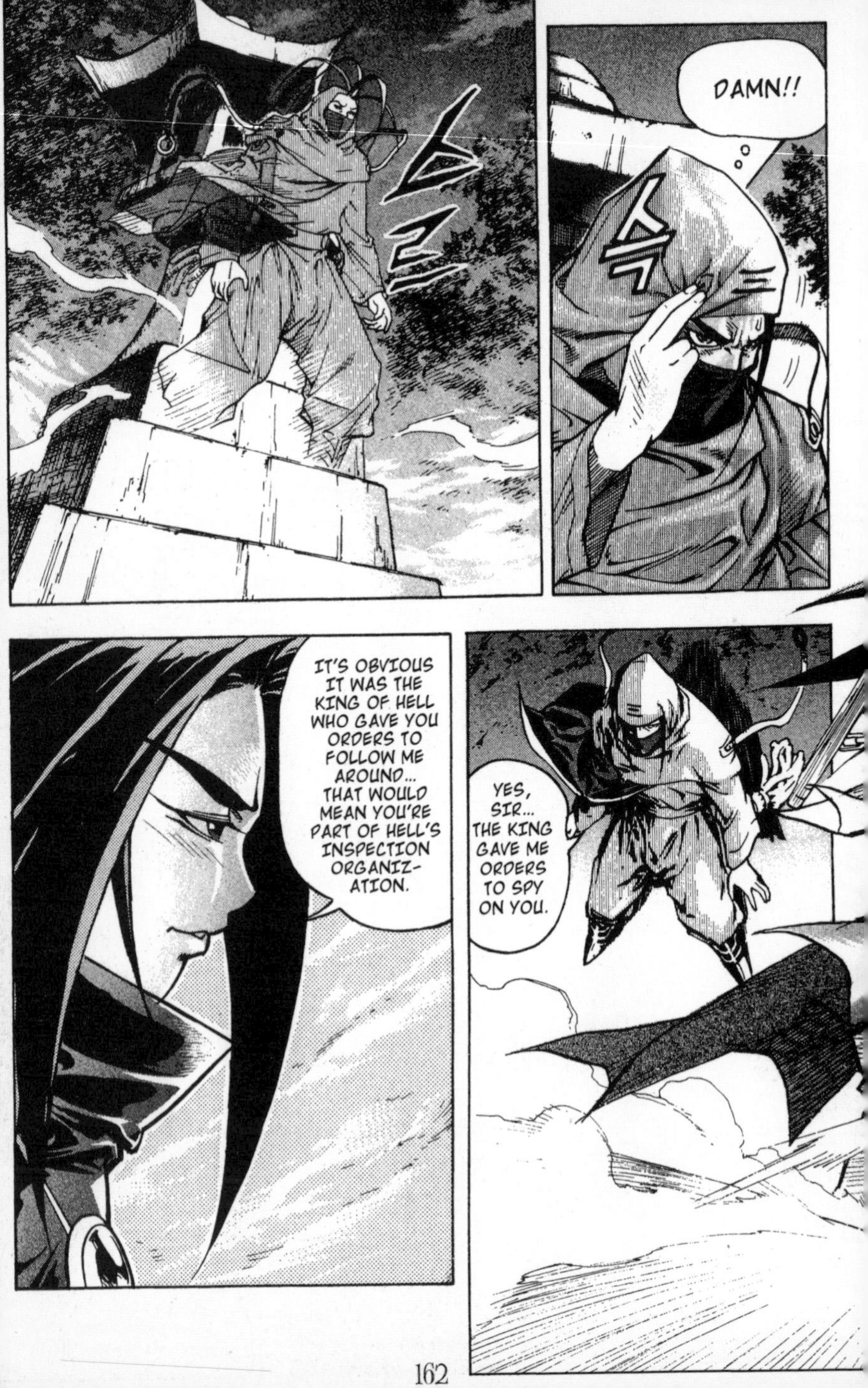
DAMN!!
IT'S OBVIOUS IT WAS THE KING OF HELL WHO GAVE YOU ORDERS TO FOLLOW ME AROUND... THAT WOULD MEAN YOU'RE PART OF HELL'S INSPECTION ORGANIZ-ATION.
YES, SIR... THE KING GAVE ME ORDERS TO SPY ON YOU.

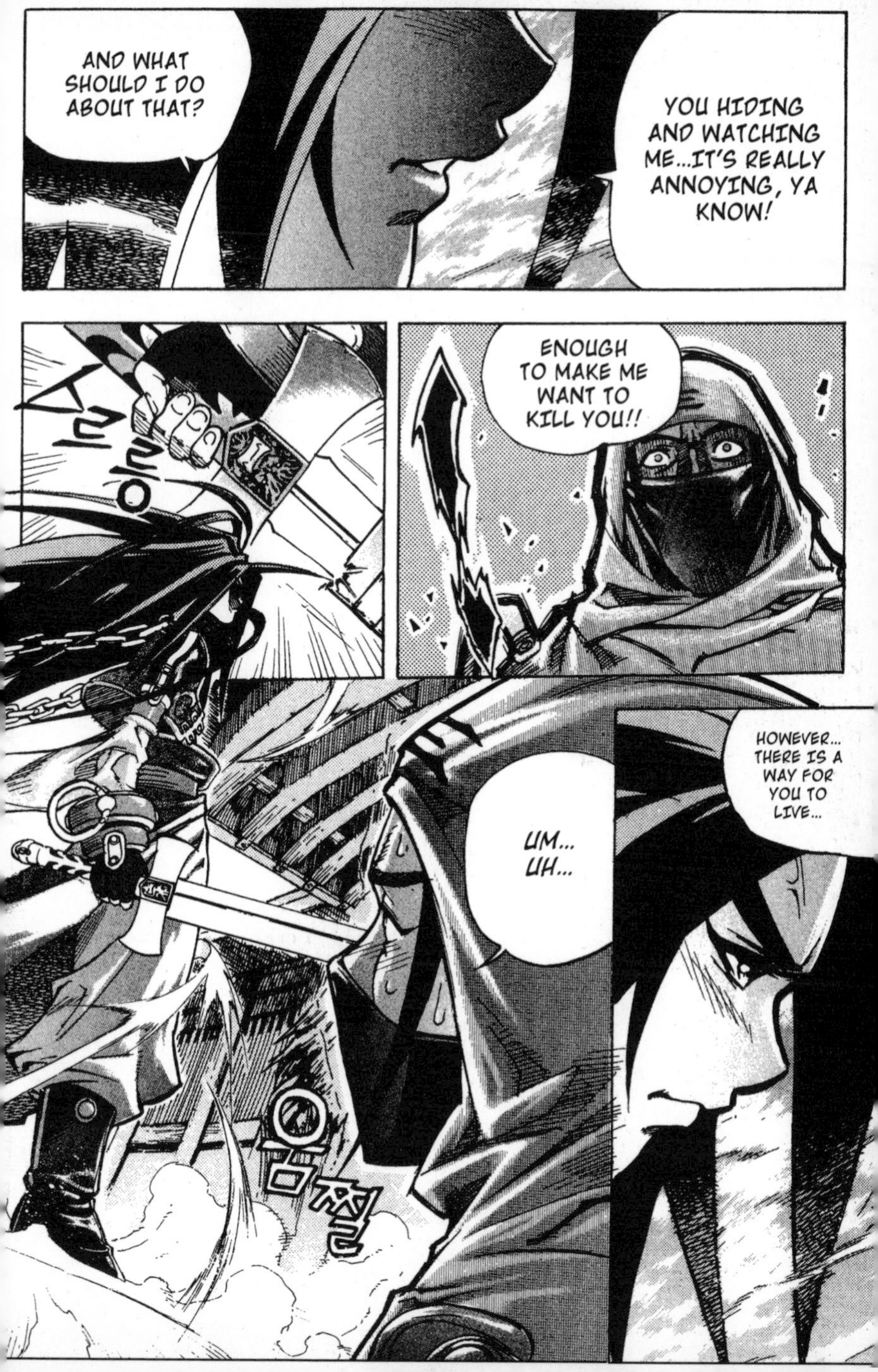
AND WHAT SHOULD I DO ABOUT THAT?
YOU HIDING AND WATCHING ME...IT'S REALLY ANNOYING, YA KNOW!
ENOUGH TO MAKE ME WANT TO KILL YOU!!
UM... UH...
HOWEVER... THERE IS A WAY FOR YOU TO LIVE...

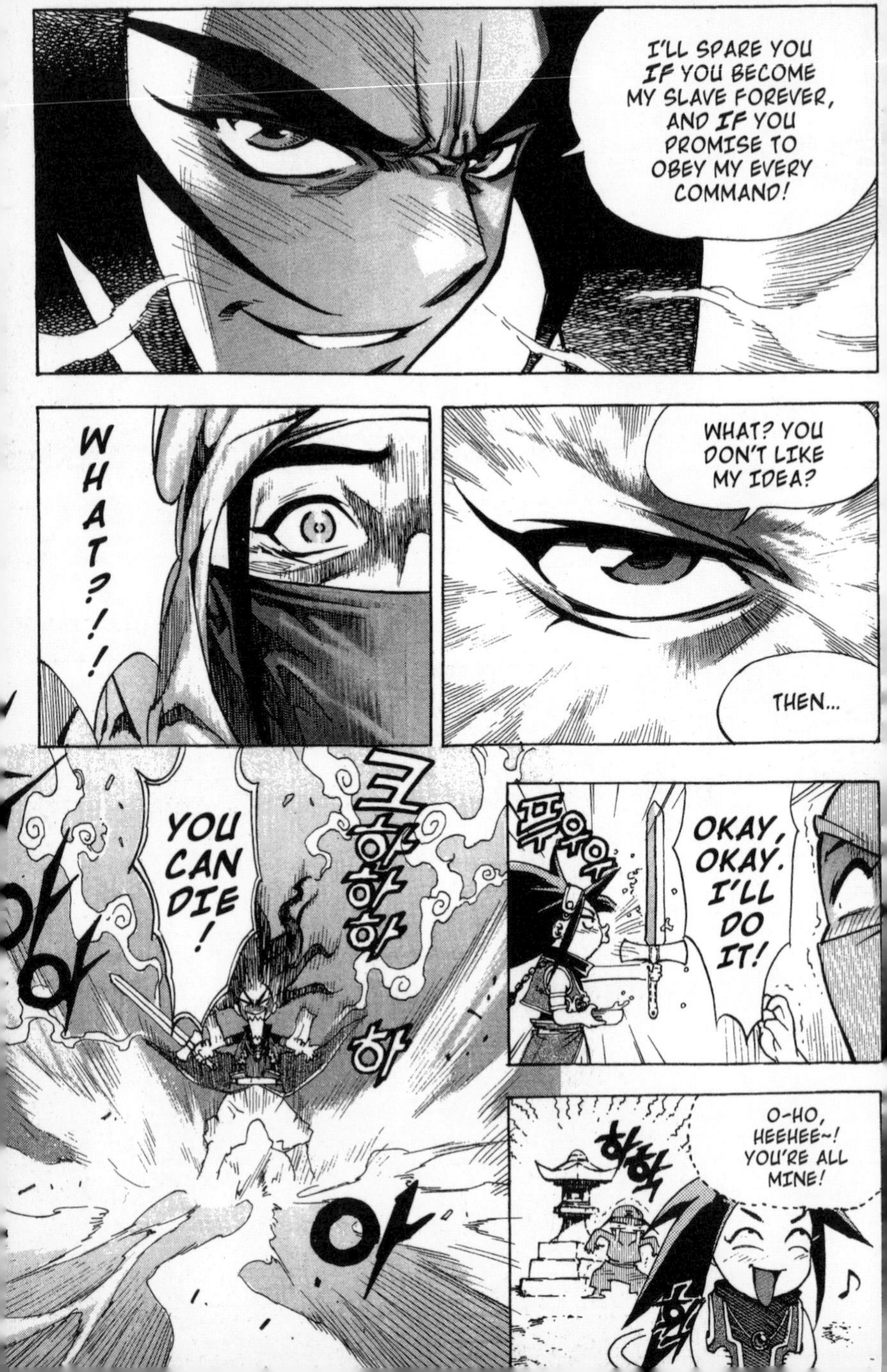

I'LL SPARE YOU IF YOU BECOME MY SLAVE FOREVER, AND IF YOU PROMISE TO OBEY MY EVERY COMMAND!
WHAT?!!
WHAT? YOU DON'T LIKE MY IDEA?
THEN...
YOU CAN DIE!
크하하하
하
아
OKAY, OKAY. I'LL DO IT!
O-HO, HEEHEE~! YOU'RE ALL MINE!
하하

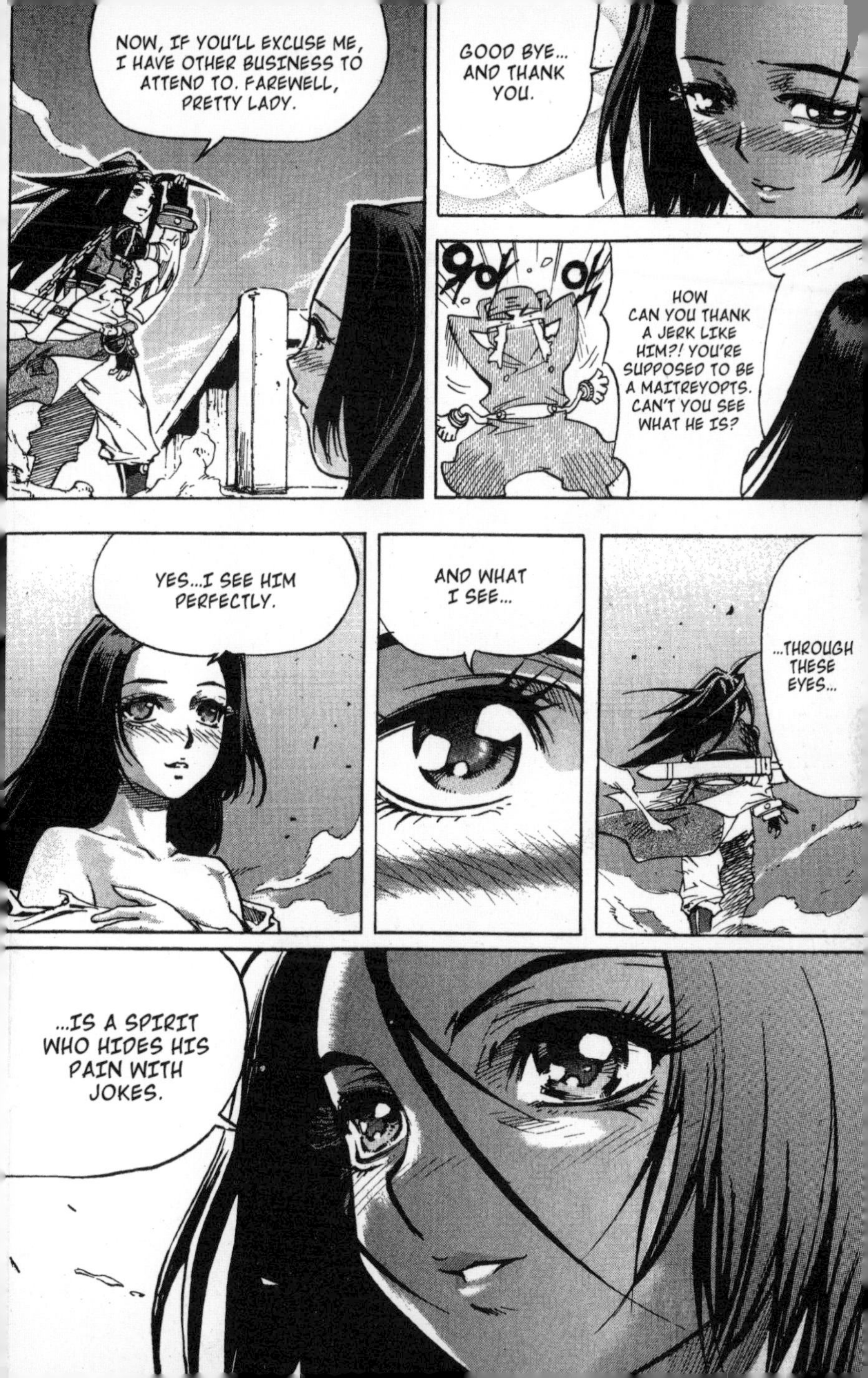
NOW, IF YOU'LL EXCUSE ME, I HAVE OTHER BUSINESS TO ATTEND TO. FAREWELL, PRETTY LADY.
GOOD BYE... AND THANK YOU.
HOW CAN YOU THANK A JERK LIKE HIM?! YOU'RE SUPPOSED TO BE A MAITREYOPTS. CAN'T YOU SEE WHAT HE IS?
YES...I SEE HIM PERFECTLY.
AND WHAT I SEE...
...THROUGH THESE EYES...
...IS A SPIRIT WHO HIDES HIS PAIN WITH JOKES.

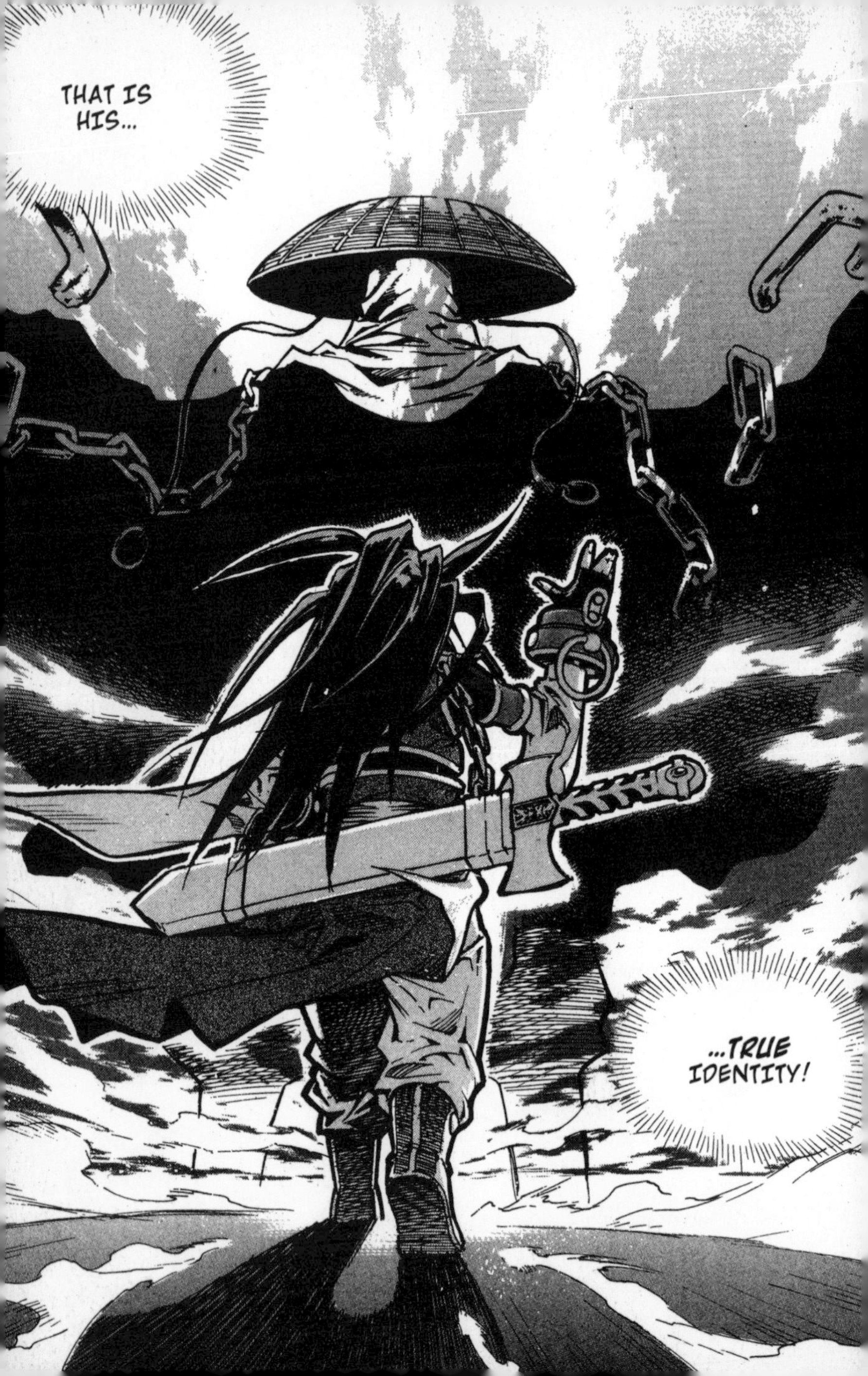
THAT IS HIS...
...TRUE IDENTITY!

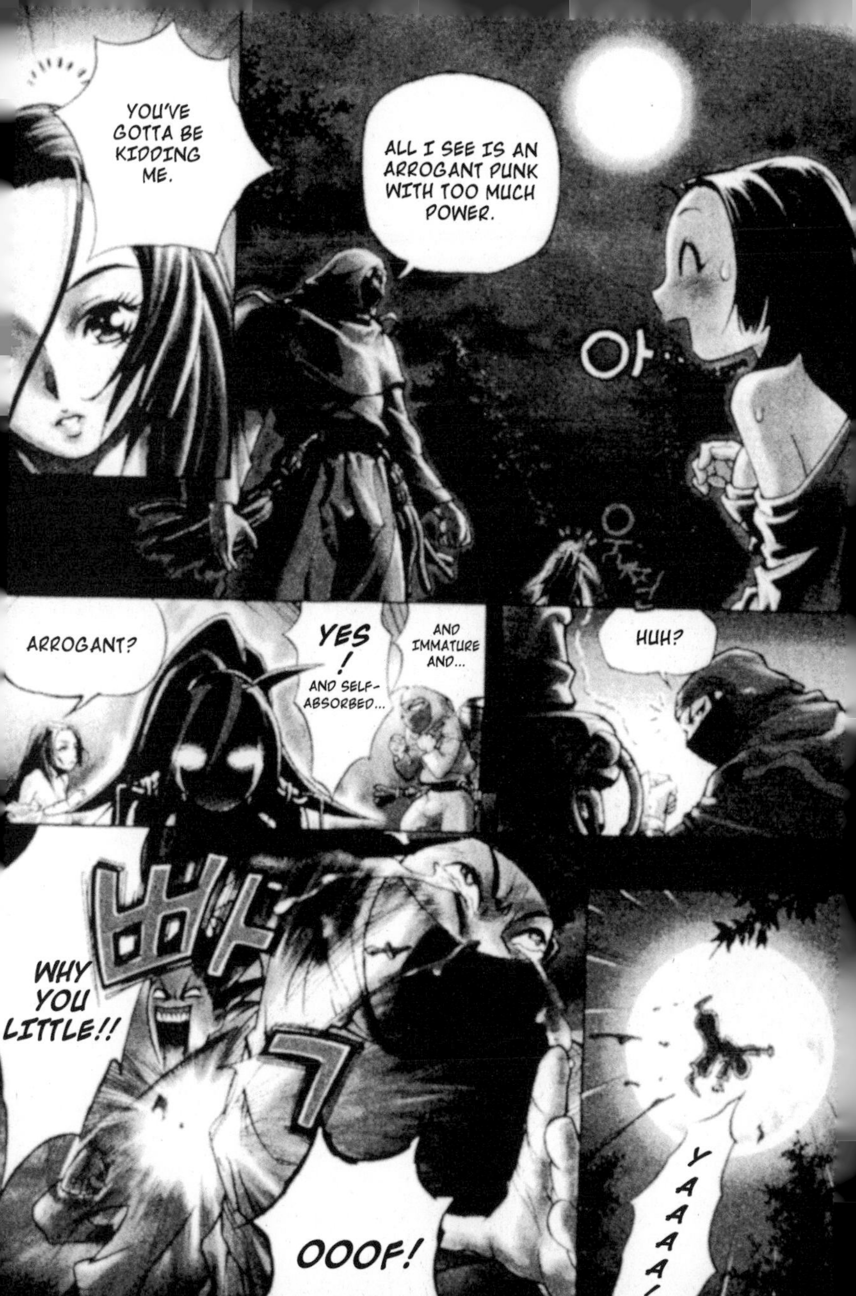
YOU'VE GOTTA BE KIDDING ME.
ALL I SEE IS AN ARROGANT PUNK WITH TOO MUCH POWER.
ARROGANT?
YES!
AND SELF-ABSORBED...
AND IMMATURE AND...
HUH?
WHY YOU LITTLE!!
OOOF!
YAAAAA!

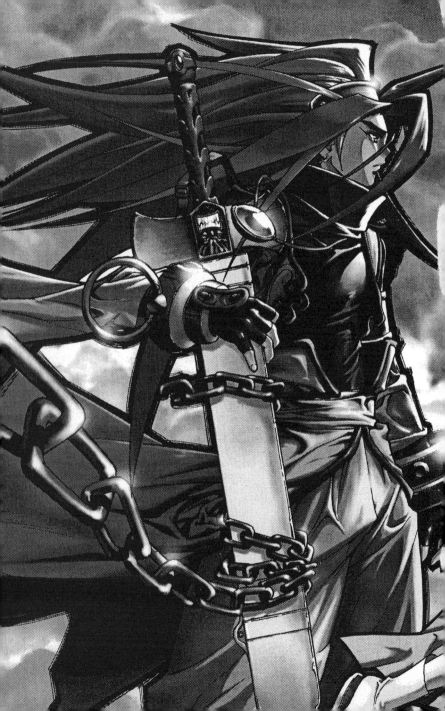

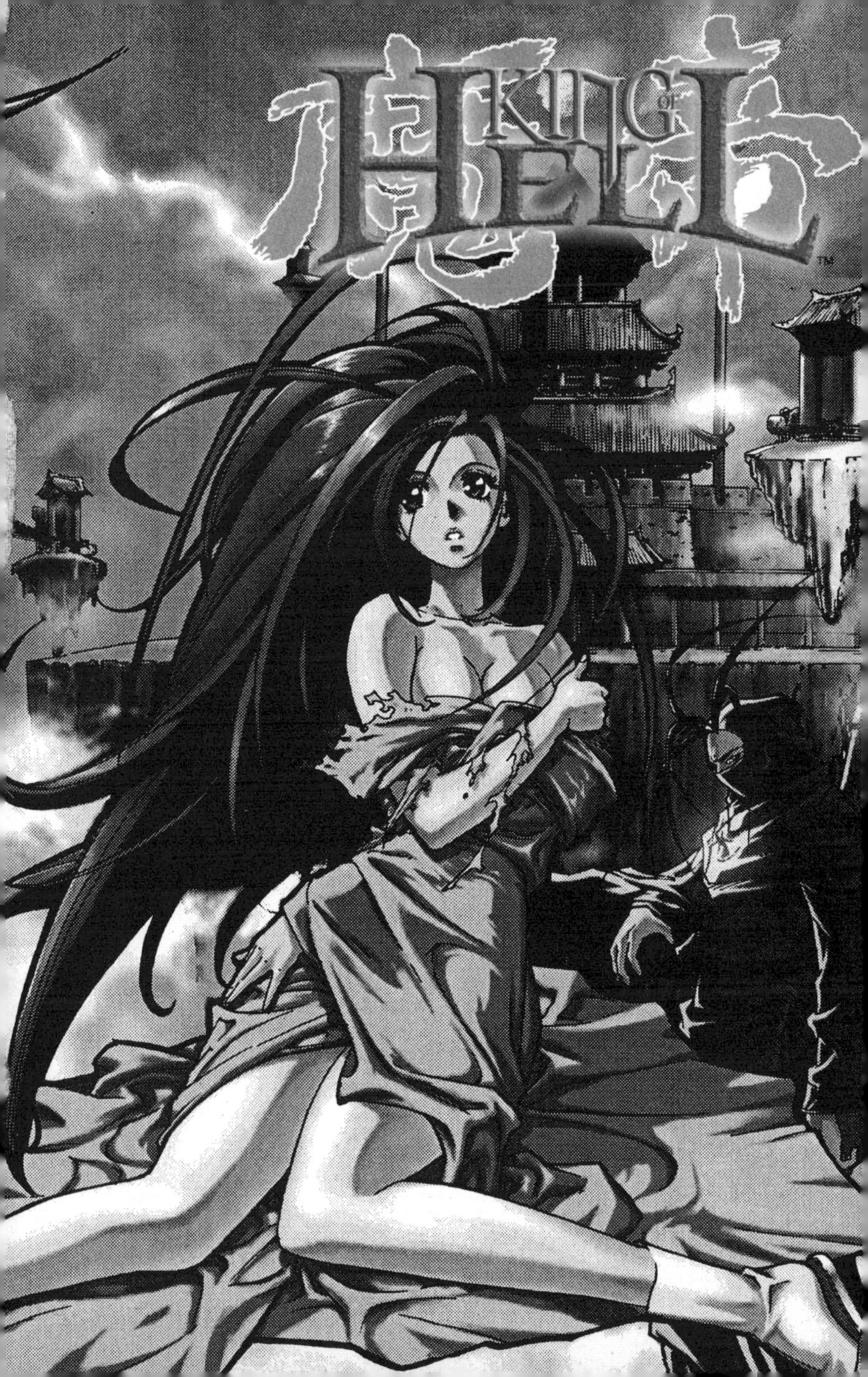
KING OF HELL

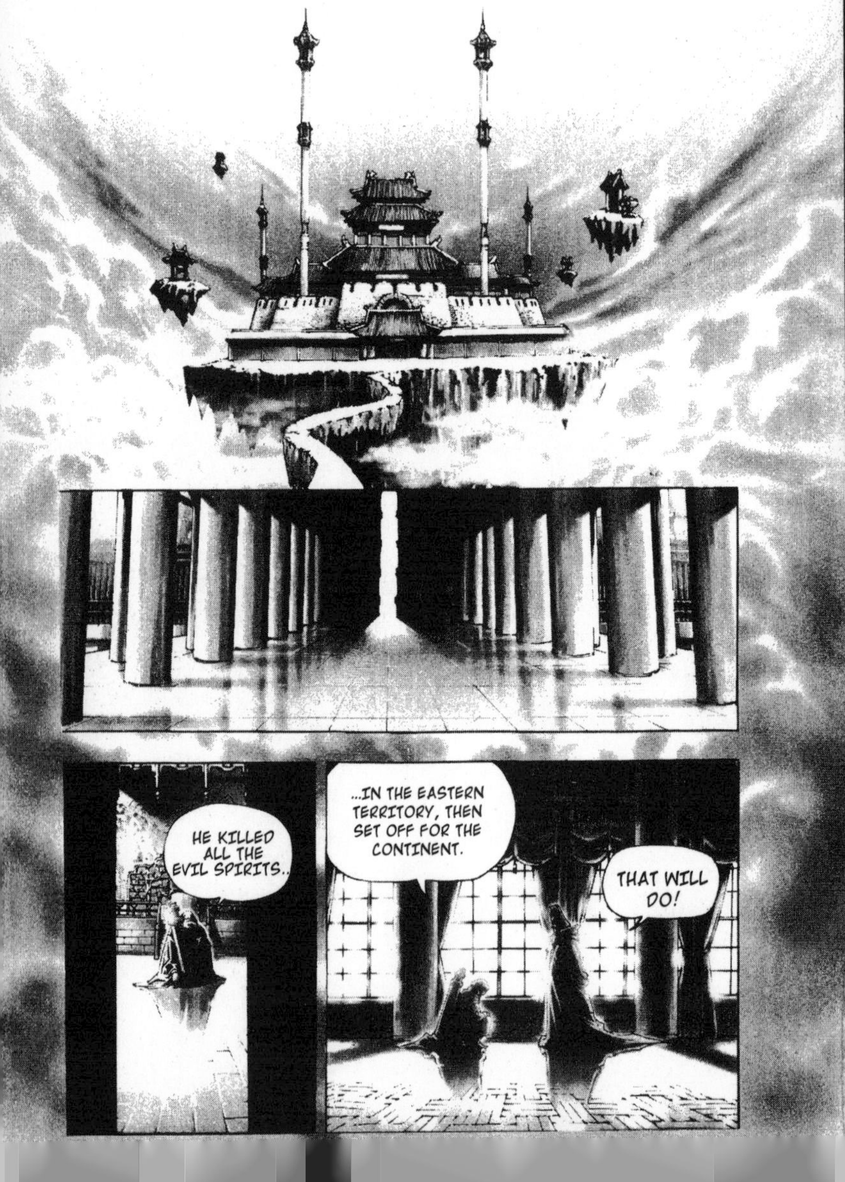
HE KILLED ALL THE EVIL SPIRITS...
...IN THE EASTERN TERRITORY, THEN SET OFF FOR THE CONTINENT.
THAT WILL DO!

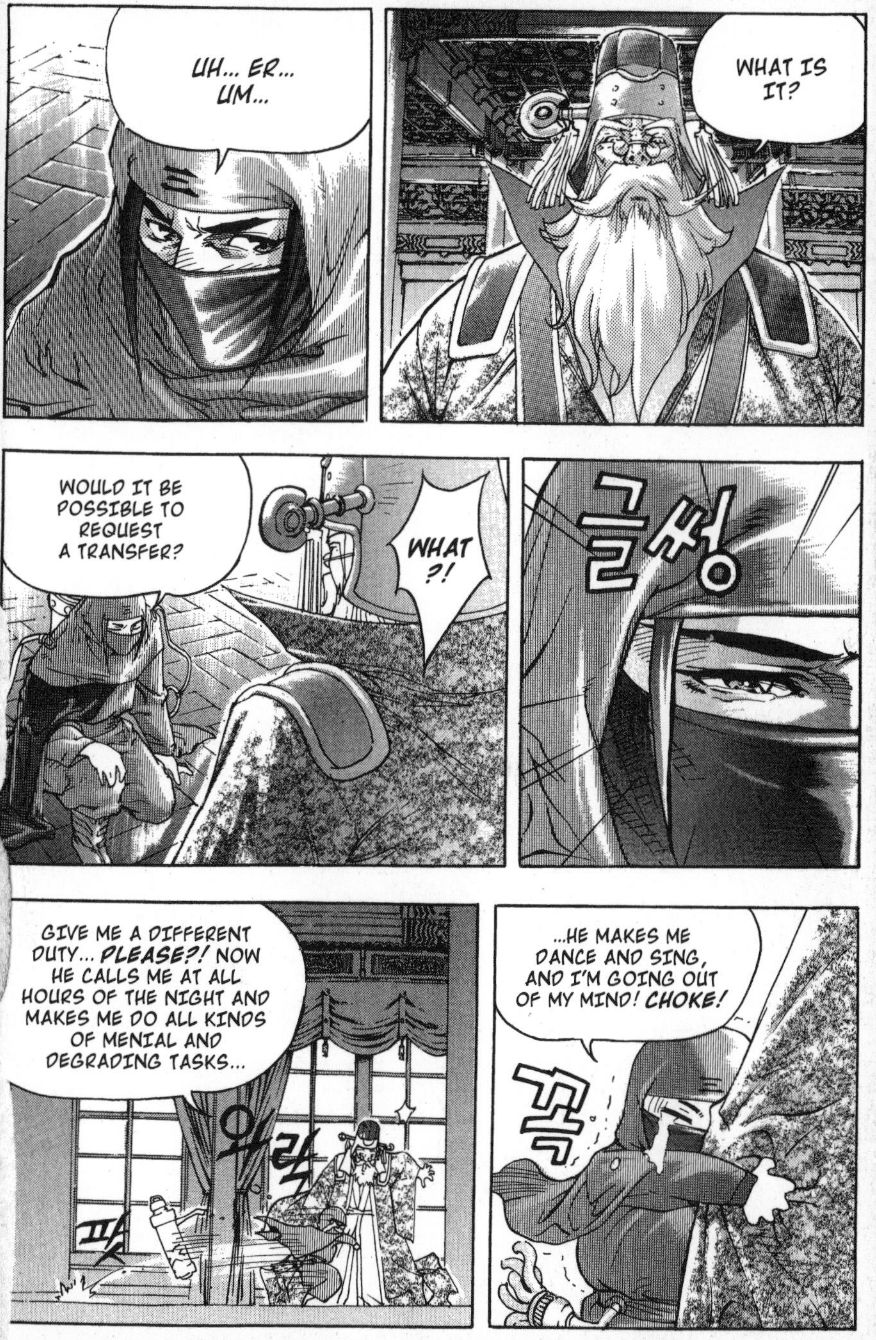
UH... ER... UM...
WHAT IS IT?
WOULD IT BE POSSIBLE TO REQUEST A TRANSFER?
WHAT ?!
GIVE ME A DIFFERENT DUTY... PLEASE?! NOW HE CALLS ME AT ALL HOURS OF THE NIGHT AND MAKES ME DO ALL KINDS OF MENIAL AND DEGRADING TASKS...
...HE MAKES ME DANCE AND SING, AND I'M GOING OUT OF MY MIND! CHOKE!

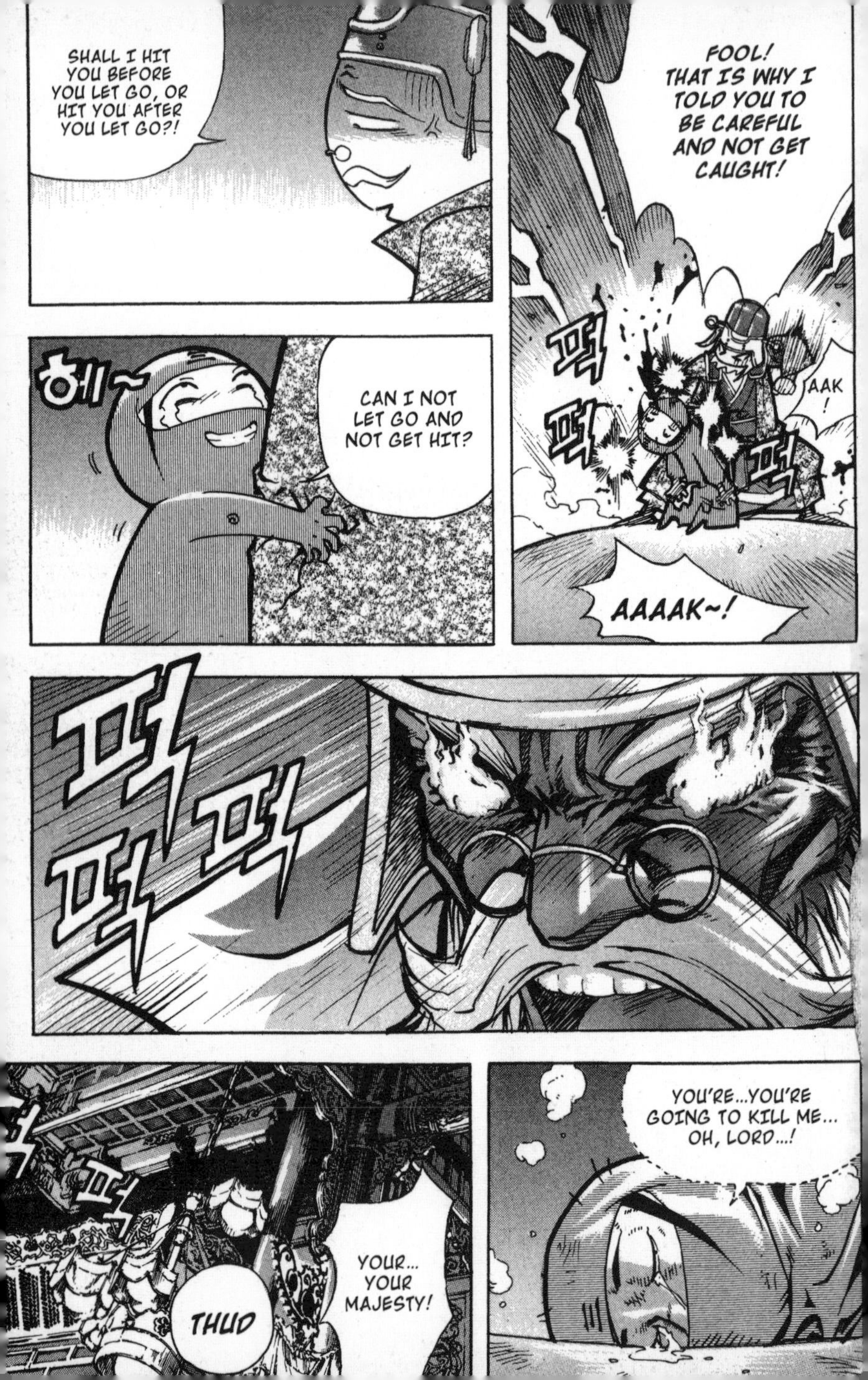
SHALL I HIT YOU BEFORE YOU LET GO, OR HIT YOU AFTER YOU LET GO?!
헤~
CAN I NOT LET GO AND NOT GET HIT?
FOOL! THAT IS WHY I TOLD YOU TO BE CAREFUL AND NOT GET CAUGHT!
퍽
퍽
퍽
AAK!
AAAAK~!
퍽
퍽
퍽
퍽
THUD
YOUR... YOUR MAJESTY!
YOU'RE...YOU'RE GOING TO KILL ME... OH, LORD...!

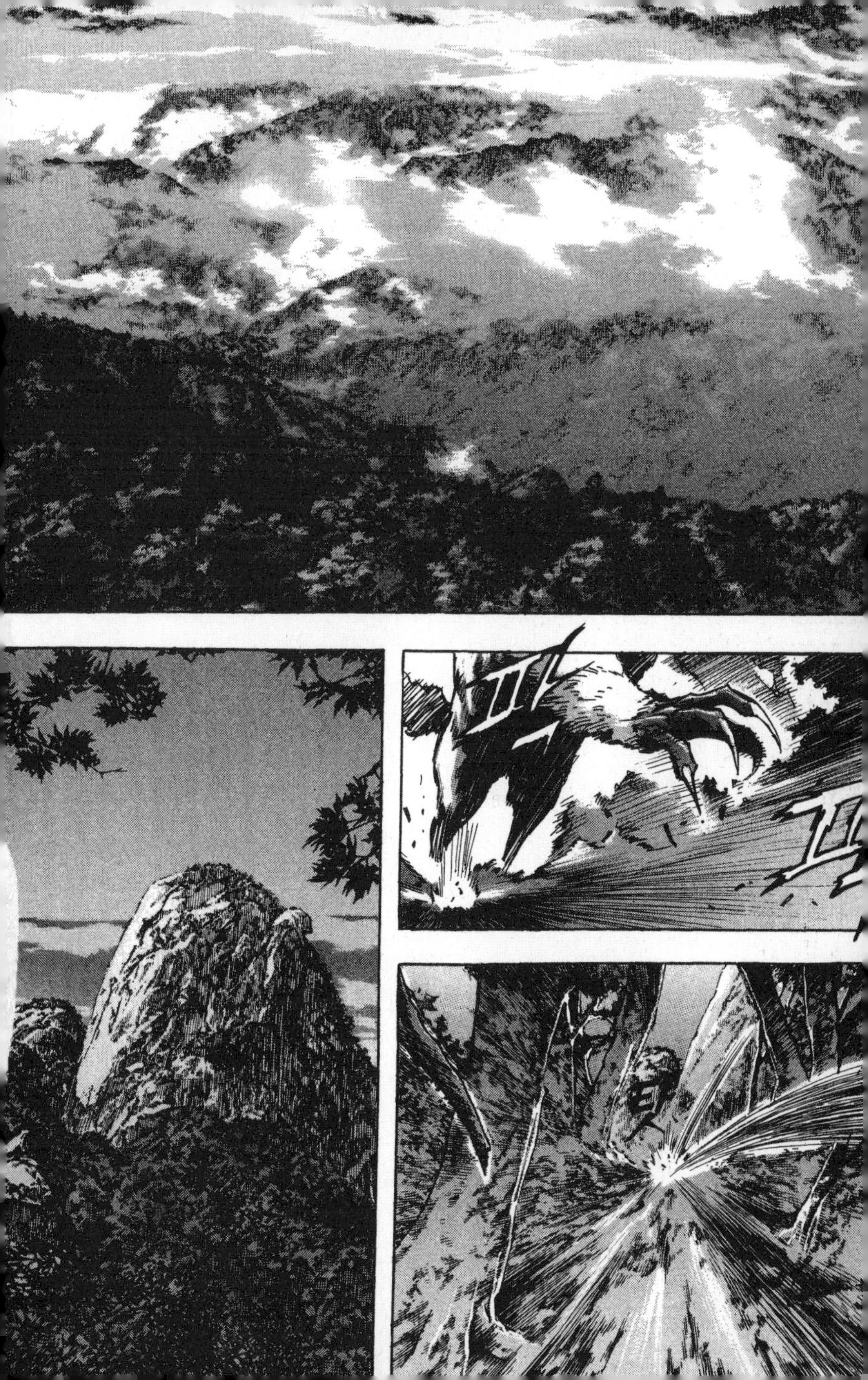

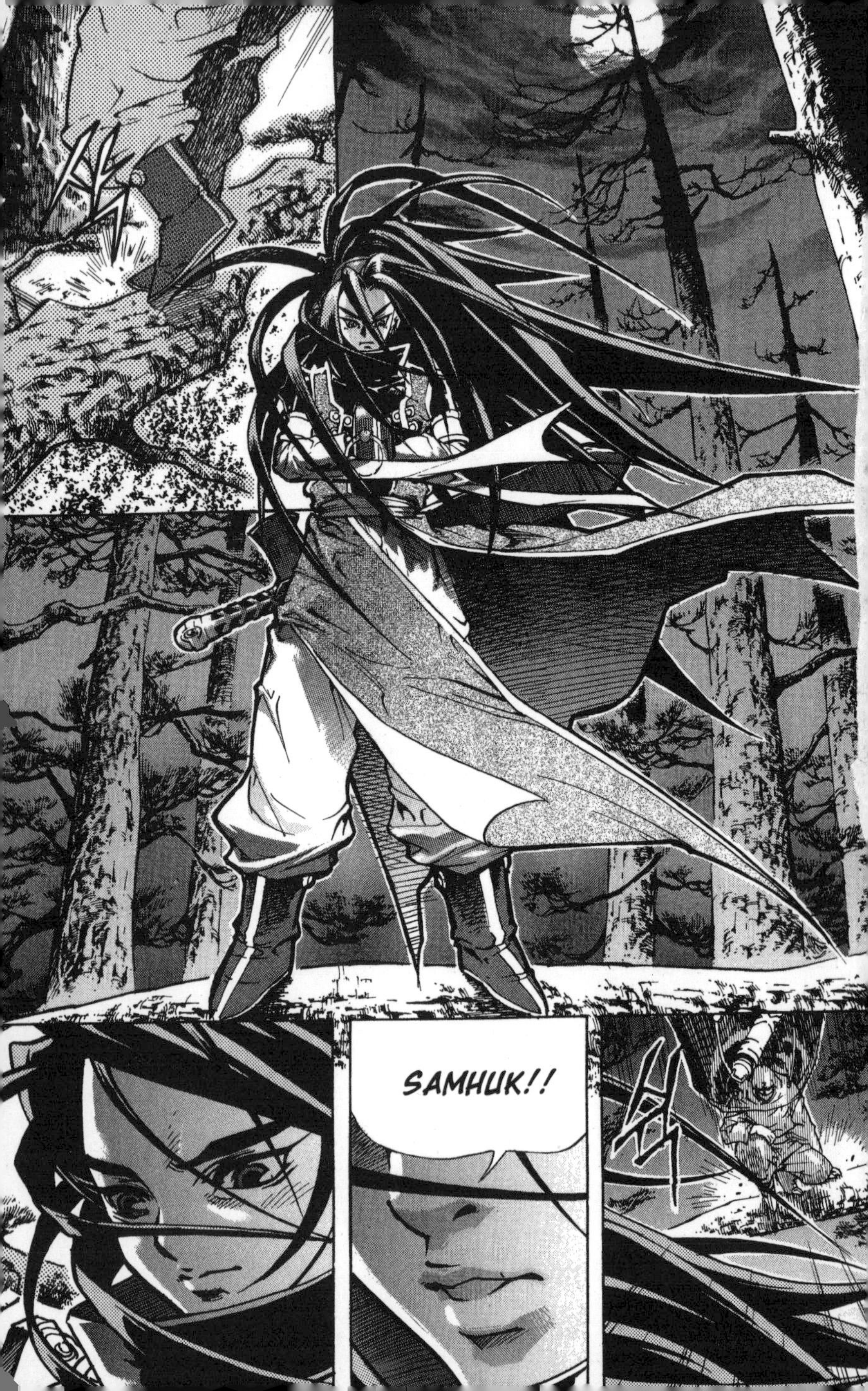
SAMHUK!!

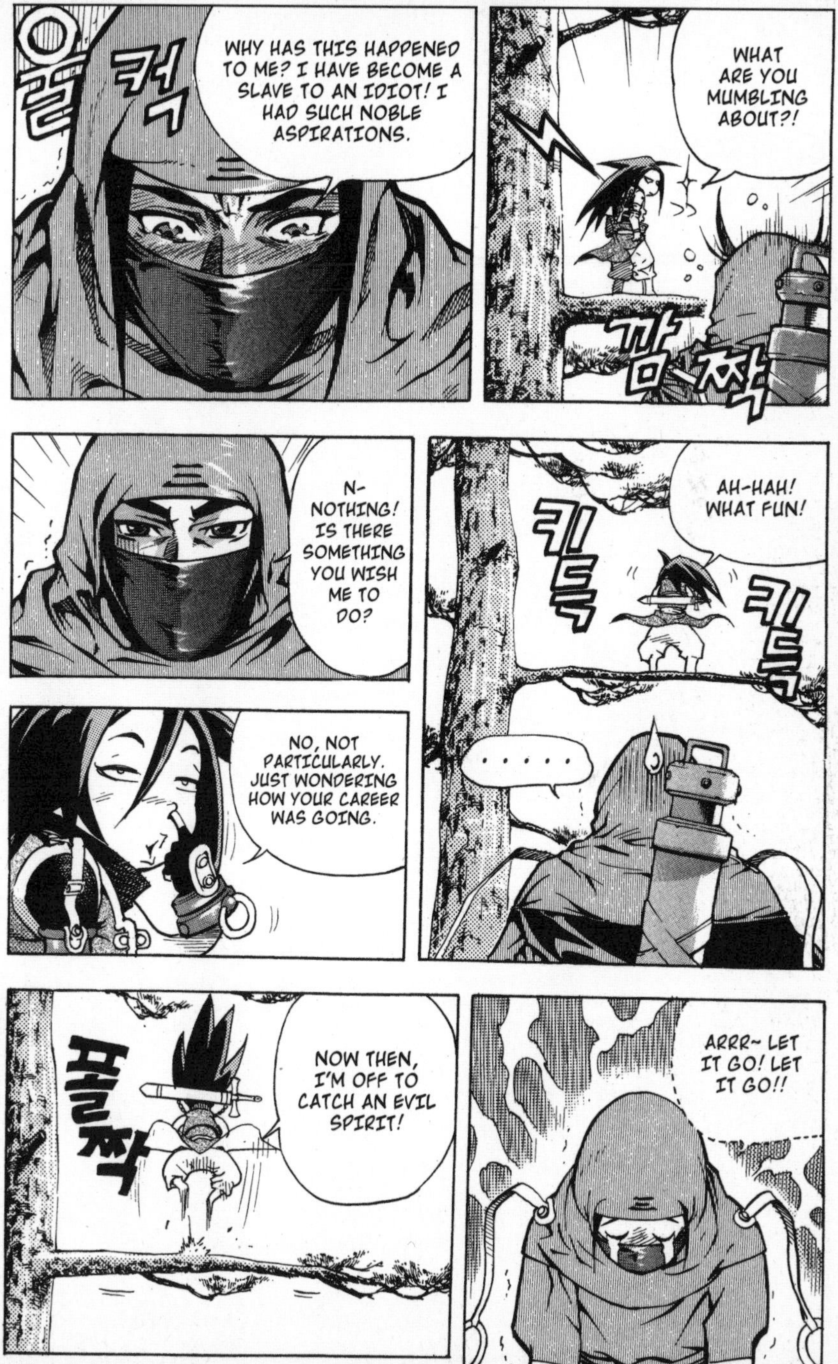
울컥
WHY HAS THIS HAPPENED TO ME? I HAVE BECOME A SLAVE TO AN IDIOT! I HAD SUCH NOBLE ASPIRATIONS.
WHAT ARE YOU MUMBLING ABOUT?!
깜~짝
N-NOTHING! IS THERE SOMETHING YOU WISH ME TO DO?
NO, NOT PARTICULARLY. JUST WONDERING HOW YOUR CAREER WAS GOING.
AH-HAH! WHAT FUN!
키득
키득
.....
폴짝
NOW THEN, I'M OFF TO CATCH AN EVIL SPIRIT!
ARRR~ LET IT GO! LET IT GO!!

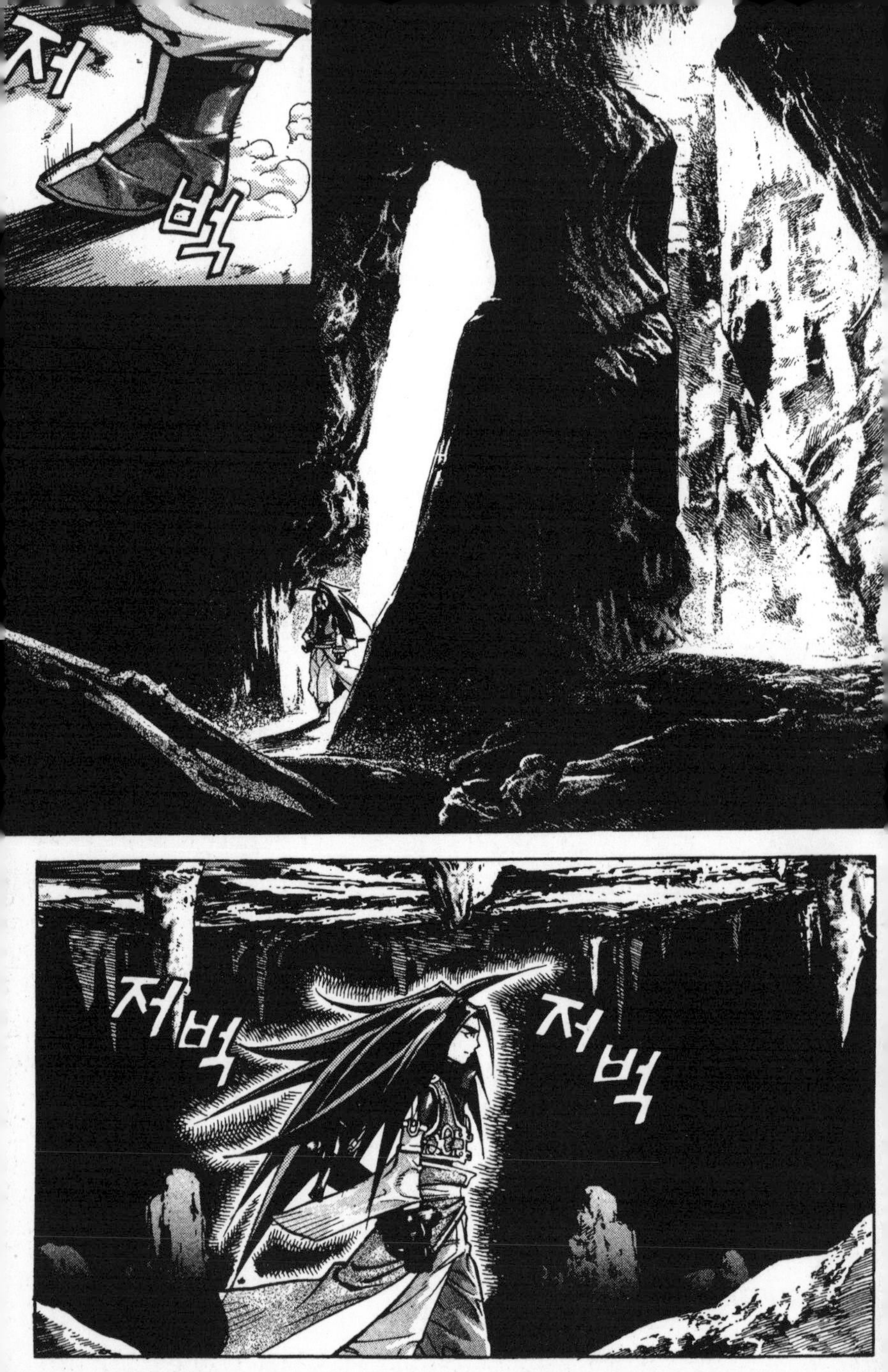
저벅
저벅
저벅

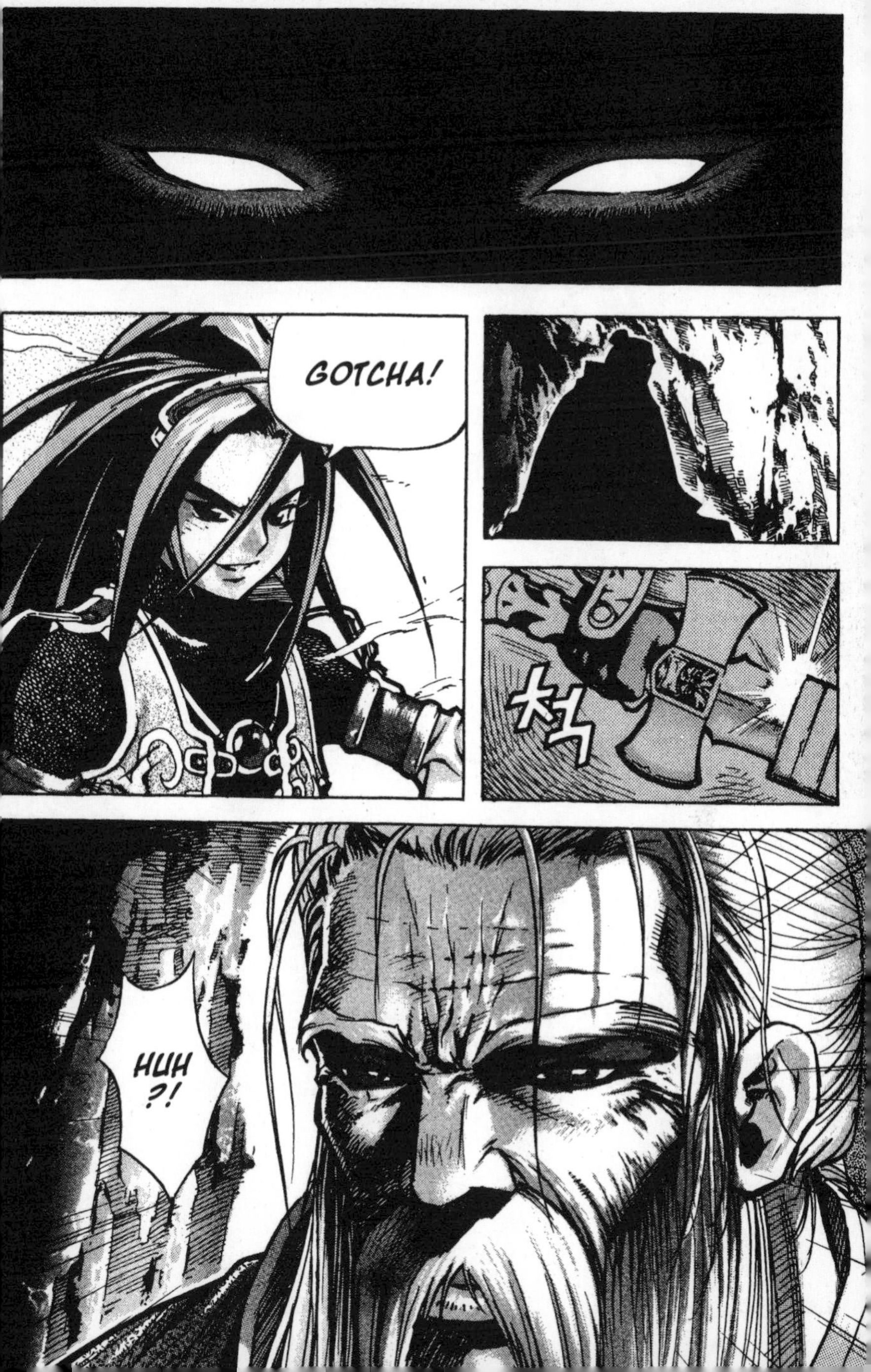
GOTCHA!
HUH ?!

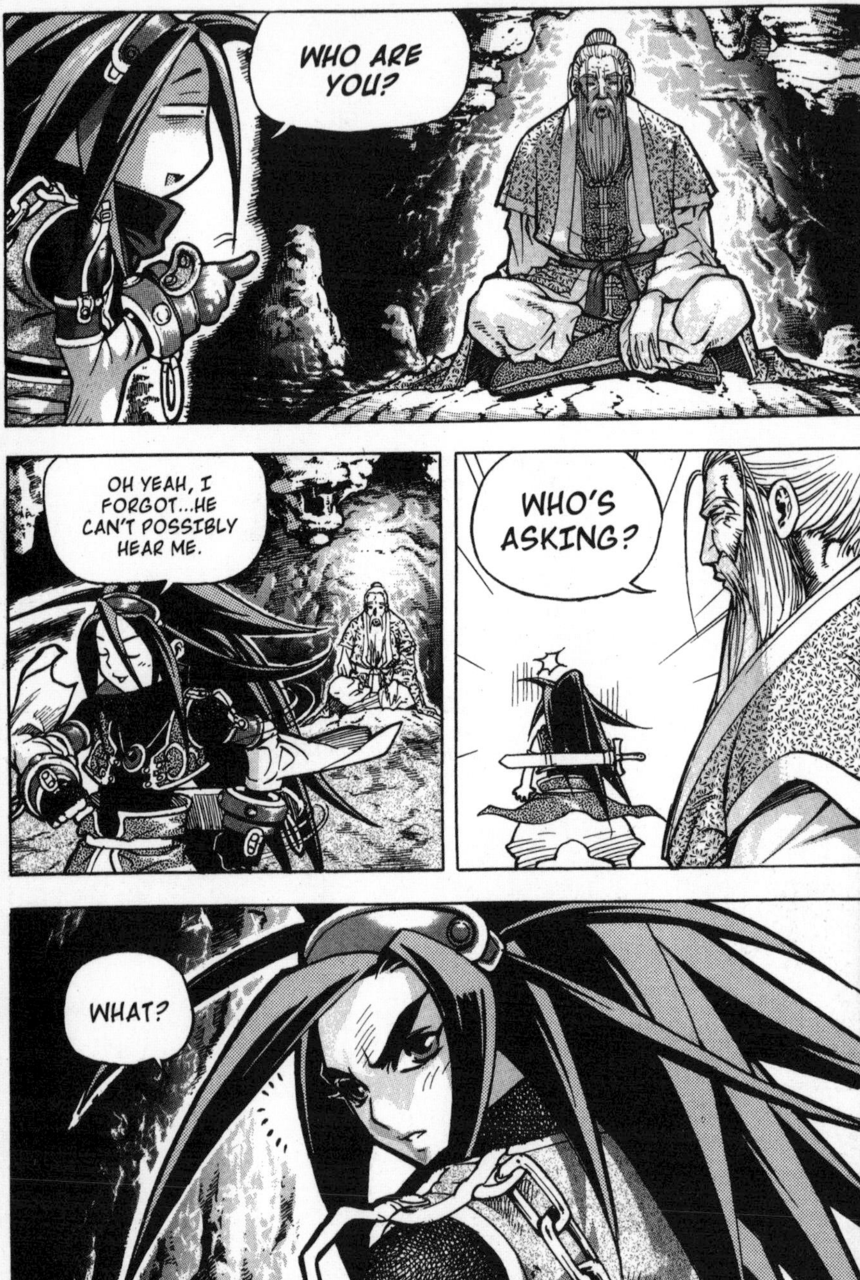

WHO ARE YOU?
OH YEAH, I FORGOT...HE CAN'T POSSIBLY HEAR ME.
WHO'S ASKING?
WHAT?

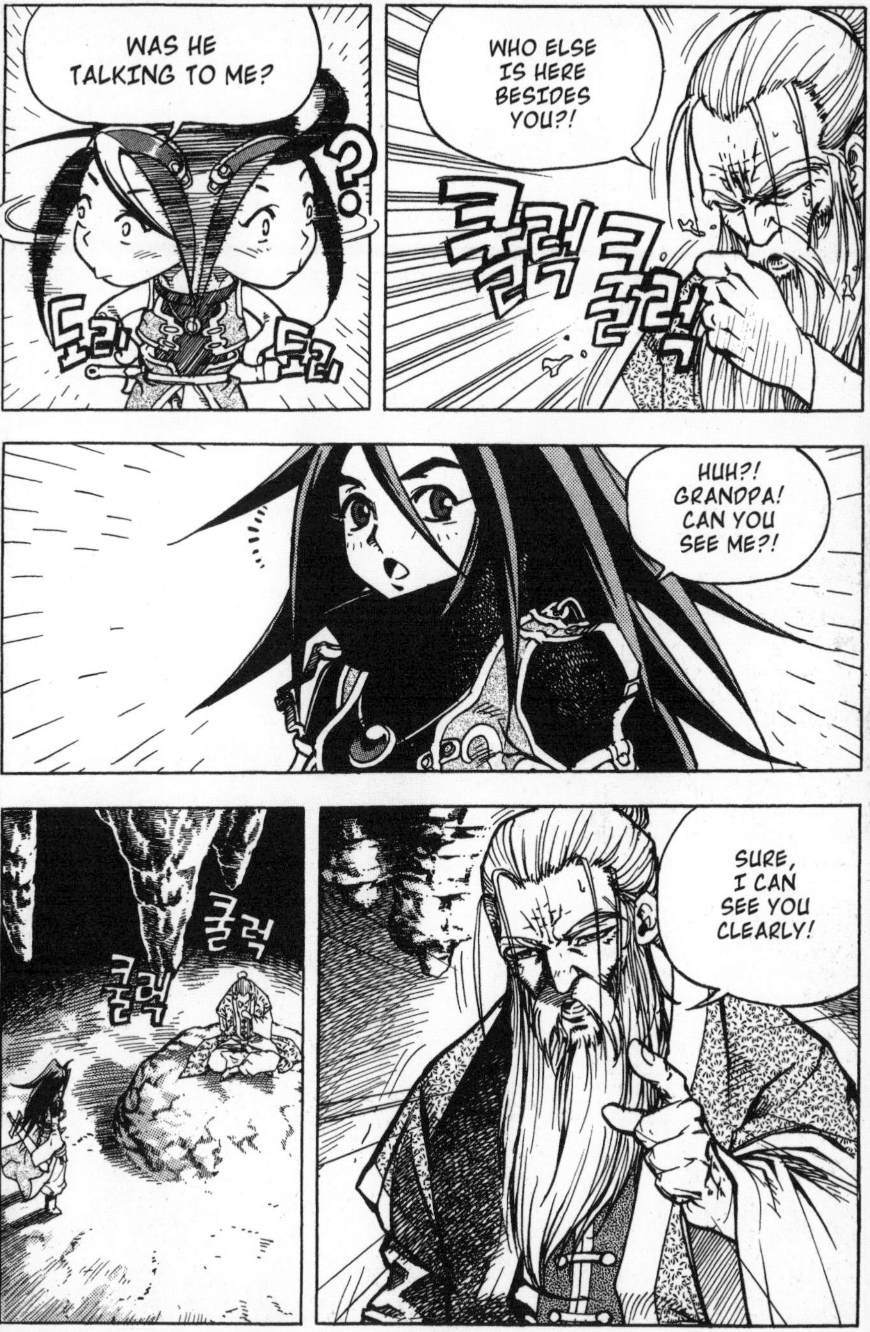
WAS HE TALKING TO ME?
?
도리 도리
WHO ELSE IS HERE BESIDES YOU?!
쿨럭 쿨럭
HUH?! GRANDPA! CAN YOU SEE ME?!
쿨럭
쿨럭
SURE, I CAN SEE YOU CLEARLY!

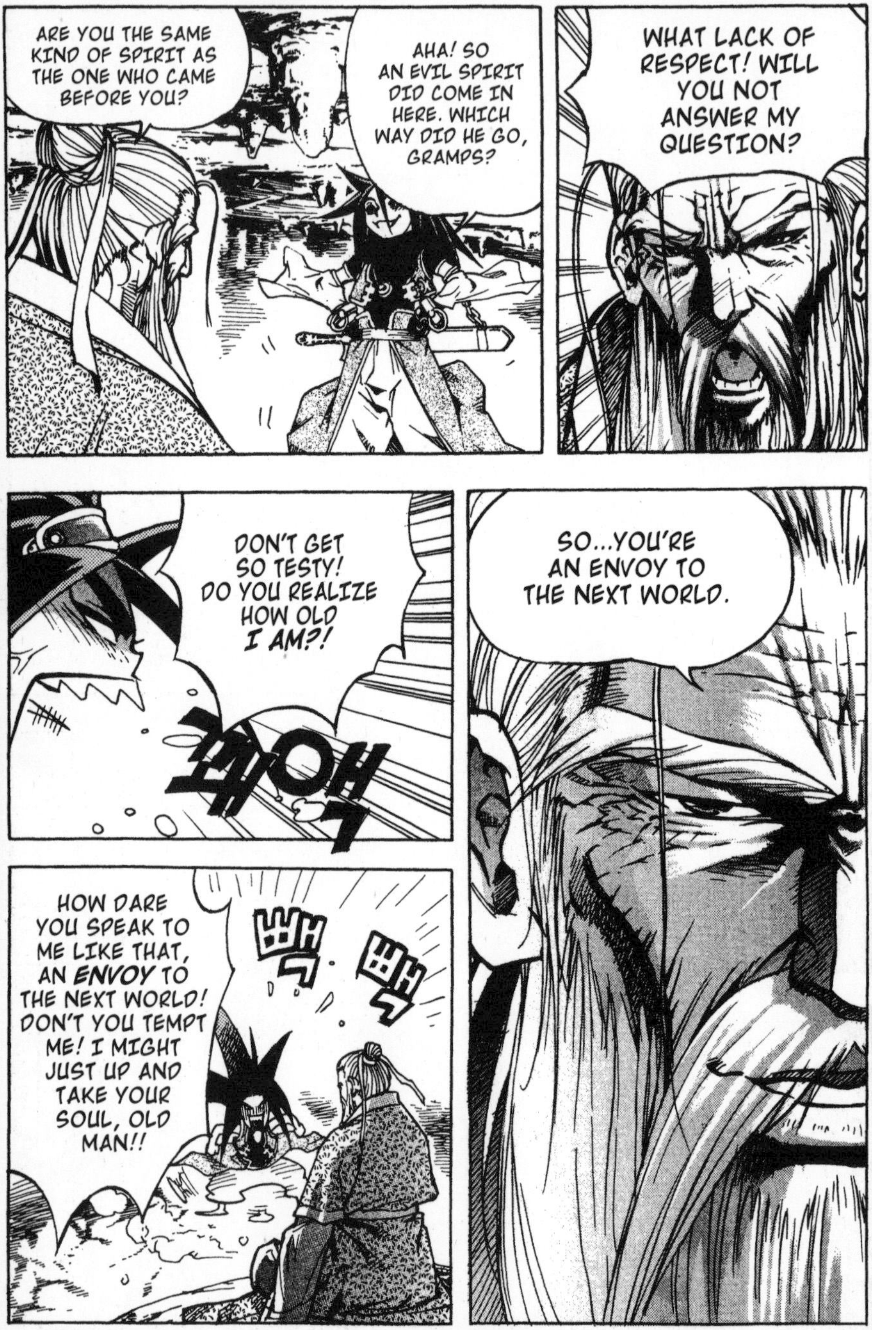
ARE YOU THE SAME KIND OF SPIRIT AS THE ONE WHO CAME BEFORE YOU?
AHA! SO AN EVIL SPIRIT DID COME IN HERE. WHICH WAY DID HE GO, GRAMPS?
WHAT LACK OF RESPECT! WILL YOU NOT ANSWER MY QUESTION?
DON'T GET SO TESTY! DO YOU REALIZE HOW OLD *I AM?!*
HOW DARE YOU SPEAK TO ME LIKE THAT, AN *ENVOY* TO THE NEXT WORLD! DON'T YOU TEMPT ME! I MIGHT JUST UP AND TAKE YOUR SOUL, OLD MAN!!
빡
빡
SO...YOU'RE AN ENVOY TO THE NEXT WORLD.

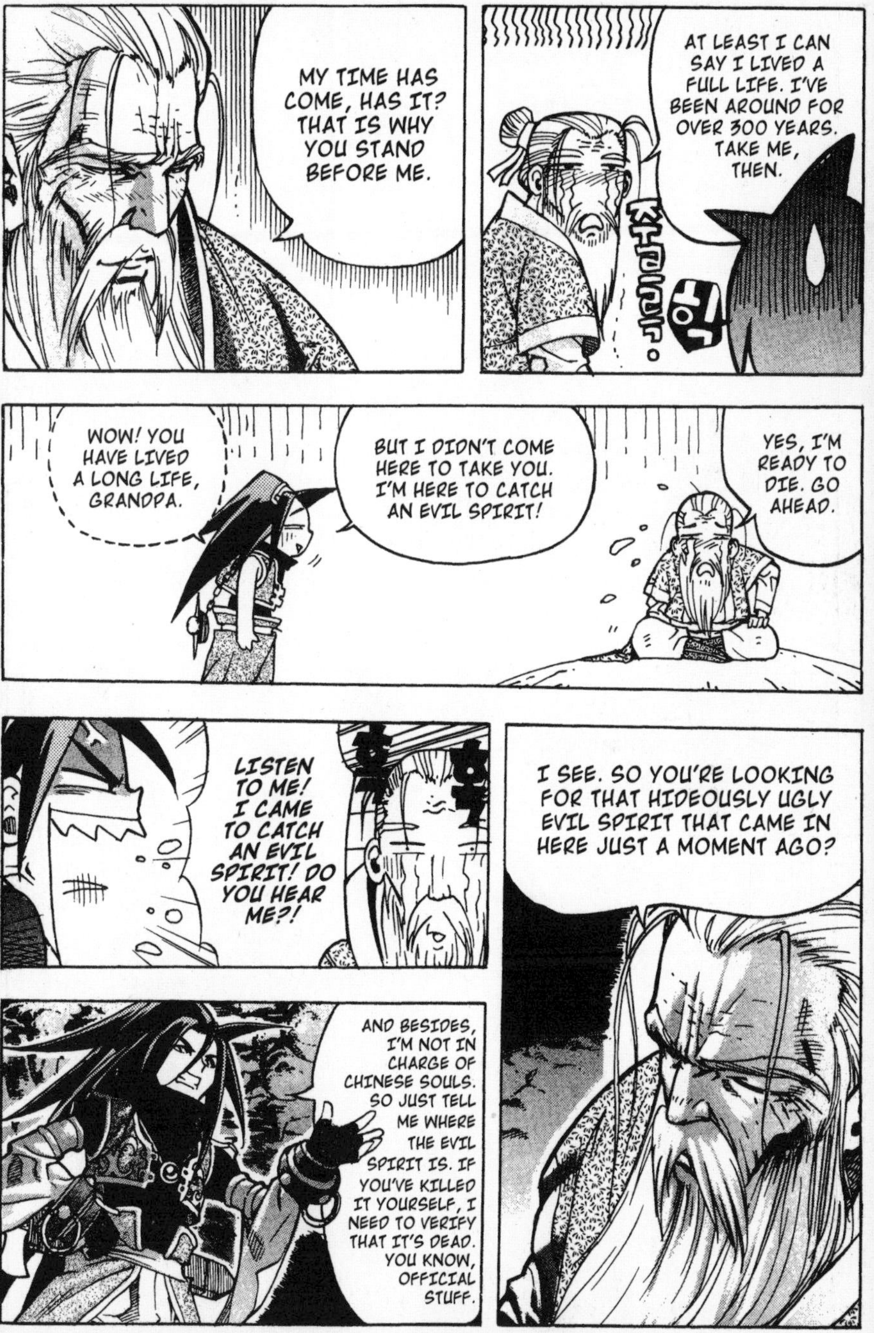
MY TIME HAS COME, HAS IT? THAT IS WHY YOU STAND BEFORE ME.
AT LEAST I CAN SAY I LIVED A FULL LIFE. I'VE BEEN AROUND FOR OVER 300 YEARS. TAKE ME, THEN.
WOW! YOU HAVE LIVED A LONG LIFE, GRANDPA.
BUT I DIDN'T COME HERE TO TAKE YOU. I'M HERE TO CATCH AN EVIL SPIRIT!
YES, I'M READY TO DIE. GO AHEAD.
LISTEN TO ME! I CAME TO CATCH AN EVIL SPIRIT! DO YOU HEAR ME?!
AND BESIDES, I'M NOT IN CHARGE OF CHINESE SOULS. SO JUST TELL ME WHERE THE EVIL SPIRIT IS. IF YOU'VE KILLED IT YOURSELF, I NEED TO VERIFY THAT IT'S DEAD. YOU KNOW, OFFICIAL STUFF.
I SEE. SO YOU'RE LOOKING FOR THAT HIDEOUSLY UGLY EVIL SPIRIT THAT CAME IN HERE JUST A MOMENT AGO?

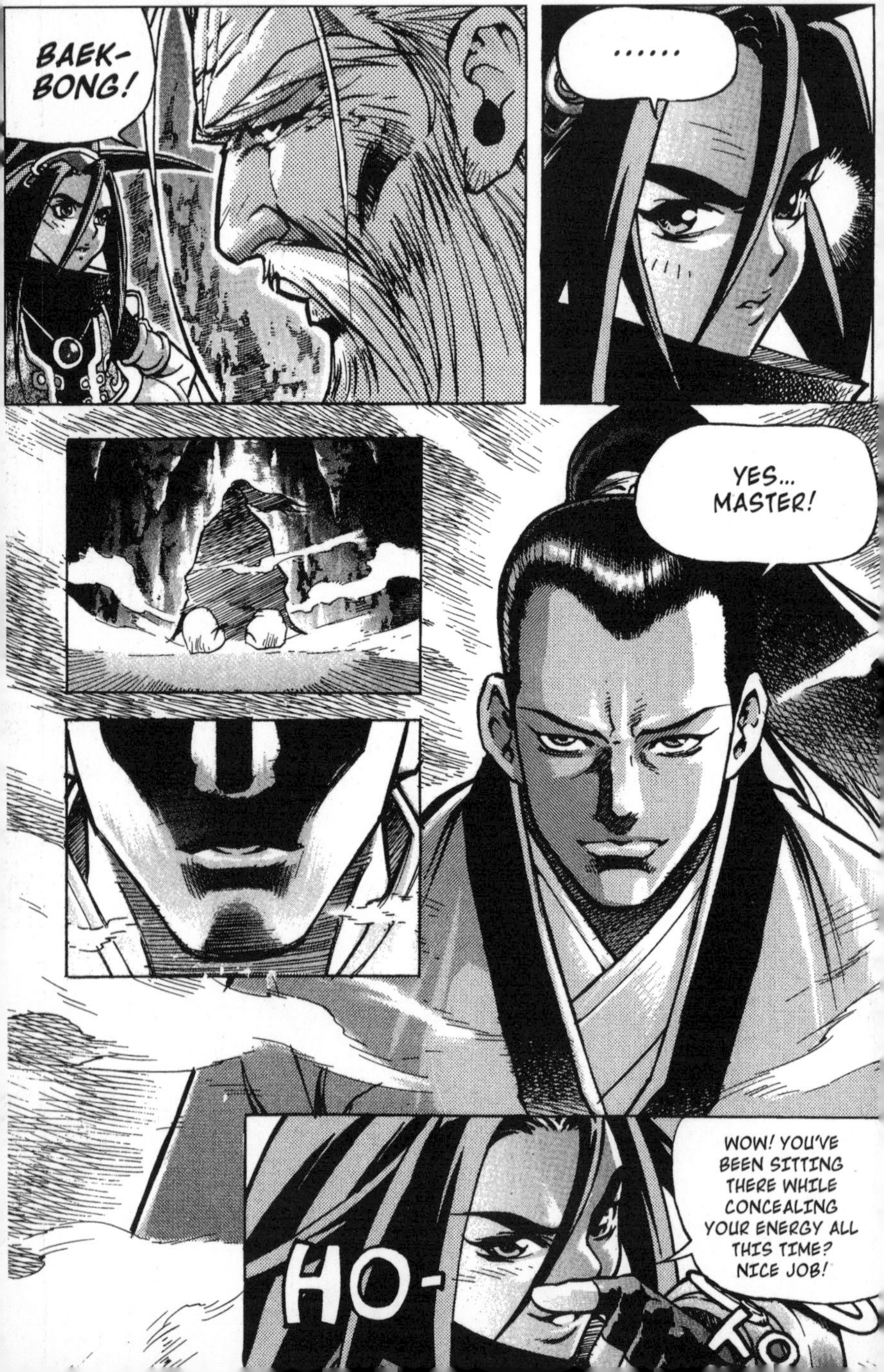
BAEK-BONG!
......
YES... MASTER!
WOW! YOU'VE BEEN SITTING THERE WHILE CONCEALING YOUR ENERGY ALL THIS TIME? NICE JOB!
HO-

WHAT HAPPENED TO THAT BEAST WHO ENTERED HERE EARLIER?

I HAVE TAKEN CARE OF HIM!

DEAD ALREADY? AWESOME. YOU SAVED ME SOME TROUBLE. I'LL BE ON MY WAY NOW. ON BREAK. UNION RULES AND SUCH.

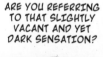

WAIT JUST ONE MOMENT~

BAEK-BONG, THERE IS A DIFFERENT ENERGY IN HERE NOW. CAN YOU SENSE IT?

ARE YOU REFERRING TO THAT SLIGHTLY VACANT AND YET DARK SENSATION?

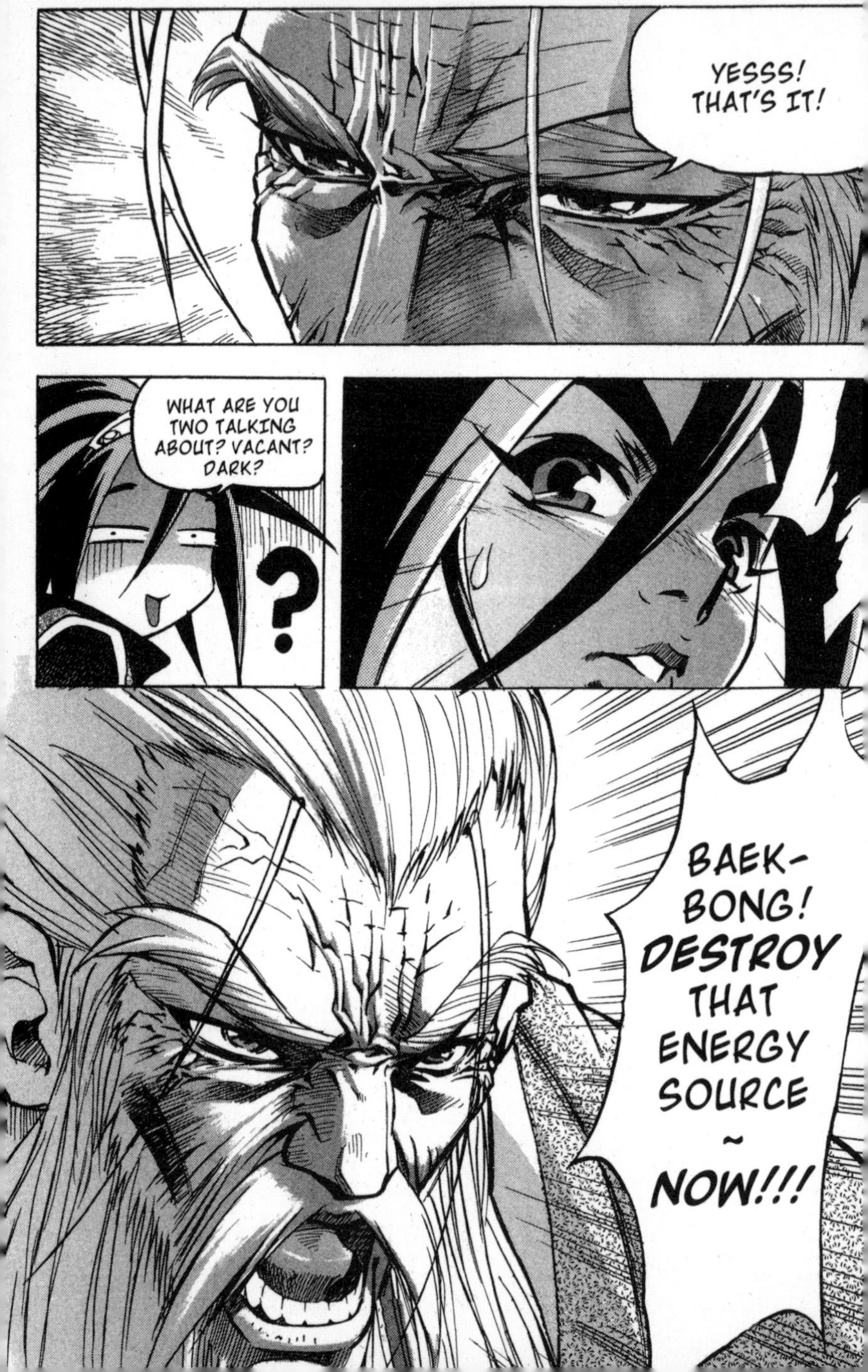
YESSS! THAT'S IT!
WHAT ARE YOU TWO TALKING ABOUT? VACANT? DARK?
?
BAEK-BONG! DESTROY THAT ENERGY SOURCE ~ NOW!!!

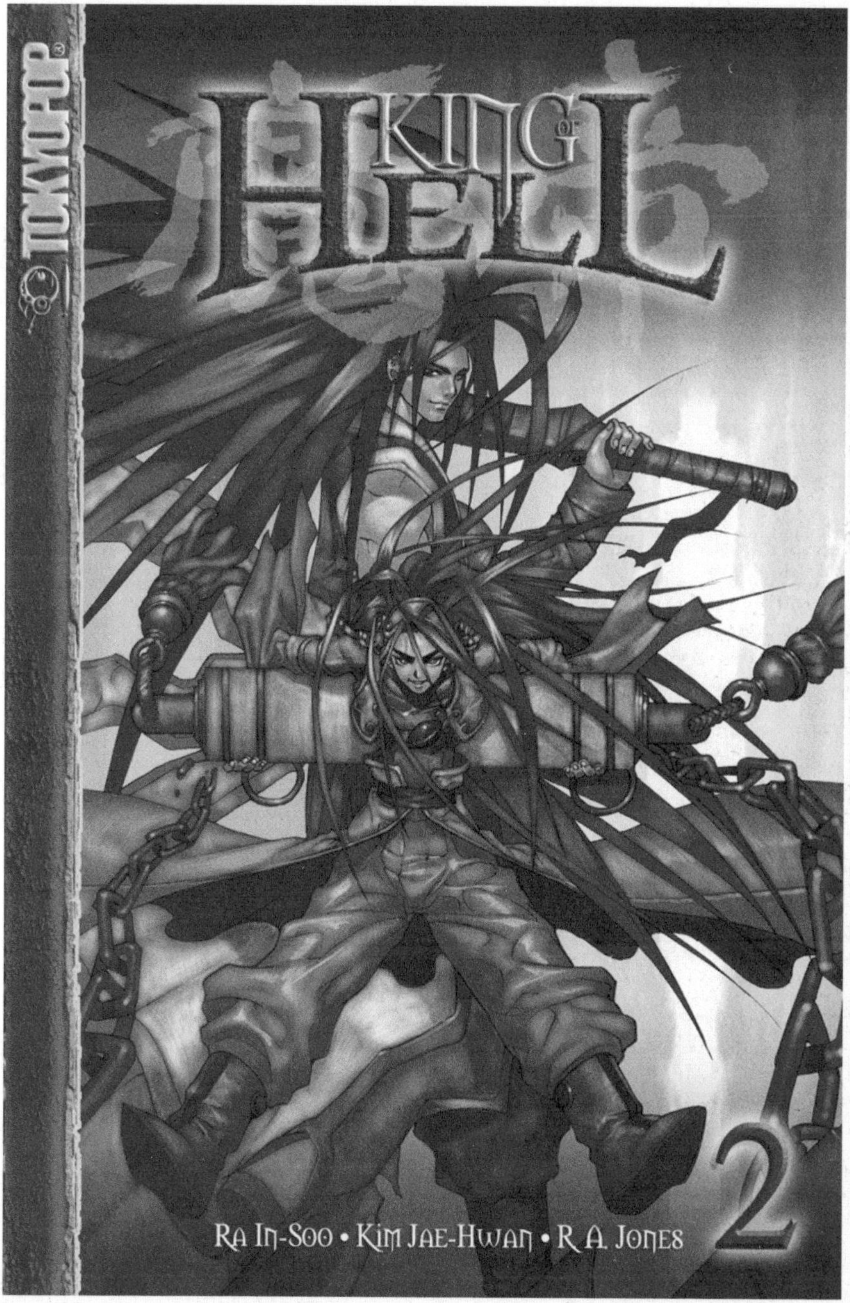
TOKYOPOP
KING OF HELL
2
RA IN-SOO • KIM JAE-HWAN • R.A. JONES

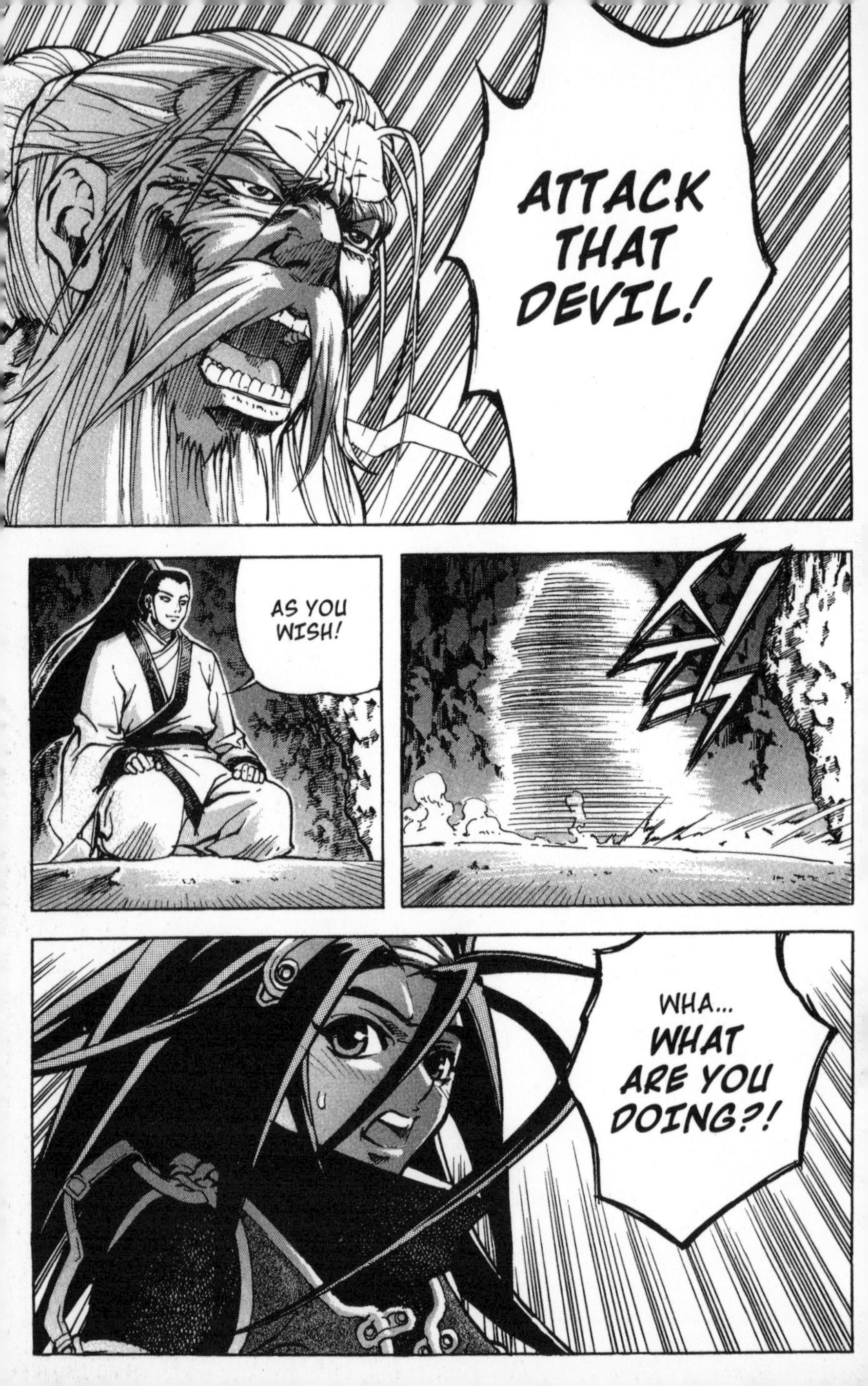
ATTACK THAT DEVIL!
AS YOU WISH!
WHA... WHAT ARE YOU DOING?!

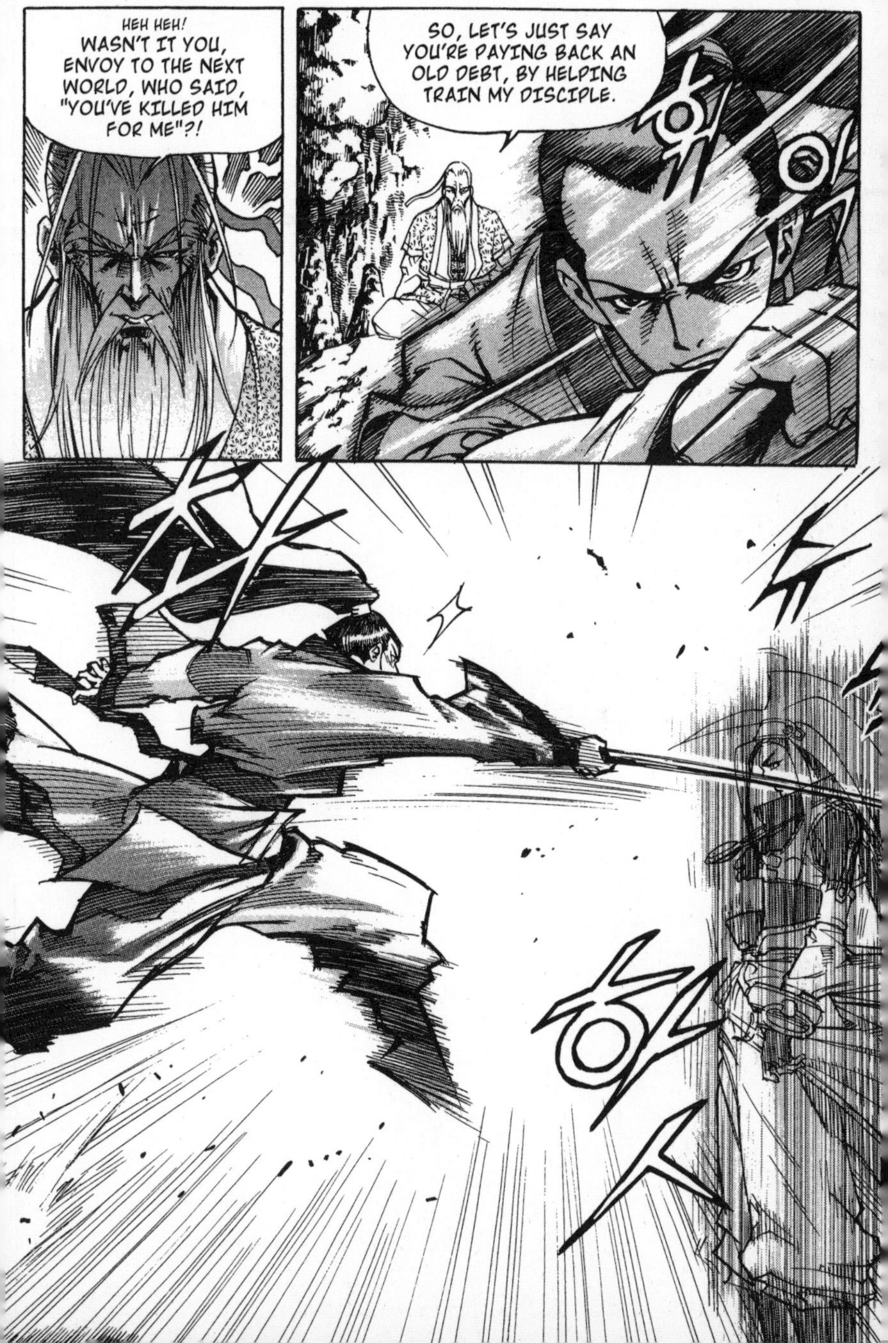
HEH HEH! WASN'T IT YOU, ENVOY TO THE NEXT WORLD, WHO SAID, "YOU'VE KILLED HIM FOR ME"?!
SO, LET'S JUST SAY YOU'RE PAYING BACK AN OLD DEBT, BY HELPING TRAIN MY DISCIPLE.

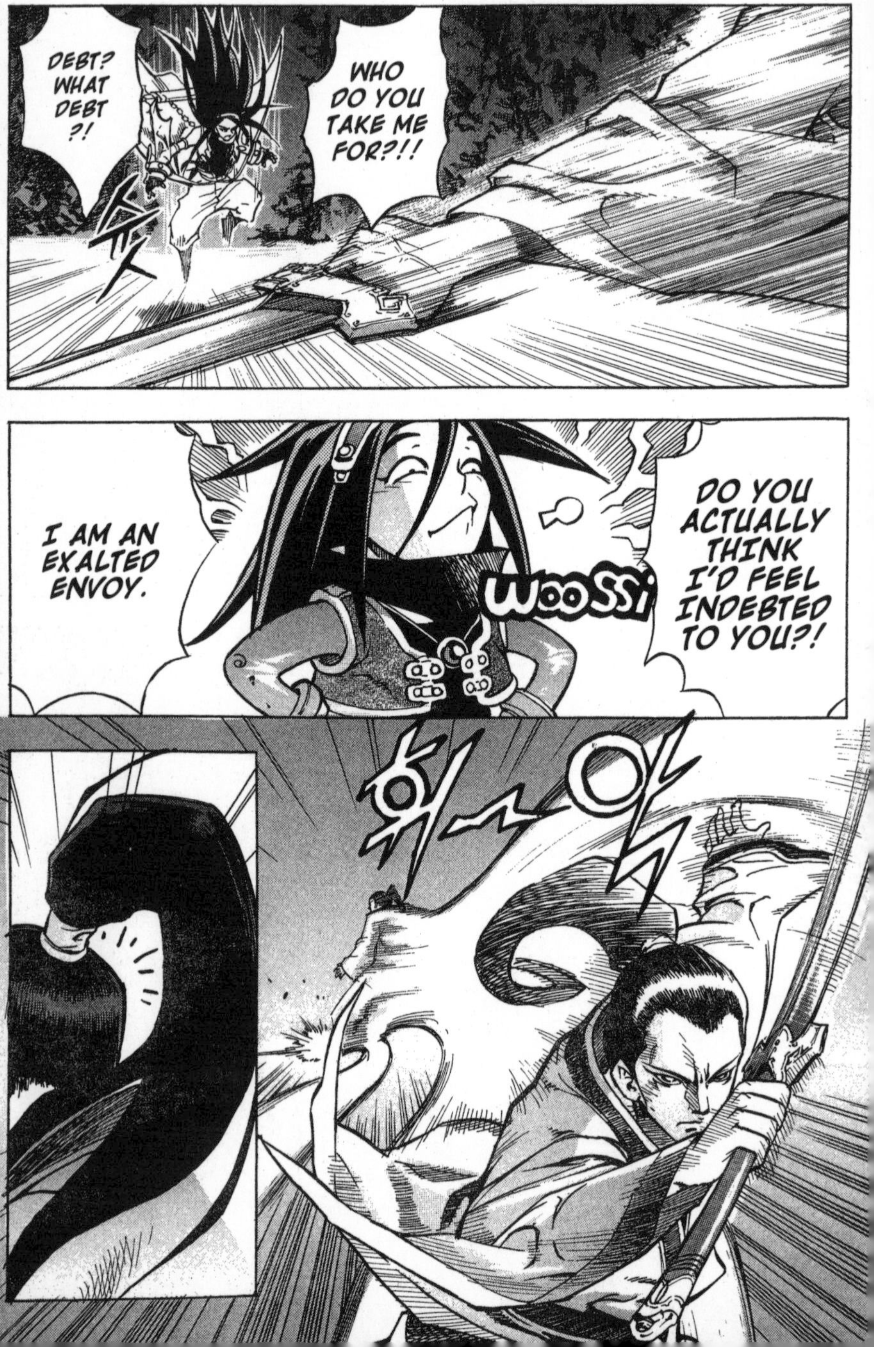
DEBT? WHAT DEBT ?!
WHO DO YOU TAKE ME FOR?!!
I AM AN EXALTED ENVOY.
WOOSSI
DO YOU ACTUALLY THINK I'D FEEL INDEBTED TO YOU?!

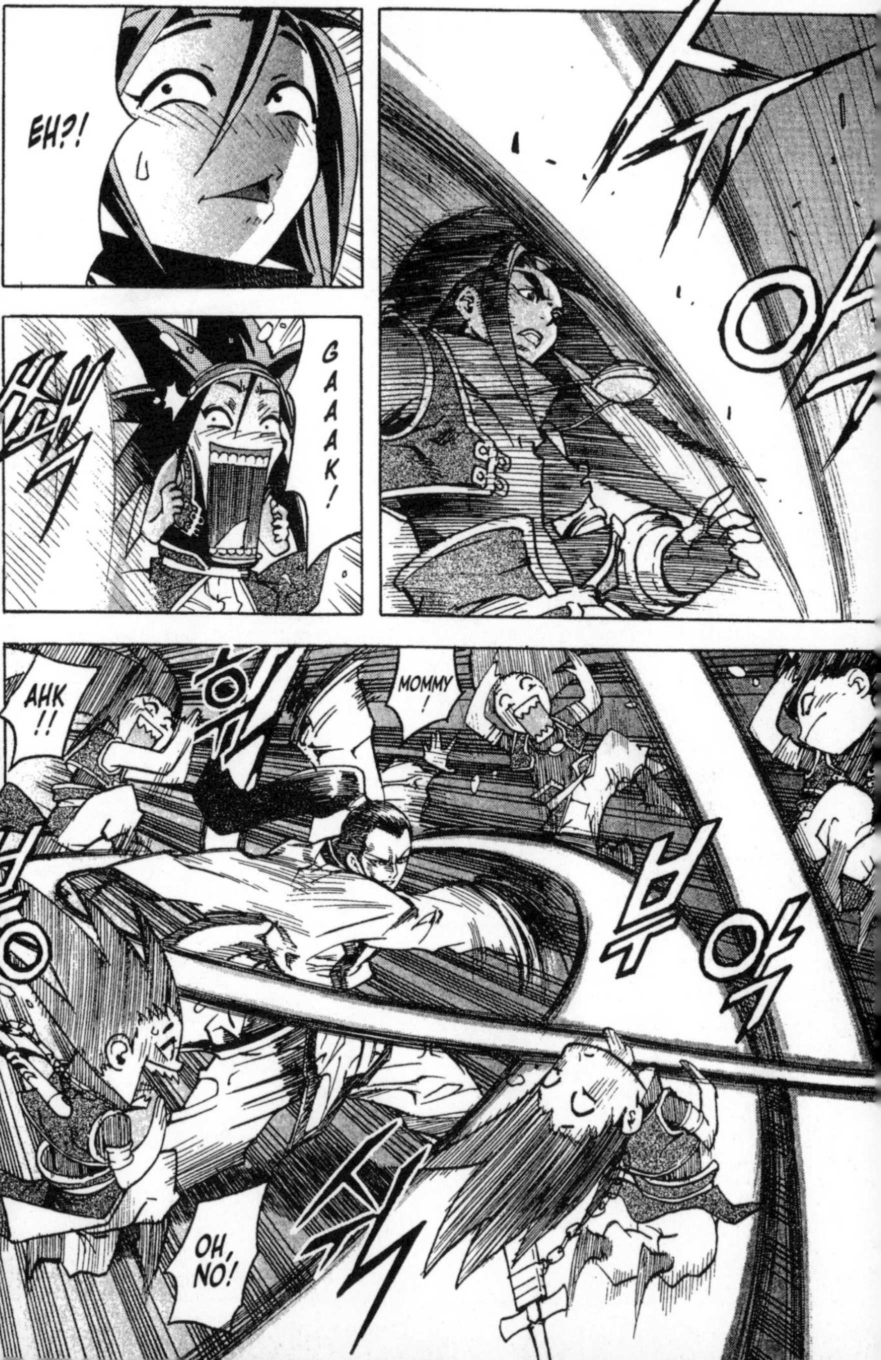
EH?!
GAAAK!
AHK!!
MOMMY!
OH, NO!

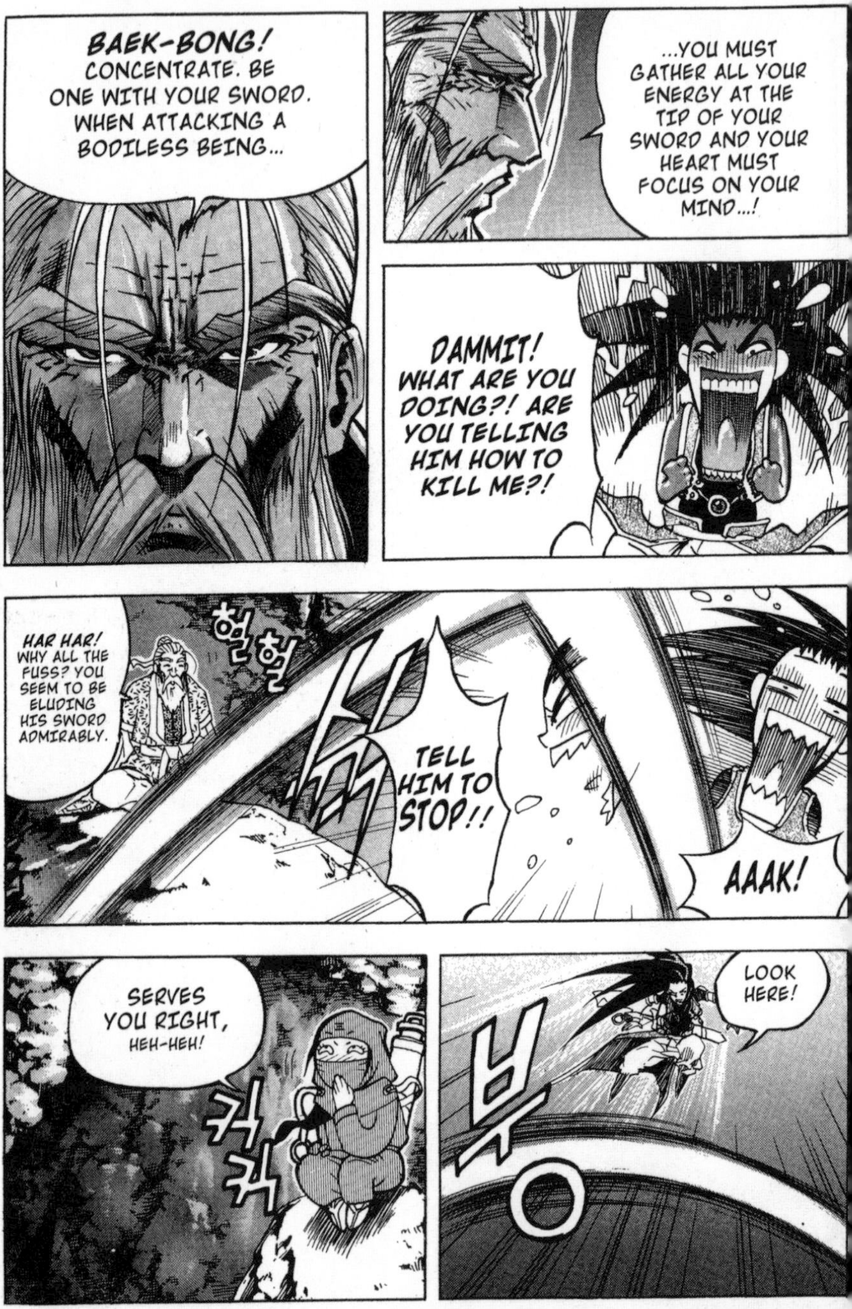
BAEK-BONG! CONCENTRATE. BE ONE WITH YOUR SWORD. WHEN ATTACKING A BODILESS BEING...
...YOU MUST GATHER ALL YOUR ENERGY AT THE TIP OF YOUR SWORD AND YOUR HEART MUST FOCUS ON YOUR MIND...!
DAMMIT! WHAT ARE YOU DOING?! ARE YOU TELLING HIM HOW TO KILL ME?!
HAR HAR! WHY ALL THE FUSS? YOU SEEM TO BE ELUDING HIS SWORD ADMIRABLY.
헐 헐
TELL HIM TO STOP!!
AAAK!
SERVES YOU RIGHT, HEH-HEH!
LOOK HERE!

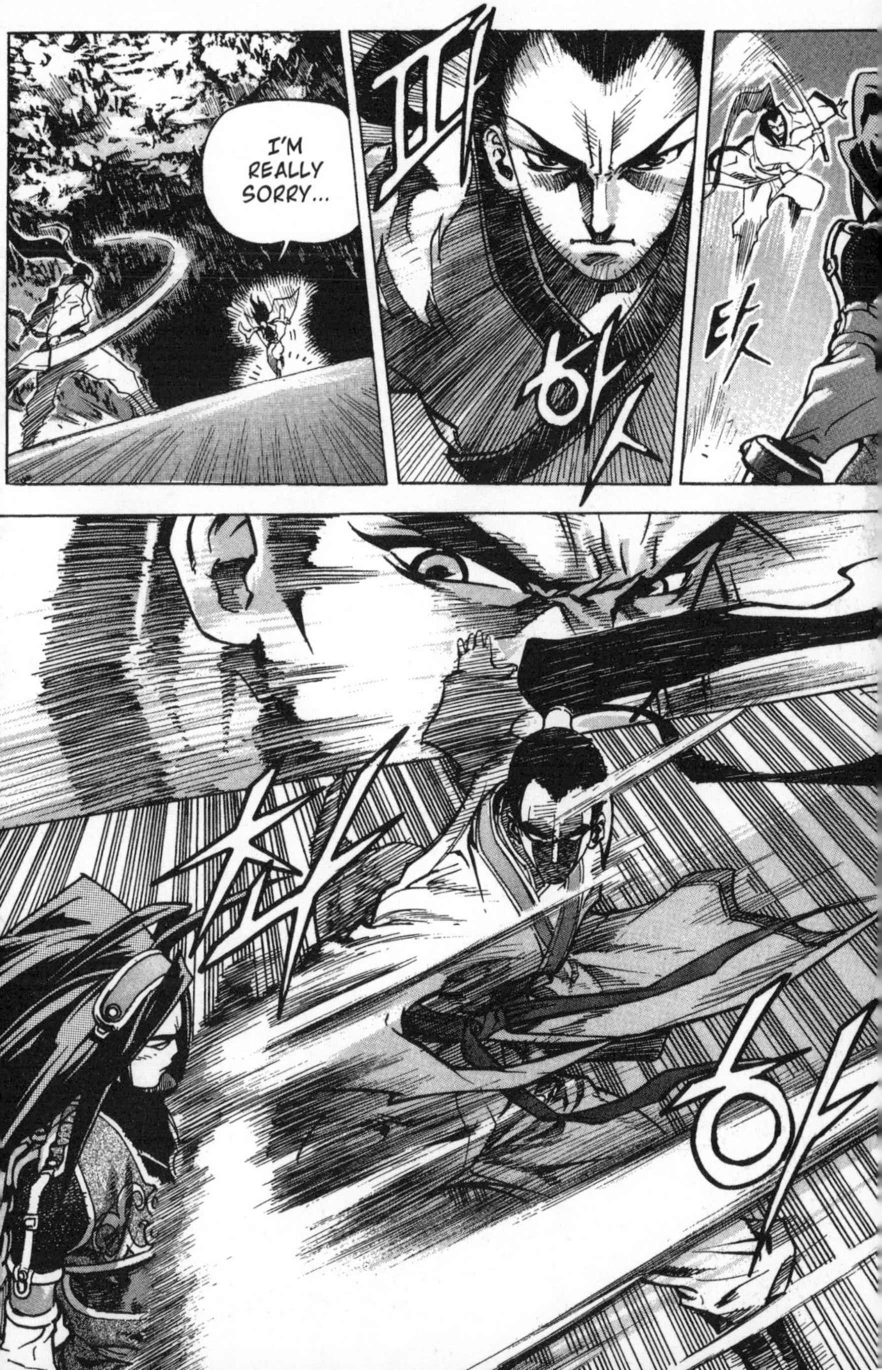
I'M REALLY SORRY...

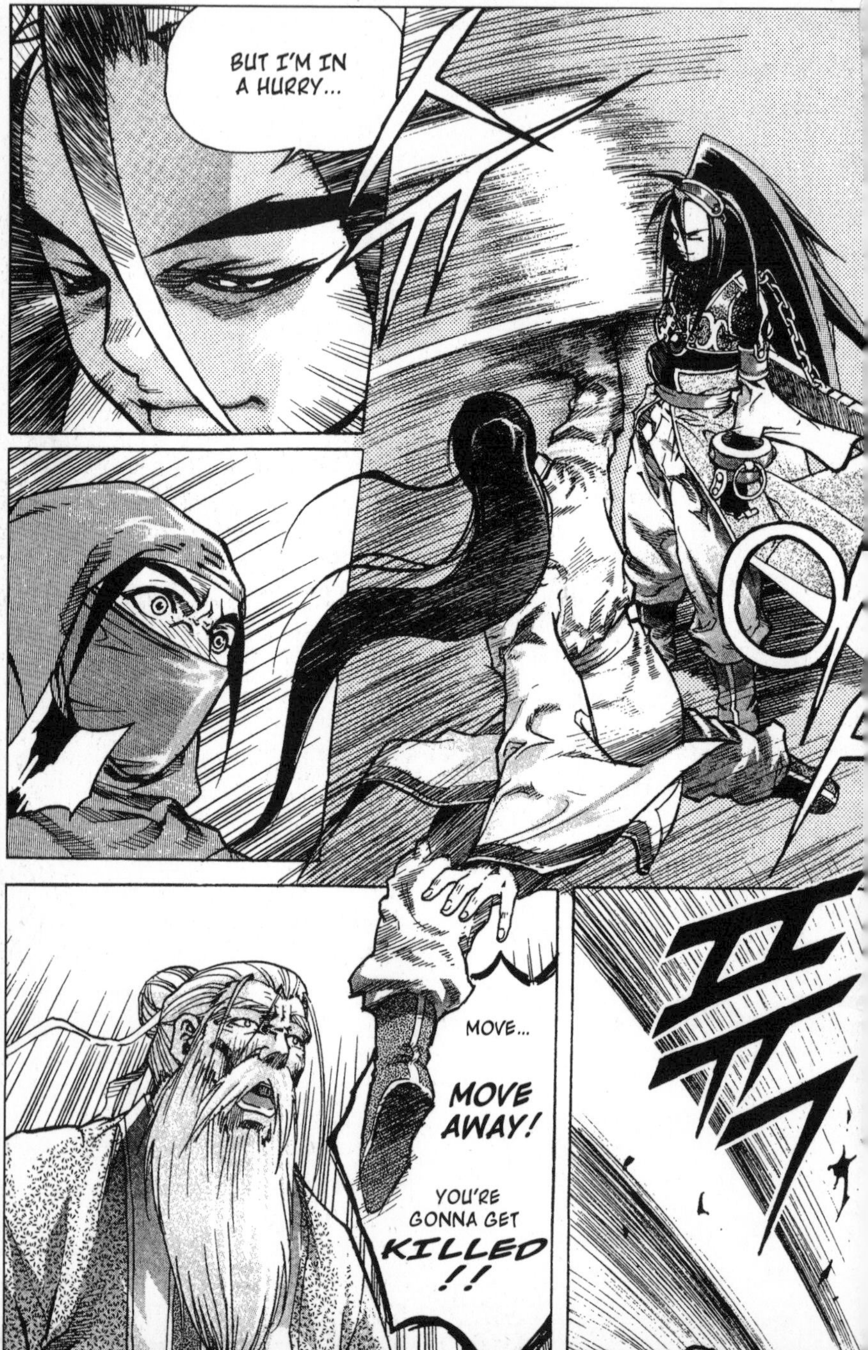
BUT I'M IN A HURRY...
MOVE...
MOVE AWAY!
YOU'RE GONNA GET KILLED!!

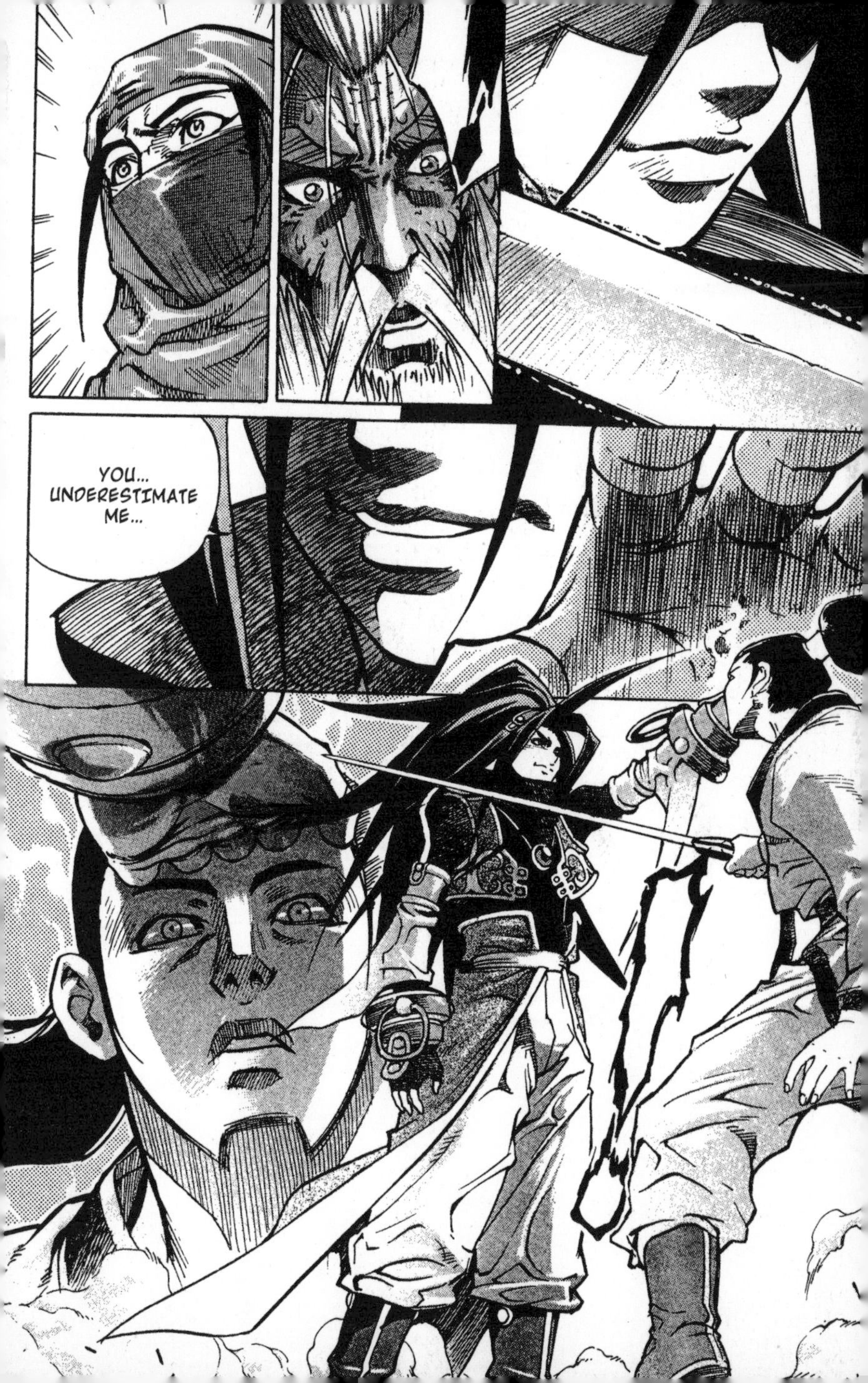
YOU... UNDERESTIMATE ME...

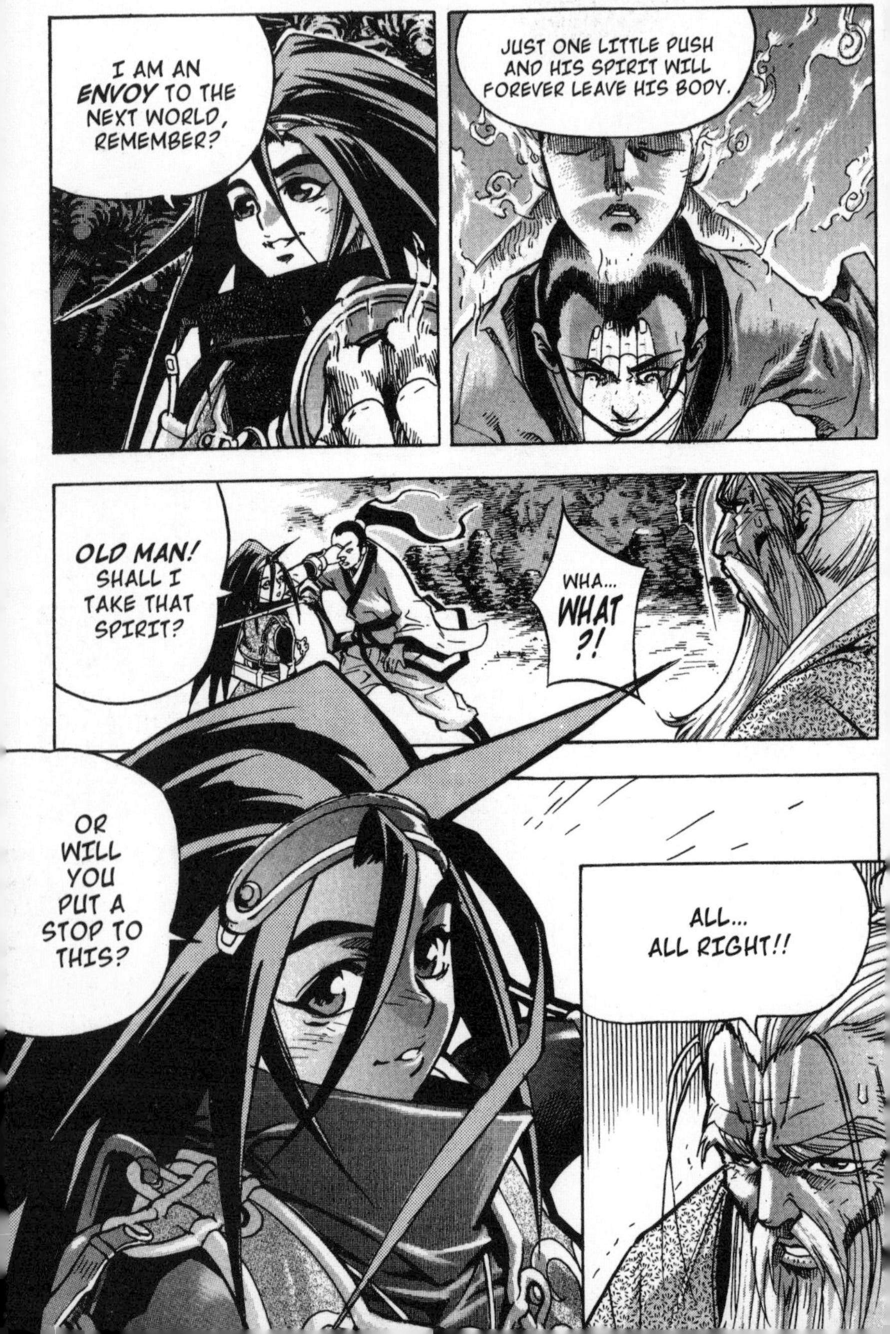
I AM AN ENVOY TO THE NEXT WORLD, REMEMBER?
JUST ONE LITTLE PUSH AND HIS SPIRIT WILL FOREVER LEAVE HIS BODY.
OLD MAN! SHALL I TAKE THAT SPIRIT?
WHA... WHAT ?!
OR WILL YOU PUT A STOP TO THIS?
ALL... ALL RIGHT!!

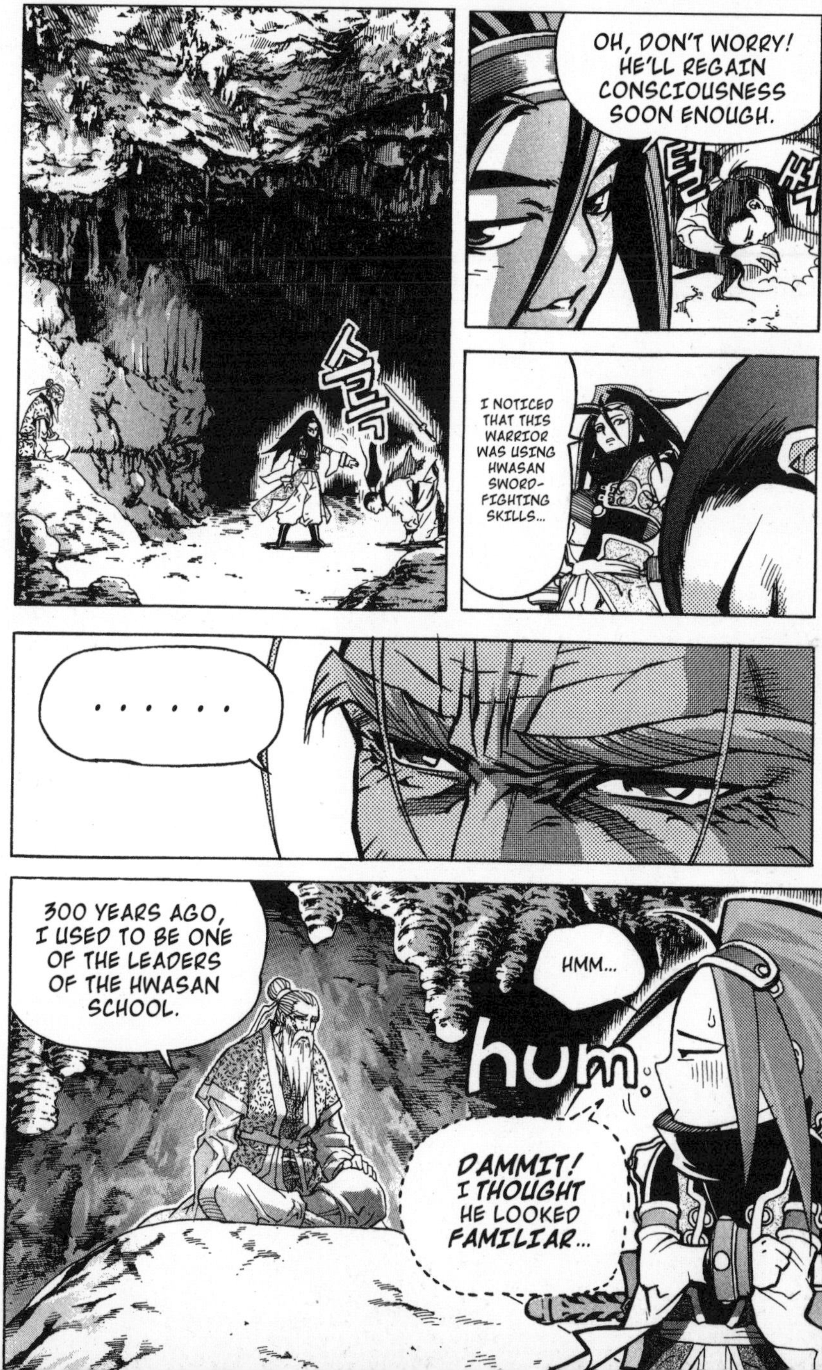
OH, DON'T WORRY! HE'LL REGAIN CONSCIOUSNESS SOON ENOUGH.
I NOTICED THAT THIS WARRIOR WAS USING HWASAN SWORD-FIGHTING SKILLS...
. . . .
300 YEARS AGO, I USED TO BE ONE OF THE LEADERS OF THE HWASAN SCHOOL.
HMM...
hum.
DAMMIT! I THOUGHT HE LOOKED FAMILIAR...

BACK THEN...

I LOST MY ARM TO **MAJEH**--A MAN WORKING FOR THE DARK SIDE.

HAR HAR HAR!

I WAS PLANNING ON TAKING MY REVENGE...

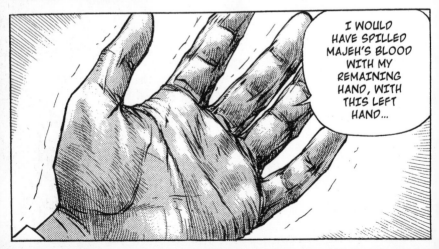

I WOULD HAVE SPILLED MAJEH'S BLOOD WITH MY REMAINING HAND, WITH THIS LEFT HAND...

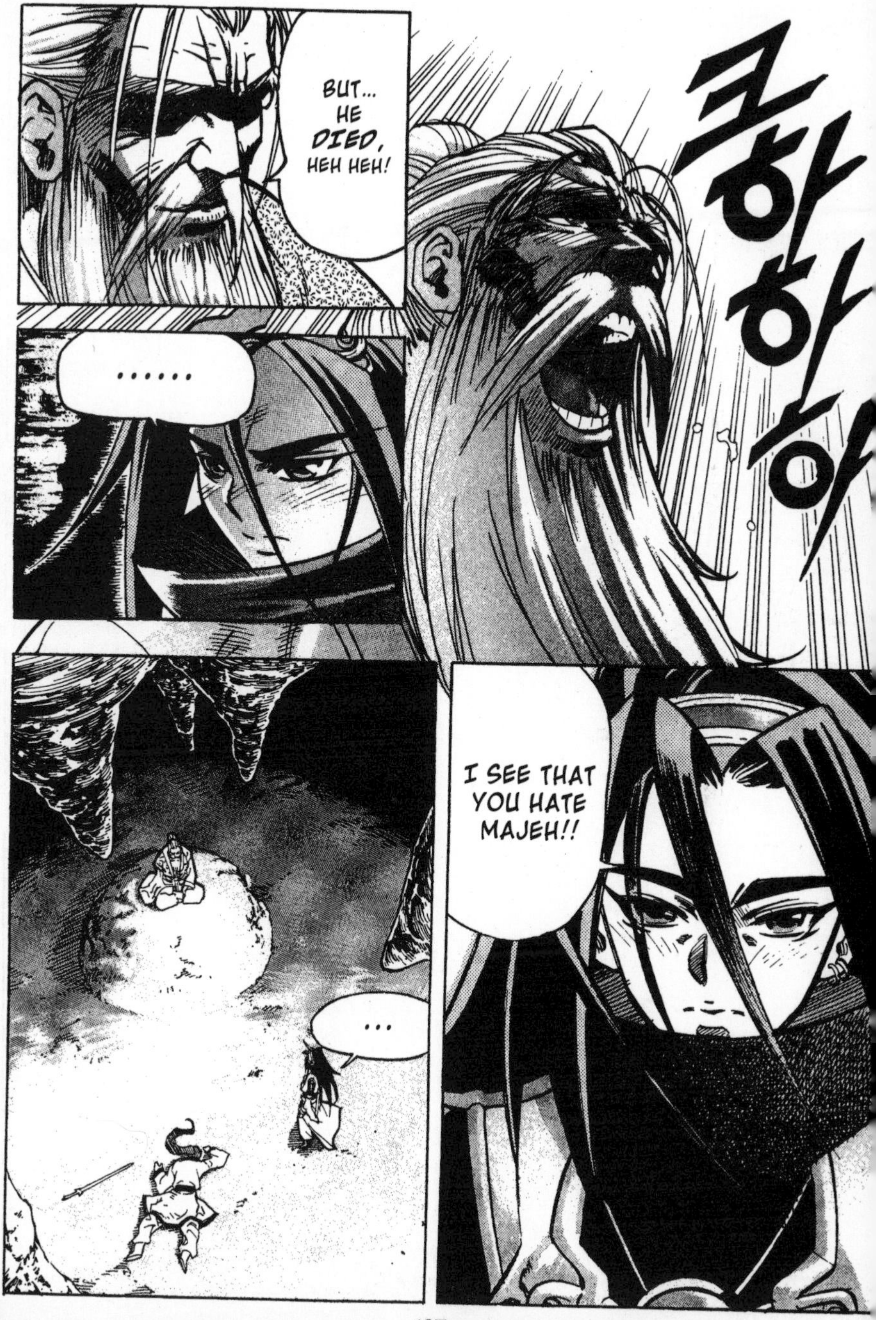
BUT... HE DIED, HEH HEH!
크하하하
......
...
I SEE THAT YOU HATE MAJEH!!

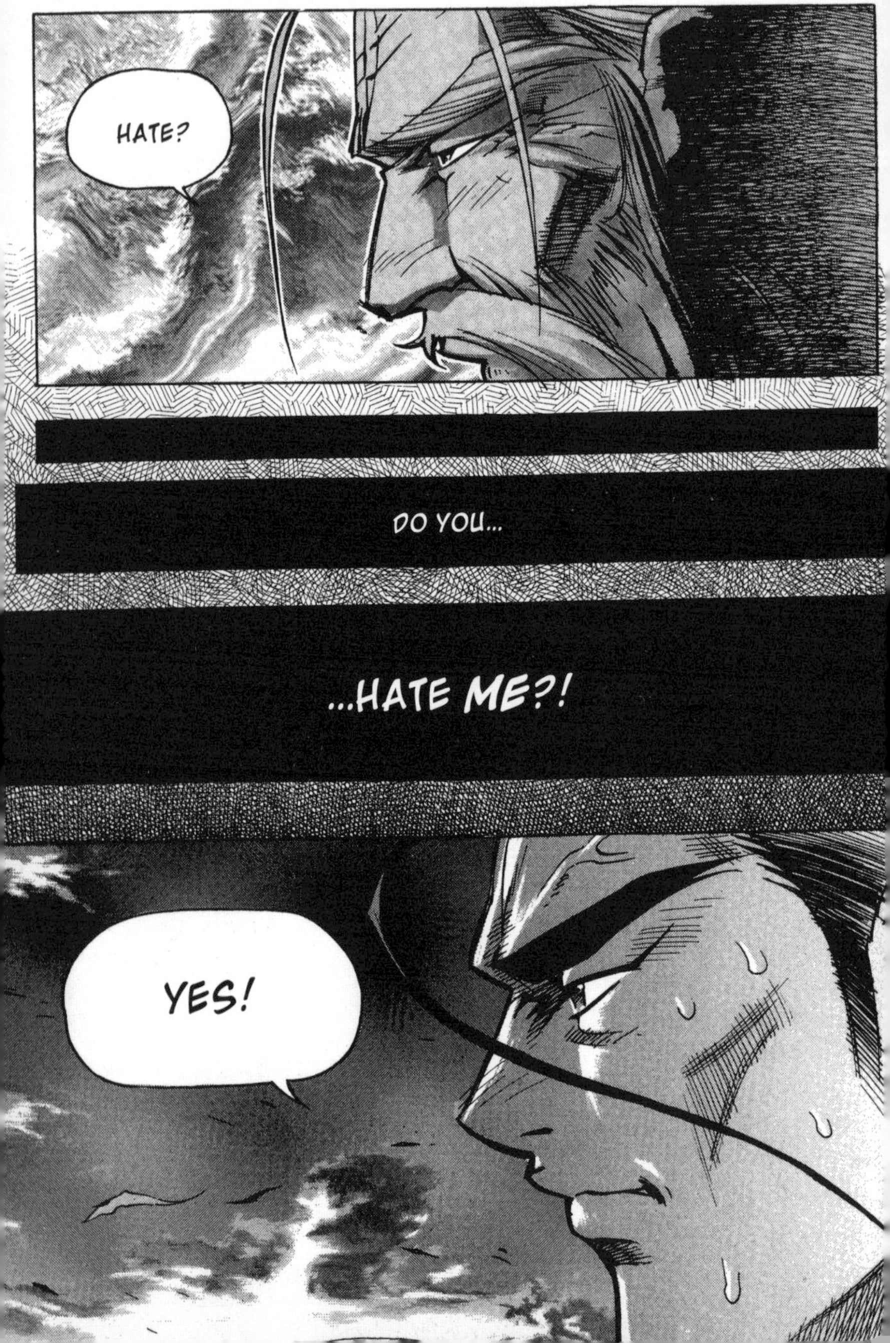
HATE?
DO YOU...
...HATE ME?!
YES!

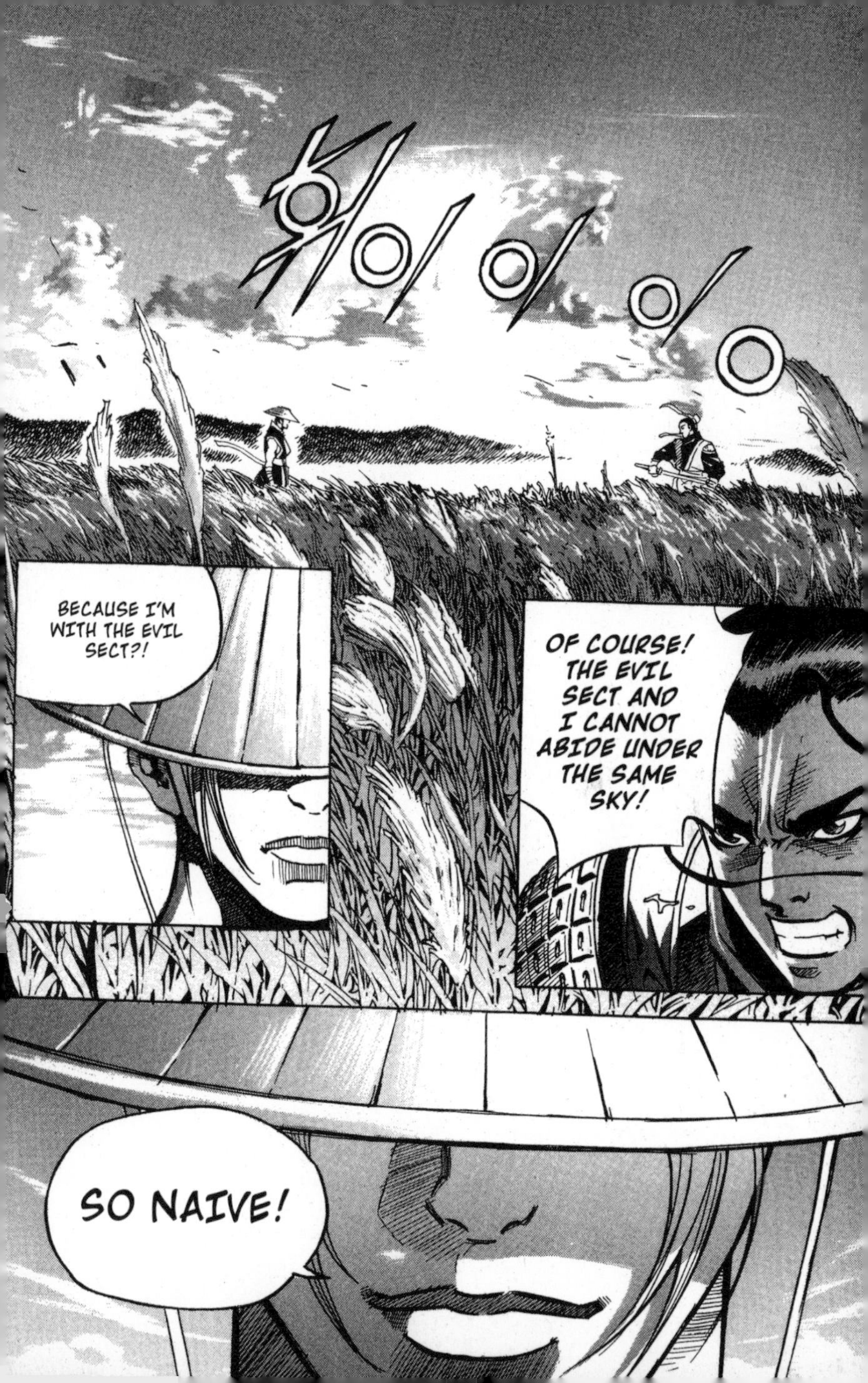
BECAUSE I'M WITH THE EVIL SECT?!
OF COURSE! THE EVIL SECT AND I CANNOT ABIDE UNDER THE SAME SKY!
SO NAIVE!

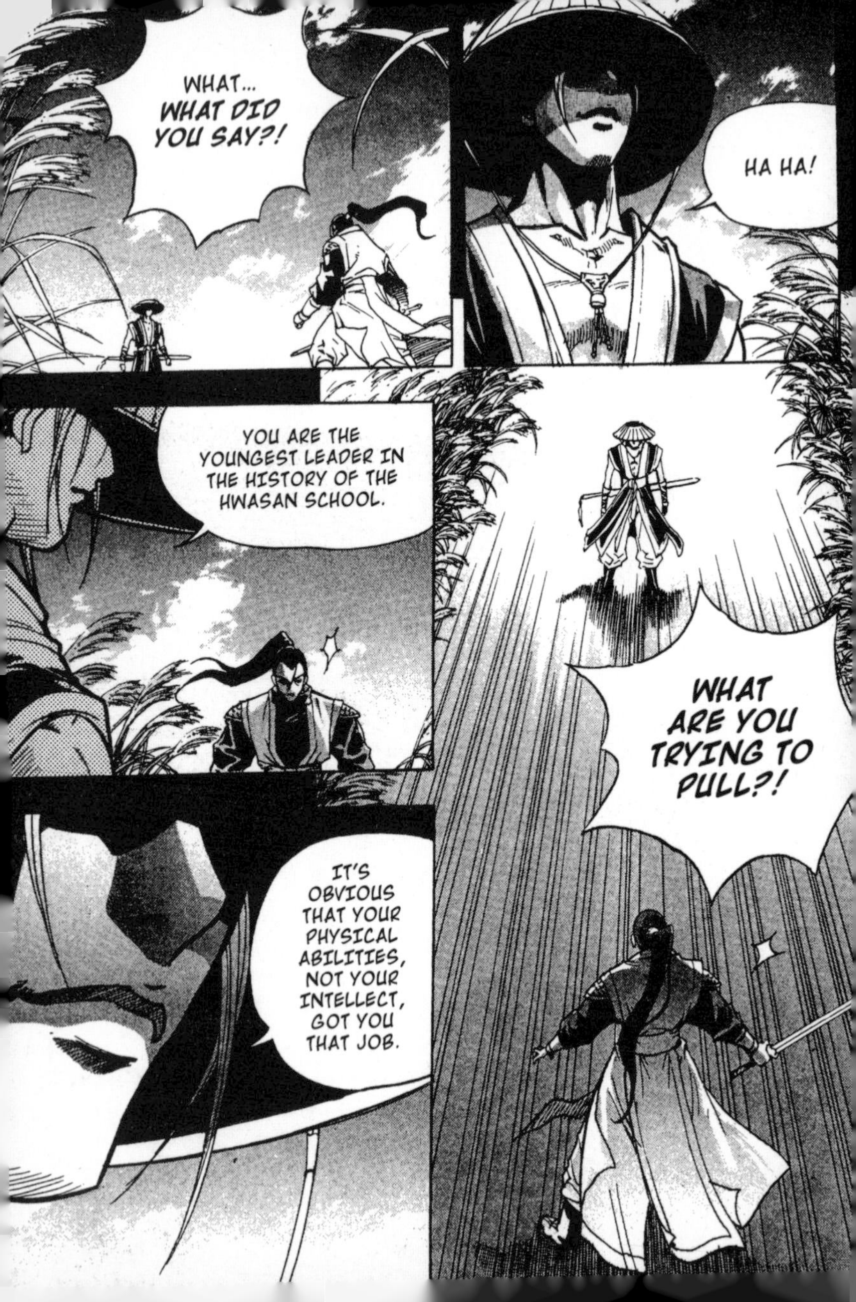
WHAT... WHAT DID YOU SAY?!
HA HA!
YOU ARE THE YOUNGEST LEADER IN THE HISTORY OF THE HWASAN SCHOOL.
IT'S OBVIOUS THAT YOUR PHYSICAL ABILITIES, NOT YOUR INTELLECT, GOT YOU THAT JOB.
WHAT ARE YOU TRYING TO PULL?!

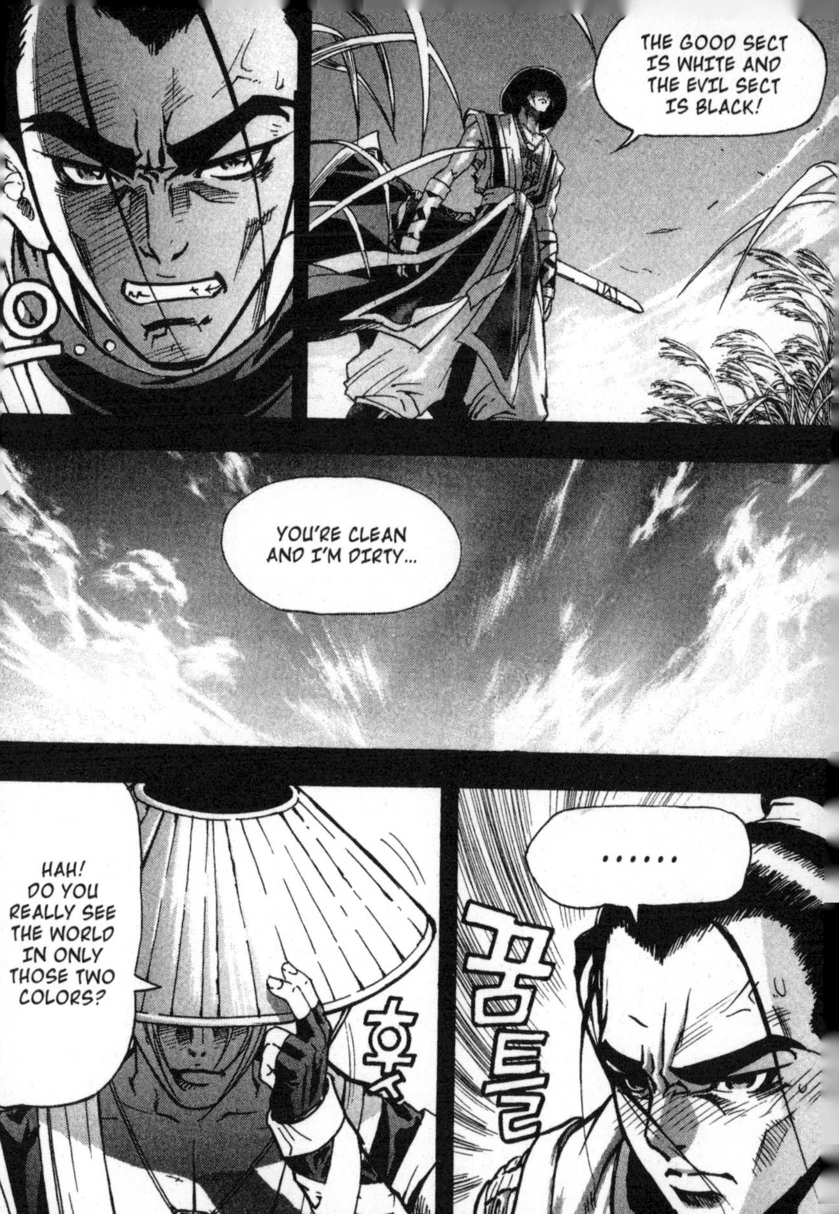
THE GOOD SECT IS WHITE AND THE EVIL SECT IS BLACK!
YOU'RE CLEAN AND I'M DIRTY...
HAH! DO YOU REALLY SEE THE WORLD IN ONLY THOSE TWO COLORS?
훗
......
꿈틀

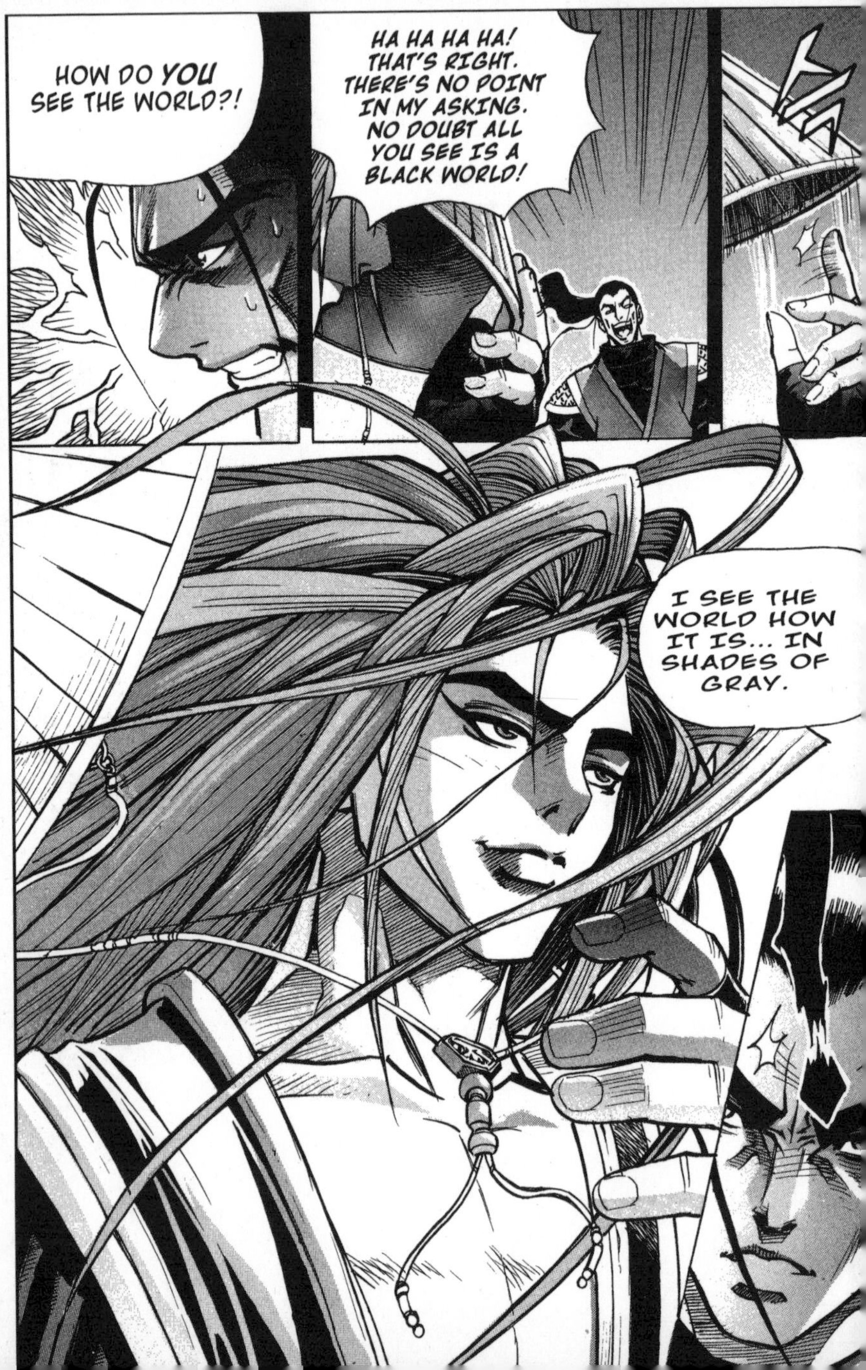
HOW DO YOU SEE THE WORLD?!
HA HA HA HA! THAT'S RIGHT. THERE'S NO POINT IN MY ASKING. NO DOUBT ALL YOU SEE IS A BLACK WORLD!
I SEE THE WORLD HOW IT IS... IN SHADES OF GRAY.

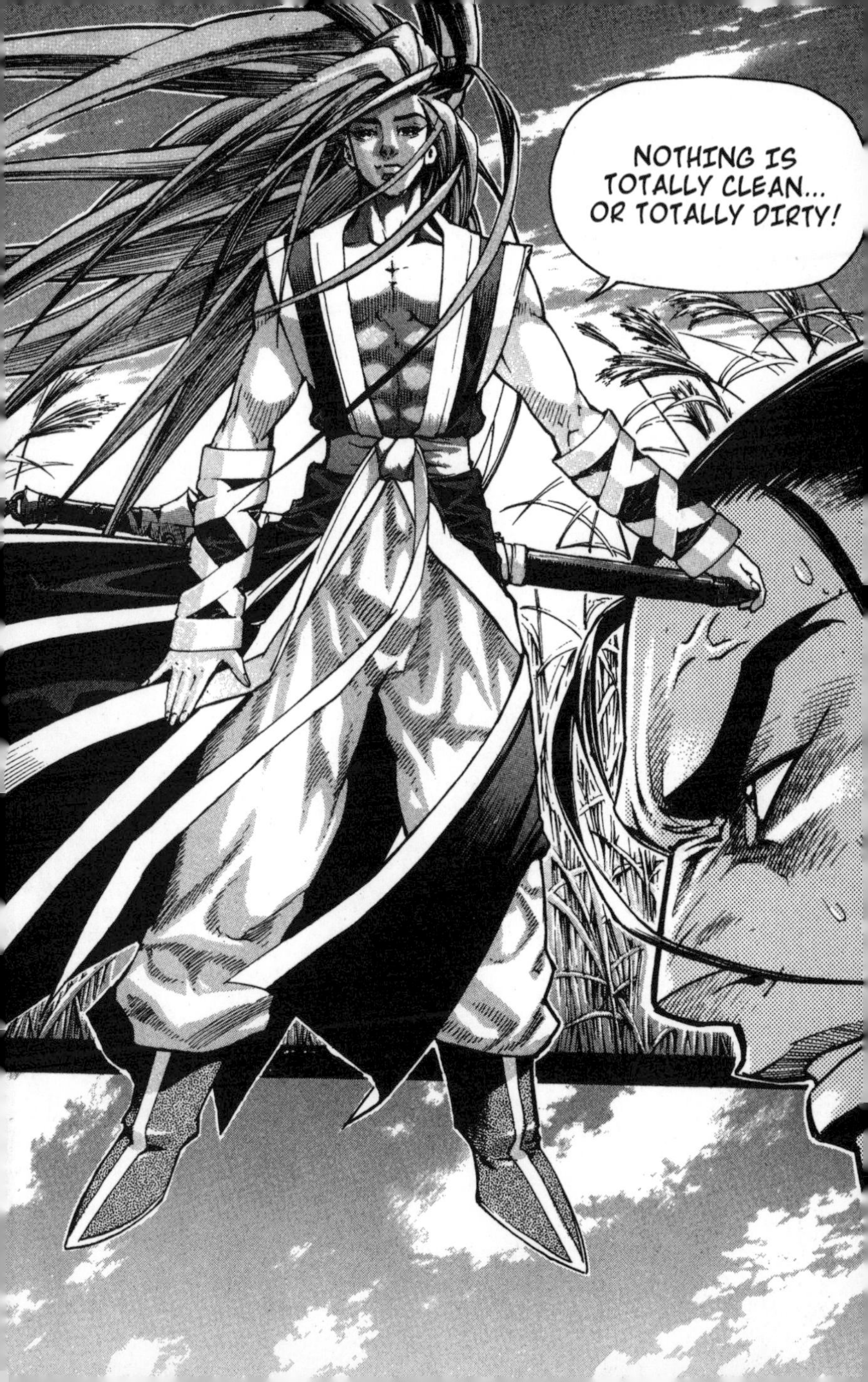
NOTHING IS TOTALLY CLEAN... OR TOTALLY DIRTY!

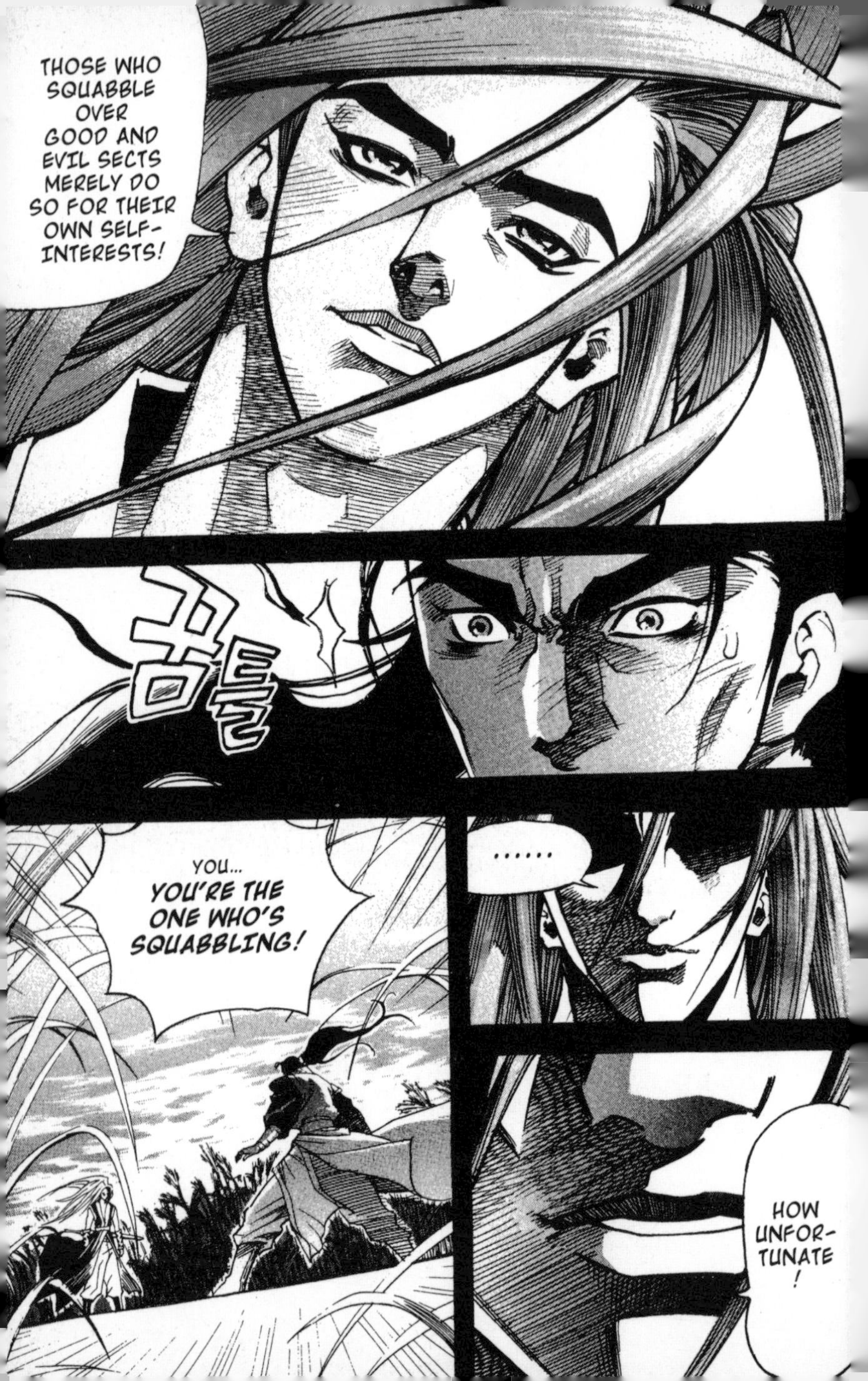
THOSE WHO SQUABBLE OVER GOOD AND EVIL SECTS MERELY DO SO FOR THEIR OWN SELF-INTERESTS!
꿈틀
YOU... ***YOU'RE THE ONE WHO'S SQUABBLING!***
......
HOW UNFOR-TUNATE!

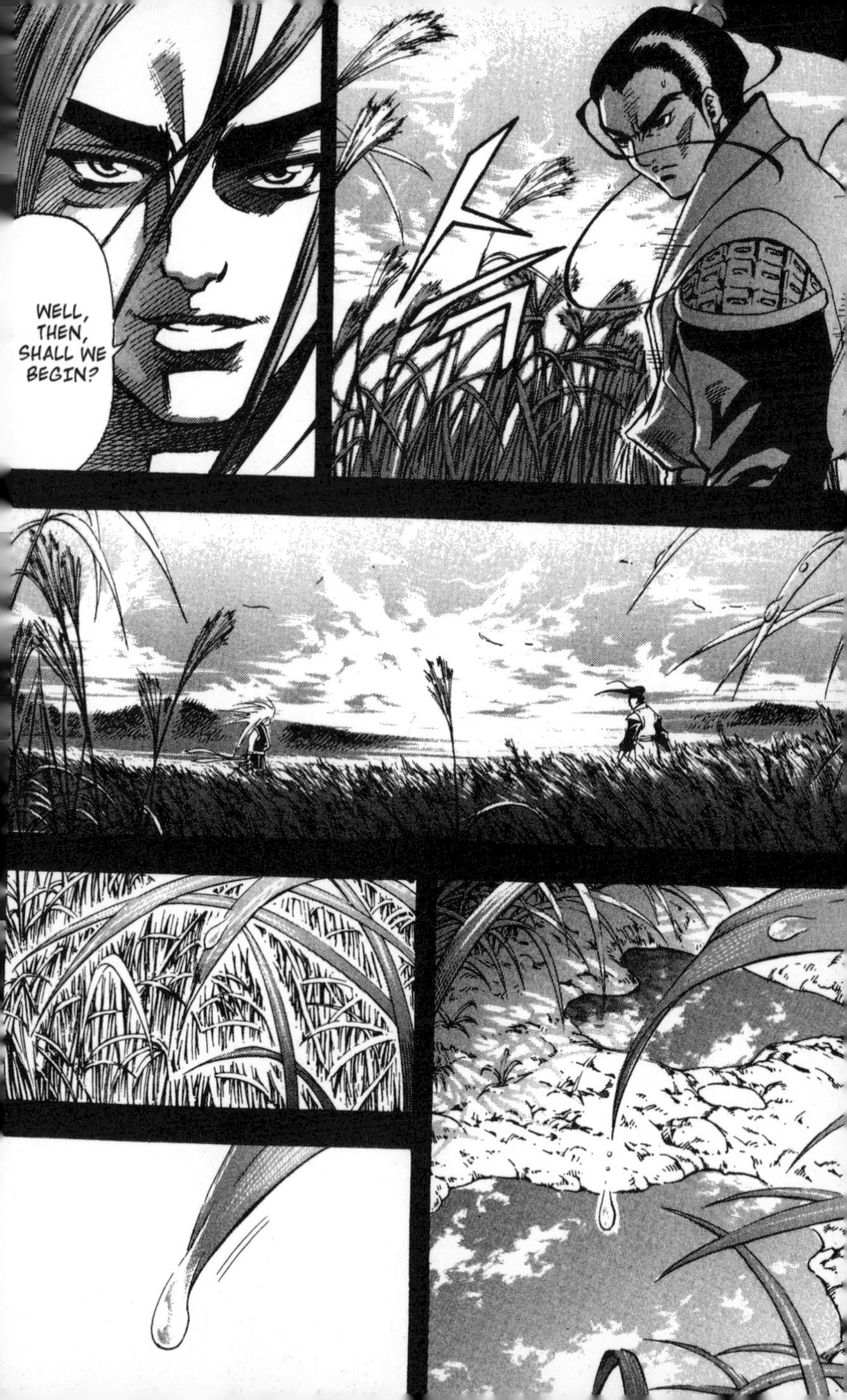
WELL, THEN, SHALL WE BEGIN?

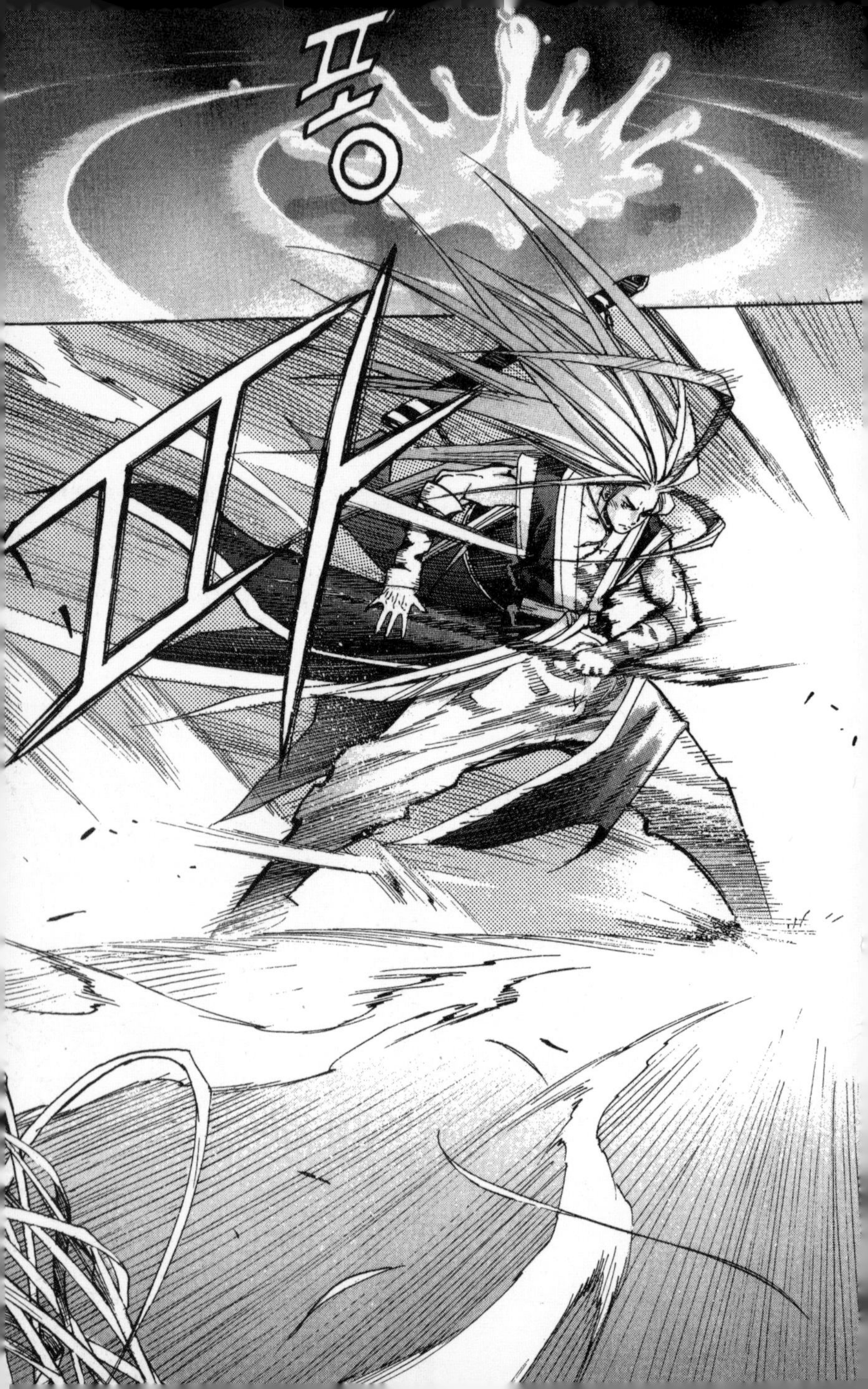
퐁

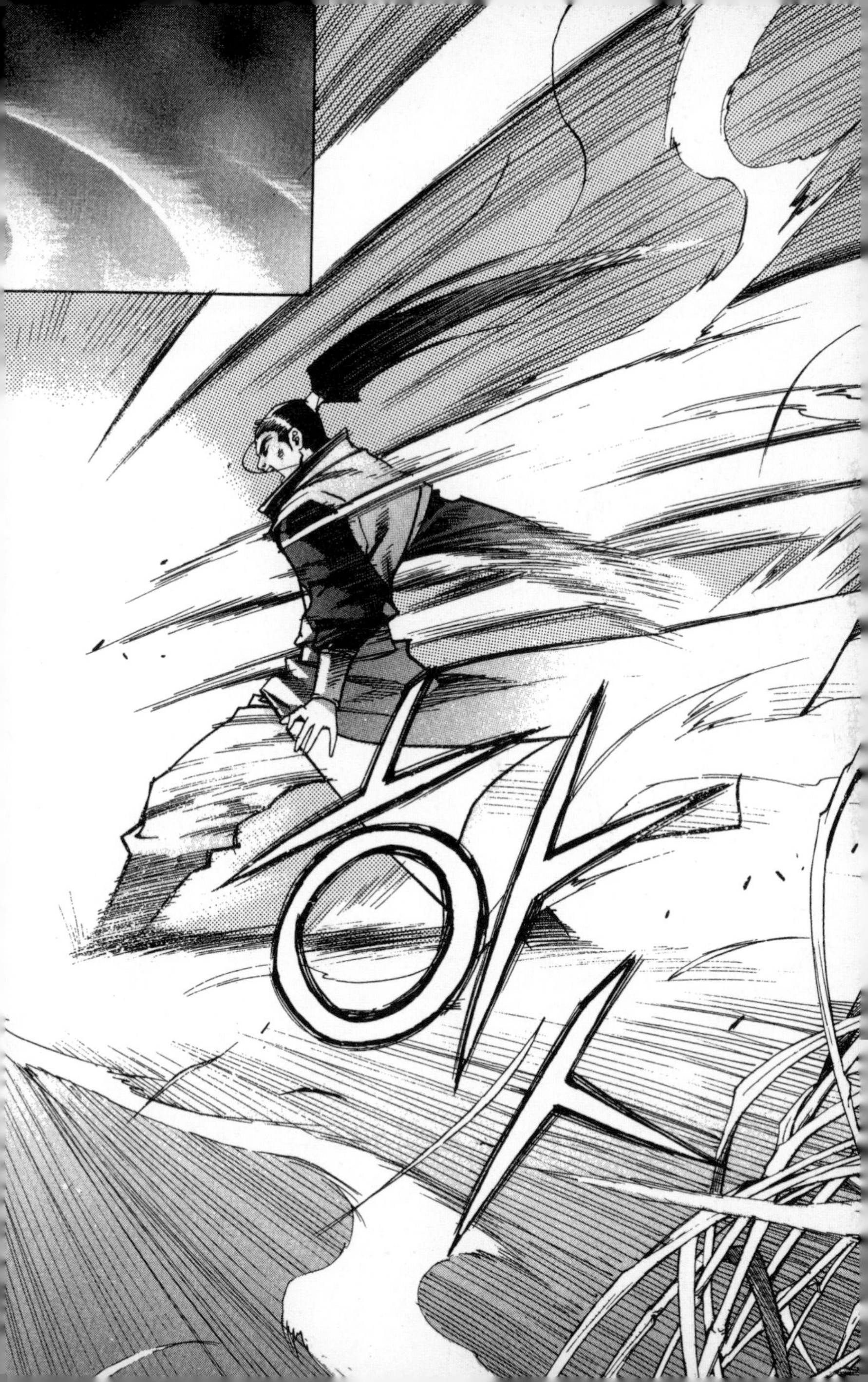

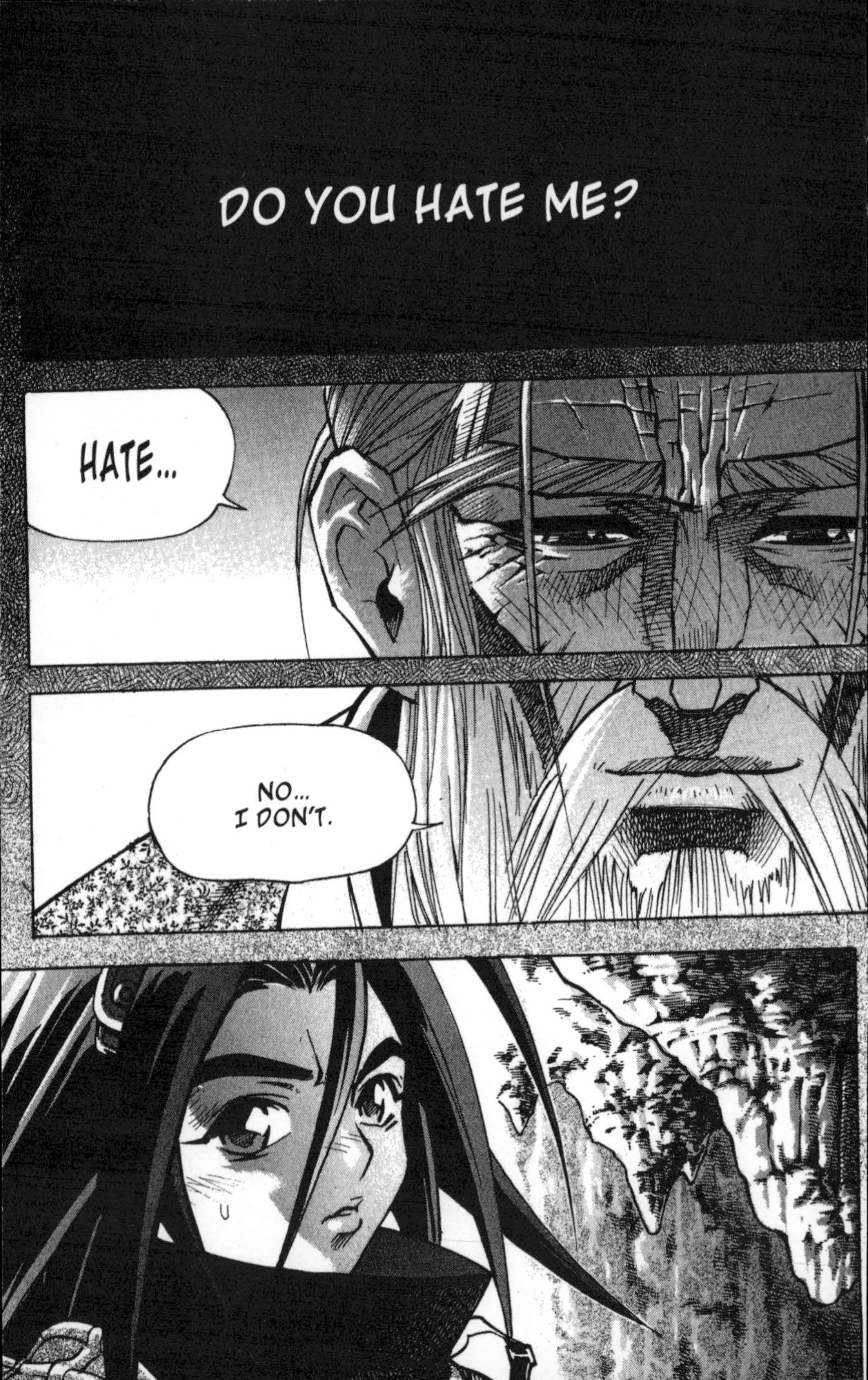
DO YOU HATE ME?
HATE...
NO...
I DON'T.

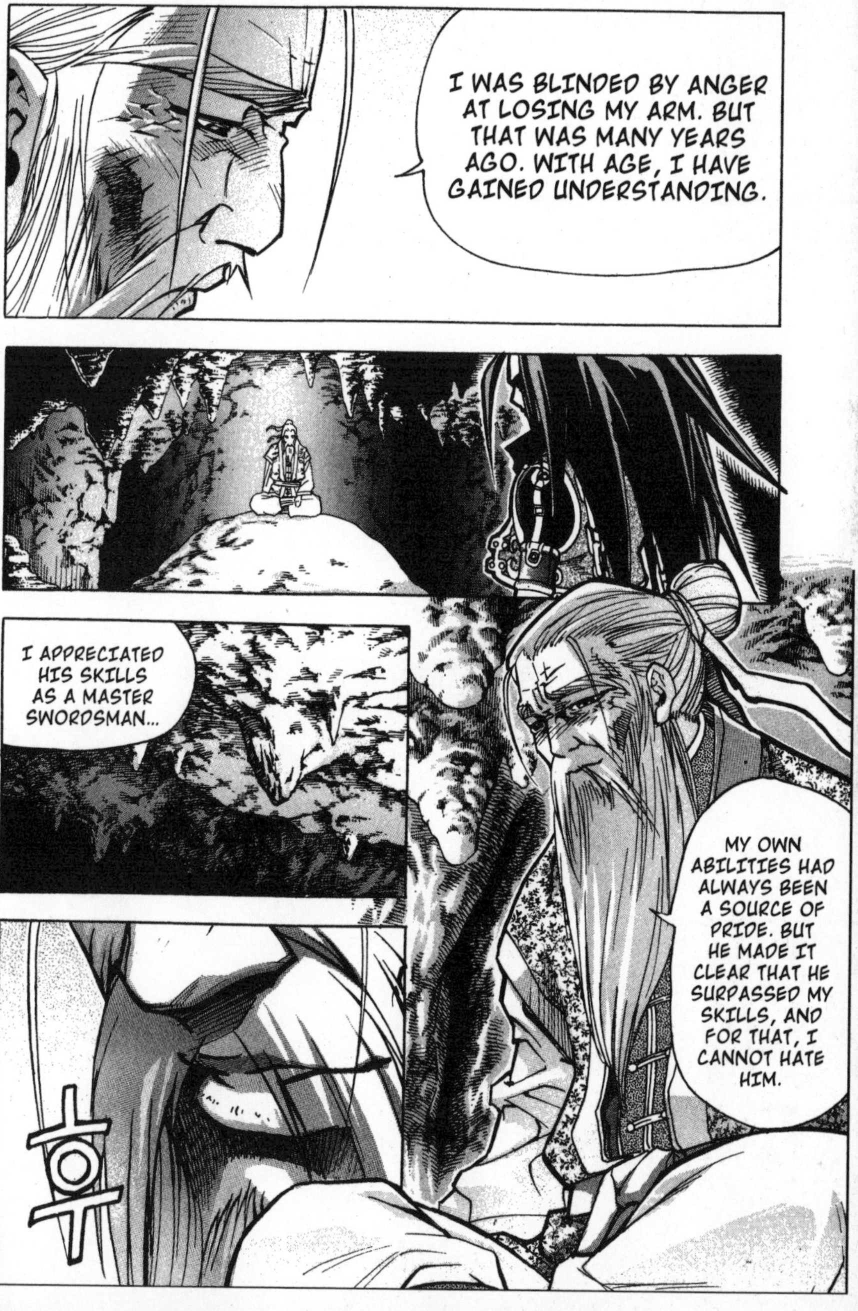
I WAS BLINDED BY ANGER AT LOSING MY ARM. BUT THAT WAS MANY YEARS AGO. WITH AGE, I HAVE GAINED UNDERSTANDING.
I APPRECIATED HIS SKILLS AS A MASTER SWORDSMAN...
MY OWN ABILITIES HAD ALWAYS BEEN A SOURCE OF PRIDE. BUT HE MADE IT CLEAR THAT HE SURPASSED MY SKILLS, AND FOR THAT, I CANNOT HATE HIM.

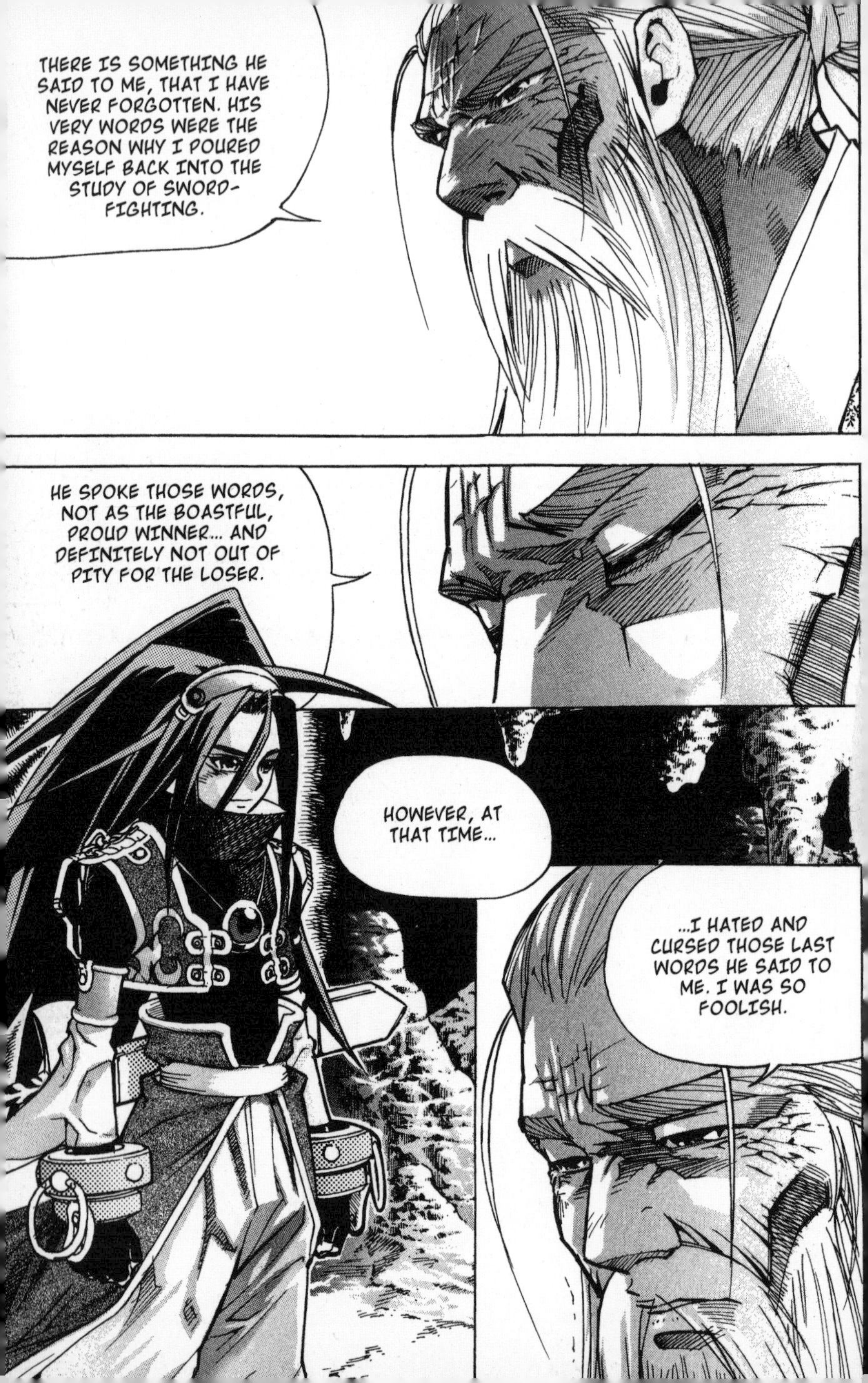
THERE IS SOMETHING HE SAID TO ME, THAT I HAVE NEVER FORGOTTEN. HIS VERY WORDS WERE THE REASON WHY I POURED MYSELF BACK INTO THE STUDY OF SWORD-FIGHTING.
HE SPOKE THOSE WORDS, NOT AS THE BOASTFUL, PROUD WINNER... AND DEFINITELY NOT OUT OF PITY FOR THE LOSER.
HOWEVER, AT THAT TIME...
...I HATED AND CURSED THOSE LAST WORDS HE SAID TO ME. I WAS SO FOOLISH.

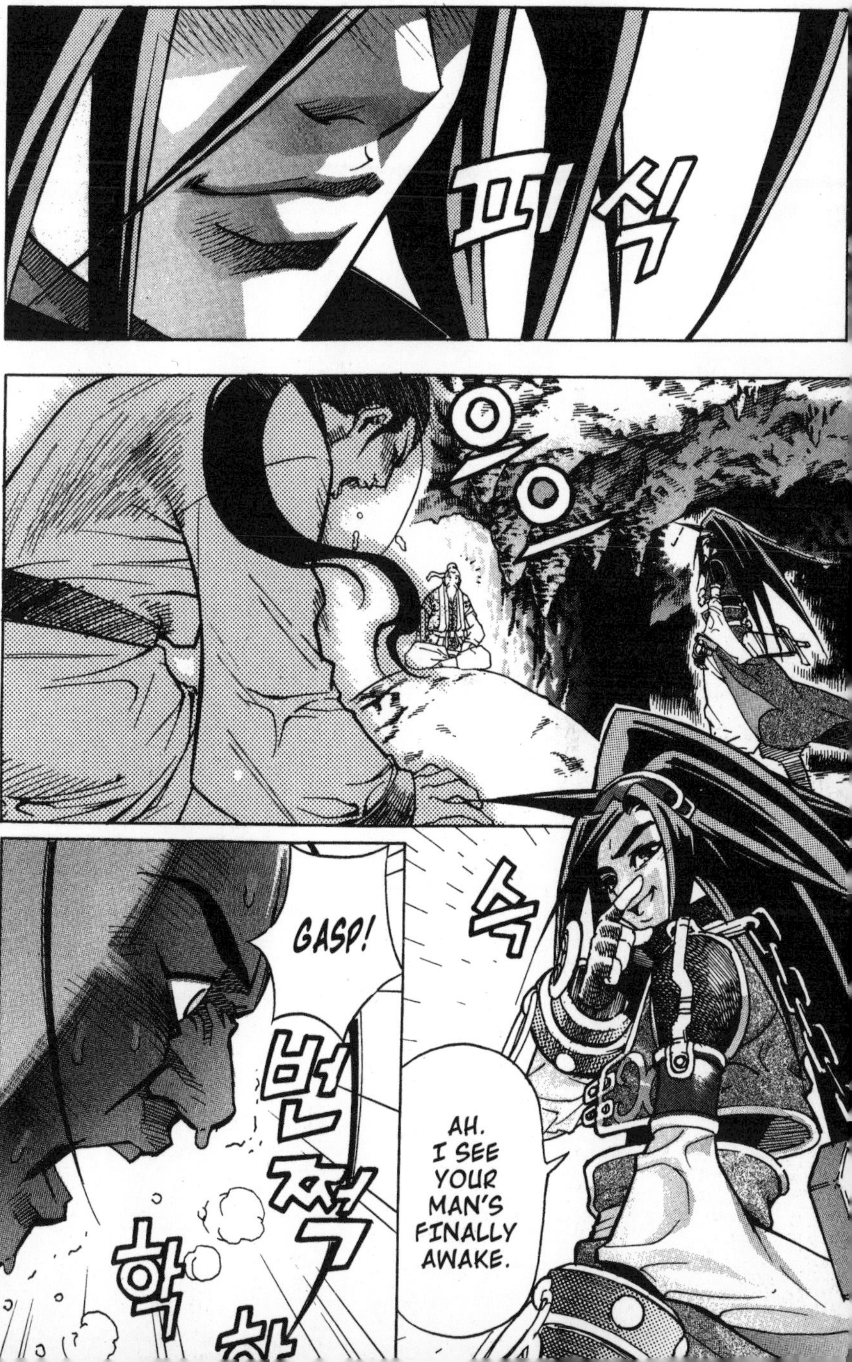
피식
으으
GASP!
번쩍
헉
슥
AH. I SEE YOUR MAN'S FINALLY AWAKE.

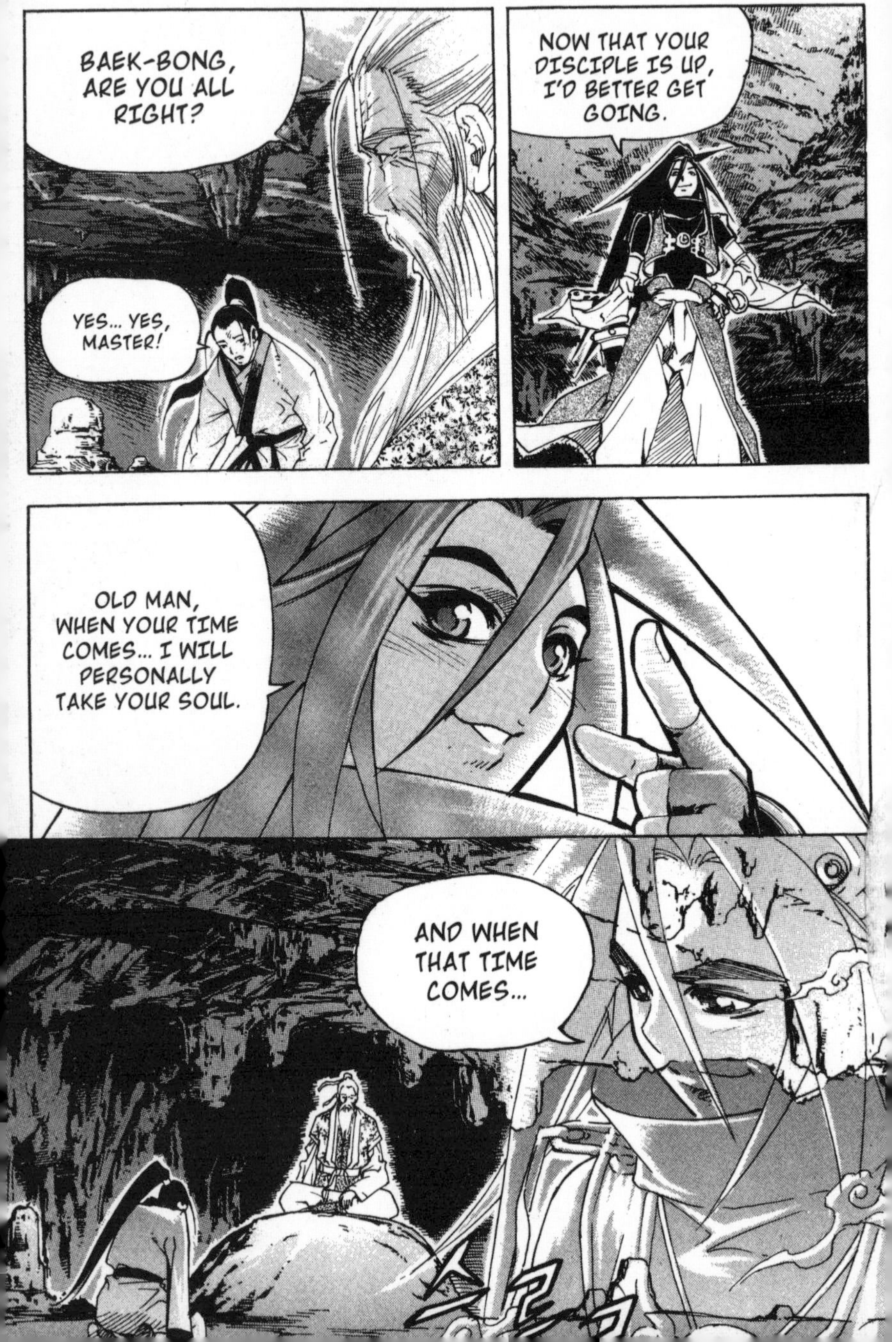
BAEK-BONG, ARE YOU ALL RIGHT?
YES... YES, MASTER!
NOW THAT YOUR DISCIPLE IS UP, I'D BETTER GET GOING.
OLD MAN, WHEN YOUR TIME COMES... I WILL PERSONALLY TAKE YOUR SOUL.
AND WHEN THAT TIME COMES...

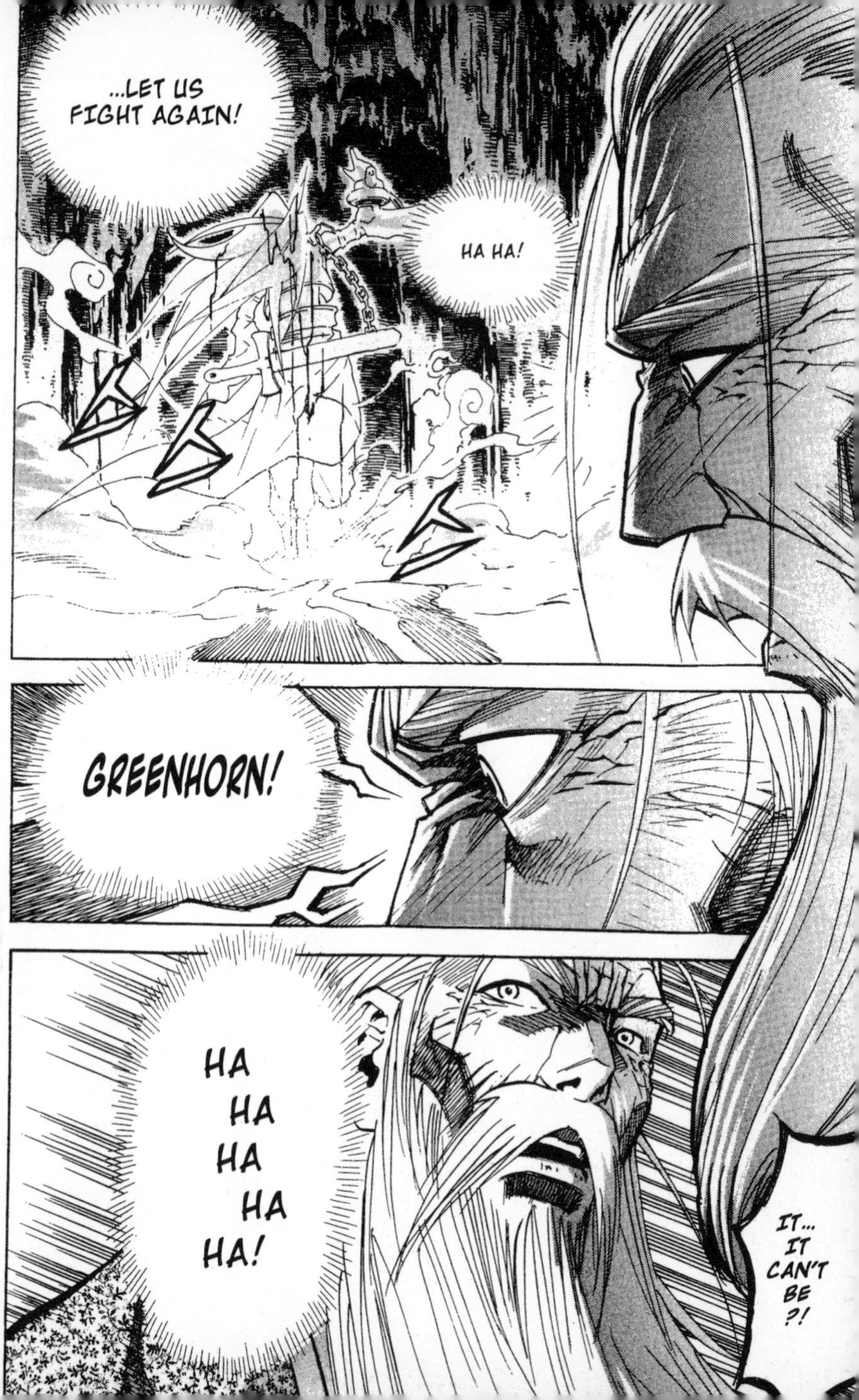
...LET US FIGHT AGAIN!
HA HA!
GREENHORN!
HA HA HA HA HA!
IT... IT CAN'T BE?!

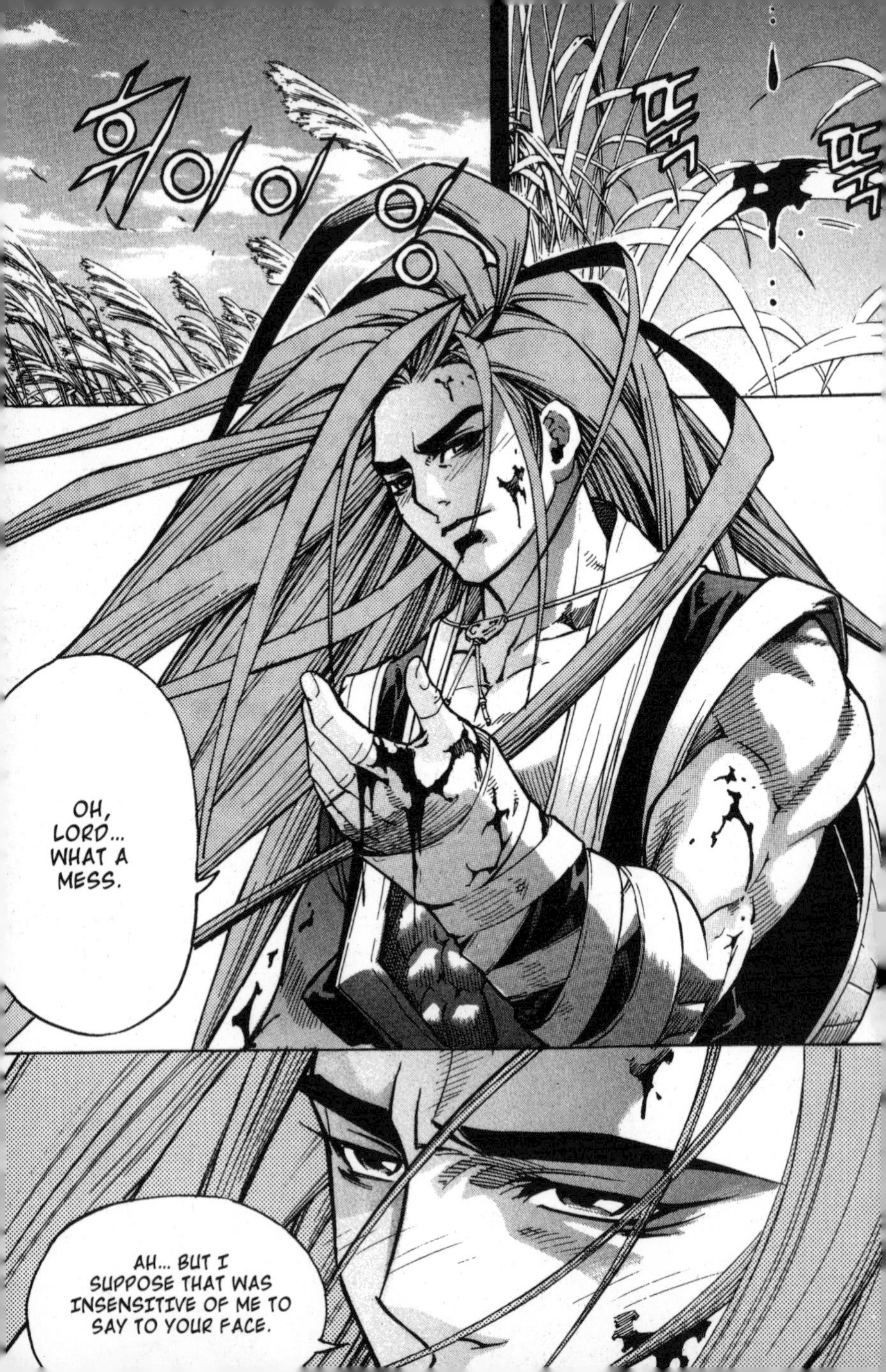

휘이이잉
뚝
뚝
OH, LORD... WHAT A MESS.
AH... BUT I SUPPOSE THAT WAS INSENSITIVE OF ME TO SAY TO YOUR FACE.

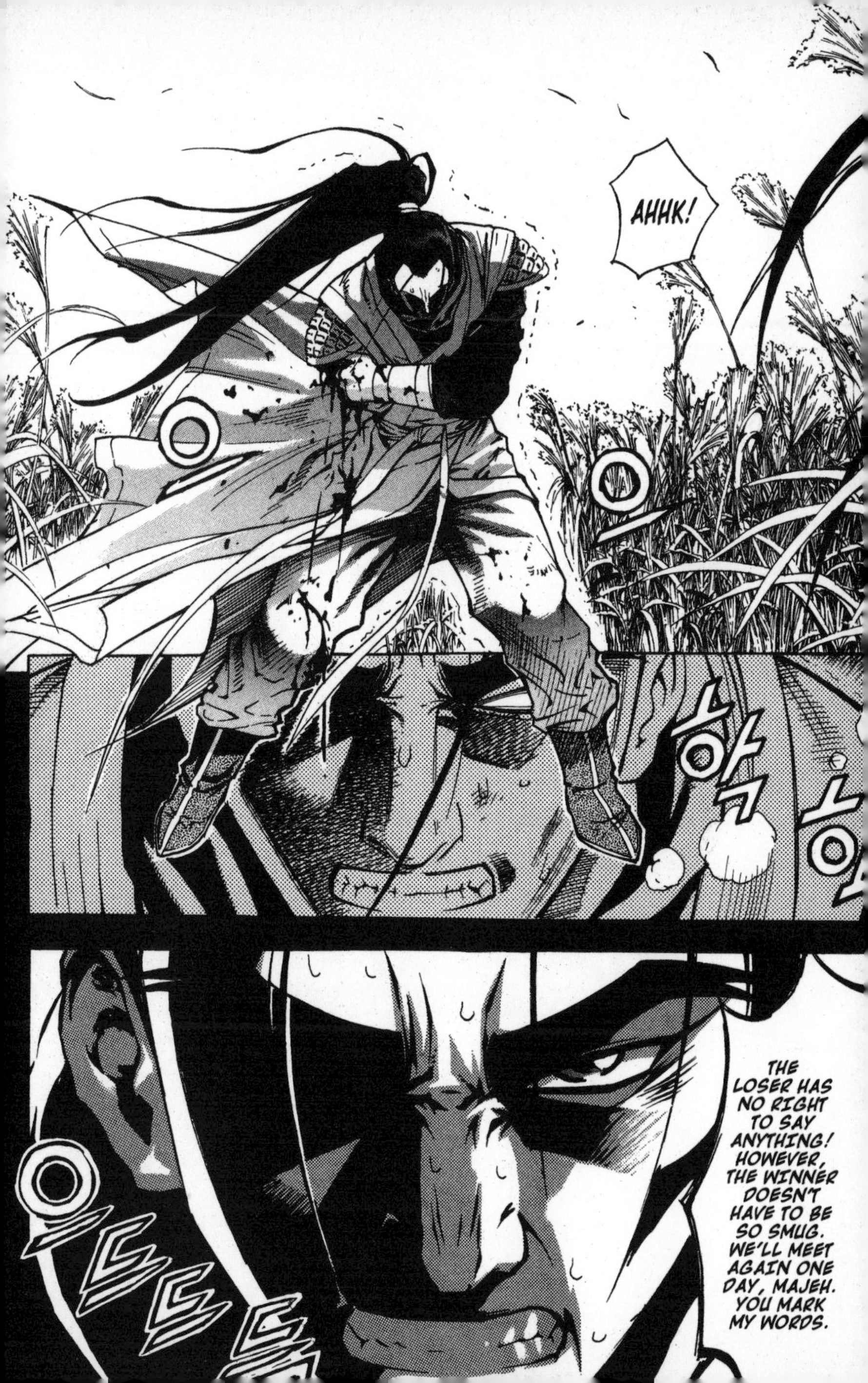
AHHK!
THE LOSER HAS NO RIGHT TO SAY ANYTHING! HOWEVER, THE WINNER DOESN'T HAVE TO BE SO SMUG. WE'LL MEET AGAIN ONE DAY, MAJEH. YOU MARK MY WORDS.

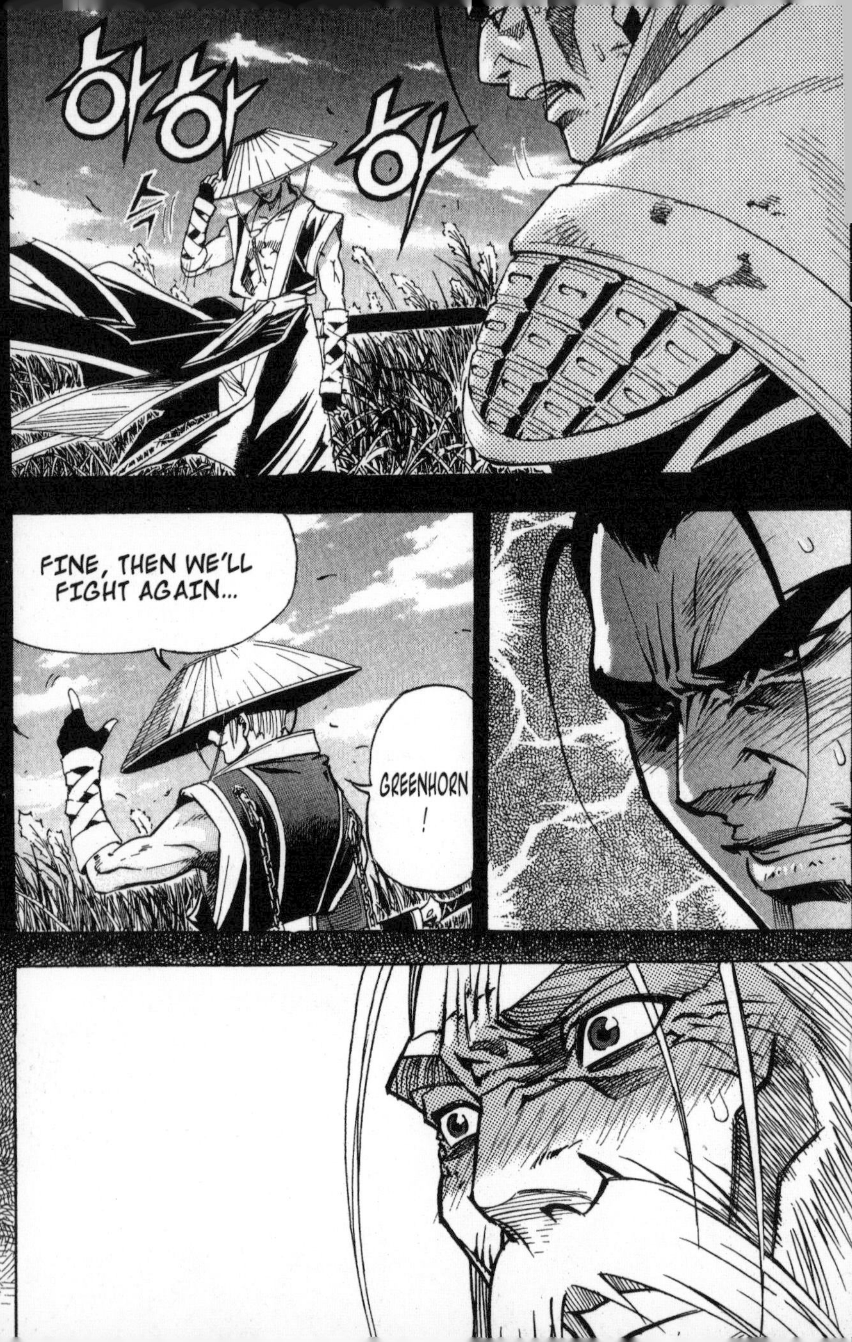
하하
하
FINE, THEN WE'LL FIGHT AGAIN...
GREENHORN!

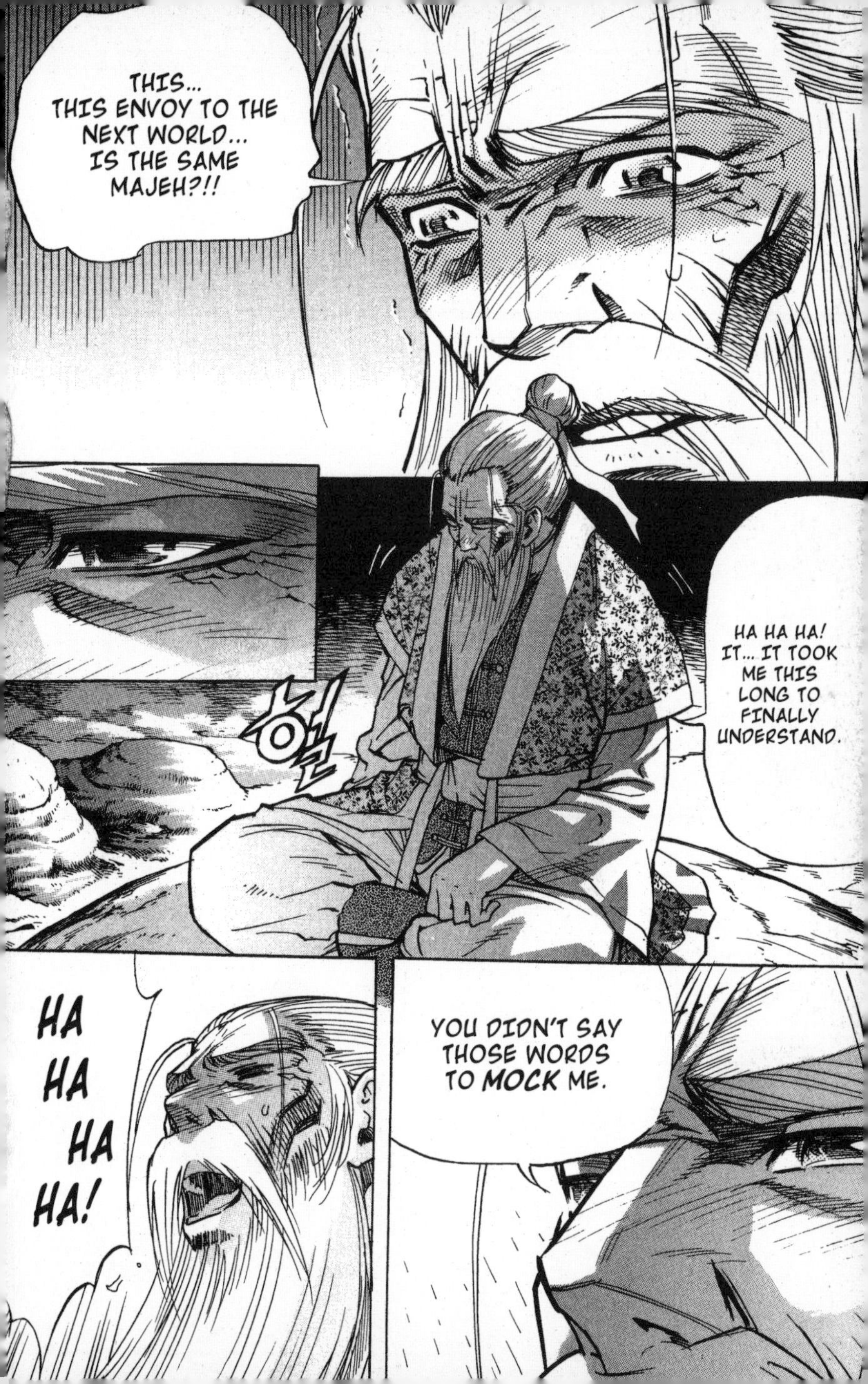
THIS... THIS ENVOY TO THE NEXT WORLD... IS THE SAME MAJEH?!!
HA HA HA! IT... IT TOOK ME THIS LONG TO FINALLY UNDERSTAND.
HA HA HA HA HA!
YOU DIDN'T SAY THOSE WORDS TO MOCK ME.

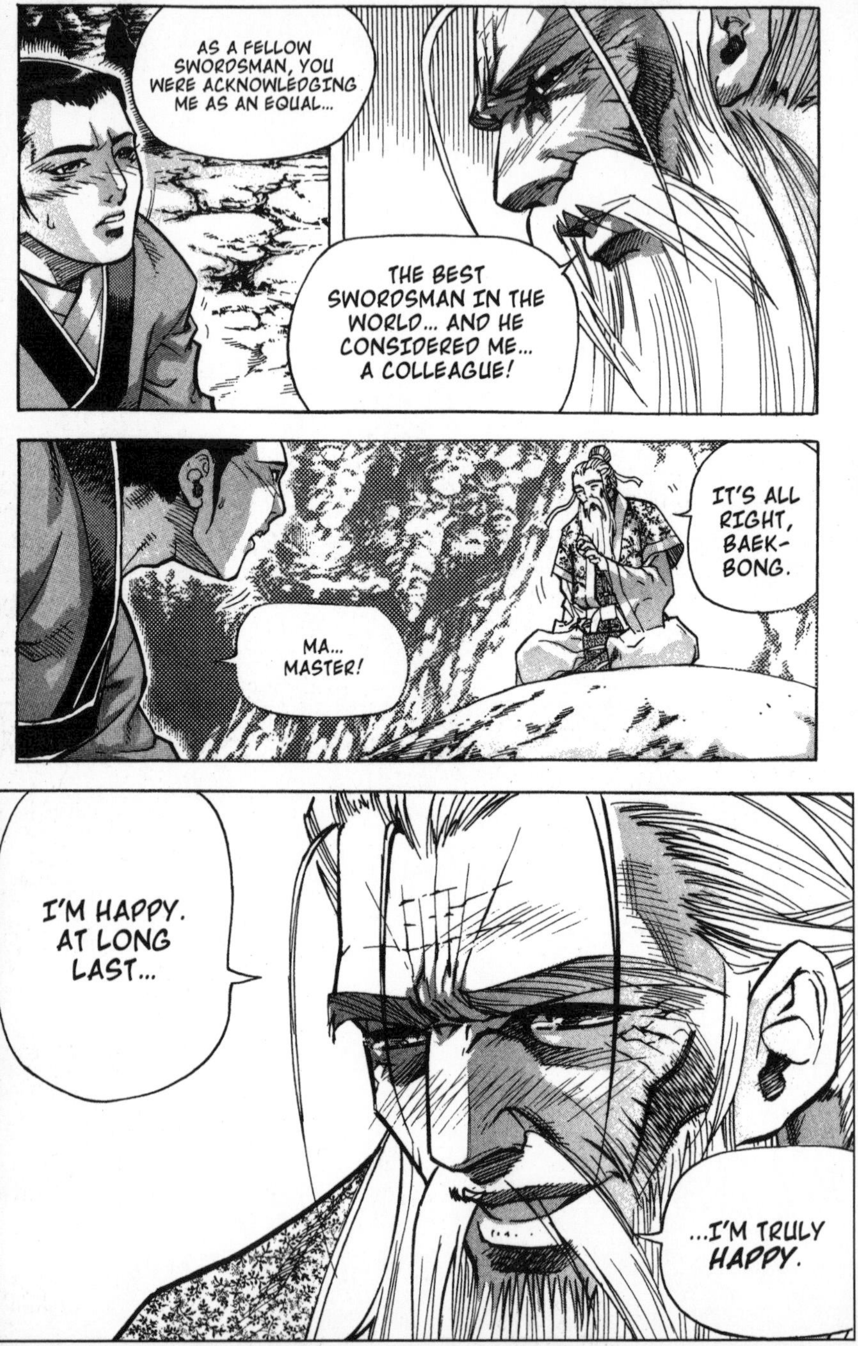
AS A FELLOW SWORDSMAN, YOU WERE ACKNOWLEDGING ME AS AN EQUAL...
THE BEST SWORDSMAN IN THE WORLD... AND HE CONSIDERED ME... A COLLEAGUE!
MA... MASTER!
IT'S ALL RIGHT, BAEK-BONG.
I'M HAPPY. AT LONG LAST...
...I'M TRULY HAPPY.

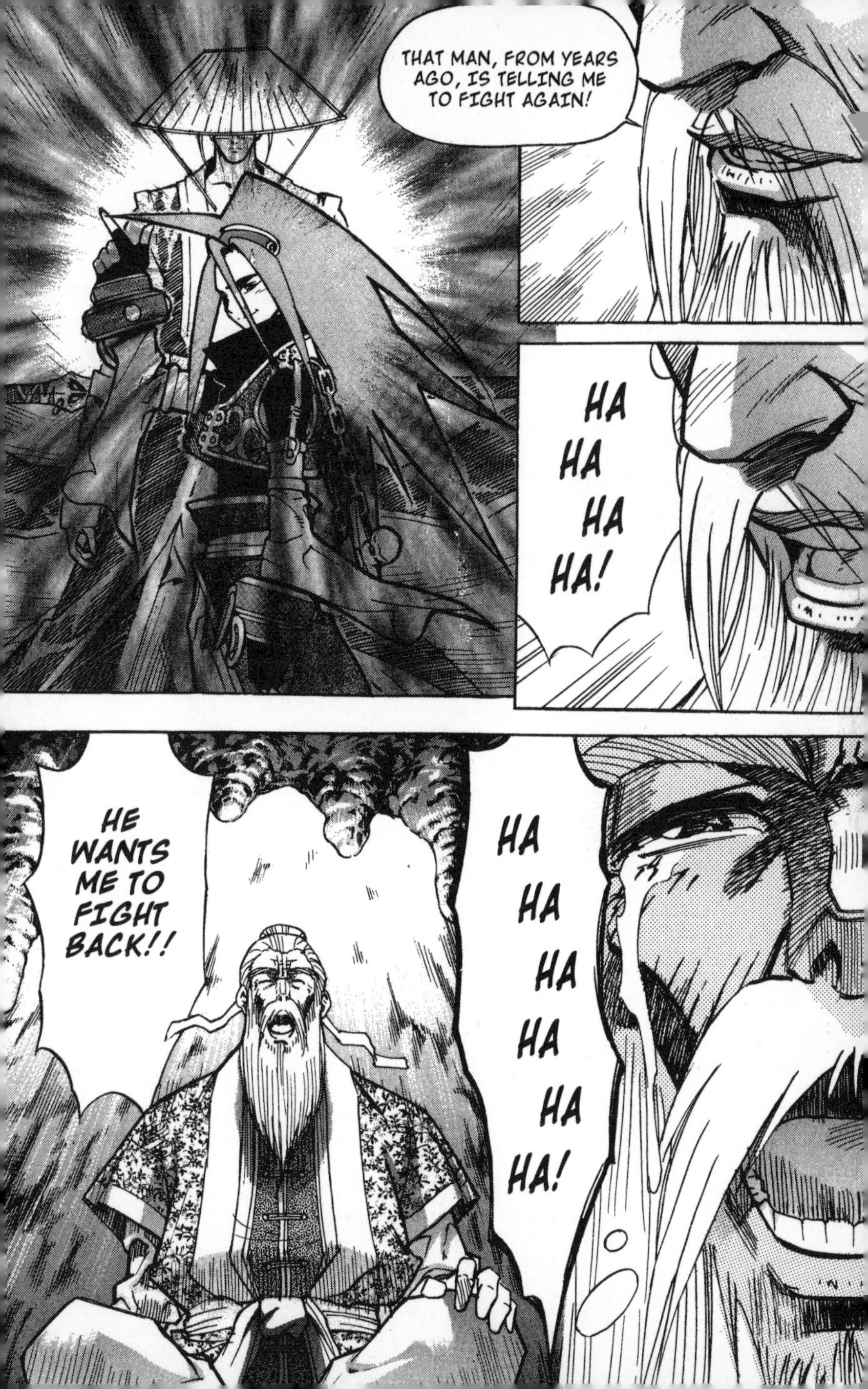
THAT MAN, FROM YEARS AGO, IS TELLING ME TO FIGHT AGAIN!
HA HA HA HA!
HE WANTS ME TO FIGHT BACK!!
HA HA HA HA HA HA HA!

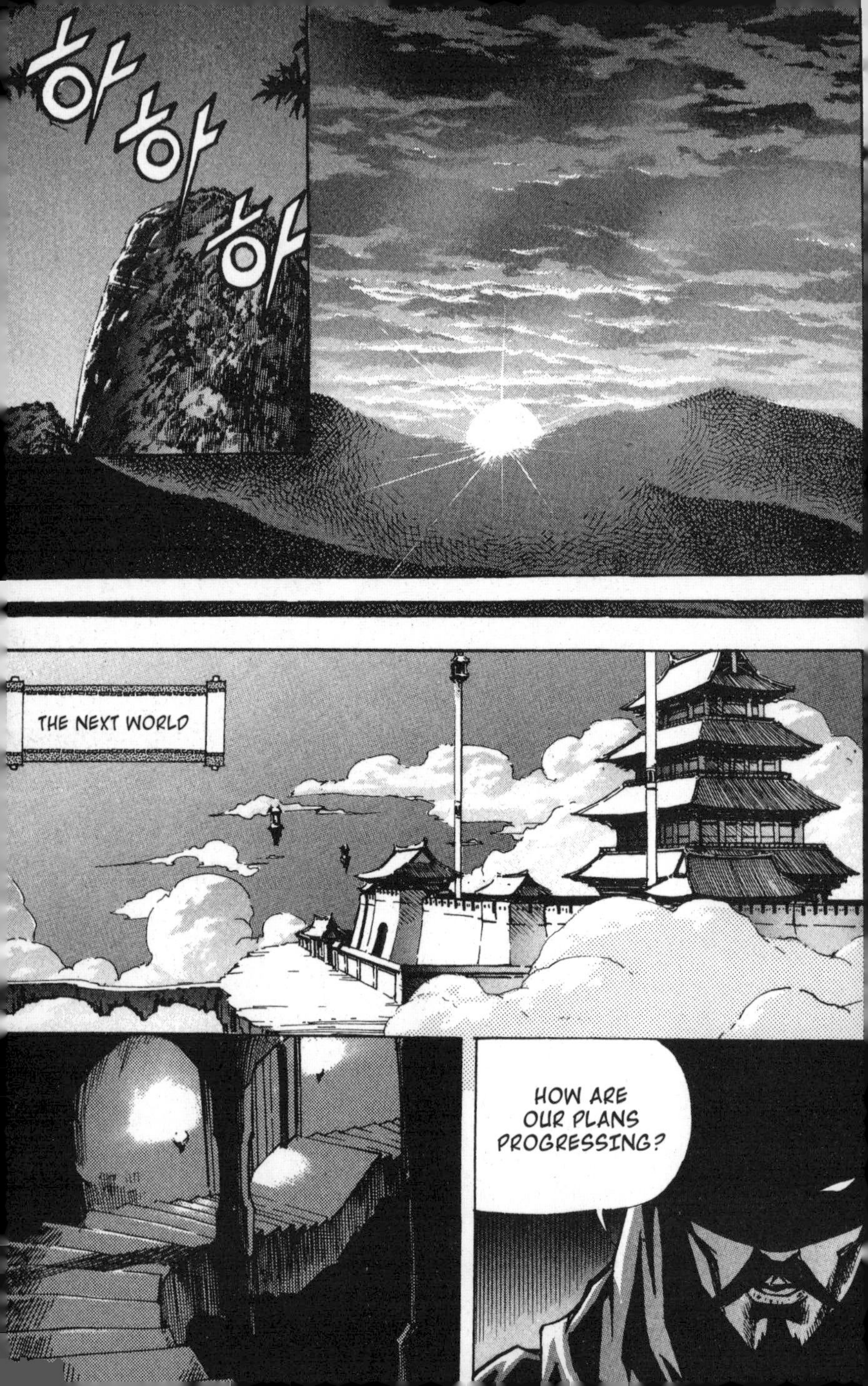
하하하
THE NEXT WORLD
HOW ARE OUR PLANS PROGRESSING?

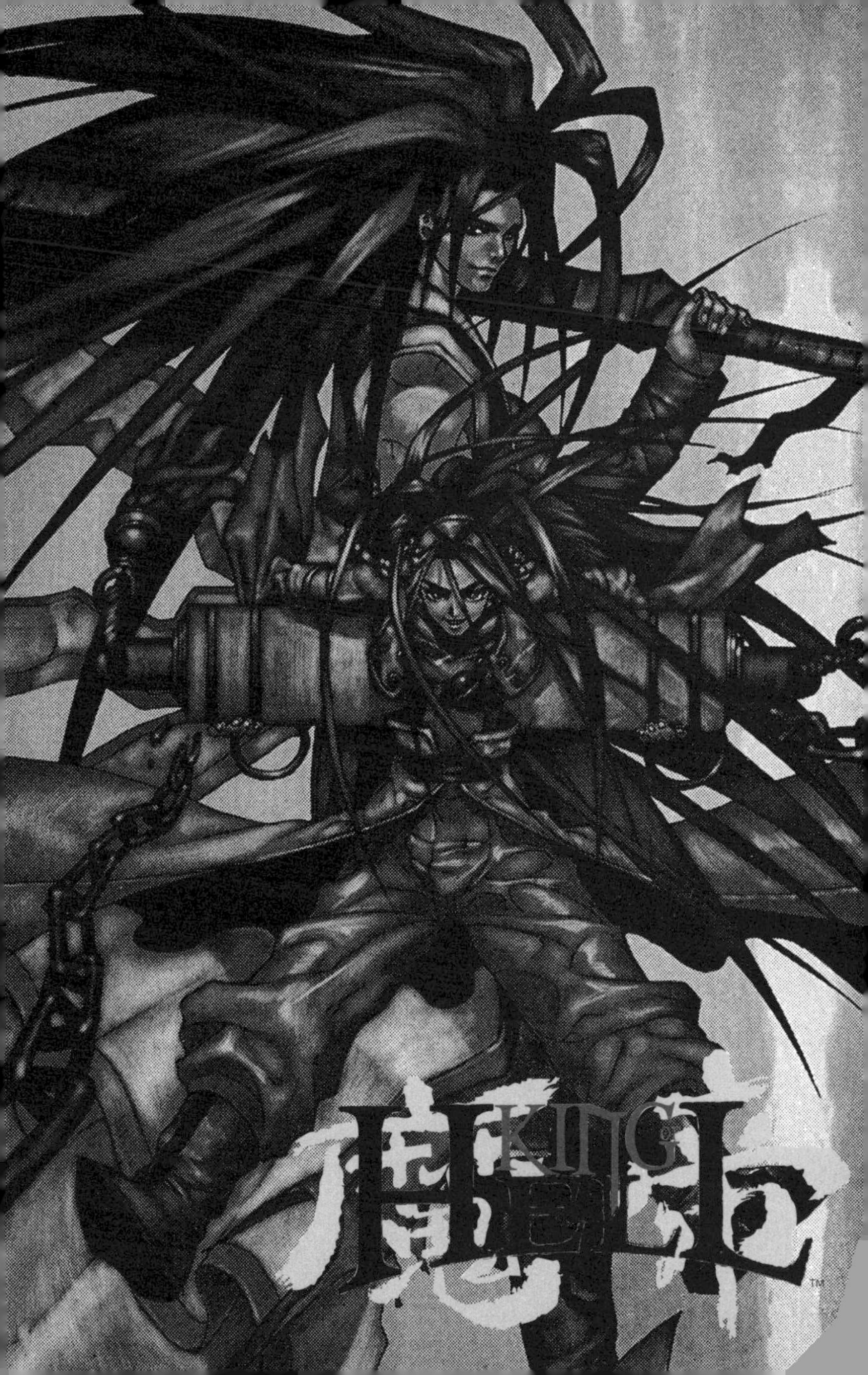
KING
HELL

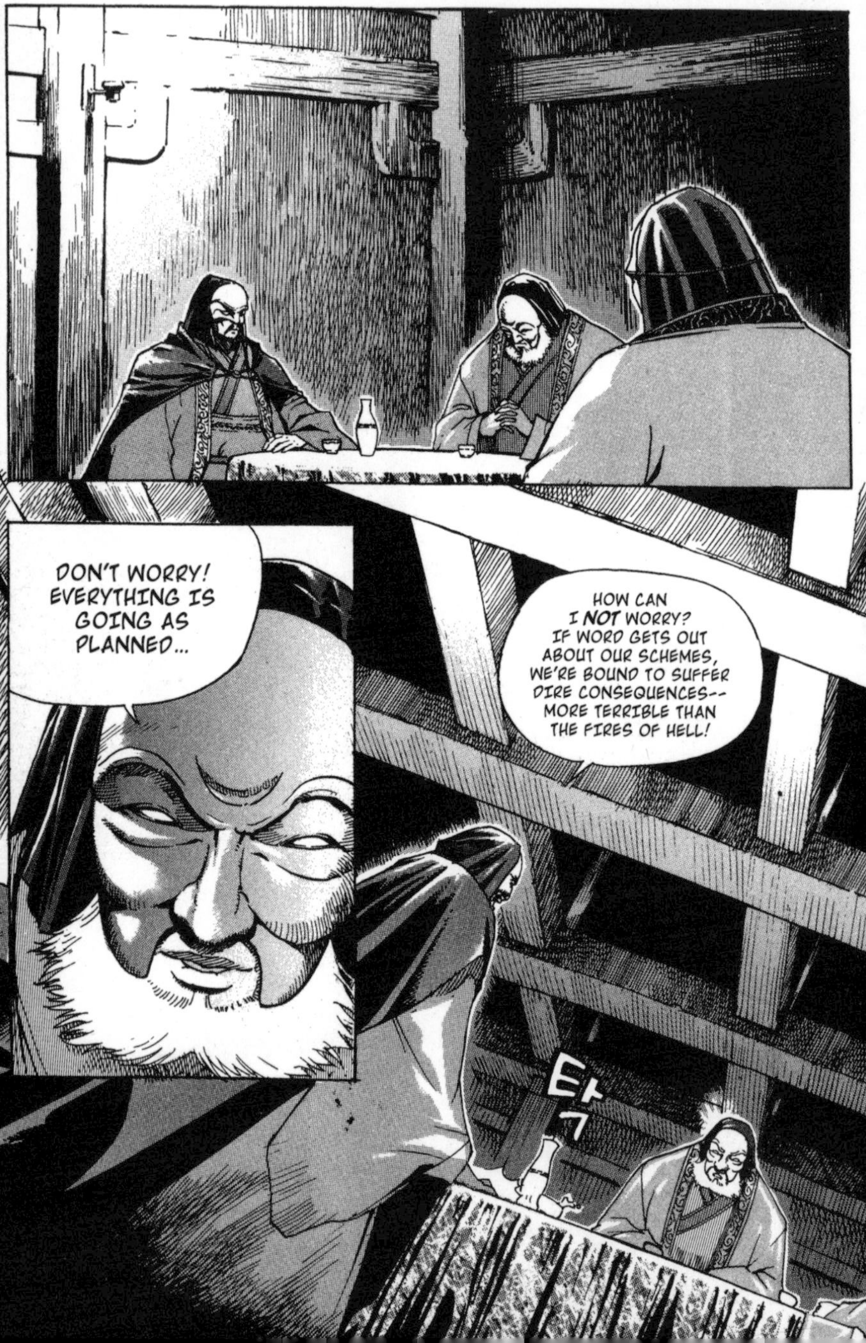
DON'T WORRY! EVERYTHING IS GOING AS PLANNED...
HOW CAN I **NOT** WORRY? IF WORD GETS OUT ABOUT OUR SCHEMES, WE'RE BOUND TO SUFFER DIRE CONSEQUENCES-- MORE TERRIBLE THAN THE FIRES OF HELL!
탁

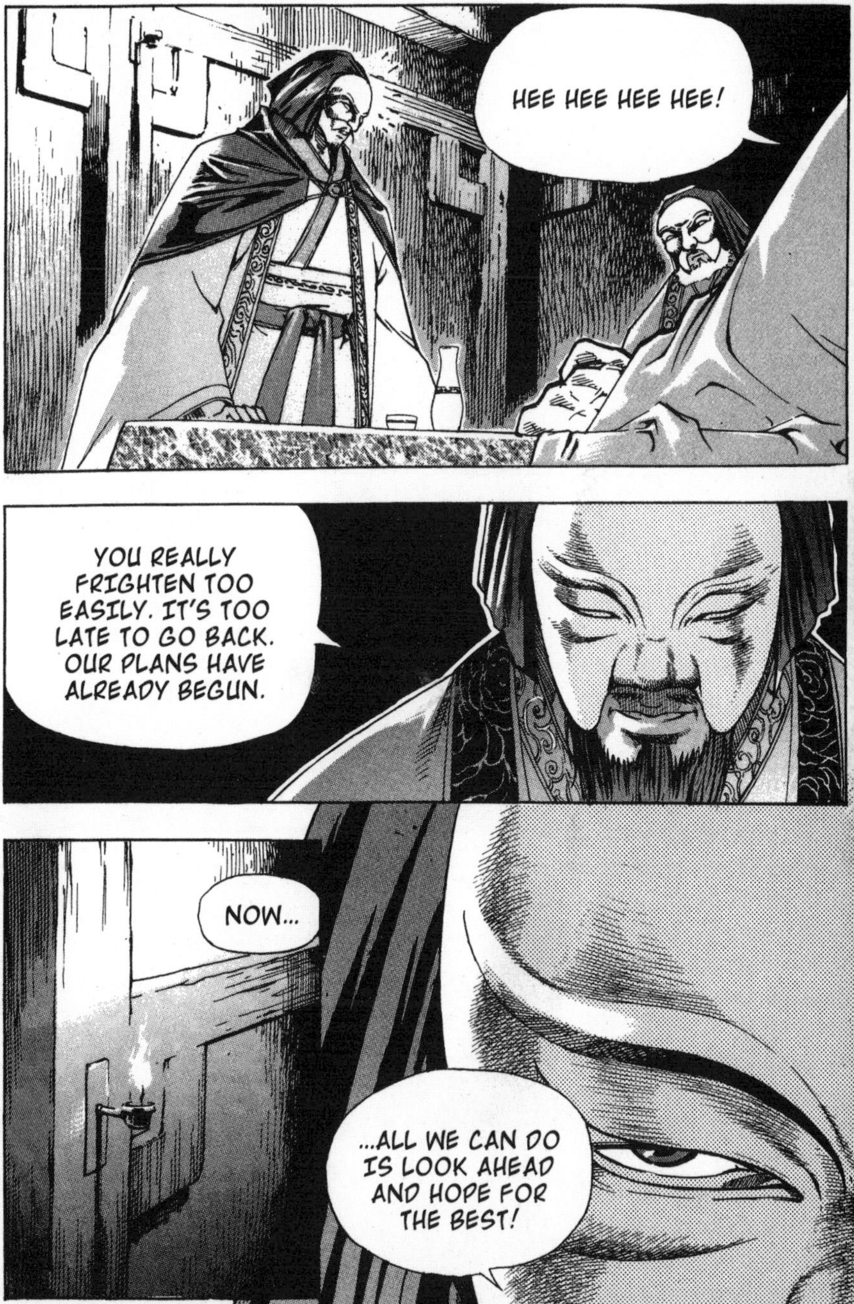
HEE HEE HEE HEE!
YOU REALLY FRIGHTEN TOO EASILY. IT'S TOO LATE TO GO BACK. OUR PLANS HAVE ALREADY BEGUN.
NOW...
...ALL WE CAN DO IS LOOK AHEAD AND HOPE FOR THE BEST!

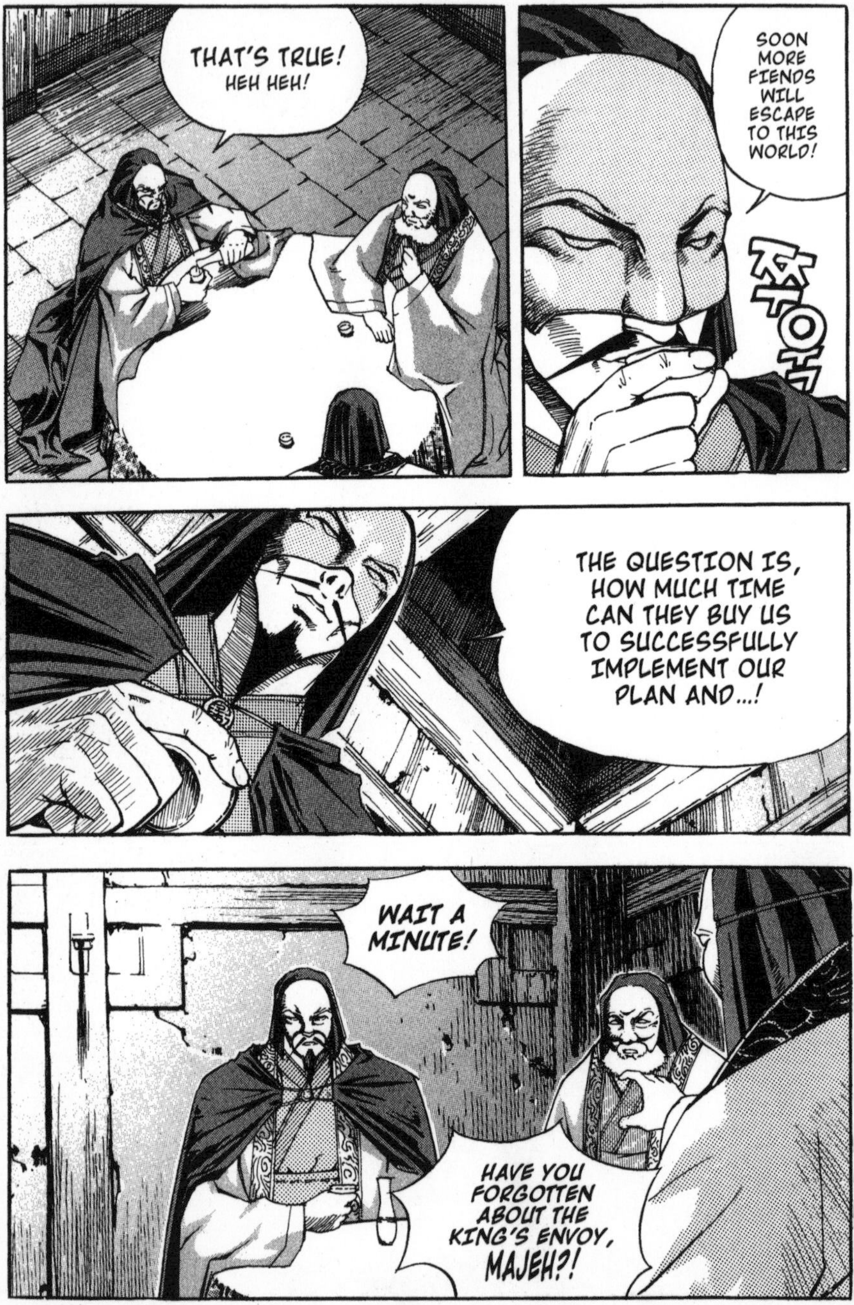
THAT'S TRUE! HEH HEH!
SOON MORE FIENDS WILL ESCAPE TO THIS WORLD!
THE QUESTION IS, HOW MUCH TIME CAN THEY BUY US TO SUCCESSFULLY IMPLEMENT OUR PLAN AND...!
WAIT A MINUTE!
HAVE YOU FORGOTTEN ABOUT THE KING'S ENVOY, MAJEH?!

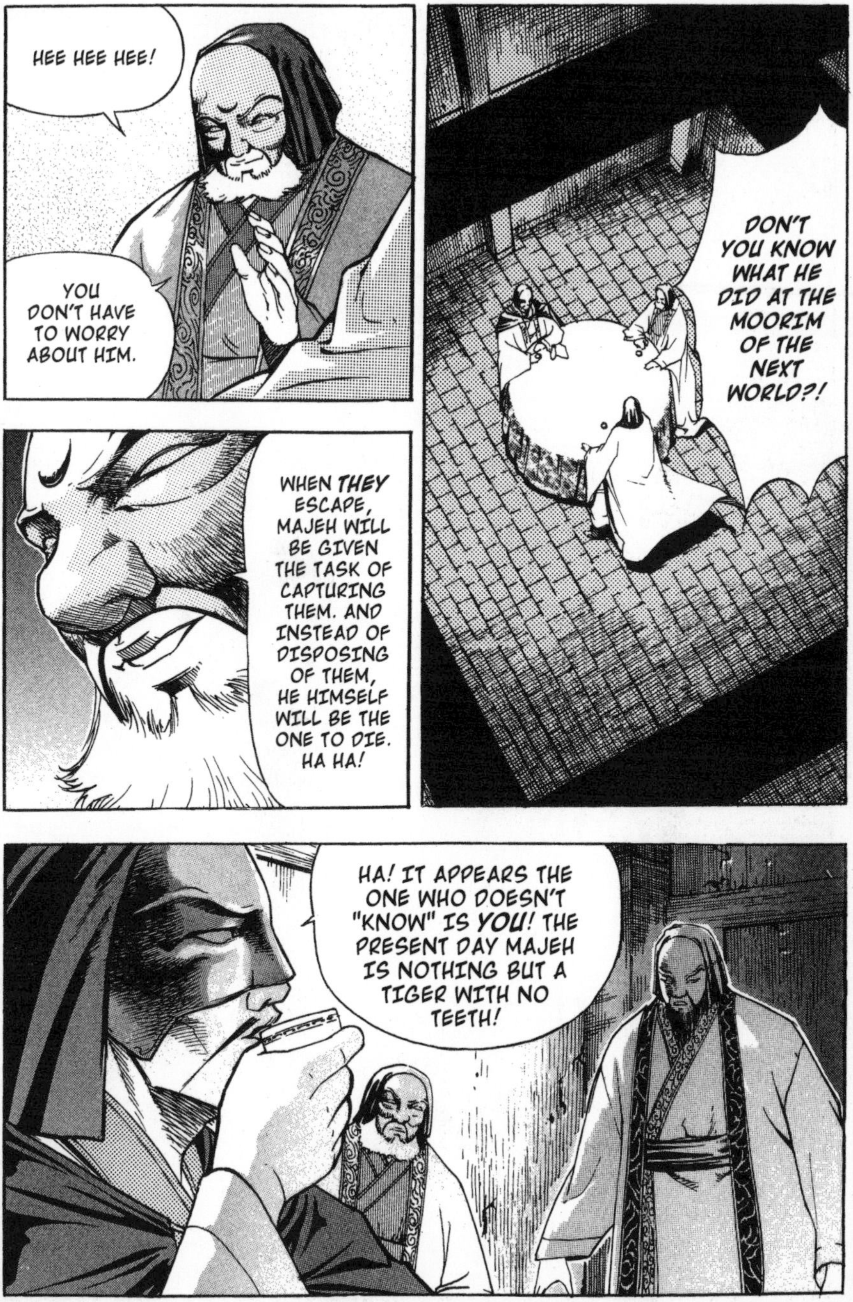
HEE HEE HEE!
YOU DON'T HAVE TO WORRY ABOUT HIM.
WHEN *THEY* ESCAPE, MAJEH WILL BE GIVEN THE TASK OF CAPTURING THEM. AND INSTEAD OF DISPOSING OF THEM, HE HIMSELF WILL BE THE ONE TO DIE. HA HA!
DON'T YOU KNOW WHAT HE DID AT THE MOORIM OF THE NEXT WORLD?!
HA! IT APPEARS THE ONE WHO DOESN'T "KNOW" IS *YOU*! THE PRESENT DAY MAJEH IS NOTHING BUT A TIGER WITH NO TEETH!

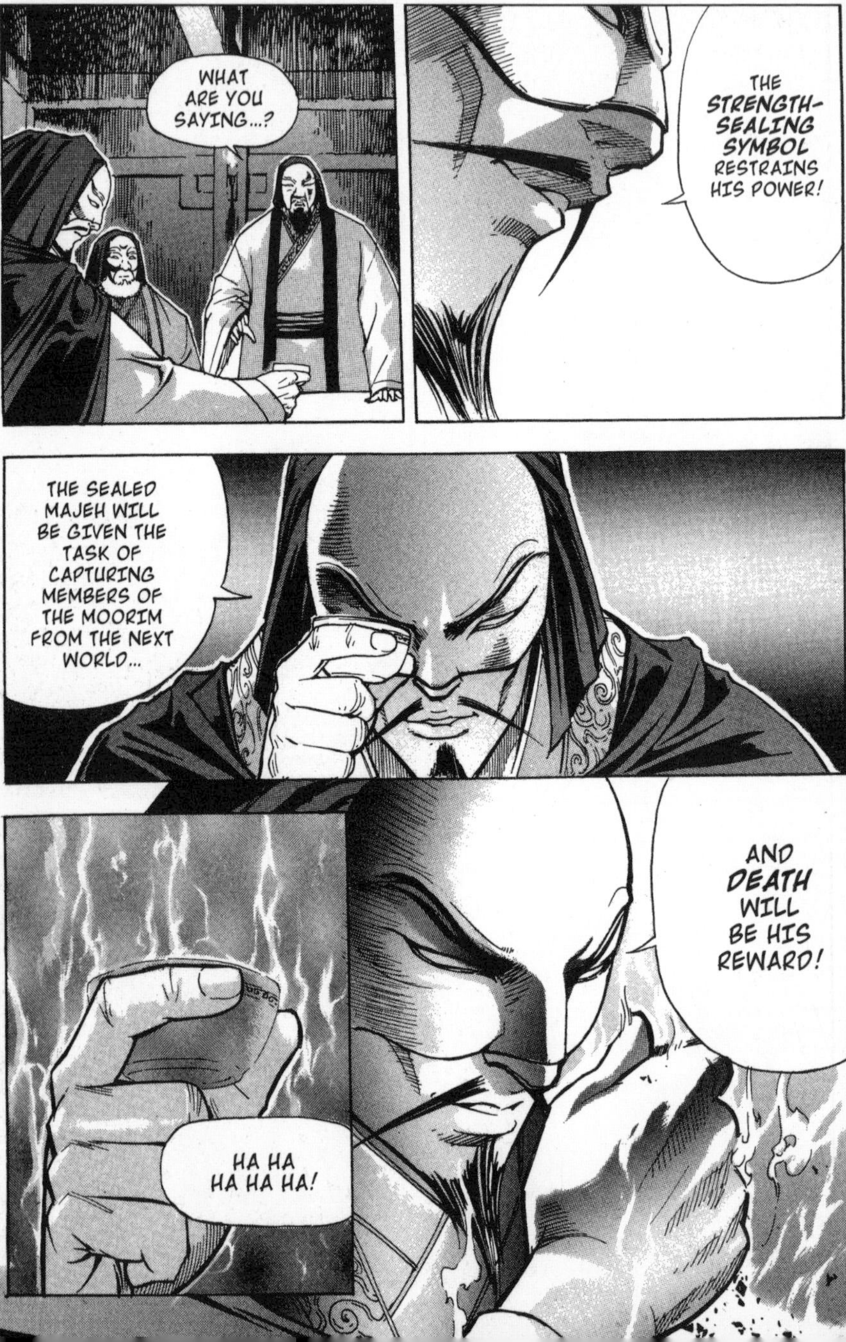
WHAT ARE YOU SAYING...?
THE STRENGTH-SEALING SYMBOL RESTRAINS HIS POWER!
THE SEALED MAJEH WILL BE GIVEN THE TASK OF CAPTURING MEMBERS OF THE MOORIM FROM THE NEXT WORLD...
AND DEATH WILL BE HIS REWARD!
HA HA HA HA HA!

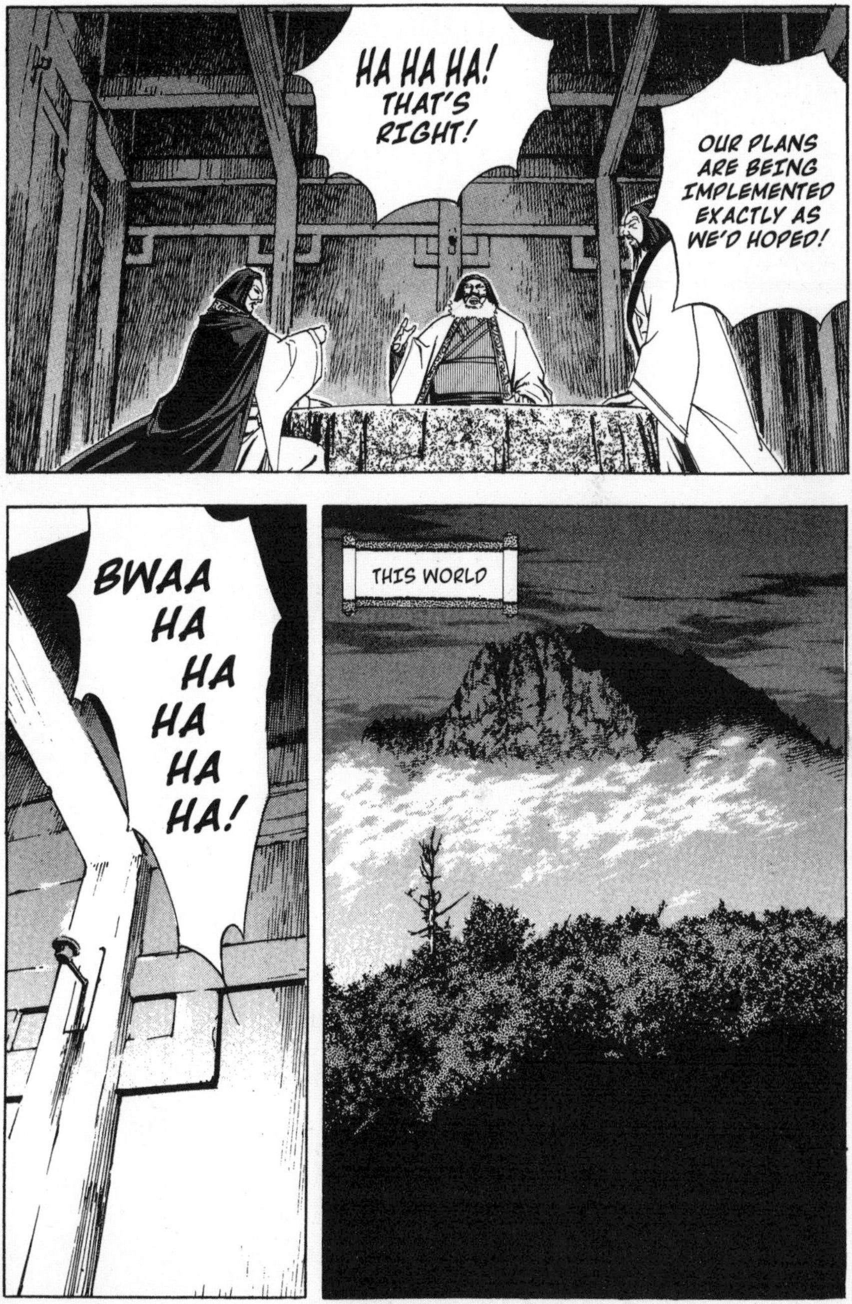
HA HA HA! THAT'S RIGHT!
OUR PLANS ARE BEING IMPLEMENTED EXACTLY AS WE'D HOPED!
BWAA HA HA HA HA HA!
THIS WORLD

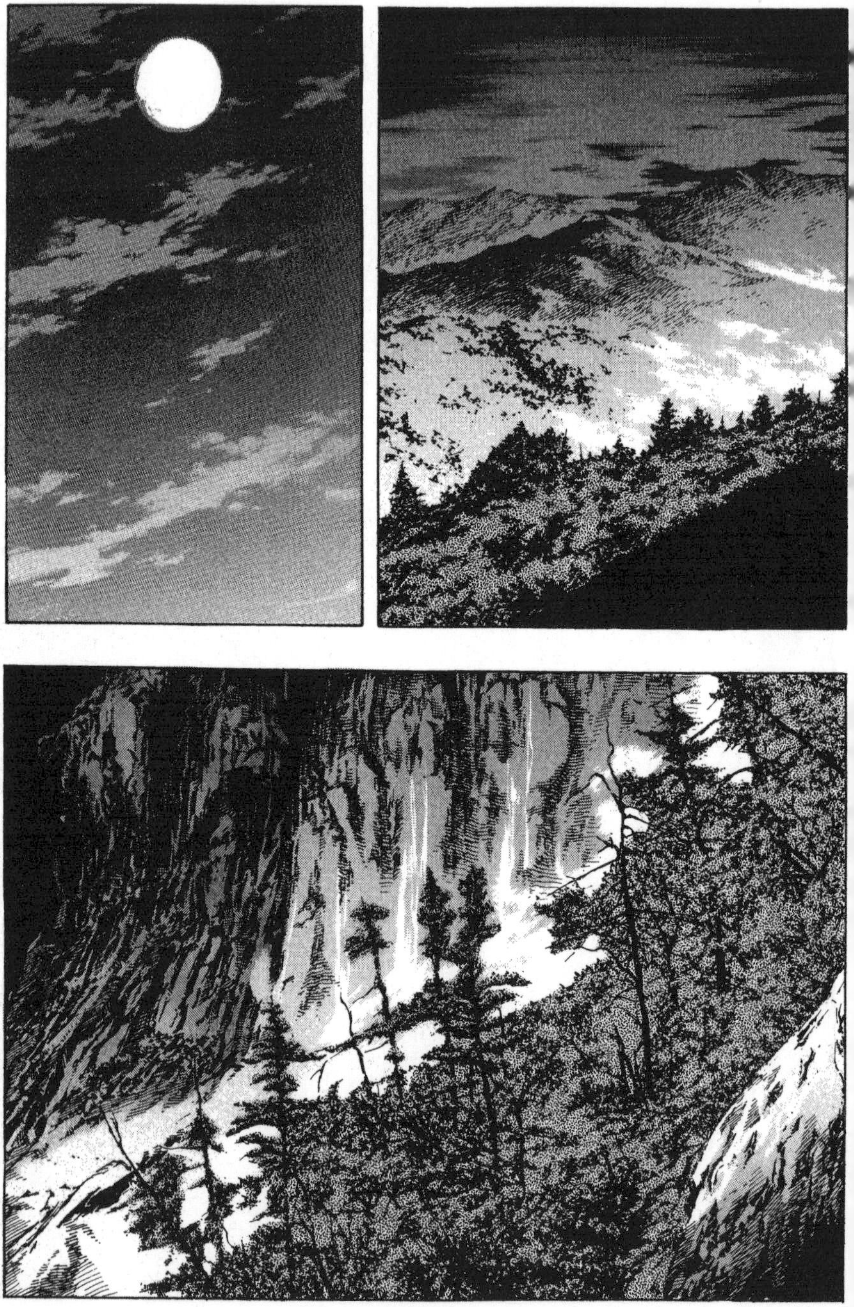

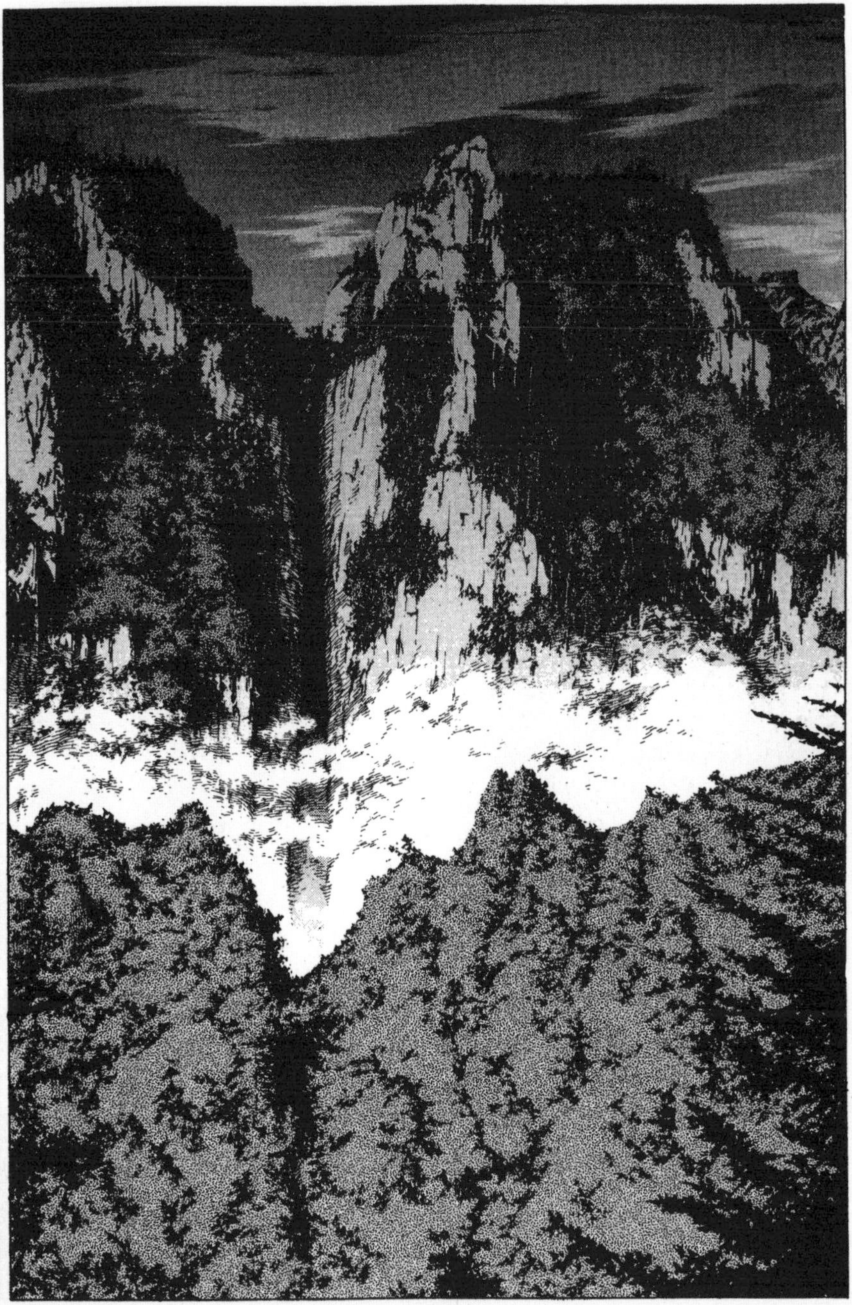

BEWARMOOYIBGOK:
"UNLESS YOU ARE A
MOON, YOU CAN
NOT ENTER"

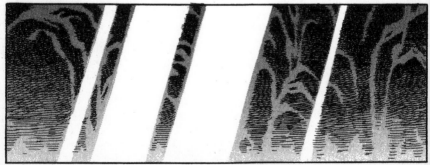

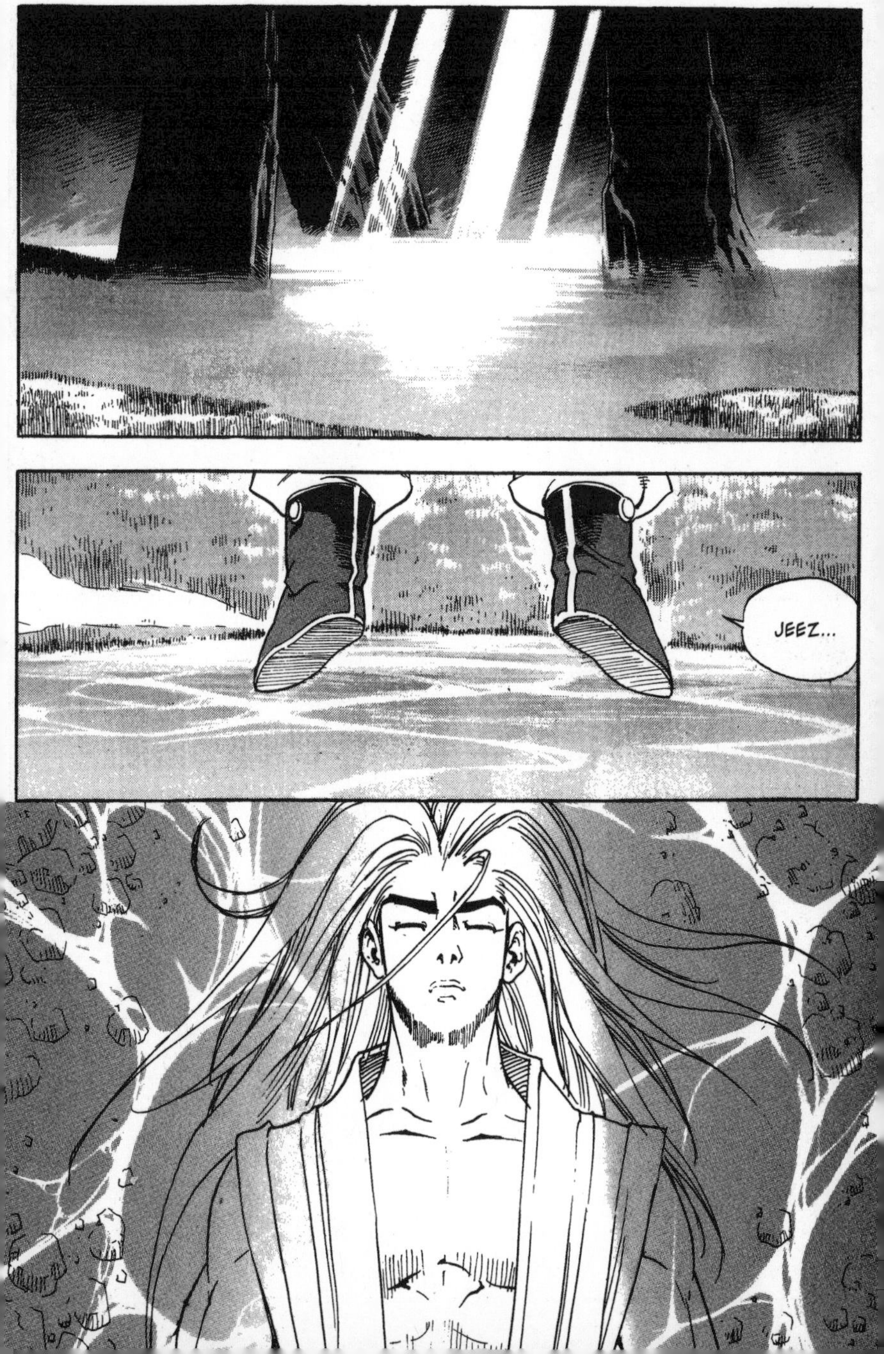
JEEZ...

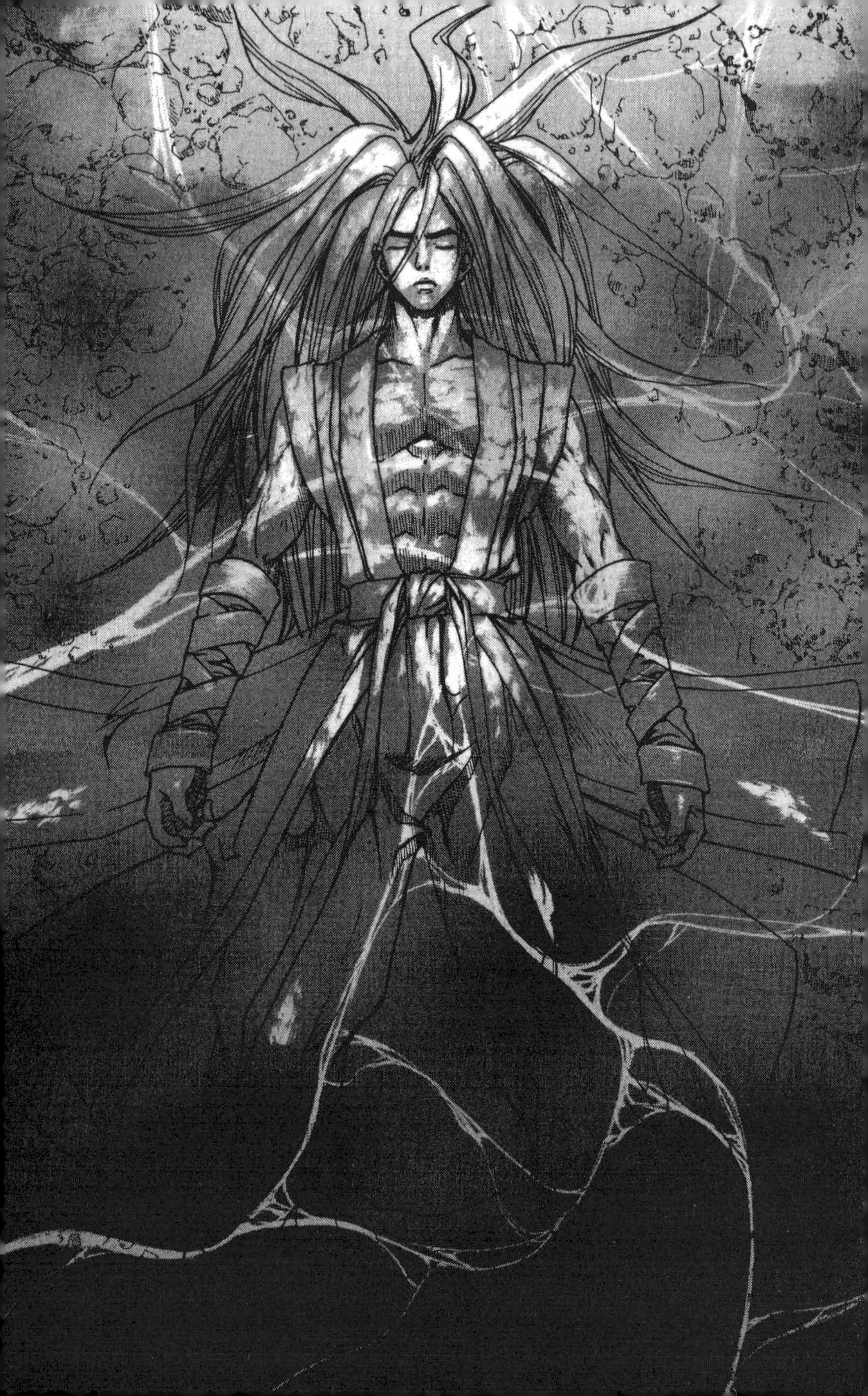

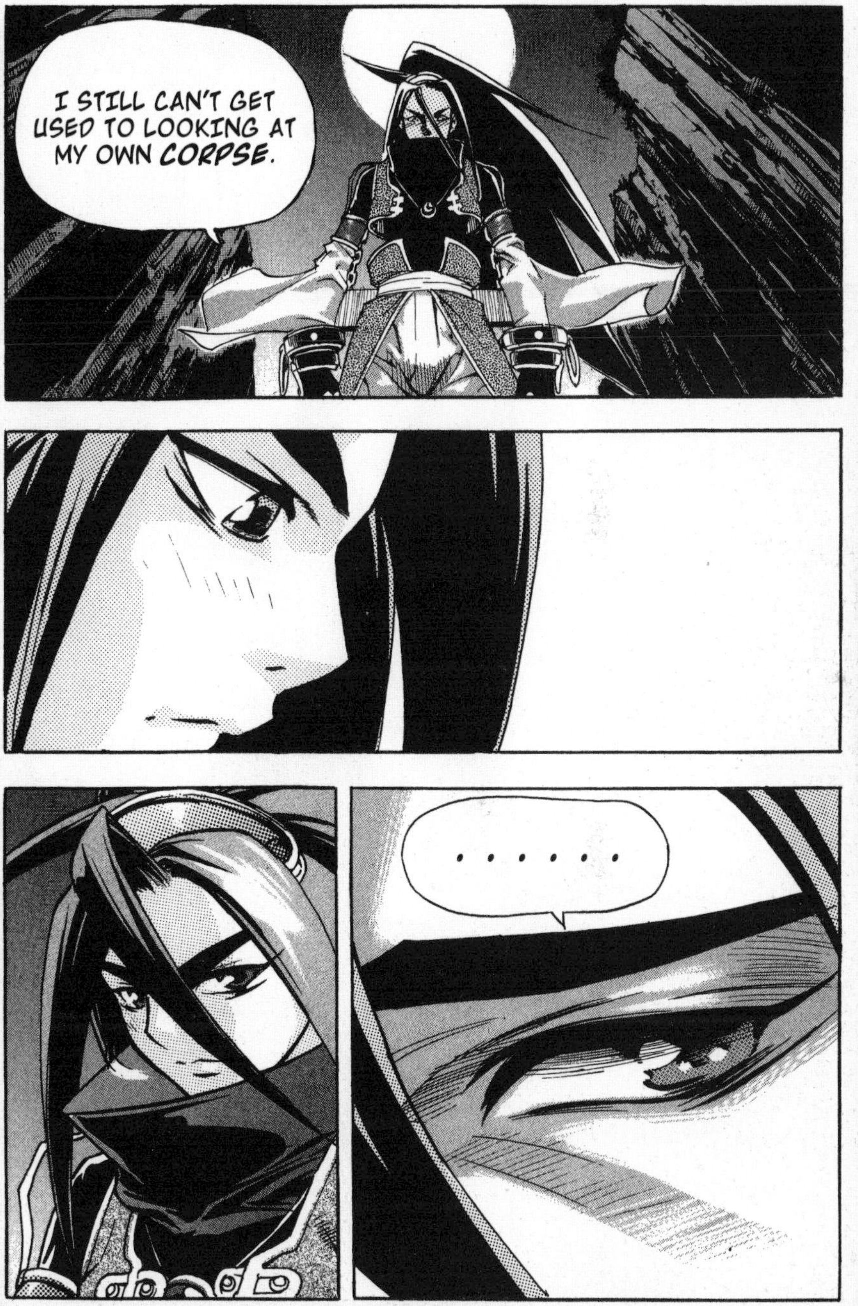
I STILL CAN'T GET USED TO LOOKING AT MY OWN CORPSE.
. . . . . .

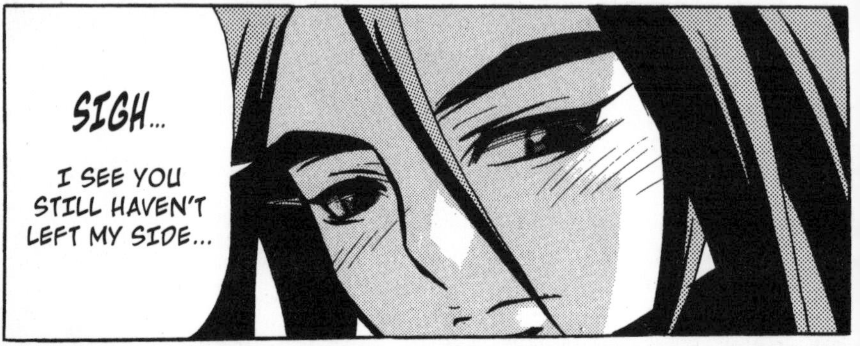
SIGH...
I SEE YOU STILL HAVEN'T LEFT MY SIDE...

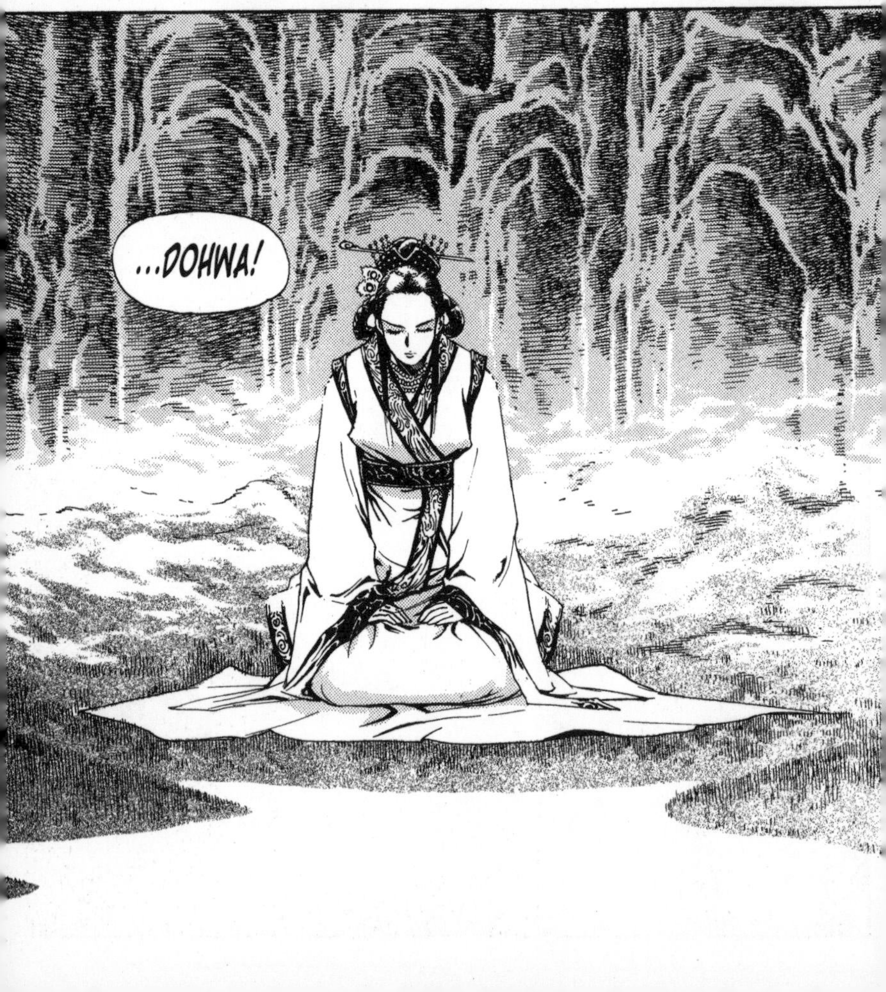
...DOHWA!

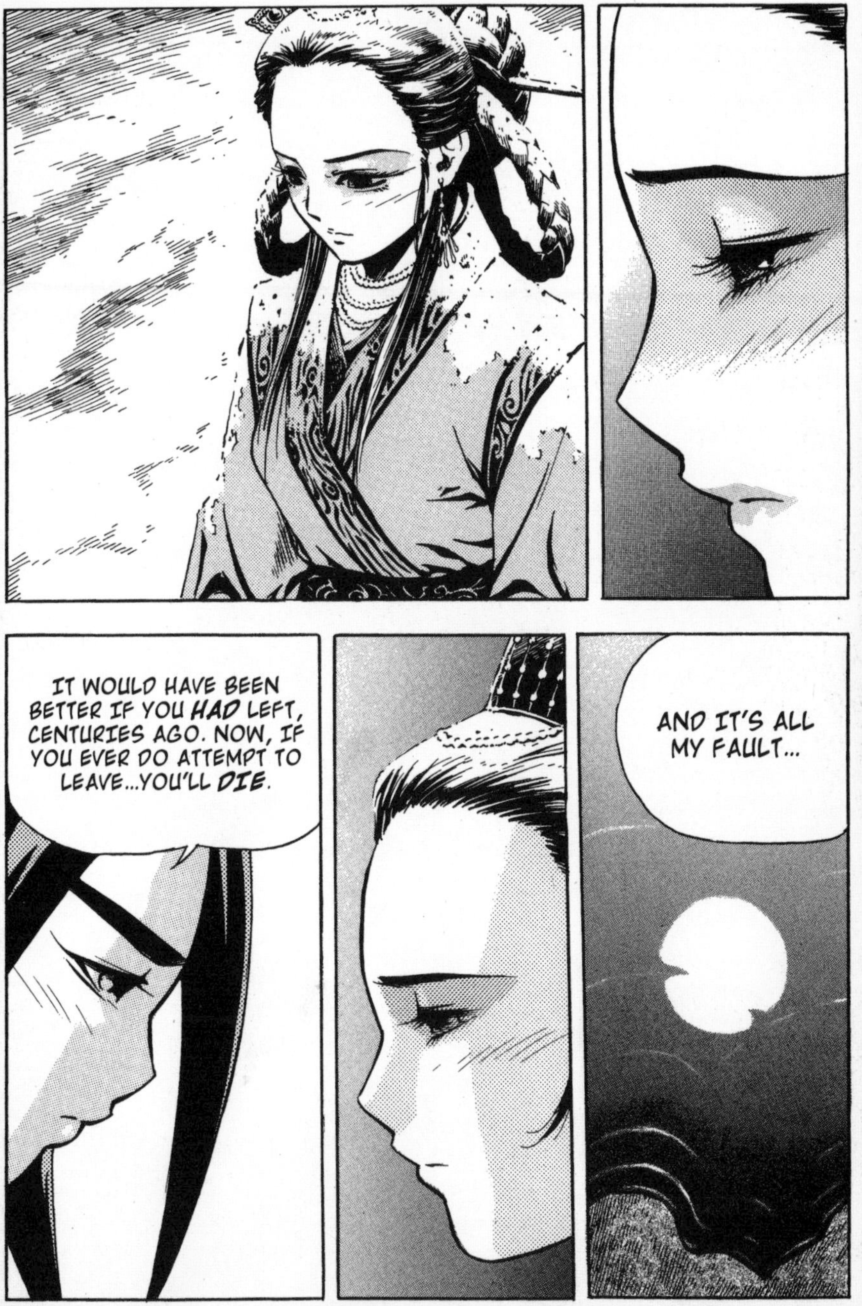
IT WOULD HAVE BEEN BETTER IF YOU HAD LEFT, CENTURIES AGO. NOW, IF YOU EVER DO ATTEMPT TO LEAVE...YOU'LL DIE.
AND IT'S ALL MY FAULT...

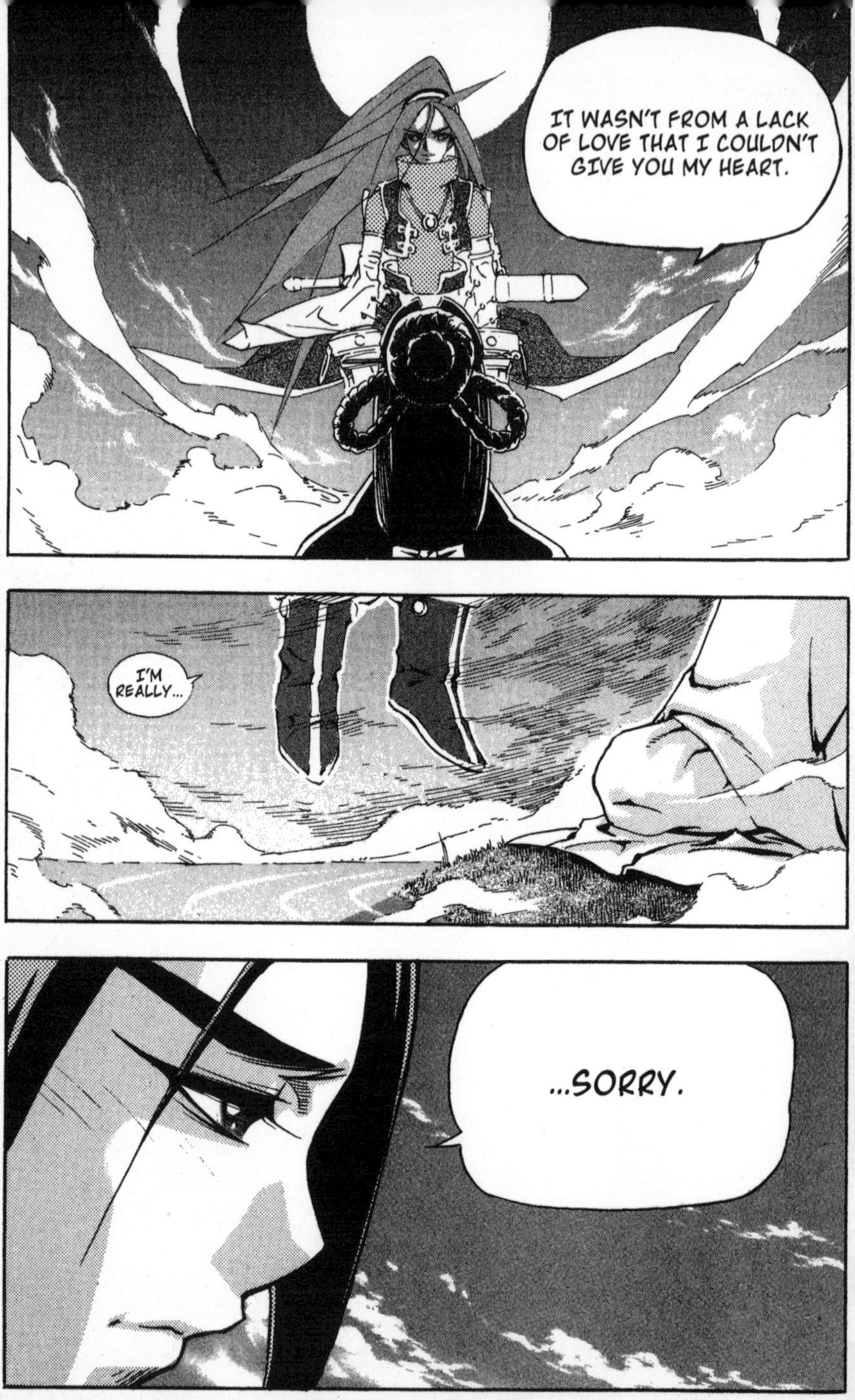
IT WASN'T FROM A LACK OF LOVE THAT I COULDN'T GIVE YOU MY HEART.
I'M REALLY...
...SORRY.

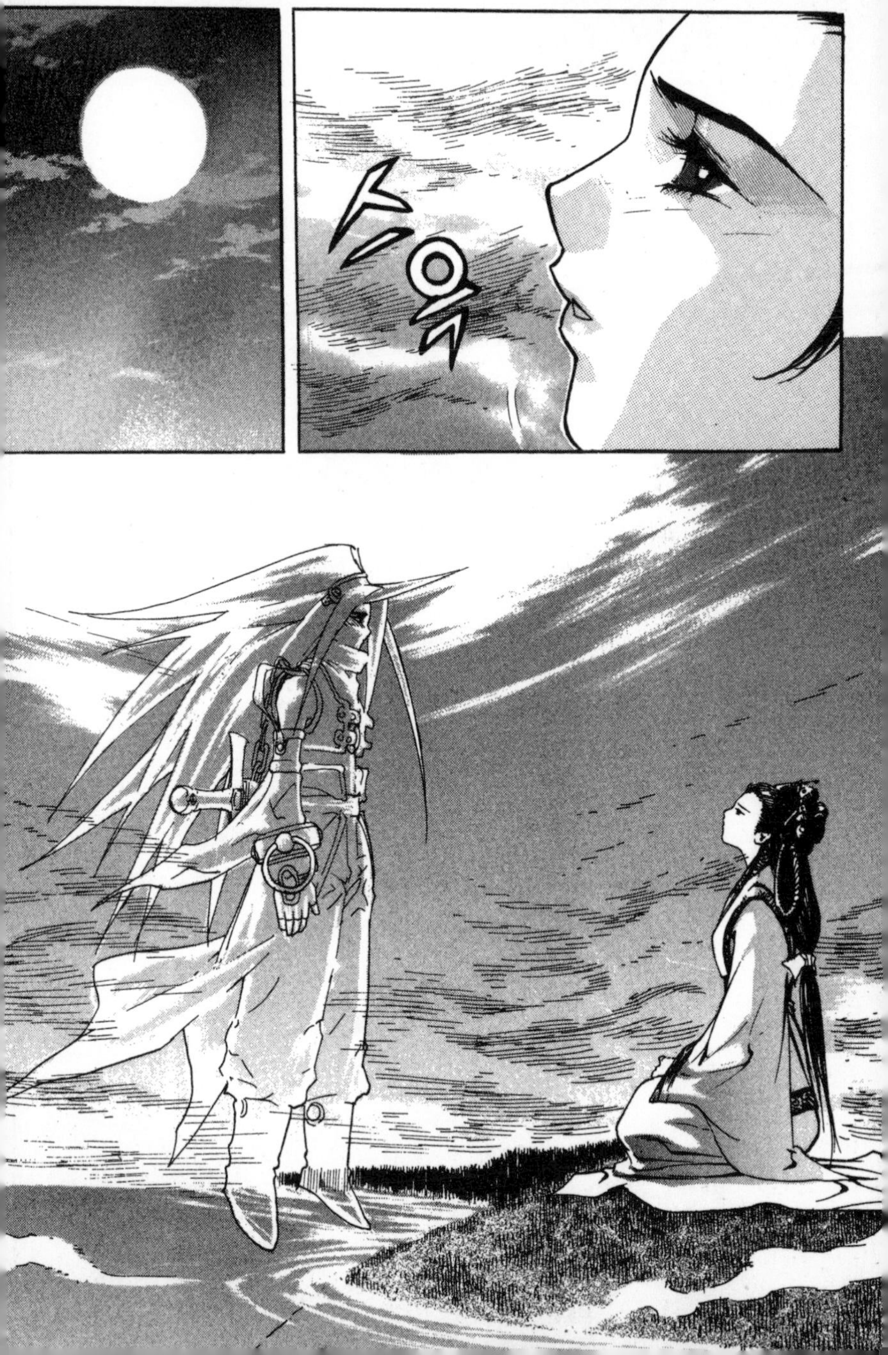

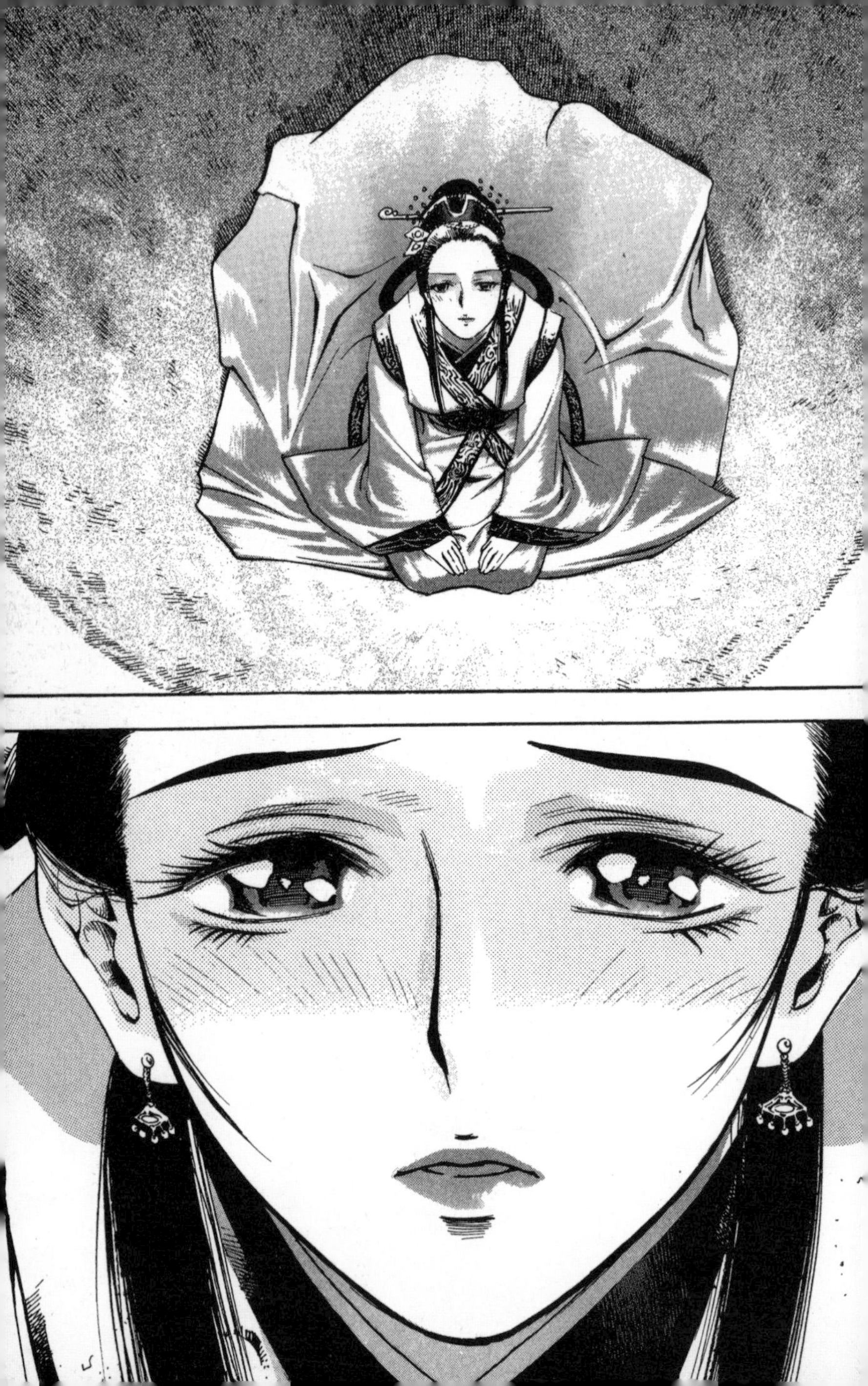

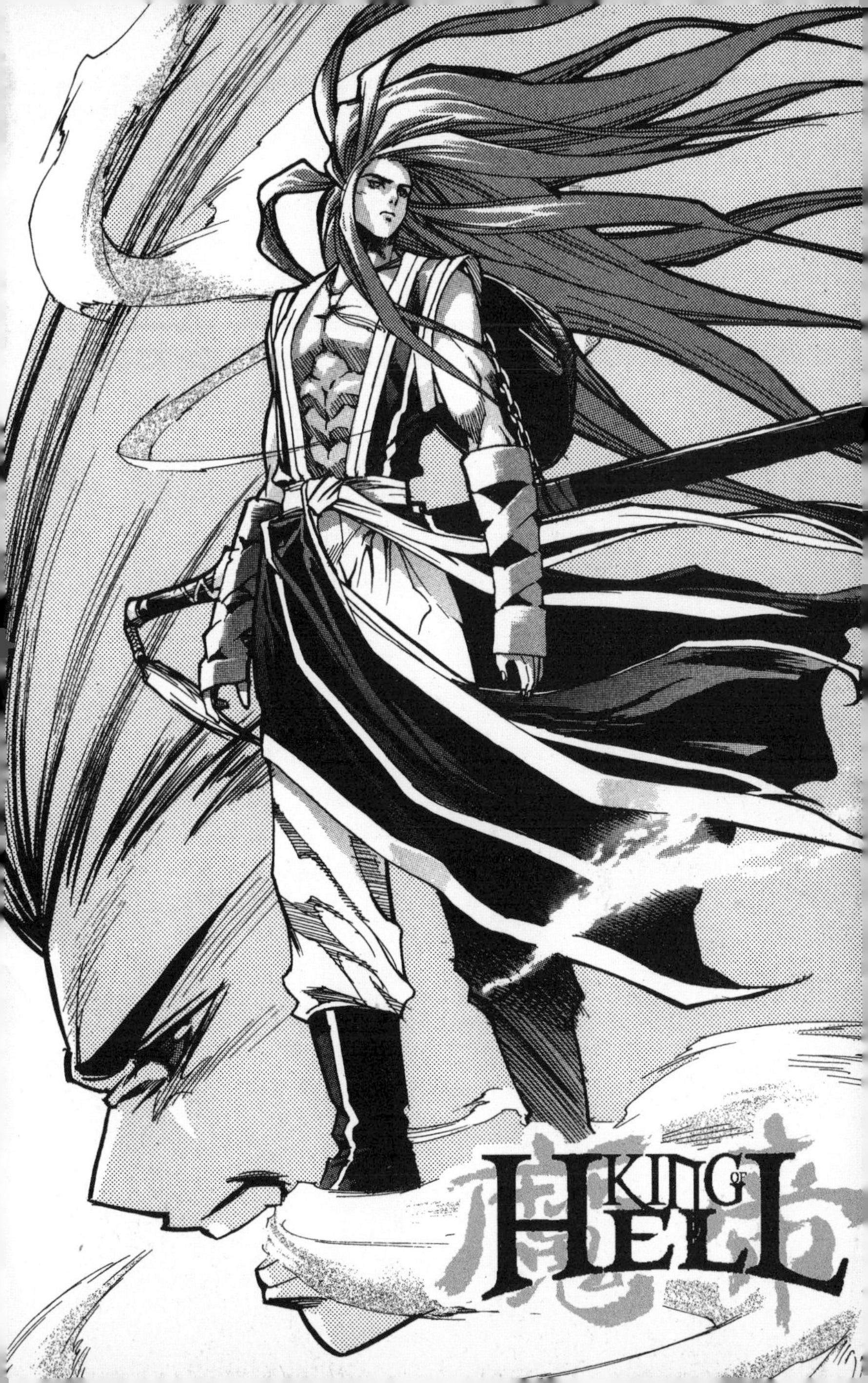
KING OF HELL

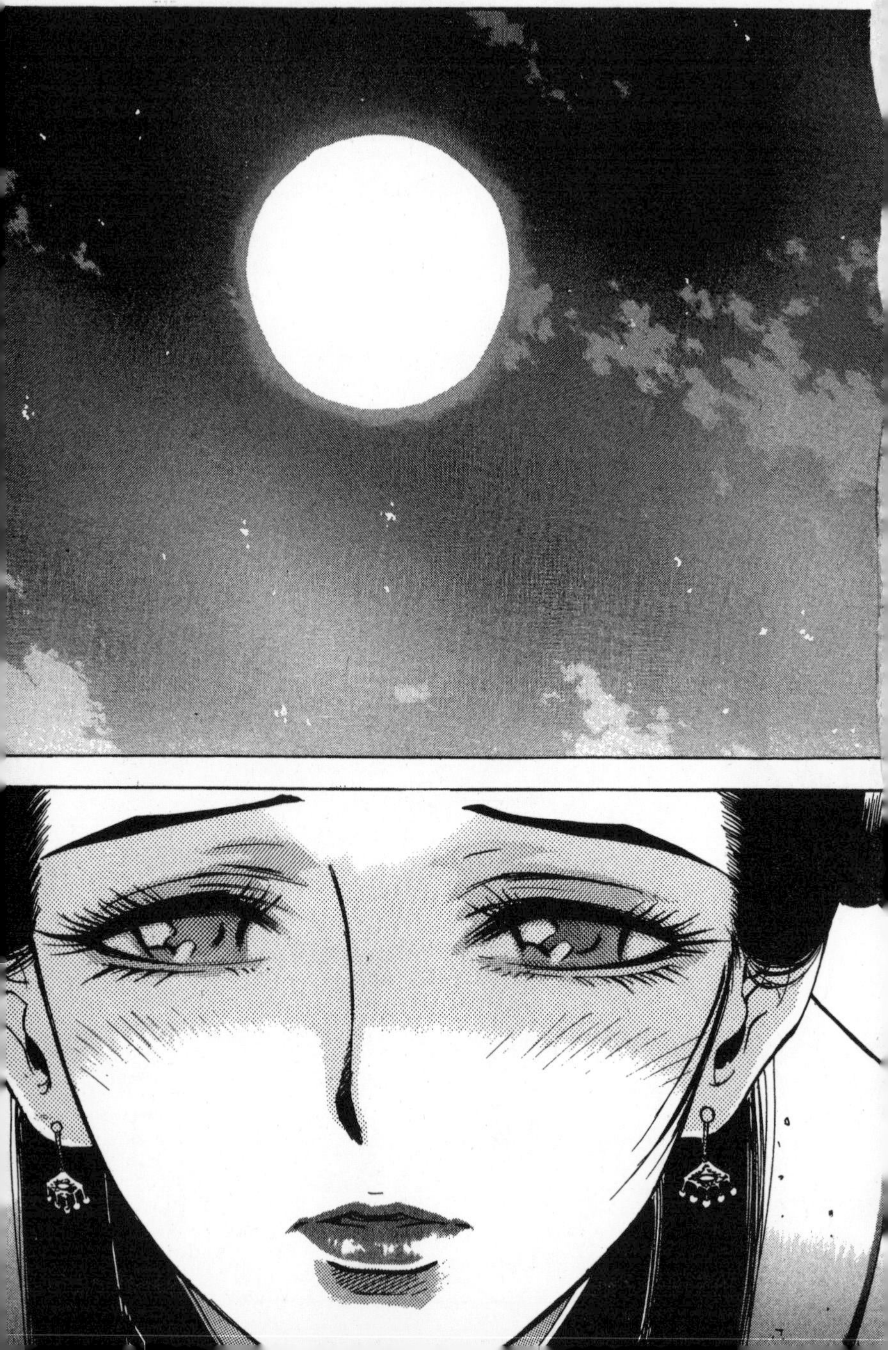

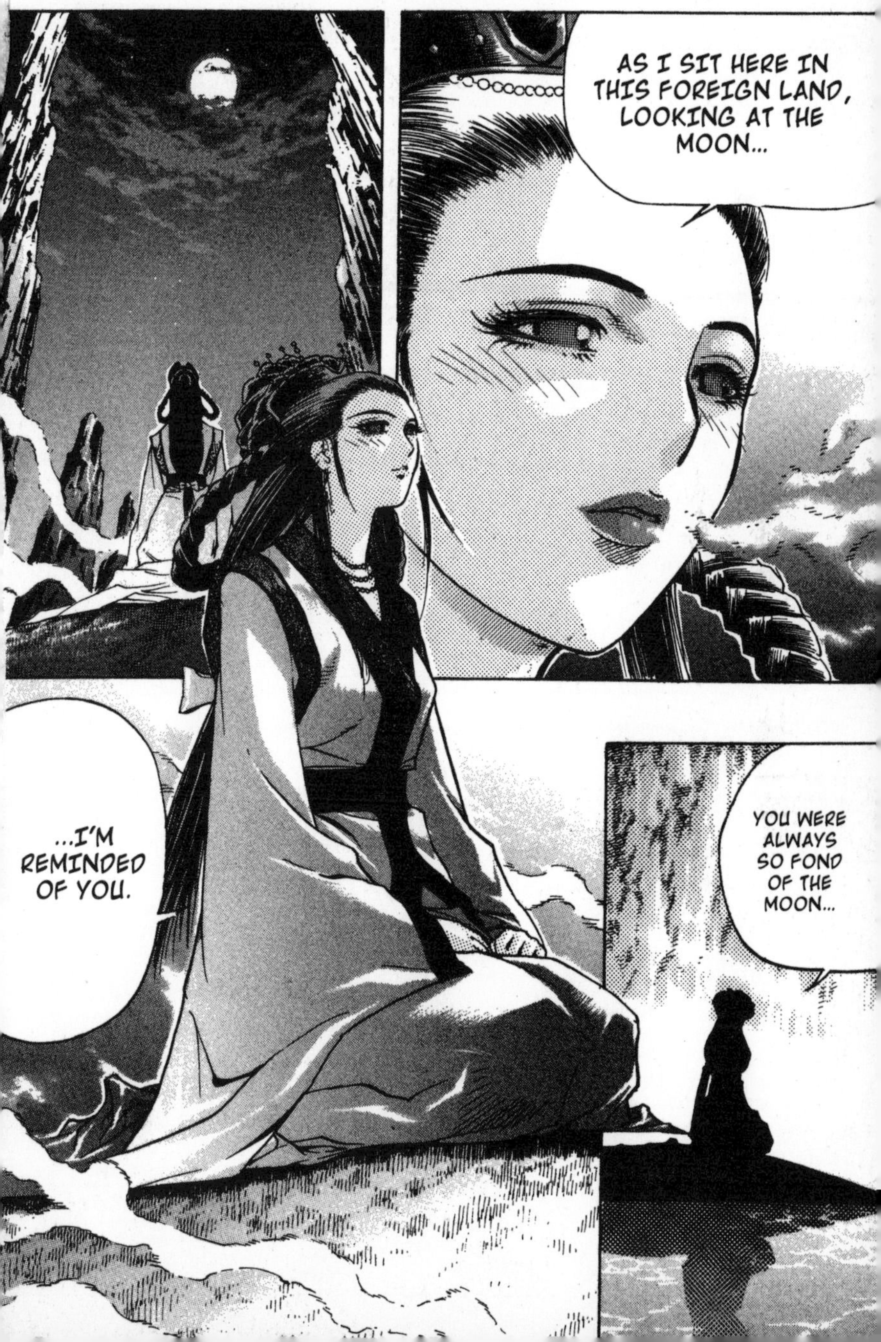
AS I SIT HERE IN THIS FOREIGN LAND, LOOKING AT THE MOON...
...I'M REMINDED OF YOU.
YOU WERE ALWAYS SO FOND OF THE MOON...

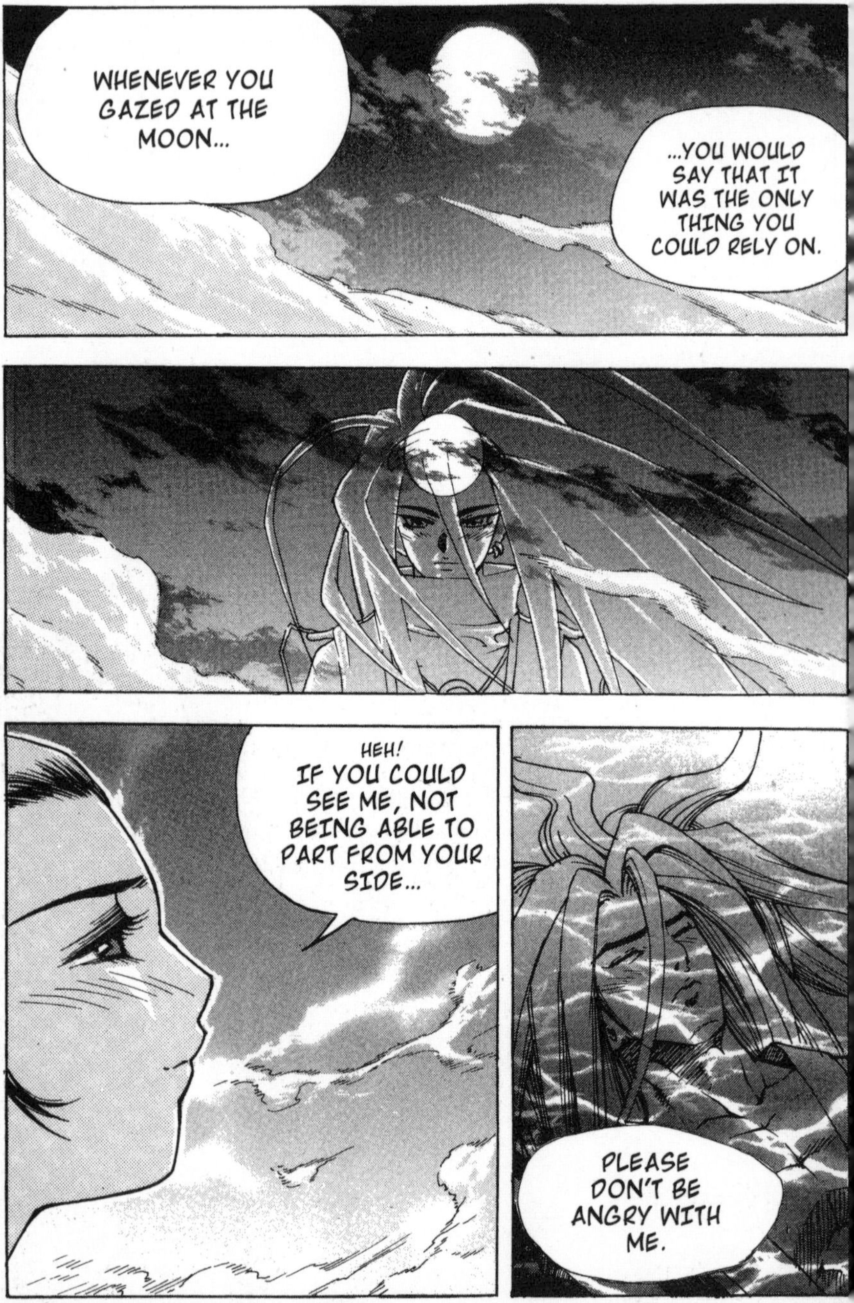
WHENEVER YOU GAZED AT THE MOON...
...YOU WOULD SAY THAT IT WAS THE ONLY THING YOU COULD RELY ON.
HEH! IF YOU COULD SEE ME, NOT BEING ABLE TO PART FROM YOUR SIDE...
PLEASE DON'T BE ANGRY WITH ME.

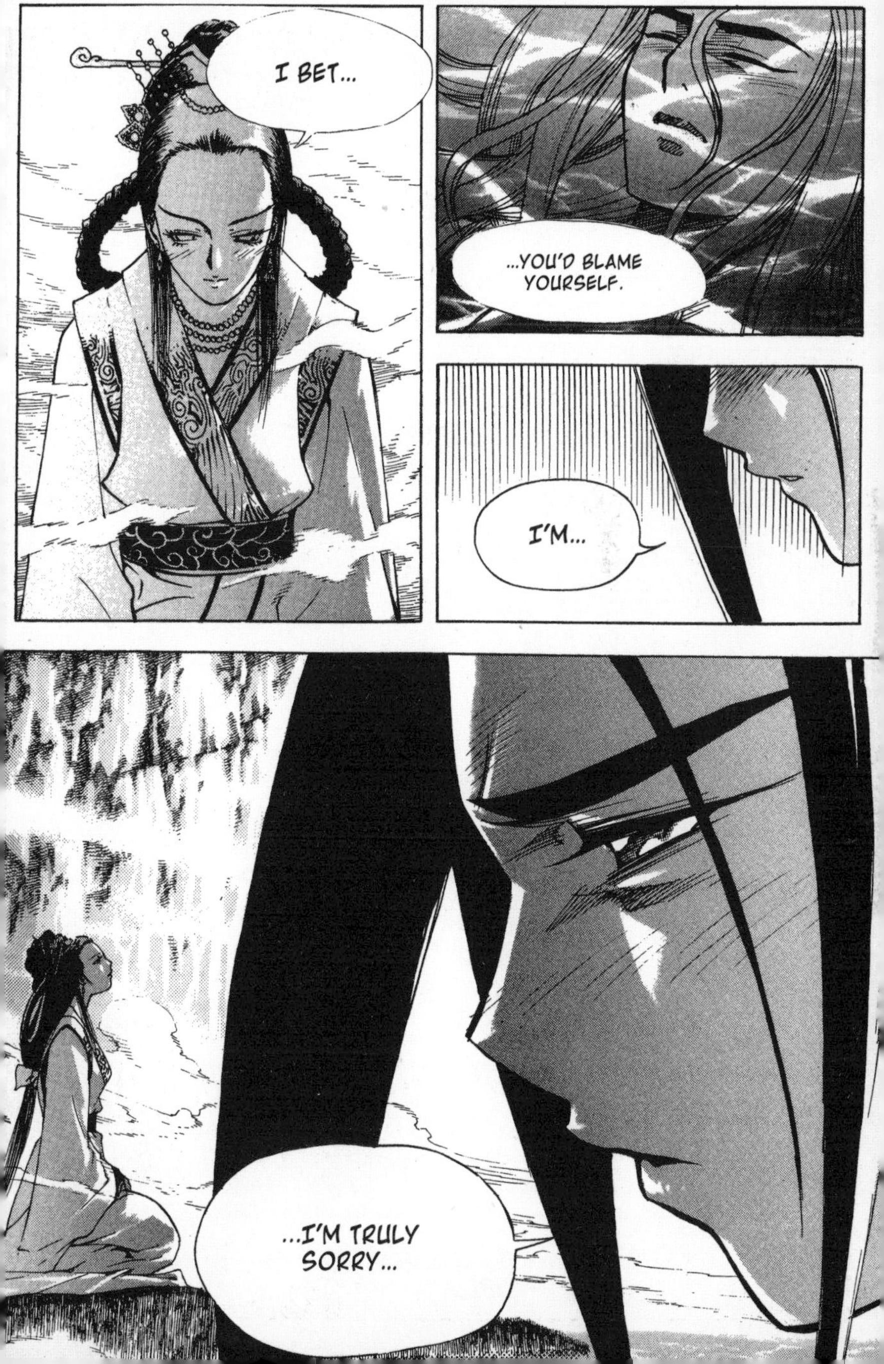
I BET...
...YOU'D BLAME YOURSELF.
I'M...
...I'M TRULY SORRY...

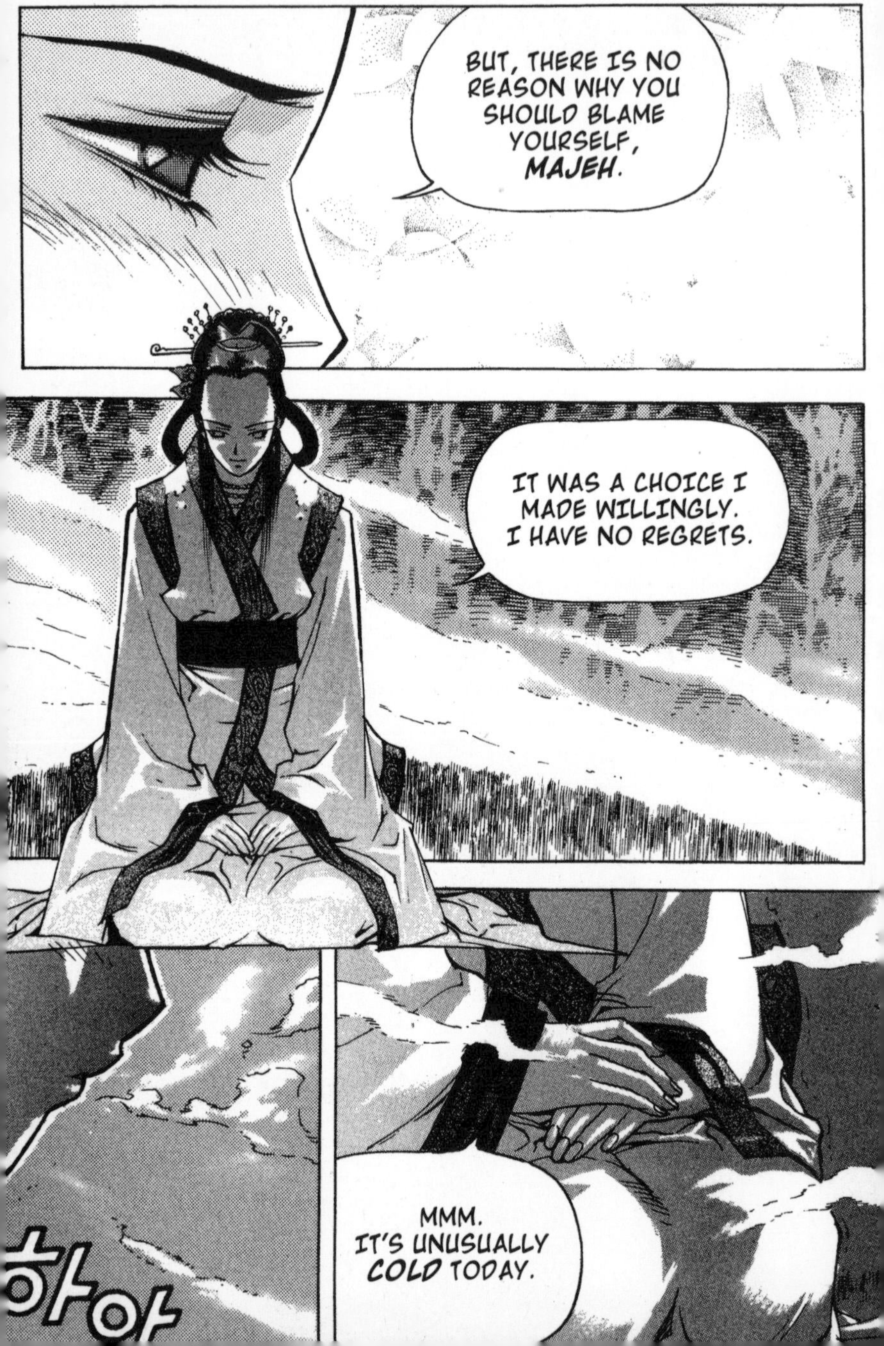
BUT, THERE IS NO REASON WHY YOU SHOULD BLAME YOURSELF, **MAJEH**.
IT WAS A CHOICE I MADE WILLINGLY. I HAVE NO REGRETS.
하아
MMM. IT'S UNUSUALLY **COLD** TODAY.

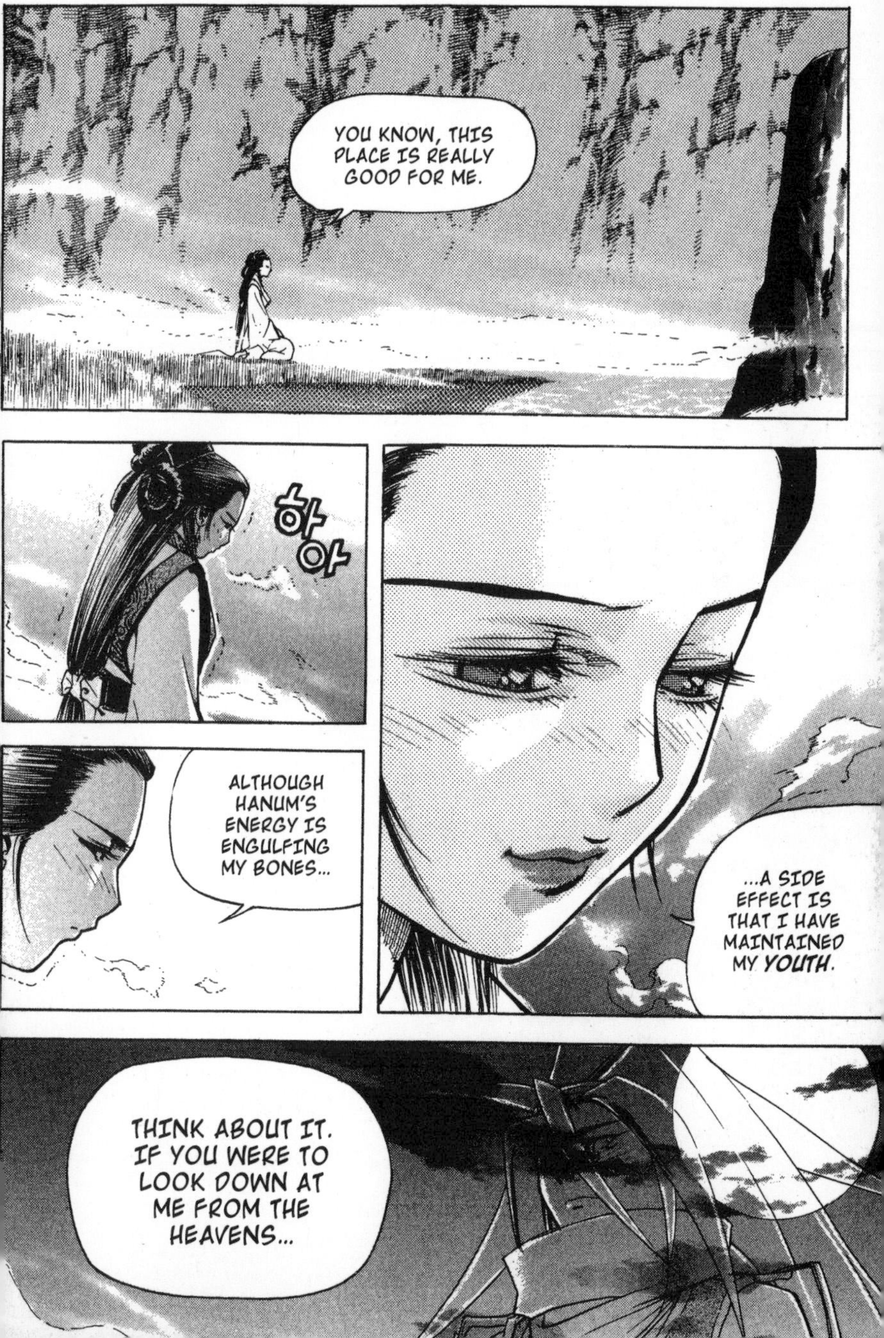
YOU KNOW, THIS PLACE IS REALLY GOOD FOR ME.
하아
ALTHOUGH HANUM'S ENERGY IS ENGULFING MY BONES...
...A SIDE EFFECT IS THAT I HAVE MAINTAINED MY *YOUTH*.
THINK ABOUT IT. IF YOU WERE TO LOOK DOWN AT ME FROM THE HEAVENS...

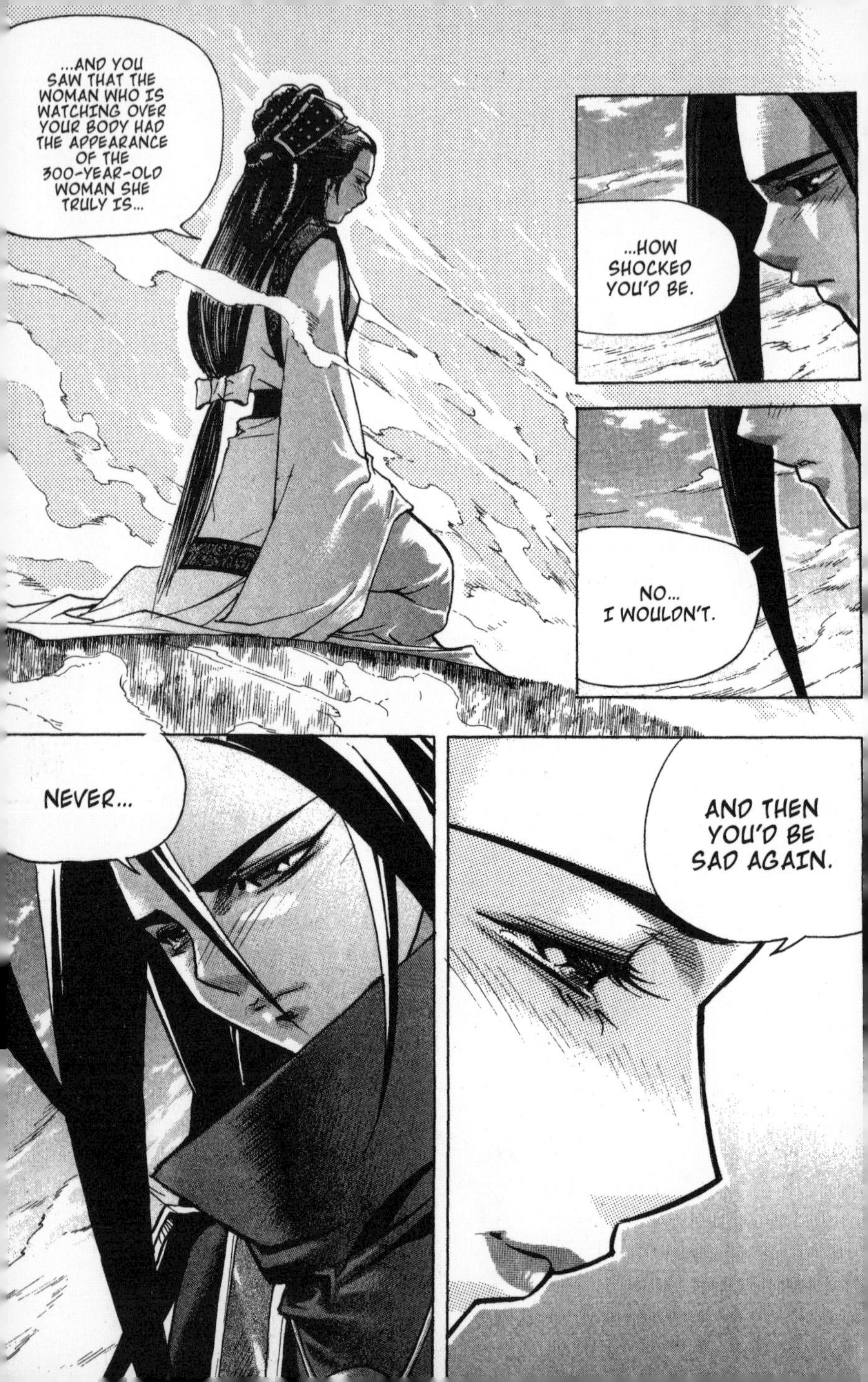
...AND YOU SAW THAT THE WOMAN WHO IS WATCHING OVER YOUR BODY HAD THE APPEARANCE OF THE 300-YEAR-OLD WOMAN SHE TRULY IS...
...HOW SHOCKED YOU'D BE.
NO... I WOULDN'T.
NEVER...
AND THEN YOU'D BE SAD AGAIN.

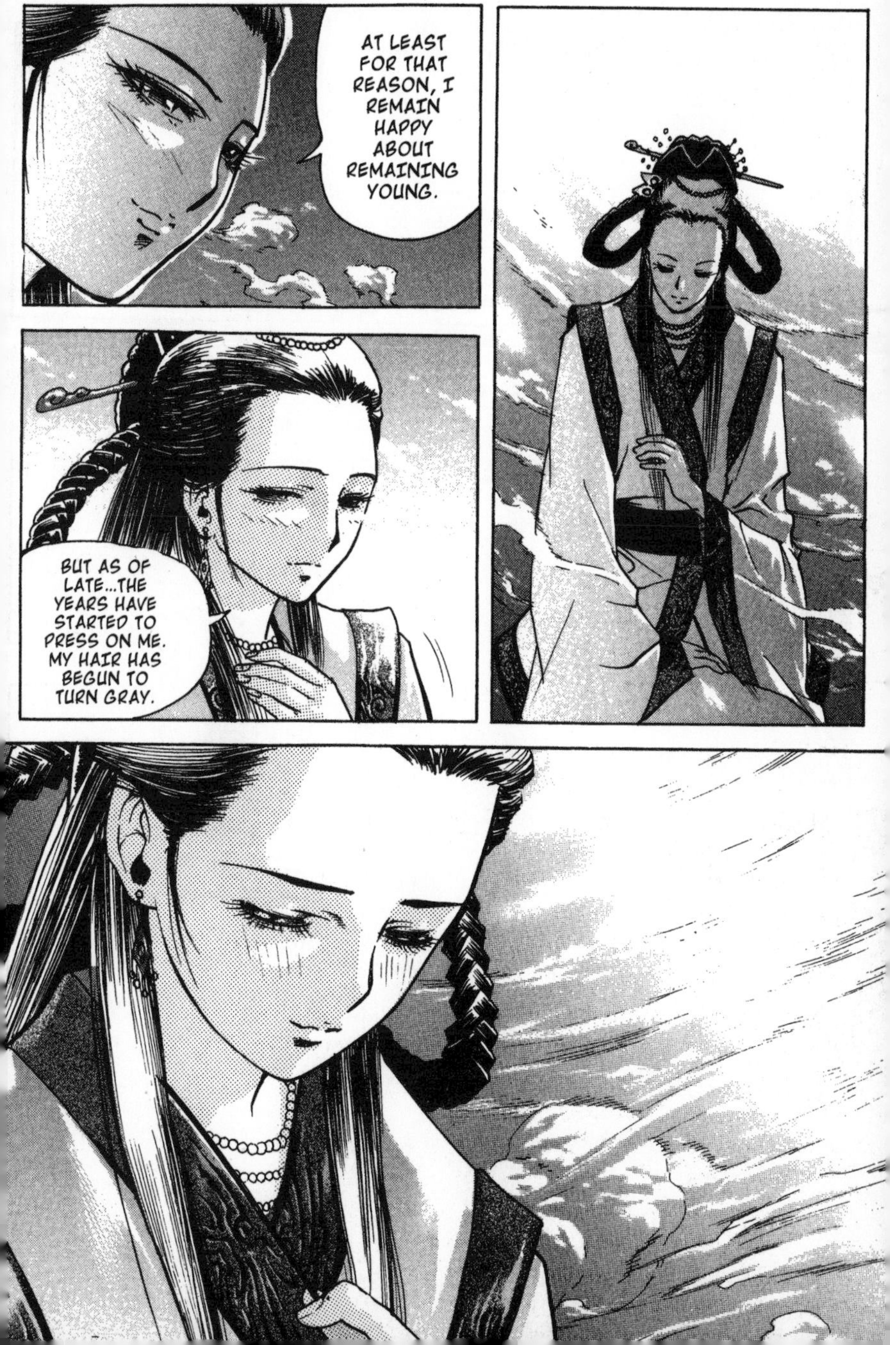
AT LEAST FOR THAT REASON, I REMAIN HAPPY ABOUT REMAINING YOUNG.
BUT AS OF LATE...THE YEARS HAVE STARTED TO PRESS ON ME. MY HAIR HAS BEGUN TO TURN GRAY.

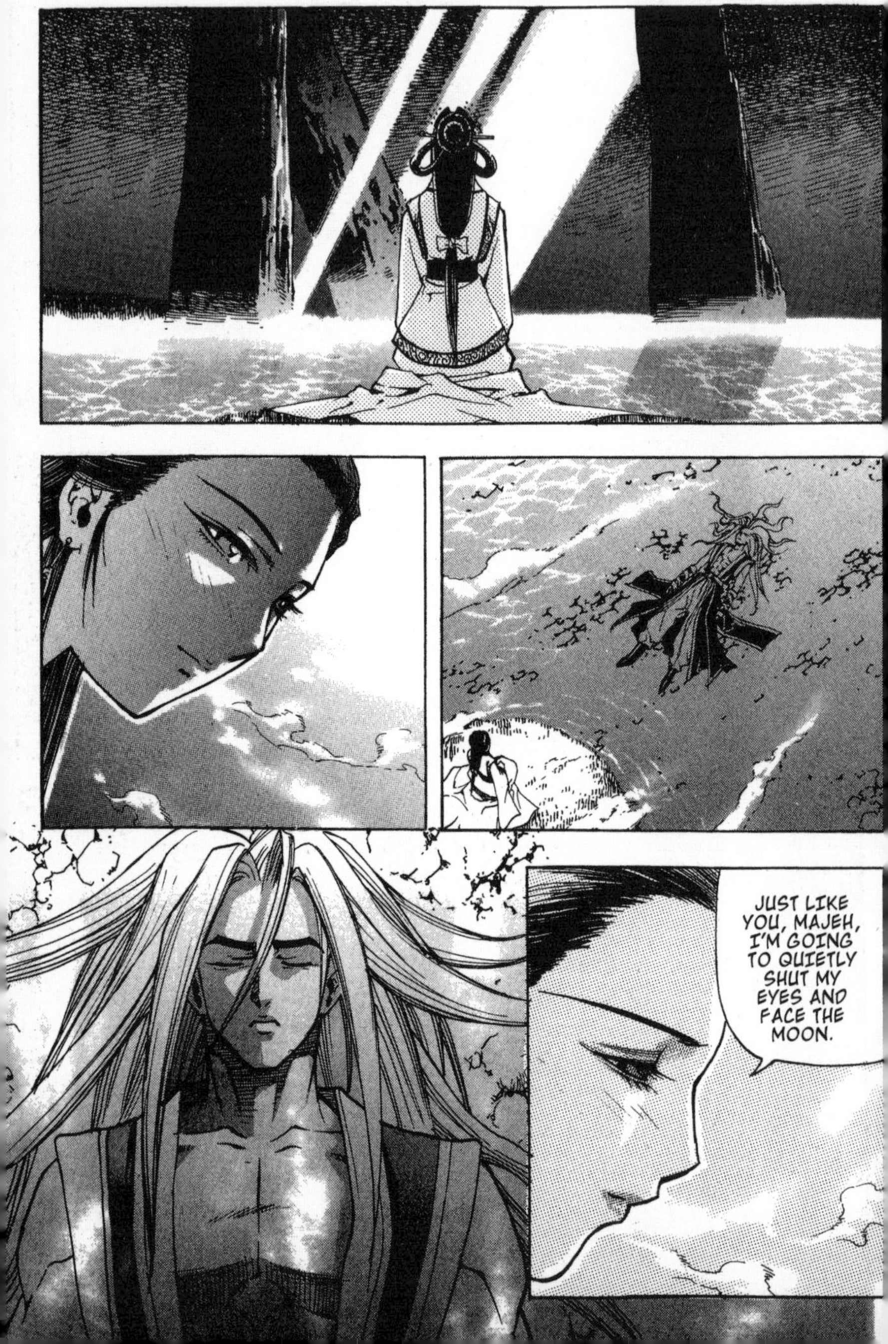
JUST LIKE YOU, MAJEH, I'M GOING TO QUIETLY SHUT MY EYES AND FACE THE MOON.

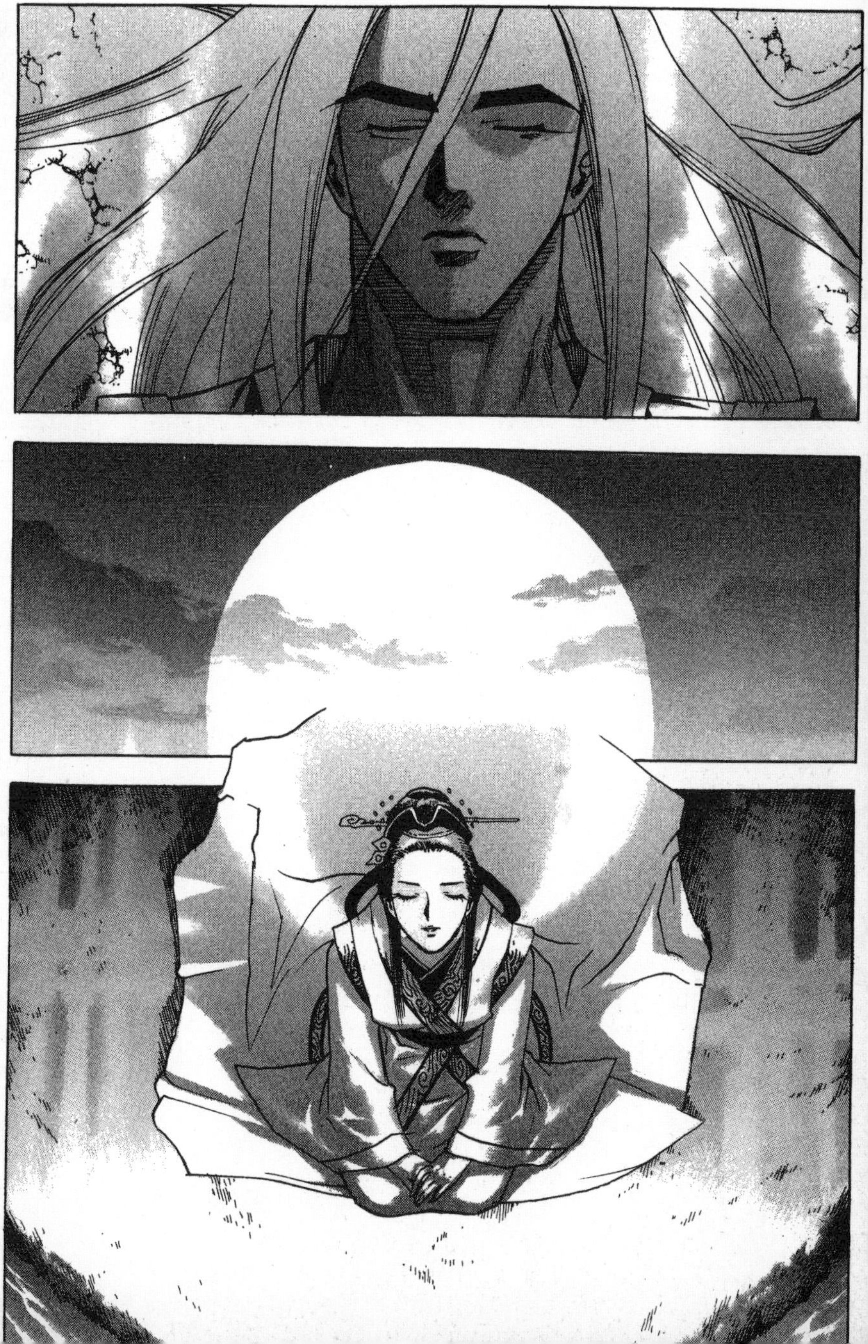

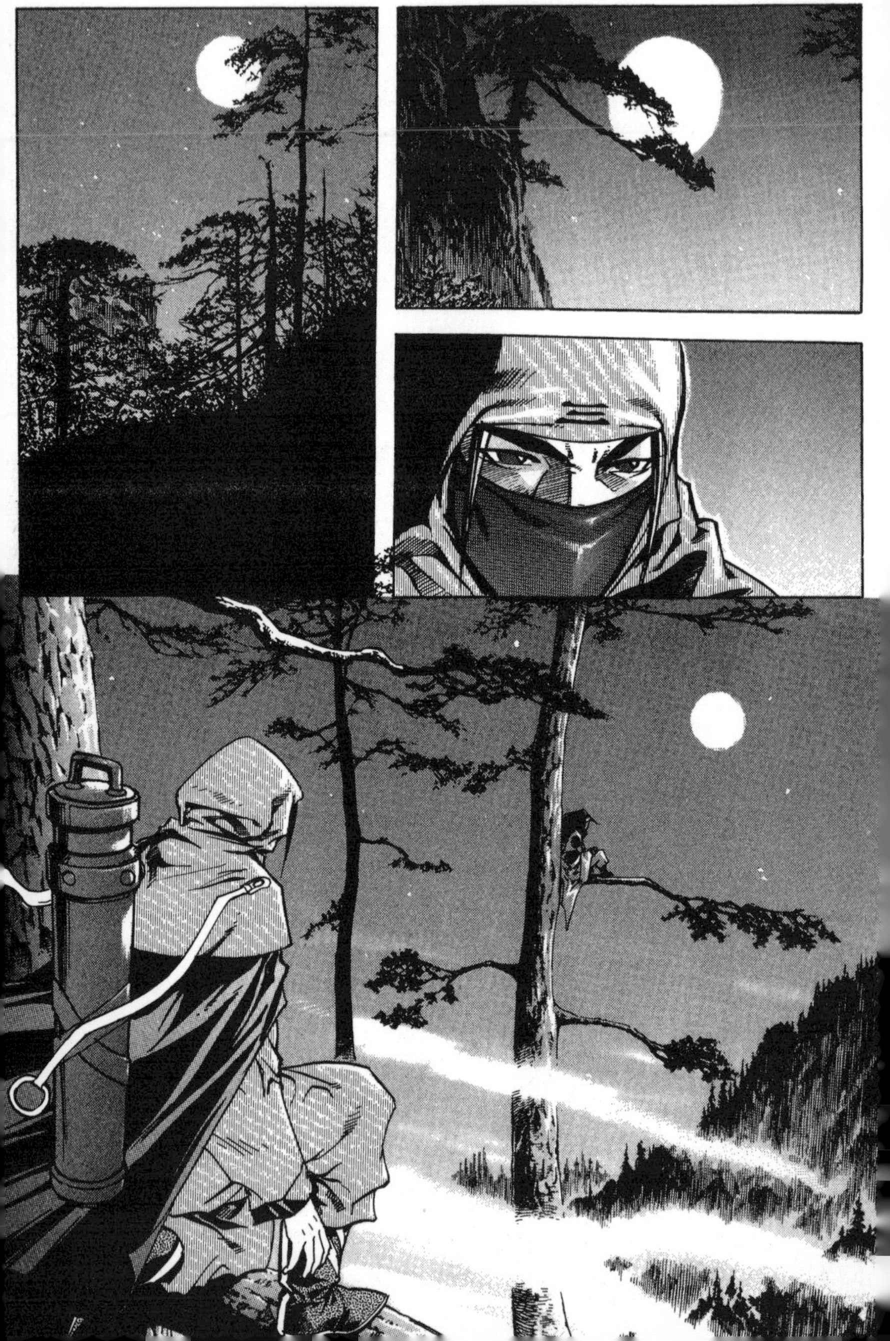

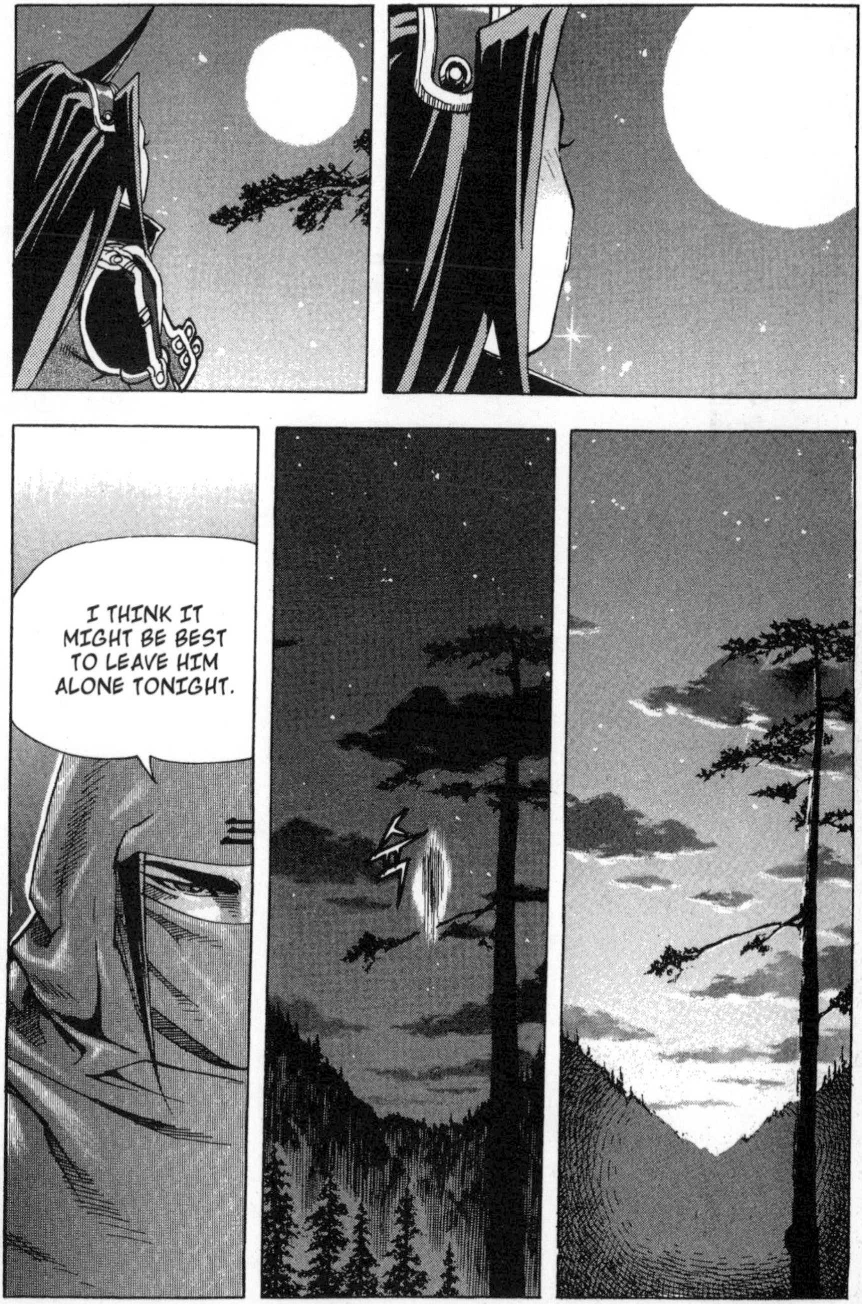
I THINK IT MIGHT BE BEST TO LEAVE HIM ALONE TONIGHT.

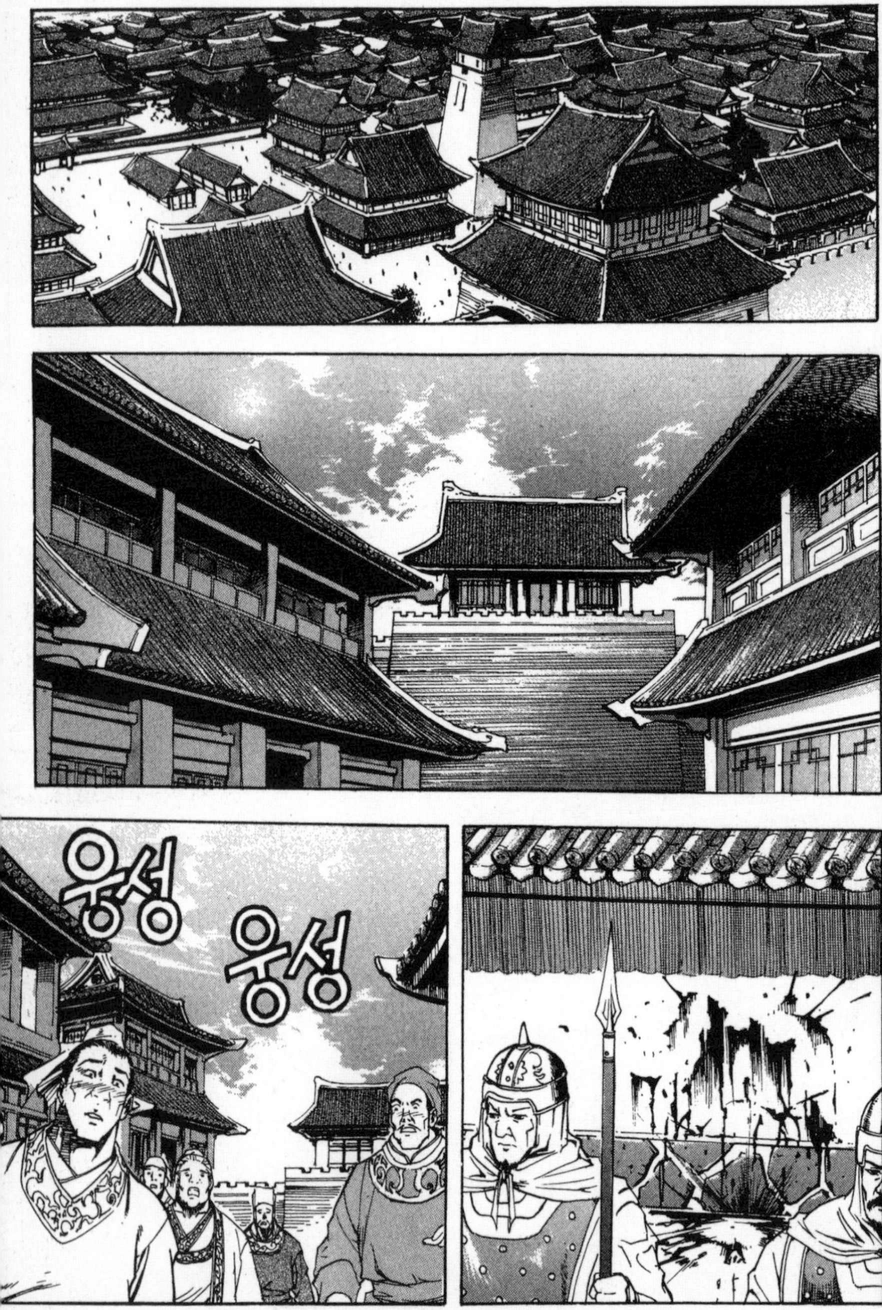
웅성
웅성

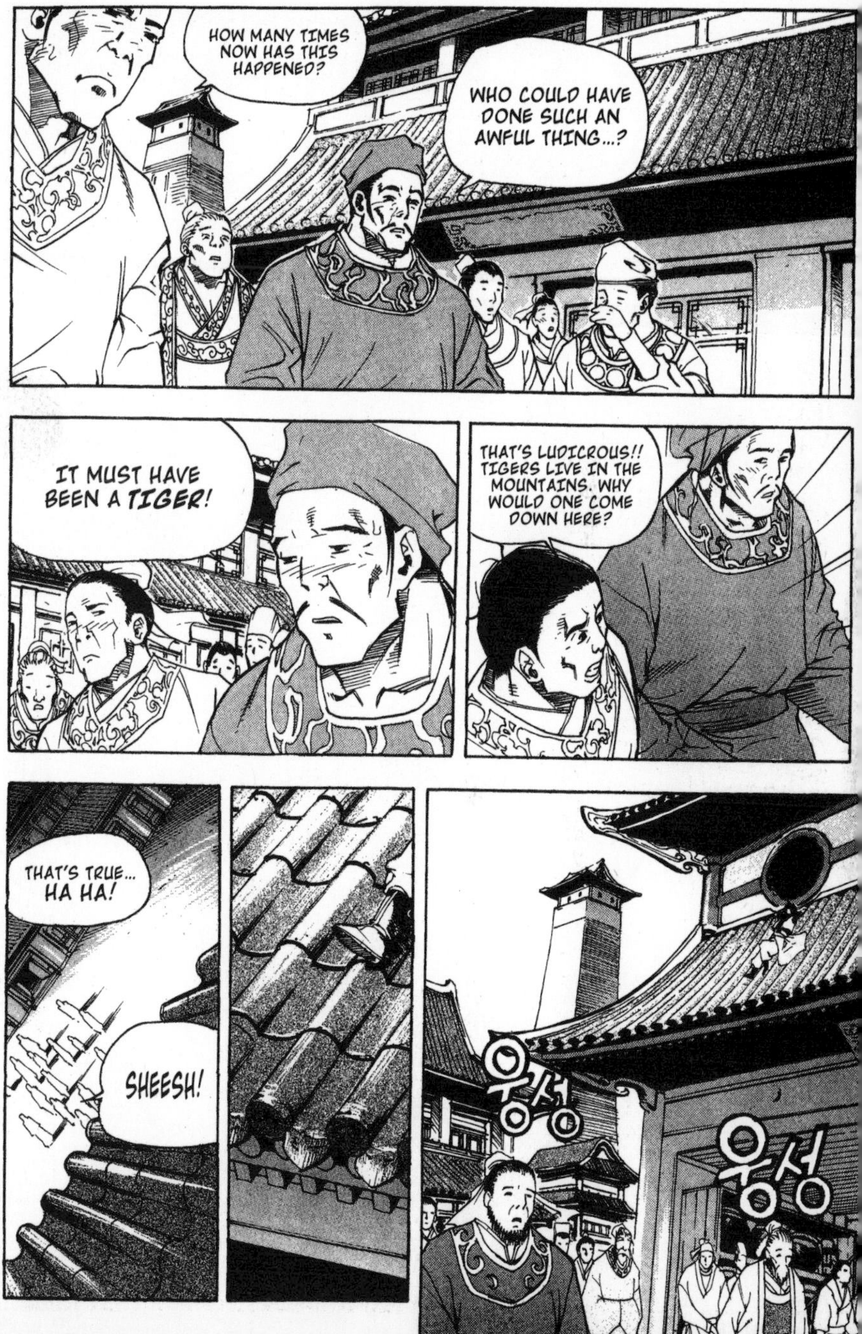
HOW MANY TIMES NOW HAS THIS HAPPENED?
WHO COULD HAVE DONE SUCH AN AWFUL THING...?
IT MUST HAVE BEEN A TIGER!
THAT'S LUDICROUS!! TIGERS LIVE IN THE MOUNTAINS. WHY WOULD ONE COME DOWN HERE?
THAT'S TRUE... HA HA!
SHEESH!
웅성
웅성

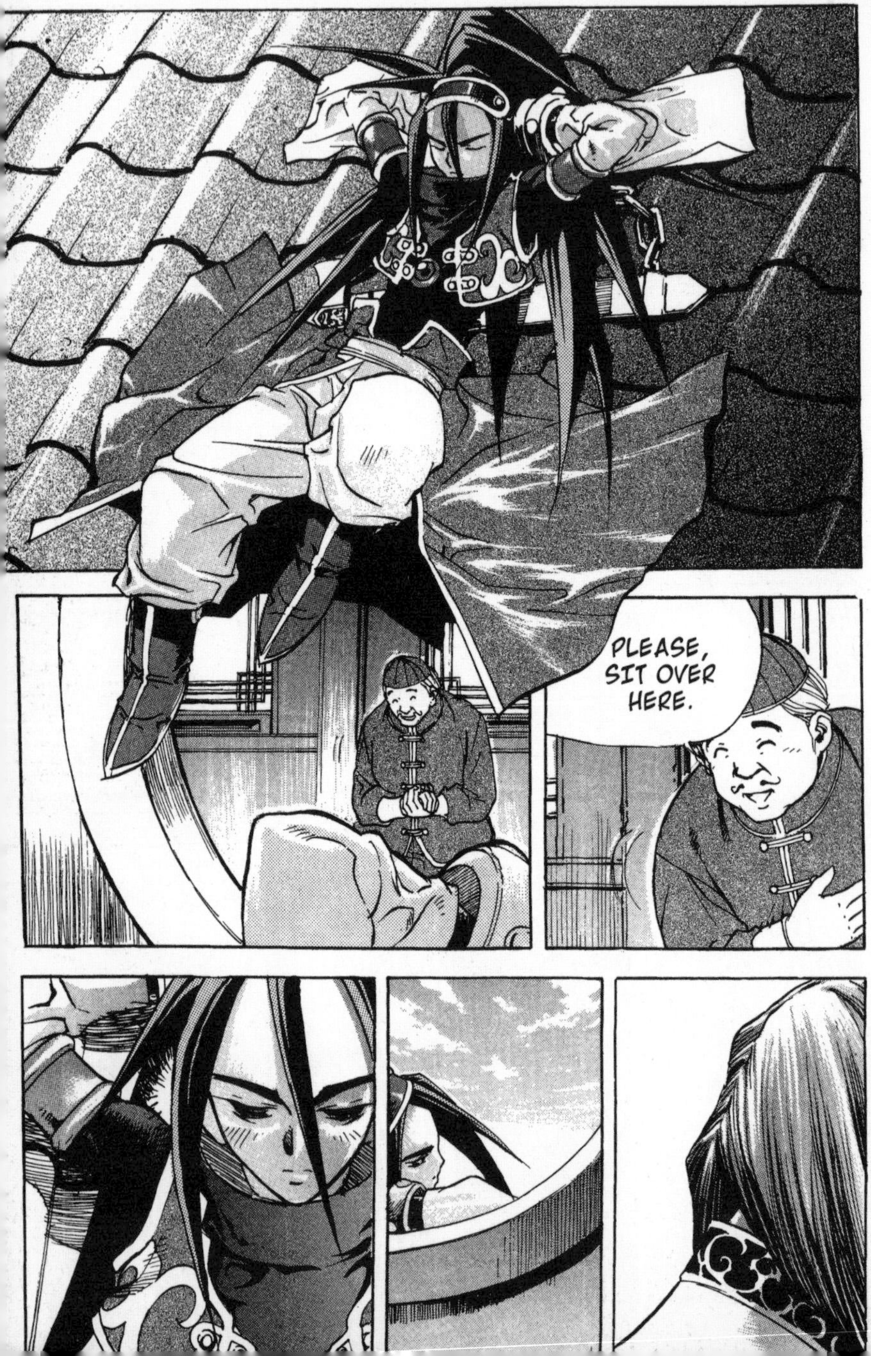
PLEASE, SIT OVER HERE.

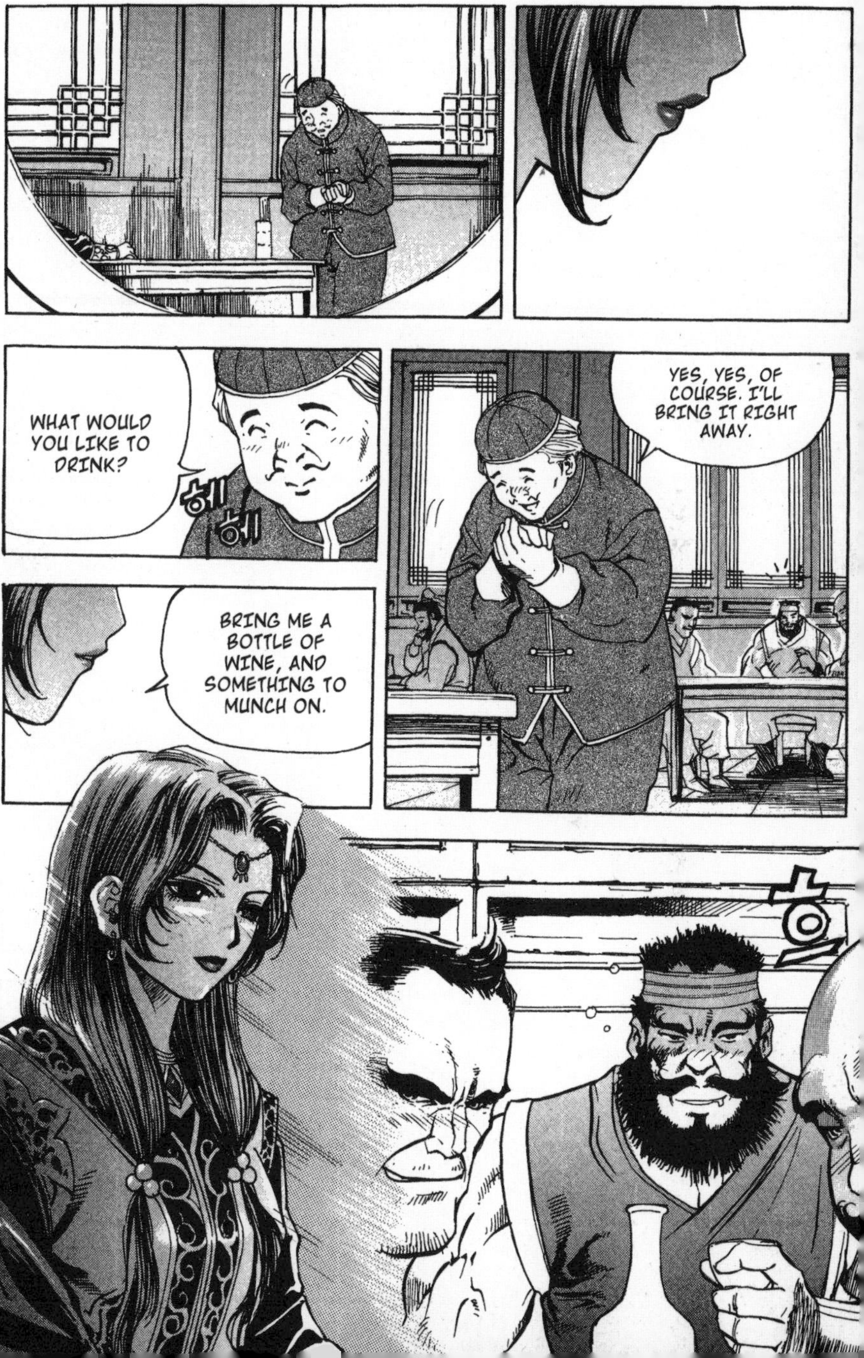
WHAT WOULD YOU LIKE TO DRINK?
헤 헤
BRING ME A BOTTLE OF WINE, AND SOMETHING TO MUNCH ON.
YES, YES, OF COURSE. I'LL BRING IT RIGHT AWAY.
흥

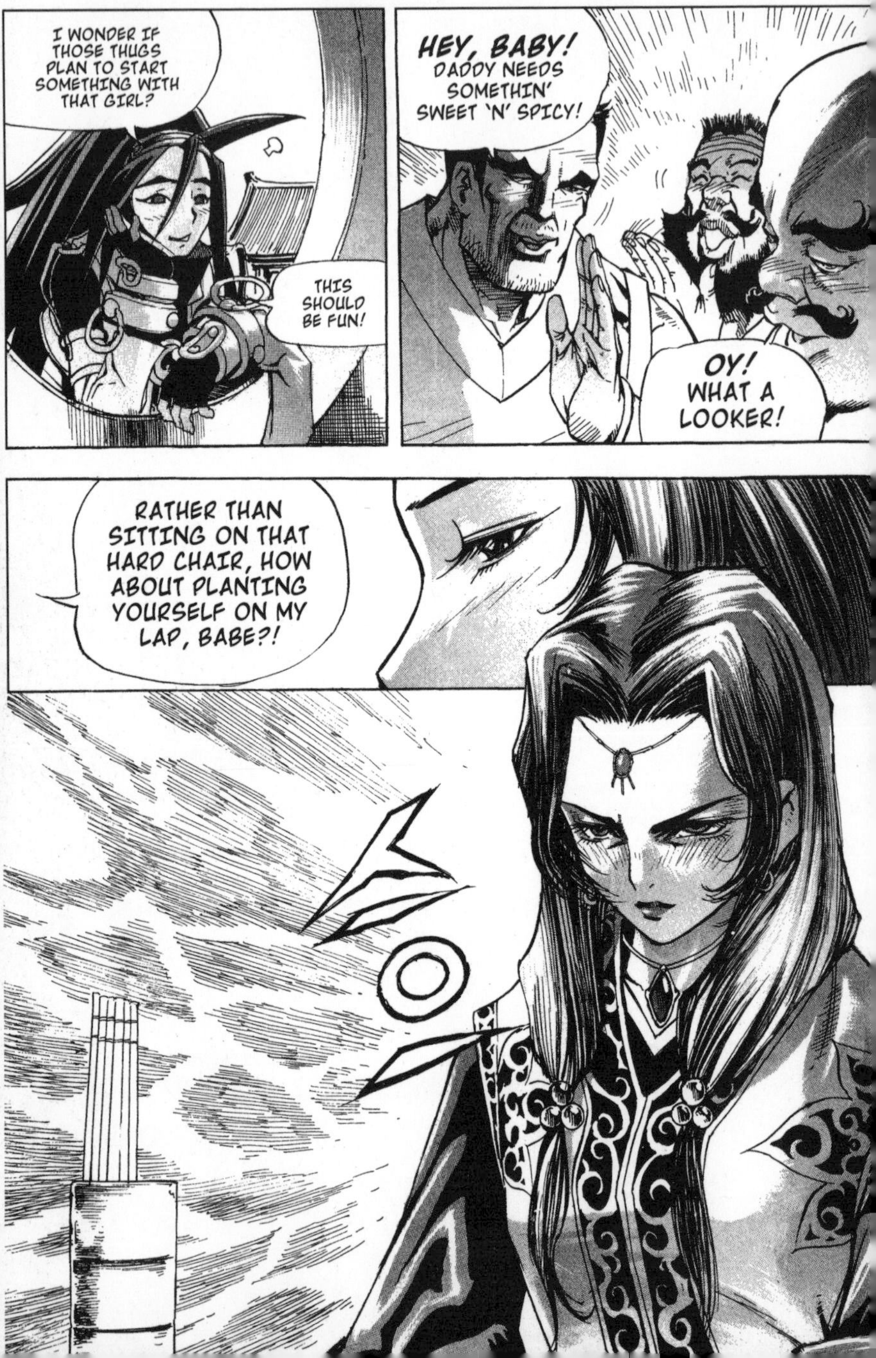
I WONDER IF THOSE THUGS PLAN TO START SOMETHING WITH THAT GIRL?
THIS SHOULD BE FUN!
HEY, BABY! DADDY NEEDS SOMETHIN' SWEET 'N' SPICY!
OY! WHAT A LOOKER!
RATHER THAN SITTING ON THAT HARD CHAIR, HOW ABOUT PLANTING YOURSELF ON MY LAP, BABE?!

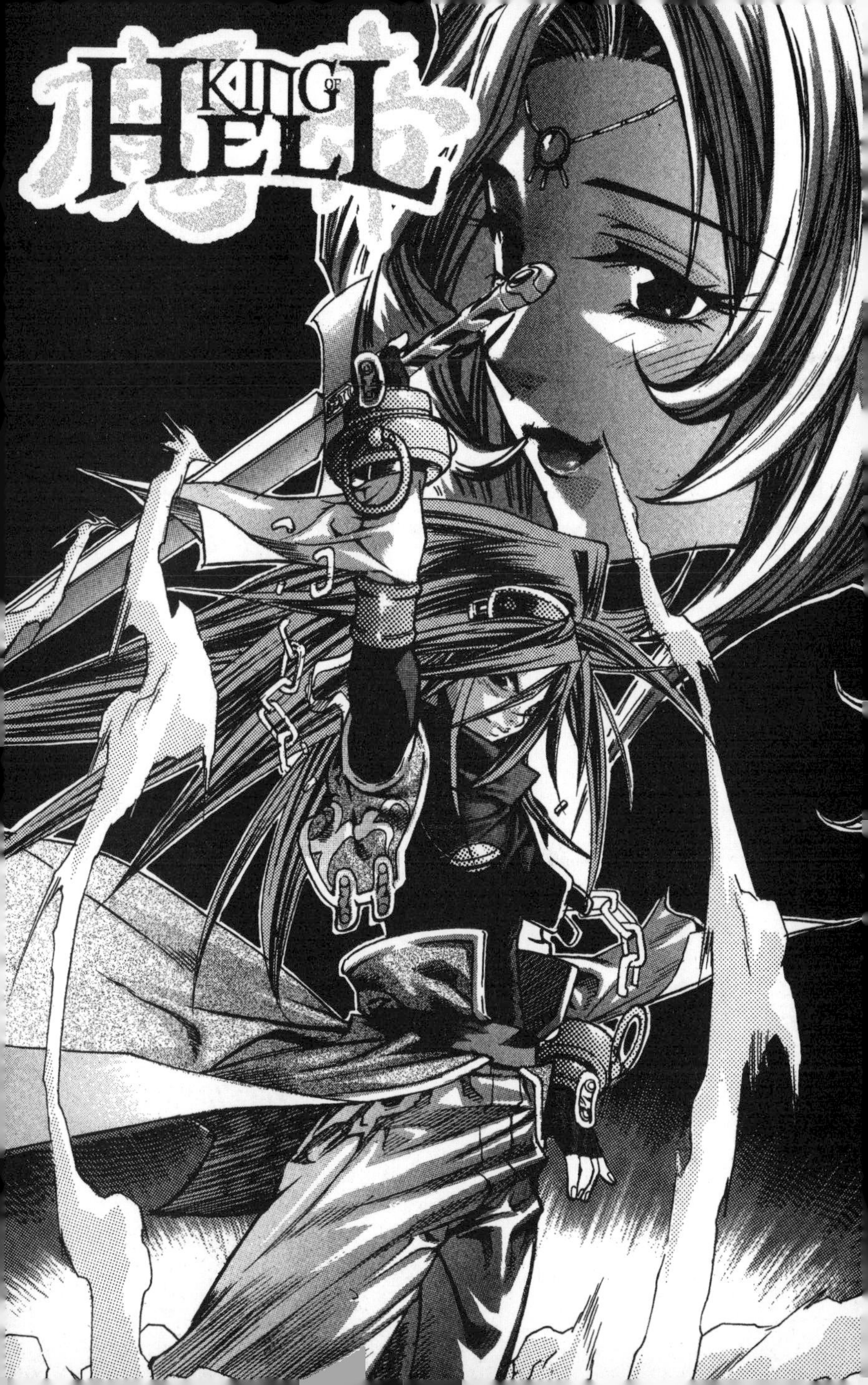
KING OF HELL

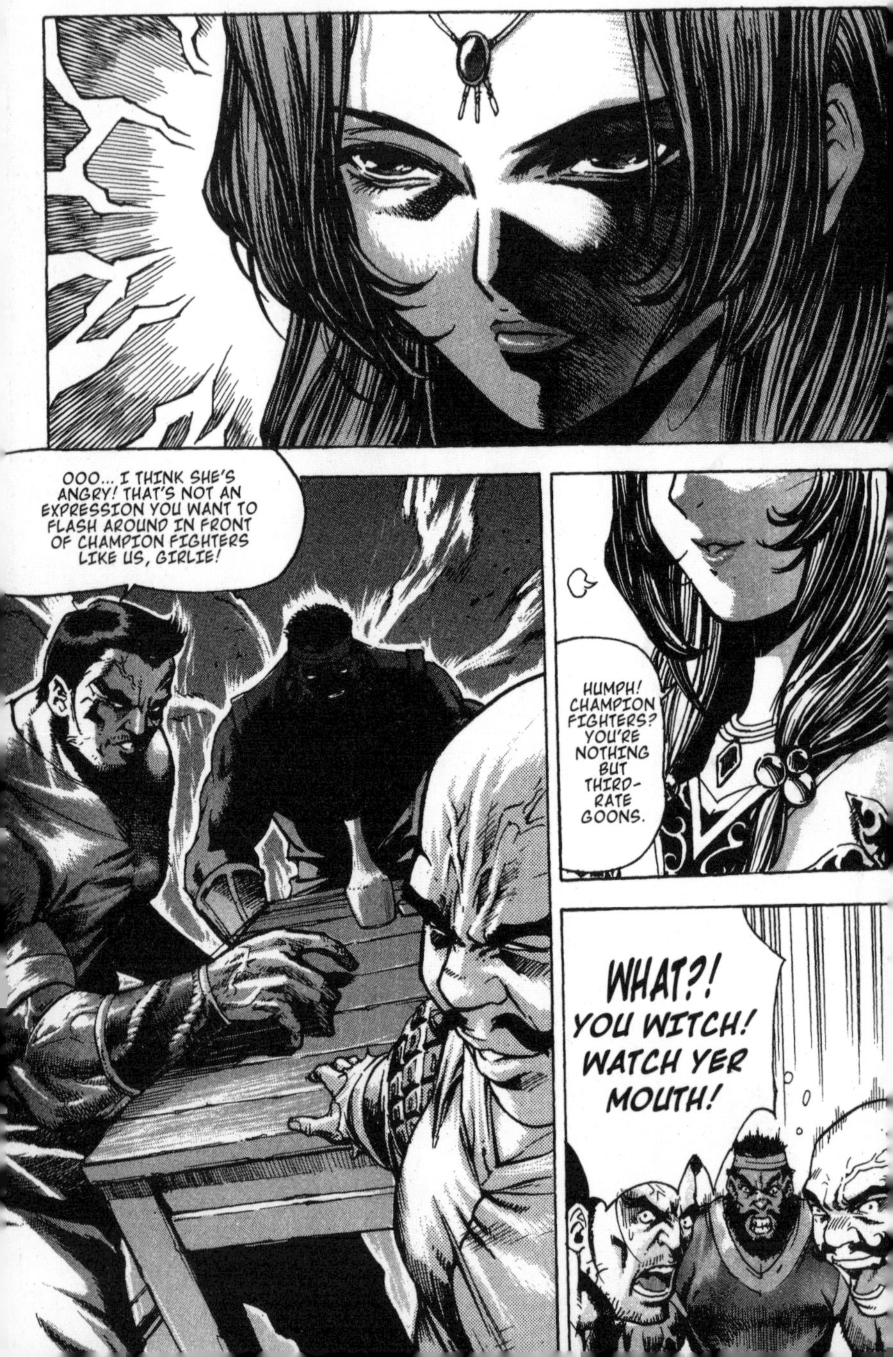
OOO... I THINK SHE'S ANGRY! THAT'S NOT AN EXPRESSION YOU WANT TO FLASH AROUND IN FRONT OF CHAMPION FIGHTERS LIKE US, GIRLIE!
HUMPH! CHAMPION FIGHTERS? YOU'RE NOTHING BUT THIRD-RATE GOONS.
WHAT?! YOU WITCH! WATCH YER MOUTH!

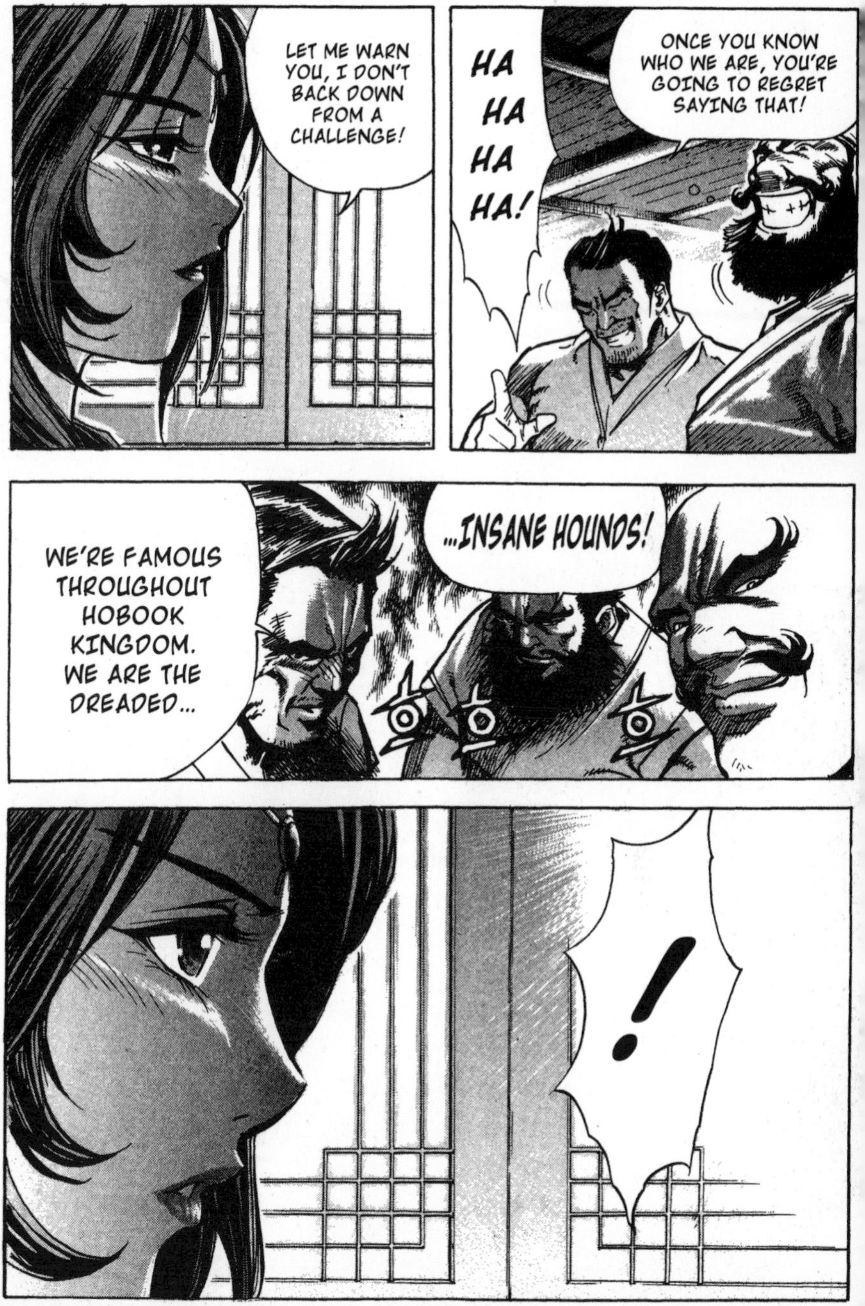
LET ME WARN YOU, I DON'T BACK DOWN FROM A CHALLENGE!
HA HA HA HA!
ONCE YOU KNOW WHO WE ARE, YOU'RE GOING TO REGRET SAYING THAT!
WE'RE FAMOUS THROUGHOUT HOBOOK KINGDOM. WE ARE THE DREADED...
...INSANE HOUNDS!
!

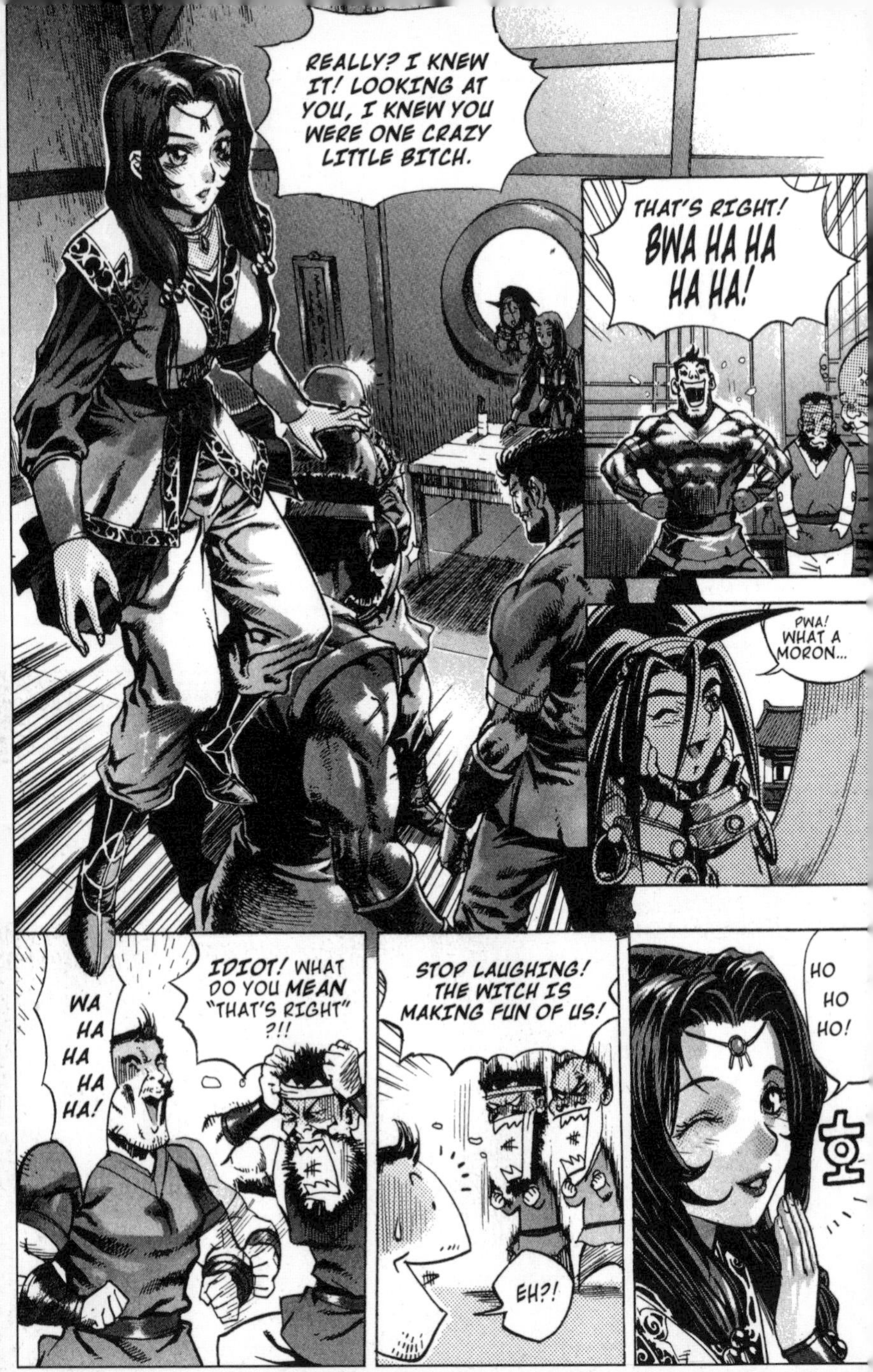
REALLY? I KNEW IT! LOOKING AT YOU, I KNEW YOU WERE ONE CRAZY LITTLE BITCH.
THAT'S RIGHT! BWA HA HA HA HA!
PWA! WHAT A MORON...
WA HA HA HA HA HA!
IDIOT! WHAT DO YOU MEAN "THAT'S RIGHT" ?!!
STOP LAUGHING! THE WITCH IS MAKING FUN OF US!
EH?!
HO HO HO!
호

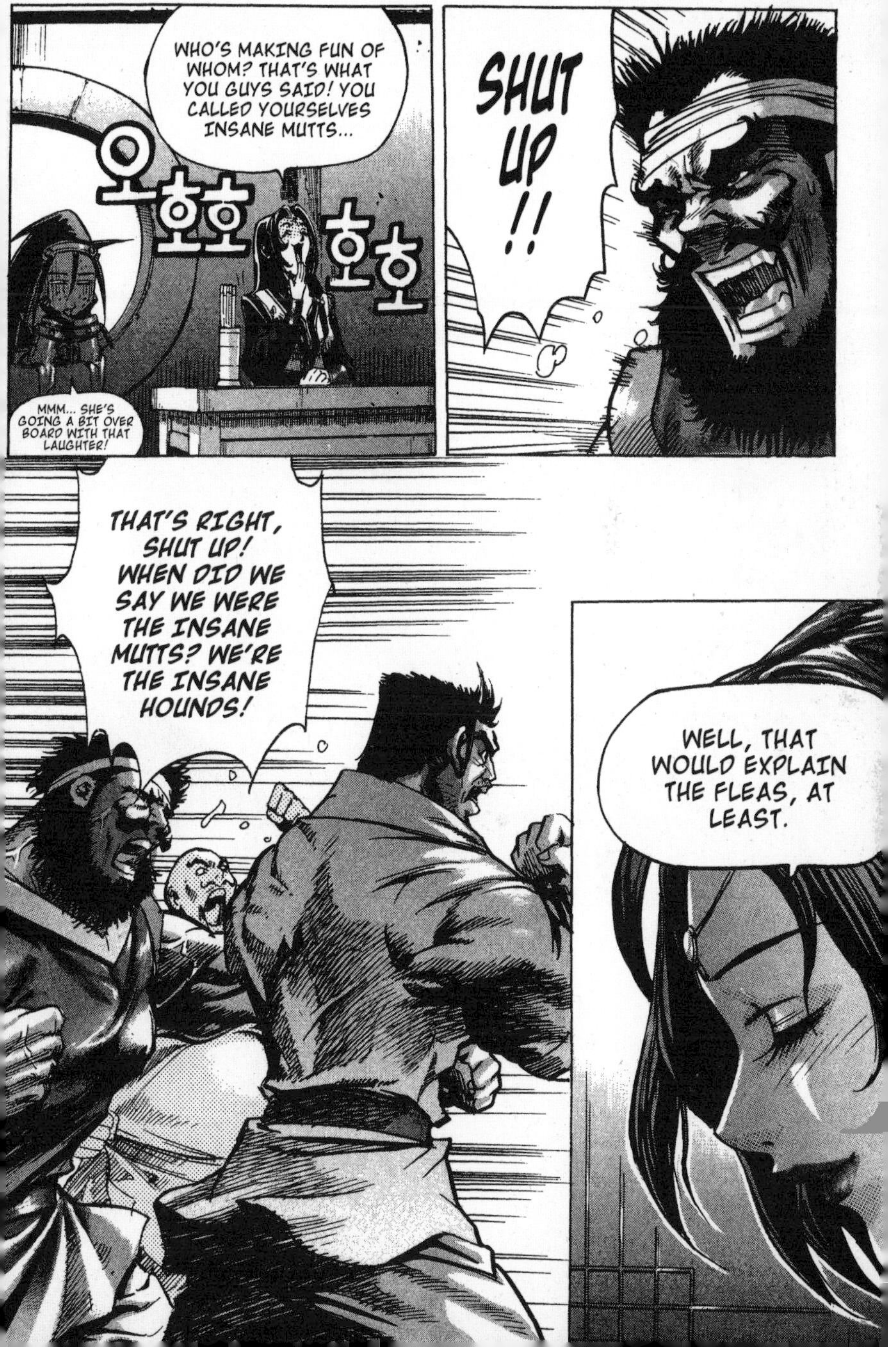
WHO'S MAKING FUN OF WHOM? THAT'S WHAT YOU GUYS SAID! YOU CALLED YOURSELVES INSANE MUTTS...
오호호 호호
MMM... SHE'S GOING A BIT OVER BOARD WITH THAT LAUGHTER!
SHUT UP!!
THAT'S RIGHT, SHUT UP! WHEN DID WE SAY WE WERE THE INSANE MUTTS? WE'RE THE INSANE HOUNDS!
WELL, THAT WOULD EXPLAIN THE FLEAS, AT LEAST.

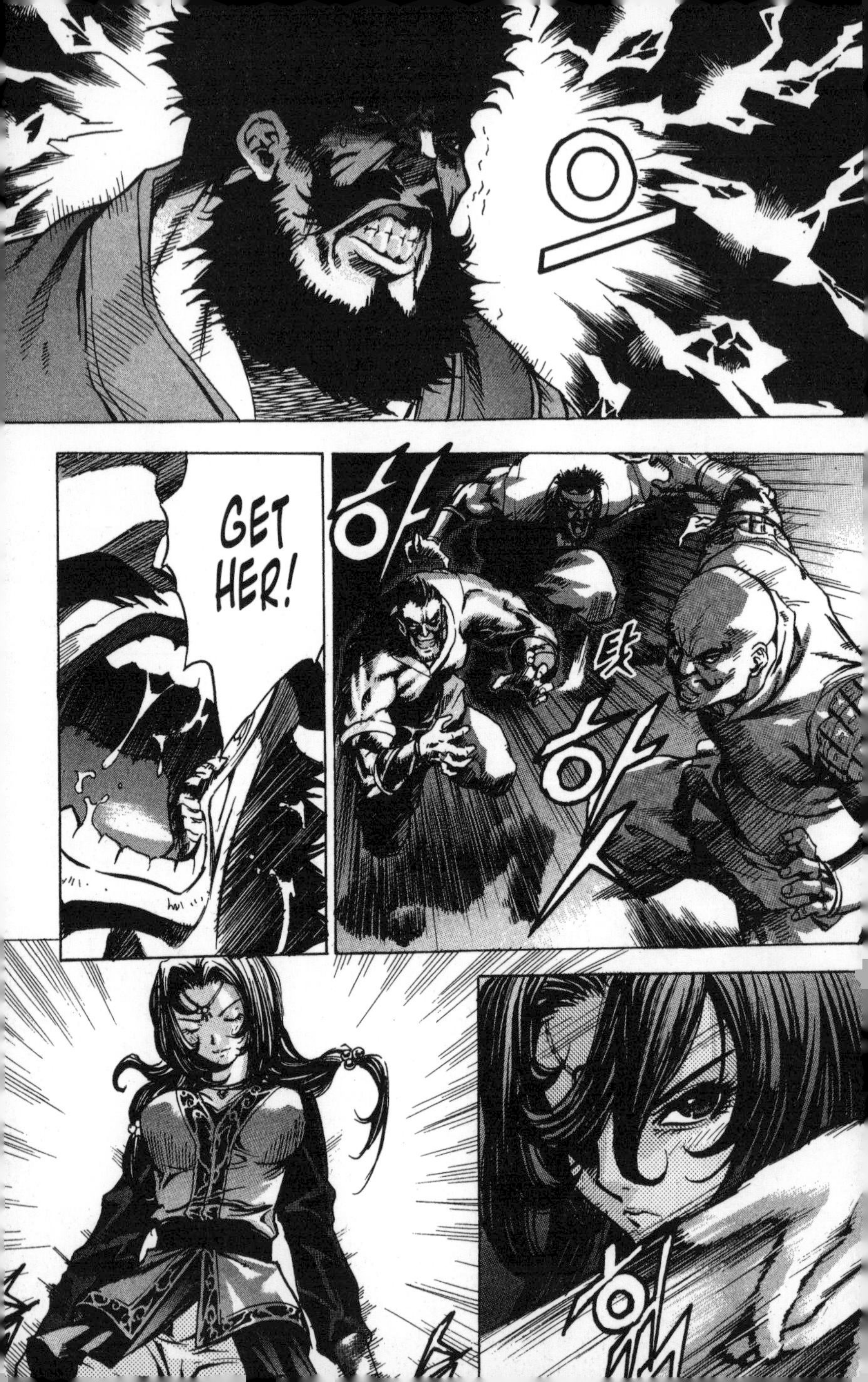
GET HER!
하
하

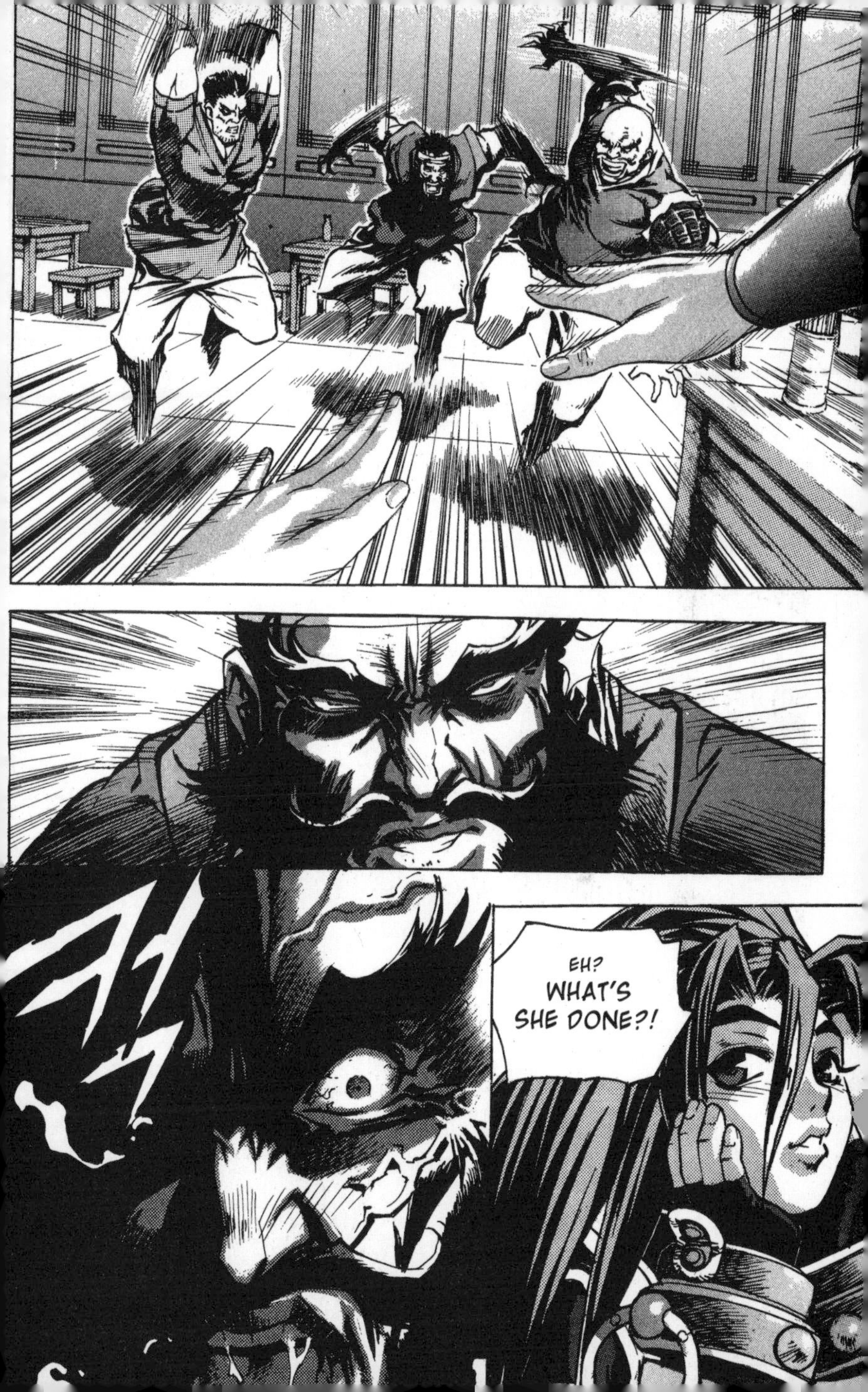
EH?
WHAT'S SHE DONE?!

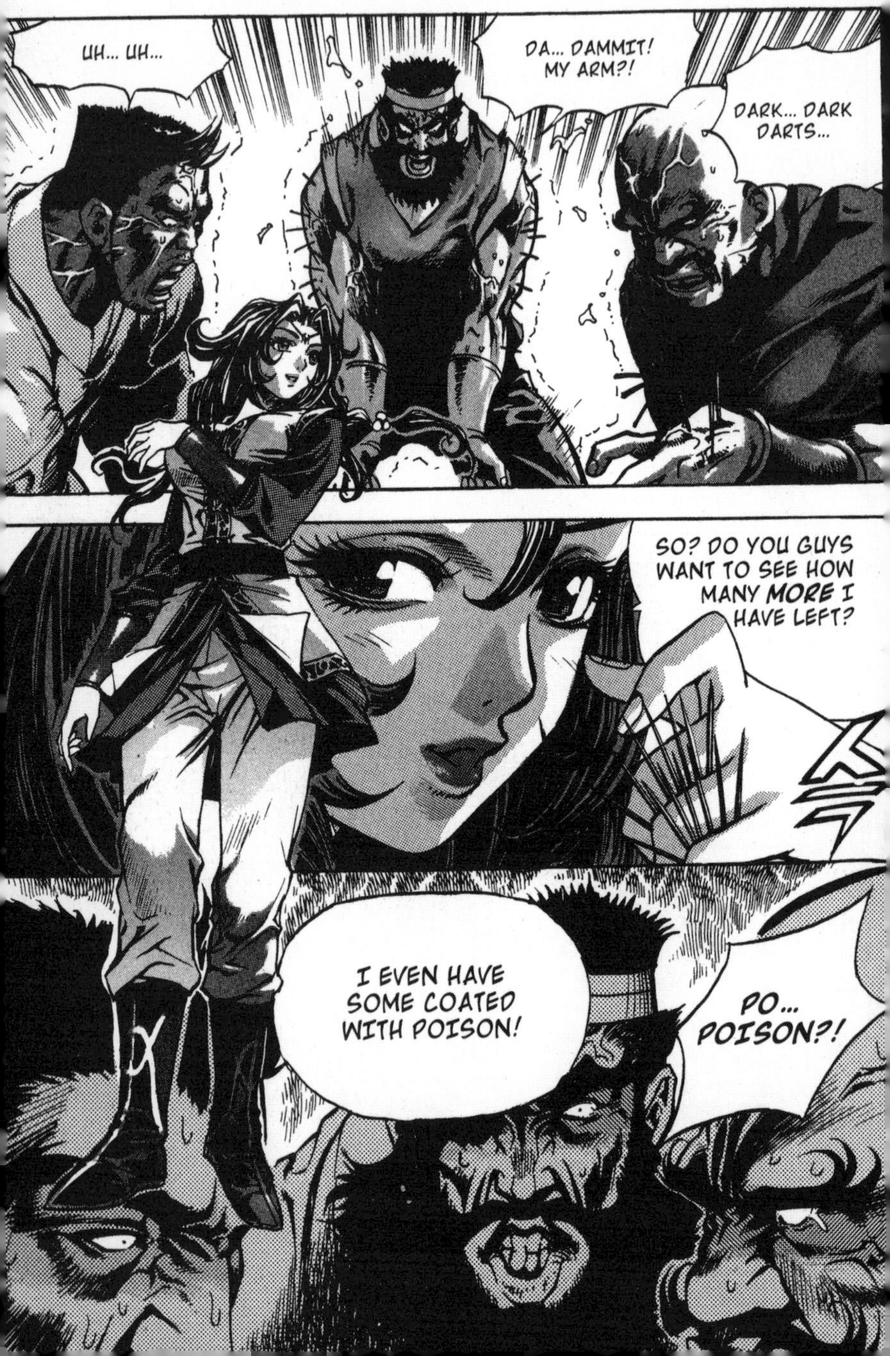
UH... UH...
DA... DAMMIT! MY ARM?!
DARK... DARK DARTS...
SO? DO YOU GUYS WANT TO SEE HOW MANY **MORE** I HAVE LEFT?
I EVEN HAVE SOME COATED WITH POISON!
PO... POISON?!

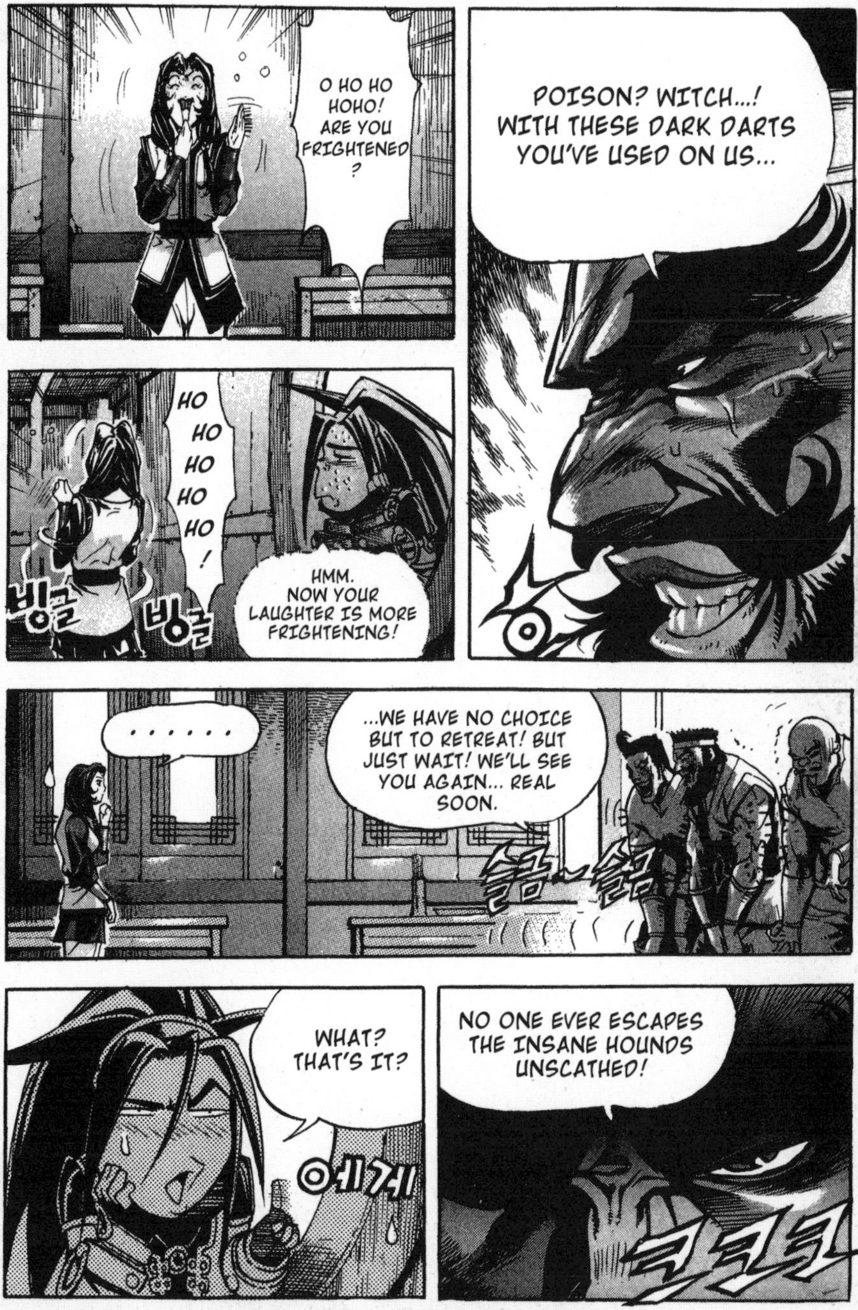
O HO HO HOHO! ARE YOU FRIGHTENED?
HO HO HO HO HO!
빙글 빙글
HMM. NOW YOUR LAUGHTER IS MORE FRIGHTENING!
POISON? WITCH...! WITH THESE DARK DARTS YOU'VE USED ON US...
......
...WE HAVE NO CHOICE BUT TO RETREAT! BUT JUST WAIT! WE'LL SEE YOU AGAIN... REAL SOON.
슬금~슬금
WHAT? THAT'S IT?
에게
NO ONE EVER ESCAPES THE INSANE HOUNDS UNSCATHED!

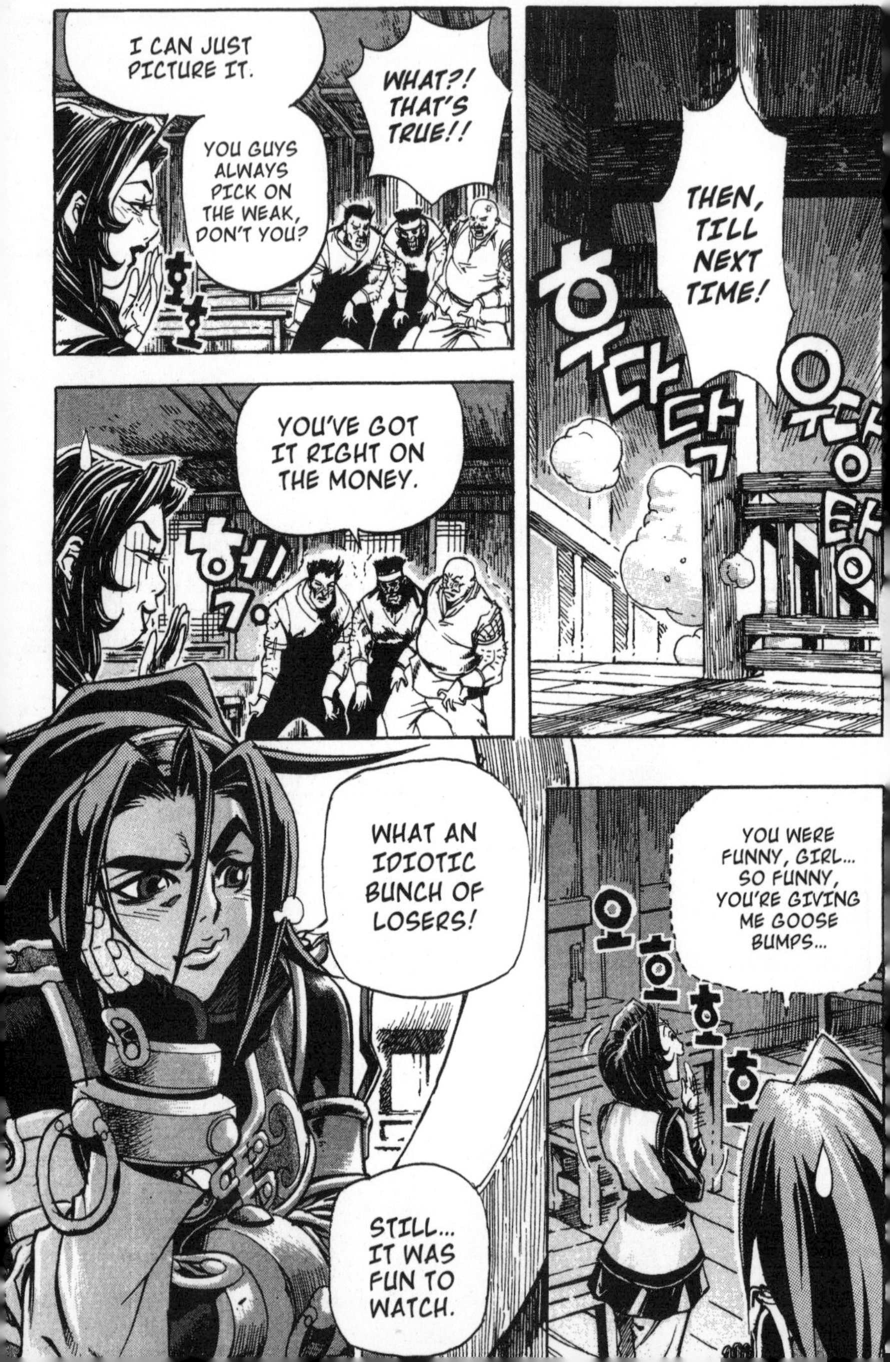
I CAN JUST PICTURE IT.
YOU GUYS ALWAYS PICK ON THE WEAK, DON'T YOU?
호호
WHAT?! THAT'S TRUE!!
YOU'VE GOT IT RIGHT ON THE MONEY.
THEN, TILL NEXT TIME!
후다닥
우당탕
WHAT AN IDIOTIC BUNCH OF LOSERS!
STILL... IT WAS FUN TO WATCH.
YOU WERE FUNNY, GIRL... SO FUNNY, YOU'RE GIVING ME GOOSE BUMPS...
오호호호

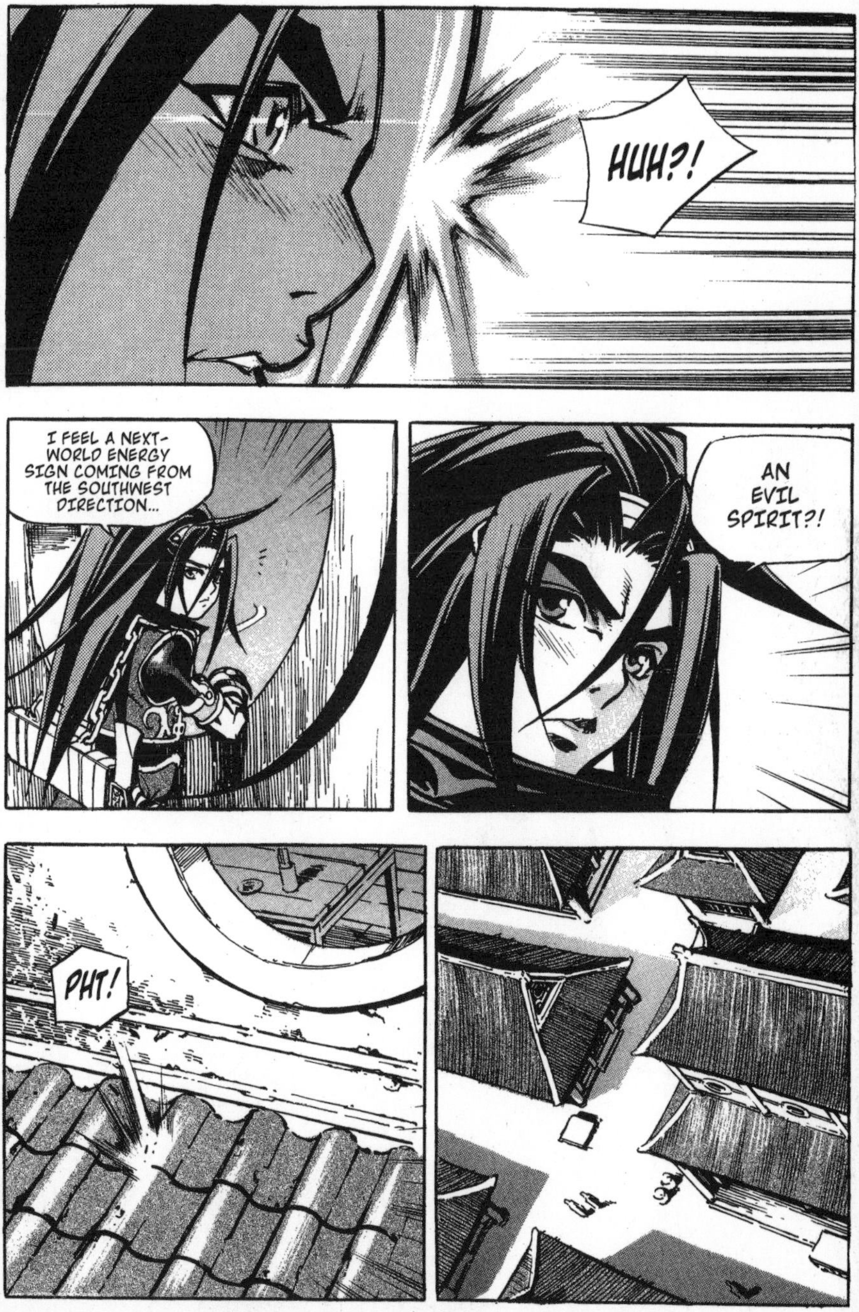
HUH?!
I FEEL A NEXT-WORLD ENERGY SIGN COMING FROM THE SOUTHWEST DIRECTION...
AN EVIL SPIRIT?!
PHT!

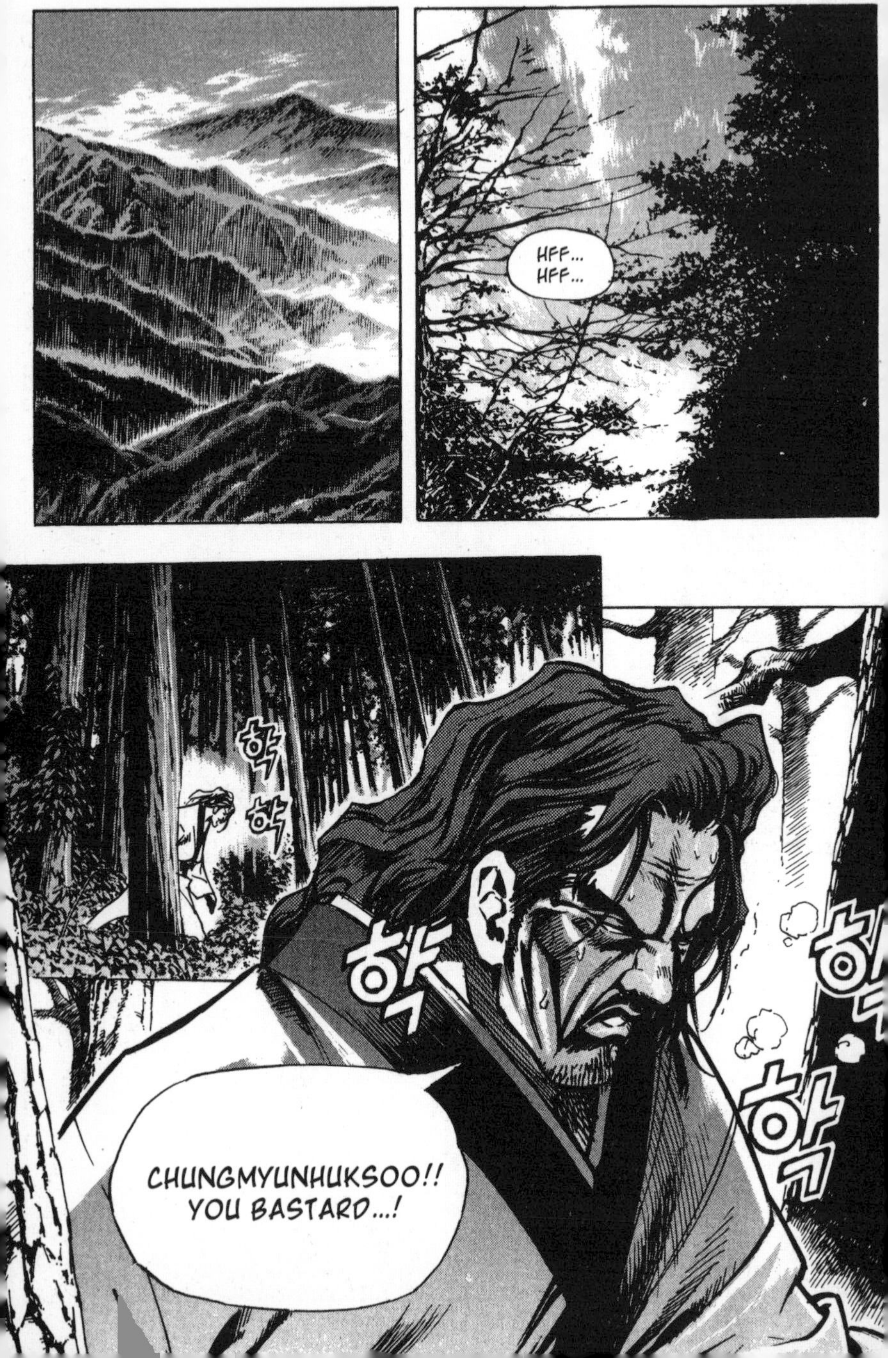
HFF...
HFF...
헉
헉
CHUNGMYUNHUKSOO!!
YOU BASTARD...!
헉
헉
헉

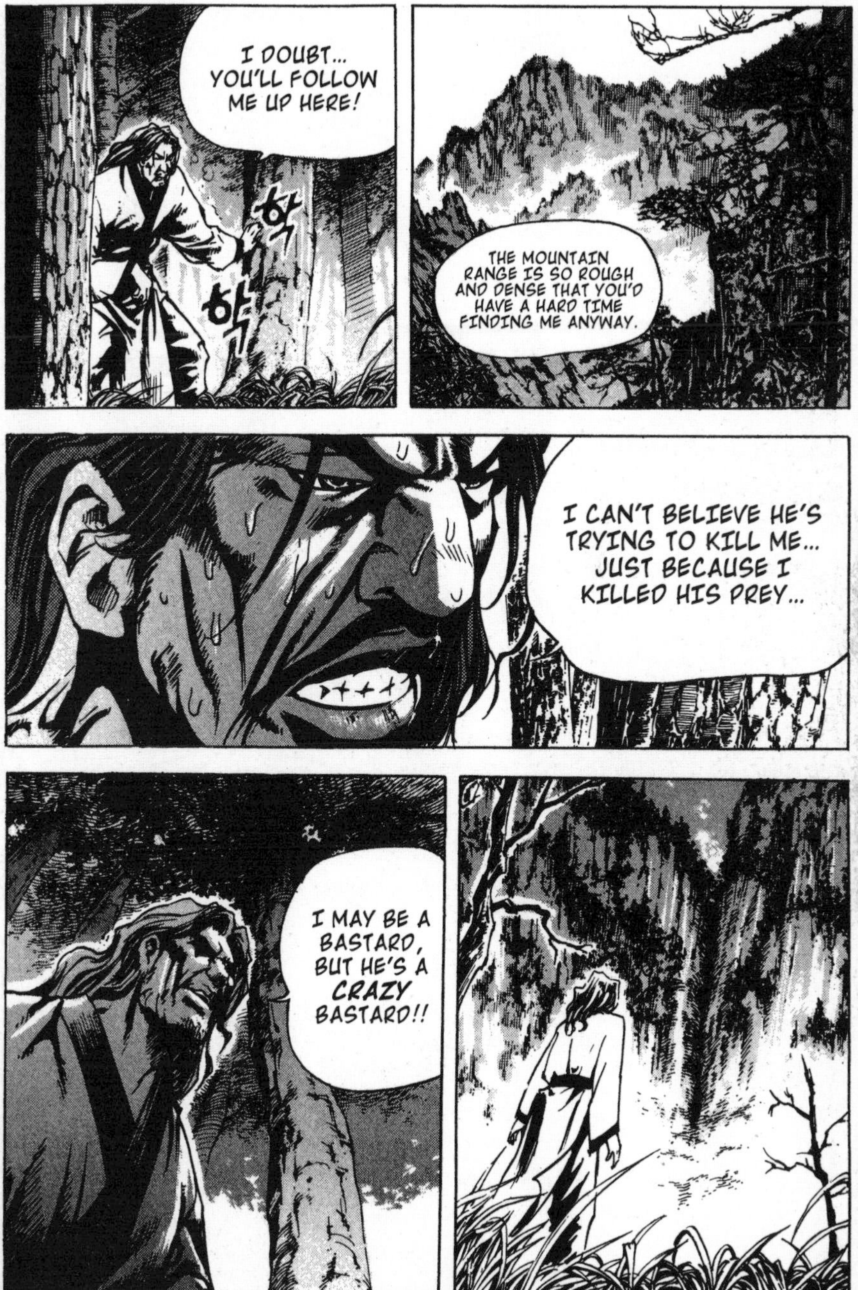
I DOUBT... YOU'LL FOLLOW ME UP HERE!
헉
헉
THE MOUNTAIN RANGE IS SO ROUGH AND DENSE THAT YOU'D HAVE A HARD TIME FINDING ME ANYWAY.
I CAN'T BELIEVE HE'S TRYING TO KILL ME... JUST BECAUSE I KILLED HIS PREY...
I MAY BE A BASTARD, BUT HE'S A *CRAZY* BASTARD!!

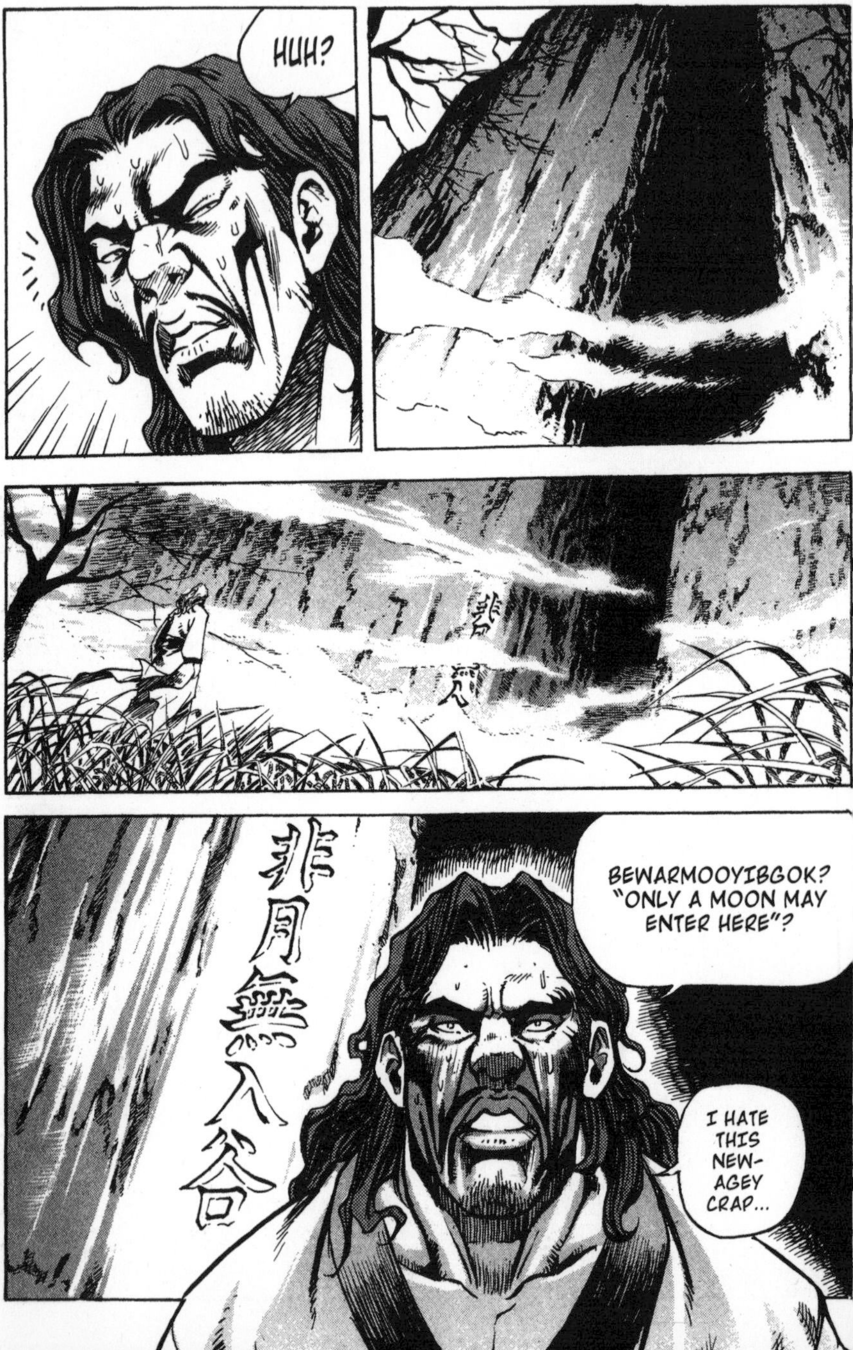
HUH?
非月無入谷
BEWARMOOYIBGOK? "ONLY A MOON MAY ENTER HERE"?
I HATE THIS NEW-AGEY CRAP...

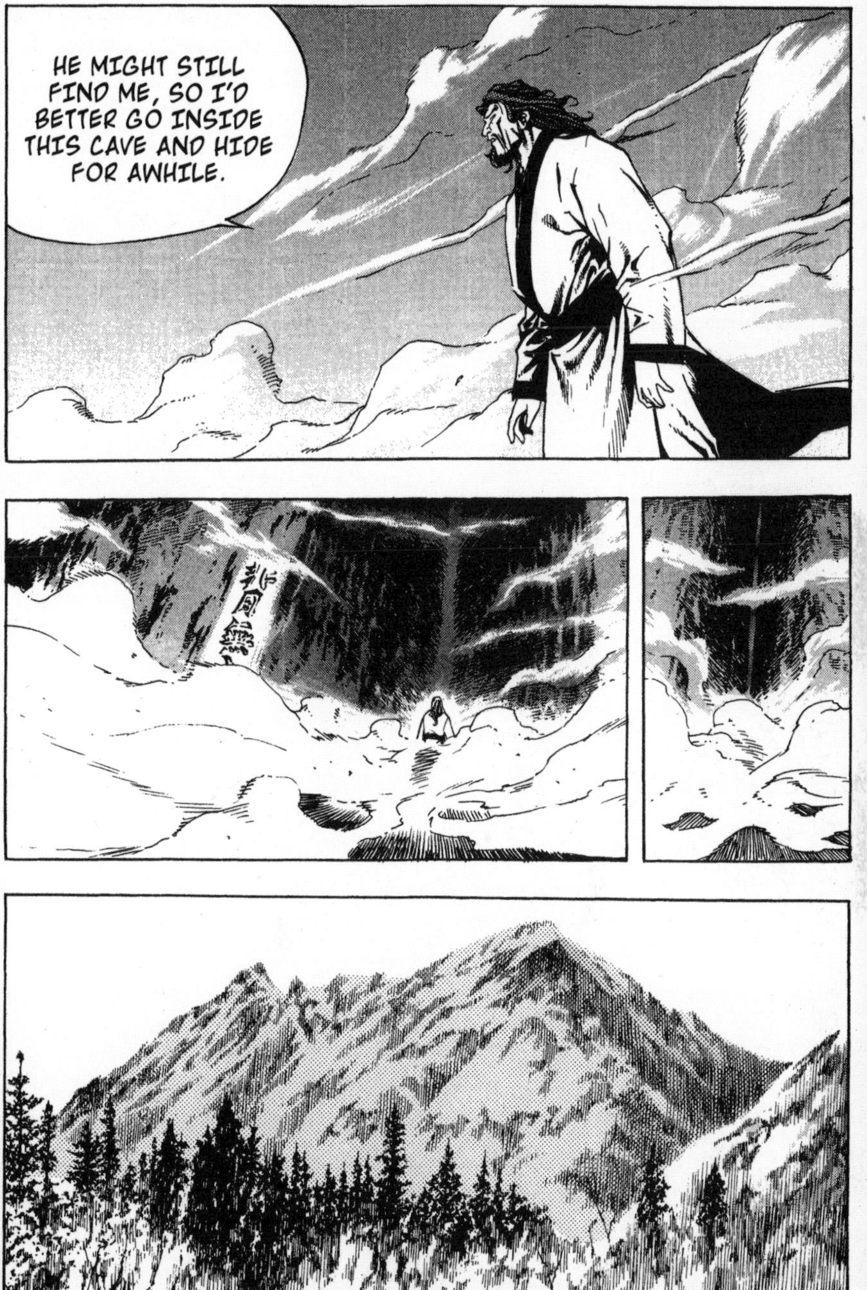
HE MIGHT STILL FIND ME, SO I'D BETTER GO INSIDE THIS CAVE AND HIDE FOR AWHILE.

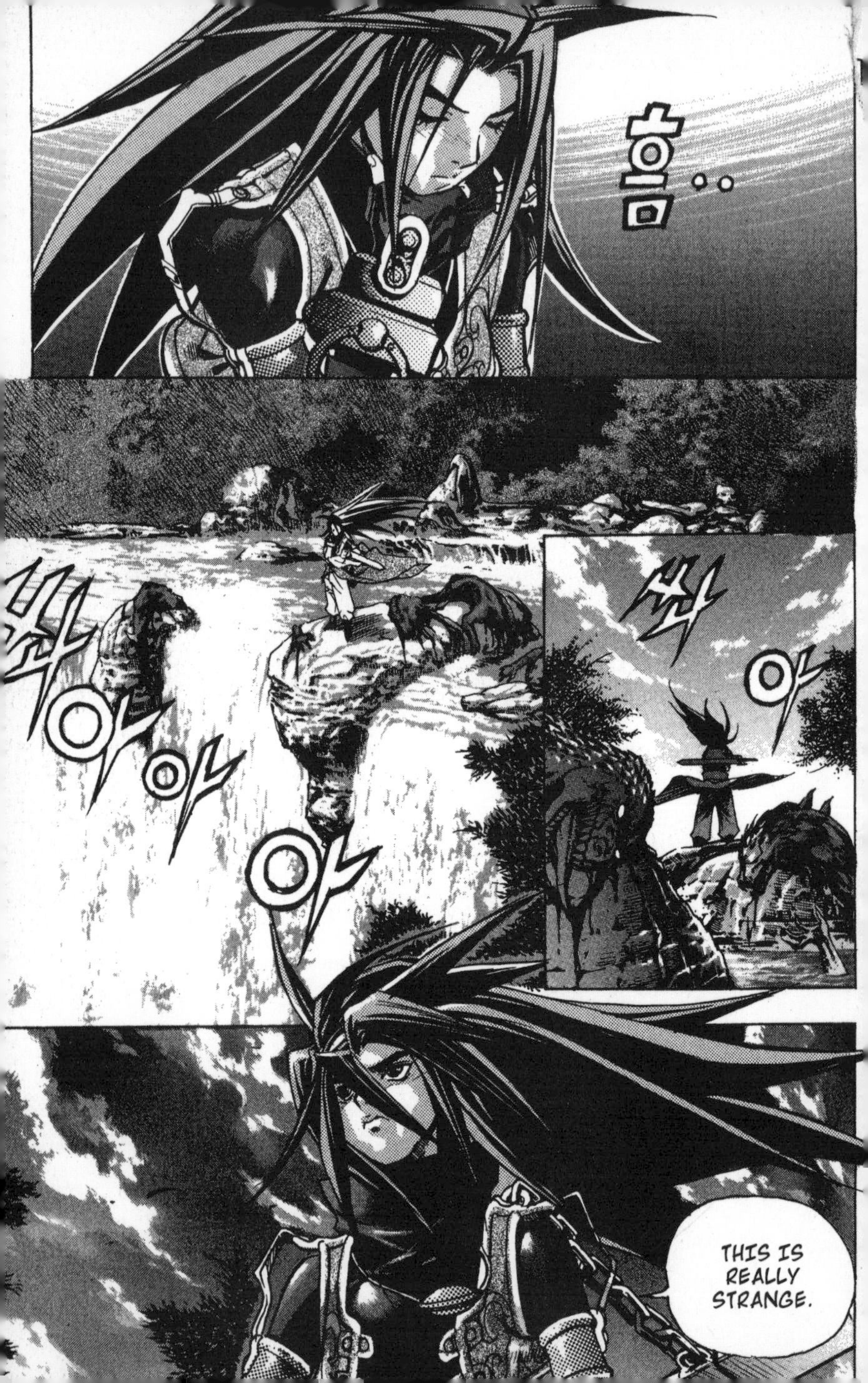
흠..
THIS IS REALLY STRANGE.

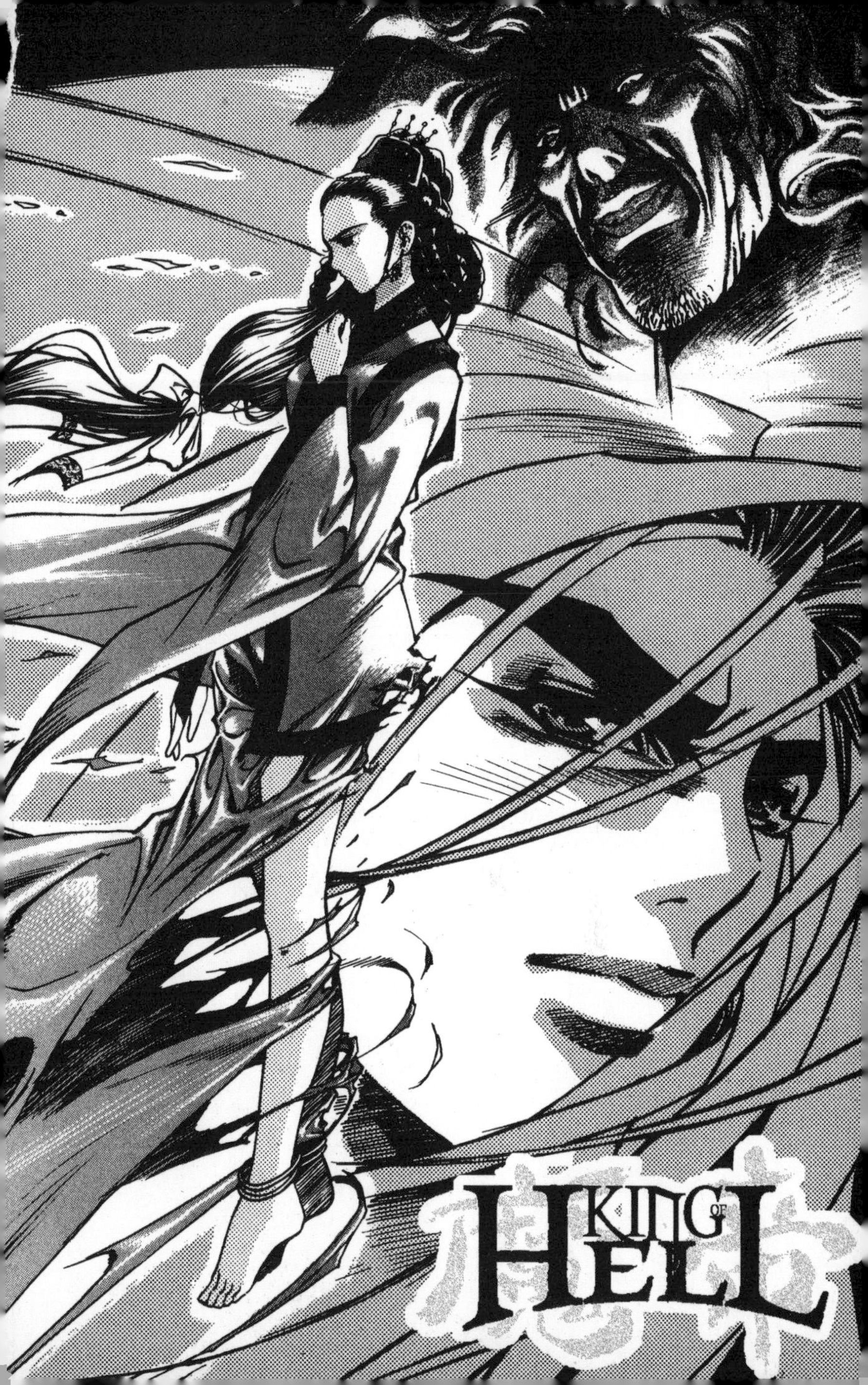
KING OF HELL

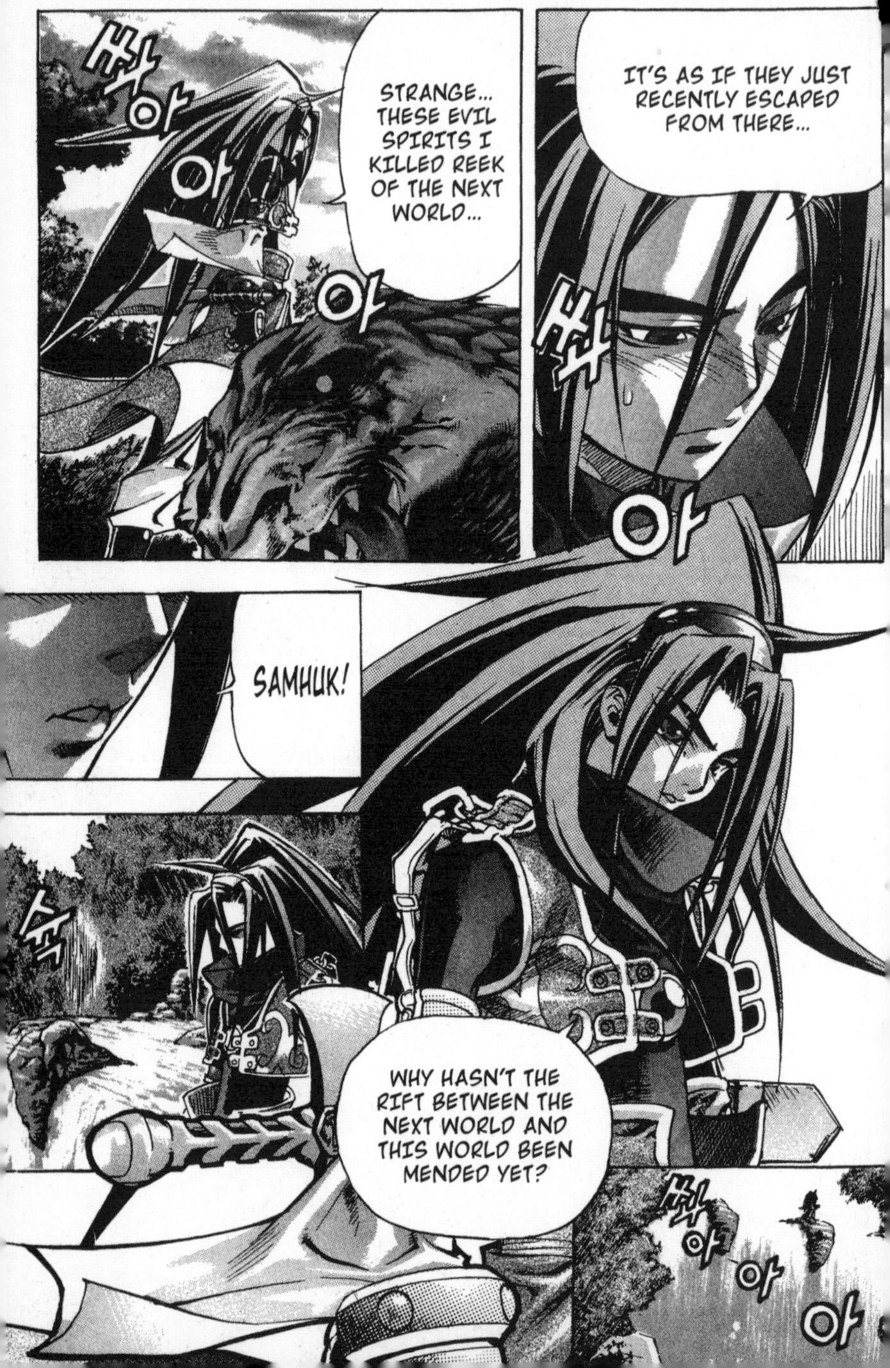
STRANGE... THESE EVIL SPIRITS I KILLED REEK OF THE NEXT WORLD...
IT'S AS IF THEY JUST RECENTLY ESCAPED FROM THERE...
SAMHUK!
WHY HASN'T THE RIFT BETWEEN THE NEXT WORLD AND THIS WORLD BEEN MENDED YET?

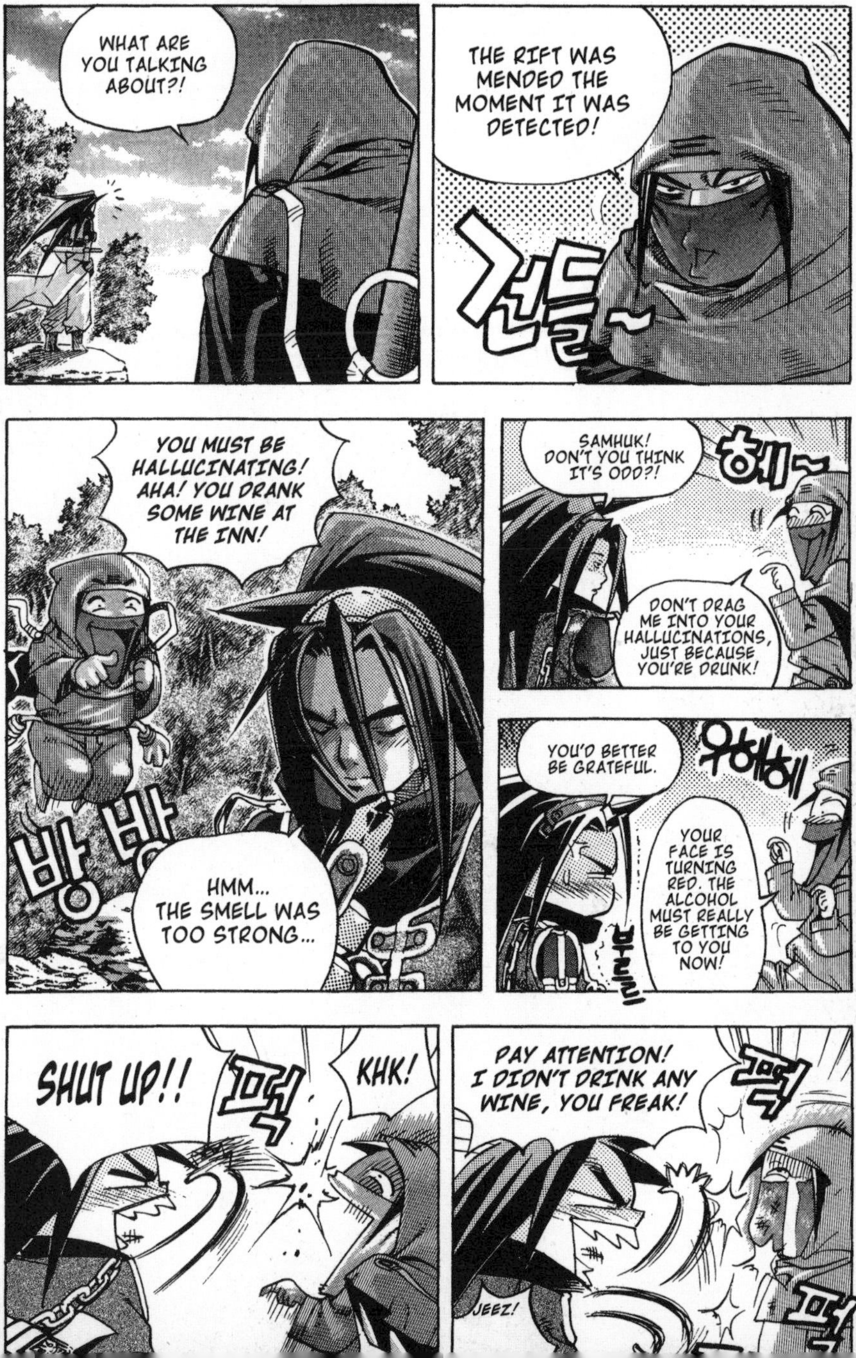
WHAT ARE YOU TALKING ABOUT?!
THE RIFT WAS MENDED THE MOMENT IT WAS DETECTED!
건들~
YOU MUST BE HALLUCINATING! AHA! YOU DRANK SOME WINE AT THE INN!
방방
HMM... THE SMELL WAS TOO STRONG...
SAMHUK! DON'T YOU THINK IT'S ODD?!
헤~
DON'T DRAG ME INTO YOUR HALLUCINATIONS, JUST BECAUSE YOU'RE DRUNK!
YOU'D BETTER BE GRATEFUL.
우헤헤
YOUR FACE IS TURNING RED. THE ALCOHOL MUST REALLY BE GETTING TO YOU NOW!
SHUT UP!!
퍽
KHK!
PAY ATTENTION! I DIDN'T DRINK ANY WINE, YOU FREAK!
퍽
JEEZ!
퍽

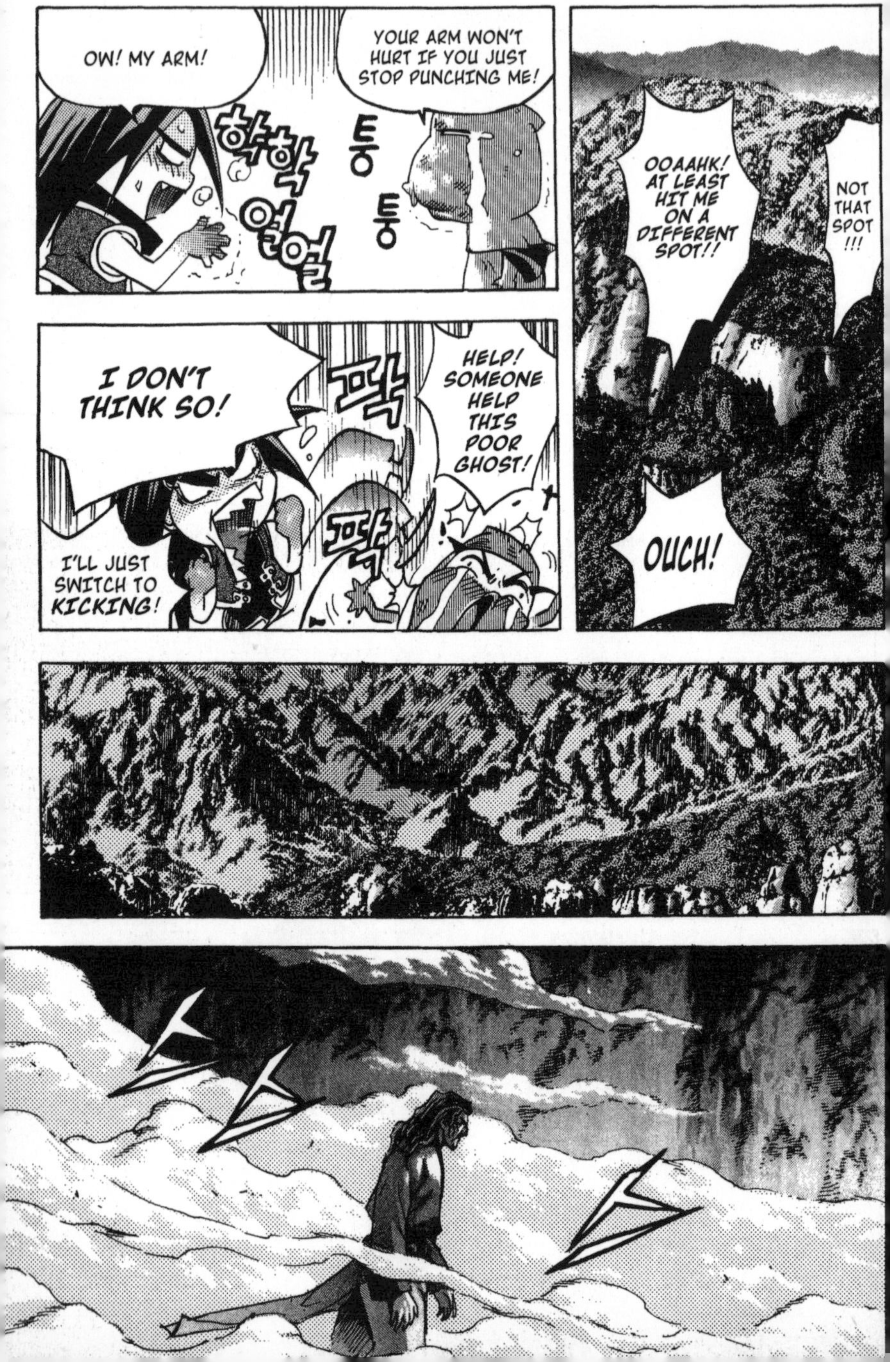
OW! MY ARM!
YOUR ARM WON'T HURT IF YOU JUST STOP PUNCHING ME!
I DON'T THINK SO!
HELP! SOMEONE HELP THIS POOR GHOST!
I'LL JUST SWITCH TO KICKING!
OOAAHK! AT LEAST HIT ME ON A DIFFERENT SPOT!!
NOT THAT SPOT!!!
OUCH!

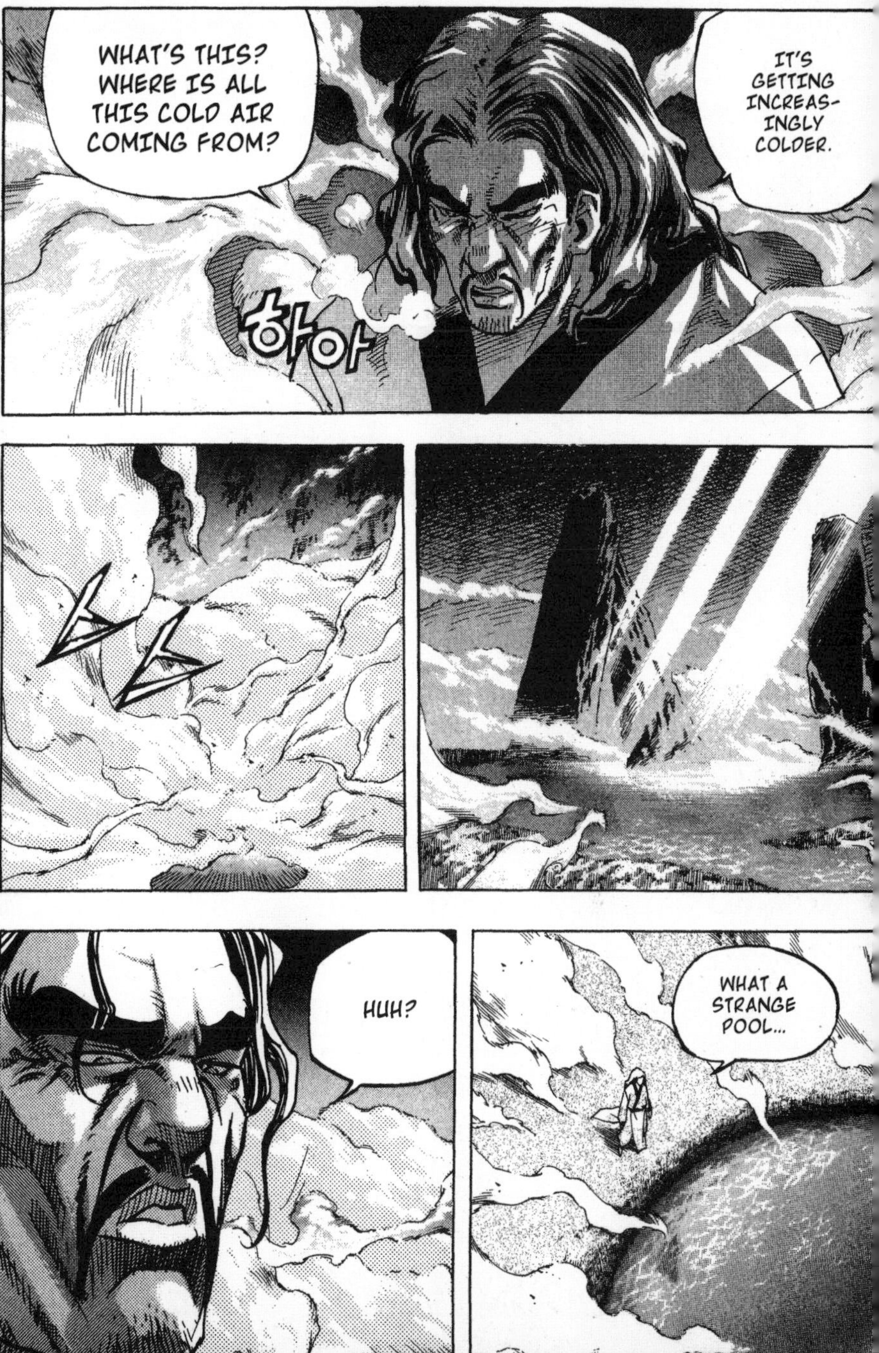
WHAT'S THIS? WHERE IS ALL THIS COLD AIR COMING FROM?
하아
IT'S GETTING INCREAS-INGLY COLDER.
HUH?
WHAT A STRANGE POOL...

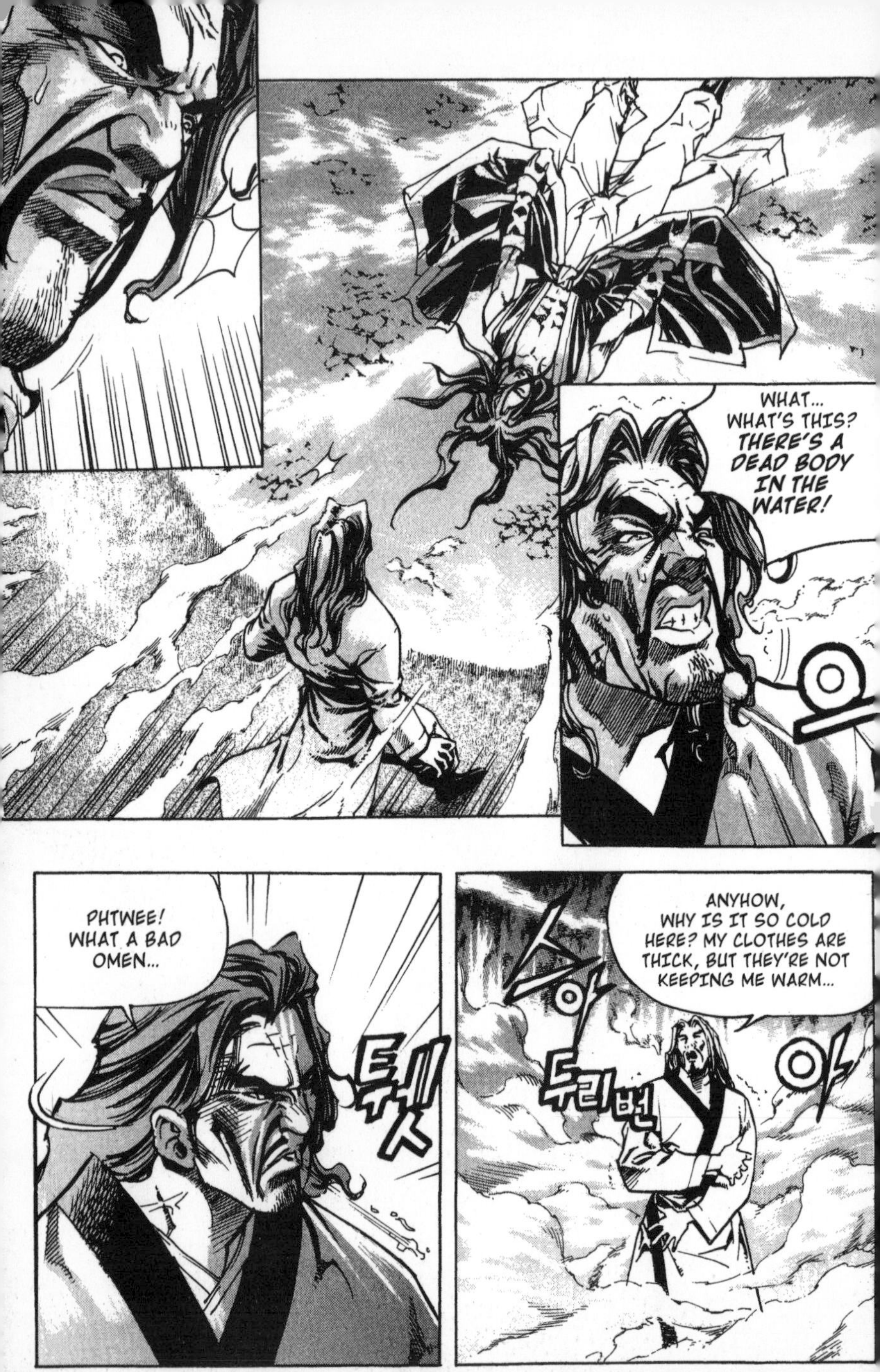
WHAT... WHAT'S THIS? THERE'S A DEAD BODY IN THE WATER!
PHTWEE! WHAT A BAD OMEN...
ANYHOW, WHY IS IT SO COLD HERE? MY CLOTHES ARE THICK, BUT THEY'RE NOT KEEPING ME WARM...
두리번

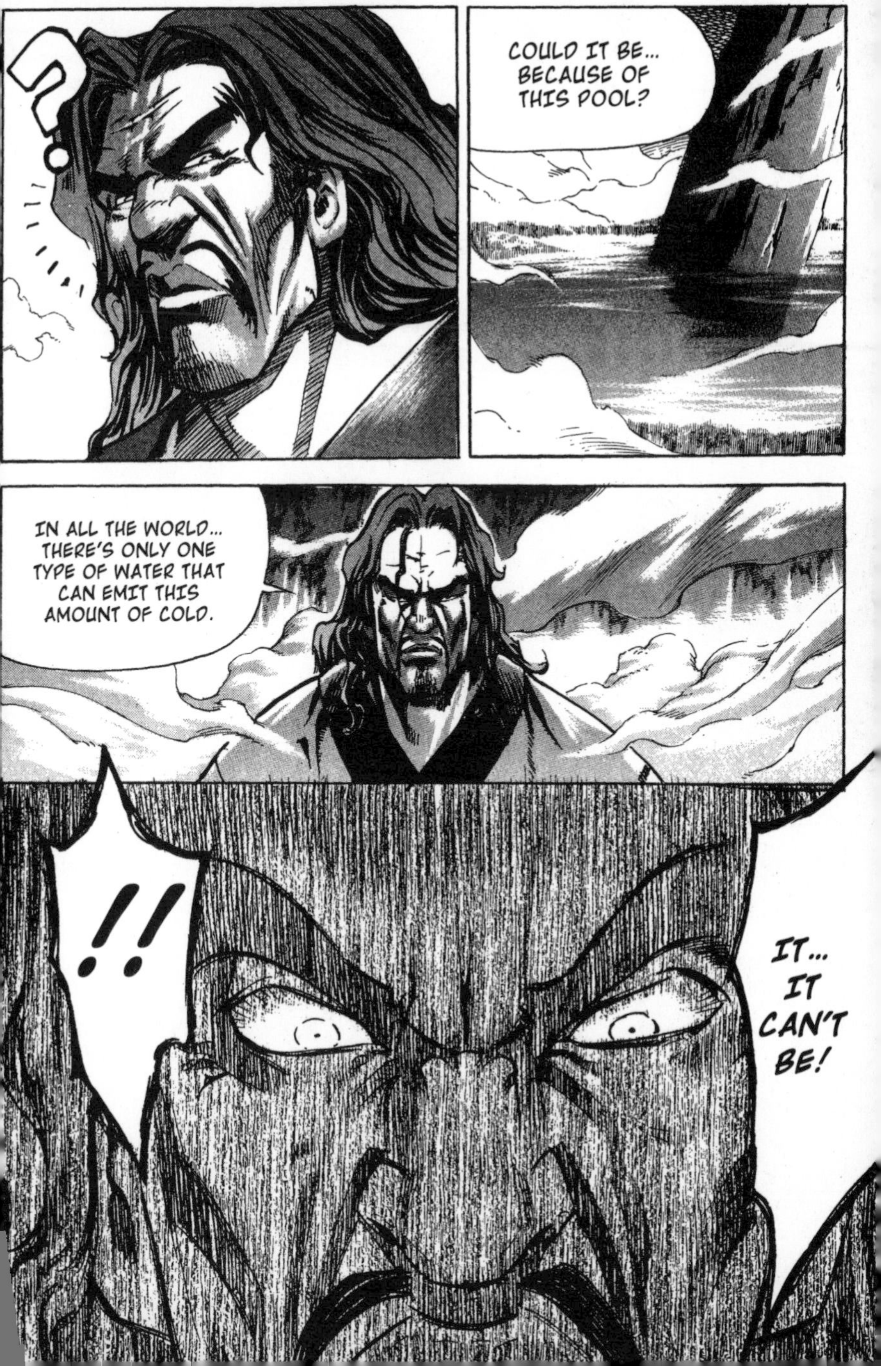
?
COULD IT BE... BECAUSE OF THIS POOL?
IN ALL THE WORLD... THERE'S ONLY ONE TYPE OF WATER THAT CAN EMIT THIS AMOUNT OF COLD.
!!
IT... IT CAN'T BE!

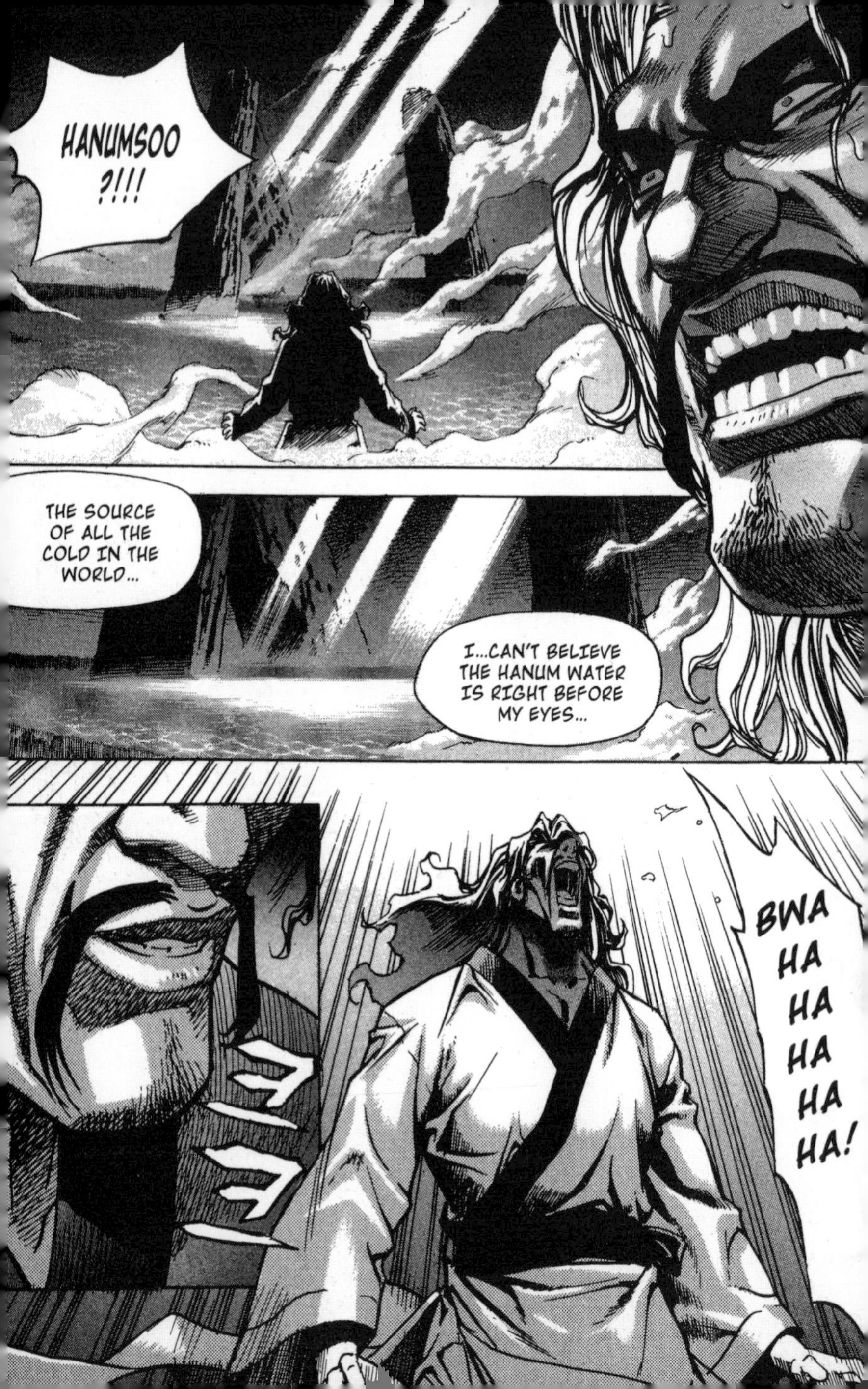
HANUMSOO ?!!!
THE SOURCE OF ALL THE COLD IN THE WORLD...
I...CAN'T BELIEVE THE HANUM WATER IS RIGHT BEFORE MY EYES...
BWA HA HA HA HA HA!

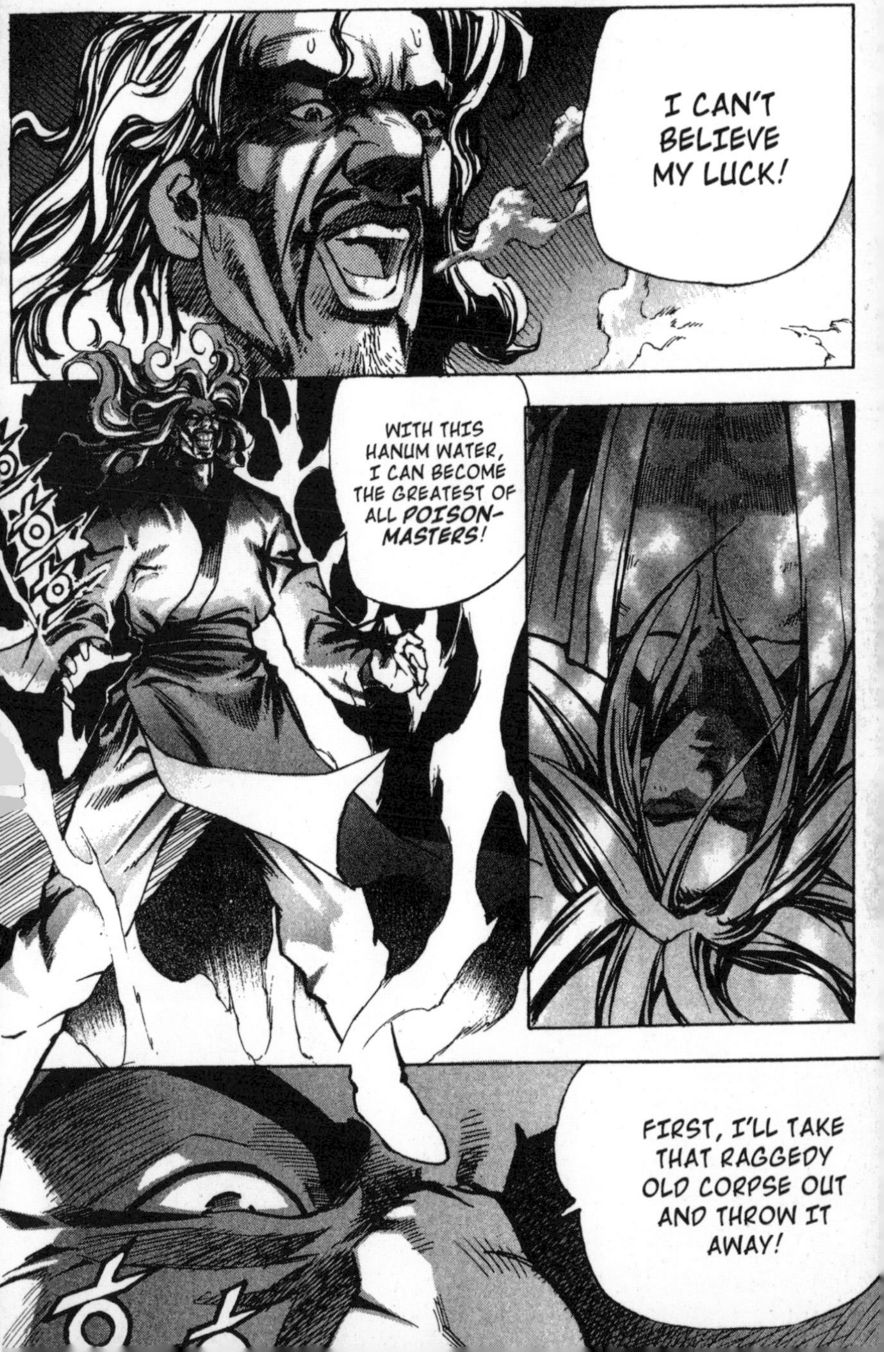
I CAN'T BELIEVE MY LUCK!
WITH THIS HANUM WATER, I CAN BECOME THE GREATEST OF ALL *POISON-MASTERS*!
FIRST, I'LL TAKE THAT RAGGEDY OLD CORPSE OUT AND THROW IT AWAY!

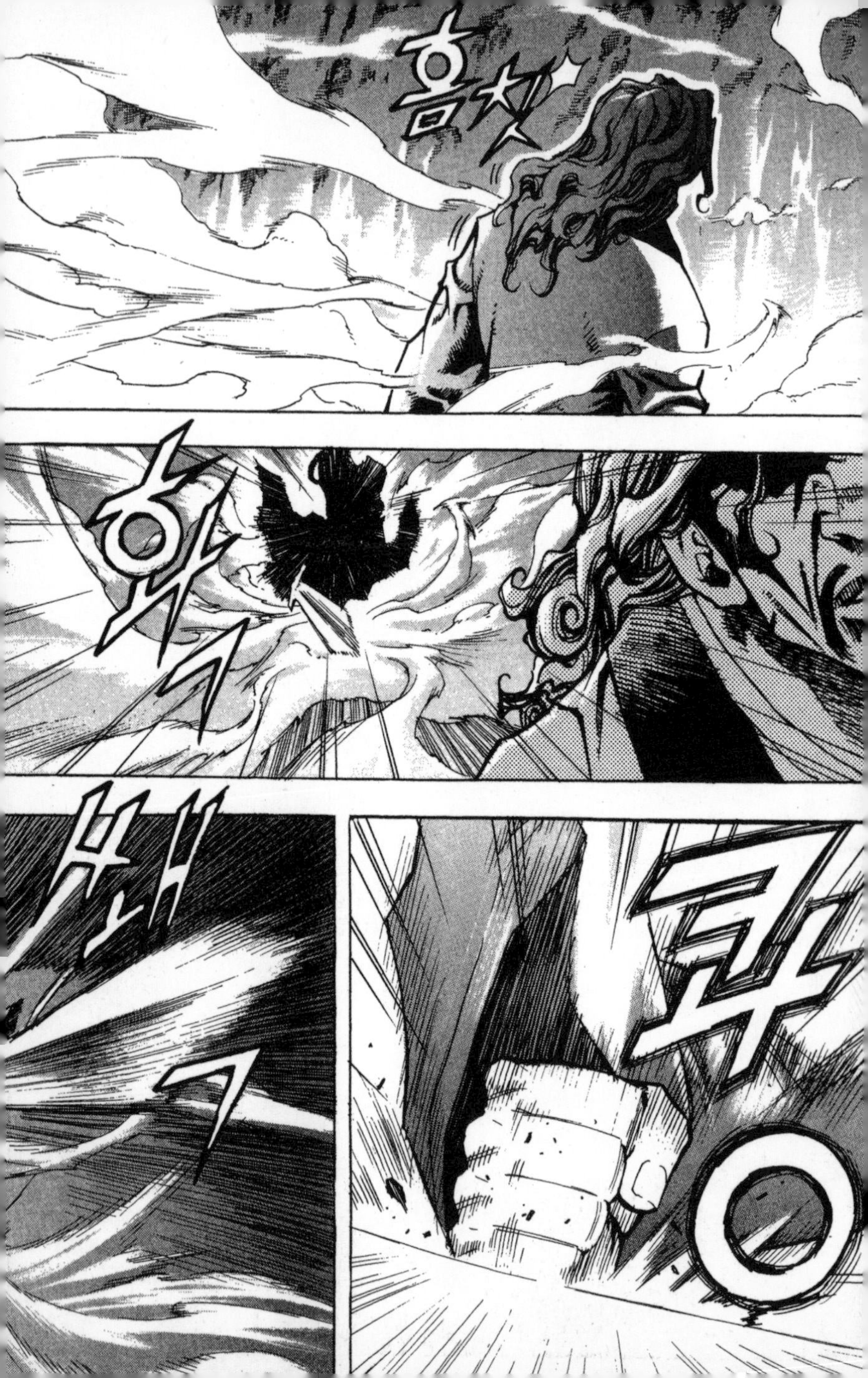
흠칫
확
쾅

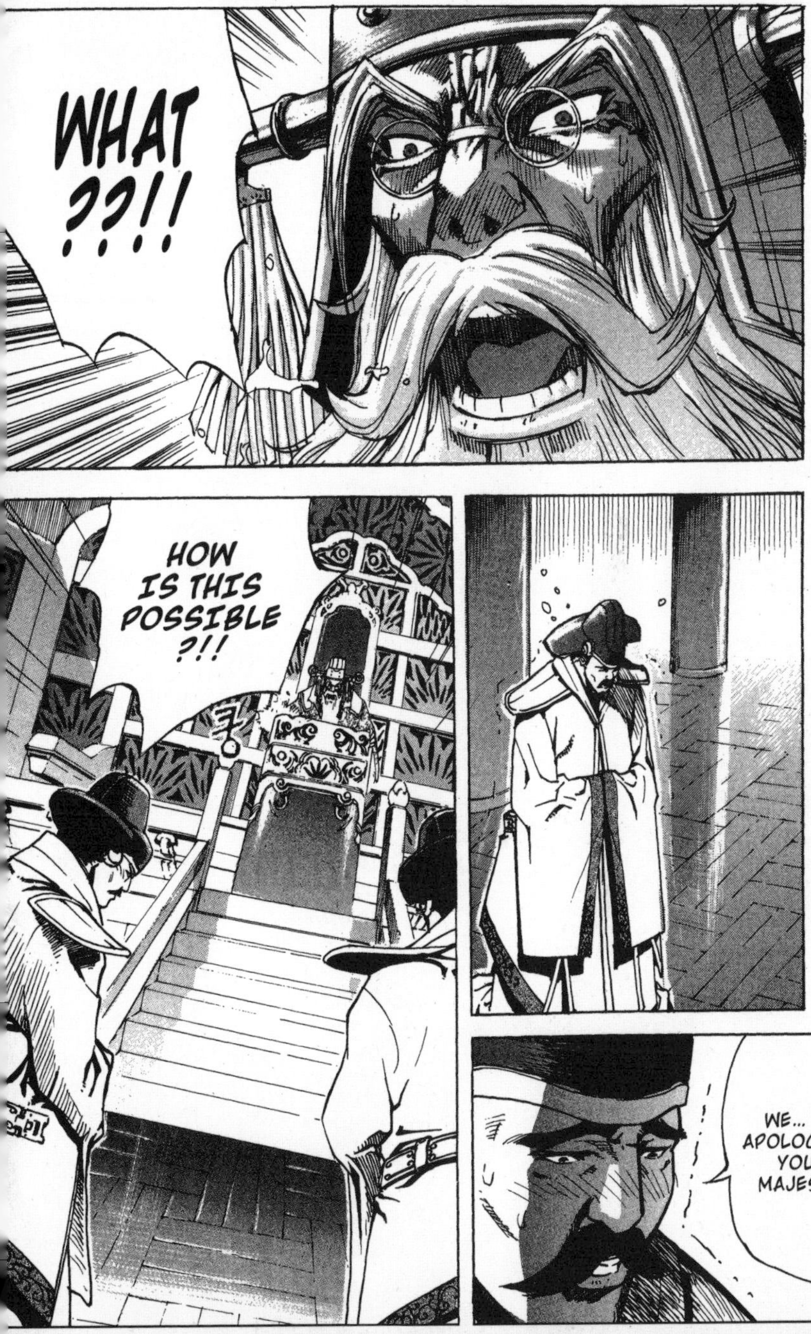
WHAT??!!
HOW IS THIS POSSIBLE?!!
WE... WE APOLOGIZE, YOUR MAJESTY.

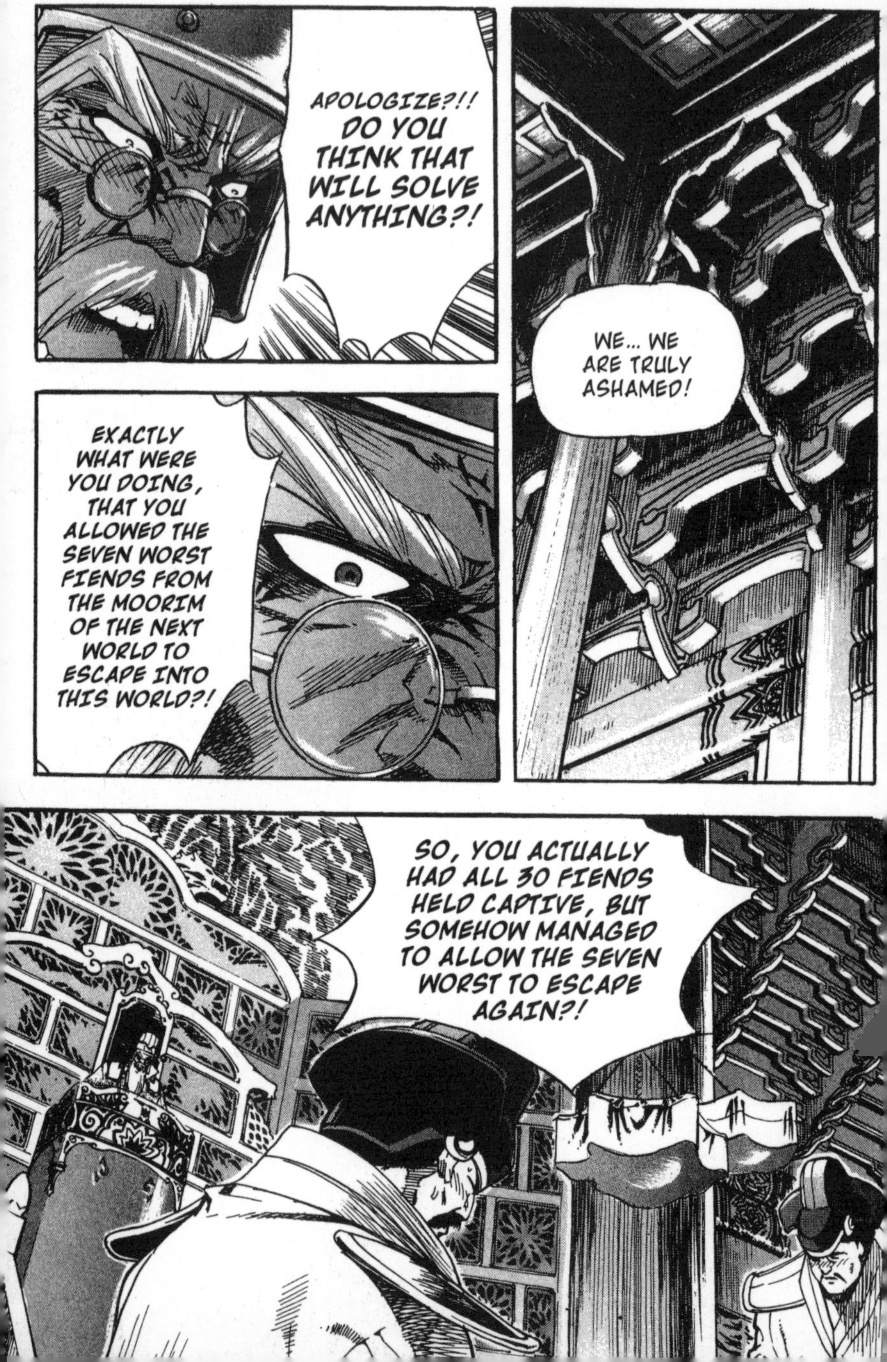
APOLOGIZE?!! DO YOU THINK THAT WILL SOLVE ANYTHING?!
WE... WE ARE TRULY ASHAMED!
EXACTLY WHAT WERE YOU DOING, THAT YOU ALLOWED THE SEVEN WORST FIENDS FROM THE MOORIM OF THE NEXT WORLD TO ESCAPE INTO THIS WORLD?!
SO, YOU ACTUALLY HAD ALL 30 FIENDS HELD CAPTIVE, BUT SOMEHOW MANAGED TO ALLOW THE SEVEN WORST TO ESCAPE AGAIN?!

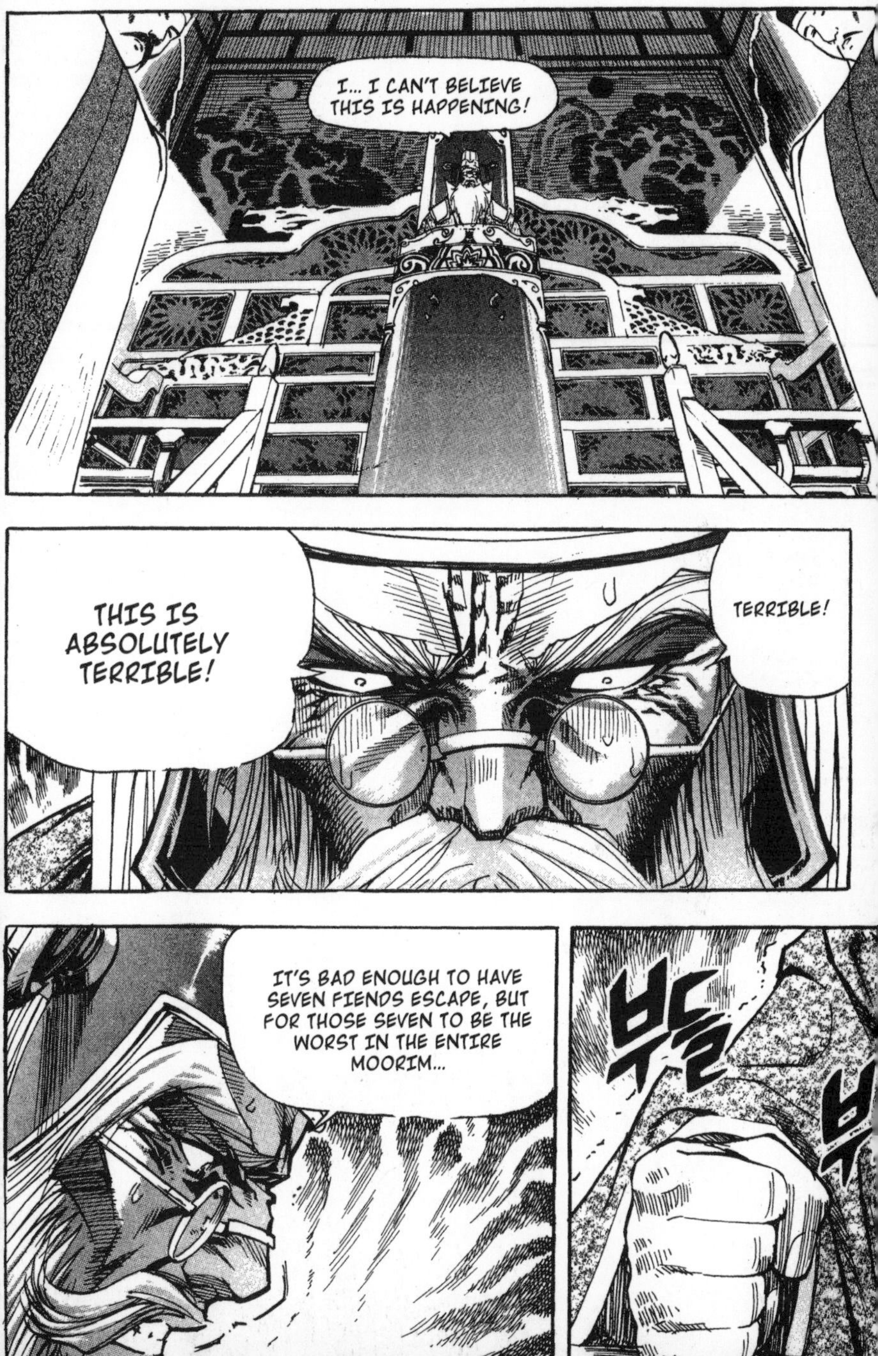
I... I CAN'T BELIEVE THIS IS HAPPENING!
THIS IS ABSOLUTELY TERRIBLE!
TERRIBLE!
IT'S BAD ENOUGH TO HAVE SEVEN FIENDS ESCAPE, BUT FOR THOSE SEVEN TO BE THE WORST IN THE ENTIRE MOORIM...
부들
부

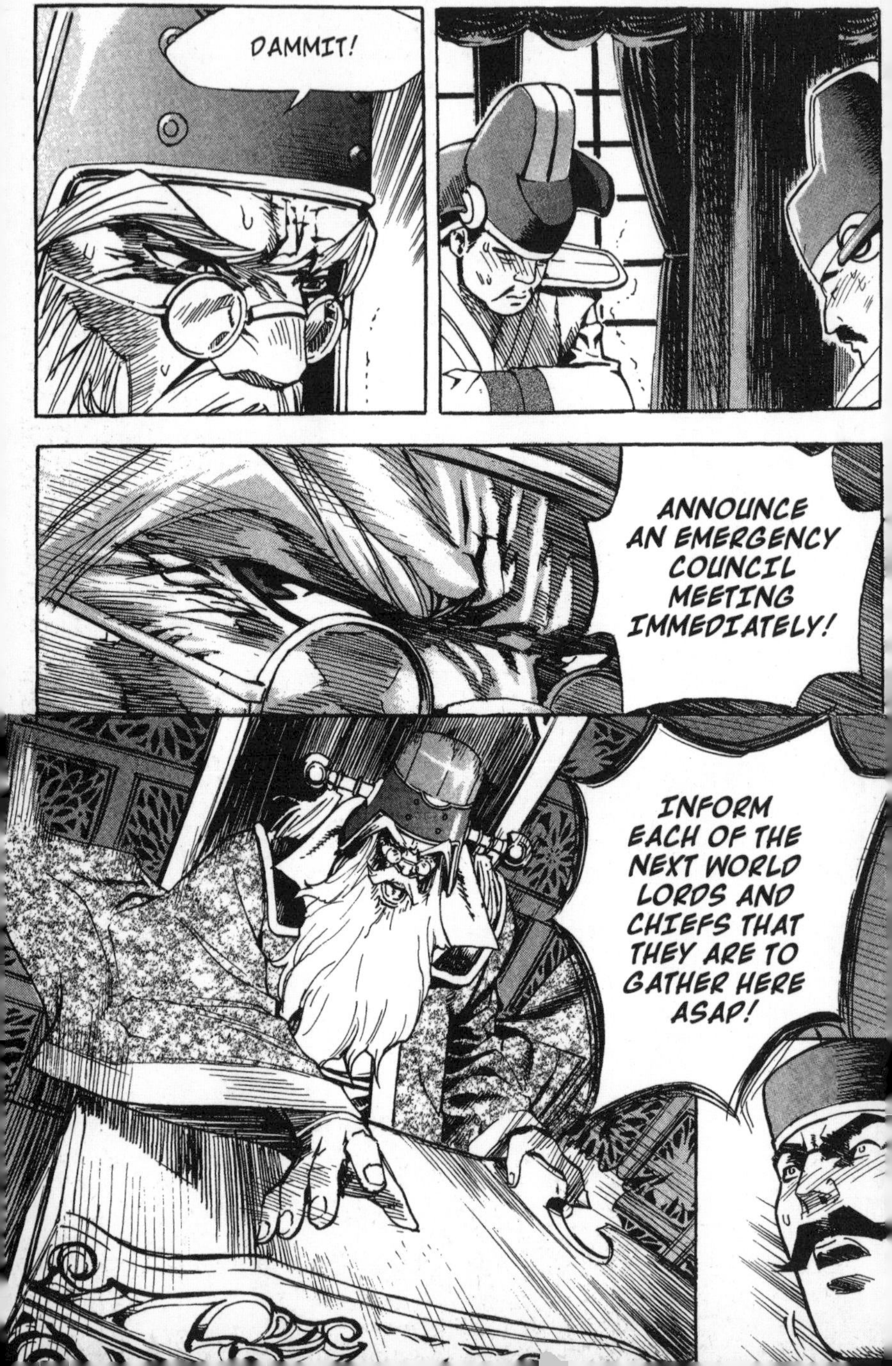
DAMMIT!
ANNOUNCE AN EMERGENCY COUNCIL MEETING IMMEDIATELY!
INFORM EACH OF THE NEXT WORLD LORDS AND CHIEFS THAT THEY ARE TO GATHER HERE ASAP!

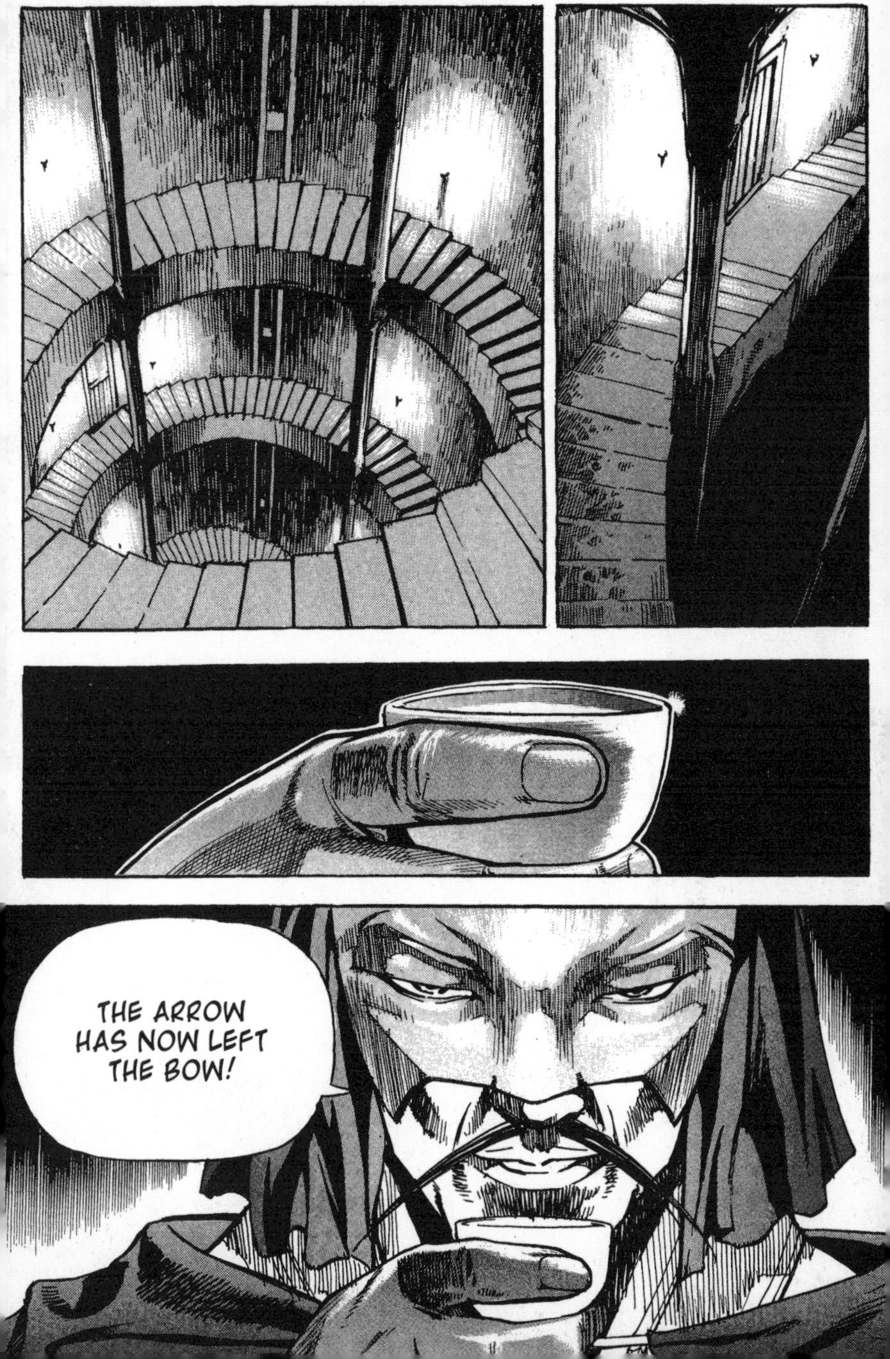
THE ARROW HAS NOW LEFT THE BOW!

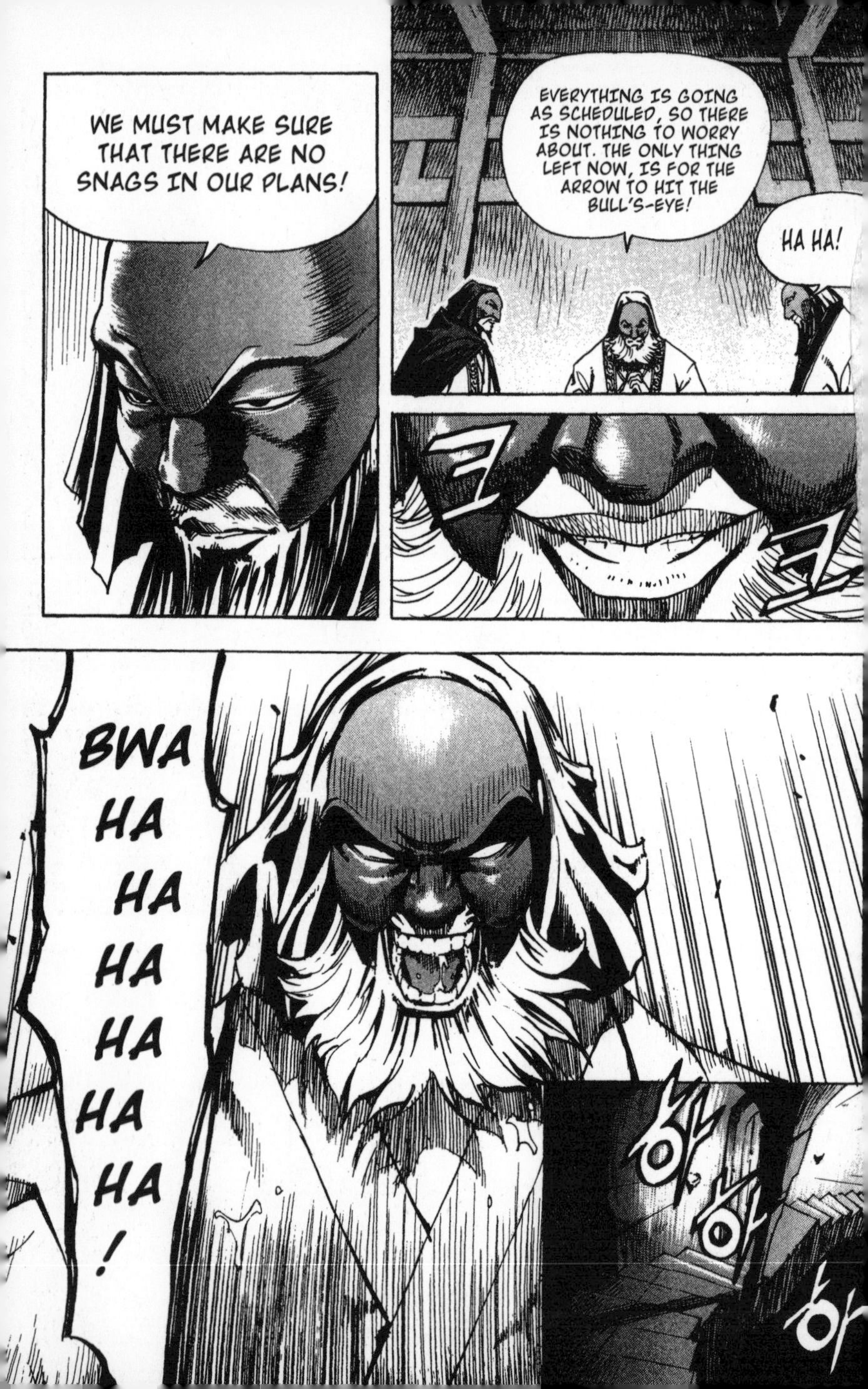
WE MUST MAKE SURE THAT THERE ARE NO SNAGS IN OUR PLANS!
EVERYTHING IS GOING AS SCHEDULED, SO THERE IS NOTHING TO WORRY ABOUT. THE ONLY THING LEFT NOW, IS FOR THE ARROW TO HIT THE BULL'S-EYE!
HA HA!
BWA HA HA HA HA HA HA!

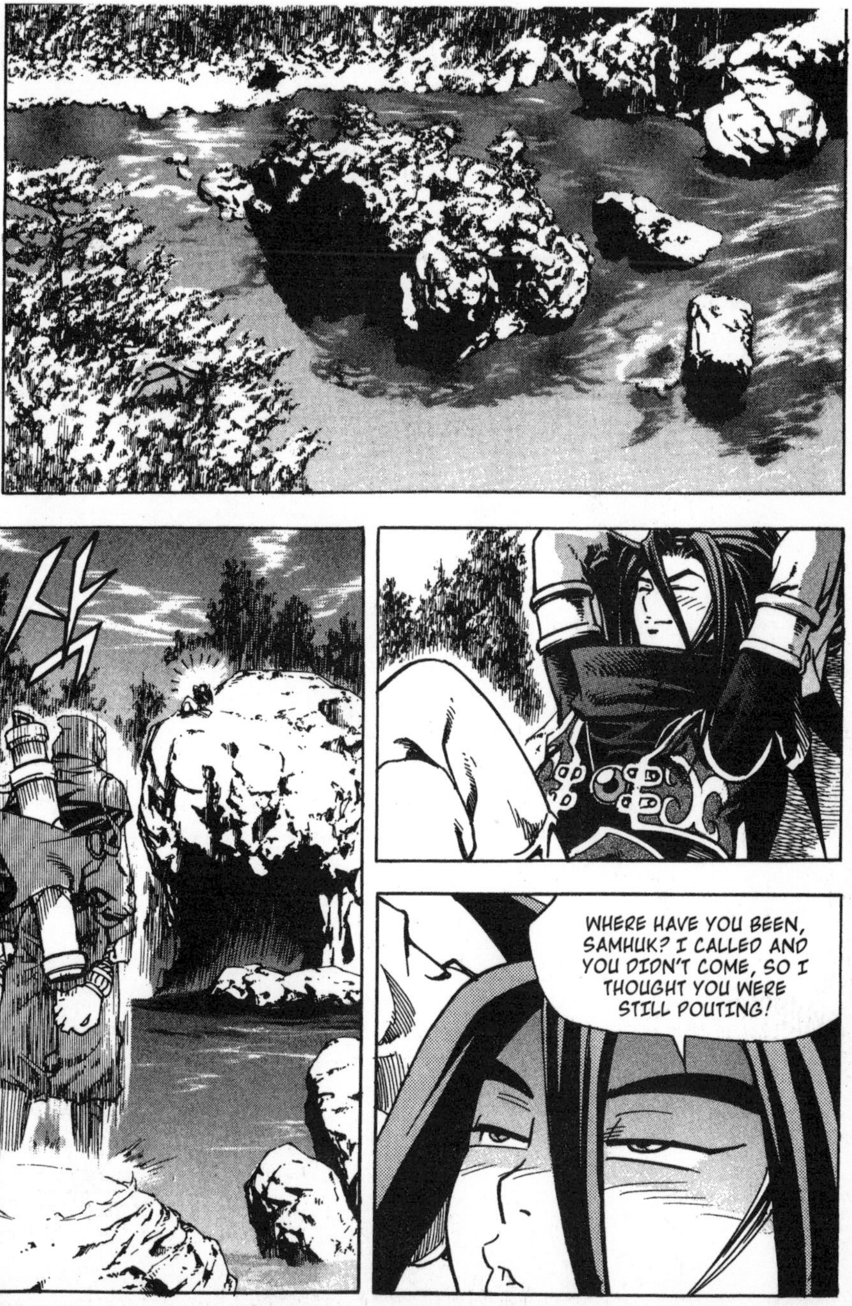
WHERE HAVE YOU BEEN, SAMHUK? I CALLED AND YOU DIDN'T COME, SO I THOUGHT YOU WERE STILL POUTING!

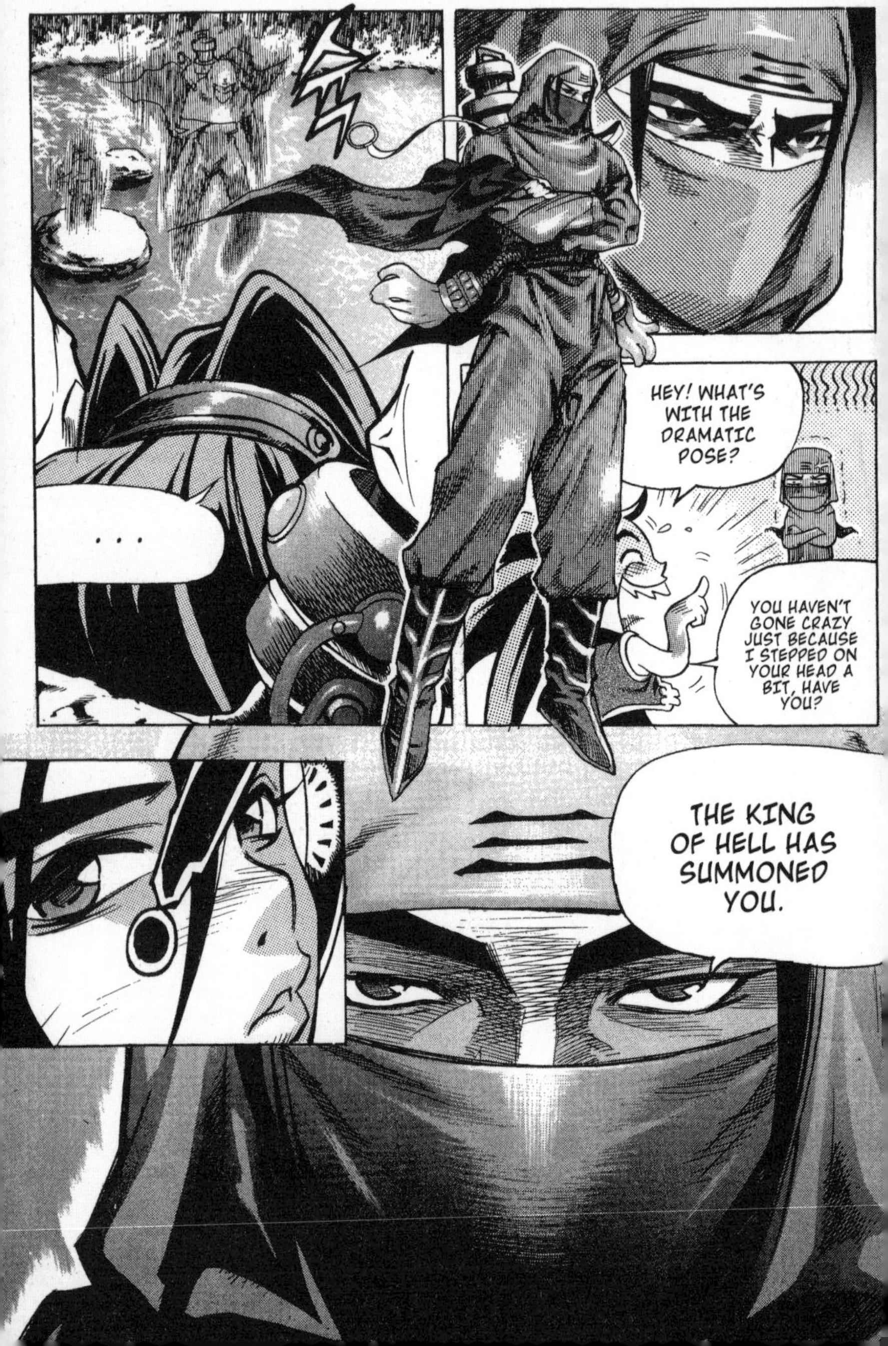
...
HEY! WHAT'S WITH THE DRAMATIC POSE?
YOU HAVEN'T GONE CRAZY JUST BECAUSE I STEPPED ON YOUR HEAD A BIT, HAVE YOU?
THE KING OF HELL HAS SUMMONED YOU.

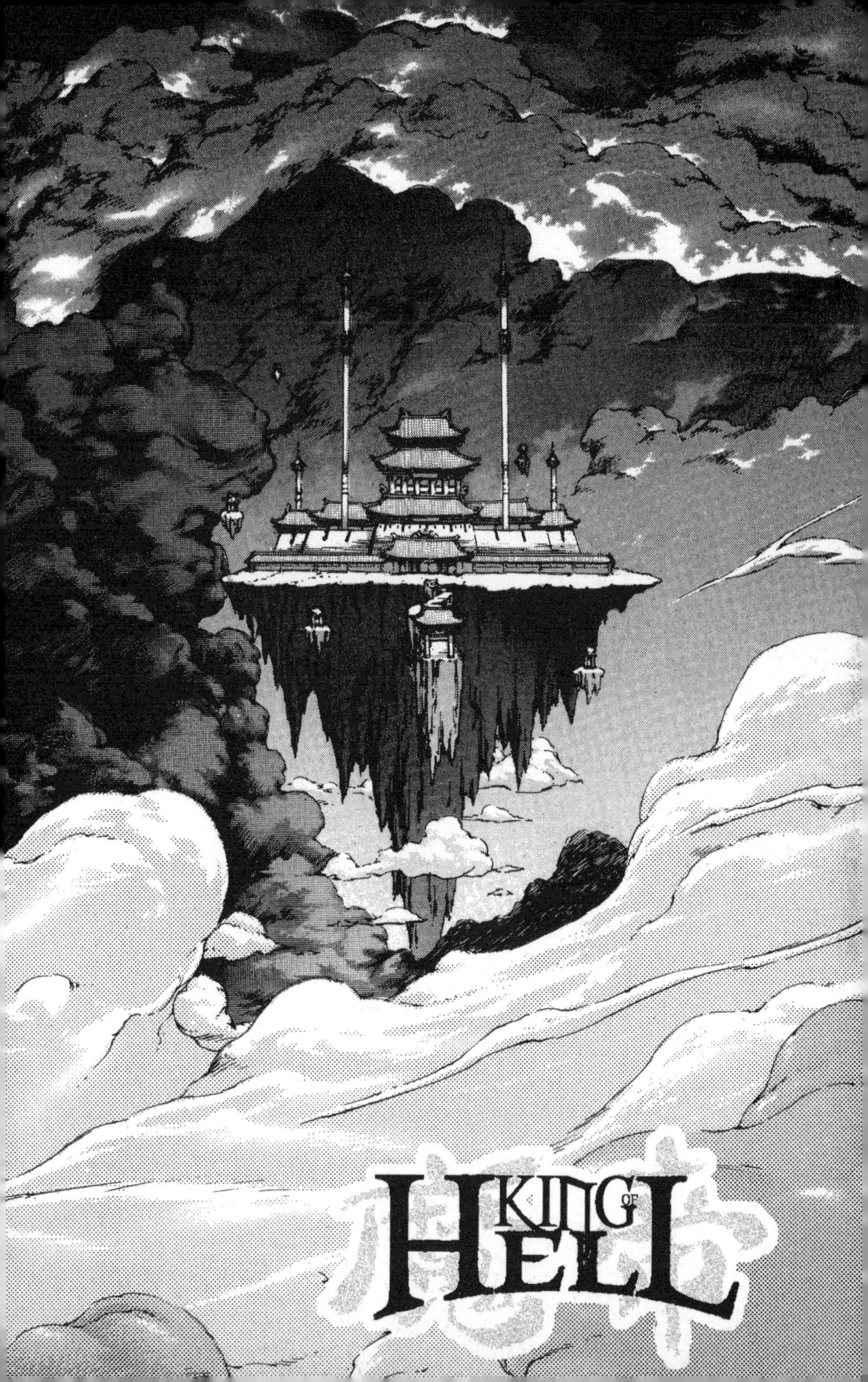
KING OF HELL

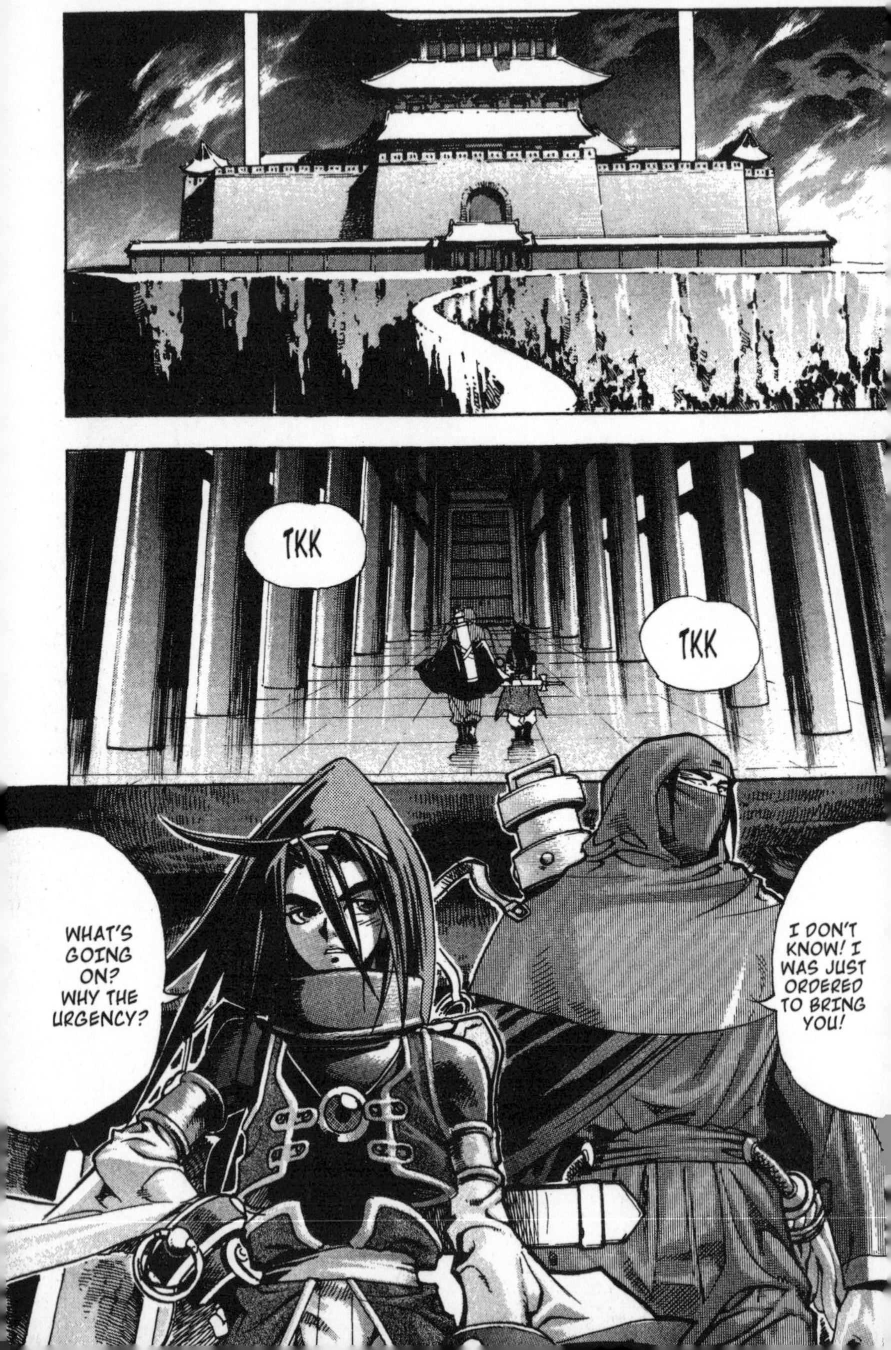
TKK
TKK
WHAT'S GOING ON? WHY THE URGENCY?
I DON'T KNOW! I WAS JUST ORDERED TO BRING YOU!

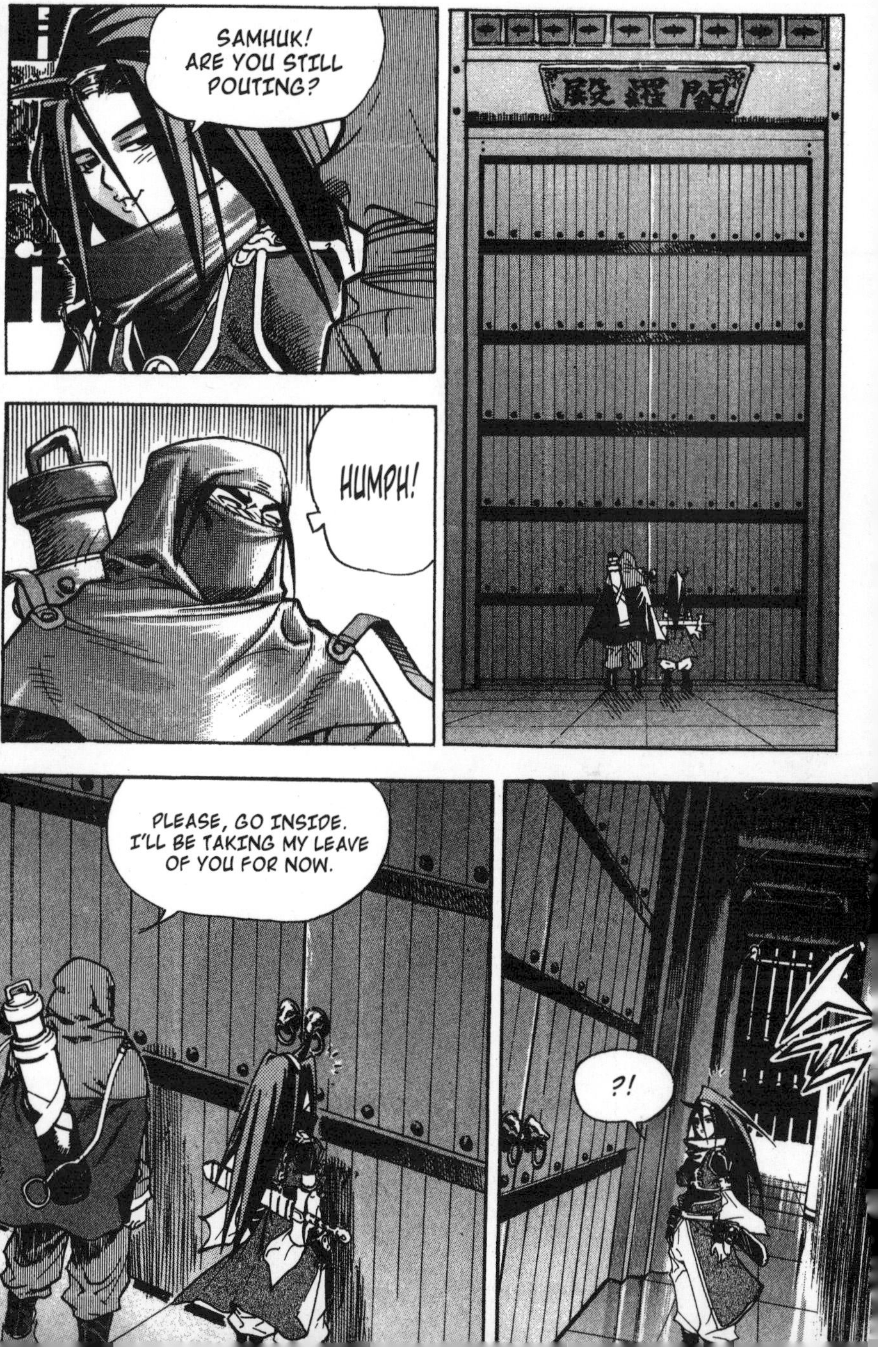
SAMHUK! ARE YOU STILL POUTING?
HUMPH!
PLEASE, GO INSIDE. I'LL BE TAKING MY LEAVE OF YOU FOR NOW.
?!

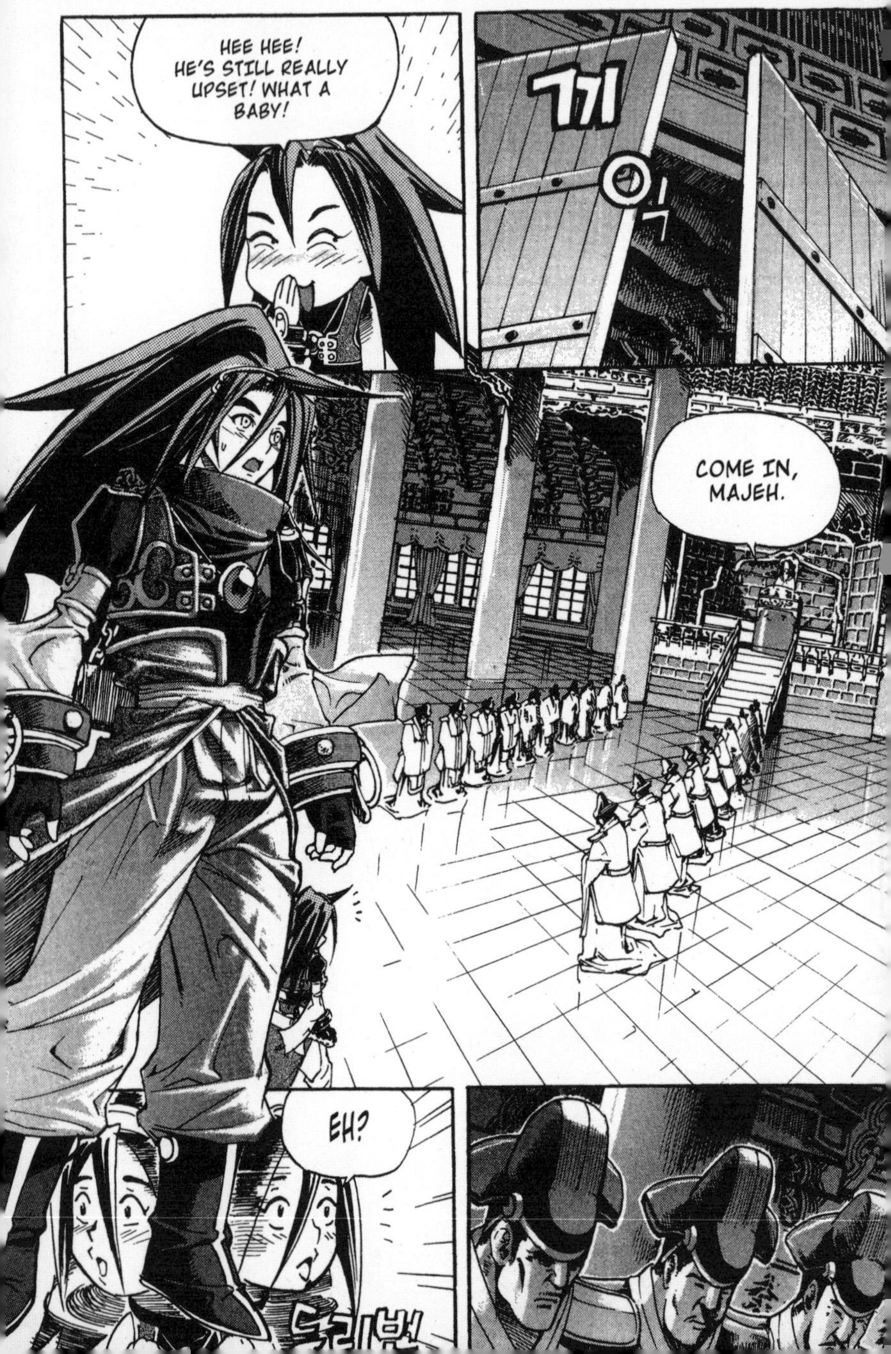
HEE HEE! HE'S STILL REALLY UPSET! WHAT A BABY!
끼
COME IN, MAJEH.
EH?
두근!번!

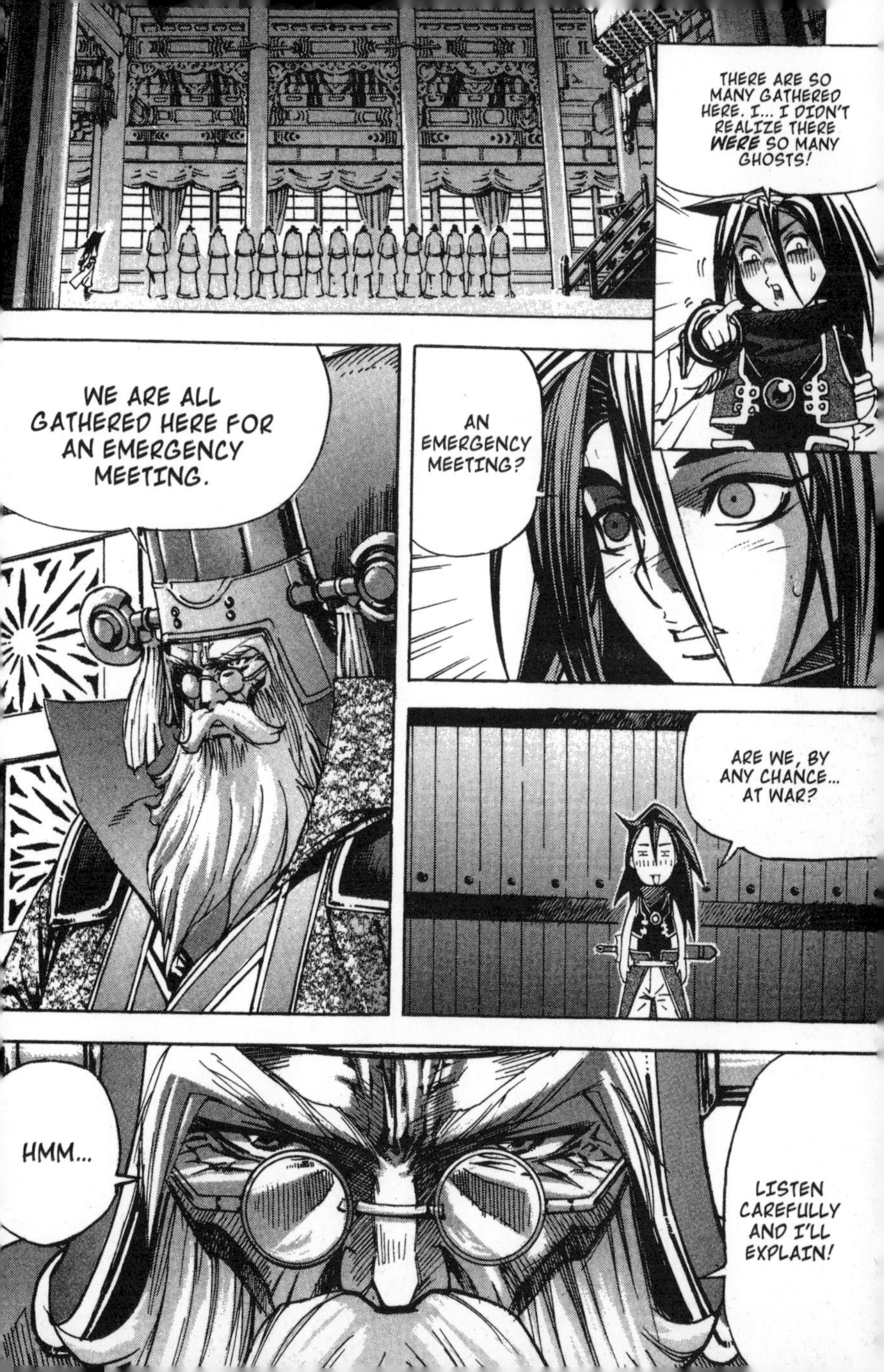
THERE ARE SO MANY GATHERED HERE. I... I DIDN'T REALIZE THERE WERE SO MANY GHOSTS!
WE ARE ALL GATHERED HERE FOR AN EMERGENCY MEETING.
AN EMERGENCY MEETING?
ARE WE, BY ANY CHANCE... AT WAR?
HMM...
LISTEN CAREFULLY AND I'LL EXPLAIN!

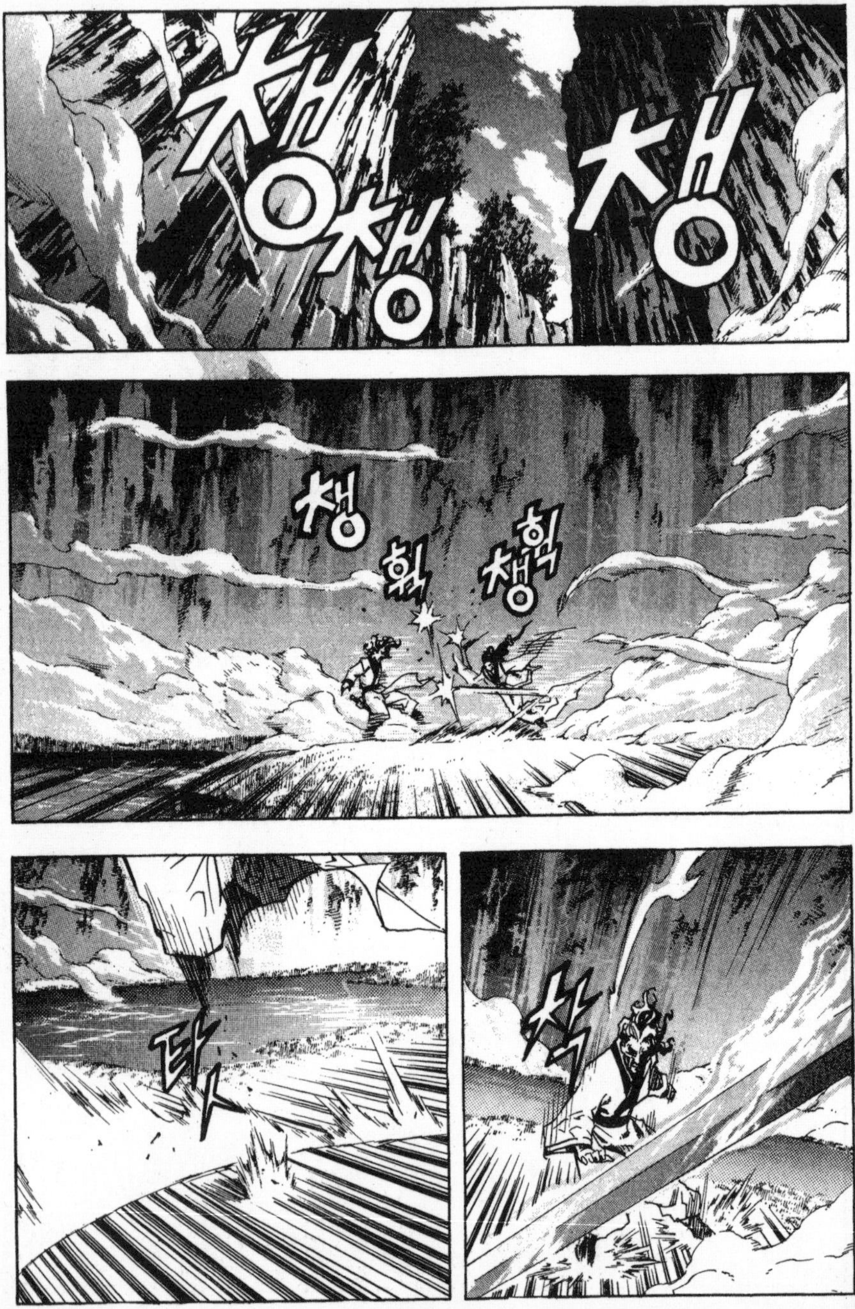
챙
챙
챙
챙
휙
챙
휙
탁
착

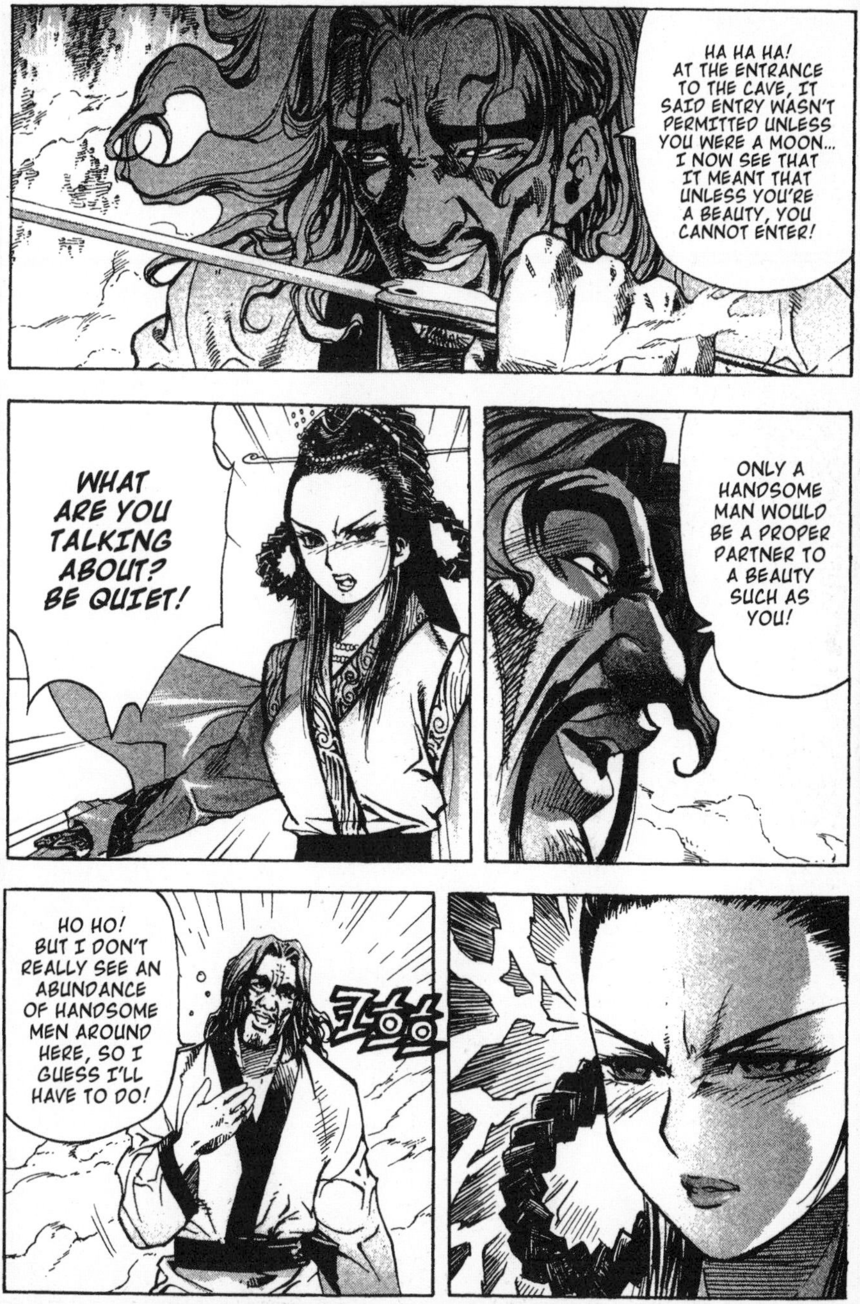
HA HA HA! AT THE ENTRANCE TO THE CAVE, IT SAID ENTRY WASN'T PERMITTED UNLESS YOU WERE A MOON... I NOW SEE THAT IT MEANT THAT UNLESS YOU'RE A BEAUTY, YOU CANNOT ENTER!
WHAT ARE YOU TALKING ABOUT? BE QUIET!
ONLY A HANDSOME MAN WOULD BE A PROPER PARTNER TO A BEAUTY SUCH AS YOU!
HO HO! BUT I DON'T REALLY SEE AN ABUNDANCE OF HANDSOME MEN AROUND HERE, SO I GUESS I'LL HAVE TO DO!

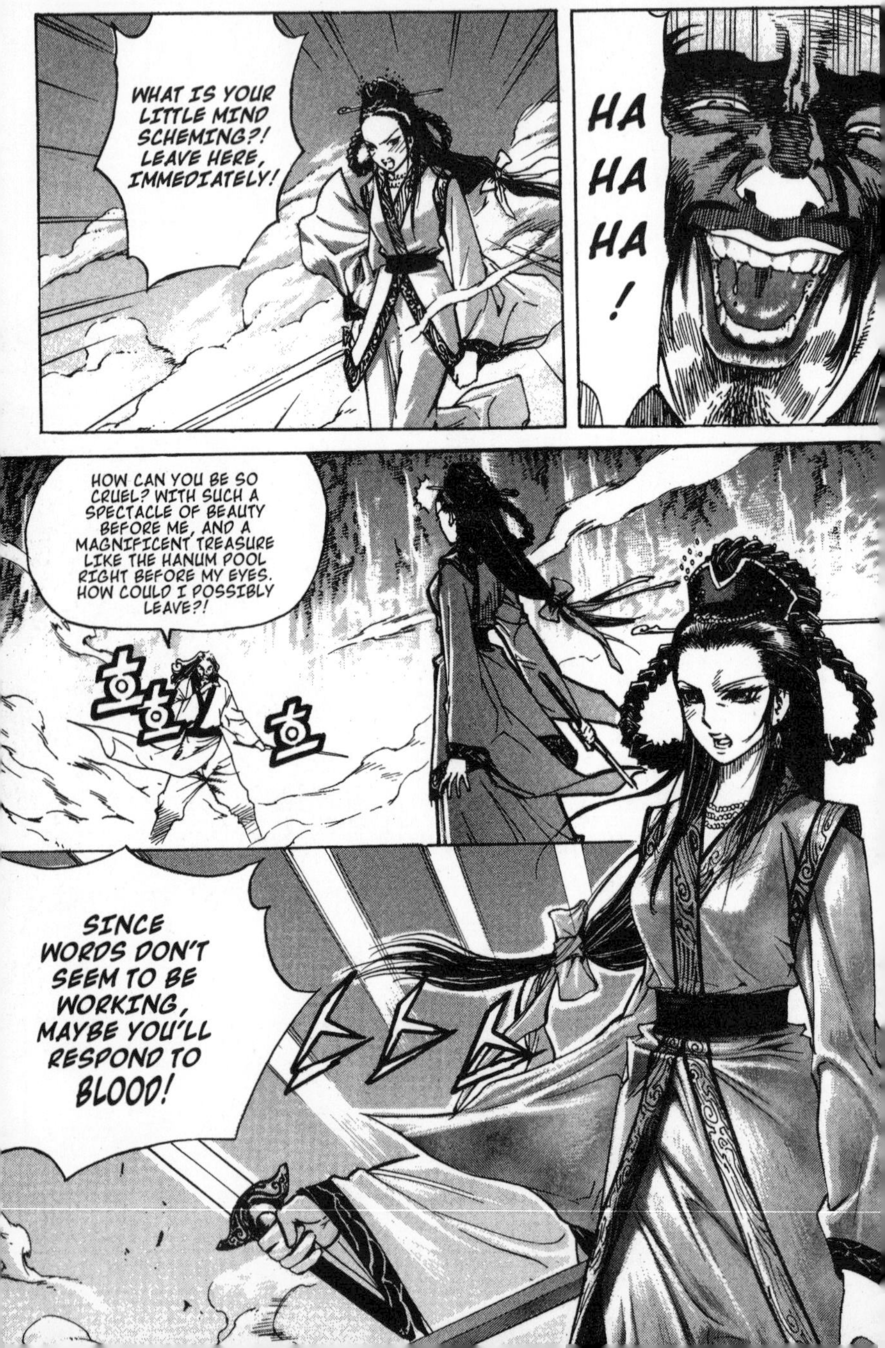
WHAT IS YOUR LITTLE MIND SCHEMING?! LEAVE HERE, IMMEDIATELY!
HA HA HA HA!
HOW CAN YOU BE SO CRUEL? WITH SUCH A SPECTACLE OF BEAUTY BEFORE ME, AND A MAGNIFICENT TREASURE LIKE THE HANUM POOL RIGHT BEFORE MY EYES. HOW COULD I POSSIBLY LEAVE?!
SINCE WORDS DON'T SEEM TO BE WORKING, MAYBE YOU'LL RESPOND TO BLOOD!

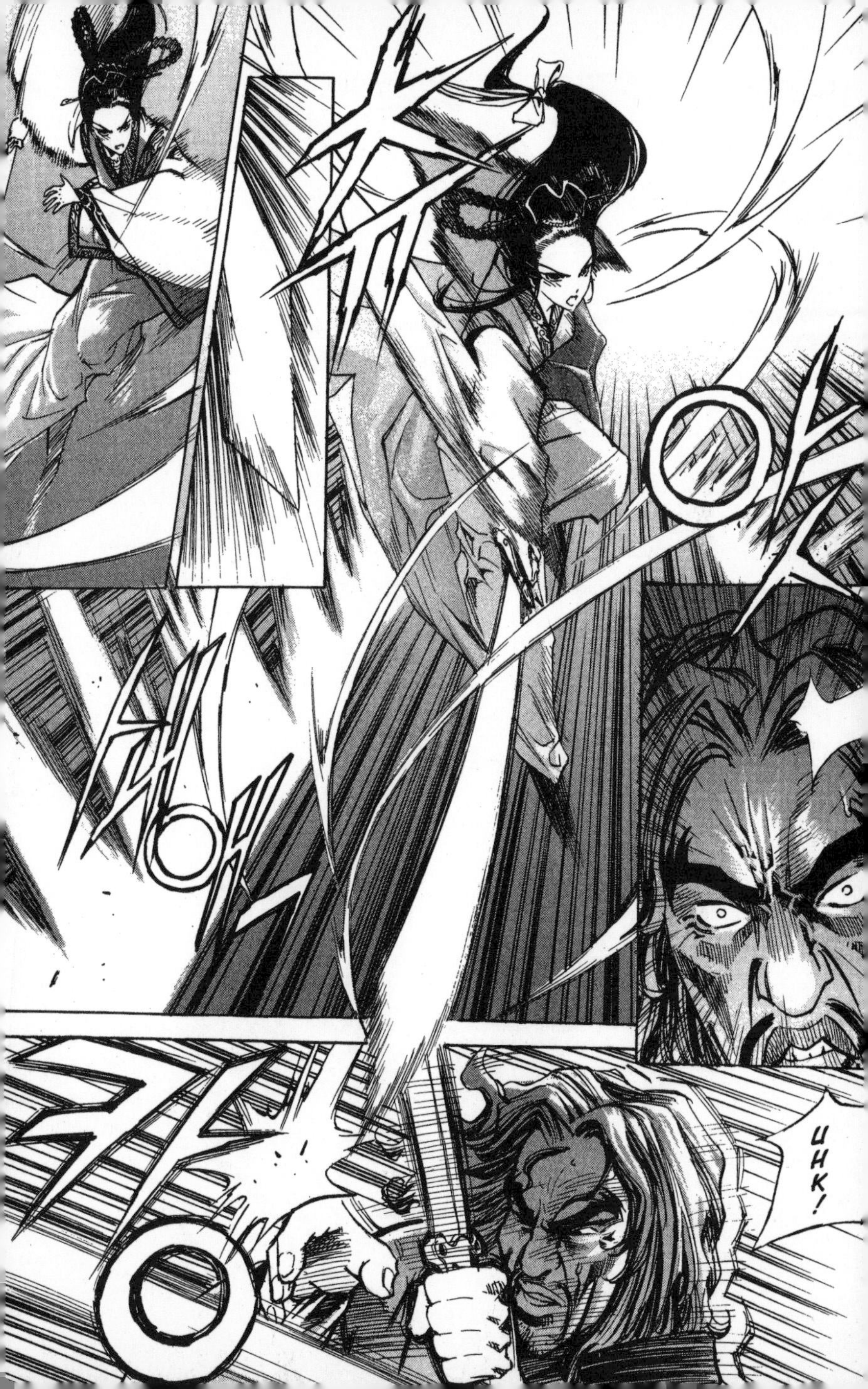
UHK!

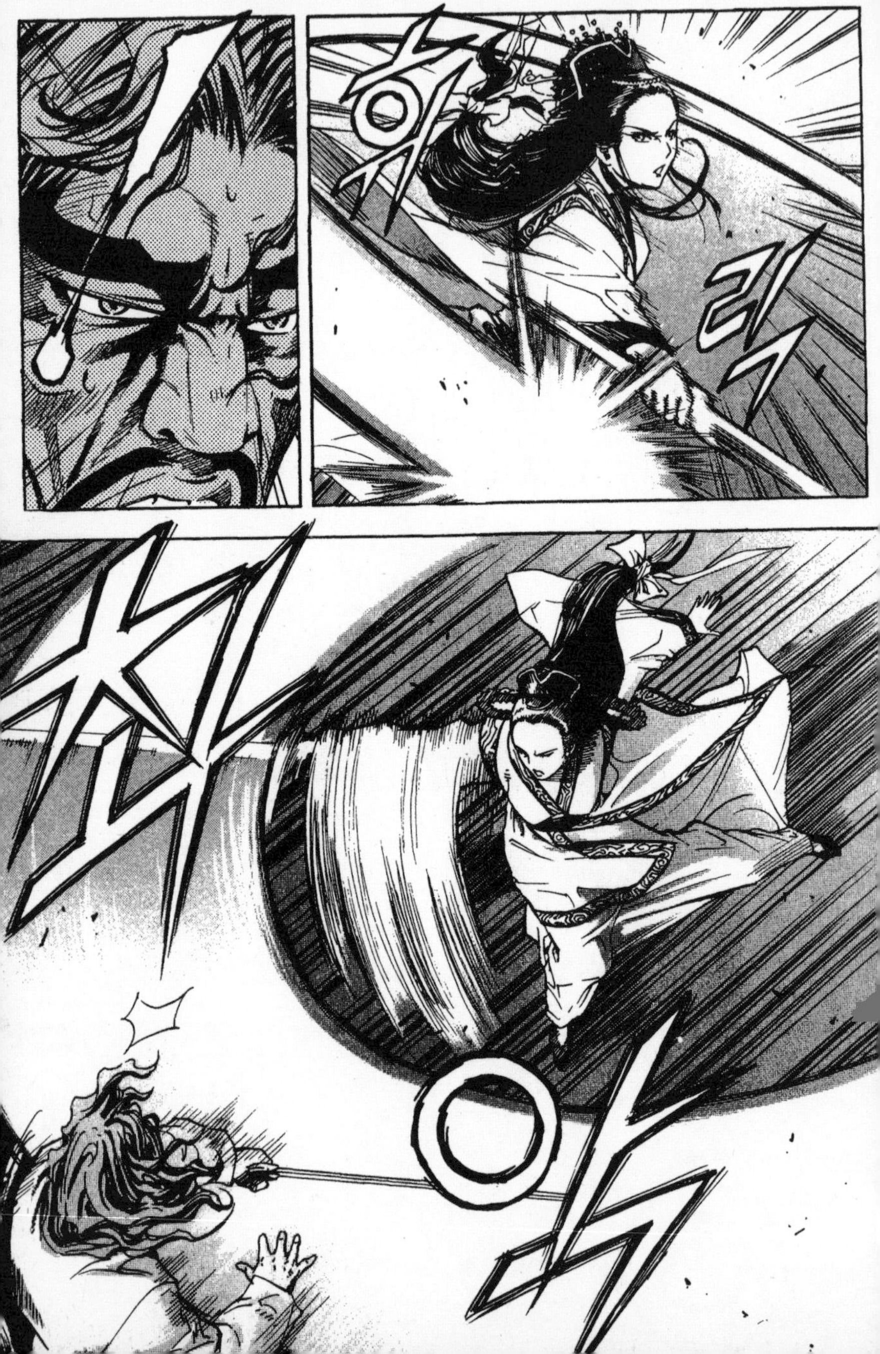

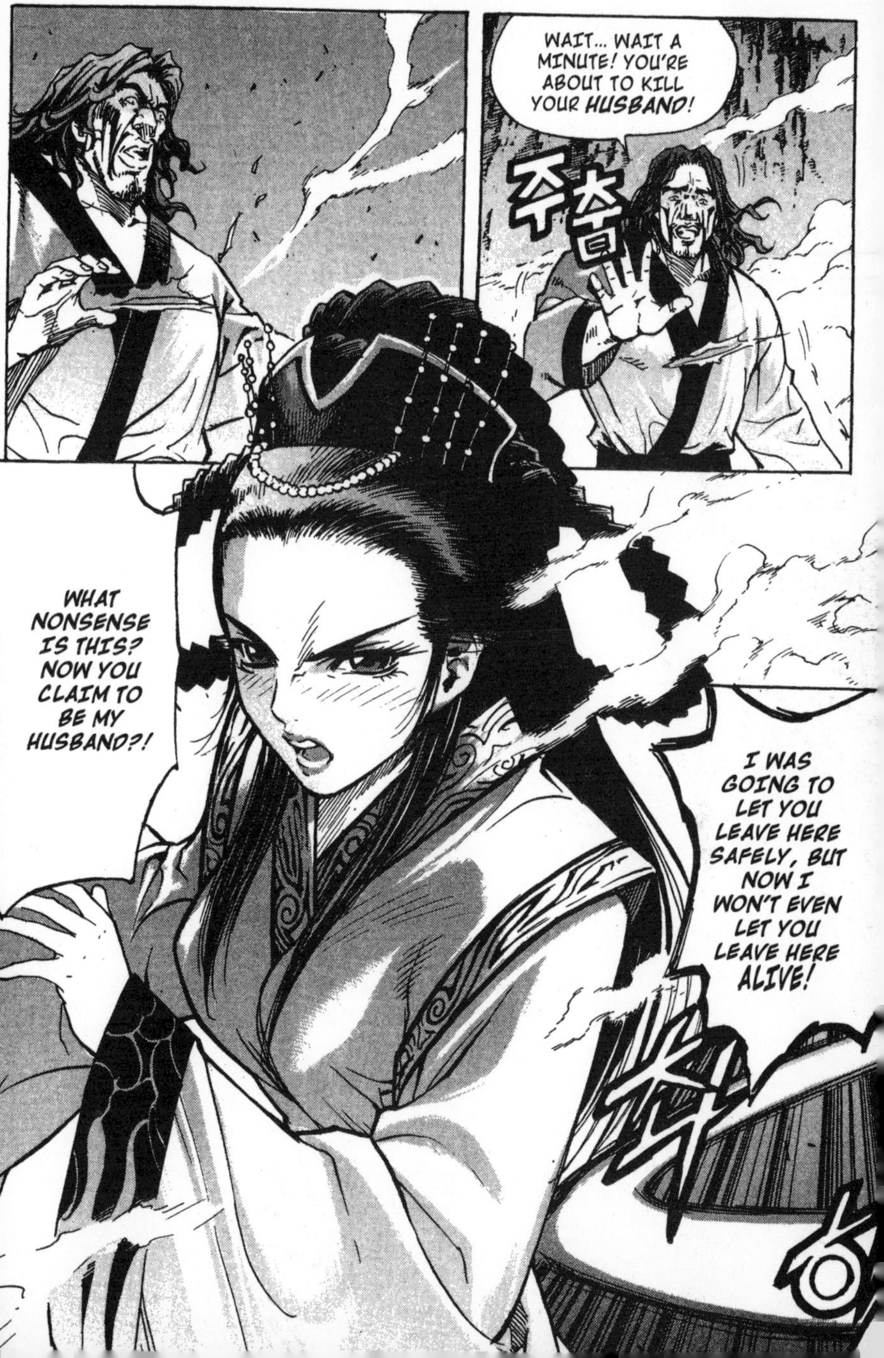
WAIT... WAIT A MINUTE! YOU'RE ABOUT TO KILL YOUR HUSBAND!
주춤
WHAT NONSENSE IS THIS? NOW YOU CLAIM TO BE MY HUSBAND?!
I WAS GOING TO LET YOU LEAVE HERE SAFELY, BUT NOW I WON'T EVEN LET YOU LEAVE HERE ALIVE!

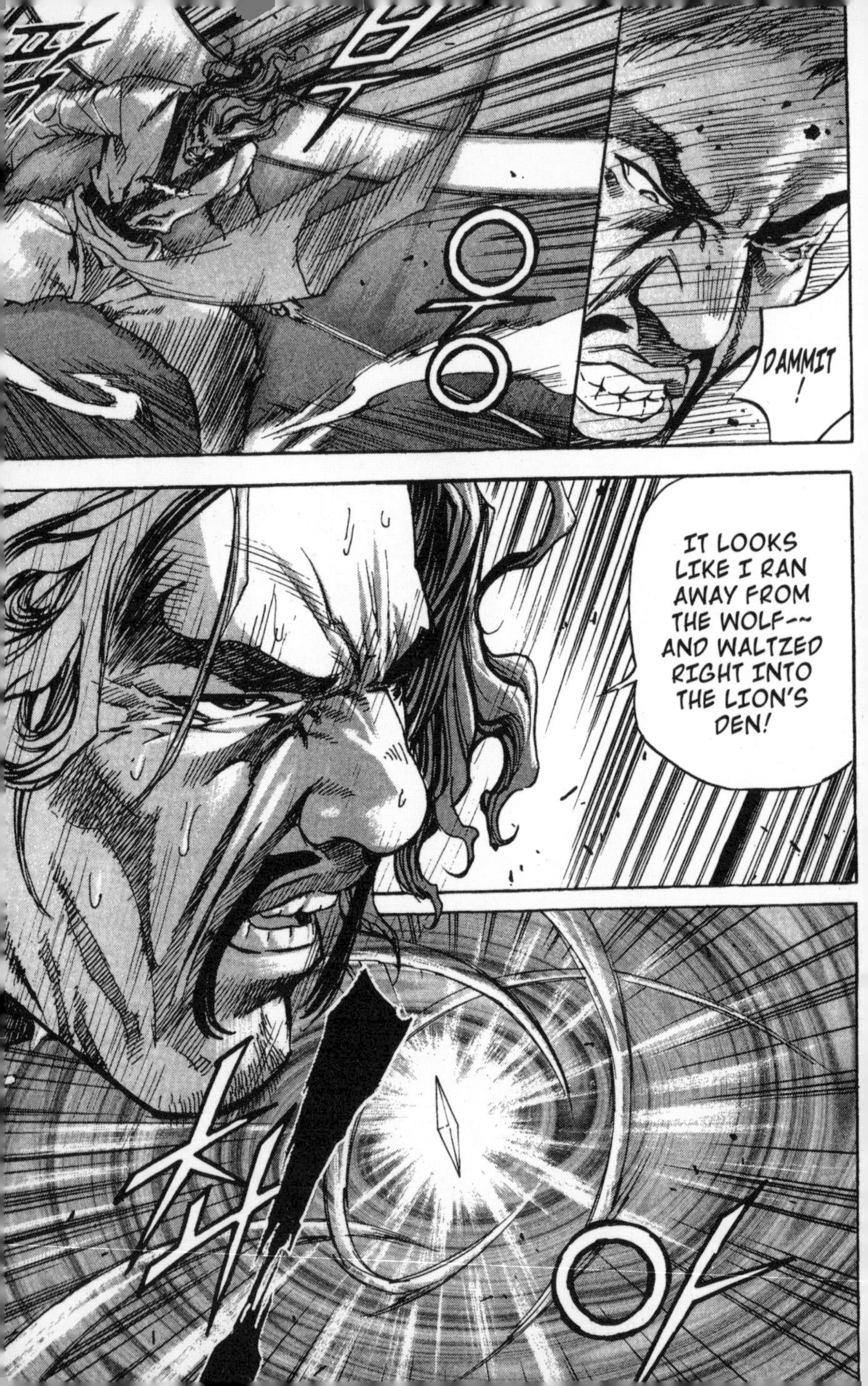
DAMMIT!
IT LOOKS LIKE I RAN AWAY FROM THE WOLF-- AND WALTZED RIGHT INTO THE LION'S DEN!

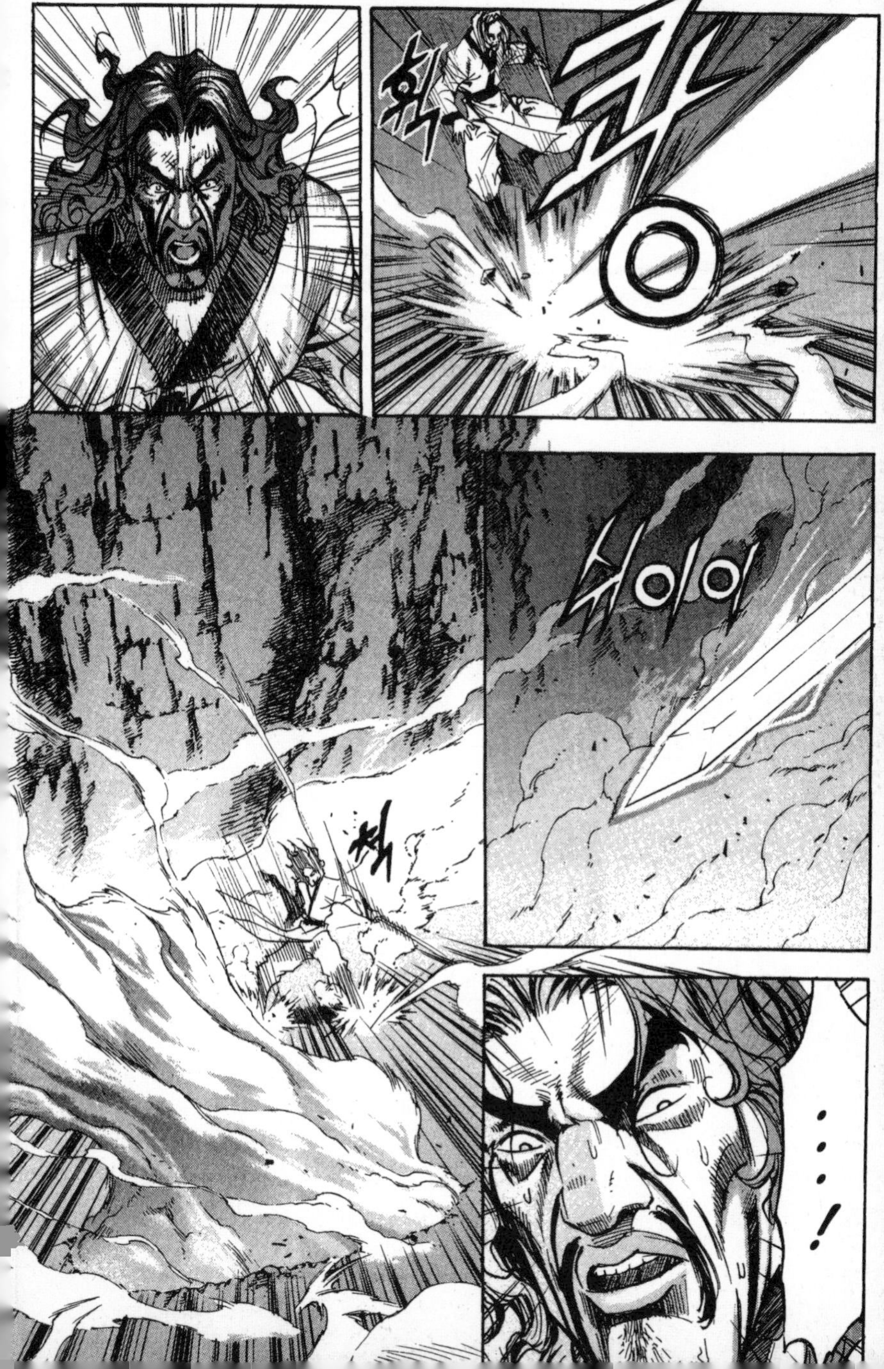
휙
쾅
척
샤이이
····!

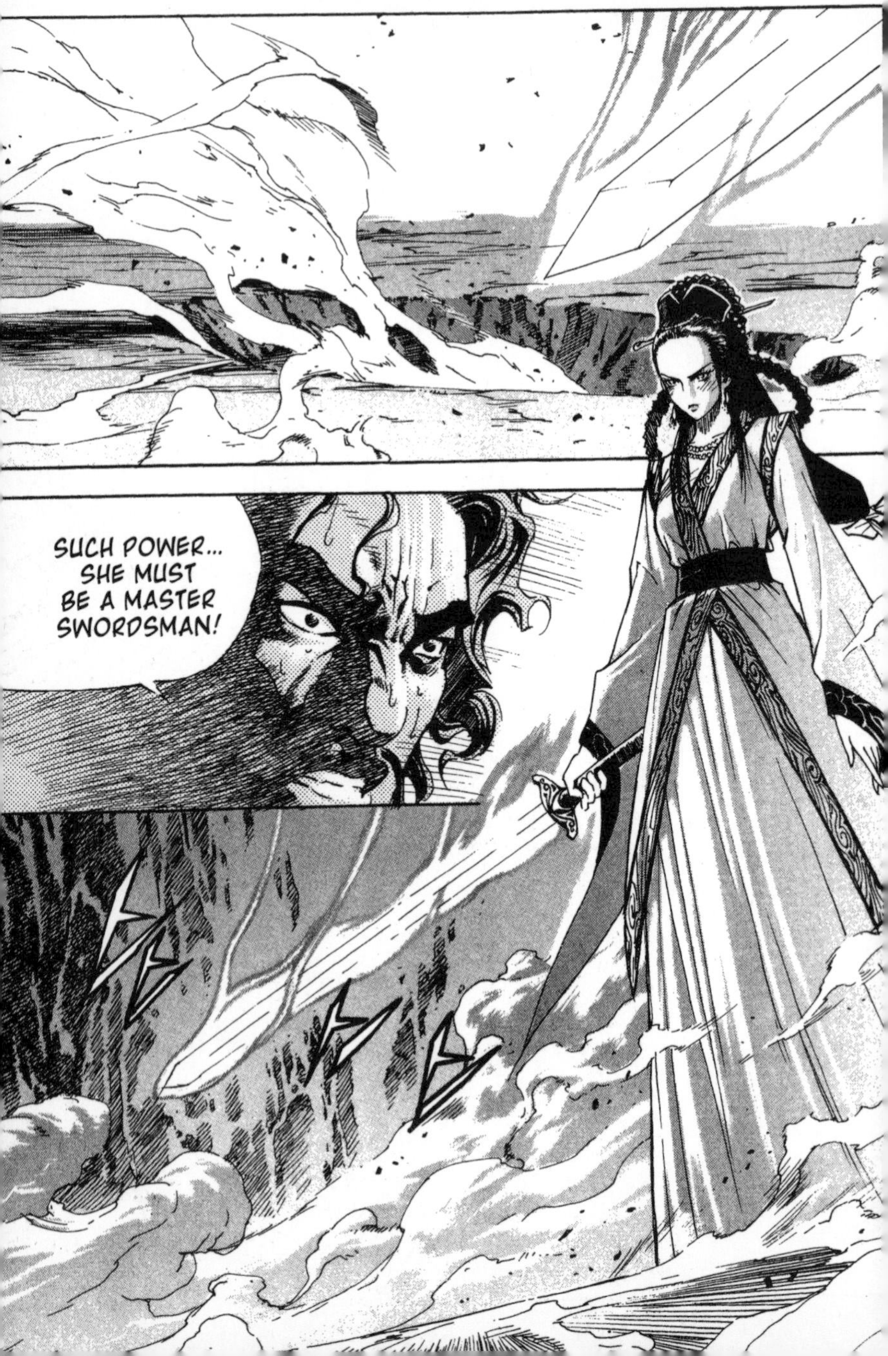
SUCH POWER... SHE MUST BE A MASTER SWORDSMAN!

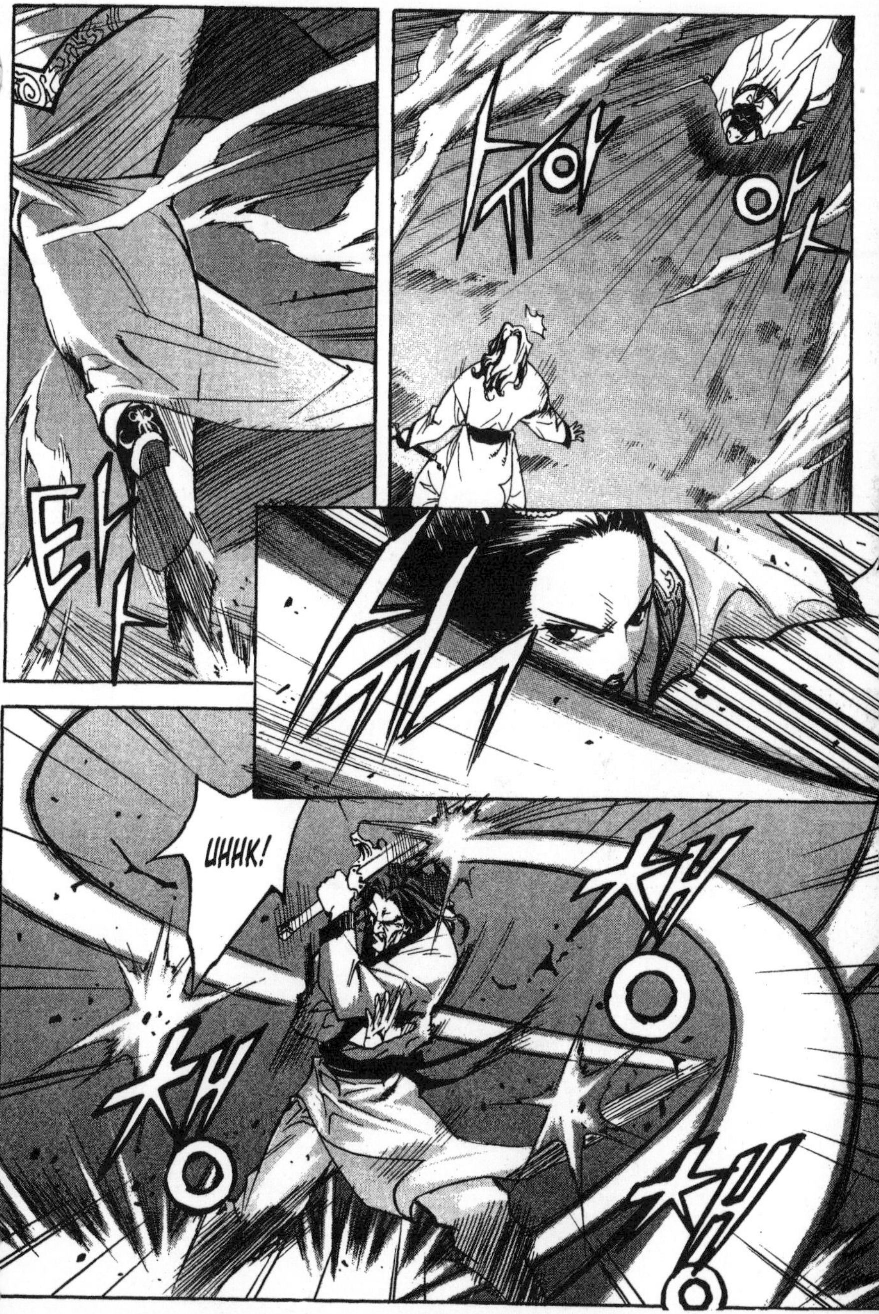

탁
파앙
파앗
쉬익
UHHK!
챙
챙
챙

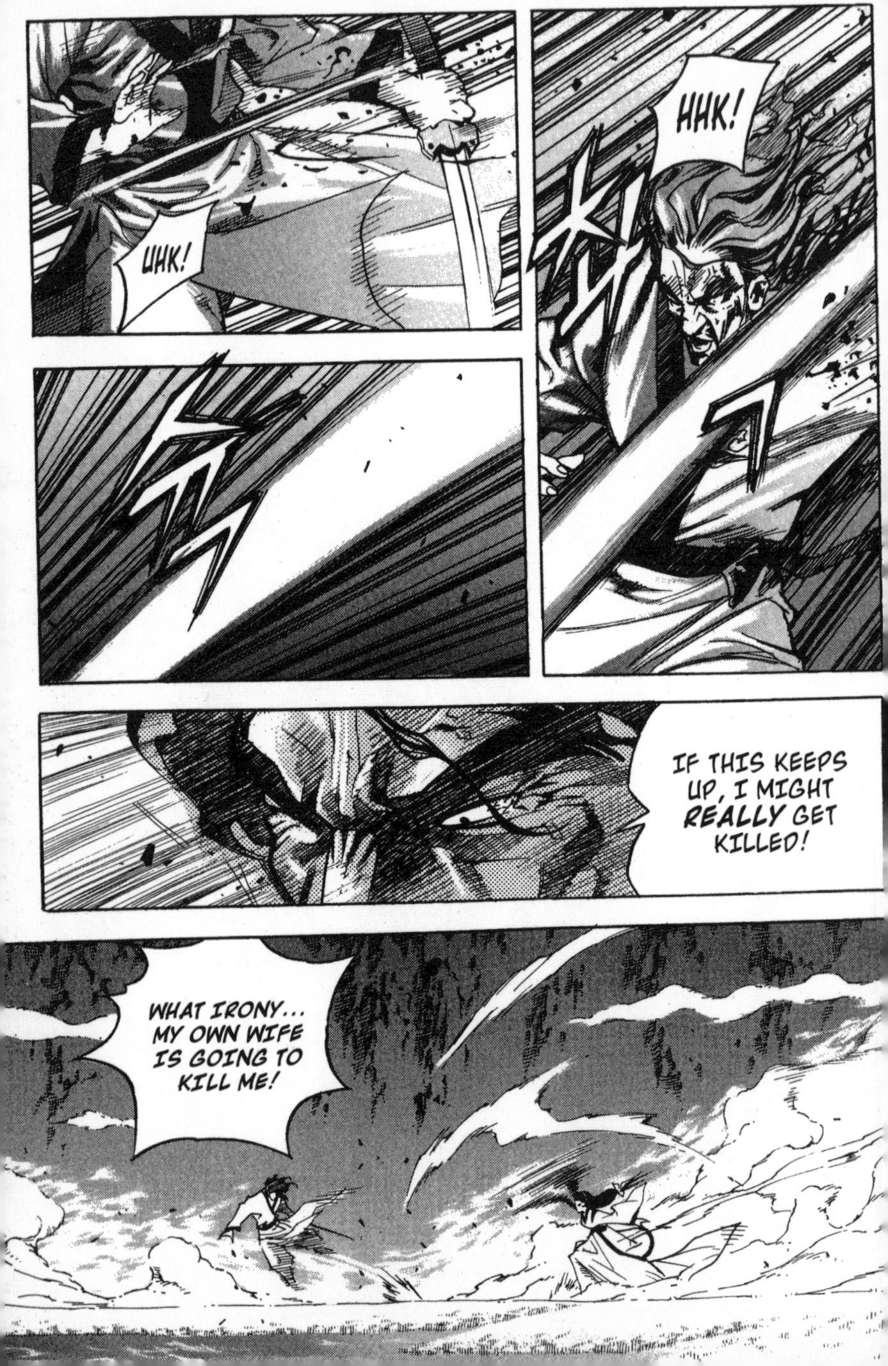
UHK!
HHK!
IF THIS KEEPS UP, I MIGHT REALLY GET KILLED!
WHAT IRONY... MY OWN WIFE IS GOING TO KILL ME!

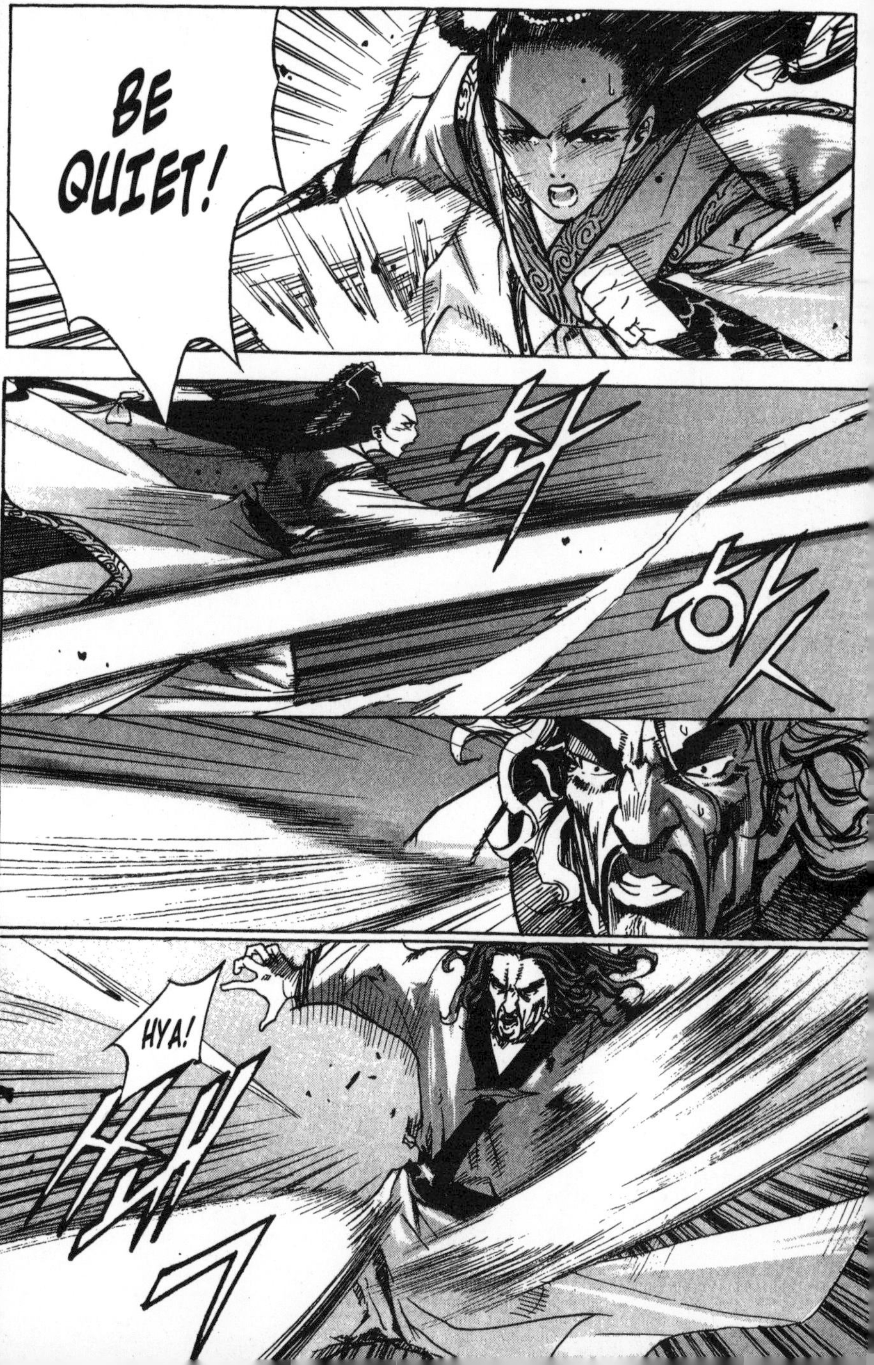
BE QUIET!
HYA!

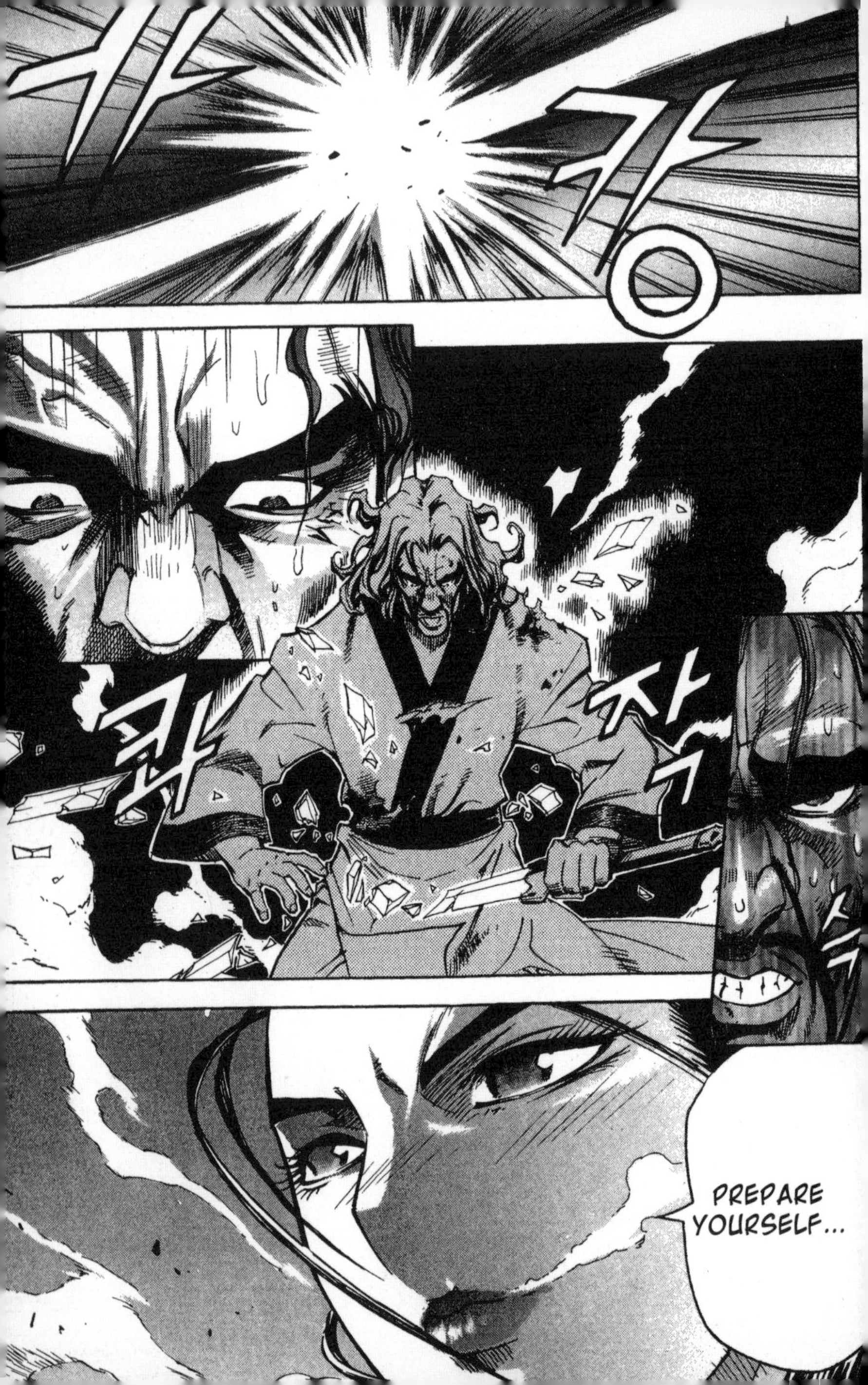
PREPARE YOURSELF...

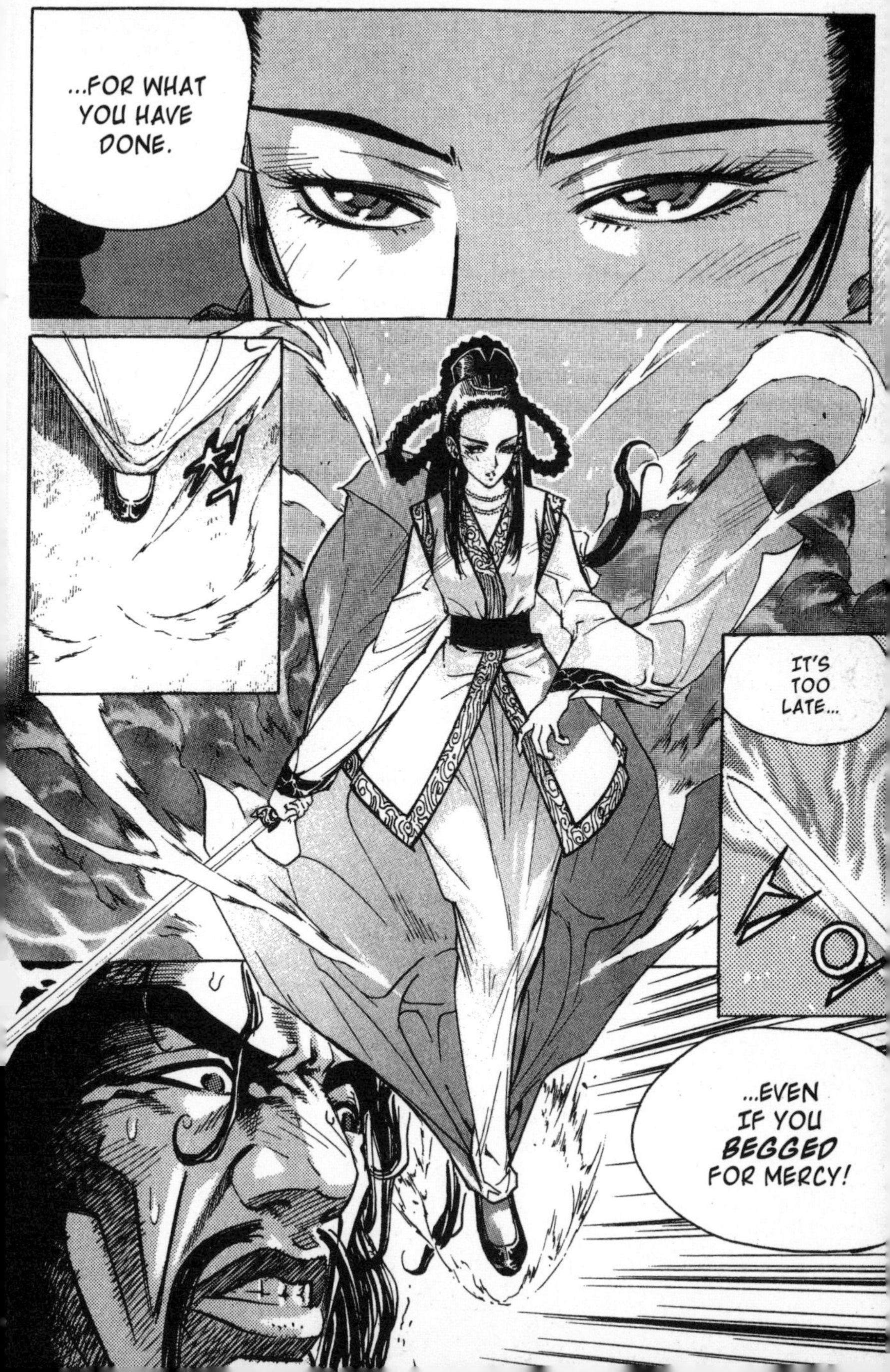
...FOR WHAT YOU HAVE DONE.
IT'S TOO LATE...
...EVEN IF YOU *BEGGED* FOR MERCY!

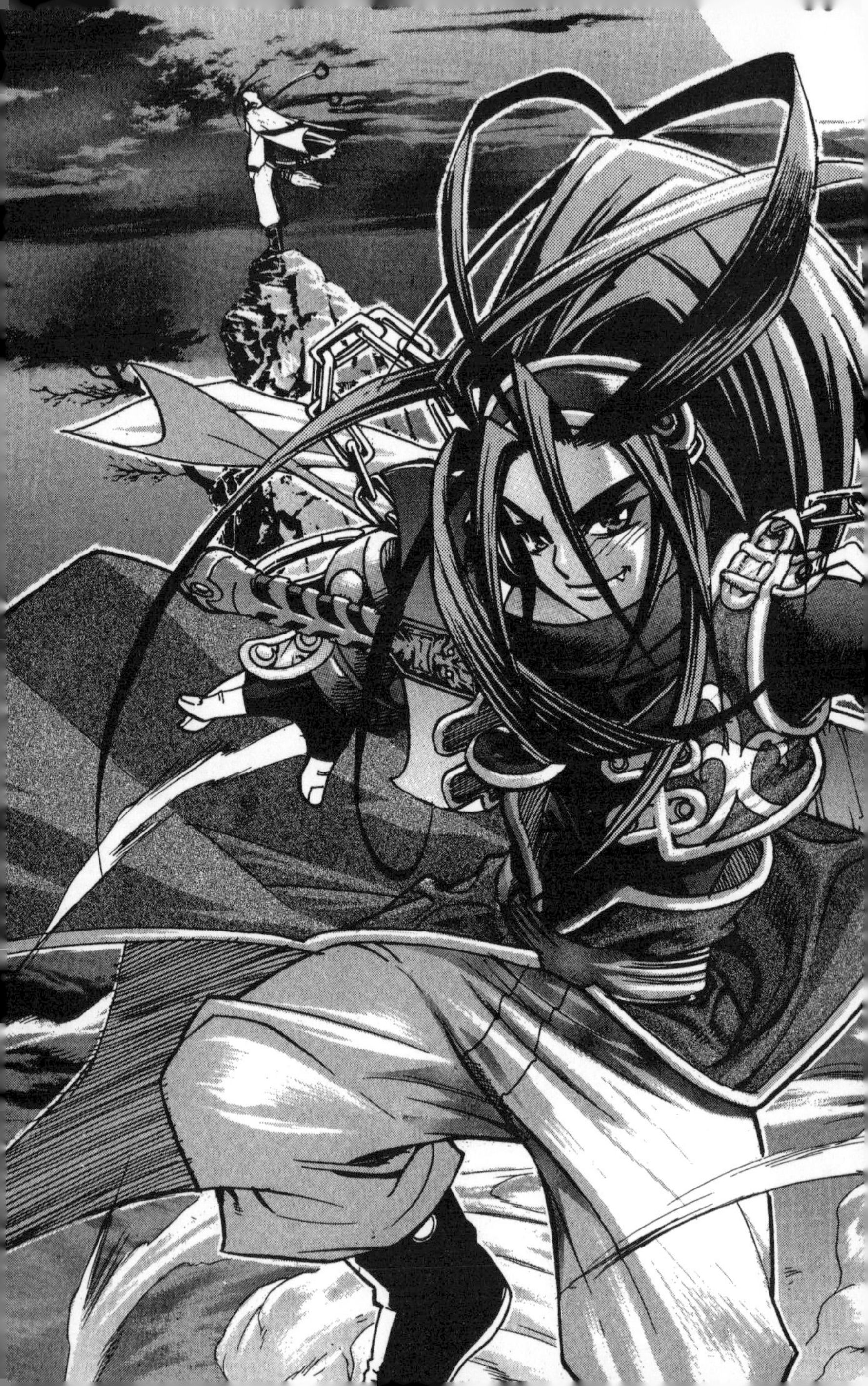

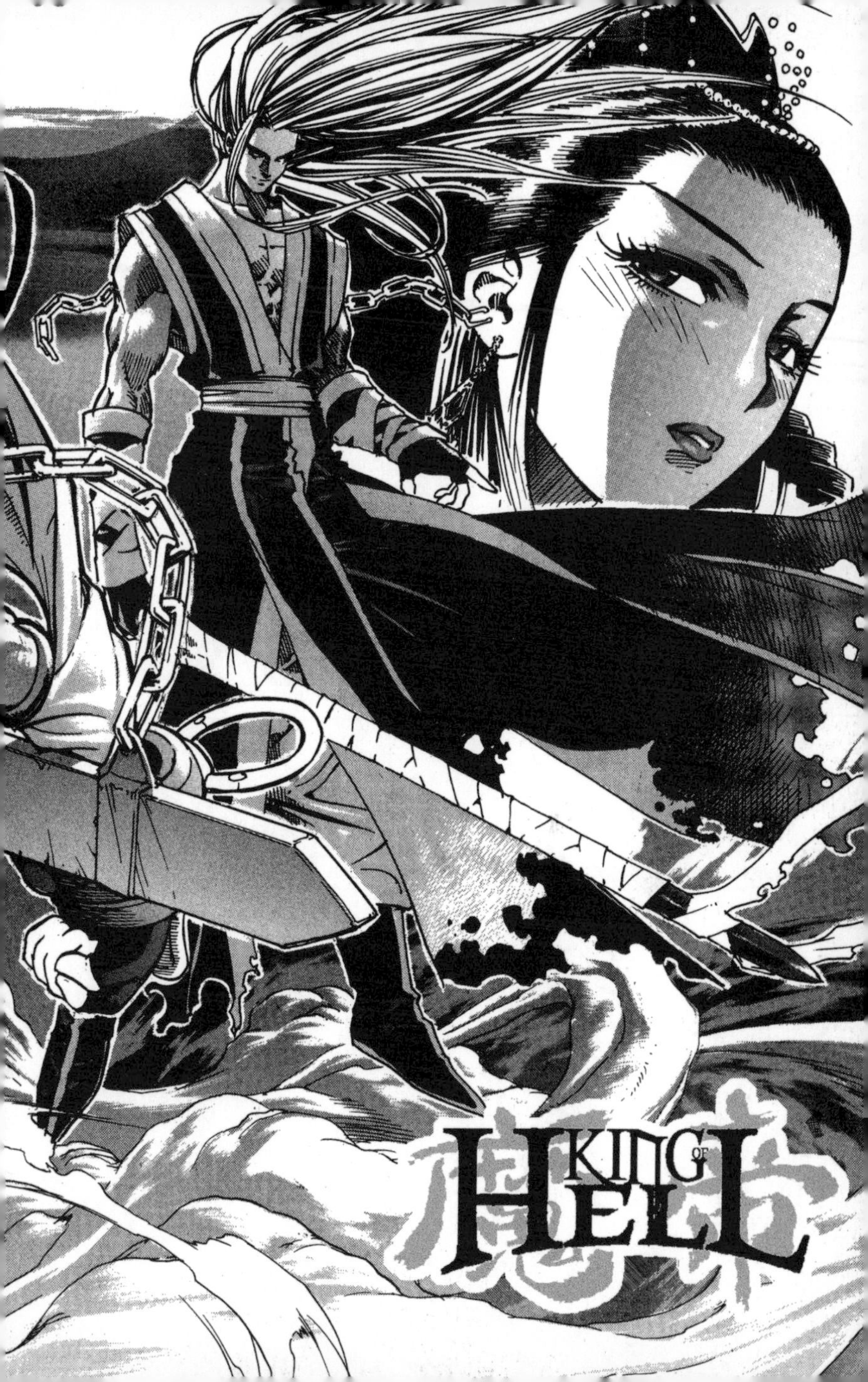
KING OF HELL

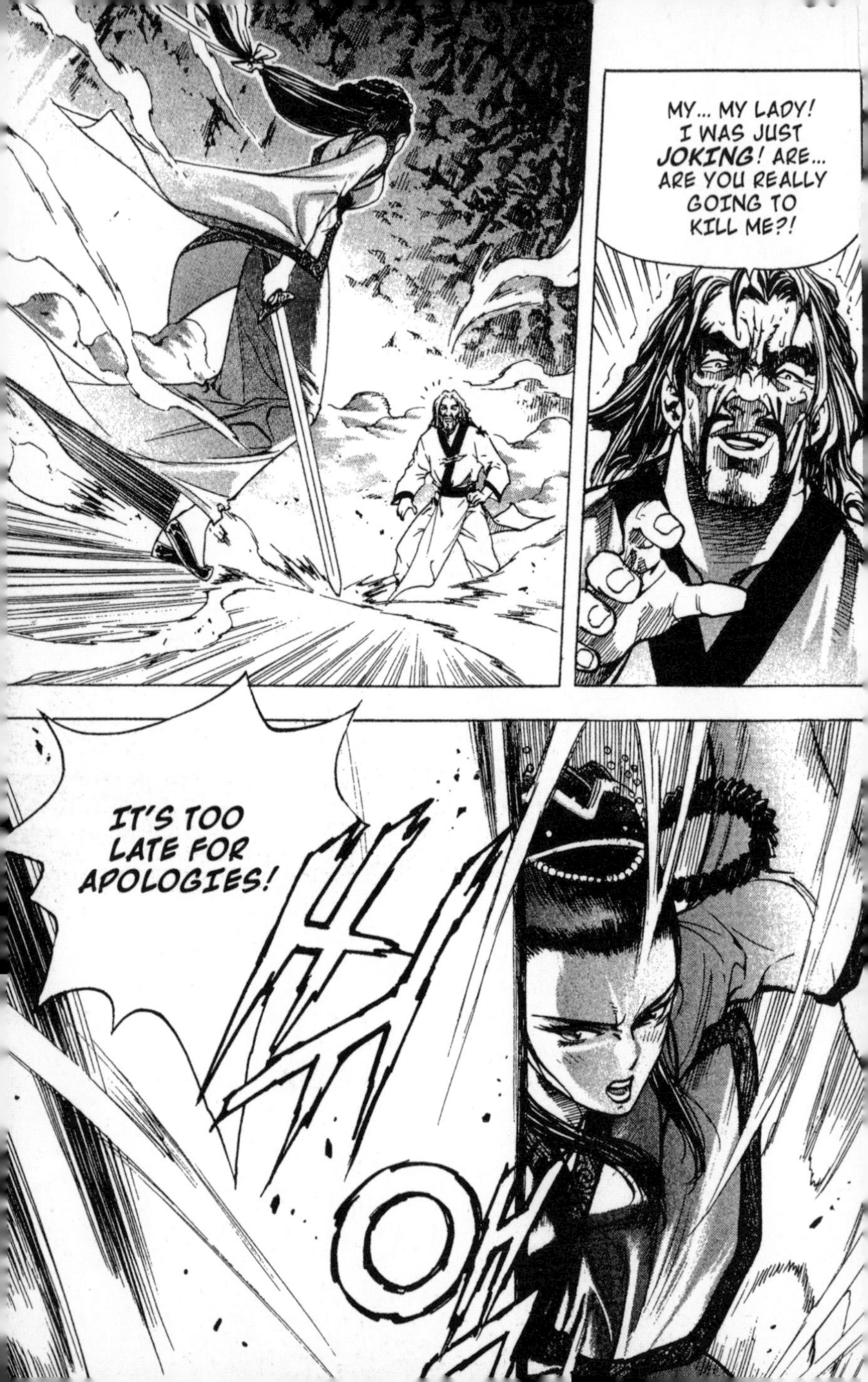
MY... MY LADY! I WAS JUST JOKING! ARE... ARE YOU REALLY GOING TO KILL ME?!
IT'S TOO LATE FOR APOLOGIES!
HHH
O

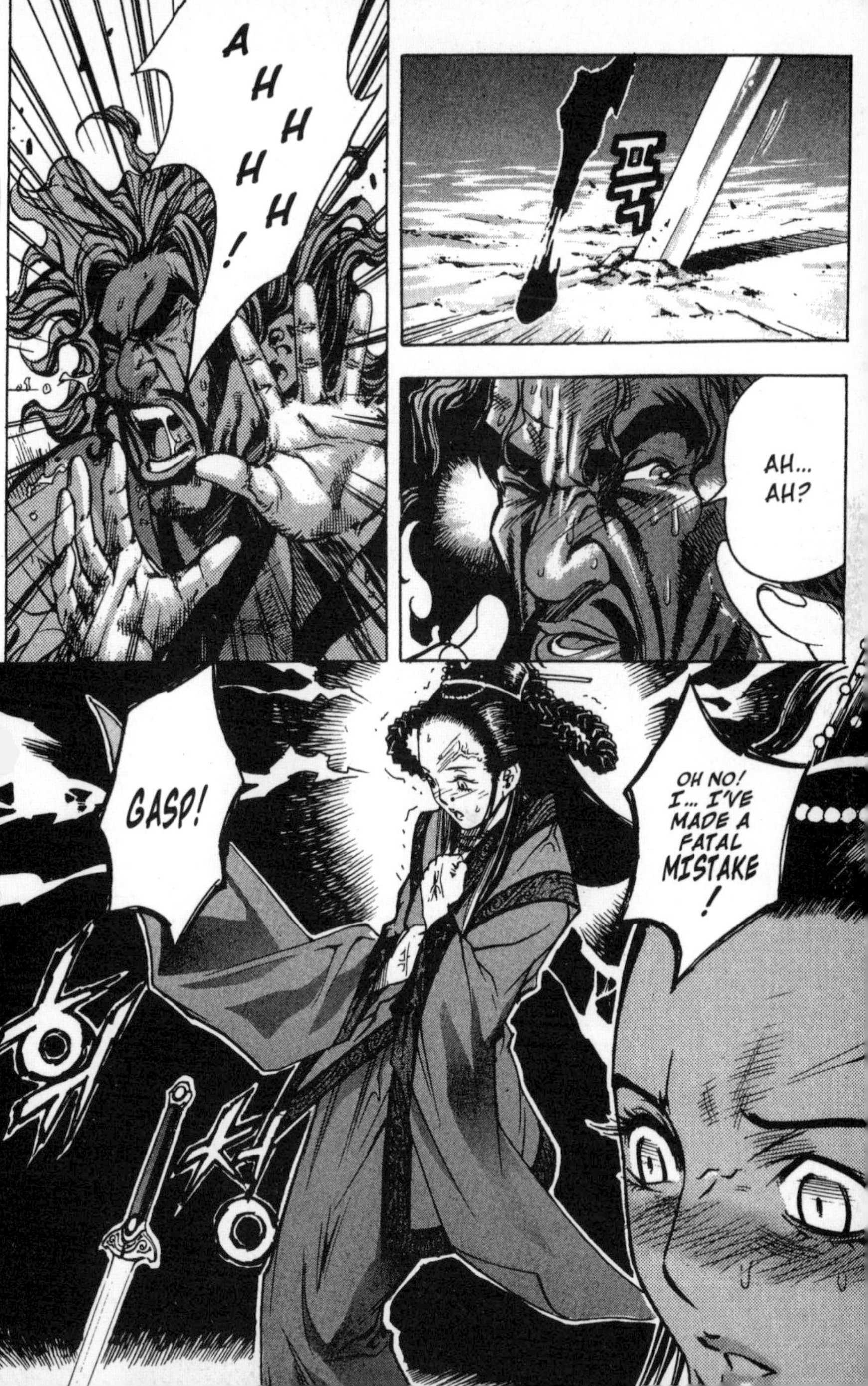
AHHHH!
AH... AH?
GASP!
OH NO! I... I'VE MADE A FATAL MISTAKE!

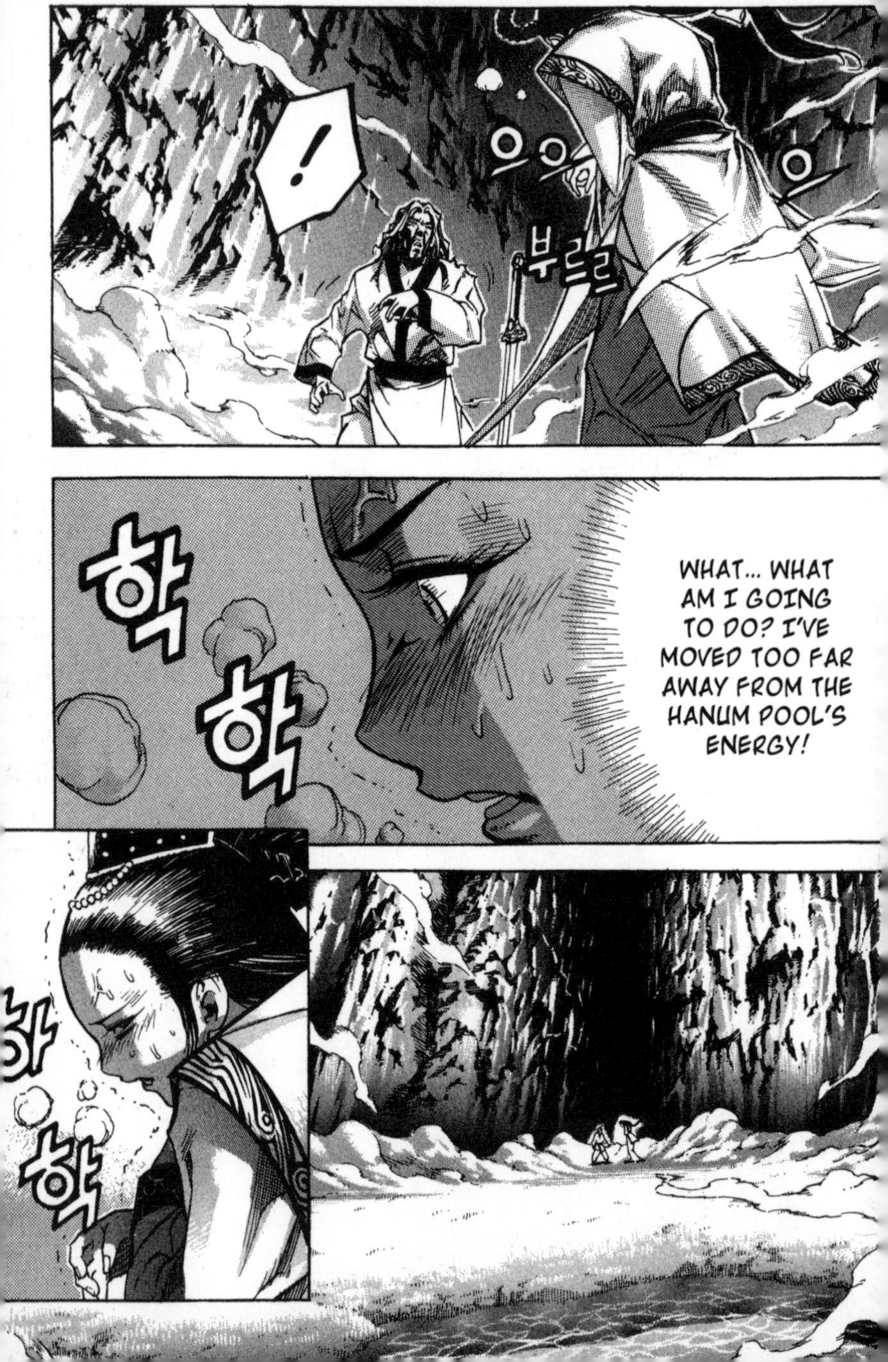
!
으으
으
부르르
학
학
WHAT... WHAT AM I GOING TO DO? I'VE MOVED TOO FAR AWAY FROM THE HANUM POOL'S ENERGY!
학
학

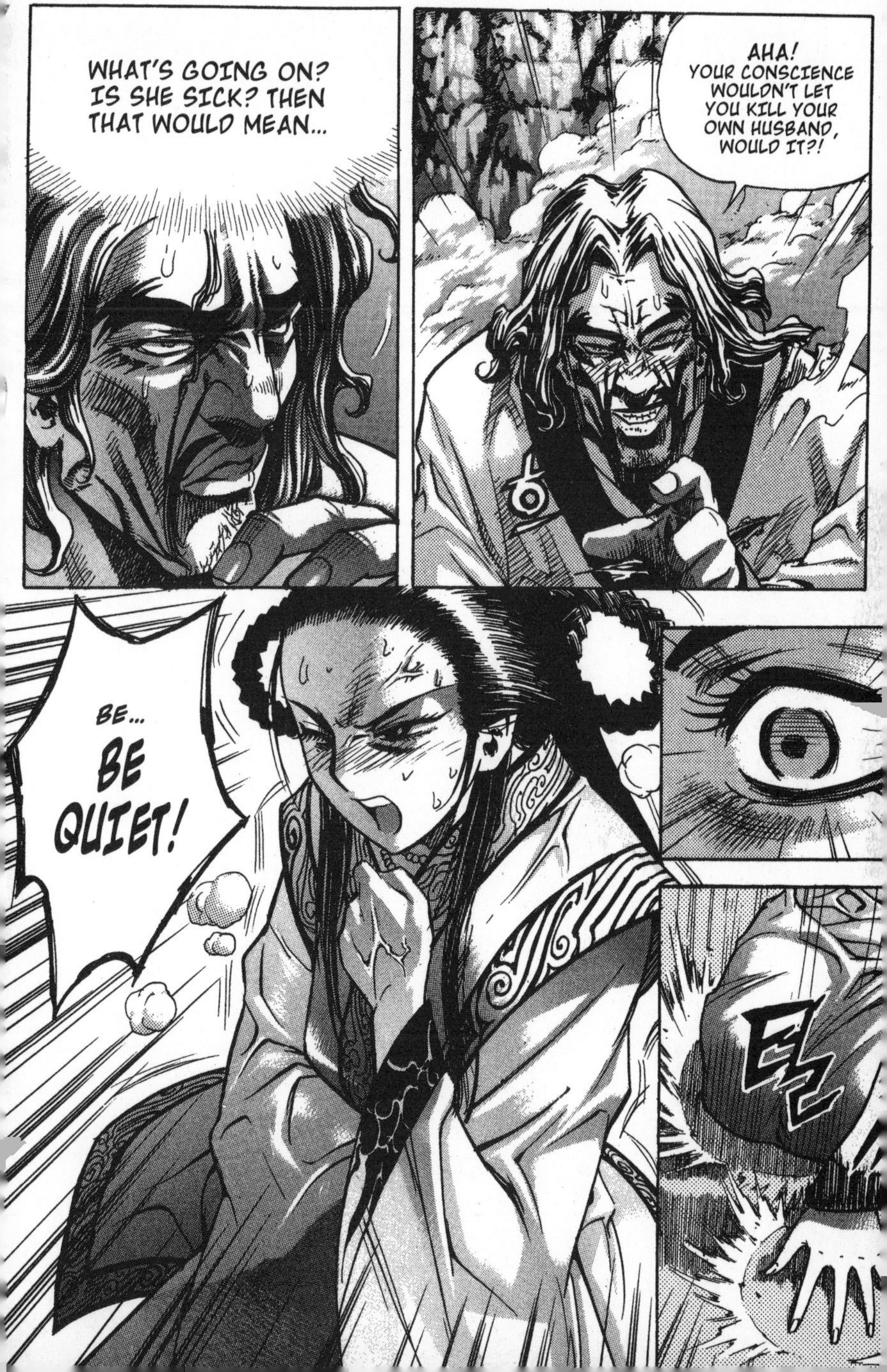
WHAT'S GOING ON? IS SHE SICK? THEN THAT WOULD MEAN...
AHA! YOUR CONSCIENCE WOULDN'T LET YOU KILL YOUR OWN HUSBAND, WOULD IT?!
BE... BE QUIET!

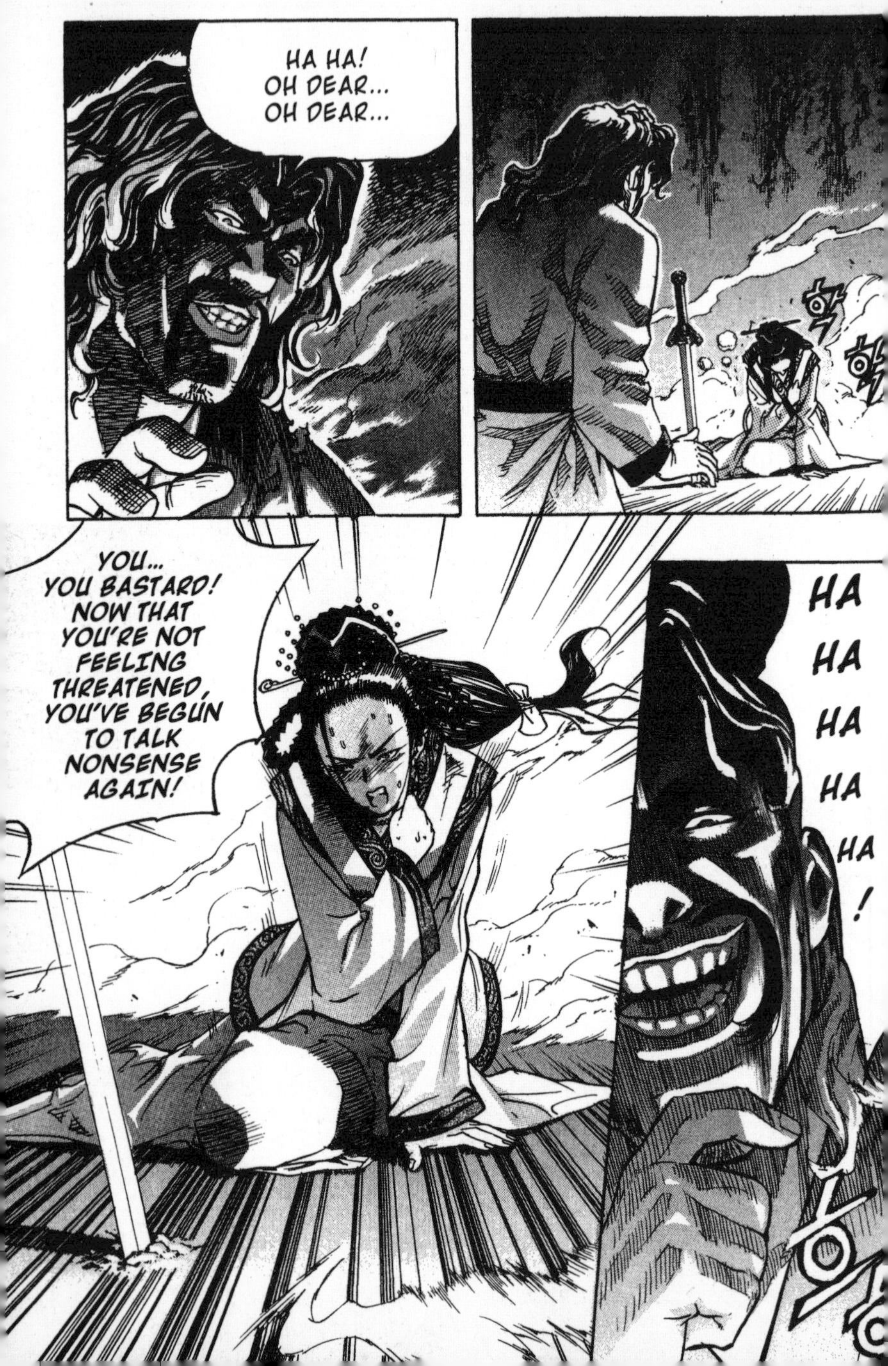
HA HA! OH DEAR... OH DEAR...
YOU... YOU BASTARD! NOW THAT YOU'RE NOT FEELING THREATENED, YOU'VE BEGUN TO TALK NONSENSE AGAIN!
HA HA HA HA HA HA!

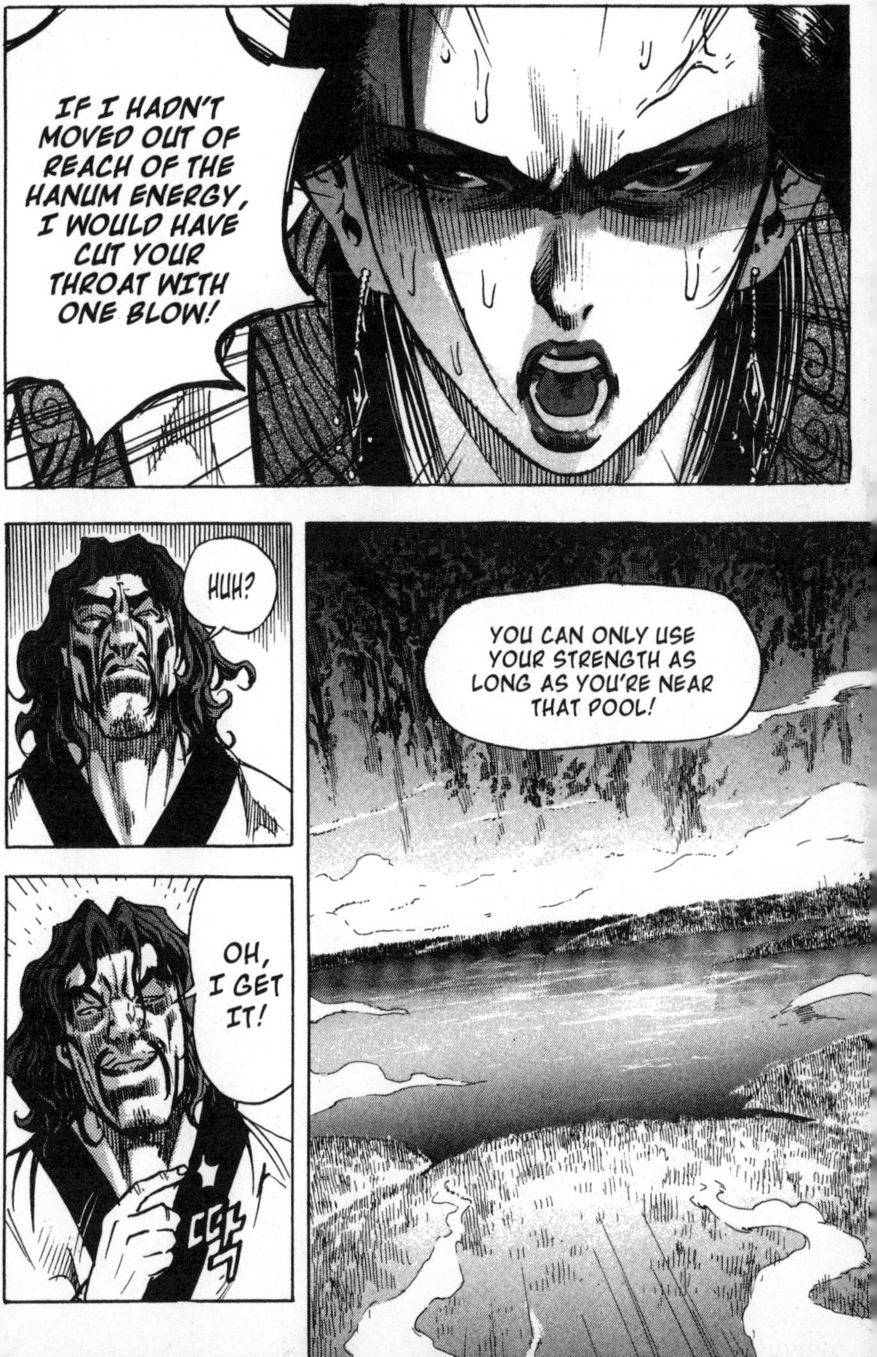
IF I HADN'T MOVED OUT OF REACH OF THE HANUM ENERGY, I WOULD HAVE CUT YOUR THROAT WITH ONE BLOW!
HUH?
OH, I GET IT!
YOU CAN ONLY USE YOUR STRENGTH AS LONG AS YOU'RE NEAR THAT POOL!

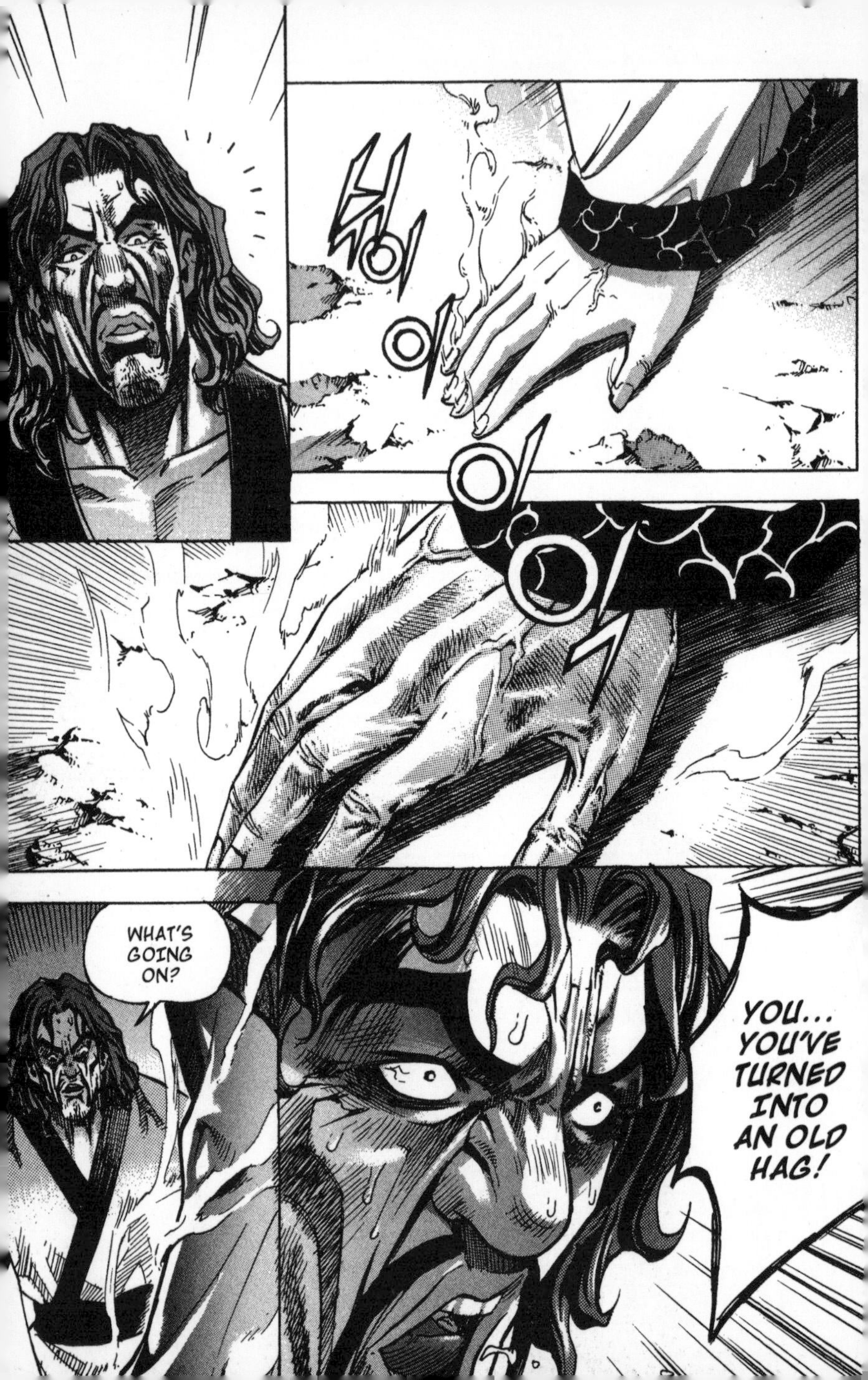
WHAT'S GOING ON?
YOU... YOU'VE TURNED INTO AN OLD HAG!

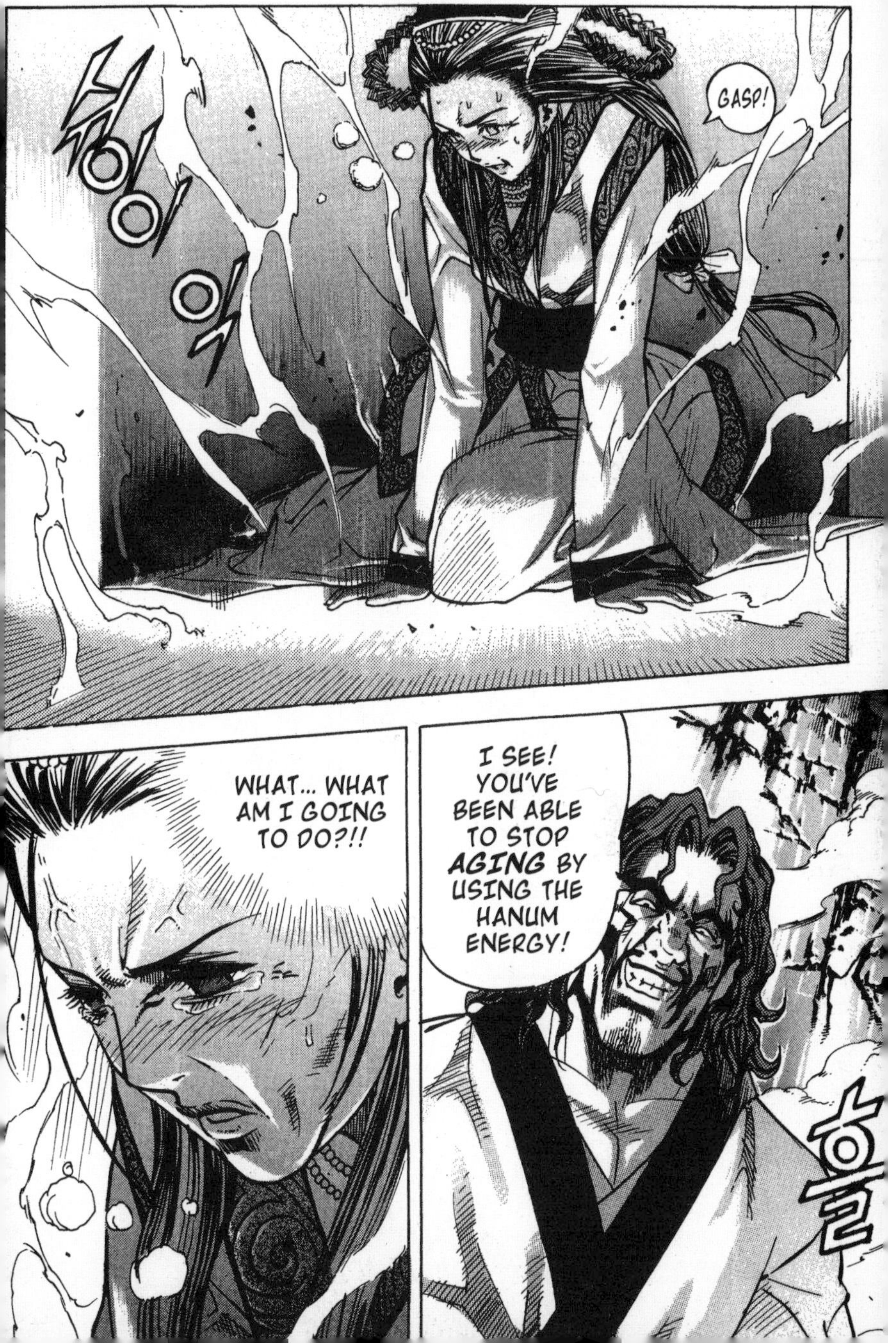
GASP!
WHAT... WHAT AM I GOING TO DO?!!
I SEE! YOU'VE BEEN ABLE TO STOP AGING BY USING THE HANUM ENERGY!

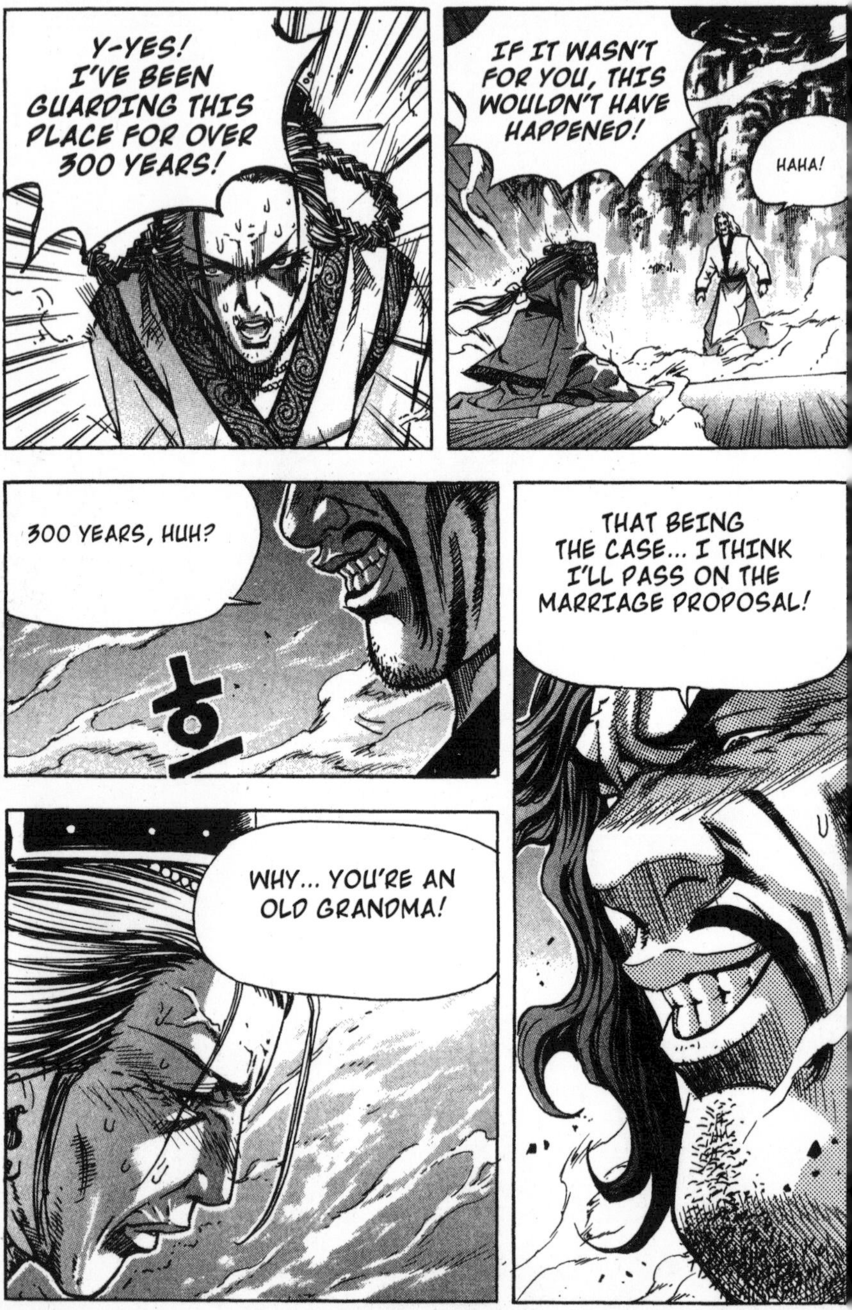
Y-YES! I'VE BEEN GUARDING THIS PLACE FOR OVER 300 YEARS!
IF IT WASN'T FOR YOU, THIS WOULDN'T HAVE HAPPENED!
HAHA!
300 YEARS, HUH?
흐
WHY... YOU'RE AN OLD GRANDMA!
THAT BEING THE CASE... I THINK I'LL PASS ON THE MARRIAGE PROPOSAL!

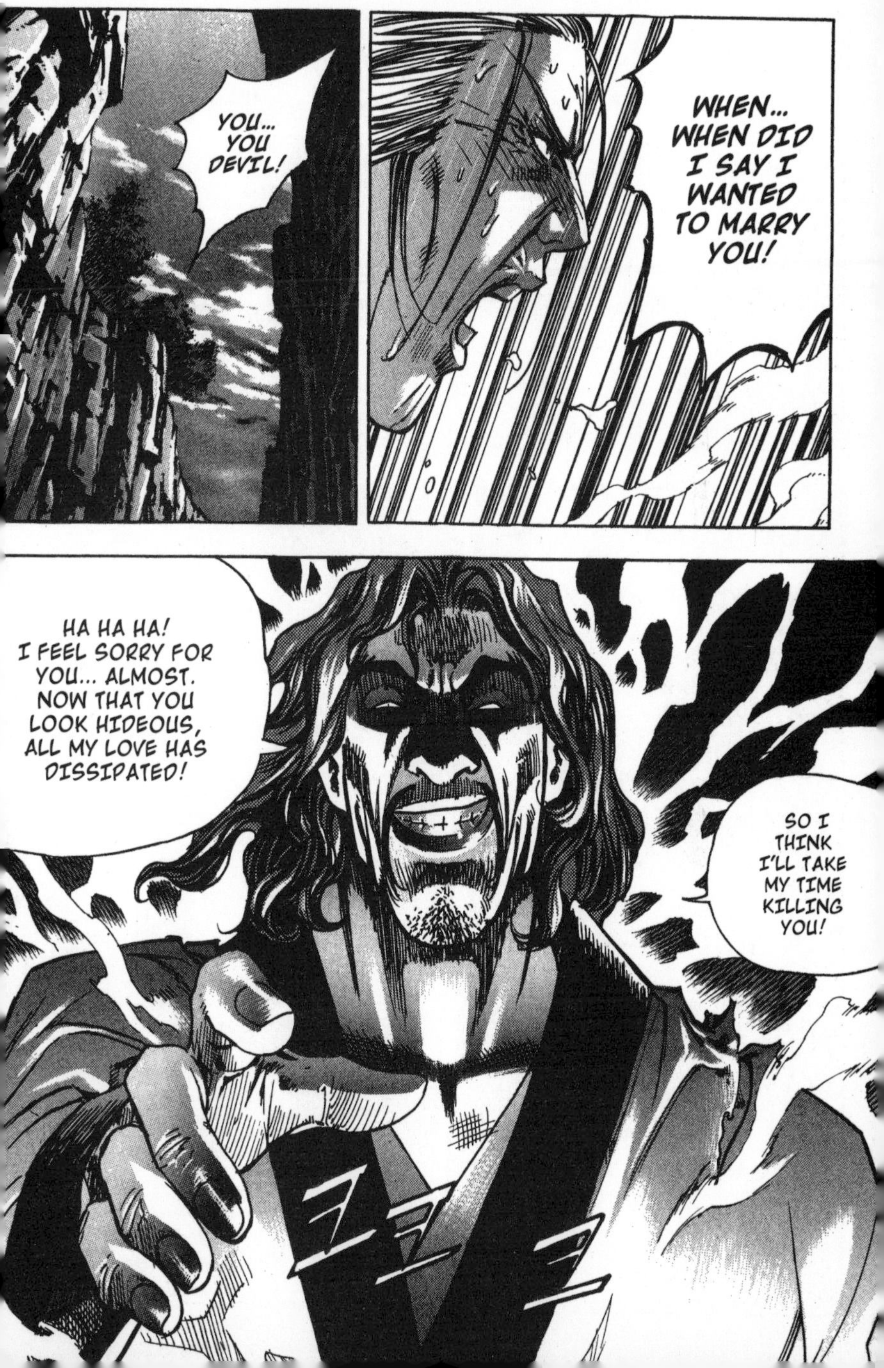
YOU... YOU DEVIL!
WHEN... WHEN DID I SAY I WANTED TO MARRY YOU!
HA HA HA! I FEEL SORRY FOR YOU... ALMOST. NOW THAT YOU LOOK HIDEOUS, ALL MY LOVE HAS DISSIPATED!
SO I THINK I'LL TAKE MY TIME KILLING YOU!

NO!

WHAT...
WHAT DID
YOU SAY??!!

I SAID NO!

322

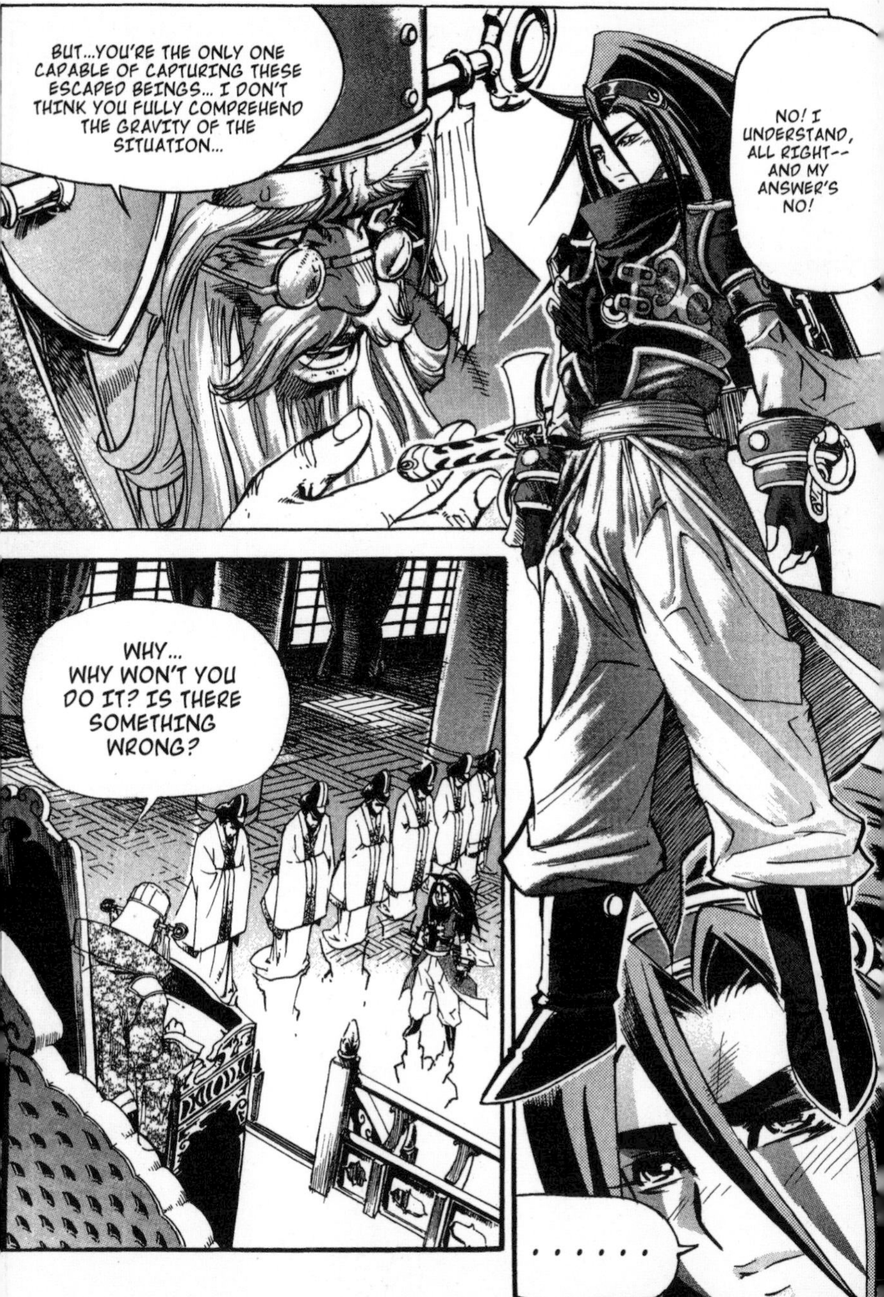

BUT...YOU'RE THE ONLY ONE CAPABLE OF CAPTURING THESE ESCAPED BEINGS... I DON'T THINK YOU FULLY COMPREHEND THE GRAVITY OF THE SITUATION...
NO! I UNDERSTAND, ALL RIGHT-- AND MY ANSWER'S NO!
WHY... WHY WON'T YOU DO IT? IS THERE SOMETHING WRONG?
......

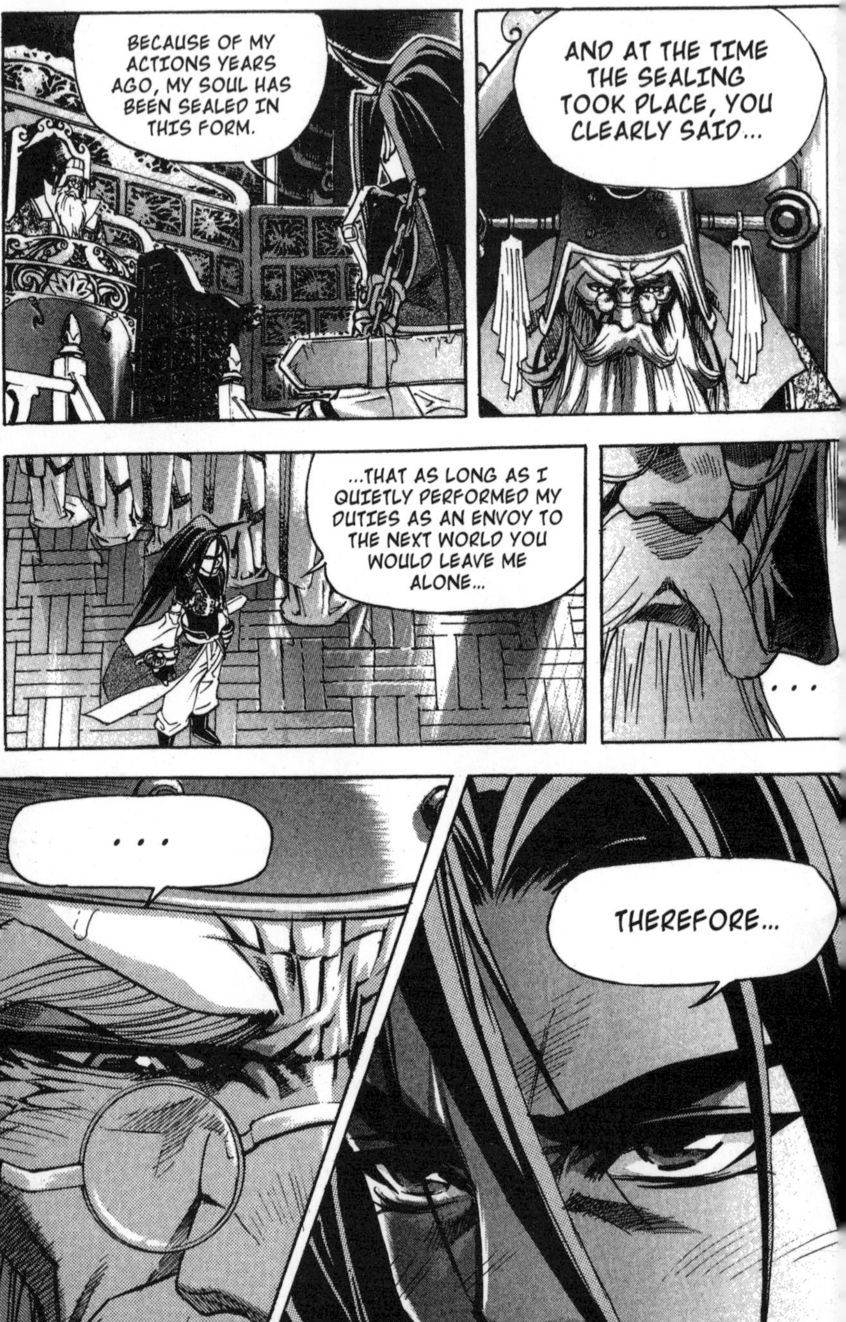
BECAUSE OF MY ACTIONS YEARS AGO, MY SOUL HAS BEEN SEALED IN THIS FORM.
AND AT THE TIME THE SEALING TOOK PLACE, YOU CLEARLY SAID...
...THAT AS LONG AS I QUIETLY PERFORMED MY DUTIES AS AN ENVOY TO THE NEXT WORLD YOU WOULD LEAVE ME ALONE...
...
...
THEREFORE...

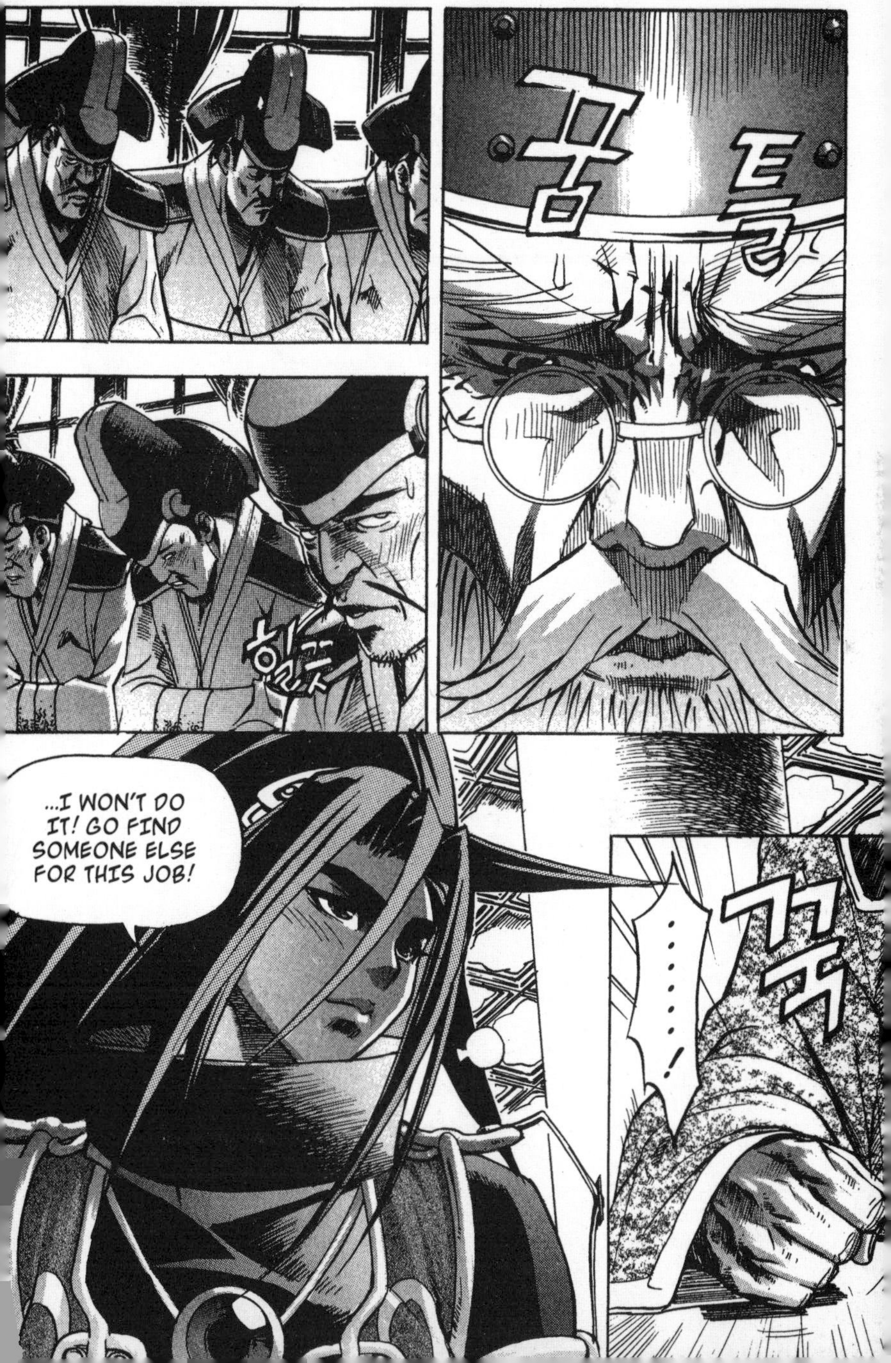

...I WON'T DO IT! GO FIND SOMEONE ELSE FOR THIS JOB!
......!

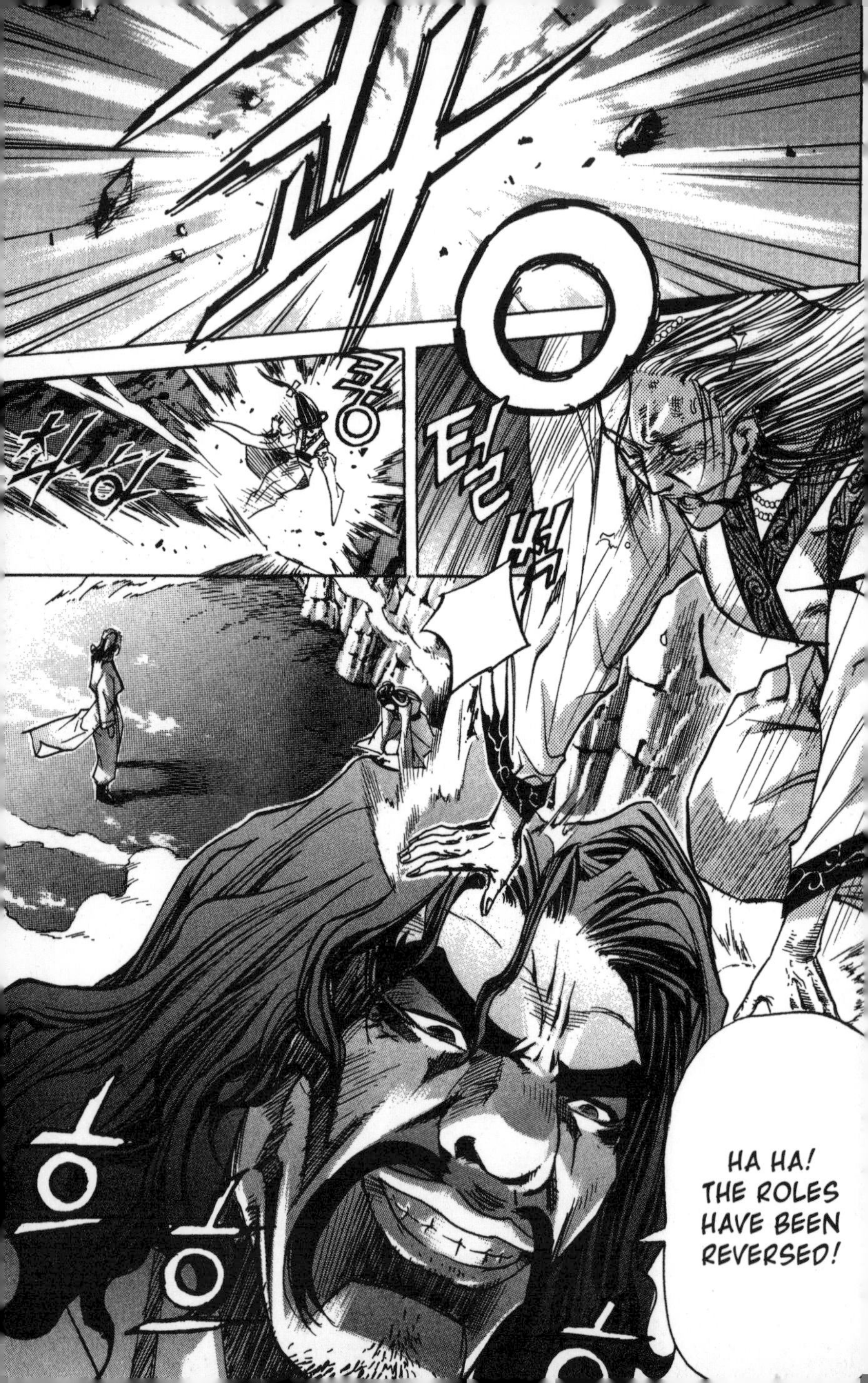
HA HA! THE ROLES HAVE BEEN REVERSED!

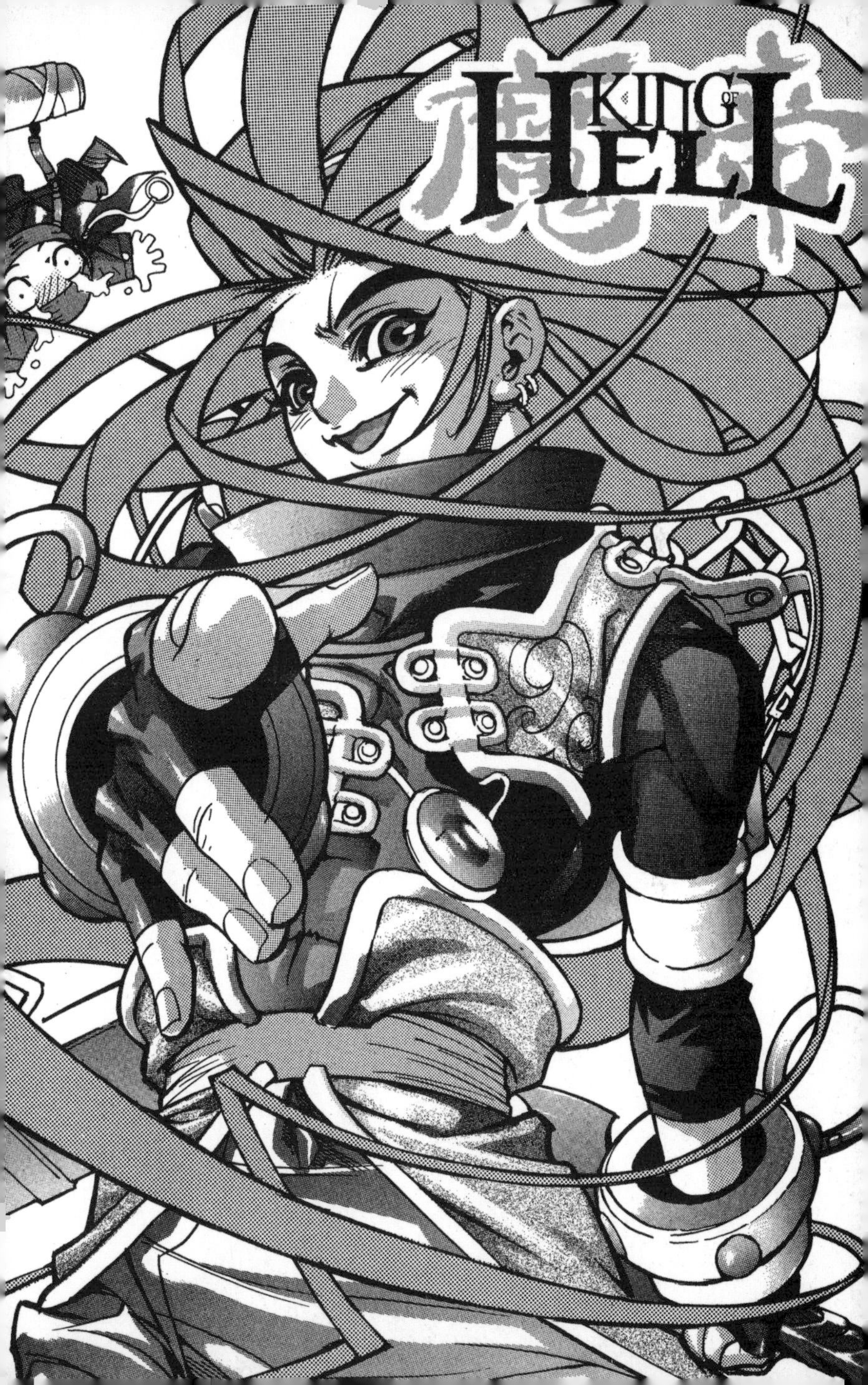
KING OF HELL

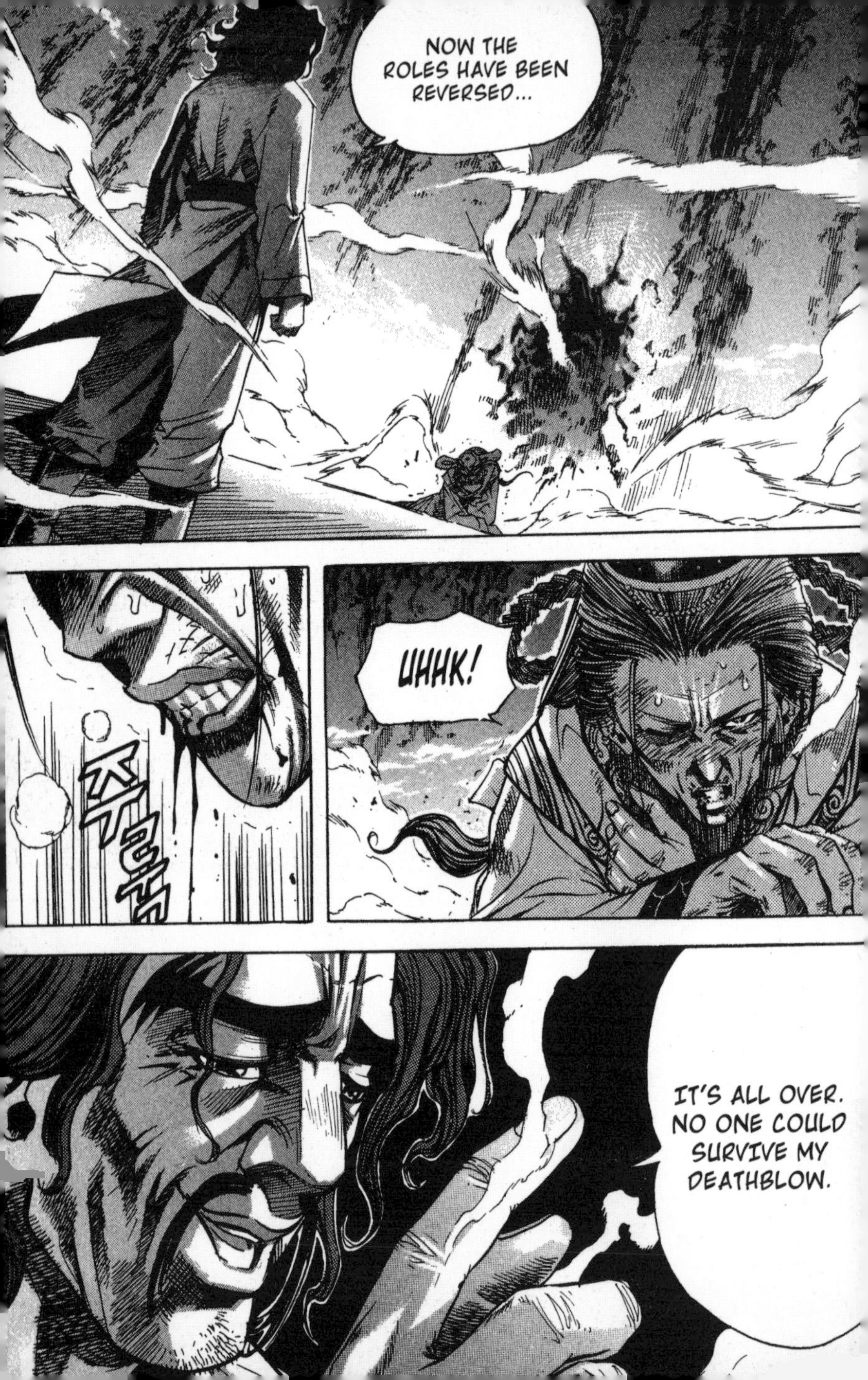
NOW THE ROLES HAVE BEEN REVERSED...
UHHK!
IT'S ALL OVER. NO ONE COULD SURVIVE MY DEATHBLOW.

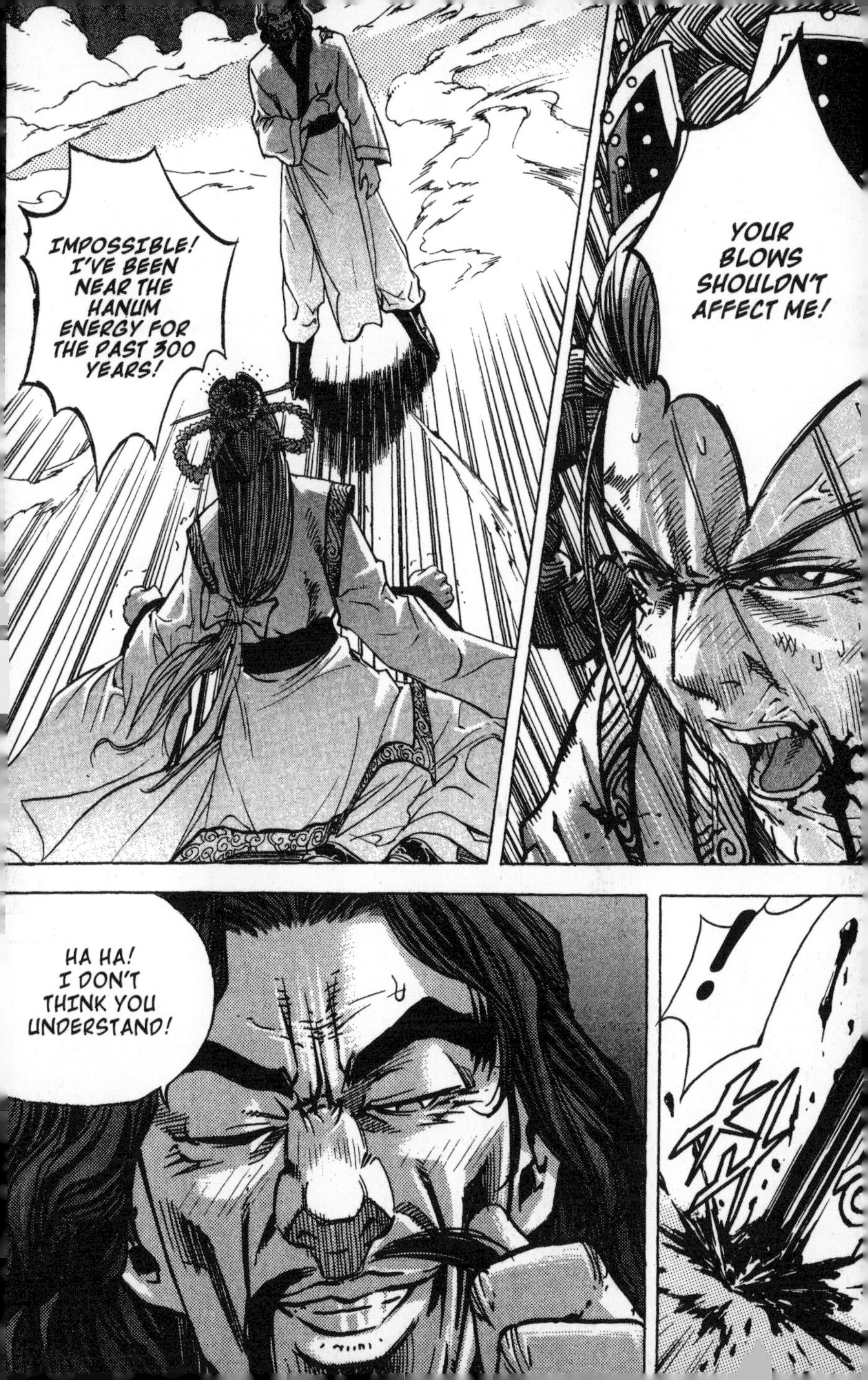
IMPOSSIBLE! I'VE BEEN NEAR THE HANUM ENERGY FOR THE PAST 300 YEARS!
YOUR BLOWS SHOULDN'T AFFECT ME!
HA HA! I DON'T THINK YOU UNDERSTAND!
!

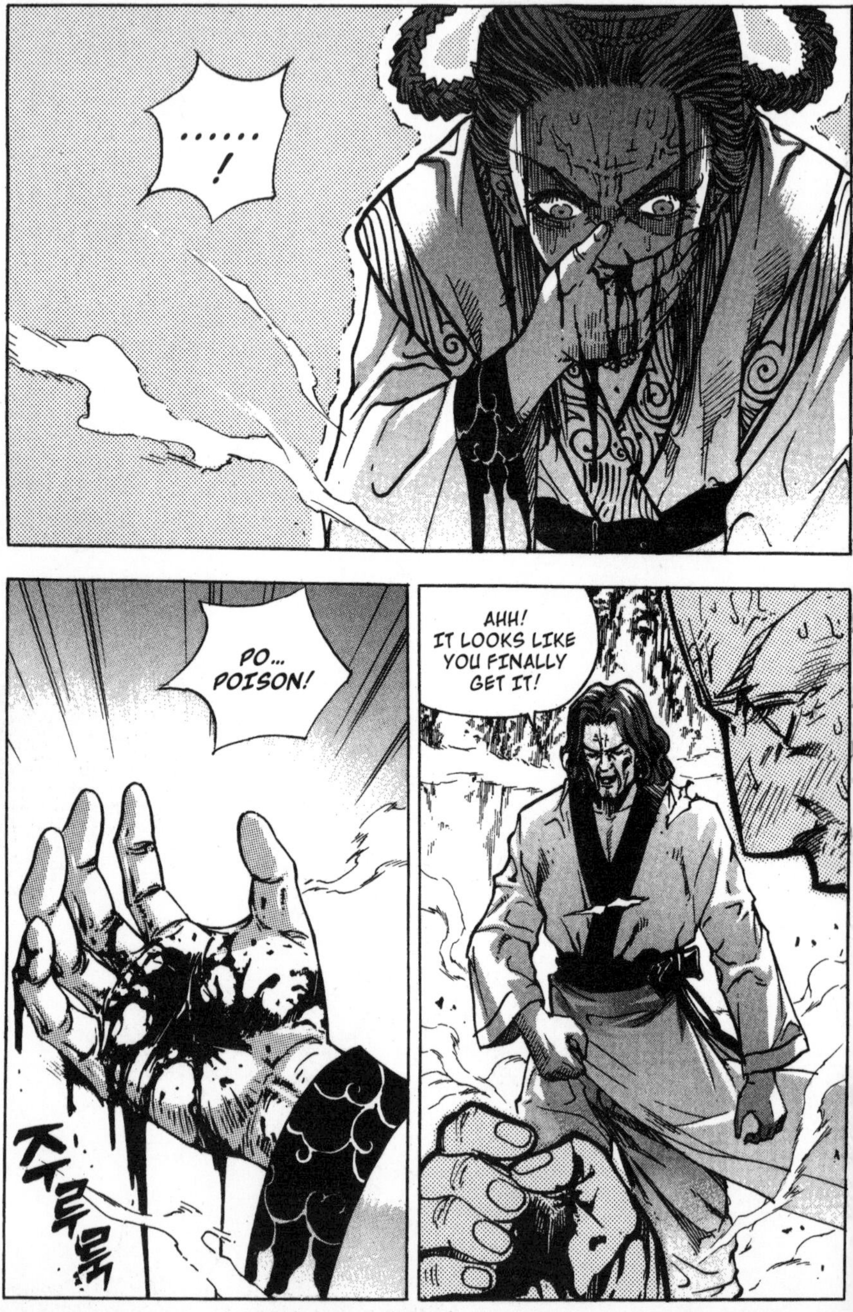
......!
PO... POISON!
AHH! IT LOOKS LIKE YOU FINALLY GET IT!

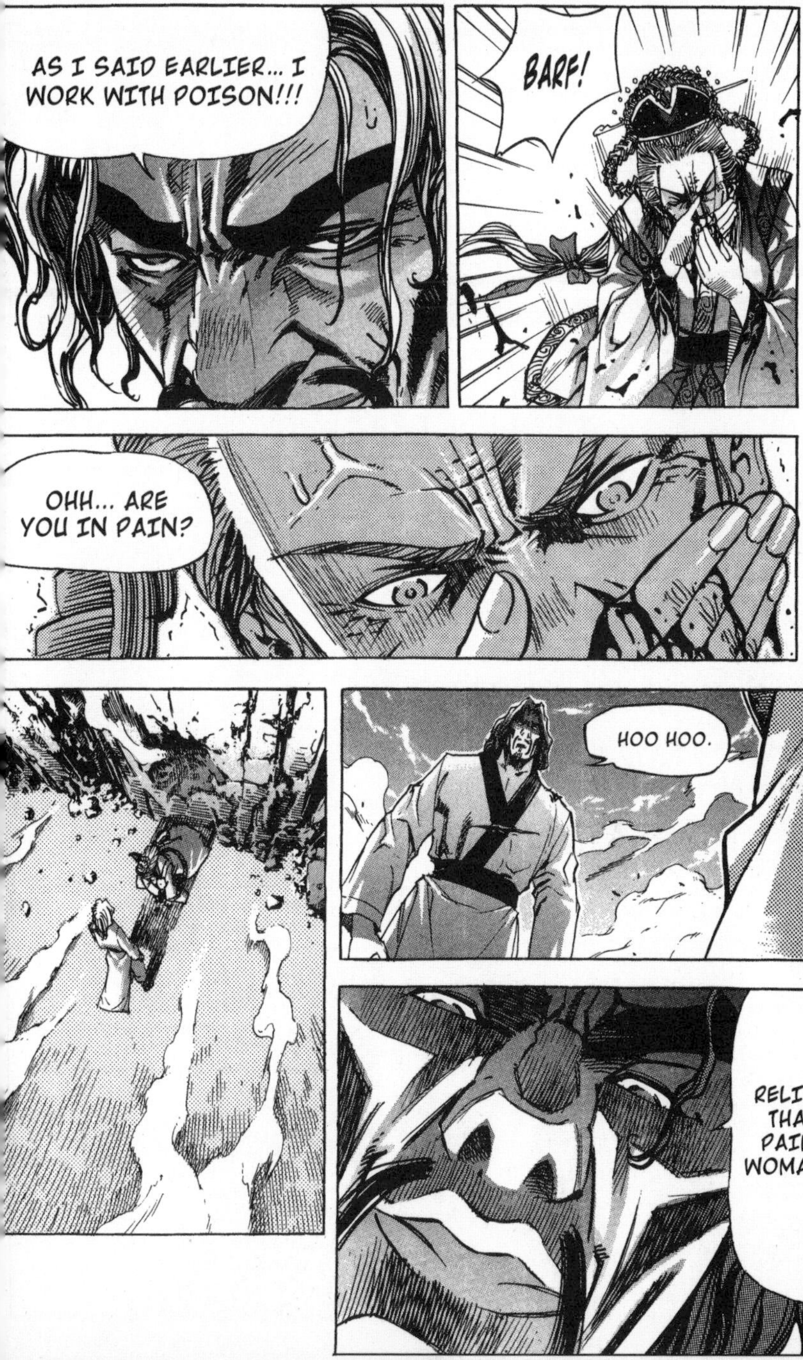
AS I SAID EARLIER... I WORK WITH POISON!!!
BARF!
OHH... ARE YOU IN PAIN?
HOO HOO.
RELISH THAT PAIN, WOMAN...

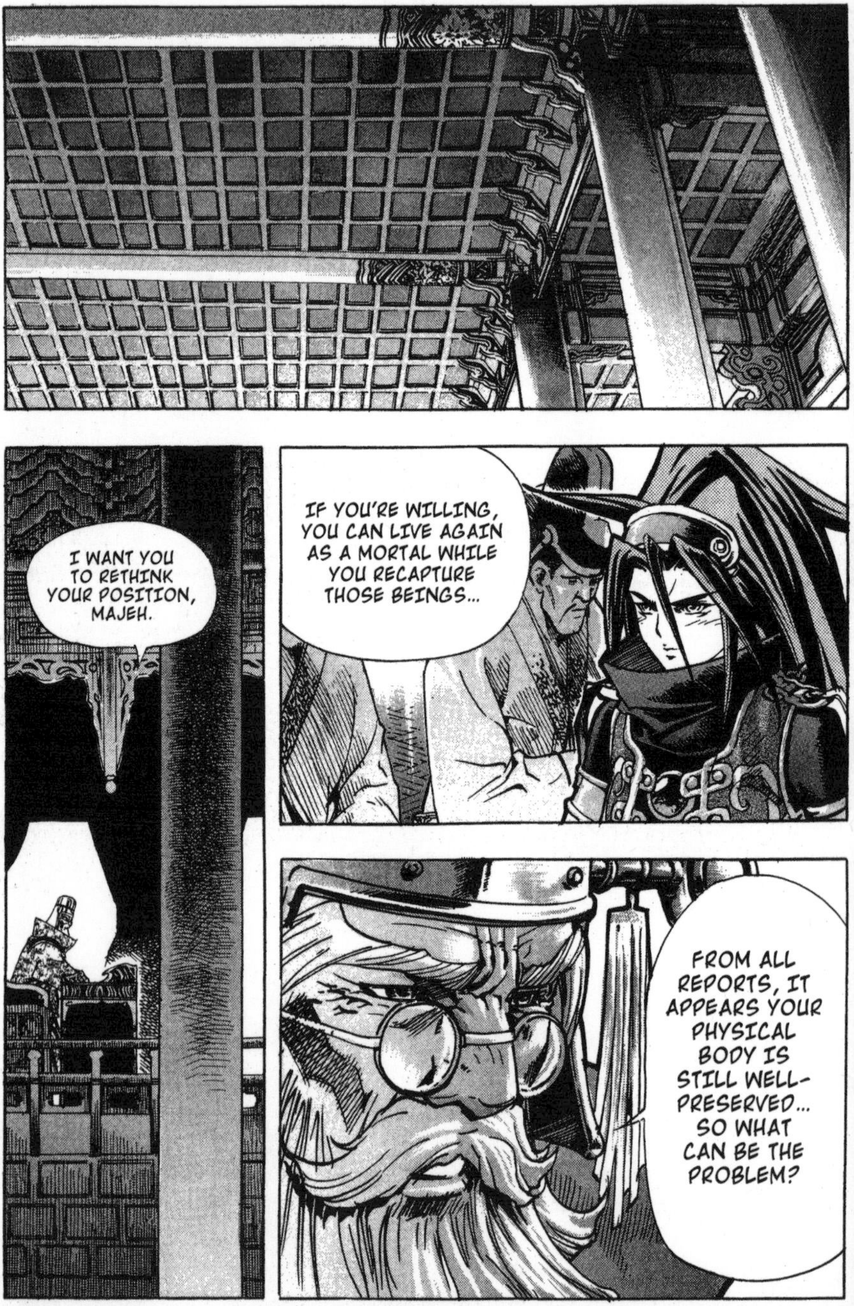
I WANT YOU TO RETHINK YOUR POSITION, MAJEH.
IF YOU'RE WILLING, YOU CAN LIVE AGAIN AS A MORTAL WHILE YOU RECAPTURE THOSE BEINGS...
FROM ALL REPORTS, IT APPEARS YOUR PHYSICAL BODY IS STILL WELL-PRESERVED... SO WHAT CAN BE THE PROBLEM?

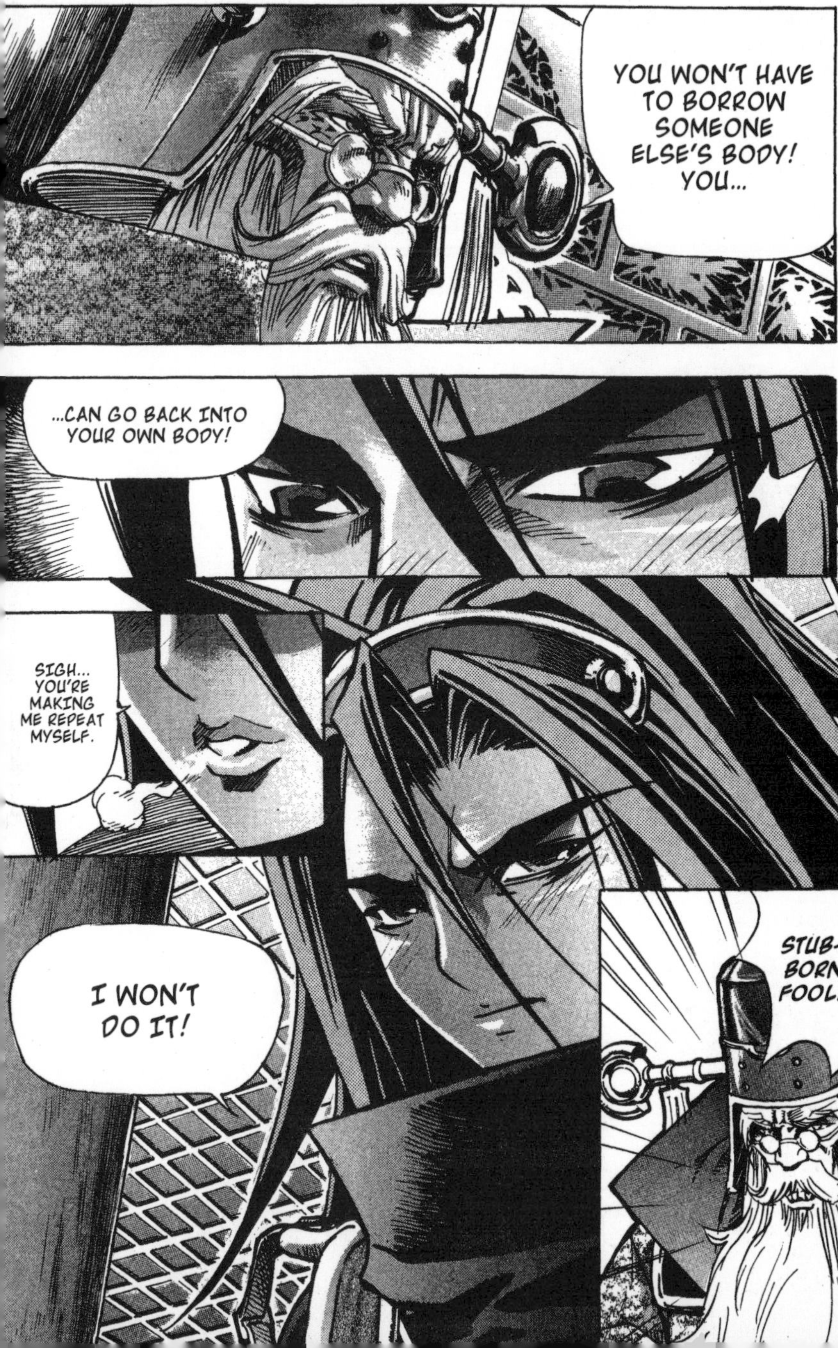
YOU WON'T HAVE TO BORROW SOMEONE ELSE'S BODY! YOU...
...CAN GO BACK INTO YOUR OWN BODY!
SIGH... YOU'RE MAKING ME REPEAT MYSELF.
I WON'T DO IT!
STUB-BORN FOOL!

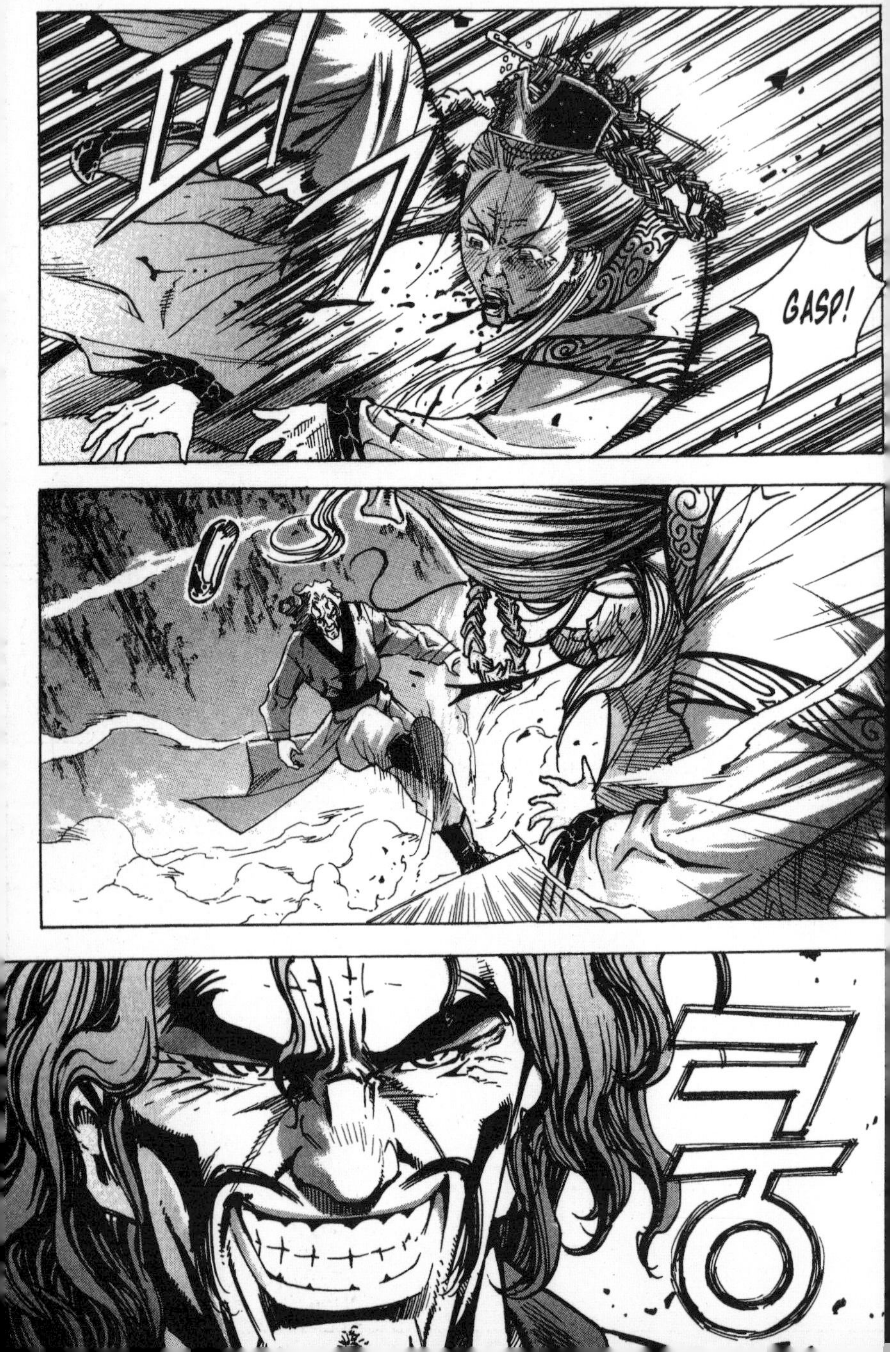
GASP!

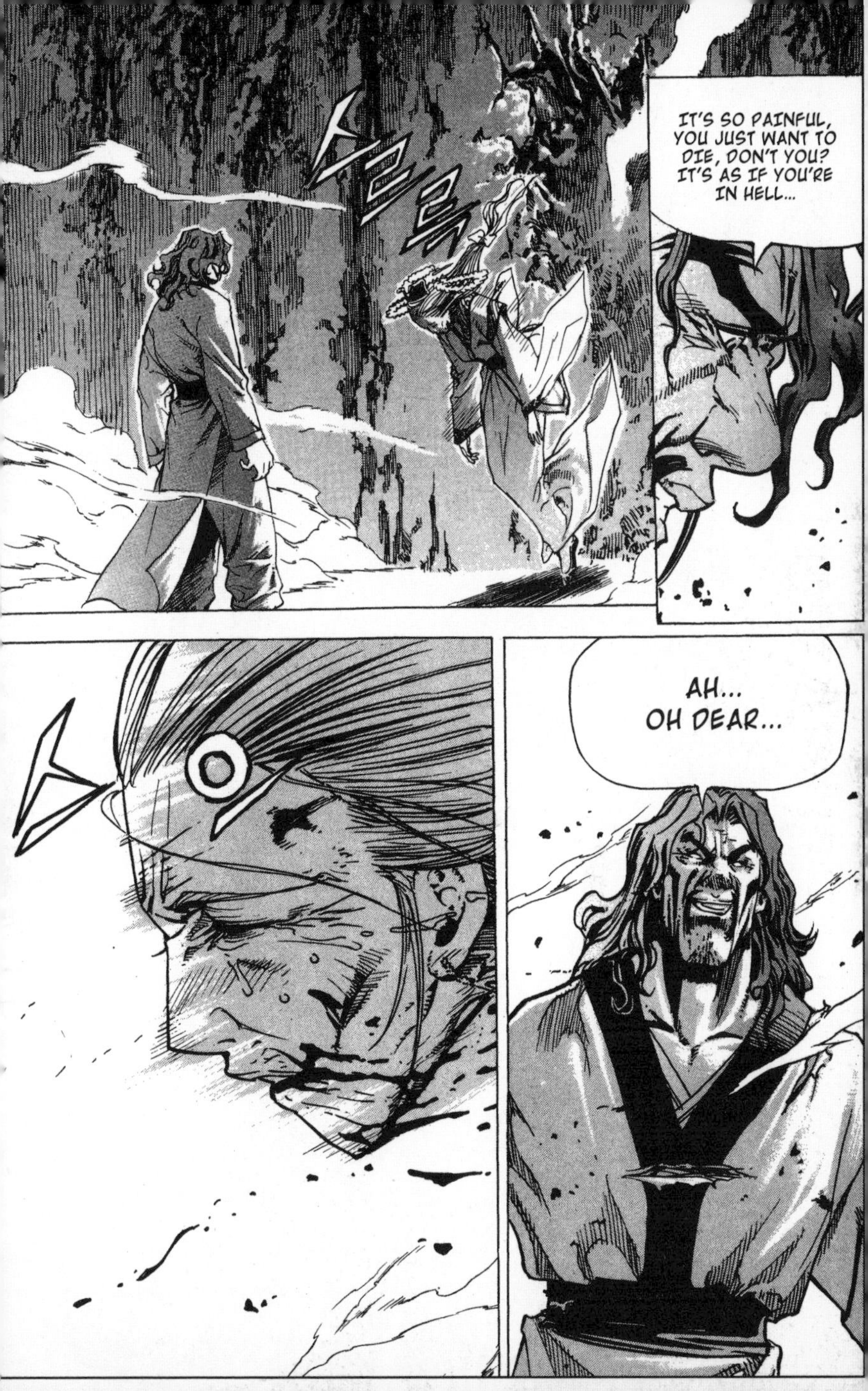
IT'S SO PAINFUL, YOU JUST WANT TO DIE, DON'T YOU? IT'S AS IF YOU'RE IN HELL...
AH... OH DEAR...

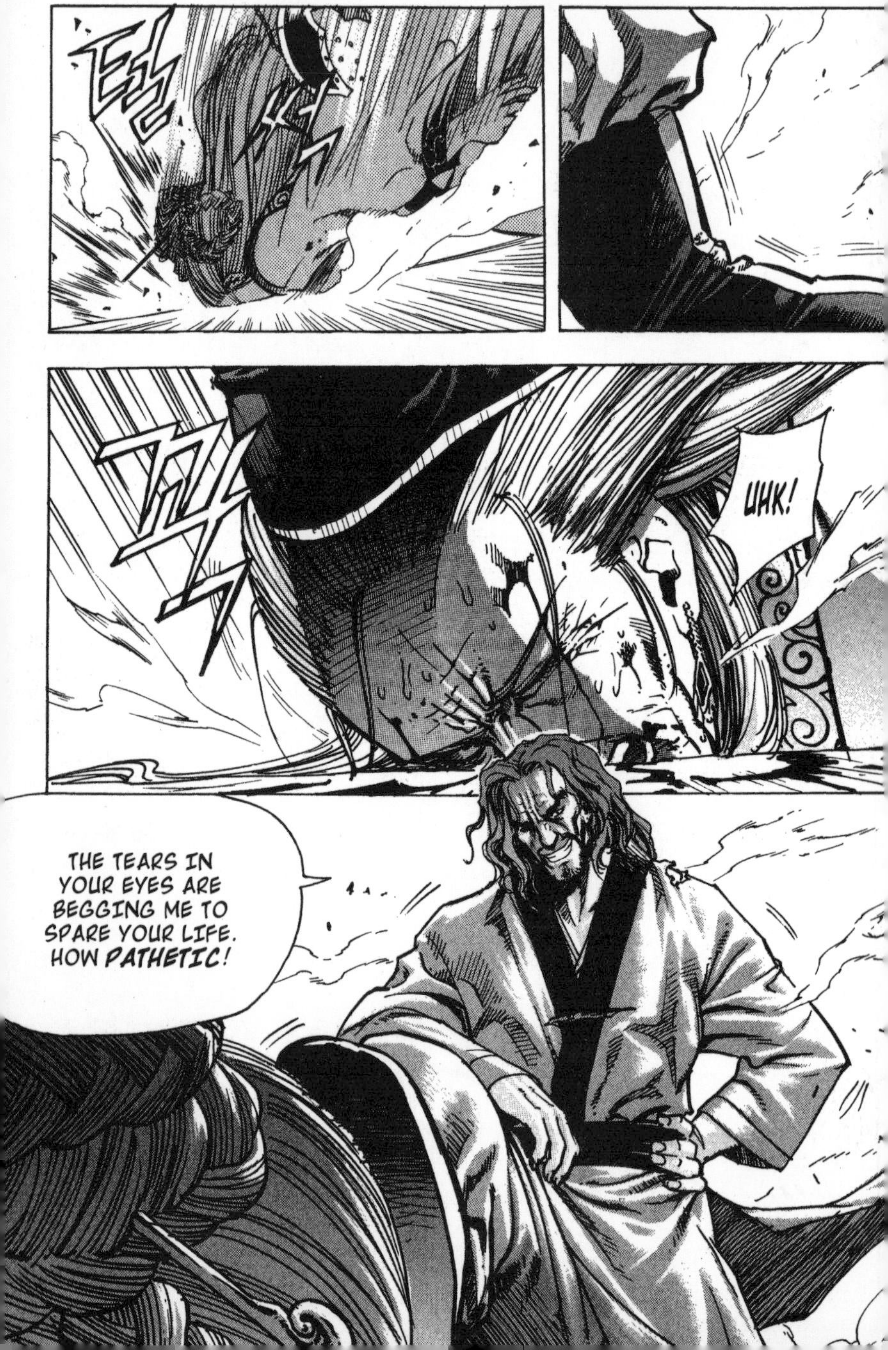
UHK!
THE TEARS IN YOUR EYES ARE BEGGING ME TO SPARE YOUR LIFE. HOW PATHETIC!

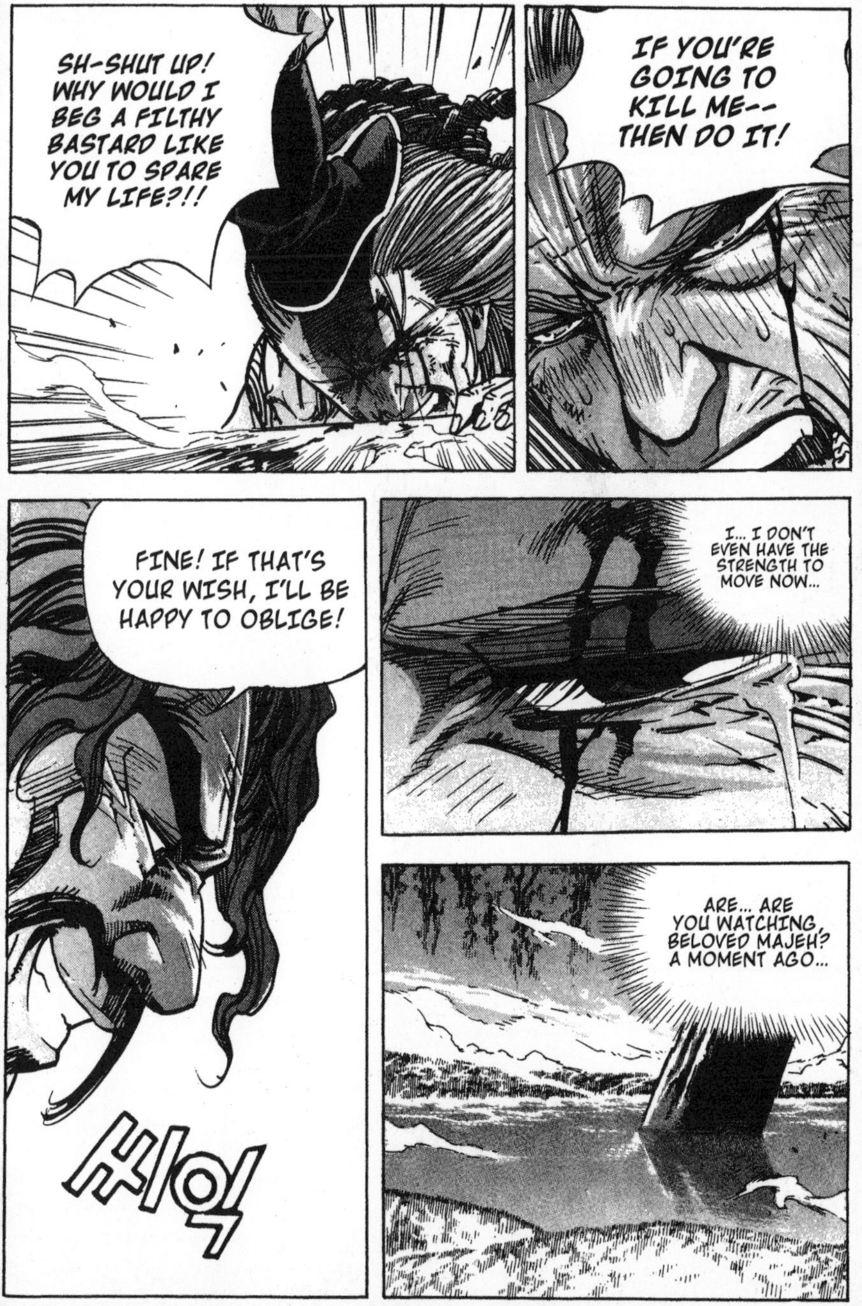
SH-SHUT UP! WHY WOULD I BEG A FILTHY BASTARD LIKE YOU TO SPARE MY LIFE?!!
IF YOU'RE GOING TO KILL ME-- THEN DO IT!
FINE! IF THAT'S YOUR WISH, I'LL BE HAPPY TO OBLIGE!
I... I DON'T EVEN HAVE THE STRENGTH TO MOVE NOW...
ARE... ARE YOU WATCHING, BELOVED MAJEH? A MOMENT AGO...

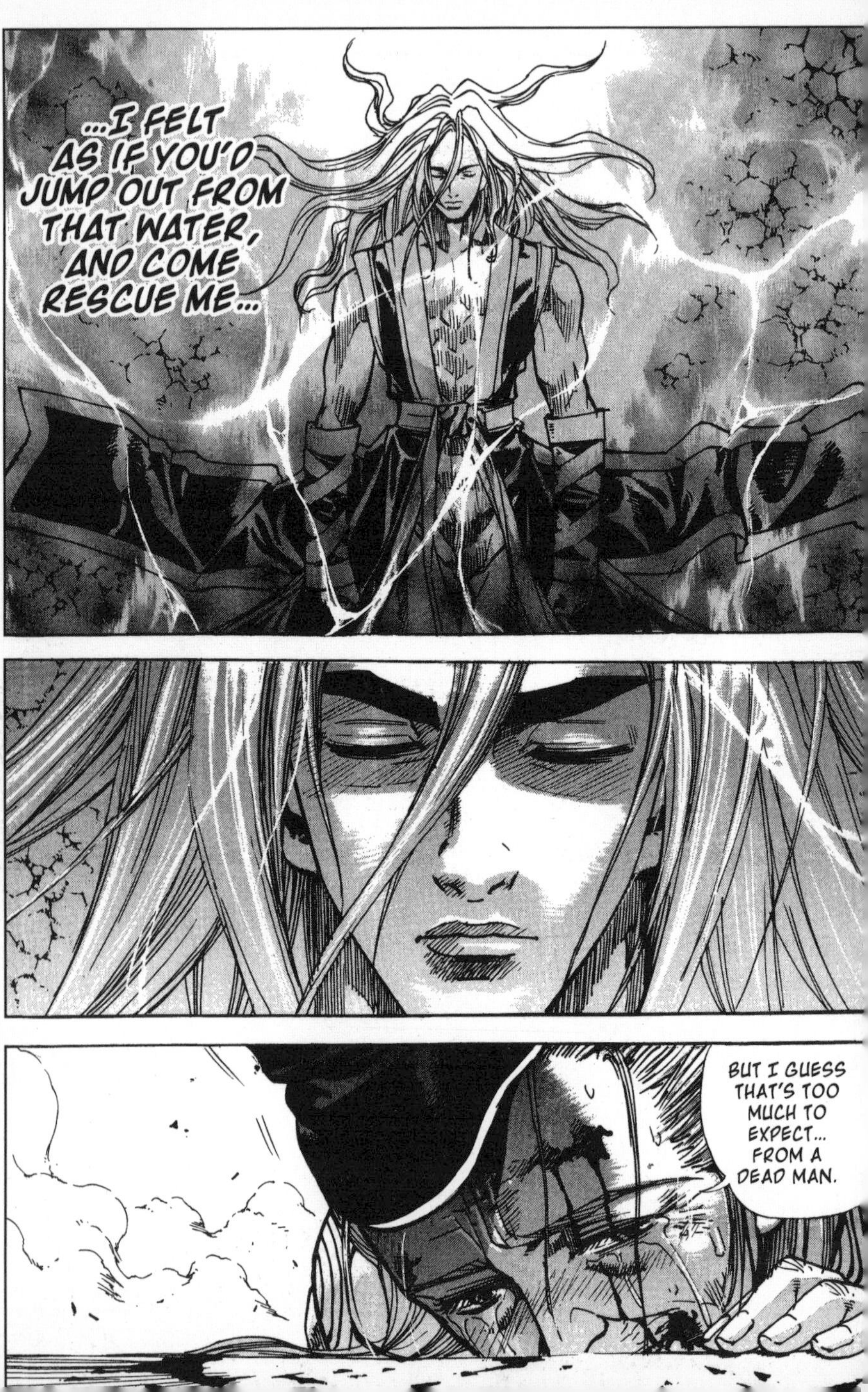
...I FELT AS IF YOU'D JUMP OUT FROM THAT WATER, AND COME RESCUE ME...
BUT I GUESS THAT'S TOO MUCH TO EXPECT... FROM A DEAD MAN.

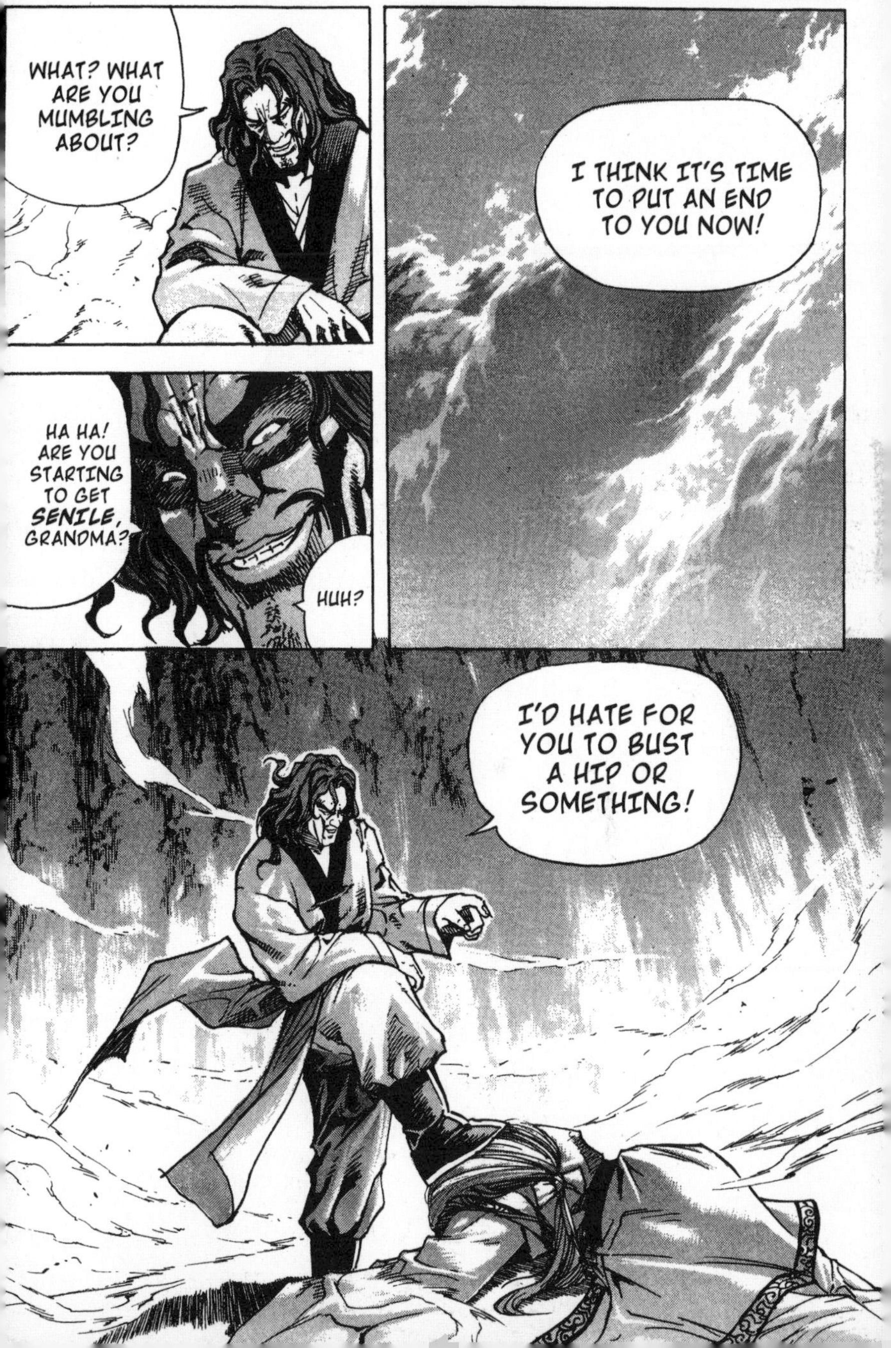
WHAT? WHAT ARE YOU MUMBLING ABOUT?
I THINK IT'S TIME TO PUT AN END TO YOU NOW!
HA HA! ARE YOU STARTING TO GET SENILE, GRANDMA?
HUH?
I'D HATE FOR YOU TO BUST A HIP OR SOMETHING!

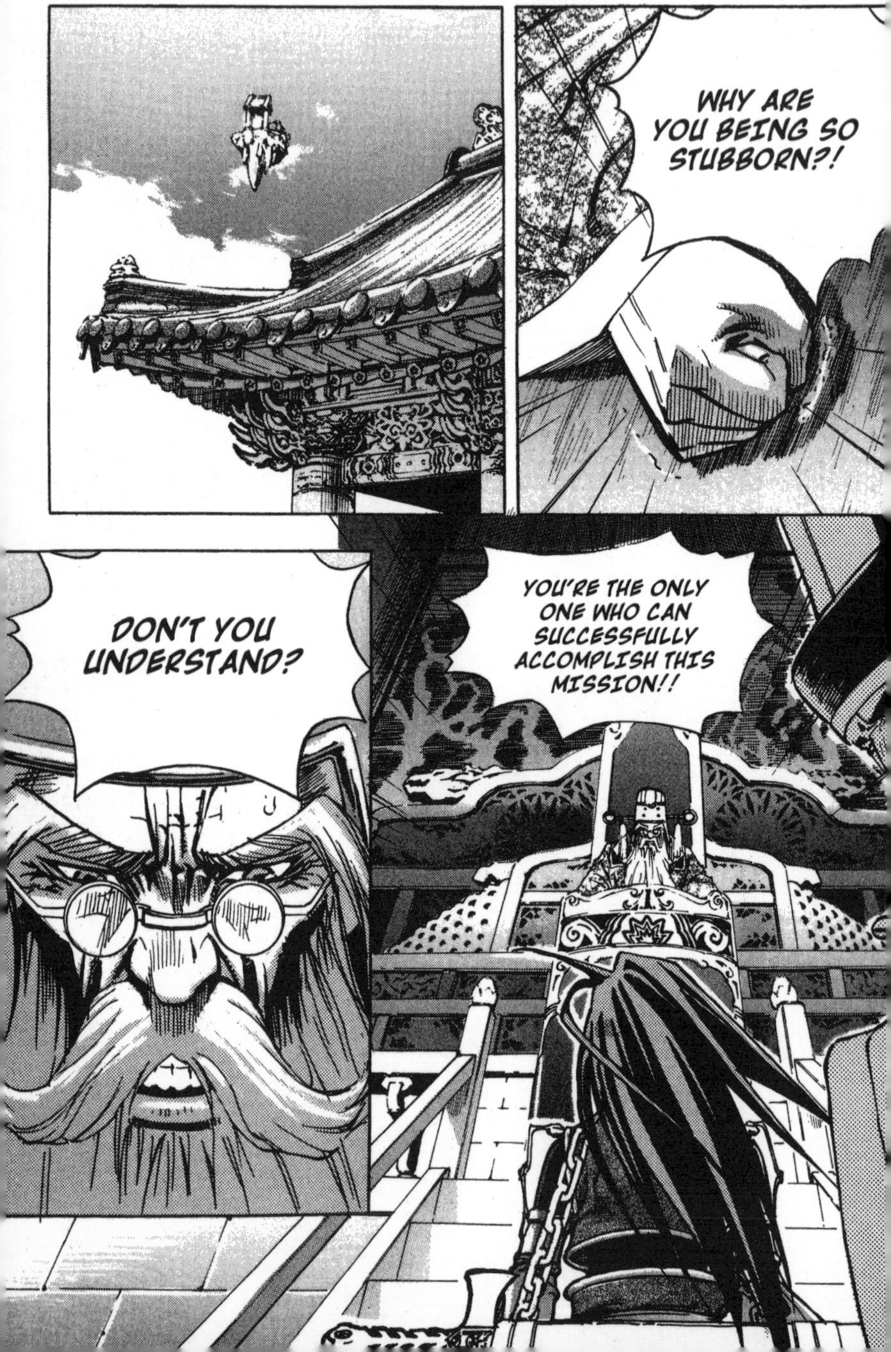
WHY ARE YOU BEING SO STUBBORN?!
DON'T YOU UNDERSTAND?
YOU'RE THE ONLY ONE WHO CAN SUCCESSFULLY ACCOMPLISH THIS MISSION!!

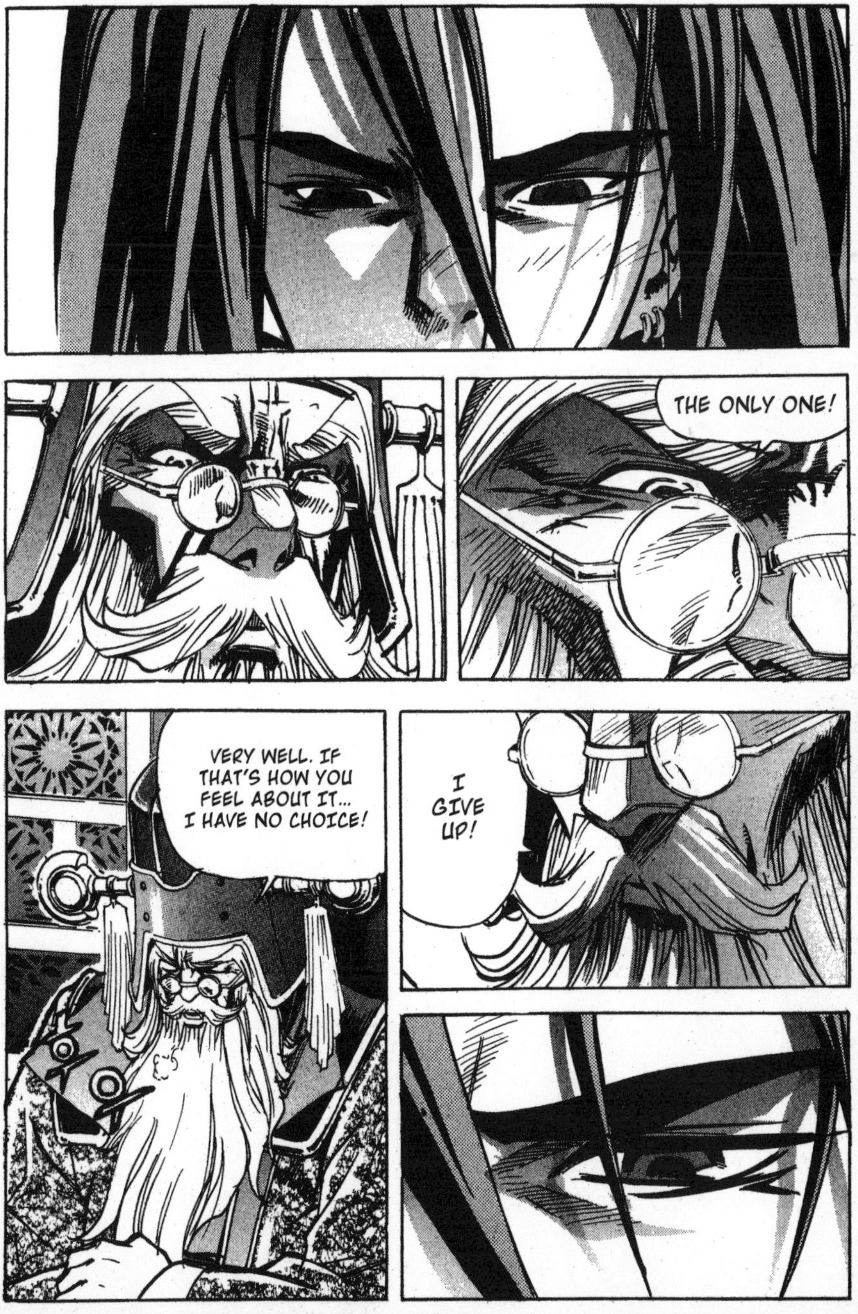
THE ONLY ONE!
VERY WELL. IF THAT'S HOW YOU FEEL ABOUT IT... I HAVE NO CHOICE!
I GIVE UP!

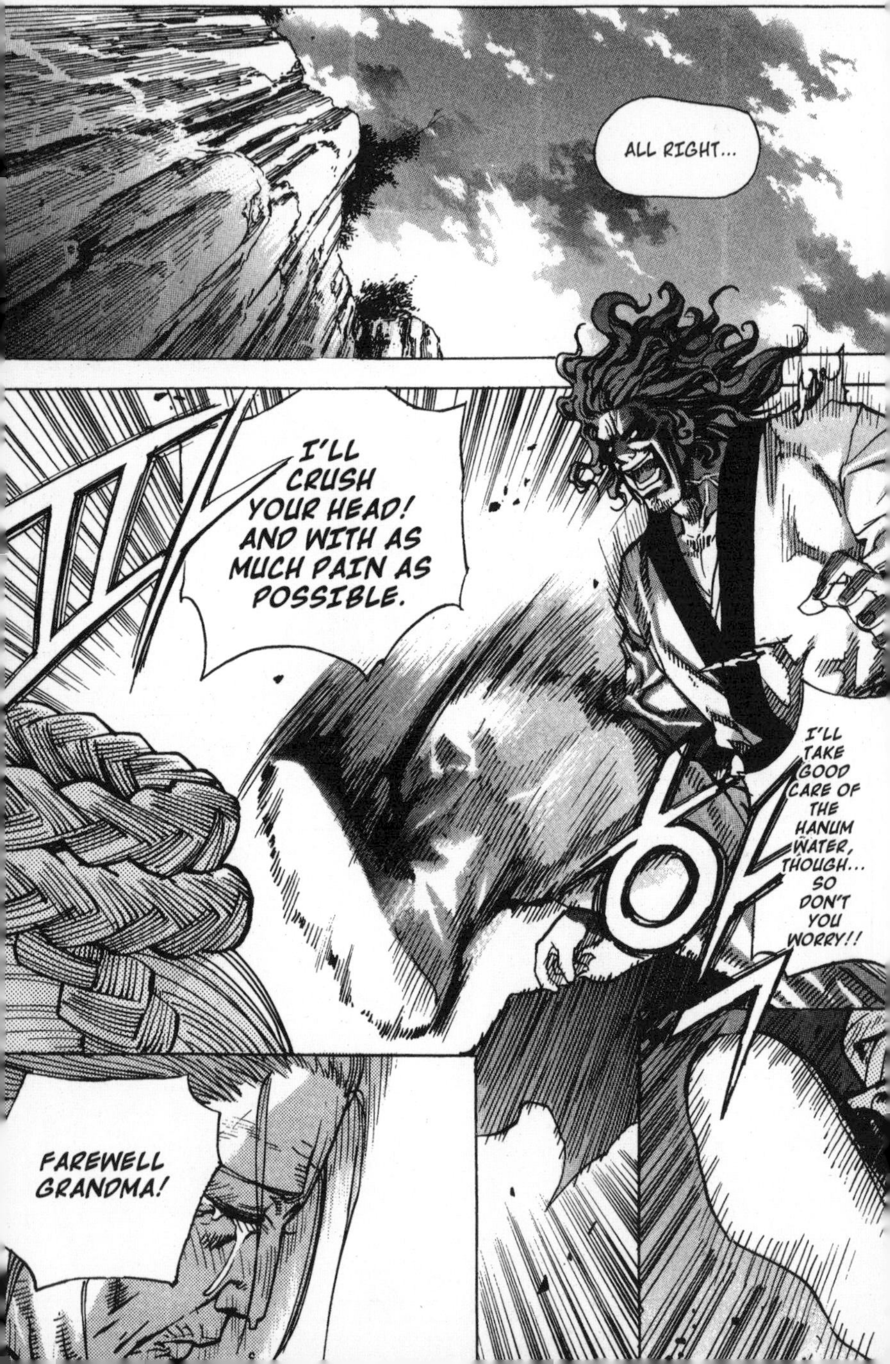
ALL RIGHT...
I'LL CRUSH YOUR HEAD! AND WITH AS MUCH PAIN AS POSSIBLE.
I'LL TAKE GOOD CARE OF THE HANUM WATER, THOUGH... SO DON'T YOU WORRY!!
FAREWELL GRANDMA!

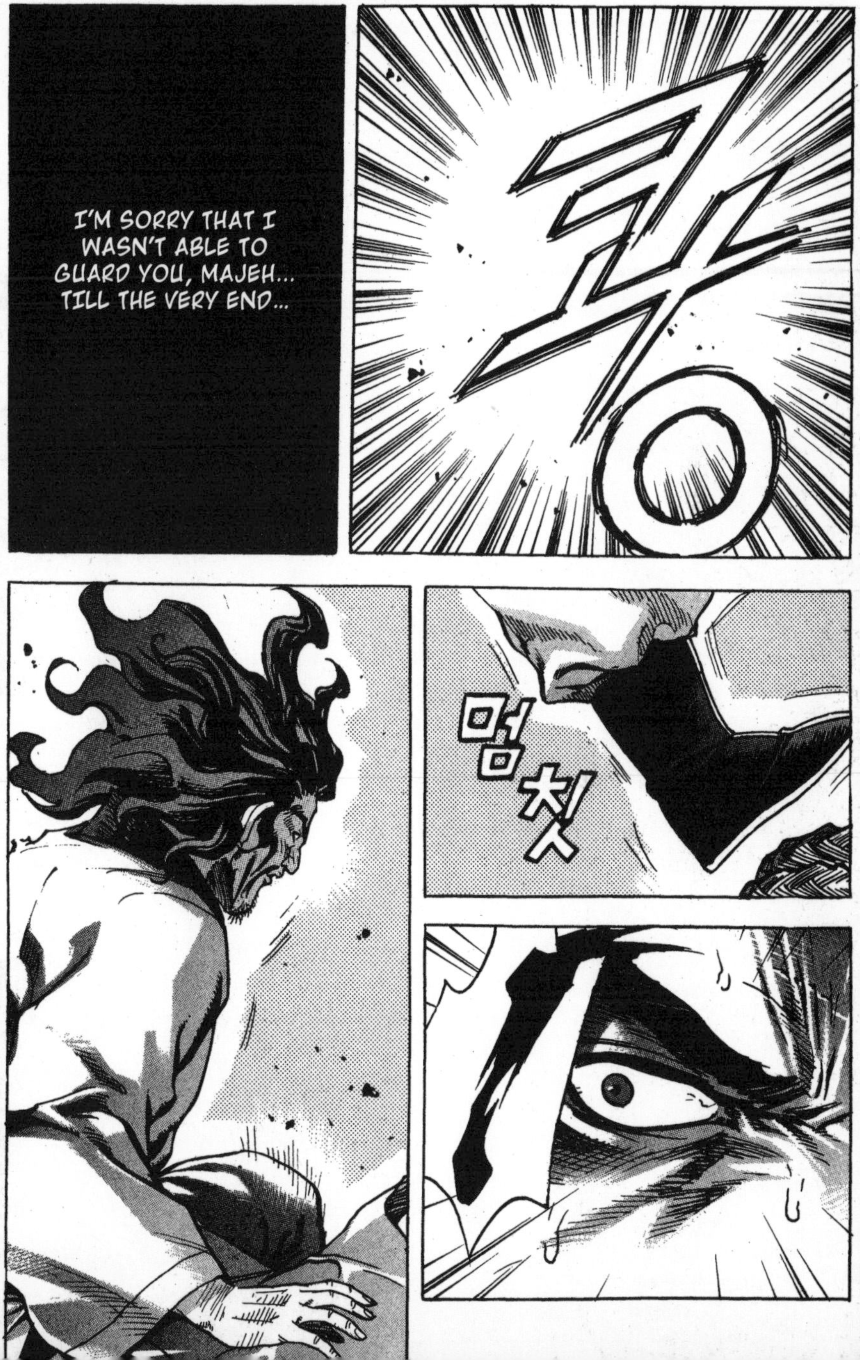
I'M SORRY THAT I WASN'T ABLE TO GUARD YOU, MAJEH... TILL THE VERY END...
멈칫

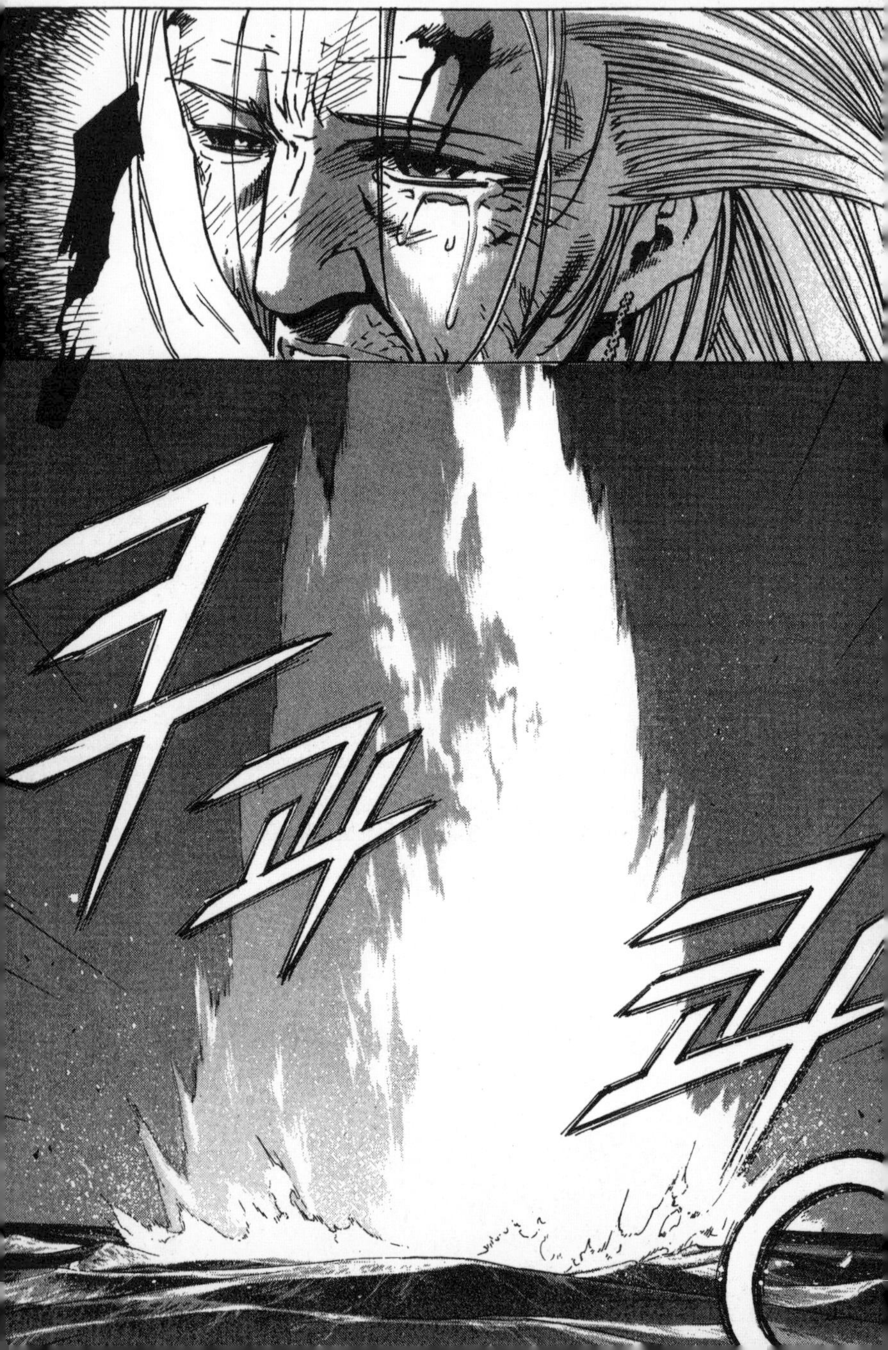

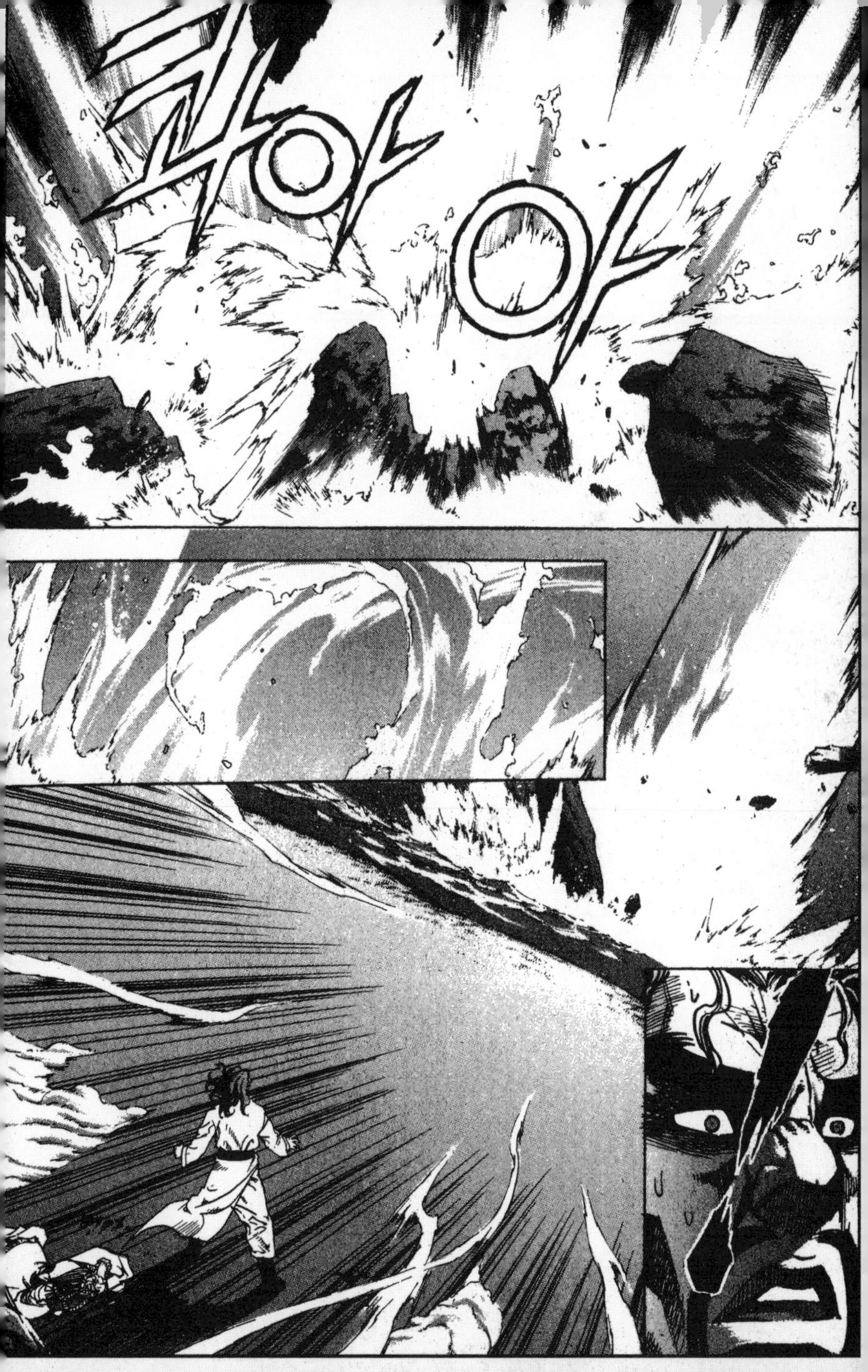

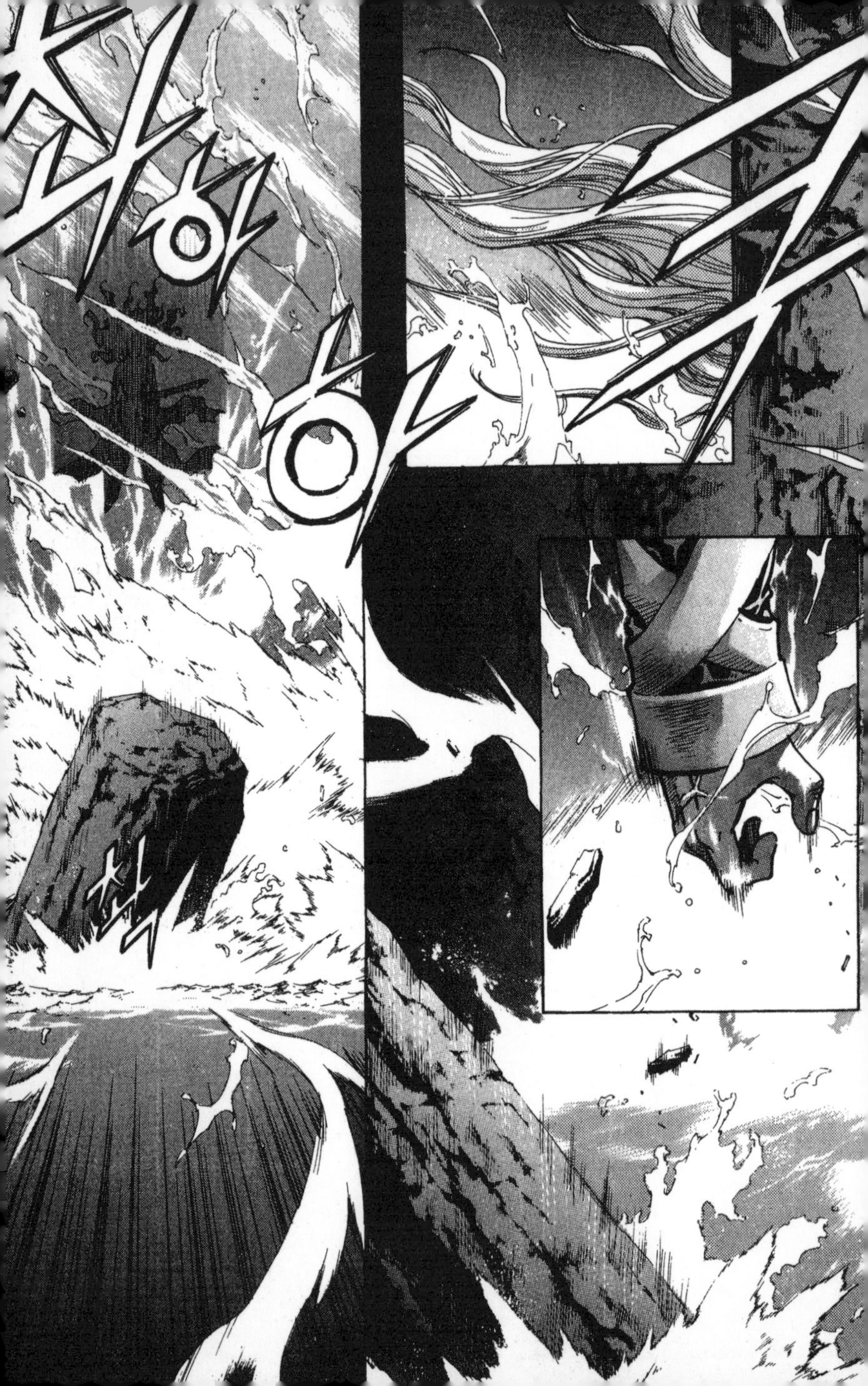
쏴아아

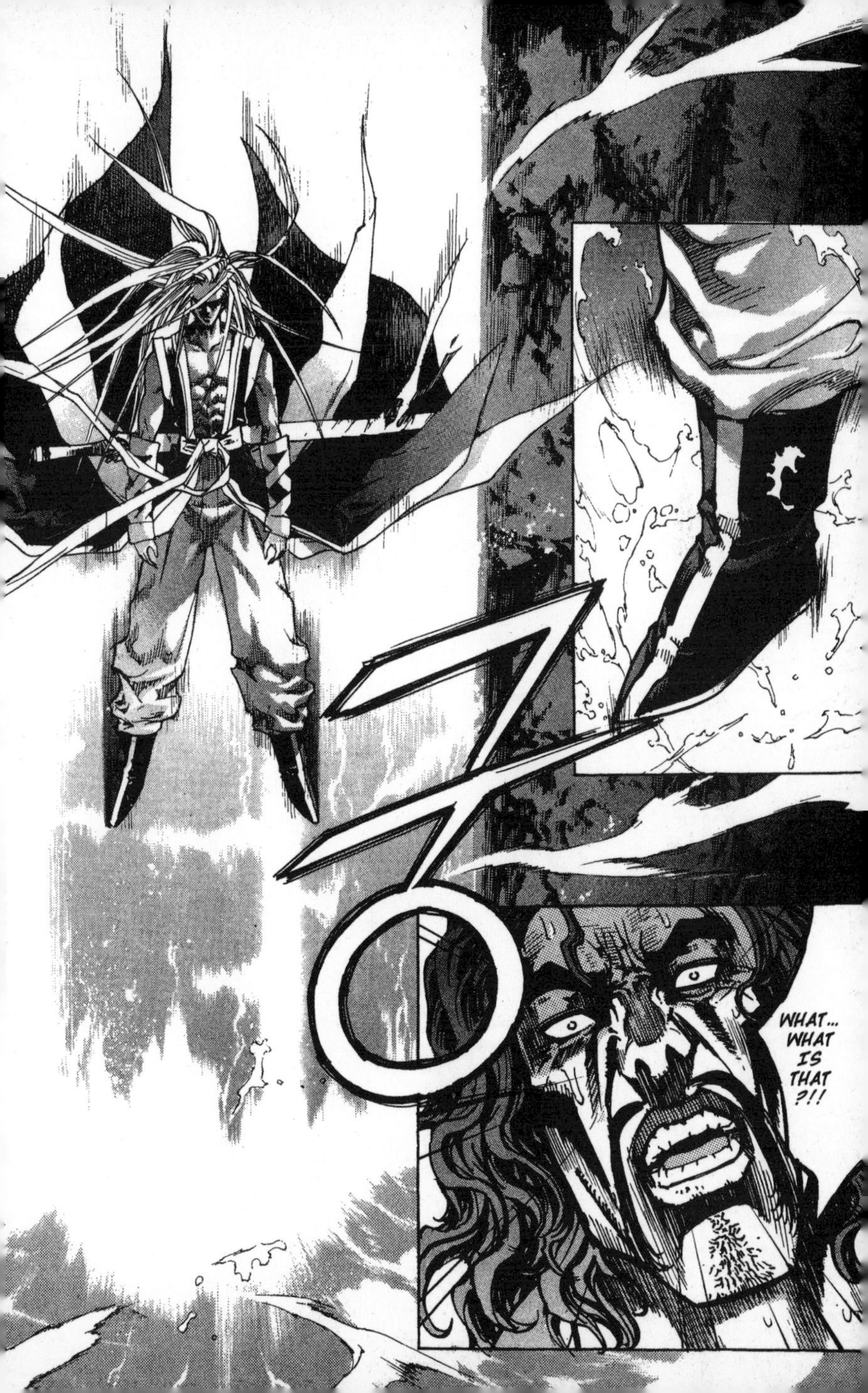
WHAT... WHAT IS THAT ?!!

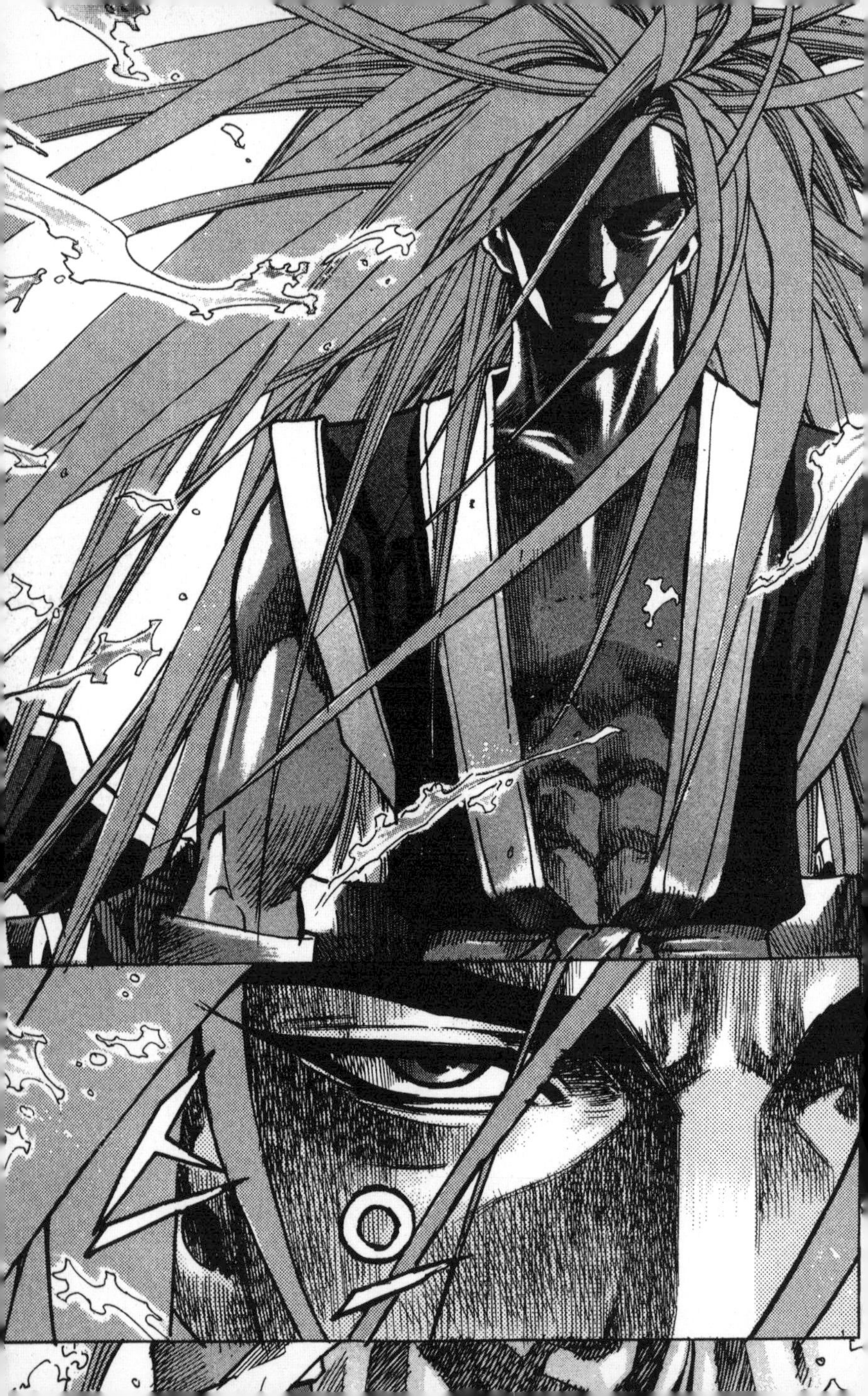

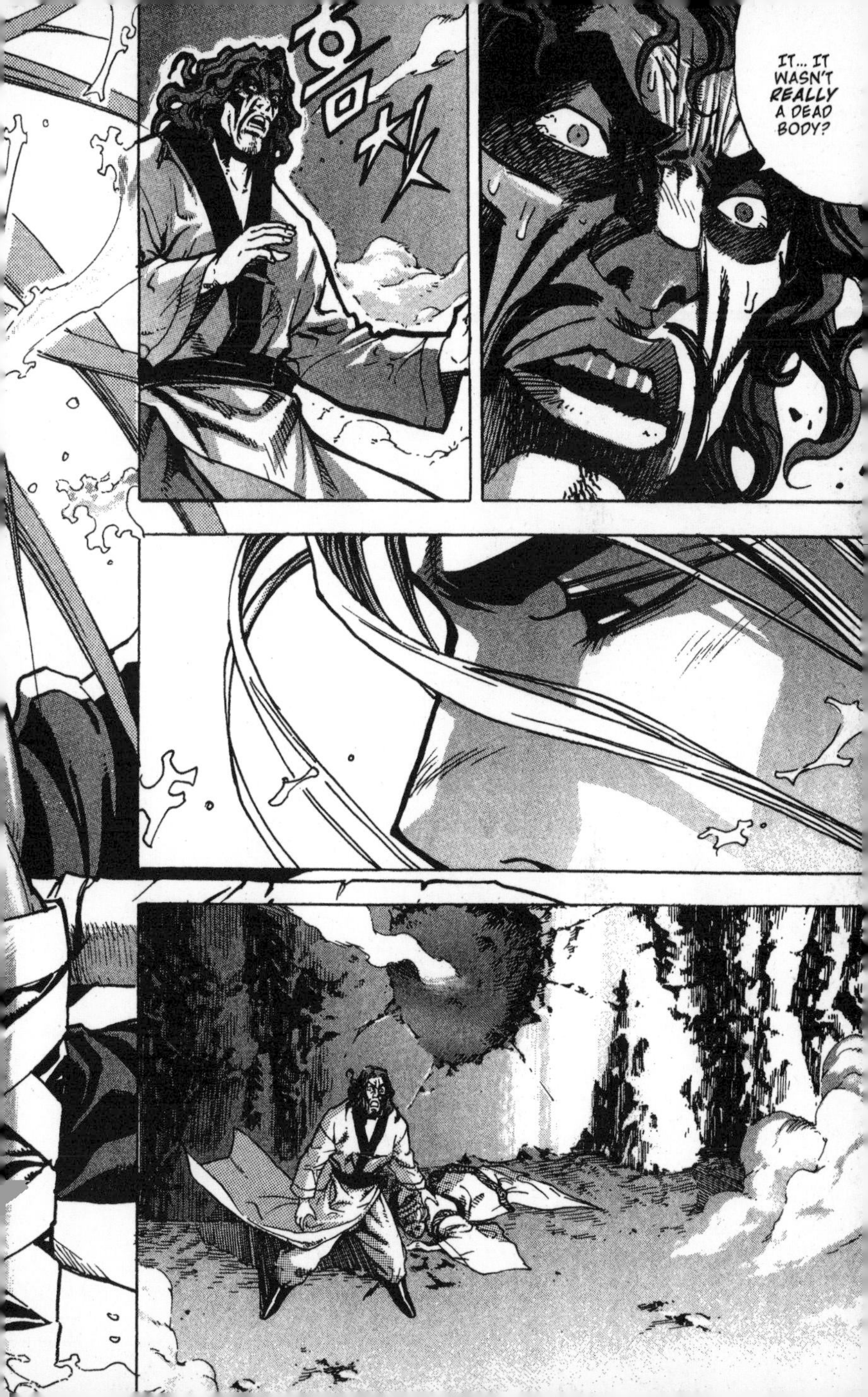
IT... IT WASN'T *REALLY* A DEAD BODY?

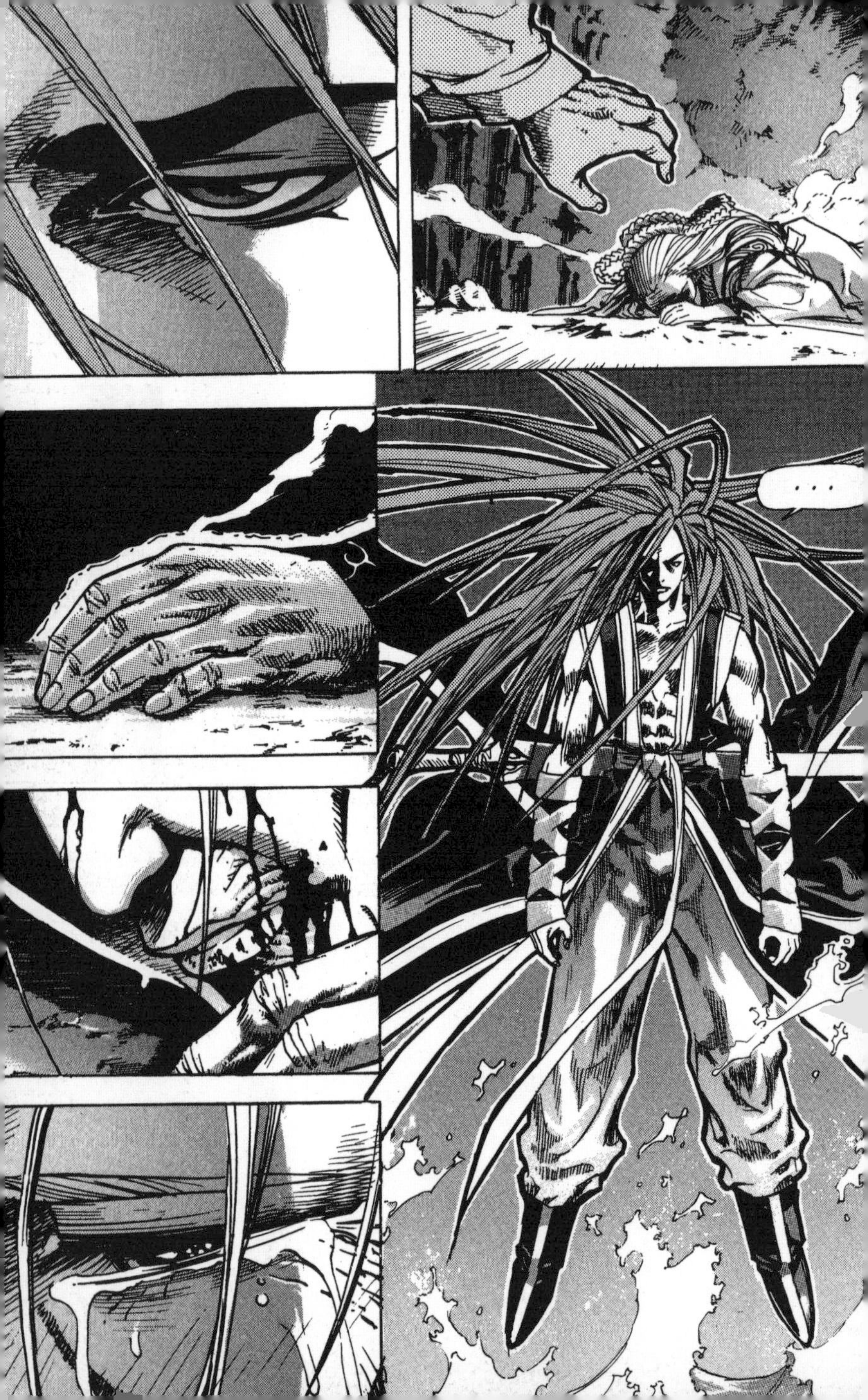
...

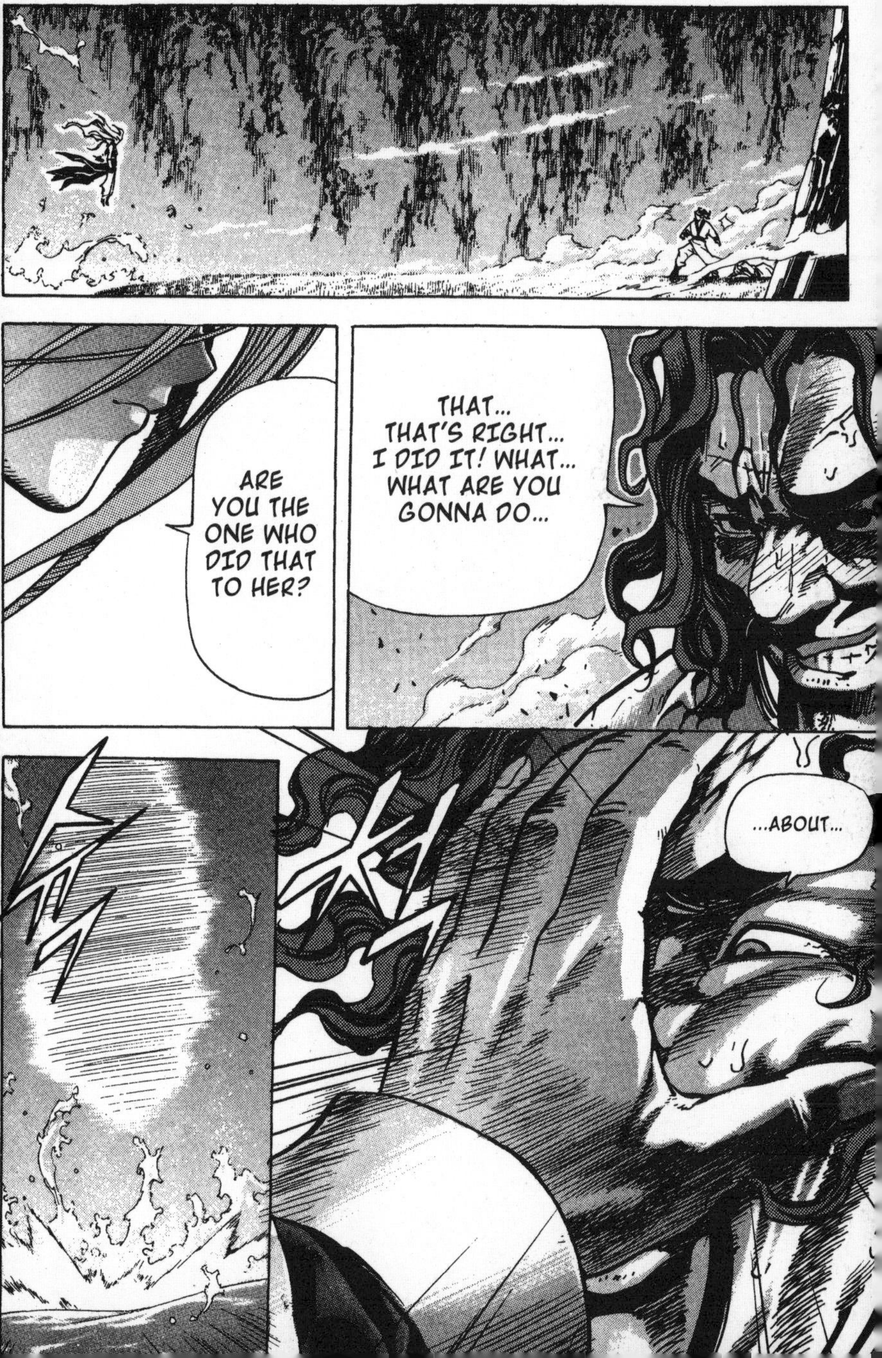
ARE YOU THE ONE WHO DID THAT TO HER?
THAT... THAT'S RIGHT... I DID IT! WHAT... WHAT ARE YOU GONNA DO...
...ABOUT...

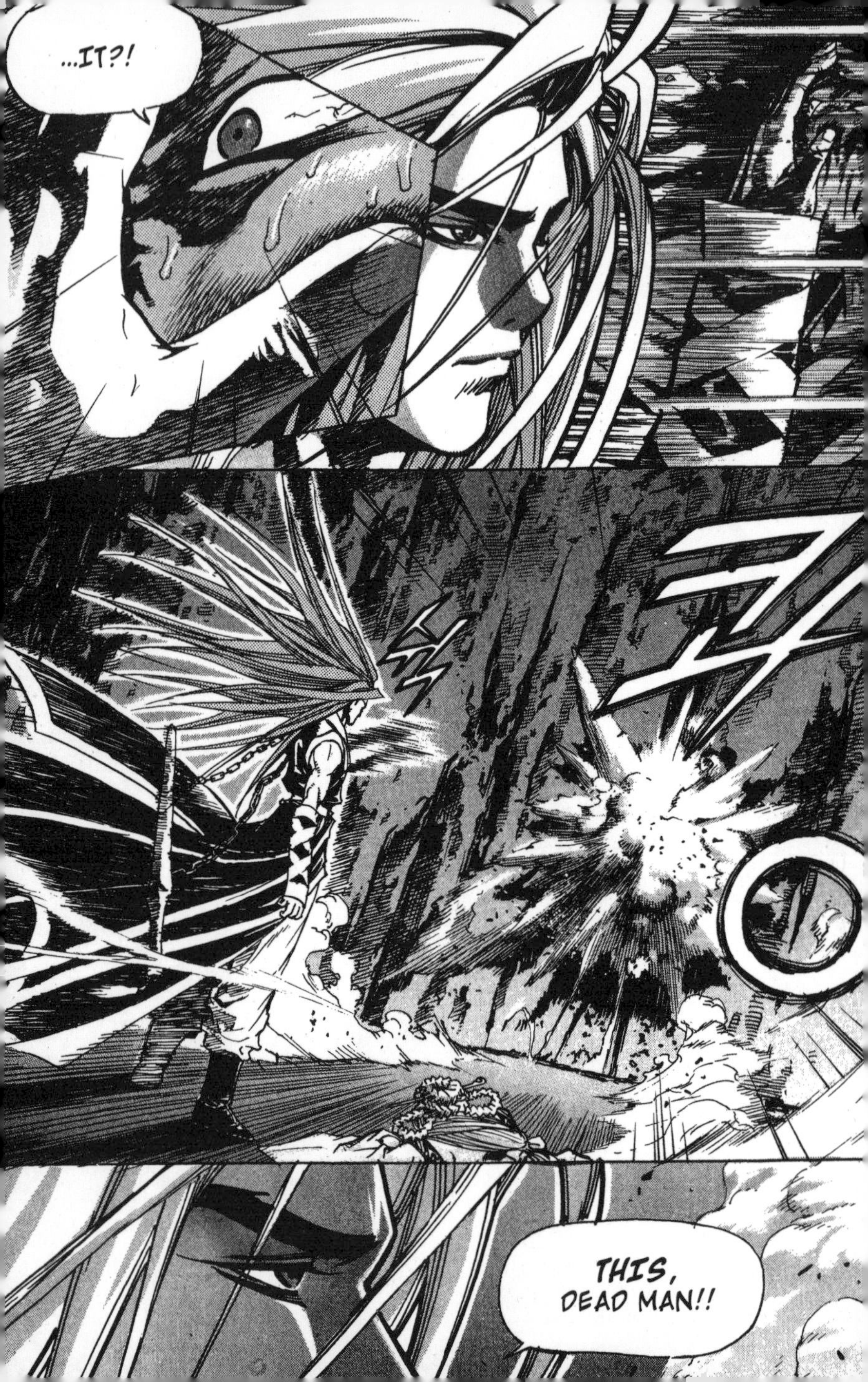
...IT?!
THIS, DEAD MAN!!

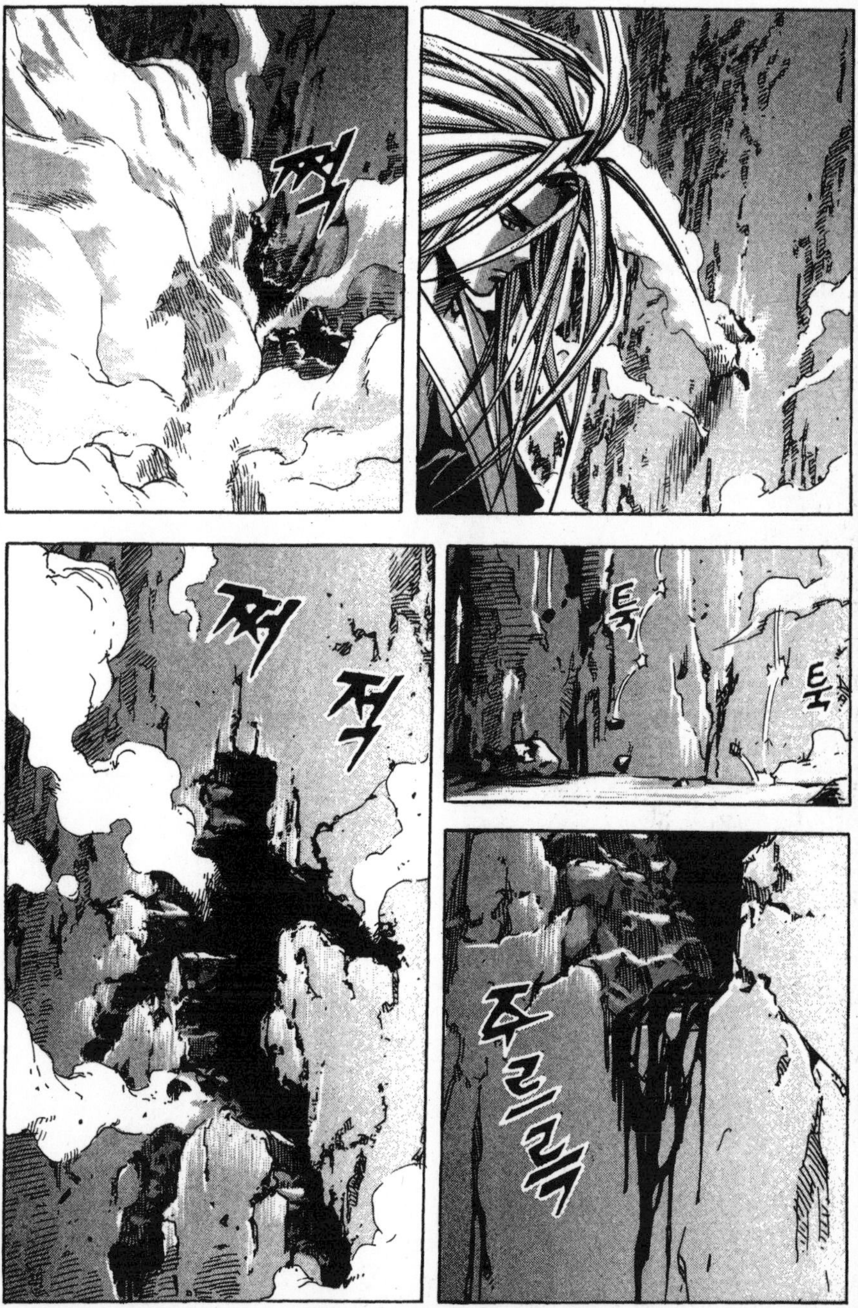
쩍
쩌적
툭
툭
주르륵

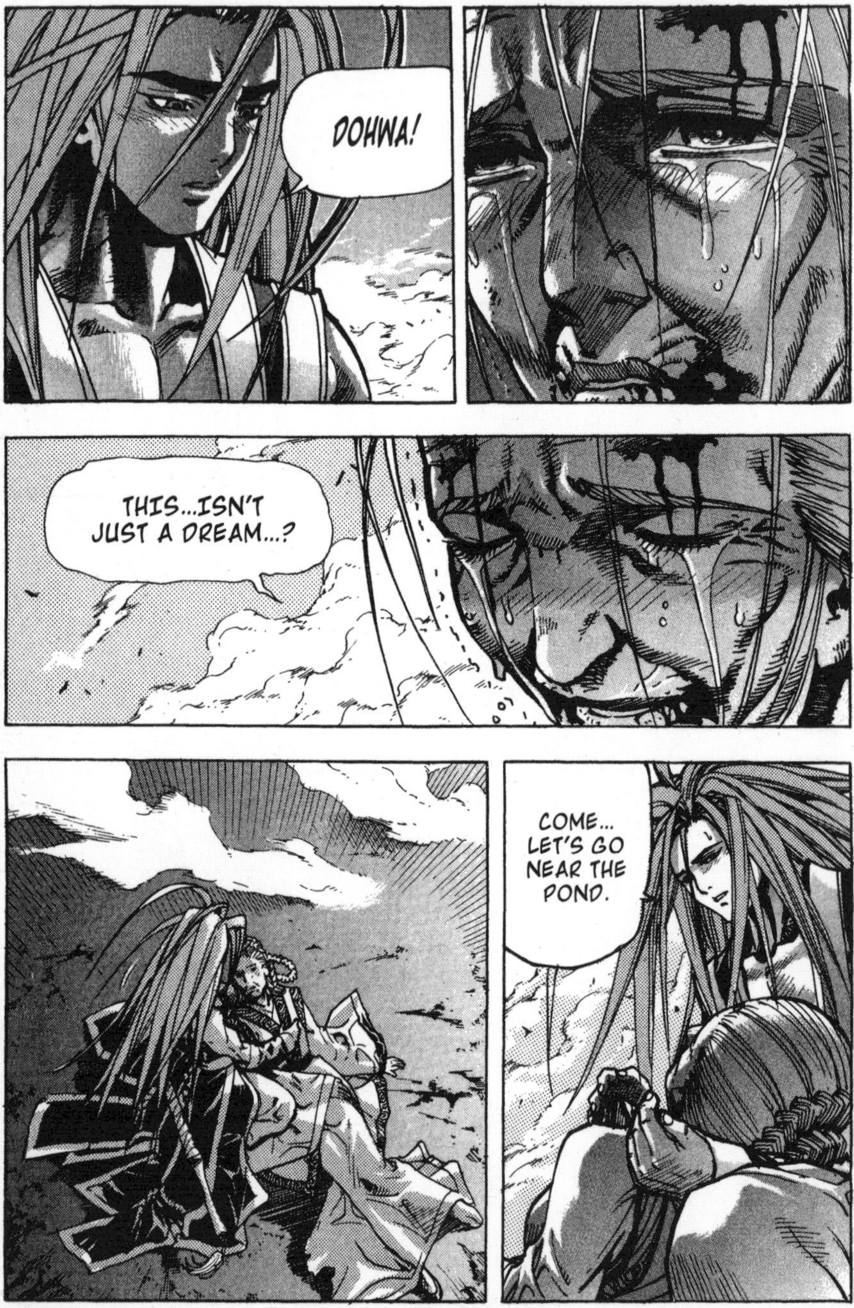
DOHWA!
THIS...ISN'T JUST A DREAM...?
COME... LET'S GO NEAR THE POND.

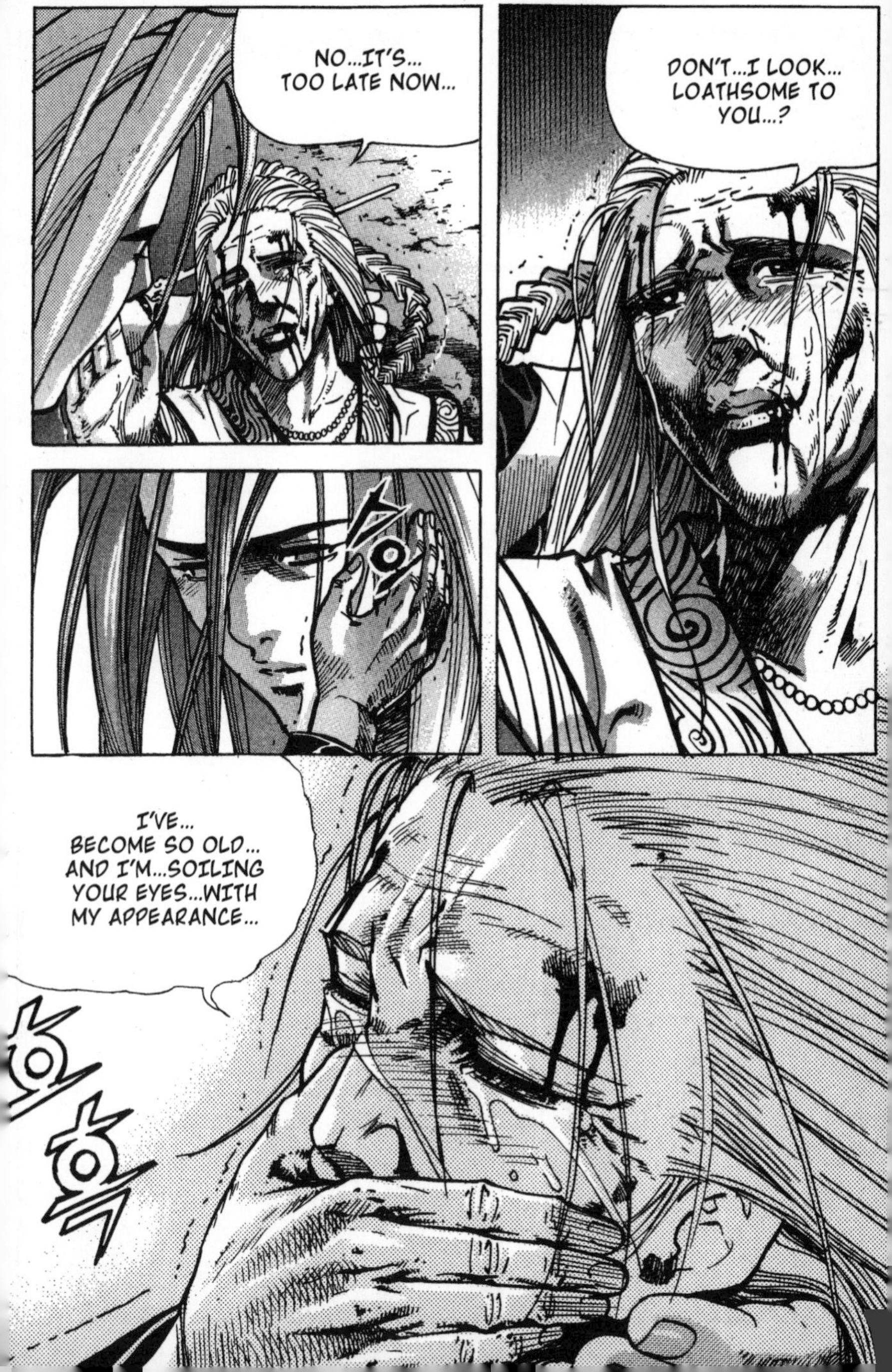
NO...IT'S... TOO LATE NOW...
DON'T...I LOOK... LOATHSOME TO YOU...?
I'VE... BECOME SO OLD... AND I'M...SOILING YOUR EYES...WITH MY APPEARANCE...

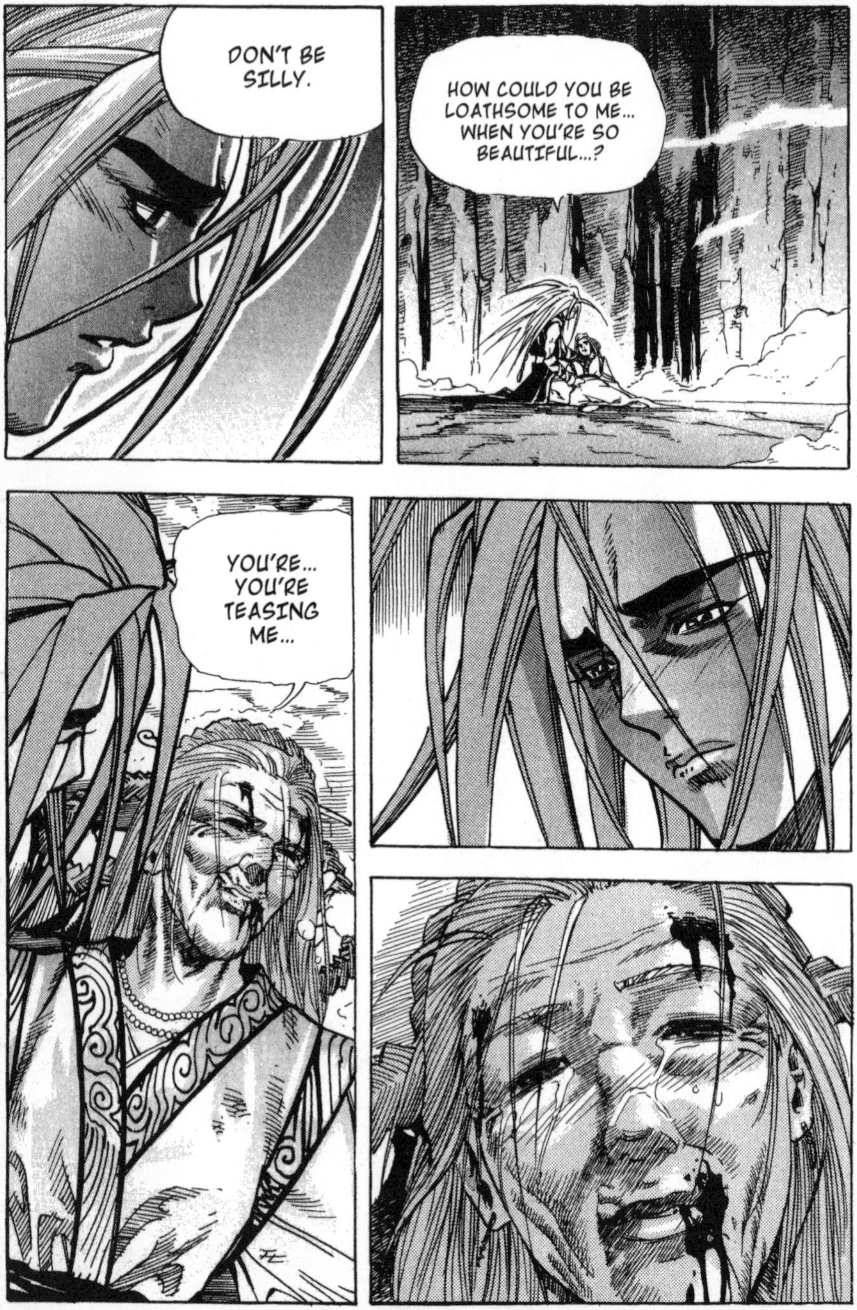
DON'T BE SILLY.
HOW COULD YOU BE LOATHSOME TO ME... WHEN YOU'RE SO BEAUTIFUL...?
YOU'RE... YOU'RE TEASING ME...

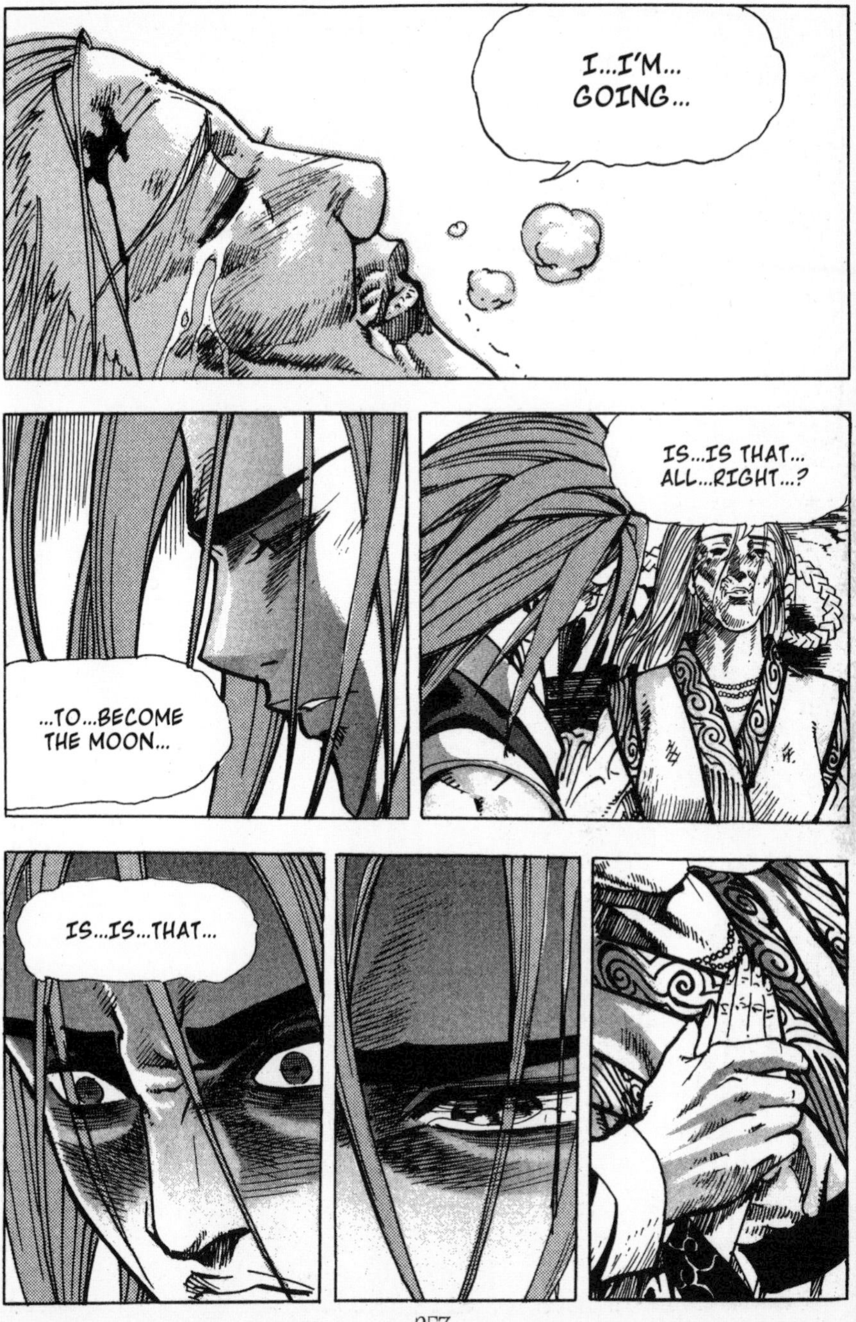
I...I'M... GOING...
...TO...BECOME THE MOON...
IS...IS THAT... ALL...RIGHT...?
IS...IS...THAT...

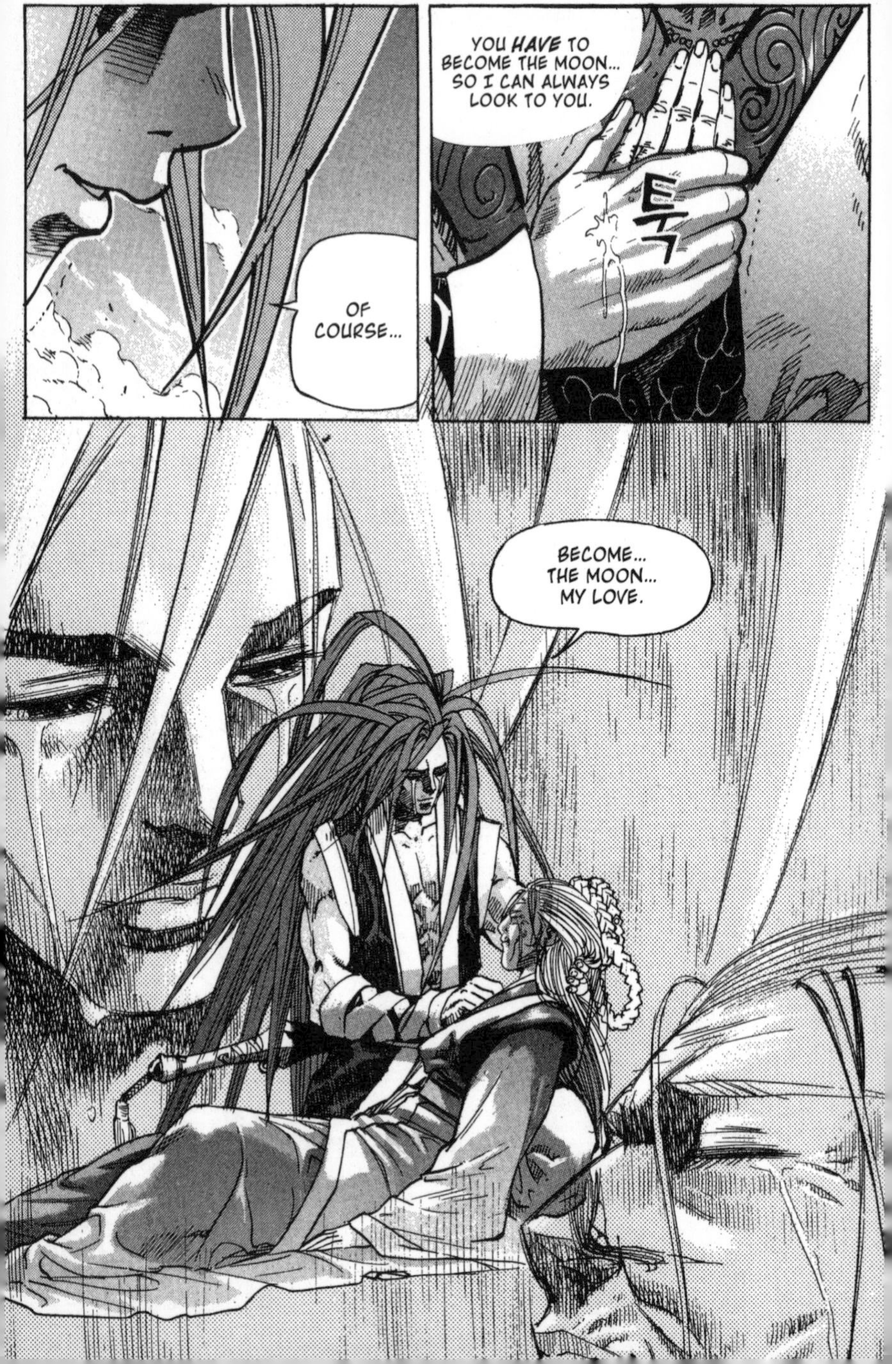
OF COURSE...
YOU *HAVE* TO BECOME THE MOON... SO I CAN ALWAYS LOOK TO YOU.
BECOME... THE MOON... MY LOVE.

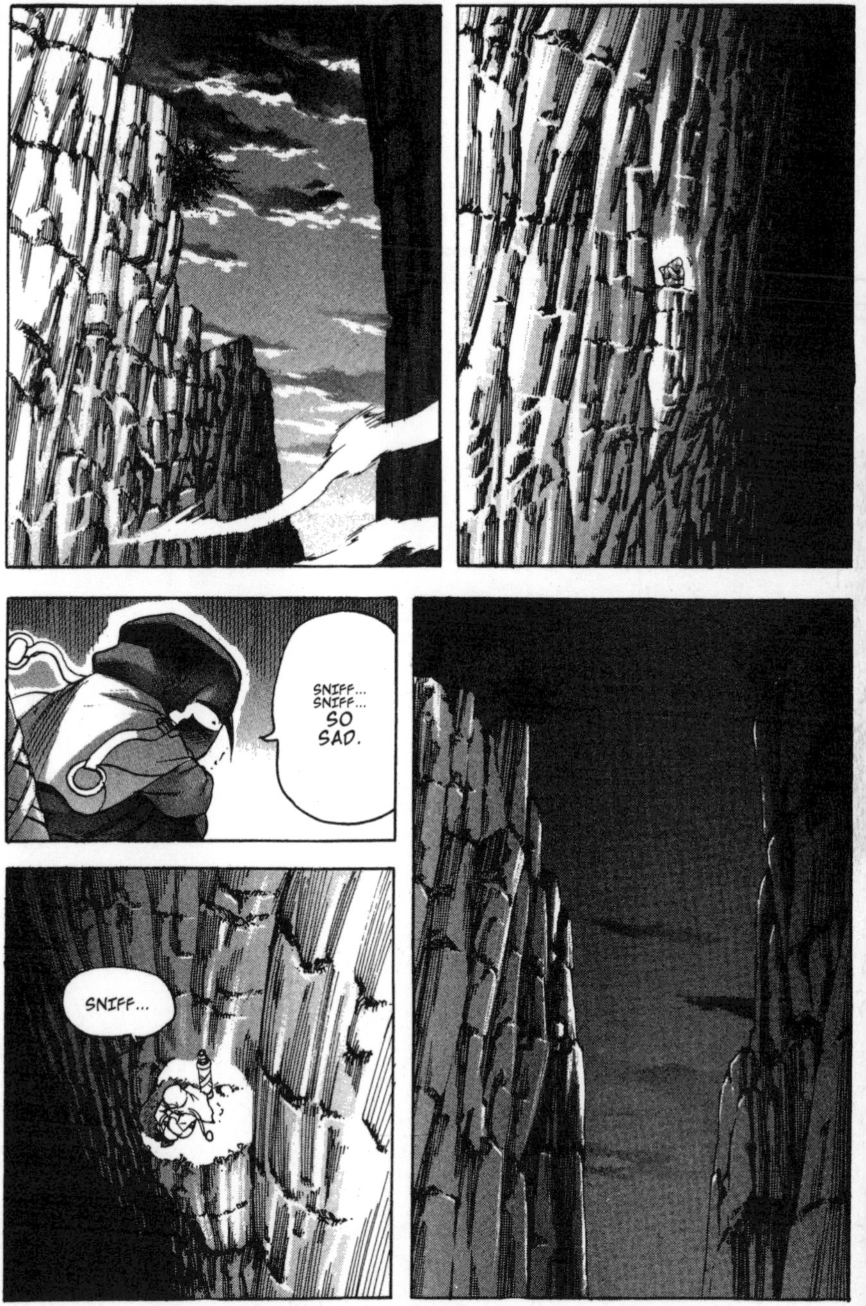
SNIFF... SNIFF... SO SAD.
SNIFF...

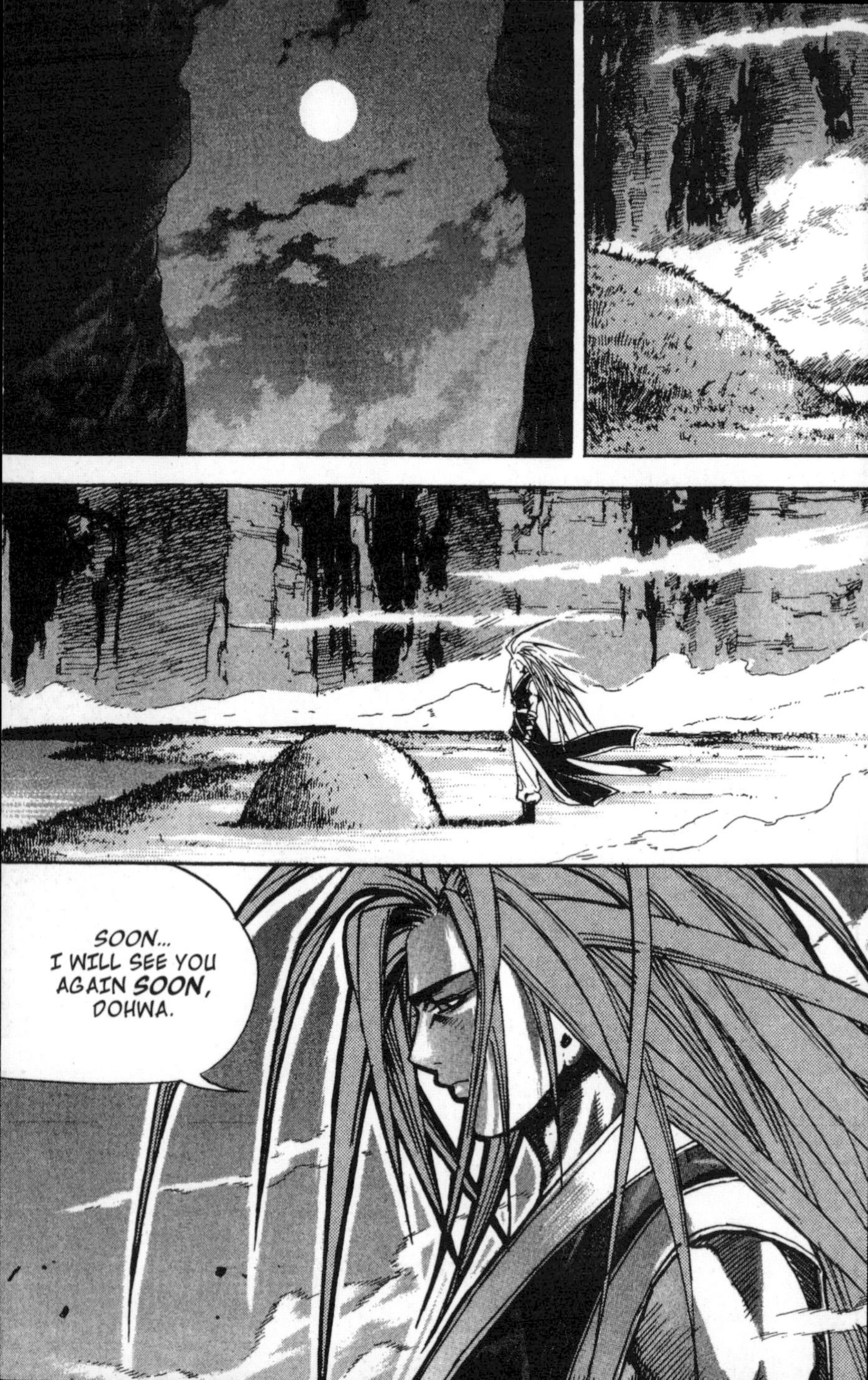
SOON... I WILL SEE YOU AGAIN SOON, DOHWA.

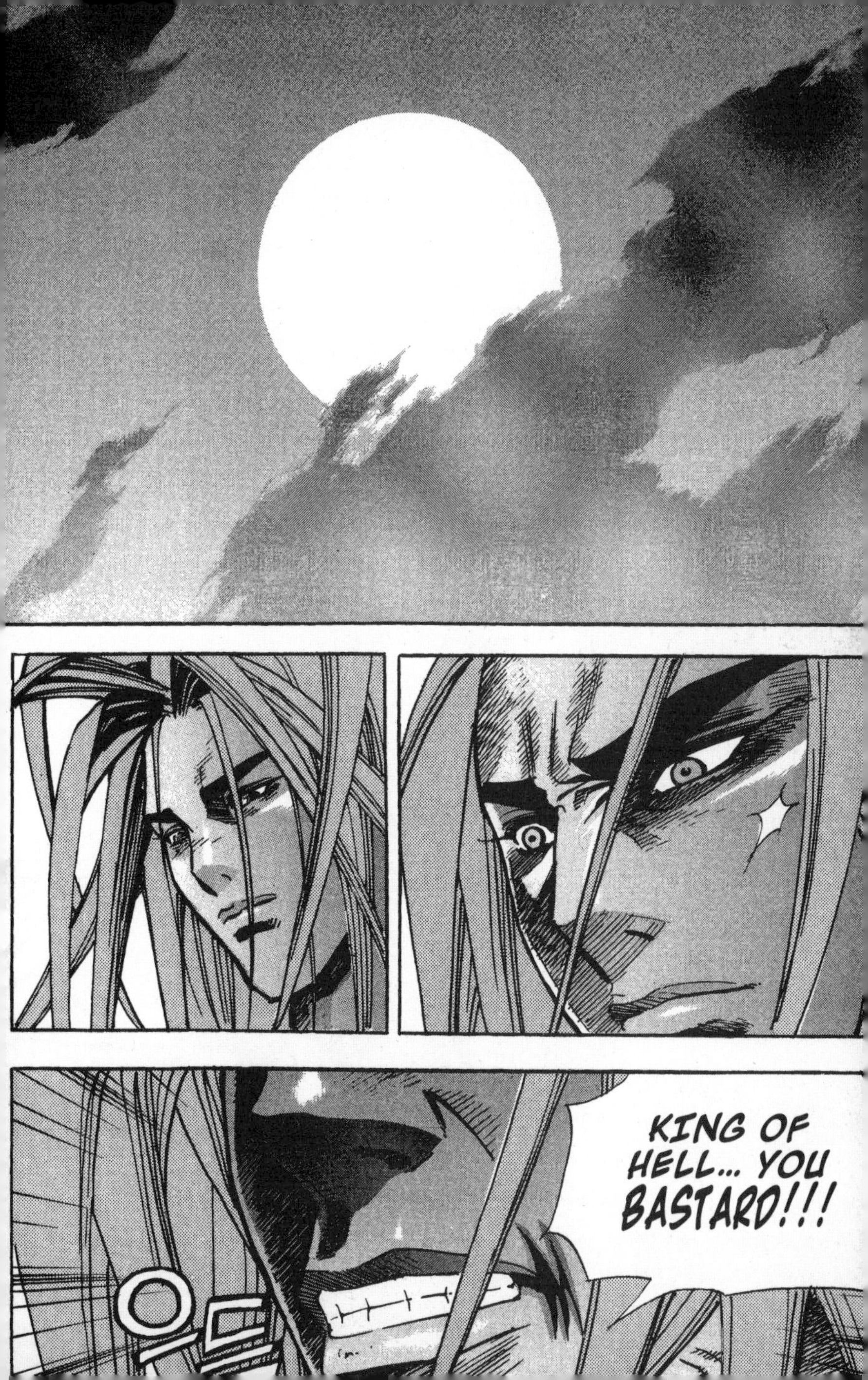
KING OF HELL... YOU BASTARD!!!

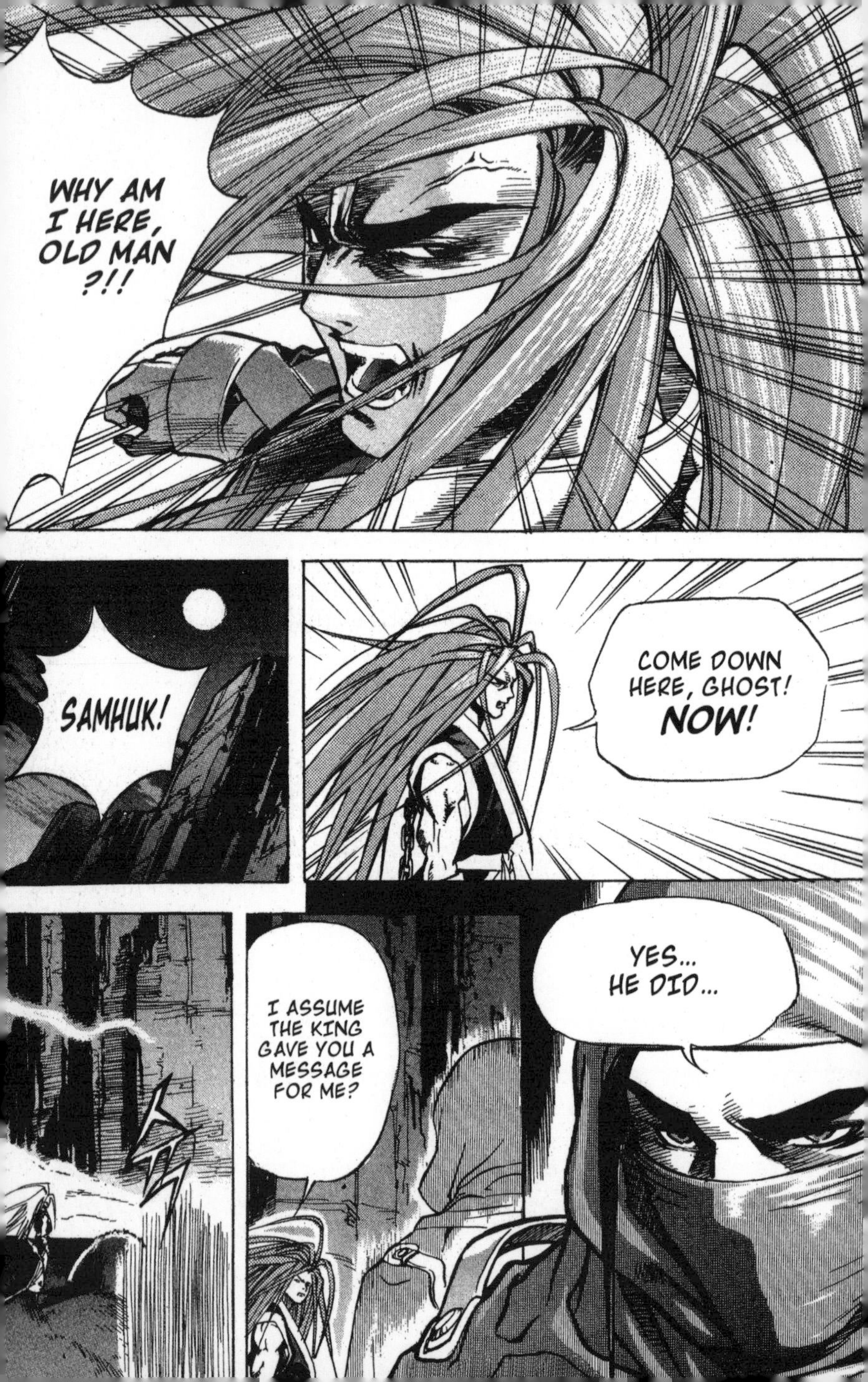
WHY AM I HERE, OLD MAN ?!!
SAMHUK!
COME DOWN HERE, GHOST! NOW!
I ASSUME THE KING GAVE YOU A MESSAGE FOR ME?
YES... HE DID...

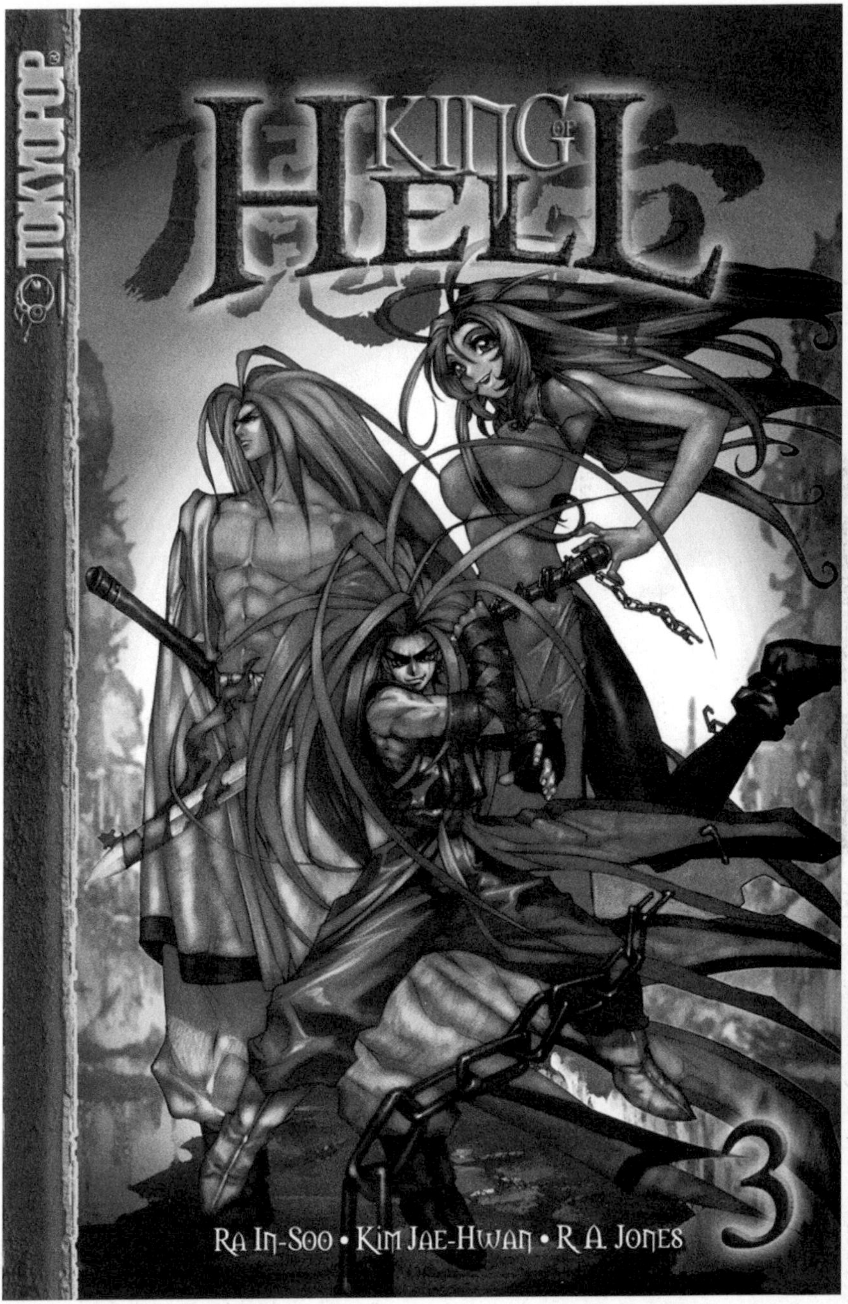
TOKYOPOP
KING OF HELL
3
RA IN-SOO • KIM JAE-HWAN • R.A. JONES

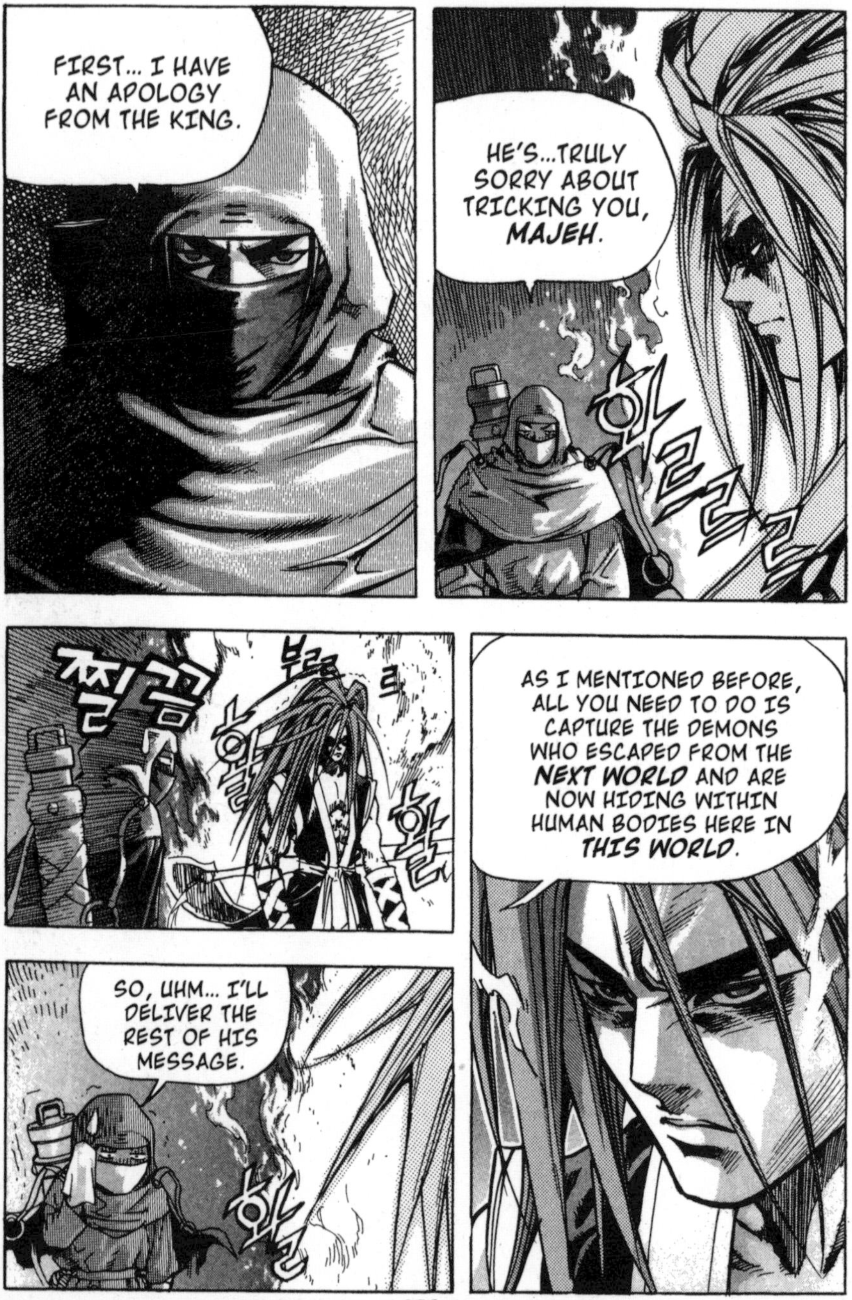
FIRST... I HAVE AN APOLOGY FROM THE KING.
HE'S...TRULY SORRY ABOUT TRICKING YOU, **MAJEH**.
찔끔
SO, UHM... I'LL DELIVER THE REST OF HIS MESSAGE.
AS I MENTIONED BEFORE, ALL YOU NEED TO DO IS CAPTURE THE DEMONS WHO ESCAPED FROM THE **NEXT WORLD** AND ARE NOW HIDING WITHIN HUMAN BODIES HERE IN **THIS WORLD**.

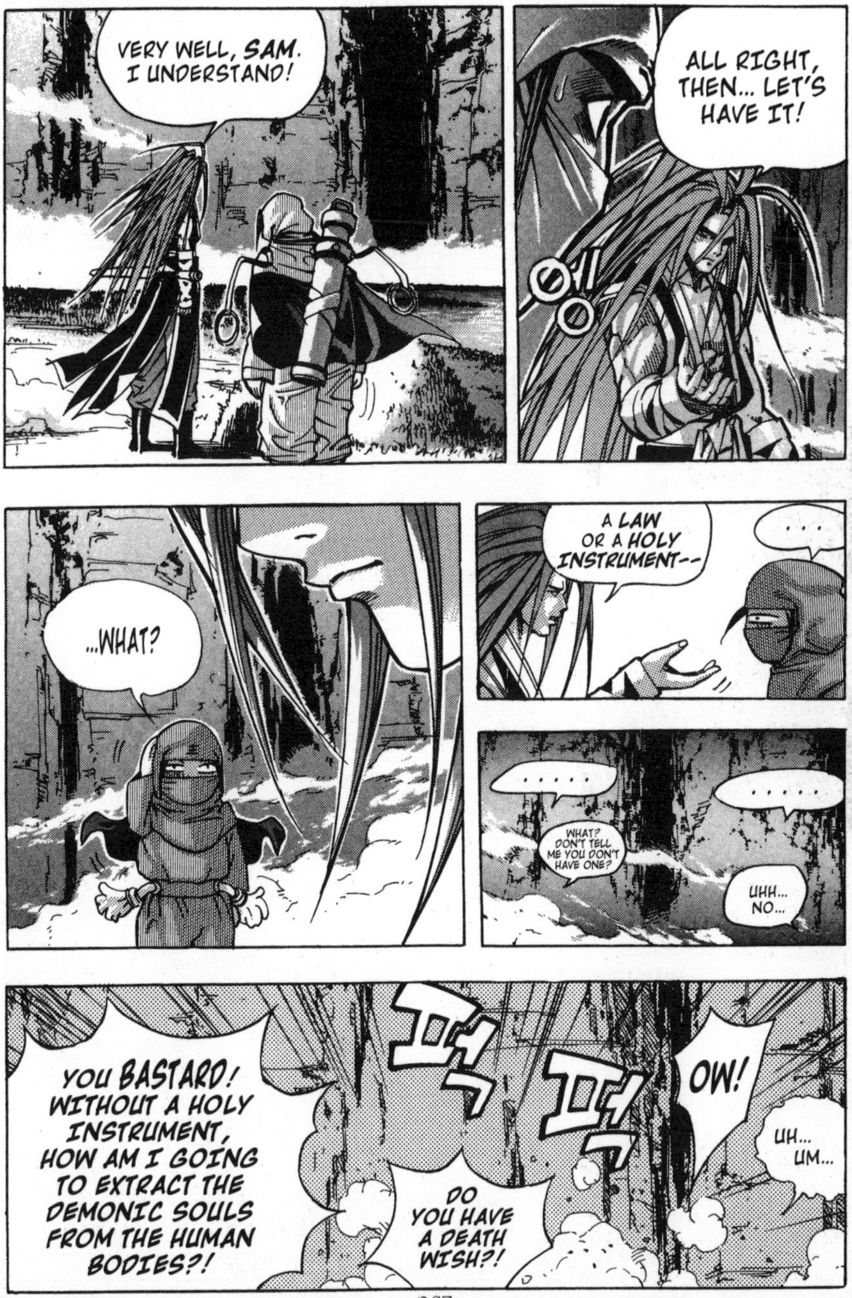
VERY WELL, SAM. I UNDERSTAND!
ALL RIGHT, THEN... LET'S HAVE IT!
...WHAT?
A LAW OR A HOLY INSTRUMENT--
...
.....
.....
WHAT? DON'T TELL ME YOU DON'T HAVE ONE?
UHH... NO...
YOU BASTARD! WITHOUT A HOLY INSTRUMENT, HOW AM I GOING TO EXTRACT THE DEMONIC SOULS FROM THE HUMAN BODIES?!
DO YOU HAVE A DEATH WISH?!
OW!
UH... UM...

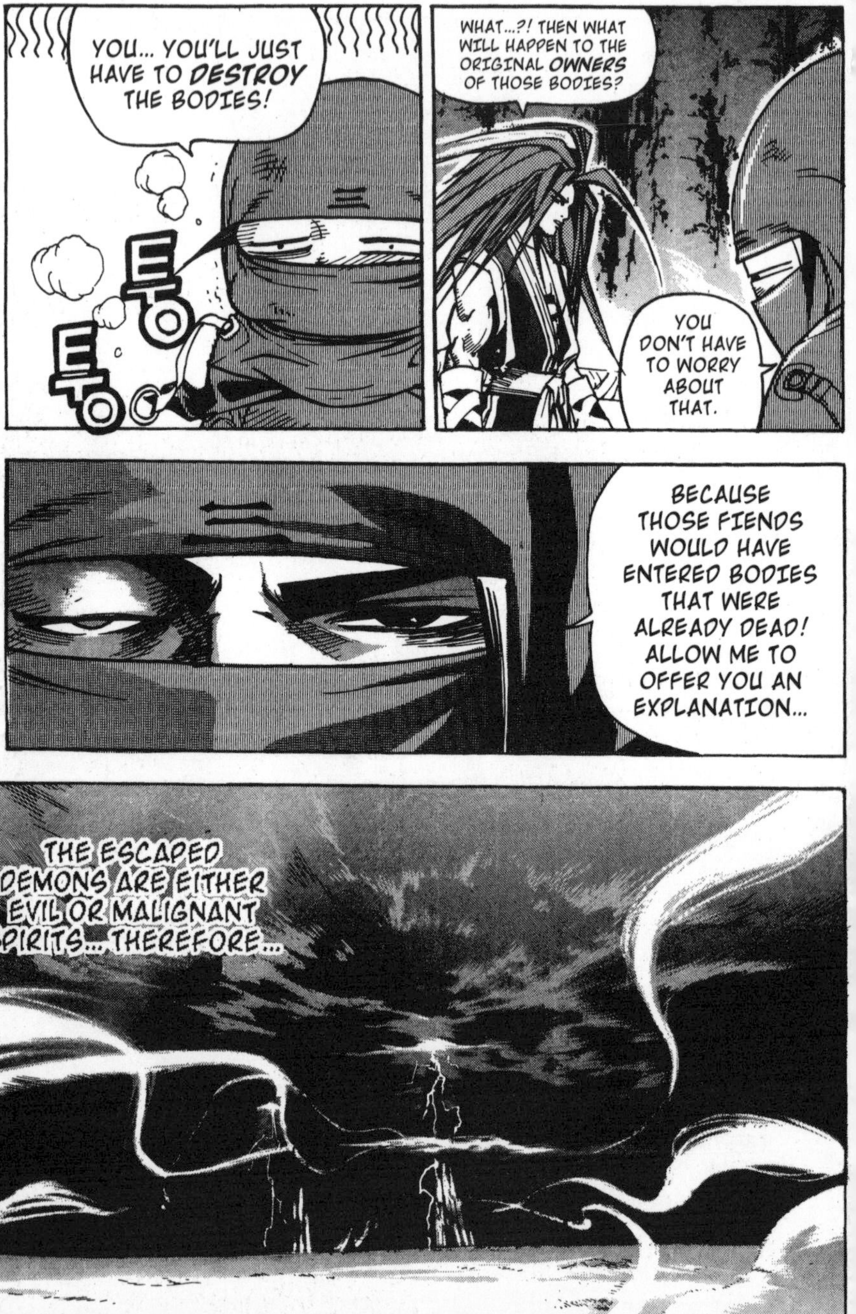
YOU... YOU'LL JUST HAVE TO DESTROY THE BODIES!
ETO
ETO
WHAT...?! THEN WHAT WILL HAPPEN TO THE ORIGINAL OWNERS OF THOSE BODIES?
YOU DON'T HAVE TO WORRY ABOUT THAT.
BECAUSE THOSE FIENDS WOULD HAVE ENTERED BODIES THAT WERE ALREADY DEAD! ALLOW ME TO OFFER YOU AN EXPLANATION...
THE ESCAPED DEMONS ARE EITHER EVIL OR MALIGNANT SPIRITS... THEREFORE...

...THEY CANNOT ENTER A BODY THAT IS STILL *LIVING*.

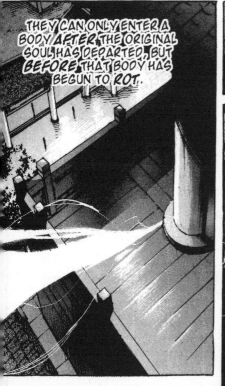

THEY CAN ONLY ENTER A BODY *AFTER* THE ORIGINAL SOUL HAS DEPARTED, BUT *BEFORE* THAT BODY HAS BEGUN TO *ROT*.

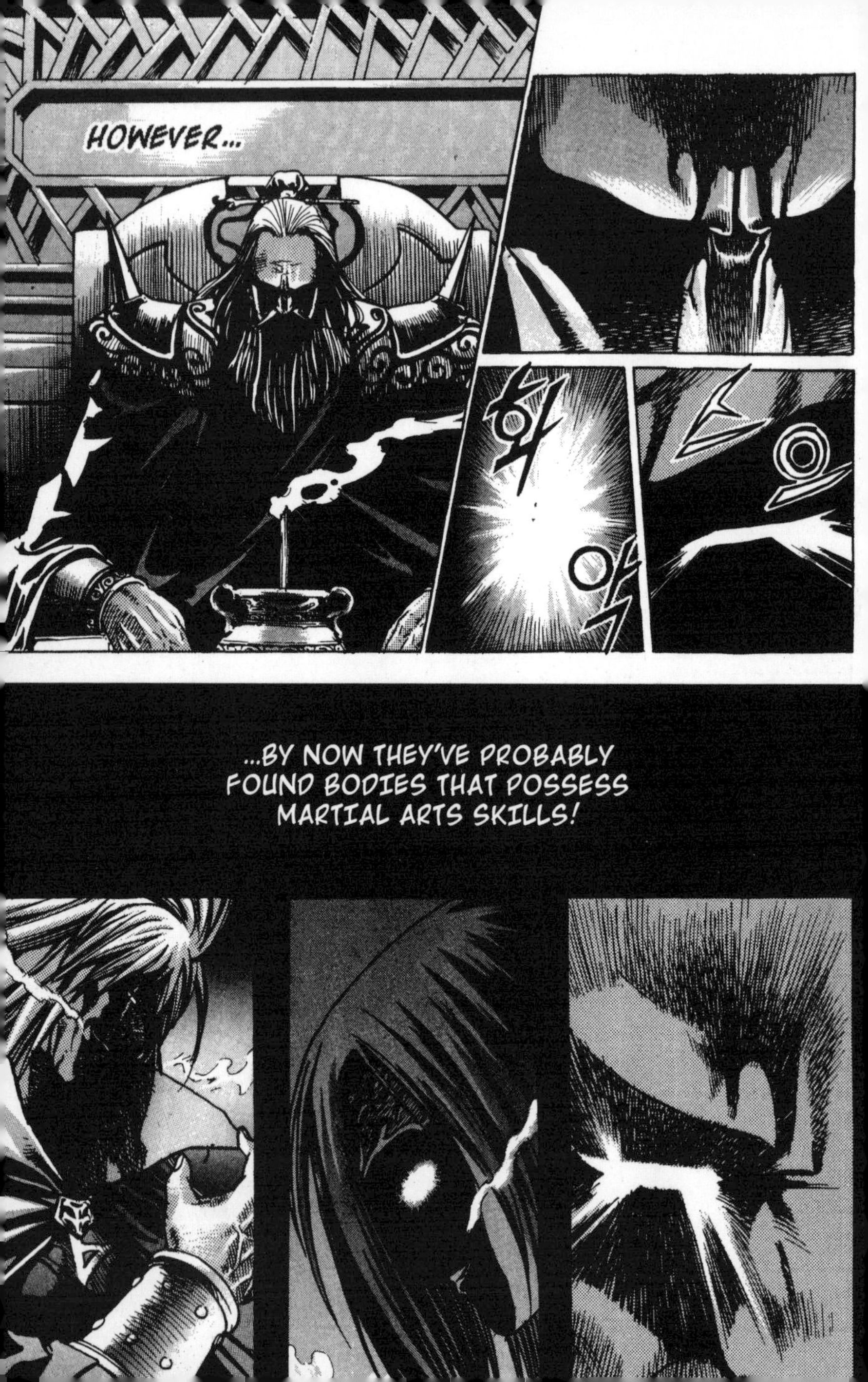
HOWEVER...
...BY NOW THEY'VE PROBABLY FOUND BODIES THAT POSSESS MARTIAL ARTS SKILLS!

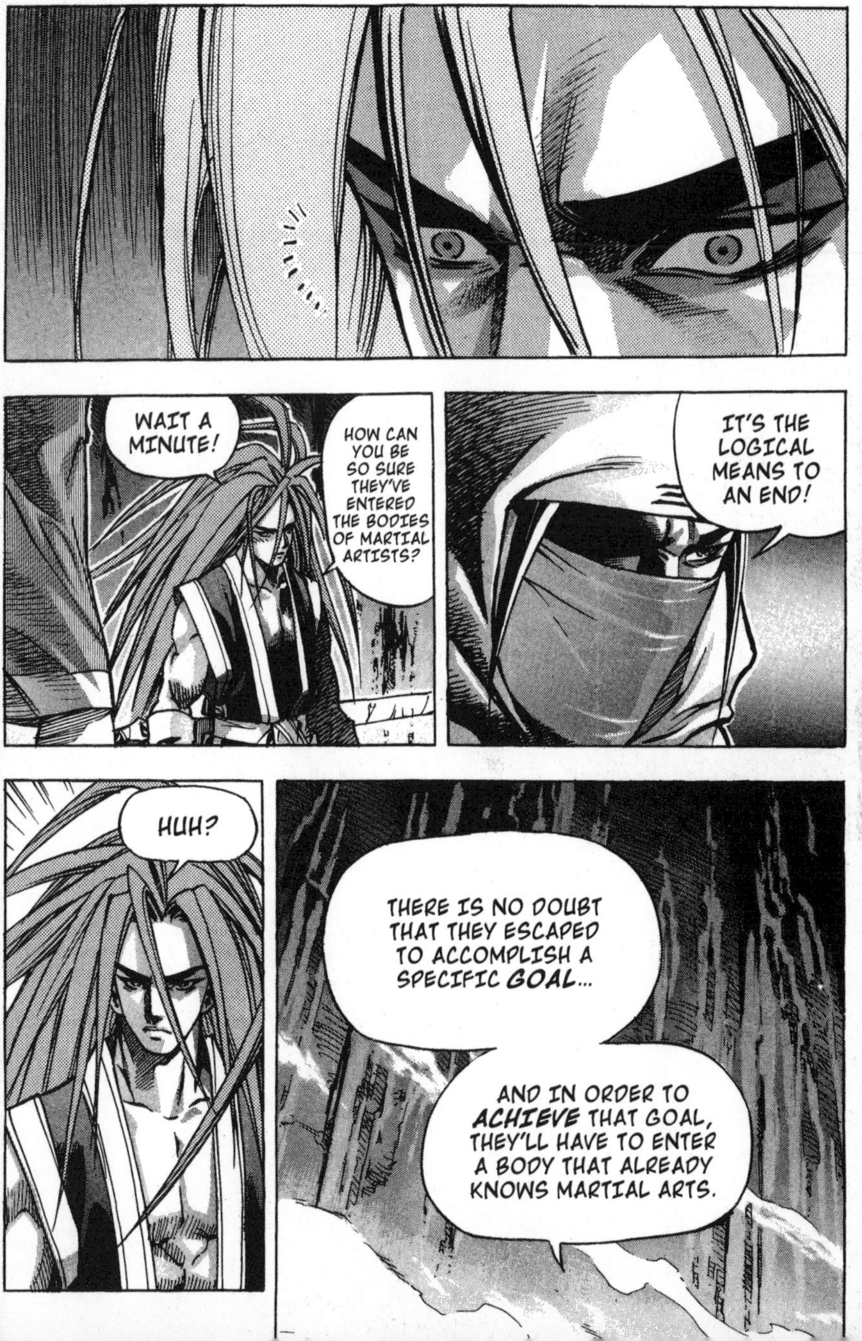
WAIT A MINUTE!
HOW CAN YOU BE SO SURE THEY'VE ENTERED THE BODIES OF MARTIAL ARTISTS?
IT'S THE LOGICAL MEANS TO AN END!
HUH?
THERE IS NO DOUBT THAT THEY ESCAPED TO ACCOMPLISH A SPECIFIC GOAL...
AND IN ORDER TO ACHIEVE THAT GOAL, THEY'LL HAVE TO ENTER A BODY THAT ALREADY KNOWS MARTIAL ARTS.

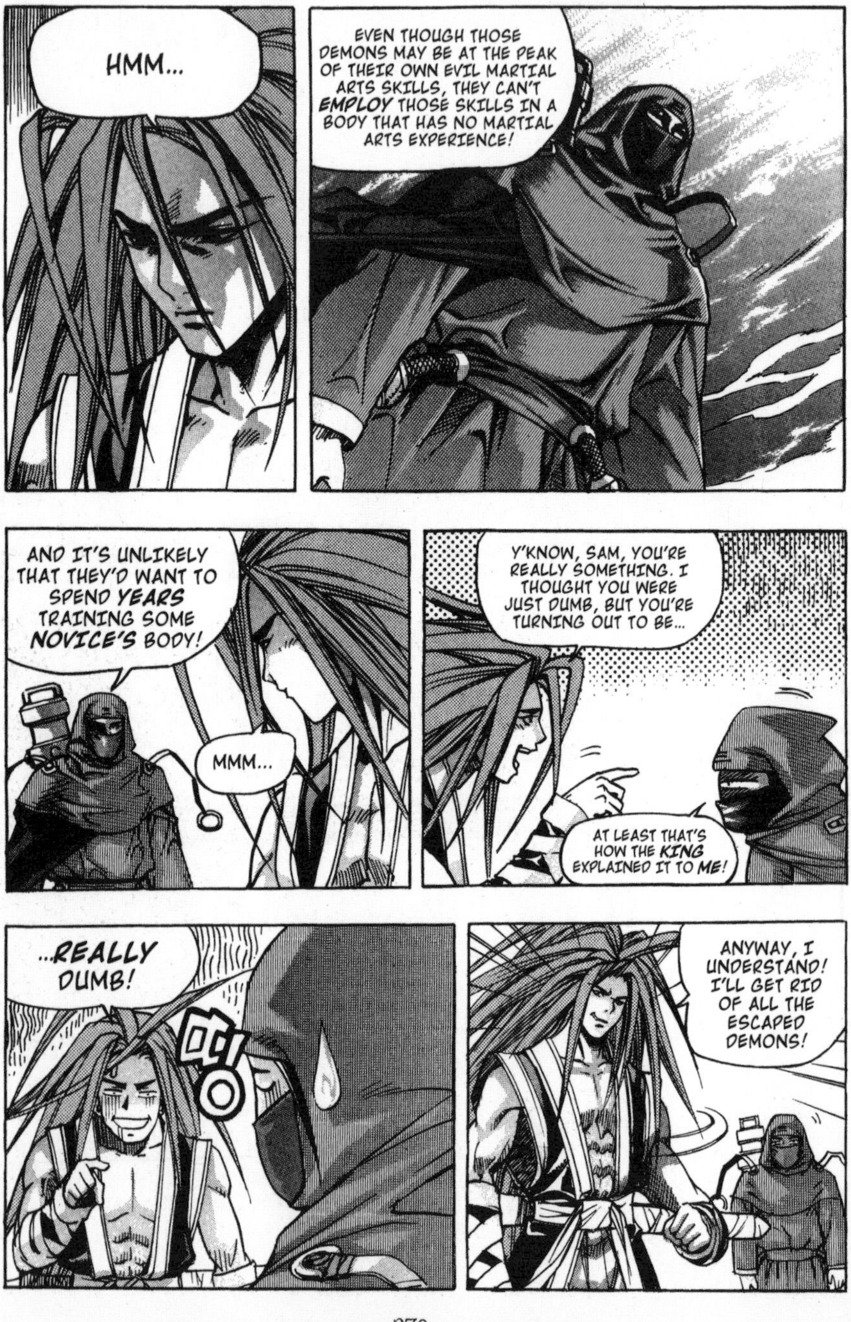
HMM...
EVEN THOUGH THOSE DEMONS MAY BE AT THE PEAK OF THEIR OWN EVIL MARTIAL ARTS SKILLS, THEY CAN'T EMPLOY THOSE SKILLS IN A BODY THAT HAS NO MARTIAL ARTS EXPERIENCE!
AND IT'S UNLIKELY THAT THEY'D WANT TO SPEND YEARS TRAINING SOME NOVICE'S BODY!
MMM...
Y'KNOW, SAM, YOU'RE REALLY SOMETHING. I THOUGHT YOU WERE JUST DUMB, BUT YOU'RE TURNING OUT TO BE...
AT LEAST THAT'S HOW THE KING EXPLAINED IT TO ME!
...REALLY DUMB!
ANYWAY, I UNDERSTAND! I'LL GET RID OF ALL THE ESCAPED DEMONS!

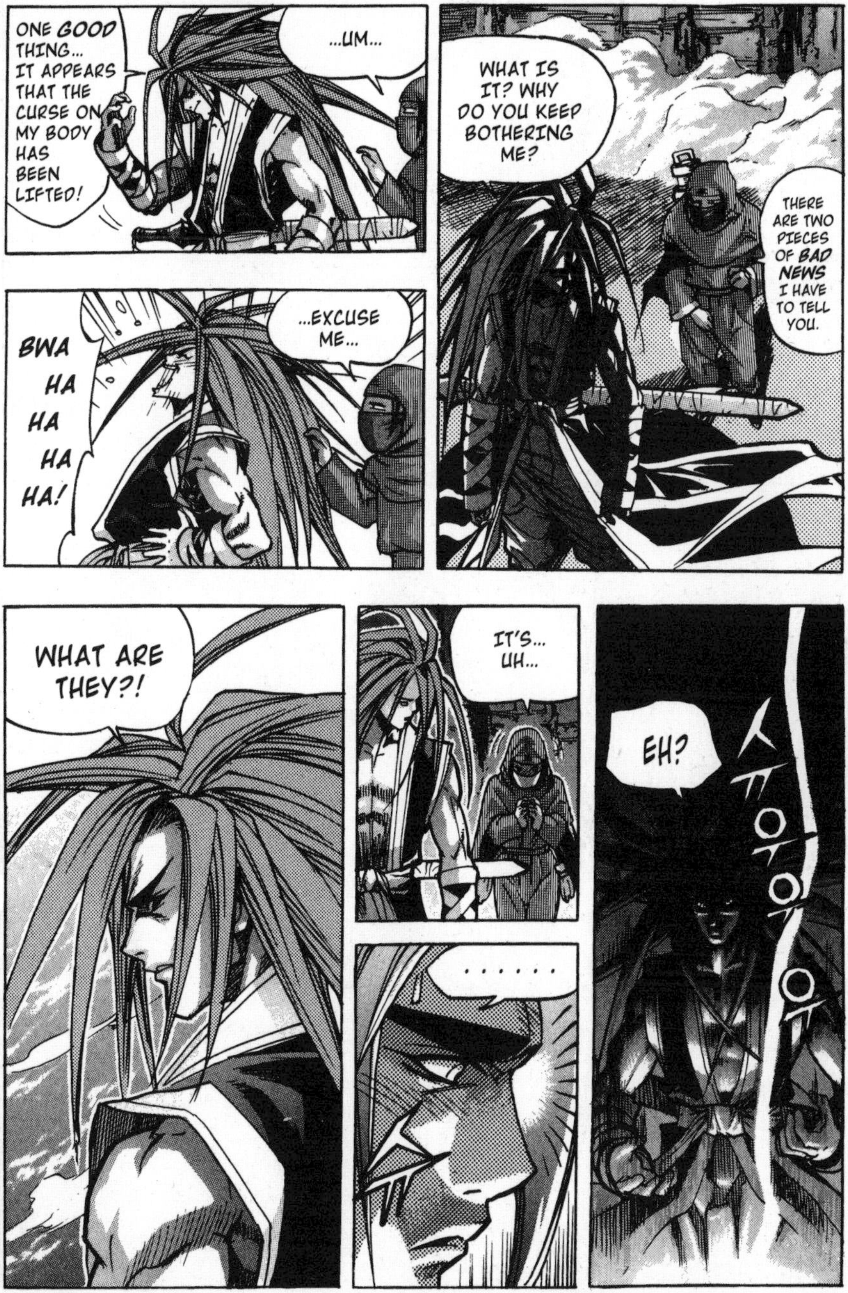

ONE GOOD THING... IT APPEARS THAT THE CURSE ON MY BODY HAS BEEN LIFTED!
...UM...
WHAT IS IT? WHY DO YOU KEEP BOTHERING ME?
THERE ARE TWO PIECES OF BAD NEWS I HAVE TO TELL YOU.
BWA HA HA HA HA!
...EXCUSE ME...
WHAT ARE THEY?!
IT'S... UH...
EH?
......

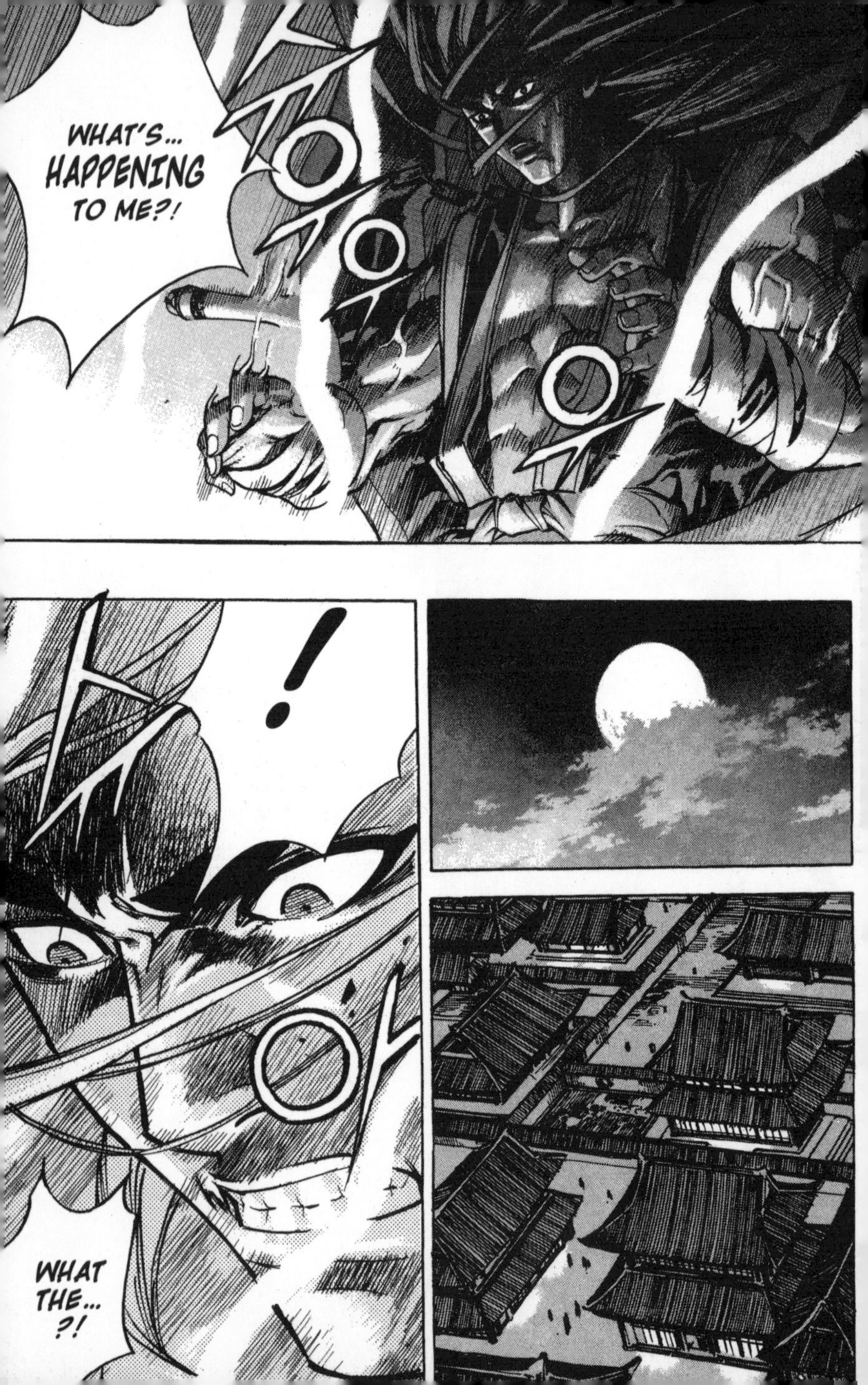
WHAT'S... HAPPENING TO ME?!
!
WHAT THE... ?!

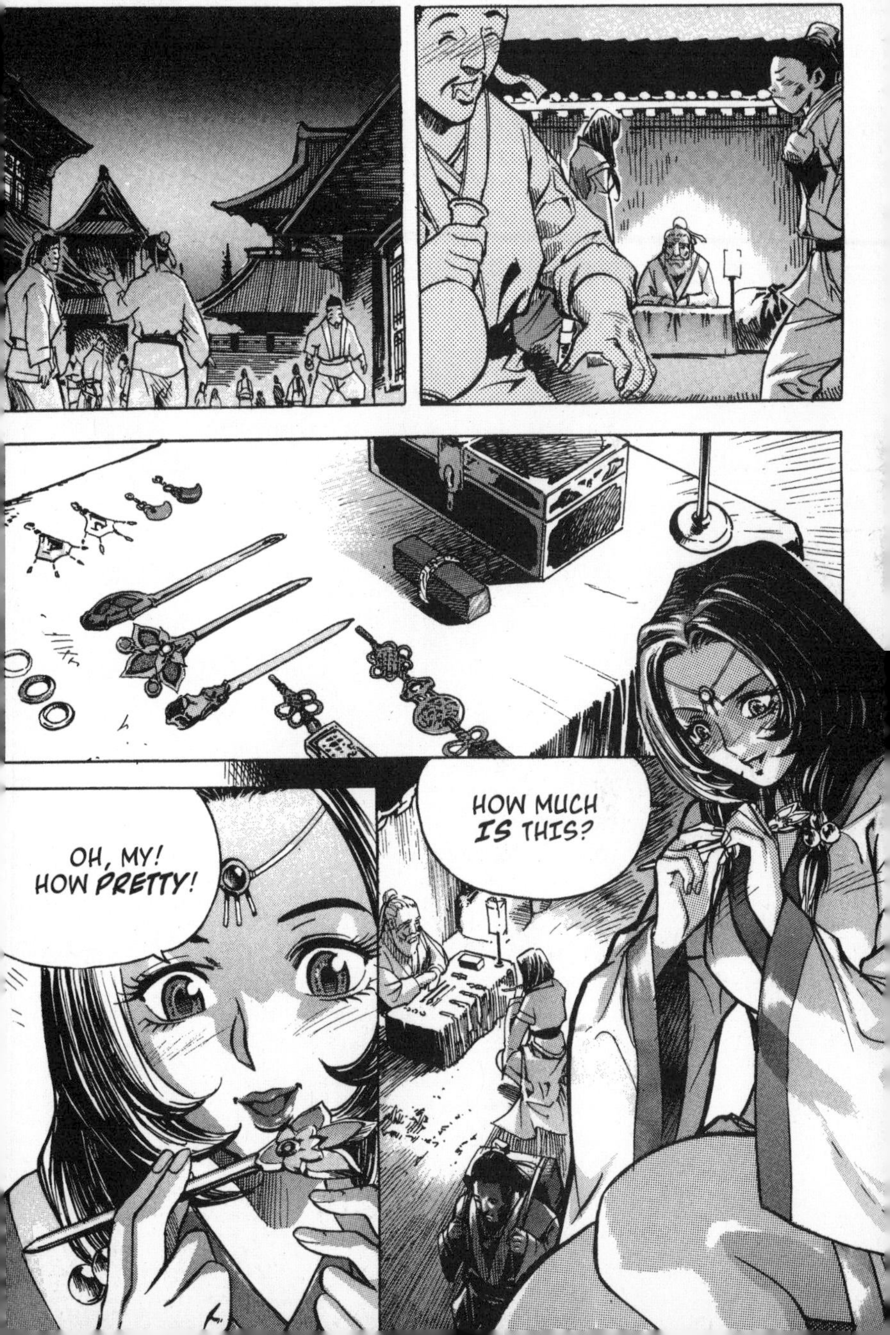
OH, MY! HOW PRETTY!
HOW MUCH IS THIS?

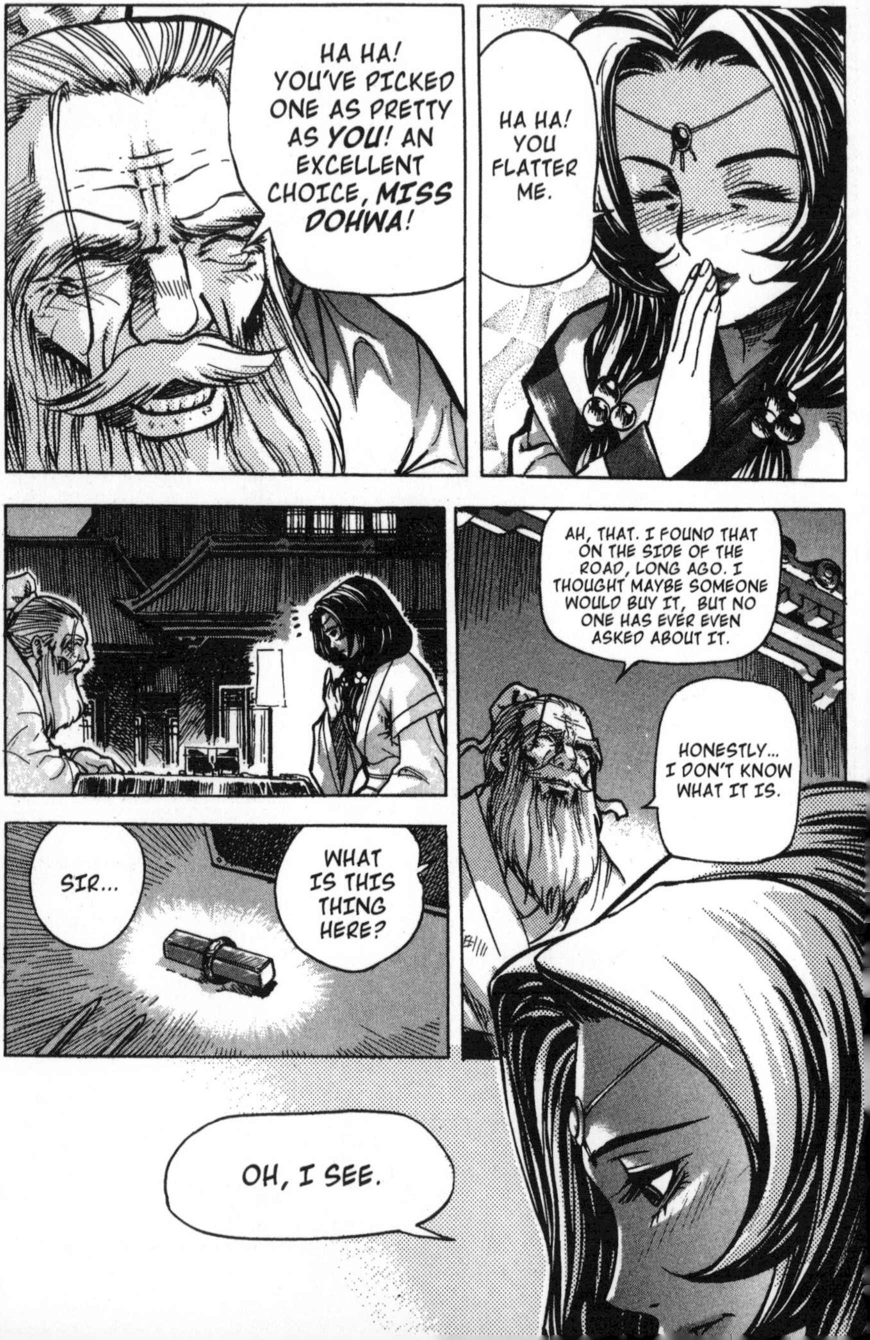
HA HA! YOU'VE PICKED ONE AS PRETTY AS *YOU*! AN EXCELLENT CHOICE, *MISS DOHWA*!
HA HA! YOU FLATTER ME.
AH, THAT. I FOUND THAT ON THE SIDE OF THE ROAD, LONG AGO. I THOUGHT MAYBE SOMEONE WOULD BUY IT, BUT NO ONE HAS EVER EVEN ASKED ABOUT IT.
HONESTLY... I DON'T KNOW WHAT IT IS.
SIR...
WHAT IS THIS THING HERE?
OH, I SEE.

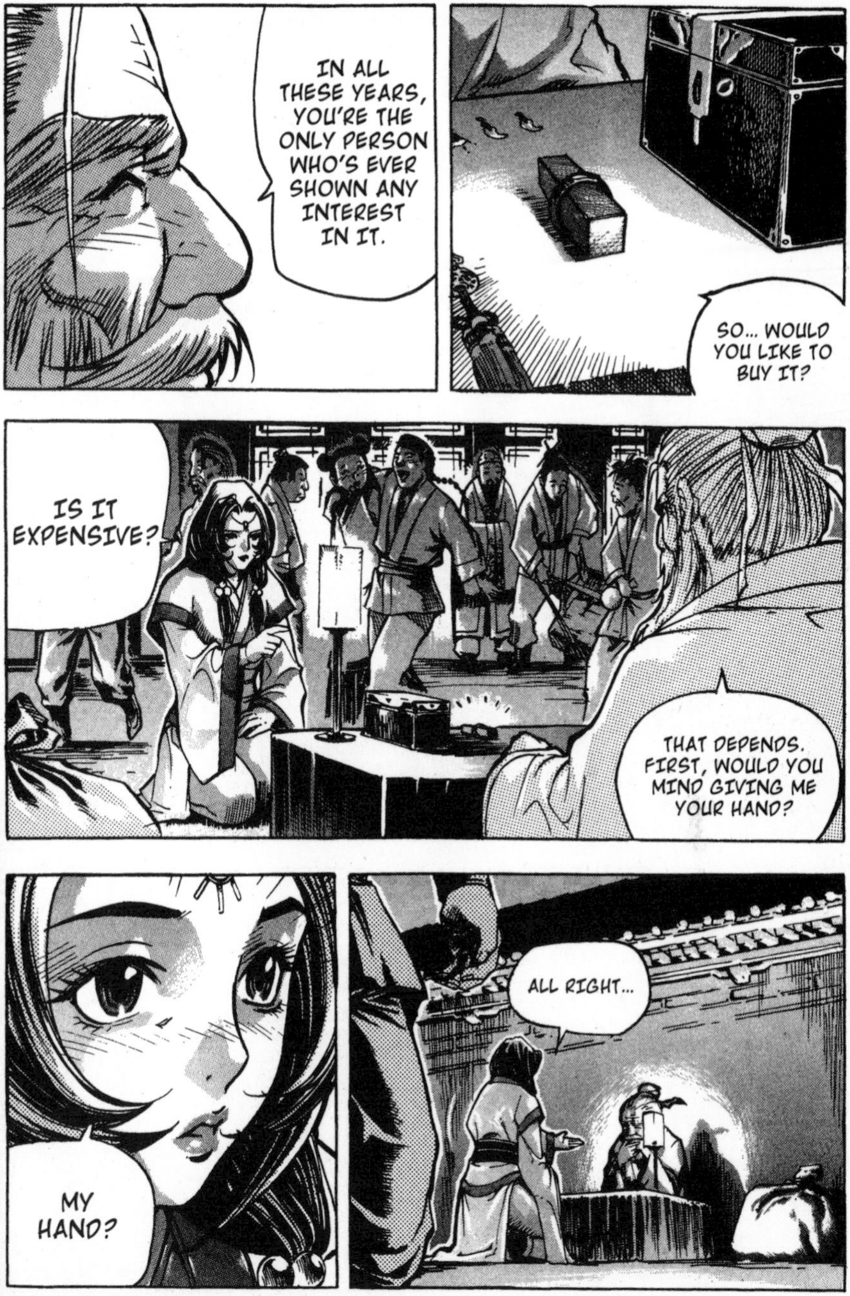
IN ALL THESE YEARS, YOU'RE THE ONLY PERSON WHO'S EVER SHOWN ANY INTEREST IN IT.
SO... WOULD YOU LIKE TO BUY IT?
IS IT EXPENSIVE?
THAT DEPENDS. FIRST, WOULD YOU MIND GIVING ME YOUR HAND?
MY HAND?
ALL RIGHT...

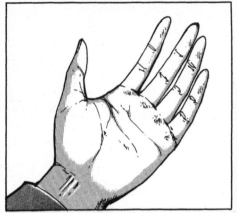

YOU HAVE TINY CALLUSES AT THE BASE OF YOUR FINGERS.

AHHH...! YOU MUST ENJOY EMBROIDERY.

HA HA...! YES, I DO.

ALL RIGHT! JUST PAY ME FOR THE HAIR CLIP AND BOTH ITEMS ARE YOURS!

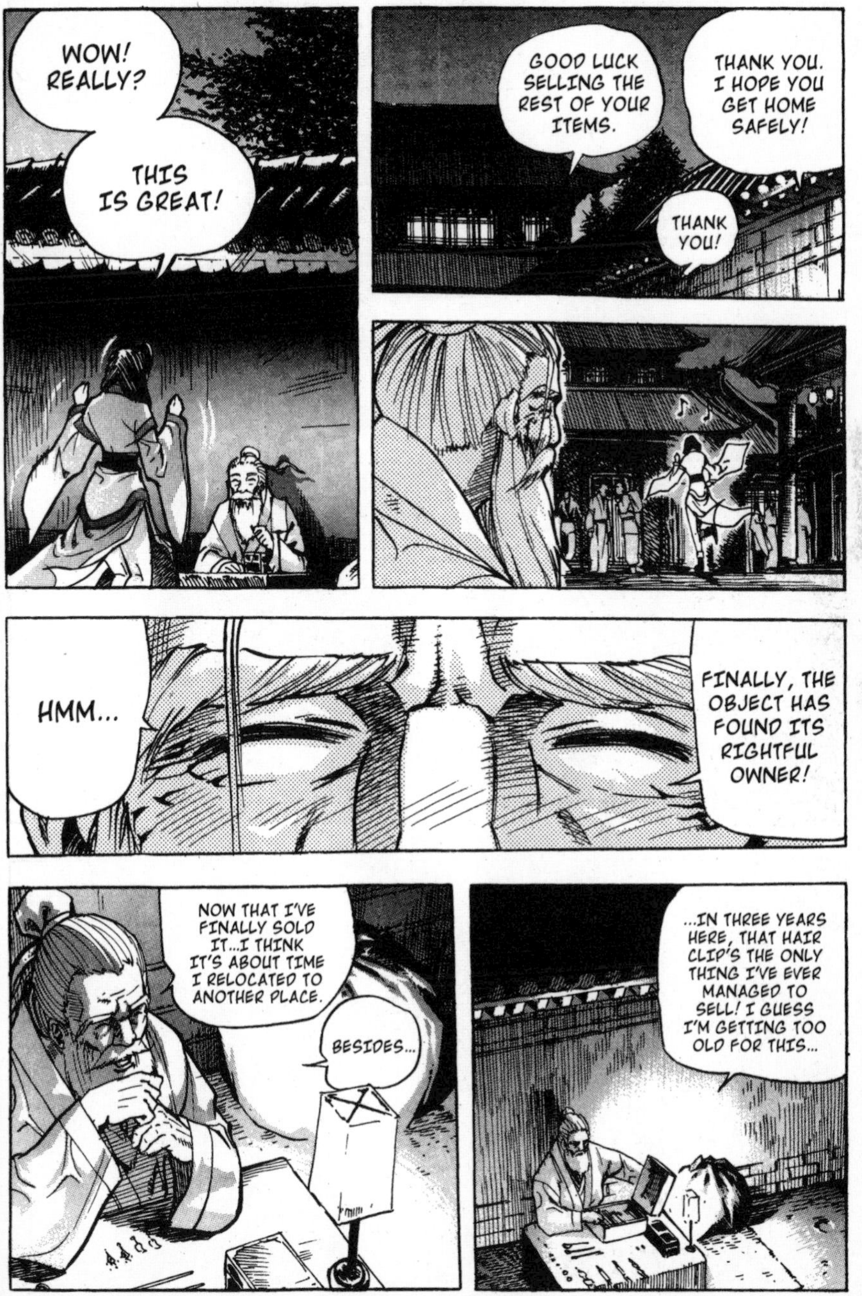
WOW! REALLY?
THIS IS GREAT!
GOOD LUCK SELLING THE REST OF YOUR ITEMS.
THANK YOU. I HOPE YOU GET HOME SAFELY!
THANK YOU!
HMM...
FINALLY, THE OBJECT HAS FOUND ITS RIGHTFUL OWNER!
NOW THAT I'VE FINALLY SOLD IT...I THINK IT'S ABOUT TIME I RELOCATED TO ANOTHER PLACE.
BESIDES...
...IN THREE YEARS HERE, THAT HAIR CLIP'S THE ONLY THING I'VE EVER MANAGED TO SELL! I GUESS I'M GETTING TOO OLD FOR THIS...

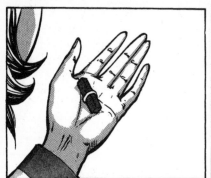

I WONDER JUST WHAT THIS IS?

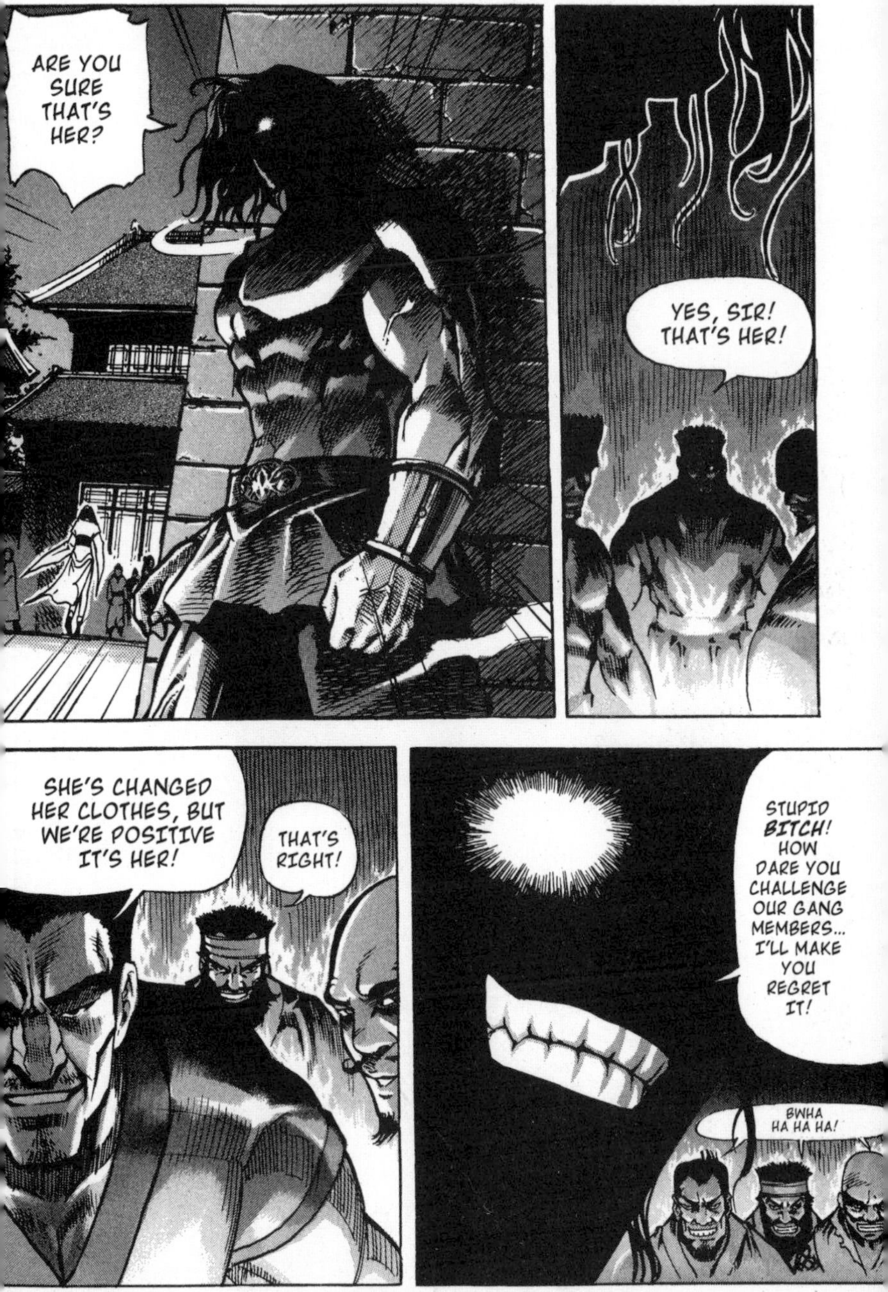
ARE YOU SURE THAT'S HER?
YES, SIR! THAT'S HER!
SHE'S CHANGED HER CLOTHES, BUT WE'RE POSITIVE IT'S HER!
THAT'S RIGHT!
STUPID **BITCH**! HOW DARE YOU CHALLENGE OUR GANG MEMBERS... I'LL MAKE YOU REGRET IT!
BWHA HA HA HA!

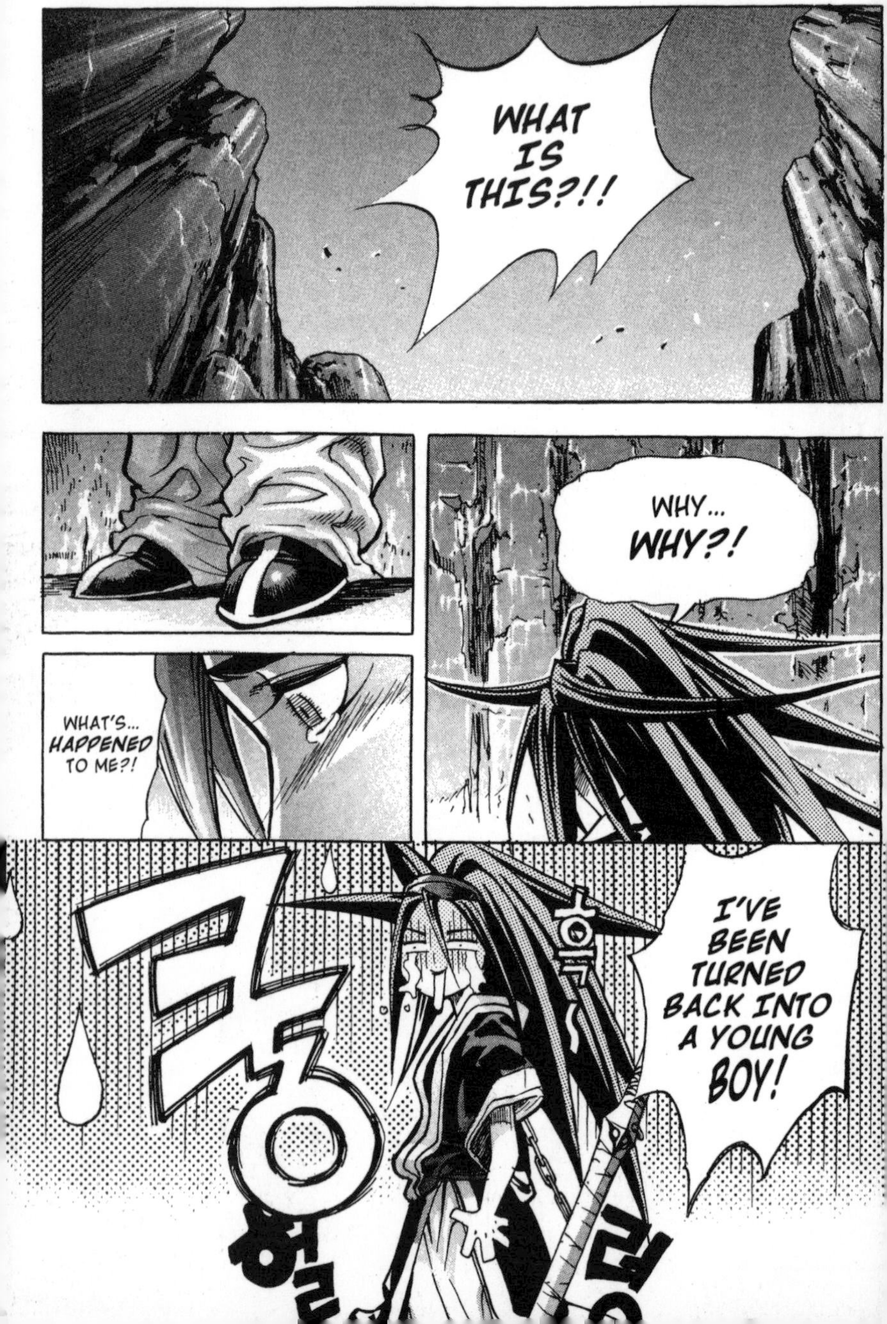
WHAT IS THIS?!!
WHAT'S... HAPPENED TO ME?!
WHY... WHY?!
I'VE BEEN TURNED BACK INTO A YOUNG BOY!

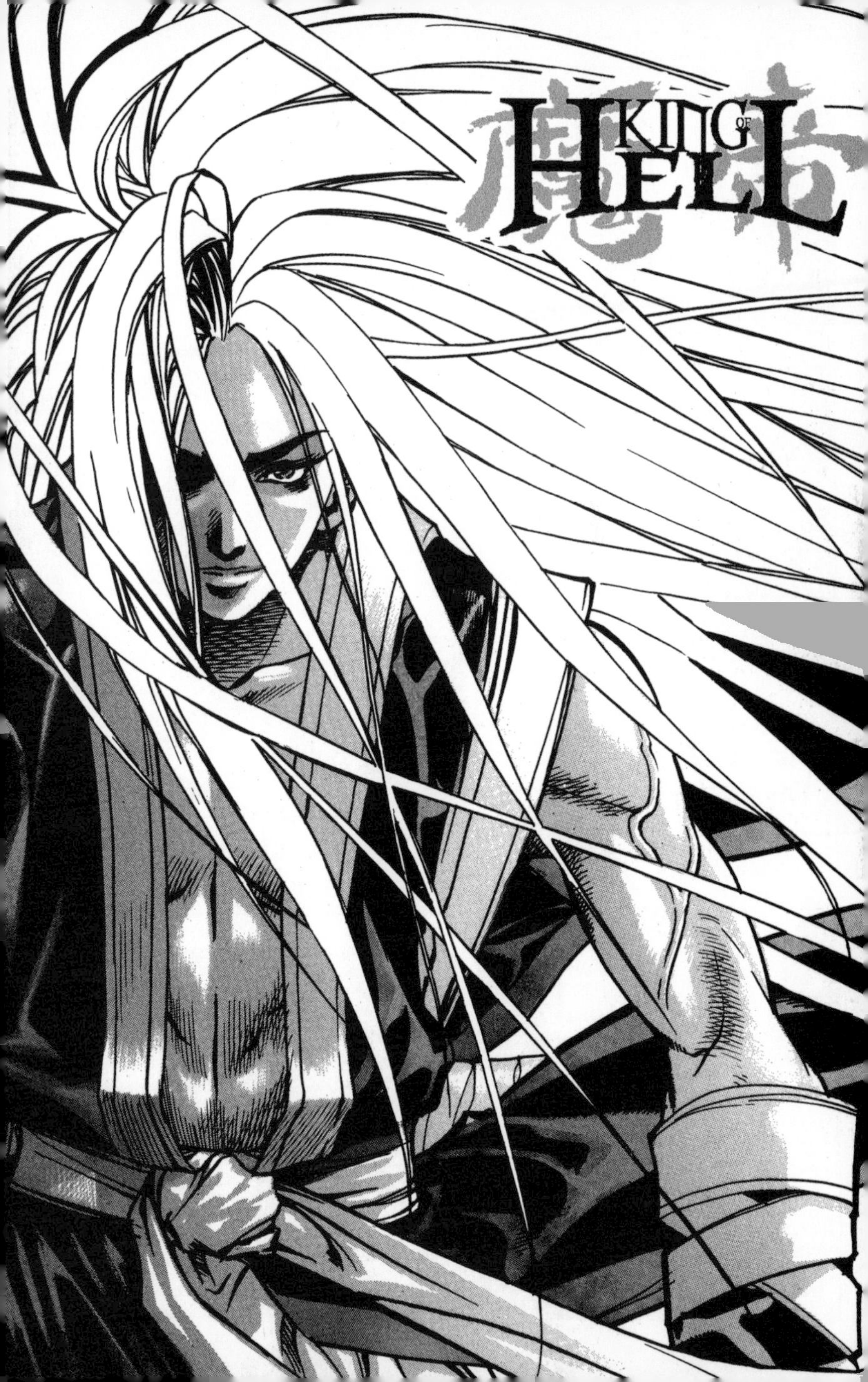
KING OF HELL
魔帝

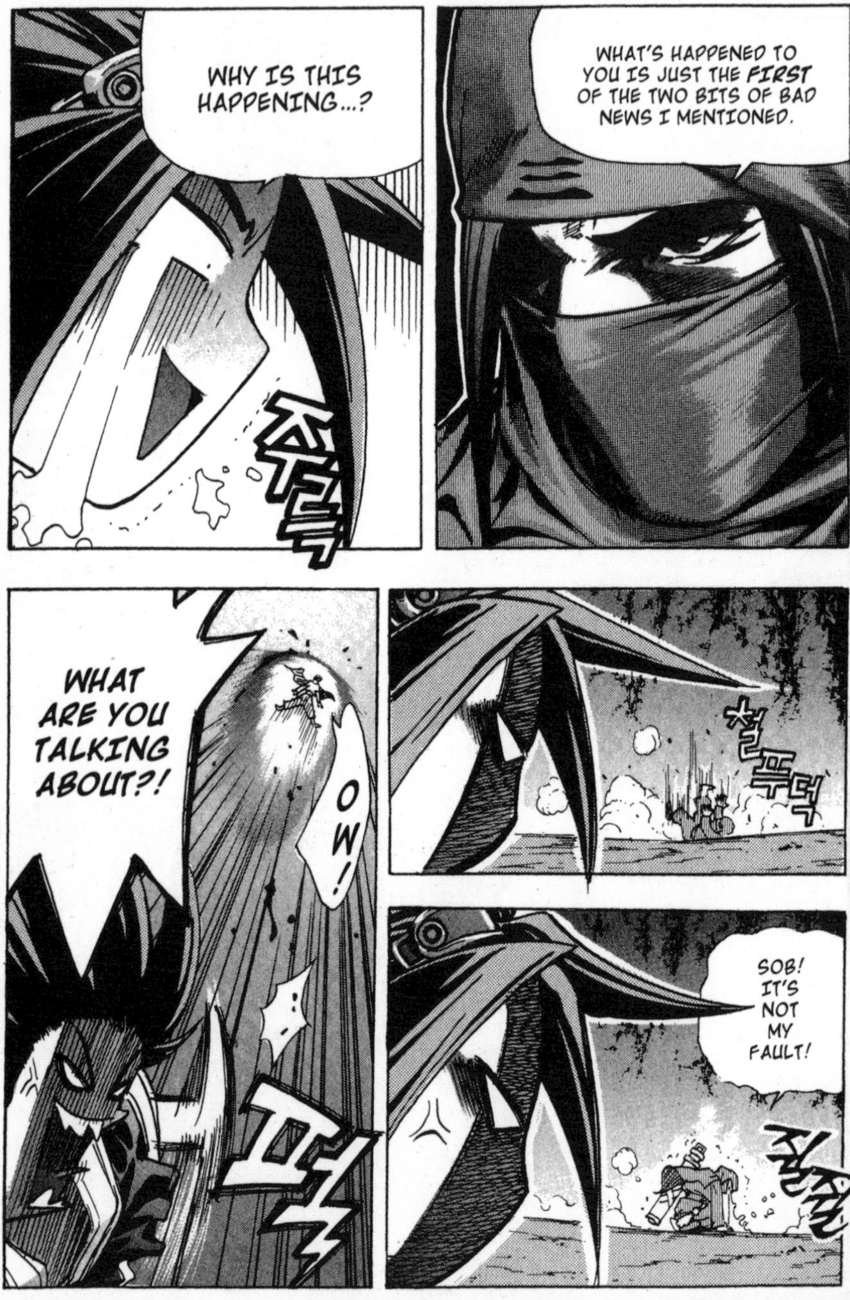
WHY IS THIS HAPPENING...?
WHAT'S HAPPENED TO YOU IS JUST THE *FIRST* OF THE TWO BITS OF BAD NEWS I MENTIONED.
WHAT ARE YOU TALKING ABOUT?!
OW!
퍽
철푸덕
SOB! IT'S NOT MY FAULT!

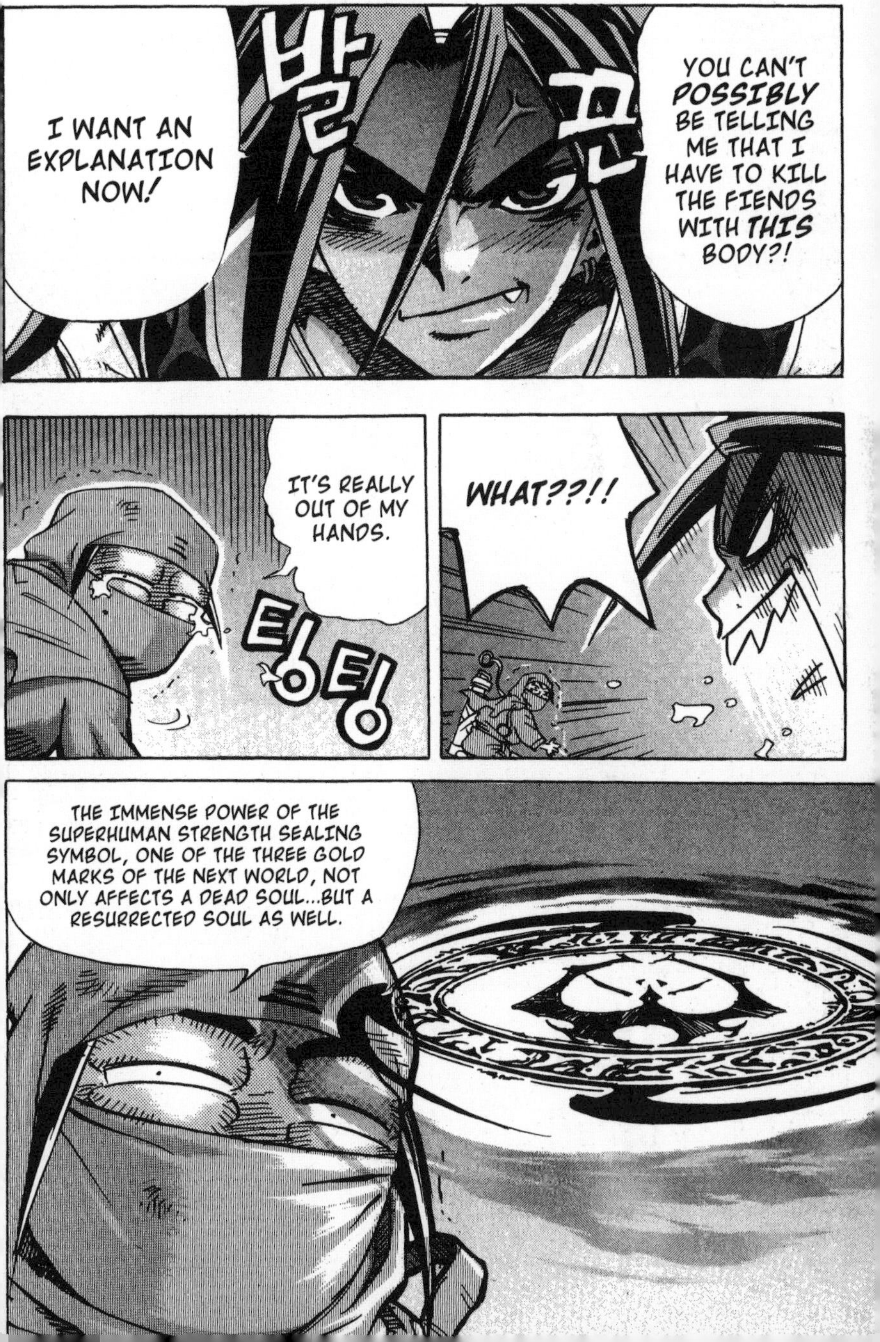
I WANT AN EXPLANATION NOW!
발끈
YOU CAN'T *POSSIBLY* BE TELLING ME THAT I HAVE TO KILL THE FIENDS WITH ***THIS*** BODY?!
IT'S REALLY OUT OF MY HANDS.
티잉티잉
WHAT??!!
THE IMMENSE POWER OF THE SUPERHUMAN STRENGTH SEALING SYMBOL, ONE OF THE THREE GOLD MARKS OF THE NEXT WORLD, NOT ONLY AFFECTS A DEAD SOUL...BUT A RESURRECTED SOUL AS WELL.

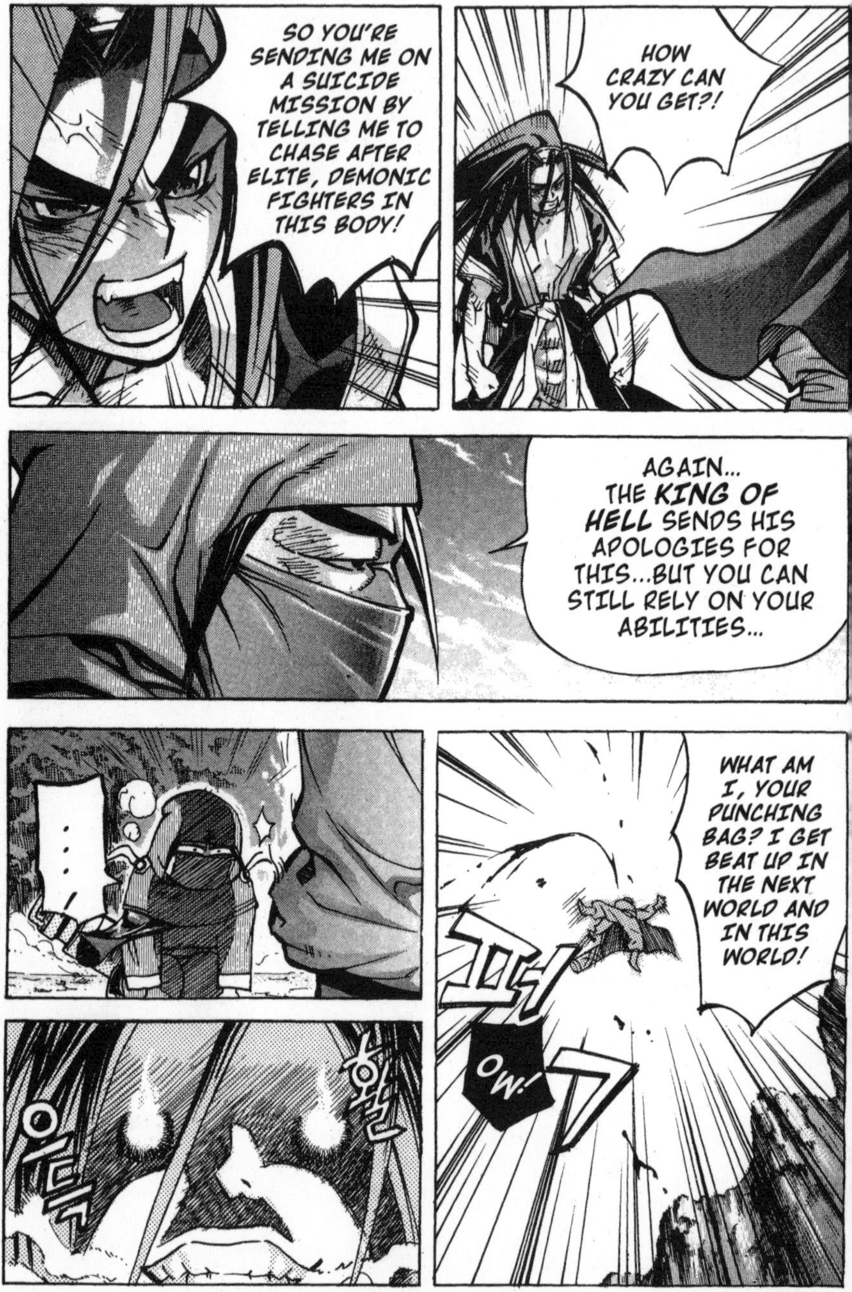
SO YOU'RE SENDING ME ON A SUICIDE MISSION BY TELLING ME TO CHASE AFTER ELITE, DEMONIC FIGHTERS IN THIS BODY!
HOW CRAZY CAN YOU GET?!
AGAIN... THE **KING OF HELL** SENDS HIS APOLOGIES FOR THIS...BUT YOU CAN STILL RELY ON YOUR ABILITIES...
...
WHAT AM I, YOUR PUNCHING BAG? I GET BEAT UP IN THE NEXT WORLD AND IN THIS WORLD!
OW!

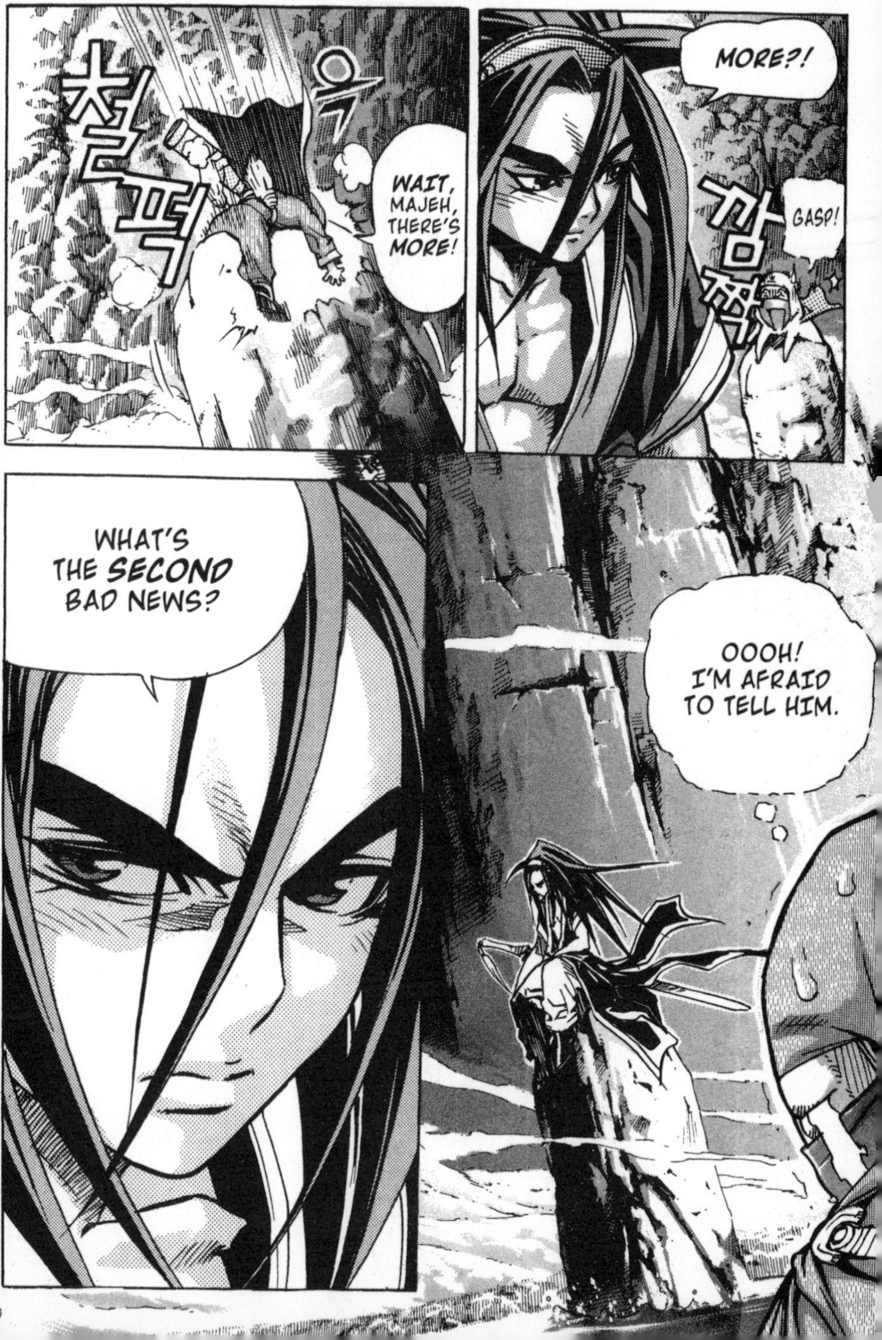
WAIT, MAJEH, THERE'S MORE!
MORE?!
GASP!
WHAT'S THE SECOND BAD NEWS?
OOOH! I'M AFRAID TO TELL HIM.

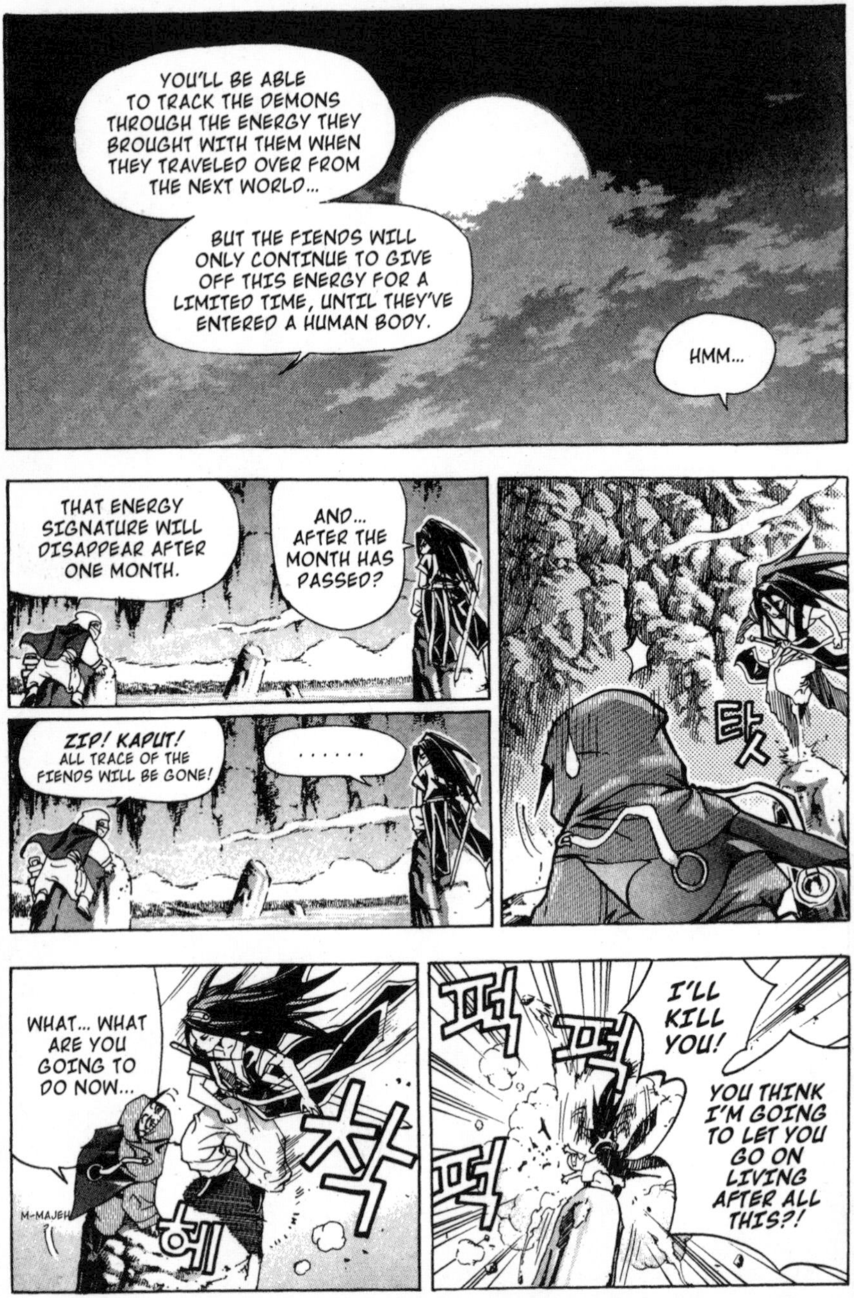
YOU'LL BE ABLE TO TRACK THE DEMONS THROUGH THE ENERGY THEY BROUGHT WITH THEM WHEN THEY TRAVELED OVER FROM THE NEXT WORLD...
BUT THE FIENDS WILL ONLY CONTINUE TO GIVE OFF THIS ENERGY FOR A LIMITED TIME, UNTIL THEY'VE ENTERED A HUMAN BODY.
HMM...
THAT ENERGY SIGNATURE WILL DISAPPEAR AFTER ONE MONTH.
AND... AFTER THE MONTH HAS PASSED?
ZIP! KAPUT! ALL TRACE OF THE FIENDS WILL BE GONE!
......
탓
WHAT... WHAT ARE YOU GOING TO DO NOW...
M-MAJEH
착
퍽
퍽
퍽
I'LL KILL YOU!
YOU THINK I'M GOING TO LET YOU GO ON LIVING AFTER ALL THIS?!

PLEASE, I'M ONLY RELAYING THE KING'S MESSAGE!

IT'S NOT MY FAULT!

.....

HERE, HOLD THIS FOR A SECOND!

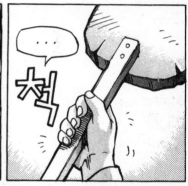

...

LIKE THIS?

YEAH... THAT'S IT.

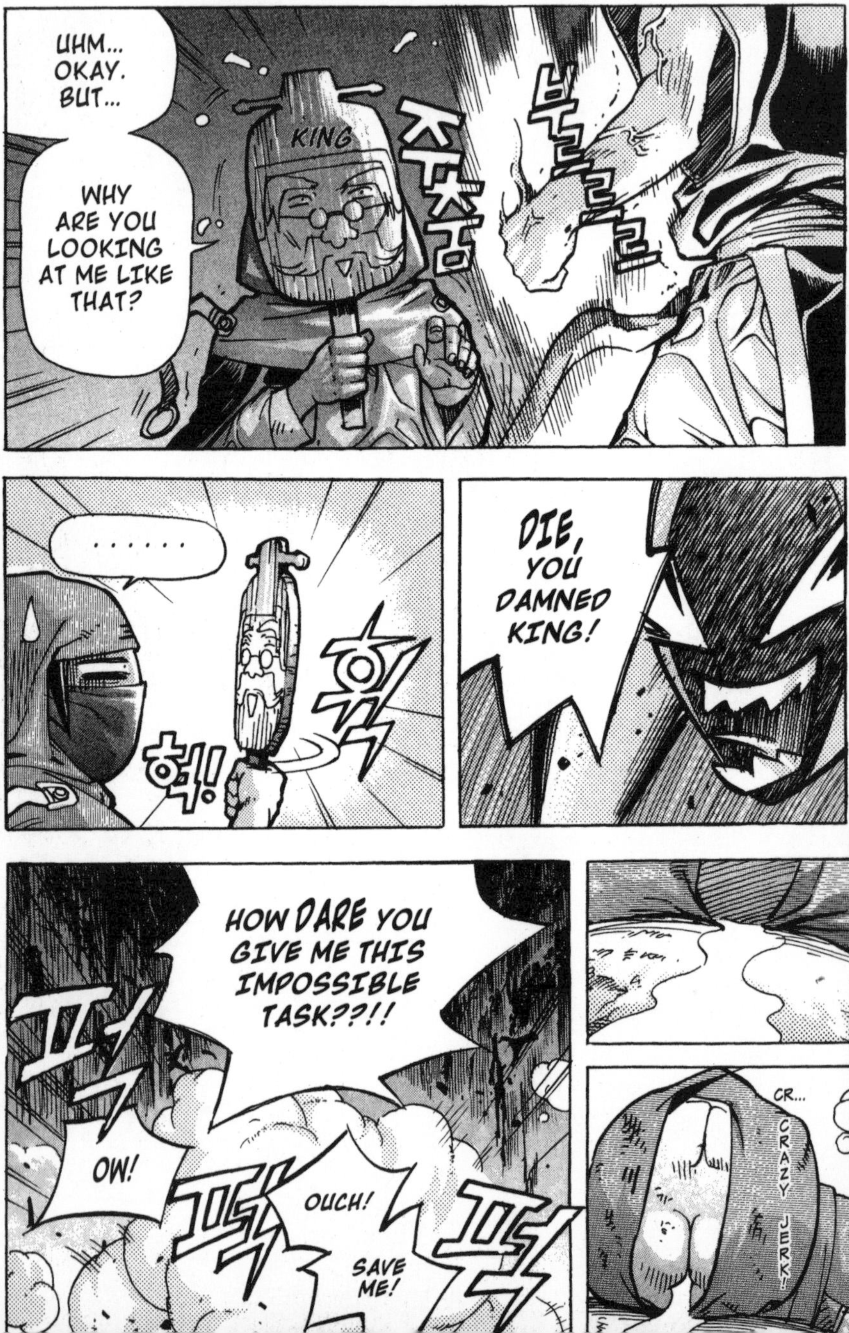
UHM... OKAY. BUT...
WHY ARE YOU LOOKING AT ME LIKE THAT?
KING
....
DIE, YOU DAMNED KING!
HOW DARE YOU GIVE ME THIS IMPOSSIBLE TASK??!!
OW!
OUCH!
SAVE ME!
CR...
CRAZY JERK!

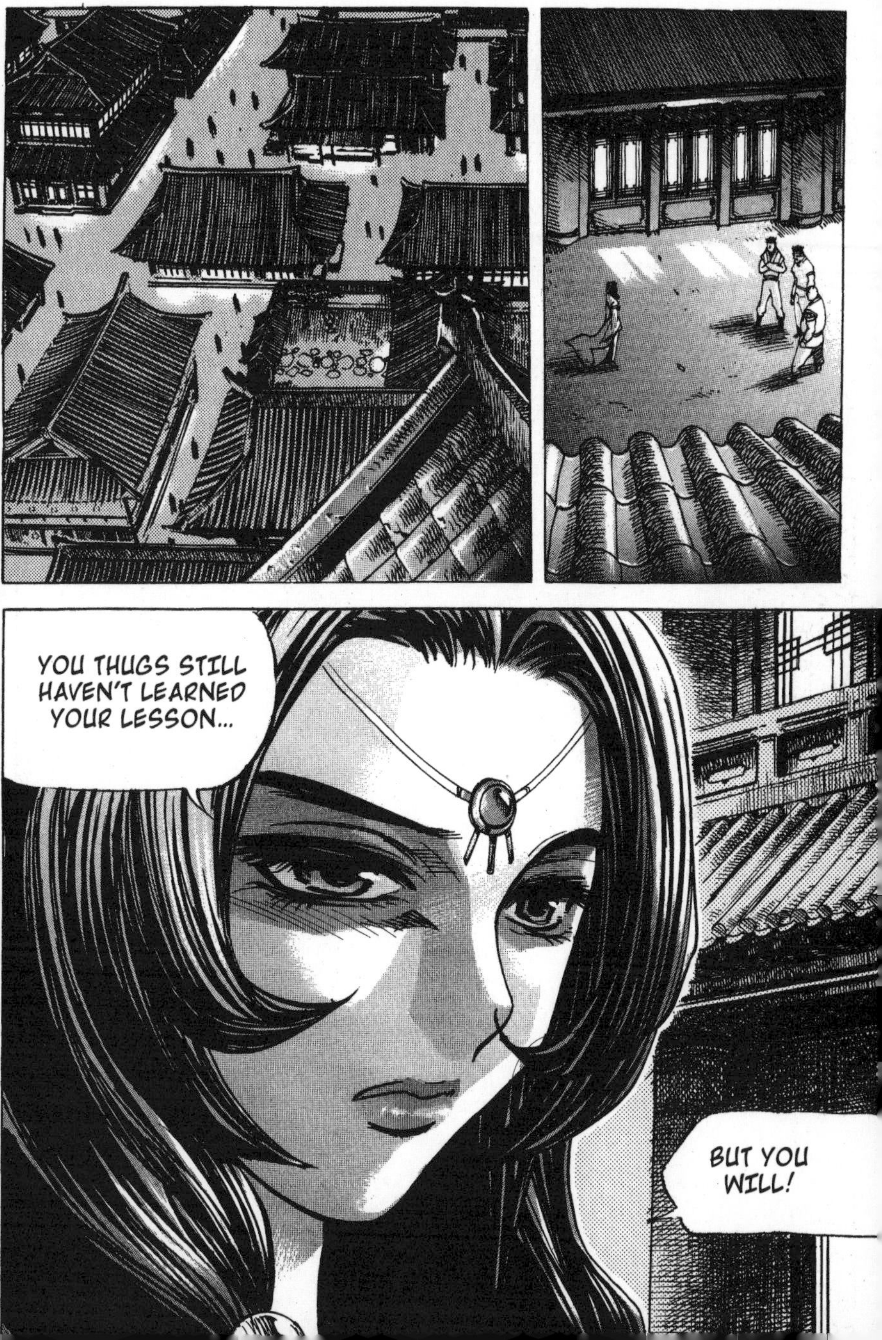
YOU THUGS STILL HAVEN'T LEARNED YOUR LESSON...
BUT YOU WILL!

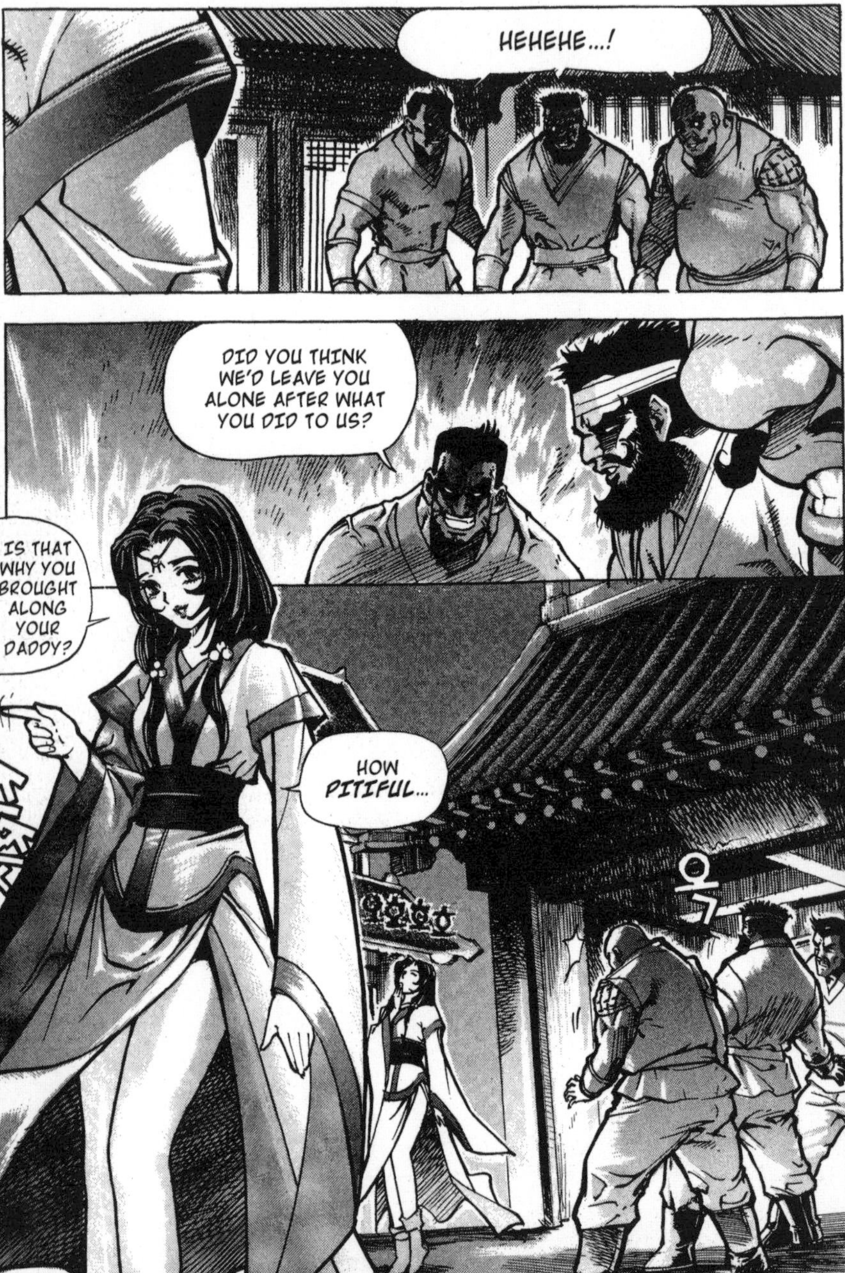
HEHEHE...!
DID YOU THINK WE'D LEAVE YOU ALONE AFTER WHAT YOU DID TO US?
IS THAT WHY YOU BROUGHT ALONG YOUR DADDY?
HOW PITIFUL...

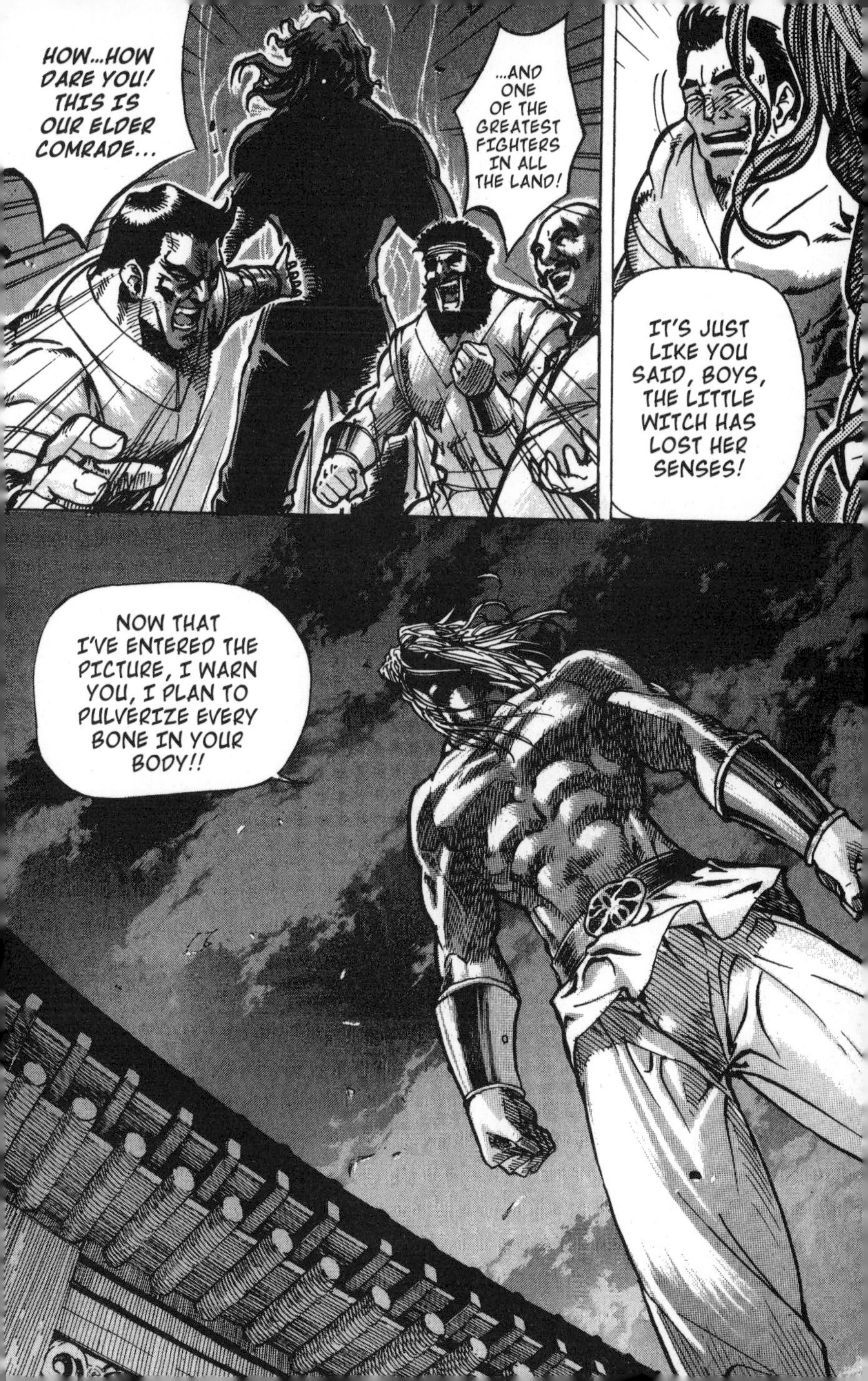
HOW...HOW DARE YOU! THIS IS OUR ELDER COMRADE...
...AND ONE OF THE GREATEST FIGHTERS IN ALL THE LAND!
IT'S JUST LIKE YOU SAID, BOYS, THE LITTLE WITCH HAS LOST HER SENSES!
NOW THAT I'VE ENTERED THE PICTURE, I WARN YOU, I PLAN TO PULVERIZE EVERY BONE IN YOUR BODY!!

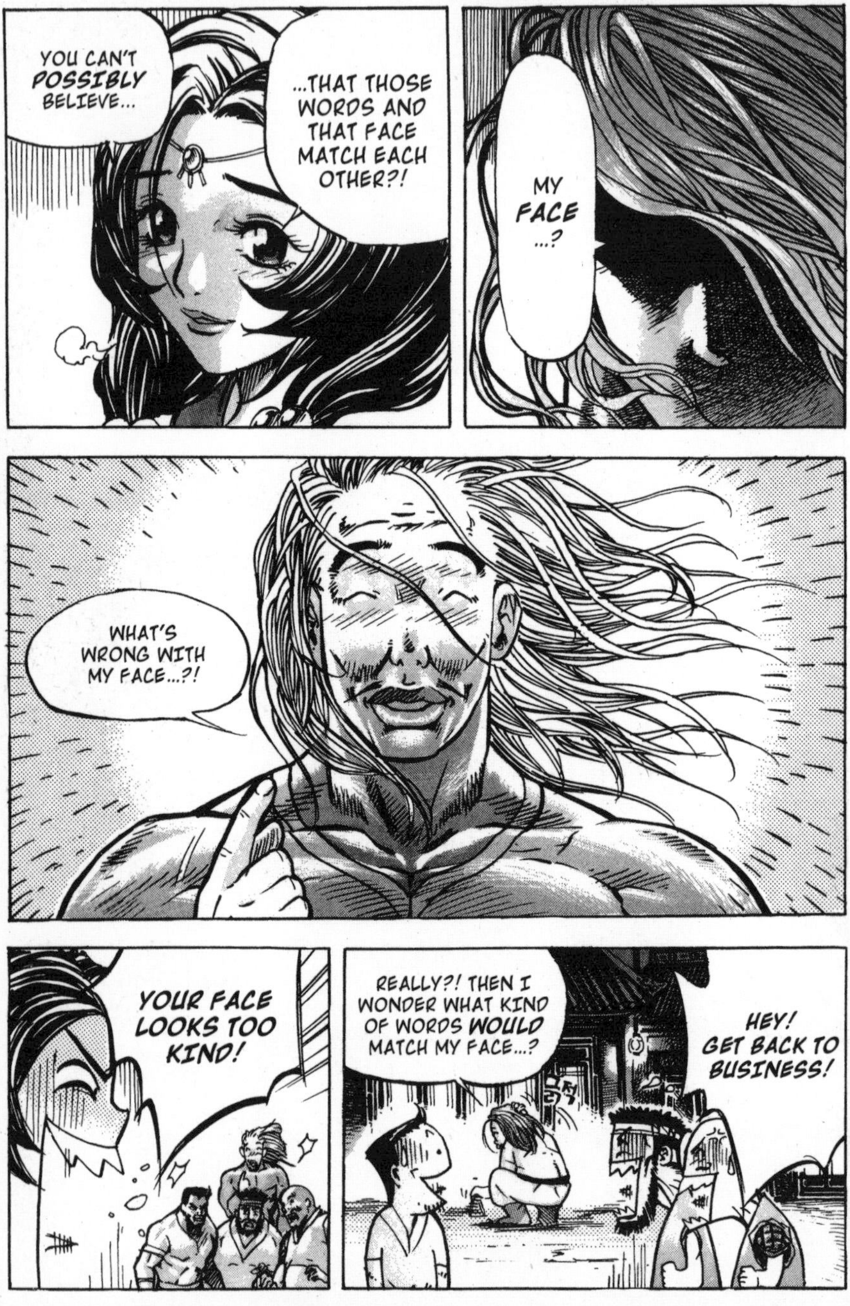
YOU CAN'T POSSIBLY BELIEVE...
...THAT THOSE WORDS AND THAT FACE MATCH EACH OTHER?!
MY FACE ...?
WHAT'S WRONG WITH MY FACE...?!
YOUR FACE LOOKS TOO KIND!
REALLY?! THEN I WONDER WHAT KIND OF WORDS WOULD MATCH MY FACE...?
HEY! GET BACK TO BUSINESS!

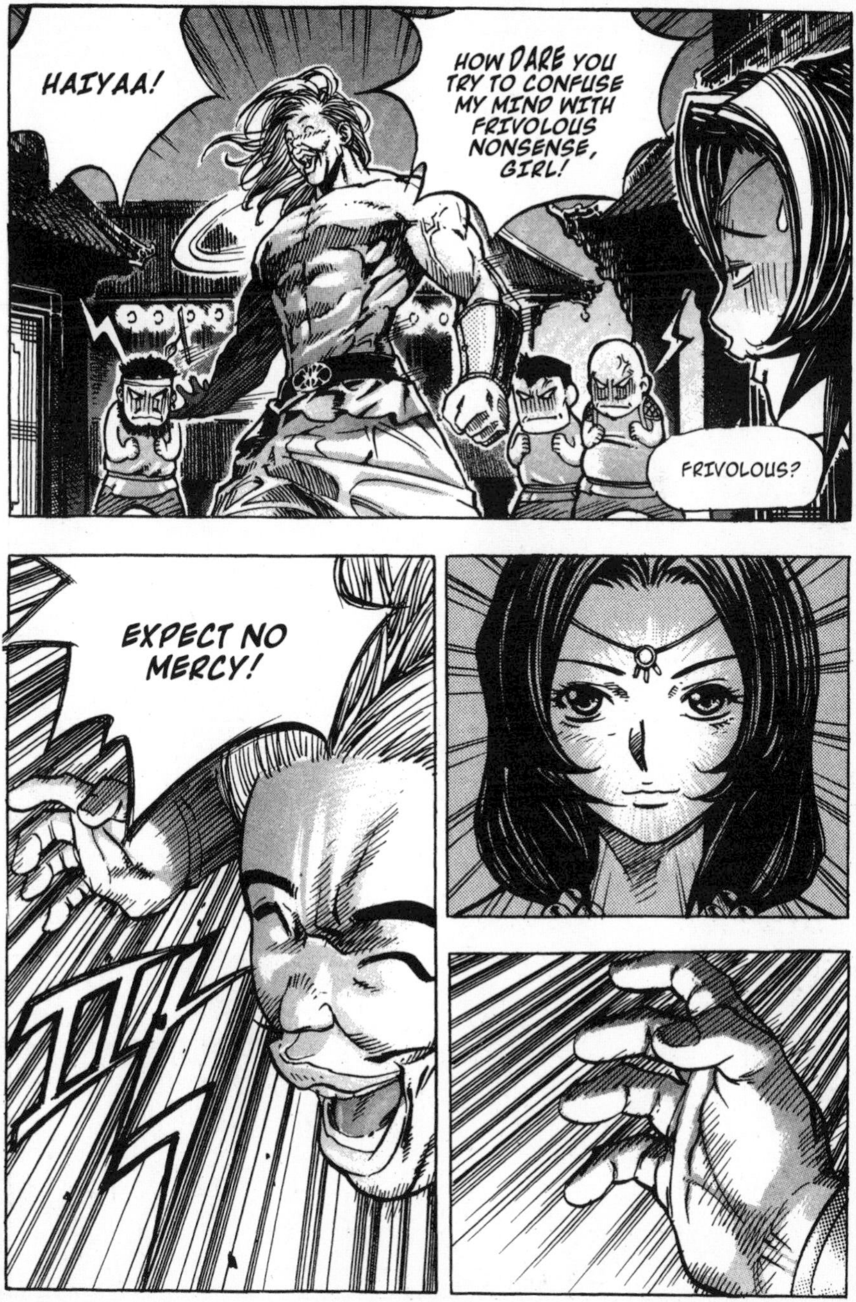
HAIYAA!
HOW DARE YOU TRY TO CONFUSE MY MIND WITH FRIVOLOUS NONSENSE, GIRL!
FRIVOLOUS?
EXPECT NO MERCY!

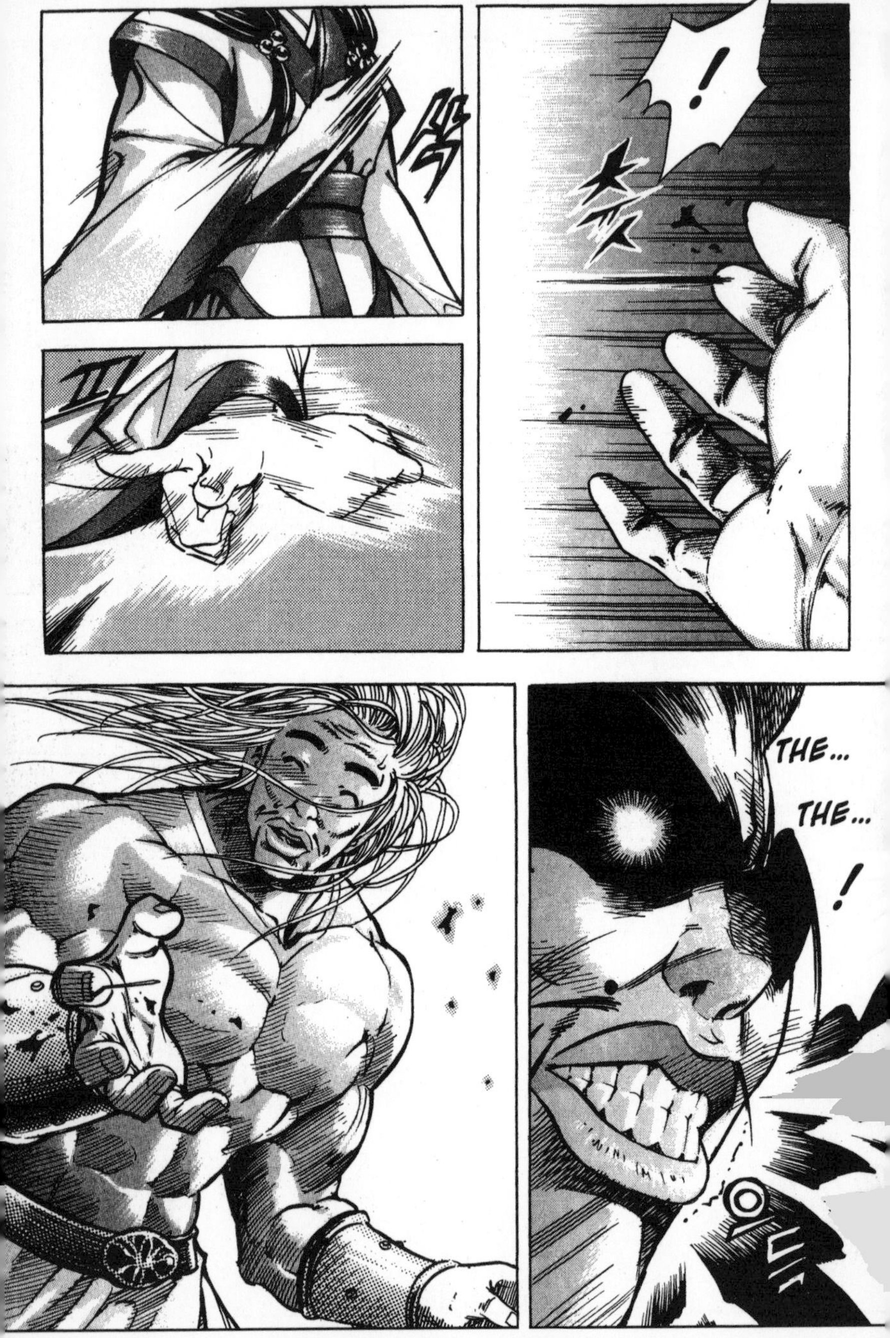
!
THE...
THE...
!

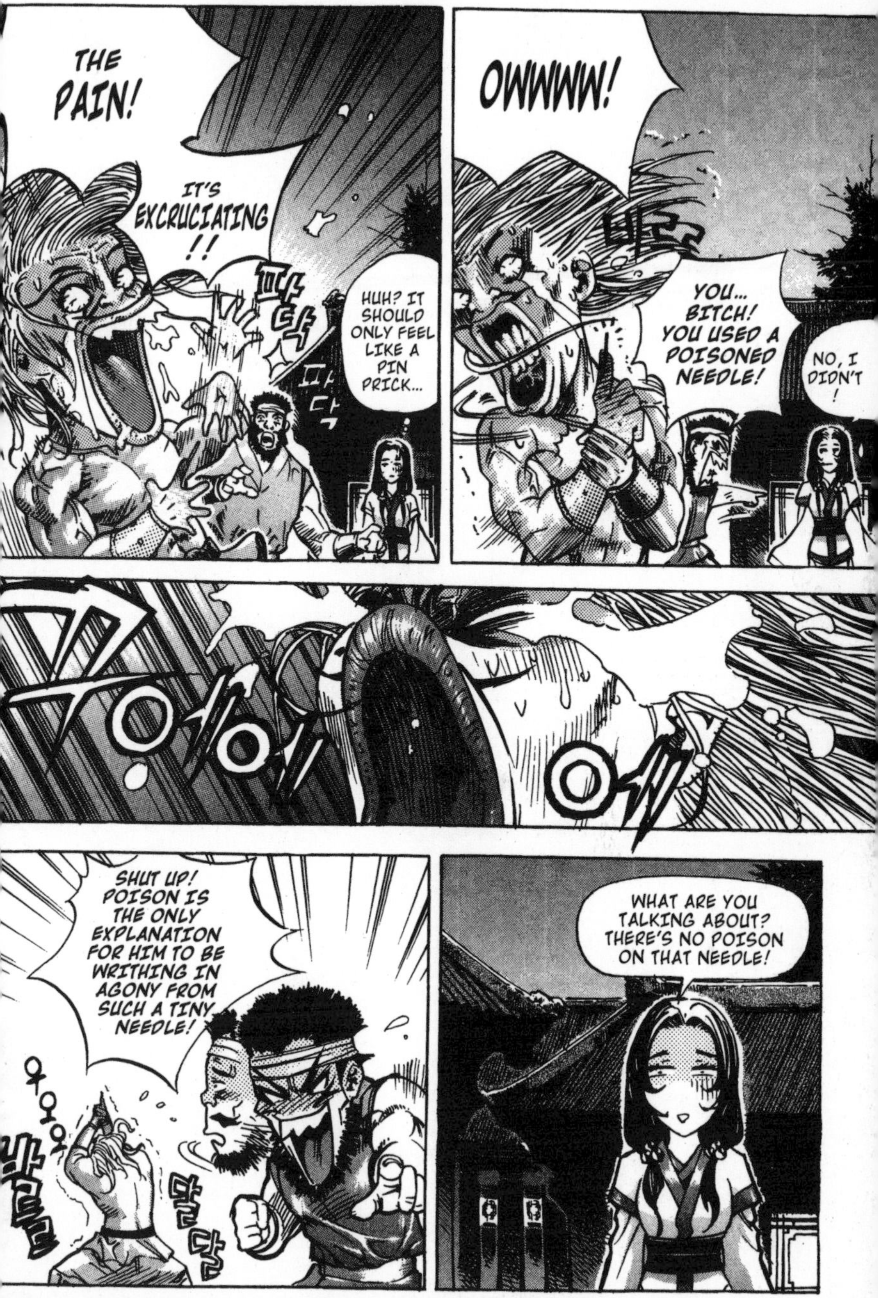
THE PAIN!
IT'S EXCRUCIATING!!
HUH? IT SHOULD ONLY FEEL LIKE A PIN PRICK...
OWWWW!
YOU... BITCH! YOU USED A POISONED NEEDLE!
NO, I DIDN'T!
SHUT UP! POISON IS THE ONLY EXPLANATION FOR HIM TO BE WRITHING IN AGONY FROM SUCH A TINY NEEDLE!
WHAT ARE YOU TALKING ABOUT? THERE'S NO POISON ON THAT NEEDLE!

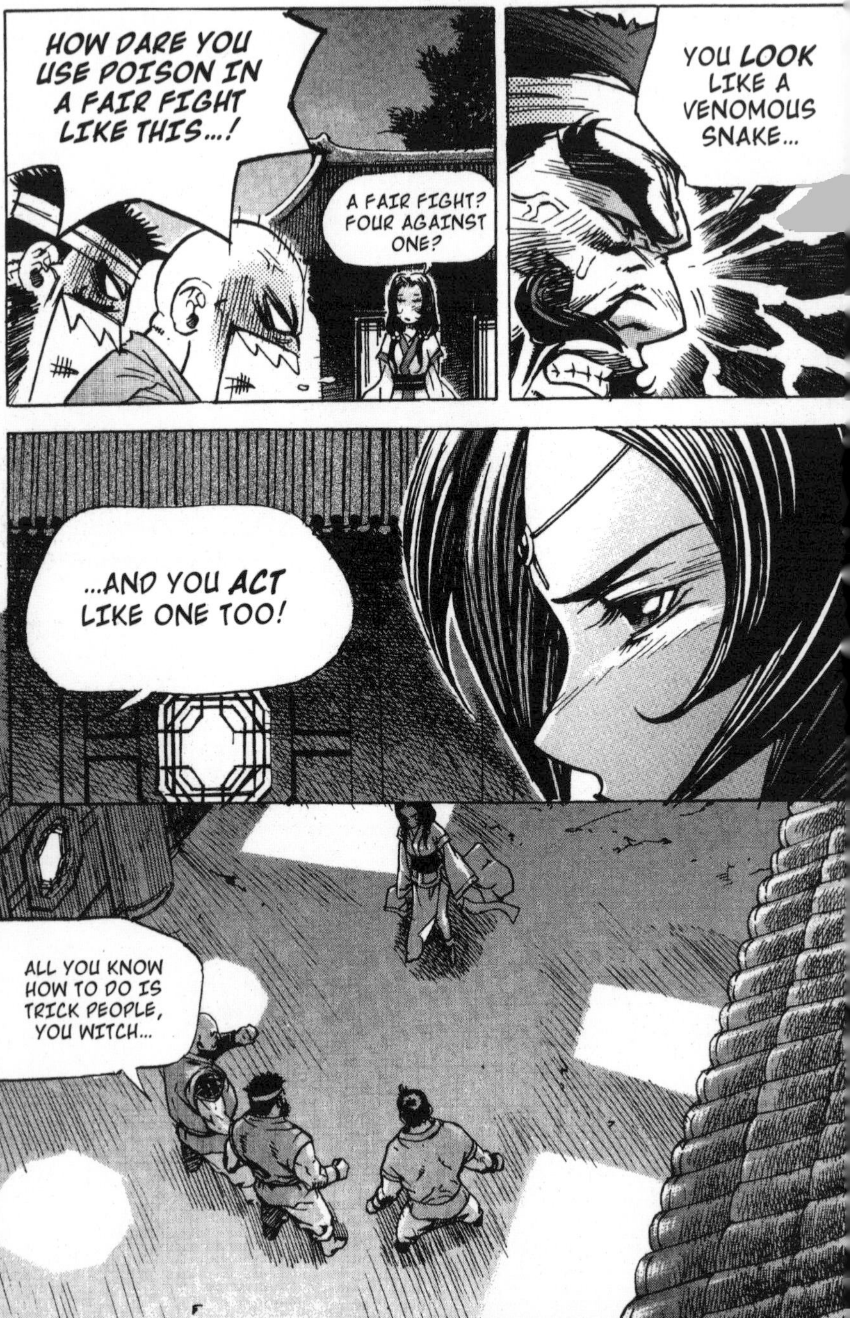
HOW DARE YOU USE POISON IN A FAIR FIGHT LIKE THIS...!
A FAIR FIGHT? FOUR AGAINST ONE?
YOU LOOK LIKE A VENOMOUS SNAKE...
...AND YOU ACT LIKE ONE TOO!
ALL YOU KNOW HOW TO DO IS TRICK PEOPLE, YOU WITCH...

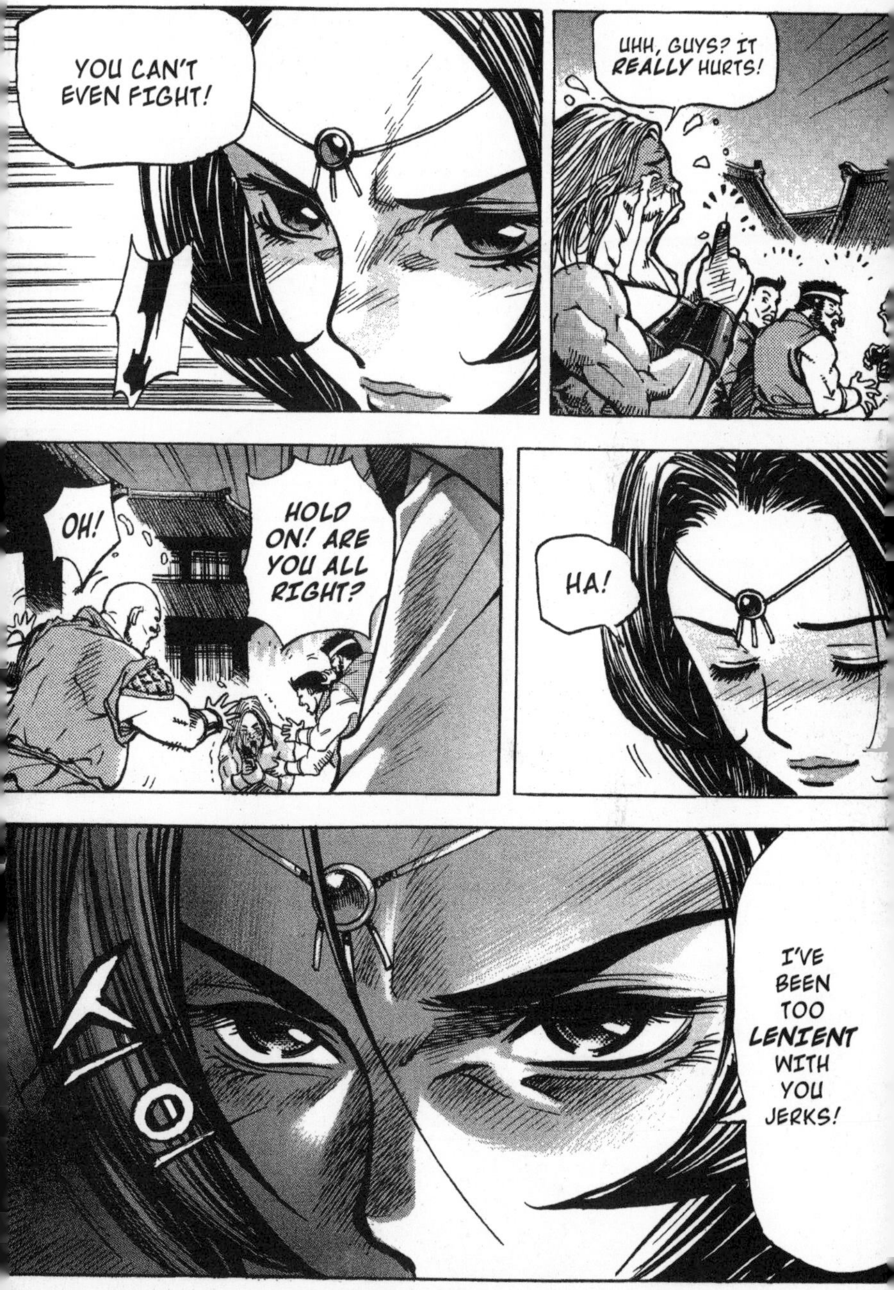
YOU CAN'T EVEN FIGHT!
UHH, GUYS? IT REALLY HURTS!
OH!
HOLD ON! ARE YOU ALL RIGHT?
HA!
I'VE BEEN TOO LENIENT WITH YOU JERKS!

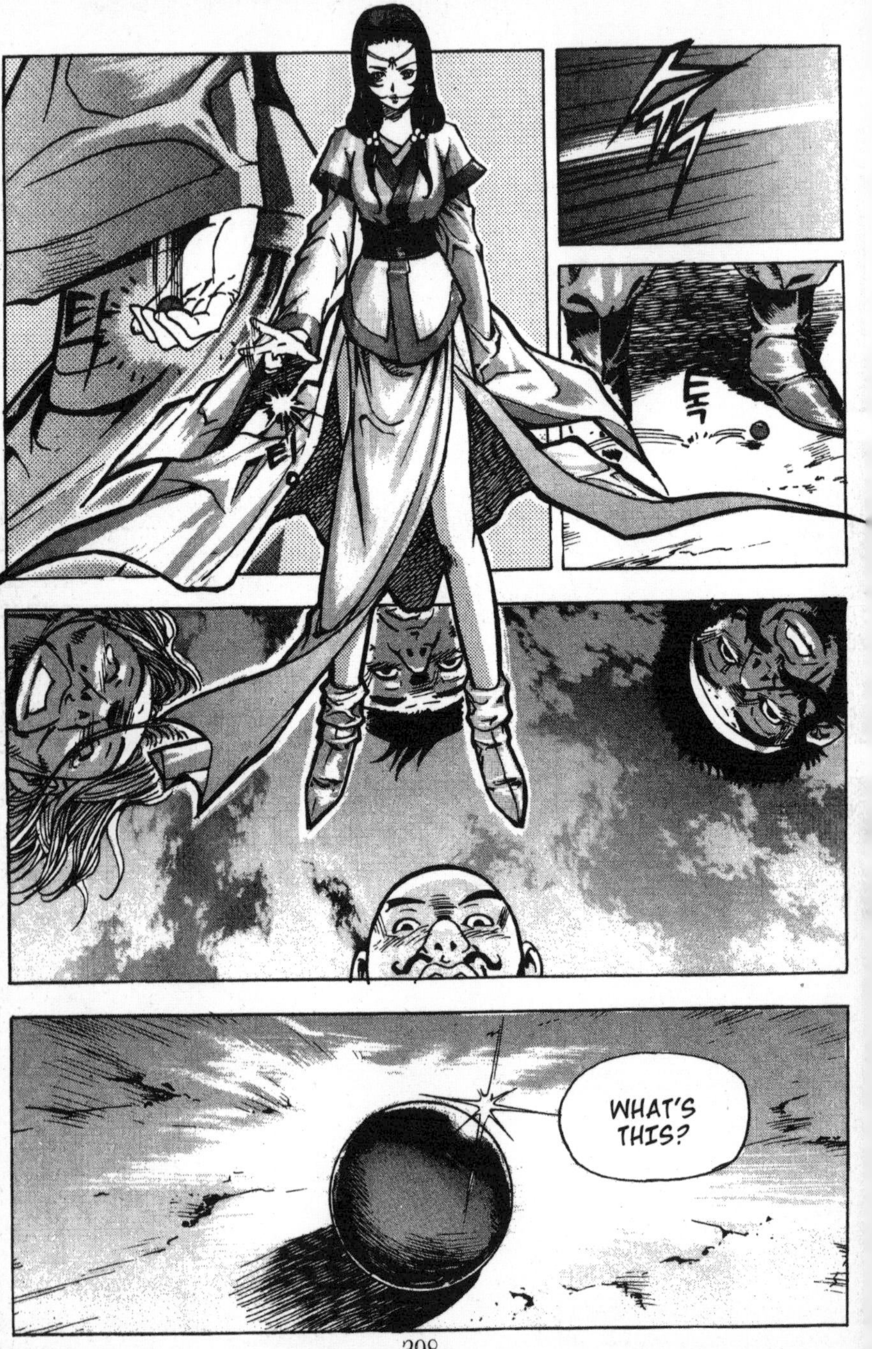
탁
틱
툭
WHAT'S THIS?

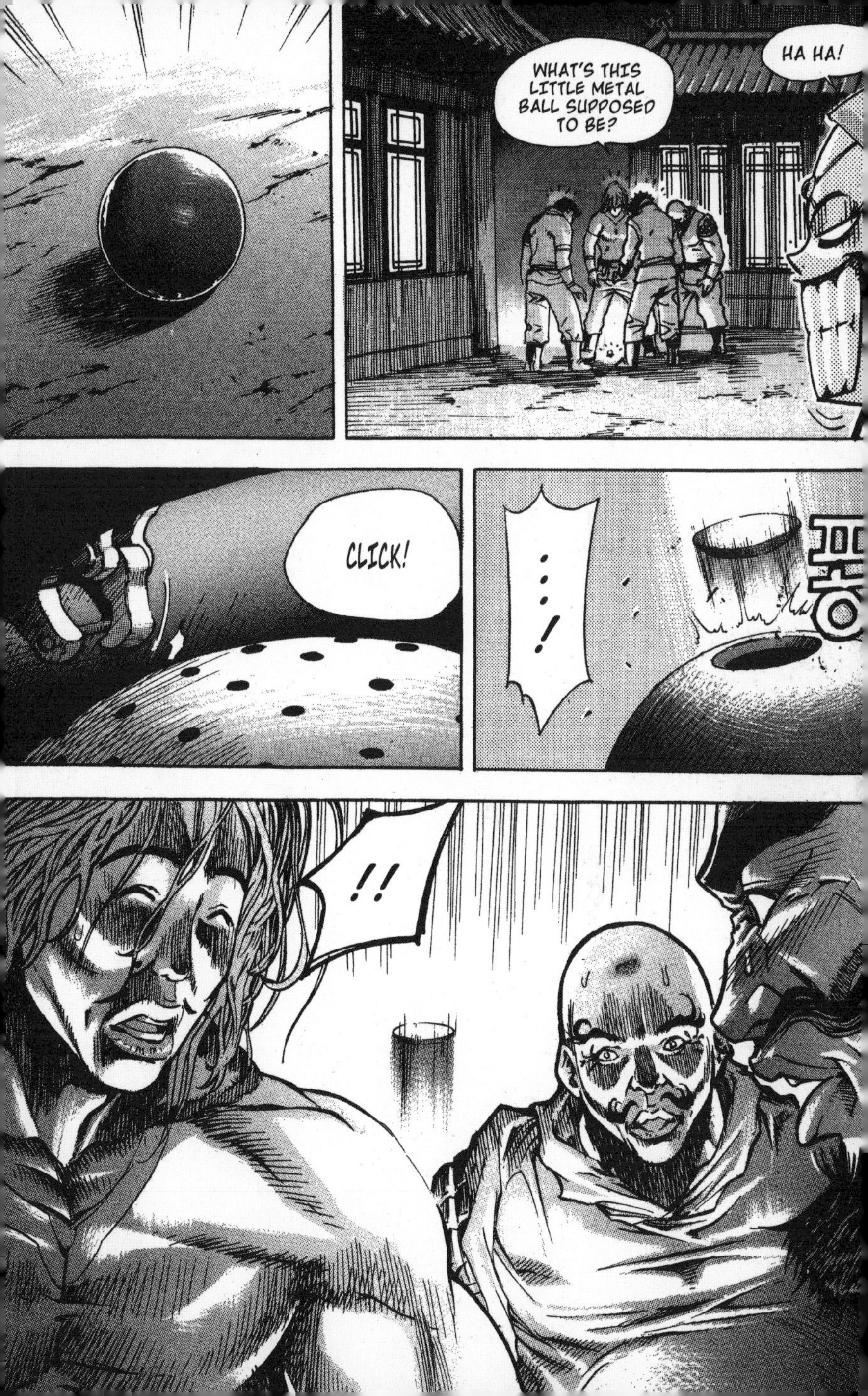
WHAT'S THIS LITTLE METAL BALL SUPPOSED TO BE?
HA HA!
CLICK!
...!
!!

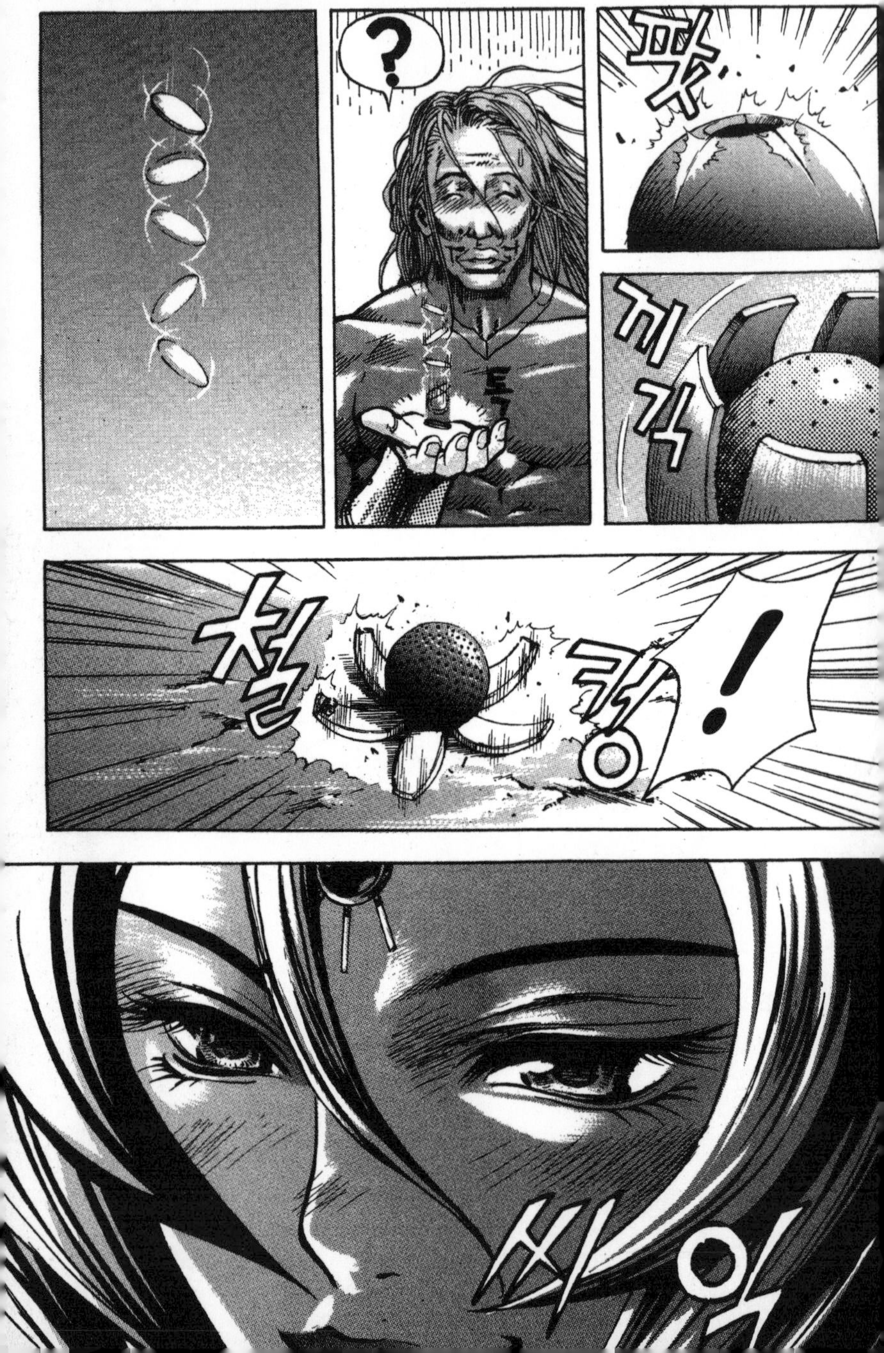
?
톡
팟
끼각
철컹
!
씨익

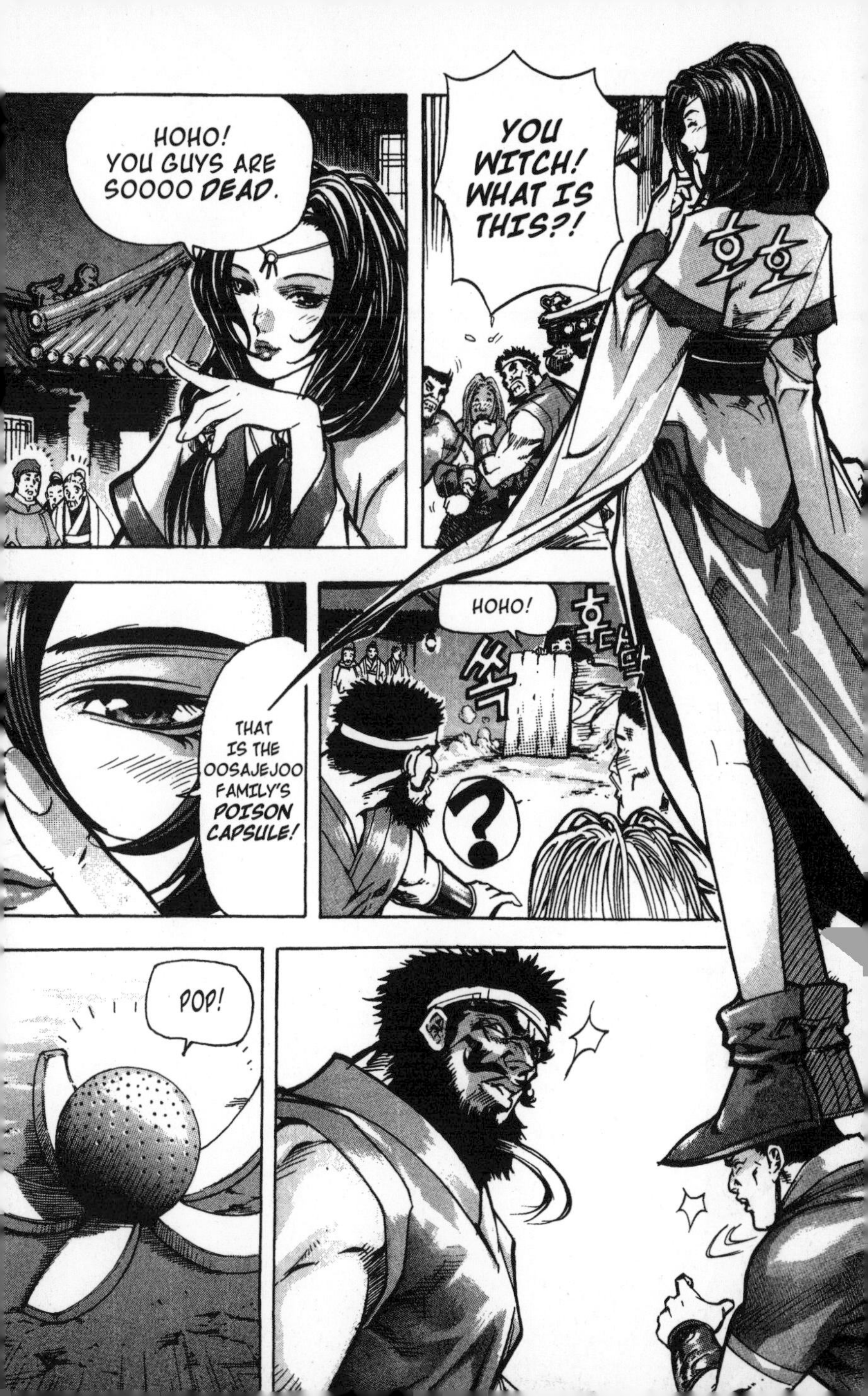
HOHO! YOU GUYS ARE SOOOO DEAD.
YOU WITCH! WHAT IS THIS?!
THAT IS THE OOSAJEJOO FAMILY'S POISON CAPSULE!
HOHO!
?
POP!

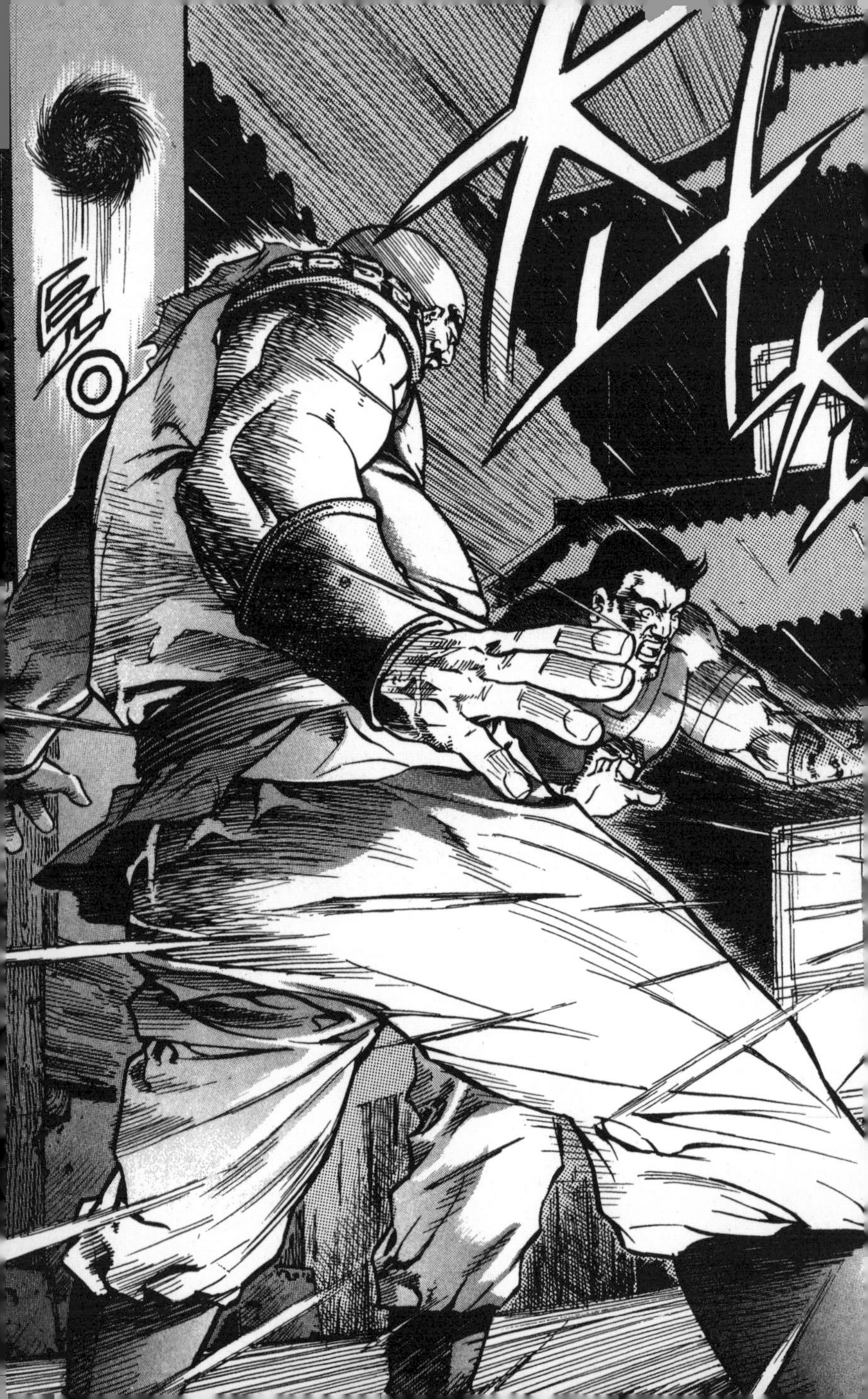

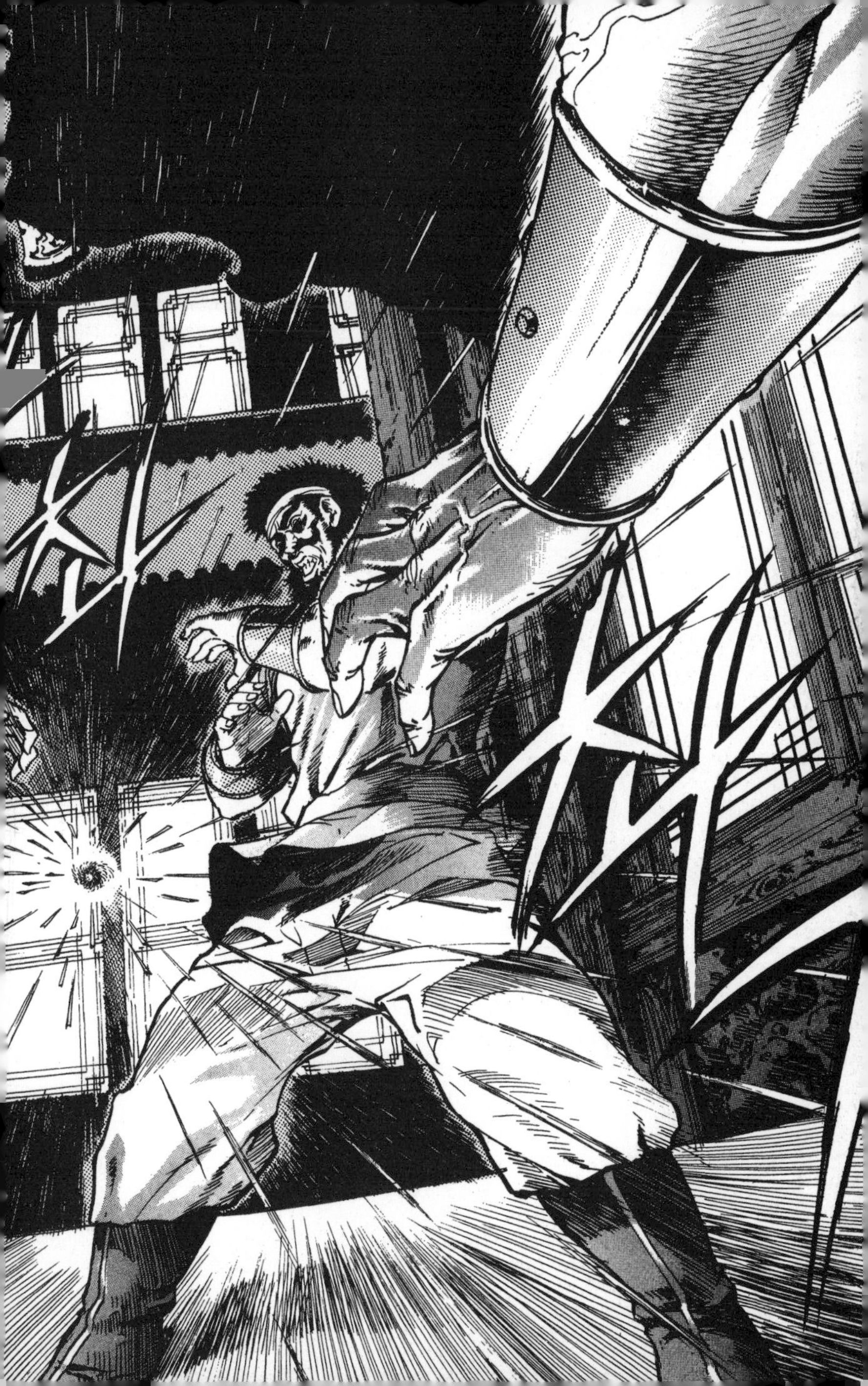

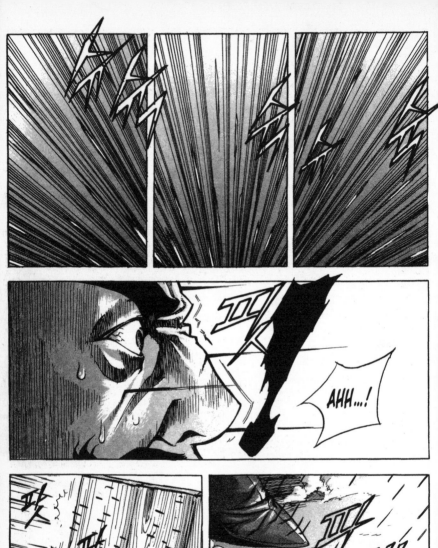

AHH...!

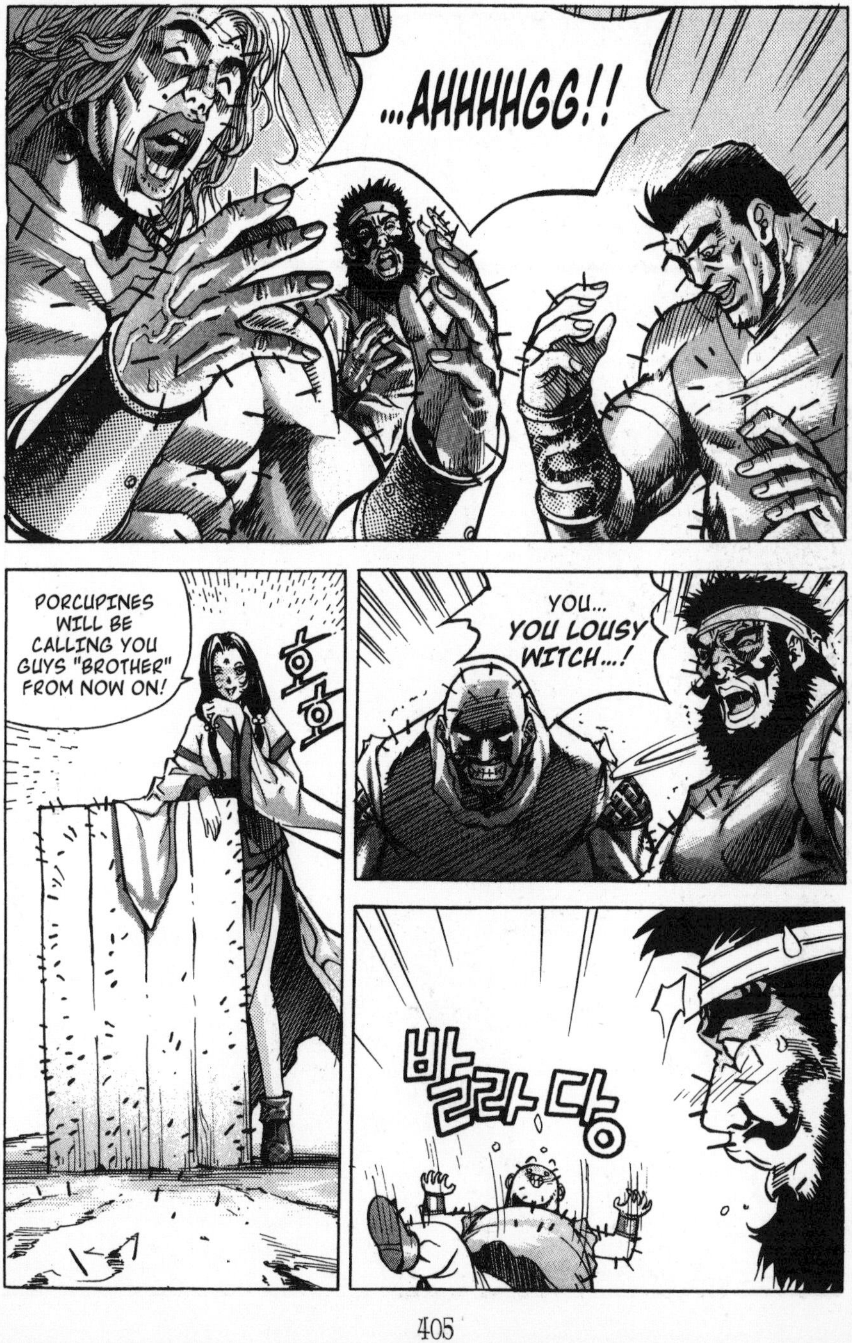
...AHHHHGG!!
PORCUPINES WILL BE CALLING YOU GUYS "BROTHER" FROM NOW ON!
호호
YOU... YOU LOUSY WITCH...!
발라당

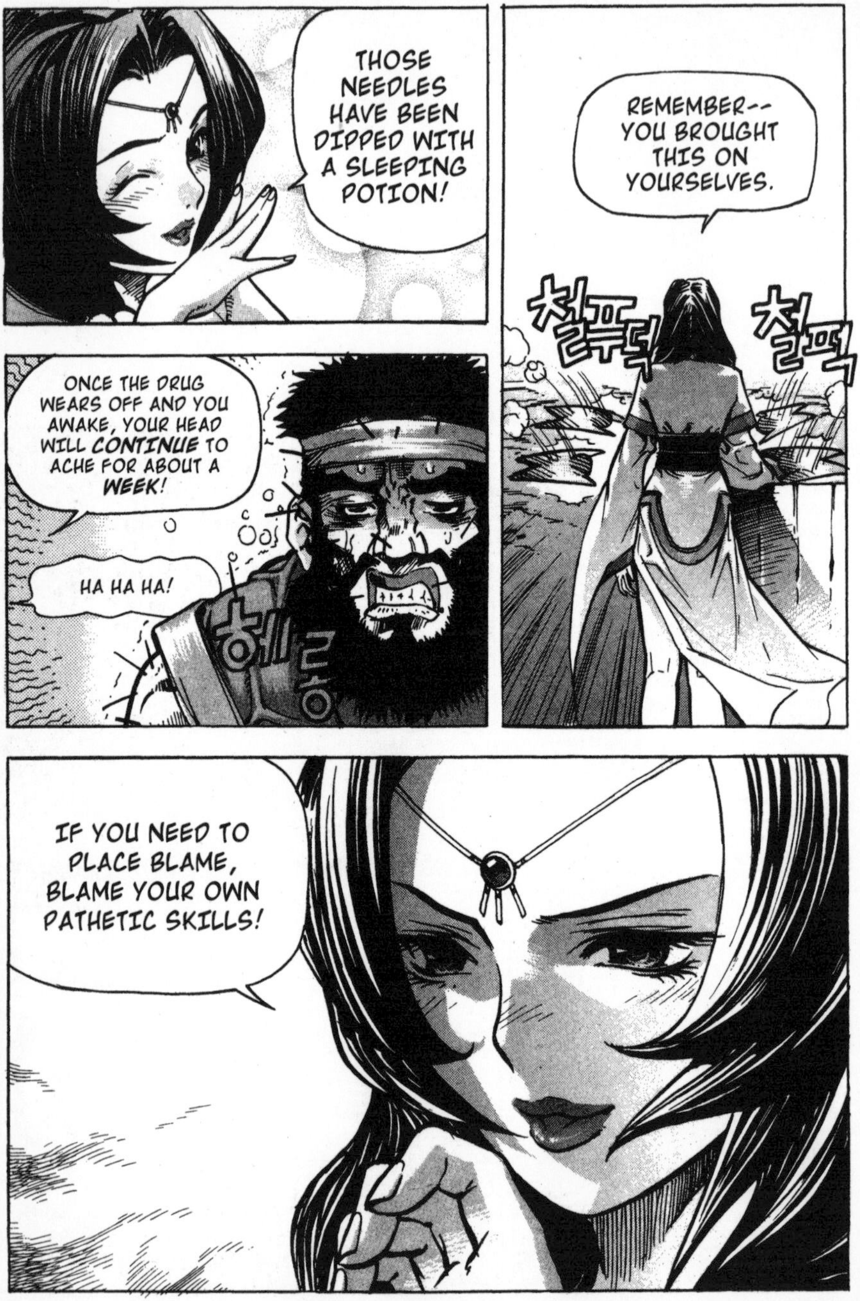
THOSE NEEDLES HAVE BEEN DIPPED WITH A SLEEPING POTION!
ONCE THE DRUG WEARS OFF AND YOU AWAKE, YOUR HEAD WILL **CONTINUE** TO ACHE FOR ABOUT A **WEEK**!
HA HA HA!
REMEMBER-- YOU BROUGHT THIS ON YOURSELVES.
철푸덕
철퍽
IF YOU NEED TO PLACE BLAME, BLAME YOUR OWN PATHETIC SKILLS!

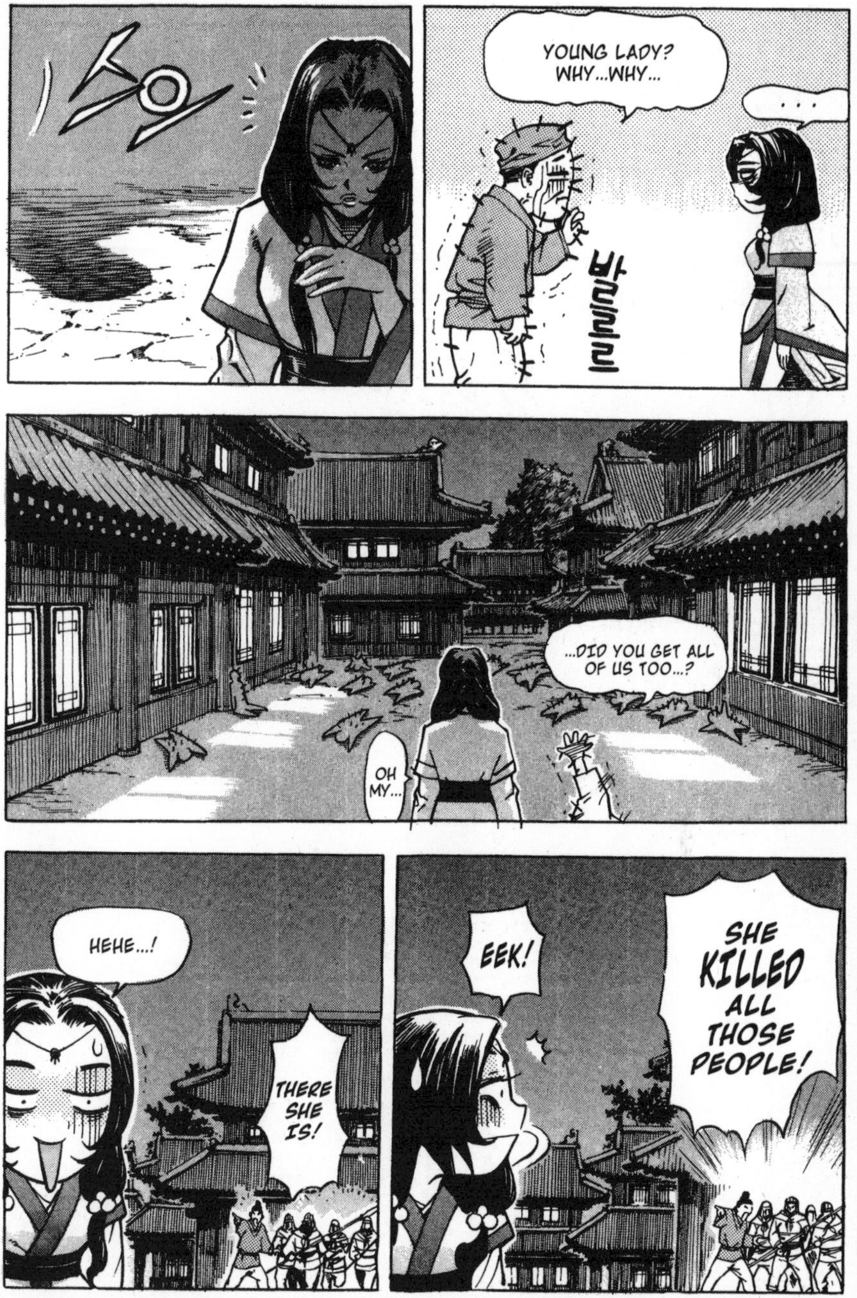
YOUNG LADY? WHY...WHY...
. . .
...DID YOU GET ALL OF US TOO...?
OH MY...
HEHE...!
THERE SHE IS!
EEK!
SHE KILLED ALL THOSE PEOPLE!

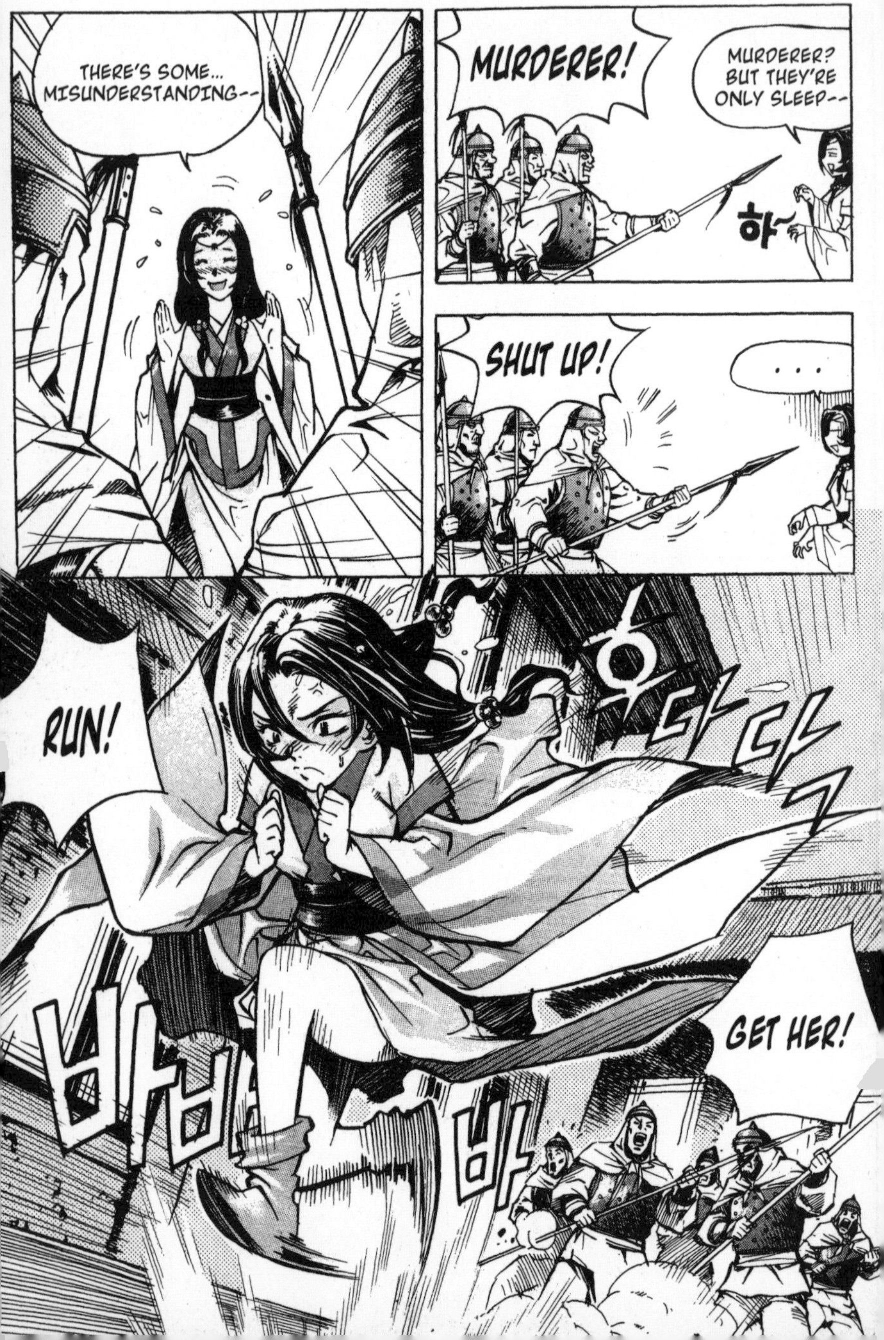
THERE'S SOME...
MISUNDERSTANDING--
MURDERER!
MURDERER? BUT THEY'RE ONLY SLEEP--
하~
SHUT UP!
. . .
RUN!
후다닥
GET HER!
바바바

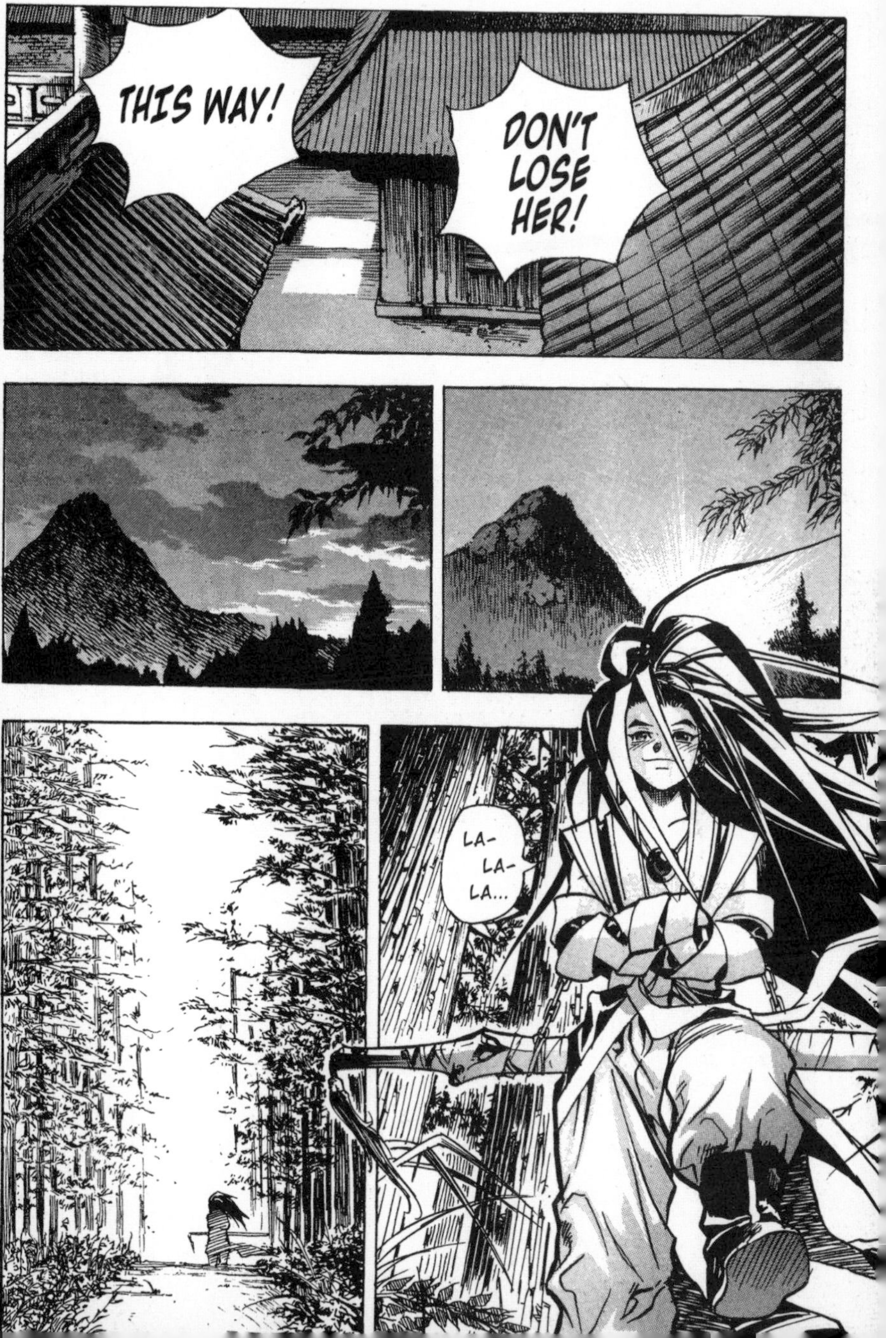
THIS WAY!
DON'T LOSE HER!
LA- LA- LA...

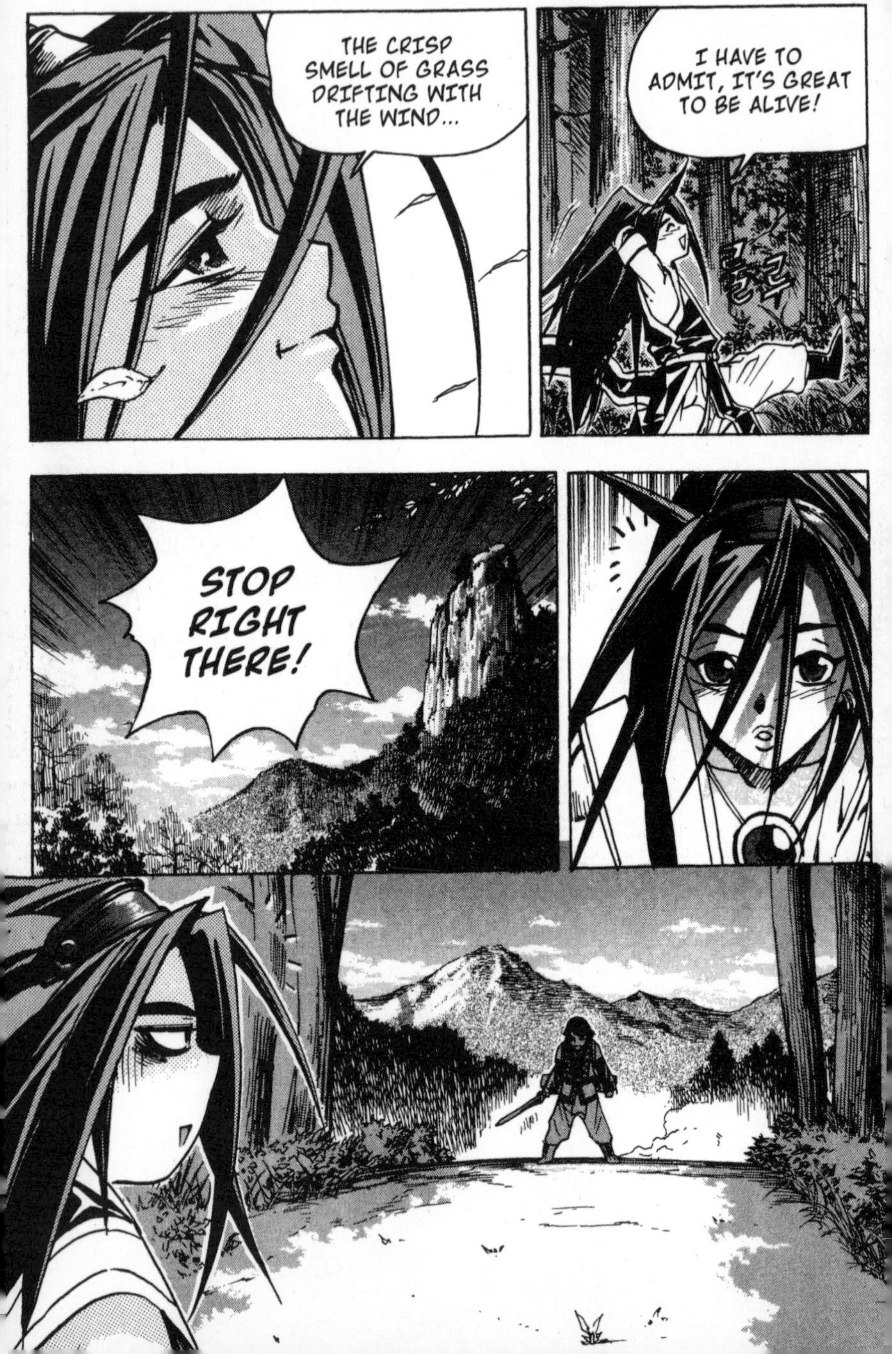
THE CRISP SMELL OF GRASS DRIFTING WITH THE WIND...
I HAVE TO ADMIT, IT'S GREAT TO BE ALIVE!
STOP RIGHT THERE!

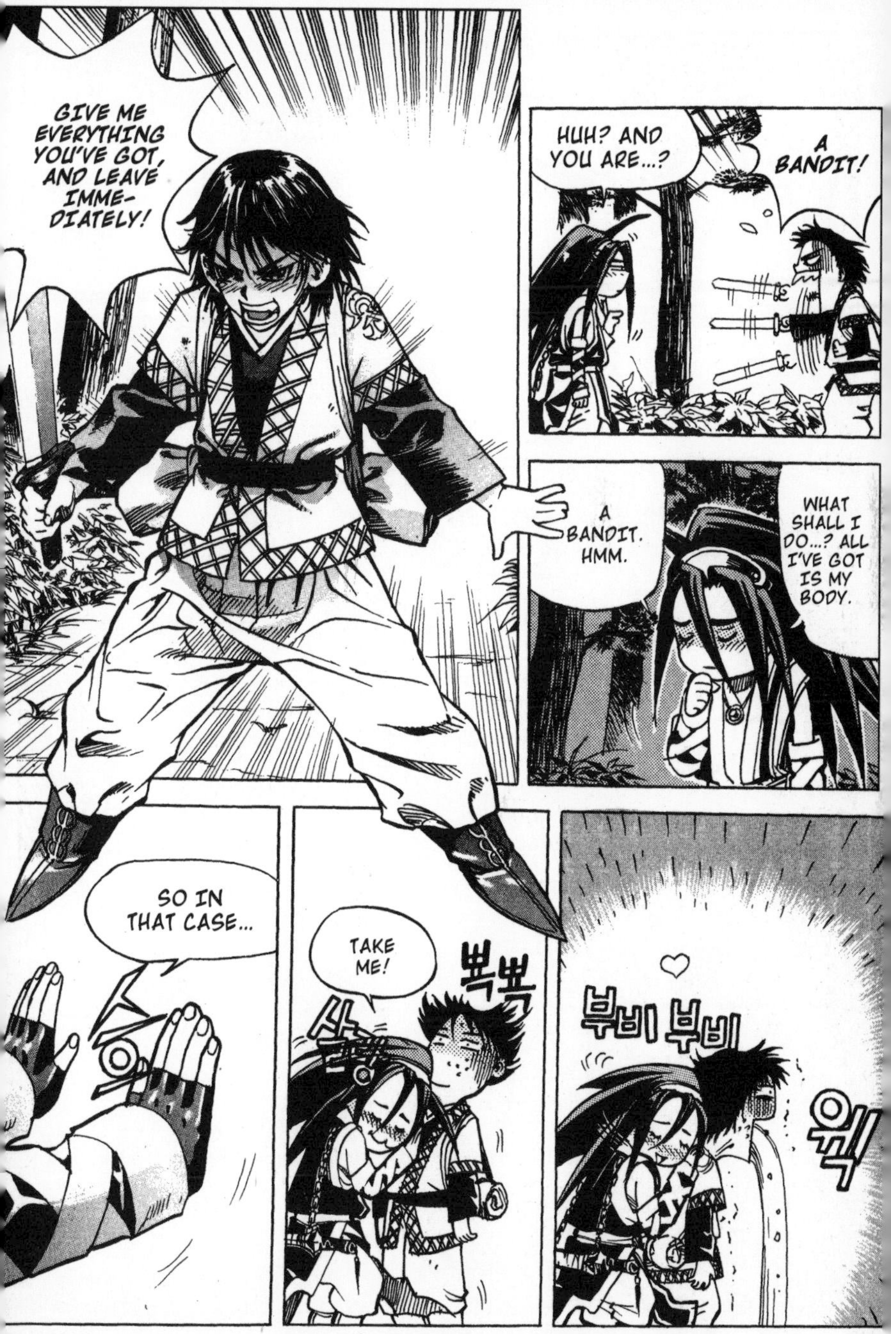
GIVE ME EVERYTHING YOU'VE GOT, AND LEAVE IMME-DIATELY!
HUH? AND YOU ARE...?
A BANDIT!
A BANDIT. HMM.
WHAT SHALL I DO...? ALL I'VE GOT IS MY BODY.
SO IN THAT CASE...
TAKE ME!
부비 부비
웩

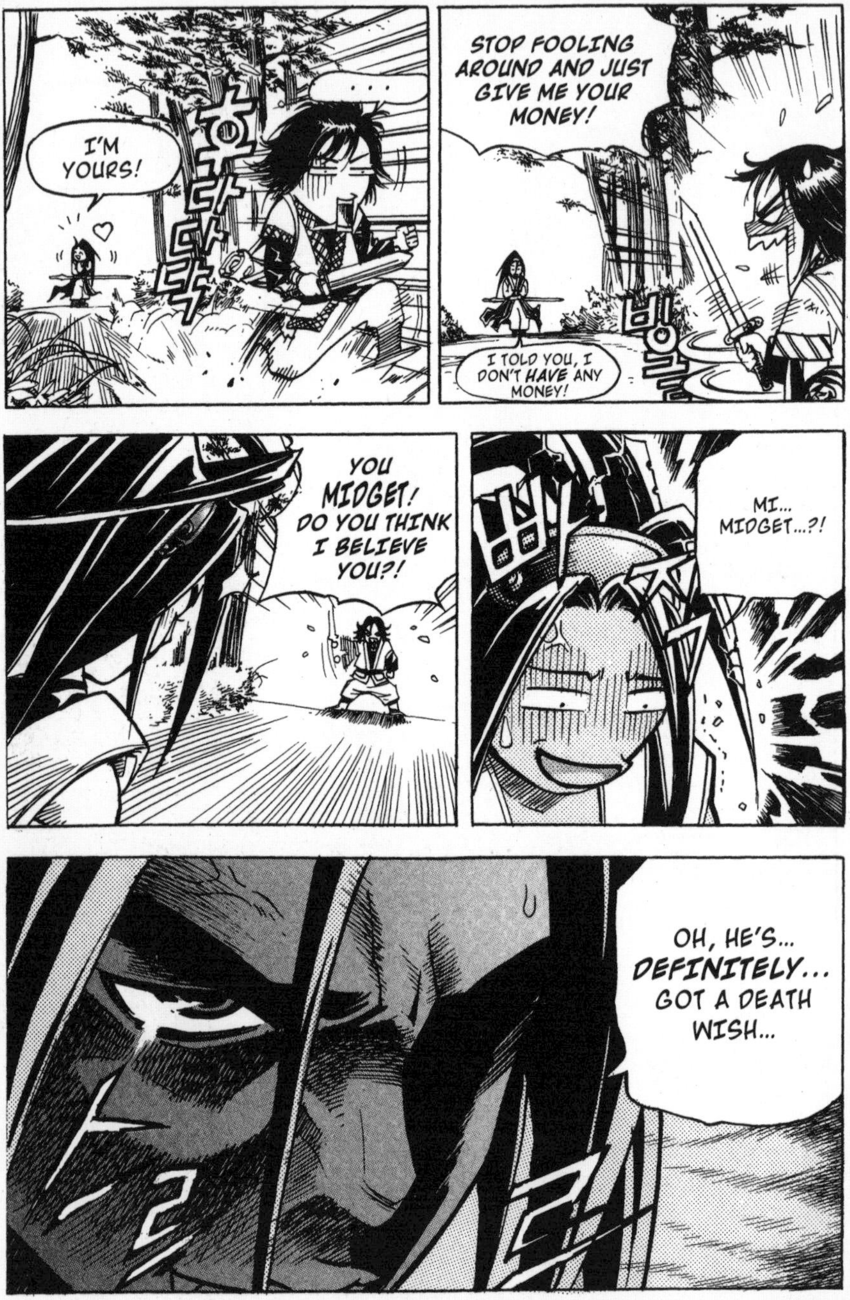

I'M YOURS!
. . .
STOP FOOLING AROUND AND JUST GIVE ME YOUR MONEY!
I TOLD YOU, I DON'T HAVE ANY MONEY!
YOU MIDGET! DO YOU THINK I BELIEVE YOU?!
MI... MIDGET...?!
OH, HE'S... DEFINITELY... GOT A DEATH WISH...

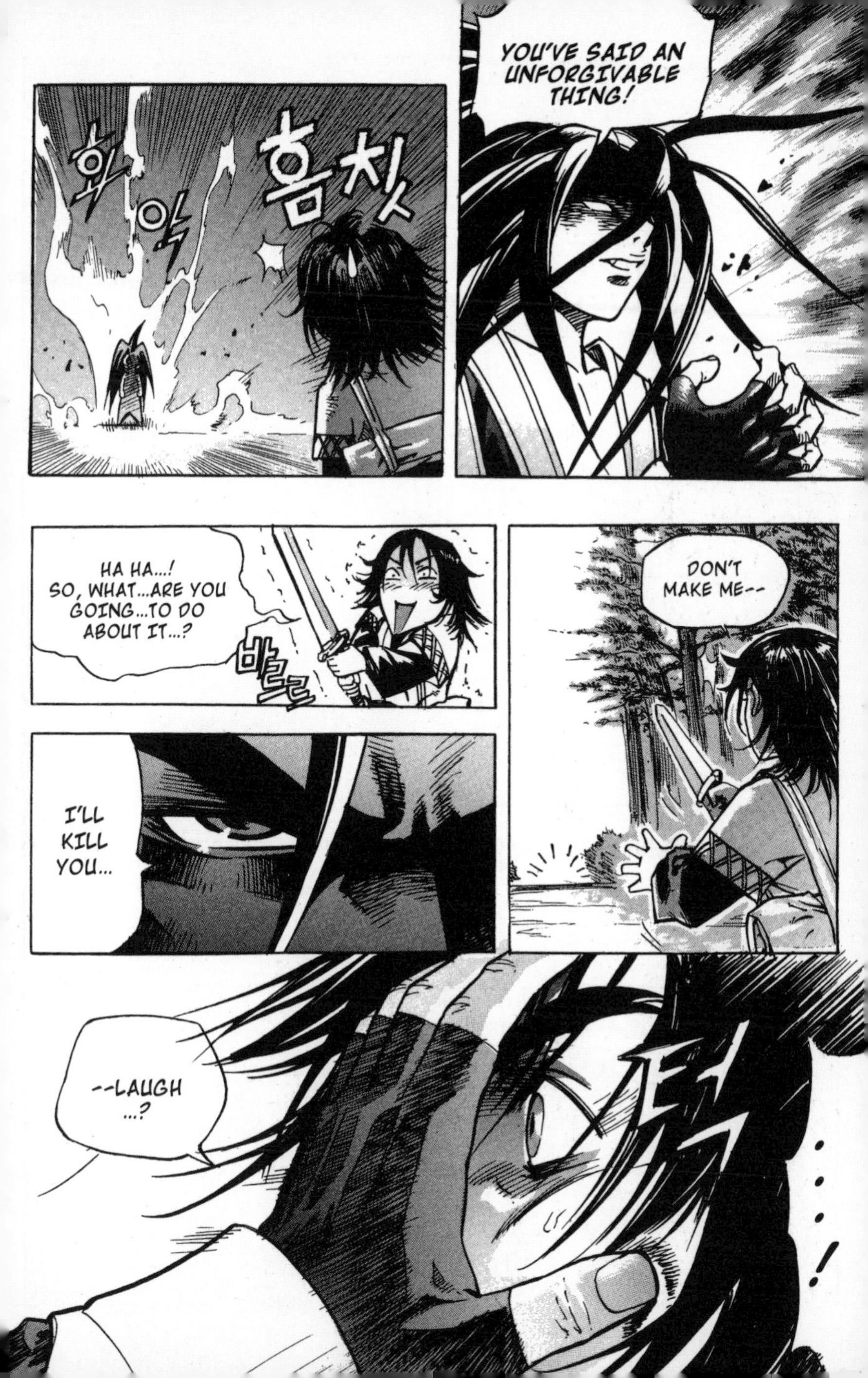
화악
흠칫
YOU'VE SAID AN UNFORGIVABLE THING!
HA HA...! SO, WHAT...ARE YOU GOING...TO DO ABOUT IT...?
바르르
I'LL KILL YOU...
DON'T MAKE ME--
--LAUGH ...?
....!

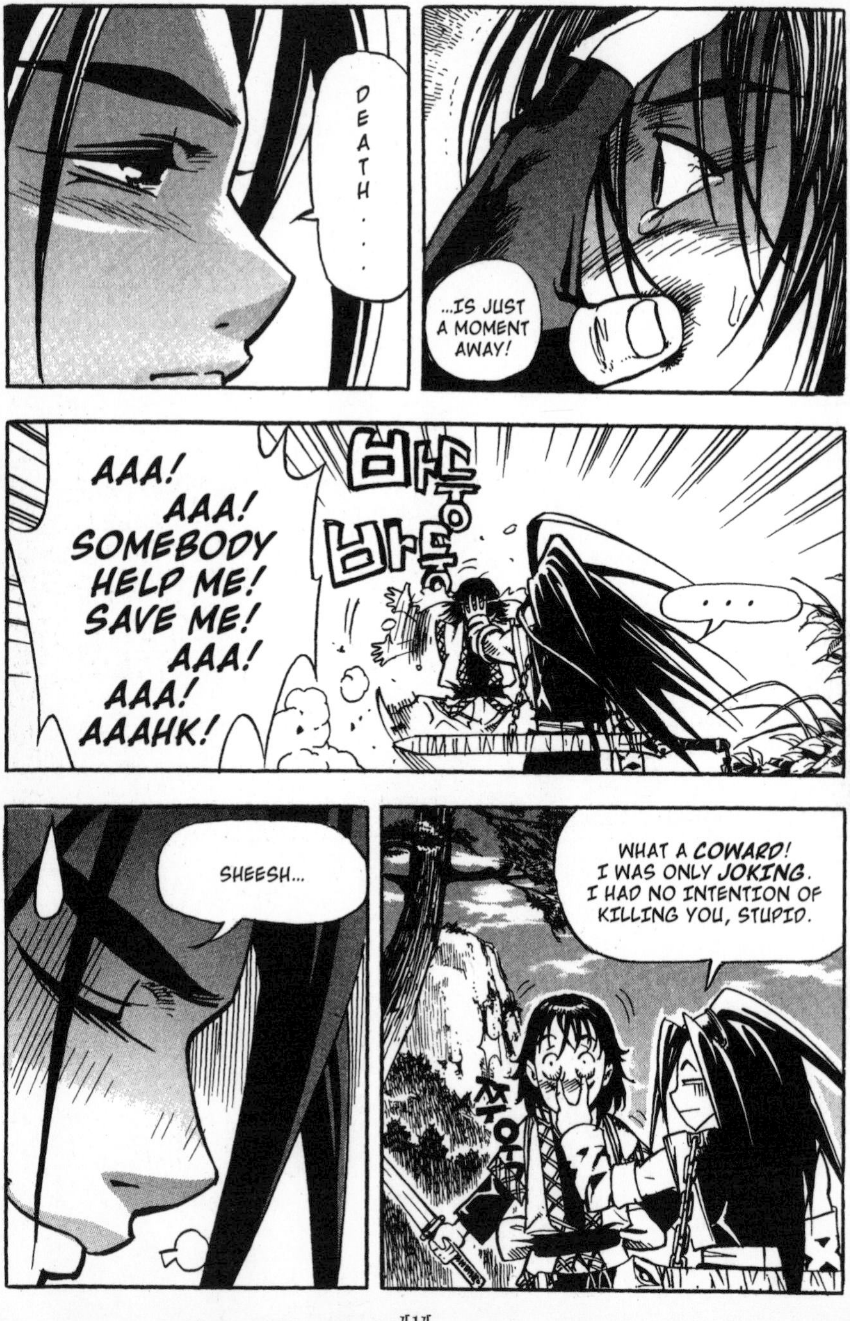
DEATH...
...IS JUST A MOMENT AWAY!
AAA! AAA! SOMEBODY HELP ME! SAVE ME! AAA! AAA! AAAHK!
...
SHEESH...
WHAT A COWARD! I WAS ONLY JOKING. I HAD NO INTENTION OF KILLING YOU, STUPID.

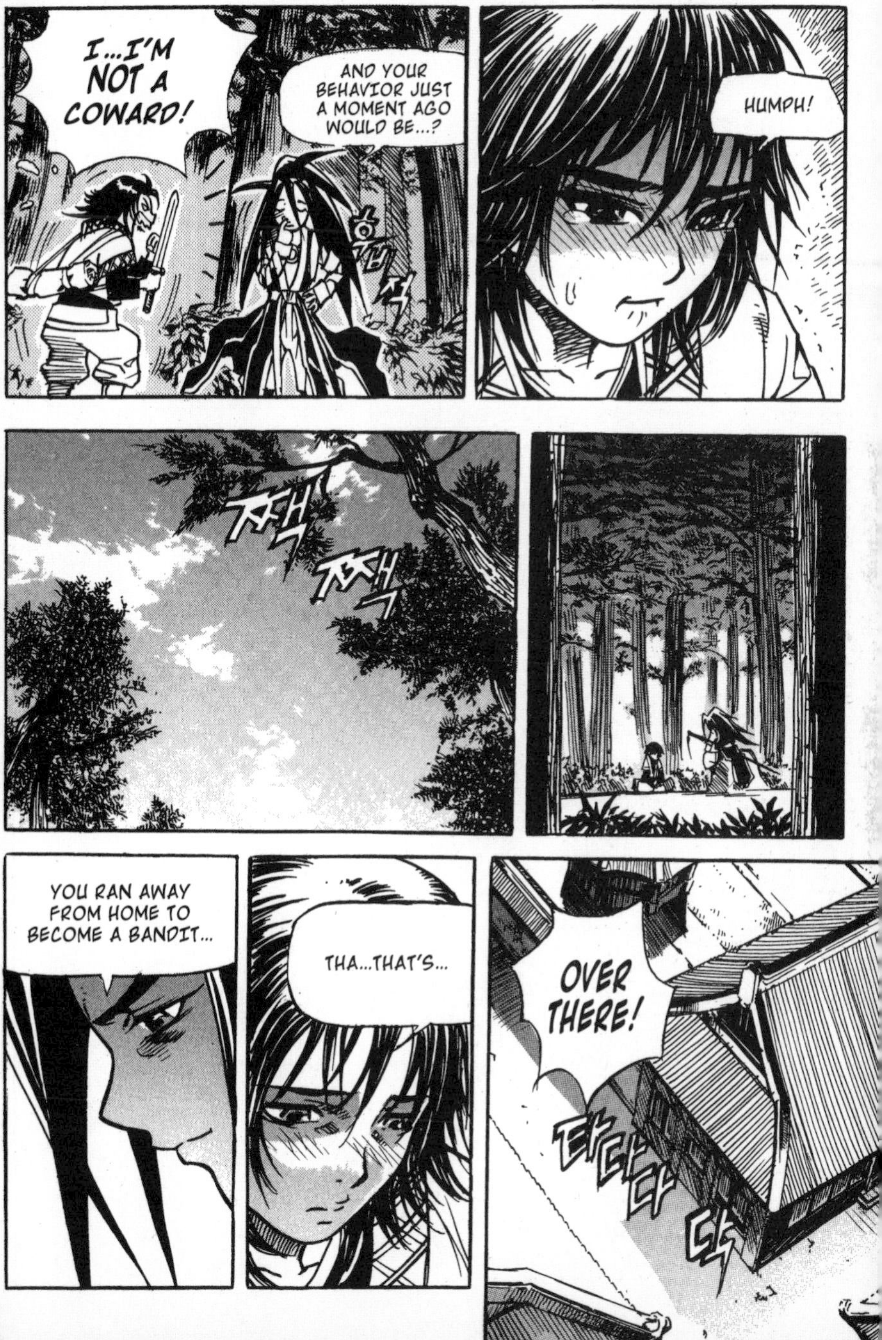
I...I'M NOT A COWARD!
AND YOUR BEHAVIOR JUST A MOMENT AGO WOULD BE...?
HUMPH!
YOU RAN AWAY FROM HOME TO BECOME A BANDIT...
THA...THAT'S...
OVER THERE!

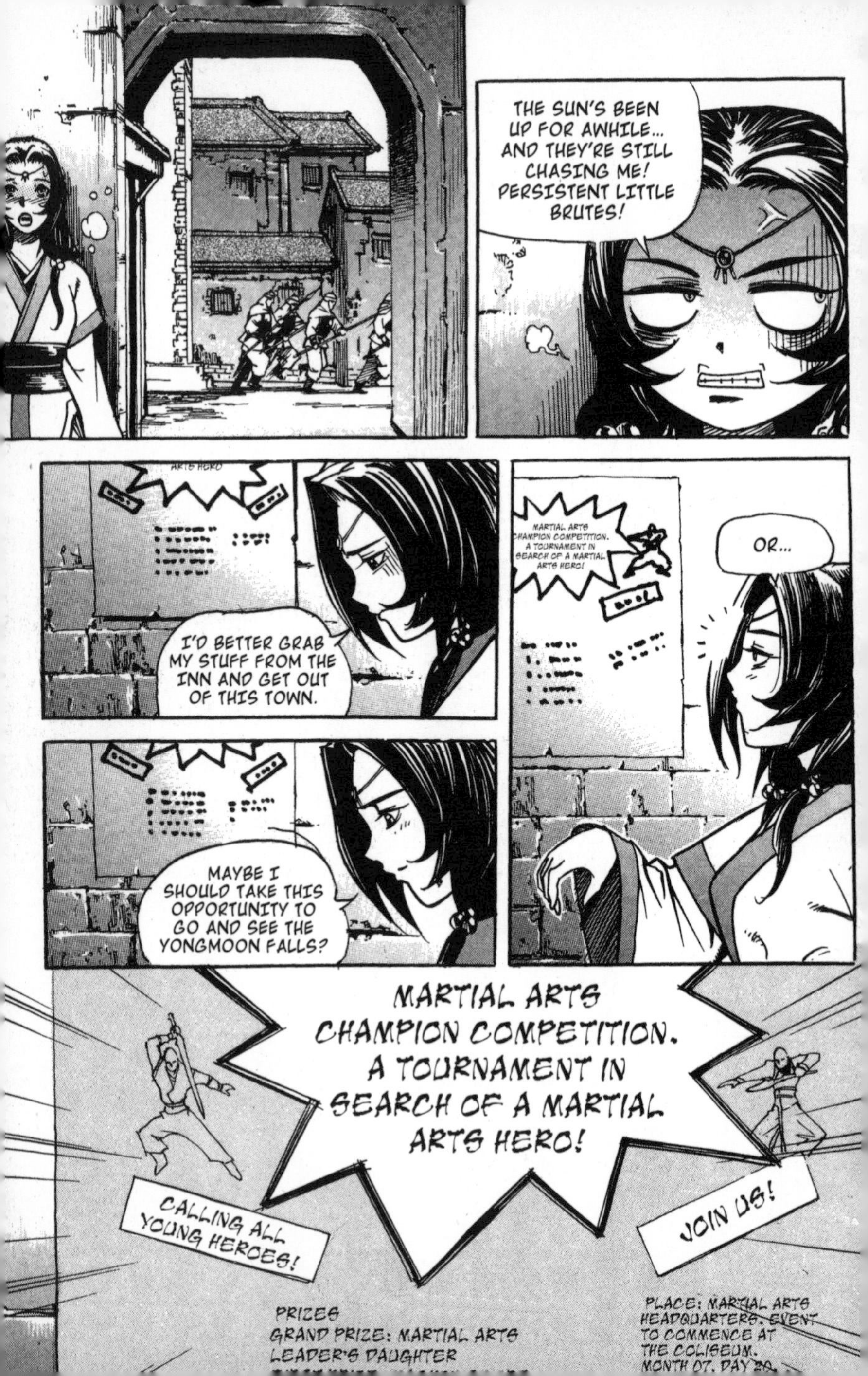
THE SUN'S BEEN UP FOR AWHILE... AND THEY'RE STILL CHASING ME! PERSISTENT LITTLE BRUTES!
I'D BETTER GRAB MY STUFF FROM THE INN AND GET OUT OF THIS TOWN.
MARTIAL ARTS CHAMPION COMPETITION. A TOURNAMENT IN SEARCH OF A MARTIAL ARTS HERO!
OR...
MAYBE I SHOULD TAKE THIS OPPORTUNITY TO GO AND SEE THE YONGMOON FALLS?
MARTIAL ARTS CHAMPION COMPETITION. A TOURNAMENT IN SEARCH OF A MARTIAL ARTS HERO!
CALLING ALL YOUNG HEROES!
JOIN US!
PRIZES
GRAND PRIZE: MARTIAL ARTS LEADER'S DAUGHTER
PLACE: MARTIAL ARTS HEADQUARTERS. EVENT TO COMMENCE AT THE COLISEUM. MONTH 07, DAY 29.

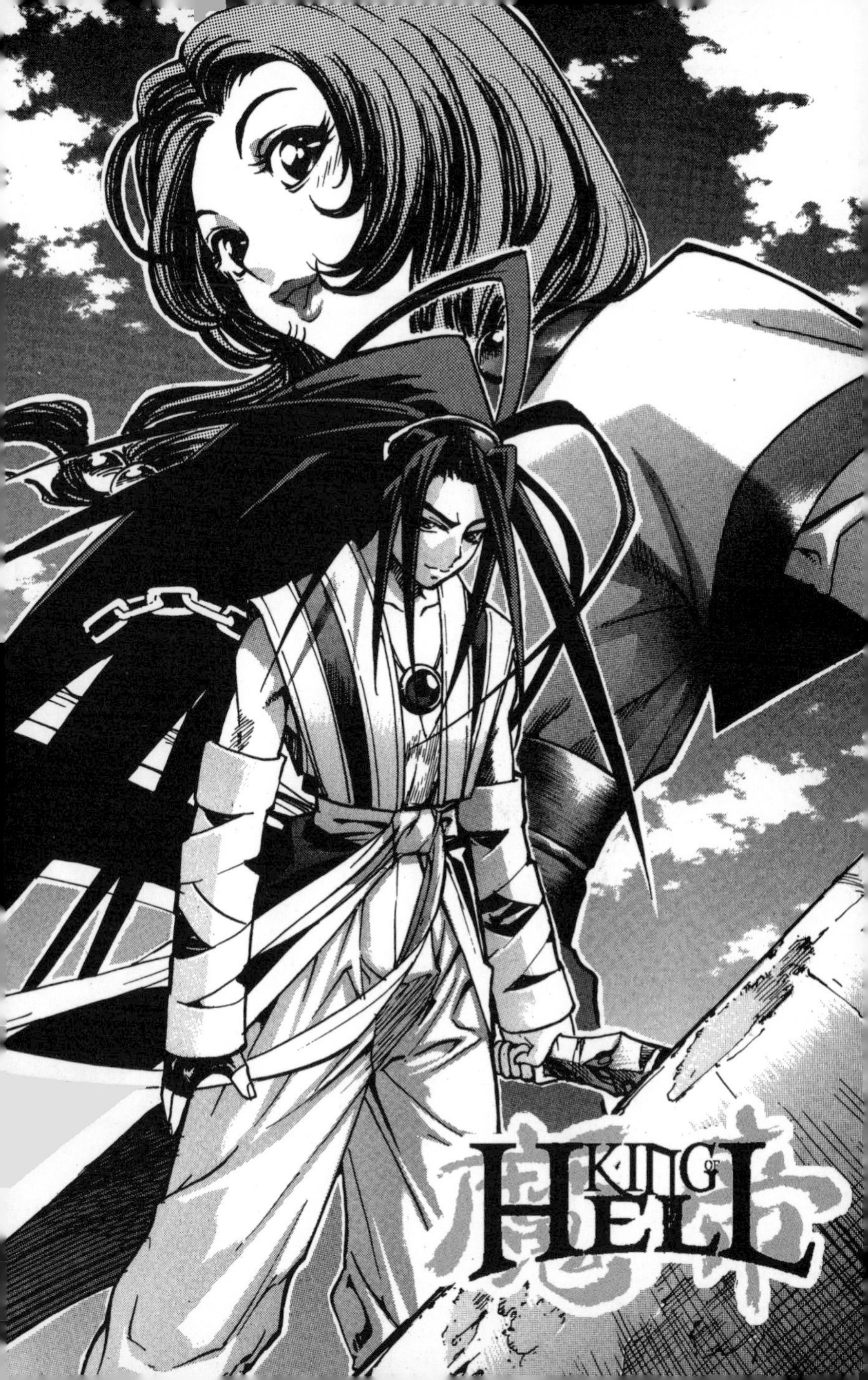
KING OF HELL

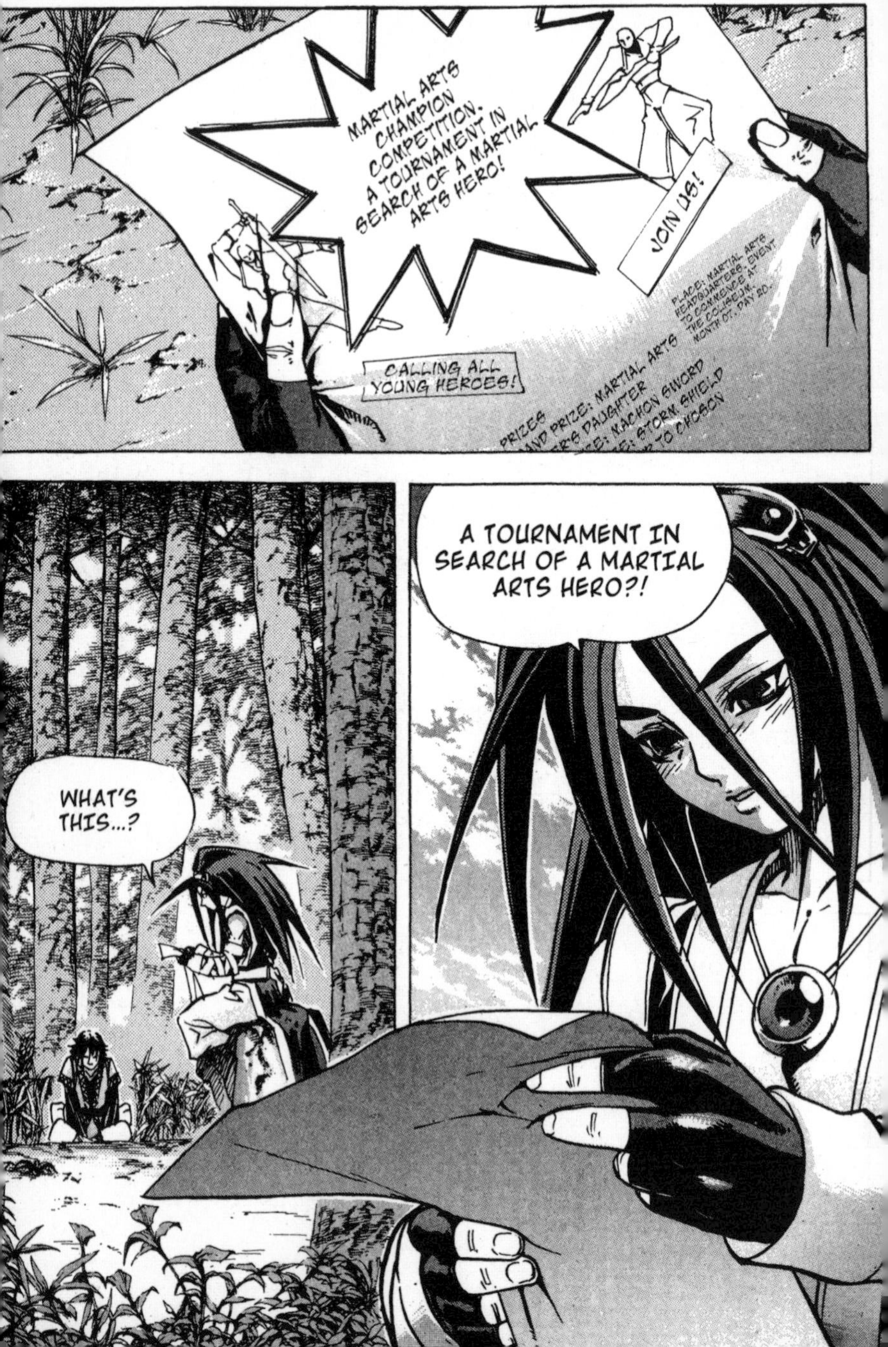
MARTIAL ARTS CHAMPION COMPETITION. A TOURNAMENT IN SEARCH OF A MARTIAL ARTS HERO!
JOIN US!
PLACE: MARTIAL ARTS HEADQUARTERS. EVENT TO COMMENCE AT THE COLISEUM. MONTH 07, DAY 20.
CALLING ALL YOUNG HEROES!
PRIZES
AND PRIZE: MARTIAL ARTS
ER'S DAUGHTER
MACHON SWORD
STORM SHIELD
TO CHOSON
WHAT'S THIS...?
A TOURNAMENT IN SEARCH OF A MARTIAL ARTS HERO?!

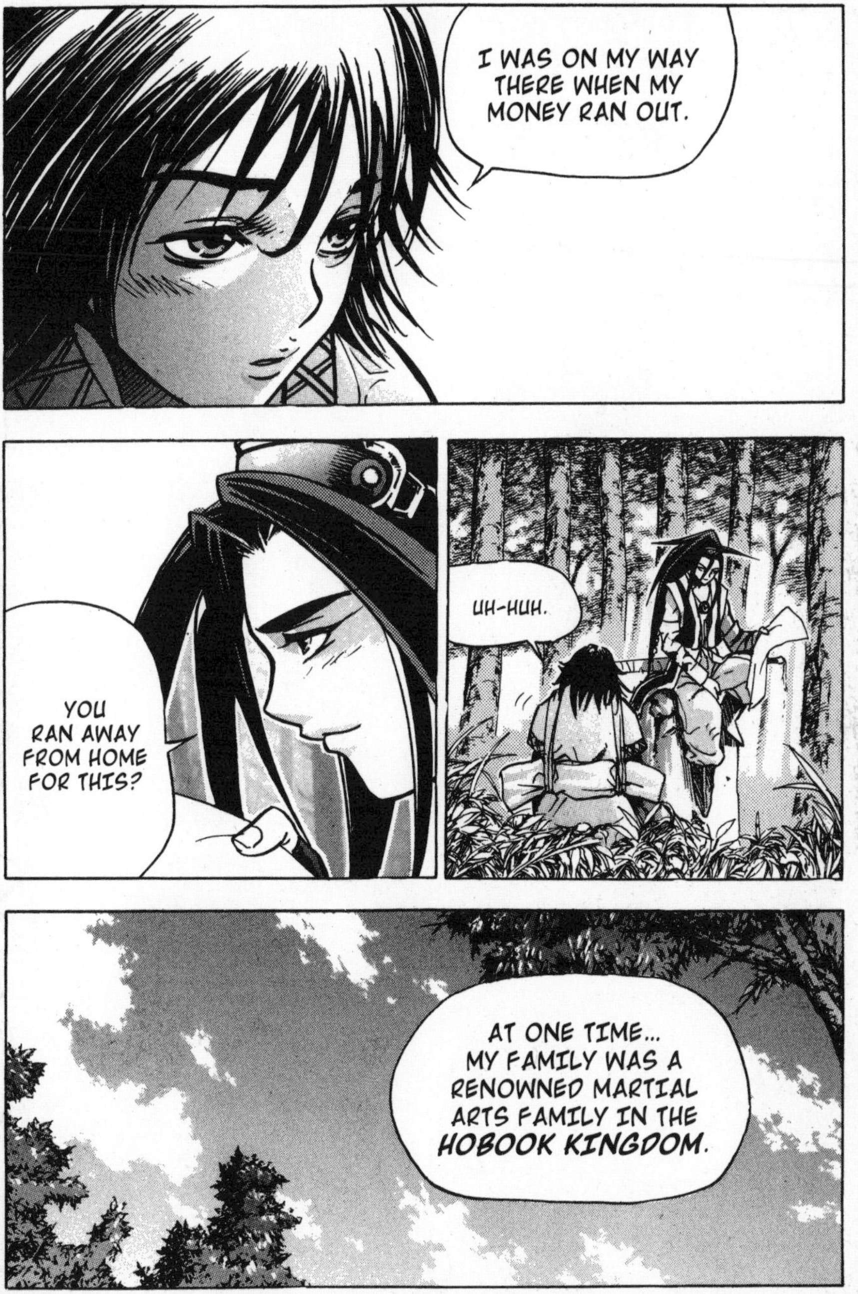
I WAS ON MY WAY THERE WHEN MY MONEY RAN OUT.
YOU RAN AWAY FROM HOME FOR THIS?
UH-HUH.
AT ONE TIME... MY FAMILY WAS A RENOWNED MARTIAL ARTS FAMILY IN THE *HOBOOK KINGDOM*.

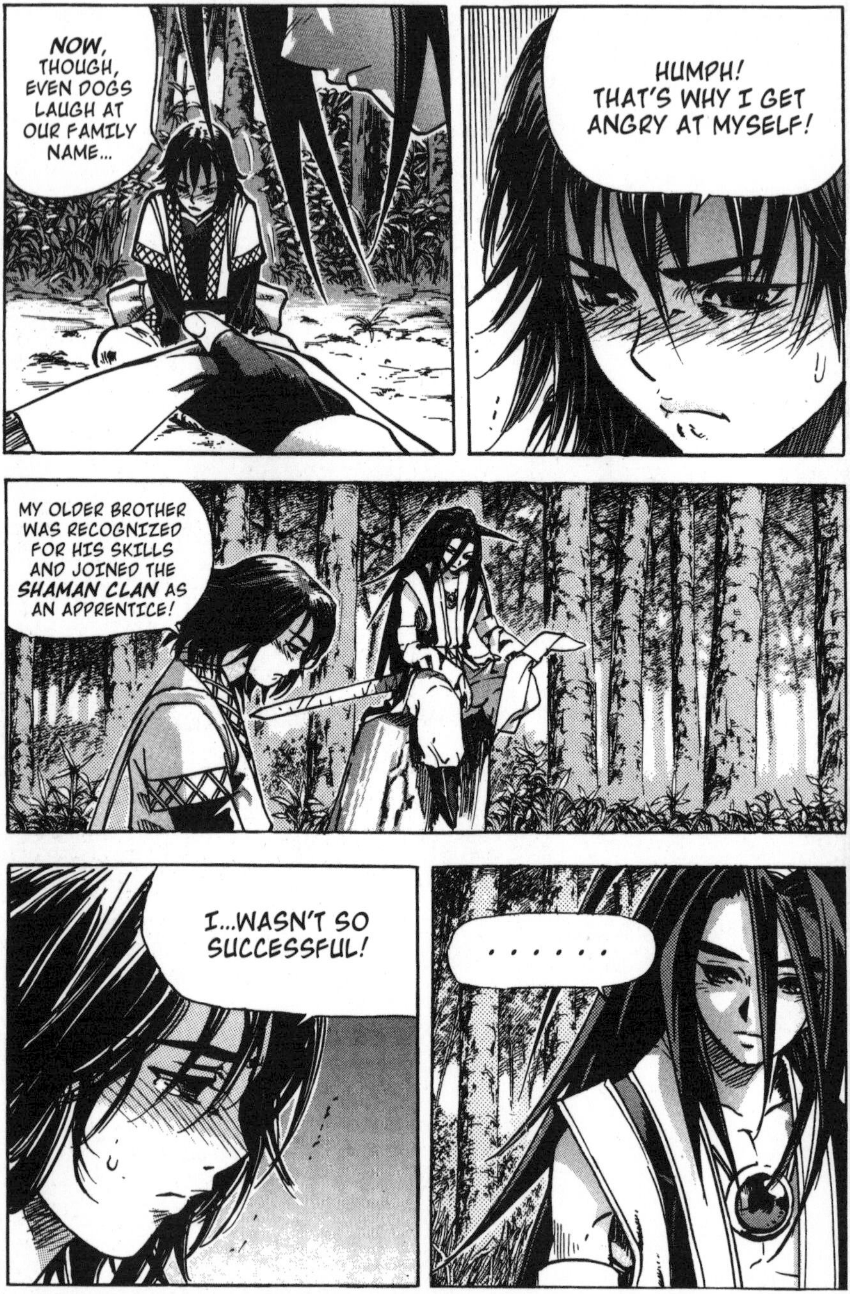
NOW, THOUGH, EVEN DOGS LAUGH AT OUR FAMILY NAME...
HUMPH! THAT'S WHY I GET ANGRY AT MYSELF!
MY OLDER BROTHER WAS RECOGNIZED FOR HIS SKILLS AND JOINED THE SHAMAN CLAN AS AN APPRENTICE!
I...WASN'T SO SUCCESSFUL!
......

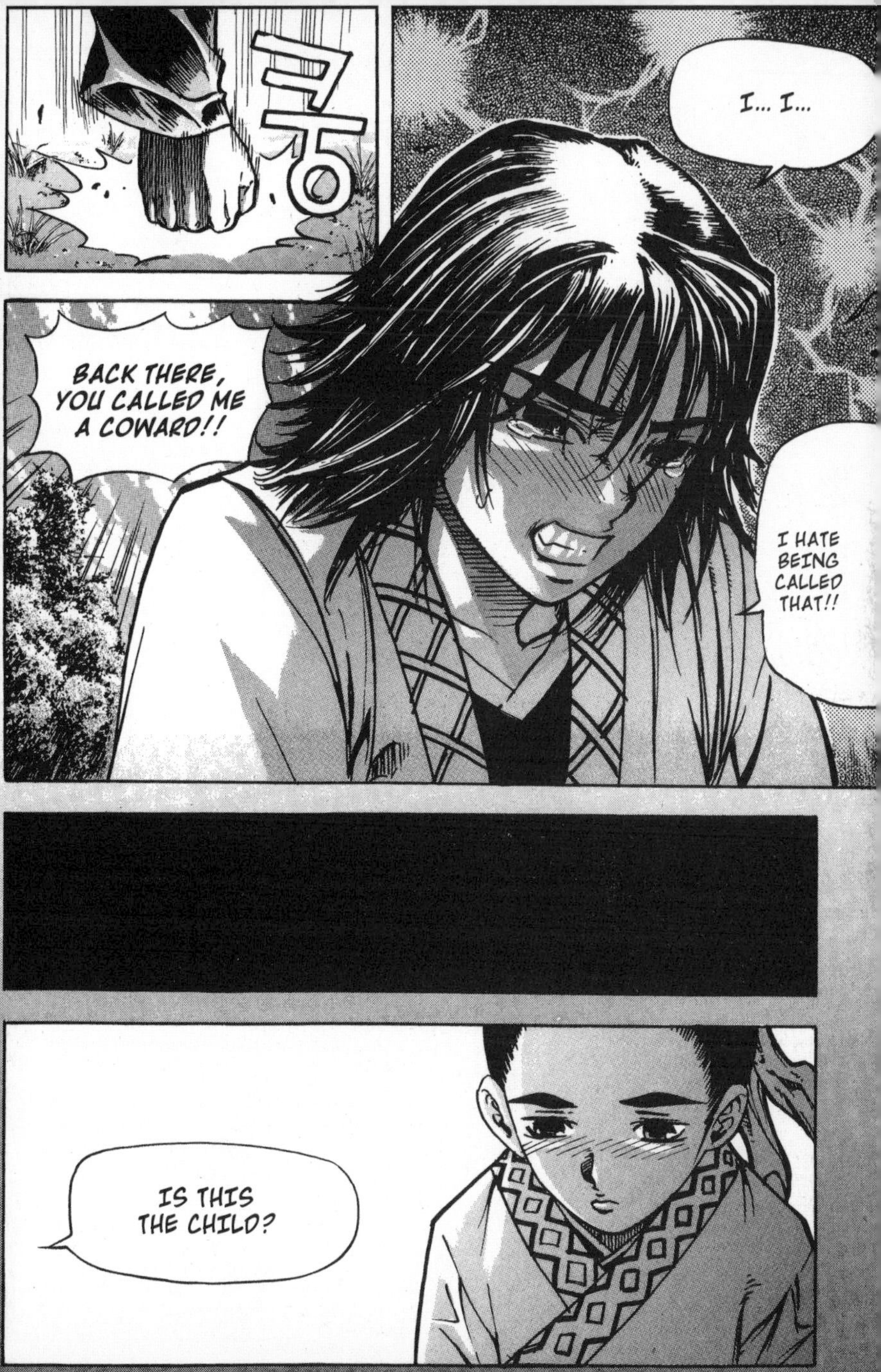
I... I...
BACK THERE, YOU CALLED ME A COWARD!!
I HATE BEING CALLED THAT!!
IS THIS THE CHILD?

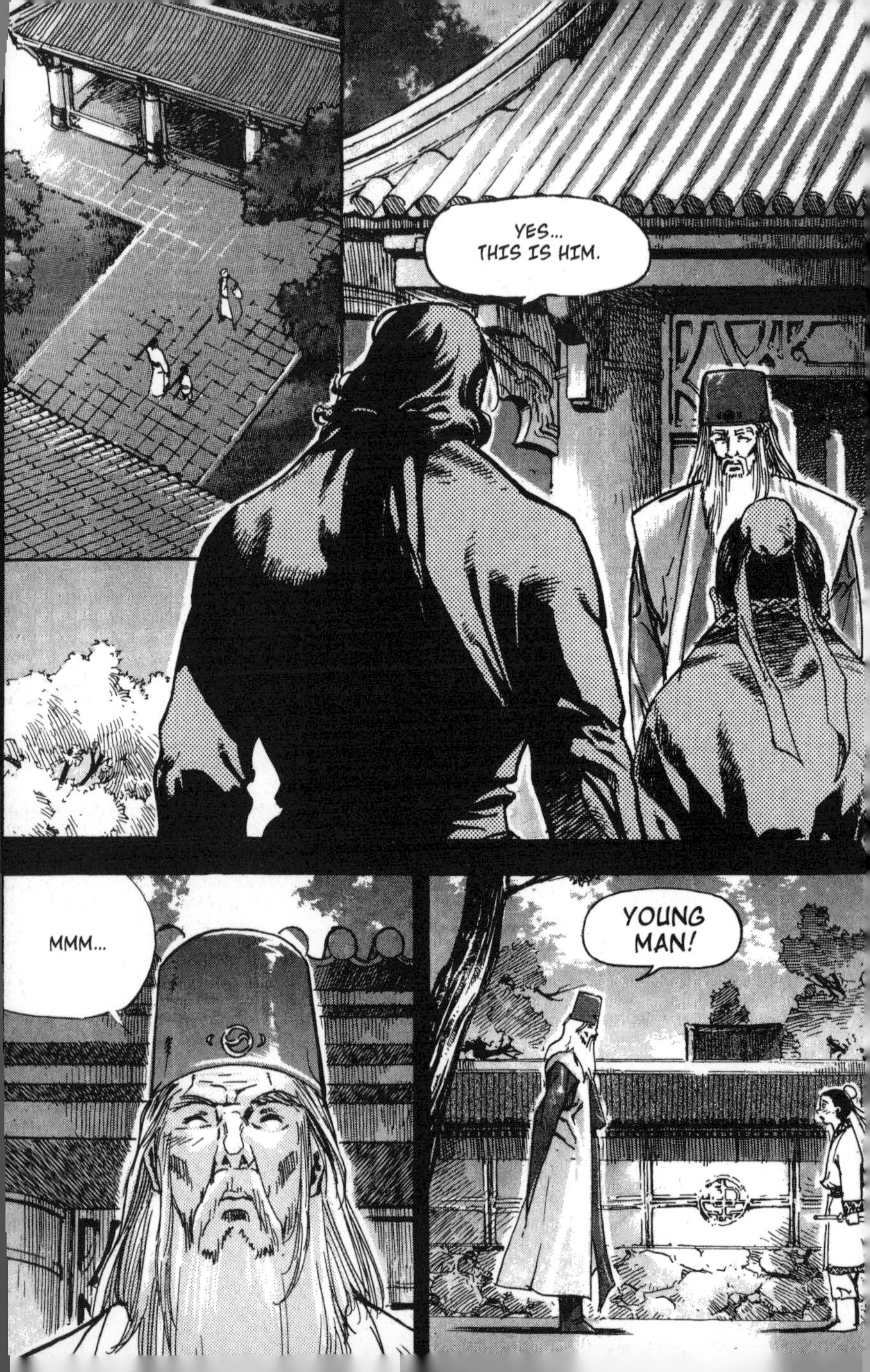
YES...
THIS IS HIM.
MMM...
YOUNG MAN!

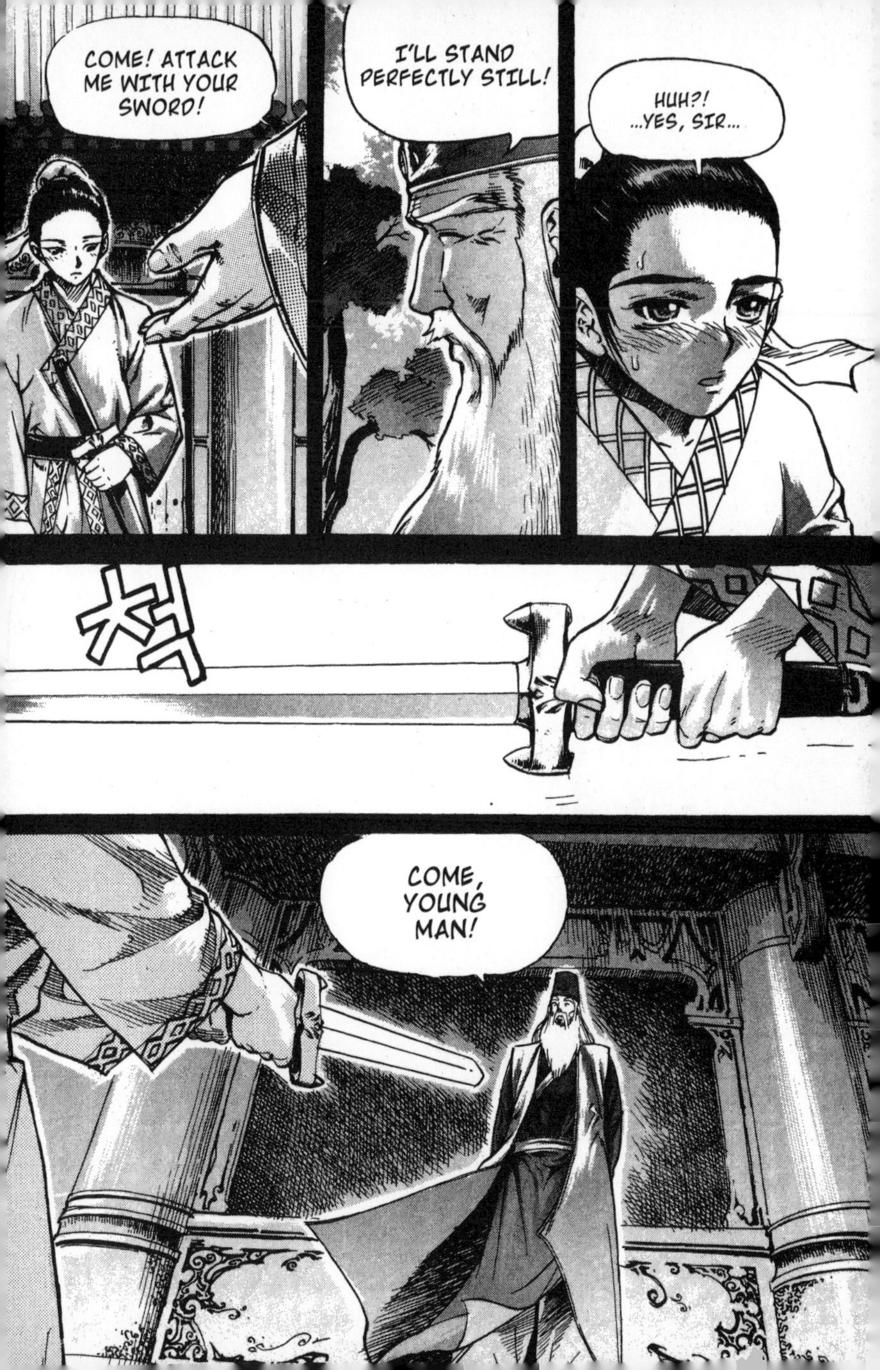
COME! ATTACK ME WITH YOUR SWORD!
I'LL STAND PERFECTLY STILL!
HUH?! ...YES, SIR...
COME, YOUNG MAN!

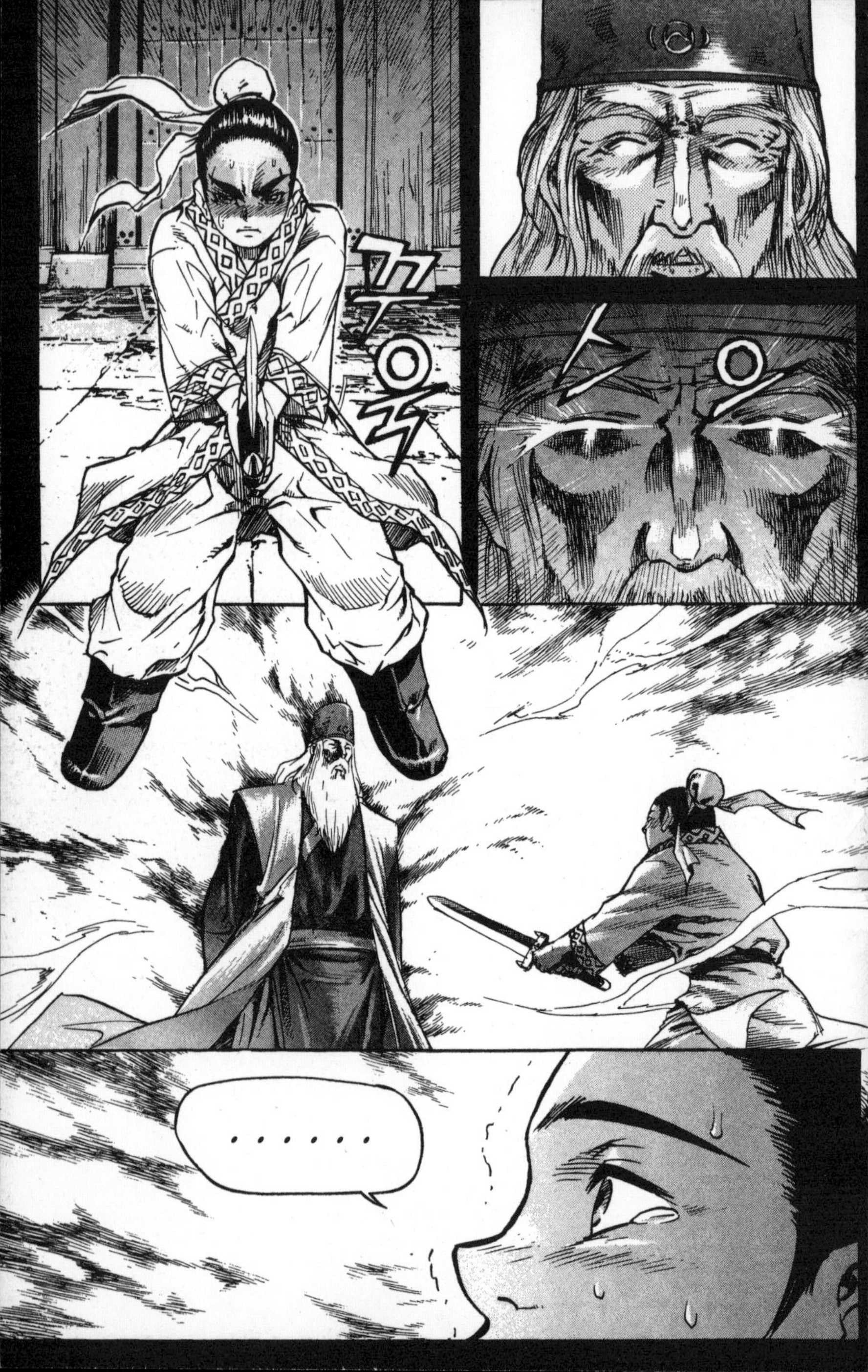
....

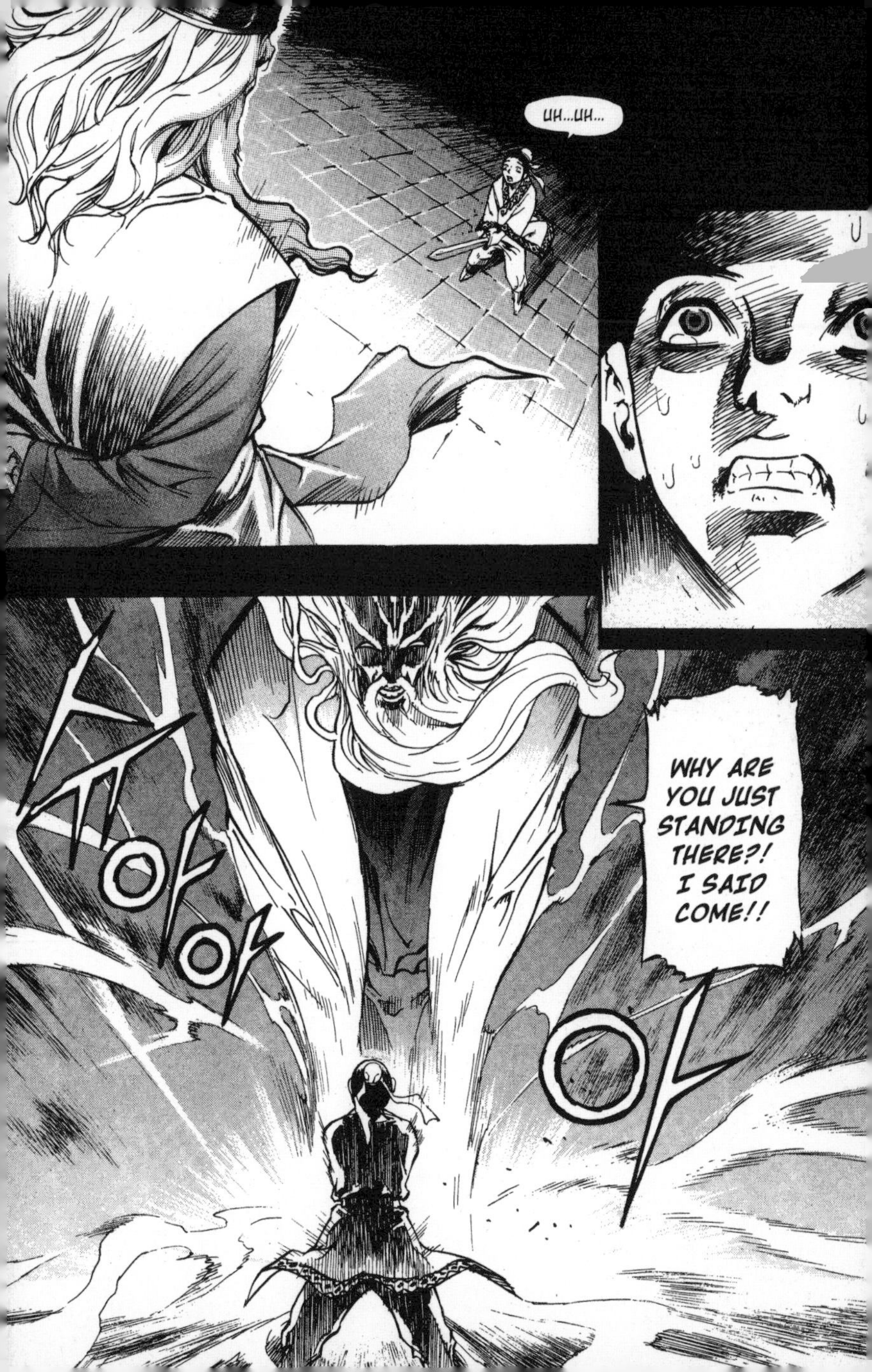
UH...UH...
WHY ARE YOU JUST STANDING THERE?! I SAID COME!!

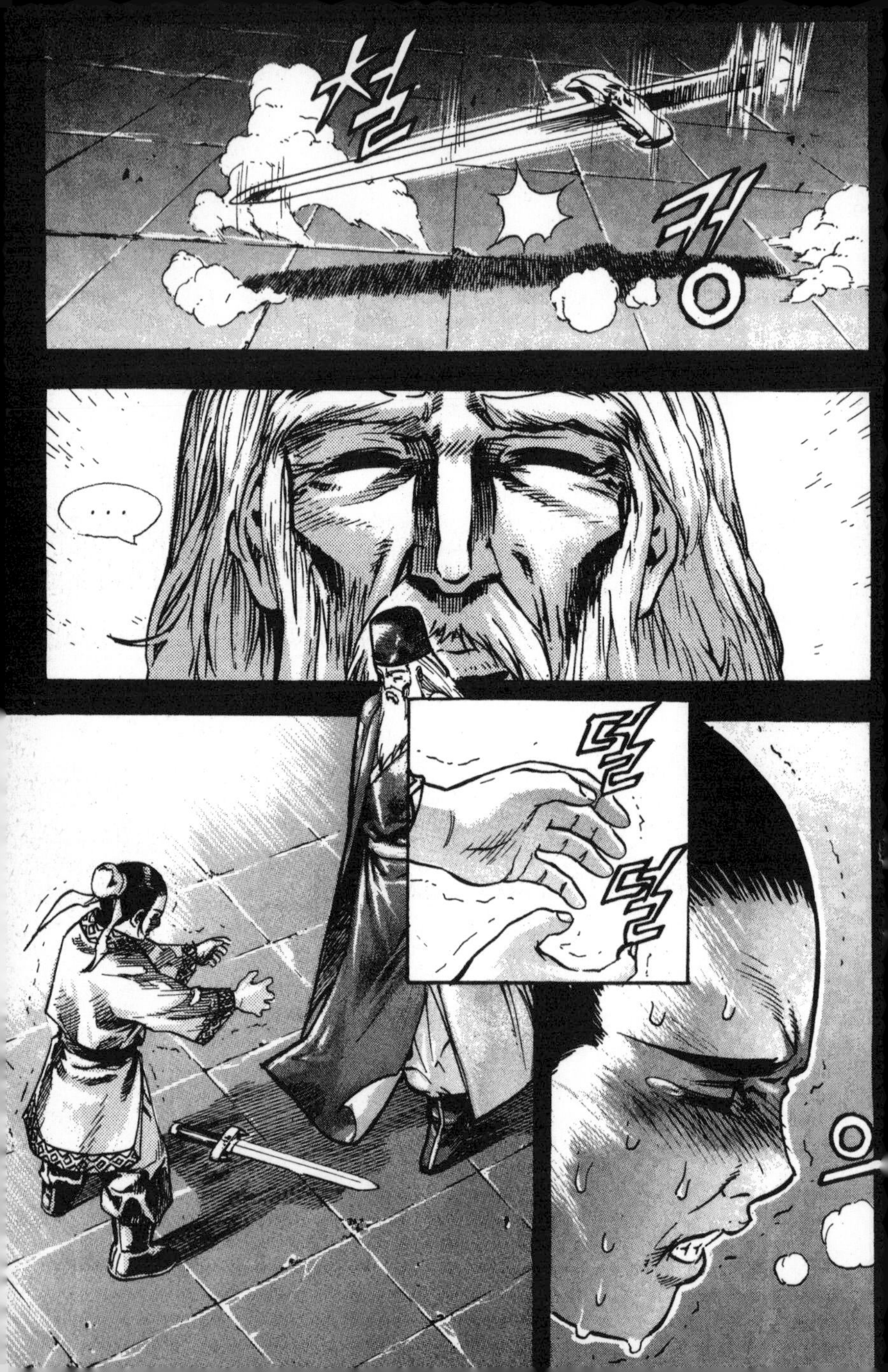
철
컹
...
덜덜
으

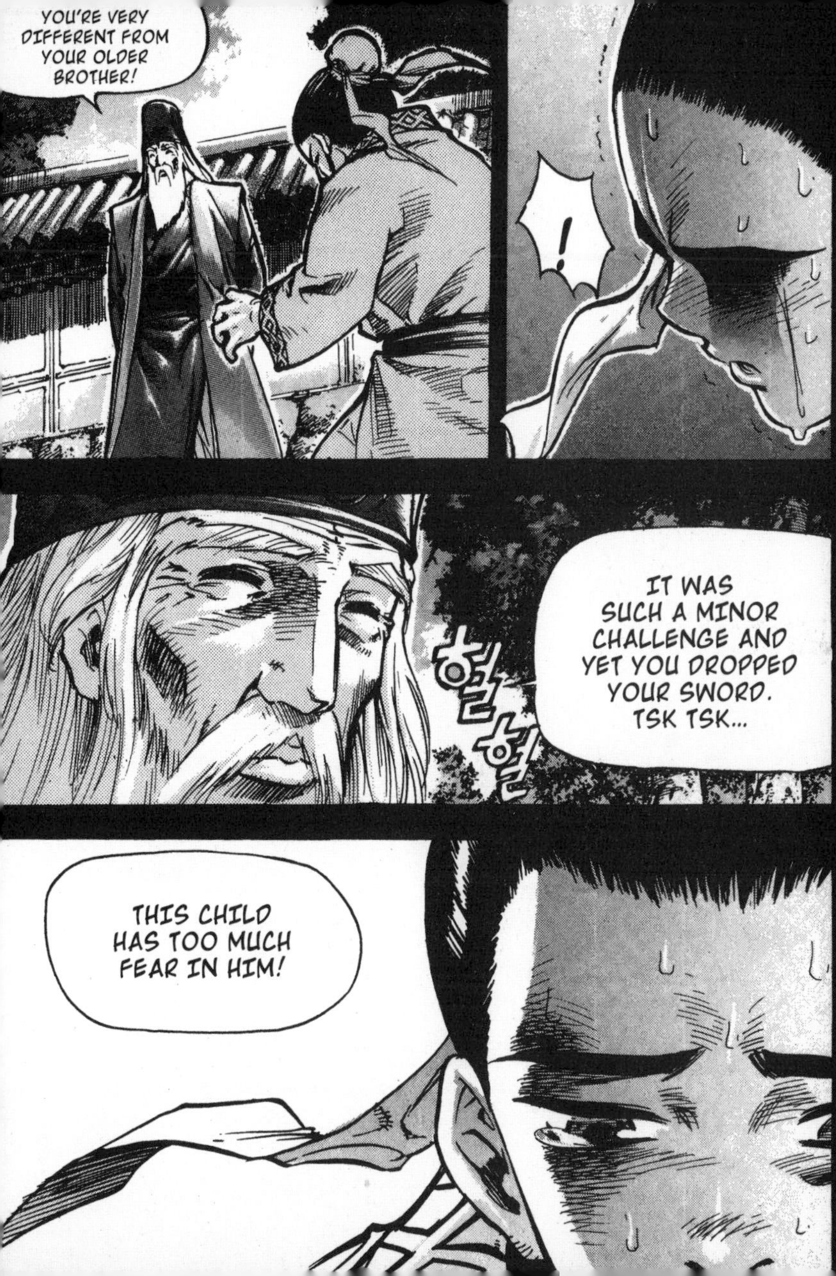
YOU'RE VERY DIFFERENT FROM YOUR OLDER BROTHER!
!
IT WAS SUCH A MINOR CHALLENGE AND YET YOU DROPPED YOUR SWORD. TSK TSK...
힐끔 힐끔
THIS CHILD HAS TOO MUCH FEAR IN HIM!

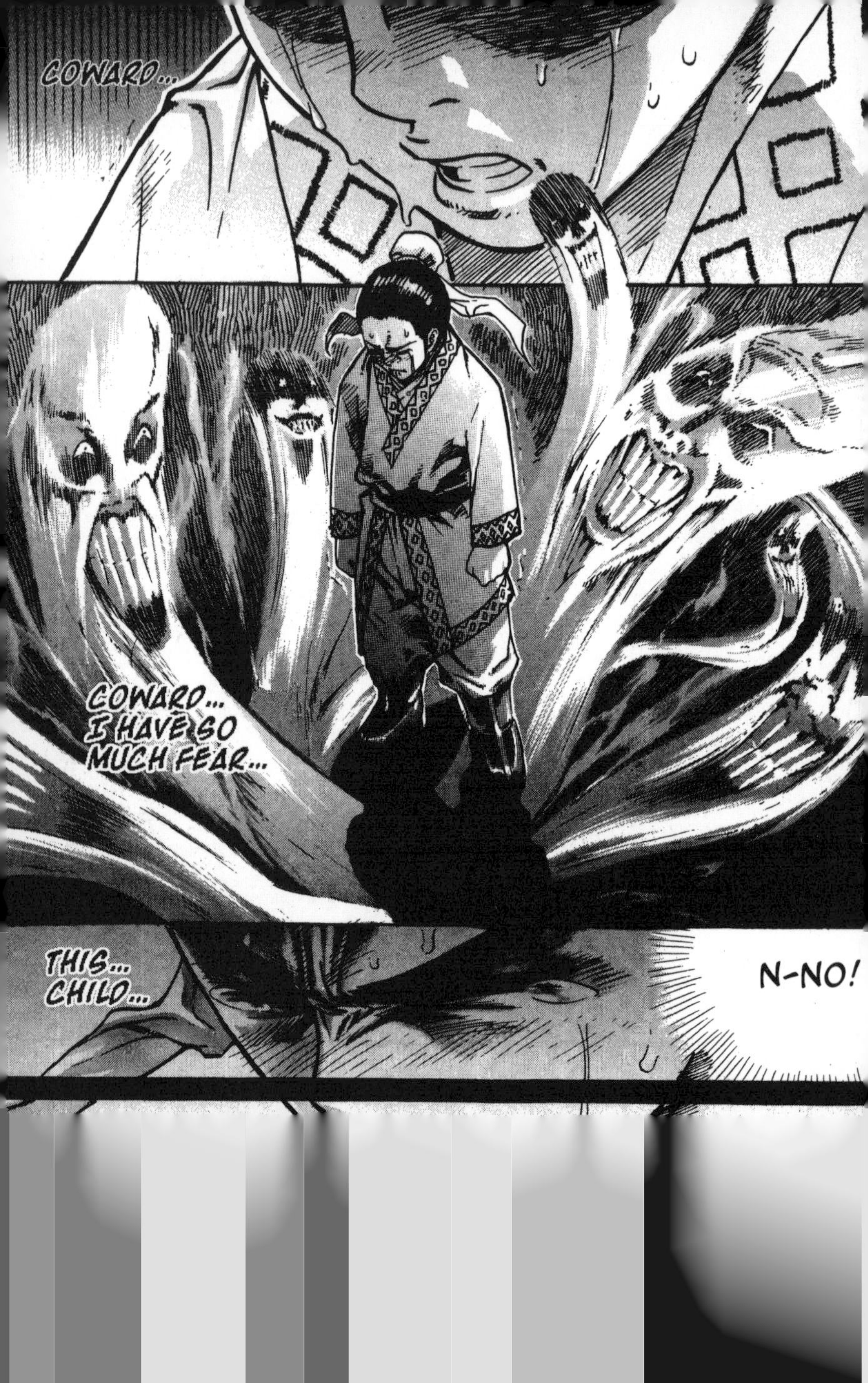
COWARD...
COWARD... I HAVE SO MUCH FEAR...
THIS... CHILD...
N-NO!

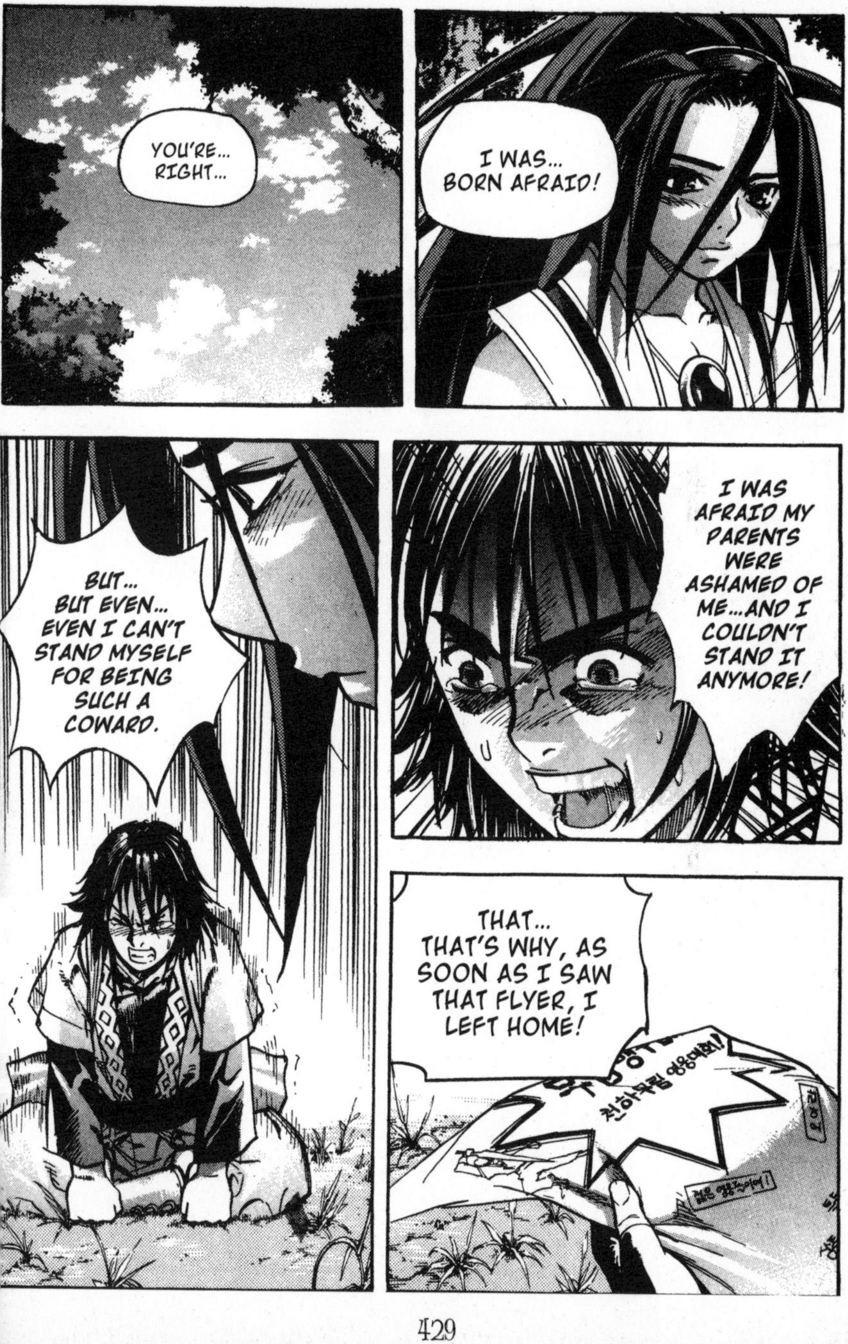

YOU'RE... RIGHT...
I WAS... BORN AFRAID!
BUT... BUT EVEN... EVEN I CAN'T STAND MYSELF FOR BEING SUCH A COWARD.
I WAS AFRAID MY PARENTS WERE ASHAMED OF ME...AND I COULDN'T STAND IT ANYMORE!
THAT... THAT'S WHY, AS SOON AS I SAW THAT FLYER, I LEFT HOME!

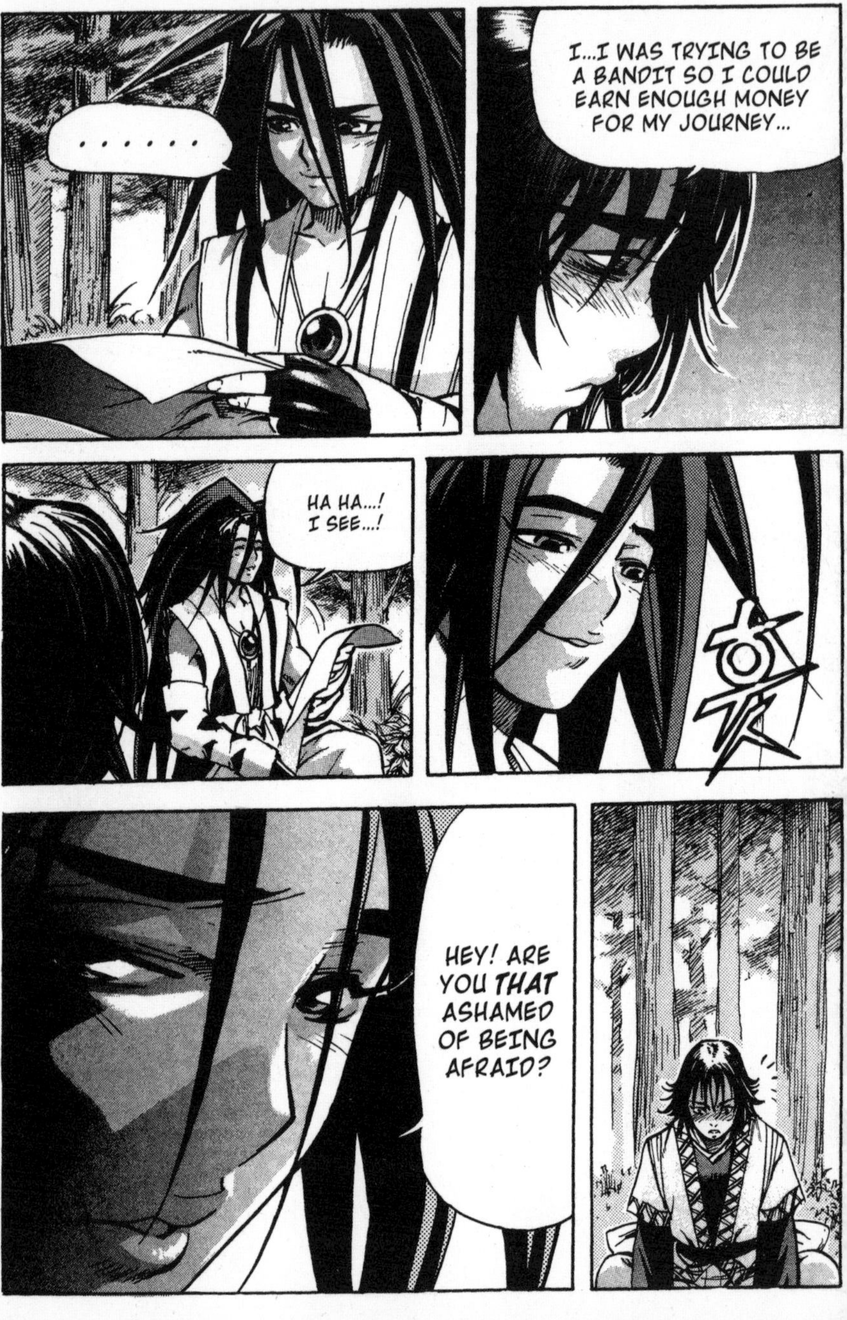
. . . .
I...I WAS TRYING TO BE A BANDIT SO I COULD EARN ENOUGH MONEY FOR MY JOURNEY...
HA HA...! I SEE...!
HEY! ARE YOU *THAT* ASHAMED OF BEING AFRAID?

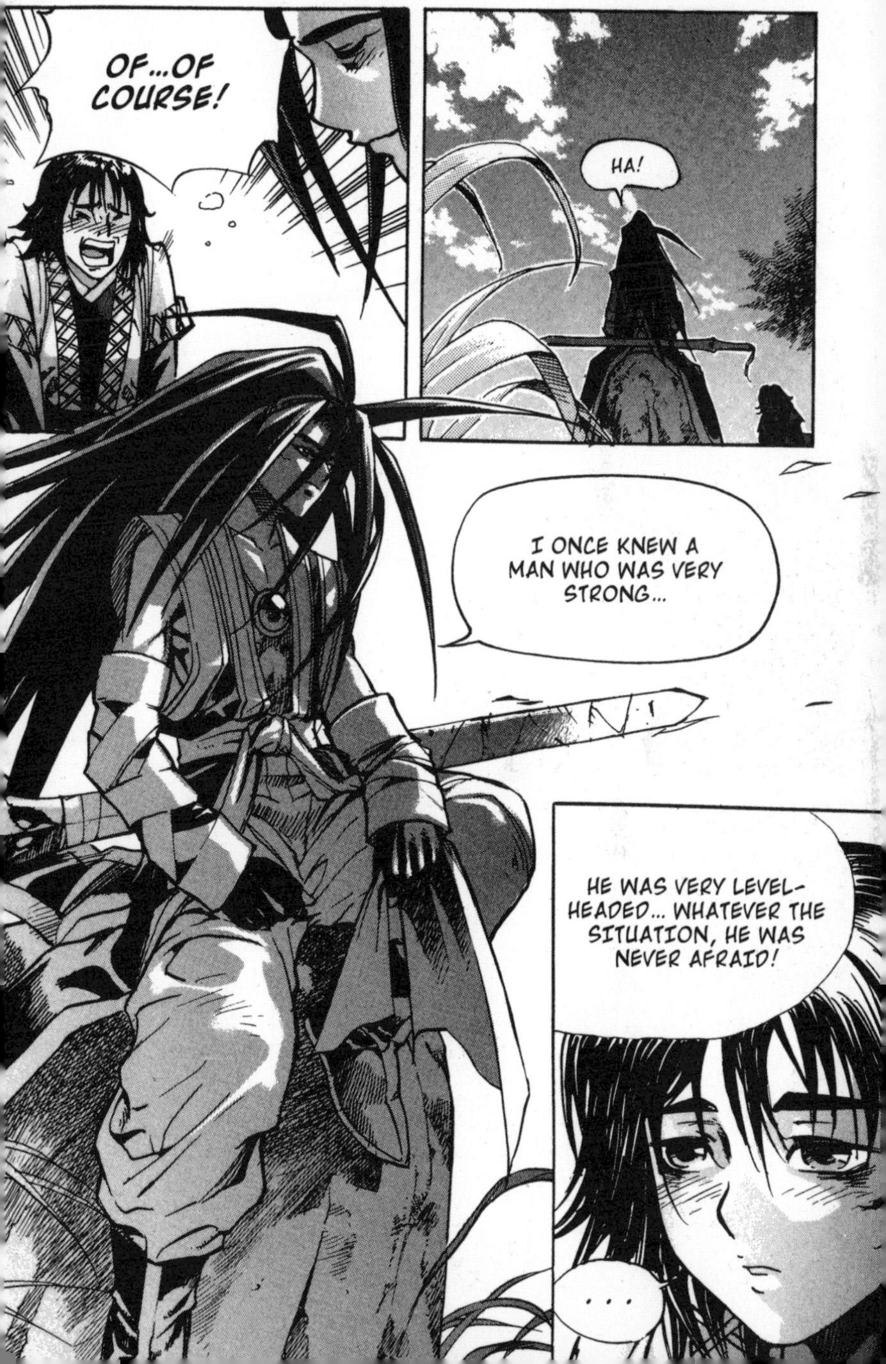
OF...OF COURSE!
HA!
I ONCE KNEW A MAN WHO WAS VERY STRONG...
HE WAS VERY LEVEL-HEADED... WHATEVER THE SITUATION, HE WAS NEVER AFRAID!
...

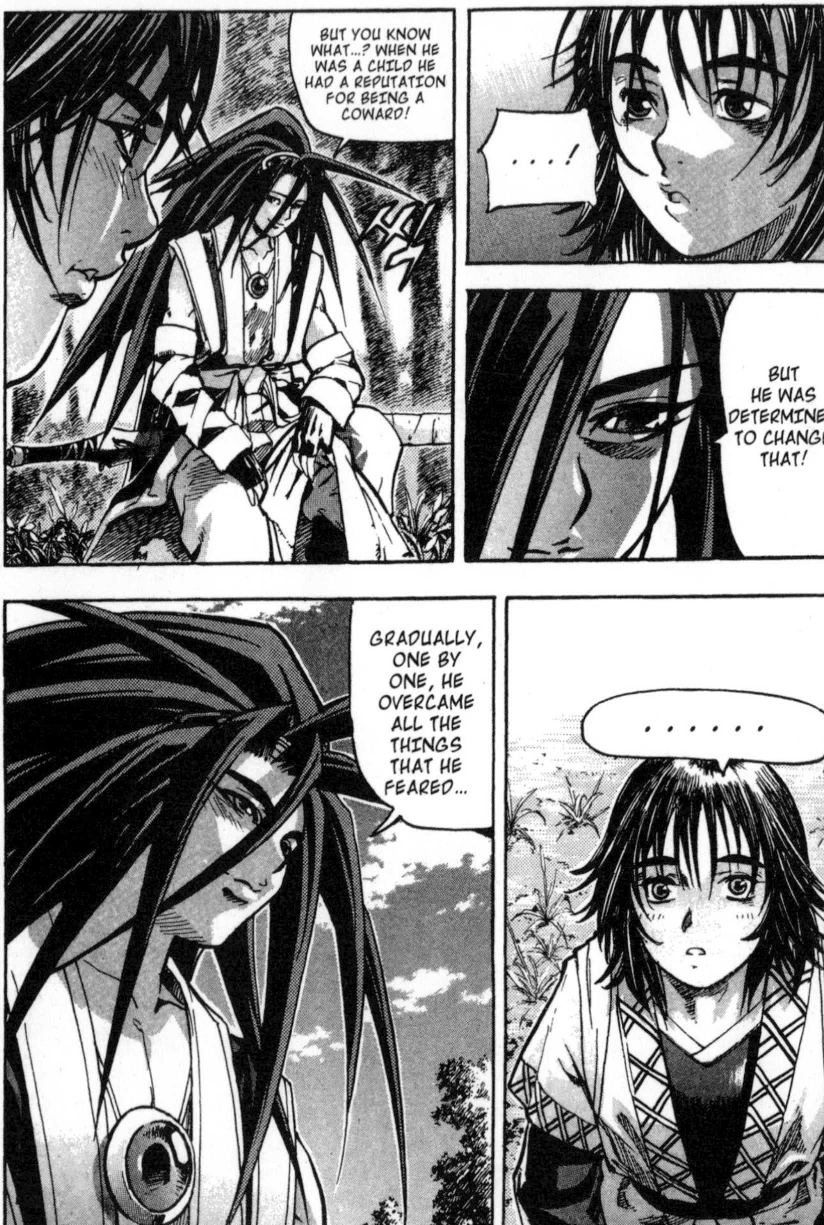

BUT YOU KNOW WHAT...? WHEN HE WAS A CHILD HE HAD A REPUTATION FOR BEING A COWARD!
...!
BUT HE WAS DETERMINED TO CHANGE THAT!
GRADUALLY, ONE BY ONE, HE OVERCAME ALL THE THINGS THAT HE FEARED...
......

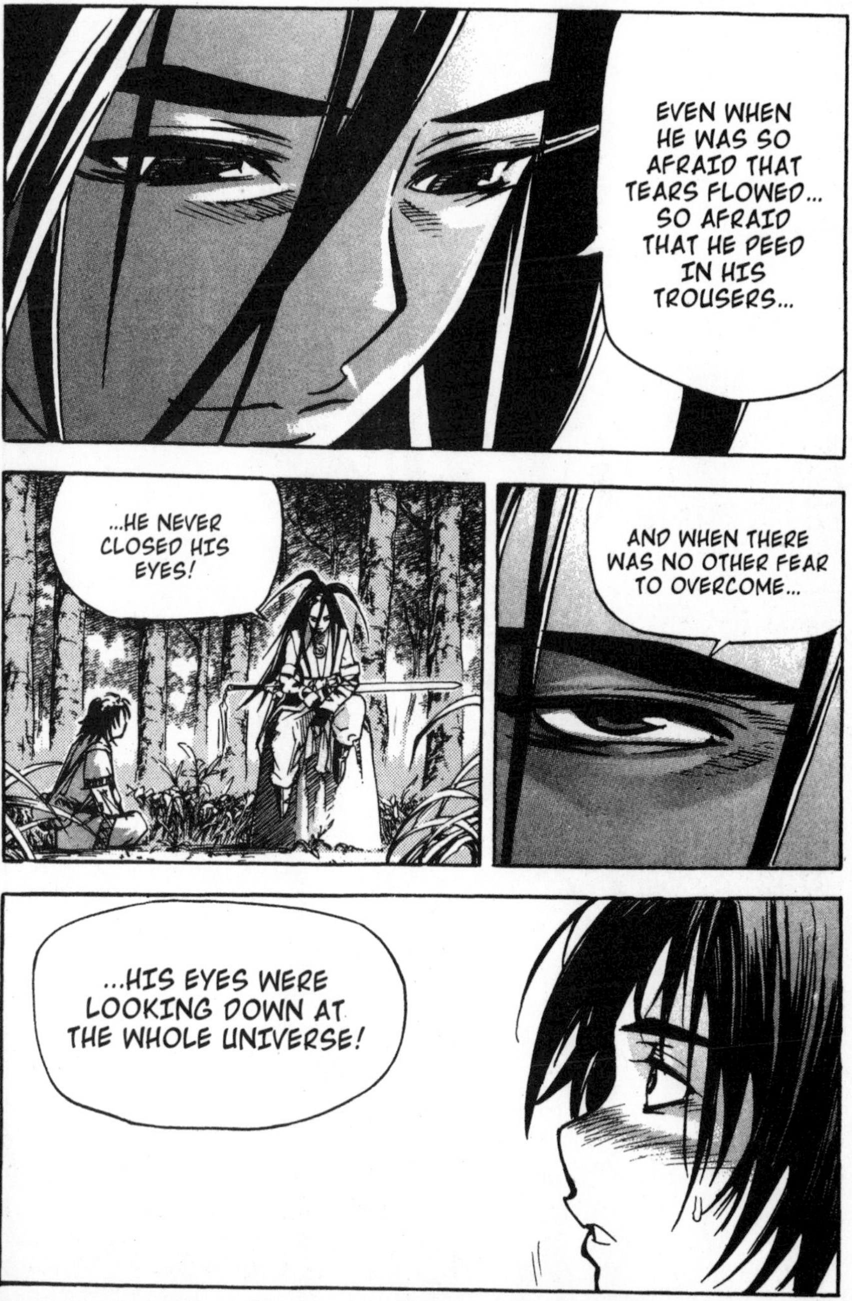
EVEN WHEN HE WAS SO AFRAID THAT TEARS FLOWED... SO AFRAID THAT HE PEED IN HIS TROUSERS...
...HE NEVER CLOSED HIS EYES!
AND WHEN THERE WAS NO OTHER FEAR TO OVERCOME...
...HIS EYES WERE LOOKING DOWN AT THE WHOLE UNIVERSE!

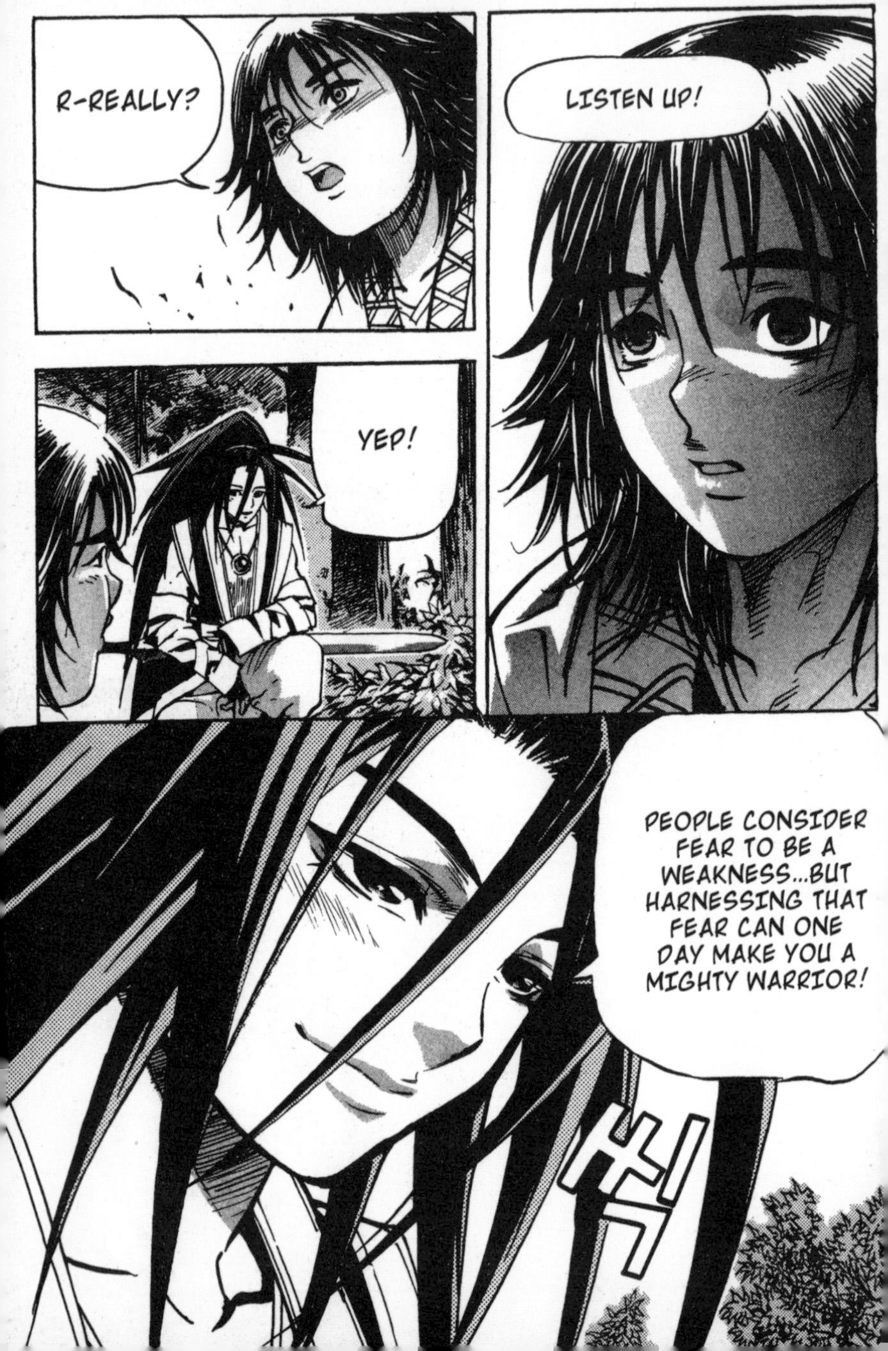
R-REALLY?
LISTEN UP!
YEP!
PEOPLE CONSIDER FEAR TO BE A WEAKNESS...BUT HARNESSING THAT FEAR CAN ONE DAY MAKE YOU A MIGHTY WARRIOR!

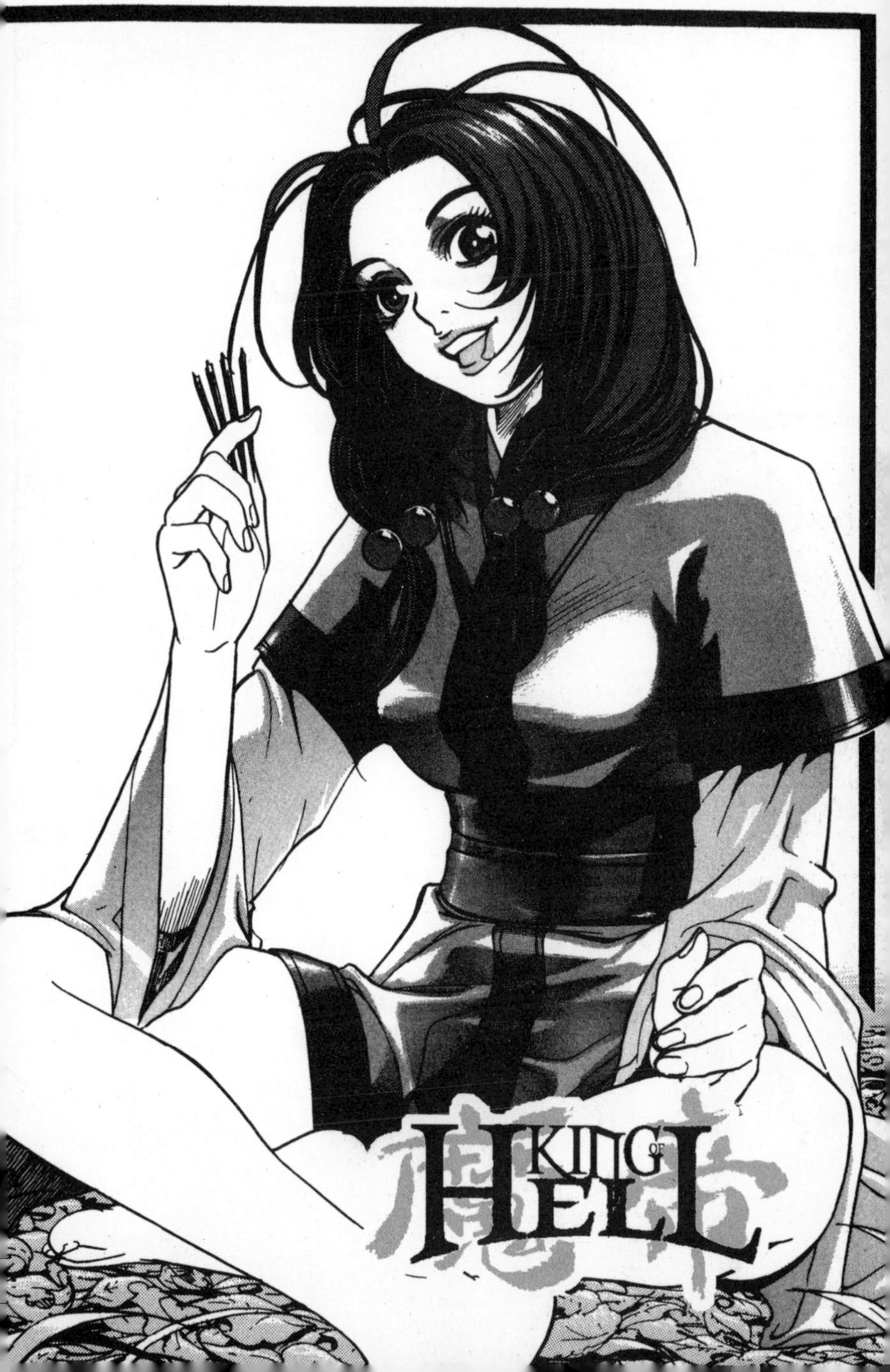
KING OF HELL

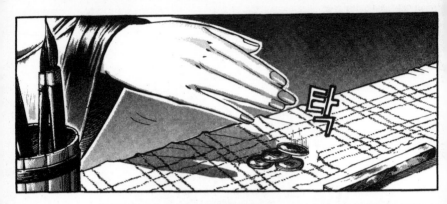

THANK YOU!
PLEASE COME
AGAIN!

GOODBYE,
DOHWA!

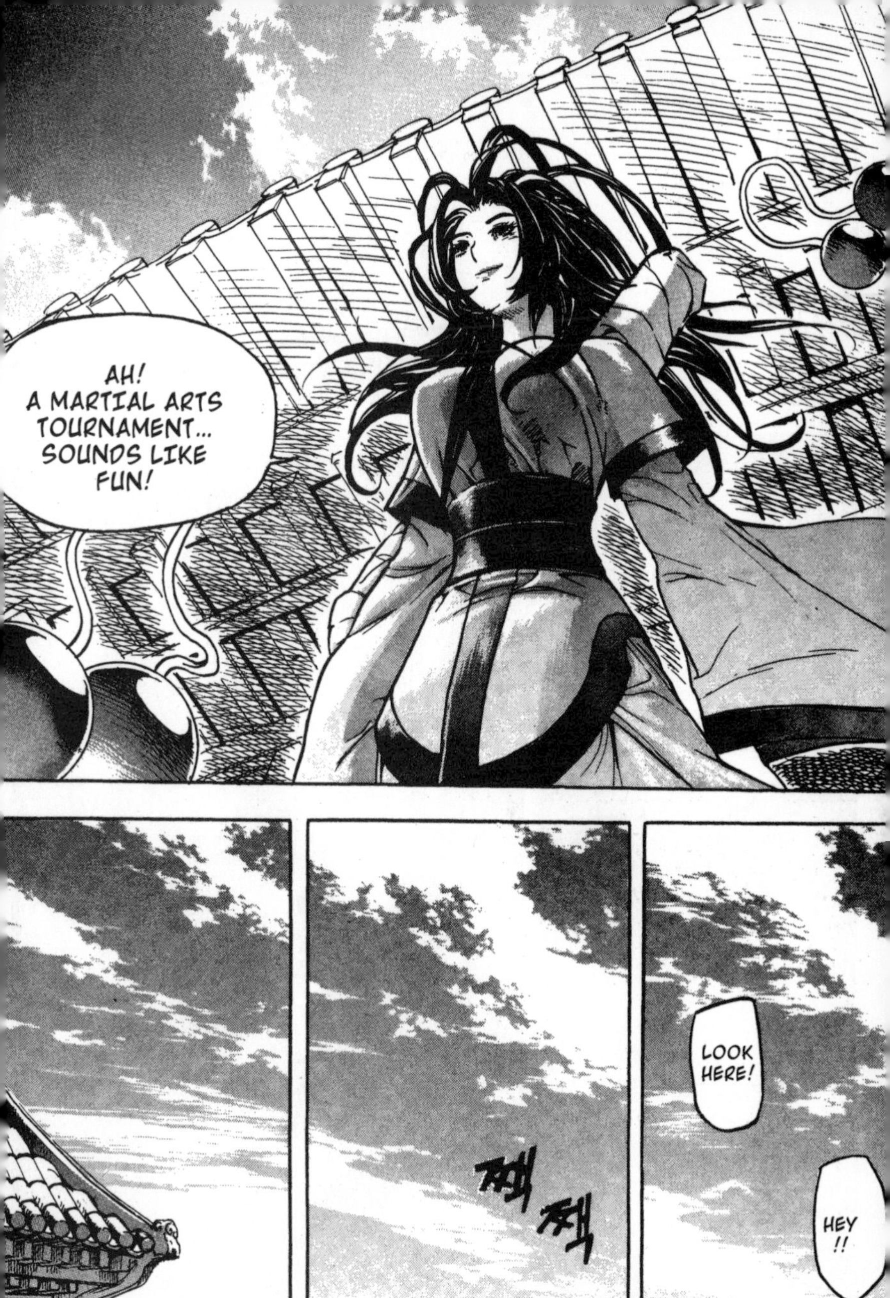
AH!
A MARTIAL ARTS TOURNAMENT... SOUNDS LIKE FUN!
LOOK HERE!
HEY !!

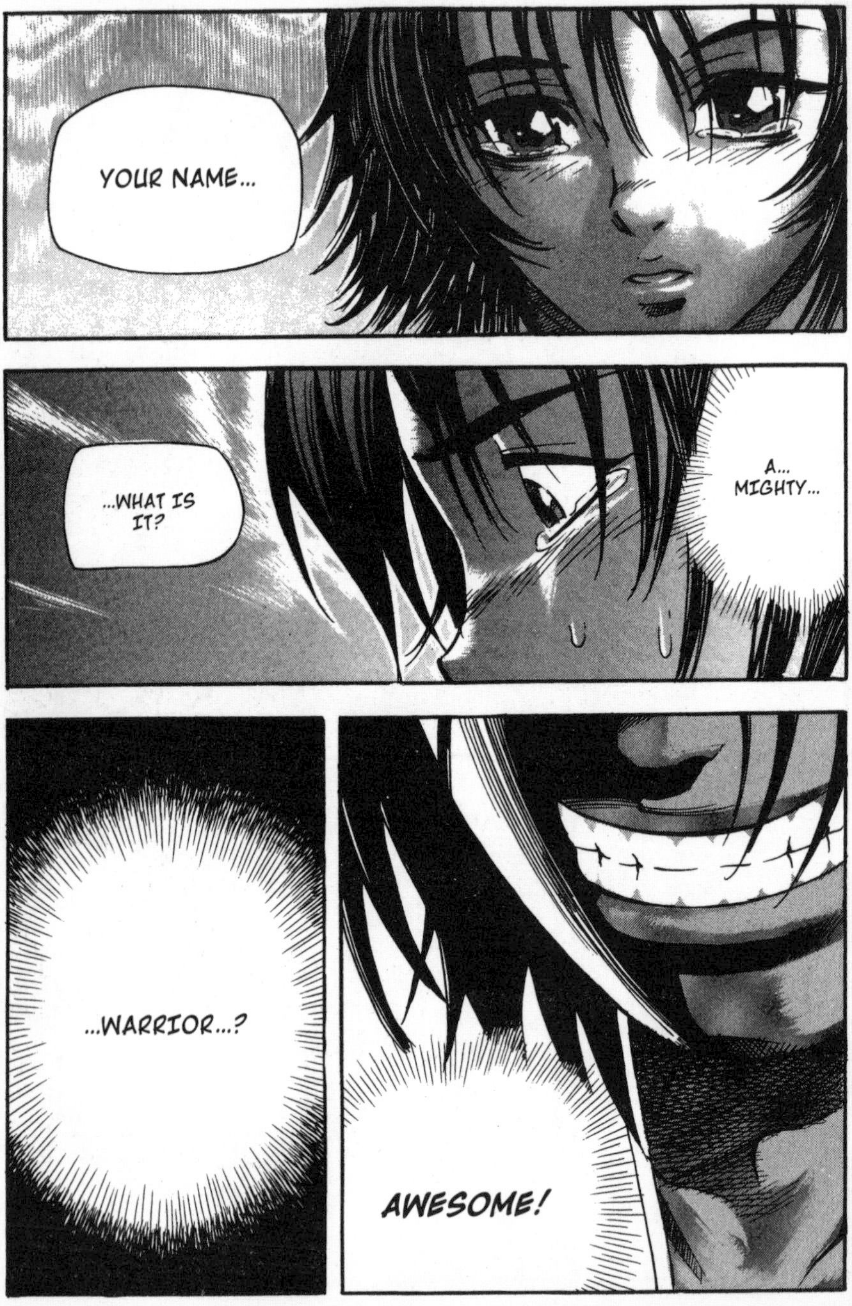
YOUR NAME...
...WHAT IS IT?
A... MIGHTY...
...WARRIOR...?
AWESOME!

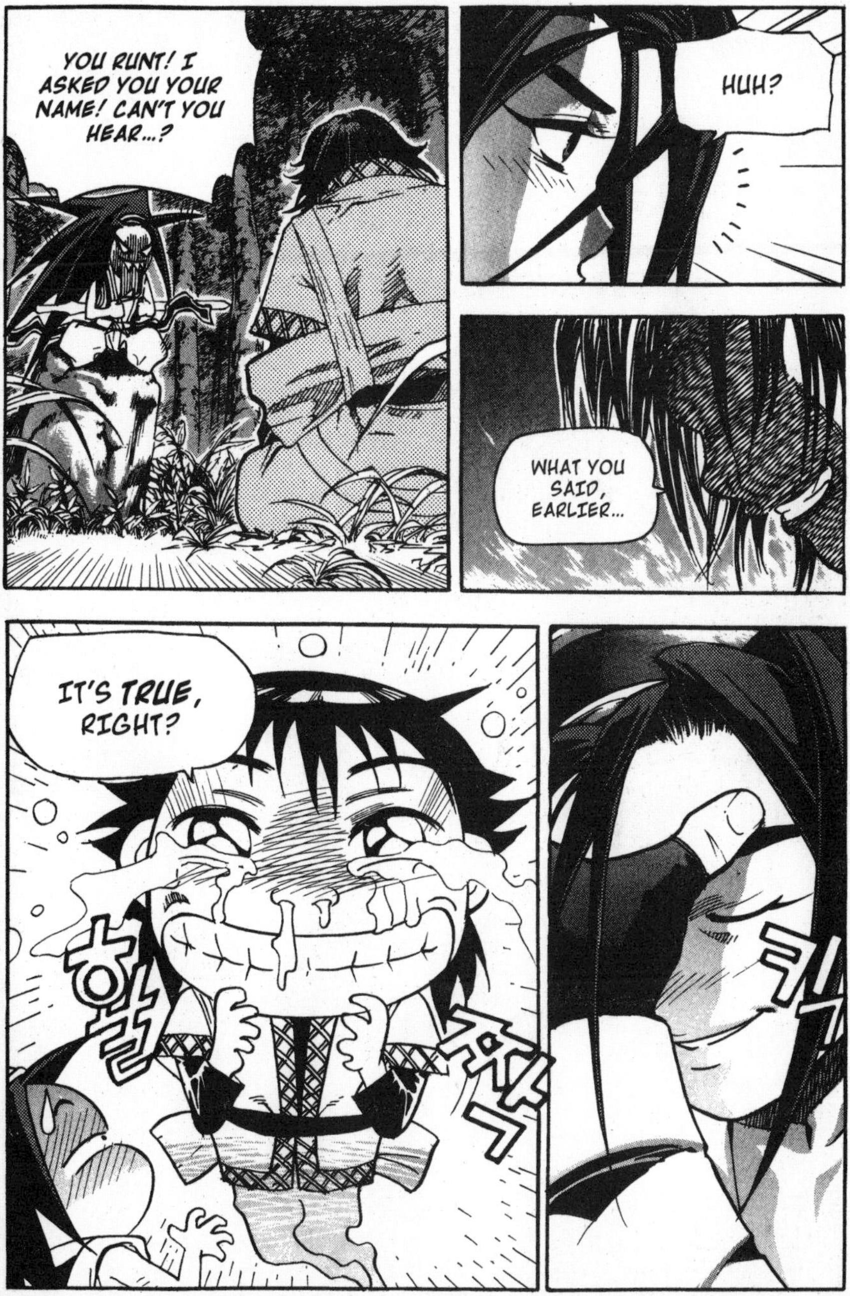
YOU RUNT! I ASKED YOU YOUR NAME! CAN'T YOU HEAR...?
HUH?
WHAT YOU SAID, EARLIER...
IT'S TRUE, RIGHT?

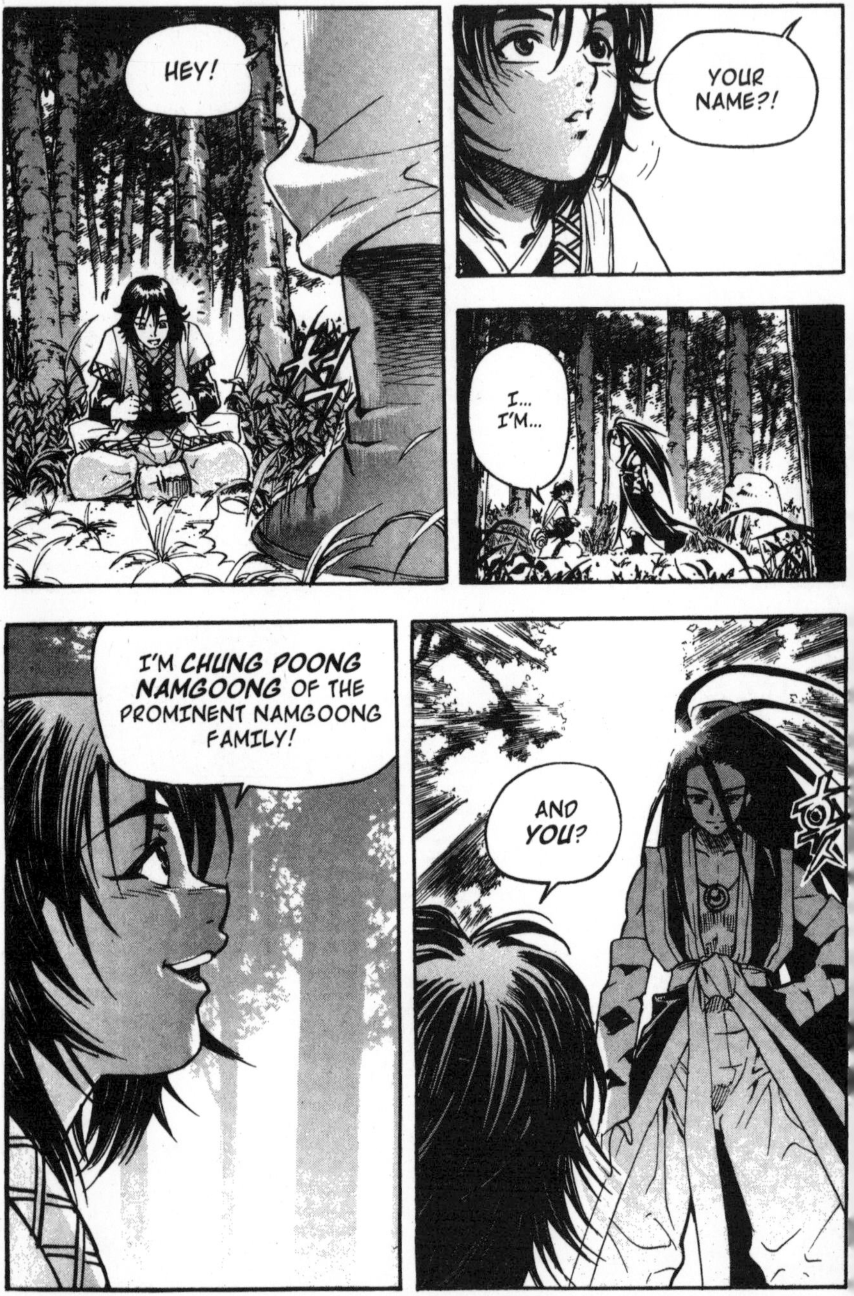
HEY!
YOUR NAME?!
I... I'M...
I'M CHUNG POONG NAMGOONG OF THE PROMINENT NAMGOONG FAMILY!
AND YOU?

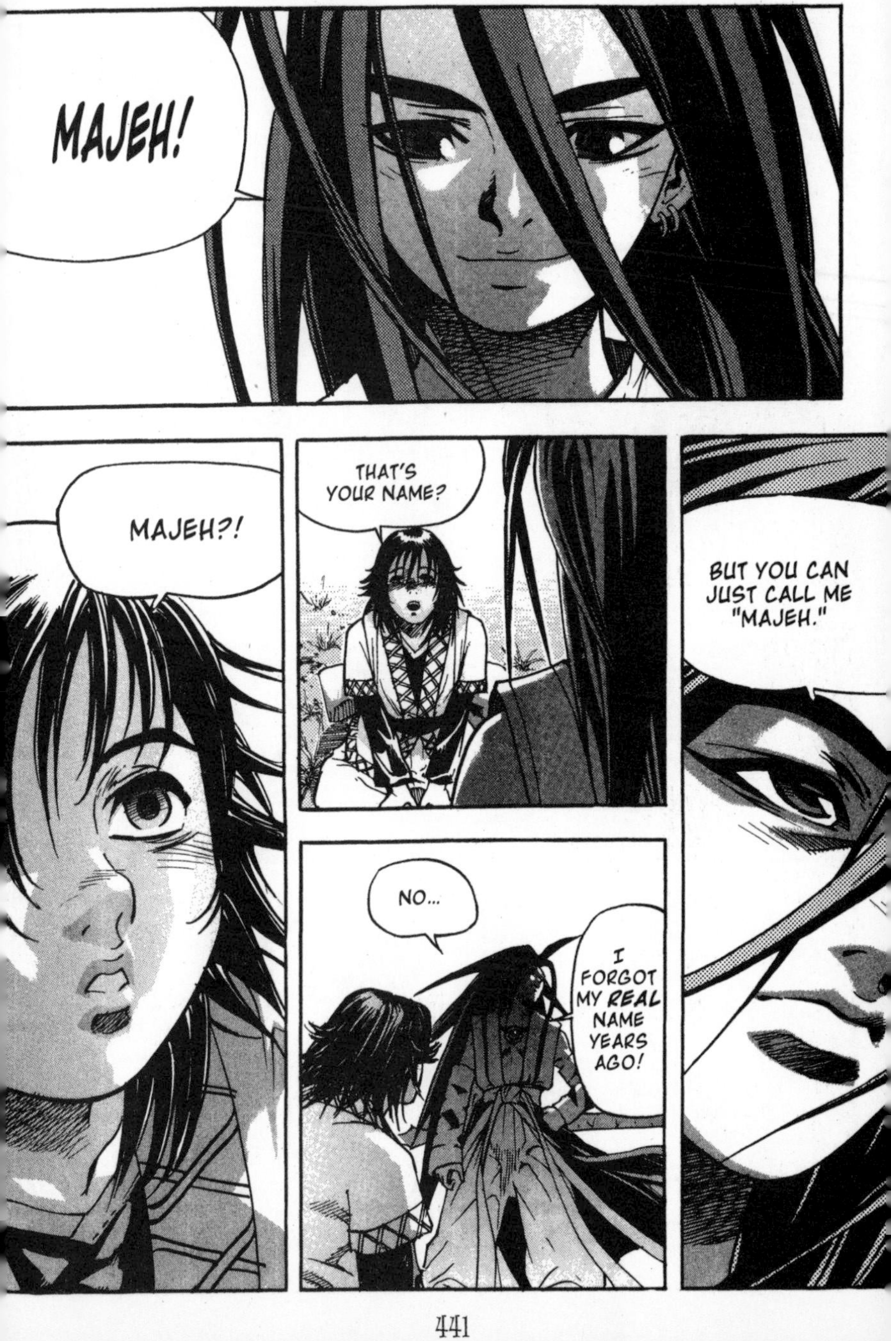
MAJEH!
MAJEH?!
THAT'S YOUR NAME?
NO...
I FORGOT MY REAL NAME YEARS AGO!
BUT YOU CAN JUST CALL ME "MAJEH."

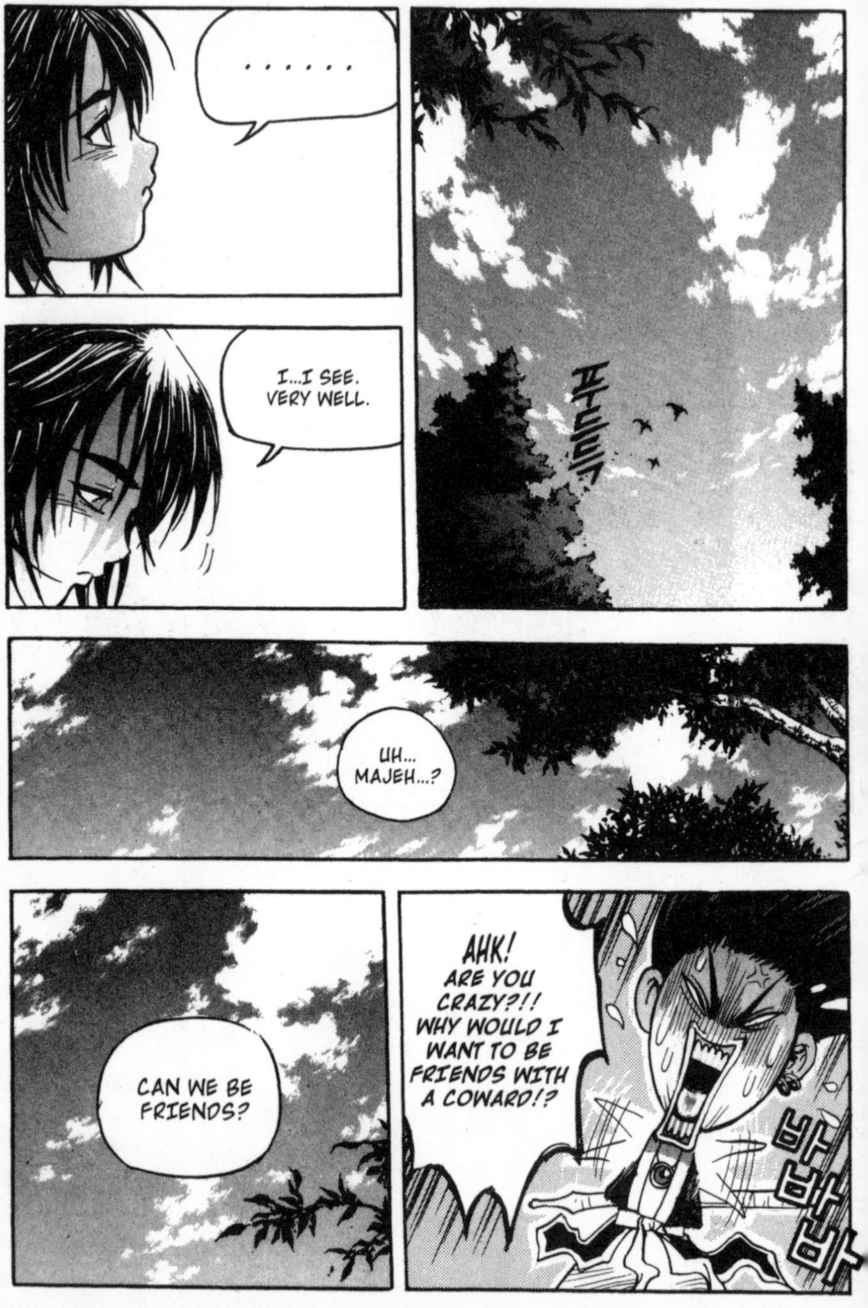
. . . .
I...I SEE. VERY WELL.
푸드득
UH... MAJEH...?
CAN WE BE FRIENDS?
AHK! ARE YOU CRAZY?!! WHY WOULD I WANT TO BE FRIENDS WITH A COWARD!?
바바바

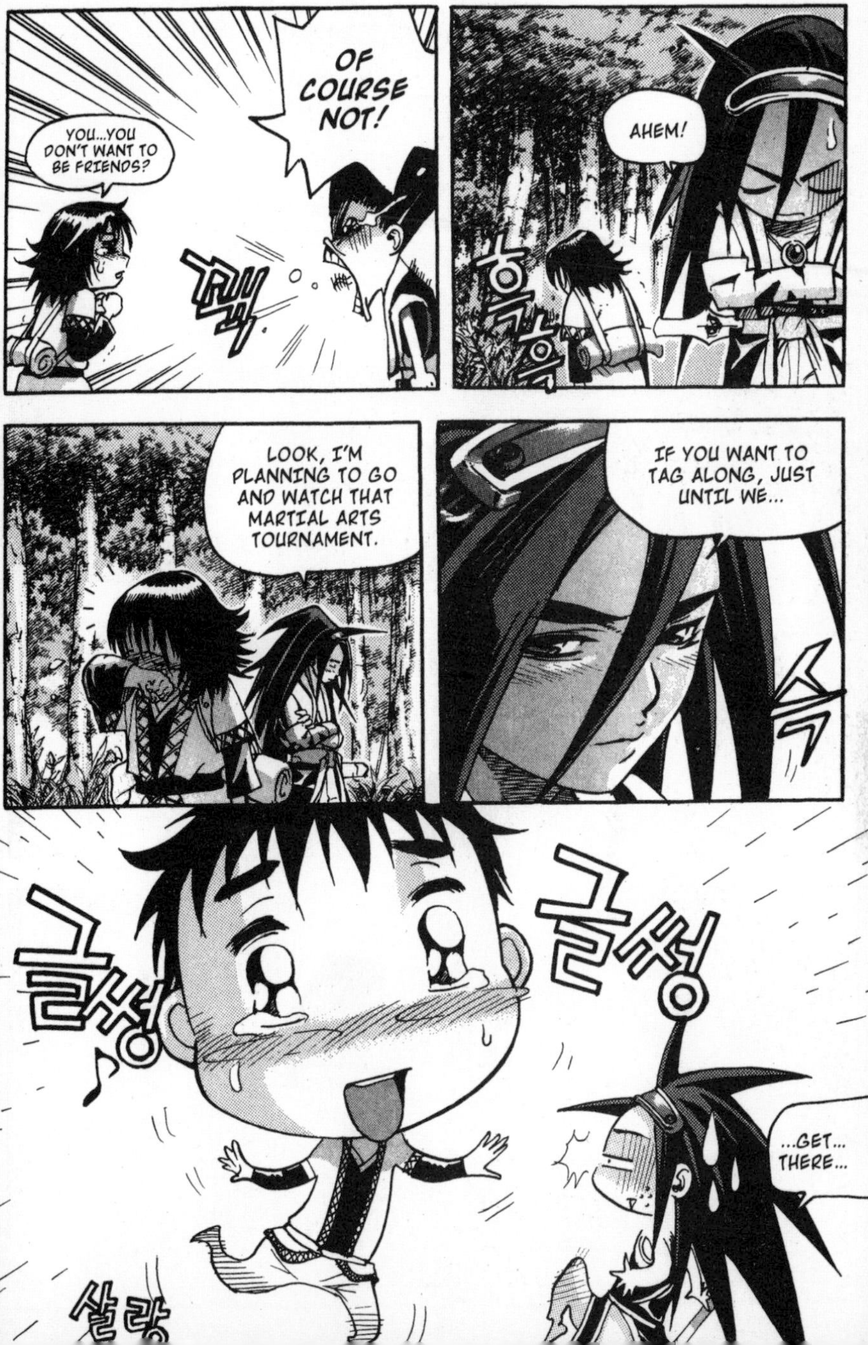
YOU...YOU DON'T WANT TO BE FRIENDS?
OF COURSE NOT!
AHEM!
LOOK, I'M PLANNING TO GO AND WATCH THAT MARTIAL ARTS TOURNAMENT.
IF YOU WANT TO TAG ALONG, JUST UNTIL WE...
글썽
글썽
...GET... THERE...
살랑

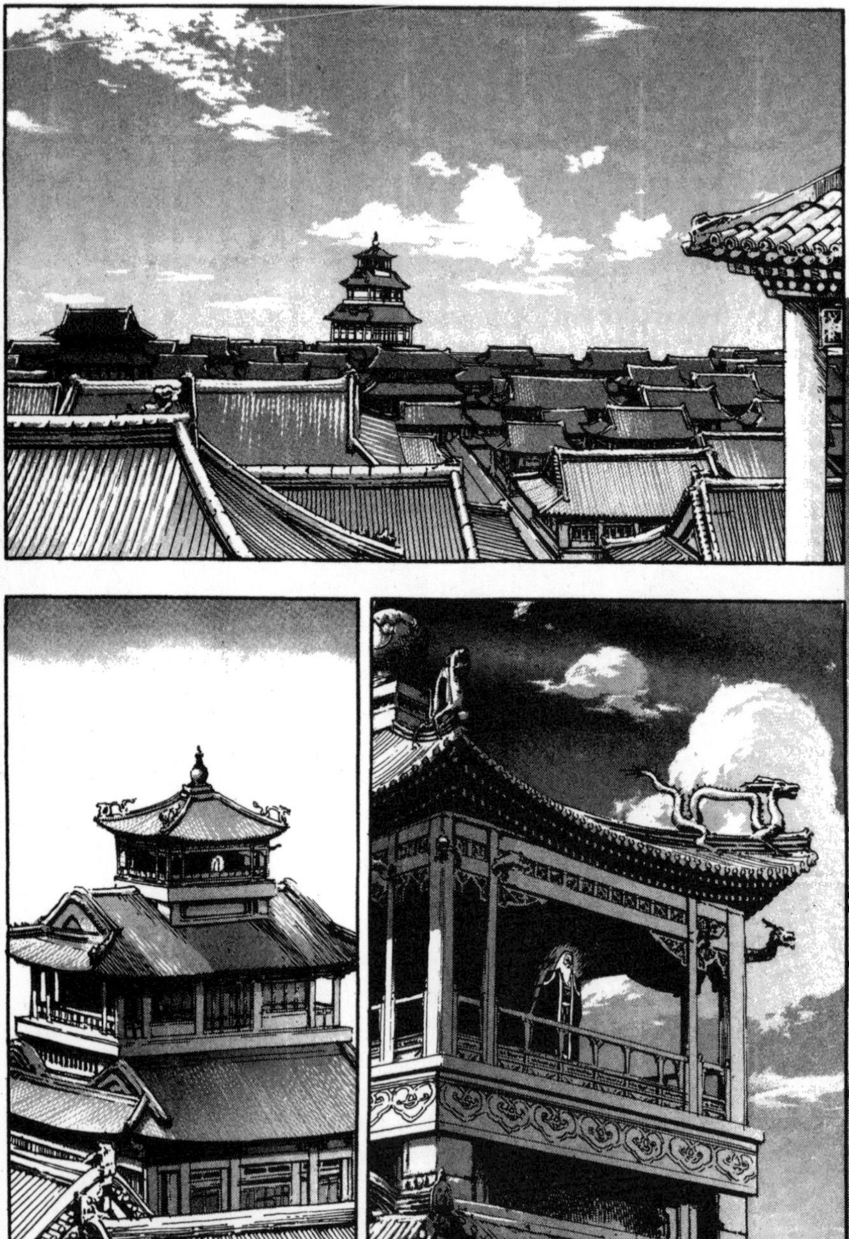

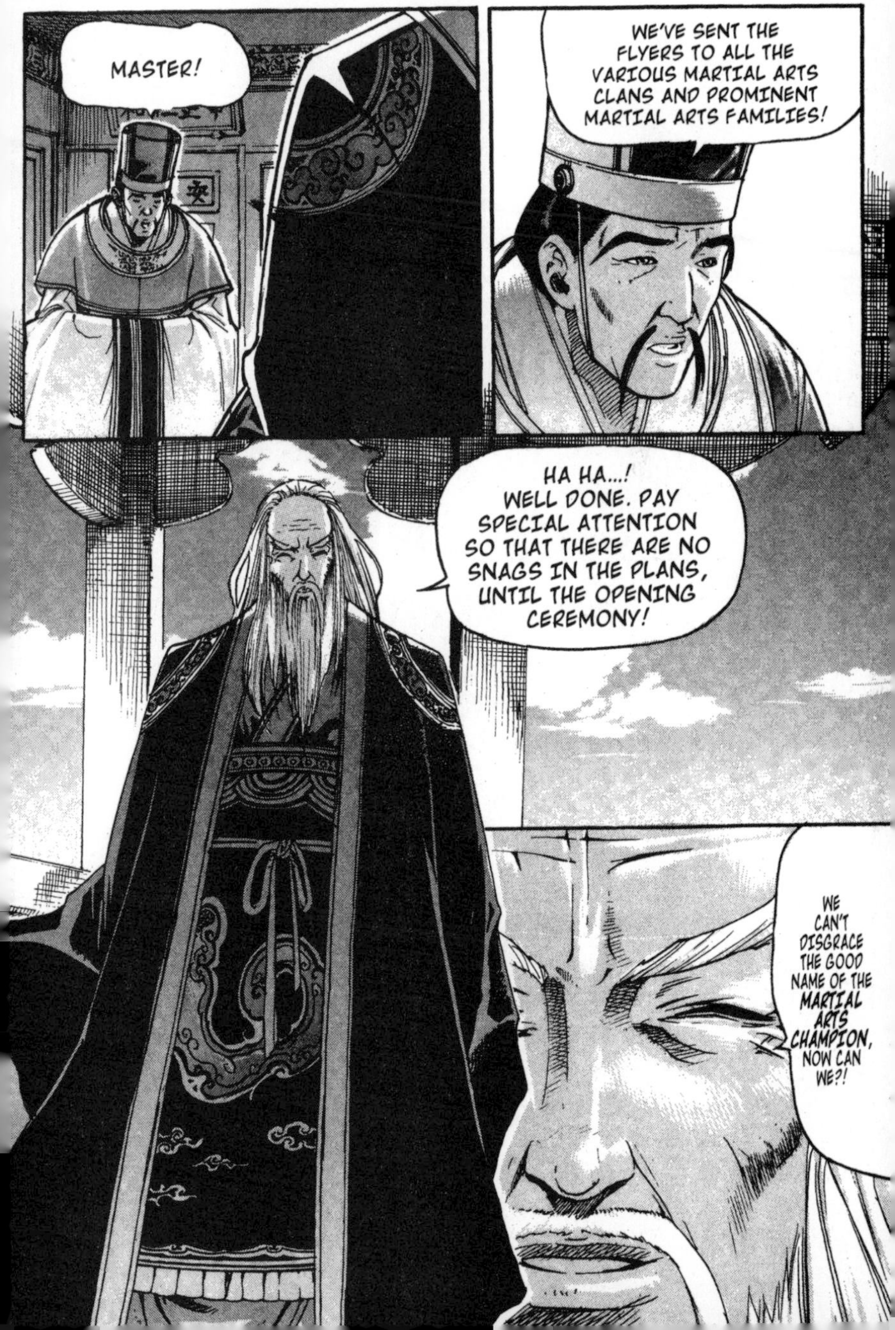
MASTER!
WE'VE SENT THE FLYERS TO ALL THE VARIOUS MARTIAL ARTS CLANS AND PROMINENT MARTIAL ARTS FAMILIES!
HA HA...! WELL DONE. PAY SPECIAL ATTENTION SO THAT THERE ARE NO SNAGS IN THE PLANS, UNTIL THE OPENING CEREMONY!
WE CAN'T DISGRACE THE GOOD NAME OF THE MARTIAL ARTS CHAMPION, NOW CAN WE?!

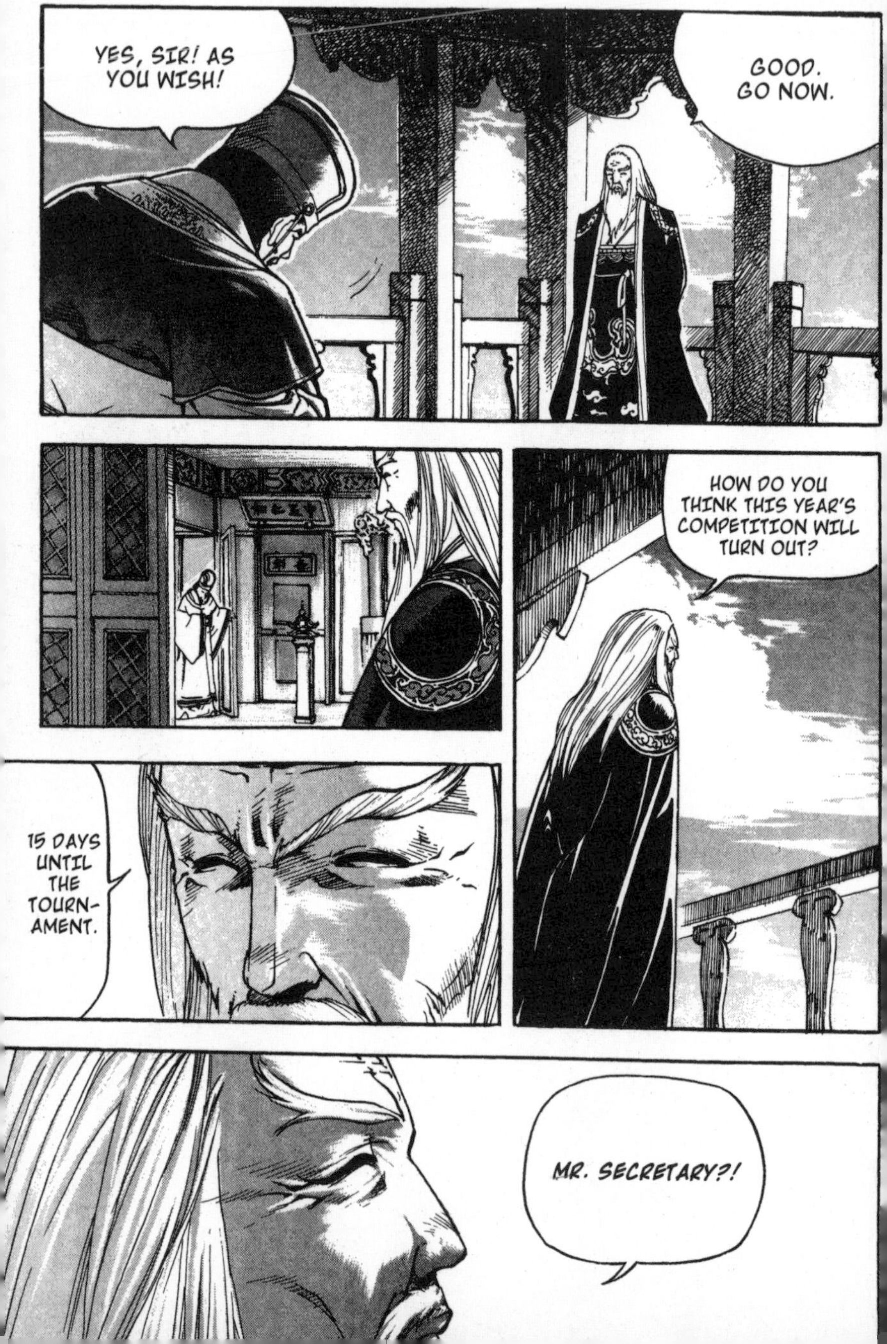
YES, SIR! AS YOU WISH!
GOOD. GO NOW.
HOW DO YOU THINK THIS YEAR'S COMPETITION WILL TURN OUT?
15 DAYS UNTIL THE TOURN-AMENT.
MR. SECRETARY?!

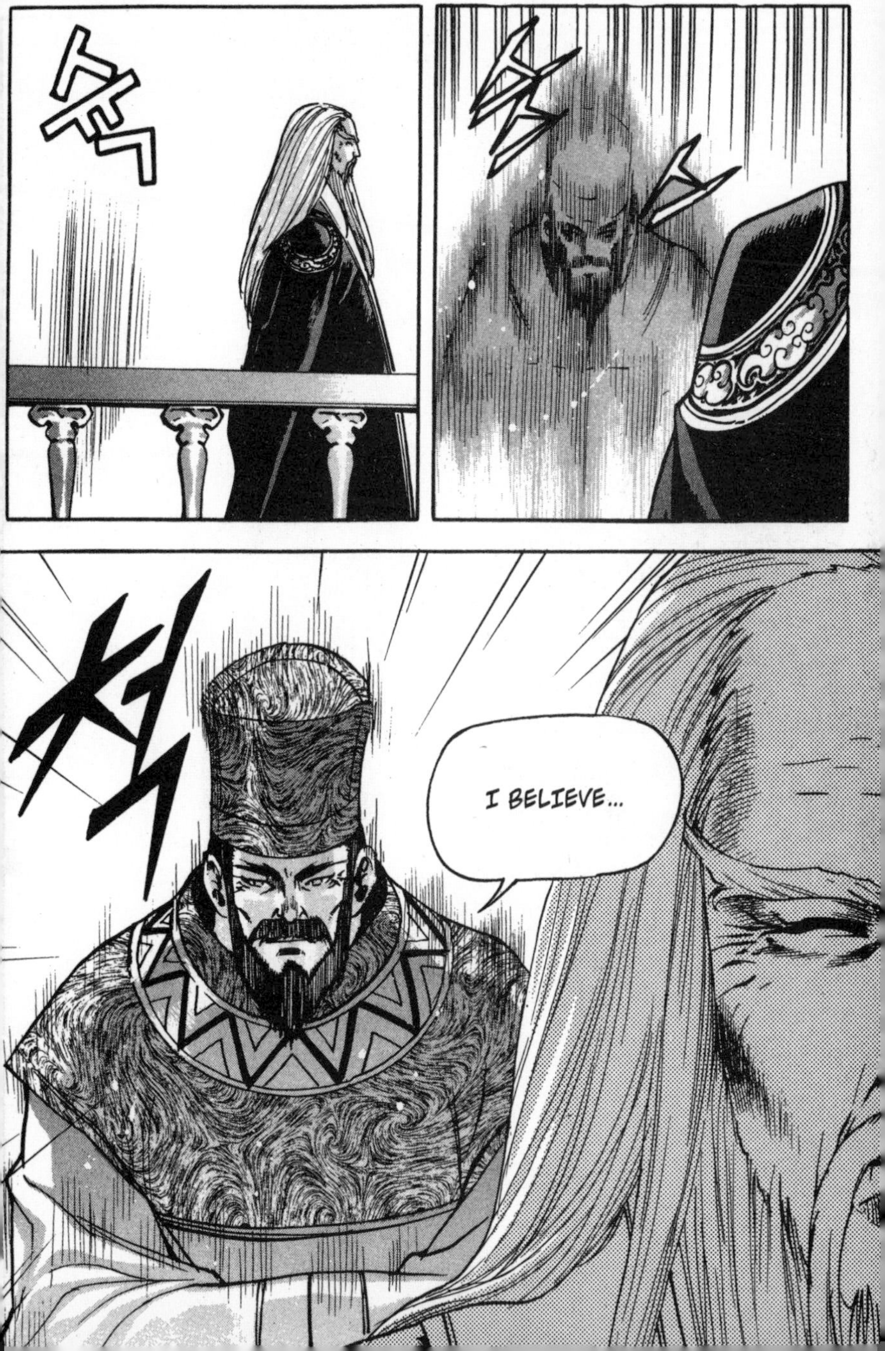
I BELIEVE...

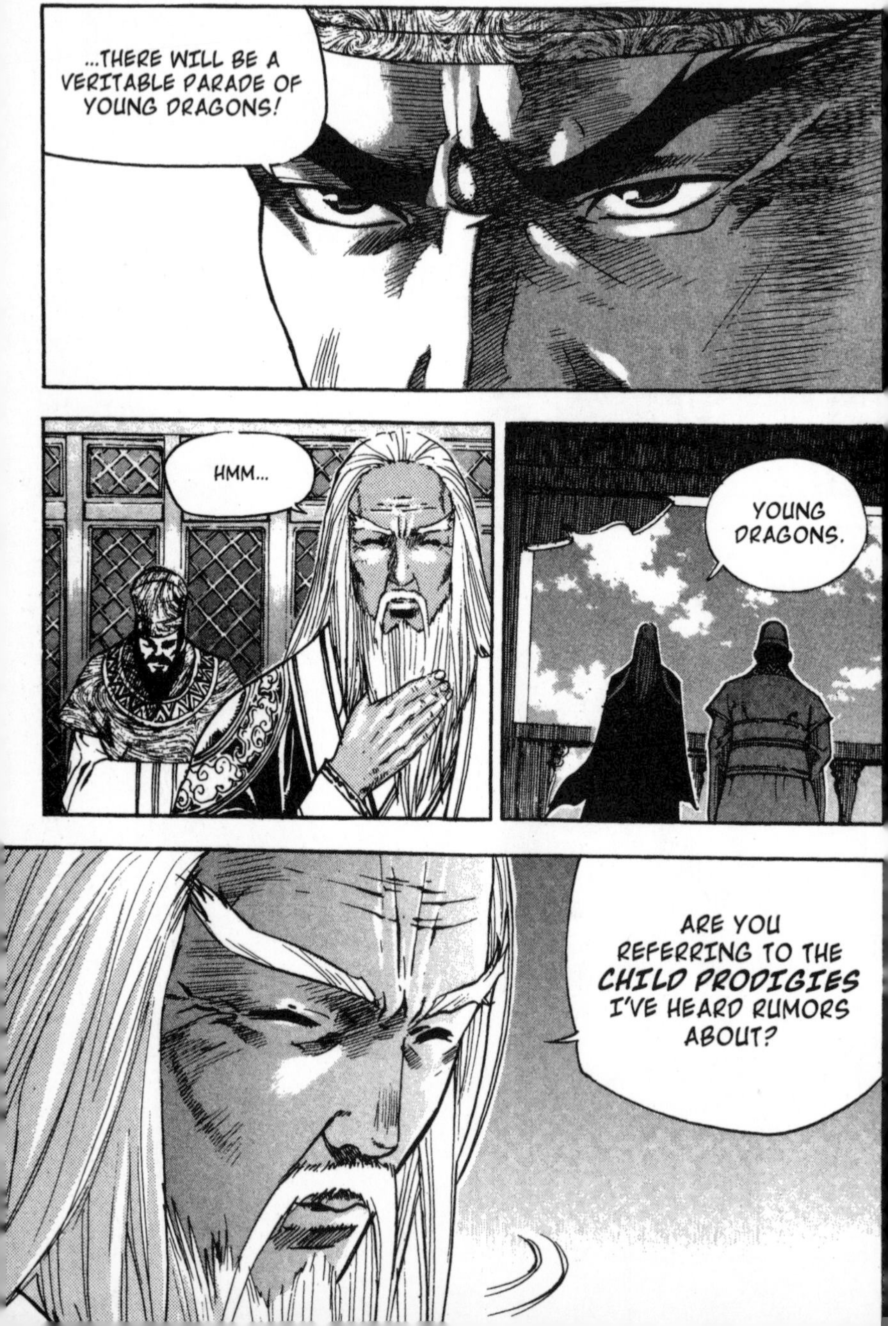
...THERE WILL BE A VERITABLE PARADE OF YOUNG DRAGONS!
HMM...
YOUNG DRAGONS.
ARE YOU REFERRING TO THE CHILD PRODIGIES I'VE HEARD RUMORS ABOUT?

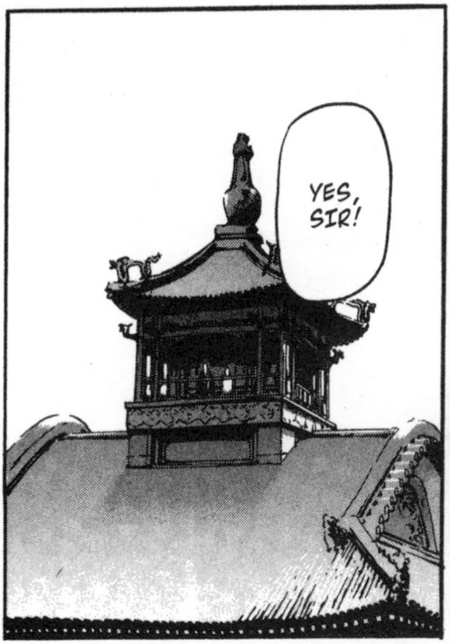
YES, SIR!
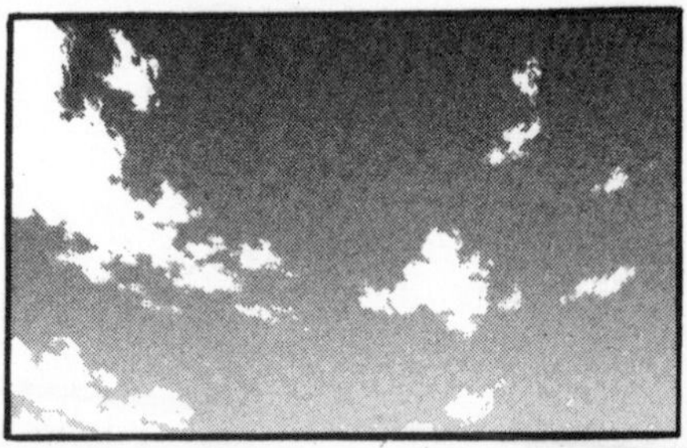
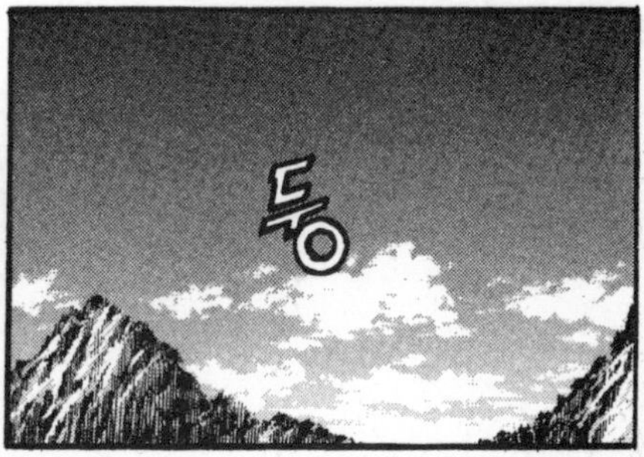
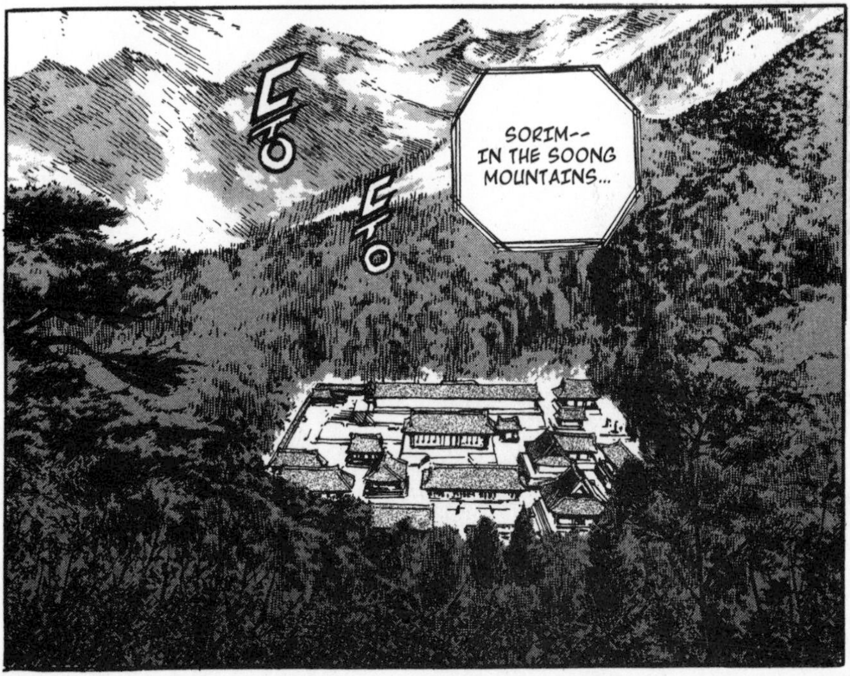
SORIM--
IN THE SOONG MOUNTAINS...

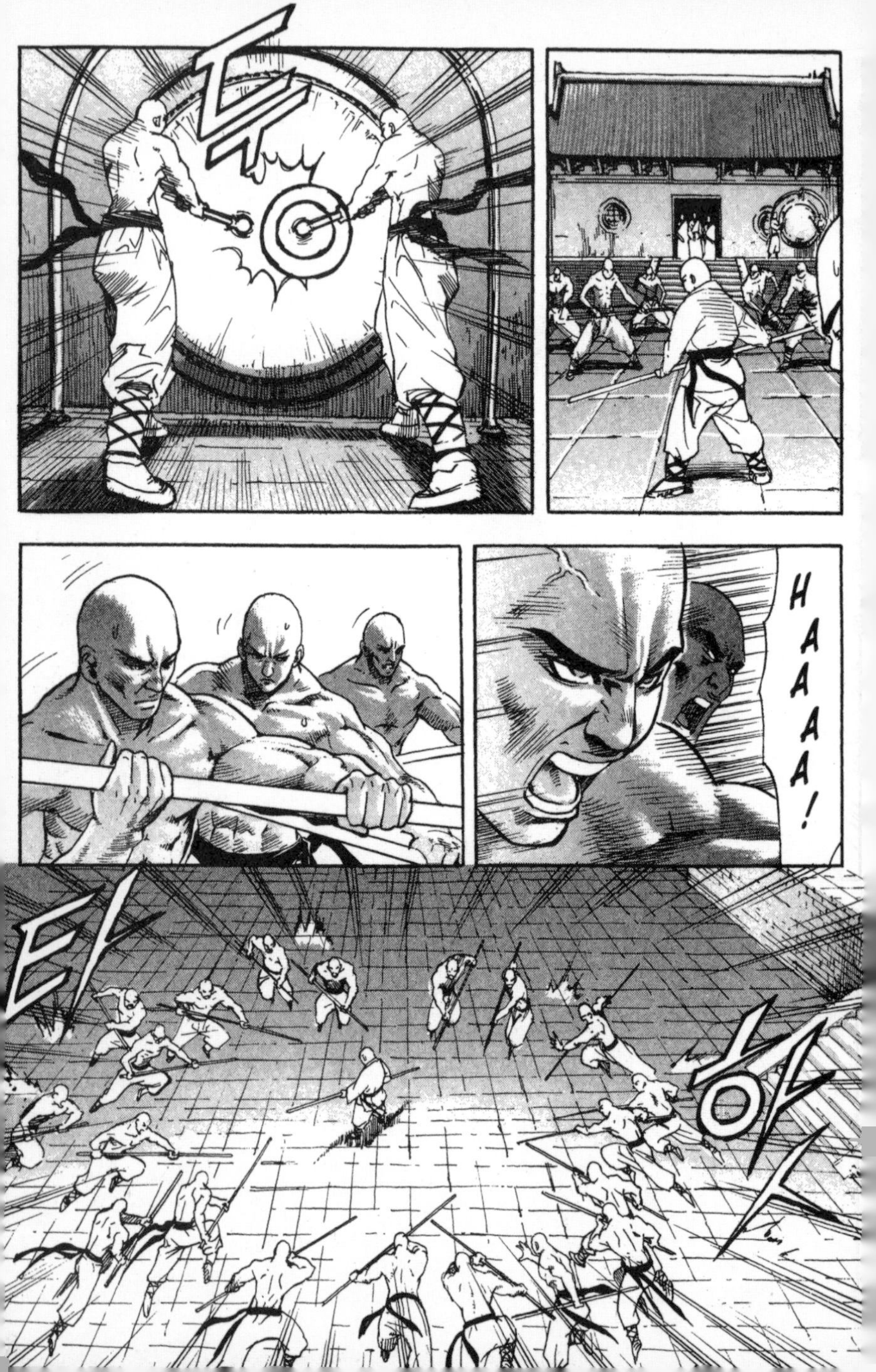
HAAAAA!

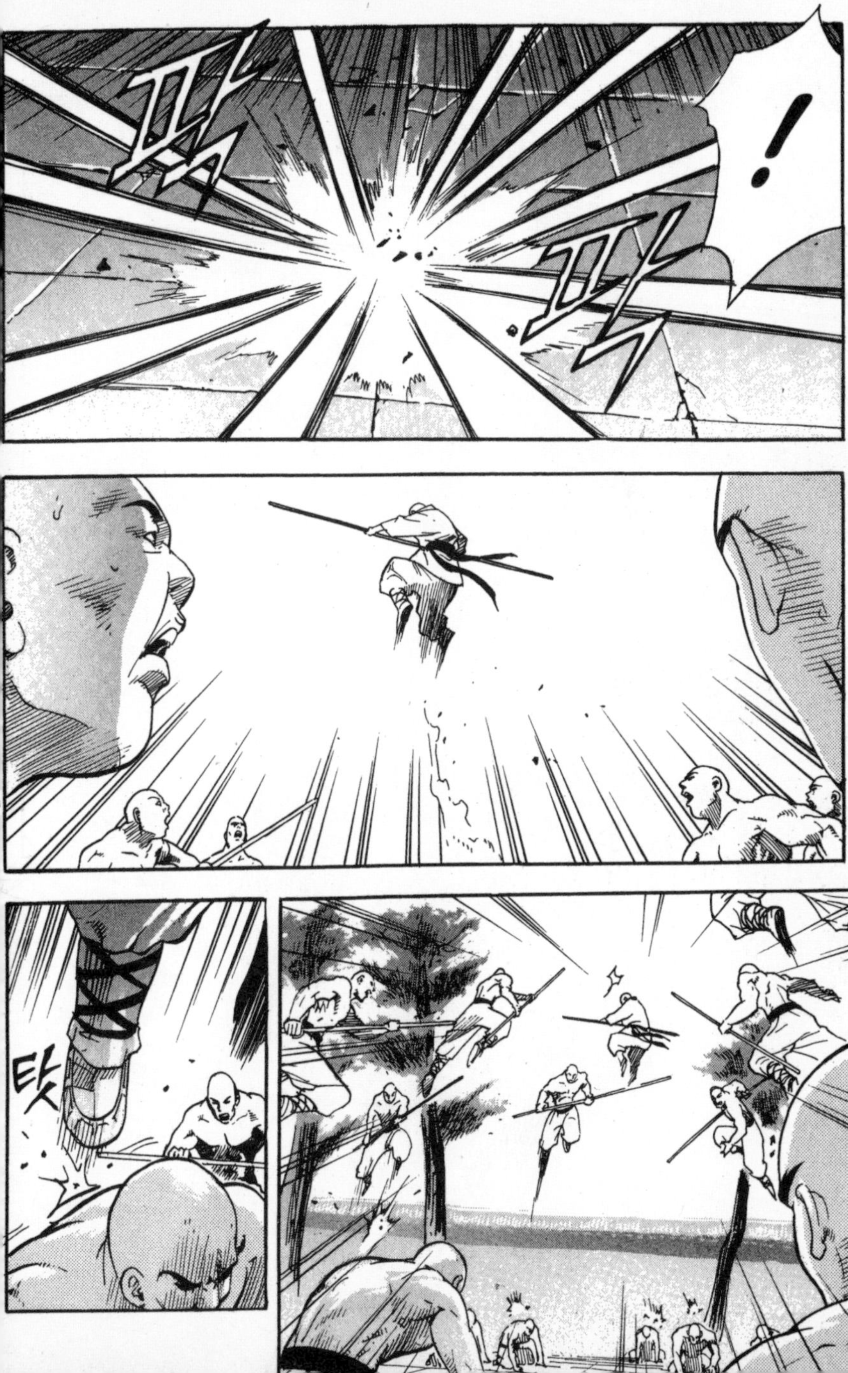
팟
!
팟
탓

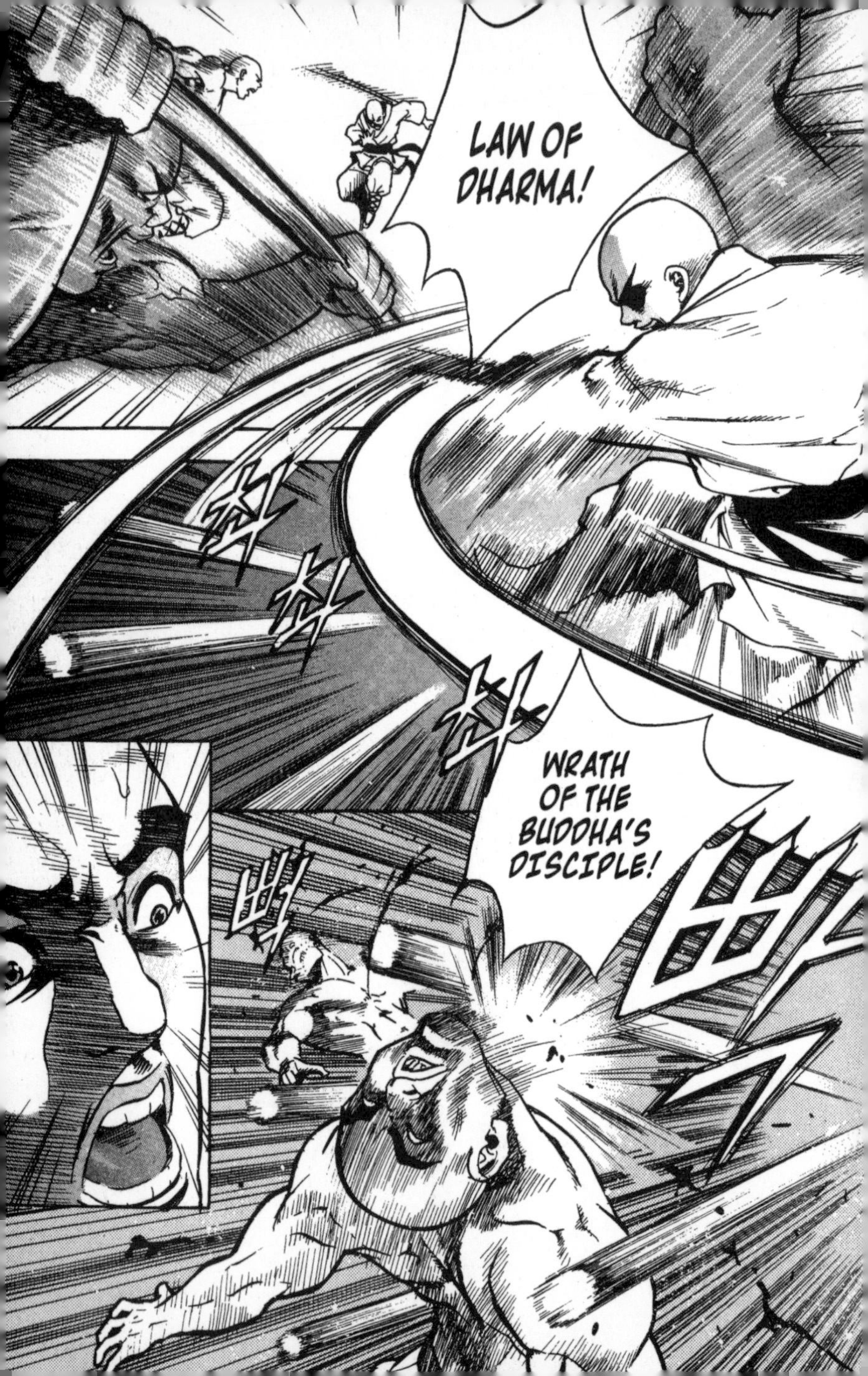
LAW OF DHARMA!
WRATH OF THE BUDDHA'S DISCIPLE!

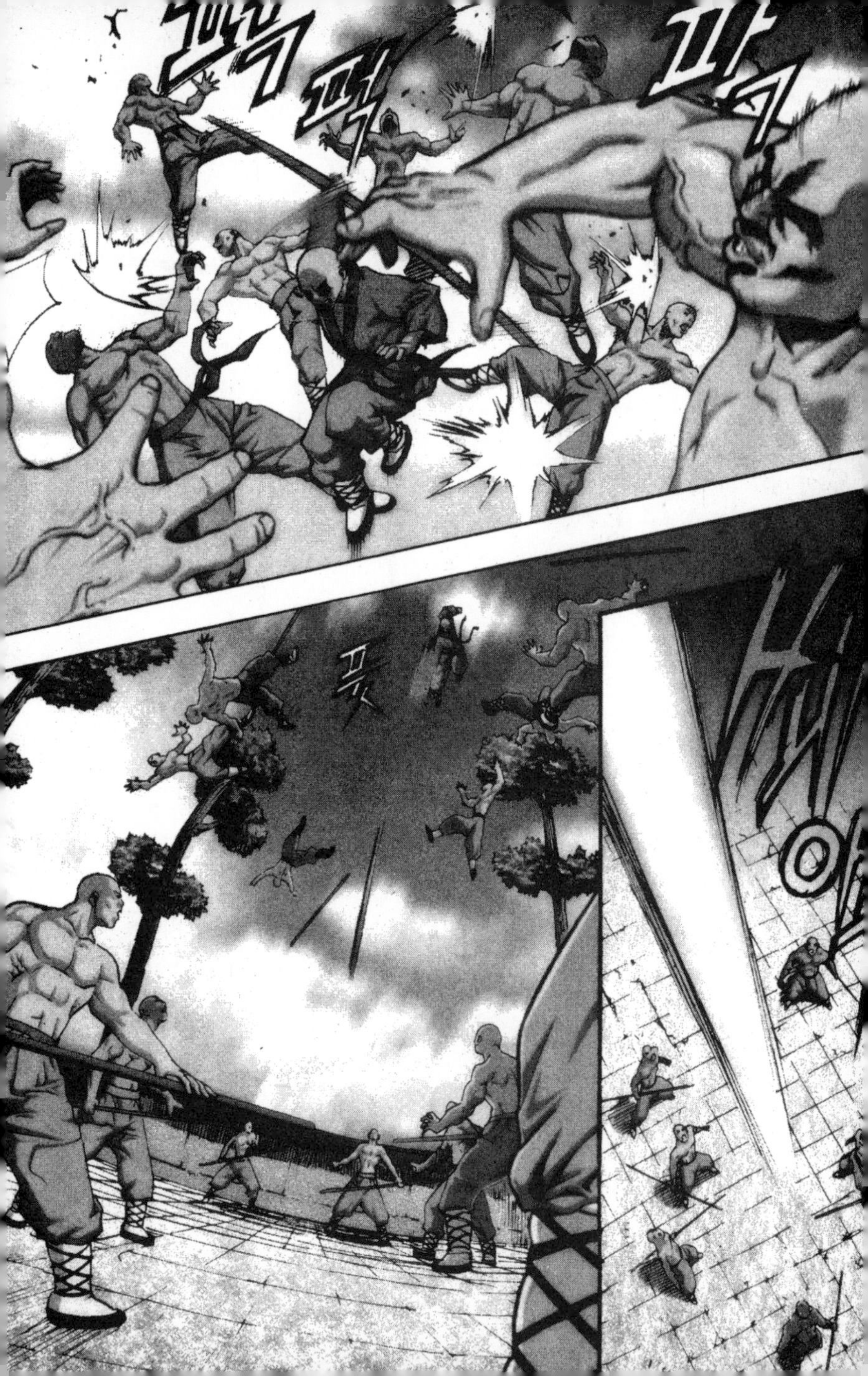

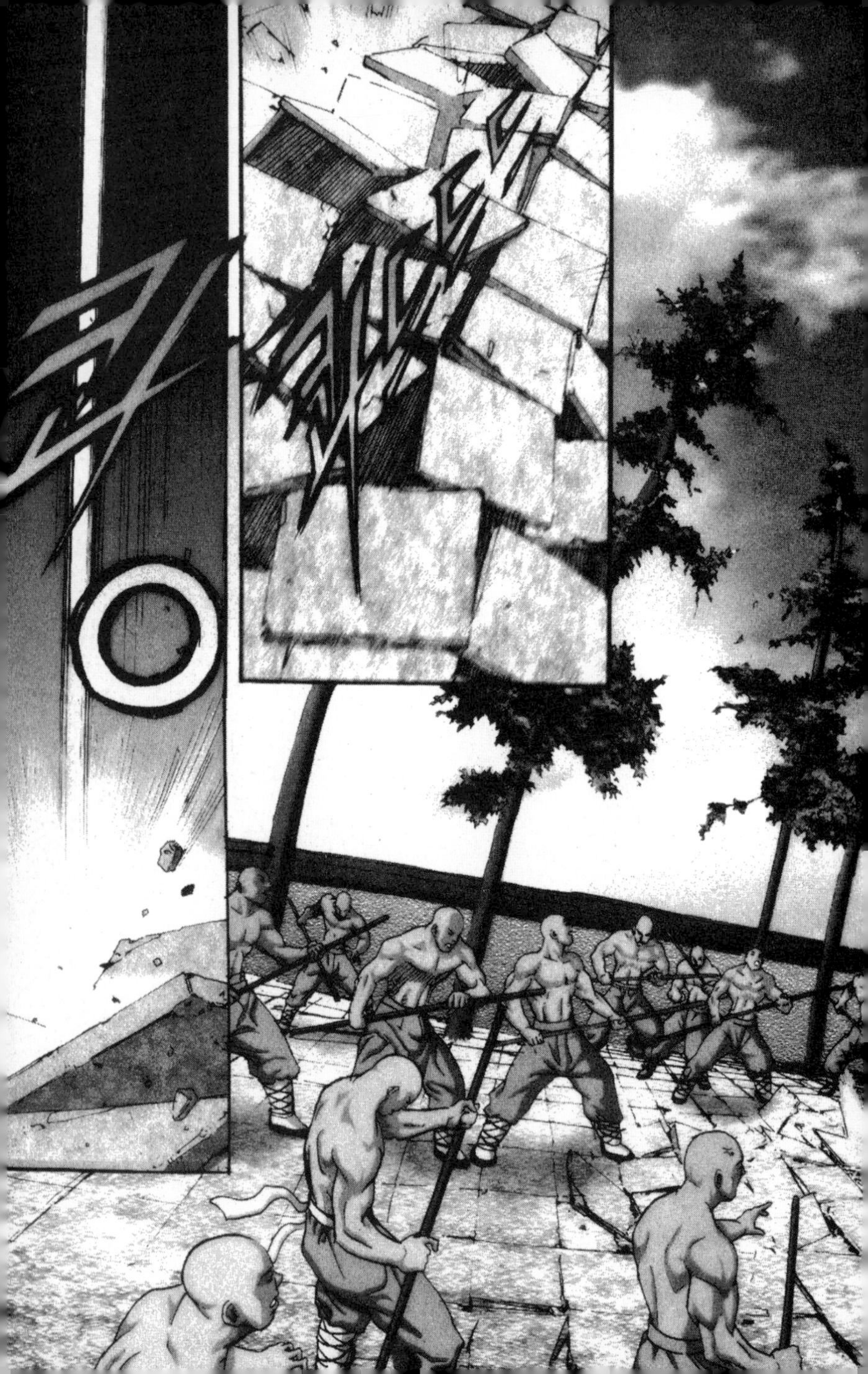

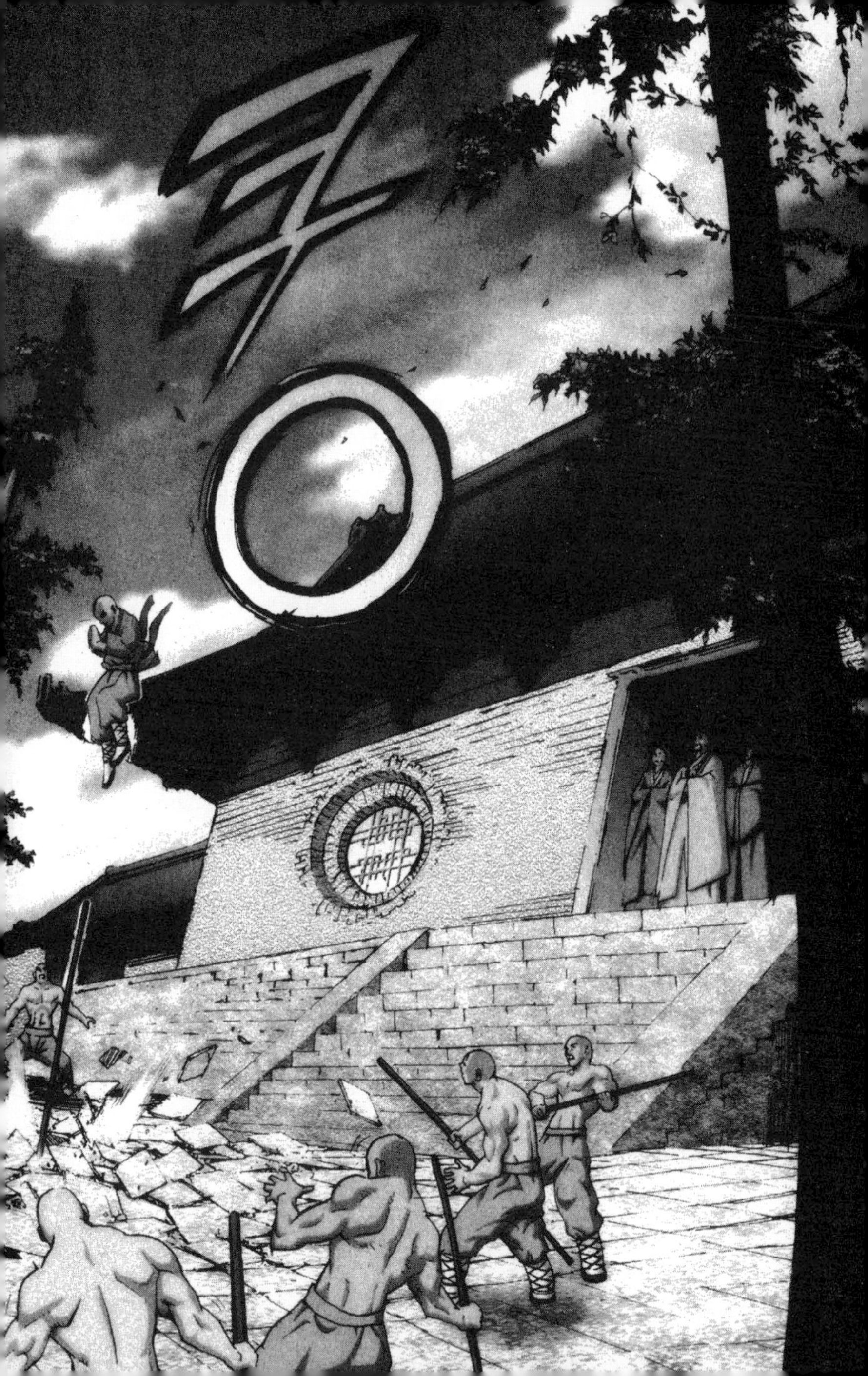

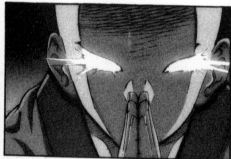

ONE THOUSAND POUND BUDDHA'S DISCIPLE!

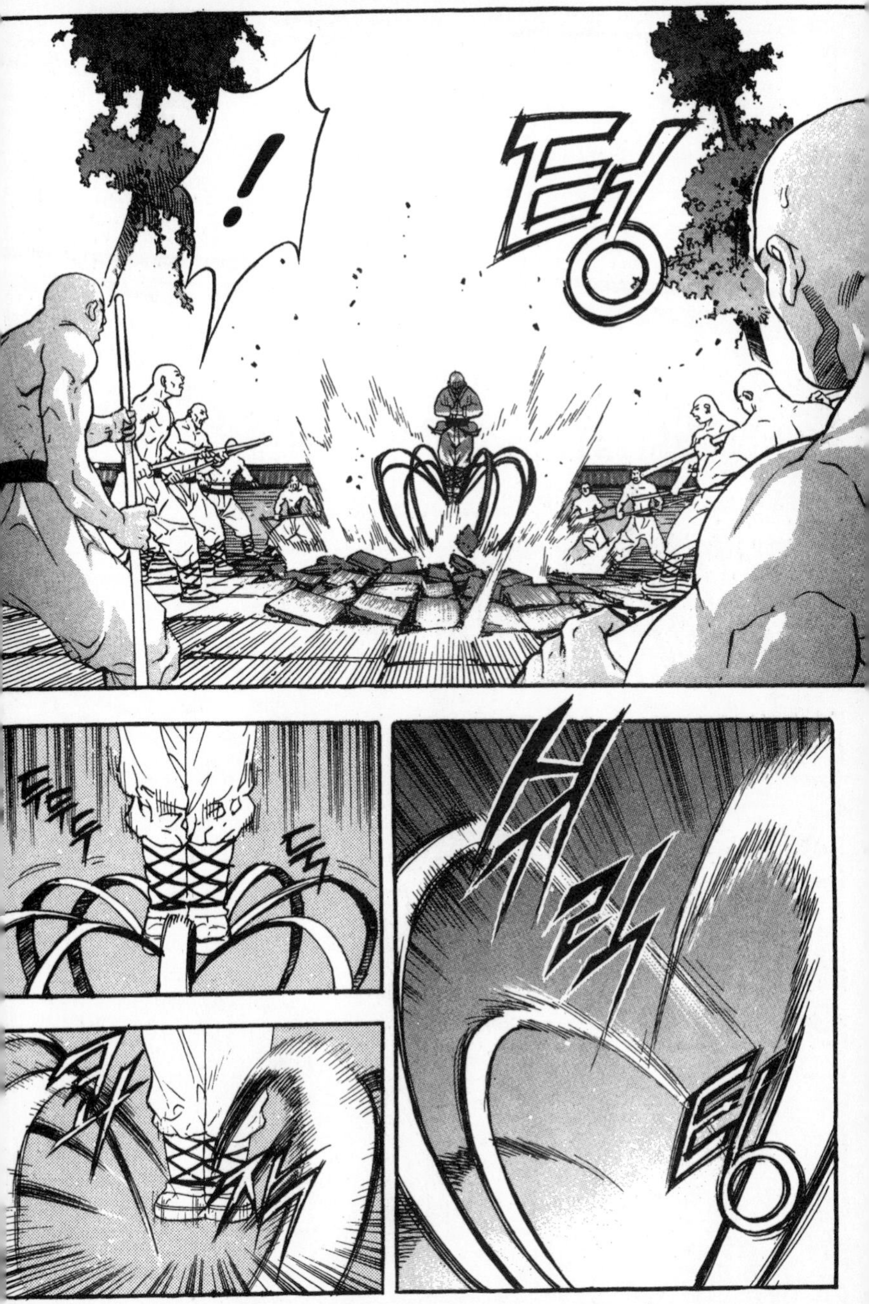
!
텅
두두두
서걱
텅

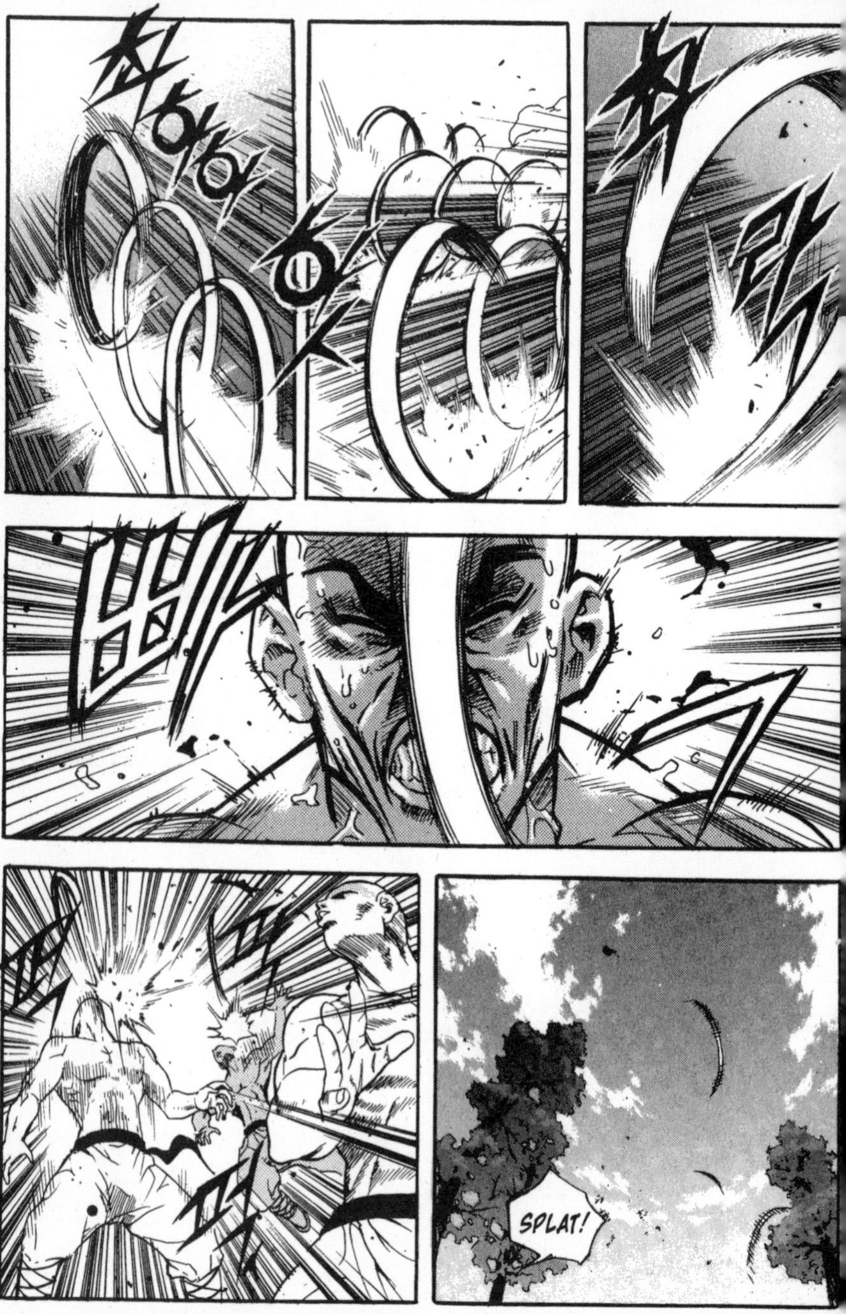
SPLAT!

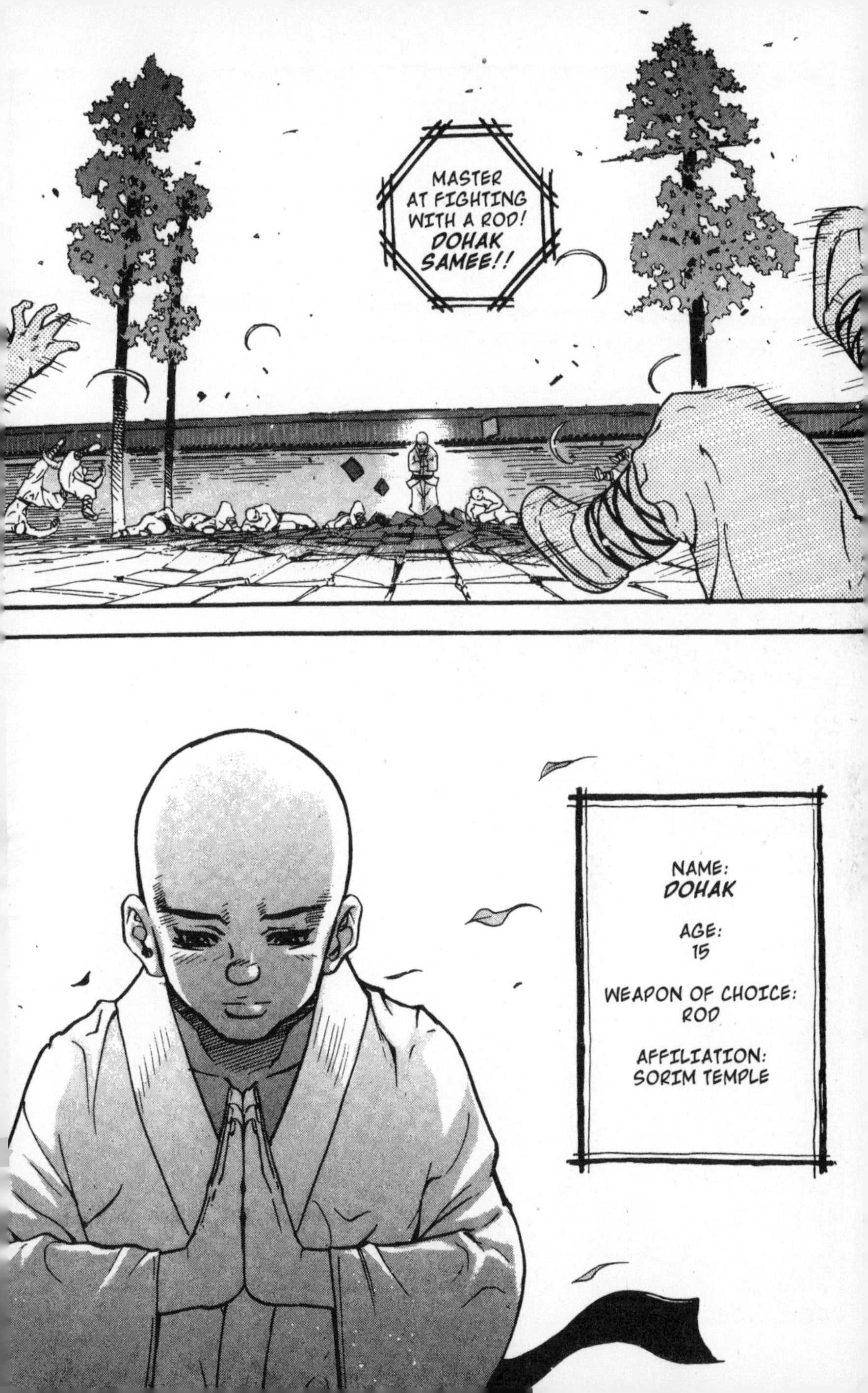
MASTER AT FIGHTING WITH A ROD! DOHAK SAMEE!!
NAME: DOHAK
AGE: 15
WEAPON OF CHOICE: ROD
AFFILIATION: SORIM TEMPLE

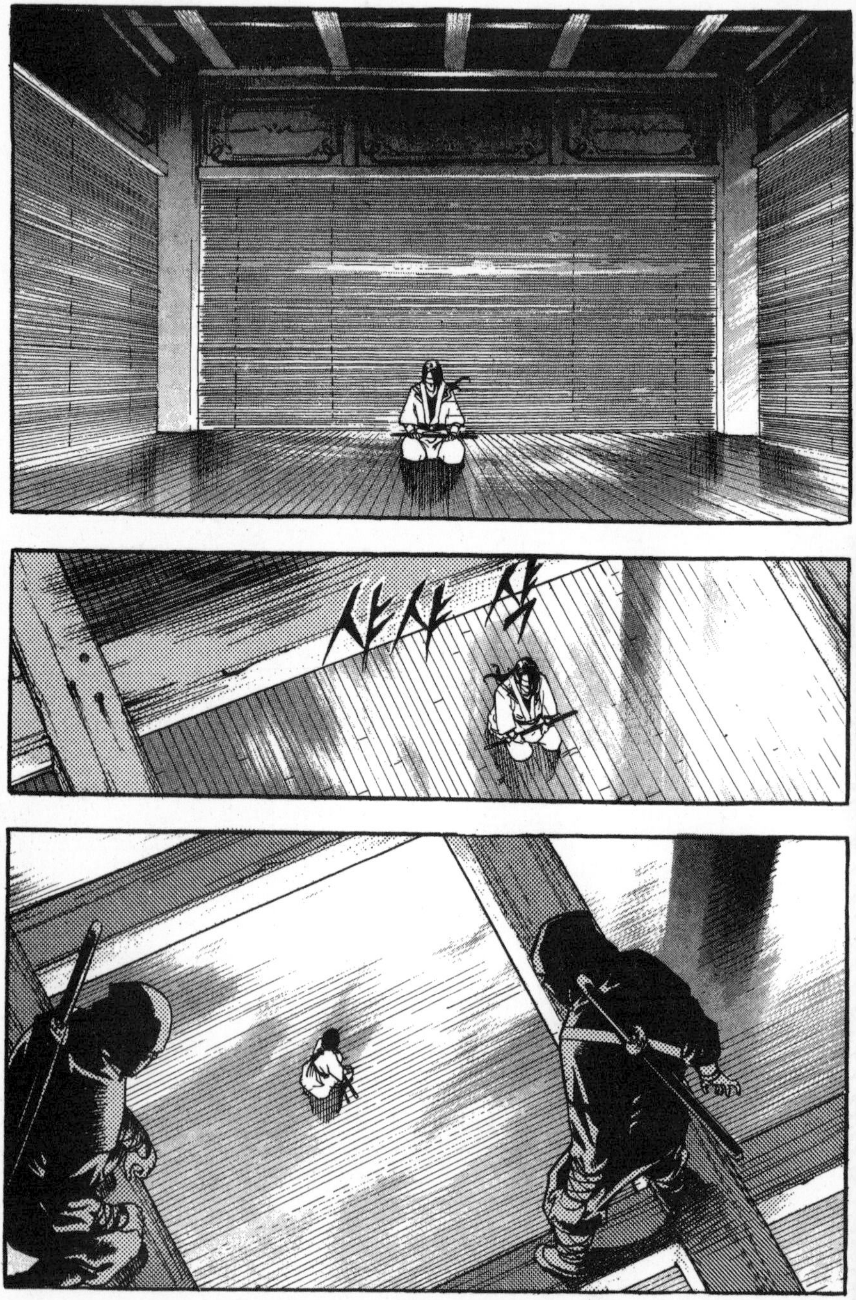
사사 삭

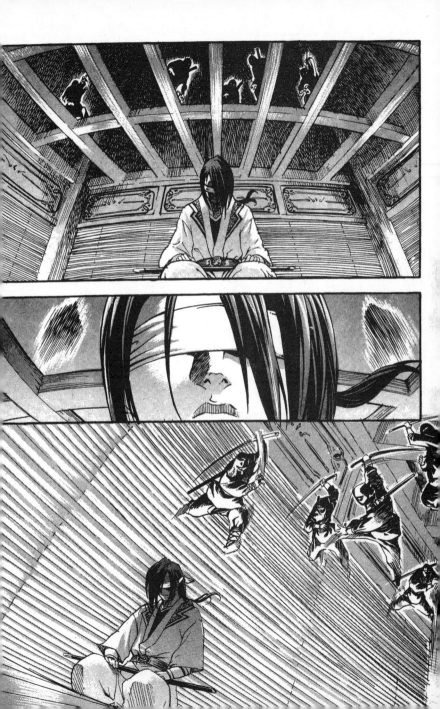

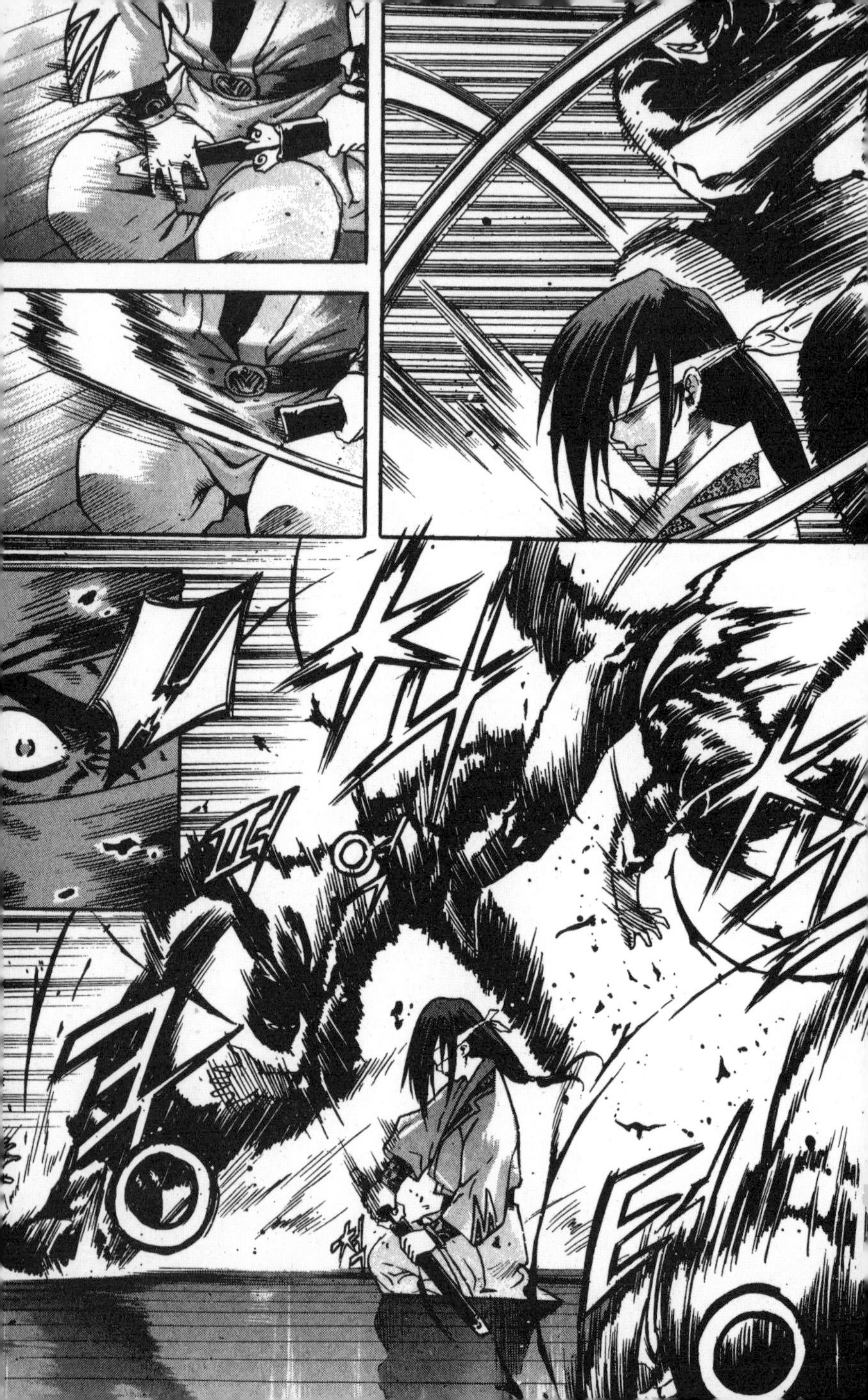

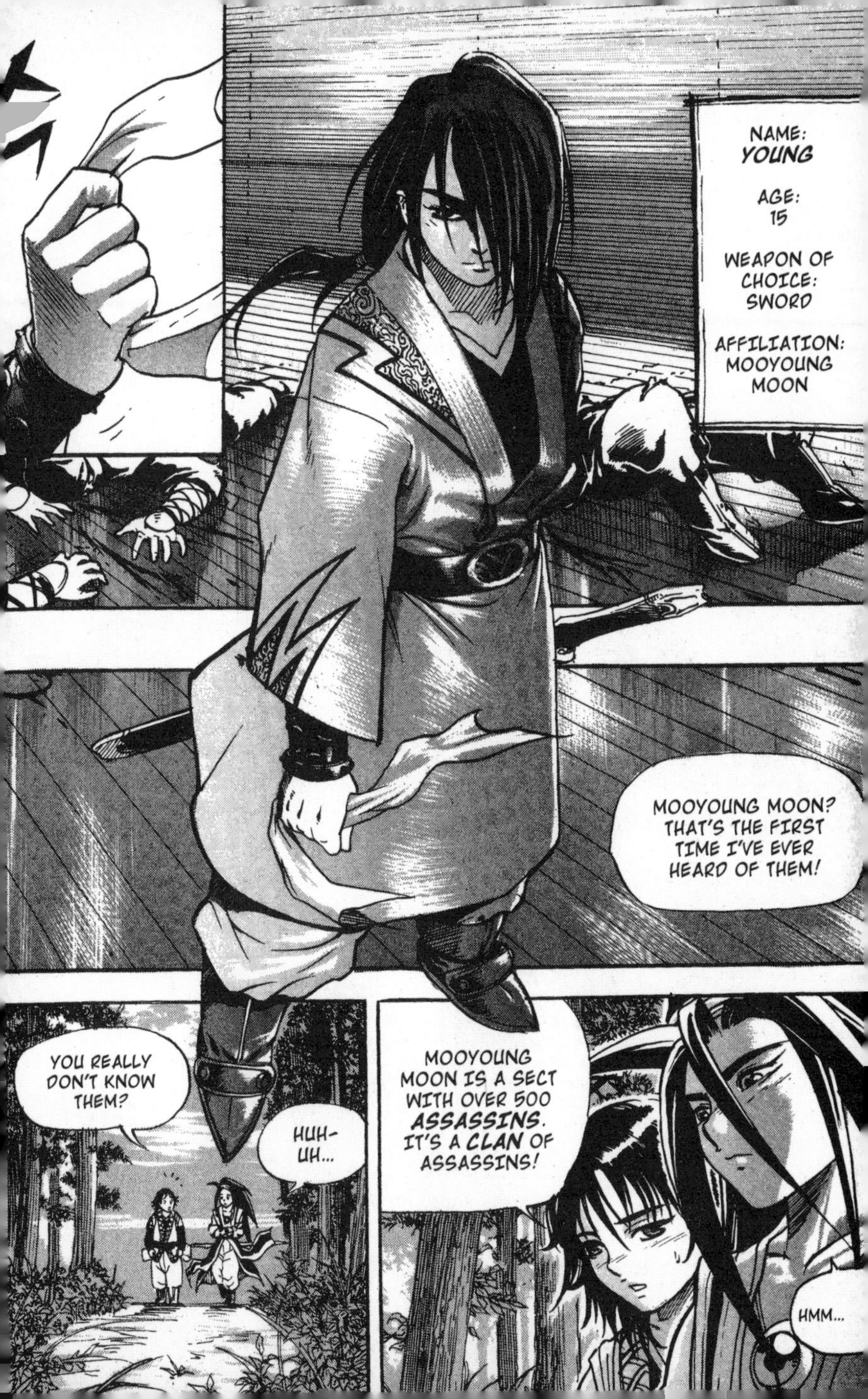
NAME:
YOUNG
AGE:
15
WEAPON OF CHOICE:
SWORD
AFFILIATION:
MOOYOUNG MOON
MOOYOUNG MOON? THAT'S THE FIRST TIME I'VE EVER HEARD OF THEM!
YOU REALLY DON'T KNOW THEM?
HUH-UH...
MOOYOUNG MOON IS A SECT WITH OVER 500 ASSASSINS. IT'S A CLAN OF ASSASSINS!
HMM...

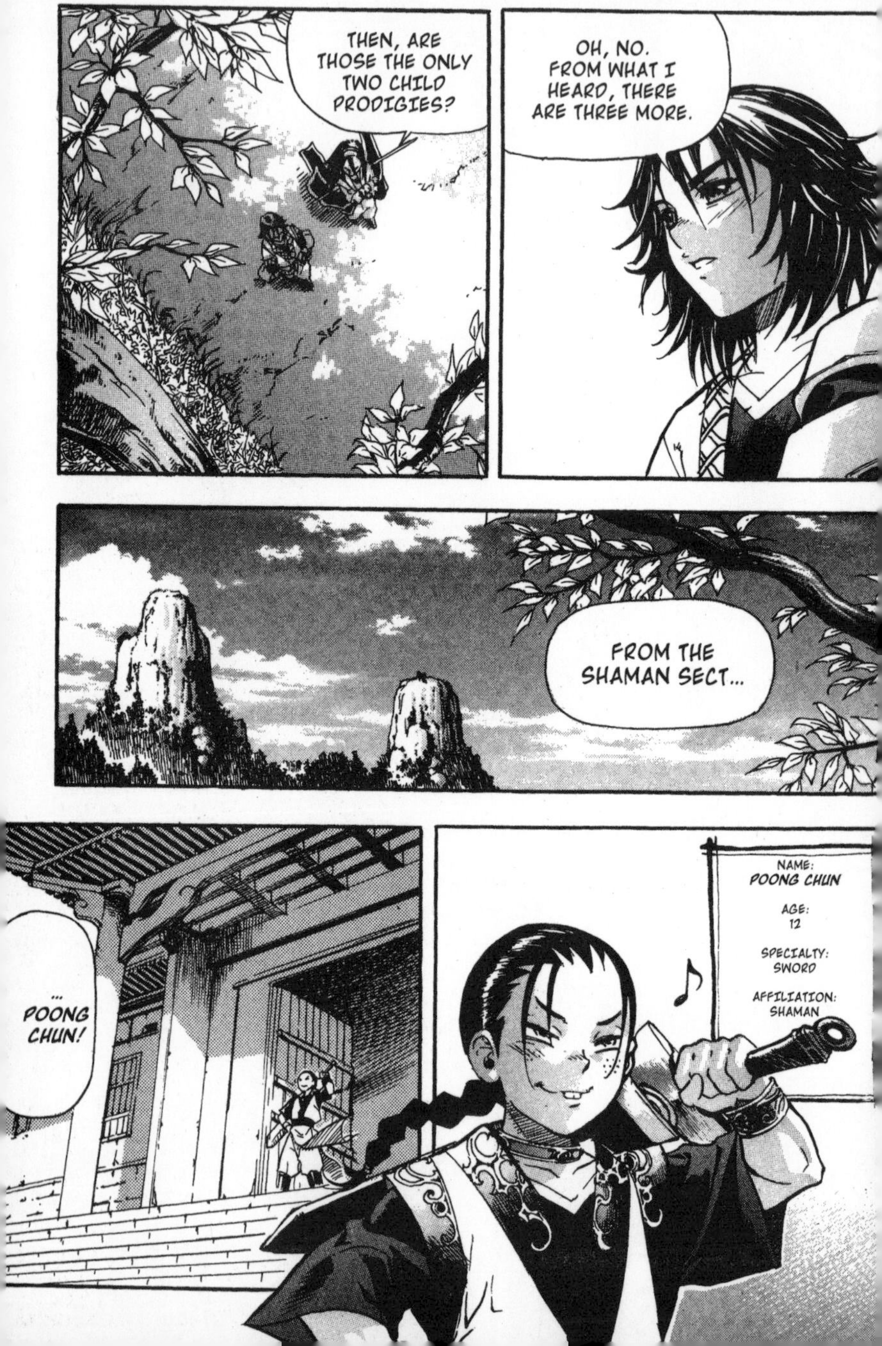
THEN, ARE THOSE THE ONLY TWO CHILD PRODIGIES?
OH, NO. FROM WHAT I HEARD, THERE ARE THREE MORE.
FROM THE SHAMAN SECT...
... POONG CHUN!
NAME: POONG CHUN
AGE: 12
SPECIALTY: SWORD
AFFILIATION: SHAMAN

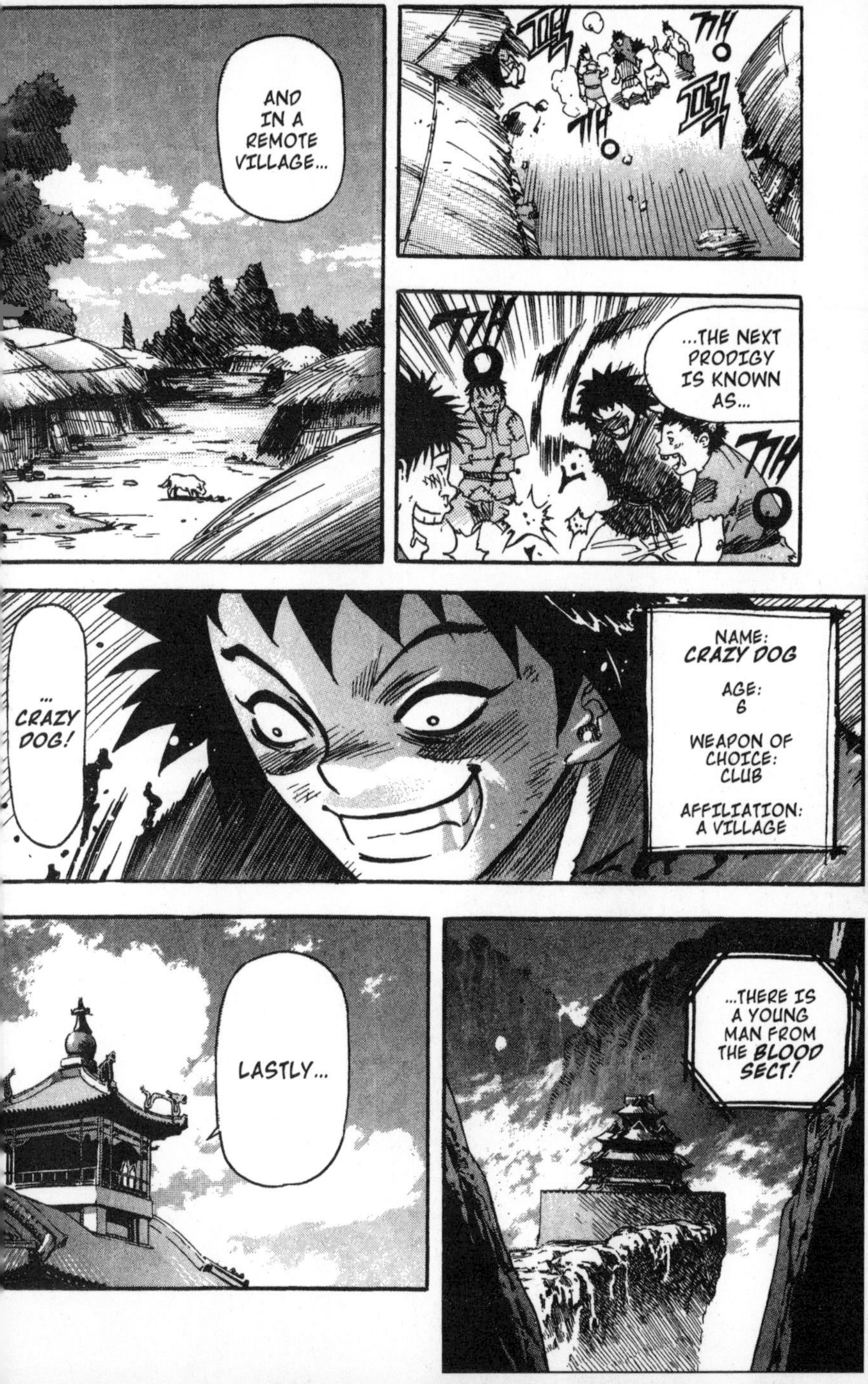
AND IN A REMOTE VILLAGE...
...THE NEXT PRODIGY IS KNOWN AS...
...CRAZY DOG!
NAME: CRAZY DOG
AGE: 6
WEAPON OF CHOICE: CLUB
AFFILIATION: A VILLAGE
LASTLY...
...THERE IS A YOUNG MAN FROM THE BLOOD SECT!

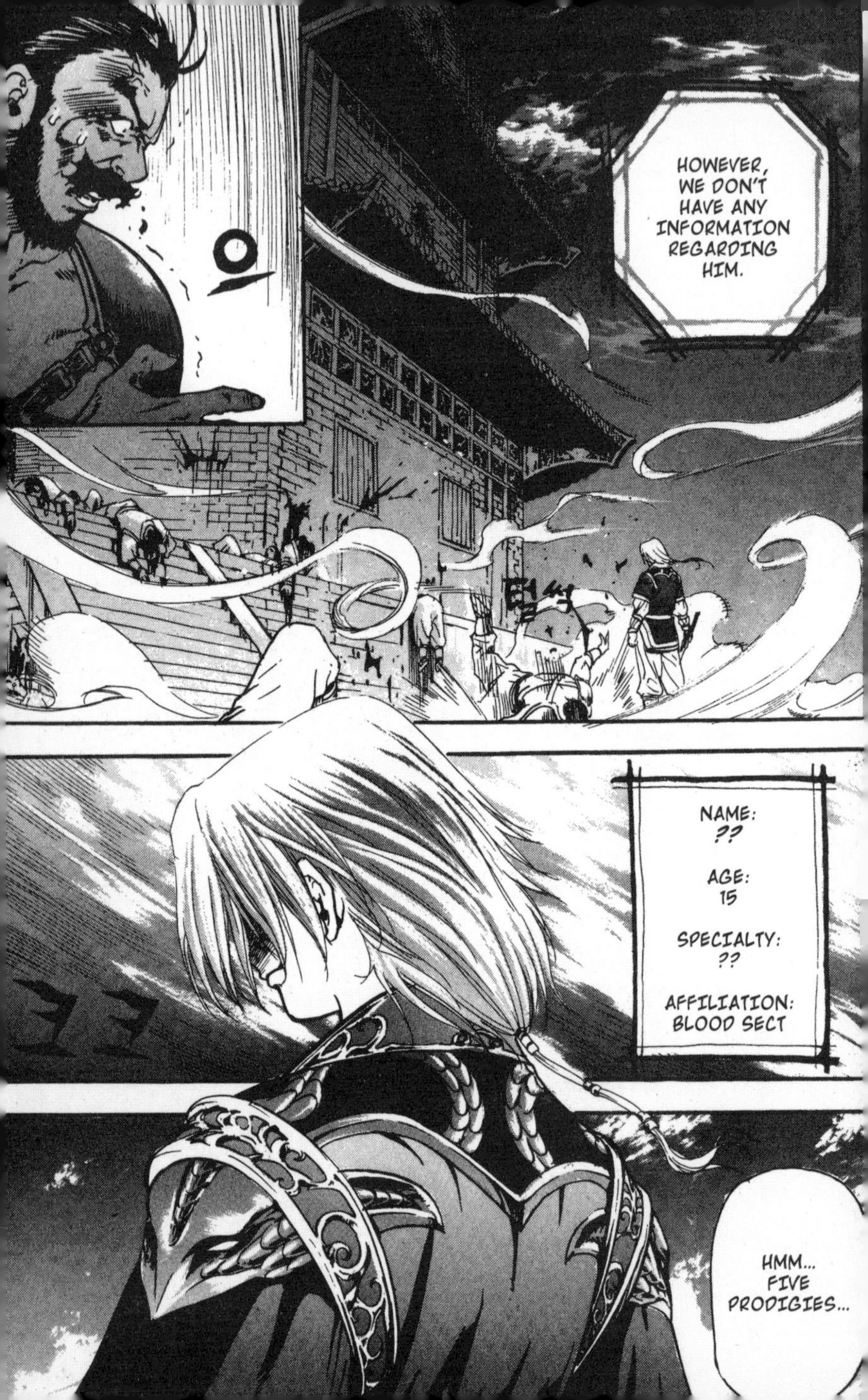
HOWEVER, WE DON'T HAVE ANY INFORMATION REGARDING HIM.
NAME: ??
AGE: 15
SPECIALTY: ??
AFFILIATION: BLOOD SECT
HMM... FIVE PRODIGIES...

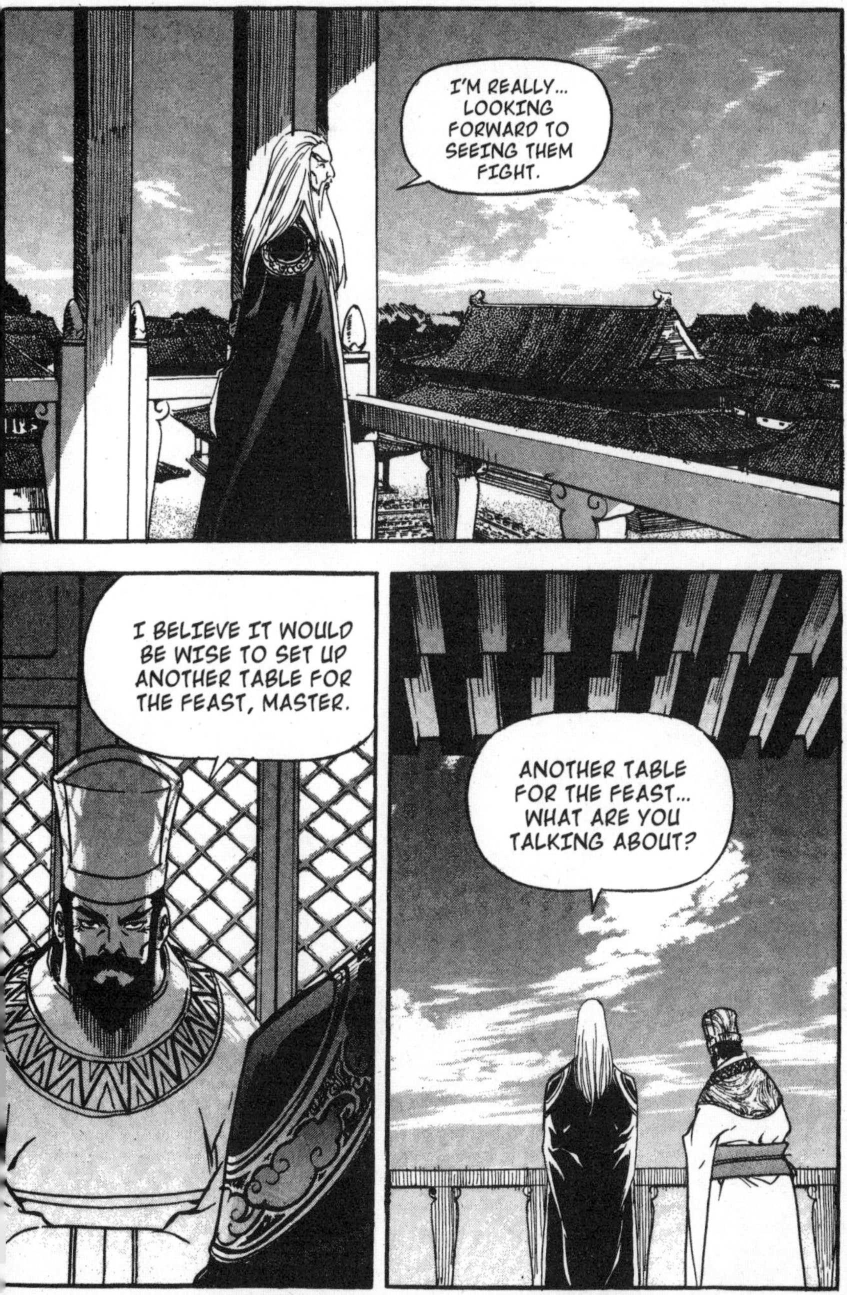
I'M REALLY... LOOKING FORWARD TO SEEING THEM FIGHT.
I BELIEVE IT WOULD BE WISE TO SET UP ANOTHER TABLE FOR THE FEAST, MASTER.
ANOTHER TABLE FOR THE FEAST... WHAT ARE YOU TALKING ABOUT?

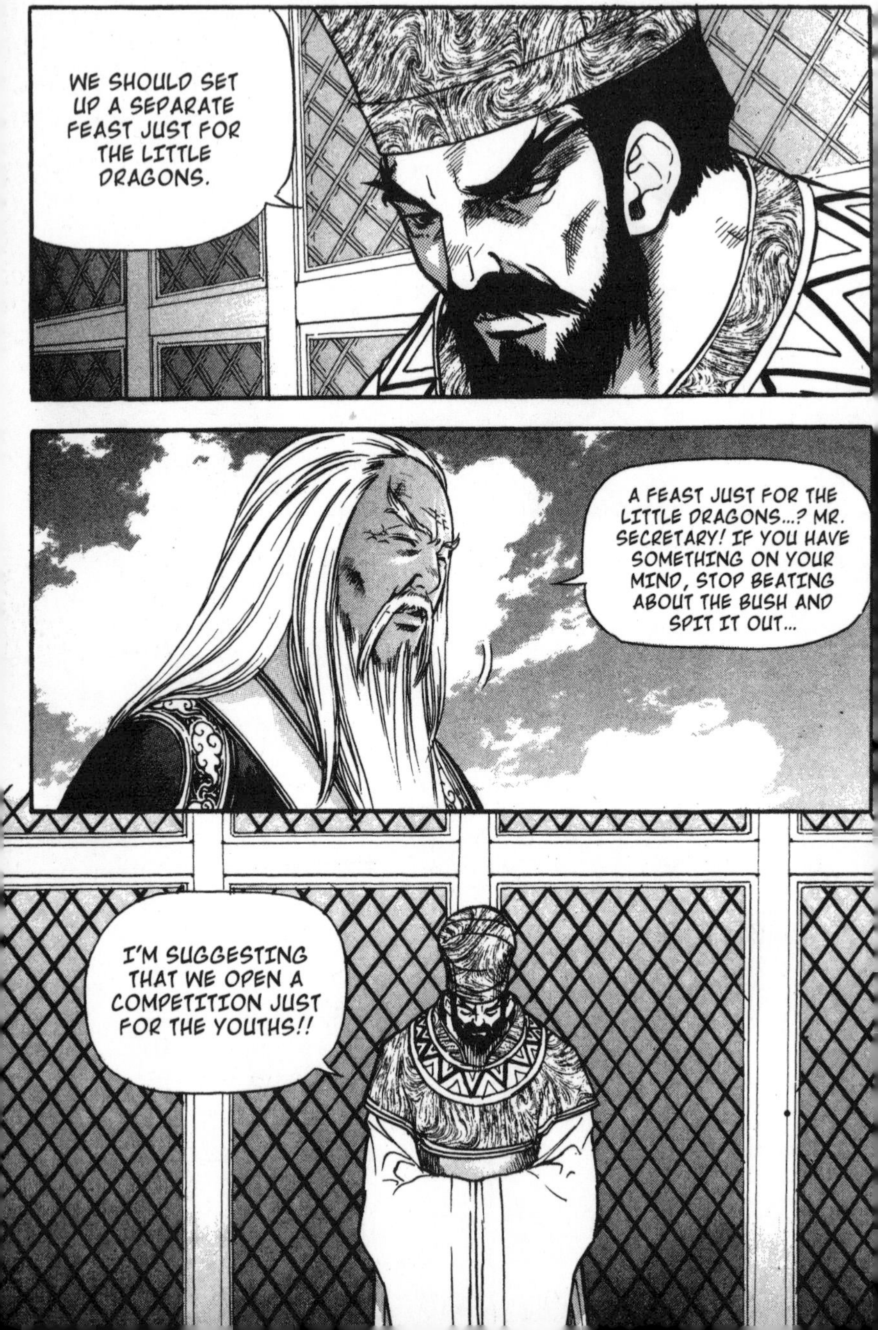
WE SHOULD SET UP A SEPARATE FEAST JUST FOR THE LITTLE DRAGONS.
A FEAST JUST FOR THE LITTLE DRAGONS...? MR. SECRETARY! IF YOU HAVE SOMETHING ON YOUR MIND, STOP BEATING ABOUT THE BUSH AND SPIT IT OUT...
I'M SUGGESTING THAT WE OPEN A COMPETITION JUST FOR THE YOUTHS!!

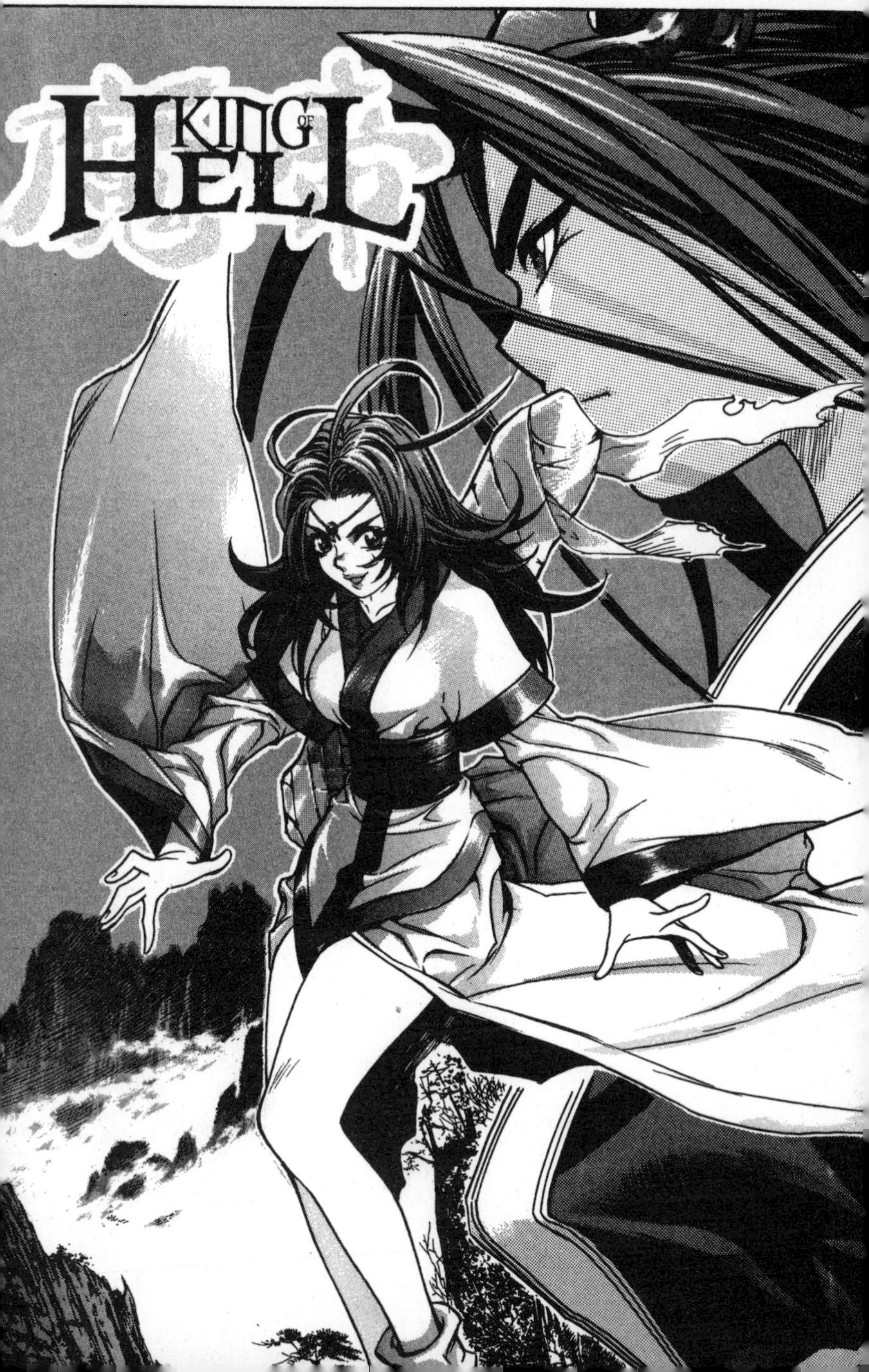
KING OF HELL

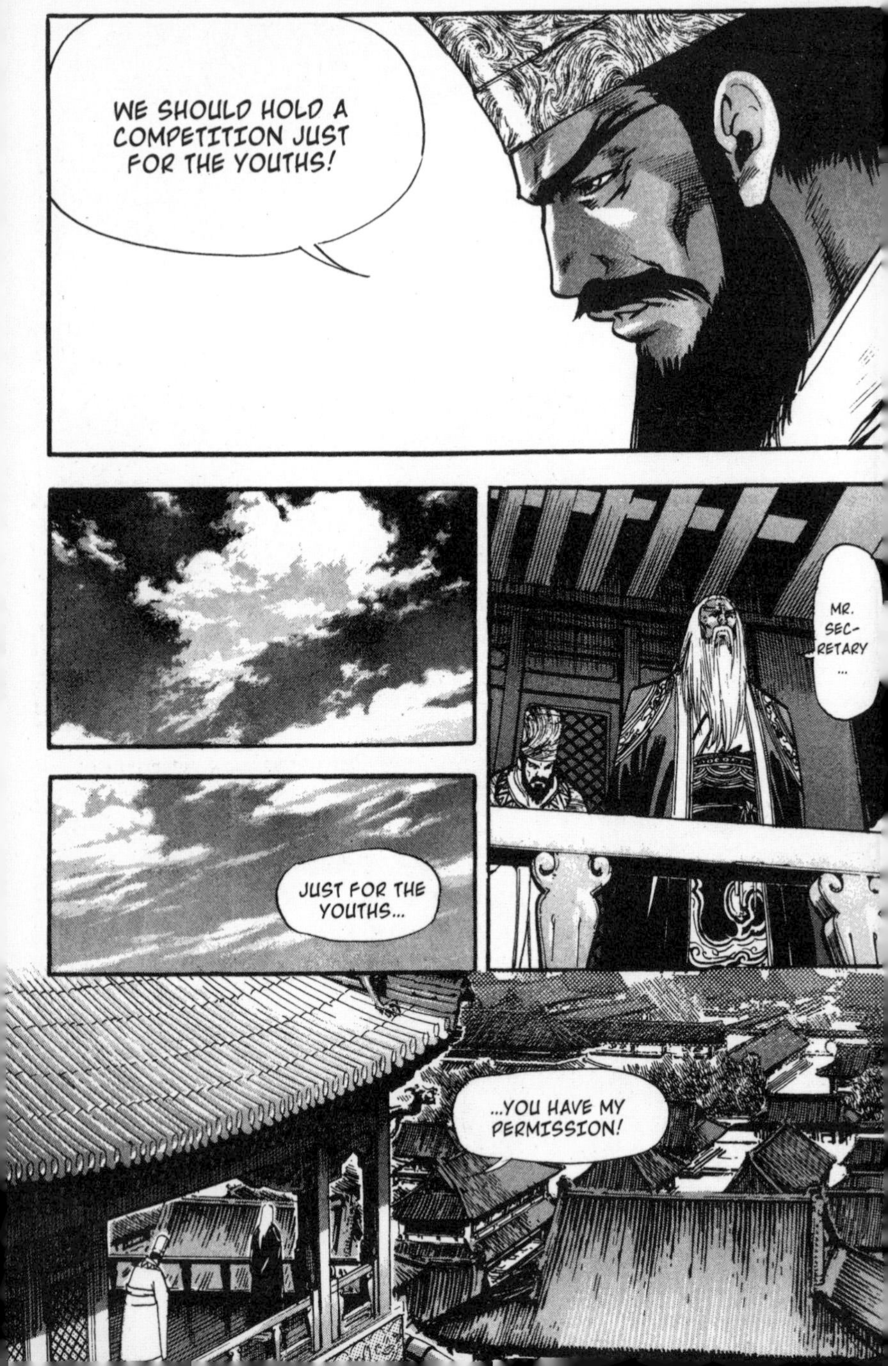
WE SHOULD HOLD A COMPETITION JUST FOR THE YOUTHS!
MR. SEC-RETARY ...
JUST FOR THE YOUTHS...
...YOU HAVE MY PERMISSION!

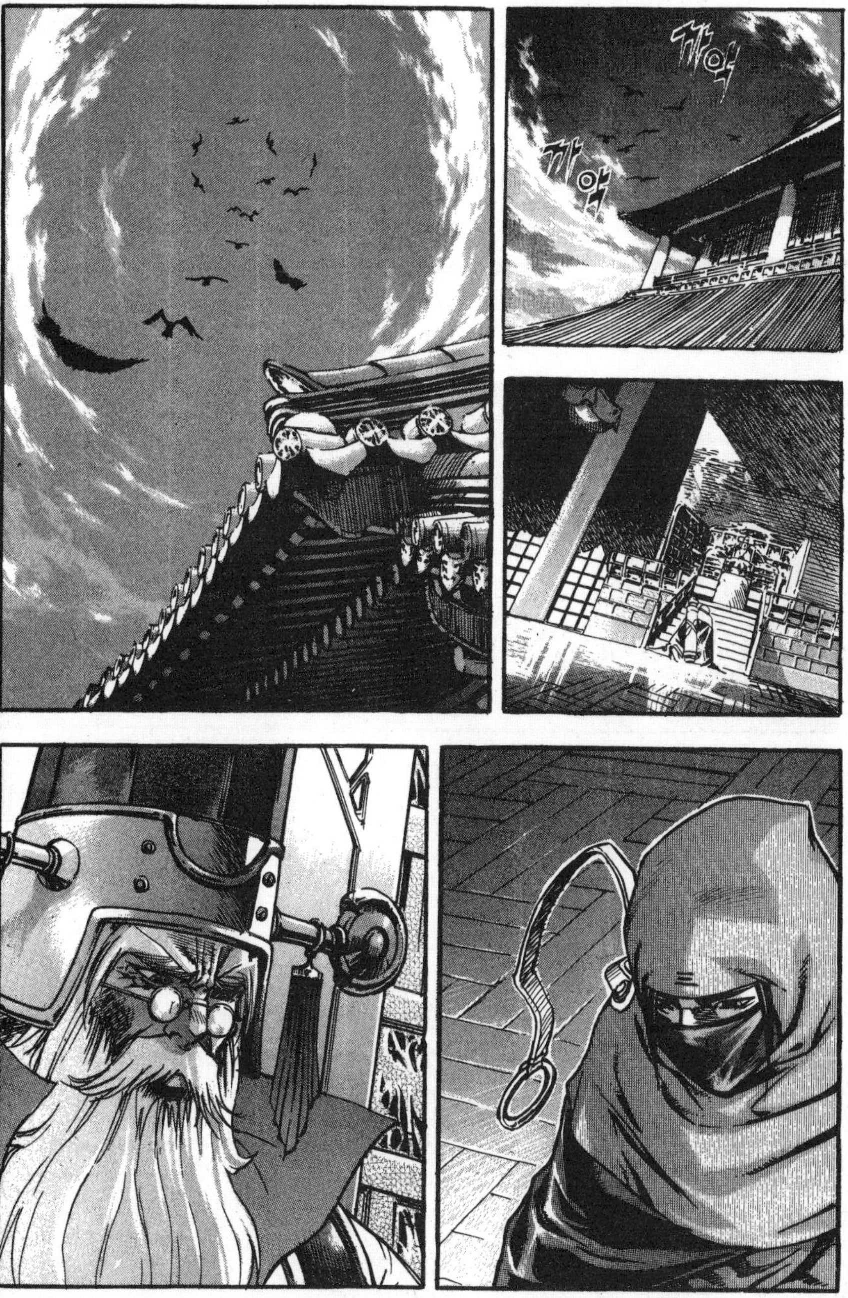
까아
까아

WHAT IS *MAJEH* DOING, SAM?

HE IS IN PURSUIT OF THE FIENDS.

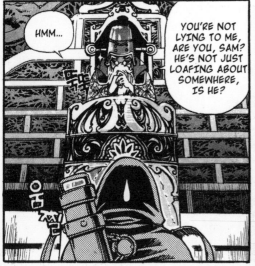

HMM...

YOU'RE NOT LYING TO ME, ARE YOU, SAM? HE'S NOT JUST LOAFING ABOUT SOMEWHERE, IS HE?

HOW...HOW CAN YOU SAY SUCH A THING, SIRE...?

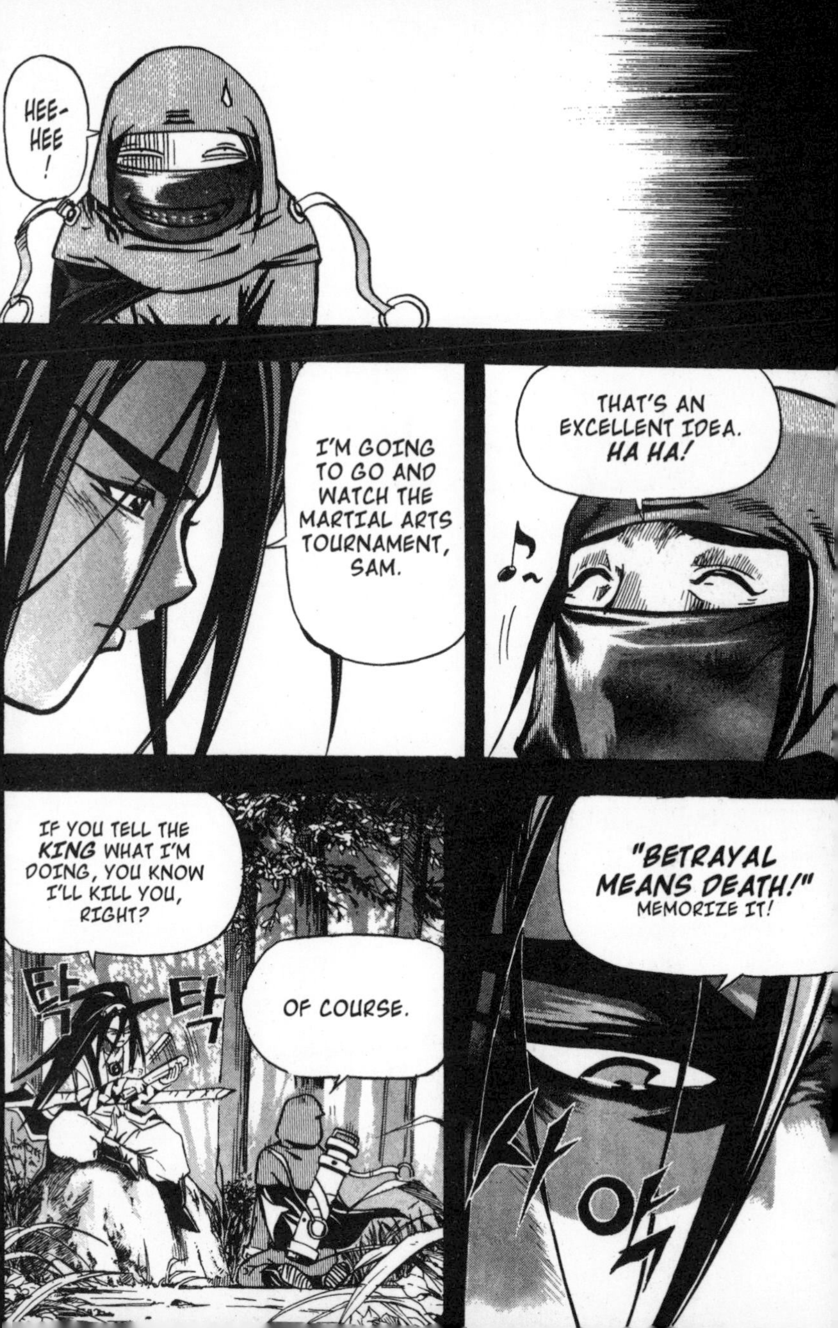
HEE-HEE!
I'M GOING TO GO AND WATCH THE MARTIAL ARTS TOURNAMENT, SAM.
THAT'S AN EXCELLENT IDEA. HA HA!
IF YOU TELL THE KING WHAT I'M DOING, YOU KNOW I'LL KILL YOU, RIGHT?
탁
탁
OF COURSE.
"BETRAYAL MEANS DEATH!" MEMORIZE IT!
아

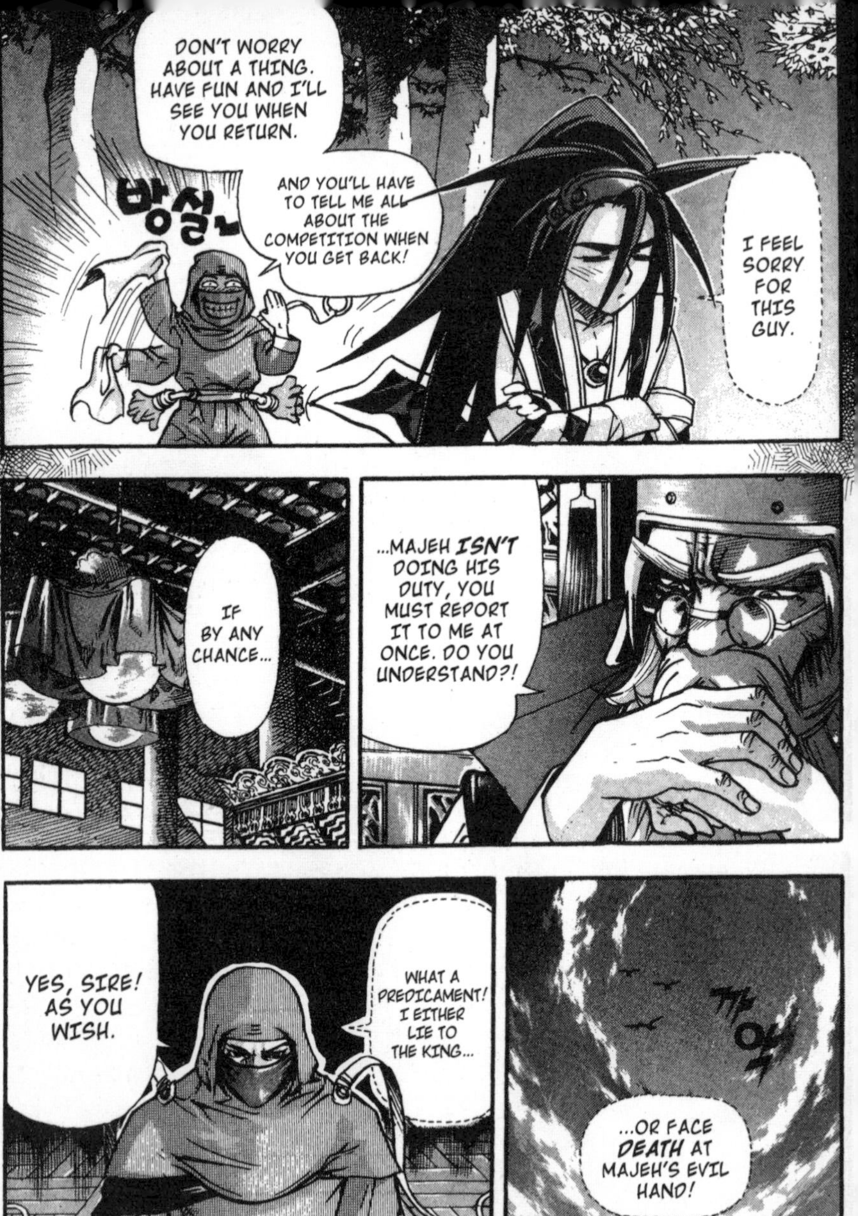
DON'T WORRY ABOUT A THING. HAVE FUN AND I'LL SEE YOU WHEN YOU RETURN.
방실
AND YOU'LL HAVE TO TELL ME ALL ABOUT THE COMPETITION WHEN YOU GET BACK!
I FEEL SORRY FOR THIS GUY.
IF BY ANY CHANCE...
...MAJEH ISN'T DOING HIS DUTY, YOU MUST REPORT IT TO ME AT ONCE. DO YOU UNDERSTAND?!
YES, SIRE! AS YOU WISH.
WHAT A PREDICAMENT! I EITHER LIE TO THE KING...
...OR FACE DEATH AT MAJEH'S EVIL HAND!

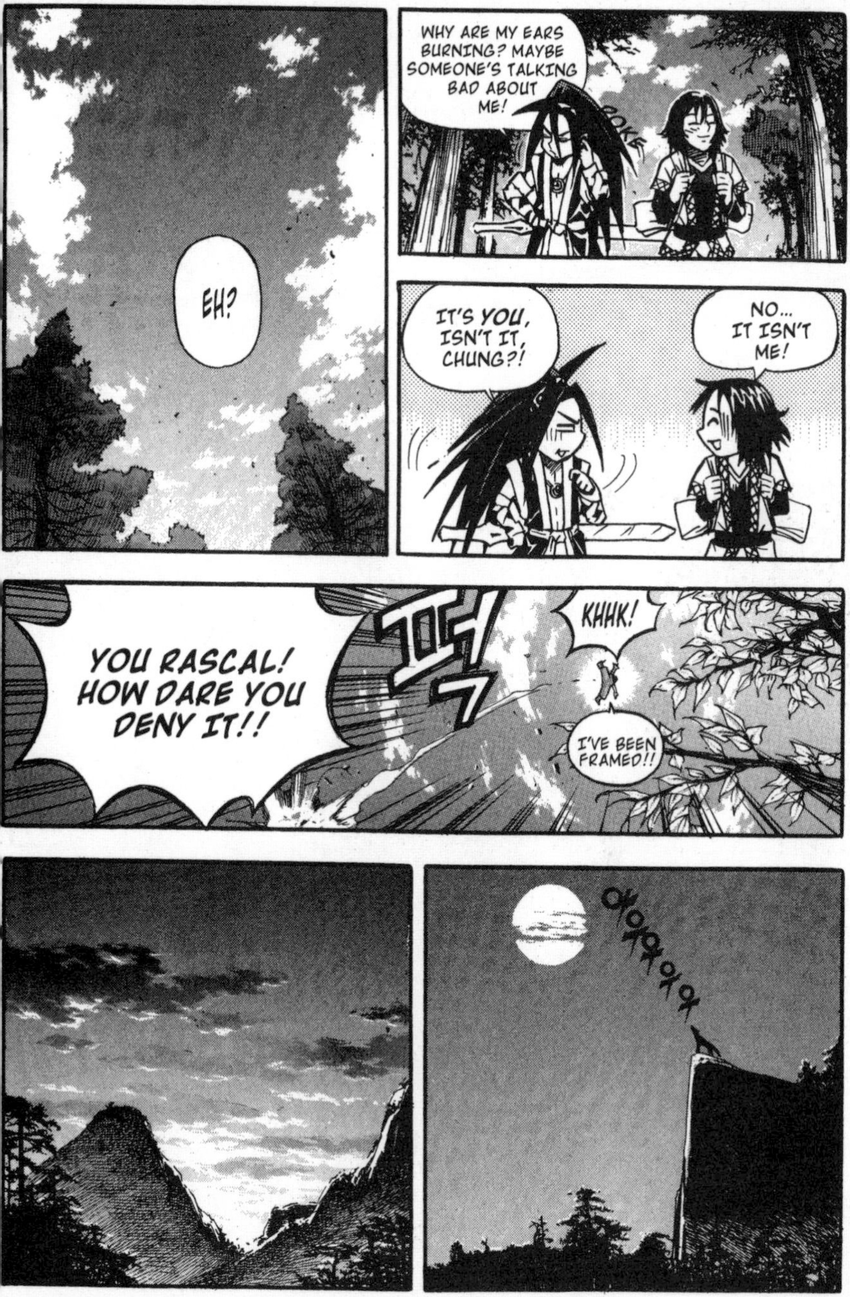

EH?
WHY ARE MY EARS BURNING? MAYBE SOMEONE'S TALKING BAD ABOUT ME!
IT'S YOU, ISN'T IT, CHUNG?!
NO... IT ISN'T ME!
YOU RASCAL! HOW DARE YOU DENY IT!!
KHHK!
I'VE BEEN FRAMED!!

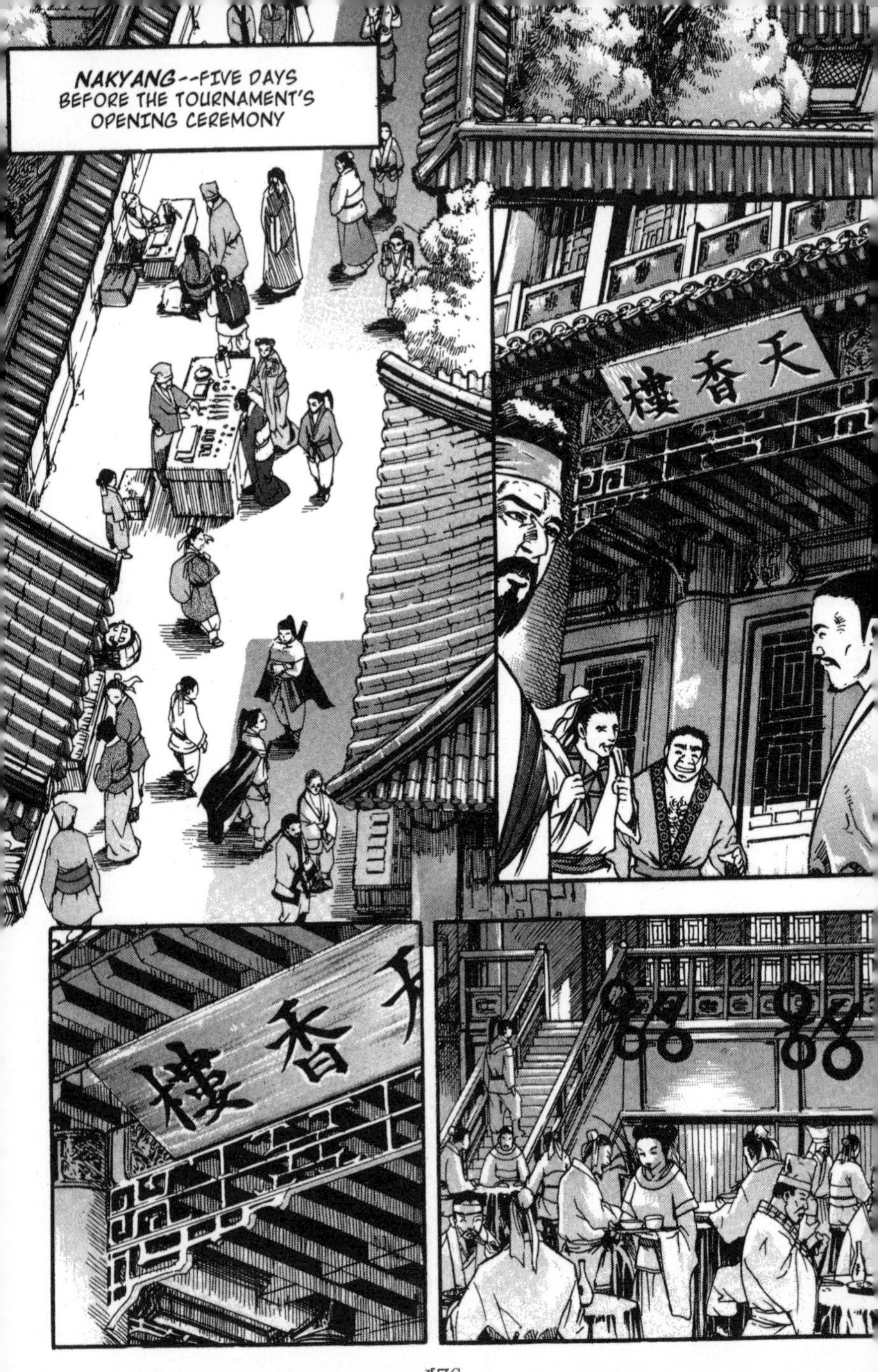
NAKYANG--FIVE DAYS BEFORE THE TOURNAMENT'S OPENING CEREMONY
天香樓
香樓

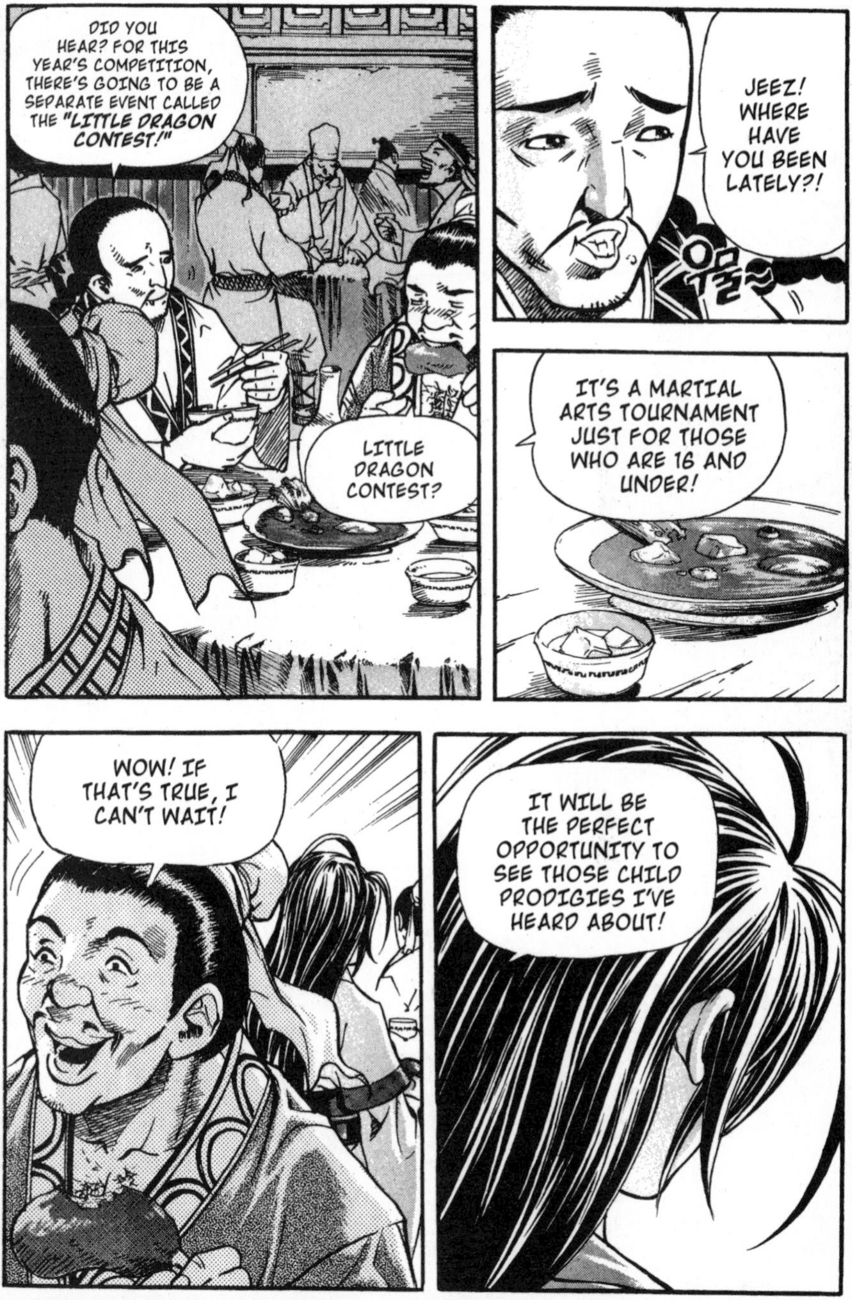
DID YOU HEAR? FOR THIS YEAR'S COMPETITION, THERE'S GOING TO BE A SEPARATE EVENT CALLED THE "LITTLE DRAGON CONTEST!"
LITTLE DRAGON CONTEST?
JEEZ! WHERE HAVE YOU BEEN LATELY?!
오물~
IT'S A MARTIAL ARTS TOURNAMENT JUST FOR THOSE WHO ARE 16 AND UNDER!
WOW! IF THAT'S TRUE, I CAN'T WAIT!
IT WILL BE THE PERFECT OPPORTUNITY TO SEE THOSE CHILD PRODIGIES I'VE HEARD ABOUT!

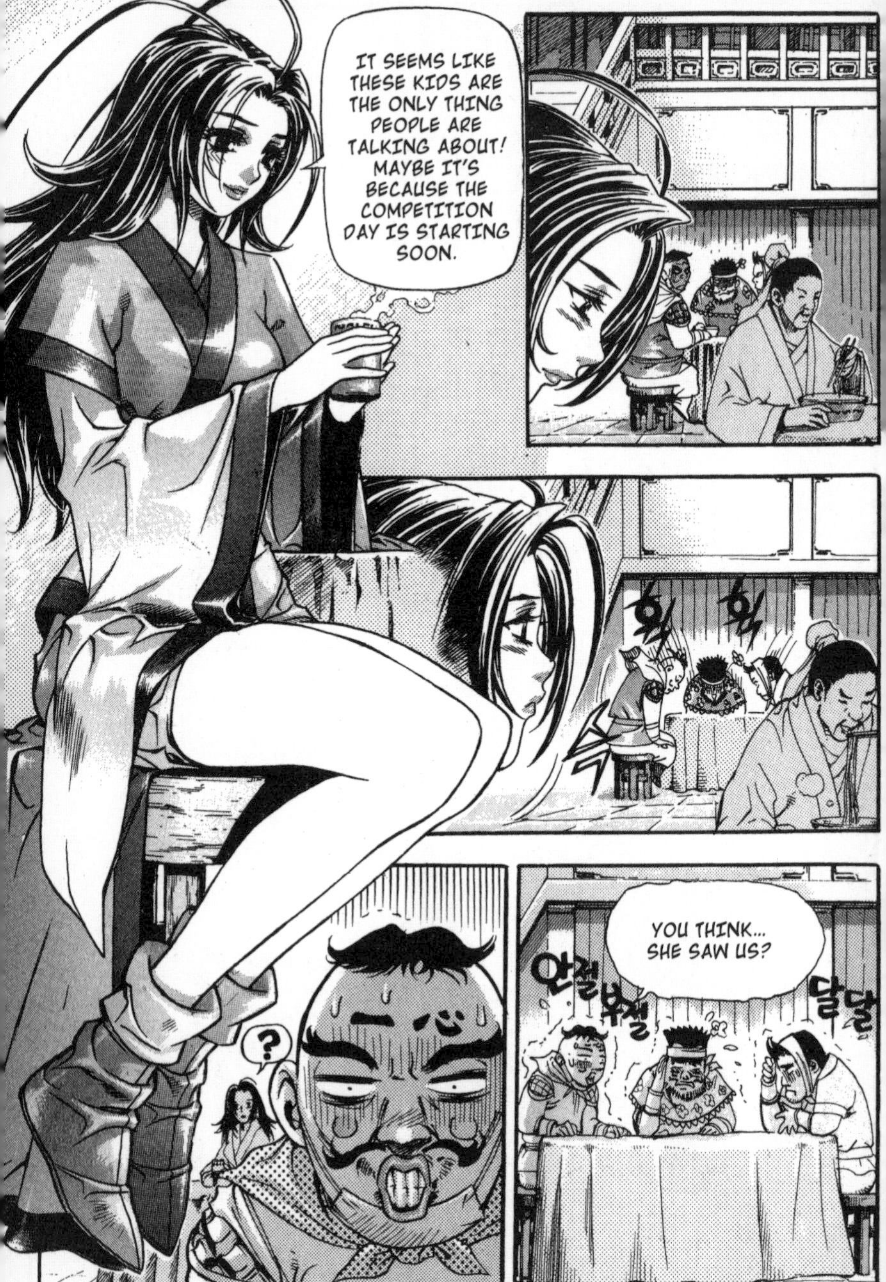
IT SEEMS LIKE THESE KIDS ARE THE ONLY THING PEOPLE ARE TALKING ABOUT! MAYBE IT'S BECAUSE THE COMPETITION DAY IS STARTING SOON.
휙 휙
?
一心
YOU THINK... SHE SAW US?
안절부절
달달

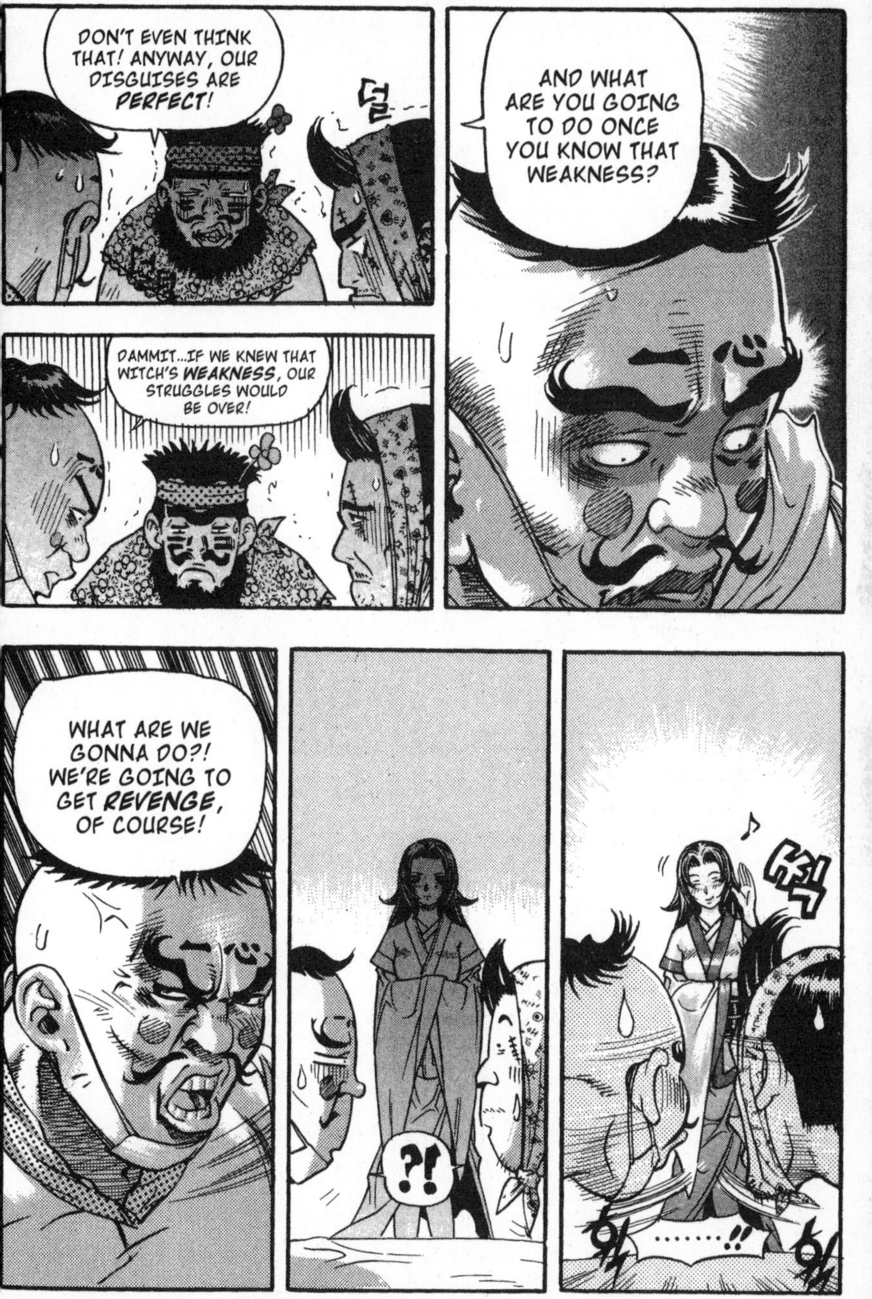
DON'T EVEN THINK THAT! ANYWAY, OUR DISGUISES ARE PERFECT!
DAMMIT...IF WE KNEW THAT WITCH'S WEAKNESS, OUR STRUGGLES WOULD BE OVER!
AND WHAT ARE YOU GOING TO DO ONCE YOU KNOW THAT WEAKNESS?
WHAT ARE WE GONNA DO?! WE'RE GOING TO GET REVENGE, OF COURSE!
?!
........!!

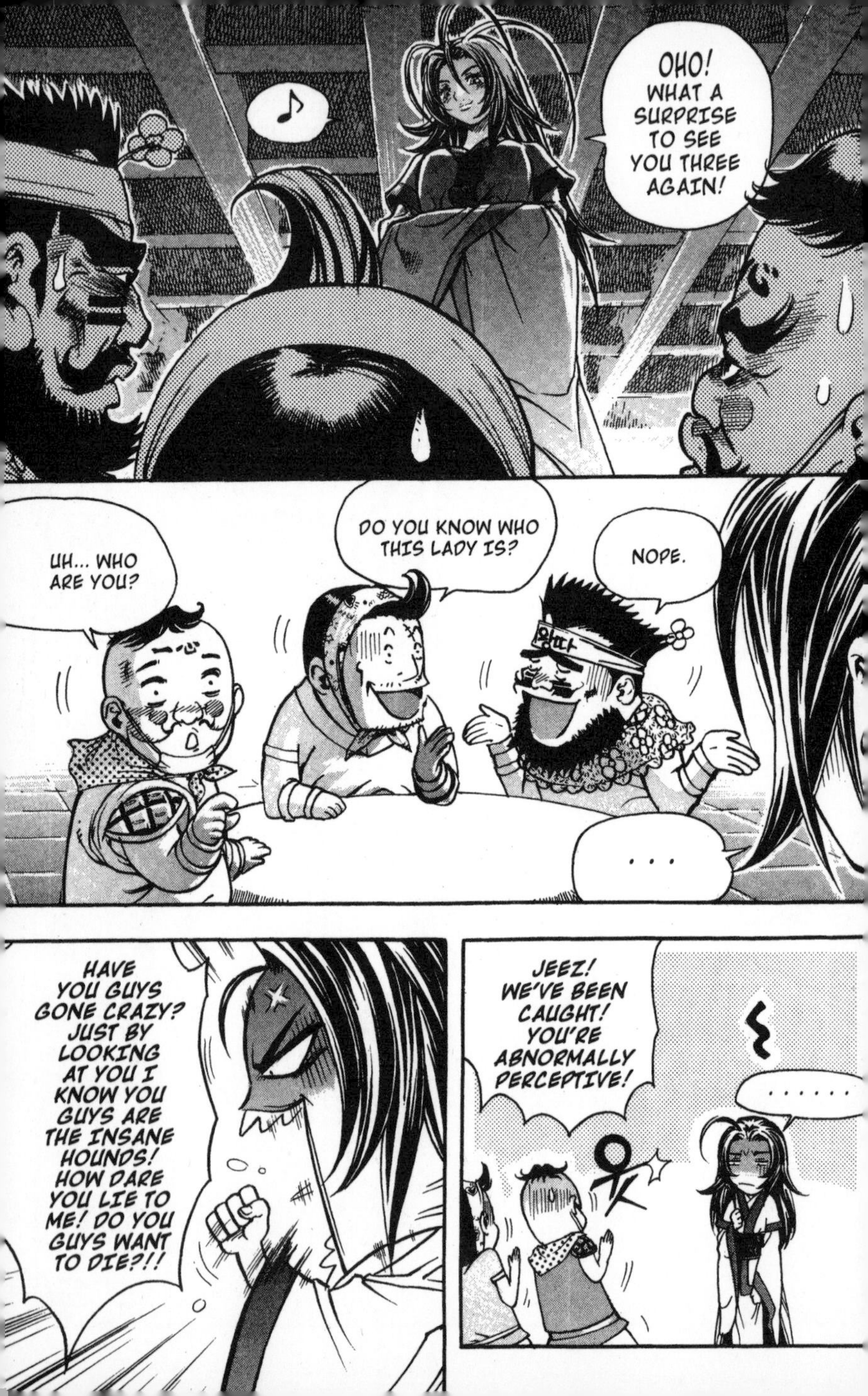
♪
OHO! WHAT A SURPRISE TO SEE YOU THREE AGAIN!
UH... WHO ARE YOU?
DO YOU KNOW WHO THIS LADY IS?
NOPE.
...
HAVE YOU GUYS GONE CRAZY? JUST BY LOOKING AT YOU I KNOW YOU GUYS ARE THE INSANE HOUNDS! HOW DARE YOU LIE TO ME! DO YOU GUYS WANT TO DIE?!!
JEEZ! WE'VE BEEN CAUGHT! YOU'RE ABNORMALLY PERCEPTIVE!
......

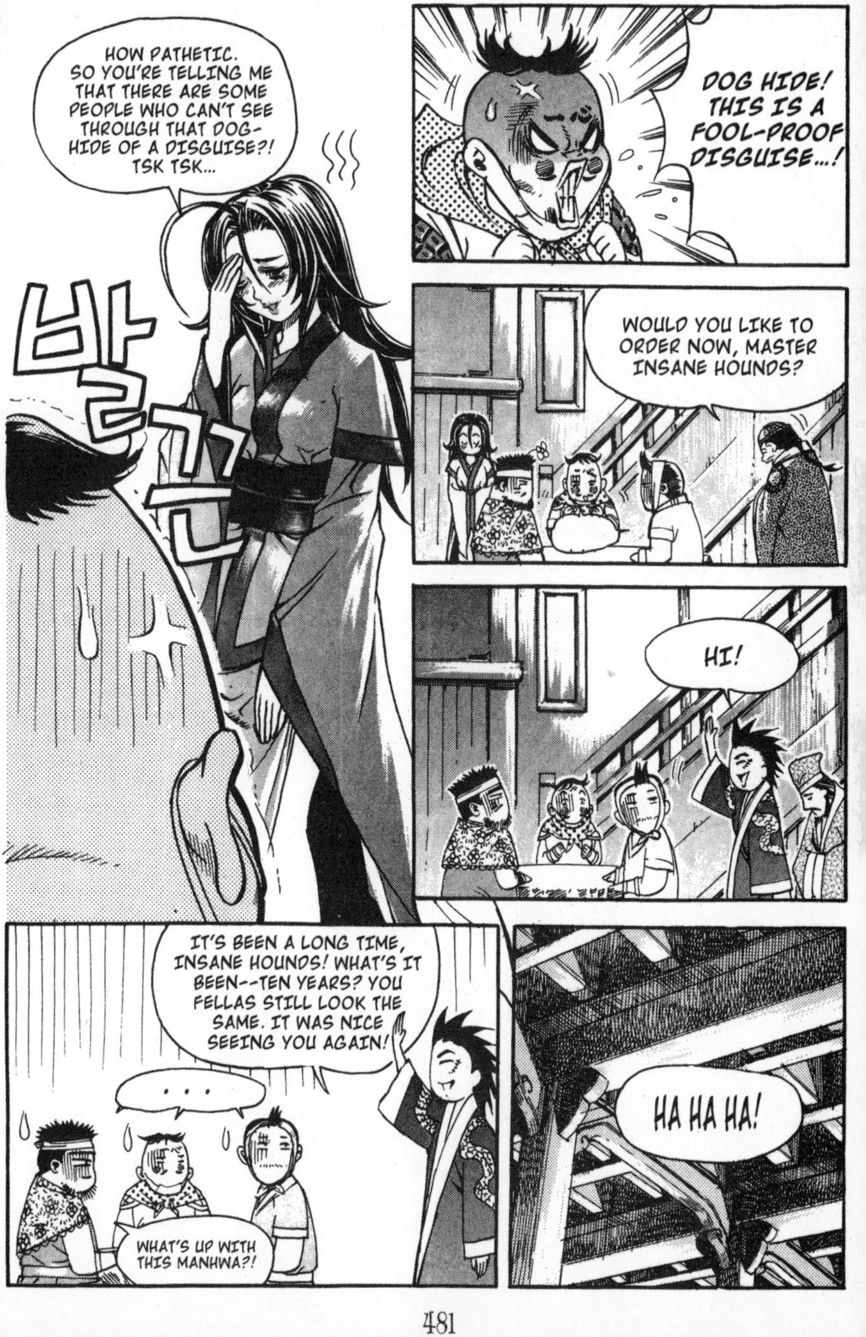
HOW PATHETIC. SO YOU'RE TELLING ME THAT THERE ARE SOME PEOPLE WHO CAN'T SEE THROUGH THAT DOG-HIDE OF A DISGUISE?! TSK TSK...
발끈
DOG HIDE! THIS IS A FOOL-PROOF DISGUISE...!
WOULD YOU LIKE TO ORDER NOW, MASTER INSANE HOUNDS?
HI!
IT'S BEEN A LONG TIME, INSANE HOUNDS! WHAT'S IT BEEN--TEN YEARS? YOU FELLAS STILL LOOK THE SAME. IT WAS NICE SEEING YOU AGAIN!
. . .
WHAT'S UP WITH THIS MANHWA?!
HA HA HA!

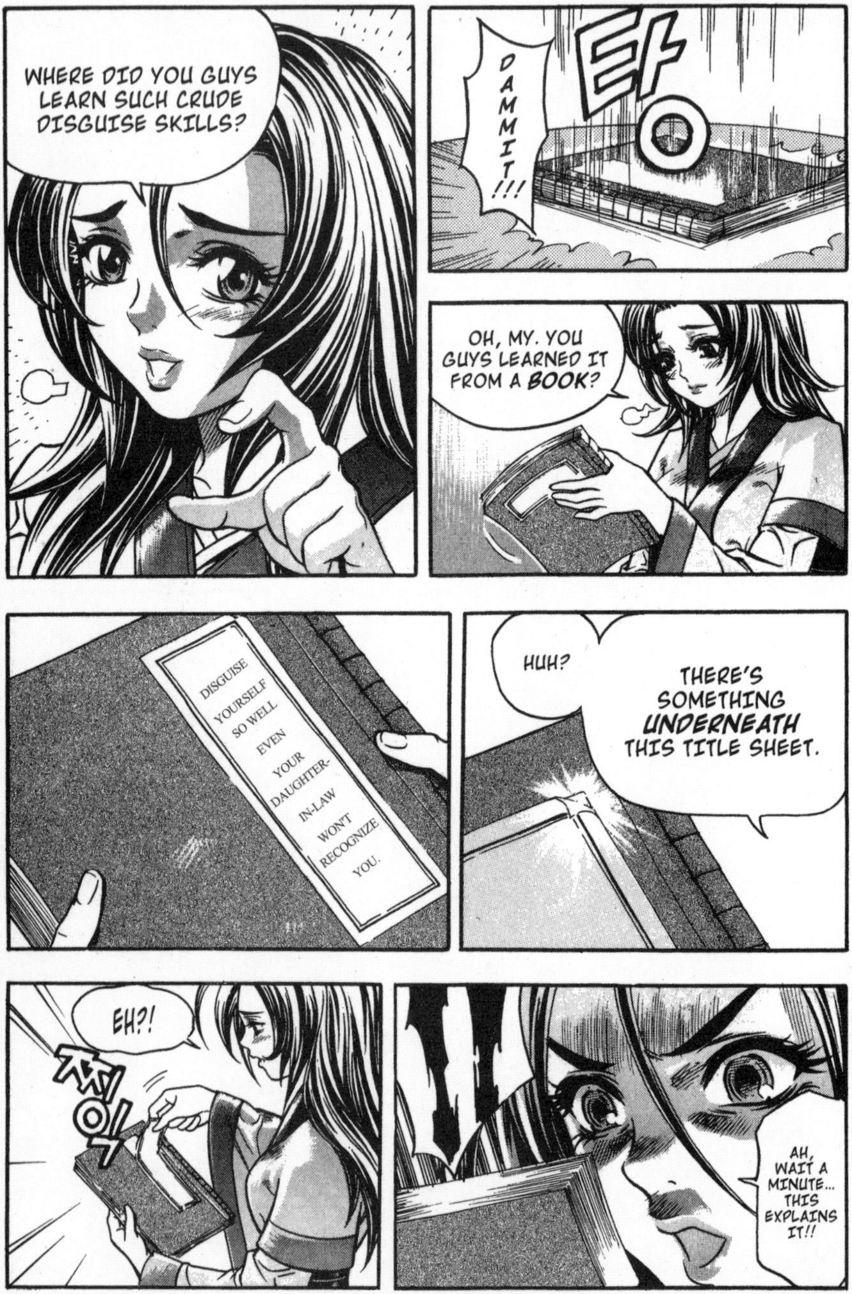
WHERE DID YOU GUYS LEARN SUCH CRUDE DISGUISE SKILLS?
DAMMIT!!!
OH, MY. YOU GUYS LEARNED IT FROM A *BOOK*?
DISGUISE YOURSELF SO WELL EVEN YOUR DAUGHTER-IN-LAW WON'T RECOGNIZE YOU.
HUH?
THERE'S SOMETHING ***UNDERNEATH*** THIS TITLE SHEET.
EH?!
AH, WAIT A MINUTE... THIS EXPLAINS IT!!

WHAT IS IT?

ARE YOU GUYS PREPARING FOR YOUR RETIREMENTS?

WHAT ARE YOU TALKING ABOUT? GIVE ME THAT!

DON'T FAINT.

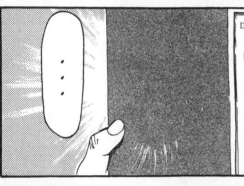

DISGUISES SO BAD ONLY YOUR DAUGHTER-IN-LAW WON'T RECOGNIZE YOU. (AN EXCERPT FROM A SENIOR'S GUIDE TO ESCAPING FROM THE HOME.)

SOMEBODY SWINDLED YOU!

THAT...THAT BOOKSTORE OWNER! I'M GONNA...

HA HA HA!

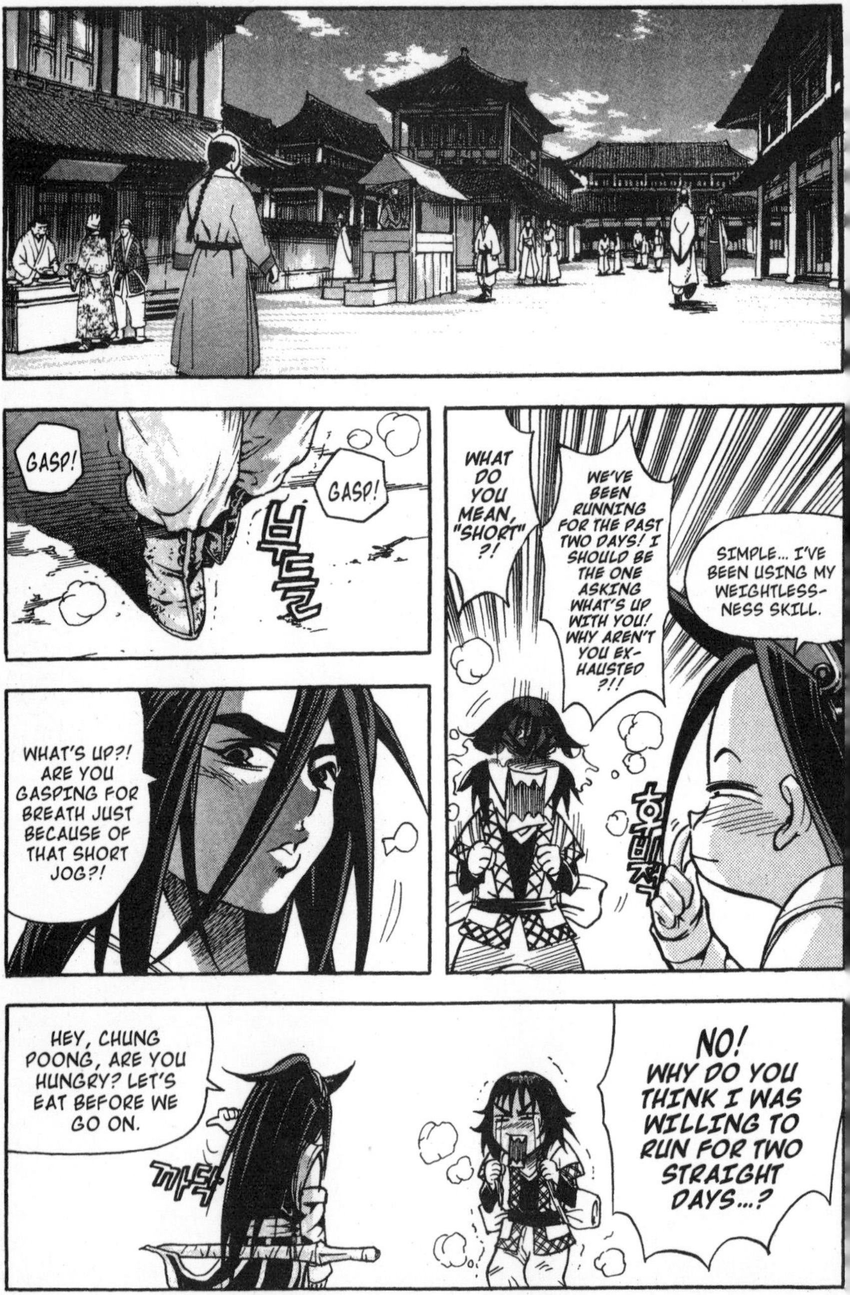
GASP!
GASP!
WHAT'S UP?! ARE YOU GASPING FOR BREATH JUST BECAUSE OF THAT SHORT JOG?!
WHAT DO YOU MEAN, "SHORT"?!
WE'VE BEEN RUNNING FOR THE PAST TWO DAYS! I SHOULD BE THE ONE ASKING WHAT'S UP WITH YOU! WHY AREN'T YOU EX-HAUSTED?!!
SIMPLE... I'VE BEEN USING MY WEIGHTLESS-NESS SKILL.
HEY, CHUNG POONG, ARE YOU HUNGRY? LET'S EAT BEFORE WE GO ON.
까딱
NO! WHY DO YOU THINK I WAS WILLING TO RUN FOR TWO STRAIGHT DAYS...?

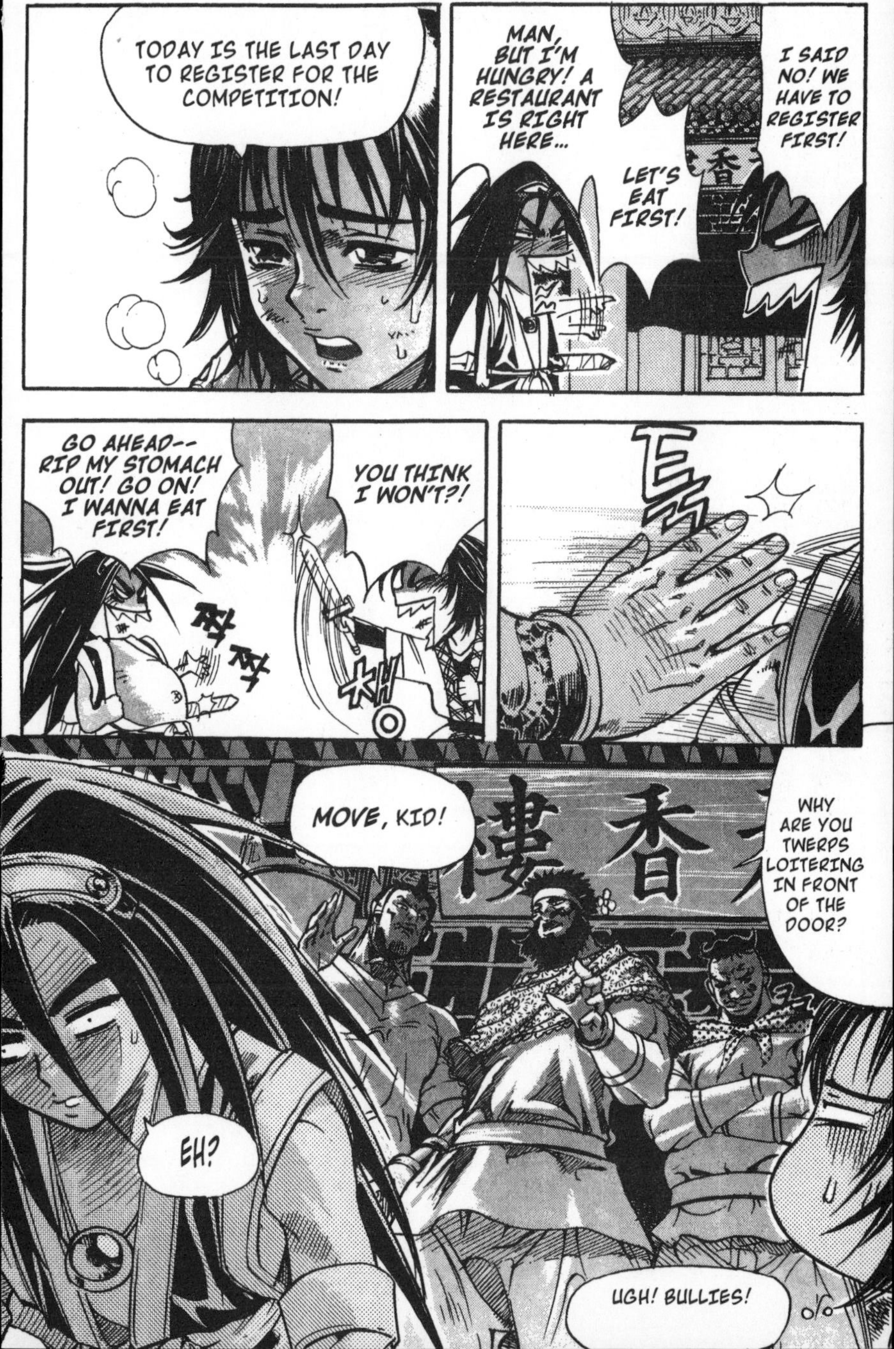
TODAY IS THE LAST DAY TO REGISTER FOR THE COMPETITION!
MAN, BUT I'M HUNGRY! A RESTAURANT IS RIGHT HERE...
LET'S EAT FIRST!
I SAID NO! WE HAVE TO REGISTER FIRST!
GO AHEAD--RIP MY STOMACH OUT! GO ON! I WANNA EAT FIRST!
짝 짝
YOU THINK I WON'T?!
MOVE, KID!
WHY ARE YOU TWERPS LOITERING IN FRONT OF THE DOOR?
EH?
UGH! BULLIES!

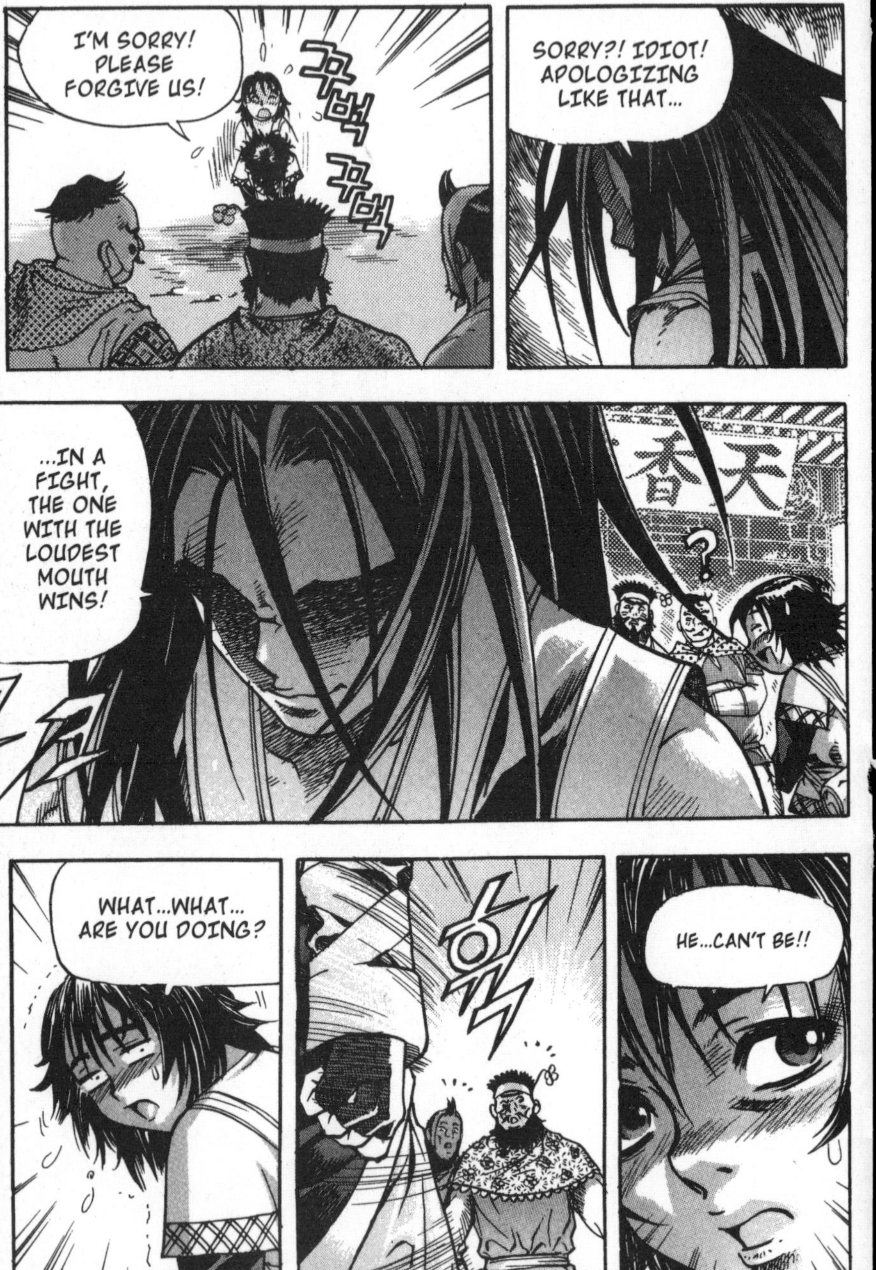
I'M SORRY! PLEASE FORGIVE US!
꾸벅
꾸벅
SORRY?! IDIOT! APOLOGIZING LIKE THAT...
...IN A FIGHT, THE ONE WITH THE LOUDEST MOUTH WINS!
香天
?
WHAT...WHAT... ARE YOU DOING?
HE...CAN'T BE!!

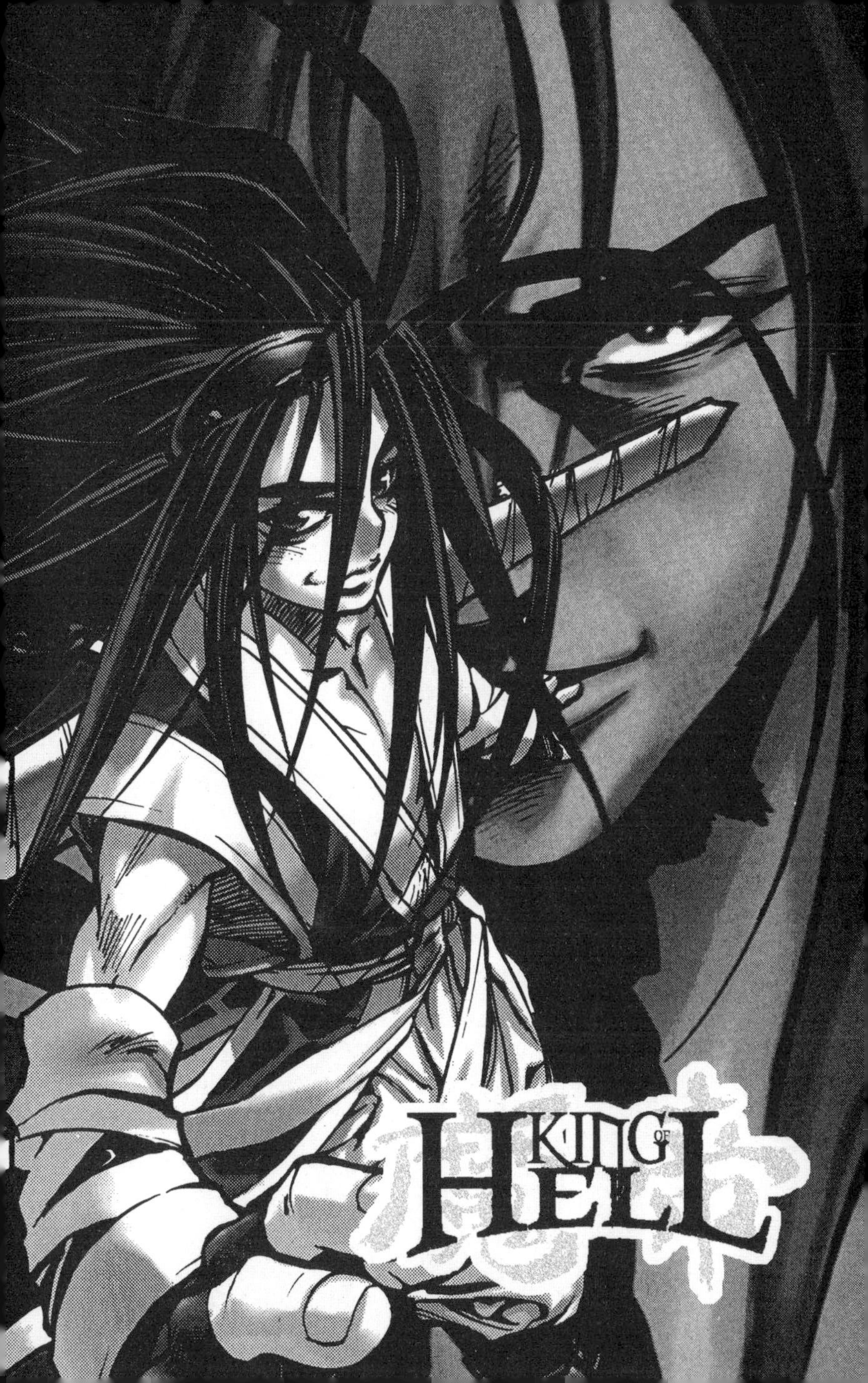
KING OF HELL

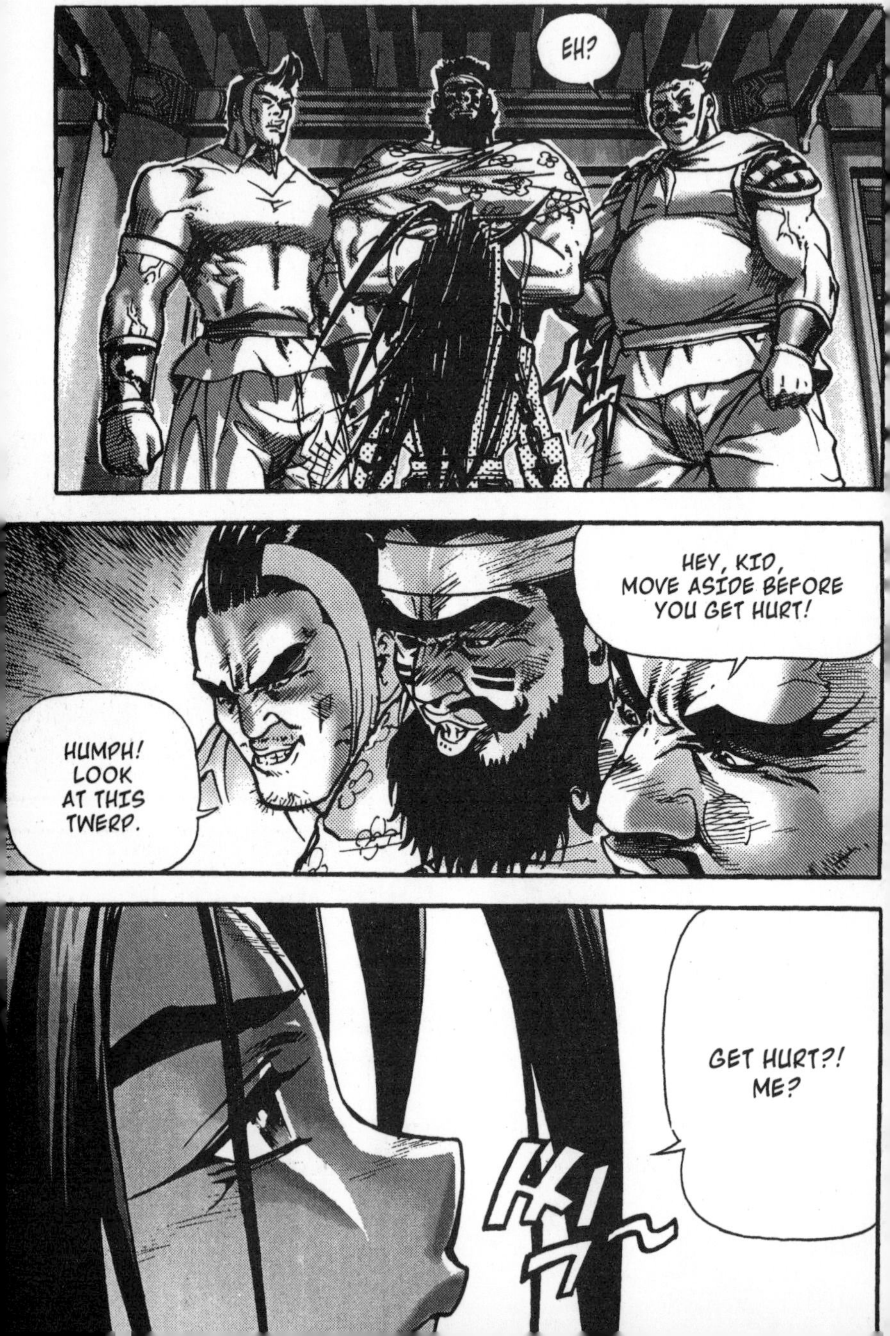
EH?
HUMPH! LOOK AT THIS TWERP.
HEY, KID, MOVE ASIDE BEFORE YOU GET HURT!
GET HURT?! ME?
KI~

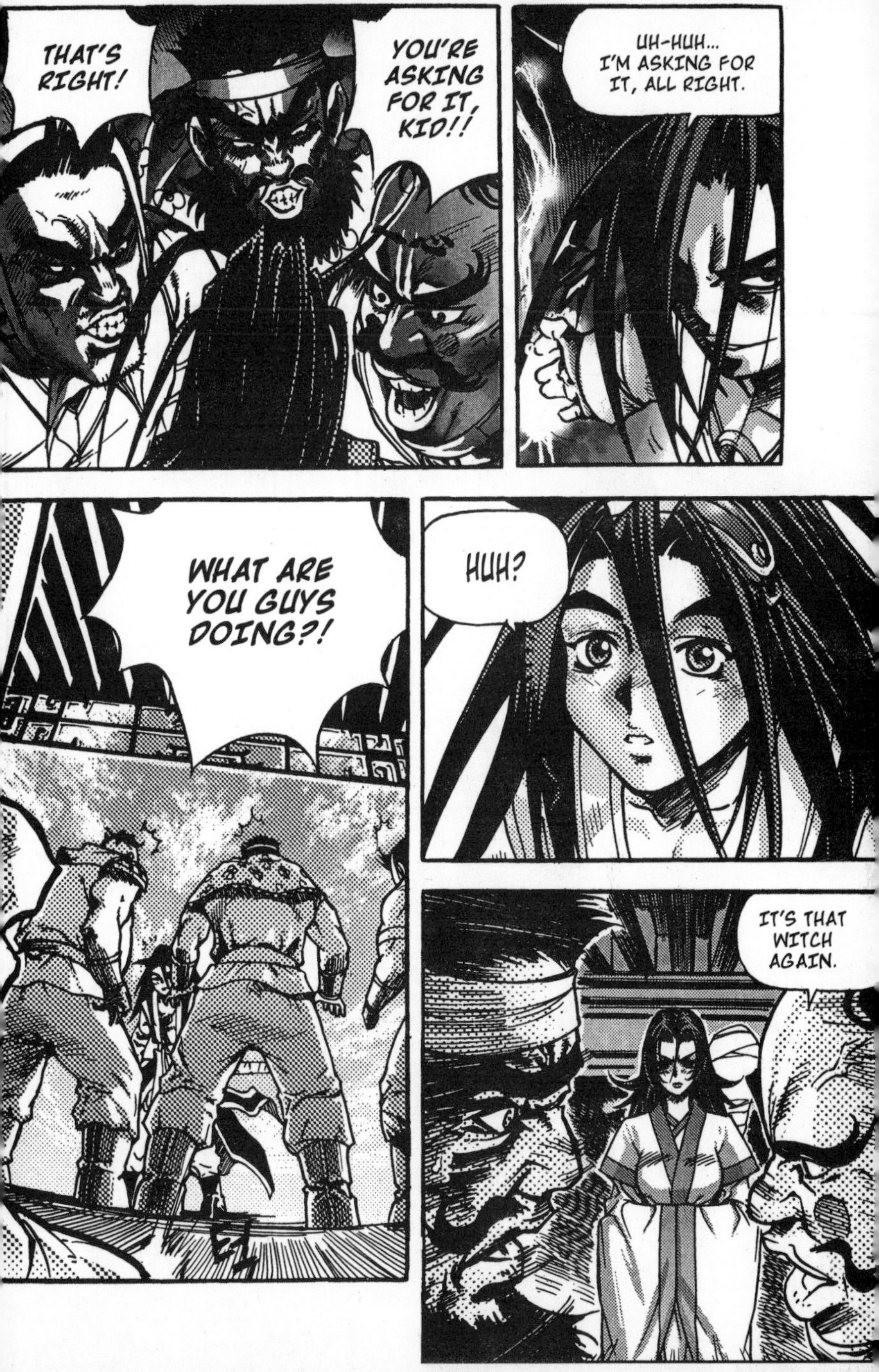
THAT'S RIGHT!
YOU'RE ASKING FOR IT, KID!!
UH-HUH... I'M ASKING FOR IT, ALL RIGHT.
WHAT ARE YOU GUYS DOING?!
HUH?
IT'S THAT WITCH AGAIN.

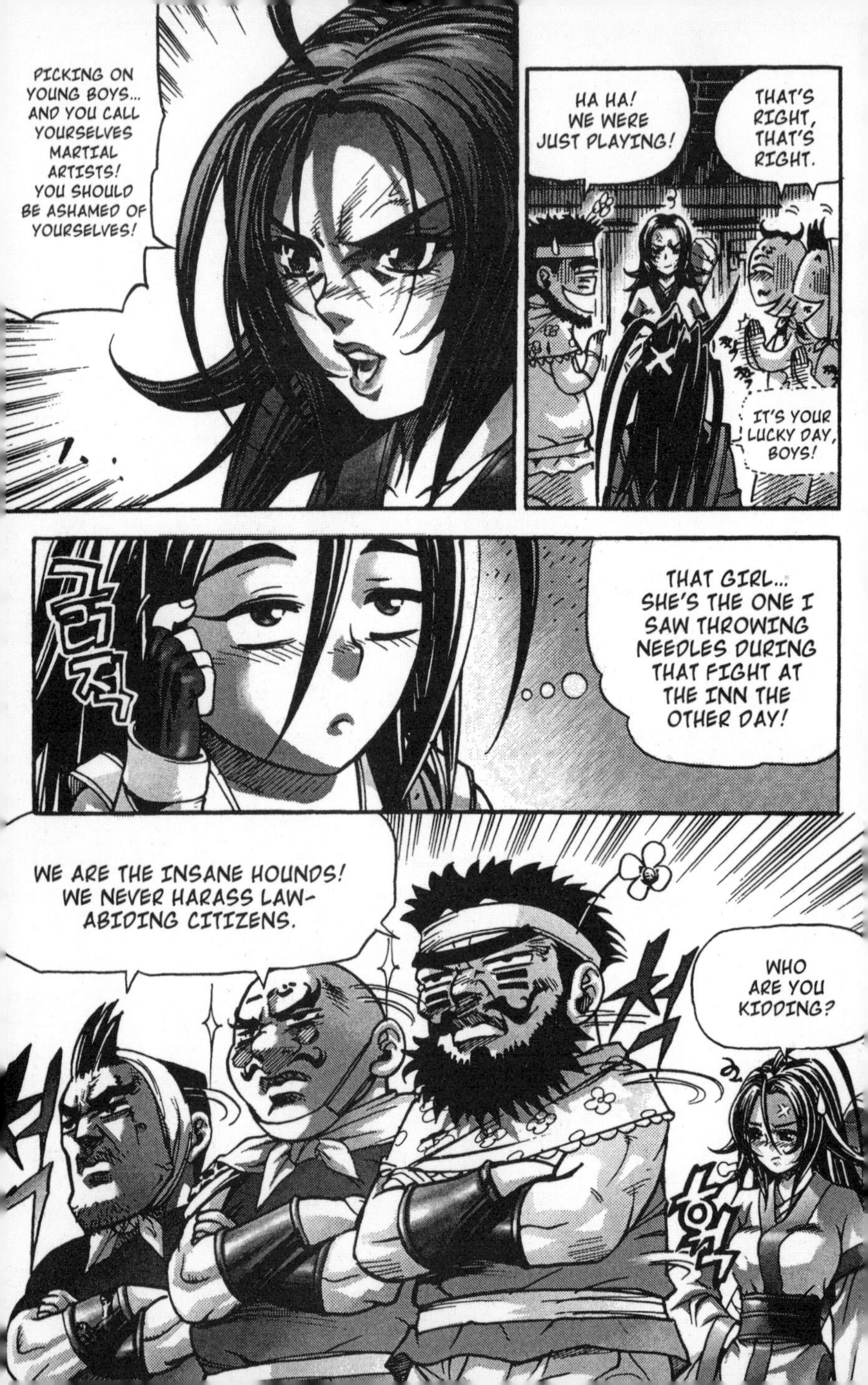
PICKING ON YOUNG BOYS... AND YOU CALL YOURSELVES MARTIAL ARTISTS! YOU SHOULD BE ASHAMED OF YOURSELVES!
HA HA! WE WERE JUST PLAYING!
THAT'S RIGHT, THAT'S RIGHT.
IT'S YOUR LUCKY DAY, BOYS!
THAT GIRL... SHE'S THE ONE I SAW THROWING NEEDLES DURING THAT FIGHT AT THE INN THE OTHER DAY!
WE ARE THE INSANE HOUNDS! WE NEVER HARASS LAW-ABIDING CITIZENS.
WHO ARE YOU KIDDING?

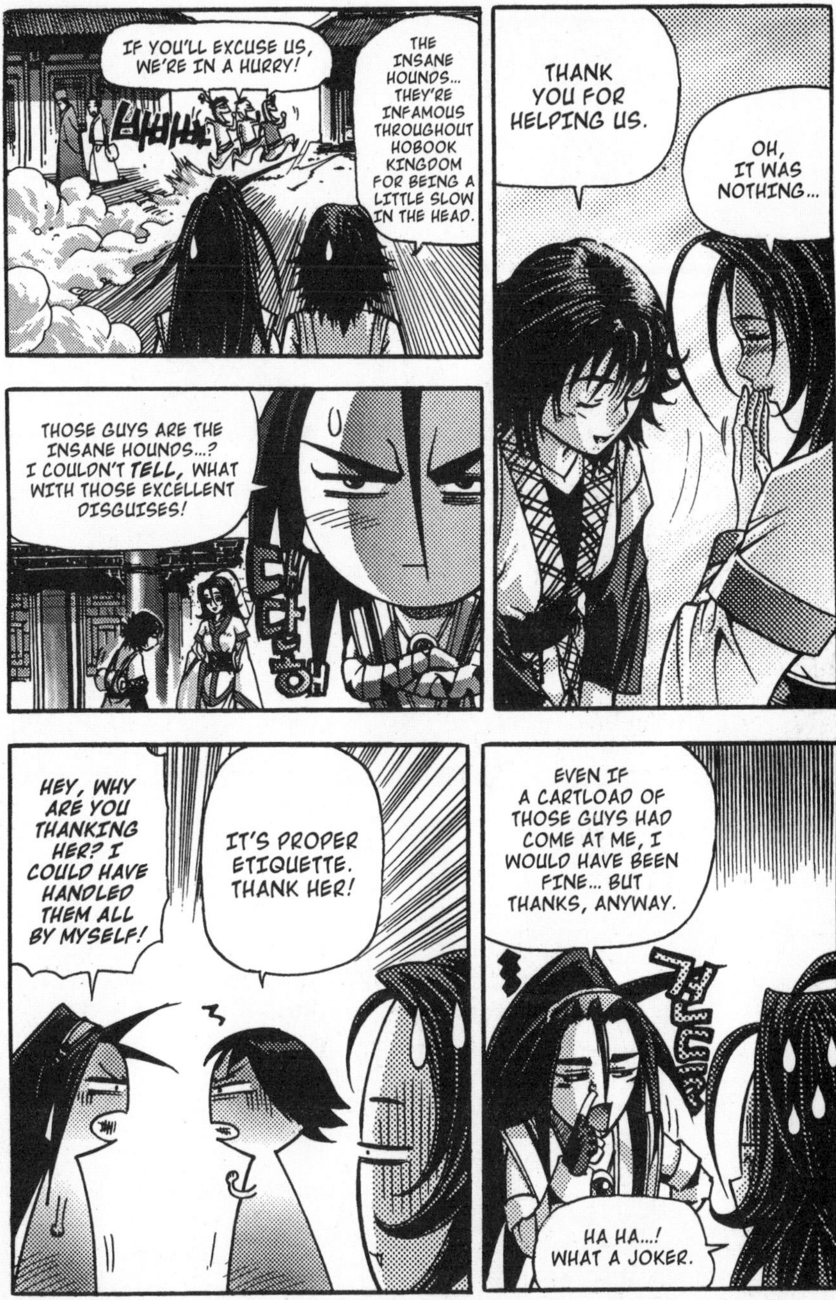
IF YOU'LL EXCUSE US, WE'RE IN A HURRY!
THE INSANE HOUNDS... THEY'RE INFAMOUS THROUGHOUT HOBOOK KINGDOM FOR BEING A LITTLE SLOW IN THE HEAD.
THOSE GUYS ARE THE INSANE HOUNDS...? I COULDN'T TELL, WHAT WITH THOSE EXCELLENT DISGUISES!
THANK YOU FOR HELPING US.
OH, IT WAS NOTHING...
HEY, WHY ARE YOU THANKING HER? I COULD HAVE HANDLED THEM ALL BY MYSELF!
IT'S PROPER ETIQUETTE. THANK HER!
EVEN IF A CARTLOAD OF THOSE GUYS HAD COME AT ME, I WOULD HAVE BEEN FINE... BUT THANKS, ANYWAY.
HA HA...! WHAT A JOKER.

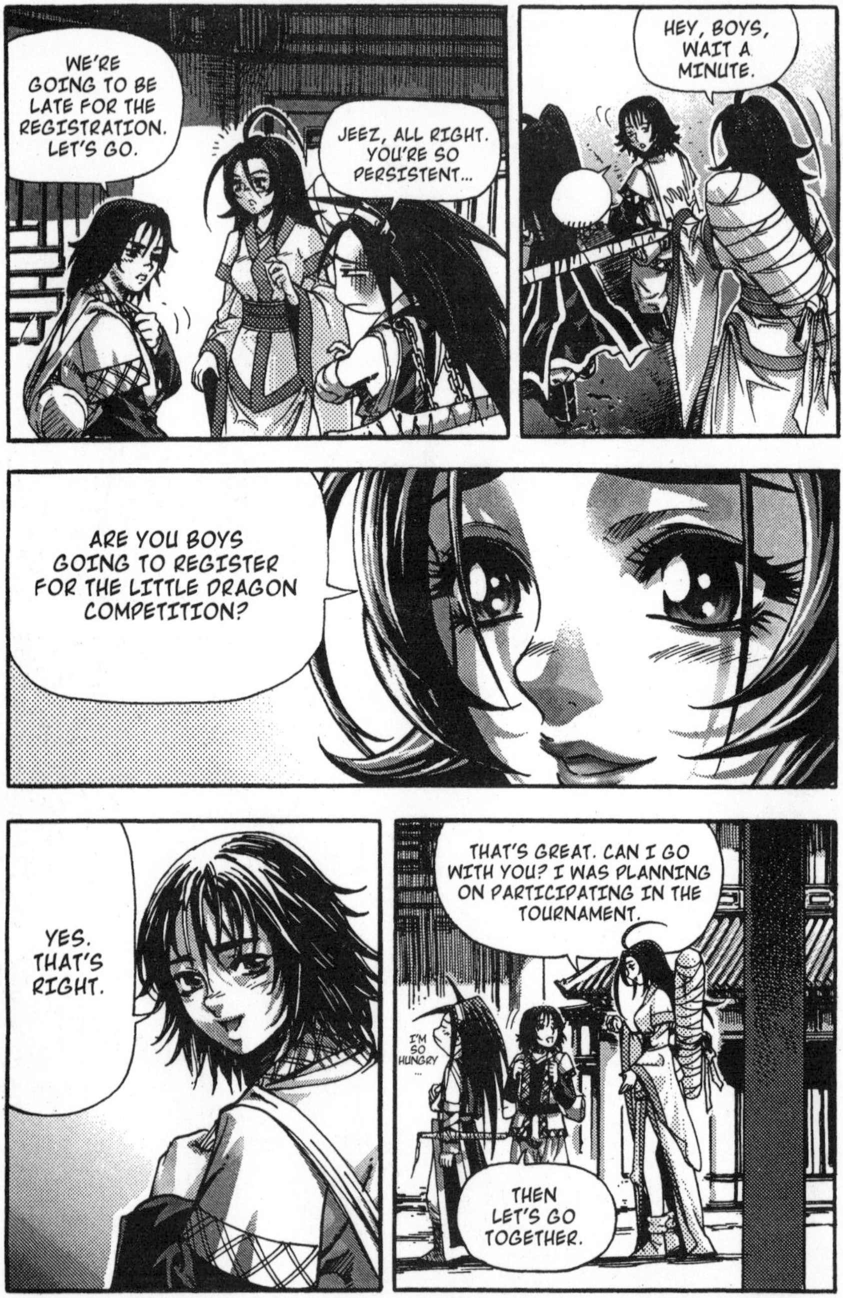
WE'RE GOING TO BE LATE FOR THE REGISTRATION. LET'S GO.
JEEZ, ALL RIGHT. YOU'RE SO PERSISTENT...
HEY, BOYS, WAIT A MINUTE.
ARE YOU BOYS GOING TO REGISTER FOR THE LITTLE DRAGON COMPETITION?
YES. THAT'S RIGHT.
THAT'S GREAT. CAN I GO WITH YOU? I WAS PLANNING ON PARTICIPATING IN THE TOURNAMENT.
I'M SO HUNGRY ...
THEN LET'S GO TOGETHER.

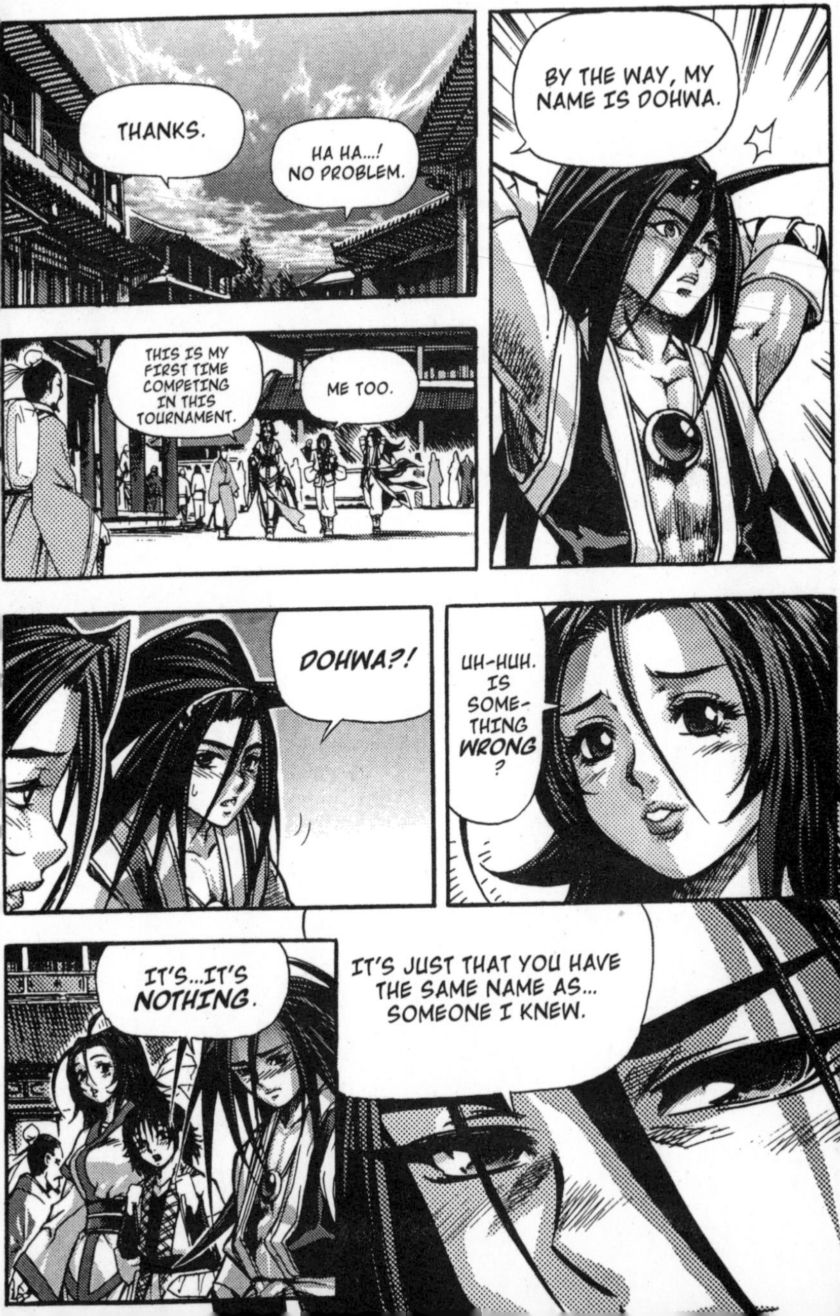
THANKS.
HA HA...! NO PROBLEM.
BY THE WAY, MY NAME IS DOHWA.
THIS IS MY FIRST TIME COMPETING IN THIS TOURNAMENT.
ME TOO.
DOHWA?!
UH-HUH. IS SOME-THING WRONG?
IT'S...IT'S NOTHING.
IT'S JUST THAT YOU HAVE THE SAME NAME AS... SOMEONE I KNEW.

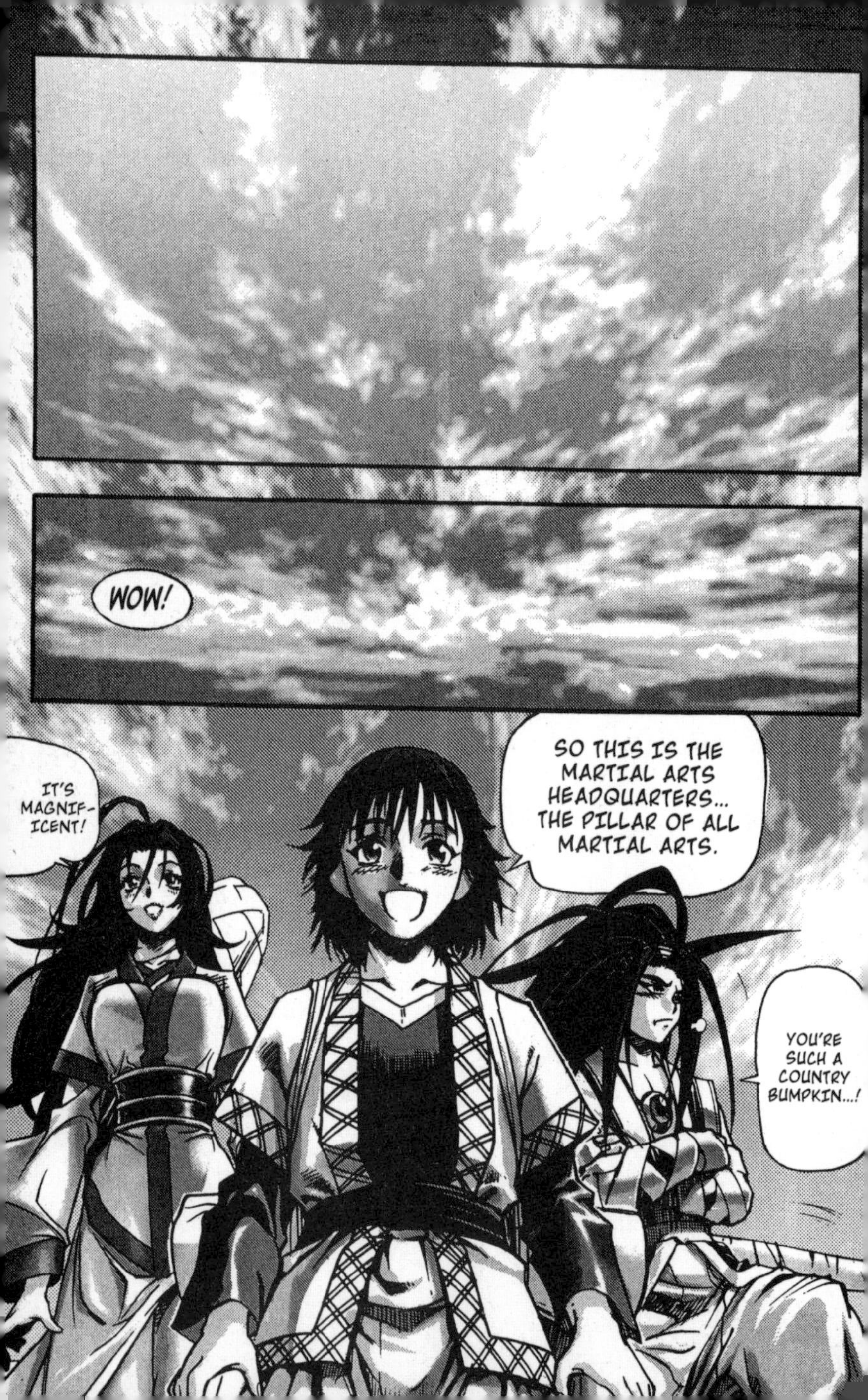
WOW!
IT'S MAGNIF-ICENT!
SO THIS IS THE MARTIAL ARTS HEADQUARTERS... THE PILLAR OF ALL MARTIAL ARTS.
YOU'RE SUCH A COUNTRY BUMPKIN...!

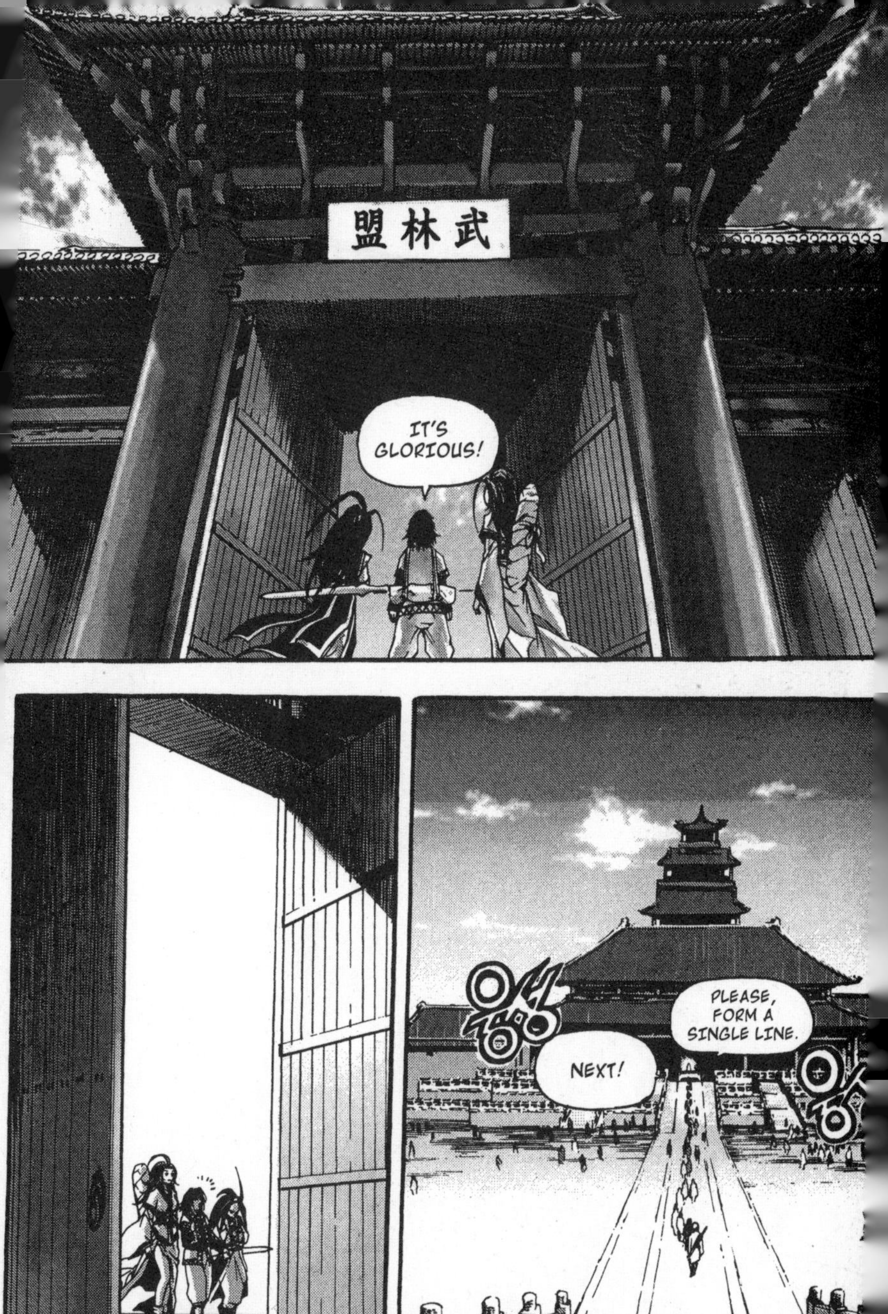
武林盟
IT'S GLORIOUS!
PLEASE, FORM A SINGLE LINE.
NEXT!

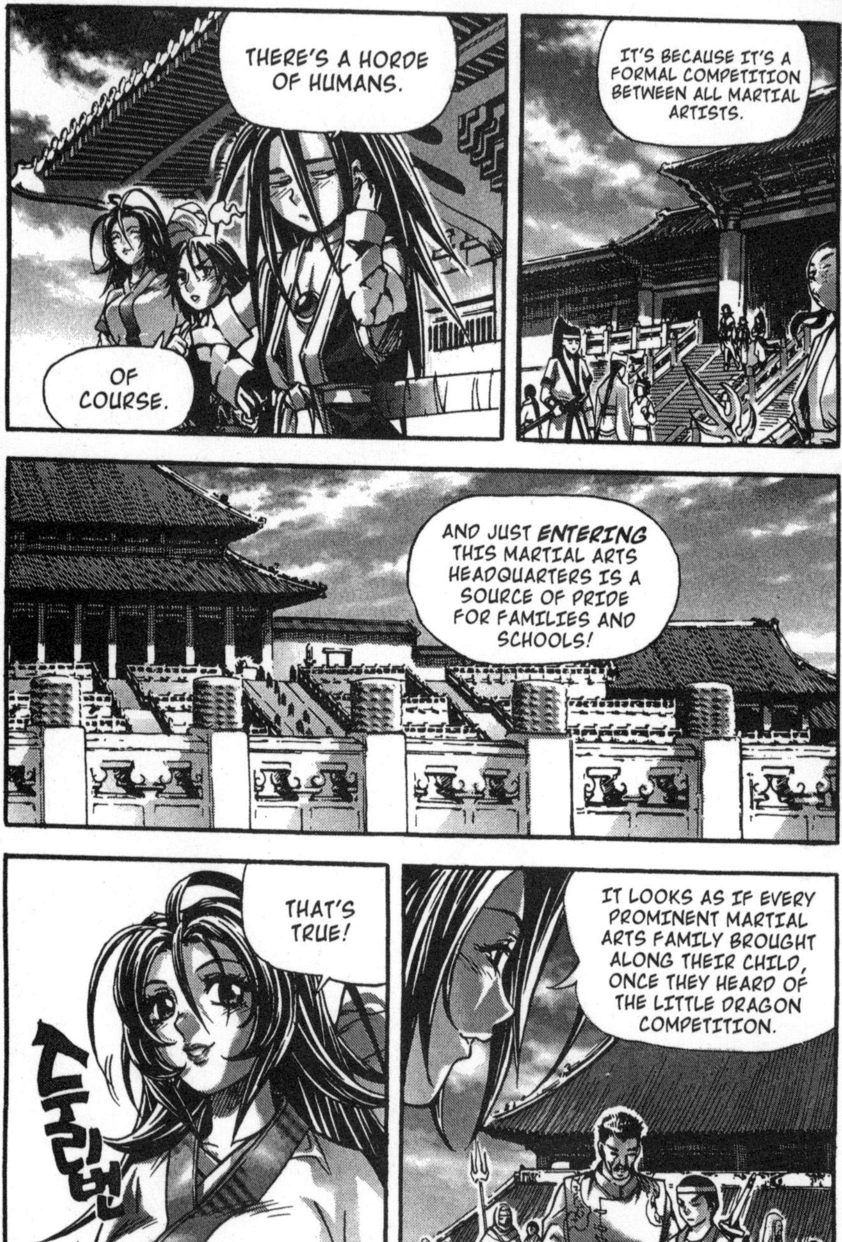
THERE'S A HORDE OF HUMANS.
OF COURSE.
IT'S BECAUSE IT'S A FORMAL COMPETITION BETWEEN ALL MARTIAL ARTISTS.
AND JUST ENTERING THIS MARTIAL ARTS HEADQUARTERS IS A SOURCE OF PRIDE FOR FAMILIES AND SCHOOLS!
THAT'S TRUE!
IT LOOKS AS IF EVERY PROMINENT MARTIAL ARTS FAMILY BROUGHT ALONG THEIR CHILD, ONCE THEY HEARD OF THE LITTLE DRAGON COMPETITION.

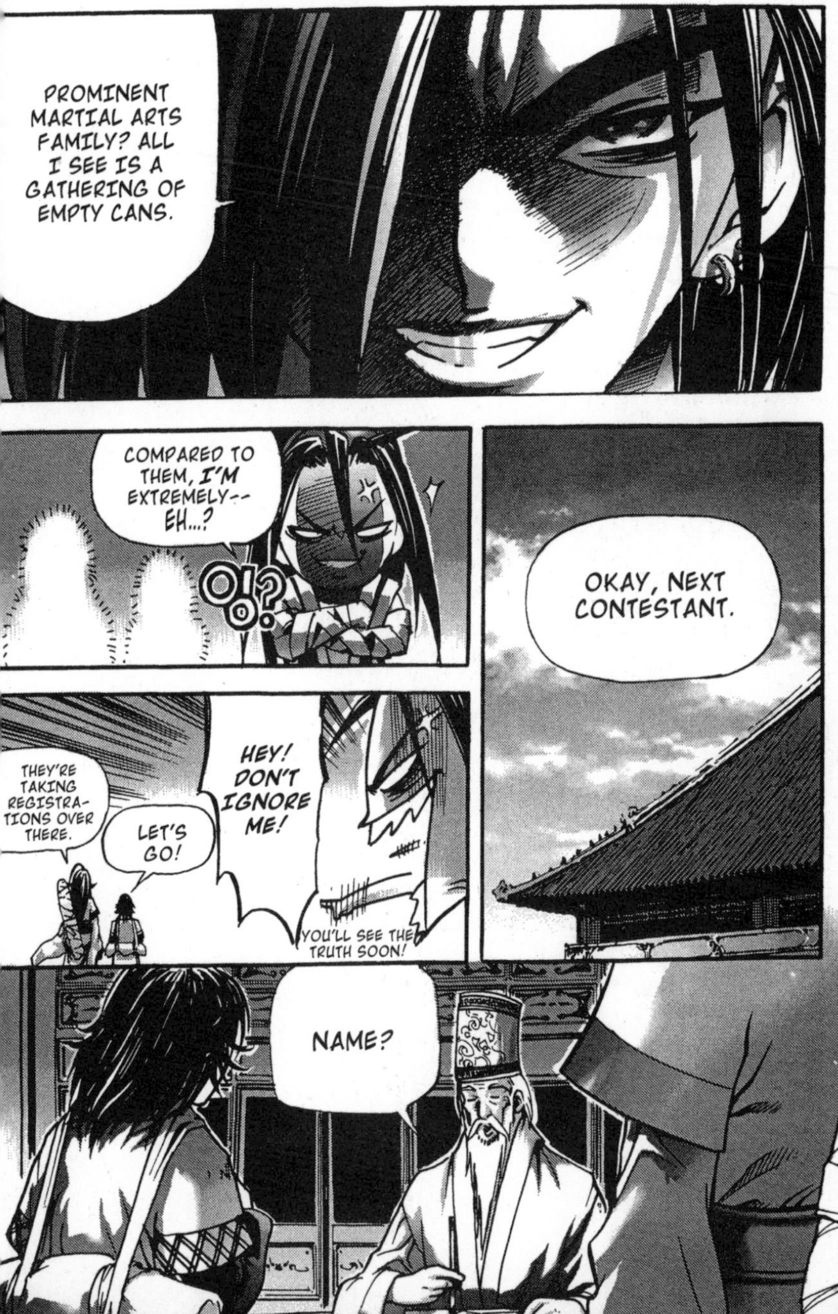
PROMINENT MARTIAL ARTS FAMILY? ALL I SEE IS A GATHERING OF EMPTY CANS.
COMPARED TO THEM, I'M EXTREMELY-- EH...?
O!?
THEY'RE TAKING REGISTRATIONS OVER THERE.
LET'S GO!
HEY! DON'T IGNORE ME!
YOU'LL SEE THE TRUTH SOON!
OKAY, NEXT CONTESTANT.
NAME?

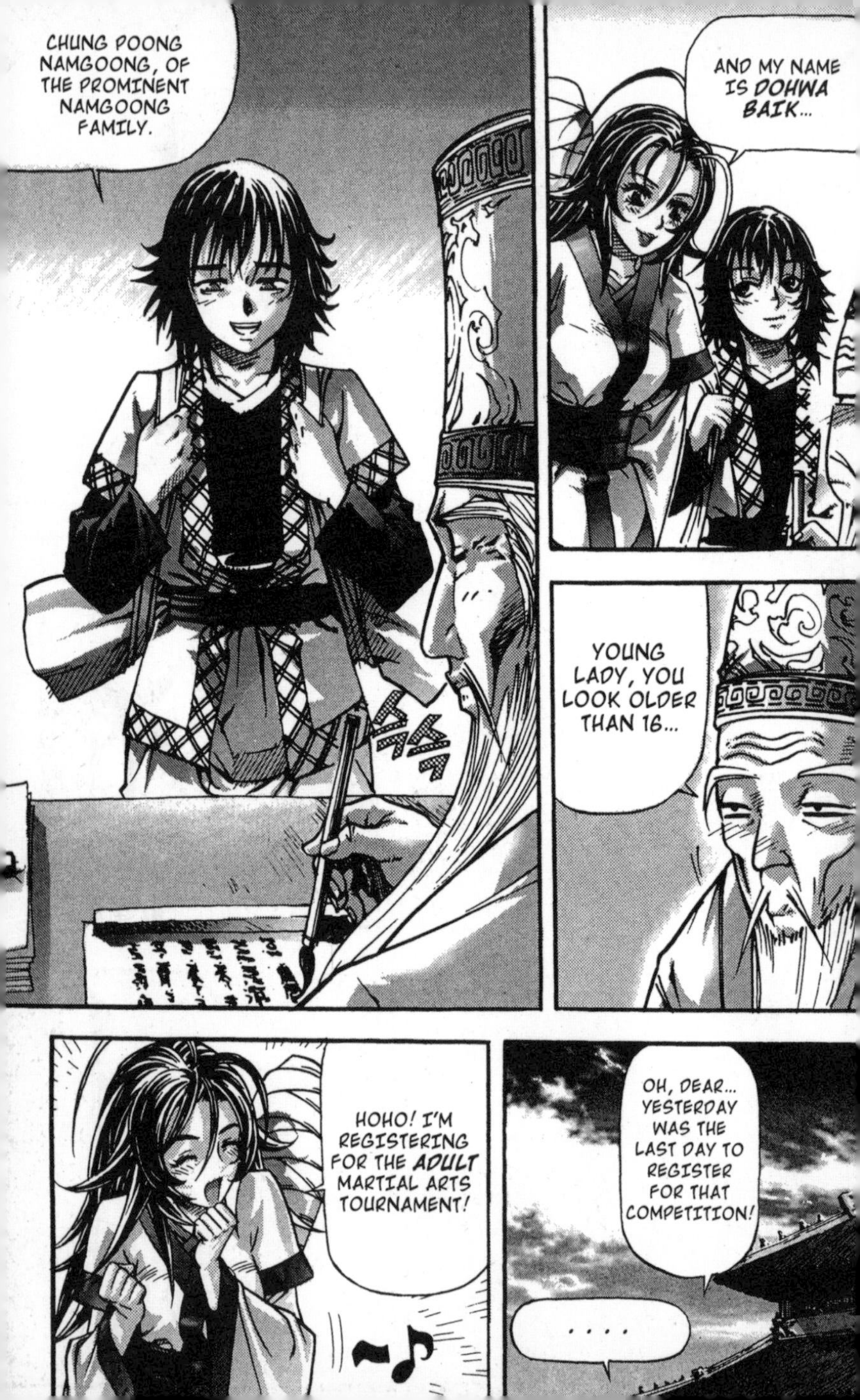
CHUNG POONG NAMGOONG, OF THE PROMINENT NAMGOONG FAMILY.
AND MY NAME IS DOHWA BAIK...
YOUNG LADY, YOU LOOK OLDER THAN 16...
HOHO! I'M REGISTERING FOR THE ADULT MARTIAL ARTS TOURNAMENT!
~♪
OH, DEAR... YESTERDAY WAS THE LAST DAY TO REGISTER FOR THAT COMPETITION!
....

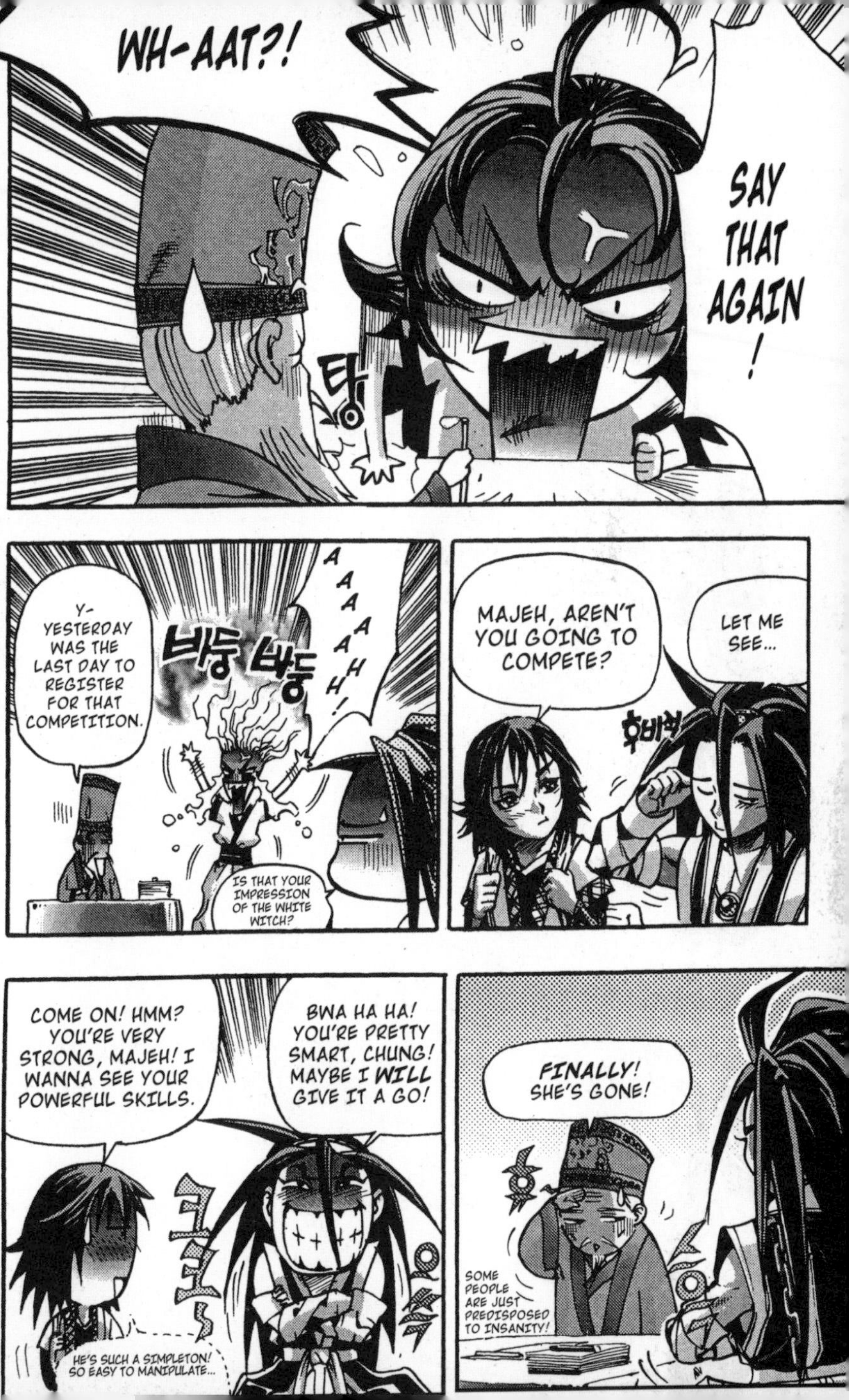
WH-AAT?!
SAY THAT AGAIN!
탕
Y-YESTERDAY WAS THE LAST DAY TO REGISTER FOR THAT COMPETITION.
바둥 바둥
AAAAAAH!
IS THAT YOUR IMPRESSION OF THE WHITE WITCH?
MAJEH, AREN'T YOU GOING TO COMPETE?
LET ME SEE...
후비적
COME ON! HMM? YOU'RE VERY STRONG, MAJEH! I WANNA SEE YOUR POWERFUL SKILLS.
BWA HA HA! YOU'RE PRETTY SMART, CHUNG! MAYBE I *WILL* GIVE IT A GO!
크크
HE'S SUCH A SIMPLETON! SO EASY TO MANIPULATE...
FINALLY! SHE'S GONE!
SOME PEOPLE ARE JUST PREDISPOSED TO INSANITY!

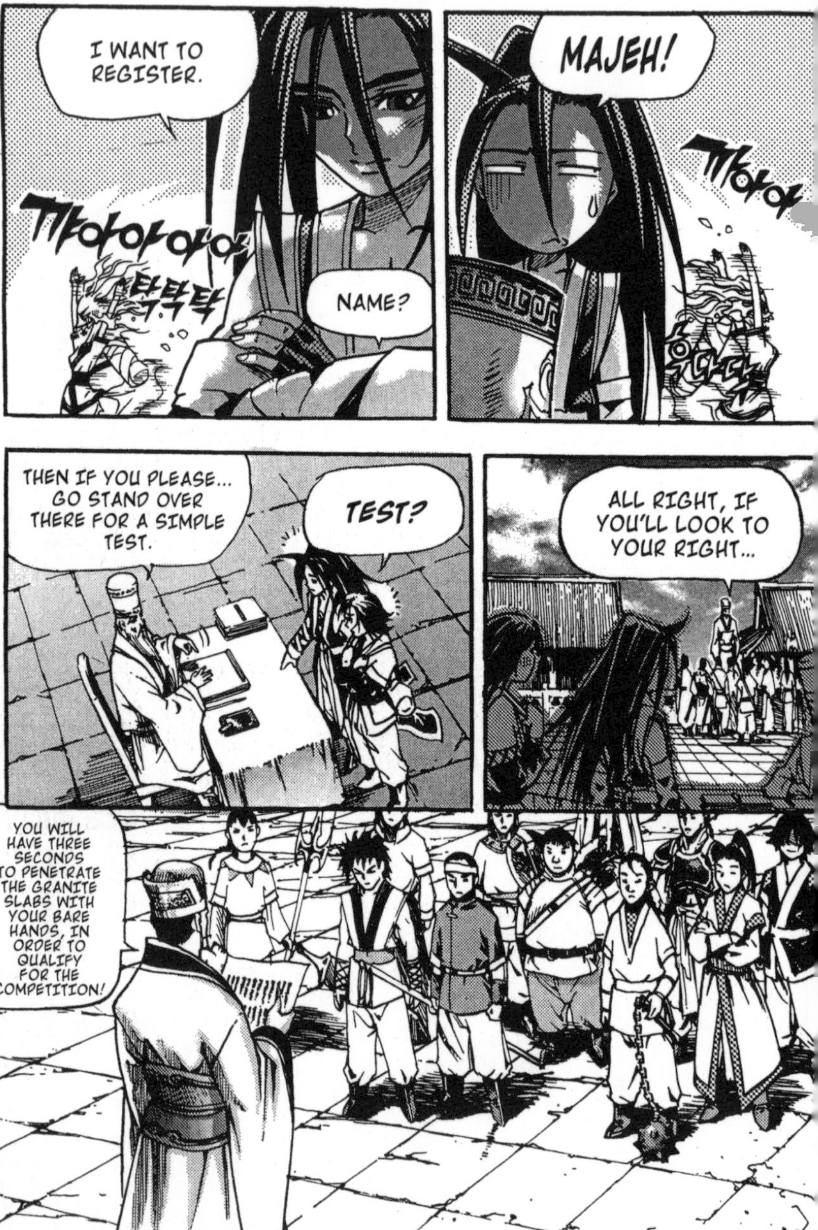
I WANT TO REGISTER.
까아아아아악
탁탁탁
NAME?
MAJEH!
까아아
THEN IF YOU PLEASE... GO STAND OVER THERE FOR A SIMPLE TEST.
TEST?
ALL RIGHT, IF YOU'LL LOOK TO YOUR RIGHT...
YOU WILL HAVE THREE SECONDS TO PENETRATE THE GRANITE SLABS WITH YOUR BARE HANDS, IN ORDER TO QUALIFY FOR THE COMPETITION!

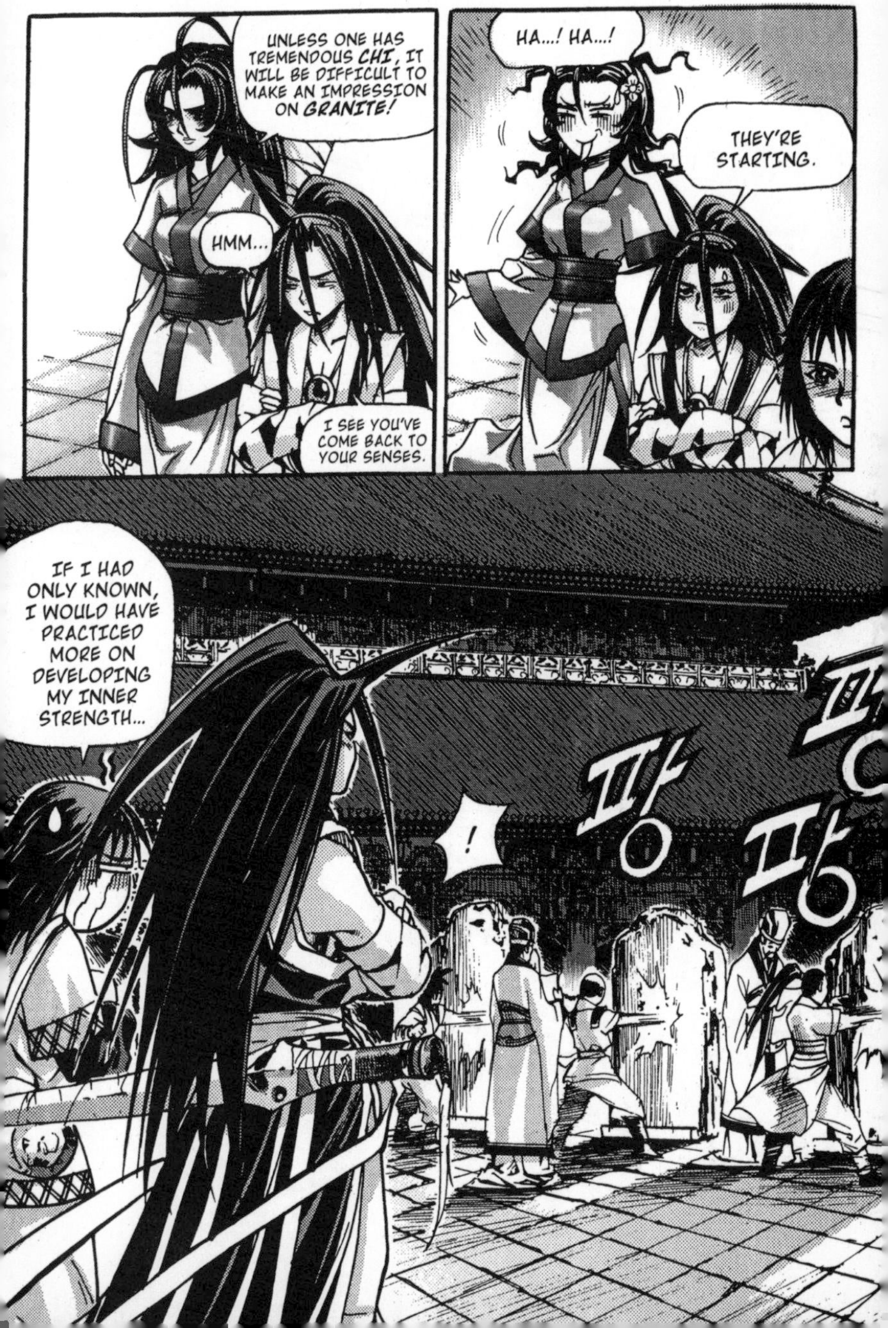
UNLESS ONE HAS TREMENDOUS CHI, IT WILL BE DIFFICULT TO MAKE AN IMPRESSION ON GRANITE!
HMM...
I SEE YOU'VE COME BACK TO YOUR SENSES.
HA...! HA...!
THEY'RE STARTING.
IF I HAD ONLY KNOWN, I WOULD HAVE PRACTICED MORE ON DEVELOPING MY INNER STRENGTH...
!

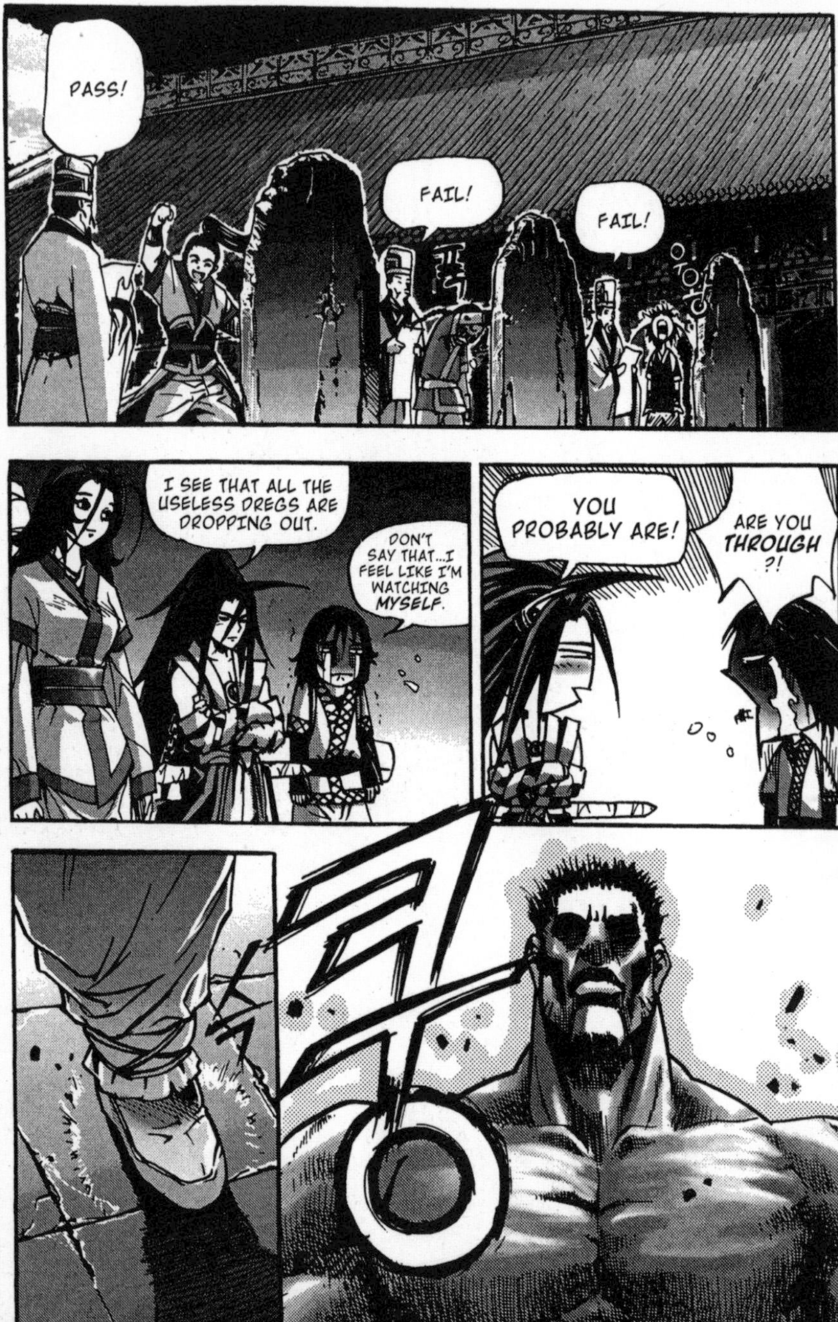
PASS!
FAIL!
FAIL!
I SEE THAT ALL THE USELESS DREGS ARE DROPPING OUT.
DON'T SAY THAT...I FEEL LIKE I'M WATCHING MYSELF.
YOU PROBABLY ARE!
ARE YOU THROUGH?!

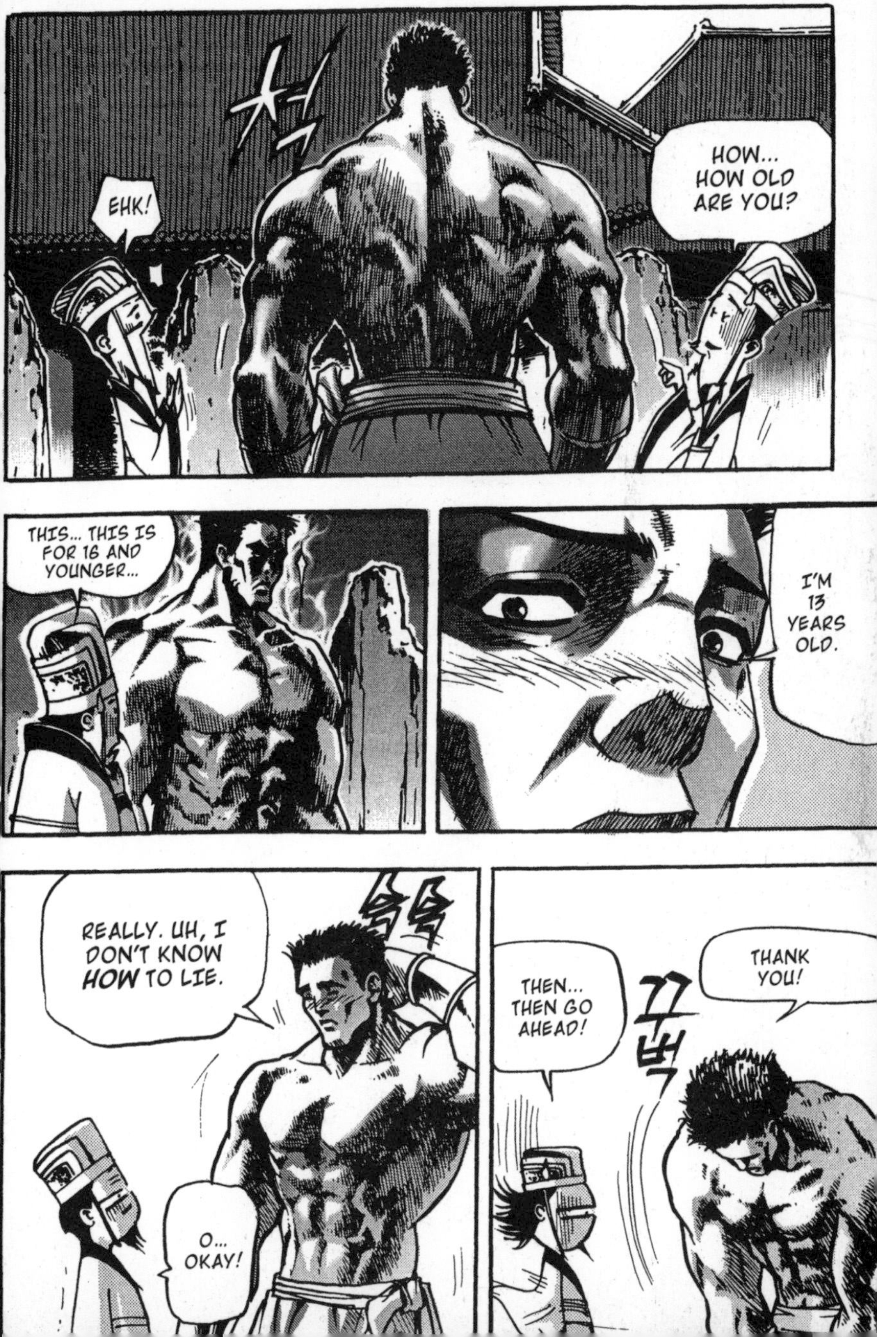
EHK!
HOW... HOW OLD ARE YOU?
THIS... THIS IS FOR 16 AND YOUNGER...
I'M 13 YEARS OLD.
REALLY. UH, I DON'T KNOW *HOW* TO LIE.
O... OKAY!
THEN... THEN GO AHEAD!
꾸벅
THANK YOU!

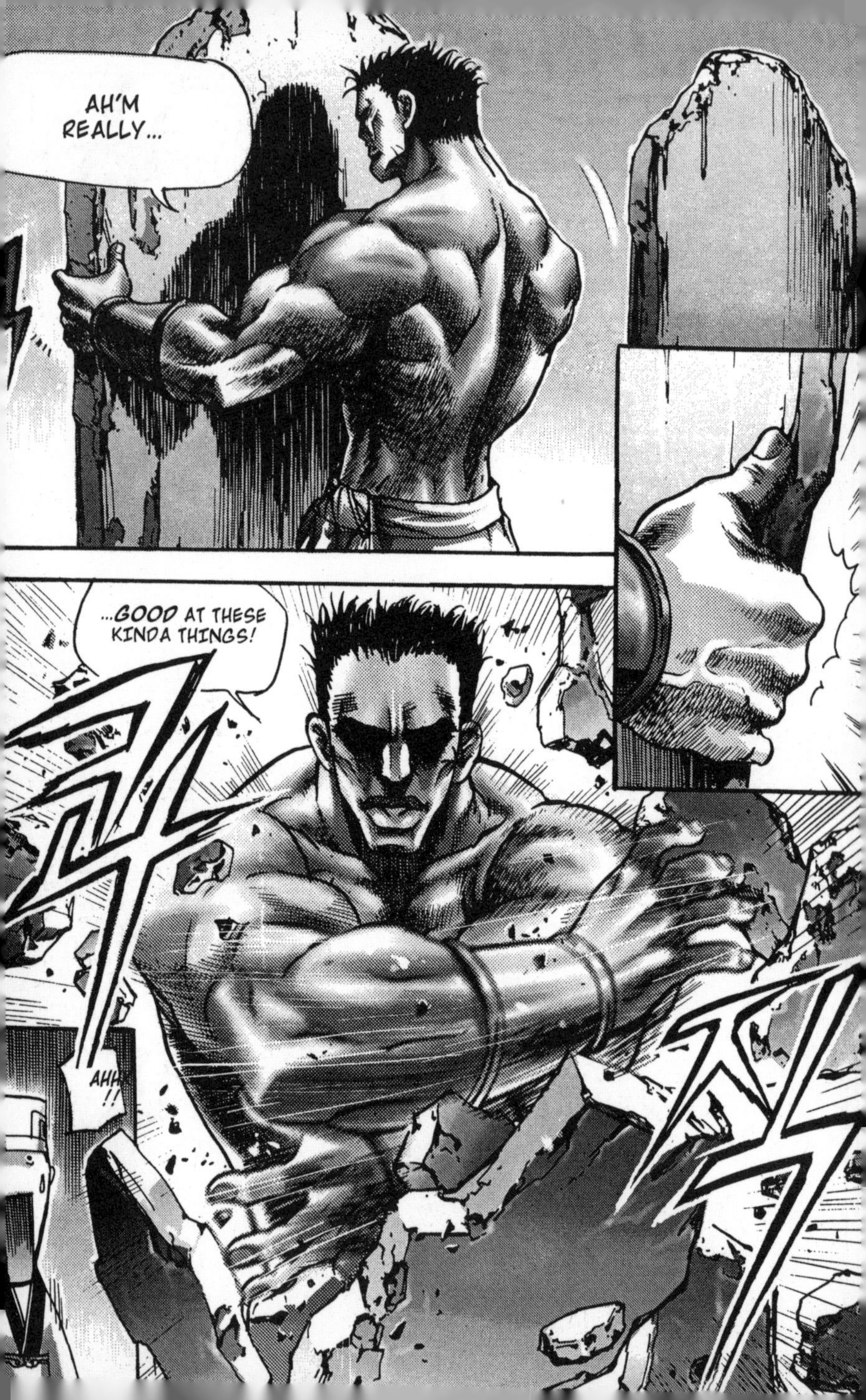
AH'M REALLY...
...GOOD AT THESE KINDA THINGS!
AHH !!

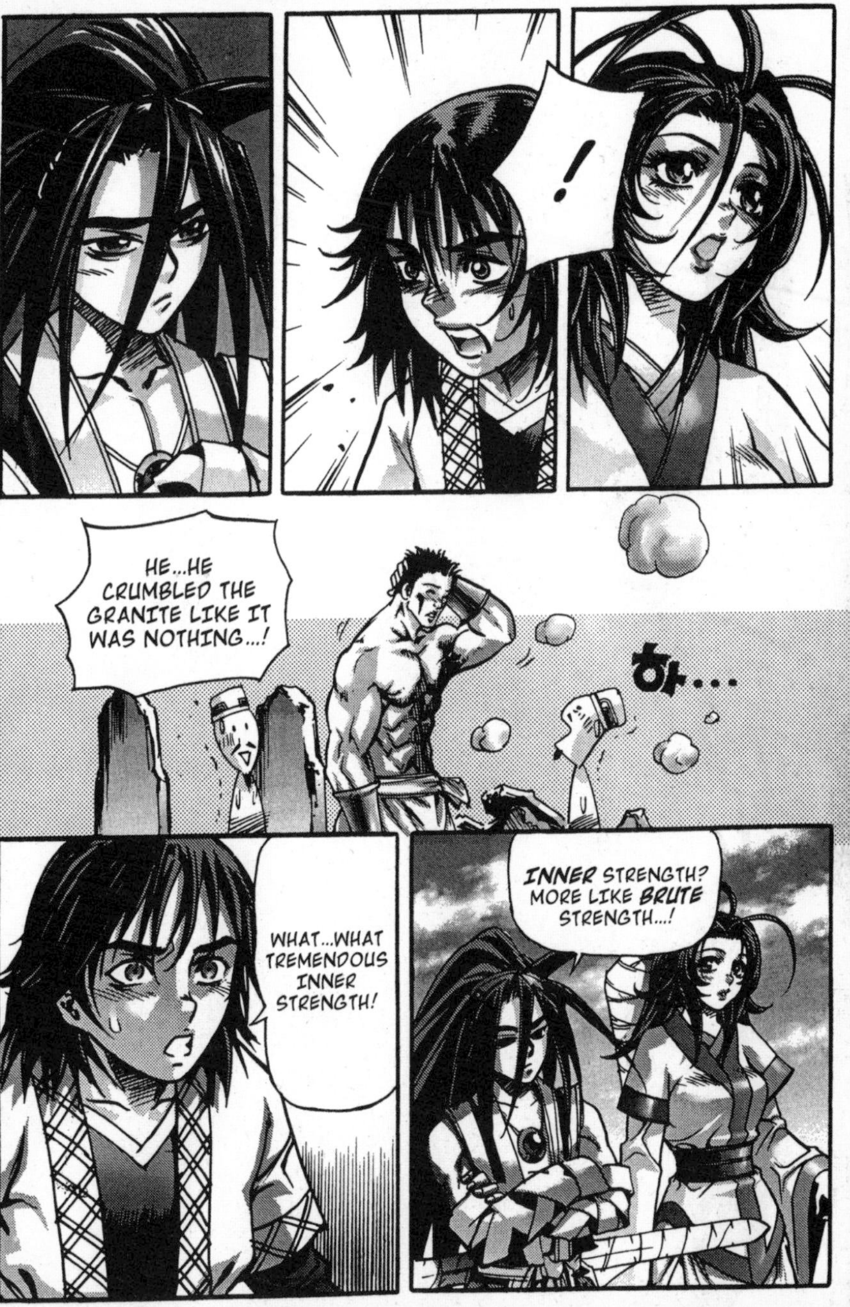
!
HE...HE CRUMBLED THE GRANITE LIKE IT WAS NOTHING...!
하...
WHAT...WHAT TREMENDOUS INNER STRENGTH!
INNER STRENGTH? MORE LIKE BRUTE STRENGTH...!

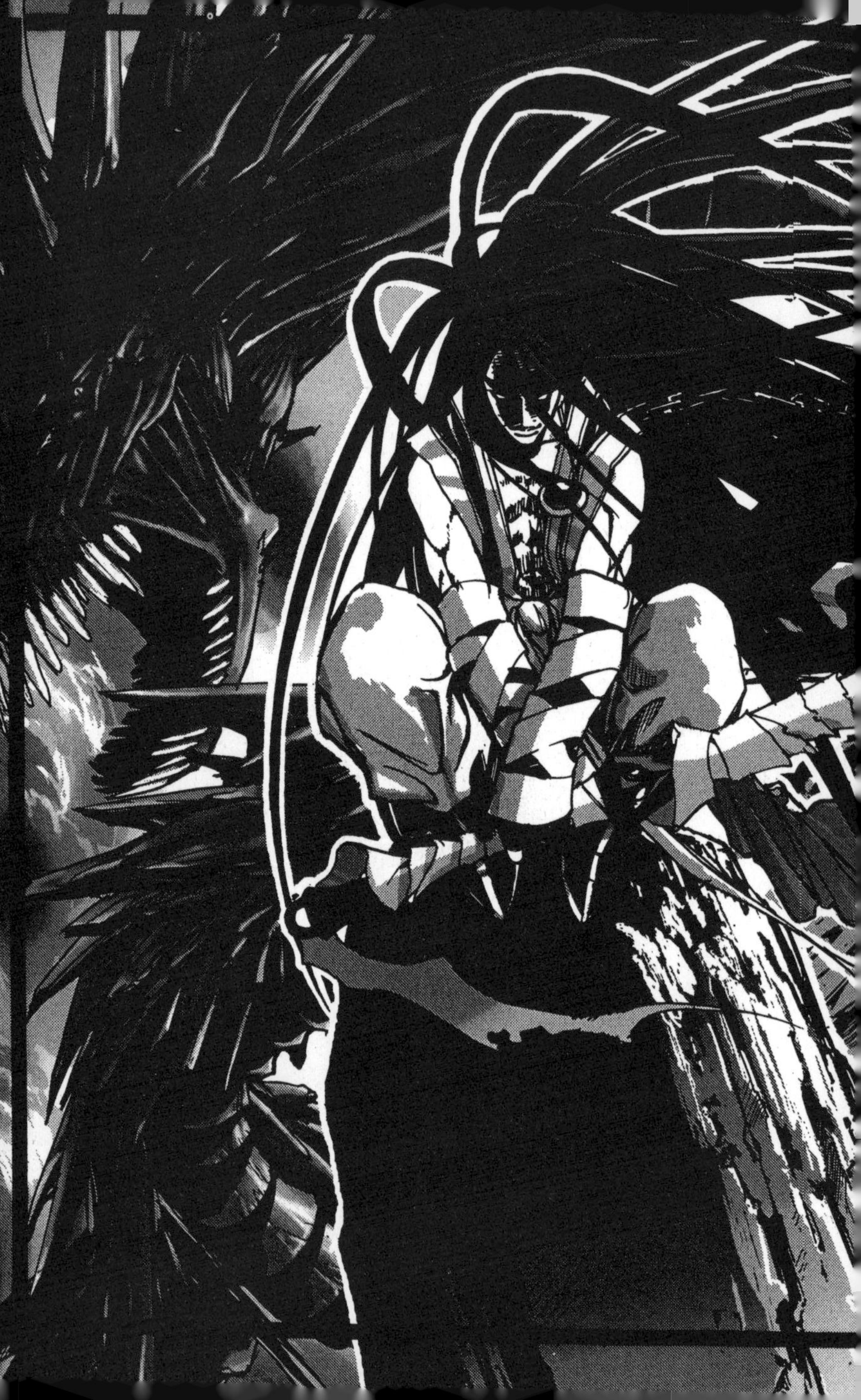

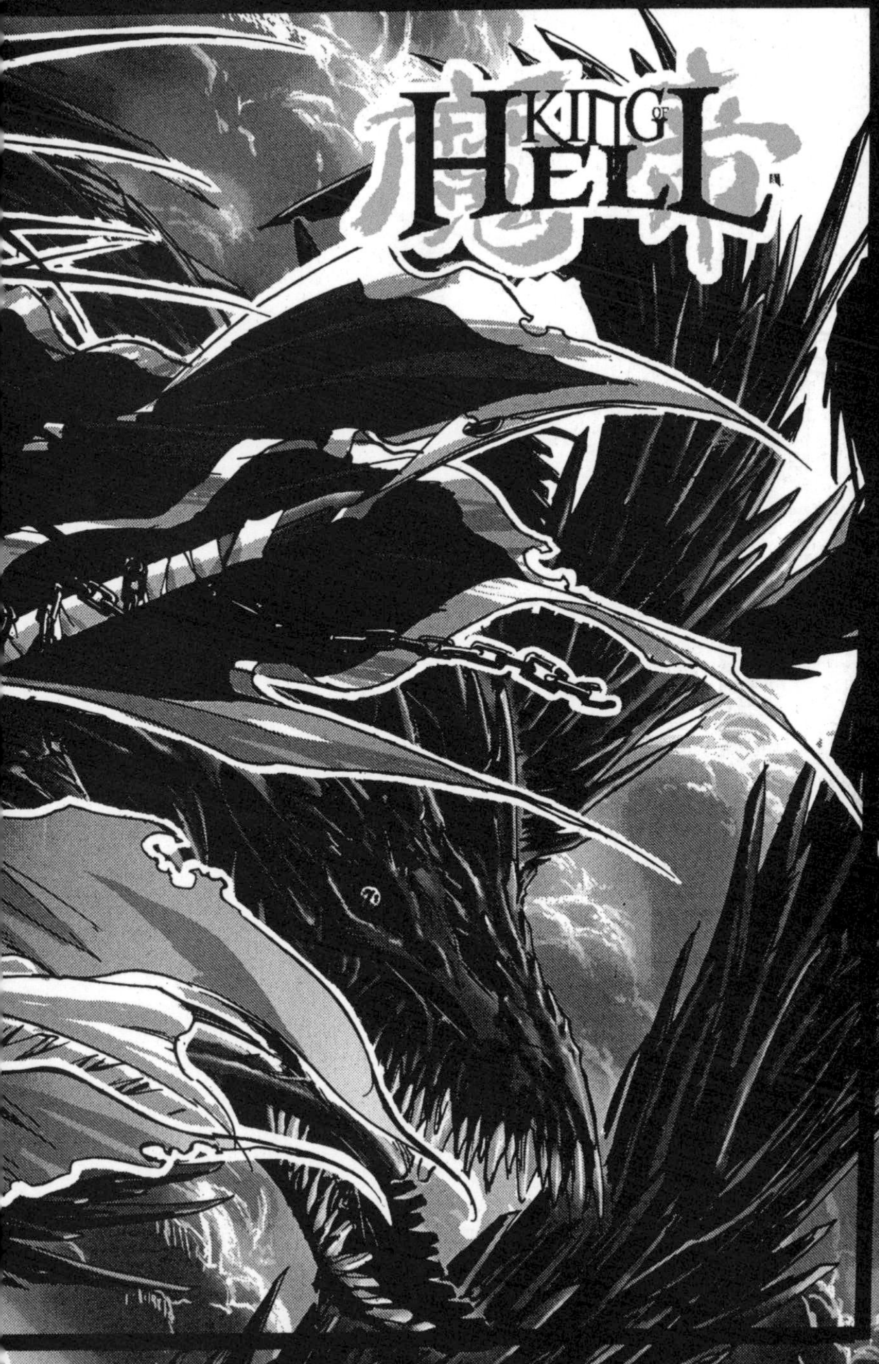
KING OF HELL

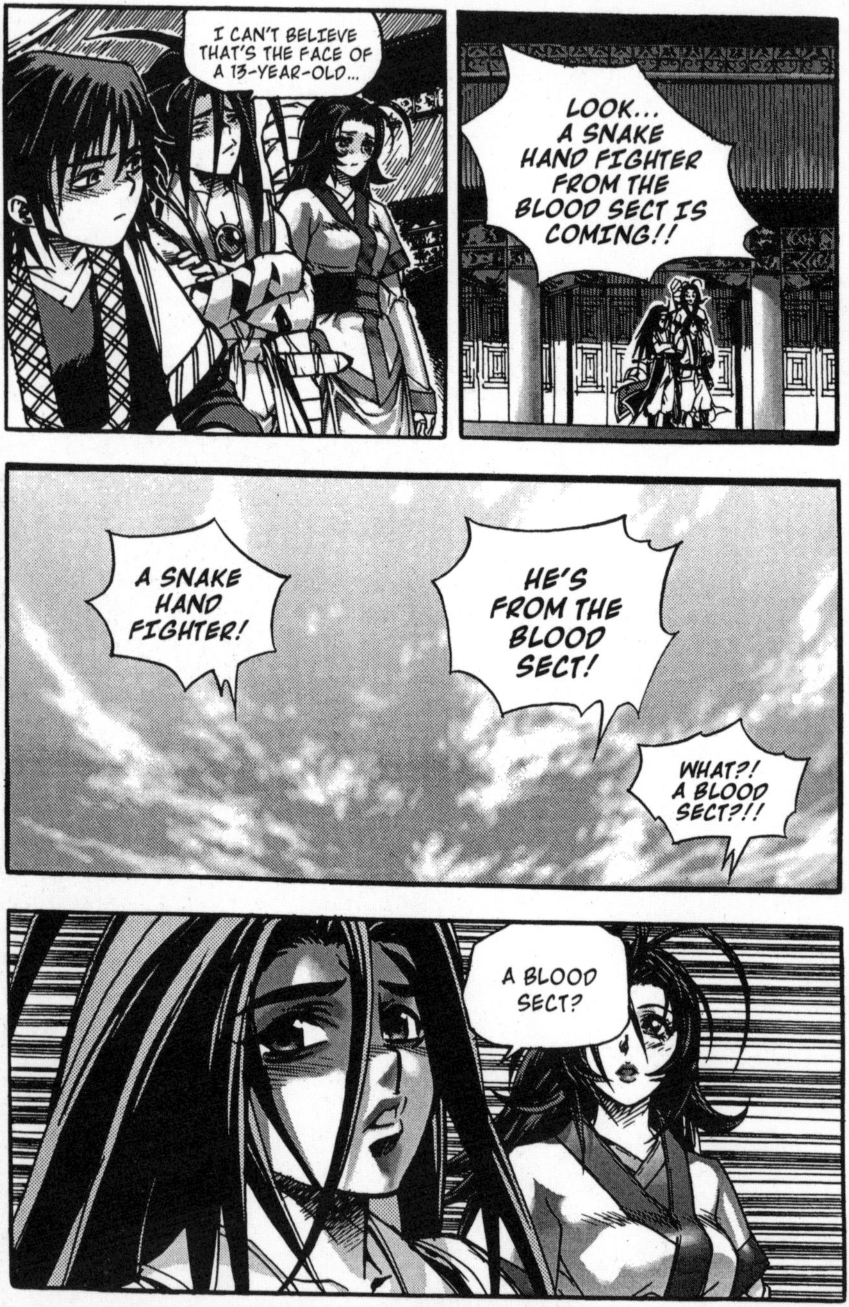
I CAN'T BELIEVE THAT'S THE FACE OF A 13-YEAR-OLD...
LOOK... A SNAKE HAND FIGHTER FROM THE BLOOD SECT IS COMING!!
A SNAKE HAND FIGHTER!
HE'S FROM THE BLOOD SECT!
WHAT?! A BLOOD SECT?!!
A BLOOD SECT?

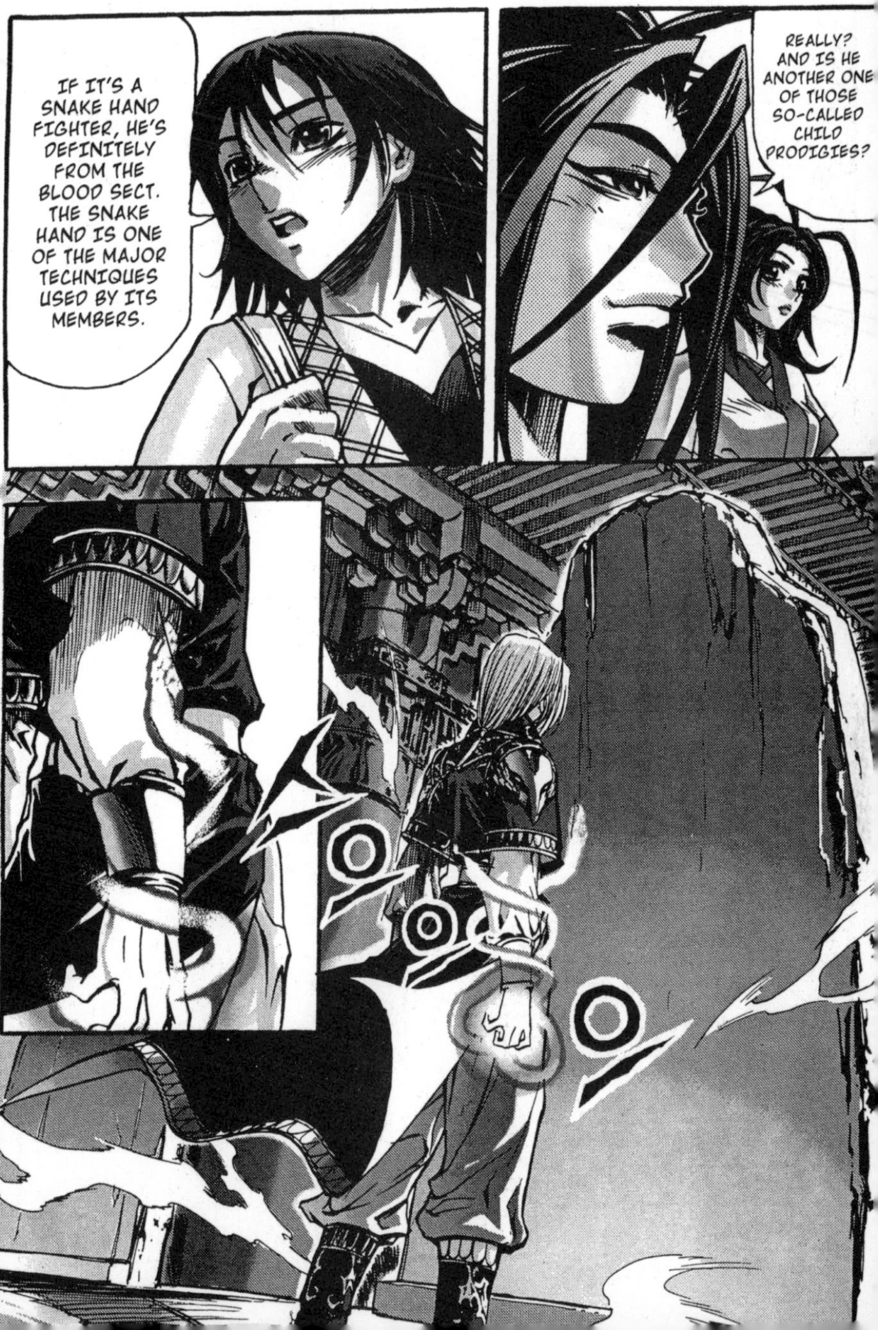
IF IT'S A SNAKE HAND FIGHTER, HE'S DEFINITELY FROM THE BLOOD SECT. THE SNAKE HAND IS ONE OF THE MAJOR TECHNIQUES USED BY ITS MEMBERS.
REALLY? AND IS HE ANOTHER ONE OF THOSE SO-CALLED CHILD PRODIGIES?

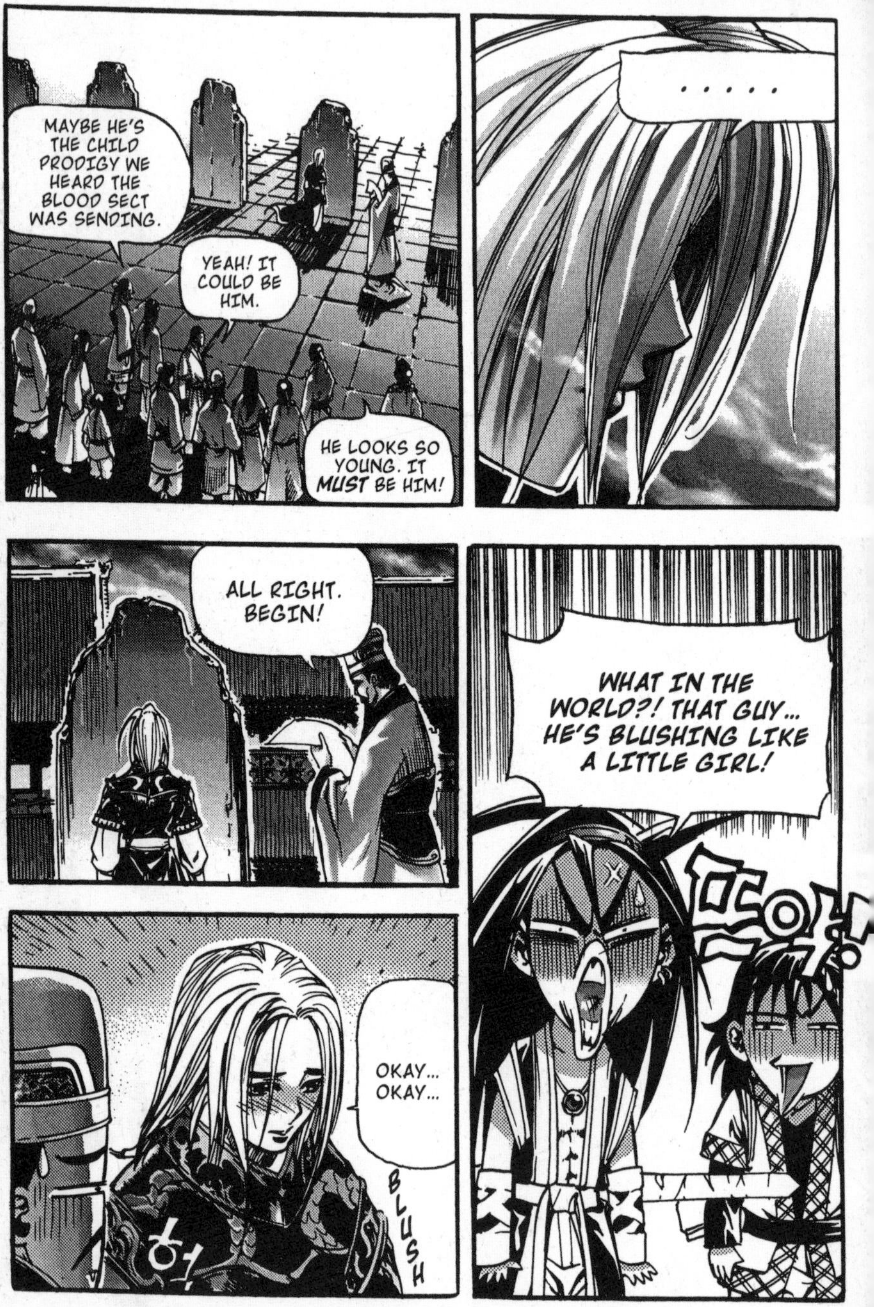
MAYBE HE'S THE CHILD PRODIGY WE HEARD THE BLOOD SECT WAS SENDING.
YEAH! IT COULD BE HIM.
HE LOOKS SO YOUNG. IT *MUST* BE HIM!
.....
ALL RIGHT. BEGIN!
OKAY... OKAY...
BLUSH
WHAT IN THE WORLD?! THAT GUY... HE'S BLUSHING LIKE A LITTLE GIRL!

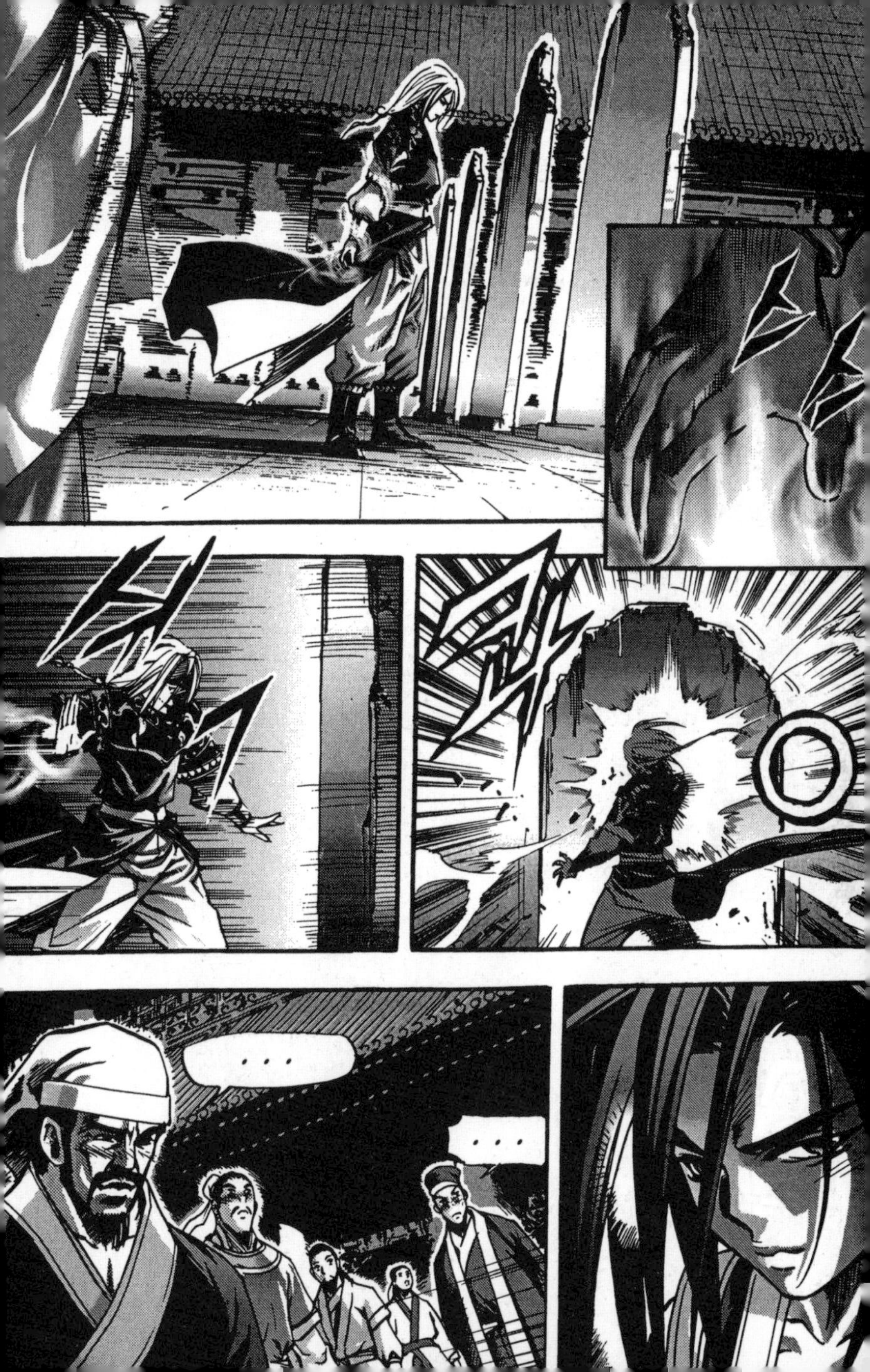
...
...

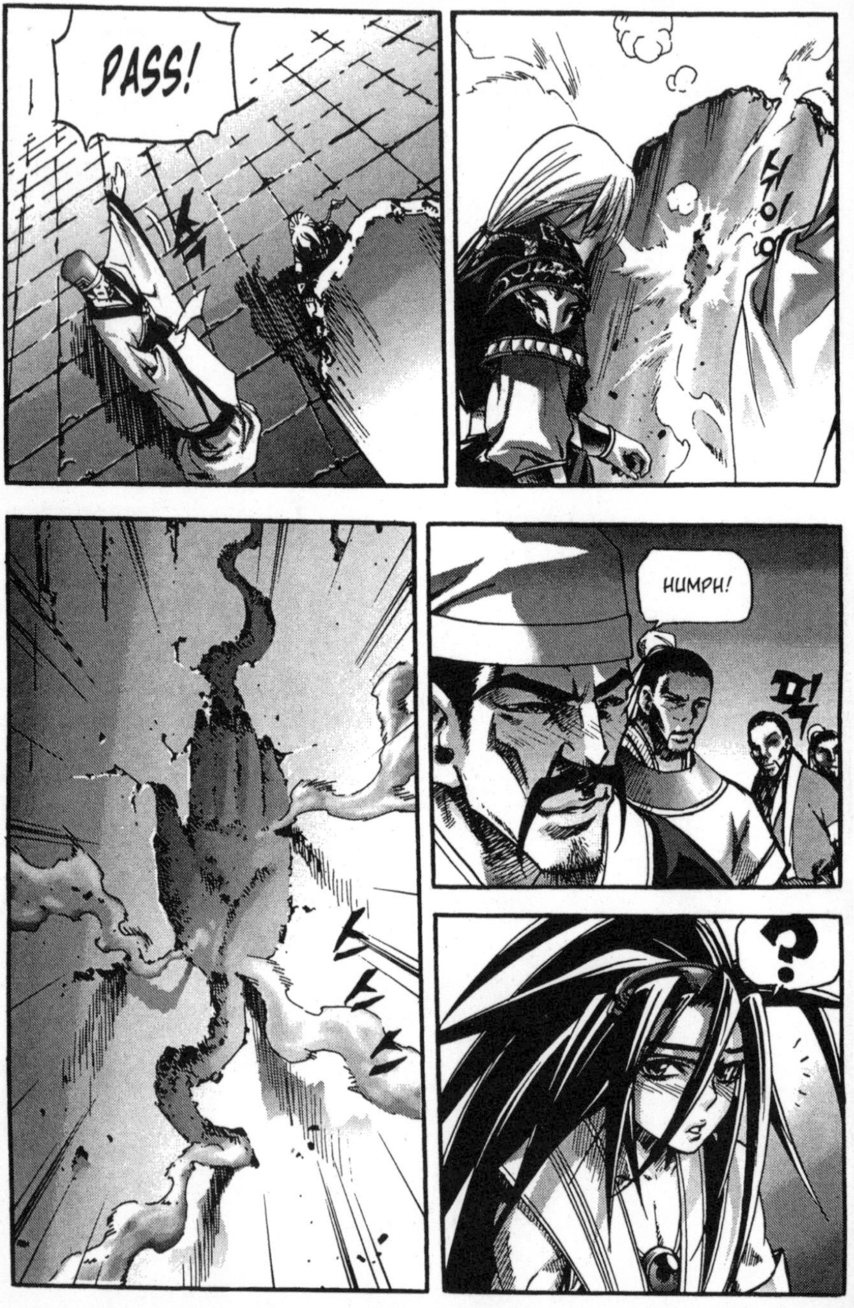
PASS!
HUMPH!
?

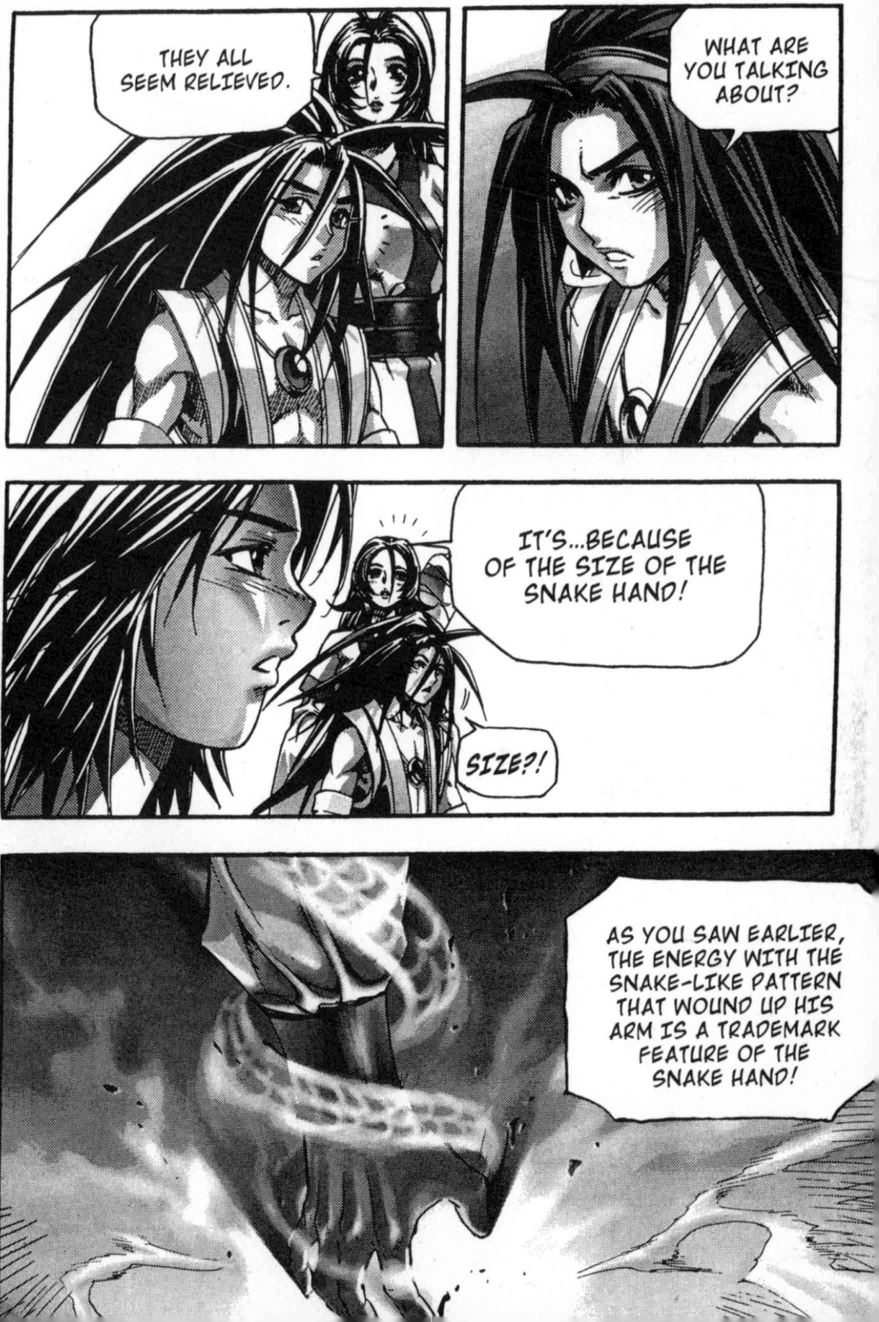
THEY ALL SEEM RELIEVED.
WHAT ARE YOU TALKING ABOUT?
IT'S...BECAUSE OF THE SIZE OF THE SNAKE HAND!
SIZE?!
AS YOU SAW EARLIER, THE ENERGY WITH THE SNAKE-LIKE PATTERN THAT WOUND UP HIS ARM IS A TRADEMARK FEATURE OF THE SNAKE HAND!

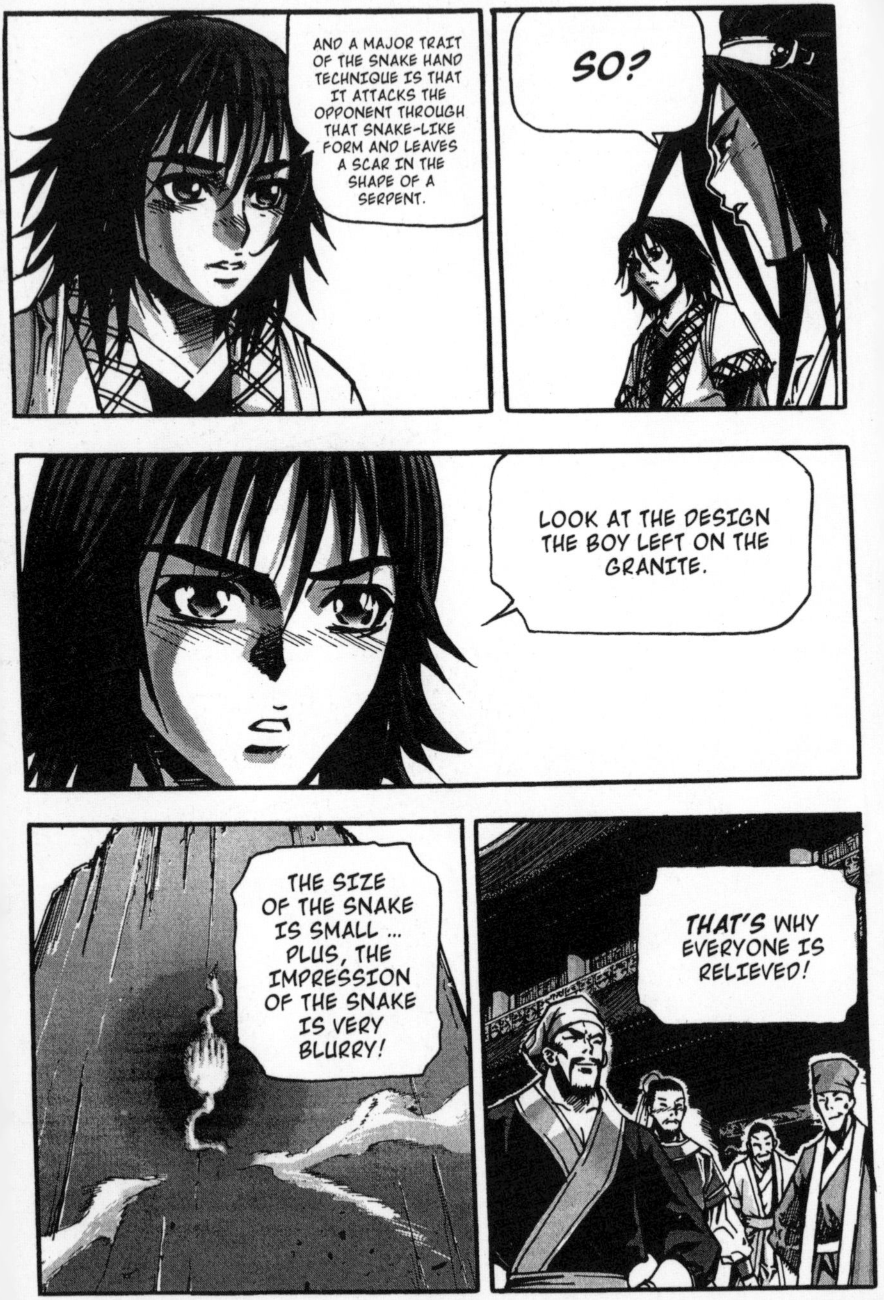
AND A MAJOR TRAIT OF THE SNAKE HAND TECHNIQUE IS THAT IT ATTACKS THE OPPONENT THROUGH THAT SNAKE-LIKE FORM AND LEAVES A SCAR IN THE SHAPE OF A SERPENT.
SO?
LOOK AT THE DESIGN THE BOY LEFT ON THE GRANITE.
THE SIZE OF THE SNAKE IS SMALL ... PLUS, THE IMPRESSION OF THE SNAKE IS VERY BLURRY!
THAT'S WHY EVERYONE IS RELIEVED!

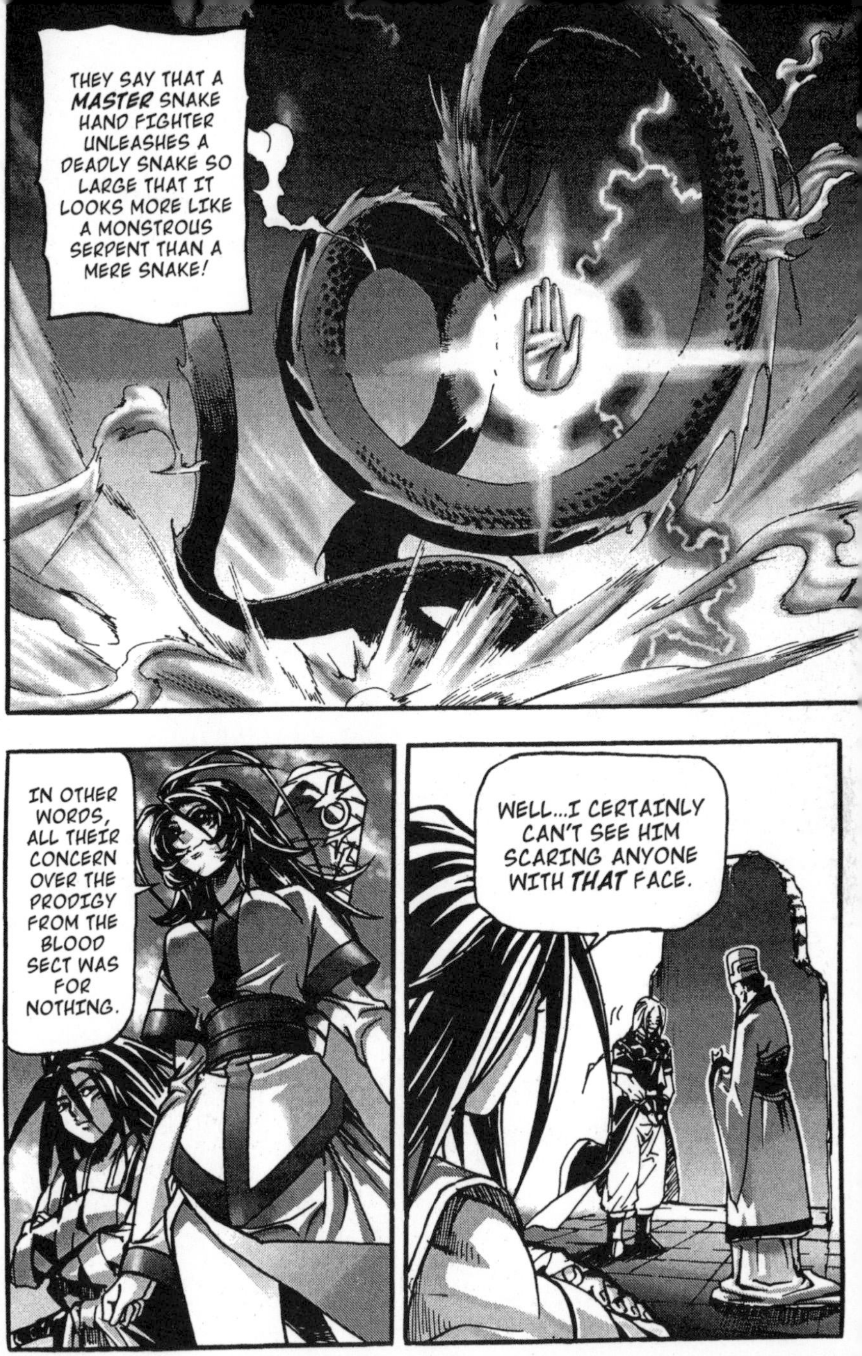
THEY SAY THAT A MASTER SNAKE HAND FIGHTER UNLEASHES A DEADLY SNAKE SO LARGE THAT IT LOOKS MORE LIKE A MONSTROUS SERPENT THAN A MERE SNAKE!
IN OTHER WORDS, ALL THEIR CONCERN OVER THE PRODIGY FROM THE BLOOD SECT WAS FOR NOTHING.
WELL...I CERTAINLY CAN'T SEE HIM SCARING ANYONE WITH THAT FACE.

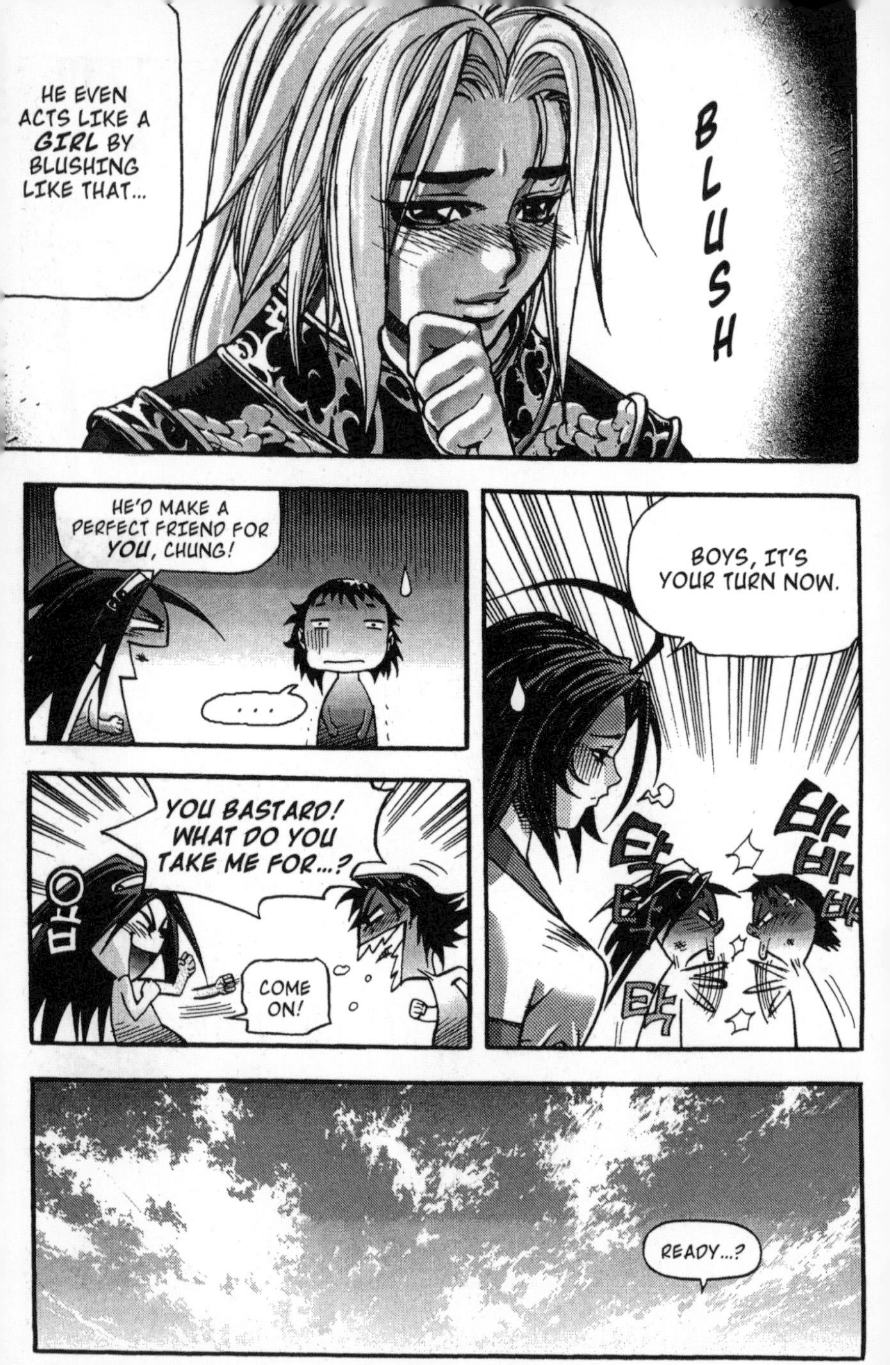
HE EVEN ACTS LIKE A GIRL BY BLUSHING LIKE THAT...
BLUSH
HE'D MAKE A PERFECT FRIEND FOR YOU, CHUNG!
...
YOU BASTARD! WHAT DO YOU TAKE ME FOR...?
COME ON!
BOYS, IT'S YOUR TURN NOW.
READY...?

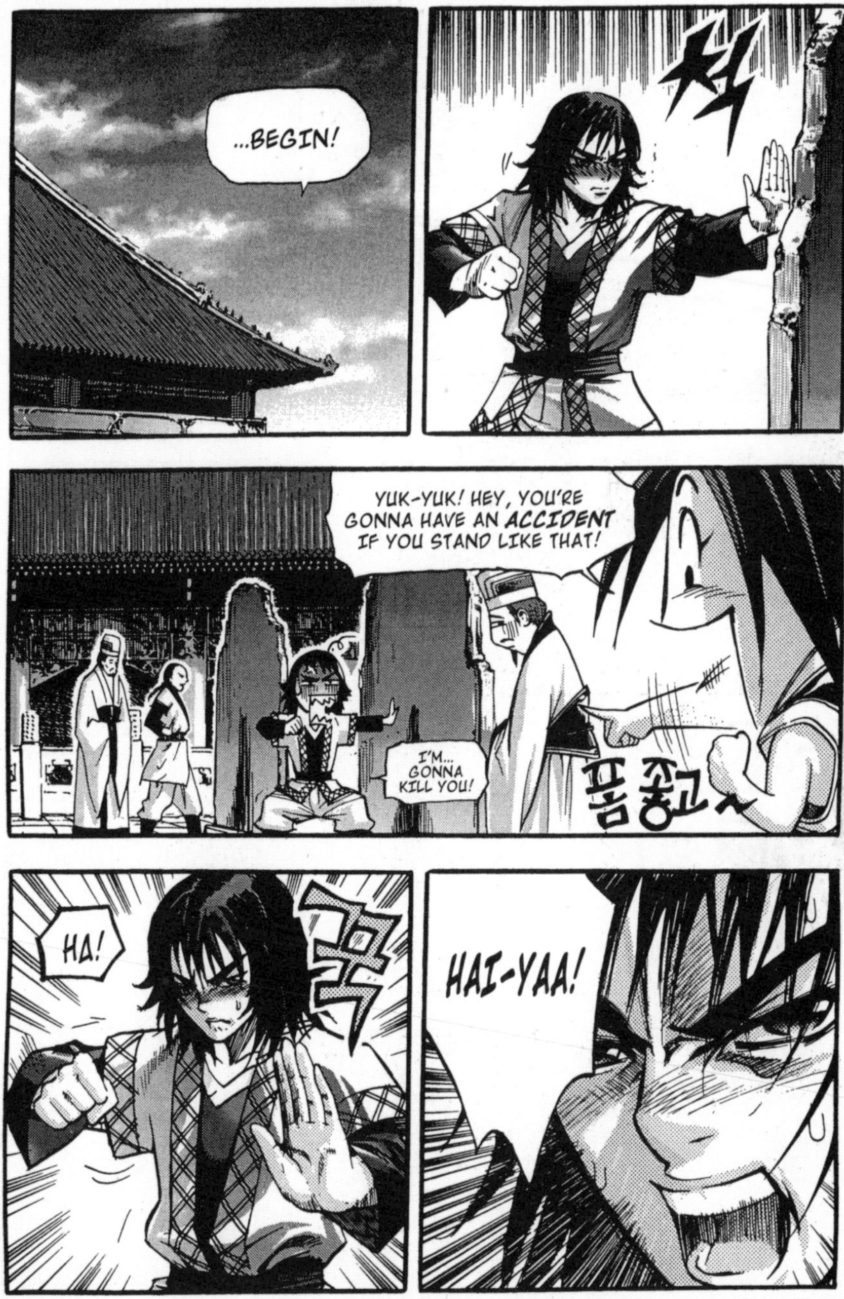
...BEGIN!
YUK-YUK! HEY, YOU'RE GONNA HAVE AN ACCIDENT IF YOU STAND LIKE THAT!
I'M... GONNA KILL YOU!
폼좋고~
HA!
HAI-YAA!

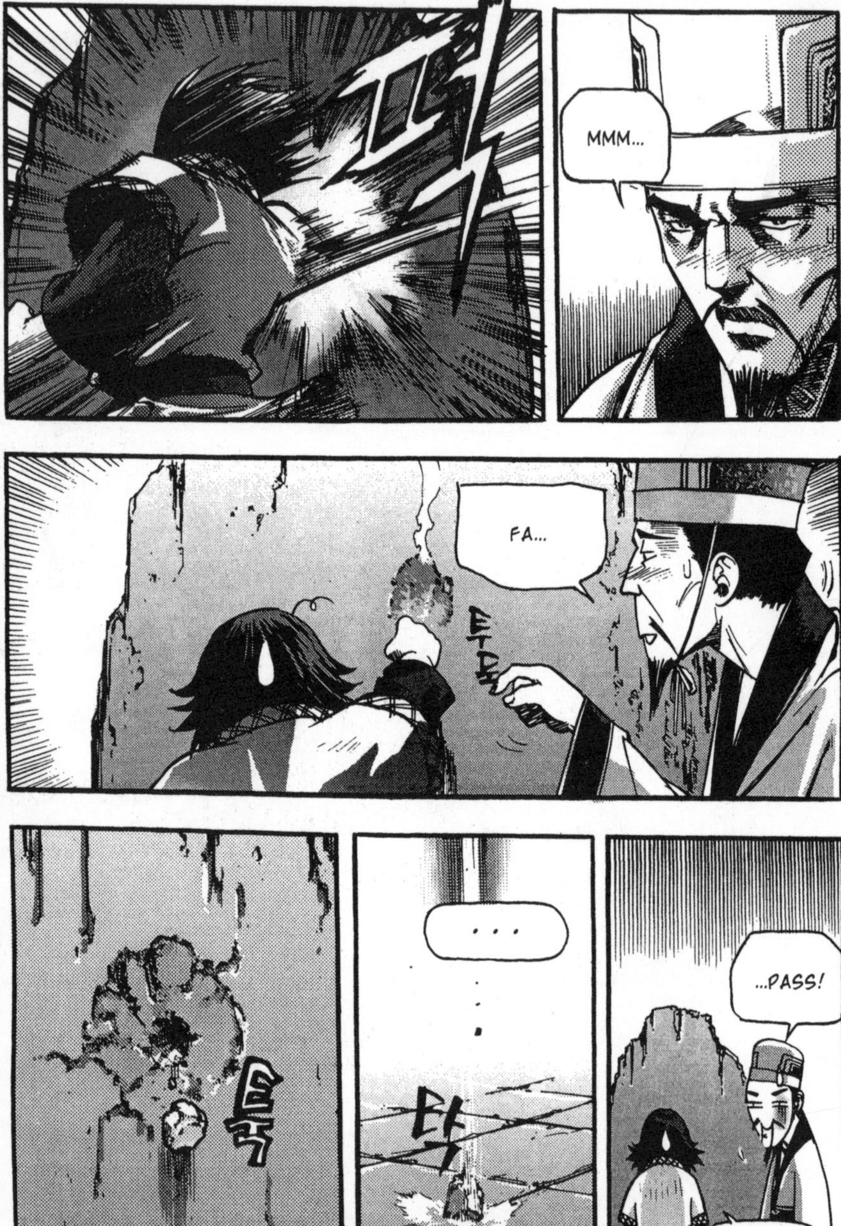
MMM...
FA...
. . .
...PASS!
...

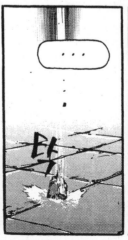

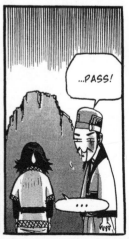

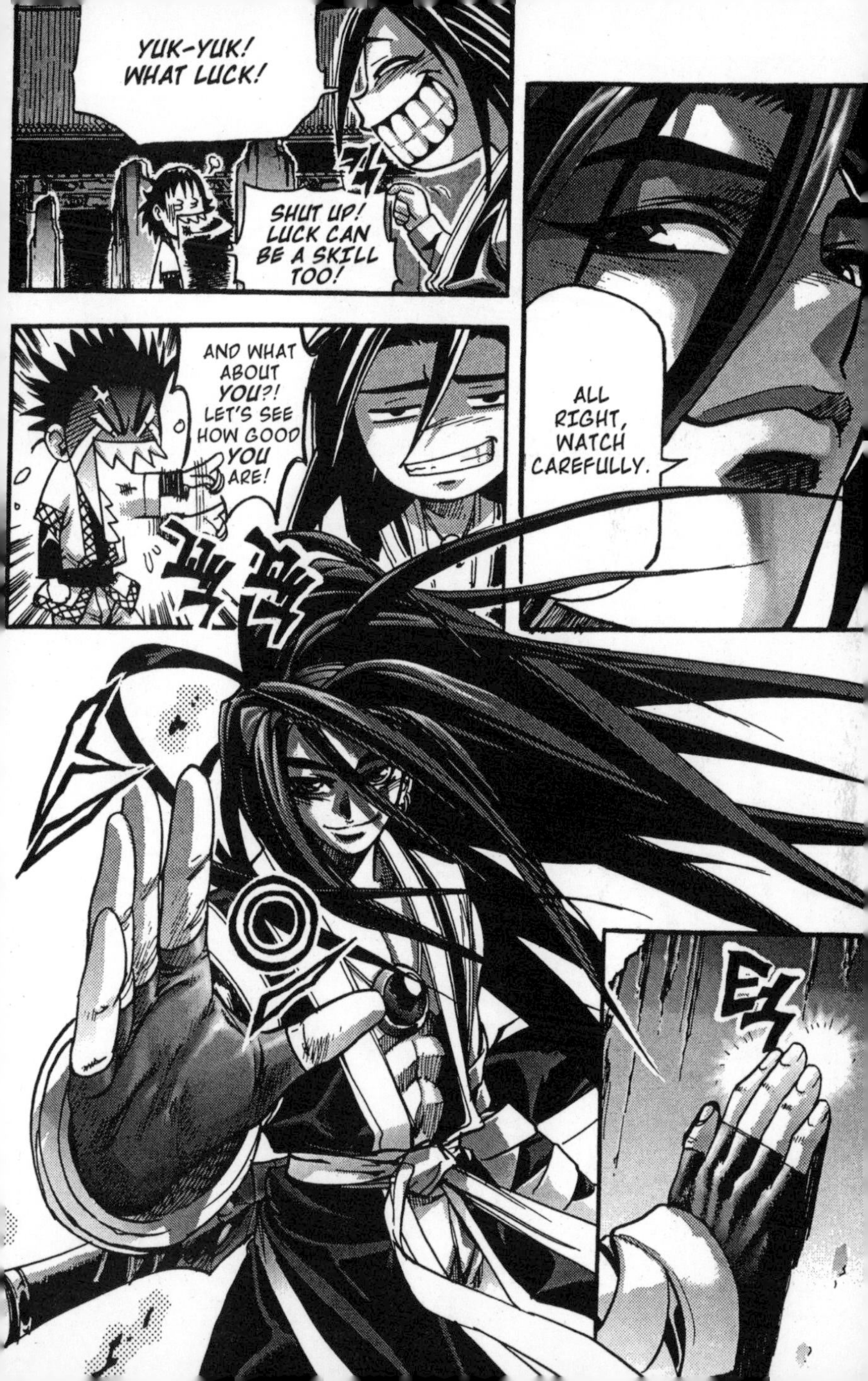

YUK-YUK! WHAT LUCK!
SHUT UP! LUCK CAN BE A SKILL TOO!
AND WHAT ABOUT YOU?! LET'S SEE HOW GOOD YOU ARE!
ALL RIGHT, WATCH CAREFULLY.

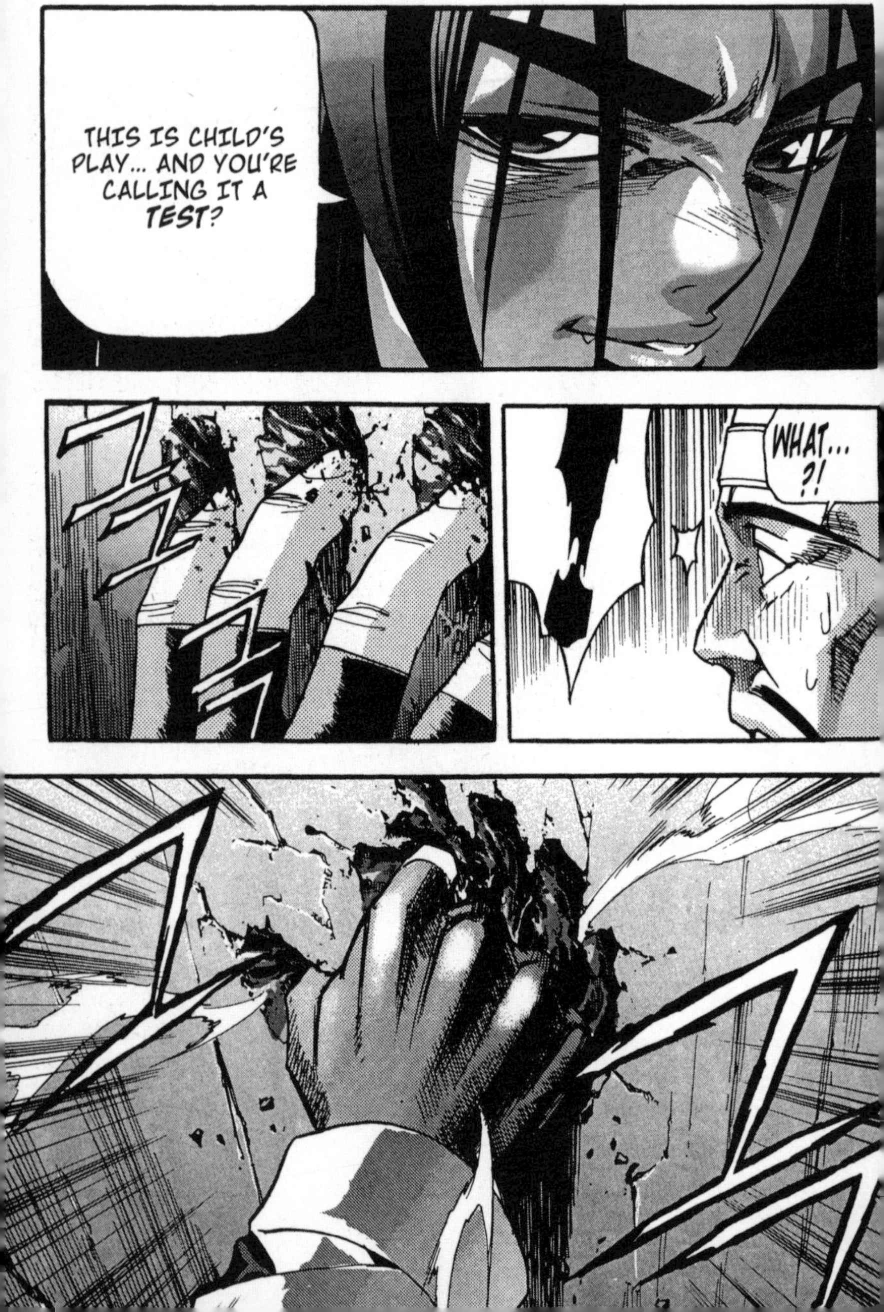
THIS IS CHILD'S PLAY... AND YOU'RE CALLING IT A *TEST*?
WHAT... ?!

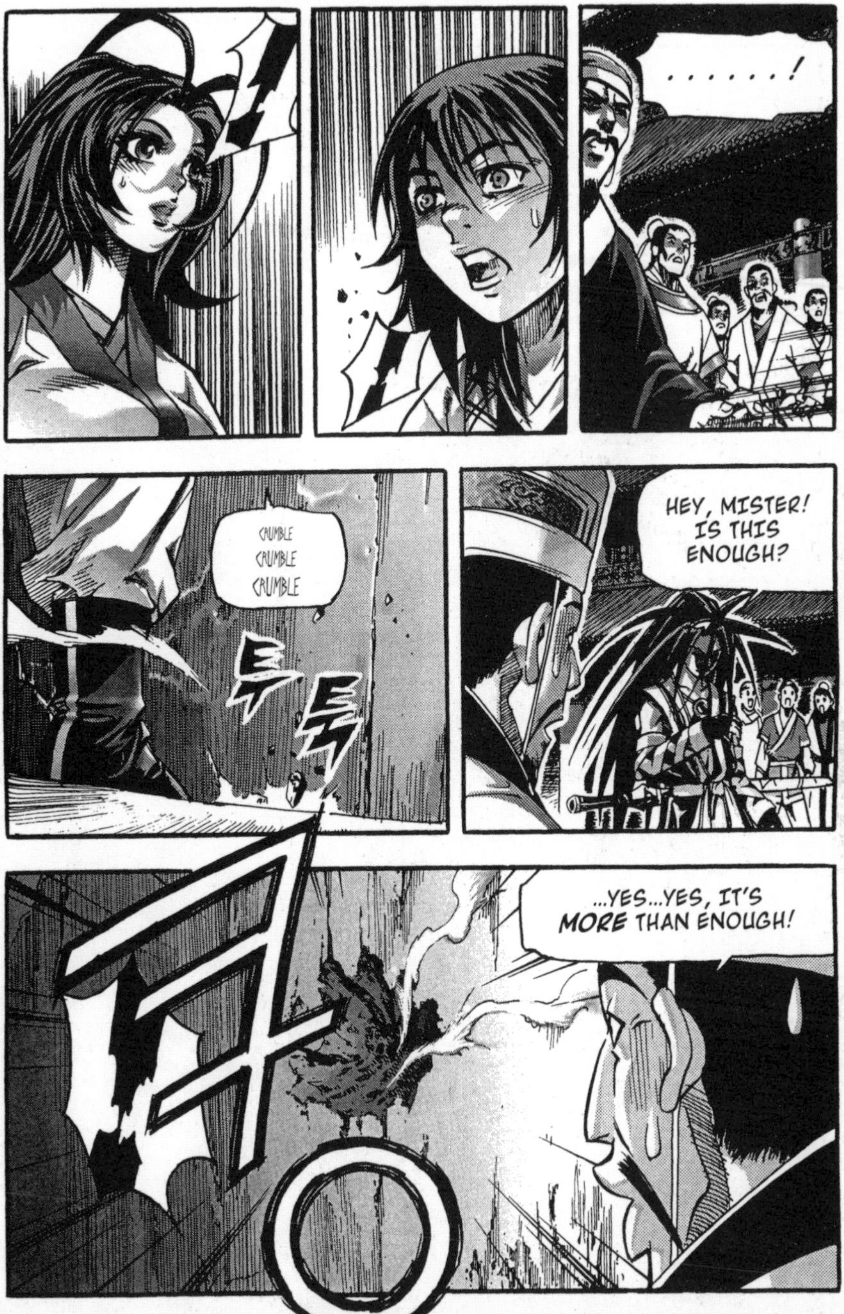
.......!
CRUMBLE
CRUMBLE
CRUMBLE
HEY, MISTER! IS THIS ENOUGH?
...YES...YES, IT'S **MORE** THAN ENOUGH!

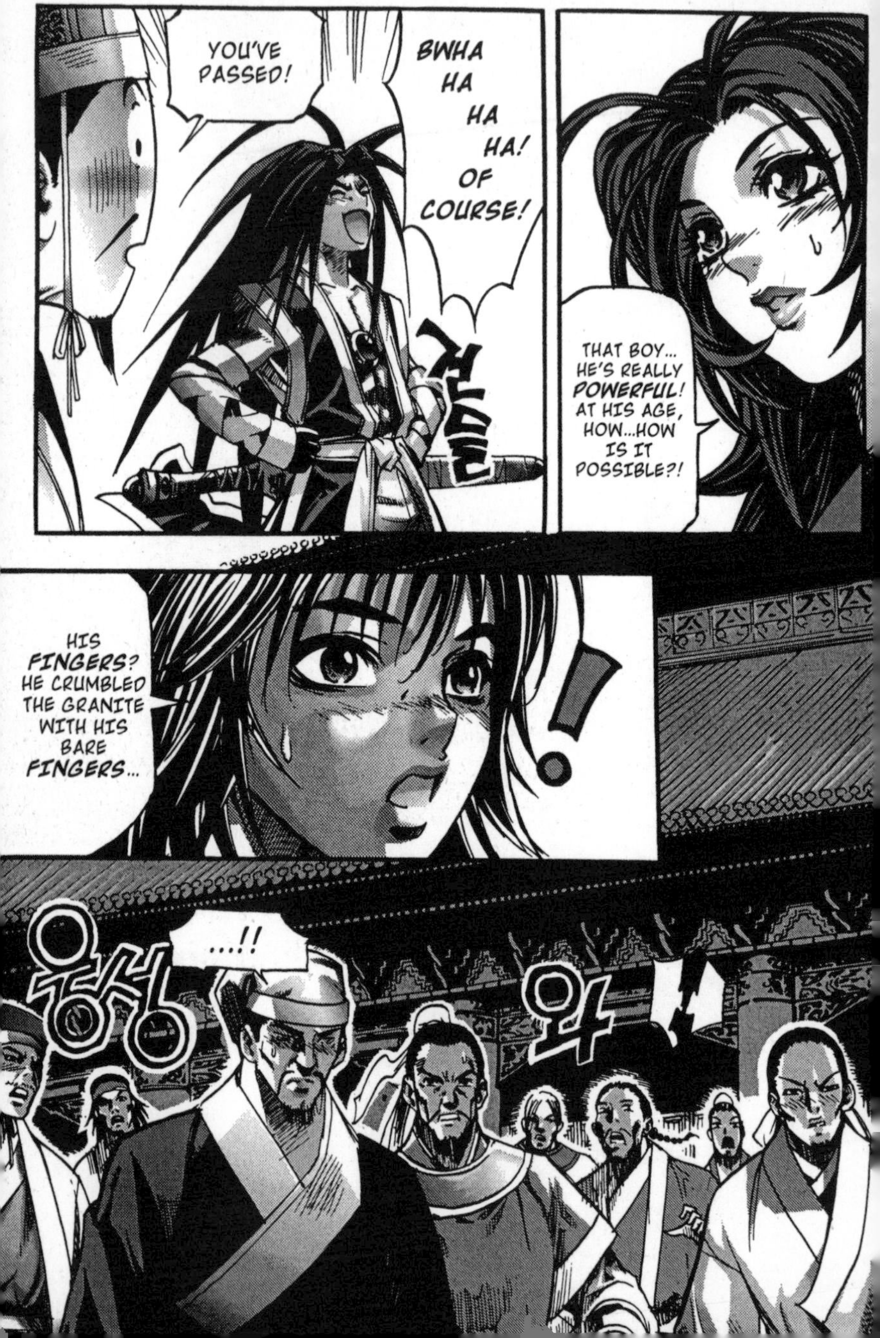

YOU'VE PASSED!
BWHA HA HA HA! OF COURSE!
THAT BOY... HE'S REALLY POWERFUL! AT HIS AGE, HOW...HOW IS IT POSSIBLE?!
HIS FINGERS? HE CRUMBLED THE GRANITE WITH HIS BARE FINGERS...
...!!

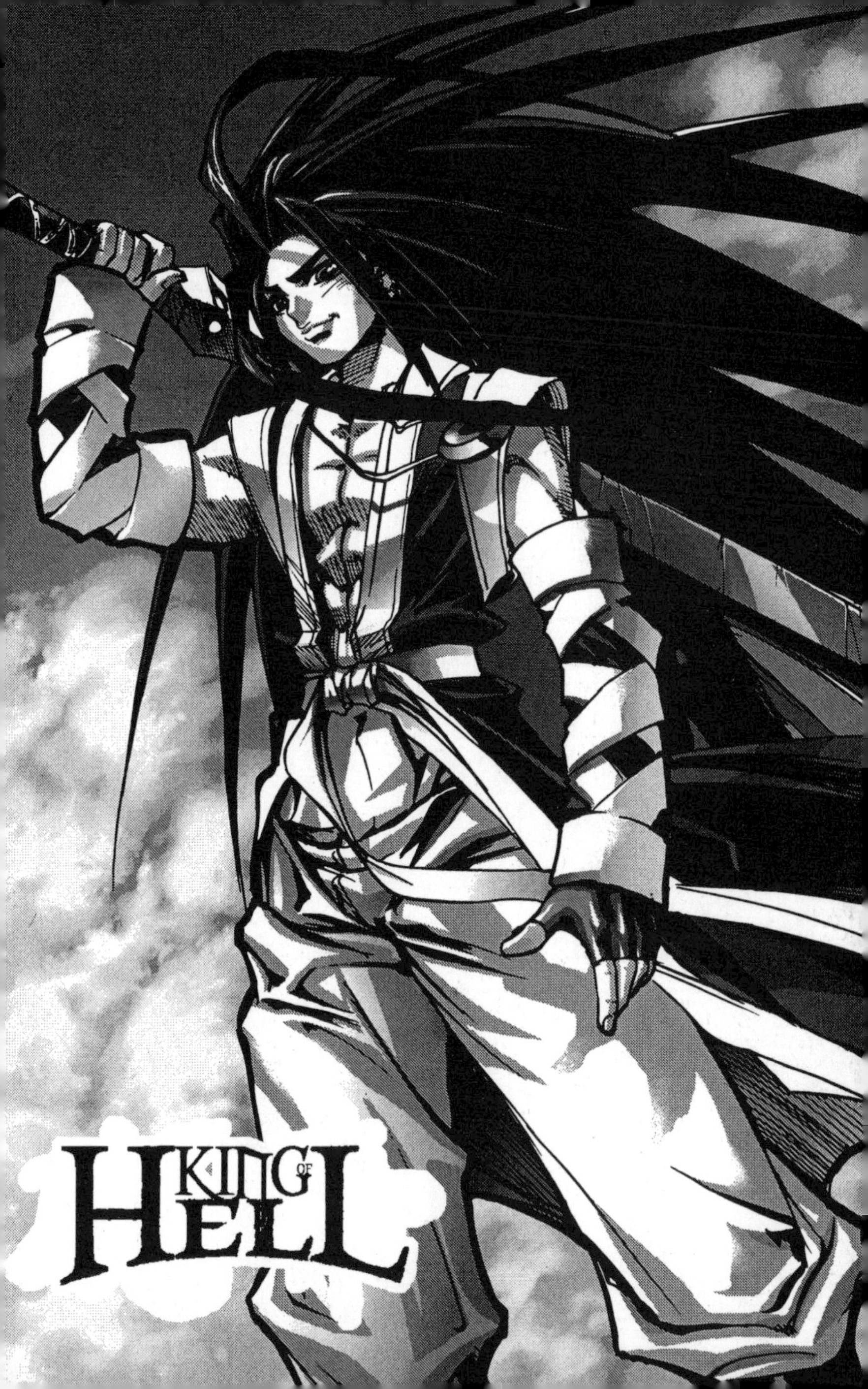
KING OF HELL

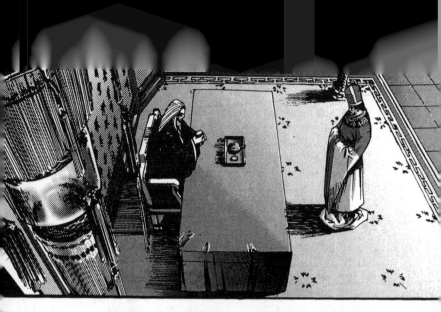

SO...HAS THE PRODIGY FROM THE BLOOD SECT REGISTERED YET?

YES, SIR. A YOUNG MAN USING THE **SNAKE HAND** HAS ARRIVED.

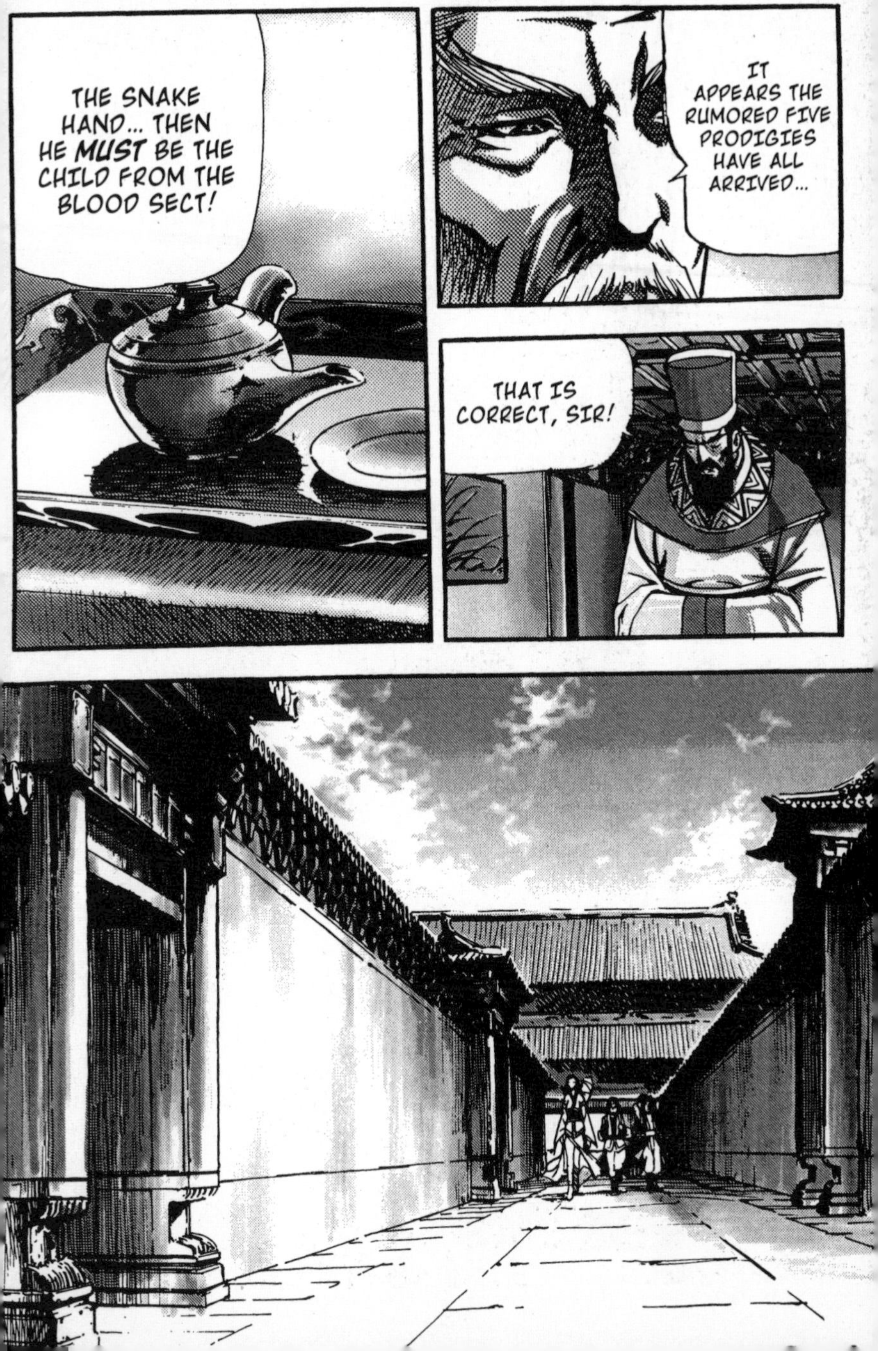
THE SNAKE HAND... THEN HE MUST BE THE CHILD FROM THE BLOOD SECT!
IT APPEARS THE RUMORED FIVE PRODIGIES HAVE ALL ARRIVED...
THAT IS CORRECT, SIR!

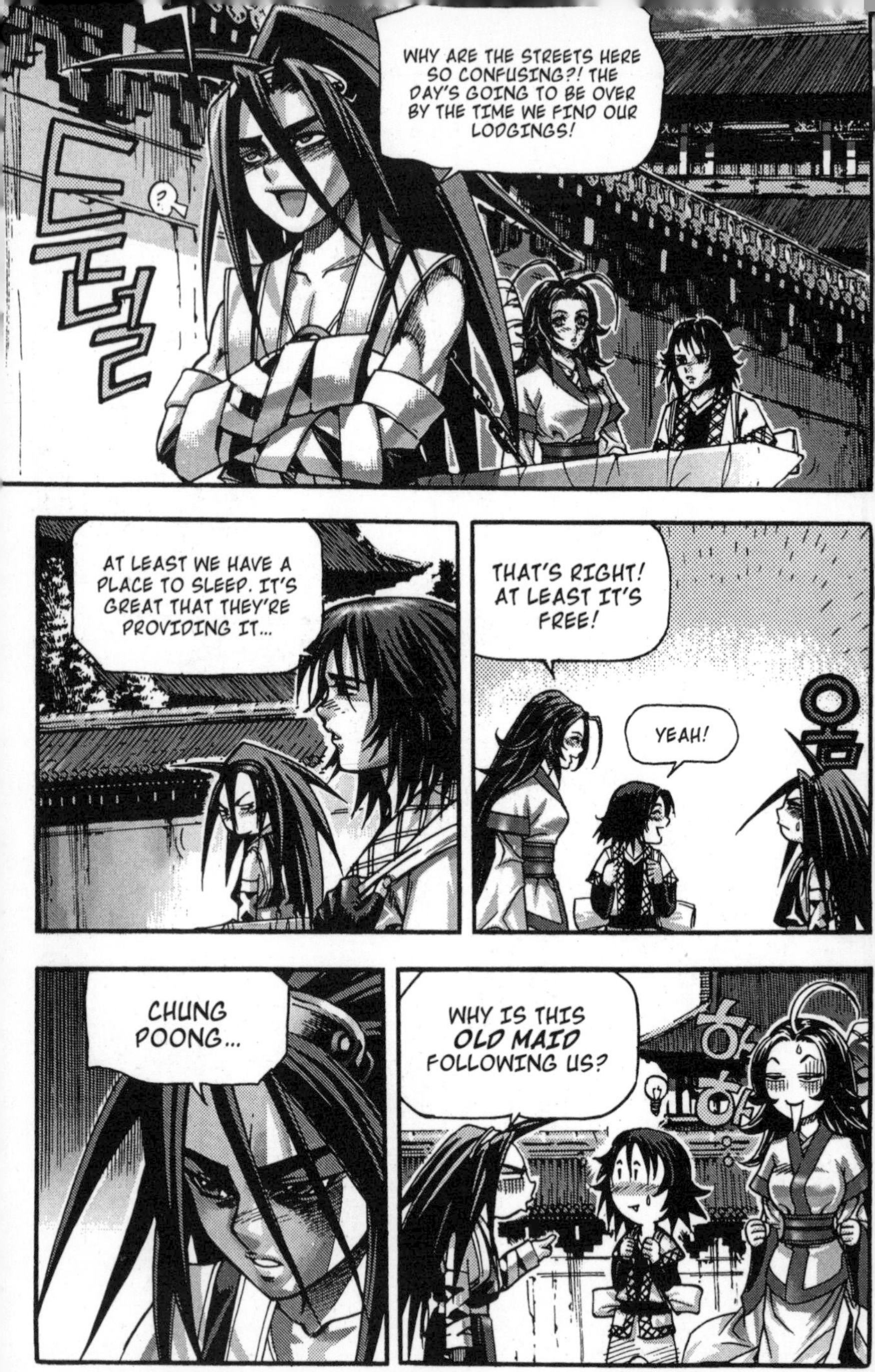
WHY ARE THE STREETS HERE SO CONFUSING?! THE DAY'S GOING TO BE OVER BY THE TIME WE FIND OUR LODGINGS!
AT LEAST WE HAVE A PLACE TO SLEEP. IT'S GREAT THAT THEY'RE PROVIDING IT...
THAT'S RIGHT! AT LEAST IT'S FREE!
YEAH!
CHUNG POONG...
WHY IS THIS *OLD MAID* FOLLOWING US?

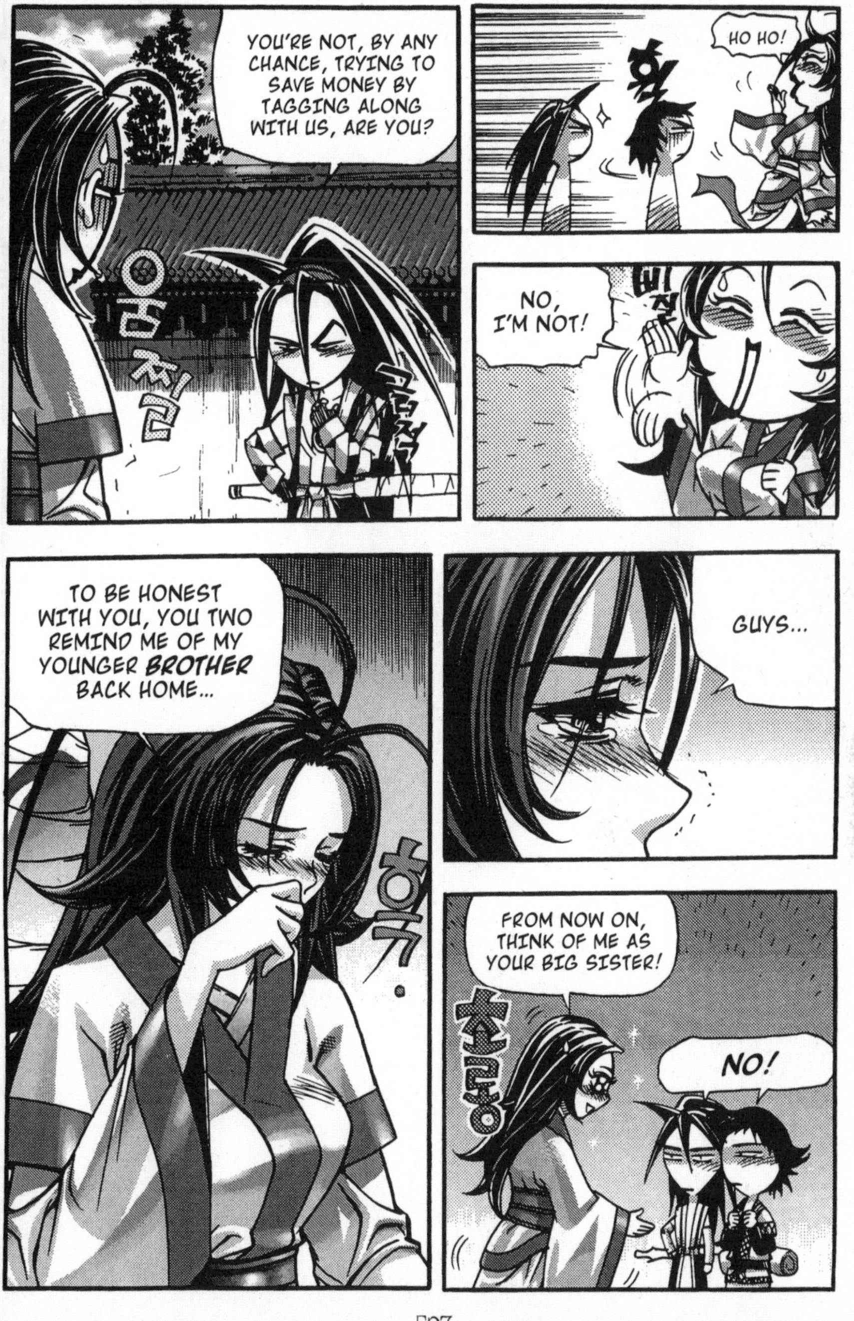
YOU'RE NOT, BY ANY CHANCE, TRYING TO SAVE MONEY BY TAGGING ALONG WITH US, ARE YOU?
HO HO!
NO, I'M NOT!
TO BE HONEST WITH YOU, YOU TWO REMIND ME OF MY YOUNGER BROTHER BACK HOME...
GUYS...
FROM NOW ON, THINK OF ME AS YOUR BIG SISTER!
NO!

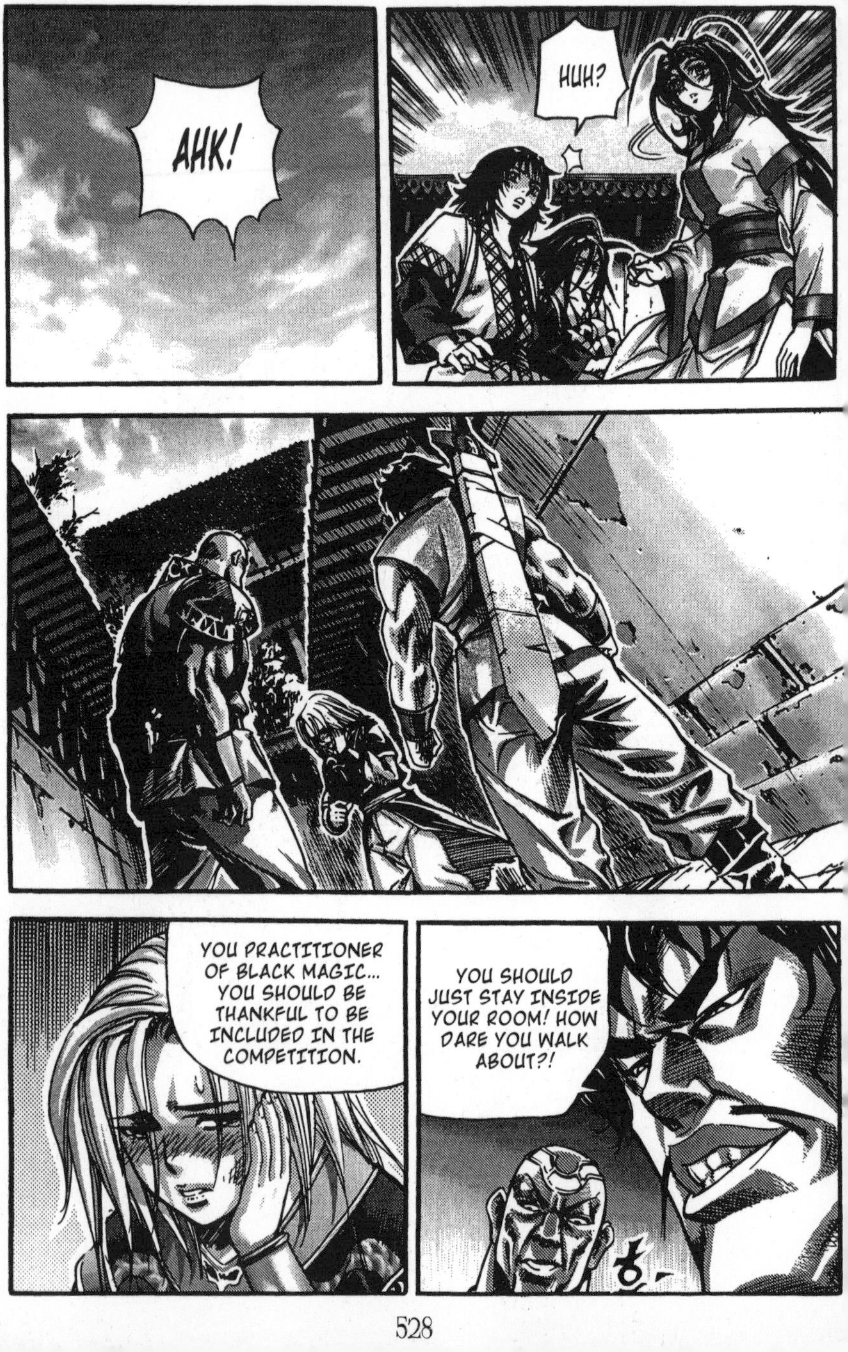
AHK!
HUH?
YOU PRACTITIONER OF BLACK MAGIC... YOU SHOULD BE THANKFUL TO BE INCLUDED IN THE COMPETITION.
YOU SHOULD JUST STAY INSIDE YOUR ROOM! HOW DARE YOU WALK ABOUT?!

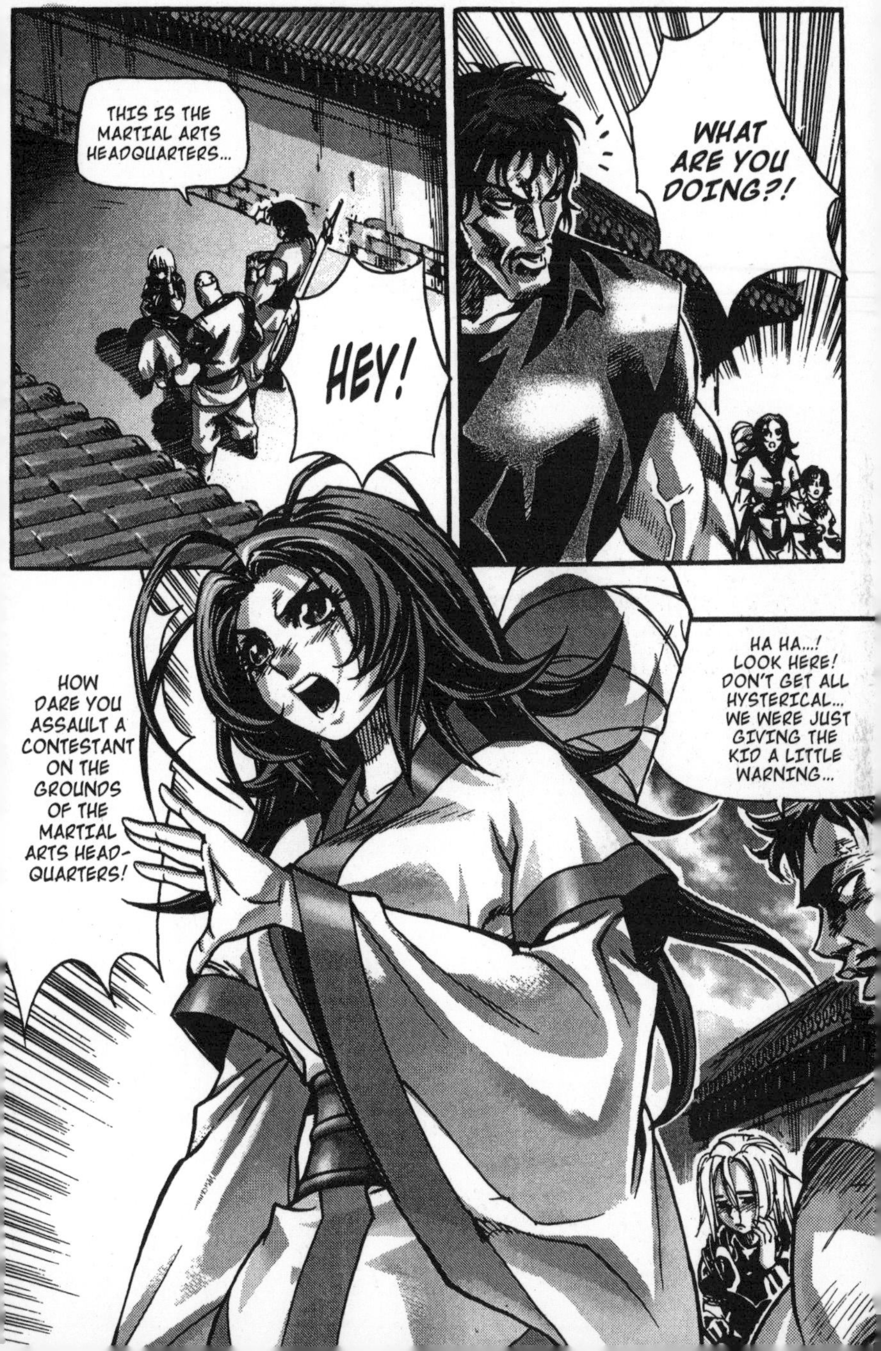
THIS IS THE MARTIAL ARTS HEADQUARTERS...
HEY!
WHAT ARE YOU DOING?!
HOW DARE YOU ASSAULT A CONTESTANT ON THE GROUNDS OF THE MARTIAL ARTS HEAD-QUARTERS!
HA HA...! LOOK HERE! DON'T GET ALL HYSTERICAL... WE WERE JUST GIVING THE KID A LITTLE WARNING...

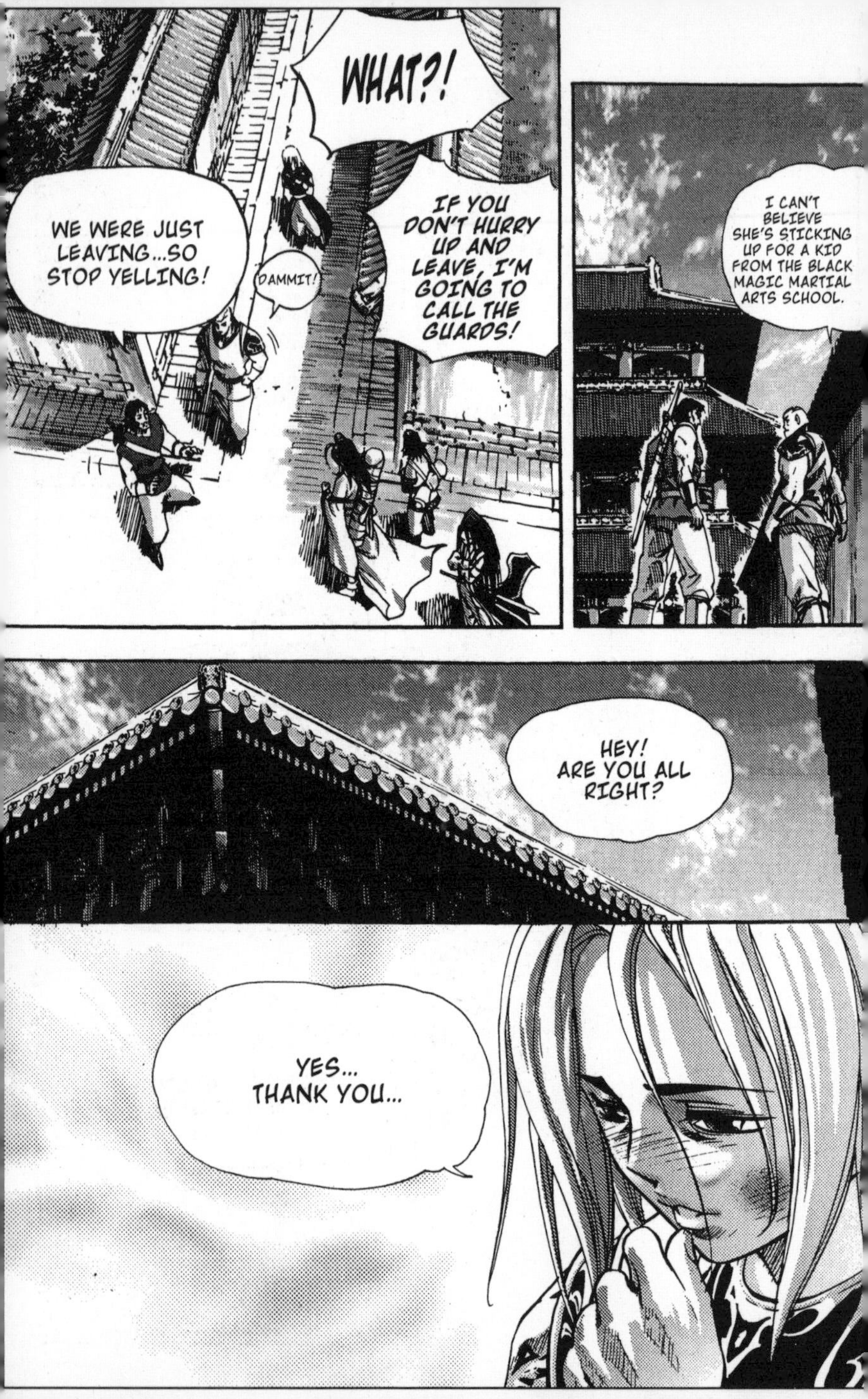
WHAT?!
WE WERE JUST LEAVING...SO STOP YELLING!
DAMMIT!
IF YOU DON'T HURRY UP AND LEAVE, I'M GOING TO CALL THE GUARDS!
I CAN'T BELIEVE SHE'S STICKING UP FOR A KID FROM THE BLACK MAGIC MARTIAL ARTS SCHOOL.
HEY! ARE YOU ALL RIGHT?
YES... THANK YOU...

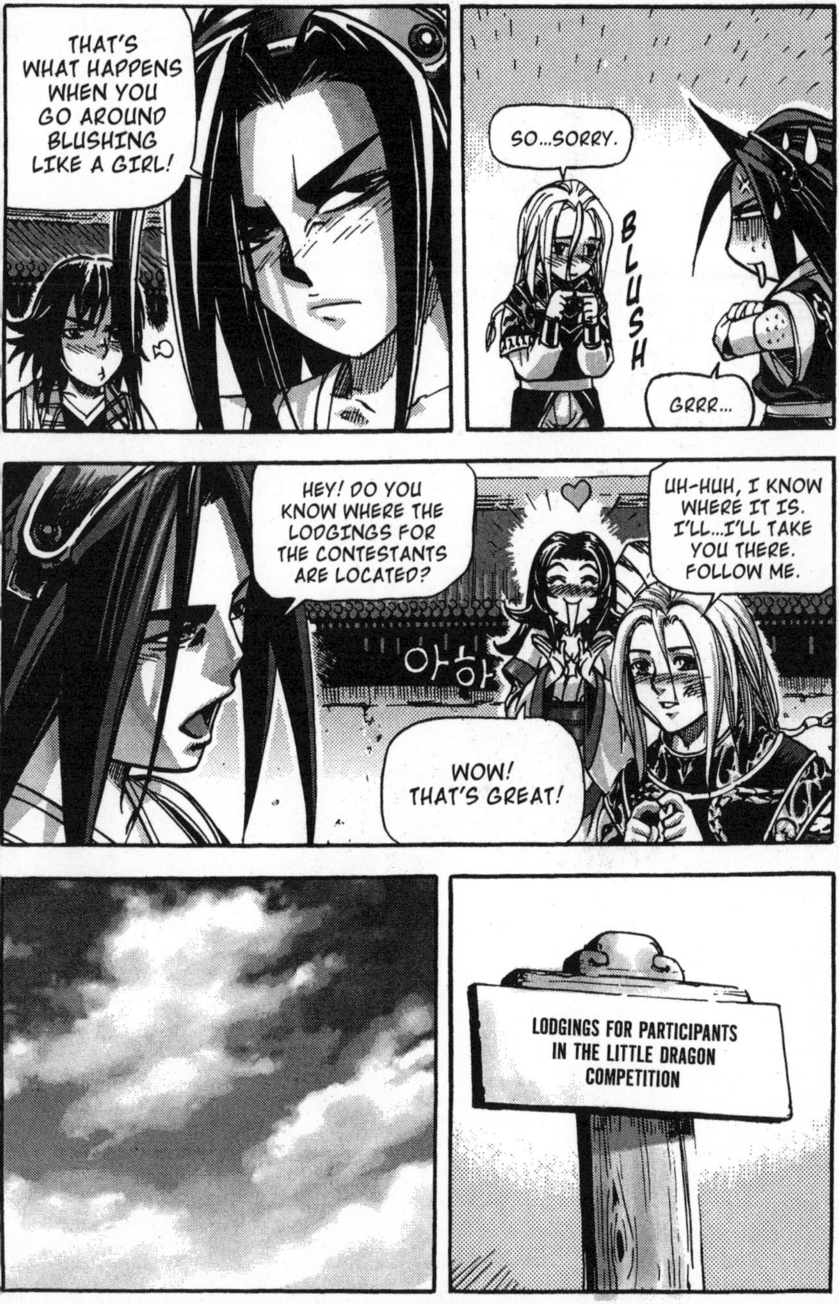
THAT'S WHAT HAPPENS WHEN YOU GO AROUND BLUSHING LIKE A GIRL!
SO...SORRY.
BLUSH
GRRR...
HEY! DO YOU KNOW WHERE THE LODGINGS FOR THE CONTESTANTS ARE LOCATED?
UH-HUH, I KNOW WHERE IT IS. I'LL...I'LL TAKE YOU THERE. FOLLOW ME.
아하
WOW! THAT'S GREAT!
LODGINGS FOR PARTICIPANTS IN THE LITTLE DRAGON COMPETITION

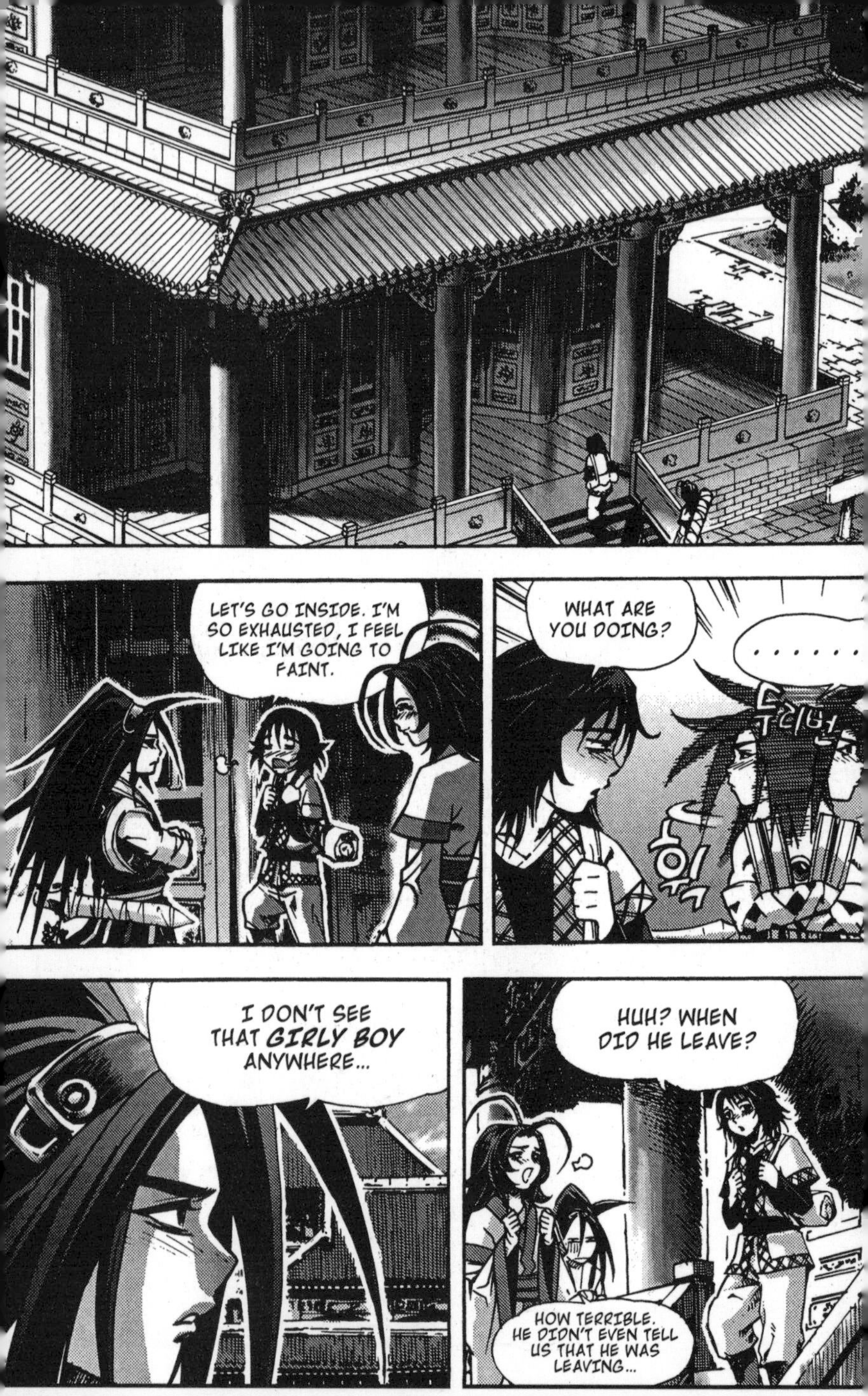
LET'S GO INSIDE. I'M SO EXHAUSTED, I FEEL LIKE I'M GOING TO FAINT.
WHAT ARE YOU DOING?
....
I DON'T SEE THAT GIRLY BOY ANYWHERE...
HUH? WHEN DID HE LEAVE?
HOW TERRIBLE. HE DIDN'T EVEN TELL US THAT HE WAS LEAVING...

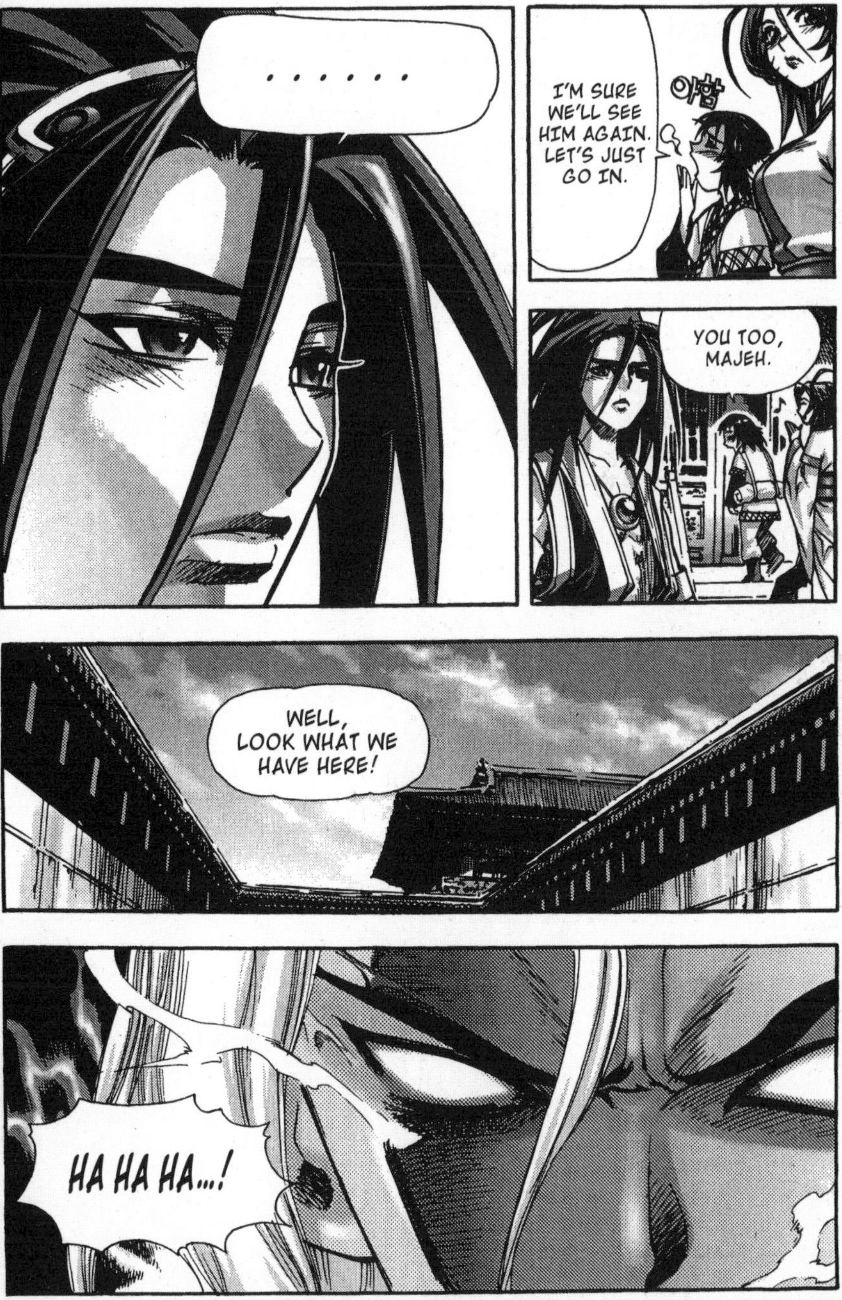
. . . . . .
I'M SURE WE'LL SEE HIM AGAIN. LET'S JUST GO IN.
아함
YOU TOO, MAJEH.
WELL, LOOK WHAT WE HAVE HERE!
HA HA HA...!

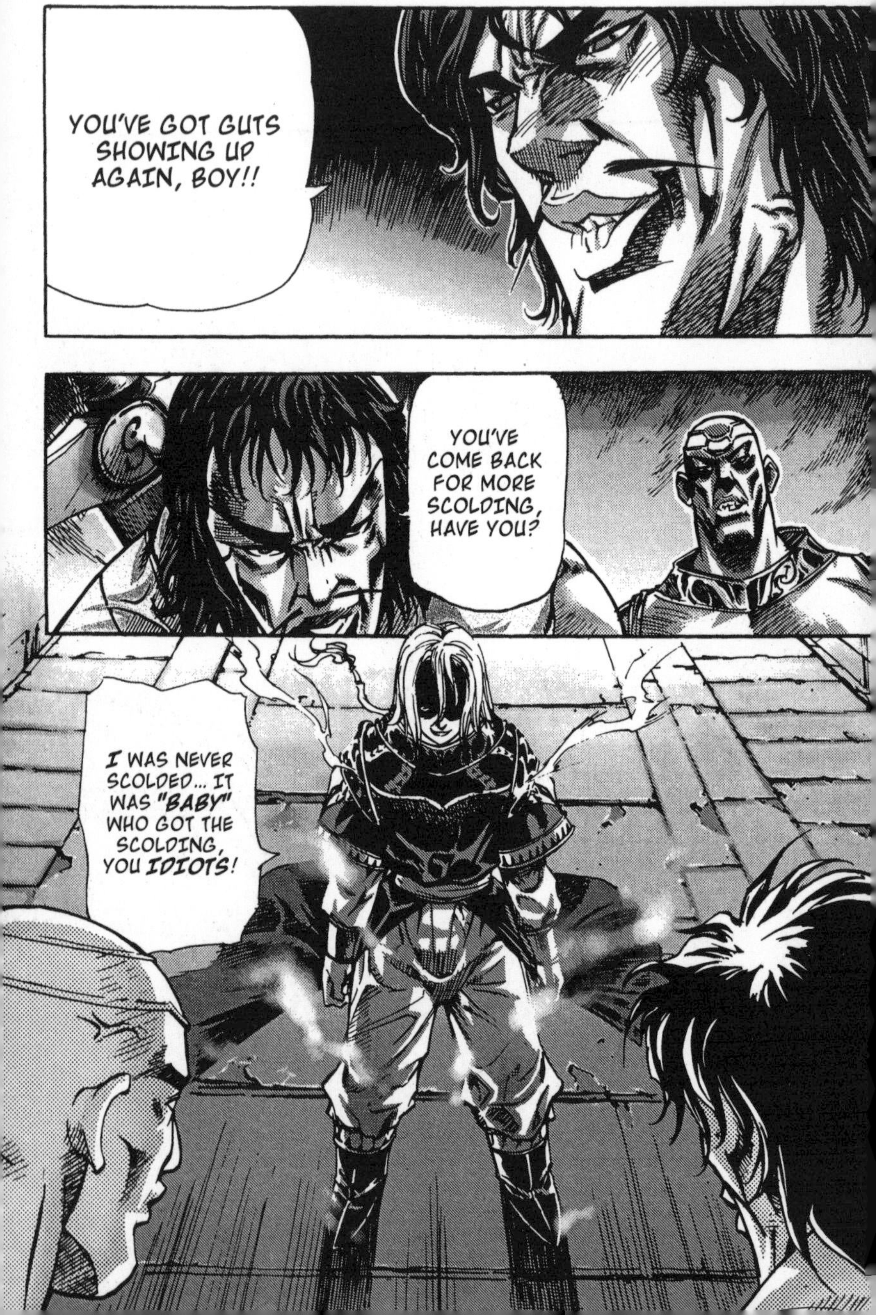
YOU'VE GOT GUTS SHOWING UP AGAIN, BOY!!
YOU'VE COME BACK FOR MORE SCOLDING, HAVE YOU?
I WAS NEVER SCOLDED... IT WAS "BABY" WHO GOT THE SCOLDING, YOU IDIOTS!

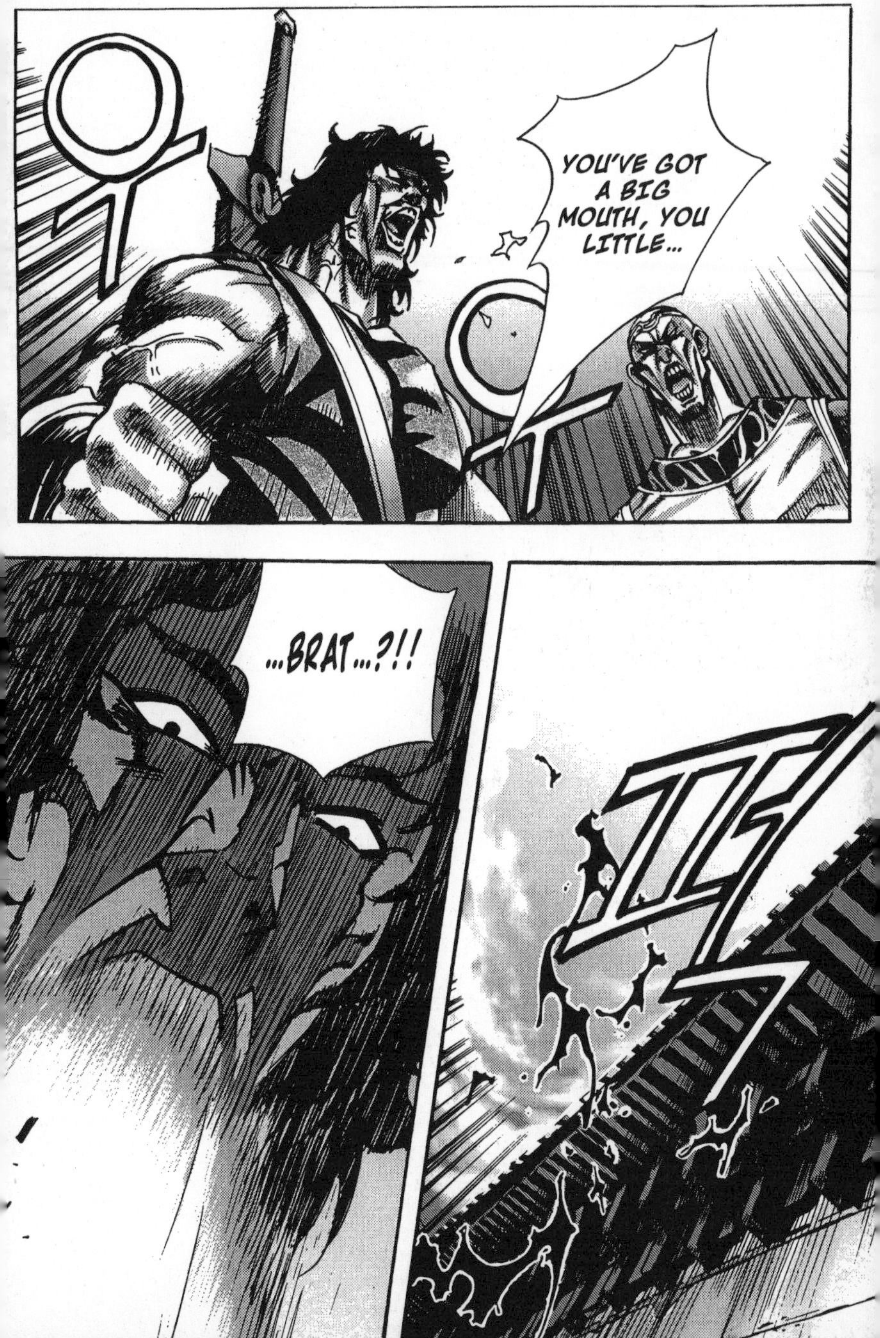
YOU'VE GOT A BIG MOUTH, YOU LITTLE...
...BRAT...?!!

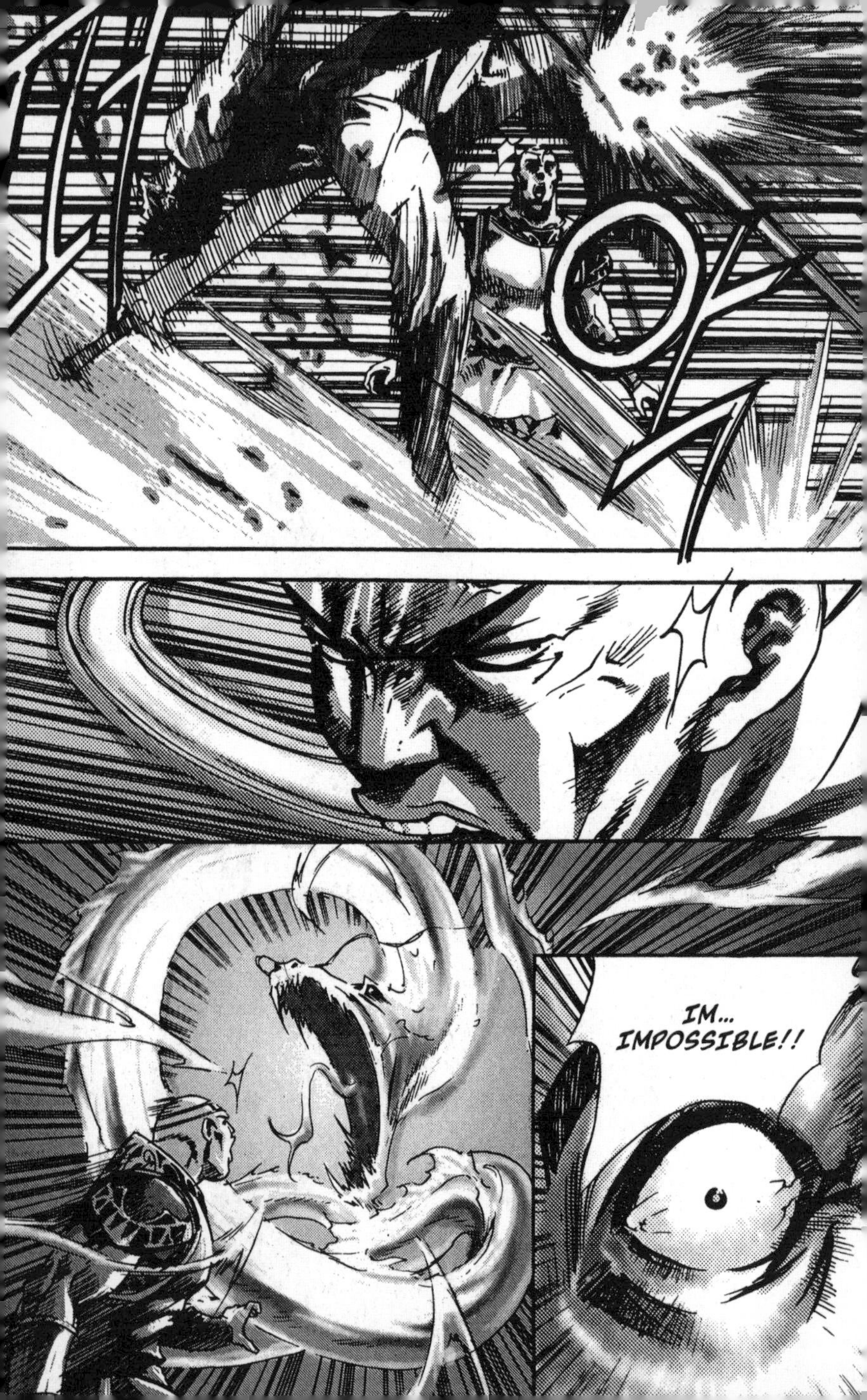
IM...
IMPOSSIBLE!!

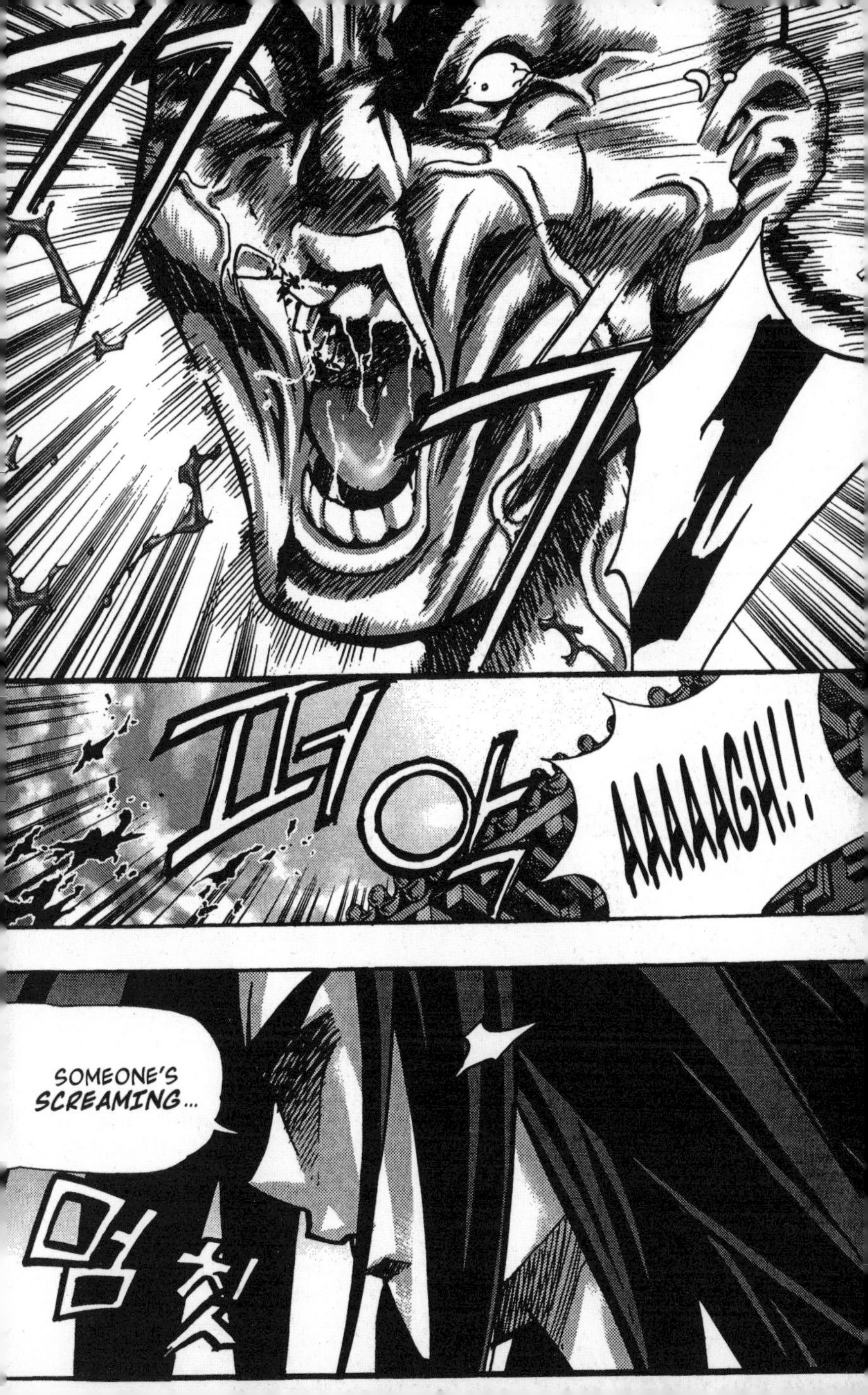
AAAAAGH!!
SOMEONE'S SCREAMING...

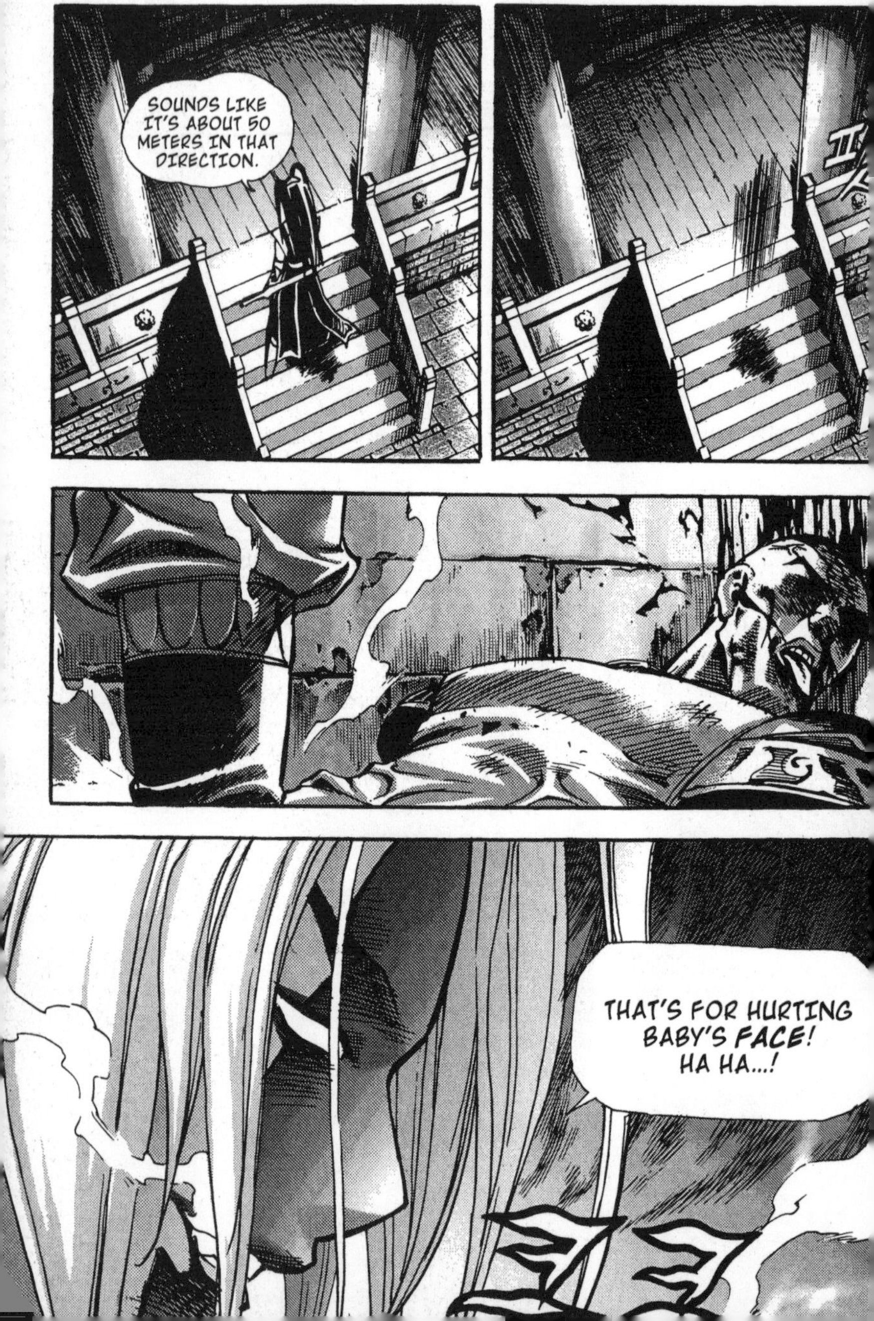
SOUNDS LIKE IT'S ABOUT 50 METERS IN THAT DIRECTION.
THAT'S FOR HURTING BABY'S *FACE*! HA HA...!

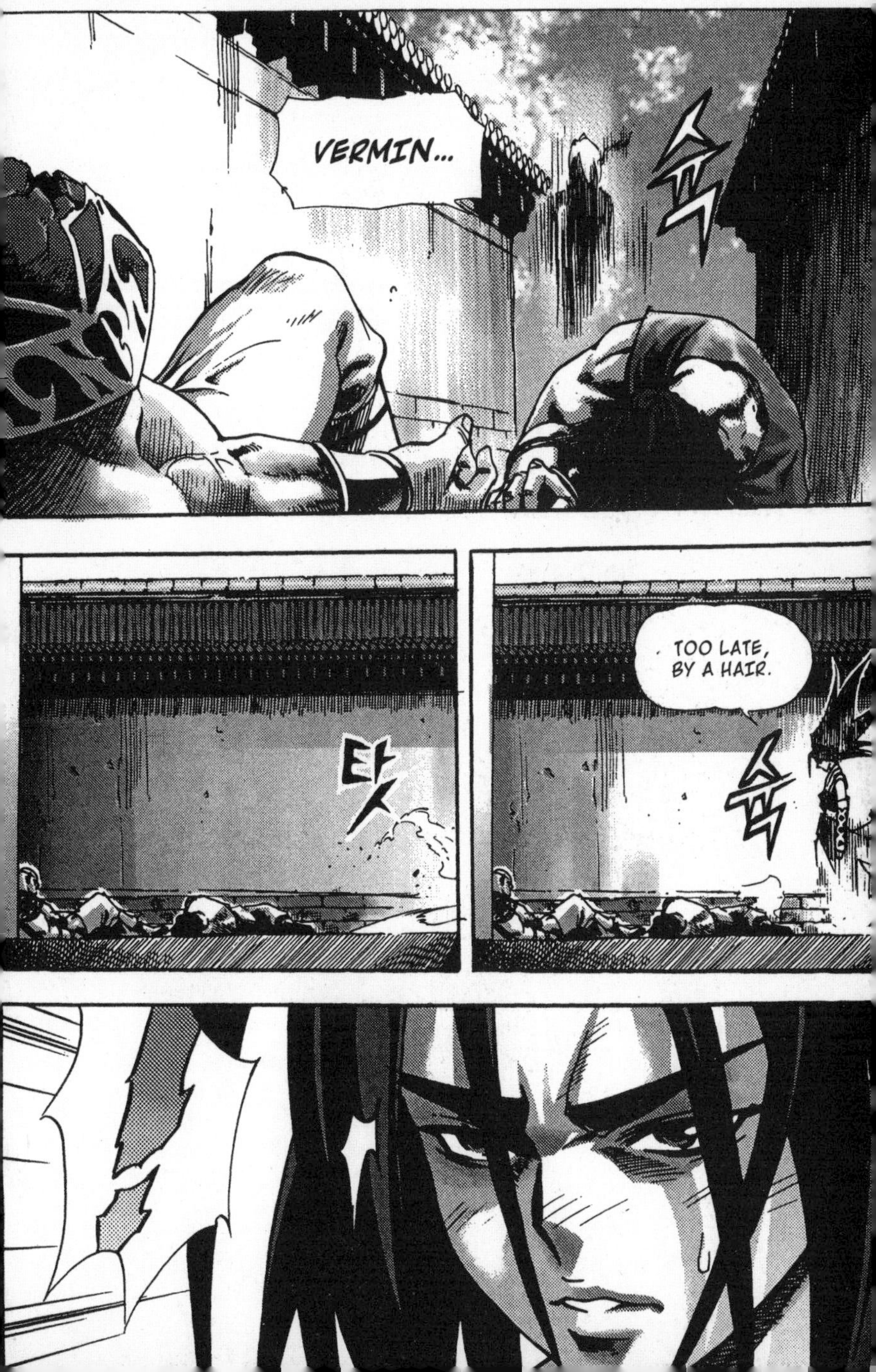
VERMIN...
TOO LATE, BY A HAIR.

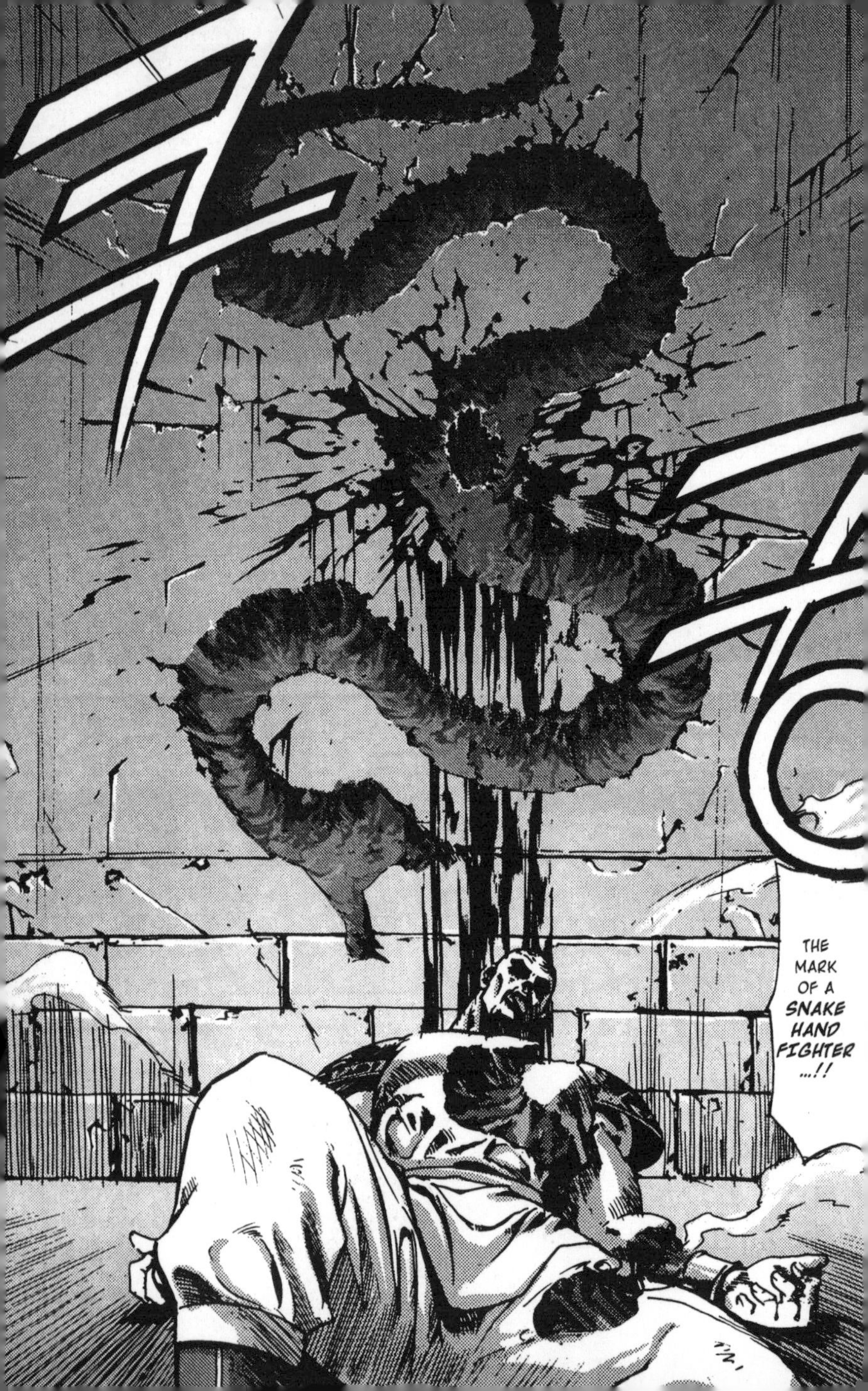
THE MARK OF A SNAKE HAND FIGHTER ...!!

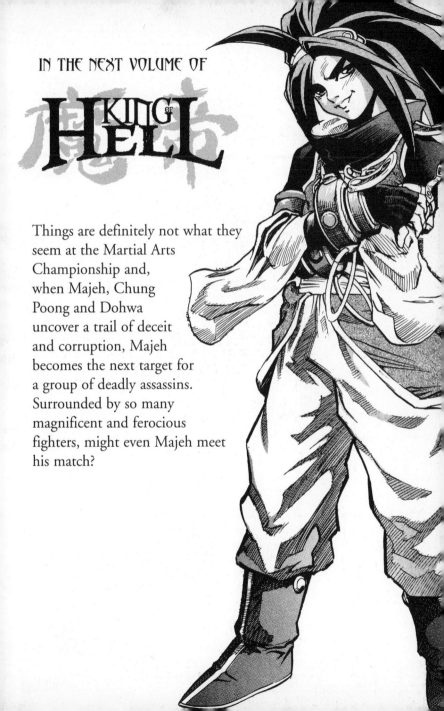

IN THE NEXT VOLUME OF

KING OF HELL

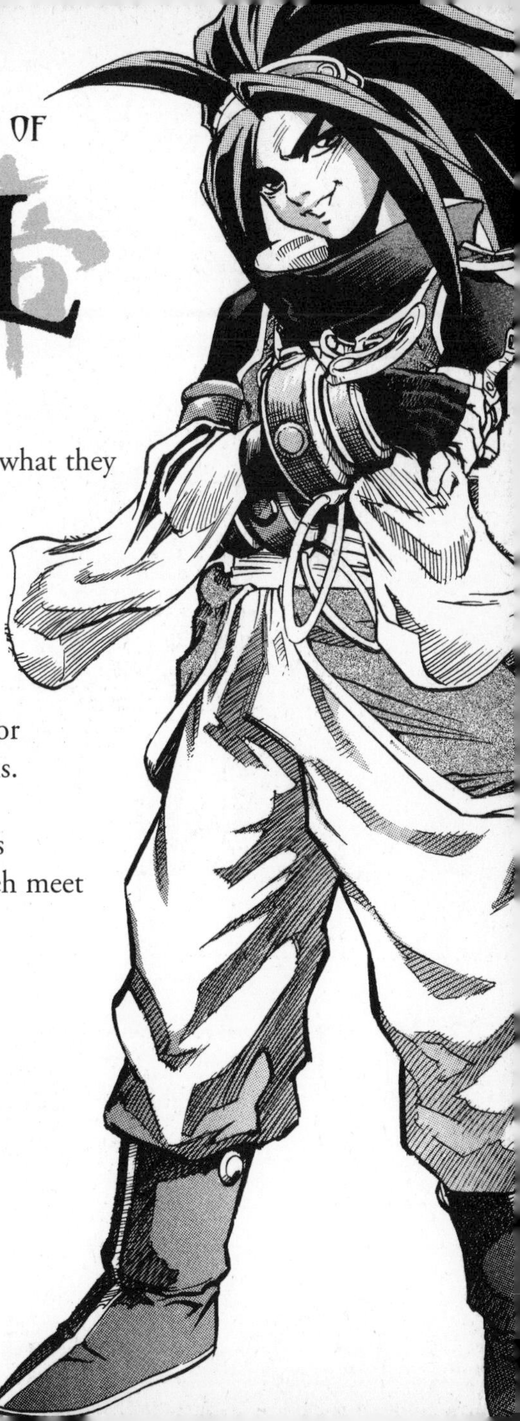

Things are definitely not what they seem at the Martial Arts Championship and, when Majeh, Chung Poong and Dohwa uncover a trail of deceit and corruption, Majeh becomes the next target for a group of deadly assassins. Surrounded by so many magnificent and ferocious fighters, might even Majeh meet his match?